MODERN PERSPECTIVES IN PSYCHIATRY

Edited by John G. Howells

2

MODERN PERSPECTIVES
IN
WORLD PSYCHIATRY

MODERN PERSPECTIVES IN PSYCHIATRY
Edited by John G. Howells

MODERN PERSPECTIVES
IN
WORLD PSYCHIATRY

Edited by
JOHN G. HOWELLS
M.D., D.P.M.

Director, The Institute of Family Psychiatry
Ipswich and East Suffolk Hospital
England

Introduced by
LORD ADRIAN
O.M.

OLIVER & BOYD
EDINBURGH AND LONDON

OLIVER AND BOYD LTD

Tweeddale Court
Edinburgh 1

39a Welbeck Street
London W.1

First published 1968

05 001611 3

Printed in Great Britain by Eyre and Spottiswoode Limited
at The Thanet Press, Margate. Kent

EDITOR'S PREFACE

Each volume in the 'Modern Perspectives in Psychiatry Series' aims to bring the facts from the growing points in a particular field of psychiatry to the clinician at as early a stage as possible. Thus, a single volume in this Series is not a textbook; a psychiatric textbook has the double disadvantage of rapidly becoming out of date and of restricting to one, or at best to a few, authors the coverage of a field as large as psychiatry. However, the eventual scope of the volumes in the whole Series is such as to constitute a complete international system in the theory and practice of psychiatry.

Contributions likely to be significant in the development of international psychiatry are selected from all over the world. It is hoped that the Series will be a factor in effecting integration of world psychiatry and that it will supply a forum for the expression of creative opinion wherever it may arise.

The present volume has benefited from the contributions of twenty-six authorities from Canada, France, Japan, Switzerland, the United Kingdom, the Union of Soviet Socialist Republics and the United States of America. Each chapter is written by an acknowledged expert, often the leading authority in his field. He was entrusted with the task of selecting, appraising and explaining his special subject for the benefit of colleagues who may be less well acquainted with it. Each chapter is not an exhaustive review of the literature on the subject, but contains what the contributor regards as relevant to clinical practice in that field. The volume will be valuable to the psychiatrist in training.

Volumes in the 'Modern Perspectives in Psychiatry Series' are complementary. Readers of this volume will find interest in the already published volume 1, '*Modern Perspectives in Child Psychiatry*' and in the next volume 3, '*Modern Perspectives in International Child Psychiatry*'. These are to be followed by '*Modern Perspectives in Psycho-Obstetrics*' and '*Modern Perspectives in Adolescent Psychiatry*'. The list of contents of the volumes already published will be found at the back of this volume. The place of the Series as an unrivalled reference source is assured by the appearance of a cumulative index in each volume.

It is with regret that we report the death of one of our contributors while the volume was under preparation; Lord Brain, F.R.S., was a distinguished and outstanding member of the medical fraternity in the

United Kingdom. His chapter in this book is his last major writing and exemplifies the high standard of his work.

The Editor wishes to acknowledge the imaginative and indefatigable work of his editorial assistant, Mrs Maria-Livia Osborn. The valuable cumulative indices are also her work.

Grateful acknowledgement is also made to the following publishers and editors of journals, and to the authors concerned, for kind permission to reproduce the material mentioned:

Lord Adrian's introduction is partly based on his address reprinted in the *British Medical Journal*, 1959, ii, 78-81.

Progress in clinical psychology, for allowing Prof. Wolpe to adapt some passages which appeared in his article 'Direct behaviour modification therapies'. Williams and Wilkins, Baltimore [Ch. III, Figs 1, 9, Plate VII (from *Strong and Elwyn's Human Neuroanatomy*, 5th ed. 1964)]; Academic Press, New York [Ch. III, Figs 3, 5, 10 (*Electron Microscope Anatomy*, 1964)]; McGraw Hill, New York [Ch. III, Figs 4 (*Cellular Fine Structure*, 1964), 11 (*The Nature of Biological Diversity*, 1963)]; W. B. Saunders, Philadelphia [Ch. III, Figs 7, 8, Plates V, XVII (*An Atlas of Ultrastructure*, 1963)]; *Journal of Cellular Biology* [Ch. III, Fig. 14 (24, 1965), Plate I (15, 1962)]; *Journal of the National Cancer Institute* [Ch. III, Fig 15, (33, 1964)]; *Bulletin of Johns Hopkins Hospital* [Ch. III, Plate II (114, 1964)]; Elesevier, Amsterdam [Ch. III, Plates III, XI, XII (*Neurohisto-chemistry*, 1965), Plates XLI, XLII, XLIII, XLIV, XLV (*Progress in Brain Research*, 1967)]; *Compte rendu de l'Academie de Science*, Paris [Ch. III, Plate IV (260, 1965)]; *Journal of Comparative Neurology* [Ch. III, Plates VI, XVIII (121, 1963)]; University of California Press, Berkeley [Ch. III, Plate VIII (*Brain Function*, 1964)]; *Journal of Neurochemistry* [Ch. III, Plate IX (6, 1960)]; John Wiley, London [Ch. III, Plates XIII, XIV, XV (*The Organization of the Cerebral Cortex*, 1956)]; *Experienta* [Ch. III, Plate XVI (21, 1965)]; *Journal of Neuropathology and Experimental Neurology* [Ch. III, Plate XIX (23, 1964)]; *Journal of Biophysics, Biochemistry and Cytology* [Ch. III, Plate XX (1, 1955)]; *American Journal of Anatomy* [Ch. III, Plates XXIII, XXVI, XXVIII, XXXI (99, 1956)]; *Science* [Ch. VIII, Fig. 4 (148, 1965), Plate X (152, 1966)]; *The American Medical Association Archives of General Psychiatry* [Ch. XI, Figs 1 (4, 55-59, 1961), 3 (81, 363-69, 1959)]; *The Annals of the New York Academy of Sciences* [Ch. XI, Fig. 2 (96, 1962)]; University of Toronto Press [Ch. XI, Fig 4 from the *Proceedings of the Third World Congress on Psychiatry* (1962)]; *Journal of Abnormal Psychology* [Ch. XI, Fig. 5 (70 1965)]; *Psychological Issues* [Ch. XVI, Table 1 (adapted from 1, 1959), Table 2, 1, 1966)].

CONTENTS

PART TWO

CLINICAL

INTRODUCTION

LORD ADRIAN
O.M., M.D., F.R.C.P., F.R.S.
Chancellor, University of Cambridge

There may still be some branches of medicine which are compact enough to be covered in full by a single author, but modern psychiatry is certainly not one of them: disorders of thought and behaviour can be viewed from too many aspects. If we are to understand the present state of psychiatric theory and practice, we must listen to a panel of experts each dealing with his own particular sector.

We shall find them dealing with a wide range of subjects, some of which had little bearing upon psychiatry until a few years ago. Today is not only a time of considerable development in psychiatry but it is also marked by spectacular progress in the 'life sciences' generally. The advance has reached down to the molecular level in biophysics, biochemistry, genetics and virology and up to that of the social behaviour of animals and men, and at every level there have been new techniques to collect the evidence as well as new ideas to explain it. We seem in fact to be on the threshold of discoveries which will give a fresh insight into some of the fundamental problems of human thinking and behaviour, discoveries in the neurophysiology of the brain, in the organization of cells and tissues, in the effects of the environment on the individual and who knows what else? New and important ideas will come whether as the result of elaborately planned research or of chance observation in the clinic or the laboratory: in either case we must be ready to make use of them, for they will certainly throw more light on mental disease.

Retrospect

This is not the first time that psychiatry has seemed to be on the verge of great advances. In this century hopes were raised when Freud's work on the neuroses suggested that some of the common types of mental disorder were caused by similar tensions and might be relieved by the psycho-analytical approach. Before that there had been Kraepelin's new classification and the periods when bacterial toxins or visceroptosis were blamed. But there have been theories of mental disease from Hippocrates onwards. Patients have been subjected to treatments of every kind: some recovered and theories would then be based on the treatment which led to the cure. The question of *post hoc* or *propter hoc* was usually left un-answered, as in so much of medical theory and practice well up to the present time.

At the end of the liberal eighteenth century, however, the treatment of mental disease had certainly changed for the better. The change had followed a new regard for the patient. Thanks to Pinel, at the head of the Bicêtre in Paris in 1793, and to Tuke, who built the Retreat at York a few years later, doctors and public alike were persuaded to show more pity in the presence of madness. They were taught that someone mentally ill should not be regarded with horror or mirth but as a sick person in a state deserving every consideration.

In spite of this in the nineteenth century psychiatry fell behind in the advance of medical science. There was little that it could gain from the progress of physiology and pathology which had begun to transform the picture of organic disease, for often in mental disturbance there were no significant pathological changes to be found in the brain or elsewhere in the body. It was no surprise that mental change occurred when the brain was injured by trauma, infected by syphilis or poisoned by alcohol, but as often as not a patient with disease of the mind would exhibit no sign of any organic disturbance.

It would not be right to imply that psychiatry made no progress throughout the nineteenth century, for the difference in status and human regard between patients with bodily and with mental disease had become progressively less. In Germany too there were university clinics where neuropathology flourished and nervous and mental diseases were studied together. In Great Britain they remained apart: the alienist had charge of the asylum for those who were classed as insane, the neurologist dealt with nervous disorders of every kind. It needed the flood of neuroses in the 1914 war as well as the theories of Freud to break the division down, to enlarge the field of psychiatry to cover the nervous patient as well as the patient of unsound mind.

War and Medical Progress

If our descendants are able to live at peace with one another, they may not realize the full effect that wars can have on medical progress. They will not be surprised at the great technological progress which came of the two world wars, but even now it is hard to recall the full force of the emotional drive which turned the world from contemplation to action in the summer of 1914.

Then and in 1939 scientists in every field lost interest in the distant target and moved heaven and earth for a chance to put their skills to practical use in the service of their ideals. And what was achieved under this emotional pressure has altered the whole pattern of scientific advance.

In physics and chemistry as well as in medicine our two great wars have encouraged practical applications and the problems which had to be solved have reacted on theory. And although some lines of scientific research have suffered, I think we should all agree that the infusion of new ideas has been to the general good.

The Neuroses Recognized

By 1914 Freud's work was already well advanced and Ernest Jones had begun to shock conventional opinion by insisting on its importance. Bernard Hart had prepared the way in 1912 by publishing a small classic *The Psychology of Insanity*, which was widely read and seemed to put psychiatry on a much more acceptable footing. But in Great Britain, until the war, the neuroses attracted little interest. The neurologists were mostly content if they could exclude organic disease, though there were a few enthusiasts to whom cases were referred for treatment. There were some reputable hypnotists and various nursing homes.

The war brought a rapid change in this neglect when 'shell shock' became an urgent problem. It was thought at first to be due to mechanical damage to the brain and was treated by rest, but the realization of its emotional content did not make its prevention easier. Within a year most of the convalescent hospitals on either side of the Channel had spectacular cases to show ranging from mutism to convulsive attacks, with all the hysterical manifestations which Charcot had found in his patients at the Salpetrière.

When the purely 'functional' origin of these symptoms was understood it seemed at first that their removal would restore the patient to health. There were various techniques for this, ranging from persuasion or hypnosis to some face-saving suggestive method, but a feature of most of them was the unrelenting pressure which was maintained until every physical symptom was abandoned. This is well described in Arthus Hurst's writings from the Seale Hayne Hospital in 1918 and in the accounts of Roussy and Lhermitte in 1917.

Unfortunately the loss of the bodily symptoms would usually cause the return of the mental distress: towards the end of the war the conversion was widely recognized and there were special hospitals close to the front line to give psychological first aid and to prevent the elaboration of the hysterical escape.

But, as the war continued, though the lengthy process of psychoanalysis was out of the question, many of those who had war neuroses to treat were beginning to find support for the Freudian outlook. The recall of distressing experiences seemed a useful, perhaps an essential step for the reassurance of the patient and it was clear that the hysterical escape from distress could only be understood in psychological terms. By the end of the war in 1918 the methods adopted in most of the special hospitals did not differ greatly from those in the war of 1939, though by then the effects of emotional disturbance were more widely understood by doctors and laymen as well.

The change in attitude to neurosis was already established by 1918. The tide was running strongly then in favour of the emotional origin and elaboration of neurotic symptoms on the lines described by Freud, though the issues had been confused by the diverging gospels of Jung and of Adler. It still runs strongly and it would need great self-assurance now to deny any value to Freud's interpretation. It has given us all a new way of regarding human behaviour from the cradle onwards, a new and coherent picture alive with details. The picture may be distorted and some of the details may have come from the mind of the painter, but it has made us consider the reasons for most of our cherished beliefs and has led to a definite change in the relations of parent and child.

The emotional stresses of war had provided a great demonstration of psychosomatic sickness, and the Freudian scheme, with its sombre interpretation of human motives, had fitted the mood of the time. Without statistics and with all the confusions of war the reported success of the treatment by abreaction was not in itself a proof of the Freudian theory, though much of the evidence concerning psycho-analysis had come from an earlier time. But the scheme is not of a kind to be readily tested and it is not surprising that different ideas have come into favour as well since the end of the First World War.

Further Progress

Much has happened, however, in medical specialization since 1918 and one of the striking changes has been the great increase in the psychiatric field. It has now extended not only to cover neuroses, but to cover much of the field of paediatrics and the field of education. Child psychiatry is now an important branch of medicine with theories and classifications of its own, and psychiatric help is expected and given for every stage of the developing mind.

There is also a striking change in the mental hospital patient. This is due in the main to the drugs which reduce disturbed behaviour and allow much greater freedom in hospital life. But apart from these general changes there have been various new developments. For the psychoses there are the new empirical treatments by physical methods or drugs and for the psychosomatic disorders there are the new ideas in theory and practice derived from the work of Pavlov.

The physical methods of treatment began from clinical observations unrelated to any theory, for Sakel found the effects of insulin coma almost by chance and Meduna tried the effect of camphor-induced convulsions because it appeared that an epileptic fit would often produce a remission of schizophrenic symptoms. The reports of the new forms of treatment in 1933 recalled the violent methods in use in the eighteenth century, but further reports were soon appearing from various mental hospitals and it was clear that the results were good.

Attention was paid to the selection of suitable cases for either treatment and the technique of convulsion therapy was further improved by the use of electrical stimulation of the brain instead of convulsant drugs. Both methods have remained in favour for over thirty years and good results have followed in thousands of patients: but how the results are caused is still completely obscure.

The surgical treatment employed by Moniz in 1936 had at least an anatomical basis. Fulton had found that in anthropoid apes neuroses caused experimentally would disappear if the frontal lobes of the brain were removed. Moniz therefore devised the operation of 'pre-frontal leucotomy' which severed the lines of communication between the frontal lobes and the rest of the brain. The operation usually succeeded in reducing emotional tension and it came into use for calming distress and aggressive or agitated behaviour. What came to be known as 'psycho-surgery' has allowed many patients to lead a more normal life but now it is rarely employed. The tranquillizing drugs have given a means of control which is much more readily graded and leaves no permanent damage.

It would be hard to over-estimate the effects of these drugs on the treatment of mental disease at the present time. By controlling abnormal behaviour they have altered the pattern of life in the wards of a mental hospital. They have made it possible to develop various kinds of training for re-entry into social life, by group discussion, wage earning employment, out-patient supervision and arrangements for after care. They have allowed many patients to live in their own homes, in the family setting, and have reduced the length of stay in the ward and the need for hospital beds.

In the subject of psycho-pharmacology, again we have mainly to deal with empirical findings. Drugs with a structure like that of Chlorpromazine (the phenothiazines) or of Reserpine (a pentacyclic compound) have been found to have some specific effects on human behaviour. Their effects on the brain have been studied and some changes in electrical activity have been found, but we know too little to say whether these are related to the calming effect on the mind.

At all events the tranquillizing drugs have succeeded insulin coma and induced convulsions as the most effective treatment for certain kinds of mental disorder and there are other drugs which are effective against depression. They free the mind from some of its troubles and their point of attack is the brain, their specific effects are presumably on neurone activity and not on conflicting ideas.

Whatever our views on the relation of mind and brain it is rational to base the treatment of mental disturbance both on a direct appeal to the mind and on the drugs and physical methods which will modify the activity of the brain. At present, however, it seems that a direct approach to the mind by psychotherapy is only possible when the disturbance of thought is slight, and that when it is severe our treatment must act on the brain. But we show our confusion by calling the slight disturbance a neurosis and the severe one a psychosis. The two great wars of Europe have added to this confusion. It is owing to them that the picture drawn by Pavlov has taken so long to come into favour in the West and that the picture drawn by Freud has scarcely begun to penetrate to the East.

Pavlov's Physiological Picture

Pavlov was an unrivalled experimenter, a skilled surgeon with abounding spirits and good health, and he took a more cheerful view of our troubles than Freud. Our anxieties are not considered as the symbolic expression of what we must not allow ourselves to think; for the mind, conscious or unconscious, has no place in his scheme. Our intelligent behaviour expresses our cerebral activity, and our troubles are due to some derangement of the processes of conditioning and of the balance of excitation and inhibition in the cerebrum. On both schemes we can blame our special troubles on the way we have been brought up, but in the East the emphasis is on the nervous connections and not on the original sin.

We must think of Pavlov's scheme as a working hypothesis for analysing behaviour from the physiological side. The picture before us is that of a nervous machine which can make intelligent decisions. The picture does not go into details, but the outlines are based on evidence which can be tested experimentally, and to that extent it has the advantage over the psychoanalytic picture of the mind. This may offer an explanation of every detail in a dream, but the evidence is seldom of a kind to give complete certainty, and it is difficult to see how the picture can be developed much further. The physiological picture is still in the making, and we have a long way to go before the advance from this side will be halted.

Prospects Today

The difficulty at present is that the advance is leading us into a wood that becomes more and more obscure because the trees are so thickly crowded. Work in the physiology and biochemistry and pharmacology of the brain has accumulated a great store of facts, and neurosurgery can now check them on the human patient. The result has been that the simple schemes which used to satisfy us are as out of date as the maps of the phrenologists, but as yet we have nothing much better to take their place. In fact, we really have no clear idea of what most of our brain does for us, of the part that much of it plays in guiding our thought and behaviour. Some areas receive signals from the sense organs or elaborate skilled movements, but there is a duplicate or even a triplicate representation, and in animals most of it can be destroyed without obvious loss. Large areas of the human cerebrum can be destroyed without making us incapable of rational thought or behaviour. The electroencephalogram seemed to herald a new way of analysing cerebral activity, but it has revealed little more than the tendency to epilepsy. Micro-electro recordings from the nerve cells of the cortex give a bewildering variety of response patterns. The search for chemical transmitters is still going on, and we await the latest reports from the neuro-surgical teams who have divided the human brain into right and left.

We still have to find whatever organic changes occur in the commoner mental disorders, but the progress of biological science has given us far more knowledge of how we should search. There are vastly improved techniques for examining structures and activities in the brain. Psychiatry can scarcely fail to profit by greater understanding of the organization of nerve cells and neuralgia, of the storage and retrieval of memories, of visual and tactile patterns in the cerebral cortex and of all the research concerning human and animal behaviour. The distinction between mind and matter may always be one of the several unsolved riddles at the boundaries of natural science, but the mind and the brain are now no longer divided by a gap which cannot be faced.

This is, of course, a most enviable position to have reached. The obscurity is a challenge. It throws no gloom on the investigator, and no one doubts that there will soon be new discoveries to bring us into the light again. Just at present, however, we seem to have gone too far to use Pavlov's formula without a good deal of revision, and we have certainly not gone far enough to be within sight of any blending of the two pictures— finding the nervous substratum of the super-ego or even of a simple conditioned reflex.

Our treatment certainly seems to be more successful. We have progressed in understanding far enough to have no further use for the methods of dealing with hysterical manifestations which were developed in the First World War. We have made our mental hospitals much more cheerful places to visit, and though they have many more patients the majority are soon able to leave. But we do not seem to have checked the incidence of disorders for which the brain or mind is mainly responsible. We are badly in need of new discoveries in the pathology of the brain and of fresh developments on the psychological side to bring the two pictures nearer together.

In fact, we have still a long way to go in the path of advance which was opened up after the war of 1914 by the shell-shocked patients, the change in our attitude to neurosis, and the theories of Freud and Jung and their fellows. Elaboration of the Freudian picture may not lead much further, but this does not mean that we cannot learn better ways of ensuring mental health, better ways of dealing with the frustrations of infancy, the revolts of youth, and the loneliness of old age. Social science, and its applications to medicine, may have been poorly served by the enthusiasts, but the medical profession has established its right to a hearing in a wide range of social problems which were formerly the exclusive province of Church and State. We must not set ourselves up to instruct the teachers, the criminal courts, and the law givers on matters about which we have no clear views ourselves, but at least we know more than they about the physics and chemistry of human behaviour and about the mental tensions which can distort it.

PART ONE

SCIENTIFIC

I

CRITICAL SURVEY OF
SCHIZOPHRENIA GENETICS

L. S. PENROSE

M.A., M.D., F.R.C.P., F.R.S.

*Emeritus Professor of Human Genetics in the
University of London*

1

Introduction

The science of genetics makes use of a large variety of techniques. In human genetics special methods have to be introduced because classical techniques, which involve experimental breeding, are not available in this field. Consequently, investigators are often obliged to use inferior tools for investigation. The results so obtained cannot then be rigidly interpreted and conclusions are indecisive. There are, nevertheless, certain branches of human genetics in which very precise results can be obtained by the analysis of family data. This occurs when the character under scrutiny is one which can be clearly defined and which is found to segregate. Examples of such characters are the blood antigens, the haemoglobins, the red cell enzymes, the serum proteins, defects of aminoacid metabolism and many other biochemical anomalies. The transmission of aberrant chromosomal patterns can also be unequivocally demonstrated. Special difficulty arises, however, when it is desired to study the genetics of human variations, which cannot be precisely defined or in which arbitrary characters or measurements have to be chosen as representative indices. Examples are stature, intelligence, hair colour and skin colour.

Provided that a trait can be expressed metrically, certain established statistical methods can be used advantageously. The correlation techniques of Galton, Pearson, Fisher and Hogben can be used to establish the degree of hereditary influence and indicate its nature. With characters that cannot be accurately measured, like peculiarities of personality, the situation is much less satisfactory. The only way of recording the trait may be by its presence or absence though, occasionally, a few degrees of manifestation are separately specified. The presence or absence of the particular quality can then be noted in all members of a family or related group and its incidence compared with that found in the general population. In some diseases, believed to be genetically controlled, the value of the observations can be greatly enhanced by investigating the age of onset of symptoms. This introduces a metrical factor which has been used in statistical analyses. Haldane and Bell have found it useful in determining the kind of genetical modifying influences which may be operative when the main hereditary factors are established.

2

Clinical Description

The study of the genetics of schizophrenia is unsatisfactory from almost every point of view. In the first place, there is no certainty that the condition can be defined or even recognized. Many different diseases are probably included under the same general diagnosis and the standards of recognition vary from one country to another because of the lack of an agreed definition. The idea of schizophrenia, as originally developed by Bleuler (1911),[2] is a philosophical concept. Kraepelin (1919)[30] defined dementia praecox in 1896 and this conception was directly clinical; it referred to an observed disease or group of diseases. Bleuler considered a much wider problem. To some extent he followed Jung's (1915)[24] principle that the psychology of patients with dementia praecox, and also those with other mental illnesses, was allied to that of dreams and Bleuler (1912)[3] called this mental process autistic thinking. However, he considered disorder of thought in dementia praecox, and consequent disruption of the personality, as the primary criterion of the disease, hence the term 'split mind' or schizophrenia. The original restriction which applied to Kraepelin's terminology, suggesting that the disease produced dementia and began in early life, was too precise for most psychiatrists to accept. This left the way open for Bleuler's much less precise terminology to pervade the whole of psychiatry and greatly to increase the difficulties for genetical investigators.

Many attempts have been made to define schizophrenia for purposes of genetical study. The characteristic psychological changes include hallucinations (especially auditory), delusions, excitement and negativism; depression, apathy and even stupor can also occur. It is nowhere stated how many of these signs must be present before the diagnosis of schizophrenia is correct. Perhaps one of the clearest definitions is that set out by Hallgren and Sjögren (1959)[14] who used the term in a narrow sense to include only those cases which have a severe and chronic course. Such restriction is necessary because, in a given patient, psychiatric diagnosis is not always constant. Indeed, a person who enters hospital with a severe mental illness is diagnosed schizophrenic only with hesitation on the first admission because of the serious prognostic implications of the diagnosis. After a prolonged period of illness with deepening mental symptoms, in the absence of physical disease with neurological changes, the diagnosis becomes almost a routine. Surveying the patients in a large mental hospital, Duncan, Penrose and Turnbull (1936)[7] found that one-third of the patients on admission to hospital had been diagnosed schizophrenic. Among patients who had been on the hospital books for twenty years, however, more than two-thirds were so diagnosed.

3

Onset

The onset of the disease can be insidious or acute and the age at which this occurs shows wide variation, ranging from five to sixty years. Onset is earlier in males than in females. Swedish investigators have shown convincingly that the mean age of onset for males is twenty-seven years and that for females, thirty-one years. The age on first admission to hospital has shown a similar sex difference. In a very large series of cases first admitted to the New York State Hospital, Malzberg (1935)[34] gave 31·8 years as the mean age for schizophrenic males and 36·5 for schizophrenic females. In a series of patients admitted to the Ontario Mental Hospitals, 1926 to 1944, each selected by having at least one relative also known to have been admitted to such hospitals, and counted once again for each affected relative, 1605 male schizophrenics had a mean first admission age of 31·4 and 1747 females a first admission age of 35·3 (Penrose 1945).[38] This implies that onset commonly precedes admission to hospital by about four years. From the point of view of genetical investigation, the age of onset data are obviously of great interest and it is astonishing that Kallmann (1938)[26] in his extensive survey, failed to make any analysis of this nor did he separate male patients from females. An important corollary to the observation of the earlier onset in males than in females is that, in instances where the disease develops very early in life (a condition known to Kraepelin as *dementia praecocissima* and, often, to the present generation, as severe autism), is more frequent in boys than in girls.

4

Relationship to Affective Psychoses

A converse picture, with respect to age of onset, is shown by the group of illnesses classified under the heading of affective psychoses. Among hospital admissions, patients with affective disorders, including manic depressive psychosis and involutional depression, constitute nearly as large a number as do those with schizophrenia. Like schizophrenia, affective states are not characteristically associated with physical illness but they involve less distortion of the personality than schizophrenia and remissions are expected. The onset tends to be about ten years later on in life than in patients diagnosed schizophrenic. Males have later onset than females and, in agreement with this fact, female patients with this diagnosis are more numerous than male patients (Malzberg, 1935).[34]

The distinction between the schizophrenic and affective types of mental disease is often supposed to be absolute but the same patient is rarely observed over a long period, say twenty years, by the same physician. Indeed it is striking how many patients who are mentally ill for very large parts of their lives come to exhibit more and more symptoms of schizophrenia, even though they may have originally been diagnosed as manic depressive.

In families investigated by pupils of Rüdin, such as Kahn (1923)[25] and Hoffmann (1921),[21] a wide spectrum of different diagnoses was found among groups of close relatives. Some later studies have tended to show that, although diagnoses overlap to some extent, there is a fairly high degree of correspondence between the type of psychotic illness which is diagnosed in sibs and in parent and child pairs. Indeed Hallgren and Sjögren considered that the occurrence of affective disease in families of schizophrenics was no more frequent than would have been expected on a chance basis. This result may depend upon the restriction of the index cases to a type which was as homogeneous as possible. If the general run of mental patients are studied and the diagnoses listed as they were made by the physicians in charge, no genetically restricted group of schizophrenics is found. Within families, disparate diagnoses are frequent. In the sample of familial instances collected from the Ontario Mental Hospitals (Penrose 1945),[38] the tendency for the same diagnosis to be made in parent and child was subject to many exceptions, as can be seen in Table 1. Similar

TABLE 1

Psychotic offspring of psychotic parents classified by diagnosis.

Parents	Schizophrenic	Offspring Affective	Total
Schizophrenic	150	34	184
Affective	205	232	437
Total	355	266	621

results have been obtained by other investigators in smaller samples (Tsuang, 1967).[46] It is also important to note that there are, proportionately, far fewer parents than offspring diagnosed as schizophrenic. This is an indication of the greatly reduced fertility of schizophrenics, that is to say of severe cases of mental illness with early onset, which has often been commented upon (Essen-Möller, 1935;[8] MacSorley, 1964[33]).

The uncertainty of diagnosis and the overlapping of symptomatology in the so-called endogenous mental illnesses has led many psychiatrists, for example Adolf Meyer, to disregard the idea that the clinical symptoms constitute diseases and to classify psychotic syndromes as types of reaction (Mayer-Gross, Slater and Roth, 1954).[35] The study of genetics in this field would then be concerned with the inheritance of reaction type. Schizophrenia in this sense is a reaction type which mainly characterizes mental illness with early onset. To a considerable extent the uncertainties of differential clinical diagnosis between schizophrenia and the affective psychoses can then be eliminated by emphasis on the age of onset of the disease. Moreover, there are some conditions of quite late onset, sometimes considered as senile psychoses, which are found in close relatives of schizophrenics and which might be regarded as genetically comparable. Analysis of likeness of diagnosis in affected relatives can thus be transposed into comparative analysis of age of onset.

5

Age of Onset Analysis

Correlations of age of onset within families were first calculated by Bell (1934)[1] for Huntington's chorea and some other neurological conditions. The value obtained for Huntington's chorea, for parent and child, was about 0·5 and Haldane (1941)[13] interpreted this as indicating that modifications causing early or late onset were genetical in character. The modifying

TABLE 2

Correlation coefficients showing degrees of likeness of onset age in pairs of psychotic relatives.

Type of pair	No. of pairs	Correlation coefficient	Standard error
Father-Son	415	0·30	0·04
Father-Daughter	422	0·33	0·04
Mother-Son	461	0·44	0·04
Mother-Daughter	430	0·39	0·04
Brother-Brother	622	0·59	0·03
Brother-Sister	1063	0·50	0·02
Sister-Sister	648	0·54	0·03
Paternal Uncle-Nephew	153	0·29	0·07
Paternal Aunt-Nephew	115	0·14	0·09
Paternal Uncle-Niece	154	0·23	0·08
Paternal Aunt-Niece	129	0·32	0·08
Maternal Uncle-Nephew	162	0·48	0·06
Maternal Aunt-Nephew	147	0·28	0·08
Maternal Uncle-Niece	148	0·41	0·07
Maternal Aunt-Niece	149	0·39	0·07

genes, however, were considered to be separate from the main hereditary cause. Haldane also pointed out that, if there were several different alleles involved, one allele causing an early onset disease type and another a late onset type, this correlation should be much higher (e.g. 0·90). It should also be noted that high onset age correlations would be obtained if entirely different diseases, each with its characteristic onset age, were grouped together in the same material.

Onset age correlations in familial mental illness, irrespective of diagnosis, were calculated (Penrose, 1945)[38] from extensive hospital records using first admission age as a substitute for age when symptoms began. The results are summarized in Table 2.

On the whole, the results are consistent with the assumption that there is one or more main hereditary factor involved and also with the assumption that there are hereditary modifying factors which influence age of onset. Since the parent-child correlations are considerably lower than the sib-pair correlations, recessivity in the inheritance of the reaction types themselves or of the modifying influence is indicated. The relatively low values of the father-son and brother-sister coefficients suggest the possibility that genes located on the X-chromosome, and possibly also on the Y-chromosome, are strong contributory influences. The high correlation values for brother-brother pairs and for sister-sister pairs also suggest that a substantial number of cases could be the result of single abnormal genes located on the sex chromosomes. The low correlation for the paternal aunt-nephew group of pairs, together with the comparatively small numbers ascertained in this relationship, supports the same conclusion. The paternal aunt and nephew can have neither an inherited X nor a Y chromosome in common. The hypothesis of sex-linked gene influence would account for the excess of male psychotics with young onset age, i.e. male cases of early schizophrenia or dementia praecocissima.

In all such analyses as these, the warning emphasized by Jackson (1960)[23] is valid, namely that familial concentration, when not demonstrably Mendelian in character, can be, to a large extent, most naturally attributed to environmental influences. Whenever there is evidence which points to genetical modification of inherited predispositions, it is likely that environment can also be an influence. A gene effect, which can be altered by the presence of another gene, may also be altered by external factors. A striking feature of the analysis of familial cases of mental illness and, in particular, the schizophrenic type, is the predominance of inheritance through the mother, shown both in the parent-child pairs and uncle-, aunt-niece, -nephew pairs. There are more cases with mental disease apparently inherited through the mother and, when so transmitted, it tends to be especially true to type. An obvious explanation of this phenomenon is to assume that the mother's mental reactions have more effect on forming those of the child than the father's. If a genetical hypothesis were sought, however, for the same peculiarity, the influence of inherited cytoplasmic factors on the mental reaction type could be considered as a rather remote possibility.

One further point about onset age and its genetical significance may be mentioned here and that is the phenomenon of anticipation in successive generations. It has been consistently found that the age of onset is later in parents, and later still in grandparents, than in the patient when more than one generation in a family is affected. The converse applies to children and grandchildren of patients. In Table 3 this effect is clearly shown if age on first admission is again accepted as a substitute for age of onset. A precise parallel to these mean ages is shown in the proportion of relatives diagnosed schizophrenic. This proportion is much smaller in members of earlier than of later generations. Formerly these phenomena were attributed to progressive worsening of the hereditary taint (Mott, 1910)[36] but this assumption is unnecessary. An inevitable tendency to ascertain pairs of affected cases during the same period of time, within a decade or two, tends to exclude examples in which the parent, uncle of grandparent has early onset and the child, nephew or grandchild has late onset (Penrose, 1948).[39] The effect is intensified by the comparatively low fertility of cases in which there is early onset of the disease, as occurs in association with the diagnosis of schizophrenia.

TABLE 3

Mean age on first admission and diagnosis of schizophrenia in different affected relatives.

Type of relative	No. of cases	No. schizophrenic	Percentage schizophrenic	Mean age on admission	S.D.
Grandfather	125	12	9·6	55·2	11·8
Father	837	72	8·6	54·0	14·0
Uncle	617	172	27·9	44·9	16·6
Brother	2307	743	32·2	38·0	16·6
Son	876	315	36·0	33·1	16·1
Nephew	577	236	40·9	30·8	13·5
Grandson	122	53	43·4	24·6	11·6
Total males	5461	1603	29·4	39·7	17·5
Grandmother	113	24	21·2	55·2	14·3
Mother	891	222	24·9	47·2	14·5
Aunt	540	150	27·8	44·7	15·5
Sister	2359	796	33·7	39·5	15·8
Daughter	852	275	32·3	35·4	15·4
Niece	580	234	40·3	32·3	13·2
Granddaughter	116	46	39·7	25·2	11·6
Total females	5451	1747	32·0	39·9	16·2

6

Familial Concentration

A common method of studying the genetics of schizophrenia has been to take a group of index cases and to find the incidence of the same condition in relatives—sibs, parents, children, uncles, aunts, etc. The incidence in each group is then compared with that in the general population. Apart from the problem of recognizing the same disease in relatives, the ascertainment of population figures presents almost insuperable difficulties. Many estimates have, however, been made of the risk of developing schizophrenia among people who live through the critical age range of fifteen to forty-five years. Usually, in such calculations, no distinction is made between the risks for males and for females and cases of early and late onset are not distinguished. Luxenburger (1936)[32] gave a general figure of 0·85 per cent for the risk and Fremming (1947)[10] gave 0·72 per cent for Germany and 0·90 for Bornholm (Denmark).

The important index which can be ascertained from this type of investigation is the ratio of the risk of the disease in patients' relatives as compared with the risk in the general population. That is to say, if the risk for a brother or sister is 10 per cent and that for the general population one per cent, the ratio, which can be called K (Penrose, 1953),[40] would be 10. Analysis can be carried out by considering separately parents, sibs, identical or fraternal twins, children or other relatives of the schizophrenic propositi. Different degrees of disease risk have been observed which correspond with different degrees of relationship. On the whole, results of surveys by a great variety of observers are fairly consistent. The examples given in Table 4 are fairly typical.

TABLE 4

Percentage incidence of schizophrenia in relatives of schizophrenics.

Source	Identical twin	Fraternal twin	Parent	Sib	Population control
Luxenburger (1936)	67	—	—	—	0·8
Kallmann (1946)	69	10	9	10	—
Slater & Shields (1953)	76	14	—	5	—
Hallgren & Sjögren (1959)	—	—	1	6	0·2
Böök (1953)	—	—	12	11	—

A genetical interpretation, which is commonly given to results of this kind, is that there is a predisposing factor which could be a single gene or a combination of genes. The hypotheses of multiple gene predisposition which have been advocated are very inexact. They do not differentiate between two and 100 loci and they neglect to explain the type of interaction of the theoretical genes. It is not known whether the genes act together additively or alternately nor whether the separate genes, which contribute, are recessive or intermediate in their effects. It is therefore reasonable, in the first instance, to see how far the hypothesis of a single gene locus is adequate and this can be done by applying simple tests.

Clearly there is no Mendelian system to be detected which will cover the majority of cases. This solution was expected by the earliest investigators of familial schizophrenia but they were soon disillusioned. Kahn (1923)[25] remarked rather pathetically that, in his material, he had not succeeded in finding Mendelian ratios. It thus became usual to assume that the gene for schizophrenia produced a predisposition. Sometimes the effect was psychotic illness. In other instances the predisposed person had a schizoid temperament only and occasionally he might be quite unaffected. The view taken by Böök (1953),[5] that the predisposition is a single gene effect with manifestation in 1/5 of the heterozygotes and all the homozygotes, can be regarded as typical. A theory which might be advanced would attribute schizophrenia to the homozygote and affective psychosis to the heterozygote of the same abnormal gene. The onset age of the homozygote would then be much earlier than that of the heterozygote. This type of inheritance has been discussed in relation to the familial incidence of diabetes, where age of onset is a critical factor. The same suggestion has never been seriously considered as an explanation of onset age variations in mental diseases. In neither diabetes nor mental illness does the theory agree very well with known facts but it may apply in some families.

A single gene recessive hypothesis is in keeping with the observation that the incidence of the disease is greater in sibs than in parents. It is also in agreement with evidence that cousin marriages in parents slightly increase the likelihood of schizophrenia in the offspring (Munro, 1938;[37] Hallgren and Sjögren, 1959;[14] Hanhart, 1965[16]). Raised parental consanguinity rates are noticeable when a recessive trait is rare, that is with a population frequency of less than 1/1000. Although consanguinity has been found to be more frequent in parents of mental hospital patients than of general hospital patients, inspection of particular cases indicates that the increase may be the result of inclusion of a few patients with rare atypical psychoses with recessive origins. If the schizophrenic reaction has its basis in a single homozygous recessive state, it is far too common to be associated with any appreciable increase of parental inbreeding.

It is worth while noting one special genetical conclusion which must follow from the recessive hypothesis. In consequence of the very low fertility of schizophrenic patients, the condition would gradually die out if the abnormal gene were not continually replaced by recurrent mutation. The rate of fresh mutation can be estimated to be between 1 in 200 and 1 in 2000 per gamete per generation (Böök, 1953;[5] Penrose, 1956[41]). This is much too high a figure to be acceptable in view of the evidence for mutation rates of other human genes which is of the order of 1 in 100,000 per gamete per generation. For this reason alone the recessive hypothesis cannot be regarded as satisfactory.

The next point to be considered is that the incidence of schizophrenia in sibs does not appear to approach the Mendelian ratio of one quarter which would be required if the disease were a homozygous condition. Figures of 5 to 11 per cent could only be consistent with this if most affected sibs had not yet developed the condition at the time of investigation. The possibility, however, should be mentioned that the observed ratios underestimate the true values because of a statistical artefact, first studied by Weinberg (1912),[47] which results from the mode of collecting the data. As Fisher (1934)[9] showed, the incidence of a familial trait in the sibs of propositi is an accurate measurement if the likelihood of the sibship's being included in the data depends upon the number of affected sibs. Otherwise it gives only a minimal estimate. Weinberg's correction may nearly double the observed value. Even if this correction were made, the estimated ratios would still not reach 25 per cent. It seems necessary, therefore, to assume that the basic hereditary predisposition is incompletely manifested.

If the assumption is made that there is a genetical causal factor, certain conclusions about its frequency in the general population can be inferred from the observation of K-values. This is a useful test because the K-value is independent of manifestation and of environmental influences for these effects can, in theory, be the same both for patients' relatives and members of the general population. On the supposition that the incidence of schizophrenia in both sibs and parents of patients is ten times that in the population ($K = 10$), the gene frequency can be inferred to be 2·7 per cent if half the heterozygotes and all the homozygotes are equally predisposed. In general, the population gene frequency is approximately $\frac{1}{4}K$. If the trait were fully dominant, the inferred population frequency would be almost the same. Recessive inheritance is suggested if the incidence in parents is lower than in sibs, as in the data of Hallgren and Sjögren. In that material the values of K are 5 and 12 for parents and sibs respectively and this would lead to an inferred gene frequency in the population of about 20 per cent.

These inferred gene frequencies imply predisposition frequencies of an order much higher than usually supposed and also exceedingly high mutation rates. They emphasize the unsatisfactory nature of any single gene explanation. Examination of the possibility of a predisposition caused by multiple additive genes leads to rather more credible results. That is to say, if K is of the order of 10 in parents and sibs, the predisposition frequency, which, for perfectly additive genes, can replace the gene frequency, must be 1·5 per cent in the population. If K were greater, the incidence of the predisposition would be lower, perhaps below 1 per cent, which approximates to the recorded observations on the incidence of the disease. However, this inference would not be satisfactory unless it were assumed that all predisposed people eventually developed the condition.

7

Twins

The study of twins has a fascination of its own besides providing a more direct attack on the problem of environmental influences than any other method. There are, however, important limitations seldom emphasized by enthusiasts. The most important of these is that twins are anomalous in themselves. Inferences which may be valid for twin pairs may not be valid for single births. However, limiting results are obtainable with some confidence. Thus, it appears that, judging from data on identical twin pairs, a significant proportion of the twins of schizophrenics are unaffected. This can be interpreted as indicating that, in general, environment certainly has a minimal effect in the aetiology of the disease. The effect may, of course, be much greater in a particular case.

The incidence of affected identical twins of index cases can be taken as a measure of manifestation of the underlying genetical predisposition. This interpretation can give additional information enabling the consistency of observed and inferred incidence figures in the general population to be checked. If it is assumed that the degree of manifestation, M, is the same for identical twins as for other relatives, the likely incidence of the disease in parents, sibs and the general population can be compared by taking any desired value for gene frequency, q. In Table 5, the general formulae for a recessive trait are given and also calculated expectations on the assumption that $M = 2/3$ and $q = 1/10$.

TABLE 5

Percentage incidence of a recessive trait with manifestation, M, in different relatives where for example, q = 1/10, M = 2/3.

Identical twin	Parent	Sib or fraternal twin	Population
$100M$	$100Mq$	$100M(1+q)^2/4$	$100Mq^2$
67	7	20	0·7

If, in the figures given by Kallmann,[27] the observed incidence is doubled, there is fair agreement. This shows that there was some formal justification for Kallmann's belief that schizophrenia could be a recessive trait provided that the necessary supplementary assumptions about manifestation and ascertainment could be upheld. No other survey results, however, can be matched in this way by such a simple assumption.

One striking piece of twin investigation, by Kallmann and Roth (1956),[28] gives much more information than usual and thus exposes complexities in the problem concealed by cruder summaries. Fifty-two index cases were selected by very young onset age, mostly between five and fourteen years. There were thirty-seven male and fifteen female index cases, showing typical male excess in that age group. Among the forty-one affected co-twins and sibs ascertained, a great majority, i.e. thirty-four, also had onset before the age of fifteen years. Of the monozygotic co-twins altogether 15/17 were affected but only 8/35 dizygotic co-twins and 18/199 sibs. The investigation strongly indicates that schizophrenia of early onset is familial. Unfortunately, the sexes of affected sibs were not listed by the writers and nothing can be inferred about the mode of any supposed inheritance.

A virtue of this study is that the age of onset is made use of as a criterion for aiding diagnosis. The more complete twin study by Slater and Shields (1953)[44] carefully separates onset age and sex of the twin propositi diagnosed schizophrenic and they came to the important conclusion that, when the disease arose late in life, it might take the form of involutional depression. Altogether the age of onset for identical twins, which had a 76 per cent concordance, had a correlation value of 0·54.

As in twin studies concerned with other diseases, the investigation of schizophrenic twins leads to the conclusion that the trait under consideration is strongly genetically determined. The twin method, however, gives no information about the type of inheritance or its mode of action. The material collected on schizophrenia has been enormous, as indicated by the summary given by Gottesman and Shields (1966),[12] but the varying 'concordance' rate of identical twins, from 25 to 30 per cent in some sources to 80 or 90 per cent in others, should warn investigators that nothing final, even about the relative significance of heredity and environment, can be established by using this method.

8

Biochemical Genetics

An entirely different approach, which may eventually solve the problem of genetics in schizophrenia, depends on the assumption that hereditary predisposition is expressed in metabolic errors. In mental deficiency, the recognition of conditions, like phenylketonuria and histidinaemia, has enabled definite genetical entities to be extracted from what was previously an undifferentiated disease group. Similar results could follow the identification of biochemical errors characteristic of mental illnesses. It can be confidently supposed that Huntington's chorea is caused by a biochemical error in which there is gradual deterioration of cerebral cells, perhaps related to the accumulation of abnormal waste products of metabolism. The Alzheimer-Pick disease group might be expected to follow the same kind of pattern. In the case of schizophrenia, however, no such immediate simplification seems possible.

In spite of an enormous number of investigations, no firm relevant biochemical discoveries have been made. This failure is partly the consequence of an orientation of investigations which is, from the genetical viewpoint, unprofitable. Thus, the monumental work of Gjessing (1947)[11] was devoted to the search for metabolic changes which were not inborn but which were associated with acute mental illness and which would disappear on recovery. Abnormal biochemistry of electrolytes in the blood, of nitrogen balance, of basal metabolism, of serum cholinesterol, or of glucose tolerance—these readings do not give direct evidence of genetical peculiarities in the manner that tests for abnormal urinary metabolites may do. Yet tests for abnormal metabolites in schizophrenics have not, so far, given very helpful information.

An interesting recent example of such an attempt concerns the so-called 'pink spot', thought to be characteristic and identified as 3,4-dimethoxyphenylethylamine (DMPE). The structure of this substance is similar to that of the hallucinogenic drug, mescaline. Subsequently, however, Kuehl, Ormond and Vandenheuval (1966)[31] showed that the compound was probably 3,4-dimethoxyphenylacetic acid, a substance excreted equally by schizophrenic patients and by normal controls. Other investigators have confirmed that it is unlikely that DMPE excretion has any significant association with schizophrenia.

There have been many other attacks on the problem of finding a specific metabolite or protein in schizophrenia. A persistent idea is that the serum of a patient must contain an abnormal substance. For example, Hoffer, Osmond and Smythies (1954)[20] believed that a naturally-occurring substance, adrenochrome, which is unstable but toxic and hallucinogenic in large quantities, might be produced in excess. No genetical studies appear to have followed from these observations and the excess in schizophrenics of this substance has not been consistently confirmed. A substance named 'taraxein', a protein fraction extractable from the serum of schizophrenics, is believed, by Heath, Leach and Byers (1963),[18] to be toxic and to cause catatonic symptoms if injected into *Rhesus* monkeys or human subjects. The substance is thought to be a special form of ceruloplasmin but, since ceruloplasmin concentration is very sensitive to the ascorbic acid level in the blood, its excess in some schizophrenics may simply be the result of dietary defect (Kety, 1960).[29] In further work, by Heath and Krupp (1967),[17] attention has been focused on the possibility that schizophrenics develop auto-immune responses to their own proteins. This idea is in agreement with that of Burch (1964)[6] who considers that somatic mutational events produce an auto-antibody which affects certain brain cells. There has been, again, no attempt to make any critical investigations into the hereditary aspects of the phenomenon.

Another approach is to search for a deficiency on the assumption that it might be the expression of inborn enzyme defect. Bogoch (1957)[4] found an inverse relationship between severity of psychotic illness and the amount of glycoprotein neuraminic acid in the CSF of schizophrenic patients but there was, naturally, no attempt made to test for neuraminic acid deficiency in relatives. Positive results would be difficult to obtain because, on recovery, the level tended to rise to normal. The blood is a tissue more suitable as a tool for genetical study than the CSF and Sullivan, Frohman, Beckett and Gottlieb (1967)[45] have investigated the ratio of lactic to pyruvic acid in chicken erythrocytes when they are metabolized with blood plasma from schizophrenic patients, from their brothers and sisters and from normal controls. Unfortunately, no peculiarities of this ratio were found in the patients' sibs although, in chronic schizophrenics, it tends to be higher than in normals.

This list of inconclusive or negative results could be continued almost indefinitely. There are, however, some interesting observations, which have not received much attention, concerning the sex hormones in schizophrenic patients. As pointed out by Hemphill (1944),[19] endocrine abnormalities can be readily demonstrated in schizophrenics. Hoskins and Pincus (1949)[22] showed that the male sex hormone level was relatively low in a series of male schizophrenic patients. The genetical significance of such findings is not clear. Noteworthy in this context is the large amount of information which has become recently available concerning the liability of patients with sex chromosome aberrations (particularly XXY and XYY males and X females) to develop mental illness. These illnesses are usually chronic and, in the absence of cytological knowledge, might easily be classified as schizophrenic in reaction type (Price, Strong, Whatmore and McClemont, 1966;[43] Hambert, 1966[15]). The study of the genetics of these cases belongs to the general field of chromosomal aberration with emphasis on non-disjunction in the paternal or maternal germ cells. At present there is very little knowledge of causes but age of the mother is one important factor (Penrose, 1964);[42] virus infections and toxic drugs are suspected in some cases as causes of non-disjunction. Thus, a powerful approach is here indicated which could lead to selection, from the undifferentiated group of patients with schizophrenic diagnosis, of some patients with specific diseases.

9

Conclusions

1. Schizophrenia is a diagnosis which is made on mental symptoms; it does not define one specific disease any more than does the diagnosis of mental deficiency or of epilepsy.
2. The schizophrenic diagnosis is a very unsuitable trait to form the basis of genetical study. By restricting the study to chronic and severe cases or to those of very early onset, useful information has been obtained.

3. The differentiation between schizophrenia, affective and other types of psychotic reaction is not precise. This difficulty can be overcome by using age of onset, which can be subjected to metrical treatment, instead of diagnosis, in family investigations.

4. Many studies have been made on twins selected by a diagnosis of schizophrenia in one or both members of the pair. Little can be directly inferred from them except that heredity and environment both enter into the causation of the diseases studied.

5. The results obtained by all the different methods of investigation employed lead to some conclusions. Strict Mendelian inheritance has not been found. In some cases, schizophrenia may be a single recessive trait. In others, the genetical background is multifactorial. Sex-linked genes probably have important effects, either as major causes in particular cases or as modifying influences.

6. Inborn biochemical errors may eventually be found which enable specific diseases which lead to schizophrenic illness to be identified. So far, the results of biochemical tests have failed to find any peculiarity which is specific to the diagnosis.

7. Sex chromosomal aberrations, such as those which produce Turner's and Klinefelter's syndromes, are occasionally found in association with mental illnesses with schizophrenic symptoms. In this way a group of cases with specific genetical predisposition has been isolated from previously undifferentiated schizophrenics.

REFERENCES

1. BELL, J., 1934. Huntington's chorea. *Treas. hum. Inherit.*, **4**, Pt 1.
2. BLEULER, E., 1911. Dementia Praecox oder Gruppe der Schizophrenine. *Aschaffenburgs Handbuch der Psychiatrie.*
3. 1912. Das autistische Denken. *Jb. f. Psychoan. Psychopath. Forsch.* **4**, 1.
4. BOGOCH, S., 1957. Cerebrospinal fluid neuraminic acid deficiency in schizophrenia: a preliminary report. *Amer. J. Psychiat.*, **114**, 172.
5. BÖÖK, J. A., 1953. A genetic and neuropsychiatric investigation of a North-Swedish population with special regard to schizophrenia and mental deficiency. *Acta genet.*, **4**, 1, 133, 345.
6. BURCH, P. R. J., 1964. Schizophrenia: some new aetiological considerations. *Brit. J. Psychiat.*, **110**, 818.
7. DUNCAN, A. G., PENROSE, L. S., and TURNBULL, R. C., 1936. A survey of the patients in a large mental hospital. *J. Neurol. Psychopathol.*, **16**, 225.
8. ESSEN-MÖLLER, E., 1935. Die Fruchtbarkeit gewisser Gruppen von Geisteskranken. *Acta Psychiat. Neurol.*, Supp. 8.
9. FISHER, R. A., 1934. The effect of method of ascertainment upon the estimation of frequencies. *Ann. Eugen., Lond.,* **6**, 13.
10. FREMMING, K., 1947. *Morbid risk of mental diseases and other mental abnormalities in an average Danish population.* Copenhagen: Munksgaard.
11. GJESSING, R., 1947. Biological investigations in endogenous psychoses. *Acta Psychiat., Kbh.*, Supp. 47, p. 93.

12. GOTTESMAN, I. I., and SHIELDS, J. (1966). Schizophrenia in twins: 16 years' consecutive admissions to a psychiatric clinic. *Brit. J. Psychiat.*, **112**, 809.
13. HALDANE, J. B. S., 1941. The relative importance of principal and modifying genes in determining some human diseases. *J. Genet.*, **41**, 149.
14. HALLGREN, B., and SJÖGREN, T., 1959. *A clinical and genetico-statistical study of schizophrenia and low grade mental deficiency in a large Swedish rural population.* Copenhagen: Munksgaard.
15. HAMBERT, G., 1966. *Males with positive sex chromatin.* Göteborg: Scandinavian University Books.
16. HANHART, E., 1965. Die genetischen Problem der Schizophrenien. *Acta Genet. Med. Gemell.*, **14**, 13.
17. HEATH, R. G., and KRUPP, I. M. (1967). Schizophrenia as an immunologic disorder. I. Demonstration of antibrain globulins by fluorescent antibody techniques. *Arch. gen. Psychiat.*, **16**, 1.
18. HEATH, R. G., LEACH, B. E., and BYERS, L. W., 1963. Taraxein: mode of action. *Serological fractions in schizophrenia.* New York: P. B. Hoebner Inc.
19. HEMPHILL, R. E., 1944. Endocrinology in clinical psychiatry. *J. ment. Sci.*, **90**, 410.
20. HOFFER, A., OSMOND, M., and SMYTHIES, J., 1954. Schizophrenia: a new approach. II. Results of a year's research. *J. ment. Sci.*, **100**, 29.
21. HOFFMANN, H., 1921. *Die Nachkommenschaft bei endogenen Psychosen.* Berlin: J. Springer.
22. HOSKINS, R. G., and PINCUS, G., 1949. Sex hormone relationships in schizophrenic men. *Psychosomat. Med.*, **11**, 10.2.
23. JACKSON, D. D., 1960. A critique of the literature on the genetics of schizophrenia. *The Etiology of schizophrenia*, p. 37. New York: Basic Books Inc.
24. JUNG, C. G., 1915. *Diagnostische Assoziationsstudien.* Leipzig: J. A. Barth.
25. KAHN, E., 1923. *Schizoid and Schizophrenie im Erbgang.* Berlin: J. Springer.
26. KALLMANN, F. J., 1938. *The genetics of schizophrenia.* New York: J. J. Augustin.
27.   1946. The genetic theory of schizophrenia. An analysis of 691 twin index families. *Smer. J. Psychiat.*, **103**, 309.
28. KALLMANN, F. J., and ROTH, B., 1956. Genetic aspects of preadolescent schizophrenia. *Amer. J. Psychiat.*, **112**, 599.
29. KETY, S. S., 1960. Recent biochemical theories of schizophrenia. *The etiology of schizophrenia*, p. 120. New York: Basic Books Inc.
30. KRAEPELIN, E., 1919. *Dementia praecox and paraphrenia.* Trs. R. M. Barclay. Edinburgh: E. & S. Livingstone.
31. KUEHL, F. A., ORMOND, R. E., and VANDENHEUVAL, W. J. A., 1966. Occurrence of 3, 4-dimethoxyphenylacetic acid in urines of normal and schizophrenic individuals. *Nature, Lond.*, **211**, 606.
32. LUXENBURGER, H., 1936. Untersuchung an schizophrenien Zwillingen und ihren Geschwistern zur Prüfung der Realität von Manifestation-schwankungen. *Zts. Neurol. Psychiat.*, **154**, 351.
33. MACSORLEY, K., 1964. An investigation into the fertility rates of mentally ill patients. *Ann. hum. Genet., Lond.*, **27**, 247.
34. MALZBERG, B., 1935. A statistical study of age in relation to mental disease. *Ment. Hyg.*, **19**, 449.
35. MAYER-GROSS, W., SLATER, E., and ROTH, M., 1954. *Clinical psychiatry.* London: Cassell & Co.
36. MOTT, F. W., 1910. The Huxley lecture on hereditary aspects of nervous and mental disease. *Brit. med. J.*, **2**, 1013.
37. MUNRO, T. A., 1938. Consanguinity and mental disorder. *J. ment. Sci.*, **84**, 708.
38. PENROSE, L. S., 1945. Survey of cases of familial mental illness. *Digest Neurol. Psychiat.*, **13**, 644.

39. 1948. The problem of anticipation in pedigrees of dystrophia myotonica. *Ann. Eugen., Lond.*, **14**, 125.

40. 1953. The genetical background of common diseases. *Acta genet.*, **4**, 257.

41. 1956. Estimate of the incidence of cases of schizophrenia and manic depressive reaction due to spontaneous mutation. *Hazards to man of nuclear and allied radiations*—Appendix E., p. 96. London: H.M.S.O.

42. 1964. Review of *Abnormalities of the sex chromosome complement in man. Ann. hum. Genet., Lond.*, **28**, 199.

43. PRICE, W. H., STRONG, J. A., WHATMORE, P. B., and McCLEMONT, W. F., 1966. Criminal patients with XYY sex-chromosome complement. *Lancet*, i, 565.

44. SLATER, E., and SHIELDS, J., 1953. Psychotic and neurotic illnesses in twins. *Med. Res. Coun. Spec. Rep. Ser.* No. 278. London: H.M.S.O.

45. SULLIVAN, T. M., FROHMAN, C. E., BECKETT, P. G. S., and GOTTLIEB, J. S., 1967. Clinical and biochemical studies of families of schizophrenic patients. *Amer. J. Psychiat.*, **123**, 947.

46. TSUANG, M.-T., 1967. A study of pairs of sibs both hospitalized for mental disorder. *Brit. J. Psychiat.*, **113**, 282.

47. WEINBERG, W., 1912. Methode und Fehlerquellen der Untersuchung auf Mendelsche Zahlen beim Menschen. *Arch. Rass. u. Ges. Biol.*, **9**, 165.

II

THE SIGNIFICANCE OF NUCLEAR SEXING

Murray L. Barr

M.D., F.R.S.C., F.R.C.P.(C)

Professor of Anatomy
University of Western Ontario, London, Canada

1

Introduction

One of the significant developments in cytology in recent years is concerned with the imprint made by the sex chromosome complex on the chromatin pattern of interphase or resting nuclei of cells. The basic observation is that in the female, whose cells have an XX sex chromosome complex, the cell nuclei contain a special mass of chromatin—the sex chromatin—which is lacking in nuclei of males, who have an XY sex chromosome complex. The usefulness of the sex chromatin as a guide to the nature of the sex chromosome complex extends beyond the normal XX and XY pairs. When sex chromosome abnormalities are included, the complex varies from XO (X-nothing) to XXXXY. The number of sex chromatin masses in a resting nucleus depends on the number of X chromosomes that are present, following the rule that one X chromosome in each nucleus is invisible, i.e. it does not appear as sex chromatin, for reasons that will be described presently. The presence or absence of a Y chromosome does not affect the sex chromatin pattern, but the clinical examination often enables one to judge whether or not the masculinizing Y chromosome forms part of the individual's sex chromosome complex.

Fortunately, the sex chromatin pattern can be determined by a simple procedure, the buccal smear test, which is applicable to large scale surveys of various kinds of populations, as well as to individuals under investigation. When a sex chromatin pattern is found that is at variance with the predominant sexual characteristics of the individual or abnormal in some other respect, the chromosomes themselves should be examined to verify the complex that is inferred from the buccal smear test in combination with the findings on clinical examination.

The principles and applications of 'nuclear sexing' are pertinent to the broad field of psychiatry because an abnormal sex chromosome complex carries with it an increased risk of mental retardation, the risk varying according to the particular sex chromosome anomaly. There are, in addition, other psychological aberrations that are in need of further study.

2

The Sex Chromatin

The intelligent use of nuclear sexing in clinical medicine, whether in the context of psychiatry, endocrinology, paediatrics or any other specialty, depends on an understanding of the sex chromatin. This has been presented by the author in some detail elsewhere.[7] The following summary will suffice to establish the significance of the sex chromatin as a diagnostic aid when dealing with certain individuals who are of interest to the psychiatrist.

Development of Nuclear Sexing Methods and Concepts

The psychiatrist may be interested in recalling that the sex difference in cell nuclei was first demonstrated in neurones, although these cells are not used in clinical studies for obvious reasons. In the course of experiments involving hypoglossal neurones in the brain stem of the cat, Barr and Bertram[8] noted that neuronal nuclei of females contained a special mass of chromatin material which was lacking in males. Within the next few years, a series of studies showed that the sex difference in cell nuclei was a cytological characteristic in various tissues and organs of carnivores and primates. Human tissues,[70] including the neurones of nervous tissues,[13, 14, 79] proved to be suitable for identification of sex chromatin as a female cytological marker, thus paving the way for the clinical application of the sex chromatin test.

Several years elapsed before the derivation of the sex chromatin was unravelled. Largely through the studies of Ohno and collaborators on dividing cells of various mammals, including man,[82] it is now clear that in the sex chromatin one is seeing an X chromosome in a highly contracted and condensed state. This means that the single X chromosome of the male's XY complex is too extended (euchromatic) to form a detectable chromatin mass in resting nuclei. The same applies to one of the two X's of the female's XX complex, the other X being, as stated, condensed (heterochromatic or heteropycnotic) and therefore responsible for the sex chromatin marker that is characteristic of cell nuclei of females. (The X chromosomes behave in this way in members of other mammalian orders such as the rodents, but identification of the sex chromatin or heterochromatic X of the female is difficult because of the coarse nature of the nuclear chromatin generally.) The dissimilar behaviour of homologous chromosomes (the XX pair) was a novel and stimulating advance in cytology and genetics. The genetic implications arise from the likelihood that a heterochromatic chromosome is to a large extent inactive, so far as elaborating messenger RNA for the synthesis of specific cytoplasmic enzymes and other proteins is concerned, unlike an euchromatc and genetically active chromosome. This led to the Lyon hypothesis,[55, 56] which deals with X chromosome genetic mosaicism among the cells of tissues and organs of females and which will be alluded to in a later section of this chapter.

Meanwhile, techniques were becoming available for the study of the chromosomes themselves in body cells of man and other mammals.[35, 43, 72, 100] Individuals with more than two X chromosomes (XXX, XXXY, etc.) were soon found; a discussion of the effect of such abnormalities on development, including mental development, will form a substantial part of this chapter. In the present context, the analysis of chromosomes and study of the sex chromatin in persons with supernumerary X's showed that the number of sex chromatin masses was consistently one less than the number of X chromosomes. This was compatible only with the single-X origin of the sex chromatin. During the past few years, nuclear sexing and chromosome analysis have become companion techniques in the study of sex chromosome anomalies.

The Sex Chromatin as Seen with the Microscope

Most nuclei contain particles of basophilic material or chromatin of varying size, in addition to the larger nucleoli. The chromatin particles represent regions here and there on the various chromosomes of the complement, these regions being dense or heterochromatic with respect to other parts of the chromosomes in resting nuclei. The chromatin particles reflect a chromosomal origin in their staining properties. They react strongly to basic dyes because of the desoxyribose (and to a lesser extent ribose) nucleic acid they contain and are stained positively by the Feulgen method, which is specific for DNA. The sex chromatin is essentially a chromatin particle or mass that is female-specific, larger than other chromatin particles and of special significance because it represents all or nearly all of a particular chromosome—one X chromosome.

The condensed X chromosome usually adheres to an intranuclear surface through unknown forces. The only available surfaces are the inner surface of the nuclear membrane and the surface of the nucleolus. The former is the usual location in those animals that have been studied, although the large nucleoli of nerve cells 'attract' the sex chromatin in some species. However, in man the sex chromatin is usually located against the inner surface of the nuclear membrane, even in neurones (Plate I).

The dense X chromosome is sufficiently 'malleable' so that the surface in contact with the nuclear membrane is often a plane one and the free surface is then convex. Its size is 1μ–$1\cdot2\mu$ in the longest dimension. Study of the same cells in the living state in cultures and then after fixation and staining shows that the sex chromatin is not affected materially as to position, size or shape by the reagents of routine fixatives. The small size of the sex chromatin and its dense straining properties make resolution of intrinsic detail difficult. In particularly favourable preparations, the sex chromatin often has an irregular outline and intrinsic pale regions. In fact, its appearance in such preparations is what one would expect of a closely coiled chromosomal thread. In electronmicrographs made from the ultra-thin sections necessary for EM work, fibres, rodlets and circular profiles, all having a diameter of about 200Å, appear to be the only components of the sex chromatin.[106] Similar components, although more densely arranged, are seen in electronmicrographs of metaphase chromosomes.

More on the Derivation of the Sex Chromatin

It was pointed out above that the sex chromatin is a single X chromosome in a tightly coiled or heterochromatic state. This is such a crucial point that elaboration of the basis for the concept seems justified.

During the first few years after the demonstration of sex chromatin, it was thought that both X chromosomes must somehow participate in its formation because dissimilar physical and functional properties between the two X's was not considered as a possibility on the basis of previous experience. However, this possibility had to be considered when Ohno and his co-workers noted that early prophase nuclei of females of several species contained one chromosome that was heterochromatic with respect to the others. This chromosome was compatible in length with an X chromosome and the prior knowledge of a special chromatin mass in resting nuclei of females made the equation of the prophase and interphase observations a logical step.

Confirmation soon came from several sources. It has already been mentioned that the results of sex chromatin tests when correlated with sex chromosome complexes in persons with supernumerary X chromosomes were compatible only with the view that one X is euchromatic and that each additional X chromosome appears at interphase as a separate mass of sex chromatin. Further confirmation came from the use of isotopes and auto-radiography. If tritiated-thymidine is made available to dividing cells in culture, the radioactive compound is incorporated into the chromosomes during the S or synthesis phase of the cell cycle, during which the chromosomes and their constituent DNA molecules replicate in preparation for the next division. In the next metaphase, chromosomes containing tritiated-thymidine can be recognized by silver grains in an overlying photographic emulsion, according to the well established technique of autoradiography. When female cells are studied in this way, one chromosome whose length is that of an X chromosome, is found to replicate later than the others. This chromosome is more radioactive or 'hot' than the remainder in cells that were exposed to tritiated-thymidine near the end of the S phase of the cycle.[40, 95] To carry this line of evidence a step further, the sex chromatin is radioactive in cells exposed to tritiated-thymidine during the latter part of the previous interphase.[16] The X chromosome of man has the same length and other structural characteristics as certain autosomes. Any doubt that the late-replicating chromosome is an X chromosome was dispelled by applying the procedures described above to cultured cells of cattle. The X chromosome of the cow can be distinguished morphologically from all other chromosomes of the complement and one of the X's is clearly the late-labelling element.[76] There seems to be doubt, therefore, that one X of the XX pair behaves differently from its partner and from the non-sex chromosomes or autosomes. This X chromosome has a propensity toward tight coiling of its constituent threads or chromonemata, this physical property being associated with late replication and a visible chromatin mass that is a female cytological characteristic. The phenomen has evolutionary and genetic implications that require some comment.

Properties of the Sex Chromosomes

The chromosome complement of a cell of a human female is illustrated in Plate II and that of the male in Plate III. The chromosomes as they appear at metaphase, or midway through cell division, are illustrated and they are arranged in a conventional manner known as a karyotype. There are twenty-two pairs of non-sex chromosomes or autosomes. They are subject to abnormalities of various kinds, the most common being the presence of an extra chromosome 21 (trisomy-21), which is the cause of mongolism or Langdon-Down's disease. However, our concern is with the sex chromosome pair and with abnormal numbers of sex chromosomes.

The two X chromosomes of the female are shown in Plate II. Each X chromosome, like the other chromosomes of the complement, consists at metaphase of two chromatids or potential daughter chromosomes. The latter are still joined at the centromere, which in the X chromosome is slightly removed from the mid-point so that one arm is longer than the other. The human X chromosome is similar morphologically, although of course not genetically or in certain other properties, with the longer members of the C group of autosomes. The Y chromosome of the male XY complex (Plate III) is much smaller than the X and the centromere is situated close to one end.

No special pair of sex chromosomes can be identified morphologically in amphibia, fish or reptiles; among the vertebrates the XX/XY sex determining mechanism is one of several special features of the mammalian class. It would appear therefore that in the dawn of mammalian evolution, early in the Cenozoic era, one pair of chromosomes became modified in a very special way. To be more precise, the major change occurred in only one member of the pair. Much of this chromosome was lost. In the persisting portion (now called the Y chromosome), genes became concentrated that cause the indifferent gonads of the early embryo to develop as testes. The latter then secrete a hormone or evocator substance which directs further development of the internal and external genitalia along male lines. The Y chromosome is therefore strongly male-determining. It probably contains other gene loci of importance for normal development of the embryo, but they have never been defined.

The chromosome destined to be known as the X chromosome was the conservative member of the pair in evolution. It remained of considerable length and is known to contain many gene loci that have nothing to do with sex determination initially or sex development thereafter. These genes have become recognized for the most part because of the occurrence of mutant gene alleles that cause one or another type of disease or developmental abnormality. It is safe to assume that the normal or wild-type genes, from which the mutants arose, have a significant bearing on development. Results of experiments on rabbit embryos[50] and inferences drawn from errors of sex development in man, indicate that in the absence of embryonal gonads (either ovaries or testes) development of the reproductive tract proceeds along female lines. This is true even though the sex chromosome complex is XY. It is clear therefore that two X chromosomes are not needed for female development in the general sense and one suspects that gene loci among the autosomes are of importance in directing the development of the genital tract in the female direction. In an XO embryo, the ovaries have a normal histological structure, with follicles, during the first half or so of gestation,[98] but follicles are usually absent after birth and such individuals are sterile, with rare exceptions. One way of interpreting the foregoing is to assume that a double dose of certain X-borne gene loci are required for normal development of the mature ovary. In the main, however, the X chromosome is apparently not much different from its premammalian precursor and from its companions in the cell among the autosomes.

X Chromosome Heteropycnosis and the Lyon Hypothesis

Thus far, we have established the appearance of the sex chromatin as viewed in microscopic preparations, together with the fact that it is a heterochromatic X chromosome and that there must be one extended X chromosome in a nucleus before X chromosome heteropycnosis can occur. Certain other facets of X chromosome behaviour are important in relation to the genetic significance of the sex chromatin.

The first points to consider are (i) when X chromosome heteropycnosis first occurs in the developmental history of the female and (ii) whether the X of paternal origin or the X of maternal origin is favoured for the heteropycnotic or heterochromatic role. In so far as primates are concerned, sex chromatin can first be detected in cell nuclei of potentially female macaque embryos between the tenth and nineteenth day of develop-

DIFFERENTIATION OF X CHROMOSOMES IN AN EARLY FEMALE EMBRYO

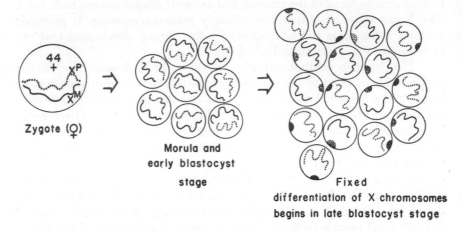

FIG. 1. Diagrammatic representation of the "fixed differentiation" of the paternal X chromosome (X^P) or the maternal X chromosome (X^M) in the early embryo.

ment. In female human embryos the first appearance of sex chromatin is between 12 and 16 days of development.[84] These primate embryos are in the blastocyst stage when one of the female embryo's two X chromosomes assumes the heteropycnotic state (Fig. 1). In the fertilized XX ovum and in the following morula and early blastocyst stage, both X chromosomes are extended, form no special mass of chromatin and are fully active genetically. The activity of both X's of very early female embryos perhaps has some significance for future development, but detailed information on this point is not available. In parenthesis, it may be pointed out that in some animals, notably the rabbit, structural and genetic differentiation between the two members of the XX pair takes place earlier than it does in the primate and can be recognized at the morula stage when the embryo consists of about 400 cells.

It is now generally accepted that either the maternal X (X^M) or the paternal X (X^P) assumes the heteropycnotic role at an early stage of embryogenesis (Fig. 1). Alternative X^M or X^P heteropycnosis, on a chance basis from cell to cell, would seem to be a necessary assumption because if either one were heteropycnotic and inactive in every cell of the body X-borne genes from either the mother or the father would be suppressed throughout the organism. The study of patterns of inheritance of X-borne genetic defects shows that this is not so. Objective cytological evidence that either X^M or X^P is the heteropycnotic, sex chromatin-forming chromosome was provided by an interesting and resourceful study.[77] The hybrid mule has 63 chromosomes, of which 32 are contributed by the maternal horse and 31 by the paternal donkey. The X chromosome of the horse and donkey can be distinguished from each other morphologically. In the female mule, the horse's X chromosome is late-labelling by the tritiated-thymidine and autoradiograph technique in about half of cultured cells and the donkey's X chromosome is late-labelling in the remaining cells.

One further point needs to be established in connection with the genetic implications of the sex chromatin. Once the 'moment of decision' has passed and an X chromosome of the early female embryo is committed to either the euchromatic and active or heterochromatic and inactive role, the X chromosome retains this property in all of its descendants through the very many cell generations that follow throughout the lifetime of the individual. This aspect of X chromosome behaviour, for which there is good cytological evidence, is known as 'fixed X chromosome differentiation'.

These cytological considerations suggest that in a sense the female is a cellular mosaic, X^M being heterochromatic in patches of cells of as yet undetermined size and X^P heterochromatic in other patches of cells. Classical work on insects and plants indicates that heterochromatic chromosomes or regions of chromosomes are genetically inert. Apparently the tight coiling of the constituent chromonemata or threads of the chromosome, perhaps with the inclusion of more than usual amounts of histones, interferes with the synthesis of messenger RNA by the genetic DNA. In any event, the concept is now taking hold that the heterochromatic X chromosome is genetically inert, although probably not entirely so. The entire concept, cytological and genetic, is known as the Lyon hypothesis because of its especially clear enunciation by Mary Lyon.[55, 56] The suppression of full genetic activity by both X chromosomes in all cells throughout the body of the female is perhaps an adjustment arrived at in early mammalian evolution. This mechanism would seem to eliminate undesirable genetic differences between the XY male and the XX female, and at the same time allow advantage to be taken of the efficient XY/XX sex determining mechanism.

What is the evidence for the hypothesis of X chromosome (X^M or X^P) functional or genetic mosaicism in females? Some of the evidence comes from animal studies. For example, X-borne mutants that affect coat colour in mice cause, in heterozygous females, a 'mottled' or 'dappled' coat with patches of normal and of mutant colour.[55] It has also been suggested that X chromosome mosaicism is in part responsible for the pattern of coat colour in calico or tortoise-shell cats (the rare tortoise-shell and infertile tomcat may have XXY sex chromosomes similar to those found in Klinefelter's syndrome in man).[81]

It is more difficult to find evidence of X chromosome mosaicism in the human female since there is no pertinent phenotypic manifestation as obvious as the coat colour of mice and cats. However, certain biochemical and histological investigations have thrown some light on the matter. Two populations of erythrocytes in the circulating blood[15] and of cells of dermal origin grown *in vitro*[26] have been described in female heterozygous carriers of the X-borne mutant gene that causes a deficiency of the enzyme glucose-6-phosphate dehydrogenase (G-6-PD). Some erythrocytes or fibroblasts are normal for the enzyme (the X with the normal, wild-type allele for G-6-PD is euchromatic and active). The remaining erythrocytes or fibroblasts are deficient in the enzyme (the recessive mutant gene is on the euchromatic X chromosome and it finds expression because the normal dominant allele is inactivated by heteropycnosis of the other X chromosome).

Additional evidence of X chromosome mosaicism comes from the study of muscle biopsies from heterozygous female carriers of the X-borne gene for Duchenne muscular dystrophy, in which gradations from normal histology to severe pathology are found.[31, 32] A possible explanation is a variation from one carrier to another, on a chance basis, in the proportion of nuclei of muscle fibres in which the X chromosome carrying the normal gene is heterochromatic, allowing the recessive mutant gene on the other X chromosome to find expression. Certain findings with respect to the blood coagulation factor IX (Christmas factor) and some forms of retinal degeneration may also be explained by X chromosome mosaicism. Curiously, studies of the Xg[a] blood group show no evidence of X chromosome mosaicism.[41] The gene locus for Xg[a] may be on a segment of the X chromosome that resists heteropycnosis.

The fact that trisomy (XXX, XXXY, XXXYY) and tetrasomy (XXXX, XXXXY) of the large X chromosome fail to be more damaging to development than they are is probably explicable on the grounds that X chromosomes in excess of one are largely inactivated in the body cells. Trisomy or tetrasomy of autosomes of comparable size appear to be lethal at a very early stage of embryogenesis.

In brief, while the sex chromatin is regarded by a cytologist working in a diagnostic laboratory as a useful clue to the number of X chromosomes in a person's cells, there are important genetic implications that need to be understood by those who work with patients who harbour a mutant gene on an X chromosome or who have supernumerary X chromosomes.

3

Correlations Between Sex Chromatin Patterns
and Sex Chromosome Complexes

Almost the entire story of the cytological significance of nuclear sexing as a guide to the nature of the sex chromosome complex is summarized in Fig. 2.[6] On scanning the figure, it will be seen that the correlations adhere to the rule that the number of sex chromatin masses is one less than the number of X chromosomes. When a normal X chromosome is paired with

CORRELATIONS BETWEEN SEX CHROMATIN PATTERNS AND SEX CHROMOSOME COMPLEXES

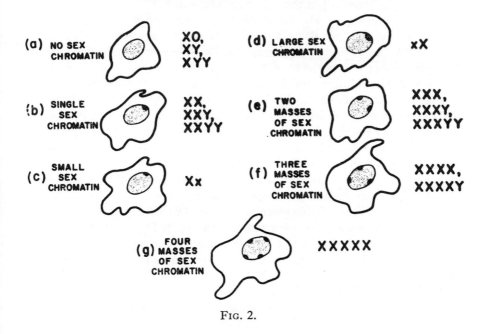

(a) NO SEX CHROMATIN — XO, XY, XYY

(b) SINGLE SEX CHROMATIN — XX, XXY, XXYY

(c) SMALL SEX CHROMATIN — Xx

(d) LARGE SEX CHROMATIN — xX

(e) TWO MASSES OF SEX CHROMATIN — XXX, XXXY, XXXYY

(f) THREE MASSES OF SEX CHROMATIN — XXXX, XXXXY

(g) FOUR MASSES OF SEX CHROMATIN — XXXXX

FIG. 2.

one that is smaller or larger than normal, because of a structural defect, the sex chromatin is slightly smaller or larger than normal (Fig. 2 c, d), although the difference is so slight as to be difficult to detect. The Y chromosome does not produce a recognizable chromatin mass and the presence or absence of the Y chromosome in no way influences the number or appearance of the heterochromatic X chromosome(s) in the interphase nucleus. With rare exceptions, an individual with a Y chromosome has testes. The results of a clinical examination, against a background of knowledge concerning the syndromes caused by abnormalities of the sex chromosome complex, combined with information obtained from examination of a buccal smear, permit a prediction of the sex chromosome complex with considerable reliability. Nevertheless, a thorough investigation must include a chromosome analysis. For example, the sex chromatin test does not distinguish between XXY and XXYY complexes and there are no distinguishing physical or mental signs that are known to be reliable at the present time. To complicate the investigation of sex chromosome abnormalities, mosaicisms of various kinds are not infrequent (XO/XX, XY/XXY and many others). When there are two populations of cells, one with two and the other with one X chromosome(s), the proportion of sex chromatin-positive nuclei in a buccal smear may be lower than when the cells all have two X chromosomes, but this does not necessarily follow. In the presence of a mosaicism of cells with different sex chromosome complexes, the phenotypic expression is likely to be that caused by the abnormal cell line in the mosaic, but there is great variability.

In considering the sex chromatin patterns shown in Fig. 2, it should be pointed out that not all cells in a buccal smear have the sex chromatin pattern that is illustrated diagrammatically. For example, in the normal XX female about 50 per cent of cells, on the average, are sex chromatin-positive. Both technical and biological factors, which need not be discussed here, contribute to this inconsistency. Similarly, when there are three X chromosomes, the buccal smear contains cells with two, one or no sex chromatin masses. The maximum number of sex chromatin masses per nucleus in a buccal smear is the significant clue to the number of X chromosomes. The representation of no sex chromatin (Fig. 2a) is accurate, however, since chromatin-positive nuclei are entirely lacking in buccal smears of persons who have a single X chromosome.

Perhaps this is a suitable place to refer briefly to the origin of anomalies of the sex chromosome complex that are shown in Fig. 2. In general, the abnormalities are the result of an error in the transfer of sex chromosomes to daughter cells during one or more cell divisions in the maturation of germ cells of one of the parents. An error at a single division (probably the reductional cell division of meiosis) is capable of producing anomalies such as XO, XXX or XXY when male and female gametes unite at conception. For the larger complexes, errors in successive cell divisions are probably involved. The diverse mosaicisms, which will not be discussed in this chapter, must be a consequence of an error in the segregation of sex chromosomes in a mitotic cell division of the zygote or early embryo. An increase in maternal age predisposes, to some extent, to certain types of sex chromosome abnormality. The mean maternal age appears to be slightly elevated for XXY males with the Klinefelter syndrome, but less so than for the trisomy-21 error of mongolism (Down's syndrome). No other factors are known to predispose to chromosomal abnormalities that are encountered clinically. The clinical conditions shown recently to be caused by chromosomal abnormalities have been known for many years and abnormalities of the chromosomes themselves have long been recognized in plants and animals, especially insects, other than man. Any recently introduced factor, such as man-made radiation, could be no more than a contributory cause at best. We are faced with the disquieting suspicion that the abnormalities result from occasional mistakes in the complicated behaviour of chromosomes that is inherent in meiosis of germ cells and that effective preventive measures may be beyond attainment in the foreseeable future. Nonetheless, the possibility that viral infections or other factors may favour meiotic nondisjunction of chromosomes should be thoroughly explored. The frequency of errors, especially autosomal errors, could be reduced if child-bearing were restricted to the young mother. Such a course of action, although laudable at first sight, imposes a loss of the vast majority of normal children who arrive late in the sequence of siblings, including many who in the light of history would be gifted.

4

The Technique of Nuclear Sexing

The buccal smear test[71] is used almost universally, in preference to the skin biopsy or blood film methods, because of its simplicity. The test is reliable in the hands of an experienced cytologist.

Epithelial cells are obtained by rubbing the mucosa of the cheek firmly with a metal spatula (the long, narrow kind used in analytical weighing). A smear of a thickness determined by practice is made on a microscope slide, which is immersed immediately in 90 per cent ethyl alcohol. After fixation for 15–30 min, the slide is immersed in absolute alcohol for 3 min and then in a 2 per cent solution of Parlodion in equal parts of alcohol and ether for 2 min. After drying briefly in air, the smear is passed through 70 per cent alcohol (5 min) and two changes of distilled water (5 min each). It is now ready for staining.

There are several suitable dyes for the staining of chromatin. Experience has shown that carbol fuchsin is reliable and it has the advantage of leaving the bacterial flora among oral mucosal cells unstained. This is of some importance when the test is used in connection with the mentally retarded with poor oral hygiene. The staining solution should be prepared as follows:

(a) Prepare a stock solution, which will keep indefinitely.

Basic fuchsin (CF-41, Coleman & Bell)	3 g
70 per cent Ethyl alcohol	100 ml

(b) Prepare a fresh supply of a working solution monthly or more frequently if many smears are being stained. Allow the solution to stand for 24 hours before using.

Stock solution	10 ml
5 per cent Carbolic acid in distilled water	90 ml
Glacial acetic acid	10 ml
37 per cent Formaldehyde	10 ml

The slide is immersed for 5–10 min in the staining solution in a Coplin jar, followed by about one minute in 95 per cent alcohol and about one minute in absolute alcohol. The exact time in the alcohols varies with the thickness of the smear. Finally, clear in xylol and apply a cover-slip with a neutral mounting medium.

Since the test depends on the accurate recognition of a nuclear component only 1μ in diameter, a good binocular microscope is required. The definitive examination of nuclei should be done with the 95X oil immersion objective and the use of a green filter is advisable when smears have been stained with carbol fuchsin. It is good practice to examine 100 nuclei carefully. Cells of the buccal mucosa vary greatly in their condition;

only nuclei with particulate chromatin are worth examining. Smears are sometimes of very poor cellular quality, especially when taken from mentally retarded children. Further smears must then be made, rubbing the mucosa more firmly in an attempt to obtain more deeply situated and healthier epithelial cells.

A chromatin-negative smear is truly negative for sex chromatin. In a positive preparation from an individual with two X chromosomes, a single mass of sex chromatin is present in 30 per cent to 80 per cent of nuclei (average 50 per cent), the exact percentage depending to a large extent on the technical quality of the preparation. If the count is less than 30 per cent, the possibility of a mosaicism or partial deletion of one X chromosome is raised and a chromosome analysis should follow. The sex chromatin is located against the nuclear membrane regularly (Plate IV), but this will not be obvious in some cells because of the orientation of the nucleus and the sex chromatin within it, in relation to the optical axis of the microscope. In view of the uniform absence of sex chromatin in buccal smears of persons with one X chromosome, it is permissible to record as positive any nucleus with a chromatin clump of about 1μ diameter, whether or not it is obviously against the nuclear membrane. While the shape is usually planoconvex, the sex chromatin sometimes appears as a narrow 'thickening' of the nuclear membrane when a disc-shaped mass of sex chromatin is viewed on edge. In some individuals of both sexes, there is a prominent mass of chromatin attached to a nucleolus. This perinucleolar chromatin can be recognized readily with experience and should not, of course, be counted.

Nuclei in other kinds of preparations are examined for sex chromatin from time to time for special reasons. A blood film will give essentially the same information as a buccal smear, but examination of a blood film is more tedious and the frequency of positive cells is low in persons with two X chromosomes. In the neutrophil polymorphonuclear leucocytes of such individuals, the sex chromatin is situated in a drumstick-shaped nuclear appendage, about $1.2\mu \times 1.6\mu$ in size, in 3 per cent of cells on the average (Plate V).[27] Nuclear appendages of that size are not present in neutrophils of persons who have only one X chromosome.

There are occasions when nuclear sexing is done on whole mounts of the amnion of spontaneous abortuses. The study of amniotic membrane is also gaining favour as a substitute for buccal smears in surveys of newborns.[93] Sections of almost any tissue or organ can be used for nuclear sexing if the occasion arises. Nuclei in sections are likely to contain coarse chromatin clumps in addition to the sex chromatin. In males, up to 10 per cent of nuclei may have a chromatin mass, presumably of autosomal origin, that mimics the sex chromatin in size and position. Tissues should be processed with special care technically if clear detail of the nuclear chromatin is to be obtained.[5]

A detailed presentation of the technique of chromosome analysis, although a matter of the most vital importance in human cytogenetics, is not directly pertinent to this chapter. The analysis is usually made on leucocytes of the peripheral blood;[60, 72] the procedure is as follows in outline.

Starting with a 5–10 ml heparinized sample of peripheral blood, the erythrocytes are separated by the addition of phytohaemagglutinin and centrifugation, and discarded. (An important role of phytohaemagglutinin is that of stimulation of cell division in the next step.) The suspension of leucocytes is incubated at 37°C for three days, during which the mononuclear leucocytes undergo frequent divisions. A colchicine preparation is added to the culture one hour before harvesting the cells, for the purpose of arresting cell divisions at metaphase. A concentration of cells is obtained by centrifugation and cell swelling to disperse metaphase chromosomes is brought about by the addition of a hypnotic solution of sodium citrate. The cells are then fixed by acetic acid and stained with aceto-orcein, carbol fuchsin or by the Feulgen method. Chromosome counts are done on well spread metaphase figures (Plate VI). Several metaphase configurations are photographed, the chromosomes are cut out of an enlarged photographic print and assembled into a conventional karyotype.

5

Clinical Conditions in Females in Relation to the Sex Chromatin Pattern and the Sex Chromosome Complex

Chromatin-negative (XO)

A syndrome in females, characterized by the triad of sexual infantilism, webbing of the neck and cubitus valgus, was described by Turner in 1938.[103] The term 'Turner's syndrome' continues to be used for patients similar to those in the original group, although their clinical delineation has changed considerably. 'Gonadal dysgenesis' is an alternative name for the disorder.

A discrepancy between the essentially female phenotype and a chromatin-negative or 'male' nuclear sex[89] drew attention to a probable genetic origin of Turner's syndrome. The XO (X-nothing) sex chromosome abnormality was established later as the most frequent sex chromosome error in the Turner patient (Plate VII).[36] Other abnormalities that cause developmental errors similar to those of Turner's syndrome are: (*i*) a mosaicism in which one cell population is XO (e.g. XO/XX and XO/XX/XXX), (*ii*) a normal X chromosome paired with a partially deleted X chromosome (Fig. 2c) and (*iii*) a normal X chromosome paired with an X-isochromosome (Fig. 2d). (If the centromere splits at the beginning of anaphase in a plane at right angles to the chromosome, one daughter chromosome consists of two short arms and the other of two long arms, of the X chromosome. An isochromosome of the long arm is found in an occasional patient with Turner's syndrome.)

XO females have the following characteristics. Growth is retarded and the height is less than five feet on attainment of full stature. The neck is usually short and in somewhat less than half of the cases there is lateral webbing of the nuchal skin. The chest is likely to be broad, with widely spaced nipples, and there is a significant increase in the frequency of congenital cardiovascular defects (usually coarctation of the aorta). Looseness of the skin of the neck and lymphoedema of the legs may call attention to the disorder in the newborn and young infant. The external genitalia are those of a normal female; uterus and tubes are present, although somewhat underdeveloped. A major defect of development involves the gonads. The ovaries of XO embryos are known to contain follicles, with oogonia, in normal numbers during the first three months of development.[98] However, follicular atresia occurs during later stages of development and the ovaries are then represented by streaks of connective tissue attached to the broad ligaments in the usual ovarian position (gonadal dysgenesis). Follicles persist in some numbers in the ovaries of a few XO females and an instance of fertility is on record. Secondary sexual development, in particular breast development, is lacking because of the deficiency of oestrogens of ovarian origin. Urinary excretion of FSH is elevated for the same reason. The accepted management includes cyclic administration of stilbesterol and progesterone. Detailed accounts of the developmental history and clinical findings in XO females are available.[3,44]

The XO chromosome abnormality is highly lethal in the first trimester of gestation and it is the most common chromosome error in spontaneous abortuses. Carr found 11 XO specimens among 200 abortuses.[18] This accounts for the low frequency of one in about 2,500 newborn females for the XO error.

With respect to the effect of this particular chromosome abnormality on intelligence, in a study of twelve girls with Turner's syndrome, eleven were found to have IQ levels between 75 and 106 and the other girl was so retarded that her IQ could not be determined.[104] In another study of thirty-seven patients, the full IQ ranged from below 50 to 125 (mean 95).[63] These results show that mental retardation is not an important sequel of the XO error, compared with some other chromosome abnormalities (see below). This is borne out by experience gained from buccal smear surveys of retardates in institutions, which rarely disclose chromatin-negative females.

The results of tests for specific factors, by Money and collaborators especially, suggest that certain psychological aberrations are present. For example, the study of thirty-seven Turner's syndrome patients mentioned above, showed that the Performance IQ (mean 86) was significantly lower than the Verbal IQ (mean 103) and that Perceptual Organization (mean 78) was significantly poorer than Verbal Comprehension (mean 112).[63] It was concluded that a degree of 'space-form blindness' is associated with the sex chromosome anomaly of Turner's syndrome. A later study showed that Freedom from Distractibility was impaired, on comparison with the scores for Verbal Comprehension.[65] The investigations cited were based on earlier work by Shaffer who concluded, following psychological testing of twenty Turner women, that there was 'a highly consistent pattern of cognitive strengths and weaknesses similar to that observed in certain types of brain damage'.[97] A defect in right-left direction sense, as measured by a road map test, has been described.[2] The relationship between a higher cognitional function and a specific chromosome abnormality is a matter of considerable interest and importance. Reading ability, as tested by the Gates Reading Survey, is reported as being normal.[1] With regard to a specific sensory system, it is of interest to note that Lindsten found that two-thirds of forty-one women with clinical signs of Turner's syndrome showed an impairment of hearing on audiometric examination, usually of a purely perceptive type.[54]

The notable shortness of stature, together with deficient development of breasts unless treated with exogeneous oestrogens, are sources of neurotic problems in some patients. XO individuals identify normally with the female gender role and the level of erotic function is average or below average.[63]

An abnormal EEG and a variety of psychiatric and neurological disorders and symptoms have been described in isolated cases of Turner's syndrome. They include schizophrenia, psychosis of undetermined type, eneuresis, anorexia nervosa, progressive cerebellar degeneration, convulsions and strabismus.[54, 59, 61, 87, 99] It is difficult to judge at this time the significance of the XO abnormality in this context. The fact remains that most XO persons are free of psychiatric manifestations.[63]

Chromatin-negative (XY)

A syndrome that occurs infrequently in females, and in which the chromosome complement is that of the male, is of interest to psychiatrists because of the light it throws on factors guiding the development of psychosexual attitudes. The syndrome, known as testicular feminization,[73] is characterized by normal female external genitalia, absence of uterus and testes within the pelvis or inguinal canals. Stature is normal and secondary female sex characteristics, including normal breast development, appear at puberty. From the time of its first recognition as a syndrome, testicular feminization was known to be hereditary because of the familial incidence of the disorder. The chromatin-negative nature of the nuclei in these patients[4] and the presence of testes suggested that the sex chromosome complex is XY; this was confirmed as soon as human chromosome analysis became practicable.[45] A mutant gene so disturbs the evocator role of the foetal testes and the end-organ response of tissues that come under the influence of this evocator and the sex hormones, that the external phenotype is entirely feminine.

The mutational genetic error which so drastically alters sex differentiation has no adverse effect on intelligence and psychosexual orientation is definitely feminine, in spite of the male XY sex chromosomes. There is no overt psychopathology, although psychological problems may ensue if the patient learns inadvertently of the true nature of her gonads. The acquisition of a distinctly feminine psychosexual outlook in such individuals seems to eliminate any important genetic influence of the sex chromosomes in moulding the gender role. The importance of environmental influences in childhood is thus emphasized since these XY individuals are quite rightly reared as girls with no thought of the obviously impossible alternative.

Other forms of male pseudohermaphroditism present a more difficult problem because the external genitalia are intersexual anatomically, rather than normally female as in the syndrome of testicular feminization. Studies of hermaphroditic children have shown that the child's gender role begins to be established between eighteen months and two years of age.[64, 66, 67] Since the external genitalia of the male pseudohermaphrodite are seldom suitable for surgical correction in the male direction, it is important in most instances that the child be reared as a girl from early infancy, in spite of the male gonads and XY sex chromosomes, and that surgical correction of the genitalia toward an acceptable female anatomy be done prior to school age. There is good evidence of 'imprinting' of the psychological aspects of gender role on an environmental basis, and this overrides genetic and gonadol factors in the child's development of psychosexual orientation.

Double Chromatin-positive (XXX)

Trisomy for the X chromosome is now a well known error.[46] A representative karyotype is shown in Plate VIII, together with the mean frequency of nuclei without sex chromatin and with one and two masses of sex chromatin in buccal smears, from sixty-one reported XXX females and five XXXY males. As noted previously, the sex chromatin pattern is unaffected by the inclusion of a Y chromosome. It has also been pointed out that the significant cell population diagnostically is the one with the maximum number of sex chromatin masses.

The triplo-X error produces either no physical defects or a variety of non-specific congenital anomalies that may be severe but are more often relatively minor, and such individuals are fertile.[28] This is at first sight surprising because of the large size of the X chromosome and its considerable genetic role, to judge from the numerous mutant genes that have been recognized as X-borne and the cause of a wide variety of hereditary, sex-linked disorders. Trisomy of an autosome of this size is generally regarded as lethal. The best explanation for the relatively less harmful effect of X-trisomy on development is that two of the three X chromosomes of each cell are rendered largely inactive through heteropycnosis to form sex chromatin. The effect on the developmental process is so variable and often so slight, so far as physical signs are concerned at any rate, that one can hardly say that there is a characteristic syndrome except in the cytogenetic sense.

Buccal smear surveys of newborn infants, followed in many instances by chromosome analysis when buccal smear findings were abnormal, resulted in a frequency of one in about 800 females.[24] XXX infants show no obvious abnormality.

Mental aspects of triplo-X females are, like the physical aspects, different from those of XO females. There is no doubt that the supernumerary X chromosome imposes an increased risk of mental retardation, but the extent of the risk cannot at present be defined. With few exceptions, the known triplo-X females (other than newborns) have been discovered during buccal smear surveys of mental retardates in institutions. The frequency of the XXX abnormality in such a population is one in about 225 females[24] and the intelligence levels vary from very low to just within the normal range. The mild nature of the retardation in many XXX females found in the above-mentioned surveys led to the suspicion that others may have a normal intellect and be free of psychopathology. This has been confirmed by detecting the error by chance on finding cells with duplicated sex chromatin in mucosal smears used for cancer detection.[22] More definite information on the bearing of the XXX error on mental retardation will be available when triplo-X infants found in surveys are studied during childhood development.

Not only do XXX and XO females differ in their risk of mental retardation but also in other psychological, and in psychiatric, manifestations. In a study of twenty-two XXX females in institutions, together with a control series matched for age and length of stay in an institution, eleven of the study group (XXX) were assessed as subnormal, i.e. with IQ less than 69.[52] The triplo-X individuals differed from the matched controls in showing more impairment of interpersonal relationships and more social withdrawal. In addition, the triplo-X patients displayed more prominently such features as psychomotor retardation, poverty of speech, persecutory ideas and ideas of reference. A wide range of psychiatric disorders was encountered in the twenty-two members of the study group. Those with IQ levels above 70 had psychiatric diagnoses that were in general typical of the mental hospital population from which they were drawn and a psychosis was superimposed on the mental retardation in five of the eleven XXX females whose IQ levels were 69 or less. Four of the study group had been diagnosed as having schizophrenia and this psychosis has been reported in isolated cases of the triplo-X error.

The information available at present conveys the definite impression that the presence of a supernumerary X chromosome predisposes the individual to abnormalities of behaviour and psychosis. The matter is in need of further study. It should be cautioned that the inclusion of an extra chromosome the size of the X chromosome, even allowing for heteropycnosis and the Lyon hypothesis, introduces a complicated situation in the disturbed genetic balance between sex chromosomes and autosomes and in other respects. The preliminary findings summarized above should not at this time be used to construct hypotheses concerning genetic predisposition to schizophrenia or other form of psychosis. One must remember that cytogenetic surveys of patients in mental institutions show that psychotic individuals, with occasional exceptions, have a normal sex chromatin pattern and sex chromosome complement.[25, 92]

Triple and Quadruple Sex Chromatin (XXXX and XXXXX)

The presence of four or five X chromosomes in females is a rare occurrence. Two adult tetra-X females are reported to be normal on physical examination and after extensive laboratory tests.[19] One of the patients has an IQ of 30 and is passive and withdrawn. The other patient has an IQ of 50; she is easily angered and shows uncontrolled acting-out behaviour. The karyotype is illustrated in Plate IX, together with the mean buccal smear findings in persons with four X chromosomes (either XXXX or XXXXY).

The only XXXXX female on record is a child with retarded physical and mental development, and several minor physical defects.[51] Mental retardation and other psychological disturbances are probably inevitable when the chromosome complement is so abnormal as to include two or three X chromosomes in excess of the two of the normal female.

6

Clinical Conditions in Males in Relation to the Sex Chromatin Pattern and the Sex Chromosome Complex

Chromatin-negative (XYY and XYYY)

The XYY sex chromosome abnormality appears to be rare; seven XYY males have been recorded in the literature since the first such individual was discovered.[94] There is no discrepancy between the sex chromatin test and the phenotype to draw attention to the sex chromosome error. Neither are there sufficiently characteristic physical signs to make the clinician suspect an XYY abnormality and ask for a chromosome analysis. For these reasons, the XYY male is likely to escape detection. Developmental anomalies reported in these males are minor and variable; the most frequent physical sign is delayed descent of the testes.

A precise statement cannot be made concerning the effect of the XYY error on intelligence, but mental retardation is probably not a highly important aspect of the condition. There are scanty, but provocative, observations on certain psychological traits. A chromosome analysis on 197 men in an institution for mentally subnormal men with dangerous, violent or criminal propensities revealed seven men (1:28) with an XYY

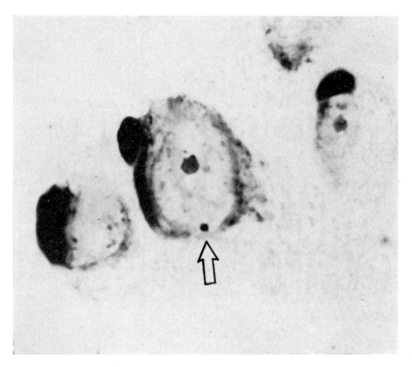

Plate I
The sex chromatin in a neurone of the cerebral cortex of a human female.

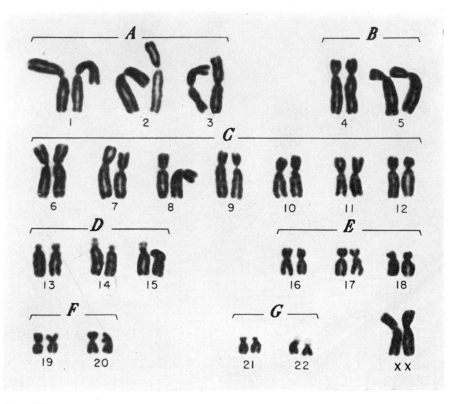

Plate II

The conventional arrangement of chromosomes, in the form of a karyotype, of a normal human female.

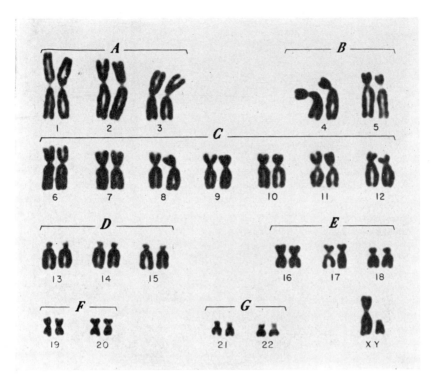

Plate III

The karyotype of a normal human male.

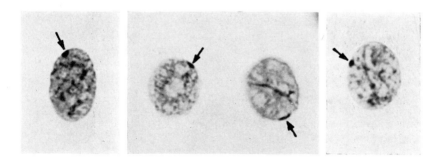

Plate IV

Chromatin-positive nuclei in a buccal smear from a normal female.

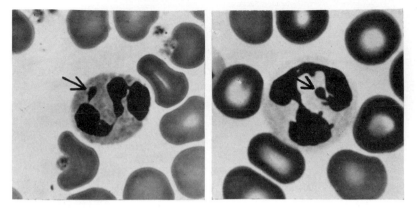

Plate V

Neutrophils from a normal female, illustrating the drumstick-shaped nuclear
appendage that contains the sex chromatin.

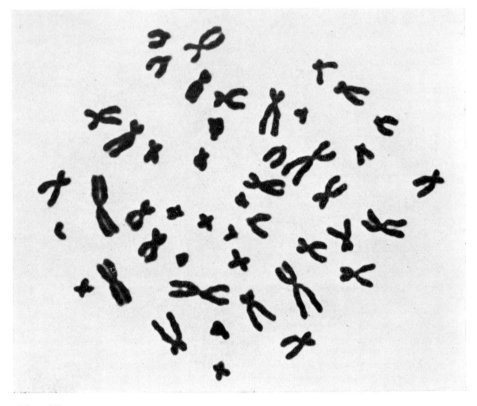

Plate VI

A metaphase configuration of chromosomes in a mononuclear leucocyte of peripheral blood.

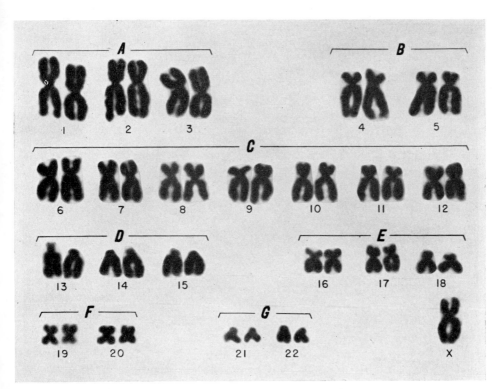

Plate VII

The XO karyotype of Turner's syndrome. All nuclei in the buccal smear are sex chromatin-negative.

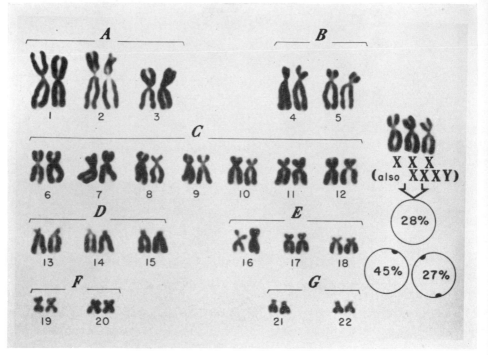

Plate VIII

Karyotype of a triplo-X female. The mean frequencies of three classes of nuclei in buccal smears of persons with three X chromosomes (XXX or XXXY) are also shown.

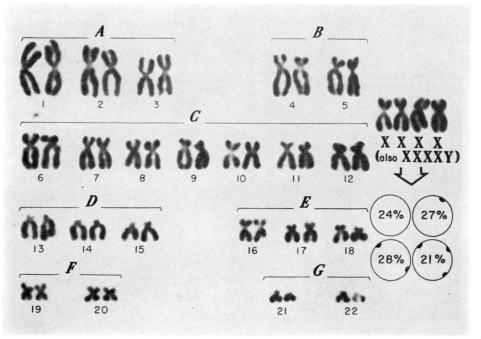

Plate IX

Karyotype of a tetra-X female. The mean frequencies of four classes of nuclei in buccal smears of persons with four X chromosomes (XXXX or XXXXY) are also shown.

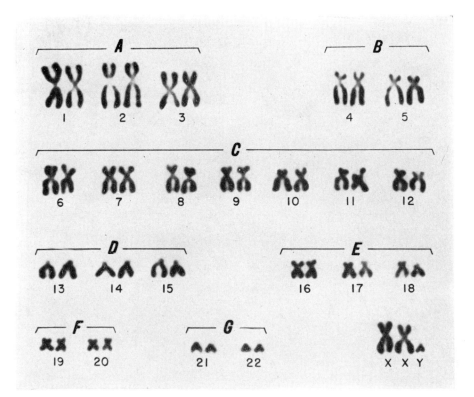

Plate X

A karyotype illustrating the most common sex chromosome abnormality (XXY) found in Klinefelter's syndrome. The buccal smear test is identical to that of a normal XX female, from 30% to 80% (av. 50%) of nuclei being sex chromatin-positive.

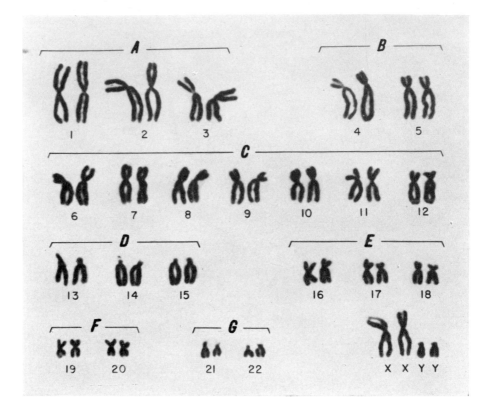

Plate XI

The XXYY sex chromosome abnormality that occurs occasionally in men with Klinefelter's syndrome. The buccal smear test is identical to that of a normal XX female or an XXY Klinefelter male.

sex chromosome complex.[47] The same investigators found only one XYY individual among 1,500 males whose chromosomes were examined for a variety of reasons, none among 266 randomly selected newborn male babies and none among 209 randomly selected adult males. (The XYY males were, incidentally, unusually tall.) The authors point out that it is not clear at present whether the increased frequency of XYY males in the institution for difficult-to-handle men is related to aggressive behaviour or mental deficiency, or both. However, XXYY males also appear to be more numerous than expected in institutions for the retarded who require special security (see below). There seems, therefore, to be a real possibility that the addition of an extra Y chromosome to the male's XY complex predisposes to significant and detrimental psychological changes. The inclusion of XYY among chromosome abnormalities found in isolated cases of childhood schizophrenia needs further study before the significance of the finding can be assessed.[96]

One instance of an XYYY abnormality was reported after Fig. 2 was prepared.[101] The patient was a five-year-old boy with IQ 80, congenital pulmonary stenosis, non-palpable right testis and slight hyperextensibility of elbows and knees. He did not differ appreciably from XYY males.

Chromatin-positive (XXY and XXYY)

There is a group of sex chromosome abnormalities which are intersexual in the sense that there are at least two X chromosomes (female) and at least one Y chromosome (male). When the buccal smear shows singly chromatin-positive nuclei, either XXY or XXYY complexes may be present, the former being much more frequent. The term intersexual is used here at some risk. It refers only to the sex chromosome complex; the patients are definitely male although the testes are pathological after puberty.

XXY and XXYY complexes (Plates X and XI), together with other intersexual complexes to be referred to later, are responsible for the well known disorder of development in the male called Klinefelter's syndrome or seminiferous tubule dysgenesis.[53, 83] The discrepancy between chromosomal and phenotypic sex was shown by finding chromatin-positive buccal smears in Klinefelter males.[88] With advances in human cytogenetics, the XXY[48] and the considerably less common XXYY[78] complexes were demonstrated. Although the majority of Klinefelter patients have an XXY complex in all cells examined in a chromosome study, a mosaic of XXY and XY cells is not uncommon. There have been about fifteen instances of the XXYY variant of Klinefelter's syndrome reported in the literature.[102]

The sequence of development leading to Klinefelter's syndrome in the adult male is briefly as follows. The XXY error does not interfere with normal intrauterine development and a male baby with this chromosome abnormality can not be recognized at birth without the aid of a buccal smear test or chromosome analysis. (The developmental history is essentially the same whether the error is XXY or XXYY and this may be borne in mind wherever XXY is mentioned in the following brief account.) Development continues to be normal during childhood except for the increased risk of mental retardation to be discussed presently. At puberty, however, testicular histopathology supervenes very quickly and this is the main, and only constant, feature of the disorder. At a time when the prepubertal seminiferous tubules should respond to pituitary gonadotrophins by enlarging because of extensive proliferation of the lining epithelium on assuming a spermatogenic function, a severe regressive change takes place instead. The normally thin connective tissue outer walls of the tubules undergo a fibrotic thickening and the epithelium concurrently becomes devoid of germ cells and contains Sertoli cells only. There is a tendency for the regressive process to proceed to complete hyalinization of tubules, which then appear as amorphous pale-staining areas in sections of the testis biopsy. Because of the small size of the pathological tubules, the Leydig cells accumulate in larger-than-normal aggregates and the testes are very small, only about 1 cm in diameter. The testicular pathology is probably the result of an abnormal end-organ response to the gonadotrophin FSH, because of the abnormal genetic coding carried by the cells of the testis.

Other physical signs of Klinefelter's syndrome are probably the consequence of a combination of genetic and hormonal influences, the latter arising in part from the low normal or below normal secretion of androgens by the Leydig cells. Patients with XXY and XXYY complexes (perhaps XXYY especially) are likely to be tall, mainly because the lower extremities are disproportionately long. Hair growth on the face is usually light and the pubic hair has a gynaecoid distribution. In the third decade, the distribution of adipose tissue tends to change to produce a somewhat feminine body contour. From the fourth decade on there are often signs of androgen deficiency, such as osteoporosis, leading to kyphosis when the vertebral column is affected, and premature senility. A greater or lesser degree of gynaecomastia is present in about half of the cases.

A reasonably accurate indication of the frequency of the intersexual sex chromosome complexes that are responsible for Klinefelter's syndrome is provided by buccal smear surveys of newborn male babies. Surveys of newborn babies in Winnipeg,[69] Berne[12] and Edinburgh[57] gave results that do not differ from each other significantly. When the three sets of data are pooled, there are thirty sex chromatin-positive male babies in a series of 14,526 male births, or one in 480. Because of the relative infrequency of the XXXY, XXXYY and XXXXY errors (see below) the nuclei are usually singly chromatin-positive. Chromosome analyses were carried out on the chromatin-positive male babies discovered in the Edinburgh survey; ten had an XXY sex chromosome complement, five showed an XXY/XY mosaicism and one had an XXYY complement. It is possible that some individuals with an XXY/XY mosaicism may not acquire the full picture of Klinefelter's syndrome at puberty. But, in general, chromatin-positive male babies may be expected to qualify for the clinical diagnosis of Klinefelter's syndrome after puberty and, since these sex chromosome errors do not impose any significant mortality risk, the figure of one in 480 may be taken as a reasonably accurate estimate of the frequency of the syndrome among adult males in general. This is borne out by finding two chromatin-positive men among 977 adult men who visited an out-patient laboratory and dental clinic.[86]

There is no question that the XXY error carries with it a higher-than-usual risk of mental retardation and persons with the XXYY abnormality fare somewhat worse. As one line of evidence, the frequency of chromatin-positive males is appreciably higher among mentally retarded patients in institutions for the retarded than it is in newborns. The combined results of four buccal smear surveys[11, 33, 58, 74] are 61 chromatin-positive males among 6,281 mental retardates, or one in 103. Similar surveys done on children attending schools for educationally subnormal children also show a greater frequency of chromatin-positive males, compared with the findings in newborns, although there is considerable variation in the frequency data from one survey to another. On the basis of the foregoing surveys and clinical experience, it is frequently stated that one in four Klinefelter subjects has an IQ below the normal range.

Most studies of intelligence levels in Klinefelter individuals have been done on groups selected with a bias of one kind or another and they give the impression that the risk of mental retardation is greater than it probably is. In a study carried out before the buccal smear test came into general use,[85] only five of 31 males with a clinical diagnosis of Klinefelter's syndrome were of normal intelligence. The average IQ of the group was 82 and none was of above average intelligence. On the other hand, clinicians who see men with the syndrome in reasonable numbers, are familiar with its occurrence in men of apparently good mental ability who occupy responsible positions in various walks of life, including the professions.

In another study of forty-seven men with the chromatin-positive Klinefelter syndrome who attended an infertility clinic,[91] two had above average intelligence and, although none had passed through college, six had completed a secondary school education.

Published comments on the mental status of Klinefelter patients, other than mental retardation, deal partly with the area of psychosexuality. Among ten chromatin-positive males discovered in the course of a buccal smear survey in an institution for the retarded, seven had a history of sex offences prior to admission.[75] The proportion with such a history was significantly higher than that found among mental defectives generally. The same study reported finding six chromatin-positive males among 600 male sexual psychopaths, a frequency of chromatin-positive males considerably higher than that of the general population. Sexual interest is directed toward the female. Although sexual drive is likely to be fairly strong in the young adult, it tends to diminish early and may progress to impotence. Incompetence in the sexual sphere, aggravated by gynaecomastia when present, may lead to neuroses, anxiety states and reactive depressions. Transvestism has been described in several Klinefelter subjects.[68] This may be a matter of coincidence rather than causal relationship since transvestites in general have a male nuclear sex.[10] In an EEG study of fourteen Klinefelter patients, only one had an entirely normal pattern; there was a typical epileptic pattern in four patients and in the others the EEG was interpreted as indicating a disturbance in the upper brain stem.[30] There is confirmation of some predisposition to EEG abnormalities and epilepsy from other sources.[37, 42]

The pattern of intellectual functioning in a series of XXY males, when analysed for the specific factors of verbal comprehension, perceptual organization and freedom from distractibility, showed no significant differences between the scores.[63] It will be recalled that the score for verbal comprehension was significantly higher than the score for the other two factors in a series of XO females.

Some authors feel that delinquency and antisocial acts are encountered more frequently in Klinefelter males, compared with the general male population.[23, 80] One study, however, based on a buccal smear survey of inmates in institutions for male delinquents and criminal offenders, did not support the view that chromatin-positive males contribute disproportionately to delinquency or felonious behaviour.[105]

In studies of the behaviour of chromatin-positive males, it is usually not known whether they are XXY or XXYY. A recent report suggests that the XXYY variant of the Klinefelter syndrome is of special significance in this context.[21] In a buccal smear survey of 942 males in hospitals for retarded persons who require special supervision and security precautions, twenty-one chromatin-positive males were found (1:45). Chromosome analysis of the chromatin-positive group followed; twelve were XXY, two had an XXY/XY mosaicism and *seven showed the XXYY variant*. It was suggested that the high incidence of XXYY males, compared with other populations that have been tested, may account for the frequency of one in forty-five for chromatin-positive males. The usual frequency of chromatin-positive males in retardates in institutions is one in about 100 male patients. It will be recalled that the XYY error was found to occur more frequently than expected in a population of mentally subnormal men with dangerous, violent or criminal behaviour.[47]

In order to maintain perspective, it is important to bear in mind that descriptions of Klinefelter patients with psychopathology or behavioural deviations are often based on biased samples derived from mentally retarded, psychotic or delinquent populations. '. . . most persons with Klinefelter's syndrome are probably stable law-abiding citizens . . .'[90]

Double Chromatin-positive (XXXY, XXXYY)

The XXXY abnormality, although now well known,[34] is comparatively rare. In our experience XXXY males do not differ materially from XXY Klinefelter individuals when both are found during buccal smear surveys of the mentally retarded in institutions.[20] However, studies of the XXX female make it very probable that the XXXY error carries an appreciably higher risk of mental retardation, and probably other psychological abnormalities, compared with the XXY error. The XXXYY abnormality appears to be very rare indeed, only one instance having been reported—in a mentally subnormal male with typical clinical signs of the Klinefelter syndrome.[17] The sex chromatin pattern in buccal smears from XXXY and XXXYY Klinefelter patients is shown in Plate VIII.

Triple Chromatin-positive (XXXXY)

The first reports[38, 39, 62] of the grossly abnormal sex chromosome complex noted above have been followed by references to some thirty patients with this error. A grouping of signs and symptoms that may be considered either as a syndrome in its own right or as a variant of Kline-felter's syndrome has emerged.[9, 29, 49] Although the patients vary from one to another, the following signs are fairly characteristic: (*i*) skeletal anomalies, including synostosis of the proximal ends of the radius and ulna, and incurving of the fifth finger, (*ii*) hypogenitalism, particularly cryptorchidism, small penis and scrotum and (*iii*) moderate to severe mental retardation. The frequency of widely spaced eyes with a mongoloid slant, depressed nasal bridge and large mouth tends to produce a characteristic face. There have been few comments on psychological disorders other than mental retardation, perhaps because most of the reported patients were young. The sex chromatin pattern in buccal smears is shown in Plate IX.

7

Conclusion

An account has been given of the sex chromatin of cell nuclei and the manner in which detection of the sex chromatin pattern in buccal smears (often called, rather inelegantly, 'nuclear sexing') gives a reasonably reliable clue as to the nature of the sex chromosome complex when clinical findings are taken into consideration. The main sex chromosome abnormalities were summarized, including the physical findings and the psychological consequences of the chromosome errors as they are known at present.

The mental effects of chromosome errors, including those of the sex chromosomes, vary with the type of abnormality. It may be said, as a generality, that the risk of mental retardation and its severity increases as the number of sex chromosomes increases above the normal two for males and females, especially when there are more than two X chromosomes. Neurotic manifestations are frequently encountered in the various syndromes described. They are partly sequelae of abnormalities in the reproductive sphere. Psychiatric disorders have been described in a sufficient proportion of persons with sex chromosome abnormalities to suggest a risk in excess of that shared by persons with normal chromosomes. Psychological and psychiatric aspects of sex chromosome cytogenetics are in need of further investigation. Prospective studies, starting with newborns who have abnormalities of the sex chromosome complex that were brought to light by routine nuclear sexing, are especially needed as a source of reliable information on the effect of sex chromosome errors on all aspects of mental development. Such studies should overcome the bias in selection of patients which now prevails.

*   *   *

Acknowledgements

I am grateful for the co-operation and assistance of Dr D. H. Carr, Dr H. C. Soltan and Dr F. R. Sergovich, who are involved in the genetic and cytogenetic research in this department. Dr Carr has kindly supplied me with the karyotypes that are illustrated in this chapter.

Our investigative work is supported by the Medical Research Council of Canada, the D. H. McDermid Medical Research Fund and an award to the writer by the Joseph P. Kennedy Jr Foundation.

REFERENCES

1. ALEXANDER, D., and MONEY, J., 1965. Reading ability, object constancy and Turner's syndrome. *Percept. Mot. Skills*, **20**, 981.
2. ALEXANDER, D., WALKER, H. T., and MONEY, J., 1964. Studies in direction sense. I. Turner's syndrome. *Archs gen. Psychiat.*, **10**, 337.
3. ASHLEY, D. J. B., 1962. *Human Intersex*. Edinburgh: E. & S. Livingstone Ltd.
4. BARR, M. L., 1954. An interim note on the application of the skin biopsy test of chromosomal sex to hermaphrodites. *Surgery Gynec. Obstet.*, **99**, 184.
5. 1965. Sex chromatin techniques. In *Human Chromosome Methodology*, edited by J. J. Yunis, p. 1. New York: Academic Press.
6. 1966. Correlations between sex chromatin patterns and sex chromosome complexes in man. In *The Sex Chromatin*, Moore, K. L. (Ed.), p. 129. Philadelphia: W. B. Saunders Company.
7. 1966. The significance of the sex chromatin. In *International Review of Cytology*, edited by G. H. Bourne and J. Danielli, p. 35. New York: Academic Press.
8. BARR, M. L., and BERTRAM, E. G., 1949. A morphological distinction between neurones of the male and female, and the behaviour of the nucleolar satellite during accelerated nucleoprotein synthesis. *Nature, Lond.*, **163**, 676.

9. BARR, M. L., CARR, D. H., POZSONYI, J., WILSON, R. A., DUNN, H. G., JACOBSON, T. S., and MILLER, J. R., 1962. The XXXXY sex chromosome abnormality. *Can. med. Ass. J.*, **87**, 891.

10. BARR, M. L., and HOBBS, G. E., 1954. Chromosomal sex in transvestites. *Lancet*, i, 1109.

11. BARR, M. L., SHAVER, E. L., CARR, D. H., and PLUNKETT, E. R., 1960. The chromatin-positive Klinefelter syndrome among patients in mental deficiency hospitals. *J. ment. Defic. Res.*, **4**, 89.

12. BERGEMANN, E., 1961. Geschlechtschromatinbeststimmungen am Neuge borenen. *Schweiz. med. Wschr.*, **91**, 292.

13. BERTRAND, I., and GIRARD, C., 1956. La recherche de la chromatine sexuelle en neuropathologie. *Bull. Acad. natn. Méd.*, **140**, 304.

14. ——— 1958. La chromatine sexuelle du neurone. *Rev. Neurol. Psychiat.*, **99**, 264.

15. BEUTLER, E., YEH, M., and FAIRBANKS, V. F., 1962. The normal human female as a mosaic of X-chromosome activity: studies using the gene for G-6-PD-deficiency as a marker. *Proc. natn. Acad. Sci. U.S.A.*, **48**, 9.

16. BISHOP, A., and BISHOP, O. N., 1963. Analysis of tritium-labelled human chromosomes and sex chromatin. *Nature, Lond.*, **199**, 930.

17. BRAY, P., and Sr. ANN JOSEPHINE, 1963. An XXXYY sex chromosome anomaly. Report of a mentally deficient male. *J. Am. med. Ass.*, **184**, 179.

18. CARR, D. H., 1965. Chromosome studies in spontaneous abortions. *Obstet. Gynec., N.Y.*, **26**, 308.

19. CARR., D. H., BARR, M. L., and PLUNKETT, E. R., 1961. An XXXX sex chromosome complex in two mentally defective females. *Can. med. Ass. J.*, **84**, 131.

20. CARR, D. H., BARR, M. L., PLUNKETT, E. R., GRUMBACH, M. M., MORI- SHIMA, A., and CHU, E. H. Y., 1961. An XXXY sex chromosome com- plex in Klinefelter subjects with duplicated sex chromatin. *J. clin. Endocr. Metab.*, **21**, 491.

21. CASEY, M. D., SEGALL, L. J., STREET, D. R. K., and BLANK, C. E., 1966. Sex chromosome abnormalities in two state hospitals for patients requiring special security. *Nature, Lond.*, **209**, 641.

22. CLOSE, H. G., 1963. Two apparently normal triple-X females. *Lancet*, ii, 1358.

23. COURT BROWN, W. M., 1962. Sex chromosomes and the law. *Lancet*, ii, 508.

24. COURT BROWN, W. M., HARNDEN, D. G., JACOBS, P. A., MACLEAN, N., and MANTLE, D. J., 1964. Abnormalities of the Sex Chromosome Complex in Man. *Spec. Rep. Ser. med. Res. Counc.* No. 305. London: H.M.S.O.

25. COWIE, V., COPPEN, A., and NORMAN, P., 1960. Nuclear sex and body build in schizophrenia. *Br. med. J.*, ii, 431.

26. DAVIDSON, R. G., NITOWSKY, H. M., and CHILDS, B., 1963. Demonstration of two populations of cells in the human female heterozygous for glucose-6- phosphate dehydrogenase variants. *Proc. natn. Acad. Sci. U.S.A.*, **50**, 481.

27. DAVIDSON, W. M., and ROBERTSON SMITH, D., 1954. A morphological sex difference in the polymorphonuclear neutrophil leucocytes. *Br. med. J.*, ii, 6.

28. DAY, R. W., LARSON, W., and WRIGHT, S. W., 1964. Clinical and cytogenetic studies on a group of females with XXX sex chromosome complements. *J. Pediat.*, **64**, 24.

29. DAY, R. W., LEVINSON, J., LARSON, W., and WRIGHT, S. W., 1963. An XXXXY male. *J. Pediat.*, **63**, 589.

30. DUMERMUTH, G., 1961. EEG-Untersuchungen beim jugendlichen Kline- felter-Syndrom. *Helv. paediat. Acta*, **16**, 702.

31. EMERY, A. E. H., 1963. Clinical manifestations in two carriers of Duchenne muscular dystrophy. *Lancet*, i, 1126.
32. —— 1964. Lyonisation of the X chromosome. *Lancet*, i, 884.
33. FERGUSON-SMITH, M. A., 1962. Sex chromatin anomalies in mentally defective individuals. *Acta cytol.*, **6**, 73.
34. FERGUSON-SMITH, M. A., JOHNSTON, A. W., and HANDMAKER, S. D., 1960. Primary amentia and micro-orchidism associated with an XXXY sex-chromosome constitution. *Lancet*, ii, 184.
35. FORD, C. E., JACOBS, P. A., and LAJTHA, L. G., 1958. Human somatic chromosomes. *Nature, Lond.*, **181**, 1565.
36. FORD, C. E., JONES, K. W., POLANI, P. E., DE ALMEIDA, J. C., and BRIGGS, J. H., 1959. A sex-chromosome anomaly in a case of gonadal dysgenesis (Turner's syndrome). *Lancet*, i, 711.
37. FORSSMAN, H., and HAMBERT, G., 1963. Incidence of Klinefelter's syndrome among mental patients. *Lancet*, i, 1327.
38. FRACCARO, M., KAIJSER, K., and LINDSTEN, J., 1960. A child with 49 chromosomes. *Lancet*, ii, 899.
39. FRASER, J. H., BOYD, E., LENNOX, B., and DENNISON, W. M., 1961. A case of XXXXY Klinefelter's syndrome. *Lancet*, ii, 1064.
40. GILBERT, C. W., MULDAL, S., LAJTHA, L. G., and ROWLEY, J., 1962. Time-sequence of human chromosome duplication. *Nature, Lond.*, **195**, 869.
41. GORMAN, J. G., DIRE, J., TREACY, A. M., and CAHAN, A., 1963. The application of $-Xg^a$ antiserum to the question of red cell mosaicism in female heterozygotes. *J. Lab. clin. Med.*, **61**, 642.
42. HAMBERT, G., 1964. Positive sex chromatin in men with epilepsy. *Acta med. scand.*, **175**, 663.
43. HARNDEN, D. G., 1960. A human skin culture technique used for cytological examinations. *Br. J. exp. Path.*, **41**, 31.
44. HAUSER, G. A., 1963. Gonadal dysgenesis. In *Intersexuality*, edited by C. Overzier, p. 298. New York: Academic Press.
45. JACOBS, P. A., BAIKIE, A. G., COURT BROWN, W. M., FORREST, H., ROY, J. R., STEWART, J. S. S., and LENNOX, B., 1959. Chromosomal sex in the syndrome of testicular feminization. *Lancet*, ii, 591.
46. JACOBS, P. A., BAIKIE, A. G., COURT BROWN, W. M., MACGREGOR, T. N., MACLEAN, N., and HARNDEN, D. G., 1959. Evidence for the existence of the human 'super female'. *Lancet*, ii, 423.
47. JACOBS, P. A., BRUNTON, M., MELVILLE, M. M., BRITTAIN, P. P., and MC-CLEMONT, W. F., 1965. Aggressive behaviour, mental subnormality and the XYY male. *Nature, Lond.*, **208**, 1351.
48. JACOBS, P. A., and STRONG, J. A., 1959. A case of human intersexuality having a possible XXY sex-determining mechanism. *Nature, Lond.*, **183**, 302.
49. JOSEPH, M. C., ANDERS, J. M., and TAYLOR, A. I., 1964. A boy with XXXXY sex chromosomes. *J. Med. Genet.*, **1**, 95.
50. JOST, A., 1947. Recherches sur la différenciation sexuelle de l'embryon de lapin. III. Rôle des gonades foetales dans la différenciation sexuelle somatique. *Archs Anat. microsc. Morph. exp.*, **36**, 271.
51. KESAREE, N., and WOOLLEY, P. V., 1963. A phenotypic female with 49 chromosomes, presumably XXXXX. *J. Pediat.*, **63**, 1099.
52. KIDD, C. B., KNOX, R. S., and Mantle, D. J., 1963. A psychiatric investigation of triple-X chromosome females. *Br. J. Psychiat.*, **109**, 90.
53. KLINEFELTER, Jr., J. F., REIFENSTEIN, Jr., E. C., and ALBRIGHT, F., 1942. Syndrome characterized by gynecomastia, aspermatogenesis without a-Leydigism, and increased secretion of follicle-stimulating hormone. *J. Clin. Endocr. Metab.*, **2**, 615.

54. LINSTEN, J., 1963. *The Nature and Origin of X Chromosome Aberrations in Turner's Syndrome*. A Cytogenetical and Clinical Study of 57 Patients. Stockholm: Almqvist & Wiksell.

55. LYON, M. F., 1961. Gene action in the X-chromosome of the mouse (*Mus musculus* L.). *Nature, Lond.*, **190**, 372.

56. 1962. Sex chromatin and gene action in the mammalian X-chromosome. *Am. J. hum. Genet.*, **14**, 135.

57. MACLEAN, N., HARNDEN, D. G., COURT BROWN, W. M., BOND, J., and MANTLE, D. J., 1964. Sex-chromosome abnormalities in newborn babies. *Lancet*, i, 286.

58. MACLEAN, N., MITCHELL, J. M., HARNDEN, D. G., WILLIAMS, J., JACOBS, P. A., BUCKTON, K. A., BAIKIE, A. G., COURT BROWN, W. M., McBRIDE, J. A., STRONG, J. A., CLOSE, H. G., and JONES, D. C., 1962. A survey of sex-chromosome abnormalities among 4514 mental defectives. *Lancet*, i, 293.

59. MELLBIN, G., 1965. Neuropsychiatric disorders in sex chromatin negative women. *Br. J. Psychiat.*, **112**, 145.

60. MELLMAN, W. J., 1965. Human peripheral blood leucocyte cultures. In *Human Chromosome Methodology*, Yunis, J. J. (Ed.), p. 21. New York: Academic Press.

61. MILCU, St. M., STANESCU, V., TONESCU, V., FOREA, I., POENARU, S., and MAYIMILIAN, C., 1964. Turner-Syndrome mit Schizophrenie und XO-Karyotypus. *Fiziologia norm. Patol.*, **10**, 139.

62. MILLER, O. J., BREG, W. R., SCHMIKEL, R. D., and TROTTER, W., 1961. A family with an XXXXY male, a leukemic male and two 21-trisomic mongoloid females. *Lancet*, ii, 78.

63. MONEY, J., 1963. Cytogenetic and psychosexual incongruities with a note on space-form blindness. *Am. J. Psychiat.*, **119**, 820.

64. 1963. Developmental differentiation of feminity and masculinity compared. In *Man and Civilization: The Potential of Women*, edited by S. M. Farber and R. H. L. Wilson, p. 51. New York: McGraw-Hill Book Company.

65. 1964. Two cytogenetic syndromes. Psychological comparisons. I. Intelligence and specific factor components. *J. Psychiat. Res.*, **2**, 223.

66. MONEY, J., HAMPSON, J. G., and HAMPSON, J. L., 1955. An examination of some basic sexual concepts: the evidence of human hermaphroditism. *Bull. Johns Hopkins Hosp.*, **97**, 301.

67. 1957. Imprinting and the establishment of gender role. *Archs Neurol. Psychiat., Chicago*, **77**, 333.

68. MONEY, J., and POLLITT, E., 1964. Cytogenetic and psychosexual ambiguity. *Archs gen. Psychiat.*, **11**, 589.

69. MOORE, K. L., 1959. Sex reversal in newborn babies. *Lancet*, i, 217.

70. MOORE, K. L., and BARR, M. L., 1954. Nuclear morphology according to sex, in human tissues. *Acta anat.*, **21**, 197.

71. 1955. Smears from the oral mucosa in the detection of chromosomal sex. *Lancet*, ii, 57.

72. MOORHEAD, P. S., NOWELL, P. C., MELLMAN, W. J., BATIPPS, D. M., and HUNGERFORD, D. A., 1960. Chromosome preparations of leucocytes cultured from human peripheral blood. *Expl. Cell Res.*, **20**, 613.

73. MORRIS, J. McL., 1953. The syndrome of testicular feminization in male pseudohermaphrodites. *Am. J. Obstet. Gynec.*, **65**, 1192.

74. MOSIER, H. D., SCOTT, R. W., and COTTER, L. H., 1960. The frequency of positive sex-chromatin pattern in males with mental deficiency. *Pediatrics, Springfield*, **25**, 291.

75. Mosier, H. D., Scott, L. W., and Dingman, H. F., 1960. Sexually deviant behaviour in Klinefelter's syndrome. *J. Pediat.*, **57**, 479.

76. Mukherjee, B. B., and Sinha, A. K., 1963. Further studies on the pattern of chromosome duplication in cultured mammalian leucocytes. *Can. J. Genet. Cytol.*, **5**, 490.

77. ——— 1964. Single-active-X hypothesis: cytological evidence for random inactivation of X-chromosomes in a female mule complement. *Proc. natn. Acad. Sci. U.S.A.*, **51**, 252.

78. Muldal, S., and Ockey, C. H., 1960. The 'double-male': a new chromosome constitution in Klinefelter's syndrome. *Lancet*, ii, 492.

79. Mylle, M., and Graham, M. A., 1954. Sex chromatin in neurons of human frontal cortex and sympathetic ganglia. *Anat. Rec.*, **118**, 402.

80. Nielsen, J., 1964. Klinefelter's syndrome and behaviour. *Lancet*, **2**, 587.

81. Norby, D. E., Thuline, H. C., and Priest, J. H., 1962. X-chromosome differentiation in relation to coat pattern in cats. *Genetics, Princeton*, **47**, 973.

82. Ohno, S., and Makino, S., 1961. The single-X nature of sex chromatin in man. *Lancet*, **1**, 78.

83. Overzier, C., 1963. The so-called true Klinefelter's syndrome. In *Intersexuality*, edited by C. Overzier, p. 277. New York: Academic Press.

84. Park, W. W., 1957. The occurrence of sex chromatin in early human and macaque embryos. *J. Anat.*, **91**, 369.

85. Pasqualini, R. G., Vidal, G., and Bur, G. E., 1957. Psychopathology of Klinefelter's syndrome. Review of thirty-one cases. *Lancet*, ii, 164.

86. Paulsen, C. A., de Sonza, A., Yoshizumi, T., and Lewis, B. M., 1964. Results of a buccal smear survey in noninstitutionalized adult males. *J. clin. Endocr. Metab.*, **24**, 1182.

87. Pitts, F. N., and Guze, S. B., 1963. Anorexia nervosa and gonadal dysgenesis (Turner's syndrome). *Am. J. Psychiat.*, **119**, 1100.

88. Plunkett, E. R., and Barr, M. L., 1956. Testicular dysgenesis, affecting the seminiferous tubules principally, with chromatin-positive nuclei. *Lancet*, ii, 853.

89. Polani, P. E., Hunter, W. F., and Lennox, B., 1954. Chromosomal sex in Turner's syndrome with coarctation of the aorta. *Lancet*, ii, 120.

90. Pritchard, M., 1964. Klinefelter's syndrome and behaviour. *Lancet*, ii, 762.

91. Raboch, J., and Sipová, L., 1961. The mental level in forty-seven cases of 'true Klinefelter's syndrome'. *Acta endocr., Copenh.*, **36**, 404.

92. Raphael, T., and Shaw, M. W., 1963. Chromosome studies in schizophrenia. *J. Am. med. Ass.*, **183**, 1022.

93. Robinson, A., and Puck, T. T., 1965. Sex chromatin in newborns: presumptive evidence for external factors in human nondisjunction. *Science, N.Y.*, **148**, 83.

94. Sandberg, A. A., Koepf, G. F., Ishihara, T., and Hauschka, T. S., 1961. An XYY male. *Lancet*, ii, 488.

95. Schmid, W., 1963. DNA replication patterns of human chromosomes. *Cytogenetics*, **2**, 175.

96. Sergovich, F. R. (Children's Psychiatric Research Institute, London, Ontario.) Personal communication.

97. Shaffer, J. W., 1962. A specific cognitive deficit observed in gonadal aplasia (Turner's syndrome). *J. clin. Psychol.*, **18**, 403.

98. Singh, R. P., and Carr, D. H., 1966. The histology of the gonads of XO embryos and fetuses. *Anat. Rec.*, **154**, 489.

99. Slater, E., and Zilkha, K., 1961. A case of Turner mosaic with myopathy and schizophrenia. *Proc. R. Soc. Med.*, **54**, 674.

100. TJIO, J. H., and LEVAN, A., 1956. The chromosome number of man. *Hereditas*, **42,** 1.

101. TOWNES, P. L., ZIEGLER, N. A., and LENHARD, L. W., 1965. A patient with 48 chromosomes (XYYY). *Lancet*, i, 1041.

102. TOWNES, P. L., ZIEGLER, N. A., and SCHEINER, A. P., 1965. An XXYY variant of the Klinefelter syndrome in a prepubertal boy. *J. Pediat.*, **67,** 410.

103. TURNER, H. H., 1938. A syndrome of infantilism, congenital webbed neck and cubitus valgus. *Endocrinology*, **23,** 566.

104. WALLIS, H., 1960. Psychopathologische Studien bei endokrin gestörten Kindern und Jugendlichen. 1. Mitteilung. *Z. Kinderheilk*, **83,** 420.

105. WEGMAN, T. G., and SMITH, D. W., 1963. Incidence of Klinefelter's syndrome among juvenile delinquents and felons. *Lancet*, i, 274.

106. WOLSTENHOLME, D. R., 1965. Electron microscopic identification of sex chromatin bodies in tissue culture cells. *Chromosoma*, **16,** 453.

III

THE CYTOLOGY OF BRAIN CELLS AND CULTURED NERVOUS TISSUES

FREDERICK H. KASTEN*
PH.D.

*Research Coordinator and Director,
Department of Ultrastructural Cytochemistry*

*Pasadena Foundation for Medical Research,
Pasadena, California*

1

Introduction

Some of the important features of brain function which dominate modern scientific interest are concerned with cortical excitability and bioelectric phenomena, information storage and retrieval, nature of the synapse, biochemical features of the nervous system and role of neuroglia. Ultimately, experimental studies of these vital problems should achieve some degree of rapport with our proliferating knowledge of the cytology of nervous elements and their fine structural features and connections laid bare by light and electron microscopy. While we are a long way from achieving this goal, the pathways are becoming clearer. The three-dimensional substrata of nervous tissues are, of course, dominated by neurons and neuroglia. Their structural interrelationships and plastic nature are enormously complex and under intensive investigation, especially at the ultrastructural level. The possibilities afforded by tissue culture techniques in studying this problem and other interesting aspects have not been overlooked. Indeed, this approach coupled with phase-contrast and time-lapse cinematography provides the only means to the direct study of living neurons, neuroglial activity, nerve fibre growth, and myelination within the confines of a relatively simple growth chamber.

Advances in neurocytology have depended on the development and successful application of new techniques. By means of special neurological

* The author holds academic appointments in the Department of Anatomy of the University of Southern California School of Medicine, and the Department of Pathology of Loma Linda University School of Medicine.

stains for Nissl substance and myelin as well as classical silver impregnation methods for axons and dendritic fibres, it has been possible to
attack and delimit the structurally complex regions of the brain. With
the post-war development and availability of electron microscopes, which
allow direct magnifications of up to 200,000 times or more with a resolving
power of 8–10 Å, it has been practical to explore the new vistas of infra-
structure. Not only has it been feasible to characterize the fine structure
of neurons and neuroglia, but more important, to detect different types
of synaptic connections and begin to understand the intricate pattern of
structural interrelations. Such knowledge subserves our comprehension
of brain function at the macromolecular level. Almost hand-in-hand with
this development and experience in interpreting electron micrographs,
there have been concomitant advances in cytochemistry.

Specialized techniques are available to fix and characterize nerve
elements with respect to the microscopic distribution of nucleic acids,
proteins, and polysaccharides, in essence the macromolecular chemical
components. It has been practicable to extend cytochemical techniques for
visualizing certain enzymes to the level of electron microscopy by employing aldehyde fixatives. These allow preservation of certain enzymes which
would be otherwise destroyed or lost by classical osmic acid fixation. By
judicious choice of reacting agents and conditions in the enzymatic test, it
has been possible to attain fine electron dense precipitates at enzyme sites
sufficient for relatively high resolution ultrastructural cytochemistry.
Examples of enzymes which can be detected in thin sections by electron
microscopy include acid phosphatase, which is associated with lysosomes,
and thiamine pyrophosphatase, restricted to the Golgi complex. A number
of good histochemistry texts are available which should be consulted by
those especially interested in this field.[2, 28, 37]

Parallel advances have been made in another branch of histo- and
cytochemistry—autoradiography, or the self-detection of radioisotopes.
The usual procedure involves the injection of a solution of a given radioactive compound into an animal. After a period of time, the animal is
sacrificed and the tissues to be investigated are fixed and prepared as for
routine sectioning. A thin layer of photographic emulsion is layered over
the section in the dark and allowed to remain in contact until there has
been sufficient exposure to the radioactive element. Following the usual
photographic processing, the preparation is stained, mounted and examined microscopically for deposits of silver grains over radioactive areas
of cells. By the use of H3-labelled compounds, which are incorporated
selectively into DNA (thymidine), RNA (uridine), and proteins (various
amino acids), it is possible to localize the intracellular site of nucleo-
proteins to approximately one micron in light microscope sections.
Essentially, the same technique may be applied with greater finesse and
control of experimental variables to cells growing in tissue culture. The
recent availability of fine grain photographic emulsions has allowed exten-

sion to ultrathin sections of tissue for examination of isotope localization by electron microscopy. In this connection, it has been claimed that it is possible to attain autoradiographic resolutions of 0·1–0·2 microns. Some of the published results are indeed impressive.

A number of other significant techniques should be mentioned. One is the use of water-soluble plastics as embedding media for ultrastructural cytochemistry. The usual epoxy resins like Epon or Araldite are very adequate for routine electron microscopy but will not allow enzymatic digestion of nucleic acids or proteins in thin sections. Such ultrastructural cytochemical procedures require the use of glycol-methacrylate (GMA) or hydroxy-glycol-methacrylate plastics. In the hands of W. Bernhard and his group, the technique has yielded valuable information about the localization of nucleic acids and proteins superimposed on usual electron micrograph images. Another method is the microdissection of single nerve cells and their morphological components. This is followed by analyses for nucleic acids using specially adapted ultramicrochemical techniques. The method was successfully applied by Hydén and Egyhàzi[21] to certain mammalian neurons, as Deiter's nucleus of the brain (Plate I). By using these specialized techniques in combination with prior learning experiments, Hydén and associates suggest that the chemical basis of memory depends on the sequential arrangement of nucleotides in RNA. Specifically, they report an increased adenine-uracil ratio in the nuclear RNA from neurons of animals trained to obtain food by balancing on a rod, compared with control animals.

By similar ultramicrotechniques, Lowry estimates the dry weight of large nerve cells to be 5,000–50,000 picograms (10^{-12} g). According to a 1966 report by Satake and Abe,[47] it is possible to extract large numbers of pure neuronal cell perikarya from rat cerebral cortex for biochemical analyses. Ultra-violet microscopy at 2600 Å, although of limited quantitative usefulness, allows the intracellular visualization of nucleic acids (Plate I), even in living cells under optimal conditions. Other microscopic techniques of value in the study of nerve cells include interference microscopy, which gives information about cellular dry mass or protein content, X-ray microscopy for elemental analyses, and polarizing microscopy for detection of molecular orientation, as in the myelin sheath around many axons. Probably the most proven quantitative cytochemical approach has been the analytical measurements of DNA in single nuclei using the Feulgen cytochemical colour reaction in conjunction with cytophotometric techniques. Equipment needs for this purpose may often be minimal to achieve reliable data. Numerous biological and medical applications of this technique are on record, which include studies of DNA content of neurons and neuroglia in different regions of the brain and in tumours. It is hoped that this brief survey of technical advances in cellular biology will indicate the basis for advances in fundamental research and their eventual tie-in with clinical practice.

It is evident that limitations of space preclude a thorough summary and review of all pertinent aspects of the subject of brain cytology. Fortunately, there are excellent texts and reviews which document the basic knowledge in this field.[15, 48, 51] The present chapter will be confined first, to a general description of neurons and neuroglia with emphasis on cortical cytology and second, to a further discussion of nervous tissues in culture and the usefulness of this dynamic approach in studies of neurocytology and function.

2

Structure of Neurons

General Features

The neuronal doctrine elaborated by Waldeyer about seventy-five years ago is still acceptable today, although it does not present the whole picture. Briefly, this doctrine states that the neuron is the structural, genetic, and functional unit of the nervous system and that all pathways consist of single neuron units organized in simple or complex circuits. Palay[35] emphasizes that this doctrine is incomplete, for it ignores the non-neuronal elements which comprise an integral part of nervous tissue—the Schwann cells in the peripheral system, oligodendrocytes and ependyma in the central nervous system, the axon sheaths, and even the blood vessels. A vast literature attests to the continuity of nerve cell and nerve fibre as a single structural unit or neuron. It has been estimated that the total volume of a large motor neuron is $0 \cdot 001$ mm^3 or 10^6 μ^3. The surface area varies within a tremendous range, according to the degree of proliferation of dendrites. In this connection, Sholl[48] estimates that the perikaryon of a cortical cell only contributes 10 per cent to the total neuronal surface. Dendritic surface projections may enlarge the surface by 90,000 μ^2. The breadth of area involved in such coverage is further grasped by one estimate that in the cerebral cortex the branches of a single nerve fibre encompass the perikarya of 5000 neurons. Fig. 1 illustrates the vast dendritic patterns in Purkinje and pyramidal cells of the brain.

In addition to processes and the cell nucleus, the neuron includes the cytoplasmic cell body or perikaryon which is essential to the function of the entire cell. The perikaryon of the neuron contains a typical accumulation of basophilic granules, which are rich in RNA and referred to as Nissl substance. There is a highly developed Golgi complex which is distributed throughout the cytoplasm. Other entities frequently observed at the light microscope level include melanin and lipofucsin granules, mitochondria, lysosomal aggregates, and neurofibrils. The axonal process is slender and usually arises from an elevation on the cell body known as the axon hillock. It frequently gives off, at a short distance from the perikaryon, several branches or collaterals at right angles to the parent fibre. Dendritic fibres are regarded as direct protoplasmic extensions of the perikaryon and con-

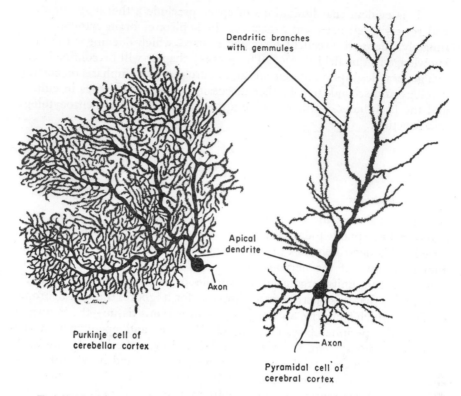

Dendritic branches
with gemmules

Apical
dendrite

Axon

Purkinje cell of
cerebellar cortex

Axon

Pyramidal cell of
cerebral cortex

FIG. 1. Scaled drawings of two principal cell types in cerebellar and cerebral cortex. Dendritic branches provide extensive area for synaptic terminals of many other cortical and subcortical neurons. Golgi preparations, monkey (from Ref. 51).

tain the same cytoplasmic organelles. In electron micrographs, smaller dendritic and axonal processes are often difficult to distinguish from one another. The nucleus of the neuron is conspicuous because of its large size, scarcity of chromatin, clear nucleoplasm, and dense prominent nucleolus. An electron micrograph of a typical neuron is shown in Plate II.

It is beyond the scope of this chapter to discuss the comparative histochemical distribution of enzymes among neurons of the central nervous system (see[1] and the chapter by McEwen in this volume). While the cerebral cortex exhibits a diffuse activity of dehydrogenase and reductase activities, the third cortical layer displays the highest activity and is in fact particularly susceptible to anoxia. Detailed cytochemical observations would suggest that in general, aerobic respiration is conducted by neuronal processes, while the perikaryon is responsible for glycolysis and metabolism through the pentose shunt. An example is presented of high dehydrogenase activity in a neuron of the hypoglossal nucleus in man (Plate III). While the neuron is a specialized cell exhibiting a high rate of protein and RNA synthesis in addition to other secretory activities, it is apparent from what was said earlier that there are distinct metabolic differences between the perikaryon and neuronal processes. It should also be emphasized that the neuron interacts metabolically with attending neuroglial cells. Hydén and collaborators showed that following stimulation of the vestibular nucleus and microdissection of its cellular components, the activity of succinic dehydrogenase and cytochrome oxidase was increased in the neurons, while a corresponding decrease in aerobic respiratory activity occurred in the surrounding neuroglia. It has been suggested that in order to conserve oxygen for the nerve cell, the neuroglial cell reverts to glycolytic metabolism.

3

Electron Microscopy of Neurons

Nucleus

The structure of the neuronal nucleus (Plate II) does not differ greatly from that of other cells. There is a sparse distribution of chromatin, usually in the form of granules of 100–200 Å size distributed irregularly or in heterochromatic patches near the nuclear envelope and *nucleolus*. Other regions of the nucleoplasm may appear somewhat empty and are likely to have lost some nuclear constituents during fixation. The nucleolus, although of great size and prominence, is undistinguished in its morphology. It consists of complex, tightly packed coils of ribonucleoprotein granules referred together as nucleonemma, some moderately dense regions (pars amorpha), and occasional vacuoles. The nucleolus maintains its integrity despite the absence of a limiting membrane. On the other hand, the nuclear envelope consists of an inner dense membrane and an outer membrane, which may connect directly at times with the membranes of the endoplasmic reticulum. The two membranes of the envelope are compressed at regular intervals to form individual pores, which are frequently in the form of a complex diaphragm. The passage of substances through such pores has been demonstrated using colloidal gold particles. This manner of communication does not exclude other means of nucleocytoplasmic interchange.

Perikaryon (See Plates V and VI)

Nissl Substance. The clumps of Nissl substance seen with the light microscope in neurons after staining with basic dyes like cresyl violet have been shown to correspond with the distribution, shape, and composition of granular or rough endoplasmic reticulum. This consists of a dense mass of parallel arrays of flattened cisternae or sacs with tubular interconnections. This endoplasmic reticular system is bounded by numerous ribosomes or ribonucleoprotein particles of 100–300 Å diameter. The ribosomes may lie attached to the membrane surfaces or free in the cytoplasm as individual particles or rosettes which are frequently called polysomes. A similar system is seen in glandular cells (pancreatic acinar cells) where high levels of protein synthesis are maintained. However, in glandular cells the ribosomes are distributed uniformly over cisternae, whereas in neurons they aggregate. It is regarded that nucleolar RNA gives rise to most of the ribosomal and free RNA of the cytoplasm and this interacts with amino acids transported to the ribosome to help synthesize new proteins. This has been confirmed for the neuron by electron autoradiography, in which newly synthesized protein first appears in the Nissl region.[10]

Golgi Complex. Palay and Palade in 1955[36] described another system of cytoplasmic membranes in neurons which is termed agranular reticulum because of the lack of associated ribosomes. The evidence is suggestive that this endoplasmic reticulum system corresponds with the classical Golgi complex. The system is complex and appears in thin sections as packed profiles of cisternae and vesicles. Although the components of the Golgi complex appear as isolated clusters, they actually comprise a network surrounding the nucleus of the neuron. In glandular cells, the complex lies between the nucleus and the secretory end of the cell and has been shown to be involved in some way with the transport of proteins first synthesized in the ribosomes. It has been seriously questioned whether the Golgi complex has the same role in neurons. However, new autoradiographic evidence by Droz[10] indicates that proteins synthesized by Nissl substance are in fact transported to the Golgi complex (Plate IV). In nerve cell injury the Golgi complex fragments and disappears.

Neurofilaments. The neurofibrils which may be observed by light microscopy have been resolved by electron microscopy into bundles of fine filaments (Plate V). Their longitudinal orientation and penetration into the axoplasm was visualized years ago by polarization microscopy. The individual neurofilaments are about 100 Å thick, appear unbranched, solid, and are of indefinite length. They are common in certain large neurons, but are rare in neurons of the cerebral cortex and granule cells of the cerebellum. They are almost always present in myelinated axons and for a short distance in dendrites of the spinal cord. During chromatolysis neurofilaments are present in greater abundance. It has been suggested that the filaments consist of structural proteins and are supporting elements, but the evidence for this is scant. Another suggestion is that the filaments play a role in impulse conduction.

Other Formed Elements of the Perikaryon. Scattered mitochondria are found throughout the cytoplasm and extend into axons and dendrites. They are small and slender, varying from 0·1–1·0 micron in diameter. Their structure is very similar to that of mitochondria in other cells; each has a relatively smooth outer unit membrane which surrounds a second unit membrane which is thrown into folds or cristae across the mitochondrial compartment. Neuronal mitochondria are noted for the fact that their cristae often run lengthwise and for the apparent absence of intramito-

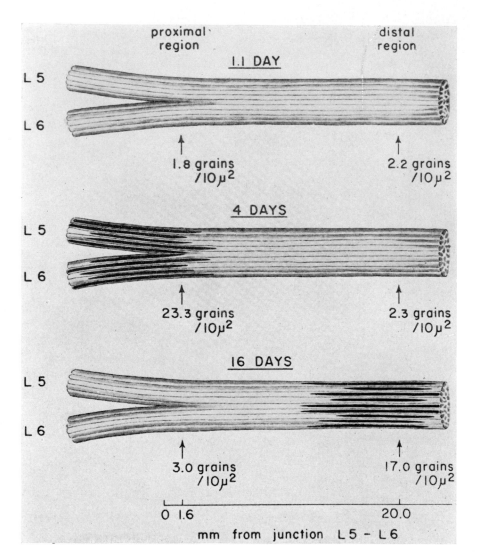

Fig. 2. Diagram representing the flow of proteins labelled with radioactive leucine from the junction of the L5 and L6 roots of the rat sciatic nerve. The heavy black lines seen in the middle diagram (four days after injection of H_3-leucine) and the bottom diagram (16 days after injection) indicate the location of the axonal radioactivity. Grain counts per $10\mu^2$ of axon are shown.
Results demonstrate a migration of radioactivity down the axon with the passage of time (from Ref. 1).

chondrial granules. Mitochondria are the sites of oxidative enzymes and function in this metabolic pathway. They are said to increase in number during chromatolysis. Recent research developments point to the presence of DNA and a protein-synthesizing system in mitochondria. Another membrane-bounded body of the same size as the mitochondria is the lysosome. It contains dense granular material in its core which consists of a dozen-odd hydrolytic enzymes as acid phosphatase and sulfatase. Lysosomes are in many types of cells and are believed to function in the degradation of phagocytosed material and during cellular degeneration. Centrioles have been observed in small granule cells of the cerebellum and ependymal cells of embryonic spinal cord but not in most neurons of adult spinal cord and brain. Since their presence is associated with mitosis, it would be surprising to find them in mature neurons. Lipid droplets, multivesicular bodies, and various ageing pigments (lipofuscin granules) have been detected in neuronal perikarya.

Axons

As has been mentioned earlier, the axon usually originates from the axon hillock or cone of origin in the perikaryon. The axon hillock is difficult to recognize in some electron micrographs, but apparently contains a reduced amount of granular endoplasmic reticulum (Plate V). The absence of Nissl substance in this region and in the axoplasm distinguishes axons from dendrites. Also, the lack of Nissl material accounts for the failure of proteins to be synthesized in the axon hillock (Plate VI). Within the axoplasm are extremely elongated mitochondria and occasional membrane-bound clear zones. Other particles are present which constitute a flowing traffic according to time-lapse film records of cultured nervous tissues (see later discussion on tissue culture). With the aid of elegant autoradiographic experiments *in situ*,[11, 50] it appears well-established that a good part of this axonal traffic is in a proximo-distal direction and consists of proteins previously synthesized in the perikaryon (Fig. 2). According to Weiss, the average rate of migration is approximately one millimetre per day. Investigations into problems associated with axoplasmic flow are ably summarized by Ochs.[34] Neurofilaments of about 100 Å diameter with a clear centre are observed to run parallel to the long axis in myelinated axons (Plate V). They may be stained collectively by argyrophilic methods and probably correspond to the neurofibrillae of silver stain preparations (Fig. 3). Neurotubules of larger diameter than neurofilaments are observed in non-myelinated axons. Axons exclusive of myelin vary in diameter from about $0.01\ \mu$ to $10\ \mu$ and may attain a length of one metre. There is no neurolemma or sheath of Schwann around axons of the CNS.

Myelin Formation. Myelin deposition is not always continuous along the course of an axon and frequently originates a short distance from the perikaryon. The myelin sheath is interrupted at intervals along the axon by constrictions, the nodes of Ranvier. Occasionally, there are defects in

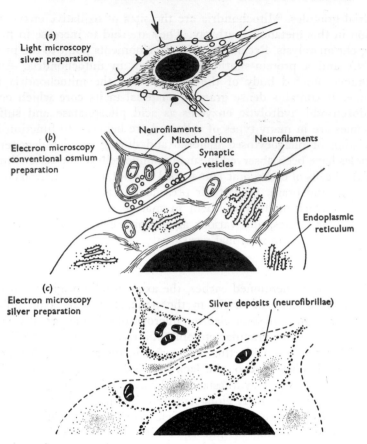

(a)
Light microscopy
silver preparation

(b)
Electron microscopy
conventional osmium
preparation

Neurofilaments
Mitochondrion
Synaptic
vesicles
Neurofilaments
Endoplasmic
reticulum

(c)
Electron microscopy
silver preparation

Silver deposits (neurofibrillae)

FIG. 3. Diagram to show the relationship between osmium-fixed boutons seen by electron microscopy (b) on the one hand, and formalin-fixed silver preparations seen by light (a) and electron microscopy (c) on the other hand. Silver neurofibrillar stains only reveal a small proportion of the presynaptic terminals actually present (from Ref. 15).

the concentric lammelae which produce visible clefts, the incisures of Schmidt-Lantermann. The nature of the formation of myelin by glia cells and attachment of myelin to the axon has been largely elucidated by electron microscopy in combination with tissue culture. In the central nervous system, myelin apparently originates with oligodendrocytes. The manner of myelin formation around axons in the CNS is believed to be the same as in the peripheral nervous system except that the Schwann cell participates in this process instead of the oligodendrocyte. There is a double-layered infolding of Schwann cell membrane, which becomes wrapped spirally around the axon in concentric layers. Another concept of myelin formation proposed in part by Luse, for which there is less evidence, is that it is formed by the apposition around the axon of multiple glial cell processes in a complex multilamellated array with subsequent flattening and fusion of these processes. A schematic drawing of myelin formation, according to the dominant spiral wrapping concept, and a comparable electron micrograph of the completed process are shown in Fig. 4 and Plate VII.

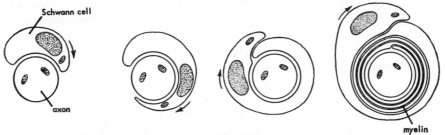

FIG. 4. Schematic representation of myelin formation by Schwann cell growth about axon. The myelin sheath is formed by a spiral infolding and fusion of the neurilemma of the Schwann cells in the peripheral nerves (from Ref. 13).

Myelin exhibits a well-known periodicity which consists of major dense lines or lamellae which are approximately 150 Å thick and are separated by interperiod lines. The material is a double refracting substance which is composed of a white lipoprotein complex organized in thin concentric sheets of protein alternating with lipids, which constitute about 80 per cent of dry weight.

Dendrites

Dendritic processes of the central nervous system are never myelinated. They are usually surrounded by glial processes and never lie directly on basement membranes. In large neurons, there may be an extension of granular endoplasmic reticulum (Nissl substance) into the dendrite. The most characteristic fine structural feature of dendrites is the presence of multiple tubules or canaliculi which lie parallel to one another and extend longitudinally through the fibre core (Plate VIII). They do not appear to be impregnated with silver and may be present in combination with neurofilaments. Dendrites also contain elongated mitochondria and membrane-bound cavities. Of special interest, are fine spinous processes or knobs which are involved in synaptic connections. They may be seen by light microscopy on the cell body and dendritic surfaces of freshly dissected nerve cells (Plate IX).

Membranes

The fine structure of cellular membranes has been shown by Robertson to consist of a triple structure after permanganate fixation, two dense lines each 25 Å thick separated by a 25Å clear zone. The total width of 75 Å is called the unit membrane and is identical whether found in mito-chondria, endoplasmic reticulum, plasma membrane, synaptic vesicles, or bounding the nucleus. It is a bimolecular lipoprotein film. On the other hand, the basement membrane which underlines many tissues is a thick sheet (100–300 Å thick) of mucopolysaccharide material. The relationship of the unit membrane to the excitable membrane of the nervous system is the subject of considerable research. While the excitable membrane was at first a physiological concept, it undoubtedly has a morphological counter-part and must be resolved in relation to ionic conduction and diffusion across synaptic clefts.

Synapses

Axons may terminate in small bulbous expansions known as end feet, boutons terminaux or synaptic boutons which are applied to the perikarya of other neurons or post-synaptic dendrites. Each bouton con-sists of a neurofibrillar loop or ring and often contains mitochondria. They are 1–2 microns in diameter and may be present in the hundreds on a single spinal cord motor cell so as to layer half the surface. The remainder of the perikaryon surface is covered with glial processes, small myelinated axons, or satellite glial cell bodies. In the cerebellum, the bouton has a characteristic mossy fibre ending. The term synapse was employed by Sherrington in 1897 to indicate a functional connection between nerve cells. In Golgi preparations, the absence of continuity between neurons supported the theory of cytoplasmic discontinuities. A comparison of formalin-fixed silver preparations and osmium-fixed boutons seen by electron microscopy is shown in Fig. 3. With the electron microscope, it has been demonstrated that there is a very constant synaptic cleft of about 200 Å. This resolves the controversy between the reticularists and the neuronists regarding the morphological relations between neurons; there is no protoplasmic continuity between synaptic elements involved in chemical transmission of the nerve impulse. Since the chemical release of transmitter substance at synapses is apparently unidirectional, it is not surprising to find synapses to be morphologically polarized.

Synaptic junctions exhibit different structural variations (Fig. 5) but retain three basic similarities: (*i*) discontinuity between cytoplasm of the two opposed membranes of a synapse; (*ii*) direct contact of the pre-synaptic (plasma membrane of an axon terminal), and subsynaptic mem-branes which are separated by a synaptic cleft of about 200 Å width; (*iii*) the presence of mitochondria, some neurofilaments, and numerous synaptic vesicles on the presynaptic side. The opposed synaptic membranes display characteristic dense and thickened patches which may appear on the postsynaptic side alone or on both sides of the cleft. It is suggested that the vesicles on the presynaptic side help elaborate neurotransmitter substances. There is apparently less morphological specialization at sites

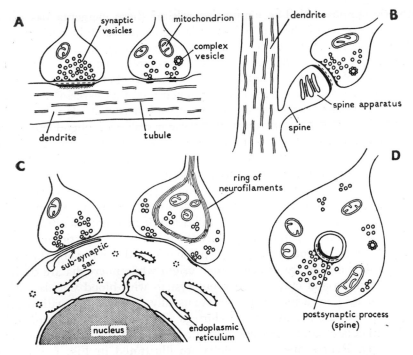

FIG. 5. Diagrams of various forms of synaptic contact illustrate differences in specialization. For example, in A at left, these synapses are restricted to dendritic trunks or their spines, whereas A at right occurs on dendritic trunks and perikarya. It has been suggested that the former are excitatory and the latter are inhibitory. The drawing at B illustrates a spine synapse which often contains an organelle termed a spine apparatus consisting of a series of sacs alternating in position with dense plates. Other details of synaptic contacts are shown in C and D. See text and original reference for further data (from Ref. 15).

where electrical transmission occurs across membranes. According to recent evidence, electronic junctions at various locations display characteristic membrane fusions with obliteration of the synaptic cleft (Plate X). Modern cell fractionation methods have permitted the isolation of different types of synaptic membranes from the brain cortex. For a concise review of the synapse, an article by Eccles in *Scientific American* is recommended.[12]

4

Cytology of Neuroglia

The importance of neuroglia in the brain and spinal cord has received greater attention in recent years, largely because these elements are recognized to constitute a more dynamic and functional system than was formerly supposed.[25] The supportive role of these elements has given way to concepts of their role in regulating neuronal fluid and gaseous interchange, formation of myelin, regeneration, phagocytosis, nutrition, and perhaps more subtle phenomena of a complex nature. The relative importance of neuroglia is underlined by the fact that in mammals only about 4 per cent of brain nuclei belong to neurons and the residual population belong largely to metabolically active neuroglial elements. The characteristic pulsations *in vitro* of Schwann cells and oligodendrocytes were documented by Pomerat and collaborators.[30, 40] The rhythmic movements are now regarded as significant characteristics of these elements although the functional interpretation is not clear. One of the 'far-out' speculations is that neuroglia which typically lie close to neuronal surfaces are involved in feeding information to the neuron essential for memory. The classification and identification of neuroglia is always open to discussion, but we will consider here the prime characteristics of macroglia (astrocytes, oligodendrocytes), ependyma, and microglia. Macroglia and ependymal cells are of ectodermal origin while microglia are derived from mesoderm and enter the nervous system with blood vessels during development. The various cell types are usually distinguished with the aid of Nissl preparations and del Rio Hortega silver preparations. Some cells are intermediate forms and are difficult to classify by light or electron microscopy. Representative neuroglia are illustrated in Fig. 6. From a cytochemical view, astrocytes contain far less activity of certain oxidative enzymes than do oligodendrocytes. Within the normal cerebral cortex, only diploid neuroglial nuclei are present, according to Feulgen cytophotometry carried out by Lapham and Johnstone.[26] They report that in the Purkinje cell layer of the human cerebellar cortex, some neuroglia are diploid while others are tetraploid; it was not possible to recognize the glial type(s). Judging from autoradiography results reported by Koenig,[24] and by Smart and Leblond,[49] using the DNA precursor H3-thymidine, oligodendrocytes are capable of division and may transform into astrocytes; whereas, astrocytes and microglia fail to synthesize DNA. It is also suggested that neuroglial cells are constantly being formed from spongioblasts.

Astrocytes

Astrocytes are branched stellate cells whose cytoplasm contains small granules known as gliosomes which are interpreted to be lipoprotein complexes. The cells exhibit abundant cytoplasm which contain the usual cytoplasmic organelles. The nucleus appears pale and contains little chromatin. The cleft of the nuclear membrane is especially prominent as are the numerous nuclear pores. Protoplasmic and fibrous astrocytes are distinguished. The former are also called mossy cells and display many branching processes (Fig. 6). They lack intracellular fibrils and are found mainly in the grey matter where they may envelop neuronal perikarya (perineuronal satellite cells). Fibrous astrocytes or spider cells have thin

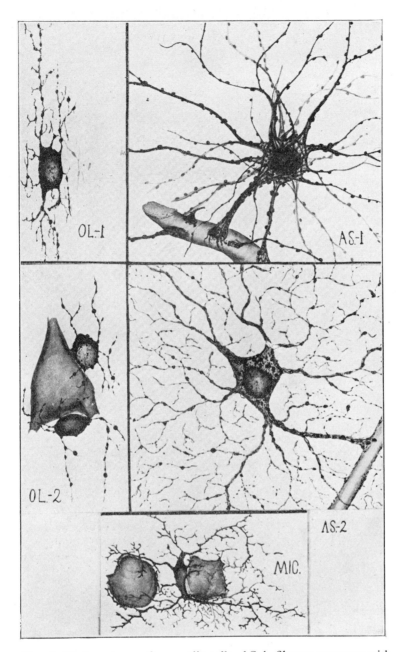

FIG. 6. Various types of neuroglia cells. AS-1, fibrous astrocyte with two processes forming foot plates against a blood vessel; AS-2, protoplasmic astrocyte with foot plate and containing gliosomes (dark granules) in its body and processes; MIC, microglia cell whose delicate spiny processes embrace the bodies of two neurons; OL-1, oligodendrocyte in the white matter; OL-2, two oligodendrocytes lying against a nerve cell (perineuronal satellites) (from Ref. 40).

unbranched processes which extend in all directions. They are derived from numerous fine gliofilaments which resemble myofibrils and tonofibrils of muscle and epithelial cells. The branched processes terminate in

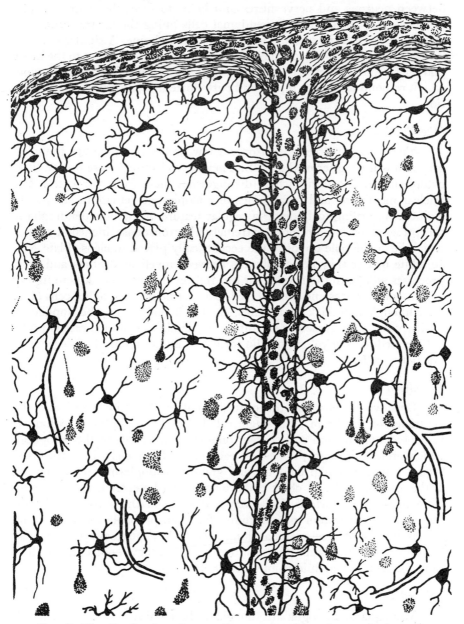

FIG. 7. The distribution of neuroglia around an incoming cerebral vessel and around capillaries in the superficial layer of the cerebral cortex. Note the glial expansion towards the pia mater (from Ref. 46).

foot plates or perivascular feet which adhere to blood vessels in the CNS (Fig. 7). They form a continuous glial membrane around blood vessels, the perivascular limiting membrane. The glial processes pack the space between neurons and nerve fibres and helps to form the neuropil. The processes also surround the ependymal cells lining the central canal and ventricles to form the internal limiting glial membrane. A similar external limiting membrane is attached by fine processes and foot plates to the inner pial surface. It is these reactive glial cells, probably of the fibrous type, which respond to surface injury and participate in healing and scar formation.

Oligodendrocytes

These are small cells with only a few processes which are found in grey and white matter of the CNS. They have electron-dense nuclei, little cytoplasm, and no fibrils which distinguishes them from astrocytes. The nuclear membrane and membranes of endoplasmic reticulum are poorly defined. According to Bodian,[3] a regular feature of the oligodendroglia is the presence of one or more extremely electron-dense inclusion bodies which lie at the pole opposite the eccentrically placed nucleus (Plate XI). In white matter they lie in columns between myelinated fibres and their processes adhere to the myelin sheath. In grey matter, they adhere tightly to neuronal surfaces and are referred to as perineuronal satellite cells (Fig. 8). Although they lack foot plates, their cell bodies may be applied to capillary walls (perivascular satellites). Their high metabolic rate is probably related to their role in myelin formation and in removal of degenerating nerve cells.

Ependyma

Ependymal cells line the central canal of the spinal cord and the ventricles of the brain as a single cell layer. They appear as columnar to cuboidal epithelium and contain bundles of filaments in the cytoplasm which project through the base of each cell. The nucleus is in the basal region while the Golgi complex and granular endoplasmic reticulum are at the opposite pole. In chick embryo spinal cord, centrioles are common close to the free surface. Cilia may project from the surface, although these are more common in embryonic life. Their probable role is in aiding the circulation of cerebrospinal fluid. Modified ependymal cells comprise the thin wall of the brain in certain locations and may modify the production of cerebrospinal fluid from vascular channels.

Microglia

Microglia or mesoglia are thought to be of fibroblastic origin which migrate into the nervous system from the connective tissue of neural blood vessels. The cells are very small and each contains a dense crenated nucleus. There is a thin rim of cytoplasm which contains densely packed

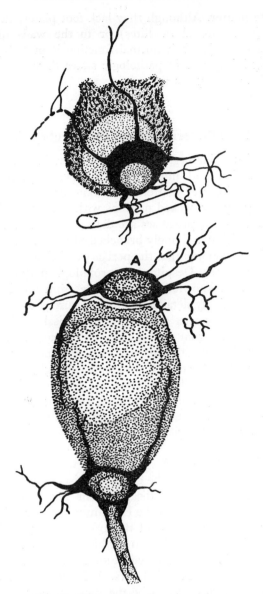

FIG. 8. Oligodendroglia in close proximity to neurons. This type of oligodendroglia is also called a perineuronal satellite cell (from Ref. 48).

ribosomes (Plate XII). With the light microscope, they may be confused with shrunken and pycnotic neurons. They are distinguished from oligodendrocytes by their smaller size, more elongated nuclei, and absence of cytoplasmic electron-dense inclusions. Microglia are observed in both grey and white matter. Although they lack foot plates, they often adhere to perikarya (perineuronal satellites) or to the walls of blood vessels (perivascular satellites). Their normal function is probably phagocytic in nature. During injury and in pathologic states they enlarge and become extremely active scavenger cells.

5

Cellular Patterns Within the Cerebral Cortex

The patterns of cellular organization of the cerebral cortex is designed for the transmission and interaction of nerve impulses. The cellular inhomogeneity of the grey matter is well-known and leads to a complex tissue containing tightly packed neurons with perikarya of different sizes. Out of these cell bodies, processes are derived which ramify for long distances. Other dendritic and finely branched fibres traverse the same areas. It is estimated by Economo that the perikarya of almost 14 billion neurons lie in the cerebral cortex. Despite the morphologic perplexity presented by the cortex, sufficient knowledge is available from special staining techniques to provide a fairly detailed cellular picture. For example, a section of the human visual cortex stained by the Nissl method (Plate XIII) reveals an outermost region almost free of neurons, a wide intermediate zone containing densely stained perikarya and neuroglia, and a lower region of white matter filled with abundant neuroglia. If a similar section is stained with a reduced silver method, the neurons with their axons and dendrites are stained (Plate XIV). Other staining methods which yield additional information about neuronal interrelationships utilize methylene blue and the so-called Golgi procedures.

Stratification Within the Cortex

There is no question that the cortex consists of a number of stratified layers. However, considerable disagreement has existed among many reputable neurocytologists as to the exact number of cortical laminations. An interesting historical resumé of this problem is given by Sholl in his monograph.[48] After a thorough study of his own, and an evaluation of the work of others, Brodmann in 1909 concluded that the cortex was built on a six-layered plan with several sub-layers. Although this view has not been universally accepted, it seems to be the most generally accepted one. A diagrammatic representation of the six cell layers and fibre arrangements is shown in Fig. 9. Proceeding downward from the cortical surface, the layers and their predominant cell types include: (*i*) the molecular or plexiform layer which contains relatively few cells—those with horizontal axons and Golgi type II cells—and a dense fibre plexus; (*ii*) the external granular layer containing numerous small pyramidal-shaped cells; (*iii*) the external pyramidal layer composed of separate layers of medium and large pyramidal neurons; (*iv*) the internal granular layer which is domina-

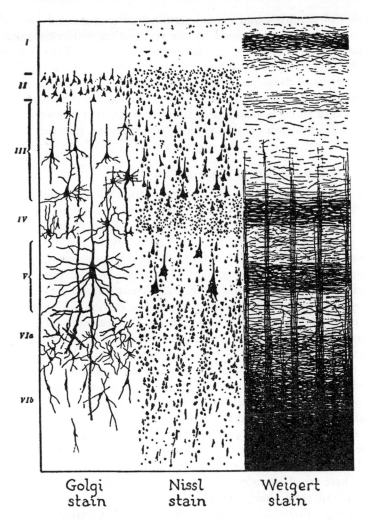

Golgi
stain

Nissl
stain

Weigert
stain

FIG. 9. The cell layers and fibre arrangement of the human
cerebral cortex. See text for details (from Ref. 51).

ted by closely-packed granule or stellate cells of different sizes; (*v*) the
internal pyramidal or ganglionic layer containing medium-sized and large
pyramidal neurons and a rich fibre plexus near the base; (*vi*) the multiform
layer or layer of fusiform cells which are spindle-shaped and perpendicular
to the cortical surface. There are many fibre bundles present as well as
some of the previously mentioned cells.

The structured pattern described above is of course incomplete and
gives no information about the intracortical conduction circuits brought
about by terminating fibres at the synaptic junctions. By using silver
impregnation methods, Cajal and later Lorente de Nó worked out the

distribution of dendritic and axonal terminals. Some general idea of the functional relationships is gained by the recognition within the cortex of three classes of nerve elements: (*i*) the endings of afferent fibres from other parts of the nervous system; (*ii*) association neurons, whose axons connect different regions of the same hemisphere or pass, as commisural fibres, to the cortex of the opposite side; and (*iii*) projection neurons whose axons conduct integrated cortical impulses to other parts of the nervous system. For further information on this subject, the reader is referred to Cajal's account of the pattern of cortical organization.[8]

Cytologic Features of Cerebral Cortical Neurons

The previous discussion on cortical stratification alluded to about seven different kinds of neurons, but this division does not exhaust the possible classifications of cortical neurons. If shape of perikarya were regarded as a legitimate basis for classification, several dozen types might be derived. According to Sholl[48] who studied Golgi preparations, there are two major cytologic divisions of neurons; these are the pyramidal and stellate cell divisions which may be further separated into a total of seven sub-groups according to the axonal pattern. For example, he suggests that one group includes pyramidal cells with axons that leave the cortex without branching, a second group comprises pyramidal cells with axons that leave the cortex and show only lateral branching, etc. In Plate XV there is illustrated a Golgi-Cox preparation of pyramidal neuron from the cat visual cortex which displays an axon with recurrent lateral processes which never pass through to the white matter. Such a cell is listed in Sholl's classification as P[4] (pyramidal cell type 4).

Pyramidal and stellate granule cells. The pyramidal neuron is the characteristic cortical cell. It appears as a pyramid in which the pointed end is directed toward the surface of the brain as the apical dendrite (Fig. 1). There are also a number of basal dendrites which emerge from the perikaryon and send their fine processes in horizontal directions. The axon is directed downward from the perikaryon and terminates in deeper layers of the cortex or passes into the white matter. Pyramidal cells have a large nucleus and prominent Nissl substance. Their perikarya vary greatly in size from 10–50 μ. However, the giant pyramidal cells of Metz in the motor area of the precentral gyrus may each be 100 μ long. The results of Hancock[16] are interesting from a cytochemical view. He finds that pyramidal nuclei from the mouse cerebral cortex incorporate H3-uridine selectively into RNA at the margins of nucleoli (Plate XVI); whereas, pyramidal nuclei in the hippocampus display a more general intracellular labelling pattern. It has been postulated that recent memory is associated with the hippocampal zone of the brain and longer term memory with neocortex. The cytochemical finding mentioned above together with biochemical evidence reinforces the idea that psychological performance is related to RNA metabolism in specific cells and layers of the brain. The stellate or granule cells are often small and have a polygonal or triangular shape. They have dark staining nuclei with little cytoplasm and are 4–8 micra in size. There are a number of dendrites extending in all directions and a short axon. In larger stellate cells, there are longer axons which invade the medullary substance.

The general ultrastructural features of neurons were discussed in an earlier section, and little additional comment is needed. As with other nerve cells, cortical neurons have large nuclei and prominent nucleoli, abundant chromophile substance composed of rough-surfaced endoplasmic reticulum and ribosomes (Nissl substance), as well as mitochondria and a Golgi complex. The axoplasm displays more neurofilaments than the perikaryon, fewer ribosomes, and no rough endoplasmic reticulum. In the molecular layer of the cortex (Plate XVII), most nerve fibres are non-myelinated and terminate in bulbous formations containing many synaptic vesicles. A few nerve fibres are myelinated and resemble those seen in peripheral nerves. The axoplasm presents a fibrous appearance which contrasts with the finely stippled components of sectioned glial processes. Rhodin in his ultrastructural atlas[46] emphasizes '. . . that the fine structure of the central nervous system has not been studied sufficiently to permit detailed interpretations of the neuroglial relationships.'

6

Cytology of the Cerebellar Cortex

The cortex is uniformly composed of three layers: (1) an outer molecular layer with few cells and myelinated fibres; (2) an intermediate single row of large, flask-shaped Purkinje cells and (3) a dense inner granular layer of cells. Many cellular details to be described are illustrated in Fig. 10.

Cytology and Distribution of Neurons

Within the molecular layer, there are a few small stellate cells with short dendrites near the surface. Closer to the Purkinje cells are larger stellate elements known as basket cells with ascending dendrites (Fig. 10). Their unmyelinated axons pass horizontally and give off collaterals which form an intricate arborization or basket around the Purkinje cell perikarya. Purkinje cells have large empty-looking nucleus with a densely staining nucleolus and concentrically arranged Nissl substance. Several dendrites are given off which extend through the molecular layer and form a rich arborization at the surface. The thinnest fibres are covered with surface knobs or gemmules. The single myelinated axon gives off horizontal collaterals which terminate on the perikarya of adjacent Purkinje cells. The main axon passes through the granular layer and enters the white matter to pass to deeper cerebellar nuclei or to other cortical areas. There may also be smaller Purkinje cells in the molecular or granular layers.

The granular layer contains densely stained nuclei which are closely

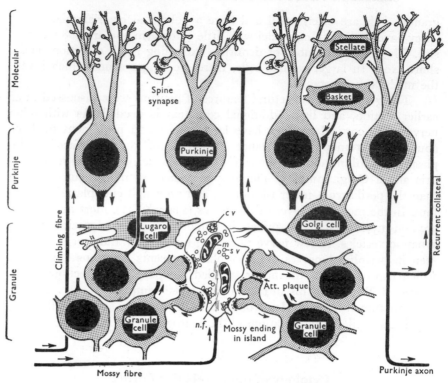

Fig. 10. Diagram of the organization of the cerebellar cortex. Labelling is as follows: cv, complex vesicle; m, mitochondria; sv, synaptic vesicle; att. plaques, attachment plaques or desmosomes; nf, neurofilament. At lower-centre, details are shown of a mossy fibre ending which is in synaptic contact with the dendritic tips of granule cells. For further details see text (from Ref. 15).

packed and constitute small multipolar cells, the granule cells (Fig. 10). They are 4–8 micra in diameter and have several dendrites which terminate in peculiar endings in open spaces known as 'islands' or 'glomeruli'. The unmyelinated axon of each granule cell ascends into the molecular layer and splits into two branches which run at right angles to the main axon. All regions of the molecular layer are covered by these tree-like extensions. Golgi type II cells are likewise scattered through the granular layer. These are intermediate in size between granule and Purkinje cells and display other cellular characteristics including vesicular nuclei and chromophilic bodies in the cell body. The dendrites of Golgi type II neurons enter the molecular layer and may pass to the surface. Each axon splits into a complex arborization which concentrates in the glomeruli. Before terminating this general sketch of the cytologic picture, it should be mentioned that there are two structural types of afferent fibres which pass into the cerebellar cortex from other regions and other parts of the cerebellum: (*i*) the

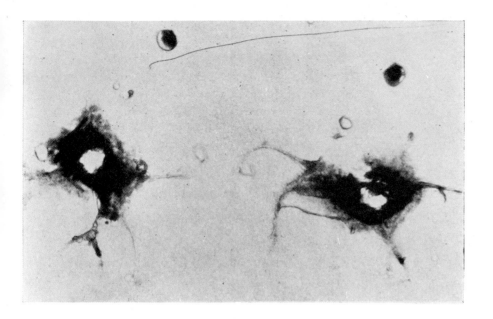

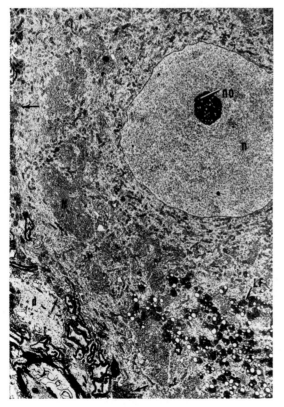

Plate I ▲

Two isolated Deiters' nerve cells, cleaned from glia and treated with phenol-water. The nucleus from each has been removed and placed above its respective nerve cell, in the centre of which is seen the corresponding hole. Photographed at 2570 Å.

◀ **Plate II**

Electron micrograph of large motoneuron of lumbar cord of the monkey. Masses of granular endoplasmic recticulum or Nissl bodies (N) tend to avoid the nuclear and cell membranes. Lipofuscin granules (LF) tend to be massed. Surrounding small myelinated fibres (f) border the perikaryon membrane which is only partly covered by synaptic boutons (arrows).

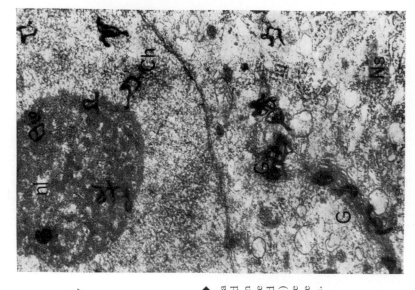

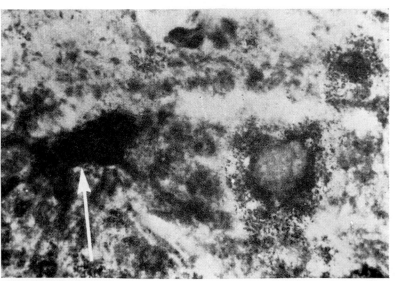

◀ **Plate III**

Neuron (arrow) in hypoglossal nucleus in man. Considerable dehydrogenase activity is exhibited here.

Plate IV ▶

Electron microscope autoradiograph of a neuron from Gasser's ganglion fixed 30 minutes after injecting H_3-leucine. In the perikaryon the silver grains are more concentrated on the vesicles and saccules of the Golgi apparatus (G) than on the Nissl substance (Ns). There is also some association with the nucleolus (nl) and the chromatin.

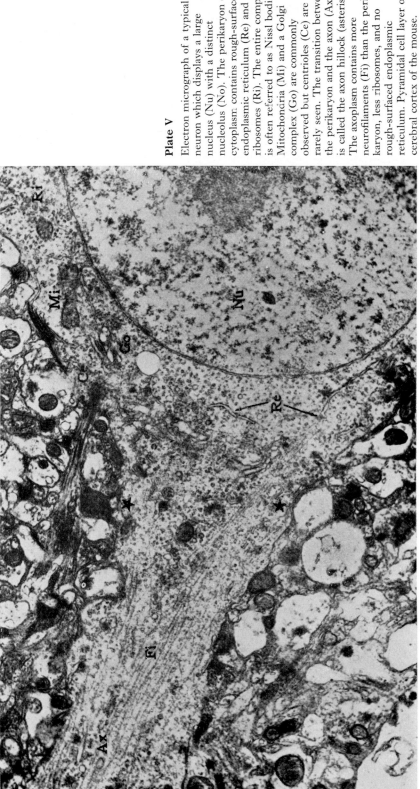

Plate V

Electron micrograph of a typical neuron which displays a large nucleus (Nu) with a distinct nucleolus (No). The perikaryon or cytoplasm contains rough-surfaced endoplasmic reticulum (Re) and ribosomes (Ri). The entire complex is often referred to as Nissl bodies. Mitochondria (Mi) and a Golgi complex (Go) are commonly observed but centrioles (Ce) are rarely seen. The transition between the perikaryon and the axon (Ax) is called the axon hillock (asterisks). The axoplasm contains more neurofilaments (Fi) than the perikaryon, less ribosomes, and no rough-surfaced endoplasmic reticulum. Pyramidal cell layer of cerebral cortex of the mouse.

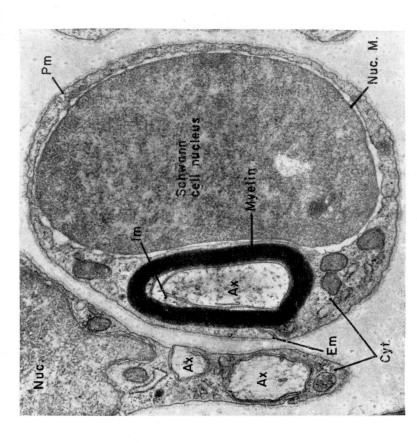

Plate VII

Electron micrograph of a small myelinated nerve fibre from rat dorsal root ganglion matured in tissue culture. The infolding plasma membrane (PM) of the Schwann cell forms an external mesaxon (Em) continuous with the outermost lamella of the myelin sheath. An internal mesaxon (Im) surrounds the axon (Ax) and is continuous with the most internal lamella of the myelin sheath. Note the small amount of Schwann cell cytoplasm (Cyt.) between the nuclear (Nuc. M) and plasma membranes. At the left are two unmyelinated axons associated with another Schwann cell.

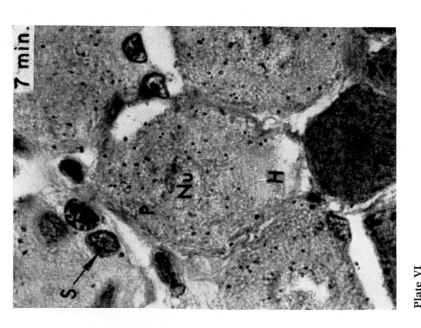

Plate VI

Autoradiograph from the semilunar ganglion of a young rat following a single injection of H_3-leucine and sacrificed after seven minutes. Silver grains reveal the sites of newly synthesized protein and demonstrate an initial synthesis over the nucleus (Nu) and perikaryon (P) but not over the axon hillock (H). A few grains are seen over satellite cells (S). After longer exposure to the protein precursor, silver grains were found to extend to the axon hillock suggesting migration of previously

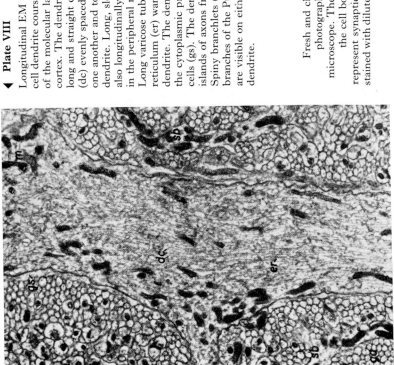

◄ Plate VIII

Longitudinal EM section of a Purkinje cell dendrite coursing through the neuropil of the molecular layer of the cerebellar cortex. The dendrite is filled with fine, long and straight canaliculi or tubules (dc) evenly spaced, and largely parallel to one another and to the long axis of the dendrite. Long, slender mitochondria (m) also longitudinally oriented, are disposed in the peripheral regions of the cytoplasm. Long varicose tubules of endoplasmic reticulum (er) wander through the dendrite. The dendrite is ensheathed in the cytoplasmic processes of neuroglial cells (gs). The dendrite is immersed in islands of axons from granule cells (ga). Spiny branchlets (sb), the terminal branches of the Purkinje cell dendrites, are visible on either side of the main dendrite.

Plate IX ▶

Fresh and cleaned Deiters' nerve cell photographed in the phase-contrast microscope. The small dense particles on the cell body and dendrite surfaces represent synaptic knobs which have been stained with dilute methylene blue solution.

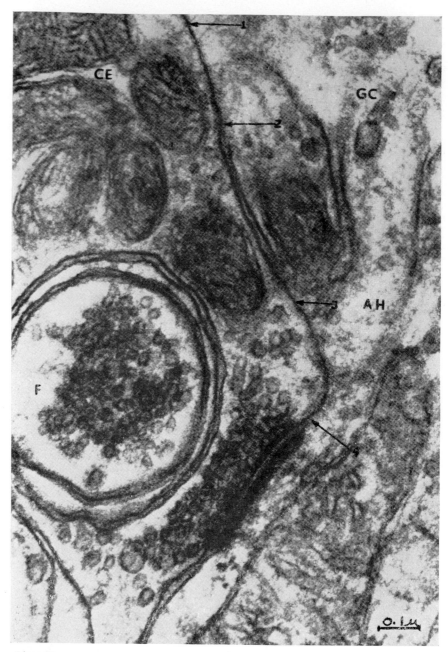

Plate X

High EM magnification of a region through the axon hillock of the chick ciliary ganglion. A tight junction or membrane fusion is located on the hillock of a post-synaptic neuron. Such electrotonic transmission is contrasted to chemical synaptic transmission. Identifications include: GC, ganglion cell; AH, axon hillock; CE, pre-synaptic calyx; F, nerve fibre containing synaptic vesicles. Arrows 1, 2, 3 and 4 indicate pre- and postsynaptic membrane specializations.

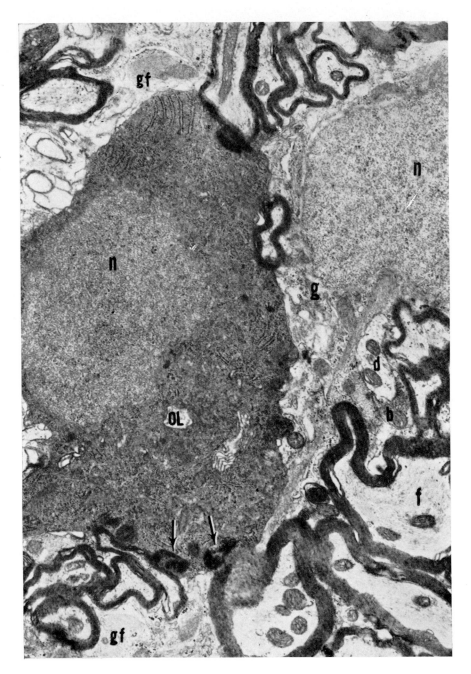

Plate XI

Electron micrograph from monkey spinal cord shows oligodendrocyte (OL) and astrocyte (g) embracing a small myelinated fibre. Glia fibrils of astrocyte (gf) are characteristic, as are the cytoplasmic dense inclusions of the oligodendrocyte (arrows).

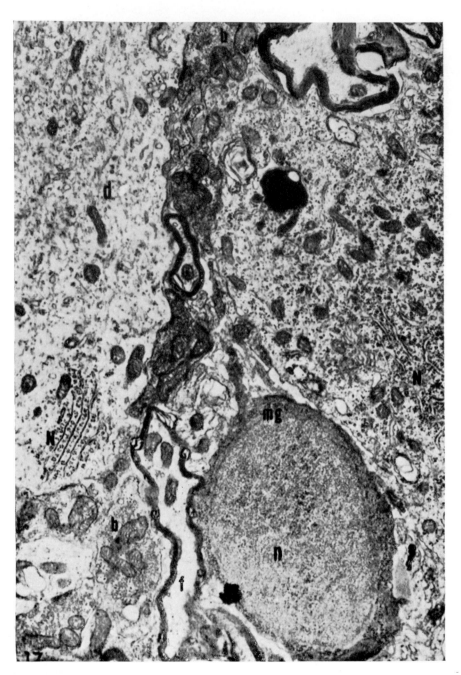

Plate XII

A probable microglial cell (mg) in region of neuropil in anterior horn of monkey spinal cord. Note small size, scarce amount of cytoplasm compared with nucleus (N), and abundance of ribosomes. Uppermost bouton (b) is in contact with neuron perikaryon on right, and dendrite (D) on left.

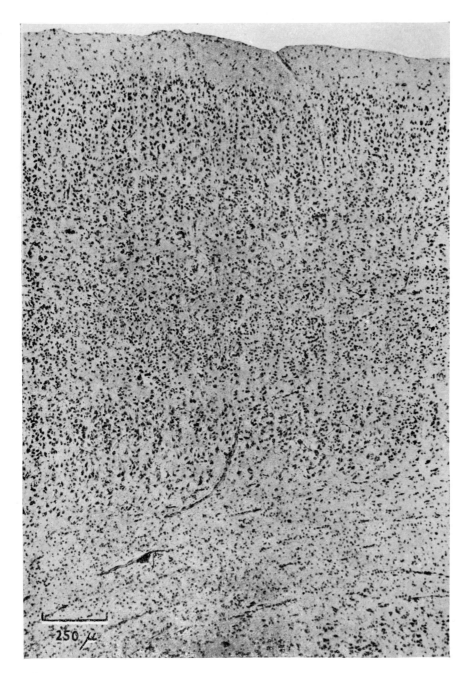

Plate XIII

A section from the human visual cortex bordering the calcarine fissure. The preparation was stained by the Nissl method and only shows the perikarya of the neurons together with neuroglial elements. The outermost region is almost free from neurons, while the lowest part shows the white matter with its abundant neuroglia.

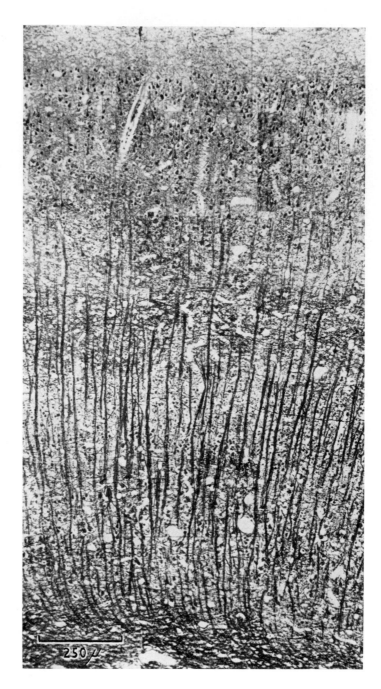

Plate XIV

A section from the same block as in Plate XIII, but stained with a reduced silver method. The neurons with their axons and dendrites are stained. The fine axons in the outermost layer may be contrasted with the thick myelinated axons of the white matter. The plexas known as Gennari's line can be seen about half-way through the cortex. The white patches in the photograph are due to blood vessels.

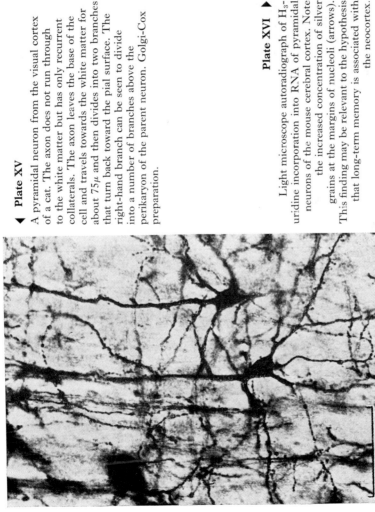

◄ **Plate XV**

A pyramidal neuron from the visual cortex of a cat. The axon does not run through to the white matter but has only recurrent collaterals. The axon leaves the base of the cell and travels towards the white matter for about 75µ and then divides into two branches that turn back toward the pial surface. The right-hand branch can be seen to divide into a number of branches above the perikaryon of the parent neuron. Golgi-Cox preparation.

Plate XVI ▶

Light microscope autoradiograph of H_3-uridine incorporation into RNA of pyramidal neurons of the mouse cerebral cortex. Note the increased concentration of silver grains at the margins of nucleoli (arrows). This finding may be relevant to the hypothesis that long-term memory is associated with the neocortex.

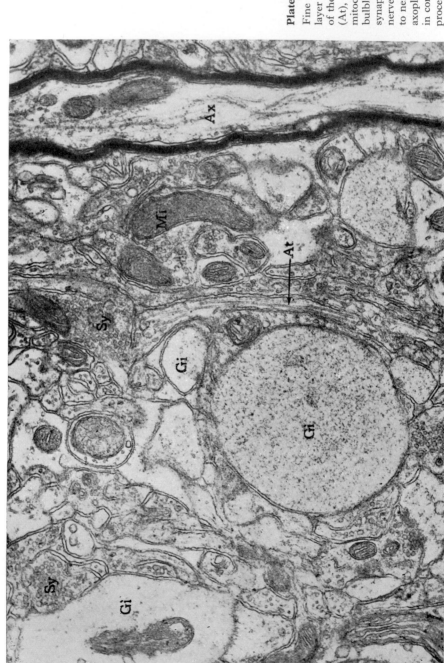

Plate XVII

Fine structural details of the molecular layer of the mouse cerebral cortex. Most of the nerve fibres are non-myelinated (At), contain fine neurofilaments and mitochondria (Mi) and terminate in bulblike formations in which numerous synaptic vesicles (Sy) can be seen. Some nerve fibres are myelinated (Ax) similar to nerve fibres in peripheral nerves. Their axoplasm has a delicate fibrous appearance in contrast to the cross-sectioned glial processes (Gi), which are finely stippled.

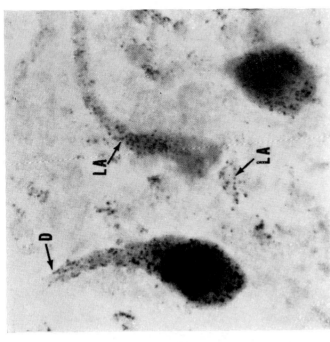

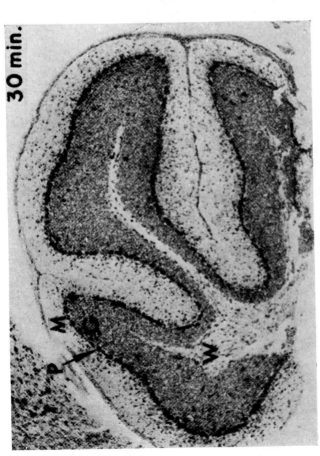

Plate XVIII

Autoradiograph of cerebellum from a young rat fixed 30 minutes after injection of H₃-leucine. Note the intense reaction over Purkinje cells (P) and moderate over granular layer cells (G). In the molecular layer (M) and in the white matter (W) the discrete reaction is due to scattered oligodendrocytes or neurons.

Plate XIX

Histochemical demonstration of acid phosphatase in Purkinje cells of the rabbit. Small granules, considered to be lysosomes, are visualized in the cytoplasm and extend for a considerable distance into the dendrites (D). The granules appear to be arranged in linear arrays (A). This is striking in the lower centre.

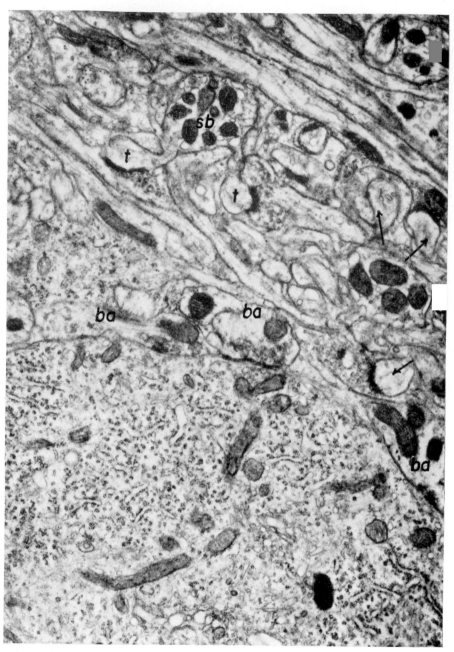

Plate XX

Electron micrograph of the region between the molecular and Purkinje cell layers. The lower part of the picture is occupied by a Purkinje cell containing a large Nissl body, Golgi apparatus, and mitochondria. Three terminals of basket cell fibres (ba) form synapses on the surface of this cell. In the molecular layer a small spiny branchlet (sb) of the Purkinje cell dendrite gives off two thorns (t) which make synaptic contact with granule cell axons nearby. Other examples of this type of contact are indicated by arrows.

Plate XXI

Four of the six-time-lapse units at the Pasadena Foundation for Medical Research. Many of the abstracts which follow in this chapter were obtained from 16 mm films made on these units. The first unit at the far left contains two phase microscopes for recording simultaneous images from two fields on the same film frame. The second unit has a gas cylinder near it for experiments in which controlled gas flows are monitored. This same unit has a TV pickup attached to allow transmission of the microscope image to a 21 inch TV screen for special monitoring. Note that all units contain incubators which are thermostatically controlled.

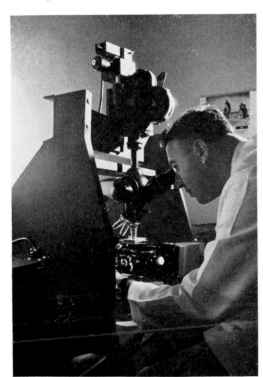

Plate XXII

The photo shows the author at another 16 mm time-lapse phase unit. This unit is built around a Zeiss Photomicroscope and allows rapid changeover from still photography (35 mm, 4 × 5 in) to 16 mm time-lapse filming or rapid scanning. The high-intensity tungsten light source provides sufficient illumination for oil-immersion phase optics and interconversion to other optics. In the photo, an external stroboscopic light source is being flashed into the system at high speed for studies of rapid axoplasmic flow.

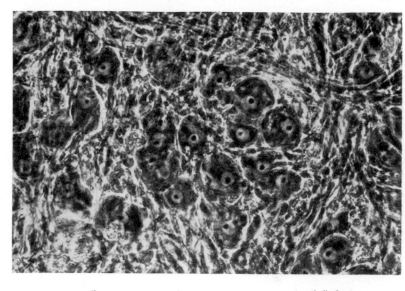

▶ Plate XXIII

The upper two photomicrographs are from sections of
newborn kitten cerebellum. Upper-left shows folia
of the type used as explants for culture after staining
by pyridine silver carbonate method. Upper right is an
area stained by hematoxylin-eosin-azure which includes
a sulcus and shows the location of Purkinje cells (P).
Lower-left shows the outgrowth from three explants
of kitten cerebellum after three weeks *in vitro*.
There is a radial emigration of cell from the explants.
Lower-right presents a cerebellar culture after seven
days of incubation showing the early development
of typical zones of outgrowth as described in Figure 13.
Preparation stained by Bodian's method.

Plate XXIV ▶

After a one-month growth in the Rose chamber a
field of healthy neurons is observed by phase
optics. Preparation from an explant of chick embryo
spinal ganglia.

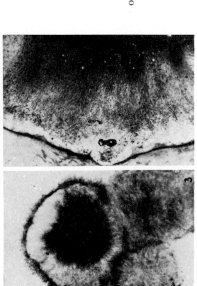

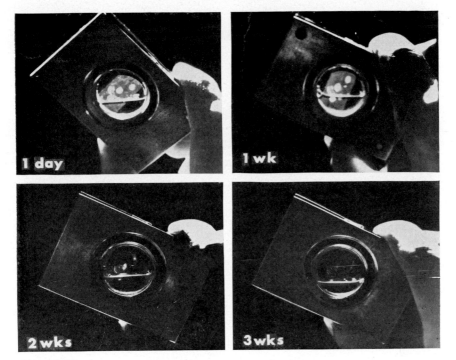

Plate XXV

This series of photos shows the macroscopic appearance of spinal cord explants when grown in the Rose chamber using an air phase over the moistened tissue. Note how the explant seems to disappear with the passage of time. Actually, neurons still remain within the original explant area as neuroglial and mesenchymal elements emigrate away.

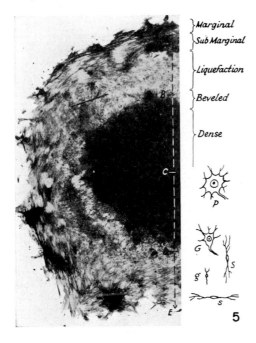

Plate XXVI

Culture of cerebellar folia from a newborn kitten showing the cellular pattern established in the outgrowth after 41 days *in vitro*. Typical cellular aggregations have been designated as zones to facilitate the description of the community of cells. The usual location of neurons has been schematized in the right portion of the photo and labelled as follows: P, Purkinje cell; g, granule cell; G, (?) Golgi Type II; s, (?) stellate cells. The cells drawn are found in the zones indicated. Preparation stained by Bodian's method.

5

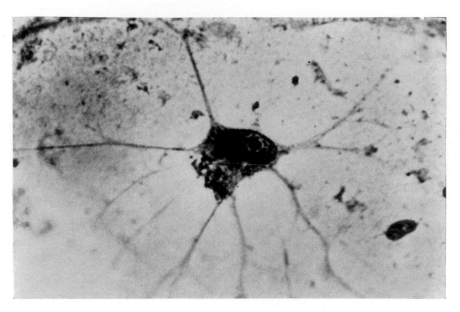

Plate XXVII

Within the bevelled zone of kitten cerebellar cultures (see Plate XXVI and Fig. 13), neurons suggestive of a Golgi type II morphology are observed. The multipolar cell shown is from a 51-day culture. Bodian preparation (unpublished data of Pomerat and Costero).

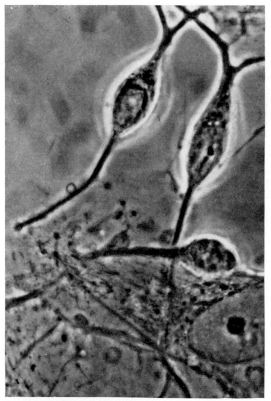

Plate XXVIII

Granule cells in a 5-day living preparation from a kitten cerebellum culture. Typical V- or T-shaped arrangement of processes at one pole and a single prolongation in the opposite direction. Phase-contrast micrograph.

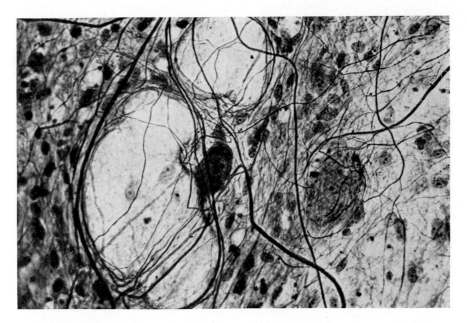

Plate XXIX

Arrangement of neurofibrils radiating from the perikaryon of a Purkinje cell following culturing for almost two months. Many thick nerve fibres are seen in the neighbourhood of the Purkinje cell. Neurofibrils impregnated with silver by Bodian's technique (unpublished data of Pomerat and Costero).

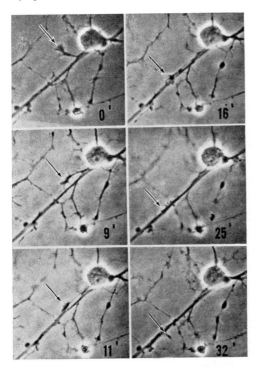

Plate XXX

Typical morphology and halo around an oligodendrocyte is shown in this series of abstracts from a phase-contrast film sequence. During the 32 minute film period, the oligodendrocytic fibres made attachment with an axon and remained attached. Note at arrow how the unusual tip of the oligo-dendrocyte fibre makes turning motions before it finally 'finds' and adheres to the axon. The resemblance to a growth cone is remarkable. Spinal cord culture grown in the Rose chamber.

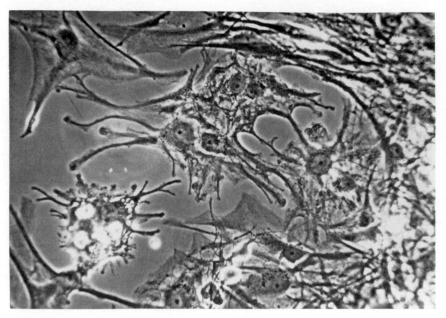

Plate XXXI

Astrocytes from loosely organized areas of the outgrowth of kitten cerebellar cultures at 41 days *in vitro*. The elements shown develop broad protoplasmic membrances. Phase-contrast photo.

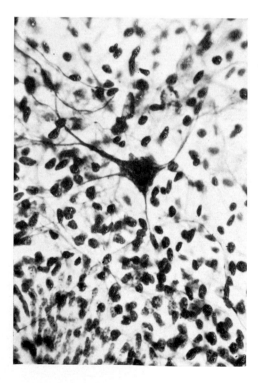

Plate XXXII

A fixed and stained preparation from cultured spinal cord displays a prominent astrocyte near a large group of ordered ependymal cells at lower-left.

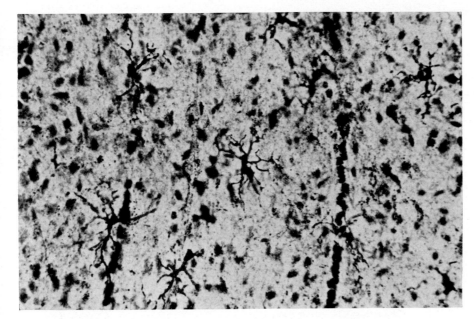

Plate XXXIII

Typical microglia are shown in this field from cultured kitten cerebellum. They are small cells with processes and are seen to be very motile when viewed by phase optics. Preparation stained with silver (unpublished data of Costero).

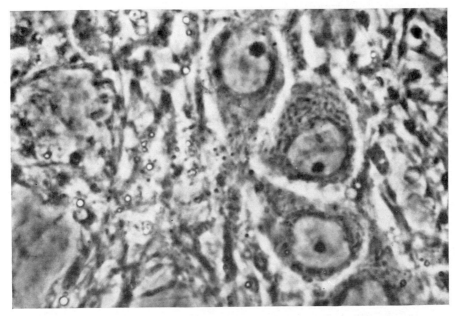

XXXIV

A triad of unipolar neurons is shown in the living state by phase optics. They are probable granule cells. Note abundant Nissl substance around the nucleus of the centre neuron. Preparation from a five-day culture of rat cerebellum cultivated in the Rose chamber.

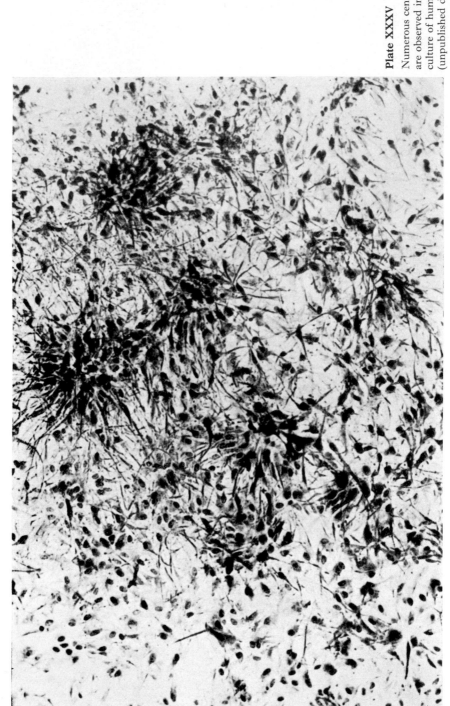

Plate XXXV

Numerous centres of neuroblasts are observed in this 45-day culture of human fetal thalamus (unpublished data of Pomerat).

Plate XXXVI
About 550 neurons are displayed in this low-power montage from a
culture of spinal ganglia. The phase-contrast image also reveals channels
which course between the cells. These contain nerve fibres which are
better seen in the silver-stained preparation of Plate XXXVII. Material
represented here provides unique opportunities to study neuronal growth
patterns under relatively flattened conditions. Tissue culture preparation
grown in the Rose chamber and derived from 10-day chick embryo.

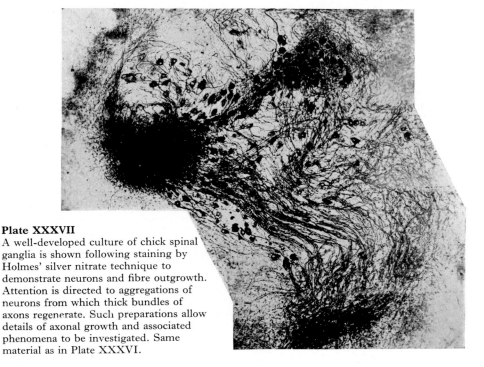

Plate XXXVII
A well-developed culture of chick spinal
ganglia is shown following staining by
Holmes' silver nitrate technique to
demonstrate neurons and fibre outgrowth.
Attention is directed to aggregations of
neurons from which thick bundles of
axons regenerate. Such preparations allow
details of axonal growth and associated
phenomena to be investigated. Same
material as in Plate XXXVI.

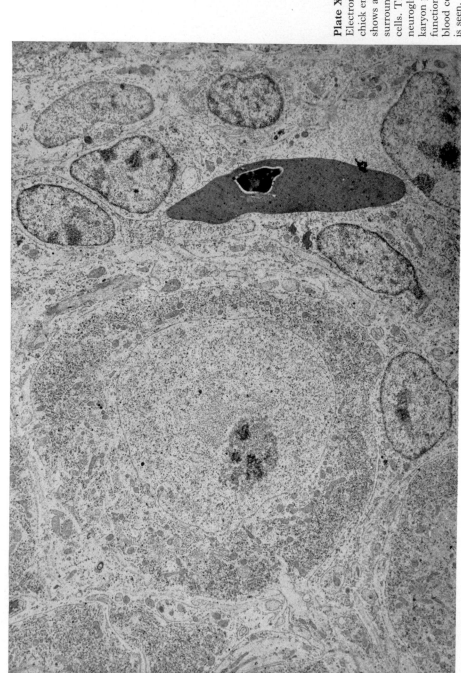

Plate XXXVIII

Electron micrograph of a section of chick embryo spinal ganglion. The field shows a large neuron in the centre surrounded by several small satellite cells. The intimate association of these neuroglial elements with the perikaryon probably serves an essential function to sustain the neuron. A blood cell with a small dense nucleus is seen,

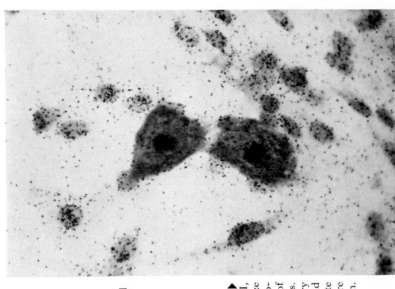

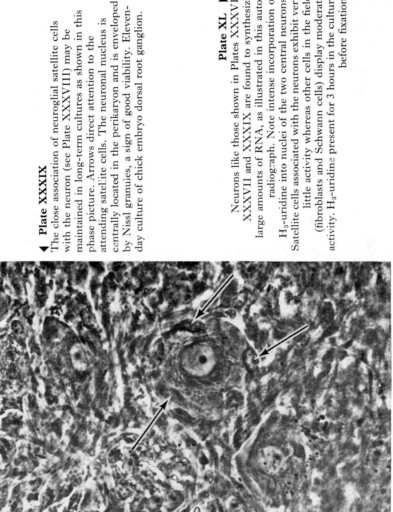

▼ Plate XXXIX

The close association of neuroglial satellite cells with the neuron (see Plate XXXVIII) may be maintained in long-term cultures as shown in this phase picture. Arrows direct attention to the attending satellite cells. The neuronal nucleus is centrally located in the perikaryon and is enveloped by Nissl granules, a sign of good viability. Eleven-day culture of chick embryo dorsal root ganglion.

Plate XL ▶

Neurons like those shown in Plates XXXVI, XXXVII and XXXIX are found to synthesize large amounts of RNA, as illustrated in this auto-radiograph. Note intense incorporation of H₃-uridine into nuclei of the two central neurons. Satellite cells associated with the neurons exhibit very little activity whereas other cells in the field (fibroblasts and Schwann cells) display moderate activity. H₃-uridine present for 3 hours in the culture before fixation.

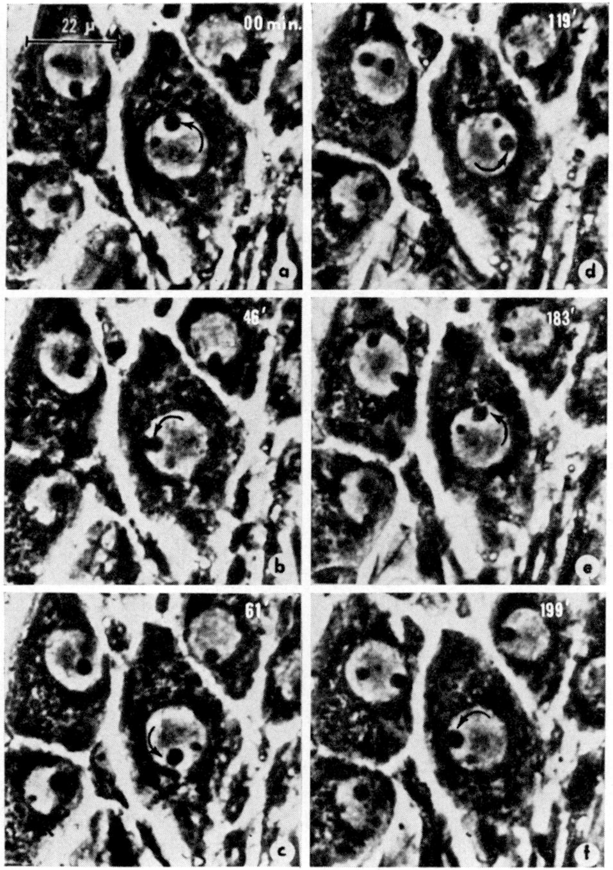

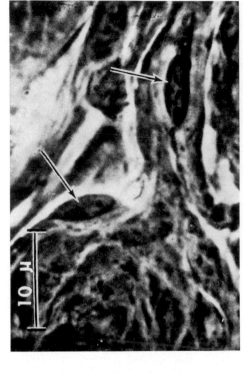

▲ **Plate XLII**

The field shows the axon hillock of a neuron at the left and two Schwann cell nuclei (arrows). The lower Schwann cell is closely attached to an axon. Phase photomicrograph from a 16-day culture of chick embryo dorsal root ganglion.

▲ **Plate XLI**

The phenomenon of nuclear rotation is demonstrated in this neuron from a 10-day culture of newborn rat dorsal root ganglion. The nucleolus (arrow) serves as an index of nuclear rotation. In this case, 1¼ rotations were completed in 199 minutes. The cell was photographed at one frame per minute. The relative time scales from one abstract to the next are shown in the upper-right corners.

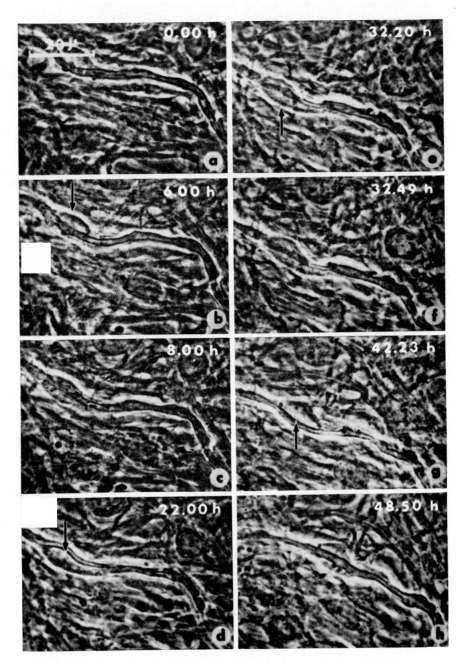

Plate XLIII
Myelination of axons of the peripheral nervous system is believed to result from the intimate binding of Schwann cells to the axon and rotational movements around the fibre. Evidence for this comes from photographic documentation of Schwann cell circumnavigation. In this series of film abstracts the nucleus of the Schwann cell lies directly under the scale marker in *a*. The nucleus (arrows) passed behind the fibre in *a* to *d*. It then proceeded (*e—g*) over the anterior edge of the fibre and reached its original position between *g* and *h*. Approximately 48 hours were required for the complete revolution. Abstracts from a two-month culture photographed at one frame every two minutes. Time scale in hours in upper-right corners. Newborn rat dorsal root ganglion.

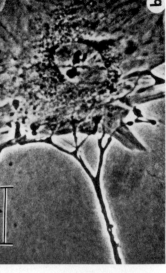

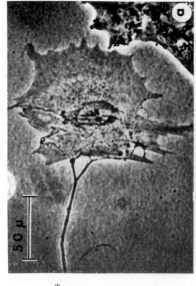

◀ **Plate XLIV**
This series of time-lapse film abstracts demonstrates the changes in configuration of a growth cone seen at the distal end of an axon. The cone was photographed at 8 frames per minute and the images were selected from a four-hour record. Note the membranous extensions which display whirling motions. The changes may occur very rapidly; for instance, 1·25 minutes separate *a* and *b*. Dorsal root ganglion of chick embryo two days in culture.

Plate XLV ▶
Surface contacts are demonstrated between growth cones from chick embryo dorsal root ganglion and an epitheloid cell. Photo *b* is a higher magnification of the same cell shown in *a*.

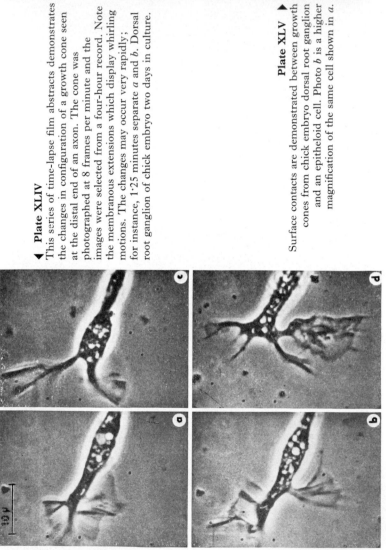

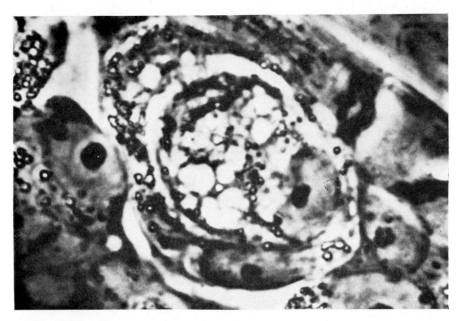

Plate XLVI
Film abstract from a 16 mm cine sequence demonstrates a newly formed meningeal whorl *in vitro*. These complex structures apparently arise by encirclement of one cell by another. The clear areas in the centre are filled with fluid. Culture derived by trypsinizing a piece of human meningioma.

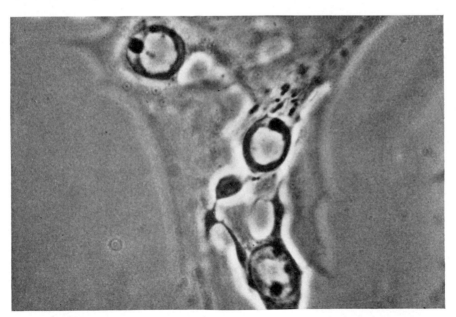

Plate XLVII
Unusual nuclear vacuoles are seen in these cultured cells derived from a human meningioma. The presence of these prominent nuclear lesions might suggest a virus involvement. Phase-contrast photomicrograph taken from a film.

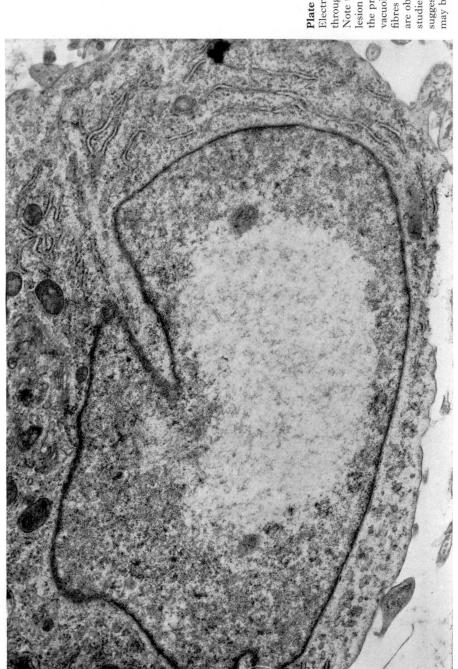

Plate XLVIII

Electron micrograph from a section through a cultured meningiomal cell. Note the resemblance of the nuclear lesion to that seen in the living cell of the preceding plate. The nuclear vacuole contains a slight residue of fine fibres and granules. No viral particles are observed in this cell or in others studied from the same tumor. It is suggested that the empty nuclear area may be a fluid reservoir in life.

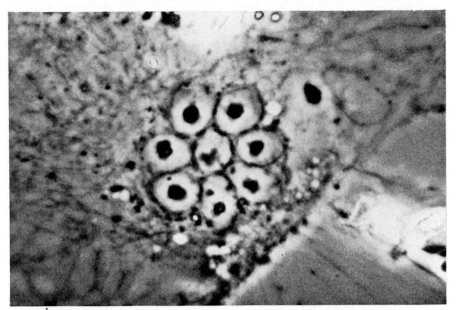

Plate XLIX
A bizarre multinucleated cell is presented here from another meningiomal tumor grown in culture. Slightly out of focus behind the rosette of eight nuclei is a dense network of mitochondria. Phase-contrast photograph taken from a film sequence.

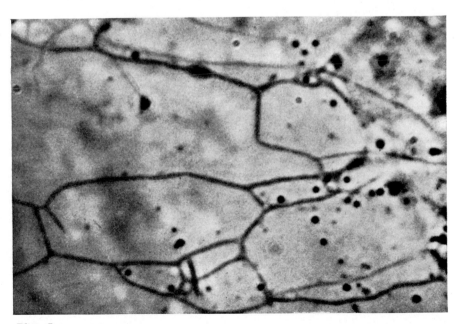

Plate L
A phase-contrast oil immersion photo demonstrates odd mitochondria from a meningioma grown *in vitro*. Characteristic closed loops are formed by connecting mitochondria. In the original film from which this photo was taken, mitochondria were seen to sever connections in one area, remain single for short periods, and eventually form new adhesions elsewhere.

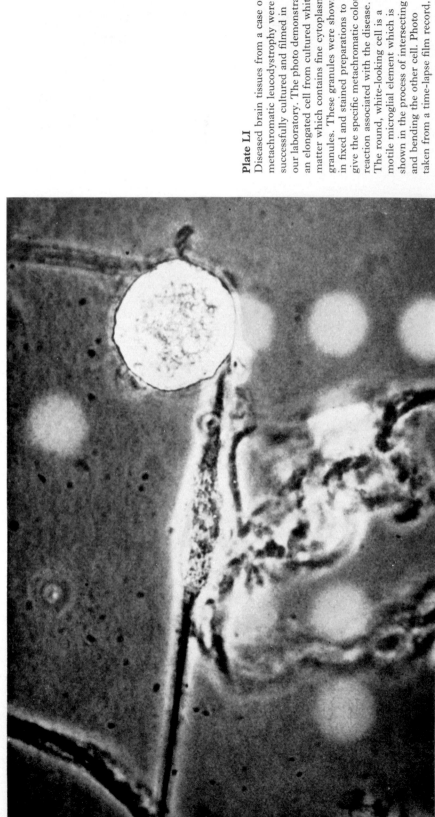

Plate LI
Diseased brain tissues from a case of metachromatic leucodystrophy were successfully cultured and filmed in our laboratory. The photo demonstrates an elongated cell from cultured white matter which contains fine cytoplasmic granules. These granules were shown in fixed and stained preparations to give the specific metachromatic colour reaction associated with the disease. The round, white-looking cell is a motile microglial element which is shown in the process of intersecting and bending the other cell. Photo taken from a time-lapse film record,

mossy fibres, which are extremely thick in the white matter and give off branches on the granular layer to terminate in the glomeruli, and (*ii*) the climbing fibres, which pass from the white matter through the granular layer and terminate in fine fibrils on the dendrites of Purkinje cells.

Special Features of Purkinje Cells

The cytologic changes in appearance of Purkinje cells during embryogenesis attracted interest, dating back to Cajal in 1929. As an outgrowth of Cajal's description, there were other unanswered questions raised

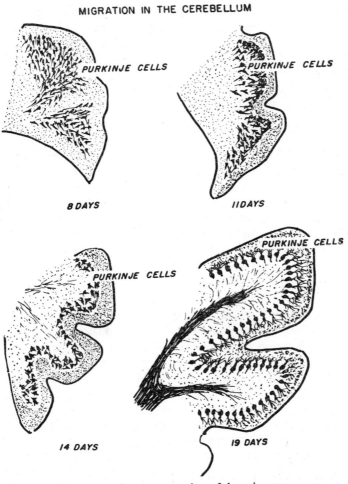

MIGRATION IN THE CEREBELLUM

FIG. 11. Diagrammatic representation of the migratory movements of the Purkinje cells in the cerebellum of the chick embryo. During early phases, they are closely packed in dense cellular rows. As they reach the cortical layer they spread in a fan-like fashion and settle in the layer which will be known as the Purkinje layer (from Ref. 27).

about the origin of these cells. Levi-Montalcini[27] demonstrated nicely with silver staining that Purkinje cells are derived from neuroblasts in the germinal layer (see Fig. 11). While in a fusiform shape, they undergo a migratory fan-like phase before settling into the characteristic Purkinje layer of the adult organism. This conclusion supports other autoradiographic studies[31, 52] in which germinal cells were labelled with tritiated thymidine and the subsequent migratory movements followed with time. From their studies on mouse embryos, Miale and Sidman[31] concluded that most Purkinje cells, Golgi type II cells and large and small neurons of the roof nuclei were formed well before birth. They postulate that extensive cell migrations during histogenesis allow particular synaptic contacts to be made and retained. Following their maturation, Purkinje cells exhibit considerable protein synthetic activities in comparison with other cells in adjacent layers (Plate XVIII), and contain high levels of enzymes. The intracellular distribution of acid phosphatase is shown in Plate XIX. The enzyme appears in the form of fine granules, probably lysosomes, in the perikaryon and the dendrites.

The fine structure of Purkinje cells and associated cellular and fibre components was studied by a number of investigators including Gray,[15] Herndon,[17] and Palay.[36] An excellent summary is given by Palay[35] in Volume 2 of *Brain Function*. The description of the Purkinje cell perikaryon, dendrites, and axon differs little from that of the generalized neuron given earlier. One important facet which has not been mentioned as yet is the ultrastructure of the neuropil with emphasis on cerebellar synaptic zones. The brief account presented below is derived from the lucid description of Palay. The network of delicate unmyelinated fibres permeating the central nervous system constitutes the neuropil. The interrelationships and connections of these fibres to form synapses may be examined in three synaptic zones of the cerebellar cortex: (*i*) synapses between the mossy fibres and the granule cell dendrites in the glomeruli; (*ii*) synapses between the granule cell axons and the Purkinje cell; and (*iii*) the synapses between the Purkinje cell axons and the basket cell axons in the granule cell layer. The axo-axonal synapse mentioned in (*iii*) above is described in detail. It should be recalled that the Purkinje cell receives information from the small basket cell neuron located horizontally in the molecular layer. Axonal collaterals from the basket cell envelop the perikaryon of the Purkinje cell (Plate XX) and continue into a brush-like formation around its axon. The endings upon the perikaryon surface form typical synaptic junctions. These synaptic endings contain the usual vesicles and mitochondria and fit tightly into discontinuities of the neuroglial sheath covering the remainder of the perikaryon. The presynaptic surface contains dense filamentous material but the postsynaptic surface appears no different from the usual neuronal plasma membrane. In Plate XX there is also seen a small branch of the Purkinje cell dendrite which gives off two thorns. These make synaptic contact with granule cell axons in the molecular layer. The termination of basket cell axons on the Purkinje cell axons is in a whorl-like pattern in which only a few make direct contact.

7
Dynamic Studies of Nervous Tissues in Culture

One of the most fascinating experimental approaches to the study of neurocytology and neurofunction lies in the domain of tissue culture. By using modified growth chambers and paying special attention to substrata and proper growth condition, it has been possible to explant and maintain the originally explanted nervous tissues *in vitro* for half a year or more despite the complexity and exacting environmental requirements. Nervous tissues *in vitro* are initially damaged when prepared as explants due to the cutting of nerve fibres. Such damaged neurons must first undergo regeneration and resynthesis of Nissl substance during the early period of culturing. Often the neuronal nucleus remains eccentric during the regenerating stage and later appears in the cell centre. Although differentiated neurons do not divide in culture, some neuroglial elements do proliferate, together with mesenchymal cells and fibroblasts. In healthy cultures, neurons frequently sprout dendrites and axons, which grow extensively, even to the extent that axons become myelinated. It is clear that this kind of a differentiated primary culture is stationary in development, especially with regard to the neuronal population, and may be expected to imitate to a large extent the complex *in situ* condition from which it was derived. The advantages of studying neurons and neuroglia in such an experimental living state, suitable in many cases for scrutiny by phase-contrast optics, is self-evident. Much of the literature on this subject has been admirably gathered together by Murray.[32] An excellent monograph by Hild, entitled 'Das Neuron',[18] is one of the valuable references in this field. Within the limitations of space afforded in this chapter it is proposed to describe briefly the current methods employed to cultivate nervous tissues and to highlight the use of this tool, hand-in-hand with ancillary techniques as time-lapse cinematography (Plates XXI, XXII), autoradiography, and electron microscopy to illustrate dynamic aspects of neurocytology. Some of the material to be illustrated was derived from the files of this laboratory under the former direction of the late Dr Charles M. Pomerat, a pioneer in the field.[23] The remainder of the material is derived from the author's current studies and from other published reports.

8
Modern Methods of Maintaining Nervous Tissue *in vitro*

There are three principal methods currently employed in various laboratories for culturing nervous tissues (Fig. 12), (*i*) the Maximow double

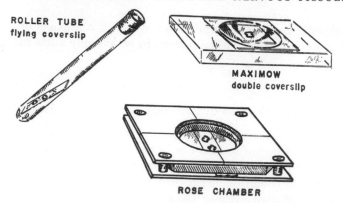

ROLLER TUBE
flying coverslip

MAXIMOW
double coverslip

ROSE CHAMBER

FIG. 12. Three methods of culturing nerve tissues are shown in the drawings. While each method is useful under certain conditions, we find the Rose chamber with its very thin coverslip to provide the only means to directly follow neuronal and neuroglial growth in the living state by phase optics and time-lapse filming. The flying coverslip in the roller tube must be removed for microscopic observations and then survives only a very short time. The Maximow chamber uses such a thick explant that only bright-field optics are usable.

coverslip assembly, in which a relatively thick tissue explant lies in a rich pool of nutrient medium, (ii) the roller tube, in which nervous tissue is supported on a so-called 'flying coverslip' while undergoing alternate immersion in nutrient fluid and exposure to air, and (iii) the Rose multi-purpose perfusion chamber, which provides for a flattened explant ideal for phase-contrast microscopy.

In each of these systems, various modifications were introduced in recent years to improve the substrate so as to facilitate growth of neuronal elements and production of myelin. Among these significant modifications were the use of a film of reconstituted collagen to replace the traditional plasma clot[5] and a cellophane dialysis membrane over the explant to apply mechanical pressure and help clear the neuronal area of migratory elements.[44]

In another procedure spinal ganglia cells were dissociated from attending satellite cells by proteinase and cultivated.[33] Although there is slight regeneration of neural processes, neurons fail to survive for longer than several days and there is a serious question about the general health of these dissociated neurons.

The roller tube method may be used to maintain tissues from the PNS as well as CNS but does not allow direct cytological observations to be made. The coverslip must be removed, remounted on a slide and sealed. Although the useful life of such remounted nervous tissues is only a few hours at the most, this has not been a severe limitation for short-term studies. Pomerat, Costero, Hogne, and Hild in various publications described the visible activities of brain cells derived from roller tubes using time-lapse photography and staining methods. Newborn kitten cerebellum provides ideal brain material for such studies.[39] In Plate XXIII are low- and high-power views of stained sections of the cerebellum prior to explantation. Following explantation into roller tubes, there are characteristic patterns of outgrowth to form typical zones (Fig. 13) in

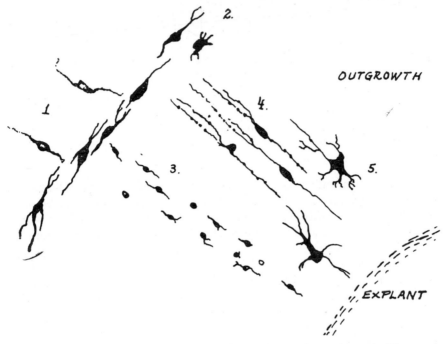

FIG. 13. Following the culturing of kitten cerebellum as shown in Plate XXIII, various neuronal types become segregated as revealed by supravital staining with methylene blue. The diagrammatic sketch suggests the presence of stellate neurons at 1, 2 and 4; granule cells are at 3, and; Golgi type II neurons are indicated at 5. Purkinje cells generally remain within the explant (unpublished data of Pomerat and Costero).

which are located stellate-type neurons, granule cells, and Golgi type II neurons. The Purkinje cells generally remain within the explant. Other features of cerebellar elements *in vitro* will be referred to later. This same system was utilized by Hild[19] in studies of myelination and bioelectric phenomena.

The thickness of tissue in the Maximow chamber precludes optimal phase-contrast microscopy. However, by judicious use of bright-field optics and follow-up procedures using embedded tissues, the Columbia group (Peterson and Murray), proved the value of the Maximow chamber for their purposes. Such tissues also were useful for direct recording of bioelectric potentials (Crain) and for ultrastructural analyses of cytologic patterns (Bunge and Bunge, Perier). A diagrammatic representation of the cellular distribution within a thick explant of spinal cord in the Maximow chamber is illustrated in Fig. 14.

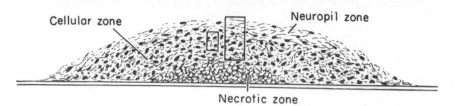

Cellular zone   Neuropil zone

Necrotic zone

FIG. 14. A diagrammatic representation of a cross-section of a rat spinal cord explant grown in the Maximow chamber. The most superficial tissue is largely neuropil; most neurons are found in a deeper broad cellular zone. A necrotic zone occupies the deepest area adjacent to the coverglass (from Ref. 7).

The Rose chamber has been favoured in our laboratory for the growth of spinal ganglia because high resolution phase observations may be made over long periods of time. A typical field of healthy neurons from such a preparation is illustrated in Plate XXIV. Long-term cine observations are carried out to document Schwann cell activity and myelination, axonal fibre manifestations, nuclear rotation in neurons, etc. A finished sound film documenting the dynamic activities of nervous tissue *in vitro* was recently produced by our group[41] in conjunction with a published review of the subject.[42] Until recently, our studies with CNS tissues were limited to roller tube preparations, but a modified procedure which proved to be a major breakthrough now allows us to maintain avian and mammalian spinal cord and brain tissue (cerebellum) in the Rose chamber.[6] Apparently, the special metabolic requirements of CNS tissue requires the presence of a substantial air phase. Continual immersion in culture medium leads to rapid degeneration, in contrast with spinal ganglia which grow well under these conditions. Instead of filling the chamber completely with fluid, less medium than normal is added so that a substantial air phase is provided over a moistened explant. Within a week or two of setup, substantial emigration of neuroglial and mesenchymal elements occurs, leaving a residue of neuron-rich tissue in the original explant (Plate XXV), which may be usefully studied by phase-contrast optics through the air phase. The new method of cultivating CNS tissues is proving extremely useful because it sustains long-term cultivation of the CNS and allows intermittent observations to be made without disturbing the culture. Also, the system allows new myelination to occur around axons. This technique may therefore be fruitful in viewing the process of myelination and in studying demyelinating diseases. Finally, it should be noted that the relative two-dimensional character of the flattened tissue still allows tissue organization patterns to be retained or to develop further, i.e., neuronal and fibre elements impinge on one another to the extent of producing synaptic junctions. Such cultures should prove useful for electrophysiological investigations in which sustained spontaneous firing patterns are followed using microelectrodes or when electrical stimuli are applied.

Cytologic Observations of Cultured CNS Tissues

Success has been achieved in growing and maintaining *in vitro* primary nervous tissues from the human cerebral cortex and mammalian hypothalamus brain stems, and cerebellum. Newborn kitten or rat cerebellum provides favourable and convenient test material for studies of nervous tissue from the brain while ten-day embryonic chicks or newborn rats are often used in studies of spinal cord.

As was indicated earlier there are typical zones of outgrowth from kitten cerebellum in which cellular components become regrouped (Fig. 13 and Plate XXVI). According to Pomerat and Costero,[39] whose work serves as a basis for the following description, the positions of cellular components *in vitro* bears a reasonable relationship to that which they might have occupied *in vivo*. At the periphery the colony is bordered by large polyhedral elements of probable pial origin. This same zone also contains stellate-type neurons which have a particular affinity for methylene blue in the living state. They are also observed in another zone closer to the explant and may correspond with Golgi type II neurons (Plate XXVII). Located between the border of the outgrowth and the dense portion of the explant in the zone of clot liquefaction are granule cells (Plate XXVIII) and Golgi type II elements. The perikarya of Purkinje cells generally remain within the area of the original explant although they may be seen in month-old cultures following thinning of the explant due to cellular emigration and the removal of debris by macrophagic activity. A better overall view of thick nerve fibres and neurofibrillar arrangements around a Purkinje cell is demonstrated in Plate XXIX. In the above study of kitten cerebellum by Pomerat and Costero healthy neurons were maintained for almost two months, a significantly longer period than that obtained with adult nervous tissues in earlier studies by these workers.

Non-neuronal elements in cerebellar cultures include oligodendroglia, astrocytes, pial elements, mesenchymal and fibroblastic cells, and macrophagic types. Oligodendrocytes are distinguished from granule cells in living preparations by virtue of the fact that the former appear to glow when studied with phase-contrast optics and contain abundant cytoplasmic granules which cast a halo around the perinuclear cytoplasm (Plate XXX). Oligodendrocytes give rise to narrow processes rather than the typical broad-based processes associated with astrocytes. By means of time-lapse cinematography, it was shown by Lumsden and Pomerat[30] that oligodendrocytes exhibit a peculiar but characteristic rhythmic pulsatile activity. The same rhythmicity is observed in these cells derived from human oligodendrogliomas. Whether or not this dynamicism is related to the myelinating function of oligodendroglia cannot be answered at present. In this connection, I recently observed an unusual time-lapse sequence in which the cell body of an oligodendrocyte was first seen attached to an axon (see Plate XXX). During the ensuing thirty-minute period of filming which was abstracted for the plate, a prominent oligodendroglial process with an active tip of unusual morphology was observed to move about violently until it made contact with the axon. It then proceeded to grow and move actively down the axon in intimate association with it. The functional significance of this unusual cellular and fibrous interaction may be related to the myelination process or to axoplasmic flow and needs to be investigated further.

In cerebellar explants and in the outgrowth, astrocytes are the most numerous cell type and are recognized by their characteristic interlacing and dense processes. Fibrous astrocytes with typical fibre branchings are illustrated in Plate XXXI. A typical stained astrocyte from the spinal cord is shown in Plate XXXII. The membranes of astrocytes are particularly active and lead to uptake of nutrient fluid in culture by pinocytosis (cell drinking). It has been suggested that glial elements *in vivo* serve for the movement of interstitial fluids and of substances in the neuroplasm.

At the marginal outgrowth of cerebellar cultures, large polyhedral elements were observed by Pomerat and Costero.[39] These were seen to contain tonofibrillae and interpreted as specialized glial cells of pial type. Other elements in the cultures undifferentiated mesenchymal cells with well-defined nucleoli, nuclear membranes, and mitochondria, as well as fibroblasts, and phagocytes including characteristic microglia (Plate XXXIII). While there has been some question raised recently about whether there is a distinct microglial cell type in the brain, there is little question about its presence and morphological distinctness in living CNS cultures.

Subsequent studies on cerebellar tissue were reported by Hild,[19] and Bornstein and Murray,[4] especially in relation to observations on myelination. In a recent well-documented study by Hild,[20] this author notes with caution that in his cerebellar cultures only Purkinje cells and large multipolar cells from the deep nuclei may be identified with a high degree of certainty. Hild claims that all other neuronal types present in the cerebellar cortex, such as basket cells, stellate cells, or Golgi type II cells, could hardly be identified as such in cultures; granule cells were curiously absent for the most part. The problems attending identification of cell type in Hild's study apparently stem from loss of special cellular characteristics and lack of functional relationships between cells. On the other hand, Hild notes that better identification was possible in the case of large unipolar neurons derived from the mesencephalic fifth nucleus and the large multipolar neurons in brain stem cultures derived from the lateral vestibular nucleus of Deiters. A triad of small unipolar neurons (probably granule cells) from one of our five-day cultures of rat cerebellum is illustrated in Plate XXXIV. Abundant Nissl substance in one of the cells testifies to its functional integrity.

Other examples could be cited of characteristic nerve elements which have been grown *in vitro* and frequently identified by their special character. For example, 45-day cultures of human foetal thalamus exhibit numerous centres of neuroblasts (Plate XXXV), spongioblasts, astrocytes, and oligodendrocytes.

Morphologic Patterns of Spinal Ganglia Cultures

The previous discussion has already provided numerous examples of how culturing of brain tissue allows display of neuronal and glial elements. Considerable work along this line has been done as well in our laboratory on nervous tissues from PNS, especially spinal ganglia. Such material may be equally instructive in understanding nerve function. The relative abundance of neurons from spinal ganglia of embryonic chick is illustrated in Plate XXXVI. This low-power montage of living cells displays about 550 well-defined neurons, usually of two size classes although this is not well seen at low magnifications. The pattern of fibre outgrowth is better seen in another preparation, fixed and then stained by Holmes' silver nitrate (Plate XXXVII). The original explants are dense and filled with neurons. Other neurons circumscribe these areas and reveal numerous nerve fibres which seemingly parallel one another to produce smooth-flowing patterns in the preparation. These fibres are large axons which have regenerated following explantation. Neuroglial and mesenchymal elements constitute the stippled background of this preparation. To present some idea of the histologic nature of chick spinal ganglia prior to explantation, the electron micrograph in Plate XXXVIII illustrates an intact neuron with its typical perineuronal satellite cells. This relationship is maintained *in vitro* (Plate XXXIX) and is probably essential for optimal growth and sustenance of the neuron. Indeed, intense RNA synthesis may be demonstrated in these neuronal nuclei (Plate XL).

The perikaryon is not seriously regarded any longer as a generator of impulses and assumes importance as the metabolic centre of the cell. The presence and regular pattern of Nissl substance is regarded as an index of neuron viability. Another criterion of good health goes hand-in-hand with the phenomenon of nuclear rotation. This was first observed by Nakai[33] in dissociated nerve cells and has been described in many other cell types in culture. In Nakai's study, 28 out of 52 neuronal nuclei rotated an average of once every hour. According to observations made in our laboratory, neither the rate of rotation nor the direction is constant. In Plate XLI, film abstracts of a cine sequence demonstrate active nuclear rotation in a neuron from a 10-day culture of rat dorsal root ganglion. In this case, a single rotation took two hours and 39 minutes. Nuclei have been shown to rotate at a similar rate for as long as 58 hours. The significance of this apparently bizarre energy expenditure may be related to intracellular circulatory pathways and propulsive mechanisms, as suggested by Pomerat.[38] We know that ribosomal ribonucleoprotein precursors originate in the nucleus. Their transport from nucleus to cytoplasm through nuclear pores would be facilitated by nuclear rotatory movements. However, the erratic nature of this movement suggests as well that this is an activity manifestation peculiar to conditions *in vitro* which may have little to do with normal cell function. The fact that such activity does occur proves the lack of direct morphologic continuity between the cytoplasmic system of membranes (endoplasmic reticulum) and the inner nuclear membrane. The energy source and manner of biochemical coupling to achieve nuclear rotation does not appear to have been investigated.

Activity of Neuroglial Cells

Considerable interest has been focused on the dynamic activities of neuroglia in culture. Such attention is warranted because of the close association of satellite cells with the neuron (Plates XXXVIII, XL), the Schwann cell with the axon and to some extent, the oligodendrocyte with the axon. It was suggested earlier, in the case of satellite cells circumscribing the perikaryon, that this relationship is of a supportive biochemical nature. Indeed, Nakai has shown that dissociated neurons lacking satellite cells survive in culture only a few days whereas histologically intact preparations may be grown for months. The metabolic interdependency of neurons and satellite cells has been demonstrated in isolated preparations by Hydén and co-workers. In recent thinking, there is a concept that glia play a role in learning behaviour. It has been suggested that they participate in the electrical response system of the brain.

Schwann cells and oligodendrocytes exhibit certain common characteristics in culture. They both are capable of dividing and exhibiting pulsatile activity. Such pulses exhibit a systole-diastole cycle of approximately 4–8 minutes. The cycle may be quantitated in developed time-lapse films by measuring the halo produced around the cell with a cadmium sulphide light detector[43] (Fig. 15). Schwann cells are known to migrate and proliferate in a chain-like fashion. This appearance coupled with their high metabolic activity has been shown by us in autoradiographs where high incorporation of tritiated uridine into nuclear RNA is observed. The role of Schwann cells and oligodendrocytes in the myelination of axons was mentioned early in this chapter (Fig. 4, Plate VII). Tissue culture played an essential part in coming to this conclusion, largely due to the work of Peterson and Murray and Hild, and testifies to the reproducibility of a complex phenomenon *in vitro*. The myelination process has already been described and is supplemented here with photographic documentation. The intimate binding of Schwann cells to axons is shown in living phase

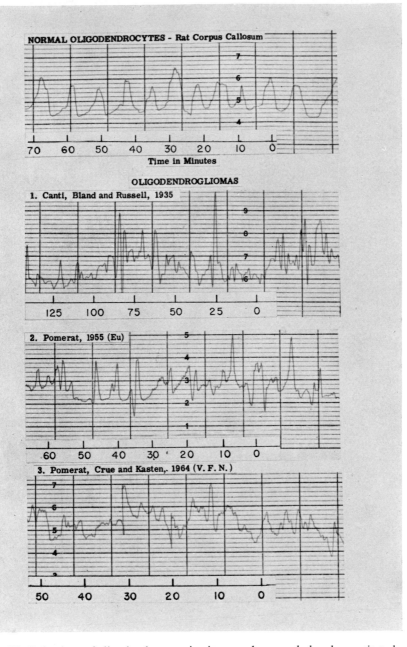

FIG. 15. Pulsations of oligodendrocytes *in vitro* may be recorded and quantitated by making strip chart recordings from cine records with the use of a cadmium sulphide scanner. A tracing from a well-isolated oligodendrocyte in a culture of the corpus callosum of a normal rat is shown in relation to data collected from film records of cells from three oligodendrogliomas. The upper graph suggests a systole-diastole cycle of approximately 4-8 minutes. The three other tracings are complex but suggest genetic similarities (from Ref. 40).

preparations (Plate XLII). Note how the Schwann cell nucleus lies directly on the axon with a thin border of cytoplasm passing directly on to the fibre. In an unusual film record reported from this laboratory and presented in abstract form (Plate XLIII), we observe apparent circumnavigation of a Schwann cell nucleus around a myelinated nerve fibre. A complete revolution was achieved in forty-eight hours. In accordance with our concepts of myelin formation, it is suggested that the turning process of the nucleus involves the Schwann cell cytoplasm as well to produce a spiral myelin configuration.

Cytologic Features of the Axon and Growth Cone in Culture

There is frequently difficulty in distinguishing and identifying neuronal processes in living cell cultures. Glial processes pervade the culture and invest the surface of perikarya and nerve fibres. The growth cone at the tip of a fibre is an aid in identifying axonal fibres. The dynamic movements of growth cones are especially well documented by abstracts of time-lapse film sequences. An example of such a sequence is in Plate XLIV from a culture of spinal ganglia. The thin membrane surface is in a constant state of motion, displaying new configurations and rapid back-and-forth undulations. The presence of pinocytic vesicles is likewise demonstrated near the growth cone. Growth cones in spinal cord cultures differ in morphology from those observed in spinal ganglia material in that the former are smaller and contain filopodia. After watching films of the 'searching' type of activities displayed by growth cones, one is often tempted to ascribe some manner of purposefulness to such movements, especially in light of the demonstration of synapses in culture. Elements of apparent non-neuronal origin may also display clear surface contacts with apparent adhesions to growth cones from axonal fibres (Plate XLV). The dynamic 'searching' type movements of growth cones seen in time-lapse films provides a note of optimism for workers attempting to achieve myoneural junctions *in vitro*.

9

Some Examples of the Use of Tissue Culture in Cytologic Studies of Diseased Nerve Tissues and Brain Tumours

While the tissue culture approach has provided excellent opportunities to investigate normal nerve tissues under relatively controlled conditions, the same possibilities have not been neglected by tissue culturists and neuropathologists for the study of material of abnormal origin. Indeed a wide range of diseased human tissues from the brain have been successfully cultivated in different laboratories.[29]

Aside from their inherent cytological interest, as with meningiomas and oligodendrogliomas, such tissues display growth patterns and cellular differences which may on occasion prove useful in the classification of tumours. The criteria for such assignment are difficult to arrive at and their prognostic value must not necessarily be taken highly. However, with further experience in this field and a willingness to desert when necessary preconceived histopathologic criteria based on fixed and stained sections, neuropathologists will undoubtedly find the combination of tissue culture and time-lapse photography an extremely practical adjunct. In addition to brain tumours, certain other biochemical disorders of the nervous system may be investigated *in vitro*, as the metabolic disease is reproduced in culture. Considerable success in this direction was achieved recently in our laboratory from a case of metachromatic leucodystrophy.

A lack of space prevents me from expanding the discussion of this important aspect of brain cytology. However, several examples will be presented largely from recent investigations in our laboratory, which illustrate some of the bizarre features of human oligodendrogliomas, meningiomas and metachromatic leucodystrophy that are reproduced in culture.

In an earlier section it was noted that oligodendrocytes *in vitro* display curious rhythmic pulsations (Plate XXX). This phenomenon occurs as well with oligodendrocytes from oligodendrogliomas. A comparison of the contraction-relaxation cycle is illustrated in Fig. 15. Admittedly, the alternating behaviour is complex and not completely repetitious with recycling, especially in oligodendrocytes from tumours. There is a suggestion of a contraction-relaxation cycle corresponding to about five minutes in glial cells from normal rat brain.

Meningiomas provide a source of particularly favourable material for investigations *in vitro*. One of the hallmarks of the disease seen in tissue sections is the presence of whorls. Fortunately, these are faithfully reproduced in culture following complete dissociation of the original tumour fragments by trypsin. It was shown by Pomerat and associates,[45] that these newly formed aggregates arise by encirclement of one cell by another, often involving numerous cells before these rotations are complete. The process involves complex circular and rhythmic motions which cause fluid displacements. An example of such a meningiomal whorl was recorded on one of our films and is presented in Plate XLVI. In addition to whorls, calcified psammoma bodies are formed *de novo in vitro*. Prominent nuclear vacuoles are seen in meningiomal cells, particularly *in vitro* (Plate XLVII). Their presence is suggestive of a viral factor, but an electron microscopic investigation by the author of one such cultured tumour, revealed faint residual fibres in the vacuolated areas (Plate XLVIII), but no recognizable viral particles. Cytoplasmic vacuoles also are observed; it may be that these cytoplasmic and nuclear regions are special fluid reservoirs involved in regulation of fluid transport at the meninges. Whether or not these cells are in fact of normal origin within the tumour requires additional study. Occasionally, multinucleated cells are observed in culture which display their nuclei in a peculiar rosette form. One such complex of eight nuclei is shown in Plate XLIX. Finally, attention is directed to the unusual arrangement of mitochondria seen in living cells from this type of tumour. Whereas typical mitochondria of many cells, including tumours, are in the form of individual filaments, those seen in meningiomas *in vitro* usually display characteristic connections with one another to form closed loops (Plate L). When followed in time-lapse films, the lattice-like effect is seen to change in dynamic fashion as individual mitochondrial elements of the network sever connections in one region and form new adhesions elsewhere. It remains to be seen whether this form of mitochondrial morphology is typical of all meningiomas. The biochemical significance of this observation needs to be elucidated.

Tissue culture offers opportunities to study biochemical disorders of the nervous system. Our laboratory was fortunate to receive several samples of tissue taken at operation from the brain and other organs of a young patient suffering with metachromatic leucodystrophy. This is a progressive, hereditary disorder in which a diffuse demyelination affects the nervous system. At the cellular level, a granular material is found in the cytoplasm of affected cells which stains metachromatically with basic dyes due to the abnormal accumulation of cerebroside sulphate esters or sulphatides.

Successful cultures were obtained from diseased white and grey matter of the brain, certain nerves, and the kidney. Time-lapse film records were obtained for the first time of the cells and we were able to detect certain cells displaying abnormal features, including the granules which were shown to be metachromatic. An abstract from one of these films (Plate LI) reveals one of the abnormal spindle-like cells which contains numerous cytoplasmic granules. A large rounded and halated microglial cell is seen to move rapidly across the field, intersect the fibrous extension of the spindle element and bend the fibre. The strength and tenacity of the cellular extensions are vividly recorded in the original film sequences as are other activity manifestations of these unusual cultures.

* * *

Acknowledgements

The author is grateful for the assistance of Mr Jon Booher in tissue culture, Miss Marci Livingstone and Mr C. George Lefeber in photography and Mrs Vivienne M. Barnes and Miss Rosemarie Bell in the capable typing of the manuscript. The original investigations reported here were supported in part by research grants to the author from the United States Public Health Service (Grant NB 03113 from the National Institute of Neurological Diseases and Blindness and Grant CA 07991 from the National Cancer Institute), a grant from the Greenville Foundation, and the American Cancer Society through an Institutional Grant to the University of Southern California.

REFERENCES

1. ADAMS, C. W. M., 1965. *Neurohistochemistry*. Amsterdam: Elsevier.
2. BARKA, T., and ANDERSON, P. J., 1963. *Histochemistry*. New York: Harper and Row.
3. BODIAN, D., 1964. An electron microscopic study of the monkey spinal cord. *Bull. Johns Hopkins Hosp.*, **114**, 13.
4. BORNSTEIN, M. B., and MURRAY, M. R., 1958. Serial observations on patterns of growth, myelin formation, maintenance and degeneration in cultures of new-born rat and kitten cerebellum. *J. Biophys. Biochem. Cytol.*, **4**, 499.
5. BORNSTEIN, M. B., 1958. Reconstituted rat-tail collagen used as substrate for tissue cultures on coverslips. *Lab. Invest.*, **7**, 134.
6. BOOHER, J., and KASTEN, F. H., 1966. A modified technique for culturing tissues of the central nervous system in the Rose chamber. *Abstracts of the 17th Annual Meeting of the Tissue Culture Association*, p. 75. San Francisco.
7. BUNGE, R. P., BUNGE, M. B., and PETERSON, E. R., 1965. Electron microscope study of cultured rat spinal cord. *J. Cell. Biol.*, **24**, 163.
8. CAJAL, S. RAMÓN Y., 1928. *Degeneration and Regeneration of the Nervous System*, vols. 1, 2. London: Oxford Univ. Press.
9. DARIN DE LORENZO, A. J., 1966. Electron microscopy: tight junctions in synapses of chick ciliary ganglion. *Science*, **152**, 76.
10. DROZ, M. B., 1965. Accumulation de proteines nouvellement synthetisees dans l'appareil de Golgi du neurone; etude radioautographique en microscopie electronique. *C.R. Acad. Sc. Paris*, **260**, 320.
11. DROZ, M. B., and LEBLOND, C. P., 1963. Axonal migration of proteins in the central nervous system and peripheral nerves as shown by radioautography. *J. Compar. Neurol.*, **121**, 325.
12. ECCLES, J. C., 1965. The synapse. *Sci. Amer.*, **212**, 55.
13. FREEMAN, J. A., 1964. *Cellular Fine Structure*. New York: McGraw-Hill Book Co.
14. GOLDFISCHER, S., 1964. The Golgi apparatus and the endoplasmic reticulum in neurons of the rabbit. *J. Neuropath. Exp. Neurol.*, **23**, 36.
15. GRAY, E. G., 1964. Tissue of the central nervous system. In *Electron Microscopic Anatomy*, Kurtz, S. M. (Ed.). New York: Acad. Press.
16. HANCOCK, R. L., 1965. Uridine incorporation into pyramidal nuclei of the mouse brain. *Experienta*, **21**, 152.
17. HERNDON, R. M., 1963. The fine structure of the Purkinje cell. *J. Cell. Biol.*, **18**, 167.
18. HILD, W., 1959. Das Neuron. In *Mollendorff-Bargmann's Handbuch der mikroskopischen Anatomie des Menschen*, **14**/4, Berlin: Springer Verlag.
19.   1964. Electrophysiological phenomena observed in single neurons and neuroglial cells in cultures of central nervous tissue. In *Brain Function*, Brazier, M. A. B. (Ed.), vol. 2. Berkeley: University of California Press.
20.   1966. Cell types and neuronal connections in cultures of mammalian central nervous tissue. *Ztsf. Zellforsch*, **69**, 155.
21. HYDÉN, H., and EGYHÁZI, E., 1962. Changes in the base composition of nuclear ribonucleic acid of neurons during a short period of enhanced protein production. *J. Cell. Biol.*, **15**, 37.
22. HYDÉN, H., and PIGON, A., 1960. A cytophysiological study of the functional relationship between oligodendroglial cells and nerve cells of Deiter's nucleus. *J. Neurochem.*, **6**, 57.
23. KASTEN, F. H., 1966. Charles Marc Pomerat—experimental biologist and humanist. *Med. Biol. Illust.*, **16**, 78.

24. KOENIG, H., 1962. Nucleic acid and protein metabolism in white matter. *Arch. Neurol.*, **6**, 177.

25. KUFFLER, ST. W., and NICHOLLS, J. G., 1966. The physiology of neuroglia cells. *Ergeb. Physiol.*, **57**, 1.

26. LAPHAM, L. W., and JOHNSTONE, M. A., 1963. Cytologic and cytochemical studies of neuroglia. 2. The occurrence of two DNA classes among glial nuclei in the Purkinje cell layer of adult human cerebellar cortex. *Arch. Neurol.*, **9**, 194.

27. LEVI-MONTALCINI, R., 1963. Growth and differentiation in the nervous system. In *The Nature of Biological Diversity*, Allen, J. M. (Ed.). New York: McGraw-Hill.

28. LILLIE, R. D., 1965. *Histopathologic Technic and Practical Histochemistry.* Third Edit. New York: McGraw-Hill.

29. LUMSDEN, C. E., 1963. Tissue culture in relation to tumors of the nervous system. In *Pathology of Tumors of the Nervous System*, Russell, D. S., and Rubinstein, L. J. (Ed.). Baltimore: Williams and Wilkins Co.

30. LUMSDEN, C. E., and POMERAT, C. M., 1951. Normal oligodendrocytes in tissue culture. *Exp. Cell Res.*, **2**, 103.

31. MIALE, I. L., and SIDMAN, R. L., 1961. An autoradiographic analysis of histogenesis in the mouse cerebellum. *Exp. Neurol.*, **4**, 280.

32. MURRAY, M. R., 1965. Nervous tissues *in vitro*. In *Cells and Tissues in Culture*, Willmer, E. N. (Ed.), vol. 2. New York: Academic Press.

33. NAKAI, J., 1956. Dissociated dorsal root ganglia in tissue culture. *Amer. J. Anat.*, **99**, 81.

34. OCHS, S., 1966. Axoplasmic flow in neurons. In *Macromolecules and Behavior*, Gaito, J. (Ed.). New York: Appleton-Century-Crofts.

35. PALAY, S. L., 1964. Structural basis for neural action. In *Brain Function*, Brazier, M. A. B. (Ed.), vol. 2. Berkeley: University of California Press.

36. PALAY, S. L., and PALADE, G. E., 1955. The fine structure of neurons. *J. Biophys. Biochem. Cytol.*, **1**, 69.

37. PEARSE, A. G. E., 1960. *Histochemistry–Theoretical and Applied.* Second Ed. Boston: Little, Brown & Co.

38. POMERAT, C. M., 1958. Cinematographic analysis of cell dynamics. *Fed. Proc.*, **17**, 975.

39. POMERAT, C. M., and COSTERO, I., 1956. Tissue cultures of cat cerebellum. *Amer. J. Anat.*, **99**, 211.

40. POMERAT, C. M., CRUE, B. L., and KASTEN, F. H., 1964. Observations on the cytology of an oligodendroglioma cultivated *in vitro*. *J. Nat. Cancer Inst.*, **33**, 517.

41. POMERAT, C. M., HENDELMAN, W. J., RAIBORN, C. W., and MASSEY, J. R., 1965. Dynamic Aspects of the Neuron in Tissue Culture. 16 mm sound film, B/W, 18 min. Pasadena Foundation for Medical Research, Pasadena, California.

42. In press. Dynamic activities of nervous tissue. In *Neurology Textbooks* Hyden, H. (Ed.). Amsterdam: Elsevier.

43. POMERAT, C. M., ROUNDS, D. E., and HUFF, W., 1964. Optical scanning and electronic recording of cellular activity. *J. Royal Micr. Soc.*, **83**, 265.

44. POMERAT, C. M., ROUNDS, D. E., RAIBORN, C. W. Jr, and POLLARD, T. D., 1964. Observations on newborn rat dorsal root ganglia *in vitro* following gamma irradiation. In *Response of the Nervous System to Ionizing Radiation*, Haley, T. J., and Snider, R. S. (ed.). Boston: Little, Brown & Co.

45. POMERAT, C. M., TODD, E. M., and GOLDBLATT, D., 1962. Activity of meningiomal whorls *in vitro*. In *The Biology and Treatment of Intercranial Tumors*, Fields, W. S., and Sharkey, P. C. (ed.). Springfield: Charles C. Thomas.

46. RHODIN, J., 1963. *An Atlas of Ultrastructure.* Philadelphia: W. B. Saunders Co.
47. SATAKE, M., and ABE, S., 1966. Preparation and characterization of nerve cell perikaryon from rat cerebral cortex. *J. Biochem.,* **59,** 72.
48. SHOLL, D. A., 1956. *The Organization of the Cerebral Cortex.* London: John Wiley.
49. SMART, J., and LEBLOND, C. P., 1961. Evidence for division and transformation of neuroglia cells in the mouse brain, as derived from radioautography after injection of thymidine-H$_3$. *J. comp. Neurol.,* **116,** 349.
50. TAYLOR, A. C., and WEISS, P., 1965. Demonstration of axonal flow by the movement of tritium-labelled protein in mature optic nerve fibers. *Proc. Nat. Acad. Sci., U.S.A.,* **54,** 1521.
51. TRUEX, R. C., and CARPENTER, M. B., 1964. *Strong and Elwyn's Human Neuroanatomy.* Fifth Ed. Baltimore: Williams and Wilkins Co.
52. UZMAN, L., 1960. The histogenesis of the mouse cerebellum as studied by its tritiated thymidine uptake. *J. comp. Neurol.,* **114,** 137.

IV

THE CHEMICAL PROCESSES
OF MEMORY

BRUCE S. McEwen

PH.D.*

Department of Zoology, University of Minnesota, Minneapolis, Minnesota.

1

Introduction

The marriage of biochemical and behavioural concepts and techniques in the search for the structural basis of memory is so recent that the reader may doubt the legitimacy of such a union. The purpose of this chapter is to demonstrate that this adventurous combination is indeed very healthy and beginning to produce some fascinating results. The origin of the active interest in this area of neurobiology must be credited to Hydén, the Swedish neurobiologist, whose elegant and audacious experiments[49, 51-53] have given many investigators the stimulus to proceed with their own experiments. Hydén must also be credited with awakening interest in the possibility that molecules in the central nervous system may in some manner 'store' memory.[47] This controversial idea will be evaluated in its current form on the basis of the available experimental evidence.

A major factor in the growing attention to the 'molecular basis' of memory is the reawakened interest in the role of the genetic material in all aspects of cell function. It is the purpose of this chapter to consider the biochemical changes associated with learning in the broader context of the biochemical plasticity of the brain. This plasticity is the direct result of the activity of genes in nerve and glial cell nuclei which are regulated by many factors in the internal and external environment, including the animal's daily experiences. In the next two sections an attempt will be made to relate biochemical plasticity of the brain to changes in gene activity.

* Present address: The Rockefeller University, New York, New York.

It will be in this context that the biochemical basis of memory will then be examined.

The reader is referred to a number of earlier review articles which cover the development of this subject and reflect various points of view.[12, 17, 29, 38, 39]

2

Changes in the Brain with Experience

An animal's brain changes chemically and anatomically as a result of its daily experience. Such changes have been carefully documented by the experiments of Bennett, Diamond, Krech, and Rosenzweig at the University of California, Berkeley.[13, 28] In their experiments two groups of adult male rats were compared with respect to the weight and the acetylcholinesterase specific activity of various regions of the brain. The two groups differed in their daily experiences for eighty days: members of one group were isolated and had 'limited experience'; members of the other group lived together in an 'enriched environment' consisting of 'toys' and various types of daily training. At the end of the eighty days the 'enriched environment' rats had a larger mass of cerebral cortex and higher cortical acetylcholinesterase activity. There were few significant differences in these parameters in other brain regions. Other experiments showed specific decreases in blinded or light-deprived animals compared to controls in the weight of the visual cortex and midbrain visual reflex centres. According to the Berkeley group, the increase in cortical mass in 'enriched environment' rats consists of an increased cortical thickness, greater in visual than in somaesthetic regions, caused by an increase in the size of cells and intercellular substances.[28] No major anatomical changes had occurred, although there may have been some increase in branching of dendrites.[28] According to the experiments of Altman and Das,[5] however, there was also an increased rate of glial cell multiplication which might account for the increased cortical mass with the 'enriched environment'. These investigators found an increased labelling of glial cell nuclei with tritiated thymidine, a precursor of DNA, in the cortices of 'enriched environment' rats.

3

Relationship Between Gene Activity and Nerve Function

In 1925, E. B. Wilson wrote in his classic book *The Cell in Development and Heredity*:[86]

'... The destructive processes and liberation of energy, as manifested by coordinated forms of protoplasmic movement, may go on for some time undisturbed in a mass of cytoplasm devoid of a nucleus. On the other hand, the building up of a new chemical or morphological products by the cytoplasm is only initiated in the presence of a nucleus, and soon ceases in its absence.'

In view of this statement and the overwhelming support and elucidation it has received from recent advances in genetics and molecular biology, the growth of the cerebral cortex and changes in chemical and morphological characteristics in an 'enriched environment' can only be regarded as the result of genes in brain cell nuclei which have been activated by the changed nervous activity in the 'enriched environment'.

Gene activity is now thought of in biochemical terms as the synthesis of messenger RNA molecules by selected regions of the DNA in the cell nucleus, followed by the synthesis of specific proteins along a template provided by the messenger RNA. Studies in Hydén's laboratory have shown that the RNA of neurons and their surrounding glial cells is very sensitive to conditions affecting nervous activity. Changes in both the amount and base composition of neuronal and glial RNA were observed as a result of drug treatment,[33, 50] and sensory stimulation,[48, 49] in diseased areas of the brain associated with Parkinson's disease,[42] and in learning experiments.[49, 51-53] Other investigators have shown that the RNA concentration in retinal ganglion cells tends to decrease in the absence of light stimulation.[16, 18, 83] These types of observations, taken together with the 'enriched environment' experiments, have suggested the hypothesis that the genetic material of neurons and glia is called upon to make adjustments to physiological changes by elaborating information for the formation of new and perhaps different protein molecules which may themselves be directly involved in the nervous activity. The protein composition and metabolism of the central nervous system will be considered in Section 6 after reviewing the evidence for the participation of RNA and protein synthesis in learning and memory.

4

Theories of the Role of Chemical Processes in Learning and Memory

According to Hebb,[45] the formation of long-term memory seems to involve diffuse structural changes in the brain. There is rather general agreement that these structural changes are concerned either with the establishment of new pathways or with the strengthening of existing pathways in the brain. However, considerable disagreement has arisen over the mechanism and nature of these structural changes. The author prefers to divide the main proposals into two groups: (*i*) One type of hypothesis states that the structural changes involve the growth of presynaptic or postsynaptic structures or changes in the level of enzymes associated with the synthesis and breakdown of transmitter substances.[12, 17] According to such mechanisms, the role of the genes would be only concerned with determining the anatomical structure of the central nervous system during embryonic development and with providing genetic information for growth or increased enzyme synthesis. (*ii*) A second group of hypotheses states that there are special molecules in the brain which influence the conducting properties of neurons or the interaction between neurons in nervous pathways.[46, 47, 81] This second type of theory proposes that the significant structural changes in memory consist of the formation of such molecules. According to the current forms of this mechanism, the genes would have (in addition to some of the functions mentioned for the first hypothesis) a role in determining the structure of these special 'memory' molecules. Each memory would not necessarily need a separate molecular type; rather, a limited number of molecular types could suffice, since the various permutations and combinations of these types taken in small groups, together with the anatomical organization of the brain, would insure that a very large number of memories could be stored.

The original proposal of Hydén that RNA stores memory is of this second type, although this hypothesis states that the base sequence of RNA is determined by electrostatic forces associated with the firing of nerve impulses, and not by the DNA.[47] Since Hydén made this proposal it has become widely accepted that the base sequence of RNA is determined exclusively by the base sequence of DNA. In order for the original Hydén hypothesis to hold, the brain would have to be an exception to this empirical rule; however, there is no evidence that brain RNA synthesis is independent of direction by DNA.[11, 23] Another hypothesis has been advanced by Gaito,[38, 39] suggesting that somatic mutations in the DNA of the brain occur during learning and provide an altered 'message' which directs the synthesis of different RNA molecules and constitutes the memory. Whereas there has been no direct test of this hypothesis, it goes very much against the widely accepted doctrine that changes in an animal's environment do not directly modify the genetic information; such modifications are thought to occur only by the random process of mutation.

Other theories of the chemical basis of memory have employed the mechanism of antibody formation as an analogy.[46, 81] In these theories it is suggested that a presynaptic neuron would secrete an antigen-like substance and that postsynaptic neurons would respond by producing antibody-like 'receptor' molecules, thereby setting up new contacts between adjacent neurons. One problem which is shared with the other theories mentioned in the previous paragraph is that there is at present no physiological information to suggest how such a mechanism would control the electrical activity of the neurons involved. Another problem with the analogy between memory and antibody formation is that many aspects of this latter process are themselves not very well understood, including the role of the genetic information in the antibody-forming cells. Thus detailed model building of a memory mechanism on the tenuous framework of even the most widely favoured schemes of antibody formation is an almost futile occupation at the present time.

These pessimistic remarks are not intended to deny that there are valuable ideas in an analogy between antibody formation and memory. Let us now consider some of the reasons for drawing such an analogy, and in so doing we shall reveal some of the important aspects of memory which future experimentation must consider. One aspect is that of the exquisite specificity in the growth of connections in the nervous system during embryonic development. Levi-Montalcini and her co-workers[85] have isolated and studied in considerable detail a growth factor which is specific for the sympathetic nervous system. Sperry[80] has discussed the incredible chemoaffinity which seems to direct the orderly growth of nerve fibre patterns and connections with end organs and other neurons. There is also evidence that some kind of highly developed chemical specificity is characteristic of different regions of the brain in the adult animal. Mihailovic and co-workers[64, 65] have published studies of the specific inhibition of electrical activity of caudate nucleus by antisera against caudate nucleus tissue which has been adsorbed by tissue from other brain regions in order to remove antibodies to common antigenic components. Such specificity may very well govern the functional connections which various brain regions and nervous pathways make with each other, and one cannot help wondering if such specificity lies at the basis of memory.

Another reason for the great interest in the process of antibody formation is that this process and the phenomenon of memory present us with an analogous situation: antibodies are formed against substances which the animal has not encountered before; memory is formed as a result of experiences which are new to the animal. Moreover, neither antibody production nor memory are carried over from the parent animal to its progeny. What then is the role of the genes in these two processes which store information about the animal's environment without apparently modifying in a direct way the hereditary material? We shall now speak only about memory. The extreme view that the genes play no part is made untenable by experimental observations, referred to in Sections 2 and 5, that growth and other forms of biosynthesis accompany learning. At the opposite extreme, the view that the genes contain in a strict sense all of the information for all of the new experiences encountered by an animal is equally unacceptable. The true role of the genes in memory must lie somewhere between these two extremes. The author believes that the two alternative hypotheses stated in the first paragraph of this section represent the most useful form of the controversy over the role of the genes. Let us now review the experimental evidence concerning the role of chemical processes in memory and see if either of these two hypotheses is strongly favoured at the present time.

5

Studies on Learning and Memory

Changes in Amount and Base Composition of Neuronal and Glial RNA during Learning

Hydén and Egyházi have published the results of two studies in which changes in both the amount and base composition of neuronal and glial RNA occurred during learning in areas of the brain which were most likely involved in the neurological activity of the task being learned.[48, 51, 52] Analyses of RNA were performed by the microtechnique developed by Edstrom.[32] The first study[48, 51] concerned the learning by hungry rats to walk up a thin wire strung between the floor and a raised platform in order to get food. Cells of the Deiters' nucleus of the brain stem were used for analysis since the rats' task was chiefly a matter of learning to balance on the wire. Functional controls consisted of vestibular stimulation by rotation in two different ways. Hydén and Egyházi found that in both learning animals and functional controls the total amount of RNA increased in Deiters' neurons compared to unstimulated, naive litter mates. However, only animals learning the task showed changes in the base composition of the RNA in the nuclei of Deiters' neurons and in the glial cells surrounding the neurons. No changes in the RNA base composition of the cytoplasm of Deiters' neurons were observed. Analyses were also performed on the neuronal RNA of the reticular formation. A small increase in total neuronal RNA content was found, but no change took place in the base composition of the nuclear RNA.

In the second study of learning,[52] Hydén and Egyházi used the ability of hungry rats to reach into a tube or dish with one front paw to obtain food pellets. Many rats show a preference to use the left or right paw when tested in an unbiased situation. Once the preference is established and the situation is changed to require the use of the opposite paw to get food, many rats will learn to use this 'non-preferred' paw. The learning will usually persist after the biased situation is removed, provided enough practice has occurred. Peterson and co-workers[70-74] have established during many years of work that a region of the frontal cortex anterior to the bregma controls the 'handedness'. Ablation of this area on the contralateral side will destroy the animal's ability to reach for food. Hydén and Egyházi found remarkable changes in the RNA of cortical neurons from this 'handedness' region when the animals learned to take food with the new paw.* The RNA content of these cells increased by as much as 100 per cent during prolonged training with the new paw, and significant changes were observed in all four purine and pyrimidine bases. In control experiments in which rats were allowed to practice with the preferred

---

* In these experiments the contralateral side to the 'preferred' paw served as a control, since the animal was using his 'non-preferred' paw exclusively.

hand, slight increases in the content of RNA per cell occurred but no changes in base composition were observed.

What is the nature of the RNA produced in neurons and glia during these learning experiments? Hydén and Lange[53] have calculated the base composition of the $\triangle$ RNA, the RNA produced in the neurons during learning. This $\triangle$ RNA has a highly asymmetric base composition in the 'handedness' experiments when the animal has had a little training, but it becomes more symmetric and 'ribosomal' in base composition with a lot of training. In the balancing experiments, an asymmetric $\triangle$ RNA was found when the learning curve tended to be linear, while a more symmetric 'ribosomal' $\triangle$ RNA was produced when the learning curve was non- linear. These calculations are subject to numerous uncertainties,[53] and only direct experiments will ever satisfactorily answer the question.

Alterations of Learning and Brain Biochemistry by Drugs

Drugs are potential tools for understanding certain aspects of the biochemistry of behaviour. But even without adding to our understanding, they offer a potential means of controlling or modifying behaviour and have therefore attracted a great deal of attention.

One of the consequences of Hydén's experiments and theory concerning the role of RNA in memory is that attempts are being made to utilize drugs which increase RNA synthesis in the brain in order to speed up learning. One such drug is 1,1,3-tricyano-2-amino-1-propene (TRIAP), shown by Egyházi and Hydén to increase the amount and change the base composition of RNA in neurons of the Deiters' nucleus and to decrease the amount and change the base composition of glial cell RNA from the same region.[33, 50] Chamberlain and co-workers[22] carried out a test of TRIAP on two learning situations in rats: (*i*) the development of a postural asymmetry;* and (*ii*) pushing a bar to avoid a shock signalled by a buzzer. TRIAP, administered in four daily injections prior to making the lesion which produces the postural asymmetry, decreased the fixation time from 45 minutes to 30 minutes; 8-azaguanine, an antimetabolite which inhibits normal RNA synthesis, increased the fixation time to 70 minutes. In the second learning situation, TRIAP administered 45 minutes prior to each daily training period decreased the mean latency to avoid shock and increased the mean number of avoidances per day. The differences between TRIAP-treated rats and controls were apparent after two days of training and very pronounced by the third day. In this second learning situation, 8-azaguanine had no effect on either parameter of learning changed by TRIAP.

---

* 'It has been shown that a postural asymmetry in the hind limbs, induced by a unilateral cerebellar or vestibular lesion, will persist after mid-thoracic spinal cord transection, providing sufficient time is allowed for this asymmetry to "fixate" in the cord before transection.' Chamberlain *et al.*[22]

Another drug, developed at the Abbott Laboratories in Chicago and called magnesium pemoline, has been reported to increase in rats both the rate of learning and the memory for a conditioned avoidance response (running to avoid a shock signalled by a buzzer).[69] Experimental animals were given magnesium pemoline 30 minutes prior to ten learning trials. Drug-treated rats learned faster and attained a much lower mean response latency than controls during the ten trials. When tested for ten trials on the following day, the drug-treated animals retained a very short latency of avoidance, which did not change, while controls showed a gradual lengthening of latency during the ten retention trials. It should be pointed out that the initial conditioning in this experiment utilized a buzzer to signal a shock; however, retention trials were run without buzzer or shock so that the animals were apparently escaping the 'memory' of unpleasant environment.

In another study of magnesium pemoline, Glasky and Simon[40] reported that the drug enhances the activity of RNA polymerase, the enzyme presumed to carry out the DNA-dependent synthesis of RNA in cell nuclei. These investigators described two types of experiments. First, they assayed brain RNA polymerase *in vitro* from rats given the drug up to two hours before sacrifice. Under these conditions their results suggest that the true RNA polymerase activity increases steadily during the two hours that the animal is exposed to the drug, while a 'pseudo-RNA polymerase' increases during the first thirty minutes and then remains constant.* In the second experiment, they added magnesium pemoline to an enzyme preparation aged for twenty-four hours at $-25°C$ and obtained evidence for the activation of the enzyme activity *in vitro*. The activation was dependent on the presence in the incubation mixture of dimethylsulfoxide, which alone had a slight effect on enzyme activity. There is as yet no information to indicate if, like TRIAP, magnesium pemoline increases the amount of RNA in brain cells.

Attempts to Transfer Specific Memory by Transferring RNA

Another direct result of the interest in RNA created by work in Hydén's laboratory has been attempts in a number of laboratories to transfer specific memory by transferring RNA molecules from the nervous system of a trained animal to a naive animal. Needless to say, the unambiguous success of such an audacious type of experiment would strongly support the theory that memory is stored in RNA. However, the experiments described so far have produced contradictory results, and it is the purpose of this section to review the various experimental approaches which have been used.

Free-living flatworms of the group called planarians have been con-

---

* True RNA polymerase requires all four nucleoside triphosphates, while 'pseudo-RNA polymerase' requires only one nucleoside triphosphate in the incubation mixture.

ditioned to contract to light as a conditioned stimulus when this is paired with electric shock as unconditioned stimulus. Planaria also possess a remarkable ability to regenerate when cut in half. McConnell and co-workers[60] reported that regenerating 'heads' and 'tails' from trained planaria showed equal 'savings' in a retesting situation. Corning and John[25] carried out regeneration experiments with ribonuclease present in the pond water. Heads regenerated with low concentrations of ribonuclease, not sufficient to affect regeneration itself, showed greater 'savings' than regenerated controls; tails regenerated in ribonuclease had less 'savings' than regenerated controls. Planaria regenerated with ribonuclease in the pond water in general required a greater number of trials to reach criterion than did planaria regenerated in the absence of ribonuclease.

In 1962, McConnell[61] published the well-known 'cannibalism' experiments with planaria. He found that untrained planaria required fewer trials to criterion when fed planaria which had been trained than when fed untrained, untreated planaria. These experiments were recently examined by Hartey and co-workers[44] who found that planaria stimulated only by light or handled, but not trained, were as effective as trained planaria in transferring 'savings' to naive planaria in the 'cannibalism' experiment. For further details of the work on planaria and the controversy over memory transfer, the reader is referred to past issues of *The Worm Runners' Digest*, edited by McConnell and co-workers.

Another controversy has arisen over recent reports that specific memory can be transferred by injections of RNA extracted from the brains of trained rats. Fjerdingstad and colleagues[34] in Copenhagen reported that rats receiving an intraventricular injection of RNA from the brain of a thirsty rat trained to run up a lighted side of a maze to get a water reward had a better performance during seven days in the same training situation than rats receiving RNA from untrained animals and rats receiving no RNA injection. In subsequent work[68, 74] this Danish group reported results of attempts to demonstrate specificity of memory 'transfer' by utilizing RNA from brains of rats trained to choose either the lighted or darkened side of the maze. 'Dark-conditioned' RNA appeared to have increased the performance in a situation where the injected rat had to choose the lighted side of the maze; 'light-conditioned' RNA appeared to improve performance to the darkened side of the maze.

Analogous experiments to those of the Danish group were carried out by a group at the University of California, Los Angeles, who injected naive rats intraperitoneally with RNA extracted from brains of hungry rats trained to approach a food cup upon hearing a signal.[9, 21] According to their results there was a highly significant improvement in performance of these rats compared to controls injected with RNA from brains of untrained rats. In subsequent work this group has presented evidence for the specificity of the memory transferred[55] and for the inter-species transfer[8] of memory from guinea-pigs to rats.

The results of these two groups of investigators have been disputed in two recent papers. Gross and Carey[43] reported their failure to reproduce the results obtained by the UCLA workers. And a group at the Universtiy of California, Irvine, has published a critical study of the experiments of both the Danish workers and the UCLA group.[59] In this study they could find no evidence for memory transfer by intraperitoneal injections of RNA in four different learning situations. However, these situations are different from the ones used at UCLA. They also reported that no radioactivity could be detected in the brain following the intraperitoneal injections of P^{32}-labelled ascites tumour and rat brain RNA. They also tested intraventricular injections of RNA in a conditioned avoidance situation and found no evidence for memory transfer.

This section would not be complete without mentioning several attempts to enhance learning and memory by administration of nonspecific RNA. In both cases, yeast RNA was used, so that specific memory transfer was not under consideration and only nutritional effects were being tested. In experiments with rats, Cook and co-workers[24] found that both learning and resistance to extinction of a conditioned avoidance response were enhanced by fifty-three daily intraperitoneal injections of yeast RNA prior to training. In an analogous study on senile human subjects, Cameron and co-workers[20] found an improvement in scores in several situations testing learning and memory, following therapy consisting of massive doses of yeast RNA given intravenously over a period of several weeks.

Attempts to Transfer Memory by Transferring Proteins or Polypeptides

There is another group of experiments involving essentially the same ideas as the RNA transfer experiments, in which the main substance being transferred appears to be low molecular weight proteins or polypeptides extracted from the brains of trained animals.

The first report of this kind, by Ungar and Oceguera-Navarro,[82] concerns the transfer of habituation from rats to mice. Extracts from brains of rats, habituated over a number of days to a 90 per cent criterion of nonresponse to the sound of a hammer striking a metal plate, were injected intraperitoneally into mice. Large differences in habituation between the experimental group and control mice injected with extracts from brains of unhabituated rats were observed over a fourteen-day testing period, which began sixteen hours after the injection of the extracts. Experimental mice showed rapid habituation (after one day) to an 80 per cent non-response level, while controls showed a gradual habituation over the fourteen days of testing to a 70 per cent non-response level.

Rosenblatt and co-workers[75-77] have recently published a group of papers concerning the transfer of various types of learned behaviour from trained to untrained rats by means of brain extracts. Both donor and recipient in these experiments were albino rats, and injections were made intraperitoneally. Five different training situations were used. Since the experiments tested many variables the main findings of these investigators will be summarized in a general way:

1. Significant transfer effects were observed from both cerebellum and cerebrum as well as whole brain.

2. Extracts in saline of brain were fractionated into four classes according to molecular weight: 1000–5000; 5000–10,000; 10,000 and above; and a particulate fraction. Only the 10,000 and above class showed no ability to produce transfer, while strongest effects were observed with the '1000–5000' and the 'particulate' fractions. Ribonuclease was without effect on the transfer activity, while chymotrypsin tended to destroy the transfer activity in the soluble fractions. Rosenblatt and co-workers suggest that the transfer factor may be a polypeptide which is normally bound to membranes or other structures.

3. A dose effect was observed; transfer of learned behaviour was not apparent if the equivalent in terms of extract of less than one brain was injected into the recipients.

4. Two experiments were designed to test for the specificity of the effect. In these experiments the experimental and control donor animals were trained on the same task but to respond to opposite cues (dark versus light). In this way the transfer effect was a measure of the dark versus light difference. In one experiment a clear difference was transferred; in the other, the transfer effect was very small and may not have been significant. However, the authors state in a general way that the transfer effects observed in all the experiments were specific.

5. Several of the experiments were designed to duplicate the extraction procedures used by Jacobson and co-workers for the RNA transfer experiments (see the previous section). Rosenblatt and co-workers suggest that protein or polypeptide in the RNA preparations may have been responsible for the transfer effects observed by both Jacobson and co-workers and by Fjerdingstad and associates.

Effects of Inhibitors of RNA Synthesis on Learning and Memory

We have so far been concerned with the possible enhancement of learning and memory by RNA or by drugs which stimulate RNA synthesis in the brain. Let us now consider experiments dealing with the possible inhibition of learning and destruction of memory by substances which inhibit brain RNA and protein synthesis.

In 1961, Dingman and Sporn[30] reported that intracerebrally-administered 8-azaguanine, an antimetabolite which inhibits normal RNA synthesis, increases the number of errors made by rats in learning a maze but has no effect on the memory for this situation. Other effects of 8-azaguanine were mentioned above in connection with the experiments of Chamberlain and co-workers[22] on the drug TRIAP. They reported that intraperitoneally-administered 8-azaguanine increases the fixation time for a neurological response analogous to learning but did not affect two parameters of behaviour in avoidance conditioning. 8-azaguanine was also utilized by Jewett and co-workers[56] in studying the learning by rats of a fixed-interval time schedule involving previously-conditioned bar-pressing for food. In addition to a decreased rate of bar-pressing indicative of lowered motor activity, the rats treated with 8-azaguanine displayed a reduced ability to discriminate the correct time interval, particularly in the latter phases of training.

Another inhibitor of RNA synthesis is Actinomycin D, which blocks the transcription of base sequences in DNA to RNA carried out by the RNA polymerase enzyme mentioned above. Barondes and Jarvik[11] achieved an 83 per cent inhibition of brain RNA synthesis with intra-cerebrally-administered Actinomycin D but could find no inhibition of learning in a simple, passive avoidance conditioning situation. However, prolonged and detailed testing of the behaviour was not attempted owing in part to the fact that the treated animals became very sick and could not be maintained on repeated doses of Actinomycin D. In a subsequent paper, Cohen and Barondes[23] found that inhibition of brain RNA synthesis by 94 to 96 per cent with Actinomycin D did not affect performance of rats in a one or two choice maze, nor did it affect memory of the training after two to four hours. Long-term effects of Actinomycin D on memory were not investigated.

Effects of Inhibitors of Protein Synthesis on Learning and Memory

In several exciting papers, the Flexners and their associates in Philadelphia have described the disruptive effects of intracerebrally-administered puromycin, an inhibitor of protein synthesis, on recent and long-term memory in mice.[35, 36] When injected into the hippocampal-temporal region, puromycin destroyed memory of recent training (3–6 days previously). Memory of training more than 3–6 days old could not be destroyed by such injections, but puromycin administered over all of the neocortex as well as the hippocampal-temporal region destroyed memory of training which had occurred three weeks previously. The distinction between recent and long term memory was illustrated in a striking experiment. Mice were trained to choose one arm of a Y maze; after several weeks they were trained to choose the other arm of the maze. Several days later, puromycin administered to the temporal hippocampal region destroyed the recent reverse learning but did not affect the older original learning. Experiments with radioactive amino acids showed that inhibition of protein synthesis in excess of 80 per cent for eight to ten hours was necessary to destroy memory.

Another inhibitor of protein synthesis, acetoxycycloheximide, has also been used by the Flexners and co-workers in their studies on memory in mice.[37] Unlike puromycin, acetoxycycloheximide did not destroy memory even though protein synthesis was inhibited to the same extent.

The authors have suggested that the explanation for the difference in effect may lie in the fact that messenger RNA is destroyed when protein synthesis is disrupted by puromycin but is conserved when it is disrupted by acetoxycycloheximide. If this explanation is accepted, one must suppose that the messenger RNA is the chemical correlate of the memory trace. Another explanation for these findings, however, is that the disruption of protein synthesis by puromycin is unrelated to its effect on memory.

Agranoff and co-workers have studied the inhibitory effects of puromycin on learning and memory in goldfish.[23, 27] Their experiments were conducted over a much shorter time period than those of the Flexners' group and reveal an entirely different and somewhat contradictory picture of the puromycin-sensitivity of memory. Puromycin injected within 60 minutes after the initial twenty trials of avoidance conditioning destroyed memory of the training as measured four days later. In these experiments, memory was found to decay linearly with time following puromycin injection. If more than 60 minutes had elapsed between the end of training and the puromycin injection, no inhibitory effect was seen on the fourth day, suggesting that there is a puromycin-sensitive 'consolidation period' for the memory which lasts several hours. This 'consolidation period' apparently took place after the fish were returned to their home tanks following training and could be delayed in time by one hour if the fish were left in the training tank with the lights off for one hour before being transferred to their home tanks.

Puromycin given one minute or 20 minutes before the initial twenty trials had no effect on that training ('short term' memory) but prevented the formation of a long term memory of the training measured on the fourth day. It should be noted that memory-disrupting doses of puromycin inhibited protein synthesis maximally three hours after injection (by 70 to 80 per cent) and that the inhibitory effect had worn off by 10 to 12 hours after injection.

According to the results from Agranoff's laboratory, there are two phases of memory in the goldfish: a puromycin insensitive phase lasting several hours leading to a puromycin-sensitive phase which also lasts for several hours and produces a permanent memory trace that does not seem to be puromycin-sensitive. These two phases of memory are consistent with the proposal of Hebb[45] that short-term memory consists of electrical activity, perhaps of a recurrent type, which leads to the development of diffuse structural changes. Many experiments have indicated that there is a brief period following training when memory is sensitive to electroconvulsive shock.[41, 73] The results from the Flexners' laboratory are not concerned with this very recent memory but concern the gradual delocalization throughout the cerebral cortex of a regionalized structural or chemical change which constitutes a long-term memory. These results contradict those of Agranoff and co-workers in that they indicate that long-term memory in the mouse can be destroyed at any time by an adequate dose of puromycin applied to the proper areas of the brain. This apparent contradiction awaits clarification by further experimentation.

6

Protein Formation in Nervous Tissue

It was pointed out at the beginning of this chapter that protein synthesis in the brain and in all other tissues is directed by RNA produced by information contained within the genes in the cell nuclei. It was also pointed out that the ultimate effect of alterations in the RNA metabolism of brain cells might be on the amount or type of protein synthesized by the very active protein metabolism of the brain. Let us now consider experiments which have been designed to relate alterations in brain protein metabolism to learning and memory.

First of all let us review the important features of cerebral protein synthesis. The reader should consult the review articles by Lajtha[57, 58] for more details on brain proteins and protein metabolism. The importance of protein metabolism for the brain and indeed for the animal is indicated by the observation that during starvation the brain is one of the few parts of the body spared from a loss of weight.[1] From the work of Richter, Waelsch, Lajtha and others[57] it is known that the protein metabolism in brain is very active even though the adult brain undergoes very little growth or cell renewal. Of the two classes of brain cells, neurons and glia, the former have by far the most active protein metabolism, and the Nissl substance of classical histology is now known to be a region of densely-packed ribosomes and very active protein synthesis. Protein formed in the neuron cell body is transported down the axon, presumably to replace protein broken down at synapses and along the length of the axon.[10, 31]

The proteins of the brain are very heterogeneous with respect to half-life, ranging from a few hours to weeks and months.[57, 63] Numerous attempts are being made to fractionate chemically the proteins of the brain,[14, 19, 67] to isolate proteins specific to nervous tissue,[66] and to study the cellular localization and metabolic turnover of various protein species.[54, 63]

In view of the net changes in brain cell RNA observed during various types of nervous stimulation (see Section 3) many investigators have looked for changes in cerebral protein metabolism by utilizing radioactive amino acids injected intraperitoneally, intravenously, and intraventricularly. In general, expectations of finding changes in amino acid incorporation with stimulation have not been realized.[58] Studies at the cellular level by quantitative autoradiography have also failed to show quantitative changes in amino acid incorporation into proteins as a direct result of brain stimulation.[5-7] Increases which have been observed[4] may be due to stress effects[5-7] or changes in cerebral circulation.[79]

Is there a Deposition of New Protein in the Brain during Learning?

The large amount of continuous protein synthesis in the brain is concerned primarily with the production of protein species of relatively short half-life, and for this reason the deposition of proteins concerned with long-term memory might be expected to result in a very small change against a large background of non-specific synthesis. However, if proteins are deposited as a permanent feature of the memory, they might be more easily detected many weeks after isotope administration when radioactive proteins not concerned with memory had been replaced with non-radioactive proteins. The author conducted some experiments[62] to test this idea by investigating protein metabolism in the cortical area controlling the 'handedness' behaviour in rats (see Section 5). The objective of the study was to see if a measurable difference in radioactive protein existed between control and experimental 'handedness' areas. In these experiments rats were given injections of tritiated leucine either preceding or several minutes following each of a series of five daily or twice-daily learning sessions. They were then placed in their cages for four to six weeks, tested for their retention of the learning, and sacrificed. The 'handedness' area of the left and right cortex was removed and analysed for radioactivity. In the experiments completed so far no difference was detected in the specific radioactivity of proteins between the two 'handedness' areas.[62]

A further refinement of these 'handedness' experiments would be to measure amino acid incorporation into proteins during learning at the cellular level. Such experiments have not yet been carried out. However, Altman and co-workers[6, 7] have reported the results of two studies in which incorporation of tritiated leucine into neurons was measured by quantitative autoradiography in groups of animals which had been subjected to two different learning situations and appropriate controls. In these experiments, isotope was given only one time, after the animals had been trained for some weeks, and thus these experiments measured only the difference in amino acid incorporating capacity between learning animals and controls after learning was essentially complete. Furthermore, sampling for radioautography was done within several hours after isotope administration, and so changes in long-lived proteins were obscured by other protein synthesis. Altman and co-workers found that the control groups in the two learning situations tended to have a higher amino acid incorporation in several brain regions.

Are New Types of Proteins Produced during Learning?

At the beginning of this chapter the hypothesis was stated that the genetic material of neurons and glia is called upon to make adjustments to physiological changes by elaborating information for the formation of new and perhaps different protein molecules which may themselves be directly involved in the nervous activity. There is presently very little experimental evidence pertaining to this possibility. However, one preliminary report by Bogoch[15] seems very promising. He and his associates have developed a technique for fractionating the soluble proteins of brain into more than 100 components by a combination of column chromatography and disc electrophoresis,[14] and have applied this technique to compare the soluble protein patterns from brain of pigeons which have experienced an 'enriched environment' (see Section 2) with patterns from pigeons experiencing a less complicated and demanding environment. The preliminary results indicate that among the more experienced pigeons, certain classes of soluble brain proteins have more components than among controls. If these results can be substantiated, the way will be opened for the isolation of these proteins which appear as a result of the increase in the animal's experience, and the relationship of these proteins to memory can then be investigated.

7

Discussion and Conclusions

Excitement over the application of molecular biology to behavioural problems may lead to hasty generalizations and rash conclusions from experiments which are taken out of context. For example, the experiments described in Section V concerning changes in RNA in neurons and glia during learning and changes in learning and memory produced by chemicals which stimulate or inhibit brain RNA and protein metabolism can lead one to the premature conclusion that mental memory is 'encoded' in RNA or protein. These experiments must be considered in the context that the brain has very active RNA and protein metabolism, which are affected by many factors not related to learning and memory. In Section 3 reference was made to the fact that alterations in brain cell RNA are observed as a result of drug administration, passive rotatory stimulation, and in Parkinson's disease; and in Section 6 there was a brief description of the high level of continuous protein synthesis in neurons concerned with renewal of proteins of short half-life which are transported down the axon. When viewed in this context such experiments on learning and memory give us a strong indication that these processes are dependent at least in part on gene activity but they do not tell us the mechanism.

We should then return to the experiments described in Sections 5 and 6 and ask if there is any evidence which would point to the mechanism of memory storage in the brain. One hypothesis (see Section 4) is that the diffuse structural changes of memory 'involve the growth of pre-synaptic or post-synaptic structures or changes in the level of enzymes associated with the synthesis and breakdown of transmitter substances'. Since growth and enzyme production are consequences of changed gene activity, most of the evidence regarding alterations in brain cell RNA in learning and the effects of drugs which stimulate or inhibit learning and memory must be regarded as consistent with this hypothesis (and equally consistent with the second, alternate hypothesis which will be discussed below). Perhaps the most compelling evidence in favour of this first hypothesis is the work of Bennett and colleagues on the consequences of an 'enriched environment' on brain structure and chemistry. It will be recalled from Section 2 that these consequences include the growth of the cerebral cortex and changes in acetylcholinesterase activity.

The second hypothesis in Section 4 states that 'there are special molecules in the brain which influence the conducting properties of neurons or the interactions between neurons in nervous pathways'. One candidate for such a class of molecules is RNA. Hydén's experiments indicate that the changes in base composition of brain cell RNA during learning may be unique, that is, not produced by control experiments which involve a similar type of nervous activity without learning. But such an assertion is very difficult to prove, since a satisfactory control experiment is very difficult to design. Another class of potential 'memory' molecules is that of proteins and polypeptides. The preliminary report of Bogoch and co-workers (Section 6), which suggests that the number of protein species in the brain increases in an 'enriched environment', points in this direction.

The successful demonstration of specific memory transfer by transferring brain RNA or protein from a trained to an untrained animal would constitute the strongest possible support for a 'molecular' hypothesis of memory. Because there are both positive and negative reports from a number of laboratories of attempts to carry out such memory transfer experiments (see Section 5), no definite conclusion regarding them can be reached at this time, but the ultimate outcome of this potentially decisive line of research must be awaited with an open mind.

REFERENCES

1. ADDIS, T., POO, L. J., and LEW, W., 1936. The quantities of protein lost by the various organs and tissues during a fast. *J. Biol. Chem.*, **115**, 111.
2. AGRANOFF, B. W., and KLINGER, P. D., 1964. Puromycin effect on memory fixation in the goldfish. *Science*, **146**, 952.
3. AGRANOFF, B. W., DAVIS, R. E., and BRINK, J. J., 1966. Memory fixation in the goldfish. *Proc. Nat. Acad. Sci., U.S.*, **54**, 788.
4. ALTMAN, J., 1963. Differences in the utilization of tritiated leucine by single neurones in normal and exercised rats: an autoradiographic investigation with microdensitometry. *Nature, Lond.*, **199**, 777.
5. ALTMAN, J., and DAS, G. D., 1964. Autoradiographic study of the effects of enriched environment on the rate of glial multiplication in the adult rat brain. *Nature, Lond.*, **204**, 1161.

6. 1966. Behavioral manipulations and protein metabolism of the brain. I. Effects of motor exercise on the utilization of leucine-H³. *Intern. J. Physiol. Behav.*, in the press.

7. ALTMAN, J., DAS, G., and CHANG, J., 1966. Behavioral manipulations and protein metabolism of the brain. III. Effects of visual training on the utilization of leucine-H³. *Intern. J. Physiol. Behav.*, in the press.

8. BABICH, F. R., JACOBSON, A. L., and BUBASH, S., 1965. Cross-species transfer of learning: Effect of RNA from hamsters on rat behavior. *Proc. Nat. Acad. Sci., U.S.*, **54**, 1299.

9. BABICH, F. R., JACOBSON, A. L., BUBASH, S., and JACOBSON, A., 1965. Transfer of learning to naive rats by injection of RNA extracted from trained rats. *Science*, **149**, 656.

10. BARONDES, S., 1964. Delayed appearance of labelled protein in isolated nerve endings and axoplasmic flow. *Science*, **146**, 779.

11. BARONDES, S. H., and JARVIK, M. E., 1964. The influence of Actinomycin D on brain RNA synthesis and memory. *J. Neurochem.*, **11**, 187.

12. BARONDES, S. H., 1965. Relationship of biological regulatory mechanisms to learning and memory. *Nature, Lond.*, **205**, 18.

13. BENNETT, E. L., DIAMOND, M. C., KRECH, D., and ROSENZWEIG, M. R., 1964. Chemical and anatomical plasticity of brain. *Science*, **146**, 610.

14. BOGOCH, S., RAJAM, P. C., and BELVAL, P. C., 1964. 'Separation of cerebroproteins of human brain. *Nature, Lond.*, **204**, 73.

15. BOGOCH, S., 1966. Summary of preliminary reports presented at Neurosciences Research Program Work Session. *NRP Bulletin*, **3**, 18 and 38.

16. BRATTGARD, S.-O., 1952. The importance of adequate stimulation for the chemical composition of retinal ganglion cells during early post-natal development. *Acta Radiologica*, Supplement 96.

17. BRIGGS, M. H., and KITTO, G. B., 1962. The molecular basis of memory and learning. *Psychol. Rev.*, **69**, 537.

18. BRODSKII, V.Ya., and NECHAEVA, N. V., 1958. Quantitative cytological research on RNA in ganglion cells of normal and exhausted retinas. *Biophysics* (Russ.), **3**, 259.

19. BRUNNGRABER, E. G., and OCCOMY, W. G., 1965. Fractionation of brain macromolecules. *Biochem. J.*, **97**, 689.

20. CAMERON, D. E., SOLYOM, L., SVED, S., WAINRIB, B., and BARIK, H., 1964. Effect of ribonucleic acid on memory defect in the aged. *Am. J. Psych.*, **120**, 320.

21. CARNEY, R. E., and JACOBSON, A. L., 1965. Transfer of learned response by RNA injection. *Science*, **150**, 228.

22. CHAMBERLAIN, T. J., Rothschild, G. H., and GERARD, R. W., 1963. Drugs affecting RNA and learning. *Proc. Nat. Acad. Sci., U.S.*, **49**, 918.

23. COHEN, H. D., and BARONDES, S., 1966. Further studies of learning and memory after intracerebral Actinomycin D. *J. Neurochem.*, **13**, 207.

24. COOK, L., DAVIDSON, A. B., DAVIS, D. V., GREEN, L., and FELLOWS, E. V., 1963. RNA: Effect on conditioned behavior in rats. *Science*, **141**, 268.

25. CORNING, W. C., and JOHN, E. R., 1961. Effect of RNAase on retention of conditioned response in regenerating planaria. *Science*, **134**, 1363.

26. DAS, G., and ALTMAN, J., 1966. Behavioral manipulations and protein metabolism of the brain. II. Effects of restricted and enriched environments on the utilization of leucine-H³. *Intern. J. Physiol. Behav.*, in the press.

27. DAVIS, R. E., and AGRANOFF, B. W., 1966. Stages in memory formation in goldfish: Evidence for an environmental trigger. *Proc. Nat. Acad. Sci., U.S.*, **55**, 555.

28. DIAMOND, M. C., KRECH, D., and ROSENZWEIG, M. R., 1964. The effects of enriched environment on the histology of the rat cerebral cortex. *J. comp. Neurol.*, **123**, 111.

29. DINGMAN, W., and SPORN, M. B., 1961. The incorporation of 8-azaguanine into rat brain RNA and its effect on maze-learning by the rate: An inquiry into the biochemical basis of memory. *J. Psychiat. Res.*, **1**, 1.

30. 1964. Molecular theories of memory. *Science*, **144**, 26.

31. DROZ., B., and LeBLOND, C. P., 1961. Axonal migration of proteins in the central nervous system and peripheral nerves as shown by radioautography. *J. comp. Neurol.*, **120–21**, 325.

32. EDSTROM, J. E., 1964. Microextraction and microelectrophoresis for determination and analysis of nucleic acids in isolated cellular units. *Methods in Cell Physiology*, vol. 1, p. 417. New York: Academic Press.

33. EGYHÁZI, E., and HYDÉN, H., 1961. Experimentally-induced changes in the base composition of the ribonucleic acid of isolated nerve cells and their oligodendroglial cells. *J. Biophys. Biochem. Cytol.*, **10**, 403.

34. FJERDINGSTAD, E. J., NISSEN, TH., and ROIGAARD-PETERSEN, H. H., 1965. Effect of RNA extracted from the brain of trained animals on learning in rats. I. *Scand. J. Psychol.*, **6**, 1.

35. FLEXNER, J. B., FLEXNER, L. B., and STELLAR, E., 1963. Memory in mice as affected by intracerebral puromycin. *Science*, **141**, 57.

36. FLEXNER, L. B., FLEXNER, J. B., ROBERTS, R. B., and DE LA HABA, G., 1964. Loss of recent memory in mice as related to regional inhibition of cerebral protein synthesis. *Proc. Nat. Acad. Sci., U.S.*, **52**, 1165.

37. FLEXNER, L. B., and FLEXNER, J. B., 1966. Effect of acetoxycycloheximide and of acetoxycycloheximide-puromycin mixtures on protein synthesis and memory in mice. *Proc. Nat. Acad. Sci., U.S.*, **55**, 369.

38. GAITO, J., 1961. A biochemical approach to learning and memory. *Psychol. Rev.*, **68**, 288.

39. 1963. DNA and RNA as memory molecules. *Psychol. Review*, **70**, 471.

40. GLASKY, A. J., and SIMON, L. N., 1966. Magnesium pemoline: Enhancement of brain RNA polymerase. *Science*, **151**, 702.

41. GLICKMAN, S. E., 1961. Perseverative neural processes and consolidation of the memory trace. *Psychol. Bull.*, **58**, 218.

42. GOMIRATO, G., and HYDÉN, H., 1963. A biochemical error in the Parkinson disease. *Brain*, **86**, 773.

43. GROSS, C. G., and CAREY, F. M., 1965. Failure of attempts to replicate learned responses by RNA injection. *Science*, **150**, 1749.

44. HARTEY, A. L., KEITH-LEE, P., and MORTON, W. D., 1964. Planaria: Memory transfer through cannibalism reexamined. *Science*, **146**, 274.

45. HEBB, D. O., 1949. *The Organization of Behavior*. New York: Wiley.

46. HECHTER, O., 1966. Reflections on the molecular basis of mental memory. Paper for a NATO Advanced Study Symposium, Oslo-Drammen, Norway, August, 1965. Academic Press, in the press.

47. HYDÉN, H., 1960. The Neuron. In *The Cell*, Brachet, J., and Mirsky, A. E. (eds.), vol. 4, p. 215. New York: Academic Press.

48. HYDÉN, H., and PIGON, A., 1960. A cytophysiological study of the functional relationship between oligodendroglial cells and nerve cells of Deiters' nucleus. *J. Neurochem.*, **6**, 57.

49. HYDÉN, H., and EGYHÁZI, E., 1962. Nuclear RNA changes of nerve cells during a learning experiment in rats. *Proc. Nat. Acad. Sci., U.S.*, **48**, 1366.

50. 1962. Changes in the base composition of nuclear ribonucleic acid during a short period of enhanced protein production. *J. Cell Biol.*, **15**, 37.

51. 1963. Glial RNA changes during a learning experiment in rats. *Proc. Nat. Acad. Sci., U.S.*, **49**, 618.

52. 1964. Changes in RNA content and base composition in cortical neurons of rats in a learning experiment involving transfer of handedness. *Proc. Nat. Acad. Sci., U.S.*, **52**, 1030.

53. HYDÉN, H., and LANGE, P. W., 1965. A differentiation in RNA response neurons early and late during learning. *Proc. Nat. Acad. Sci., U.S.*, **53**, 946.

54. HYDÉN, H., and MCEWEN, B., 1966. A glial protein specific for the nervous system. *Proc. Nat. Acad. Sci., U.S.*, **55**, 354.

55. JACOBSON, A. L., BABICH, F. R., BUBASH, S., and JACOBSON, A., 1965. Differential approach tendencies produced by injection of RNA from trained rats. *Science*, **150**, 636.

56. JEWETT, R. E., PIRCH, J. H., and NORTON, S., 1965. Effect of 8-azaguanine on learning of a fixed-interval schedule. *Nature, Lond.*, **207**, 277.

57. LAJTHA, A., 1964. Protein metabolism in the nervous system. *Int. Rev. Neurobiol.*, **6**, 1.

58. 1964. Alterations in brain protein metabolism. *Int. Rev. Neurobiol.*, **7**, 1.

59. LUTTGES, M., JOHNSON, T., BUCK, C., HOLLAND, J., and MCGAUGH, J. An examination of 'transfer of learning' by nucleic acid. *Science*, **151**, 834.

60. MCCONNELL, J., JACOBSON, A. L., and KIMBLE, D. P., 1959. The effects of regeneration upon retention of a conditioned response in the planarian. *J. Comp. Physiol. Psych.*, **52**, 1.

61. MCCONNELL, J., 1962. Memory transfer through cannibalism in planarians. *J. Neuropsych.*, **3**, Suppl. 1, S42.

62. MCEWEN, B., and HYDÉN, H., 1965. Unpublished experiments.

63. 1966. A study of specific brain proteins on the semi-micro scale. *J. Neurochem.*, in the press.

64. MIHAILOVIC, LJ., and JANKOVIC, B. D., 1961. Effects of intravenously injected anti-nucleus caudatus antibody on the electrical activity of the cat brain. *Nature, Lond.*, **192**, 665.

65. 1965. Effects of anticerebral antibodies on electrical activity and behaviour. *Neurosci. Res. Prog. Bull.*, **3**, 8.

66. MOORE, B. W., 1965. A soluble protein characteristic of the nervous system. *Biochem. Biophy. Res. Commun.*, **19**, 739.

67. MOORE, B. W., and MCGREGOR, D., 1965. Chromatographic and electrophoretic fractionation of soluble proteins of brain and liver. *J. Biol. Chem.*, **240**, 1647.

68. NISSEN, TH., ROIGAARD-PETERSEN, H. H., and FJERDINGSTAD, E. J., 1965. Effect of RNA extracted from the brain of trained animals on learning in rats. II. *Scand. J. Psychol.*, **6**, 265.

69. PLOTNIKOFF, N., 1966. Enhancement by magnesium pemoline of acquisition and retention of conditioned avoidance response in rats. *Science*, **151**, 703.

70. PETERSON, G. M., and DEVINE, J. V., 1963. Transfers in handedness in the rat resulting from small cortical lesions after limited forced practice. *J. Comp. Physiol. Psych.*, **56**, 752.

71. PETERSON, G. M., and FRACAROL, LA. C., 1938. The relative influence of the locus and mass of destruction upon the control of handedness by the cerebral cortex. *J. Comp. Neurol.*, **68**, 173.

72. PETERSON, G. M., and BARNETT, P. E., 1961. The cortical destruction necessary to produce a transfer of a forced-practice function. *J. Comp. Physiol. Psych.*, **54**, 382.

73. QUARTERMAIN, D., PAOLINO, R. M., and MILLER, N. E., 1965. A brief temporal gradient of retrograde amnesia independent of situational change. *Science*, **149**, 1116.

74. ROIGAARD-PETERSEN, E. J., FJERDINGSTAD, and NISSEN, TH., 1965. Facilitation of learning in rats by intracisternal injection of 'conditioned RNA'. *Worm Runner's Digest*, **7**, 15.
75. ROSENBLATT, F., FARROW, J. T., and HERBLIN, W. F., 1966. Transfer of conditioned responses from trained rats to untrained rats by means of a brain extract. *Nature, Lond*, **219**, 46.
76. ROSENBLATT, F., FARROW, J. T., and RHINE, S., 1966. The transfer of learned behavior from trained to untrained rats by means of brain extracts, 1. *Proc. Nat. Acad. Sci., U.S.*, **55**, 548.
77. 1966. The transfer of learned behavior from trained to untrained rats by means of brain extracts, II. *Proc. Nat. Acad. Sci., U.S.*, **55**, 787.
78. ROSS, R. B., 1964. Facilitation of maze learning in rats with strychnine sulfate. *Nature, Lond.*, **201**, 109.
79. SOKOLOFF, L., and KETY, S. S., 1960. Regulation of cerebral circulation. *Physiol. Rev.*, **40**, Suppl. 4, 38.
80. SPERRY, R. W., 1963. Chemoaffinity in the orderly growth of nerve fibers and connections. *Proc. Nat. Acad. Sci., U.S.*, **50**, 703.
81. SZILARD, L., 1964. On memory and recall. *Proc. Nat. Acad. Sci., U.S.*, **51**, 1092.
82. UNGAR, G., and OCEGUERA-NAVARRO, C., 1965. Transfer of habituation by material extracted from brain. *Nature, Lond.*, **207**, 301.
83. UTINA, I. A., NECHAEVA, N. V., and BRODSKII, V. Ya., 1960. RNA in the ganglion cells of the frog retina in the dark and illumination with constant and flickering light. *Biophysics* (Russ.), **5**, 749.
84. WESTERMAN, R. A., 1963. Somatic inheritance of habituation of responses to light in planarians. *Science*, **140**, 676.
85. WHIPPLE, H. E., (Ed.), 1964. Symposium on the nerve growth factor. *Ann. N.Y. Acad. Sci.*, **118**, Art. 3, 147.
86. WILSON, E. B., 1925. *The Cell in Development and Heredity*. New York: Macmillan.

V

THE MEANING OF MEMORY

Lord Brain

F.R.S., M.A., D.M., F.R.C.P.

In ordinary conversational usage to remember something means to be able to recall it: forgetting is the inability to recall. But even in everyday usage memory may apply to a number of different things. One may be said, for example, to remember an event or a fact or a name or a face, or how to get to a place, or how to ride a bicycle. Though all these forms of memory have in common an element of recall, they differ considerably in respect of what is recalled. In some instances what is recalled has been learned, for example, a name or a fact, or riding a bicycle, but an event which we recall is not something we should ordinarily say we have learned. But if we study the process of learning in animals, it seems to cast doubt on this distinction. The only way in which we can test memory in animals is to expose them to experiences, and see how their subsequent behaviour is modified by those experiences. If so, they are said to have learned something from the experiences, and in that sense these experiences are 'remembered', whether consciously or not. Using such methods of investigation it can be shown that exposure to a single experience may modify the animal's subsequent behaviour, so that it may be said to have learned from one experience. This casts a doubt on whether there is a physiological basis for our verbal distinction between remembering the Coronation and how to ride a bicycle, and it would seem that any consideration of memory will have to take into account what is known about the process of learning in animals. Learning, therefore, may be defined as the process by which experience is stored and becomes capable of influencing subsequent behaviour, and memory may be defined as the conscious awareness of such past experience.

1

The Fundamental Nature of Memory

We are still ignorant of the fundamental nature of the process whereby past experience (information) is stored, how it can influence subsequent behaviour, and how it can be recalled to consciousness. We shall be considering later the parts of the brain concerned in this process, but in this section we shall be dealing with the physical process of the storage of information.

The structure of the nervous system is such that as far as we know, all the experiences of organisms which possess nervous systems influence those nervous systems in the same fundamental way. Receptors, which are sensitive to various kinds of physical stimuli, when stimulated excite nerve impulses. These are conducted along the corresponding sensory neurons to the central nervous system where they enter into relationship with a vast number of other neurons, which they can influence only by exciting changes at their synaptic junctions. This part of neural activity, therefore, is electrical, and has to be thought of in terms of the frequency and rate of conduction of nerve impulses and their temporal relationships. Until comparatively recently, little more than this was known about the activity of the nervous system except that nerve impulses were capable of causing chemical changes at the synaptic junctions. It was natural, therefore, that neurophysiologists who possessed only these basic facts should think of memory storage in terms of nerve impulses and their accompanying electrical changes alone. This led to the view that memory might be due to continuously reverberating electrical circuits of great complexity in the brain (Lorente de Nó[17, 18, 19]). However, the hypothesis of reverberating electrical networks as the sole basis of memory is no longer acceptable in view of the fact that memories are retained after hypothermia, electroconvulsive shocks, and narcotics, all of which abolish such electrical activity.

Eccles[8] to overcome this objection invokes prolonged plastic changes at synapses. He seeks to explain conditioned reflexes (a form of learning) by supposing that the association of the conditioned stimulus with the unconditioned stimulus leads to the development of synaptic knobs, and hence facilitates synaptic transmission. Eccles admits that the experimental demonstration of changing synaptic efficacy requires thousands of impulses, or relatively prolonged periods of disuse, whereas conditioned reflexes are established by relatively few presentations of the conditioned stimulus together with the unconditioned stimulus, and unique events can be remembered for a whole lifetime. He seeks, therefore, to combine his synaptic facilitation theory with reverberatory circuits in the nervous system, as a result of which he suggests that a single event may activate each link in a spatio-temporal pattern thousands of times within a few seconds.

During recent years, however, the study of the process of protein synthesis and its application to the storage and release of genetic information has given rise to new hypotheses about the possibility of the molecular storage of memory. This theory perhaps derives an *a priori* plausibility from its application to the development of the individual organism from the fertilized ovum. Since all the information necessary for this extremely complex process can be stored in the form of molecular structure, and since this process leads in the development of the individual to the structure of the nervous system itself, it would seem not improbable that a similar process should be at work in the most fundamental functions of the nervous system. However, if that is the case, we are still far from understanding it. The subject has recently been discussed in considerable detail by Hydén[13] and Roberts[29] and Schmitt[35]. If changes in molecular structure do constitute the basis of memory it is probable that ribonucleic acid (RNA) plays an important part in this. Neurons may contain large amounts of RNA and Hydén has observed that a quantitative increase in the amount of RNA in nerve cells may be correlated with learning.

But even if the storage of memory does depend upon molecular changes in neurons, it is still necessary to explain how these changes are produced by the arrival of electrical impulses at synaptic junctions, a question discussed by Schmitt[35]. We have also to explain how particular patterns of experience are distributed to the neurons for molecular storage and how the same particular combination of neurons is called upon again when the specific memory needs to be evoked. These complex questions are discussed by Schmitt, and the molecular basis of memory in a *Lancet* leader.[14] There are interesting parallels, not only between memory and genetics, but also between psychological memory and immunological 'memory'. We seem to be approaching the standpoint of Samuel Butler who, in 1882, said: 'I have for some years . . . urged . . . that the connection between memory and heredity is so close that there is no reason for regarding the two as genetically different, though for convenience' sake it may be well to specify them by different names.' (Butler.[6])

Even though memory cannot be attributed entirely to reverberating neural circuits, there is abundant evidence of the wide spread through the brain of the neural impulses which underlie learning and memory. Russell and Ochs[31] showed experimentally that memory traces are normally stored in both cerebral hemispheres in the rat. Using the method of induced spreading depression—a reversible method of eliminating cortical function—they showed that temporary abolition of the function of one hemisphere did not impair learned performance. If, however, a memory trace was established in one hemisphere only no spontaneous transfer to the other hemisphere subsequently occurred, but in such circumstances one reinforced response when both hemispheres were active led to immediate transfer to the opposite hemisphere. Similarly Morrell[22] found that an epileptogenic lesion induced in the cortex of one cerebral hemisphere gave rise to a mirror focus in the opposite hemisphere, and this secondary lesion showed paroxysmal self-sustaining epileptiform discharge, and the 'learned' behaviour of the secondary lesion was 'remembered' even after months of inactivity.

Conversely, the effect on visual learning of dividing the optic chiasma or the connections between the two cerebral hemispheres has been studied by Myers,[24] who has shown that in such circumstances, each cerebral hemisphere behaves as a unit independent of the other, and the recent observations of Gazzaniga, Bogen and Sperry[11] have confirmed this for man.

The many different experimental approaches to the subject of learning have recently been reviewed by Galambos and Morgan,[10] and many electro-encephalographic studies of conditioned reflexes are reported in the Moscow Colloquium on Electro-encephalography of Higher Nervous Activity.[23]

Lashley[15] was one of the earliest workers in this field. Discussing experiments on learning, he says that they seem to rule out the motor cortex or Betz cell area as containing any part of the conditioned reflex arc. He thinks that the associative connections for memory traces of the conditioned reflex do not extend across the cortex as well defined arcs or paths. Such arcs are either diffuse through all parts of the cortex, passed by relays through lower centres, or do not exist. Memory disturbances of simple sensory habits follow only upon very extensive experimental destruction, including almost the entire associative cortex. Small lesions embracing no more than a single associative area do not produce loss of any habit: large lesions produce deterioration which affects a variety of habits, irrespective of the sensory-motor elements involved. There is therefore no evidence of any restricted localization of specific memory changes in the cortex.

There is, however, another element in memory besides the specific memory traces, however these may be distributed in the cortex. Galambos and Morgan[10] point out that besides what happens in the cortex there is a second class of neural events in learning, which consists of those that prime or prepare the brain for the durable change it will undergo. Among these are the so-called 'motivational' and 'attentive' states that commonly precede and accompany the learning process, and without which learning is unlikely or impossible. Lashley[15] also alludes to this when he says: 'I believe that the evidence strongly favours the view that amnesia from brain injury rarely, if ever, is due to the destruction of specific memory traces; rather the amnesias represent a lowered level of vigilance, a greater difficulty in activating the organized patterns of traces, or a disturbance of some broader system of organized functions.'

2

The Anatomy of Memory in Man

During the last decade there have been a number of observations on the effects upon memory of localized lesions of the human brain. A critical review of the literature of this subject has been published by Ojemann.[25] Scoville and Milner[36] reported loss of recent memory in ten cases after bilateral hippocampal excisions. There was no deterioration of intellect or personality. Milner[21] reported memory loss in two patients following excision of the left hippocampal region only. She assumed that the opposite side had previously been damaged. These two patients exhibited a retrograde amnesia for four years and three months respectively and gross loss of recent memory, there being a retention defect cutting across any distinction between verbal and perceptual material and sense modalities. (See also Penfield and Milner.[28]) Walker[45] reported recent memory impairment after unilateral temporal lobe lesions in four cases. There was a loss of recent memory in all, but the capacity for immediate recall was intact. Walker asked why this symptom occurred only in 10–15 per cent of patients who had had operations on the temporal lobe, either the dominant or non-dominant one, and suggested that differences might depend upon the varying use of imagery. He put forward the view that the hippocampal area might be a mechanism controlling the fixation and availability of memories stored elsewhere. Bickford, et al.[4] reported three patients in whom memory disturbances resulted from electrical stimulation below the cortical surface of the temporal lobe. In two, stimulation in the general region of the posterior part of the middle temporal gyrus below the surface produced a syndrome of loss of memory for recent events up to several days, with normal recall for events preceding the amnesia. The severity of the amnesia depended on the duration of the stimulation, and complete recovery occurred in from one minute to two hours.

The evidence based upon surgical resection of the whole or part of one or both temporal lobes seems to be that gross impairment of recent or 'ongoing' memory results from bilateral lesions of the anterior two-thirds of the hippocampus, especially the region from 5 to 8 cm from the tip of the temporal lobe (Fig. 1). Bilateral removal of the uncus and amygdala does not have this effect. Nor as a rule do unilateral lesions of the significant area. Though this has been reported in some cases, it has been thought that there might also have been unsuspected lesions of the remaining temporal lobe. Unilateral excision of the temporal lobe does not usually have lasting effects on recent memory.

Penfield (Penfield and Jasper,[27] Penfield[26]) has reported a number of instances of the evocation of memories of past events, often with hallucinatory vividness, by the electrical stimulation of the temporal cortex in patients operated upon under local anaesthesia.

So far we have considered the effects upon memory of lesions of the

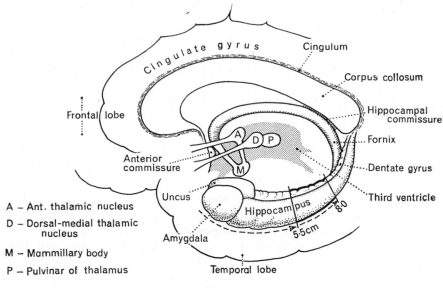

FIG. 1.

temporal lobe only. A number of workers attach importance to a bilateral pathway which, beginning with the hippocampus, passes by way of the fornix through the mammillary bodies, thence to the optic thalamus and finally to the cingulate gyrus (Fig. 1). The evidence for the importance of the fornix, reviewed by Ojemann, appears inconclusive. Certainly it has been divided on both sides, and also been congenitally absent, without any impairment of memory. (See also Sweet et al.)[37]

In this context the site of the lesions found in Korsakoff's syndrome are important since loss of recent memory is a characteristic feature of that syndrome. Adams, Collins and Victor,[1] and Victor[43] report that the only constant lesions are to be found in the medial parts of the medial dorsal, pulvinar and antero-ventral nuclei of the thalamus, the mammillary bodies and the terminal portions of the fornices (Fig. 1). Barbizet[3] regards the mammillary bodies as important in relation to memory defect.

Finally, Whitty and Lewin[46] have described loss of recent memory in the confusional state following cingulectomy.

3

The Pathology of Lesions Responsible for Impairment of Memory

From what has just been said, it will be clear that the pathology of lesions responsible for impairment of recent memory will be that of the processes which are likely to damage the hippocampal gyri, possibly the fornices and certainly the mammillary bodies and optic thalami, and probably the cingulate gyri bilaterally. Much of the information cited in the previous section was derived from surgical operations on one or both temporal lobes, or the cingulate gyri, for the treatment of epilepsy or behaviour disorders.

Similar effects may be produced by intracranial tumours, and a study of 180 patients with intracranial tumour by Williams and Pennybacker[47] showed that memory disturbances were most likely to occur and to be most specific when the lesion involved the floor or walls of the third ventricle, an experience confirmed by Delay, Brion and Derouesné.[7]

Vascular lesions are of special interest. Victor, Angevine, Mancall and Fisher[44] have reported a case of severe loss of recent memory associated with bilateral infarctions in the infero-medial portions of the temporal lobes and related structures, more specifically in the hippocampal formation, fornix and mammillary bodies. The uncus, amygdaloid body and terminal digitations of the hippocampus were unaffected on either side. The affected areas are supplied by the posterior cerebral arteries, and there was other evidence of ischaemia within their distribution in their patient, and indeed a general vertebro-basilar ischaemia. The importance of this case lies not only in the evidence it affords as to the localization of the lesions responsible for loss of recent memory but also because it draws attention to the fact that impairment of memory may be a symptom of vertebro-basilar insufficiency.

Victor[43] believes that Wernicke's encephalopathy and Korsakoff's syndrome are identical, when they are due to nutritional deficiency. The qualification is important because Korsakoff's syndrome can also be used to describe a symptom complex which may be due to other causes. The Wernicke-Korsakoff syndrome is due to thiamine deficiency, the commonest cause of which is alcoholism. The pathological changes related to the loss of memory as mentioned above are located in the optic thalami, the mammillary bodies and the terminal portions of the fornices.

Acute encephalitis may be followed by persistent memory defect as reported by Rose and Symonds.[30] It was concluded that temporal lobe lesions were present in these cases.

The above seem to be the principal pathological processes which may selectively affect the parts of the brain specifically concerned with memory. Of course many diffuse processes may incidentally do so, for example, head injury, and various toxic, metabolic, infective and degenerative conditions, such as hypoxic encephalopathy, subarachnoid haemorrhage, neurosyphilis, both meningo-vascular and dementia paralytica, and meningitis, both pyogenic and tuberculous. For reasons previously given, it is impossible to locate the pathological processes which involve remote rather than recent memory, but as might be expected, these seem usually to be of a diffuse kind, whether vascular or degenerative.

4

Post-Traumatic Amnesia

The types of amnesia which may occur after a head injury are of both practical and theoretical importance. They are divided into post-traumatic amnesia, PTA, which is the loss of memory for events occurring subsequently to the injury, and retrograde amnesia, RA, amnesia for events which occurred before the injury. Both have been studied by Russell and his collaborators (Russell and Nathan,[33] Russell,[32] Russell and Smith[34]). As Russell has pointed out, the duration of PTA can be estimated accurately only after the patient has recovered from even slight degrees of confusion. It will then usually remain relatively constant and form a permanent index of the duration, not of unconsciousness, but of impaired consciousness. The duration of PTA, as we shall see, provides some indication of the severity of the brain injury. Sometimes, PTA is delayed, being separated from the actual injury by a lucid interval which the patient is able to recall. Loss of memory for events during the time covered by PTA is not always uniformly complete. The patient subsequently may be able to recall islands of memory; for example, after a motor car accident he may remember something of an ambulance ride to hospital, though he does not remember being put into the ambulance nor subsequent events in hospital for perhaps two or three days. After a mild head injury, such as concussion on football field, the victim may go on with the game, although subsequently this period is subject to post-traumatic amnesia.

During PTA the patient may confabulate, and if the subject of his confabulation relates to the accident, which he knows he has had, he may give an entirely misleading account of it. In this context Russell[32] makes an interesting observation, to which we shall return later. He quotes the case of a man who had an accident, but subsequently gave an account of it which showed that he was confusing it with a previous accident which had occurred two years before. This confabulation, as Russell points out, was 'clearly due to failure to localize his memories of the more recent injury'.

In a more recent study, Russell and Smith[34] have analysed the data relating to PTA in a series of 1766 cases of closed head injury. They divided their patients into four groups. _A_ was an acute group with admission to hospital within three days of the injury, _B_ a subacute group with admission within three weeks, _C_ a chronic group, admitted more than three weeks after the injury; and _D_ a similar chronic group, differing from _C_ only in that patients were selected on account of substantial injuries and symptoms. The period of PTA was classified as follows: nil, less than one hour, one to twenty-four hours, one to seven days, more than seven days. It was found that there were six signs or symptoms, the incidence of which consistently increased with longer PTAs in all four groups. These positively correlated features were: skull fracture, motor disorder, anosmia, dysphasia, memory and/or calculation defect, and retrograde amnesia over thirty minutes. On the other hand, there were three clinical features which showed a consistently random relationship to the duration of the PTA, namely anxiety and depression, giddiness without vertigo, and headache (never or acute only). In both Russell and Smith's series and in a series of 1000 cases, details of which were provided for them by Lewin, it was found that the incidence of long PTA systematically increased with age in each of the four populations, and that the interaction of age and the duration of PTA provided a more reliable assessment of the severity of closed injury than when one of the two factors alone was taken into consideration. The difference between the symptoms and signs which correlated positively with the duration of the PTA in all four groups, and those which did not, was correlated with that between organic and non-organic aetiology. Russell and Smith concluded that, out of approximately 100 different signs and symptoms, PTA emerged as a most sensitive and reliable index of severity for cases of head injury without signs of focal damage, such as depressed fracture or intracranial haemorrhage.

5

Retrograde Amnesia

Retrograde amnesia is extremely common after a head injury, which causes loss of consciousness, but may also occur after electro-convulsive therapy, status epilepticus, meningitis, acute cerebral anoxia, as in hanging, CO poisoning, and severe loss of blood. RA is most easily studied when it occurs after head injury. Russell and Nathan[33] investigated 1029 cases of accidental head injury, excluding gunshot wounds, and observed that there was no RA in 133, there was RA lasting under 30 minutes in 707 and over 30 minutes in 133. In fifty-six cases there was no record. Thus in 840 cases out of 973, there was either no RA, or it was under 30 minutes in duration. Russell and Nathan point out that, when a patient says that he remembers an accident, it may wrongly be concluded that there is no RA because the head injury may have been caused, not by the accident which the patient remembers, but by his hitting the ground a second or two later, which may have caused a momentary RA. Patients with PTA lasting from one to seven days may frequently have only a short RA, but on the whole an RA of more than twelve hours is likely to be associated with a PTA of more than seven days.

Russell and Nathan found that in 186 cases of gunshot wound of the brain or skull, with a definite period of PTA, there were no fewer than sixty-five with no RA; that is to say, the patient remembered his head being struck by the missile. This in their view must be connected with the more focal type of injury. They suggest that perhaps some diaschisis effect causes the disturbance of consciousness, and, if so, the memory of the injury is registered and retained before the trans-neuronal shock effect spreads to prevent further remembering.

During the period of gradual recovery of consciousness after a head injury, while the patient is still confused, the RA is often very long. This may lead the patient to give the date as several years previously, with a corresponding reduction in his age. This long RA slowly shrinks, but the PTA may end long before the RA shrinks to its final duration. During this period of shrinking amnesia, Russell and Nathan point out, the patient is unable to recall an important group of memories which, as later recovery shows, were well registered. Recovery of memory occurs not in order of importance, but in order of time: long past memories are the first to return, and the temporary blocking of relatively recent memory may be so marked that several years of recent life may be entirely eliminated. During recovery the RA shrinks at a varying rate to a point where memory of subsequent events ceases abruptly. This usually leaves the duration of RA clearly indicated, but this can be estimated accurately only after full recovery of consciousness. By the time the RA has shrunk to a few minutes or less, the patient has usually fully recovered consciousness, and, indeed, a brief RA is often an accurate indication of mental normality.

Nathan made the interesting experiment of testing the effect of barbiturate hypnosis on RA and PTA. In twenty-eight out of forty cases investigated, both remained unchanged. In the remaining twelve cases, however, some additional memory was recovered, though this was sometimes insignificant. These investigations confirmed the view that both the RA and the PTA are in most cases the result of injury to the brain, and not hysterical.

Russell and Nathan make the important observation that while RA for a large part of previous life may be observed during the stages of recovery before confusion has disappeared, they have never observed an RA to extend over many months permanently, except in hysteria or gross traumatic dementia.

Russell[32] points out that there must be some neurological difference between the brief RA and the RA which may last for several days in some cases of severe head injury with a long PTA. Such prolonged RAs may include the memory of important events. When such events are obliterated from memory after head injury, they are usually for relatively recent happenings. Recent memories are therefore more vulnerable than those that are remote. This long RA differs from the memory disorders of organic dementia, in which not only are recent memories lost but the ability to recall events from day-to-day is lost as well: whereas in most cases of head injury this faculty returns to normal after recovery from the confusion. The nature of RA is considered later.

6

Amnesia for Current Events

There is as yet no generally accepted term for the syndrome to be described in this section. The essence of it is that the patient, though conscious, and capable of experiences from moment to moment, is unable to remember them as soon as they are past. The term 'loss of recent memory' is an unsuitable one because that applies also to retrograde amnesia, an entirely different condition. Korsakoff's syndrome includes as a cardinal symptom loss of memory for current events, but it usually includes other symptoms to be described below. Moreover, Korsakoff's syndrome has a number of causes, and is therefore no more well defined as a pathological than as a clinical entity. The term Korsakoff-Wernicke syndrome—a term used by Victor—is equally unsatisfactory. Wernicke's syndrome is a well-defined pathological and nosological entity, but it is only one of a number of causes of Korsakoff's syndrome and Korsakoff's syndrome is not necessarily an ingredient of Wernicke's encephalopathy. Hence it seems best to isolate the symptom, amnesia for current events, and go on to consider its clinical and pathological associations. The essence of this disorder is an inability to retain current experiences in the mind for more than a very short time. It would be difficult to improve on the description given by Milner[21] of the two patients with bilateral hippocampal lesions whom she studied. In both of these cases the symptom was produced by surgery. The patients, she says, 'show a very gross impairment of memory for all events subsequent to operation, and they are unable to recall test material after a lapse of five minutes or less, if their attention has been diverted to another topic in the meantime. The retention difficulty is not specific to any one kind of material, but is quite general, affecting stories, drawings and numbers, and cutting across any distinction between verbal and perceptual material or between one sense modality and another'. Neither patient showed any defect of attention, concentration, or reasoning ability, and neither had aphasia. Both of them continued to earn their living, one as a glove-cutter and the other as a draughtsman, their professional skills being well maintained. A very similar account is given of the patient studied by Victor et al.[44] They say 'The patient's ability to recall recent events and to learn and retain new factors were both seriously affected. He would ask the same question over and over again. He spent hours watching baseball on television, but as soon as the set was turned off, he was unable to remember the score or any other detail of the game. However, he was able to recall correctly the highlights of games that had been played many years before. He could not remember whether he had smoked a cigarette or simply put it away. He would forget simple instructions given by his wife, when she left for work, and would neglect to read notes which had been left to reinforce his memory. During this period he was still able to play bridge adequately, and actually taught his nephew the game of solitaire, but he was unable to learn new card games, such as canasta.' This patient had other psychological disabilities owing to widespread cerebral arteriosclerosis. Nevertheless, 'the impairment of general intelligence was mild in degree, in contrast to the impairment of memory function measured by the Wechsler Memory Scale.' Later it was reported of the same patient of his response to psychometric tests that 'his general intellectual functions were still at a "bright normal" level. There was the same mild impairment of certain cognitive functions as before; once again the striking failure was demonstrated by the Wechsler Memory Scale, particularly the difficult word association test.'

The amnesia for current events, though profound and continuous, is not, however, always absolute. Thus the niece of the patient of Victor *et al.* came to visit him for several days and stayed on for two months, and for many months afterwards, the patient could recall this event and appreciated its humorous aspect. A patient of my own spontaneously mentioned a similar occurrence. Though normally quite unable to remember anything that had happened to him for more than a minute or two, he was able to recall the details of his wife's terminal illness and death which occurred after he had developed his amnesic state, and which upset him very much. It would seem, therefore, that emotion may temporarily overcome the defect. The memory of events long past is unimpaired, though when the amnesia develops abruptly, there may be a period of retrograde amnesia immediately antedating its onset. Thus Milner's patients both showed some retrograde amnesia for a period before the operation, four years in one case and three months in the other. Skills acquired by the patient before the onset of the amnesia are also unimpaired, but he cannot acquire new skills because he cannot retain the necessary experiences. But if his occupation depends upon old skills he can still carry it on, and in one such case, that came to my notice, a business man with complete amnesia for current events was nevertheless able to direct his business, relying on his memory of the past, combined with an elaborate system of card indices and notebooks, which enabled him to keep current events in his mind long enough to make the necessary decisions.

It follows from what has been said that we are dealing here with a highly specific defect which can occur in isolation from any other disorder of psychological function, and which has no other consequences than those which follow naturally from the inability to acquire and retain new memories.

It is only rarely, and almost exclusively when the symptom follows surgical excision of the relevant areas of one or both temporal lobes, that the symptom occurs in its pure form. I have, however, seen an example following acute encephalitis, when in all other respects, recovery was complete. Other causal conditions have been enumerated above (see p. 118), but such disorders as cerebral arteriosclerosis, vitamin B1 deficiency due to chronic alcoholism or other causes, acute encephalitis, and anoxia are very likely to involve other structures besides the relevant part of the hippocampal gyrus. In such cases there may be other psychological disorders. But study of amnesia for current events in its pure form shows that no more symptoms can be attributed to it than those just described, and therefore this amnesic syndrome itself is not due to mental confusion, inattention, an intrinsic disturbance of the time sense, etc. If such disorders are also present they must be attributed to other lesions than those responsible for the amnesic syndrome.

7

Korsakoff's Syndrome

Korsakoff's syndrome is a form of mental disorder characterized by a group of symptoms of which the most striking are amnesia for current events, and confabulation. The subject has recently been reviewed by Lewis.[16]

Clinical Features

The amnesia for current events, which occurs in Korsakoff's syndrome, is similar to that described above, the patient having no recollection of what has recently happened to him. Confabulation describes his attempt to fill the gap in his memory by giving an account of events which have not happened or, at any rate, have not happened when he says they did. Whitty and Lewin,[46] studying the post-cingulectomy confusional state, bring forward evidence suggesting that the confabulation is not pure invention, but is the result of misplacing memories in time. What the patient alleges to have happened recently has in fact happened in the past, but not at a time when he supposes it to have happened. As mentioned above, Russell has put forward a similar explanation of confabulation in the post-traumatic amnesic syndrome. Lewis draws attention to the dream-like quality of confabulation in some cases of Korsakoff's syndrome, and also the importance of emotional factors in distorting or repressing memories. Temporal order and temporal relationships are invariably disturbed, and perceptual disturbances have been noted by Talland[38, 39] and Talland and Ekdhal.[42] (See also Talland.)[40, 41]

Aetiology and Pathology

Korsakoff's syndrome may be the result of a large number of pathological disorders, the best known of which is chronic alcoholism, in which the causal factor appears to be vitamin B1 deficiency, and the pathological changes identical with those of Wernicke's encephalopathy (Victor).[43] Other causes include head injury, anoxia, carbon monoxide poisoning, epilepsy, electro-convulsive therapy, acute encephalitis, dementia paralytica and other forms of dementia, intracranial tumour, cerebral arteriosclerosis, and the operation of cingulectomy. As stated above, the lesions responsible for the Korsakoff-Wernicke syndrome are situated in the medial parts of the medial, dorsal pulvinar and antero-ventral nuclei of the thalamus, the mammillary bodies and the terminal portion of the fornices.

The Nature of Korsakoff's Syndrome

Since, as we have seen above, amnesia for current events can occur in complete isolation from the other psychological disturbances with which it is associated in Korsakoff's syndrome, it seems reasonable to conclude that such other symptoms are not the result of the amnesia, nor can they be its cause. The perceptual disorders, disordered time sense, and confabulation would therefore appear to be independent results of the rather diffuse changes which are present in Korsakoff's syndrome. The significance of this will be further discussed below.

8

Transient Global Amnesia

Fisher and Adams[9] have recently drawn attention to a syndrome not hitherto generally recognized. They reported seventeen patients, seen over the previous seven years, who had all experienced a sudden episode of temporary amnesia, usually of a few hours' duration, after which there was complete restoration to the previous state of health. Unassociated, they say, with any focal motor or sensory neurological deficit or with overt seizure activity, the clinical manifestations of the attack consisted for the most part of a disorder of mentation, in which a defect of memory, involving the events of the recent past and the present, but leaving personal identification intact, was the most definite feature. I have myself seen a number of cases of this kind.

Thirteen of Fisher and Adams' patients were men, and four were women. All were middle-aged or elderly, their ages ranging from 55 to 60 years. One of their patients gave a history of three attacks in the previous six years, the remaining sixteen patients experienced only one attack each. Certain precipitating factors have been noted; two female patients in Fisher and Adams' series developed their symptoms shortly after bathing in the cool waters of the Atlantic Ocean, and two men had taken shower baths. In my own series, the amnesia occurred after bathing in three patients, two male and one female, and in the female two attacks each followed bathing. Two of Fisher and Adams' patients, and one of mine, developed the amnesia after sexual intercourse. In no case was there any impairment of consciousness. The mental disturbance may be noticed spontaneously by the patient himself or by those who are with him at the time. Conversation with the patient revealed that at the onset of the attack there was an amnesia, often patchy, for the events of the previous days or weeks, months, or even years. Usually during the episode he or she sat quietly with a puzzled expression: some appreciated that something was wrong and repeated questions over and over again, or expressed the fear that they were suffering from a stroke.

Negative features were the absence of any symptoms suggesting an epileptic attack. There was no weakness or paralysis or sensory disturbance related to the limbs; behaviour during the attack was always quiet, and there was no restlessness or automatic activity. On clinical examination there was no evidence of any organic neurological disorder related to the attack. Such routine laboratory investigations as were carried out were normal. In Fisher and Adams' series an electro-encephalogram was obtained after the end of the amnesia in thirteen cases and was interpreted as normal in eight. In the remaining five a variety of diffuse or focal EEG abnormalities were observed.

Fisher and Adams discuss the possible pathogenesis of this syndrome. They begin by noting that 'the episodes, by virtue of their brevity, transiency, reversibility, and associated suspension of memory recording, bear a close resemblance to the amnesic spells described in temporal lobe seizures'. After reviewing the literature of amnesia in relation to epilepsy, however, they come to the conclusion that 'even if epilepsy is the basis, the literature on the subject does not record similar examples. One might suppose that the cases represent the discharge of a focus which lies so completely within the neural apparatus subserving the recording and remembrance of events that only memory is affected and no other symptom or sign manifests itself. The 'amnesic episode' could result from either ictal discharge or post-ictal disturbance akin to the phenomenon known as Todd's paralysis.' As Fisher and Adams point out, however, if a seizure discharge is the basis of these attacks, then the nature of the focus remains obscure. There may be no evidence of a further attack, and none of any causal lesion, over a subsequent period of years.

Fisher and Adams next consider the possibility that these episodes are caused by either transient focal cerebral ischaemia or by a 'small stroke'. Nevertheless, the search should continue for cases in which a localized ischaemia has been proved by clinical and post-mortem examination capable of eliciting a pure memory disorder.

Amnesia of psychological origin is a well recognized form of memory loss of a global type, but Fisher and Adams consider that there is very little, or no, resemblance between the type of amnesia they describe and amnesia of psychological origin.

They summarize the features of psychogenic amnesia as follows: (*i*) men and women are approximately equally affected; (*ii*) 95 per cent of patients are under the age of fifty; (*iii*) the loss of memory typically involves personal identification. In addition, recollection for what transpires in a circumscribed period is often lost and occasionally the patient remembers nothing at all; (*iv*) the amnesia usually develops when the patient is away from home or alone, and he finds himself wandering in the street, or a public place, hotel, or railway station; (*v*) the memory span, i.e. memory recording during the attack may be normal or above normal; (*vi*) the attack clears only after the patient is taken into custody or applies for medical care; (*vii*) automatic confused behaviour is virtually unknown;

(*viii*) the questions asked by the patient are few, simple and stereotyped, for he does not know what questions a truly amnesic patient might ask; (*ix*) the cause of the amnesia is usually discovered in psychological stresses; (*x*) pre-amnesia personality disorders are the rule; (*xi*) during the amnesic period the emotional attitude varies with the cause of the attack; the malingering and hysterical groups are often unconcerned, although mild depression or agitation occurs too; the psychotic group behave in accordance with their basic psychiatric illness; (*xii*) recovery tends to be abrupt and is often markedly influenced by suggestion.

The possibility that any transient amnesic episode is psychogenic needs to be considered, but I agree with Fisher and Adams that the differences between transient global amnesia and psychogenic amnesia are so marked that confusion between them is unlikely to arise if due attention is paid to the differentiating features.

Other possible causes of transient amnesia could be rejected. There was no evidence of head injury or drug or alcoholic intoxication, nor of hypoglycaemia.

A study of the reported cases, and my own experience of nine patients, suggests that transient global amnesia may include two distinct clinical pictures. There are patients whose behaviour at the time of the episode is noticeably abnormal. For example, one of mine, after coitus one night remembered nothing more until he awoke at 5 a.m. the next morning. Between the act of coitus and going to sleep he had been confused, called the cat in by the name of a former cat, asked his wife why his daughters had not come in, though they were not living in the house, and why they were sleeping in that particular room, though it was the one they usually slept in. When he awoke the next morning, he was mentally normal, and had no recollection of what had happened. In another category, however, falls another patient who, on two occasions had no recollection of the events of several hours, although during both periods he had been working in his office and his secretary had noticed nothing abnormal about him. McCulloch[20] quotes a dramatic example of this kind of disturbance. A man, eighty years old, attended a meeting of a board of directors lasting eight hours. McCulloch says: 'His judgement was remarkably solid. The amount of detail involved in the transaction was enormous, and it actually took over six hours to get all of the requisite details on the map. He summarized that detail at the end of the meeting, in a period of half an hour, very brilliantly, and when he came out, he sat down, answered two letters that were on his desk, turned to his secretary, and said: "I have a feeling that I should have gone to a board of directors' meeting." He was not then, or at any later time, able to recall one iota of that meeting, and he was in that state for nearly a year before he died.' The patient who is confused, and is subsequently unable to recall the events which occurred during his period of confusion, in this respect resembles a patient with post-traumatic amnesia. The situation is different with the patient who was mentally normal during the period which he cannot remember. Something causes him to have a retrograde amnesia for this period of time.

9

Specific Memory Defects

As was said earlier, memory necessarily enters into all learned behaviour. Focal disturbances of such behaviour, therefore, can be described in terms of loss of memory for the function or skill acquired by learning. In this sense, all forms of aphasia, agnosia, and apraxia can be attributed to loss of memory for particular forms of language recognition or action, though such disorders are not usually classed with disorders of memory. Certain varieties of them, however, need to be mentioned, partly because by common usage they are apt to be regarded as specifically related to the function of memory, and partly because for that reason their focal character may not be recognized, especially when they occur in the elderly. *Loss of topographical memory* is characterized by inability to describe accurately routes familiar to the patient and to visualize familiar scenes. This disorder may occur independently both of other forms of visual disorientation and of loss of memory for objects. Loss of topographical memory appears usually to be the result of a left occipital lesion, the left being the dominant cerebral hemisphere for this function, though the right may be so occasionally. *Visual object agnosia* may be regarded as loss of memory for objects; a special form of it, inability to recognize faces, is known as *prosopagnosia*. *Loss of visual imagery for objects* is a rare disorder in which the patient cannot visualize his relatives or his home or familiar objects. He may therefore be said to be unable to remember what they look like. (For a further discussion of these topics and relevant references see Brain.)[5]

10

Memory Disorders in the Elderly

Any of the disturbances mentioned in the previous section may occur in the elderly as a result of cerebrovascular disease or presenile or senile dementia. Some difficulty in remembering names is so general that it may perhaps be regarded as a normal accompaniment of ageing rather than the result of any pathological process. Pathological disorders of memory in the elderly and aged tend to impair recent memory more than memory for the remote past, and a severe amnesia for current events is not uncommon. In severe dementia both forms suffer severely. Chronic amnesic syndromes in the elderly are discussed by Allison[2] and in addition to those already mentioned, he adds the failure to employ memory as a tool, which he describes as 'amnesic indifference'.

11
The Neurology of Memory

In conclusion, let us see how far it is possible to fit together the varied facts and hypotheses, which we have been considering, into a consistent theory of the neurology of memory. It is as well to begin with the statement that there are four elements in memory, registration, retention, recall and recognition. As we shall see, it is not always easy to decide which one or more of these factors is at fault in a particular case.

Let us begin with the fact of retrograde amnesia occurring after a head injury. During the period of retrograde amnesia, the patient until he received his head injury was in normal health. His capacity for experience was normal and, presumably, the experiences which he has forgotten were normally registered. The period of retrograde amnesia is usually short. Why can the patient not remember the events which took place at this time? Russell[32] puts forward an interesting explanatory hypothesis. 'The almost constant occurrence of RA after concussion,' he writes, 'indicates that the injury, though it cannot have time to prevent what is last seen or heard from reaching the sensorium, does completely prevent its retention for future recall. The latter process presumably requires a few seconds of time for completion. The occasional occurrence of a vision of events within the RA indicates that in these cases some form of registration has occurred with great vividness which, though it can never be properly retained for later recall, can reproduce itself from a relatively low level in the form of a momentary "vision". The injury in such a case appears to have blocked the process of retention halfway. The variations in the RA during recovery of full consciousness seems to be specially significant. Distant memories return first, and loss of memory for the previous few years may, for a time, be so complete that the patient believes himself to be several years younger. After severe injury there may be a permanent RA of several days' duration which may include events of great importance to the patient. . . . We are therefore forced to the conclusion that as memories become older they become more strongly established, irrespective of their importance to the individual, while recent memories are relatively liable to traumatic extinction, however important they may be. . . . It seems likely that memory of events is not a static process. If it were, then distant memories would surely fade gradually and would be the more vulnerable to the effects of injury. On the contrary, when the brain is injured, these distant memories are the least vulnerable. It seems that the mere existence of the brain as a functioning organ must strengthen the roots of distant memories. The normal activity of the brain must steadily strengthen distant memories so that within the passage of time these become less vulnerable to the effects of head injury.' Russell concludes that memory depends on an active neuronal mechanism which never rests.

Russell's views, therefore, involve two hypotheses. The first is that immediately after experiences occur they go through a process lasting a few seconds which is necessary for their retention for future recall. Traumatic retrograde amnesia is attributed to interference with this process by the concussion. The second hypothesis is that some process of continuous reinforcement of memory occurs in the brain, and the survival of older memories better than more recent ones is put down to the fact that this reinforcing process has had longer to operate in the case of older memories.

There is, however, an alternative view which has the advantage of involving only one hypothesis, which would explain all the facts relating to amnesia after head injury. The fact that our memories are arranged in a serial order, which corresponds to the temporal order of the events which they represent, surely implies that they are recorded in the nervous system, in some way not yet understood, in which succession in time is represented by spatial order. Gooddy[12] has likened the process of memory to the operation of a tape-recorder, upon which current events make a permanent impression, which is then stored. He goes on to suggest that if the area of the tape, which at the moment is recording, is exposed to an unusually violent electrical disturbance, this would spread along the tape into the area on which the most recent record has been made, and obliterate this. The resulting loss, he suggests, is analogous to retrograde amnesia. Gooddy might then have gone further by pointing out that if the electrical disturbance damaged the part of the tape upon which future recordings were to be made so that these were not properly recorded, this would be analogous to the state of the brain responsible for post-traumatic amnesia. All the features of retrograde amnesia could be satisfactorily explained by translating Gooddy's analogy of the tape-recorder into neurophysiological terms. We must suppose that a head injury affects the process of recording experiences maximally as it is occurring at the time, and that the disturbance is then transmitted by a form of diashisis or neural shock along the pathways concerned with the recording of previous experiences, but in diminishing force the further it spreads. This hypothesis would explain the greatest vulnerability of the most recent memories, and the fact that, in general, the more severe the head injury, judged by the duration of the PTA, the longer the RA is likely to extend into the past. It would also explain the shrinkage of the RA by the fact that the shock-wave would temporarily put out of action many more neuronal connections than it actually destroyed. Those least damaged would be those representing events furthest in the past, and these therefore would be the first to recover, until at the end of recovery the patient is left with a period of retrograde amnesia representing neuronal connections absolutely destroyed. Old memories would survive, not because they are continuously being reinforced, but because they lie so far away in terms of the spatio-temporal organization of the nervous system that even the most severe shock-wave is unlikely to reach them.

The fact that the capacity for recent memory may be completely and permanently abolished by selective lesions of part of the hippocampal gyrus seems to indicate that this circumscribed region of the brain plays an essential part in the process whereby current experiences are translated into memory. There is no reason to suppose that memories are stored in the hippocampal gyri, indeed, all the evidence is to the contrary. They are, as it were, a physiological gate through which the experiences must pass if they are to become memories. What happens to them there we do not know.

The evidence cited at the beginning of this chapter indicates that other diencephalic structures and the cingulate gyri probably also play a part in this process, though again we are ignorant as to its nature. Nor do we know much about the relationship between memory, awareness of its temporal organization, and our appreciation of time itself. Such evidence as there is suggests that the cingulate gyri may have an important part to play in this.

As for the storage of memory, all the physiological evidence suggests that this involves extensive areas of the brain, and pathology reinforces this by associating impairment of memory for remote events with diffuse cerebral disorders rather than with focal lesions. How memories are stored we do not know.

REFERENCES

1. ADAMS, R. B., COLLINS, G. H., and VICTOR, M., 1962. Troubles de la memoire et de l'apprentissage chez l'home. *Physiologie de l'Hippocampe*, p. 273. Paris: Editions du Centre National de la Recherche Scientifique.
2. ALLISON, R. S., 1961. Chronic amnesic syndromes in the elderly. *Proc. Roy. Soc. Med.*, **54**, 961.
3. BARBIZET, J., 1963. Etudes Cliniques sur la Mémoire. *J. Neurol. Neurosurg. Psychiat.*, **26**, 127.
4. BICKFORD, R. C., MULDER, D. W., DODGE, H. W., JR., SVIEN, H. J., and ROME, H. P., 1958. Changes in memory function produced by stimulation of the temporal lobe in man. *Proc. ARNMD*, **36**, 227.
5. BRAIN, 1965. *Speech disorders*, pp. 172–76. London: Butterworth.
6. BUTLER, S., 1916. *The Notebooks of Samuel Butler*, p. 57. A. C. Fifeld.
7. DELAY, J., BRION, S., and DEROUESNÉ, C., 1964. Syndrome de Korsakoff et etiologie tumorale. *Rev. Neur.*, **111**, 97.
8. ECCLES, J. C., 1953. *The neurophysiological basis of mind*, pp. 219–27. Oxford.
9. FISHER, C. M., and ADAMS, R. D., 1964. Transient global amnesia. *Acta Neurol. Scandin. Neurol. Suppl.*, 9, **40**.
10. GALAMBOS, R., and MORGAN, C. P., 1960. The neural basis of learning. *Handbook of physiology*, Section 1, Neurophysiology, III. p. 1471. Ed. John Field. Washington: American Physiological Society.
11. GAZZANIGA, M. S., BOGEN, J. E., and SPERRY, R. W., 1965. Observations on visual perception after disconnection of the cerebral hemispheres in man. *Brain*, **88**, 221.
12. GOODDY, W., 1964. Some comments on the significance of retrograde amnesia with an analogy. *Brain*, **87**, 75.

13. HYDÉN, H., 1964. Introductory remarks to the session on memory processes. *Neuro-Sciences Research Programme Bulletin*, **2**, 23.
14. LANCET, 1965. Memory molecules, ii, 1281.
15. LASHLEY, K. S., 1950. In search of the engram. *Symp. Soc. Exp. Bill.*, **4**, 454, and 1960, *The neuropsychology of Lashley*, p. 482, *et sec.* Eds. Beach, F. A., Hebb, D. O., Morgan, C. G., and Nissen, H. W. New York, Toronto, London: McGraw-Hill Book Co. Inc.
16. LEWIS, A., 1961. Amnesic syndromes. *Proc. Roy. Soc. Med.*, **54**, 955.
17. LORENTE DE Nó, 1933. Studies on the structure of the cerebral cortex. I. The area entorhinalis. *J. Psych. Neurol.*, **45**, 381.
18. ——— 1934. Studies on the structure of the cerebral cortex. II. Continuation of the study of the ammonic system. *Ibid.*, **46**, 113.
19. ——— 1943. In *Physiology of the nervous system* by J. F. Fulton, p. 274. Oxford.
20. McCULLOCH, W., 1951. Why the mind is in the head. *Cerebral mechanisms in behaviour*, p. 58–59. Ed. by L. A. Jeffress. New York: John Wiley & Sons, and London, Chapman & Hall.
21. MILNER, B., 1958. Psychological defects produced by temporal lobe excision *Proc. ARNMD*, **36**, 244.
22. MORRELL, F., 1961. Lasting changes in synaptic organisation produced by continuous neuronal bombardment. *Brain mechanisms and learning*, p. 375. Eds. J. F. de la Fresnay, A. Fessard, R. W. Gerard and J. Konorsky. Oxford: Blackwell Scientific Publications.
23. Moscow Colloquium on Electroencephalography of Higher Nervous Activity, 1960. Eds., Jasper, H. H., and Smirnov, G. D. Supplement No. 13. Int. Journal of Electroencephalography and Chemical Neurophysiology. Montreal, Canada.
24. MYERS, R. E., 1956. Function of corpus callosum in interocular transfer. *Brain*, **79**, 358.
25. OJEMANN, R. G., 1964. Correlations between specific human brain lesions and memory changes. *Neuro-Sciences Research Programme Bulletin*, **2**, 77.
26. PENFIELD, W., 1958. The role of the temporal cortex in the recall of past experience and interpretation of the present. *Neurological Basis of Behaviour*, p. 149. Eds. Wolstenholme, G. E. W., and O'Connor, C. M. London: J. & A. Churchill Ltd.
27. PENFIELD, W., and JASPER, H., 1954. *Epilepsy and the functional anatomy of the Human Brain*, p. 125. London: J. & A. Churchill Ltd.
28. PENFIELD, W., and MILNER, B., 1958. Memory deficit produced by bilateral lesions of the hippocampal zone. *Arch. Neur. Psychiat.*, **79**, 475.
29. ROBERTS, R. B., 1964. Self-induction and memory. *Neuro-Sciences Research Bulletin*, **2**, 39.
30. ROSE, F. C., and SYMONDS, C. P., 1960. Persistent memory defect following encephalitis. *Brain*, **83**, 195.
31. RUSSELL, I. S., and OCHS, S., 1963. Localization of a memory trace in one cortical hemisphere and transfer to the other hemisphere. *Brain*, **86**, 37.
32. RUSSELL, W. R., 1959. *Brain memory learning*. Oxford.
33. RUSSELL, W. R., and NATHAN, P. W., 1946. Traumatic amnesia. *Brain*, **69**, 280.
34. RUSSELL, W. R., and SMITH, A., 1961. Post-traumatic amnesia in closed head injury. *Arch. Neurol.*, **5**, 4.
35. SCHMITT, F. O., 1964. Molecular and ultrastructural correlates of function in neurons, neuronal nets and the brain. *Neuro-Sciences Research Programme Bulletin*, **2**, 43.
36. SCOVILLE, W. B., and MILNER, B., 1957. Loss of recent memory after bilateral hippocampal lesions. *J. Neur. Neurosurg. Psychiat.*, **20**, 11.

37. SWEET, W. H., TALLAND, G. A., and ERVIN, F. R., 1959. Loss of recent memory following section of fornix. *Trans. Amer. Neur. Ass.*, **76**.
38. TALLAND, G. A., 1958. Psychological studies of Korsakoff's psychosis in perceptual functions. *J. Nerv. Ment. Dis.*, **127**, 197.
39. 1959. The interference theory of forgetting and the amnesic syndrome. *J. abnorm. Soc. Psychol.*, **59**, 10.
40. 1960a. Psychological studies of Korsakoff's psychosis. V. Spontaneity and activity rate. *J. Nerv. Ment. Dis.*, **130**, 16.
41. 1960b. Psychological studies of Korsakoff's psychosis. VI. Memory and learning. *Ibid.*, 366.
42. TALLAND, G. A., and EKDAHL, M., 1959. Psychological studies of Korsakoff's psychosis in the rate and mode of forgetting narrative material. *J. Nerv. Ment. Dis.*, **129**, 391.
43. VICTOR, M., 1965. The effects of nutritional deficiency in the neurons system. A comparison with the effects of carcinoma. *The remote effects of cancer on the nervous system*, p. 134. Eds. Lord Brain and Norris, F. H. New York and London: Grune and Stratton.
44. VICTOR, M., ANGEVINE, J. B., JR., MANCALL, E. L., and FISHER, C. M., 1961. Memory loss with lesions of hippocampal formation. *Arch. Neur.*, **5**, 244.
45. WALKER, A. E., 1957. Recent memory impairment in unilateral temporal lesions. *Arch. Neurol. Psychiat.*, **78**, 543.
46. WHITTY, C. W. M., and LEWIN, W., 1960. A Korsakoff syndrome in the post-cingulectomy state. *Brain*, **83**, 648.
47. WILLIAMS, M., and PENNYBACKER, J., 1954. Memory disturbance in third ventricle tumours. *J. Neurol. Neurosurg. Psychiat.*, **17**, 115.

VI

CORPOREAL AWARENESS
(BODY-IMAGE; BODY-SCHEME)

MacDonald Critchley

C.B.E., M.D., F.R.C.P.

Hon. Consulting Physician, National Hospital, Queen Square, London.

The modern interest in body-image really began with the writings of the otologist Bonnier[1] (1893–1905) who introduced the term 'schematia' to indicate a composite sensory experience embracing the complete anatomical make-up of an individual. With greater precision, Henry Head and Gordon Holmes[11] in 1911–12 first drew attention—in not very clear language—to the mental idea which a person possesses as to his own body and its physical and aesthetic attributes. In their own words:

'The final product of the tests for the appreciation of posture or passive movement rises into consciousness as a measured postural change. For this combined standard, against which all subsequent changes of posture are measured before they enter consciousness, we propose the word 'schema'. By means of perpetual alterations in position we are always building up a postural model of ourselves which constantly changes. Every new posture or movement is recorded on this plastic schema. . . .'

As practical and authoritative neurologists, Head and Holmes never for a moment realized that they had opened a Pandora's box which let loose a spate of metaphysics, much of it sheer verbiage. The next and very important intervention was made by P. Schilder[16] who, in 1923, brought out his work *Das Körperschema*. Twelve years later it was expanded in his English monograph *The image and appearance of the human body*. Elsewhere I have described this book as a *chef d'oeuvre manqué*, a work which just falls short of being one of the great monographs of neurology. Like other famous precedents it began well but tailed off feebly.

The immediate post-Schilderian conceptions of the body-image focus around the monograph of J. Lhermitte[12] (1939). In 1949 Critchley[3] lectured on the topic of 'the body-image in neurology' and wittingly or not, this article when it appeared in print in 1950, triggered off a fresh mass of written material upon this subject at the hands of psychiatrists, neurologists, paediatricians, psychologists and philosophers, much of which was of very dubious value.

The topic began to get out of hand. Terminology blossomed so that terms like 'body image', 'body schema', 'corporeal schema', 'image de soi' were employed more or less interchangeably. It soon became obvious that thinking was becoming so muddled that the various expressions were made to stand in the literature for wholly different ideas at different times by different writers. At one moment the idea was perceptual; at another it was a conceptual one. Part of the trouble was due to a lack of clear definition, the one put forward by Head and Holmes being more elucidatory than hermeneutic.

1

Definition and Terminology

Obviously this chaotic state of affairs is untenable. Even though it may require later to be modified, some tentative definition should be advanced, as for instance 'the idea which an individual possesses as to the physical properties of his own anatomy, and which he carries over into the imagery of his self'.

The notion is a complex one, for it includes such activity as the imagery which one possesses and utilizes during states of rumination or brooding, including the predormitum, and also states of dreaming. This is a purely conceptual matter. But in addition it includes actual bodily sensations which may be perverted in kind or natural, arising from part or perhaps the whole of the anatomy. An obvious example is the phantom limb, or the feeling of intactness which an amputee experiences as regards his missing segment. But the two notions, however cognate, are actually disparate. The former is imaginal, the latter mainly perceptual in nature, and yet both stand within the fabric of the terms 'body-image' or 'body-schema'. Smythies has attempted to correlate body-image with the former and body-schema with the latter aspect of the problem. This, however, was a retrospective attitude, and however commendable the purpose, remains unacceptable. Clearly an all-embracing term is needed; one which combines conceptual with the more tangible perceptual components. The author therefore puts forward a plea for the acceptance of the less definitive term 'corporeal awareness' to replace both body-schema and body-image.

It becomes important to determine the physiology of this idea of corporeal awareness and to trace its ontogeny. It is not an inborn entity but is one which grows up slowly as the child becomes older, though always tagging after to some extent.[6] The development proceeds in a step-like rather than uniform fashion, advancing abruptly between the seventh and eighth year of age. Chief among the formative factors are the visual, the tactile and the labyrinthine components. The visual factors are twofold in character. In the first place they comprise the information which the adolescent subject steadily accumulates from inspection of his own anatomy. This particularly applies to the body-segments which are ordinarily exposed, e.g. the hands. In some primitive communities within the tropics, the body surface which is ordinarily exposed may be more extensive. The face occupies a special niche. It is an area of the body which is out of the range of sight of the individual. His only clue to his own facial appearance is afforded by inspection by way of reflection in a looking-glass or the surface of a pool. Opportunities for self-inspection are not always available, though there may be exceptional instances as in the case of an actor. Moreover the reflected image is in many ways an artificial simulacrum, for as soon as an individual gazes in a looking-glass, he strikes an attitude. The manifold facial mannerisms and little grimaces cease, and the mirror reflection is often merely a stylized and immobile still-life edition of what every bystander realizes as something quite different. As Oscar Wilde put it '*Il ne faut regarder que dans les miroirs. Car les miroirs ne nous montrent que des masques*'.

We must remember too that the visual knowledge of one's self is never complete, whether by way of direct gaze or mirror-reflection. Certain areas remain *terrae incognitae*, for they cannot be inspected either directly or by any optical device, e.g. the occiput, the nape of the neck, and the interscapular area.

Ordinarily too the growing individual receives information from the visual observation of other persons. He learns to realize the standard height, the common facial delineaments, the postures, attitudes and gaits of others, and the abundance of man's gestural world. Even two-dimensional representations in the way of photographs, portraits, and illustrations add their important quota to the visual component of one's own corporeal awareness. By determining a mean he can draw certain conclusions as to his own facial and bodily appearance.

The tactile factors which lead to the development of corporeal awareness consist in the proprioceptive impulses from the joints and muscles, especially in the course of vigorous movement. To these must be added the sum-total of exteroceptive data, e.g. the touch, painful, thermal messages ascending from part or whole of the body-surface. Other sensory components are made up of the complex of visceral sensations, both physiological and pathological.

Labyrinthine factors constitute the third constituent which builds up the body-image. Bonnier was indeed inspired by the considerable upsets in bodily feelings occurring in states of vertigo, and he spoke of the vestibular constituent of the eighth cranial nerve as *le nerf de l'espace*. However. these factors are not as important as the foregoing, which contribute more to the growth of an adult type of body-image.

An individual's body-image is by no means in the nature of a naked mannikin or homunculus. Not only is it ordinarily clad but, according to the immediate circumstances, it may spread so as to involve inanimate objects which are in contact or in close proximity. The body-image of a motorist, an air-pilot, an equestrian, temporarily includes part at least of the automobile, the aircraft, or the horse. A surgeon with his probe, a blind man with his white stick, for the time being are endowed with an extension of corporeal awareness. This is the phenomenon sometimes spoken of as the 'Phantom Body' or better still *Le Spatialité de Situation* (Merleau-Ponty).[13]

The importance of each of these factors can be well realized in those instances of deprivation of special sense modalities since birth. For example the congenitally blind child year by year develops corporeal awareness in the absence of visual factors. Not only does he have no opportunity of studying his own anatomy or his own mirror-image, but he cannot observe the appearance of others around him. His sole means of acquiring knowledge as to the shape and surface of himself and others is through manual contact.

It is not surprising, therefore, that when a congenitally blind subject makes a drawing or plasticene model of a man, odd deformations are displayed. This is particularly the case when the congenitally blind victim is of mediocre intellectual calibre. Those parts of the anatomy which are of special personal significance are apt to loom unduly large and therefore to take a conspicuous part in the drawings and models. For example, the hand with the sensitive fingers constitutes not only a manual tool, but also an organ of perception for making contact with the external world, animate and inanimate. A blind child may therefore when asked to draw a man, pay particular attention to the fingers and hands, which may be of inordinate development and size to the detriment of the face and body. In the case of clay models of the head and neck, the mouth may occupy a predominant role, for it is by way of the lips, tongue and oral cavity that the blind person speaks, feeds, breathes, and even in certain circumstances makes tactual exploration. In the models collected by von Stockert[21] executed by children of rather low intelligence, born blind, practically nothing existed except a sphere for the head, and a huge crater with everted lips representing the mouth. Eyes, ears, nose, neck and so on, took little part in the art-form of such children.

2

Phantom Phenomena

Similarly in persons deprived of a limb, corporeal awareness continues to operate so as to produce a phantom limb, which represents not the activity of severed peripheral nerves, but rather the body-image which continues to operate as though the individual were intact. One recalls the difficulty with which painful phantom limbs are ablated. Indeed nothing short of a cerebral insult whether it be the intervention of a cerebro-vascular lesion causing a hemiplegia or the surgical operation of parietal-cortical topectomy, stands any chance of ridding the patient of the painful phantom. The phantom limb may alter in size, shape, motility and position in space with the passage of time, but it remains in some form or other a constant manifestation of the will for integrity. Even mental defectives who lose a limb develop a phantom for a while at any rate, indicating that past sensory input is more important than high cognitive levels (M. L. Simmel).[18]

There is a certain difference, however, in the degree of vividness of phantom limbs according to whether the segment has been lost surgically or through the slow intervention of disease. This is well illustrated in the case of patients with leprosy.[17] Here progressive necrosis of the phalanges may lead to miniature stumps representing all that is left of the adult fingers, but in such cases a phantom finger does not follow. However, should the leper lose his arm either as the result of trauma or surgery, then a phantom arm will appear. Moreover, if the gangrenous stumps are amputated surgically, a phantom will follow representing the original intact fingers, and not the mere stumps (Critchley, Simmel).

It is of particular interest to enquire whether these phantom phenomena apply only to the extremities as Leriche affirmed. Can it be demonstrated that phantom segments sometimes occur after injury or surgical excision of other parts of the anatomy? Thus after removal of the nose, ear, breast, penis, do phantom organs follow? The question cannot be answered positively because the situation varies from one individual to another, and also depends upon the segment which is involved. Certainly loss of the anus after an abdomino-perineal excision of the rectum may be followed by a phantom orifice, ready for the passage of matter or gas. A phantom nose, a phantom penis, and even possibly a phantom eye, have been described in the literature in a plausible fashion. Loss of an ear, however, is less assured and further enquiry along such lines would be rewarding. Riddoch[15] stated that it was a question of prominence or protrusion of segments of the body which determines whether or not a phantom develops after surgery. The question of phantoms following the surgical loss of a breast is more complicated. For example the awareness of the existence of a breast is not ordinarily a conspicuous perceptual experience and it is at first sight not easy to decide what type of enquiry to pursue after mastectomy. However, feelings are commonly referred to the breast or nipple in pregnancy, during menstrual periods, and in the course of sexual stimulation. These may well continue to appear after the surgical loss of one mamma. M. L. Simmel[20] has recently studied a series of seventy-seven post-mastectomy patients and obtained some evidence of a phantom in about 40 per cent, especially among the younger, more intelligent and more introspective subjects.

Another point of interest about phantom phenomena concerns the age at which phantom limbs appear; or rather, how often phantom limbs appear in the case of young subjects who have lost a limb through disease in early childhood and infancy. The results of enquiry establish that a body-image may be present at an earlier age than is commonly imagined, so that the loss of an arm or a leg in very early childhood may well be followed by an unequivocal phantom image. In my series a child of three and a half years was endowed with a vivid phantom image of a limb lost two years previously. But in very young amputees the phantoms may be transient and afterwards be forgotten altogether (M. L. Simmel).[19] The situation is probably very different in cases of congenital absence of limbs, as for example in thalidomide babies. Such children as they grow to adulthood might not be expected to possess what might be called a phantom limb, in other words, an engram resulting from years of sensory stimulation. On the other hand it may happen that on the conceptual plane of corporeal awareness, the thalidomide victim of amelia, especially when older in years, may during his day-dreaming state, or when planning future activities in which he visualizes himself as participating, may possibly regard himself not as a creature apart, devoid of arms and legs, but as an orthodox member of the community, of average height, stature, and endowed with limbs. Thus E. Weinstein and E. A. Sersen,[23] using a special 'playing game' technique have claimed that five out of thirty amelic children possessed phantoms. This observation suggested there might exist in such young persons a sort of built-in frame-work of the body-schema. Perhaps the presence or absence of phantom limbs in congenital amelics depends upon whether cortical and spinal neurons exist corresponding with the musculature of the missing bodily segments. This topic is one which merits further enquiry.

Phantom limbs may also occur, not after surgical intervention, but after paralytic disease, due to lesions at various levels of the nervous system. For example a patient paralysed as the result of a transverse lesion of the spinal cord, whatever the cause, and completely insensitive from the waist downwards, may not feel himself sawn across the middle like a conjuror's partner, but may experience some vague impression of his lower limbs. But the idea which he may entertain as to the length or posture of the limbs may be at complete variance with reality. Thus he may imagine his paralysed legs as being unusually short, or with the middle segments missing, so that the feet seem to be attached to the thighs. Or it may seem to him that the paralysed extremities are flexed at the hip and knees, whereas actually they lie in extension; or it may be the other way round. Phantom limbs can follow lesions of the nervous system not only at the spinal level, but even higher. Perhaps the most likely situation for such a phenomenon to develop is an abrupt vascular lesion deep in one or other parietal lobe. The resulting clinical picture will be that of a contralateral hemiplegia and hemianaesthesia, but the patient in his imagery may conceive of a phantom supernumerary limb, lying in an attitude quite other than is actually the case. The phantom third arm, for example, may seem to be in full extension and abduction at the shoulder, and not folded across the chest as the paralysed limb actually is. Or at times it may appear to move of its own accord, the true paralysed limb being devoid of volitional power. If, however, the paralysed limb be passively placed in the posture occupied by the phantom limb, then the two may merge, and the supernumerary limb for the time being disappears. In one case at least, the patient characteristically personified the phantom, calling it 'the intruder' or 'that fellow'.

3

The Body-Concept

That the phantom limb is something more than a mere concept and possesses many perceptual properties is shown by the fact that it can share in sensorial alterations along with the rest of the body. Thus when the patient is cold and shivering the phantom limb too may seem to be subjected to goose-flesh. In more pathological conditions an amputee who develops peripheral neuritis may experience pains, tingling, and pins and needles in all extremities including the phantom limb. The itching of a generalized irritative dermatitis may also be experienced in the phantom limb. According to Ekbom,[9] the syndrome of restless legs probably does not extend to a missing lower limb, though the stump may be involved in uncomfortable dysaesthesiae.

Some of the foregoing remarks may be exemplified in the following:

1. A patient with traumatic paraplegia with a level at Th. 8. was given an instillation of intrathecal alcohol. Thereafter, spasticity was replaced by flaccidity, and both legs were placed in an attitude of extension and abduction. The legs would now feel heavy and very hot, and as if they were tightly touching each other.

2. A case of traumatic paraplegia with complete transverse lesion below Th. 7. Though the lower limbs were insensitive the patient was aware of their existence but felt as though the legs were all the time crossed.

3. An amputee with a phantom foot later developed a generalized peripheral neuritis of a painful character. These pains were especially marked in the phantom foot.

4. A German prisoner of war sailor had lost his right arm. Later he developed diphtheritic polyneuritis following which he experienced constant dysaesthesiae in his extremities including the missing hand.

5. A Parkinsonian developed tingly discomfort, stiffness and awkwardness of the right (actual) arm and also in his phantom left limb, which had followed an amputation. The patient began steadily to rely more on the phantom left arm, as the right arm became more and more useless.

6. An elderly man who had lost both legs in the First World War

developed phantom feelings of both feet sometimes with pain. After a right-sided hemiparesis due to a stroke the patient completely lost the phantom sensation on both sides.

Turning for the moment to the more conceptual aspect of corporeal awareness, and dealing with one's own notion of self in certain situations past and future, we may find considerations of considerable interest. A striking lack of correspondence may be met with in the discrepancy between the true appearance of the anatomy as obvious to everyone around, and the notion which the individual himself entertains. The two may be entirely different. Although on an intellectual plane the patient may quite well realize and be able to express graphically the fact that he is bald-headed and grey haired, wrinkled, cadaverous, bowed in stance, and altogether changed, nevertheless he rarely for a moment regards himself in that way when he is thinking about his recent activities or what he was doing in the remote past, nor when he comes to project his thoughts into future plans. When he visualizes himself on a projected holiday or business trip, the body image that he nurses in such circumstances is that of an individual considerably younger than the actual one. In other words, the body-image does not keep pace with the increasing alterations in the features and build so obvious to others, but it lags behind. The degree of difference varies; first of all according to age, the gap becoming wider and wider as the years go by; and secondly according to the state of the individual's well-being. If he should happen to feel well and vigorous, healthy and refreshed, then his body-image becomes that of his far younger self. However, if the contrary is the case, and the ageing individual feels tired, depressed, or in pain, it is more likely that his corporeal awareness will conform closely to that of his actual appearance. A discrepancy between image and reality is often strikingly brought home to the person concerned when he inspects snapshots which were taken of him by other members of the family, and with which he expresses rather shocked dissatisfaction, protesting perhaps that the photograph is a bad one and is nothing like him.* It also is apt to show itself at a reunion of alumni, where his class-mates at college who qualified together and then parted, meet at some function twenty or thirty years later. Each individual probably looks at the others and thinks to himself how old his contemporaries are looking, never for a minute realizing that he too appears to them at least as changed.

Another interesting discrepancy probably occurs between persons who are markedly unconventional in body-build, height, or appearance. Such crippled or deformed persons may in an intellectual fashion be able to describe precisely their configuration, but not for a moment do they

---

* D'Annunzio wrote in his old age 'I have just received the photograph which was taken yesterday. It is ruthless, for it shows me as I am, and my face just as it is. Nevertheless, whilst riding today, I experienced inexplicably youthful sensations'. (Quoted by J. Todd and K. Dewhurst.)[22]

visualize themselves as such in their browsing or day-dreaming moments. The stunted achondroplasiac; the man who is unduly tall or grossly over-weight; the individual who has been disabled from old poliomyelitis and is left with a withered limb; the albino; the man with a grotesque rhinophy-ma; and the old pottique stunted from extreme scoliosis, may not for a moment imagine himself as being different from anyone else, although in his sober moments of cold reflection he knows full well the extent of his anomaly. This particularly applies to those who are well below the average height—the midget, the achondroplastic dwarf, and the victim who has lost both legs at the hip-joints. If we accept for a moment the notion put forward by Claparède[2] that the focus of most vivid imagery lies at a point somewhere between the two eyes, and that one looks out on to the world from such a height, then the midget must be someone quite different. In his ordinary waking moments instead of inspecting his entourage from a height of five to six feet, he is always peering upwards. But what about his times of loneliness, as for example when dropping off to sleep at night? Does he in thinking forward or reminiscing backward, still gaze up at a world of pseudo-giants; or does he imagine himself an equal? It is probable that at such times he does, and that the discrepancy for the moment does not exist.

Some inkling as to the nature of the body-image in the crippled may be discovered through the medium of a 'draw-a-man' test. A child with cerebral palsy is liable to omit one or more limbs. One of my patients who had been afflicted with alopecia drew an elaborate figure of a man, but omitted the usual scribble depicting hair.

Another consideration regarding the body-concept concerns its location in outer space with reference to the actual body. A difference probably occurs according to whether one thinks forward or thinks backward. Perhaps it can be said that when an individual indulges in a reverie and broods upon some past event in which he has participated, then the imagery becomes concentrated on himself, and he stands entirely within his own self and looks around. In other words his own body-image occupies the central or nodal point whereby he looks upon himself as an actor and not an onlooker. However, when the individual switches from the past and looks into the future, in order to plan some activity—a voyage, a piece of work, a social occasion—then he probably sees himself as a participant, looking upon himself not from afar, but as an *alter ego* standing close by, perhaps to one side of the imagined actor in the future scene.

These statements may hold for conditions which are more or less normal. If, however, one considers the situation when the subject is not in vigorous health, but very unwell, then the situation might be different indeed. Even with the normal person, subjected temporarily to a state of ecstacy, as for example when passively or actively participating in music, there may occur an intense depersonalization leading to a wide dislocation between the actor and the onlooker. The singer who is carried away by his song, may visualize himself as from the back of the theatre. The same applies to an orchestral conductor who, as the music sweeps him on, seems to drift further and further into the distance, looking on at a midget performer. Something comparable may occur in orgasmic experiences. The relevant literature contains one piece of fine writing on the part of a female observer . . .'Gradually there is a very acute awareness of every individual component of my body as if each part had a separate longing of its own. All these longings gather together, drawn towards my innermost being, and then fall away from my insignificant matter. A state of fluidness seems to supervene and I discover to my great delight that my body does dissolve and that I can, and have escaped. For a brief moment I know myself without a body—only thus can this experience be described—and, on one or two occasions, from my exalted position, which is always to the left diagonally from and facing the body, I have been able to look down upon my shell. Surely the reality must be that complete self which has flown so swiftly out of the body, for it is *that* self which gazes so confidently upon what had seemed to be such a disordered array of meaningless parts each with its own sensation striving to assert itself, and which now lies immobile, inanimate and totally unaware of the immense change that has overtaken it. It is only the material tool of my true reality.

'On reflection, when the excitation has receded, I often wonder, provided consciousness could be retained, if dying would produce a similar experience. Fainting, a bodily lapse I have experienced a few times, has nothing in common and is certainly very dull and unpleasant when compared with the exhilaration of a being set free.

'To a minor degree, I have felt a similar exhilaration, like a "walking on air" feeling, when listening to music, i.e. the Fifth Symphony by Sibelius, Beethoven's Pastoral, piano music of Chopin, and a Bach organ fugue. Wagnerian compositions and similar music give me a very real feeling of evil as if in giving myself to it completely I would awake to find I had sold my soul to the devil.'

4

Heautoscopy

There is a phenomenon which approaches closely to this physiological phenomenon, namely the rare and very interesting instances of specular hallucination or heautoscopy, whereby an individual experiences not a vivid image but a veritable visual hallucination of himself. This is a theme which, originally mentioned by Aristotle when writing of Antipheron, has since become dear to the writers of romantic literature even more than to neurologists and psychiatrists. The circumstances in which a veritable heautoscopy can occur—as apart from fictional notions—are states of ecstacy; of confusion; as well as during epileptic or migrainous equivalents.

The first reference in pathology is perhaps that of the Swedish naturalist Linnaeus who from time to time had a very vivid image of himself, situated in natural circumstances and behaving in a natural fashion. Once he entered his study to find the image of himself seated in a chair writing or reading. Or as he would wander through his garden studying a plant or picking a blossom here and there, he might see some little distance away his *alter ego* performing the same actions, stopping to gaze at a flower and pluck it.[14]

5

Corporeal Image in Various Disease-States

The notion of body-image is very much influenced by intercurrent physical disease, not necessarily neurological. Thus in almost any condition of localized pain the segment involved may obtrude itself unduly into the patient's awareness, and may be inescapable from the imagery. For example the pain of a fractured wrist may cause the affected arm to appear too big, too heavy, or too long. The same applies to other regions of the body other than the limbs. Again during states of diarrhoea the focus of attention may be somewhere perineal. In dyspepsia, or even in the physiological circumstances of hunger, thirst, undue coldness, uncomfortable heat, sexual arousal, the body-image may show a more or less local enhancement. This would correspond with what Bonnier termed 'hyperschematia' (or 'macrosomatognosia'). Something similar is also met with in patients afflicted with states of partial paralysis. A limb which can be moved only with difficulty may appear unduly awkward, cumbersome, too long, too broad, and excessively heavy. Phenomena of this order are commonly experienced by patients with disseminated sclerosis. On the other hand, there may be a contrary state of affairs whereby a segment of the anatomy may seem to shrink, and even drop out of awareness. This is particularly so when a limb is completely paralysed and insensitive. Thus a patient with a total paralysis due to a brachial plexus injury may feel that the affected limb is shrunken and excessively light. He may or may not have a phantom limb as well. In some cases of hemiplegia, especially when the lesion lies in the non-dominant hemisphere, the affected limb may seem to the patient to be withered, and too light (and yet at other times too heavy). These phenomena correspond with a 'hyposchematia' or 'microsomatognosia'. Something like this may be vividly experienced during states of vertigo. The famous surgeon John Hunter, who was liable to Ménière-like attacks, described in arresting language how he would seem to shrink at such times and recede into the distance. In those rare conditions where the victim suffers generalized pain as opposed to localized pain, something similar may occur. The trauma of severe electric shock represents one of the few circumstances where pain is universally experienced, and there are vivid descriptions on record of how the electrocuted individual seems to shrivel up and almost attain the dimensions of a doll or puppet. In other pathological circumstances there may occur not so much an enhancement, nor yet a decrement of the body-image, as a distortion which cannot strictly speaking be described in terms of plus or minus. Some of the most telling descriptions of this dysschematia, as we may call it, or deformation of the body-image, are to be met with in the delirious states due to certain drug intoxications. Here mescalin and LSD are particularly potent, and the literature on this subject is rich in incisive descriptions of the personal feelings of distortion.

A few clinical instances can be quoted in illustration:

1. During the acute symptoms of his cardiac infarction the patient felt as though he had become elongated and was twelve feet high. This lasted two hours.

2. In each attack of migraine one hand would seem to be a very long way off.

3. A woman of forty-one with a left hemiparesis due to a fractured skull sustained when she was five also developed post-traumatic epilepsy. For the past two years she has had epileptic equivalents in which she would feel as if she were in two halves which would not connect. If she were to try and clap her hands they would miss each other. 'I have to keep moving my left arm and leg to make sure that these limbs are part of me.'

4. A woman of 57 sustained temporal lobe attacks. '. . . My head does not seem to be on my body any more and the right side of the head is not there. The feeling is as if I were in the air, seeing my body lying on the bed, and I say to myself "get back there".'

5. Following childbirth a woman of twenty-eight sustained a sudden dysphasia and right-sided mild hemiparesis with severe right hemi-hypaesthesia. Lying relaxed in bed she would feel as though there was nothing there on the right side—even when she tried to move the paretic limbs.

6. A patient with a left parietal meningioma had life-long attacks of migraine. In each of these the right side would feel bigger and swollen, as if there were a sharp line down the middle. The left side, however, would remain 'calm, cool and collected, while the right side would be tense, anxious, agitated and highly-strung'.

6

Corporeal Over-Awareness: Narcissism, Self-Portraiture

The body-image experience is, of course, a perfectly natural and normal one, but ordinarily it is by no means obtrusive, and is more likely to loom only in states of solitude when the lonely individual is cogitating about his actions past or his future activities. It is a notion which possibly may elude the descriptive powers of one who is not of high intelligence or whose vocabulary is limited. Therefore it is more likely to be comprehended by those of some intelligence, particularly introspective psychopaths of high intellectual calibre, where we find perhaps the most flamboyant descriptions of all. In one particular psychiatric anomaly, body-image is all-important. I refer of course to states of narcissism. Here the subject takes an inordinate and unconscionable interest in his bodily appearance and his subjective sensations and he may constantly alter his activity so as to check up his appearance, or to embellish it or to commit it to posterity. Mirrors and portraits may occupy an unduly important role. He or she may adorn the visage with cosmetics to an inordinate degree. The male may indulge in elaborate and unconventional hair-styles and grow whiskers, beards and other facial adornments as if obeying some urge to express his odd personality. Elaborate headgear may be an instance of narcissism and may play an important and deliberate role in the scheme of things. During the German occupation of France some women were able to express their personalities only by wearing the most outrageous headgear which became more and more complicated and extraordinary as the restrictions of the invader increased. Narcissism may be exemplified in primitive persons by deliberate deformation of the anatomy. For example scarifying the body, tattooing the face, inserting discs of wood into the lips or into the lobes of the ears, or transfixing the nose with skewers. A pathological state of the body-image can also be pointed to in the well-known case of the ageing beauty which might be called the 'Miss Haversham phenomenon' after Charles Dickens. The old lady who although a recluse continues to wear the most elaborate clothing and to indulge in extreme make-up and coiffure, but conforming with the fashion of decades ago is an instance in point. Such persons as the Comtesse de Castiglione, and Lady Wilde, the mother of Oscar, are recalled in this context. Another fantastic example of a narcissistic self-preoccupation is to be met with in the auto-reproduction carried out by the Japanese Ito Hamashi, who constructed a life-size model of his nude body, with every surface marking, every vein, artery and tendon faithfully depicted. Every wrinkle was there in place, and the head and body were likewise adorned with hair plucked from appropriate areas of his own anatomy. Yet another classic case is that of Beatrice Turner, a young girl who grew up in a strict puritan family who kept her more or less a prisoner so that she should not be sullied by masculine influences. Year after year she remained at home and painted. In due course her parents died and the ageing Beatrice Turner continued with her art. After she too had succumbed in her late sixties, the house was found to be filled with hundreds of paintings of herself, all in the guise of a beautiful young woman in her early twenties. Latterly the portraits were of herself as a nude.

This leads us to the topic of self-portraiture among artists, one which would merit a serious neuro-psychological study. Some painters have indulged in this practice; others have not. In some instances it was perhaps a question of economy, for a mirror-image is a cheaper model than one who is hired by the hour. But in some cases the question of finance did not enter into the problem. Some artists seem to have specialized in self-portraiture as for example Rembrandt (nearly 100 instances), Cézanne (40), Picasso (30), Delacroix, von Marées, Max Liebermann, Levis Corinth, Max Beckman, O. Kokoschka, and Edvard Munch. As we have already mentioned, the mirror-image of a person possesses certain important anomalies and this can often be depicted in an artist's self-portraiture. A number of artists have employed the device of inserting themselves as a minor item within a major work, like certain film directors. This *Assistinzbild* as it is called, is currently represented in many of the portraits executed by Annigoni. It is striking how often an artist's auto-representation has been macabre or grotesque (*vide* Caravaggio who depicted himself in the severed head of Goliath, and Michelangelo whose *Last Judgment* shows his face in St Bartholomew carrying his own flayed skin). The factor of supreme narcissism in self-portraiture is shown in the frequency with which the artist paints himself in some expansive or over-ornate fashion. Thus Dürer, in the third of his self-portraits, identified himself with Christ. The other interesting factor is that of distorted corporeal awareness. Munch in his picture *Between clock and bed* painted in his seventy-eighth year, shows himself as a much younger man. On the other hand Vallotton's almost photographic self-portrait, painted when he was seventeen, shows himself looking far older.

Max Friedlander[10] in his *Art and Connoisseurship* has graphically described the problem from a layman's point of view:

'The self-portrait provides the psychologist with an opportunity for stimulating speculation. Externally it may be recognized through the glance directed decisively at the speaker—since the painter looked at himself in the mirror, and the attention, seemingly addressed to us, was devoted to his own appearance. This entails a self-revelation, an emergence from the picture to a degree which usually is not characteristic of portraits. Man does not take up a neutral or objective attitude towards his own appearance; his participation is coloured more by his "will" than by his "idea". Self-portraits do not confirm the view that we know ourselves better than others. They are not in a particularly high degree "good likenesses". Observation is interfered with by vanity, by ambition. The painter wants to cut a figure; he takes himself over-seriously, portrays himself in a definite situation, namely, as gazing, with open eyes, in tension and action. The ordinary sitter on the other hand, the person whose portrait is being painted, gets tired and bored. For this reason self-portraits are aggressive and dramatic, and not infrequently theatrical. They convey to us less what the painter looked like than what he wanted to look like. One may speak of a rhetoric of the self-portrait.'

7

Disorders of Corporeal Awareness and Parietal Disease

The story of the manifold anomalies of corporeal awareness which may follow brain-disease has often been told and is now familiar to neurologists and psychiatrists. For this reason the various disorders may merely be enumerated. At one end of the scale of defect is simple passive neglect of one limb during what should have been a bimanual activity. More pathological is the syndrome of active unilateral neglect whereby the patient fails to wash, dry, make-up, or clothe one side of the anatomy. When hemiparesis is a conspicuous feature, the patient may display various degrees of awareness. There is anosognosia which though strictly speaking indicates lack of knowledge of the defect, is often extended to the more grave condition of denial of paralysis. Intermediate reactions include illusory projection of the defect on to some unimportant peripheral disorder (e.g. a sprain, rheumatism, etc.). Another is met with in an unexpected lack of concern over the fact of paralysis (anosodiaphoria). Patients who display deeper levels of disintegration may go so far as to deny the ownership of the paralysed limb, and indulge in fantastic confabulation. Quite different is the case where awareness of hemiplegia exists but with a morbid and almost illusory reaction towards the paralysed limb. This misoplegia or hatred of paralysis may be associated with the idea that the palsied arm is shrivelled, ugly, claw-like. Much commoner is the attitude of the chronic hemiplegic who may come to look upon his affected limb as if it were a puppet or play-thing, in a sort of playful semi-detachment. This so-called personification of the paralysed limb is illustrated by the patient's facetious or semi-serious habit of endowing it with a nick-name.

It is conventional to regard these organic anomalies of corporeal awareness as the expression of disease of the non-dominant parietal lobe. Although the volume of clinical supporting evidence is impressive, there are other attitudes which merit serious consideration. Briefly, the current hypotheses comprise the following:

1. That corporeal awareness is a faculty localized within the non-dominant parietal lobe.

2. That it is a parietal faculty in essence, but that lesions of the dominant hemisphere preclude the demonstration of defects, owing to concomitant aphasia.

3. That the various types of unawareness are not necessarily parietal symptoms, but may occur with lesions of the brain in any situation. This is the 'denial syndrome' of Weinstein and Kahn.

4. That the reaction of a patient towards his hemiplegia is the resultant of his previous personality.

5. That the demonstration of these various types of unawareness is

largely an iatrogenic clinical artefact, the product of the peculiar interpersonal relationship as between doctor and patient.

Space will not permit full discussion of these points. Suffice it to say that these foregoing hypotheses are not mutually exclusive.[4, 5, 7, 8]

REFERENCES

1. BONNIER, P., 1905. L'Aschématie. *Rev. neurol.*, **13**, 605–09.
2. CLAPARÈDE, E., 1924. *Arch. Psychol.*, *Genève*, **19**, 172.
3. CRITCHLEY, M., 1950. The body-image in neurology. *Lancet*, i, 335–41.
4. 1953. *The Parietal Lobes.* Arnold. London.
5. 1955. Personification of paralysed limbs in hemiplegics. *Brit. med. J.*, ii, 284.
6. 1955. Quelques observations relative à la notion de la conscience du moi corporel ('corporeal awareness'). *L'Engephale*, **44**, 501–31.
7. 1957. Observations on Anosodiaphoria. *L'Encephale*, **46**, 540–546.
8. 1965. Disorders of corporeal awareness in parietal disease. In *The Body Precept*. Ed. Wapner, S., and Werner, H. New York: Random House.
9. EKBOM, K. A., 1961. Restless legs in amputees. *Act. med. Scand.*, **169**, 419–21.
10. FRIEDLANDER, M. *Art and Connoisseurship*. Oxford: Bruno Kassirer Ltd.
11. HEAD, H., and HOLMES, G., 1911–12. *Brain*, **34**, 102–254.
12. LHERMITTE, J., 1939. *L'image de notre corps*. Paris: Nouvelle Revue Critique.
13. MERLEAU-PONTY M., 1945. *Phénoménologie de la Perception*. Paris: Gallimard.
14. OLSSON, T., 1949. En Linnean om Linné Svenska Linné-sallakapets *Årsskrift*, **32**, 68–70.
15. RIDDOCH, G., 1941. Phantom limbs and body shape. *Brain*, **64**, 197–222.
16. SCHILDER, P., 1935. *The image and appearance of the human body*. London: Kegan Paul, Trench, Trubner.
17. SIMMEL, M. L., 1956. Phantoms in patients with leprosy and in elderly digital amputees. *Amer. J. Psychol.*, **69**, 529–45.
18. 1959. Phantom experiences in mental defective amputees. *J. abnorm. soc. Psychol.*, **50**, 128–30.
19. 1962. Phantom experiences following amputation in childhood. *J. Neur., neurosurg. psych.*, **25**, 69–78.
20. 1966. A study of phantoms after amputation of the breast. *Neuropsychol.*, **4**, 331–50.
21. STOCKERT VON, F. G., 1952. Storungen der Darstellungsfunktion bei Sinnes-defekt. Gleichzeitig ein Beitrag zum Agnosie-Problem. *Nervenarzt*, **23**, 121–26.
22. TODD, J., and DEWHURST, K., 1955. The double: its psycho-pathology and psycho-physiology. *J. nerv. ment. Dis.*, **122**, 47.
23. WEINSTEIN, E., and SERSEN, E. A., 1961. Phantoms in cases of congenital absence of limbs. *Arch. neur. psych.*, **111**, 905–11.

VII

THE PHENOMENA OF HYPNOSIS

Stephen Black

M.R.C.S., L.R.C.P.

Director of a Research Unit in Psychophysiology under the Nuffield Foundation at 43 Wilton Crescent, London, S.W.1 and former grant holder in the Division of Human Physiology of the Medical Research Council

1

Introduction

The Problem of Defining Hypnosis

Since we have no definite knowledge as to the nature of the hypnotic state, it is easier to describe the phenomena of hypnosis than to define hypnosis itself. We can, of course, diagnose hypnosis, although without forewarning to include it in the differential diagnosis, this might not be all that easy. And because hypnosis is apparently a physiological state induced by psychological means, we may describe it as *psychophysiological* and thereby postulate some interaction between mind and body. But we lack any unifying theory as to the nature of mind and matter—or indeed any theory as to the nature of life itself—and as pointed out by Cullen (1960)[25] our concepts of *psyche* and *soma* are dominated by seventeenth-century cartesian dualism. While our thinking in terms of physiology is entirely mechanistic, our ideas on the psyche are, *faute de mieux*, exclusively pyschological—or related to observations of behaviour. Although a reasonably ordered system as the specialty of *psychiatry* has nevertheless been developed, we are not yet agreed on what we mean by 'mind' and we cannot even prove its existence without resorting to the doubtful evidence of extra-sensory perception (Beloff, 1962).[4]

By *genetic* definition, hypnosis is a state of *decreased consciousness which occurs as a result of constrictive or rhythmic stimuli*. But such a definition may not adequately distinguish hypnosis from sleep and since, as we shall see, hypnosis is definitely not sleep, we must abide by the logic of Aristotle and a definition *per genus et differentiam*—which is to make a statement and qualify it in terms of peculiarities.

Many of the peculiarities of hypnosis which most clearly distinguish it from sleep can be conclusively demonstrated only in man, yet to limit hypnosis to the species *Homo sapiens* would be an error, since a state of decreased consciousness which is not sleep can be demonstrated as a result of appropriate stimuli in a wide variety of phyla. Consequently our definition must include the negative qualification that the state of decreased consciousness is sleepless—and further *differentiae* to substantiate this can then be added as we see fit. The more obvious peculiarities which distinguish hypnosis from sleep are therefore considered in the historical order of their scientific investigation.

2

History of Hypnosis Relevant to its Definition

In his *Deliciae physico-mathematicae*, Schwenter[108] reported in 1636 that if the head of a chicken is pressed to the ground and a chalkline drawn forward from the immobilised beak, the bird will remain transfixed without restraint, until roused by some clearly defined stimulus. Kirscher[65] (1646) independently described the same phenomenon, which he claimed as his own *experimentum mirabile*, but his conclusions, like the title of Schwenter's work, largely reflected the scientific climate of the time. Although he postulated 'fantasy constriction' by the chalkline, he also included the effects of 'cosmic magnetism'. In historical order, however, the *catatonia* by which a chicken is immobilised in this way should stand as the first peculiarity which distinguishes hypnosis from sleep—and *constriction* as the first class of stimulus by which hypnosis is produced.

The approach to hypnosis as a biological phenomenon amenable to investigation by animal experiments was interrupted for two hundred years—owing partly to the historical development of science and partly to the publication by Mesmer in 1766 on the medical applications of hypnosis in man.[83] With the advent of a more biological climate in the nineteenth century, interest in 'animal hypnosis' was renewed—mainly by Czermak (1856), who demonstrated hypnosis in many species.[26] The cause of the implied decreased consciousness as the *immobility of catatonia* was first identified by Preyer (1878)—who ascribed this to a fright response[96] which was the view taken by Darwin (1884).[27] Fabre then reported that immobility could be produced in most avian species—simply by swinging the bird to and fro and tucking its head under its wing.[41]

Animal hypnosis is well reviewed by Völgyesi.[121] He points out that although Mesmer emphasised the psychosomatic effects of hypnosis, he described it as 'animal magnetism' and by so doing implied a phenomenon common to all animals, with man included. It has now been shown that catatonic states can be produced by constrictive or rhythmic stimuli in insects, spiders, crustacea, fishes, amphibia, reptiles, birds and in many different species of mammal. However, the reports of these experiments suggest that the term 'constrictive stimulus' should be widely interpreted here to include *disorientation*—as in Fabre's experiments with birds— while in many animals the degree of catatonia may be minimal and *amenability to control* a more accurate description of the resulting state. Many wild animals become only mildly catatonic, but generally amenable if hooded—as in falconry.

Amenability to control raises the element in hypnosis of a second individual being involved—*in effect 'the hypnotist'*—and the degree to which hypnotic states can or cannot be produced without this. Our cartesian concepts of mind and matter, with which Kirscher was also entangled, tend here to confuse the issue and even good Pavlovians like Völgyesi are apt to introduce such terms as 'psychic control' in an effort to bridge the semantic gap. In animal hypnosis some awareness of the environment is maintained even in extreme catatonic states, as evidenced by eye and head following of the hypnotist's movements. In man, this *relative degree of awareness* and the so-called *rapport with the hypnotist* are two of the most significant characteristics which distinguish hypnosis from sleep.

The stimuli producing hypnosis can be imparted by animals of both the same or different species—hypnosis is both intra and interspecific. Moreover, interspecific hypnosis as a form of control of one species of animal by another, is a common phenomenon in nature—as with rodents by reptiles. But intraspecific hypnosis also occurs outside man, as exemplified in breeding habits among the *arachnidae*. Evidence of *autohypnosis* among animals as well as man, without any apparent previous 'hypnotic instruction' raises important issues with regard to the phylogenetic etiology of the hypnotic state. Associated with catatonia, hypnosis is common among many species as an aid to protection by cryptic coloration and mimicry, as exemplified in widely different phyla by the stick mimicry of insects like the mantis *Dixippus* and the wind-mimicry of the bittern *Botaurus*.[121]

Kirscher's suggestion that *magnetism* might be involved in hypnotic induction was an attempt to explain an otherwise inexplicable biological phenomenon in terms of a natural force which was not only equally inexplicable at the time, but was apparently without other biological effects. Given the Newtonian concept that all nature could be explained in the materialistic terms of energy, this was not indeed all that unreasonable. Even today, the fact that unlike such energetic systems as heat, light, sound and electricity, magnetism plays apparently only a meagre biological role, if any, is a current subject for research.

It seems probable that the idea of magnetism in association with hypnosis was fostered as a result of the traditional technique by which the magnetism of one piece of metal is transferred to another—namely by stroking. And this process, moreover, can be accomplished without physical contact, although less effectively. Whatever the facts here, the 'magnetic passes' of Mesmer introduced a new concept to the technique of hypnotic induction—and thereby added *rhythmic stimulation* to constriction as the second class of stimulus by which hypnosis is produced. With his metal tub around which the patients sat holding hands, Mesmer clearly believed that, as with the magnetisation of metals, physical contact produced the most effective results—and he was right, although for the wrong reasons. Current research on hypnotic induction has established beyond question that the best results are achieved if physical contact is made with the subject.[14]

Disentangling hypnosis from magnetism, Braid (1843)[18] then showed that induction could be carried out by eye fixation alone and introduced most of the modern terminology: including the confusing word hypnosis—implying 'sleep' from the Greek *hypnos*—together with 'hypnotism', 'hypnotise' and, most significantly, 'suggestion'. This idea of the role of suggestion which parallels amenability to control, was quickly adopted in France and the concept of *hypnosis as a state of increased suggestibility* was established by Liébeault[72] and then developed by Bernheim at Nancy.[5] It is against this background that the therapeutic effects of suggestion alone, particularly autosuggestion—presumably without autohypnosis—were applied by Coué.[24]

Meanwhile, the use of hypnotic suggestion for both the relief and production of physical symptoms in the form of paralyses, anaesthesias and contractures—localised catatonia—was theatrically demonstrated by Charcot in his clinic at the Salpêtrière hospital in Paris—where Freud attended as a student in 1885. It is now recognised that these famous demonstrations by Charcot were carried out with only a limited *côterie* of patients, whom he had diagnosed as suffering from an ill-defined clinical entity which he described as *hysteria*. With his background in pathological anatomy, Charcot then attempted to explain this condition in terms of somatic peculiarities.[21] As a result, Charcot established *an association between hypnotisability and hysteria* which is still prevalent today.

It is, however, the finding of this author that patients with well-defined physical symptoms of hysterical origin can only rarely be effectively hypnotised—a fact explained by Stafford Clark[113] in terms of a 'diminished capacity for rapport on the part of the patient secondary to an abnormally excessive investment of unconscious mechanisms in the creation of symptoms'. In view of this, one is led to the conclusion that either the diagnostic meaning of hysteria has been changed, or to the unsympathetic deduction that Charcot's 'patients' were more demonstration hypnotic subjects than anything else. On present evidence it would be unreasonable to include any association with hysteria, or the hysterical personality, as further qualification in our definition of hypnosis—even limiting this to the phenomenon in man.

Before leaving Paris, Freud tried unsuccessfully to interest Charcot in the psychological significance of his work, such as the meaning of 'glove and stocking' anaesthesia produced by either hypnotic suggestion or hysteria. But according to Freud's own account, he had himself at that time no hint as to the unconscious etiology involved.[45] It was not until watching Bernheim's experiments at Nancy in 1889, that Freud first 'received the profoundest impression of the possibility that there could be powerful processes which nevertheless remain hidden from the consciousness of man'. As a result of this experience, Freud started his work with Breuer in Vienna, which was eventually to establish the role of the *unconscious mind* in both hypnosis and hysteria and to lay the foundations of psycho-analysis by free association.[44] Almost by definition, therefore, when speaking to a deeply hypnotised subject we are *in direct contact with the unconscious mind of the Freudians.*

The cartesian dichotomy of mind and body eventually divided the *subjective* investigators such as Freud from the *objective* investigators like the physiologist Pavlov—with supporters on both sides, like Adler and Jung on the one hand and the *behaviourist psychologists*, Morgan and Watson, on the other. Already largely denying the philosophical concept of 'consciousness', the behaviourists were from the outset handicapped in the investigation of any state of decreased consciousness, howeverproduced, and their contributions to the study of hypnosis are accordingly minimal. Pavlov's purely physiological approach, however, was more successful.

Having established the existence of *the conditioned reflex*, Pavlov—like Preyer and Darwin—interpreted the phylogeny of hypnosis, and the frequently accompanying catatonia, as an ecological defence mechanism and introduced the concept of a process of *protective inhibition*. But since this resulted from *cortical irradiation of inhibition* and such was already his explanation of sleep, Pavlov failed to make any sharp distinction between the two states.[93]

The conditioned reflex, however, is of importance to our definition because it may explain so much about hypnosis, including the mechanism of induction by rhythmic stimulation. In man, at least, from our earliest days, rhythmic movements are used by the mother to establish a first order conditioned reflex inducing sleep—in which *fatigue* is the unconditioned stimulus, *sleep* the unconditioned response and stroking or patting—with physical contact—as well as rocking and even a lullaby, are the *rhythmic* conditioned stimuli. Phylogenetically, however, *constriction* apparently also constitutes an unconditioned stimulus producing the unconditioned response of *hypnosis*. It is therefore possible that through the *constriction of swaddling in infancy*, a second conditioned reflex is set up in which *rhythmic* stimuli, especially in the absence of fatigue, take over from constriction to induce *hypnosis as the conditioned response*. From this simple system the whole technique of hypnotic induction from Mesmer onwards may be derived.

Whether swaddling in infancy does in fact produce a degree of hypnosis remains in question, although the highly constrictive swaddling practiced among primitive peoples certainly maintains a more relaxed state than is common among European infants. And whether the corollary holds good that hypnotic induction is *therefore* easier among primitive peoples, must await a more controlled investigation of the ecology of hypnotisability. Esdaile's Indian series (1850) of 2,000 surgical operations under hypnotic anaesthesia might support such a hypothesis,[39A] while hypnosis is certainly a common phenomenon in the cults of the African witch doctors.

But the academic question then arises as to whether the stimulus of constriction in producing hypnosis should rightly be described as 'unconditioned', or whether we are not dealing here with a conditioned reflex established in the course of ontological development. Conditioned reflexes can be set up in simple organisms of ancient phylogeny, such as the platyhelminthes, as demonstrated by McConnell with *Planaria* (1962).[86] During development of the embryo, whether *in utero* or *in ovo*, the organism is physically constricted and even in later stages relatively immobile as a result, although some sensibility if not awareness of the environment can be demonstrated. With the organism confined in this way, the primary conditioned reflex of all experience may therefore be set up. Post natally, the conditioned stimulus constriction then produces a conditioned response in the form of the relative immobility and partial sensibility of foetal life—which we observe as the catatonia of hypnosis. It is, of course, possible that foetal immobility is not entirely due to physical constriction and that a degree of endogenous catatonia is essential to survival—although such foetal catatonia is unproven. However, the spontaneous catatonia of animal hypnosis is of the type *flexibilitas cerea* by which the foetus could be safely moulded to its environment—and in support of the general hypothesis, the spontaneous hypnotic posture of most animals is certainly foetal.

3

The Definition of Hypnosis

The various qualifications of the hypnotic state which differentiate it from sleep can now be listed in an historically based definition: *Hypnosis is a sleepless state of decreased consciousness which occurs in most animal phyla as a result of constrictive or rhythmic stimuli usually imparted by another organism and which may be distinguished from sleep by the presence of catatonia, relative awareness or increased suggestibility and in which direct contact is made with the unconscious mind in man.*

4

Induction, Trance Depth and the Form of Suggestion

Hypnotic Induction

The technique of hypnotic induction follows logically from the definition. Confining ourselves to man, the best results will be obtained by a combination of constriction with the conditioned reflexes presumably established in infancy regarding sleep.

Ideally, the subject should therefore be well tucked in with a blanket, lying supine on a comfortable couch with a low, soft pillow, in a silent, warm and darkened room. All anxiety having been relieved by previous discussion, eye fixation should then be established on a suitable object and the increasing suggestibility utilised in an induction monologue overtly suggesting sleep as a euphemism for hypnosis. When the eyes closed, the hypnotist should then stroke the subject's forehead and the monologue be continued with suggestions of deepening sleep—by association with heaviness of the limbs, further relaxation and lowering of the respiration rate. A sample induction monologue on these lines is given by Mason.[80]

By so-called 'post-hypnotic suggestion' (PHS)—which is hypnotic suggestion of responses post hypnosis—any hypnotisable subject can be 'coded' so that induction follows immediately on a single word from the hypnotist—or even a single action. In experimental hypnosis, for instance, the author uses the Greek letter of the subject's first initial and by further suggestion blocks any possibility of it being employed by anyone else, or by the subject, or the letter having any special significance outside the hypnotic situation. It will be noted that since it is essential to relieve anxiety to induce hypnosis, the first answer to the question 'Can a person be hypnotised against his will?' is in the negative. On the other hand, with regard to a subject well-conditioned to go into a deep trance on use of a code, the answer is affirmative.

Trance Depth

In the British population, 5 per cent can be hypnotised into a *deep trance*, following which there is spontaneous amnesia for the period of hypnosis, together with retrograde amnesia for some seconds before induction; 35 per cent can be hypnotised into a *medium trance*, without any subsequent amnesia, but where many of the phenomena of hypnosis can be demonstrated; and the remaining 60 per cent can be only lightly hypnotised. There are probably no psychologically healthy individuals who cannot be hypnotised at all, so that failure to produce hypnosis is likely in itself to be evidence of hysteria—or failure on the part of the hypnotist to relieve the normal anxiety about being hypnotised, or create the right environment.

Whatever the etiology of hypnosis as evoked by suggestions of sleep the response of the *deep-trance subject* to the appropriate stimuli takes place on first induction within about ten seconds. This reaction, indeed is, so immediate that it almost seems to imply the genetic inheritance of a psychophysiological mechanism unrelated to any system of early conditioning—whether in infancy or *in utero*. But although there is some evidence that deep-trance subjects run in families,[121] such subjects are only rarely, if ever, discovered *ab initio* in the elderly—which would indicate a conditioned reflex with protracted Pavlovian decay, unless reinforcement has been provided by hypnosis when younger. Contrary to much of the literature [121, 40] there is in any case no substantial evidence of correlating somatic, or for that matter psychic characteristics with hypnotisability, which would be expected in the presence of a genetic etiology.

While there are elaborate scoring systems for recognition of trance depth,[28, 70] the classification given above has the virtue of simplicity. It may be argued that the diagnosis of amnesia is never easy, but under the controlled conditions of the hypnotic situation, this is not really so difficult: one simple device is to take the subject's wristwatch and subsequently ask the time. Nevertheless, even in these circumstances, the final diagnosis must depend on clinical judgement.

Although there are many deepening techniques described[127, 35, 130] it is not the experience of the author that any medium-trance subject can ever be made into a deep-trance subject. However, there appear to be levels of trance depth for the deep-trance subject—as evidenced by the effectiveness of suggestions of psychophysiological responses—while trance deepening can always be effectively applied to medium and light-trance subjects. Repetition of a code word with suggestions of deepening sleep is a useful method of increasing trance depth, while the 'split suggestion' technique of Mason and Black is of particular value. It involves the deliberate creation of conflict which is followed by deepening of trance as soon as this is relieved and may thereby constitute a further stimulus producing summation.[8]

The Form of Suggestion

The suggestions given to the subject can be of three kinds:

1. Direct Suggestion Under Hypnosis (DSUH).
2. Indirect Suggestion Under Hypnosis (ISUH).
3. Post-hypnotic Suggestion (PHS).

In assessing the significance of any psychophysiological phenomenon produced by hypnotic suggestion, it is important to clarify which of these systems has been employed. DSUH is supposed to imply that the subject's response is a direct result of the suggestion and unrelated to any associated emotional modality. On the other hand, ISUH takes into account the psychophysiological responses to emotion. Thus the suggestion: 'You are hot' is intended as DSUH and investigation of, for example, forearm bloodflow following this suggestion, will produce little or no result. The suggestion: 'You are hot because the house is on fire' is clearly liable to evoke the emotion of anxiety and the plethysmograph record is likely to indicate blood flow changes.[9] The effects of PHS can be both linked with emotion as in ISUH or aimed to avoid this as in DSUH.

To what degree it is ever really possible to impart suggestion under hypnosis without involving some emotional reaction is questionable, but at least the introduction of this terminology by Black[7] has helped to explain much of the confusion evidenced in the early experimental literature. It should be emphasised, however, that with deep-trance subjects at least, the degree of control by the hypnotist would seem to be considerable and that in the experimental situation dealing with problems of mind and body, DSUH as a research tool can produce remarkably consistent results.

5
Classification of Hypnotic Phenomena

All the phenomena produced by hypnosis may be classified as *Psychological* or *Physiological*. In trance, hypnosis *per se* produces those signs by which we distinguish it from sleep, together with the additional phenomena of respiratory changes and possibly tunnel vision. The subsequent effects of hypnosis *per se*—that is, effects post hypnosis—are entirely psychological and limited to the amnesia of the deep-trance subject and a degree of *rapport* with the hypnotist in all subjects. All other phenomena of hypnosis are produced by suggestion.

Not all the spontaneous phenomena are always apparent: thus some respiratory change is always observed—usually as a change in rate, but sometimes only of depth—but catatonia only rarely occurs in response to induction by suggestions of sleep. Although we have every reason to assume increased suggestibility in hypnosis *per se*, it requires suggestion to elicit this, while the demonstration of tunnel vision necessitates not only opening the eyes under hypnosis following suggestion—a feat only per-formed without waking by deep-trance subjects—but specific instructions with regard to the test procedure.

The phenomena produced by hypnosis are thus (A) *Spontaneous* or (B) *In Response to DSUH*, and are either *Psychological* or *Physiological*.

(A) Spontaneous Phenomena
Psychological
(i) Increased suggestibility.
(ii) Rapport.
(iii) Deep-trance amnesia.
(iv) Contact with the unconscious mind.

Physiological
  (v) Relative awareness compared with sleep.
  (vi) Catatonia.
  (vii) Respiratory changes.
  (viii) Tunnel vision.

(B) Phenomena in Response to DSUH

Psychological
  (ix) Amnesia.
  (x) Emotional changes.
  (xi) Perceptual changes.
  (xii) Psychological age-regression.

Physiological
  (xiii) Neuro-sensory.
  (xiv) Neuro-motor.
  (xv) Autonomic.
  (xvi) Epitheliological.

Although the phenomena under (B) are listed as being produced by DSUH, they can occur in response to ISUH, or PHS. The *biochemical*, *endocrinological* and *immunological* effects produced by DSUH are considered as they may be related to the autonomic and epitheliological phenomena. The hypothesis that hypnosis may also have a role in *oncology*, although by no means untenable, is omitted here in the absence of sufficient evidence to this effect, in spite of a considerable literature on the subject, most of which is reviewed by Kroger.[69, 97]

6

(A) Spontaneous Phenomena of Hypnosis

Spontaneous Psychological Phenomena

Increased suggestibility. A suggestible person as defined, is one who responds to implication in the absence of a rational need for response. A state of *increased suggestibility* should therefore involve a decrease in the ability of a subject to assess the rational need for response. The concept of suggestibility in hypnosis thus implies some limitation of the cerebral mechanisms concerned with the analysis of stimuli, but we have as yet no objective evidence to substantiate this. The EEG record of intrinsic cerebral rhythms under hypnosis is apparently identical with that in the relaxed state,[2 36,] while without suggestion, no change in the pattern or amplitude of evoked potentials can be recorded over any part of the cerebral cortex (Black and Walter).[17]

The clinical evidence, however, is clear, even the evidence of the stage hypnotists: under hypnosis, by DSUH, the subject can easily be persuaded to perform acts which go beyond the rational need for response. With some cunning and ISUH, the deep-trance subject could in fact be made to follow almost any suggestion within his powers: and the truthful answer to the other old question 'Can the hypnotised subject be made to perform acts contrary to his moral code?' is a qualified *affirmative*. Numerous statements in the literature taking an opposite view would seem to be more a public relations campaign by hypnotists than a scientific observation. But leaving aside the individual nature of the relationship between the Freudian censor and the id, there are in any case varying depths of even deep-trance hypnosis, and if the subject is not deep enough, or this inadvisable experiment is inadequately designed, the most likely result is the elegant creation of an experimental neurosis.

Rapport. Freud eventually interpreted *hypnotic rapport* in terms of the positive transference of psychoanalysis, relating it to the Oedipus and Electra complexes,[46, 98] while Watkins[126] suggests that hypnosis occurs spontaneously in analytic sessions. Whether identical with the positive transference or not, the rapport of hypnosis evokes the dependence of the child-parent relationship and the normal erotic attachments of the Freudian family drama. As both Breuer and Freud found, it is the doctor's dilemma when practising hypnosis, that in a manner eschewed by the psychoanalysts, he must create an intimate environment and include with it a degree of physical contact, if he is to be sure of achieving maximum results. Failure to do so may result in failure of treatment and the general use of hypnotherapy is not therefore to be recommended. With the five per cent of deep-trance subjects, on the other hand, such is the degree of suggestibility that adequate control of rapport can in fact be maintained.

Deep-trance Amnesia. The spontaneous amnesia of the deep-trance subject only relates to the experience under hypnosis, while under hypnosis there is no amnesia either for previous hypnotic experience or for experience in the waking state. Indeed, there is much to suggest that under deep-trance hypnosis there is little amnesia concerning our dreams. Hypnosis would therefore seem to be a level of consciousness in which all recorded experience may be amenable to recall.

In diagnosing the spontaneous amnesia of the deep-trance, given the ideal induction environment and the most effective technique, some degree of rapport is liable to be established in a single session with even a light-trance subject—let alone a medium-trance subject. Since the subject may be aware that spontaneous amnesia has been taken as a criterion of deep-trance, this immediate development of *rapport* is liable to evoke a desire to please with pretence of amnesia. This is important in research when screening for deep-trance subjects for experimental purposes, and also in the application of hypnosis to medicine. Given control provided by the deep-trance, the physician may for example be prepared to take on management of an asthmatic case in such a way, but a simple error in the diagnosis of hypnotic amnesia could make this a task for which he is unprepared.

Contact with the Unconscious Mind. Deep-trance hypnosis provides the most useful means available for immediate demonstration of the existence of the unconscious mind. The spontaneous amnesia of the deep-trance is alone indicative of a level of experience of which we have no conscious memory, while the recall of procedures under hypnosis from one session to another, without any conscious memory of these procedures in between or afterwards, is particularly convincing. When this is combined with the effects of PHS that the subject will behave in a particular way, the evidence is irrefutable—especially as the subject will frequently explain an apparently anomalous action with an immediately available *rationalisation*.

Existence of the unconscious is still questioned in some circles— notably among behaviourist psychologists—and demonstrations of this kind might usefully be included in the curriculum of medical training. But it is significant that the existence of the unconscious as revealed in this way, often produces a degree of resistance in the audience and a consequent search for rationalisation, no doubt unconsciously motivated. Phylogenetically it is not without reason that the greater part of the mind remains unconscious and the revelation that in such a simple manner contact can immediately be made with this part can be disturbing.

Many phenomena of hypnosis are best explained by this direct contact with the unconscious. Given the supposition that a large part of *conscious motivation* is of unconscious etiology and the power of hypnotic *rapport*, if instruction is given to the unconscious either by DSUH, ISUH or PHS, it is not surprising, for example, that individuals can be motivated to concentrate on the process of *learning*[119]—or that a supposed *accuracy in time judgement* can be produced.[114] The validity of time judgement phenomena, however, should be carefully checked against time judgement in the waking state *in an environment entirely devoid of distraction*—which is the environment obtaining for the hypnotised subject.

Spontaneous Physiological Phenomena

Relative awareness compared with sleep. In light and medium-trance subjects, conversation with the hypnotist, or even with a third person present, is immediately possible, but with deep-trance subjects the ability to speak itself may require initial suggestion and the subject is nearly always spontaneously 'deaf' to anything but the voice of the hypnotist, unless told otherwise. When light and medium-trance subjects are instructed to open their eyes, they usually wake up as a result—even when suggestion is given to the contrary. But following DSUH to open the eyes, the deep-trance subject will respond and remain hypnotised without qualifying instruction. In some subjects a state of apparent wakefulness can be created in this way if the blanket suggestion is given that the subject will 'see, hear and feel' as if awake, but remain 'asleep'. Such individuals evidence a 'withdrawn' appearance strikingly reminiscent of schizophrenia —an appearance which may also occur in some subjects post-hypnosis when unacceptable PHS has been given.

Catatonia. Although spontaneous catatonia rarely occurs in response to induction by suggestion of sleep, this has nevertheless been seen as *flexibilitas cerea* in naive deep-trance subjects who have not had the opportunity of observing or learning about hypnosis. Such individuals are now rare in Britain—if only because of television and a copious popular literature—and the author's two cases were both young nurses in PTS, Irish and Indian. Spontaneous catatonia which is not always wax-like, can, however be readily observed in hypnosis as induced by rhythmic stimuli in the rituals of primitive peoples—a fact which may have led to the erroneous diagnosis of many such cataleptic states in trance as the tetany of alkalemia due to hyperventilation without reference to hypnosis.

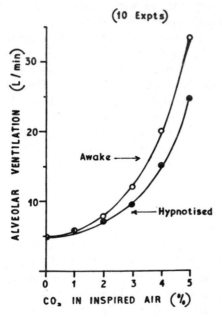

Mean alveolar ventilation
vs.
Percent CO_2 in inspired air
for deep trance subjects

(10 Expts)

FIG. 1. The effect of hypnosis *per se* on respiration: breathing 5 per cent Co_2, there is a drop of 32 per cent in the alveolar ventilation. (Black and Pugh.)

Among the Yoruba in Nigeria, the author has observed a sacrificial ritual by the Sopono smallpox cult, in which five out of some forty women present ended in trance with catatonia—which was then rendered wax-like through passive arm flexion by the 'witches' in charge. In the Aladura church, six in a hundred went into trance but without catatonia. In both instances, subsequent screening for hypnotisability under clinical conditions, revealed that these eleven women were all deep-trance subjects, while in random control groups from both cults, only light or medium-trance subjects were discovered.

Respiratory changes. Since a lowered respiration rate occurs in sleep, it is not surprising that hypnotic induction by suggestions of sleep should have a similar effect. Doust[34] has shown that the level of arterial oxygen saturation is a function of trance depth: anoxaemia increases as trance deepens. Black and Pugh measured the alveolar ventilation at different concentrations of carbon dioxide in the inspired air—and the effects of hypnosis on breath holding.[14] Breathing five per cent carbon dioxide, deep-trance subjects when hypnotised showed a drop of 33 per cent in the alveolar ventilation. They could also hold their breath longer under hypnosis.

These results suggest some decrease in sensitivity of the respiratory mechanism similar to that which occurs in sleep as well as in hibernation and aestivation.

Tunnel vision. Although this phenomenon might well be classified as *perceptual*, it can at least be demonstrated by the clinical confrontation test of the visual fields, whatever the subjective element involved in this procedure. Since deep-trance subjects alone can open their eyes under hypnosis without waking, the phenomenon can only be effectively demonstrated under such conditions, although medium-trance subjects told to

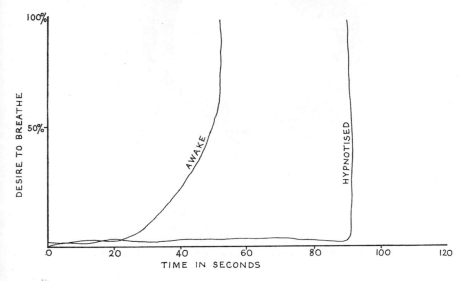

FIG. 2. Under hypnosis the subjective experience of any experiment can be re-lived by the subject through appropriate time regression. This graph plotting the subjective desire to breathe against time was drawn by a deep-trance subject after breath-holding experiments—a hundred per cent 'desire to breathe' being the point on the ordinate when a breath had to be taken. (Black and Pugh.)

open their eyes, may still evidence some narrowing of the visual fields even if apparently awake. It is the author's view that minor degrees of hypnosis may affect vision in this way when driving and that this phenomenon is of importance to road safety, given rhythmic stimulation from the engine and eye fixation on a straight road with white lines, or 'cat's eyes' at night.

In the deep-trance subject hypnotised with eyes open, visual field testing with a perimeter elegantly demonstrates the delicacy of research into hypnotic phenomena in general. While the clinical confrontation technique nearly always produces evidence of tunnel vision, the result with a perimeter may depend on the position of the hypnotist and the semantics of the test instruction. If the hypnotist does not sit immediately in front of the seated subject, both fields will tend to expand so as to take in an area at the side which includes his presence. Moreover, the instruc-

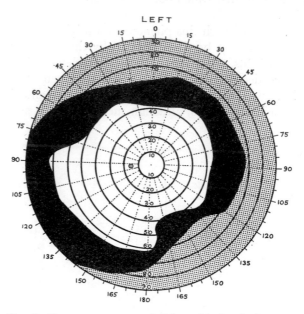

FIG. 3. Spontaneous tunnel vision of a deeply hypnotised subject as measured with a perimeter. Owing to the complications of this test and the semantics involved the constriction recorded in this way is never as great as in the simple 'confrontation' test of the clinicians. (Black.)

tion: 'Tell me when you see *this object* appear' may produce only limited evidence of tunnel vision, whereas the instruction: 'Tell me when you see *anything* appear' may produce evidence of visual field constriction by as much as two thirds. The subjective report describes this phenomenon as akin to intense concentration on the centre of the visual field without any precise blocking of peripheral vision. It may be, therefore, that the *test instruction* of eye fixation evokes the phenomenon by suggestion—in which circumstances, of course, the tunnel vision of hypnosis should not really be classified as spontaneous.

7

(B) Phenomena in Response to DSUH

Psychological Phenomena by DSUH

Amnesia. Subsequent amnesia for the period of the hypnotic trance can be induced in good medium-trance subjects by DSUH—a fact which has no doubt contributed to confusion as to the proportion of deep-trance subjects in the community: a figure frequently given as being around 20 per cent for European stock.[69, 80] Some amnesia, indeed, for past events prior to the hypnotic session may also be produced in medium-trance subjects in this way, but the responses in both instances are always more ambiguous than with deep-trance subjects.

Taking the phenomenon of amnesia as produced in deep-trance hypnosis as our model, the spontaneous amnesia of the deep-trance can immediately be relieved *in toto* or in part by DSUH in the course of a session—the subject can be made to remember everything that happened while under hypnosis, or to recall only isolated material. Moreover, this relief of deep-trance amnesia can apply to previous hypnotic sessions—and even hypnotic sessions by another hypnotist. If an attempt to 'block' such recall has been made by the previous hypnotist with DSUH, the ability of the subject to overcome this would then seem to depend upon the relative degrees of rapport involved.

The amnesia for events prior to the hypnotic session which can be produced by DSUH in deep-trance subjects, can be apparently quite complete and diagnostically difficult to distinguish from amnesia of organic origin without other signs—or an appropriate history. Single events of only a few seconds duration and whole periods up to many years can be wiped from the subject's memory, while total amnesia to simulate a case of memory loss, as in an hysterical fugue, may be created at will. All such hypnotic amnesia can immediately be relieved by the hypnotist—even with the blanket 'clearing' suggestion: 'Everything is now quite normal again.'

Experimental studies on the *depth of hypnotic amnesia*, using the stylus maze, are reported by Coors[23] and the *quantity of amnesia* was investigated by Strickler.[116] Taking the view of Dorcus[32] that amnesia is the reverse of learning, Scott[107] set up conditioned reflexes with a buzzer as the conditioned stimulus, in subjects both waking and hypnotised. He showed that production of the conditioned reflex is potentiated by hypnosis. Pavlov had previously shown that extinction can result from hypnosis in dogs[120] and in general it was shown by Paterson *et al*[90] that most of the phenomena of the conditioned reflex are potentiated by appropriate DSUH, including the 'forgetting' of extinction.

We still have no real knowledge as to the degree of total experience recorded and even after 300 years there is little to challenge the *tabula rasa* of Locke. But the evidence of psychoanalysis indicates at least the degree to which things can be forgotten—and why—and the amnesia produced by

DSUH supports this. The therapeutic applications, however, are limited, bearing in mind the psychodynamics of Freudian forgetting and the role of repression in the etiology of neurosis Whatever the nature of a traumatic experience, the temptation to relieve immediate suffering by hypnotic amnesia should be resisted—even for short periods

Emotional Changes. The most easily demonstrated of all hypnotic phenomena is control of emotion by DSUH. Emotional sensitivity to the ambient emotional climate is the basis of social intercourse and under hypnosis this is exaggerated. Even without DSUH the subject may respond spontaneously to the emotions of the hypnotist without his knowing it—so that however well the hypnotist may have thought to conceal, for example, his depression, a similar state is later reported by the subject. It is unwise to embark on induction unless in an equable state of mind and to hypnotise when ill is always liable to produce complications.

By DSUH in all healthy subjects, variations in the emotional modality can virtually always be obtained and it is tempting to think that agitated, depressed or anxious patients could easily be helped in such a way. But once again, the use of hypnosis is disappointing. As with all hypnotic phenomena, the resulting effect is a function of the depth of trance and even with a deep-trance subject, although apparent relief may be obtained in trance, the effect rarely persists for more than a few days after waking —and usually only hours—following which the state of the patient is liable to be worse than before. Lacking, of course, is the essential process of interpretation of unconscious material at the conscious level which is the basis of psychoanalysis.

Even when a distressing emotional state is entirely rational in origin— as in the bereaved or with those crossed in love—although in a deep-trance subject both DSUH and ISUH may be employed to create a new outlook and to encourage belief in the healing quality of time, this also is not advisable and may produce later complications. The catharsis of grief is no doubt of value in itself and patients treated in such a way often find it difficult to make the readjustment of their lives necessary to find subsequent happiness.

Without getting too lost in the nature of 'reality' in the terms of Locke or other English empiricists—or entangled with Kant and Hegel—it is commonsense to question the *reality of hypnotic phenomena* and aware as we all are of the theatrical tradition that 'the show must go on', the emotional changes produced by DSUH are no exception. In this respect, however, an objective physiological change is always a help to the philosopher, although the complications of dealing with human emotion as an experimental entity are legion. Black and Friedman investigated variations in the plasma cortisol levels (hydrocortisone) as produced by changes in the emotional modality following DSUH in deep-trance subjects.[15] Their evidence shows that although forceful DSUH of fear, anxiety and tension may produce rises in the plasma cortisol—sometimes by 50 per cent—DSUH of happiness and elation have no effect. Black, on the other hand, has shown that the flicker-fusion frequency threshold rises with DSUH of happiness,[13] but this was apparently unchanged following suggestions of unhappiness possibly less heroic than those in the Black and Friedman experiments. In any case not all subjects in either of these experimental series provided positive data, but if we recognise that it is

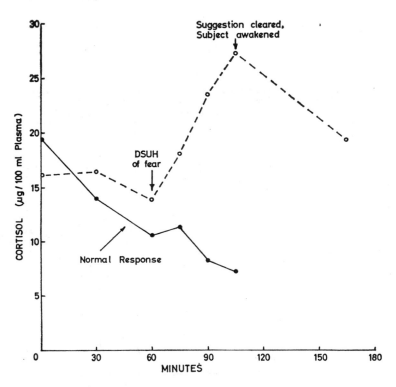

FIG. 4. From 09.00 hours there is a steady drop in the plasma cortisol level (hydrocortisone), but DSUH of 'fear' at 15.00 hours produces a sharp rise lasting 45 minutes. (Black and Friedman.)

always easier for a subject to accept suggestions of happiness than to experience fear or anxiety which is more real than histrionic, it may be concluded that while the plasma cortisol level is *in fact* unchanged on DSUH of elation, the effect of depression on the flicker-fusion threshold remains equivocal.

Perceptual changes. Here the philosophical problem of reality obtrudes more than ever, for we are dealing with subjective experience. If we define perception as the central organisation of peripheral sensory data, a distinction can be made between the perceptual changes produced by DSUH and the neuro-sensory phenomena discussed later. However, the effects in both are profound and this classification may be largely academic: if the sensory data are rendered erroneous at any level, their organisation is likely to produce perceptual errors, whatever the categorical analysis.

We all desire magic and even more than the rarely achieved instant cure of hysterical symptoms, the perceptual changes of hypnosis seem magical in the extreme. The subjective evidence indicates that a perceptual

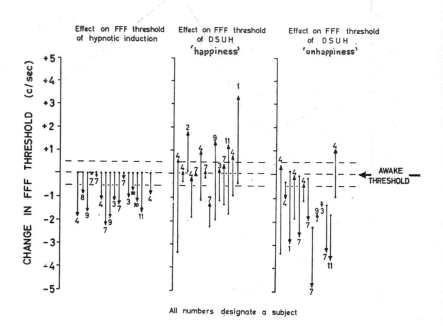

CHANGES IN FLICKER FUSION FREQUENCY (FFF) THRESHOLD
AFTER INDUCTION OF HYPNOSIS
AND AFTER DIRECT SUGGESTION UNDER HYPNOSIS (DSUH)
OF MOOD CHANGES
(43 Expts)

FIG. 5. The FFF shows evidence of a spontaneous drop on hypnotic induction and is raised by DSUH of 'happiness'. The results of DSUH of 'happiness' are, however, equivocal. (Black.)

change involving any sensory modality can be produced by DSUH. Such responses can refer to the *special senses* and to *all other modes of sensibility* of the peripheral nervous system. The result in each case is essentially an *hallucination*, which may be either *positive*, in the sense that perception is present without sensory data, or *negative* in the sense that perception is absent in the presence of sensory stimuli.

In response to DSUH the deep-trance subject will report seeing, hearing, smelling and tasting in the absence of appropriate stimuli, as well as any experience usually derived from peripheral stimulation, both cutaneous and deep. These responses may be produced individually or together—and indeed, according to the subjective report, there seem to be few limits to the hallucinatory experience of hypnosis, especially when ISUH is employed in motivation.

Taking visual perception as a model, in response to DSUH, a deep-trance subject will report seeing virtually anything the hypnotist suggests. Thus a suggestion may be given that somebody known to the subject is sitting in an empty chair and apparently in a manner similar to the technique of 'in-lay' in television production—a person in one studio is super-imposed against a background in another—the hallucinated image is displayed against an appropriate area of background which in turn is negatively hallucinated.

Such hallucinations can be produced with the eyes closed or open—and also by PHS. By further DSUH of aural hallucination, the subject will carry on conversation with the image and the *histrionic* and remarkably *creative quality* of the experience becomes apparent—especially when suggestion of the hallucinated individual is deliberately vague, or un-structured. In this fantasy situation, not all subjects speak aloud and await an unheard reply, but may 'carry on the conversation' in silence before reporting.

Just as negative hallucination of the background is implied in positive hallucination, so the background seems to be positively hallucinated in negative hallucination. When DSUH is given that a third person present, is absent—or has never existed—the subject's visual perception in the positively hallucinated area obscured by the third person, can be tested. If a hand is held in this obscured area, it is said to be invisible by the subject—but if the subject is then asked how many fingers are extended, although the first guess may be disconcertingly right, repetition soon demonstrates the absence of magic. But the important point here is the depth of our desire for magic and the remarkable degree to which a serious academic audience may seem to expect otherwise—no doubt also influenced by unconscious identification with the subject. Of interest too is the disturb-ing subjective experience of the negatively hallucinated individual himself.

By DSUH normal sleep can be induced in the course of a hypnotic session—as demonstrated by EEG evidence of sleep spindles. In such sleep, or indeed in normal sleep at night, specific dreams can then be produced by PHS. Meares[82] utilises this fact in hypno-analysis while Kroger suggests that hallucinated material of all kinds following unstruc-tured suggestions, can be of value after the manner of play-analysis in child psychiatry.[69] Such unstructured hallucinations certainly throw light on the subject's unconscious motivation, although this is often coloured by the effects of *rapport*—but since the technique must apply to only 5 per cent of the population, it can hardly have any serious therapeutic applica-tion.

Anterior Cortical Responses to Peripheral Stimuli
Average of 12 Presentations.

(a)   Click only.

(b)   Flash only.

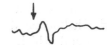

(c)   Click only, after 48 present-
       ations, showing Habituation.

(d)   Flash only, after 48
       presentations,
       showing Habituation.

(e)   Irregular Click followed regularly by Flash (as Flicker
      at 15 c.p.s.) showing Contingent Habituation.

(f)   Contingent Habituation accentuated by Motor Response.

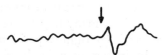

(g)   Return of Flash Response on withdrawal of Click.

Calibration.   20μV

◄─ 1 sec ─►

FIG. 6. *Objective Evidence of Cortical Changes in the Presence
of Hypnotic Hallucination.* (Black and Walter.)
The Phenomenon of 'Contingent Habituation'. Averaged evoked
potentials in anterior non-specific cortex to clicks and flashes
are shown at (a) and (b) and the responses after monotonous
repetition at (c) and (d)—where the negative component
(upwards) is diminished by 'habituation'. (e): irregular
presentation of click S_1 followed regularly by flash S_2 maintains the negative spike of S_1, but diminishes or abolishes this
negative component in the response to S_2 by *contingent
habituation*, a process augmented but not dependent upon an
operant response at S_2 (f). On withdrawal of irregular click
(S_1), the response to the irregular flash (S_2) returns.

Plate I

Demonstration by the author of *flexibilitas cerea* in a hypnotized rabbit. Although the spontaneous hypnotic posture is foetal with flexed limbs, on passive extension these remain in the position shown. Hypnotic induction is by simple constriction of the animal on its back, with one hand over the eyes (Photo: K. Black).

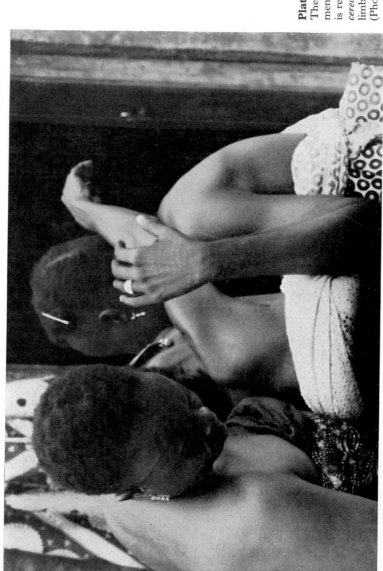

Plate II
The spontaneous catatonia of a hypnotized member of the Sopono cult in Nigeria is rendered wax-like to produce *flexibilitas cerea* through passive flexion of the limbs by the 'witches' in charge (Photo: **P.** Daly).

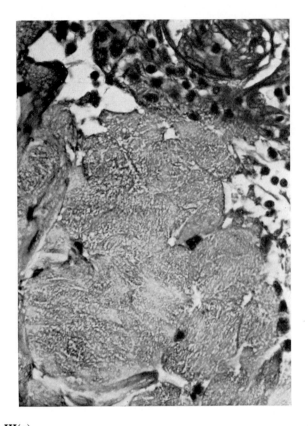

Plate III(a)

Detail of connective tissue of hypodermis close to a blood-vessel showing the loose reticular structure of the collagen in the normal uninhibited response to P.P.D. in a tuberculin-sensitive subject, giving a clinical/Mantoux-positive reaction (X 645).

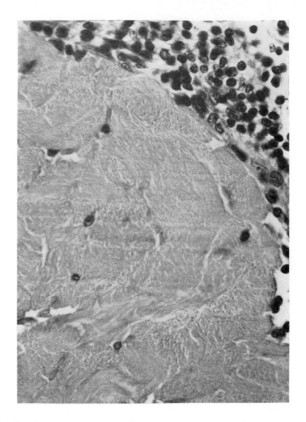

Plate III(b)

Detail similar to that in (*a*) showing the compact character of the collagen in the inhibited response of a tuberculin-sensitive subject, giving a clinically Mantoux-negative reaction following DSUH 'not to react'. This histological evidence suggests that a vascular constituent of the reaction is involved in the mechanism of inhibition by DSUH (X 645).

Histrionic versions of perceptual symptoms in neuropsychiatry can be demonstrated in suitable subjects by DSUH, while reports of paraesthesiae and pain are easily elicited. Such effects may occur spontaneously in response to ISUH and Black has noted the significant *precordial pain* often reported when attempted DSUH of nothing but 'unhappiness' is given and its likely relation to this common psychosomatic symptom.[14]

The Effects of Dilution of Probability on Anterior Cortical Responses.

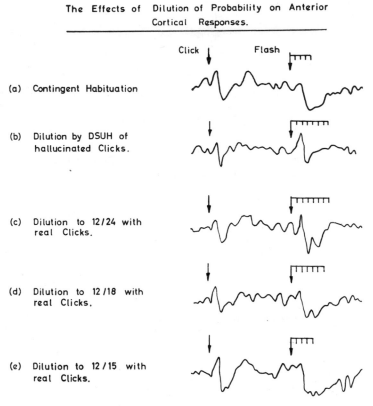

FIG. 7. *Effects of Probability on Contingent Habituation.* When the probability of association between S_1 and S_2 is 'diluted' by DSUH of additional *hallucinated* and unassociated clicks, the negative component in the response to S_2 returns (b). This also occurs when dilution is carried out with *real* additional and unassociated clicks (c) and the magnitude of the negative component in the response to S_2 is shown to be a direct function of the degree of dilution – or an inverse function of the probability.

None of these phenomena, however, prove convincing to the discerning neurologist and a relatively central rather than a peripheral change is always implied.

Electro-neurophysiological investigation shows alpha-blocking following DSUH of hallucination, as with any process demanding attention. However, objective evidence of *cortical changes related to the nature of the hypnotic hallucination* was found in 1963 by Black and Walter.[17] Using electronic averaging of EEG records, they investigated the effects on evoked potentials in the anterior non-specific cortex of variations in the probability of association between stimuli. When two stimuli of the same

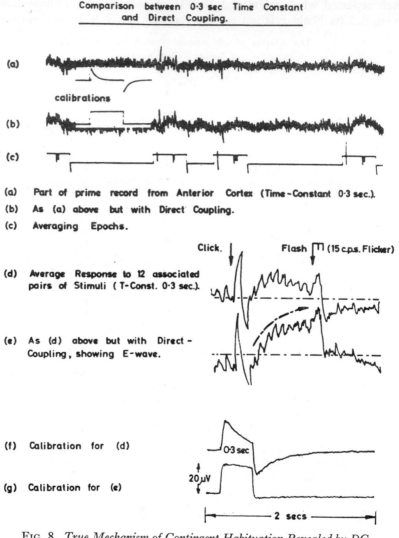

Comparison between 0·3 sec Time Constant and Direct Coupling.

(a)

calibrations

(b)

(c)

(a)   Part of prime record from Anterior Cortex (Time-Constant 0·3 sec.).

(b)   As (a) above but with Direct Coupling.

(c)   Averaging Epochs.

Click.   Flash ⊓ (15 c.p.s. Flicker)

(d)   Average Response to 12 associated pairs of Stimuli (T-Const. 0·3 sec.).

(e)   As (d) above but with Direct - Coupling, showing E-wave.

(f)   Calibration for (d)

0·3 sec

20 µV

(g)   Calibration for (e)

|←   2 secs   →|

FIG. 8. *True Mechanism of Contingent Habituation Revealed by DC.* Prime records from anterior non-specific cortex are shown at (a) with 0·3 second time constant and at (b) with directly coupled amplifiers. At (d) using a 0·3 second TC, contingent habituation is present and at (e) the true mechanism of this effect is revealed by DC as a slow contingent negative variation (CNV)—Expectancy Wave or E-wave. Thus with a 0·3 sec. TC the negative component in the response to the flash (S$_2$), is engulfed in this transient DC shift. It was in this way that the CNV was discovered.

or different modalities are associated in time, interaction results from irregular presentation of the first (S_1), followed regularly by the second (S_2). By such 'contingent habituation' the negative component in the non-specific cortical response to S_1 is maintained, while that to S_2 is diminished: an effect augmented, but not dependent upon inclusion in the experimental design of an operant response at S_2 (Walter, 1964).[123]

Working with this phenomenon, Black and Walter based their experimental design on the hypothesis that the amount of information received by an organism about its environment would be—according to information theory—a function of the improbability of the events detected by the senses. They showed that when the probability of association between clicks (S_1) and flashes (S_2) was diluted with frequent hallucinated, additional and unassociated clicks reported by the subject to have been produced by DSUH, contingent habituation was abolished—and the negative component in the response to S_2 reappeared. This also occurred when the probability of association was diluted with real, additional and unassociated clicks. By dilution with varying proportions of such real clicks, the magnitude of the negative component in the response to S_2 was found to be a function of the degree of dilution—thus supporting the hypothesis. Significantly, however, no effect was produced unless the diluting stimuli were identical with S_1.

Black and Walter repeated this work with a number of different sensory modalities and concluding that their results suggested one way in which hypnotic suggestion may influence the perception of reality, the cortical mechanisms involved were investigated further. Recording with directly coupled amplifiers (DC), it was demonstrated that in contingent habituation there is a slow 'contingent negative variation' (CNV) in which the negative component in the response to S_2 appears to be engulfed: thereby explaining how it comes to be abolished in recordings with a short time-constant. As expected, this CNV was then found to disappear as contingent habituation was abolished by DSUH of diluting hallucinated clicks, while dilution with varying proportions of real clicks showed that its magnitude was an *inverse* function of the degree of dilution (Walter *et al.*, 1964[125]; Walter, 1965[124]).

For some years confusing artefacts due to eye movements threw justifiable doubt on the validity of the CNV, but not on the effects of either real or hypnotic dilution on contingent habituation. In 1966, however, this cerebral phenomenon was finally confirmed by Low *et al.*[74]—principally by demonstration in a subject with enucleated eyes—although their interpretation appeared to put undue emphasis on the effects of an operant response at S_2. Basically a transient DC shift in the standing potential and alternatively described as the 'expectancy wave' or E-wave, the CNV is therefore a cerebral mechanism which is amenable to change following DSUH of a precisely defined hallucination. It thereby provides objective evidence of the subjective hallucinatory experience and indicates

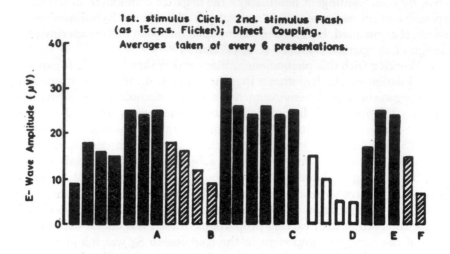

Amplitude of Expectancy Wave and Dilution of Probability of Associations.

1st. stimulus Click, 2nd. stimulus Flash
(as 15 c.p.s. Flicker); Direct Coupling.

Averages taken of every 6 presentations.

(i) Probability undiluted giving 42/42 at A.

(ii) Diluted giving 24/48 at B.

(iii) Undiluted giving 36/36 at C.

(iv) Extinction, Clicks only 24 at D.

(v) Undiluted giving 18/18 at E.

(vi) Diluted giving 12/24 at F.

FIG. 9. *Effects of Probablity on the CNV.* The magnitude of the CNV or Expectancy Wave is shown to be a direct function of the probability of association between paired stimuli (S_1) click and (S_2) flash, when S_1 is irregularly presented, followed regularly by S_2 – or an inverse function of the degree of dilution of probability with additional, real and unassociated clicks. At (A), (C) and (E) the probability of association between S_1 and S_2 is taken by the anterior non-specific cortex as a hundred per cent $(p = 1)$; at (B), $p = 0.5$; at (D), p is approaching zero; at (F), $p = 0.5$ again. Clearly the cortex takes previous experience into account so that the response to $p = 1$ immediately after (B) $(p = 0.5)$ is very large and continues so to (C), while at (D) there is still minimal expectancy following the 102 presentations up to (C). Dilution with unassociated clicks hallucinated by DSUH produces precisely these same effects and the CNV therefore provides objective evidence of the subjective hallucinatory experience.

the degree to which an hallucination can accurately imitate reality—indeed, the effects on the CNV of hallucination and reality appear to be identical.

Psychological Age-regression. The 'genuineness' of this phenomenon has been debated in the literature,[32, 69, 80] although the meaning of 'genuine' in this instance is ill-defined. When DSUH is given to 'go back in time' to a particular age or date, the deep-trance subject will behave in the appropriate manner. Regressed to childhood the subject will talk in a childish voice, behave childishly and write as a child. There are many records in the literatures of handwriting tests from the age of three onwards, carried out in this way.

Dorcus[32] accepts as 'genuine' a state of age-regression in which absence of any knowledge, skills or even reflexes acquired subsequent to the age of regression can be demonstrated—and on this basis there is no argument. Subjects regressed to infancy should be incontinent and lose rapport with the hypnotist—which is not the case. The most thorough investigation here is by Orne.[88] The analysis of drawings made by subjects regressed to childhood showed in fact only 'sophisticated over simplification', while a series of Rorschach studies revealed no consistent change other than a lowering of the 'form level': a feature of the Rorschach record most subject to conscious control and mood. He concluded that the personality organisation may change, but it remains that of the adult. In any case, simple tests of the day of the week on certain dates easily demonstrates the confabulation involved in age-regression.

Much play has been made with the *Babinsky reflex* elicited in subjects regressed to an age younger than six months, as demonstrated by Gidro-Frank and Buch[47] and confirmed by True and Stevenson.[117] The phenomenon can certainly be reproduced with consistency. First, it is the view taken here that no relevance one way or another, should be attributed to the demonstration of this phenomenon in medically trained subjects—students and nurses being standard source material—for there is no evidence that the anatomist with hysterical anaesthesia of hand and forearm, produces anything other than the expected glove distribution. Secondly, the *Babinsky reflex can be elicited in sleep although not in hypnosis per se*, and since we may presume that regression to infancy implies a sleeping infant—evidenced indeed by the subject's behaviour—and sleep can so easily be induced under hypnosis, *spontaneous sleep* may well be the explanation of this much debated phenomenon.

Under stress we all regress to the emotional, if not the intellectual climate of childhood. Given the concept of physiological *hysteresis* and the ability of the unconscious to create that 'running together in time and space' noted by Freud, it is conceivable that the psychological regression of hypnosis is in part physiologically based. The hypnotic subject may thus draw upon consciously forgotten material of many 'memory modalities' to create the appropriate mood in which to confabulate a super-structure of detail. For there are striking anecdotes in this field. The author has regressed three overtly dextral deep-trance stammerers to the day when they 'first learned to write' and found each of them anxious, or even agitated with an imaginary pencil in the left hand—and apparently being instructed to use the right. A psoriasis patient whose condition followed upon a BCG inoculation at 14 years, when regressed to the moment of the injection, first produced a convincing display of childish response to pain in the left arm. But he did better than that: at 48 hours the nursing sister at his factory—quite unaware of the situation—telephoned that she had inspected the 'injection area on his left arm' of which he was complaining and that this now seemed 'rather inflamed' and asked for him to be seen. Unfortunately, by the time he arrived, this only example of the phenomenon of *hypnotic stigmata* ever encountered by this author, had been relieved—because, as the subject put it under hypnosis, 'I was coming to see you'.

Physiological Phenomena by DSUH

Neuro-sensory. These can apparently involve any part of the nervous system, but as with all neurological phenomena produced by DSUH, the changes are essentially those of the so-called *hysterical conversion symptoms* and perhaps the only genuine neurological distinction possible is between the sensory and motor effects as given. Sensory changes in the CNS can be either *positive* or *negative*—in as much as the subject may respond in the absence of stimuli, or fail to respond when stimuli are present.

The most significant *peripheral sensory phenomenon* produced by DSUH is the negative change of *anaesthesia*. Compared with other hypnotic phenomena, both this and hyperaesthesia are relatively independent of trance depth. Light-trance subjects in whom virtually no other hypnotic phenomena can be demonstrated, easily lose cutaneous sensibility to pain in response to hypnotic suggestion. Nevertheless it requires a good medium-trance subject—with stoical disposition at that—to achieve a depth of anaesthesia under which even minor surgery can be carried out. But in the deep-trance subject, complete and lasting anaesthesia can easily be produced and there are many records in the literature of major surgical operations performed in this way—including mammaplasty[80] and caesarian section,[68] as well as procedures involving the peritoneum such as hysterectomy[68] and appendicectomy.[121]

Given modern techniques in anaesthesia and the fact that hypnosis is applicable in this way to only one in twenty in the population, any genuine indication for the substitution of chemical anaesthesia by hypnosis must be very rare indeed and major operations performed under hypnosis today are likely to be more experimental than in the best interests of the patient. However, hypnosis may be usefully combined with chemical anaesthesia to produce relaxation before induction,[77] while its general application in obstetrics cannot be far removed from the techniques of Dick Read.[99] Since, moreover, even the light-trance subject responds well in this respect and motivation is so important, it is not surprising that hypnosis can be useful in a casualty department,[48] in dentistry[84] or in general practice.[101] In the management of amputees suffering phantom limb pain and in terminal cases, especially those with knowledge of their condition, it is well to remember the outside chance that the patient may be a deep-trance subject and the remarkable relief of suffering which can then be achieved. Hypnotic screening of all such patients is therefore indicated.

As noted by Freud, local anaesthesia in forearm or leg produced by DSUH is of the glove or stocking distribution and anywhere else in the body is quite unrelated to the anatomical distribution of sensory nerves. In this respect, the deep significance attached by the unconscious mind to the *semantics of hypnotic instruction* is revealing: a supine subject with hands clasped over the abdomen, for example, may respond to the suggestion 'You can feel no pain *below* your wrists' with bilateral anaesthesia of

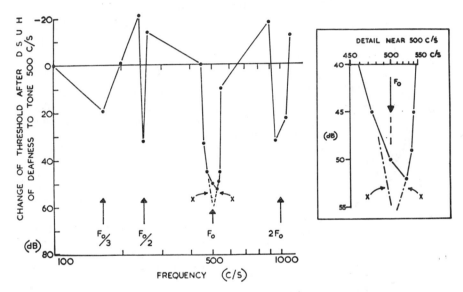

FIG. 10. Audiogram, following DSUH of frequency selective deafness to pure tone of 500 c.p.s. (F_0), using the hypnotic instruction 'You will not hear this *sound*'. There is partial 'deafness' at $F_0/3$, $F_0/2$, and $2F_0$. Detail near F_0 shows the surprising accuracy of frequency judgment at a reduction in amplitude between 50 and 55 dB. (Black and Wigan.)

forearm from wrist to elbow. This individualistic sensitivity of the unconscious to some literal interpretation of the hypnotist's words is obviously important in any clinical application—especially in obstetrics where the instruction 'You will feel no pain' may sometimes be interpreted as 'There will be no baby either' and uterine inertia in the second stage.

In the *special* senses, apparent *total deafness* can be produced in deep-trance subjects by DSUH, as reported by Pattie,[92] but it is well to warn the experimenter in this field of the danger of losing rapport if a tactile code to clear the suggestion is not first established. Early work is reviewed by Hilgard and Marquis (1945)[59] who suggest that the conditioned responses to auditory stimuli shown to be absent following DSUH of deafness by Fisher (1932)[42] and Erickson (1938 b)[38] can be voluntarily inhibited.

Black and Wigan (1961)[7] investigated *frequency selective deafness* and found that in certain subjects the resulting apparent selective deafness sometimes included not only the test frequency, but also half and twice this frequency—and in one subject, one third the frequency. Their evidence indicated that such variations were once again related to the semantics of hypnotic suggestion—in this instance an unconscious distinction between the words 'note' and 'sound'. Of interest too, was a constant associated loss of peripheral vibratory sense to the same frequency as the test tone. Black and Wigan also established conditioned reflexes, using tone of specific frequency as the conditioned stimulus, electric shock as the unconditioned stimulus and the resulting increased heart rate as the conditioned response. Following DSUH of deafness to the tone, heart rate remained normal, but after clearing the suggestions of selective deafness, the conditioned reflex was still present.

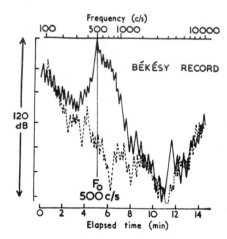

Fig. 11. Bekesy audiogram following DSUH of deafness to tone of 500 c.p.s. As the frequency changes automatically from a 100 to 10,000 c.p.s., the amplitude or the sound delivered is governed by the subject with a spring loaded pressure control in one hand. Instruction is given to keep the level so that the tone can 'just be heard'—thus providing a continuous record of the hearing threshold. The dotted tracing gives the normal threshold ante-hypnosis. (Black and Wigan.)

The literature on the physiology of hypnotic sensory loss in genera was reviewed by Gorton (1949).[50] Later Dawson (1958b)[29] proposed that there might be attenuation of the afferent sensory volley at a subcortical level through centrifugal impulses in fibres from the cortex to synapses in sensory pathways. He showed, for example, that the post-synaptic response to stimulation of a rat's forepaw could be reduced by 50 per cent in the presence of a preceding stimulus to the contralateral area of the sensory cortex—and this was confirmed by Satterfield (1962) in the cat.[104] Livingstone (1959) concluded that centrifugal control is probably exerted on most of the sensory input in this way.[73]

But direct stimulation is not always necessary to demonstrate this effect. Recording from the cochlear nucleus of the cat, Hernández-Péon, Scherrer and Jouvet (1956)[55] showed that responses to click stimuli were diminished when the cat's *attention* was distracted by concomitant stimuli in other modalities—a finding repeated when recording from the cat's

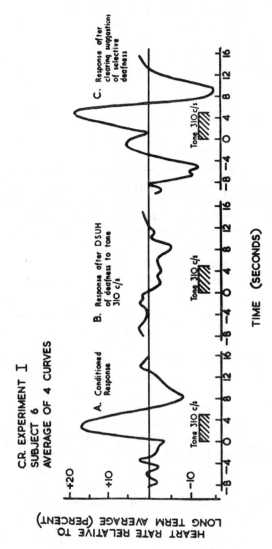

Fig. 12. Increased heart rate is the conditioned response and tone of 310 c.p.s. the conditioned stimulus in this conditioned reflex demonstration of frequency selective deafness produced by DSUH. (Black and Wigan.)

optic tract (Hernández-Péon *et al.* 1957).[56] Aspects of this work were criticised by Horn and Blundell (1959)[60] and Hugelin, Dumont and Paillas (1964)[62] but Hernández-Péon and Donoso (1957)[57] also recorded evoked responses to flashes in waking patients with electrodes implanted in the occiputal lobe and found the evoked potentials to vary in size with 'attention to the stimulus'. When the patient concentrated on arithmetic or recalled a visual image, the response was reduced or abolished.

As Halliday and Mason (1954)[52] point out, these findings establish a *prima facie* case that efferent signals in the *absence of attention* are attenuated at synapses in ascending pathways. On the hypothesis that similar attenuation of the afferent volley might be involved in hypnotic sensory loss, they investigated the effects on cortical evoked potentials of DSUH of local anaesthesia and total deafness in the presence of appropriate stimuli. Recording with a short time constant, they found that when either anaesthesia or deafness was reported to be present by the subjects, the evoked non-specific cortical responses were apparently normal—a finding confirmed by Black and Walter (1965)[17] also using a short time constant. Halliday and Mason suggested on such evidence that no part of hypnotic sensation loss can be attributed to attenuation in afferent pathways, as is apparently the case with 'inattention'.

Nevertheless, Black and Wigan[7] had already shown that increased heart rate as the conditioned response was abolished in hypnotic selective deafness and to Black and Walter—in view of their own findings—this indicated that the level where hypnotic blockade of hearing takes place probably does lie at some point *below* centripetal projection of the input to non-specific frontal cortex, but above heart regulating centres in the medulla. On first principles, attention to a stimulus implies an assessment of its information content or improbability, and obversely, inattention implies that the stimulus is probable. If afferent signals are attenuated in the absence of attention by impulses in centrifugal fibres, initiation of this mechanism could depend on the non-specific cortical assessment of probability demonstrated to occur by Black and Walter—and then shown as the CNV to be a transient DC shift in the standing potential. The negative finding by Halliday and Mason certainly demonstrated the complexity of experimentation in this field, but they were not using direct coupling—or even a long time constant. In any case, if the electro-neurophysiology of sensation really involves not only the receipt of data, but constant data processing in terms of most if not all contingent probabilities, more sophisticated experiments than any designed up to date are probably required to clarify this phenomenon of hypnotic sensory loss.

Hypnotic blindness raises as many philosophical and electro-neurophysiological problems as hypnotic deafness. The most accurate description is an 'inability to see'. Although tunnel vision occurs spontaneously and negative hallucination can so easily be induced, *total blindness* is more difficult and even in deep-trance subjects may require several sessions before 'complete blackness' is reported—and the phenomenon is not therefore of much value in pure research. Given total hypnotic blindness, although the blink reflex may be absent in response to sudden bright light, pupillary constriction and alpha blocking can be demonstrated—as well as alpha following to a stroboscope (Barber, 1961).[2] Apart from *selective visual blocks* to provide apparent hemianopias and scotomata, *colour blindness* can also be produced—and is difficult to demonstrate as an hysterical-type phenomenon by the Ishihara plates. Erickson[39] suggested hallucination of bright colours and then found that *after images* in appropriate complementary colours were reported by unsophisticated subjects—a finding confirmed by Rosenthal and Mele[103] and by Dorcas,[31] but questioned by Barber (1964).[3]

Neuro-motor. Although hypnotic catatonia may only rarely occur spontaneously in man, it can easily be produced by DSUH. In deep-trance subjects, complete catalepsy follows immediately on the suggestion 'You will be quite stiff and unable to move'—thus providing the stage hypnotist with dramatic suspension of the hypnotised subject between two chairs—and the unfounded implication of increased muscular power.

Such catatonia can be converted at once to *flexibilities cerea*, although this may not be easy *ab initio*, owing, no doubt, to the complexity of the semantics involved. But following a demonstration of *flexibilities cerea* in one subject, this is readily created in another by suggestions which imply imitation. As among the Yoruba, forced passive flexion of the catatonic limb may also produce wax-like mobility throughout the body, presumably by implication.

Like the sensory phenomena, these motor effects are hysterical in nature and the inactivated muscles are not therefore related to motor nerve distribution. An attempt to produce the *spastic paralysis* of an upper motor neurone lesion results in a most unconvincing neurological picture—although, by suggestions of imitation, a superficial rendering of spasticity may be created. More confusing to the neurologist is the *flaccid paralysis* induced by the simple suggestion of inability to move a limb. In these circumstances, tendon reflexes can be strikingly diminished, if not entirely abolished. In many subjects, DSUH of *total inability to move* induces deep sleep—a fact which may suggest some explanation of hypnotic palsy. Since in sleep the jerks are diminished, but not in hypnosis *per se*, the possibility arises that the flaccid paralysis of an isolated limb produced by DSUH is something akin to 'localised sleep'—or a Pavlovian spread of inhibition to appropriate parts of the cortex.

With regard to increased capacity for muscular work, Nicholson 1920)[87] demonstrated this in the middle finger following DSUH, using the Mosso ergometer—a finding confirmed by Williams (1929)[128] and Rousch.[100] Probably increased motivation is the real explanation here—and an ability to withstand the discomforts, or even pain of muscular fatigue. In any isometric muscular performance, temporary catatonia is almost certainly involved. The use of hypnotic motivation in athletic training has been widely applied, but since all effects are likely to be a function of trance depth, it is not surprising that the results are only anecdotal. The general findings on muscular function support Kennedy's view that after suitable training ergometric and dynamometer tests are not likely to indicate any increase in performance following DSUH.[64]

Autonomic. It is one view that psychosomatic disorders result from sympathetic-parasympathetic imbalance and since in any case the emotional modality can so easily be altered by hypnotic suggestion, autonomic responses are to be expected—and it is the limitations of *direct* suggestion in this respect which are of most interest. The copious literature on *positive effects* reports little of significance, especially in the absence of any distinction between ISUH and DSUH. Heyer (1925)[58] and Heilig and Hoff (1925)[53] demonstrated gastric peristalsis and tonicity by fluoroscopy, when suggestions concerning food were made to starved subjects, while Scantlebury and Patterson (1940)[105] produced cessation of such gastric movement following hypnotic suggestion of eating. Using a balloon-manometer, Lewis and Sarbin (1943)[71] confirmed these findings and included as a control 'imagined feeding' in the waking state, which was not found to inhibit hunger contractions. On *gastric secretion*, Delhougne and Hanson (1927)[30] showed that specific enzymes were secreted for suggested specific food substances.

In the genitourinary system, most functions are amenable to hypnotic control in suitable subjects (Dunbar, 1954,[35] Kroger, 1963[69]) and this includes sexual excitement and the menses. From the clinical point of view, hypnosis can therefore be applied in the treatment of psychological amenorrhea, dysmenorrhea, frigidity and impotence—but while the results will be a function of trance depth, the transference may be relatively independent of this and least amenable to control in the light-trance subject.

Hudgins (1933)[61] claims to have *conditioned the pupillary reflex to voluntary control* by DSUH. On the suggestion 'contract' given to a group of hypnotised subjects, light stimulation was administered as the unconditioned stimulus and auditory stimulation by a bell as the conditioned stimulus. Eventually the pupils of the group contracted without light or bell—and *even* at the thought of the word 'contract'. However, this work is of no great significance, since it can easily be shown that the pupils contract anyway on intense 'thought'—and indeed vary continuously in size according to the emotional modality of the moment.

Some significant *negative effects* have been established in the *cardiovascular system*. While ISUH readily produces tachycardia—and in anxious subjects, a relative bradycardia—DSUH of 'slow heart beat' in relaxed subjects is notably ineffective. Moreover, Black *et al.* (1963)[10] used plethysmography to investigate DSUH of thermal stimuli on forearm and hand circulation. They showed that suggestions of local or whole body heating or cooling, produced only small changes unrelated to the thermal suggestion—but ISUH of heating produced marked changes of emotional type. These findings supported those of Doupe *et al.* (1939).[33]

Epitheliological. An abundant clinical literature makes plain the degree to which epithelial tissues in general can suffer pathological change in response to psychic factors—reminding us perhaps of the ectodermal

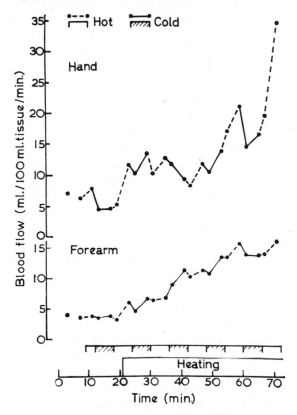

FIG. 13. Forearm and hand bloodflows as measured by plethysmography in the presence of whole body heating and alternate DSUH of heat and cold as indicated. Whole body heating starts at 21 minutes, after which the average bloodflow in hand and forearm increases. Although the bloodflow tends to change on DSUH of either heat or cold, the response is apparently unrelated to the nature of the suggestion. (Black, Edholm, Fox and Kidd.)

origin of skin and nervous system, but nevertheless posing scientific and philosophical questions which are as yet largely unanswered. Epithelial effects produced by DSUH can be positive as well as negative: pathological change of skin and mucosae can be created or inhibited. The literature on *positive epithelial phenomena* is impressive and has been reviewed by Barber (1961).[2] An hysterical patient previously cured of blindness by

DSUH produced multiple herpetic blisters 25 hours after ISUH of being 'run down and debilitated' (Ullman, 1947)[118]—a finding already reported by Heilig and Hoff (1928)[54] who also determined the opsonic index in such subjects and found that 'physiological resistance was reduced' after the experiment.

But if the evocation of viral activity is as yet inexplicable, the induction of *local non-herpetic blisters* by DSUH is even more challenging. Patti (1941)[91] reviews the significant literature on such examples of *the phenomenon of hypnotic stigmata*. The general experimental design is to touch the subject's arm with a piece of metal at room temperature while DSUH is given that the metal is red hot. Hadfield (1917)[51] produced by this means a blister surrounded by inflammation at 36 hours, but intriguingly both Jendrassik (1888)[63] and Smirnoff (1912)[110] found that blisters formed in other parts of the body. Other variations of this type of experiment are recorded by many authors, including Krafft-Ebing (1889).[67]

In this author's view the experimental design required to create the illusion presumably essential to the production of such phenomena—and especially under controlled and repeatable experimental conditions—is both practically difficult and ethically questionable. The deep-trance subject places complete trust in the hypnotist and rapport even under hypnosis rapidly deteriorates at the slightest suspicion that this is being betrayed. To obtain maximum effects from DSUH, maximum rapport is necessary—and the suggestion 'I am now going to touch your arm with a red hot iron', if believed, is likely to challenge even the strongest transference. A negative result of such an experiment will not therefore prove anything about the phenomena of hypnotic stigmata—and both negative and positive results could seriously damage the subject.

The negative epithelial effect is, on the other hand, a mechanism practically as well as ethically suitable for experimental investigation: and the literature here is no less impressive. Epithelial pathology amenable to treatment by DSUH is *both congenial and acquired*—and Mason's[78] controlled cure by DSUH of Brocq's congenital ichthyosiform erythrodermia highlights more than ever the cartesian complex in our thinking. And to Mason's admittedly anecdotal, but nevertheless significant result, can be added treatment by DSUH of congenital linear naevus by Gordon and Cohen (1952)[49] and pachyonychia congenita by Mullins *et al.* (1955).[85]

It is in the field of apparently *acquired epithelial conditions*, however, that the clinical use of hypnosis is most widely reported—including the successful treatment of all the overtly allergic forms of dermatitis, the urticaries and atopic eczemas, as well as many skin conditions of less clearly defined etiology, such as psoriasis, acne, rosacea, lichen planus and alopecia areata. In addition many mucosal pathologies such as peptic ulcer and ulcerative colitis have been relieved, if not cured by DSUH. The use of hypnosis in this way was reviewed by Dunbar (1954)[35] and later by Kroger (1963).[69] Undoubtedly the best controlled clinical experiment was conducted by Sinclair-Gieben and Chalmers (1959)[109] who treated warts by DSUH and successfully produced involution of the warts on the 'treated' side of nine patients out of ten, while warts on the control 'untreated' side remained unchanged. In the unsuccessful case, involution of warts occurred on *both* sides.

Writing on Mason's cure of Brocq's ichthyosis, Bettley (1952)[6] rightly commented that this alone 'demands a revision of current concepts on the relation between mind and body', but in fact the whole picture of psychic control of epithelial function indicates the inadequacy of our present approach. At what point then can this complex problem be attacked? In peptic ulcer at least, a clear cut neurological effect is implied, but if we allow for the well-known psychosomatic phenomenon of *symptom migration*, even a stomach ulcer becomes mysterious when it appears after relief by DSUH as an attack of atopic asthma. Such migration suggests, however, that although the physical channel for emotional outlet is not necessarily related to the nature of the psychopathology, for each individual there is in effect a pecking order of psychosomatic responses— and the evidence indicates that allergy tops the list in the majority of people.

Keeping to the inhibition of noxious responses, we have thus in the allergic individual a most useful experimental animal and if such an individual happens then to be a deep-trance subject, the experimental situation should be ideal. But deep-trance subjects are only one in twenty and it is not surprising therefore, that the clinical uses of hypnosis and controlled clinical trials on the treatment of such conditions as asthma, have tended to produce equivocal results.

The early literature is reviewed by Barber (1961)[2] and by Kroger (1963),[69] but most of the evidence is anecdotal although not lacking in enthusiasm. Magonet (1955),[75] Ambrose and Newbold (1958)[1] and Meares (1960)[82] have all claimed good symptomatic relief for severe asthma and Stewart (1957)[115] reported nine complete remissions in twelve cases. In 1960, however, Smith and Burns carried out a controlled clinical trial in which a group of 25 children was treated for one month by 'hypnotic suggestion'—*and the result was negative*. In a longer trial, Maher-Loughnan et al. (1962)[76] found that 'hypnosis, supplemented by daily autohypnosis effectively relieved the subjective symptoms'—but noted that marked variations occurred between different centres. In 1967, the British Tuberculosis Association Research Committee[20] also reported on a statistically controlled, one year trial with follow up, in which 127 patients —who turned out to include seven deep-trance subjects—were treated for asthma by DSUH and 'autohypnosis', while 125 were given breathing exercises. Subjective 'diaries' were kept by both groups and monthly recordings made of the FEV and VC, as well as the eosinophil counts in blood and sputum. It was concluded that 'hypnosis was of value in treating various types of asthma'—but marked improvement in many of the controls on *breathing exercises alone* was also noted.

There is a discrepancy here between the enthusiastic anecdotes and the more sober reports on the results of statistically analysed trials—and a hint in both that the use of hypnosis in the treatment of anything, and allergy in particular, creates a vested interest in its effectiveness. But none of this detracts from the value of hypnosis as a research tool in the investigation of allergic phenomena and it is as well therefore to have the immunological and psychophysiological background clearly defined.

The existence of a psychological factor in the etiology of any skin condition was first recognised by Wilson (1856)[129] with reference to eczema and the term 'allergy' was later coined by von Pirquet (1906).[122] By injection of his 'allergen' in the form of Koch's old tuberculin, von Pirquet established the role of immunological mechanisms in the acquired delayed-type hypersensitivity (DTH) of tuberculosis. That skin-sensitizing antibodies were present where an immediate-type hypersensitivity (ITH) response could be elicited in congenital as well as acquired skin conditions, was then demonstrated by Prausnitz and Küstner (1921)[94] by passive transfer from the allergic to the non-allergic subject. Coca and Grove (1925)[22] later described this kind of hypersensitivity as 'atopy'. The pathology of many non-dermatological conditions was soon shown to be allergic, or atopic in nature—like asthma and hayfever—and their treatment by immunological techniques was widely investigated (Freeman, 1950).[43] But the continued clinical recognition of psychological factors in the allergic reaction also led to treatment by psychotherapy—and the initial dichotomy of opinion concerning the best treatment which eventually stimulated development of psychosomatic medicine. Since it is now recognised that all physical illness has concomitant psychological complications and all psychological illness produces its own physical symptoms, any distinction between psychosomatic and general medicine should surely be considered academic.

Accepting that allergy can be relieved by DSUH in suitable subjects, Mason and Black (1958)[79] investigated the psychophysiology of what they took to be a recognised clinical phenomenon and treated by DSUH a deep-trance subject with a long history of seasonal asthma and hayfever. Strong rapport with the hypnotist was established prior to the seasonal onset, so that a successful clinical result was almost guaranteed. In the course of treatment, weekly skin tests of the ITH response showed the patient's decreasing sensitivity to the known allergens, but when finally there were no symptoms or skin responses, the Prausnitz-Küstner (PK) reaction was demonstrated by intradermal injection of the patient's serum into a non-allergic subject. Here then was one answer: such passive transfer of skin-sensitizing antibodies indicated that whatever the mechanism of allergic inhibition by DSUH, the systemic serological picture remained unchanged.

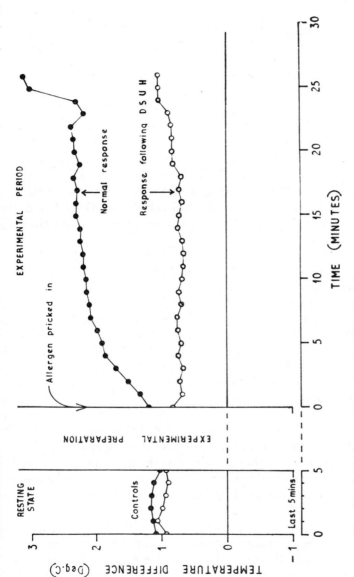

Fig. 14. *Inhibition of Allergy by DSUH.* (Black.)
Instant inhibition of the immediate-type hypersensitivity response. The temperature changes of this inflammation-like reaction were recorded with thermocouples in the waking state on one arm, and again on the other arm after DSUH 'not to react'. The upper curve shows the normal temperature change following inoculation of the allergen and the lower curve the response on the opposite arm after instant inhibition of the allergic reaction had been produced by DSUH.

Using healthy hypnotic subjects in whom the ITH response to known allergens could be elicited, Black (1963a)[8] then carried out a series of laboratory experiments under controlled conditions. The ITH response was measured in the waking state on one arm, and again on the other arm after DSUH 'not to react': temperature changes of the inflammation-like response were recorded with thermocouples, the oedema with skin-fold-thickness calipers and the colour changes by colour photography. The results showed varying degrees of *instant inhibition* in eight subjects out of twelve, five of whom were deep-trance subjects and one a medium-trance subject with a history of successful treatment of hayfever by DSUH. Follow-up on one subject showed that such instant inhibition continued without further suggestion for 54 days and that this could not be reversed by clearing suggestion and DSUH of reversal at 68 days. A subject who failed to produce instant inhibition was given repeated DSUH over 10 days: at 2 days, evidence of inhibition appeared and then increased throughout treatment. It was concluded that *instant inhibition of the ITH response* can be produced in certain individuals by DSUH and that *eventual inhibition* might be produced in a larger proportion of individuals if treatment were continued.

Here then was another answer: the effects of DSUH on the ITH response can be 'instant'—as well as accumulative as in clinical practice—and may occur within seconds after suggestion has been given. To examine this phenomenon further and to eliminate the possibility of immunological desensitization of the subject by preliminary experimental innoculations, Black (1963b)[9] next investigated the effect of DSUH on the dose-response curve of the PK reaction. Noting the probable role of trance depth in producing positive results in his previous experiment, Black controlled the effects produced in seven deep-trance subjects against those in seven medium-trance subjects. Statistically significant shifts in the dose-response curve were reported in both groups, but the shift was greater with deep-trance subjects and it was concluded that the degree of shift was very probably a function of trance depth. More significantly perhaps, these results suggested a further answer: that the mechanisms involved in the hypnotic inhibition of allergy could be independent of the presence of circulating antibodies and could act locally on a skin area sensitized by the donor's serum.

The ITH response as elicited in skin tests reaches a maximum at about 15 minutes and usually disappears within 30. No information is likely to be obtained, therefore, from cytological examination of skin biopsies. However, von Pirquet's original allergic reaction is a relatively slow process and the DTH response is maximal at 48 hours and may continue for several days. In 1959 Mason and Black investigated inhibition of the Mantoux reaction by DSUH (Mason, 1960)[81] and Black et al. (1963)[11] studied this effect in four hypnotic subjects from whom full-thickness skin biopsies were taken for histological examination. The result showed that the tuberculin reaction as observed clinically in the Mantoux test using PPD, was inhibited by DSUH and that while histologically there was no observable change in the degree of cellular infiltration, there was evidence that the exudation of fluid had been inhibited. It was concluded that the Mantoux-positive reaction can be inhibited by DSUH to give a clinically Mantoux-negative result and that a vascular constituent of the reaction is probably involved in the mechanism of inhibition.

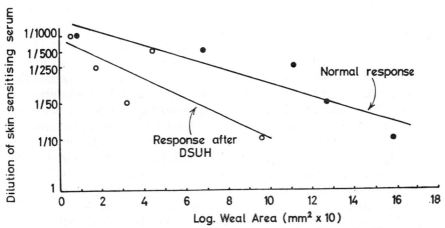

FIG. 15. Shift in the dose-response curve of the Prausnitz-Küstner reaction following DSUH not to react: mean of 7 deep-trance subjects. Such inhibition of the PK reaction in general following only passive transfer of skin-sensitizing antibodies, not only suggests a systemic mechanism, but indicates that this can operate in the absence of circulating antibodies.

Obermeyer (1955)[89] reviews psychosomatic aspects of skin allergy and Spector (1960)[112] suggests that histamine and possibly 5-hydroxytryptamine may be involved in the ITH response—but it is the initiation and in particular the inhibition of the mechanism which really poses our problem. Although Black's immunological work may have established some facts concerning the inhibition of allergy by DSUH, it really contributes little to the clinical observation that allergy is influenced by psychic factors. However, Prausnitz-Giles (1963)[95] concluded from this work that whatever the neurological or immunological explanation, the results 'opened up a wide new field of research'.

It is obvious, however, that such research need not always be conducted with the aid of hypnosis and the psychodynamics of the psychophysiology may be as revealing as the physiology alone—as was shown by Kissen (1958).[66] By statistical analysis he found that 62 per cent of 303 cases of clinical tuberculosis, emotional factors precede onset of disease and 90 per cent of such factors were due to 'a break in a love link'. Establishing on these findings a 'tuberculous personality' with an 'inordinate need for affection', he then showed clear-cut evidence of this personality in 100 per cent of tuberculous patients, as against 16 per cent of controls.

Psychophysiological mechanisms to explain the inhibition of allergy by DSUH were discussed in the *BMJ* (1964).[19] Citing Rosenblueth and Cannon (1934)[102] on the one hand, neurovascular mechanisms were proposed on evidence by these workers of antidromic impulses in afferent nerves during peripheral vasodilatation in emotionally disturbed dogs. On the other hand, it was suggested that 'tissue permeability can be altered by adrenocortico hormones, the secretion of which is controlled by the anterior pituitary and hence governed by the hypothalamus and all nervous mechanisms working thereon'. However, Doupe *et al.* (1939)[33] and Black *et al.* (1963)[10] showed that DSUH of thermal stimuli produces no variation in forearm and hand blood flow—a finding which probably suggests that neurovascular mechanisms do not play a part in allergic inhibition by DSUH. With regard to the action of adrenocortico hormones, Black and Friedman (1965)[16] estimated plasma cortisol levels (hydrocortisone) in two deep-trance hypnotic subjects during production of a shift in the dose-responsive curve of the PK reaction by DSUH. In addition, by forceful DSUH of fear, a rise in the plasma cortisol level of one subject was produced in order to assay the maximum psychophysiological level which might be expected to occur. By intravenous titration, the dose of ACTH required to produce this level was then determined—and adrenal function stimulated in both subjects with intravenous ACTH in the appropriate dosage while the effects on the dose-response curve of the PK reaction were observed.

The results showed that during a shift in the dose-response curve of the PK reaction by DSUH, there was *no significant change in the plasma cortisol levels*—while there was also *no shift in the dose-response curve* when a rise in plasma cortisol occurred as a result of adrenal stimulation by ACTH in dosage within the psychophysiological limits. It was concluded that a shift in the dose-response curve of the PK reaction by DSUH does not involve stimulation of adrenal function by the hypothalamic-pituitary-adrenal axis to produce a rise in plasma cortisol levels—and that cortisol is therefore unlikely to play any part in the inhibition by DSUH of allergic skin reactions in general.

8

Conclusions

Obviously the problems presented by the phenomena of hypnosis are far from solved and the evidence suggests that it is not only the dichotomy of mind and matter in our thinking which creates the difficulties: it is probable that our basic concepts on the nature of living things are also inadequate.

For three hundred years science was mainly advanced by an investigation of nature in terms of energy—a process which culminated in Einstein's equivalence of mass and energy according to his equation $E=mc^2$. It was tempting to think, therefore, that if most universal phenomena could be explained in terms of energy, then *all* phenomena should be explicable in this way—with both life and mind included. But no satisfactory explanations of either life or mind in these terms are yet forthcoming and our difficulties with the phenomena of hypnosis may also derive from this important gap in scientific knowledge.

In attempting to determine the nature of mind, we are concerned with a biological parameter the dimensions of which are apparently not a function of energy—and there is much to suggest that this is also true of life itself. In 1929 Szilard[116A] interpreted information as negative entropy and on this basis in 1944, Schroedinger[106] proposed that by the receipt of information living things extract order from the relative disorder of their inorganic environment and thereby exist as metastable improbabilities in the general probability trend of the universe towards more probable states. In Schroedinger's terms life 'feeds on information' within the constraints of energy and since this hypothesis was put forward, many major discoveries in molecular biology alone have tended to confirm it. At a fundamental level the role of DNA itself indicates the significance of information in the chemistry of life and demonstrates what might be called the cybernetic rather than the energetic nature of the processes of biological change.

If then both life and mind are manifestations of matter in response to its informational qualities as distinct from its energetic constraints, it is no longer all that surprising that the transfer of information in the form of hypnotic suggestion can have profound effects which appear to be relatively independent of those biological processes already interpreted in terms of energy. Perhaps more conclusive results concerning the phenomena of hypnosis might be obtained if more of our experiments could be designed according to hypotheses based on such ideas.

REFERENCES

1. AMBROSE, G. J., and NEWBOLD, G., 1958. *A handbook of medical hypnosis.* London, Baillière, Tindall and Cox.
2. BARBER, T. X., 1961. Physiological effects of 'Hypnosis'. *Psychol. Bull.*, **58**, 390.
3. BARBER, T. X., 1964. Hypnotically hallucinated colors and their negative after-images. *J. Am. Psychol.*, **77**, 313–18.
4. BELOFF, J., 1962. *The Existence of Mind.* London, MacGibbon and Kee.
5. BERNHEIM, H., 1884. *De la suggestion dans l'état hypnotique et dans l'état de veille.* Paris: Doin.

6. BETTLEY, F. R., 1952. *Brit. med. J.*, ii, 996.
7. BLACK, S., and WIGAN, E. R., 1961. An investigation of selective deafness produced by direct suggestion under hypnosis. *Brit. med. J.*, ii, 736.
8. BLACK, S., 1963a. Inhibition of immediate-type hypersensitivity response by direct suggestion under hypnosis. *Brit. med. J.*, i, 925.
9. BLACK, S., 1963b. Shift in dose-response curve of Prausnitz-Kustner reaction by direct suggestion under hypnosis. *Brit. med. J.*, i, 990.
10. BLACK, S., EDHOLM, O. G., FOX, R. H., and KIDD, P. J., 1963. The effect of suggestion under hypnosis on the peripheral circulation in man. *Clin. Sci.*, **25,** 223.
11. BLACK, S., HUMPHREY, J. H., and NIVEN, JANET S. F., 1963. Inhibition of Mantoux reaction by direct suggestion under hypnosis. *Brit. med. J.*, i, 1649.
13. BLACK, S., 1963. M. R. C. Colloquium.
14. BLACK, S., 1964. The use of hypnosis in the treatment of psychosomatic disorders. *Proc. Soc. Psychosom. Res. Conference 1962.* Oxford: Pergamon Press.
15. BLACK, S., and FRIEDMAN, M., 1964. Unpublished work.
16. BLACK, S., and FRIEDMAN, M., 1965. Adrenal function and the inhibition of allergic responses under hypnosis. *Brit. med. J.*, i, 562.
17. BLACK, S., and WALTER, W. G., 1965. The effects on anterior brain responses of variation in the probability of association between stimuli. *J. Psychosomat. Res.*, **9,** 33.
18. BRAID, J., 1843. *Neurohypnology or the rationale of nervous sleep considered in relation with animal magnetism.* London.
19. *Brit. med. J.*, 1964. i, 1129.
20. British Tuberculosis Association Research Committee Report, 1967. *Hypnosis for asthma—a controlled trial.* In press.
21. CHARCOT, J. M., 1878. Contracture hystérique et aimant: catalepsie provoquée artificiellement. Zoopsie. Catalepsie chez animaux. *Gaz. Hôp.*, Paris, **51,** 1073, 1097, 1121. *C.R. Soc. Biol.*, **5,** 119, 230.
22. COCA, A. F., and GROVE, E. F., 1925. *J. Immunol.*, **10,** 445.
23. COORS, D., 1928. *A determination of the density of post-hypnotic amnesia for the stylus maze.* Wisconsin: Madison Univ. Press.
24. COUÉ, E., 1922. *Self-mastery through conscious autosuggestion.* London: Allen.
25. CULLEN, J. H., 1960. In *Progress in the biological sciences in relation to dermatology.* Ed. A. Rook, p. 197. London: Cambridge Univ. Press.
26. CZERMAK, J. M., 1856. Eine neurophysiologische Beobachtung an einem Triton cristatus. *Z. Zool.*, **7.**
27. DARWIN, C., 1872. *The expression of the emotions in man and animals.* London: Murray.
28. DAVIS, L. W., and HUSBAND, R. W., 1931. A study of hypnotic susceptibility in relation to personality traits. *J. Abnorm. Social Psychol.*, **26,** 175–82.
29. DAWSON, G. D., 1958. The central control of sensory inflow. *Proc. roy. Soc. Med.*, **50,** 531–35.
30. DELHOUGNE, F., and HANSEN, K., 1927. Die suggestive Beeinflussbarkeit der Magen und Pankreassekretion in der Hypnose. *Deut. Arch. Klin. Med.*, **157,** 20.
31. DORCUS, R. M., 1937. Modification by suggestion of some vestibular and visual responses. *Am. J. Psychol.*, **49,** 82–7.
32. DORCUS, R. M., 1956. *Hypnosis.* New York: McGraw-Hill.
33. DOUPE, J., MILLER, W. R., and KELLER, W. K., 1939. Vasomotor reactions in the hypnotic state. *J. Neurol. Psychiat.*, **2,** 97.

34. Doust, J. W., 1953. Studies on the physiology of awareness. Oximetric analysis of emotion and the differential planes of consciousness seen in hypnosis. *J. Clin. Exp. Psychopath.*, **14**, 113.
35. Dunbar, F., 1954. *Emotions and bodily changes.* N.Y.: Columbia Univ. Press.
36. Ellingson, R. J., 1956. Brain waves and problems of psychology. *Psychol. Bull.*, **53**, 1–34.
37. Erickson, M. H., 1938. *J. gen. Psychol.*, **19**, 127, 167.
38. Erickson, M. H., 1938. Experimental findings on hypnotic deafness with a conditioned response technique. *J. gen. Psychol.*, **19**, 151-67.
39. Erickson, M. H., 1939. The induction of colour blindness by a technique of hypnotic suggestion. *J. gen. Psychol.*, **20**, 61–89.
39a. Esdaile, J., 1850. *Mesmerism in India.* Hartford, England: Andras.
40. Eysenck, H. J., 1947. *Dimensions of personality.* London: Kegan Paul.
41. Fabre, I. M., and Kafka, G., 1913. *Einführung in die Tierpsychologie.* Leipzig: Barth.
42. Fisher, V. E., 1932. Hypnotic suggestion and the conditioned reflex. *J. exp. Psychol.*, **15**, 212-17.
43. Freeman, J., 1950. *Hayfever.* London: Heinemann.
44. Freud, S., and Breuer, J., 1892. *Freud's Collected Papers.* London: Hogarth.
45. Freud, S., 1935. *An Autobiographical Study.* International Psycho-analytical Library, No. 26.
46. Freud, S., 1949. *Standard edition of the complete psychological works of Sigmund Freud,* Vol. XIV, p. 7 (trans. Strachey). London: Hogarth Press.
47. Gidro-Frank, L., and Buch, M. K. B., 1948. A study of the plantar response in hypnotic age regression. *J. Nerv. Ment. Dis.*, **107**, 443-58.
48. Goldie, L., 1957. Medical Use of Hypnotism. *Brit. med. J.*, ii, 823.
49. Gordon, H., and Cohen, K., 1952. Case of congenital linear naevus treated by hypnosis. *Int. Derm. Congr.*, **10**, 376.
50. Gorton, B. E., 1949. The physiology of hypnosis. A review of the literature. *Psychiat. Quart.*, **23**, 317–43, 457–85.
51. Hadfield, J. A., 1917. The influence of hypnotic suggestion on inflammatory conditions. *Lancet*, ii, 678.
52. Halliday, A. M., and Mason, A. A., 1964. The effect of hypnotic anaesthesia on cortical responses. *J. Neurol. Neurosurg. Psychiat.*, **27**, 300.
53. Heilig, R., and Hoff, H., 1925. Beitraege zur Hypnotischen Beeinflussung der Magenfunktion. *Med. Klin.*, **21**, 162.
54. Heilig, R., and Hoff, H., 1928. Ueber Psychogene Entstehung des Herpes labialis. *Med. Klin.*, **24**, 1472.
55. Hernández-Péon, R., Scherrer, H., and Jouvet, M., 1956. Modification of electric activity in cochlear nucleus during 'attention' in unanaesthetized cats. *Science*, **123**, 331–32.
56. Hernández-Péon, R., Guzman-Flores, C., Alcaraz, M., and Fernandez-Guardiola, A., 1957. Sensory transmission in visual pathway during 'attention' in unanaesthetized cats. *Acta neurol. Lat. amer.*, **3**, 1–8.
57 Hernández-Péon, R., and Donoso, C. M., 1957. Subcortical photically evoked electrical activity in the human waking brain. *Excerpta Medica,* 4th int. Congr. Electroenceph. clin. Neurophysiol. p. 155.
58. Heyer, G. R., 1925. Psychogene Funktionsstoerungen des Verdaungstraktes. In *Psychogenese und Psychotherapie koerperlicher Symptome.* Ed. Schwartz, O. Vienna: Springer.
59. Hilgard, E. R., and Marquis, D. G., 1940. *Conditioning and learning.* New York: Appleton-Century.
60. Horn, G., and Blundell, J., 1959. Evoked potentials in visual cortex of the unanaesthetized cat. *Nature, Lond.*: **184**, 173–74.

61. HUDGINS, C. V., 1933. Conditioning and voluntary control of pupillary light reflex. *J. gen. Psychol.*, **8**, 3.
62. HUGELIN, A., DUMONT, S., and PAILLAS, N., 1960. Tympanic muscles and control of auditory input during arousal. *Science*, **131**, 1371–72.
63. JENDRASSIK, E., 1888. Einiges ueber suggestion. *Neurol. Zbl.*, **7**, 281.
64. KENNEDY, A., 1960. As quoted A. A. Mason. Ref. 80.
65. KIRSCHER, A., 1646. *Ars magna lucis et umbrae*. Romae. Libr. II, Pars. 1, p. 154.
66. KISSEN, D. M., 1958. *Emotional factors in pulmonary tuberculosis*. London: Tavistock.
67. KRAFT-EBING, VON, R., 1889 *Eine experimentelle Studie auf dem Gebiete des Hypnotismus*. Enke: Stuttgart.
68. KROGER, W. S., and DeLEE, J. B., 1957. The use of hypoanaesthesia for caesarean section and hysterectomy. *J. Am. med. Assn.*, 9 Feb. 1957.
69. KROGER, W. S., 1963. *Clinical and experimental hypnosis*. Philadelphia and Montreal: J. B. Lippincott.
70. LeCRON, L. M., and BORDEAUX, J., 1947. *Hypnotism today*. New York: Grune and Stratton.
71. LEWIS, J. H., and SARBIN, T. R., 1943. Studies in psychosomatics. *Psychosomat. Med.*, **5**, 125.
72. LIÉBEAULT, A. A., 1886. *Du sommeil et des etats analogues consideres, surtout au point de vue l'action du moral sur le physique*. Paris: Masson.
73. LIVINGSTON, R. B., 1959. Central control of receptors and sensory transmission systems. In *Handbook of physiology*: Section 1. Neurophysiology, vol. 1, pp. 741–60. Washington: American Physiological Society.
74. LOW, M. D., BORDA, R. P., FROST, J. D., and KELLAWAY, P., 1966. *Neurology*, **16**, 771.
75. MAGONET, A. P., 1955. *Hypnosis in asthma*. London: Heinemann.
76. MAHER-LOUGHNAN, G. P., MACDONALD, N., MASON, A. A., and FRY, L., 1962. Controlled trial of hypnosis in the symptomatic treatment of asthma. *Brit. med. J.*, ii, 371.
77. MARMER, M. J., 1959. Hypnoanalgesia and hypnoanesthesia for cardiac surgery. *J. Amer. med Assn*, **171**, 512–17.
78. MASON, A. A., 1952. A case of congenital ichthyosiform erythrodermia of Brocq treated by hypnosis. *Brit. med. J.*, ii, 422.
79. MASON, A. A., and BLACK, S., 1958. Allergic skin responses abolished under treatment of asthma and hayfever by hypnosis. *Lancet*, i, 877.
80. MASON, A. A., 1960. *Hypnotism for medical and dental practitioners*. London: Secker and Warburg.
81. MASON, A. A., 1960. Hypnosis and suggestion in the treatment of allergic phenomena. *Acta allergolica*, **7**, 332.
82. MEARES, A., 1960. *A system of medical hypnosis*. Philadelphia: Saunders.
83. MESMER, F. A., 1766. *Dissertatio Physico-Medica de Planetarium influxu*. Vindobona.
84. MOSS, A. A. 1952 *Hypnodontics., or Hypnosis in dentistry*. Brooklyn, N.Y.: Dental Items of Interest Publishing Company.
85. MULLINS, J. F., MURRAY, N., and SHAPIRO, E. M. 1955. Pachyonychia congenita treated by hypnosis. *Arch. Derm., Chicago*, **71**, 264
86. McCONNELL, J. V., 1962, and THOMPSON, R. U. Texas.
87. NICHOLSON, N. C., 1920. Notes on muscular work during hypnosis. *Bull. John Hopkins Hosp.*, **31.**
88. ORNE, M. T., 1951. The mechanisms of hypnotic age regression: An experimental study. *J. abnorm. soc. Psychol.*, **46**, 213.
89. OBERMEYER, M. E., 1955. *Psychocutaneous medicine*. Springfield, Ill.

90. PATERSON, A. S., PASSERINI, D., BRACCHI, F., and BLACK S., 1962. Etude de l'hypnose et de l'effet des drogues ataratiques au moyen de la méthode des réflexes conditionnés chez l'homme. *Proc. Congrès des Médecins Aliénistes et Neurologistes, Montpellier 1961.*

91. PATTIE, F. A., 1941. The production of blisters by hypnotic suggestion: a review. *J. abnorm. soc. Psychol.*, **36**, 62.

92. PATTIE, F. A., 1950. The genuineness of unilateral deafness produced by hypnosis. *Am. J. Psychol.*, **63**, 84–86.

93. PAVLOV, I. P., 1953. *Ueber die sogenannte Tierhypnose.* Berlin: Ausgewaehlte Werke.

94. PRAUSNITZ, C., and KÜSTNER, H., 1921. *Zbl. Bakt.*, **86**, 160.

95. PRAUSNITZ GILES, C., 1963. Correspondence in *Brit. med. J.*, i, 1287.

96. PREYER, W., 1873. Ueber eine Wirking der Angst bei Thieren. *Zentralbl. f. med. Wissenschaften*, **11**, 177.

97. *Proc. 4th International Conference on Psychosomatic Aspects of Neoplastic Disease*, Turin, 9.6.65.

98. PUNER, H. W., 1947. *Freud. His Life and Mind.* New York: Grosset and Dunlap.

99. READ, G. D., 1943. *Revelation of Childbirth.* London: Heinemann.

100. ROUSCH, E. S., 1951. Strength and endurance in waking and hypnotic states. *J. Appl. Psychol.*, **3**, 404.

101. RYDE, D. H., 1966. The curious art of thumb gazing. *J. Col. Gen. Practit.*, **12**, 3.

102. ROSENBLUETH, A., and CANNON, W. B., 1934. *Amer. J. Physiol.*, **108**, 599.

103. ROSENTHAL, V. G., and MELE, H., 1952. Validity of hypnotically induced colour hallucination. *J. abnorm. soc. Psychol.*, **47**, 700–04.

104. SATTERFIELD, J. H., 1962. Effect of sensorimotor cortical stimulation upon cuneate nuclear output through medical lemniscus. *Cat. J. nerv. ment. Dis.*, **135**, 507–12.

105. SCANTLEBURY, R. E., and PATTERSON, T. L., 1940. Hunger motility in a hypnotised subject. *Q. J. expt. Physiol.*, **30**, 347.

106. SCHROEDINGER, E., 1944. *What is Life?* Cambridge: Univ. Press.

107. SCOTT, H. D., 1930. Hypnosis and the conditioned reflex. *J. gen. Psychol.*, **4**, 113.

108. SCHWENTER, D., 1636. *Deliciae physico-mathematicae.* Nürnberg.

109. SINCLAIR-GIEBEN, A. H., and CHALMERS, D., 1959. Evaluation of treatment of warts by hypnosis. *Lancet*, ii, 480.

110. SMIRNOFF, D., 1912. Zur Frage der durch hypnotische Suggestion hervor-gerufenen vasomotorischen Stoerungen. *Z. Psychother. med. Psychol.*, **4**, 171.

111. SMITH, J. M., and BURNS, C. L. C., 1960. *Brit. J. Dis. Chest.* **54**, 78.

112. SPECTOR, W. G., 1960. *Progress in the biological sciences in relation to dermatology.* Cambridge: Univ. Press, p. 295.

113. STAFFORD CLARK, D., 1966. Personal Communication.

114. STALNAKER, J. M., and RICHARDSON, M. W., 1930. Time estimation in the hypnotic trance. *J. gen. Psychol.*, **4**, 362.

115. STEWART, H., 1957. *Brit. med. J.*, i, 1320.

116. STRICKLER, C. B., 1929. A quantitative study of posthypnotic amnesia. *J. abnorm. soc. Psychol.*, **24**, 108.

116a. SZILARD, L., 1929. *C. Physik.*, **53**, 840.

117. TRUE, R. M., and STEPHENSON, C. W., 1951. Experiments correlating E.E.G., pulse and plantar reflexes with hypnotism, age regression etc. *Personality*, **1**, 252.

118. ULLMAN, M., 1947, Herpes simplex and second degree burns induced under hypnosis. *Amer. J. Psychiat.*, **103,** 828.
119. UHR, L., 1958. Learning under hypnosis. *J. Clin. expt. Hypnosis*, **6,** 121.
120. VÖLGYESI, F. A., 1938. Pavlov and hypnosis. *J. Phys. U.S.S.R.* Vol. XXIV.
121. VÖLGYESI, F. A., 1966. *Hypnosis of man and animals*. London: Baillière, Tindall and Cassell.
122. VON PIRQUET, C., 1906. *Münch. med. Wschr.*, **53,** 1457.
123. WALTER, W. G., 1964. The convergence and interaction of visual, auditory, and tactile responses in human non-specific cortex. *Ann. N.Y. Acad. Scil.*, 112-320.
124. WALTER, W. G., 1965. Effects on anterior brain responses of an expected association between stimuli. *J. Psychosom. Res.*, **9,** 45.
125. WALTER, W. G., COOPER, R., ALDRIDGE, V. J., McCALLUM, W. C., and WINTER, A. L., 1964. Contingent negative variation: an electric sign of sensori-motor association and expectancy in the human brain. *Nature Lond.*, **90,** 203–380.
126. WATKINS, J., 1954. Trance and transference, *J. Clin. expt. Hypnosis*, **2,** 284.
127. WEITZENHOFFER, A. M., 1957. *General techniques of hypnotism*. New York: Grune and Stratton, p. 213.
128. WILLIAMS, G. W., 1929. The effect of hypnosis on muscular fatigue. *J. abnorm. soc. Psychol.*, **24,** 318-27.
129. WILSON, E., 1856. *Diseases of the skin*. London: Churchill.
130. WOLBERG, L. R., 1948. *Medical hypnosis*, **1,** 116. New York: Grune and Stratton.

VIII

SLEEPING AND DREAMING

Ian Oswald
M.D.

Senior Lecturer in Psychiatry, University of Edinburgh

1

Introduction

A sufficiency of recent sleep is essential for both mental and physical health. I shall here briefly review some of the recent developments in our understanding of sleep mechanisms and then deal with sleeping and dreaming as they concern particularly the practising clinician. Comprehensive technical reviews of the literature are available in the books of Kleitman[67] and Oswald,[91] a less technical but more modern presentation being that of Oswald.[93]

The Cerebral Basis of Sleep

In the years after World War I the epidemic of encephalitis lethargica provided an opportunity for post-mortem examinations on patients who had recently shown severe sleep disturbance. Von Economo[27] was led to attribute the abnormal sleep to inflammation within the central brain stem. Neurologists later pointed out that space-occupying lesions of the upper cervical spinal cord do not disturb consciousness, whereas lesions in the mid-brain and diencephalon frequently cause states resembling sleep.[15] Likewise, compression of the mid-brain at the tentorial opening by herniation of temporal lobe or because of haemorrhage within the posterior fossa[58] leads to drowsiness passing into stupor.

The prime importance of brain-stem function in controlling sleep and wakefulness was further demonstrated in the work of Hess[50] who carried out electrical stimulation of parts of the cat's thalamus and reported that apparently natural sleep ensued. A truly notable landmark was the report by Moruzzi and Magoun[85] that electrical stimulation of the reticular formation in the central core of the cat mid-brain regularly caused an abrupt transition from the appearances of sleep to those of wakefulness. It was out of this last work that there grew the concept of the brain-stem reticular activating system—a central core extending from the medulla to the posterior hypothalamus and certain of the thalamic nuclei, and from which non-specific nerve impulses ascended to the cortex and descended to the spinal cord.

The impulses were non-specific in that they did not convey information specific to any particular sensory mode but had the function of facilitating the responsiveness of the cortex on the one hand or the spinal cord on the other, so that when the flow of non-specific impulses was high the organism was able to deal effectively with life events: it was awake. Drowsiness and sleep were envisaged as periods during which the flow of non-specific activating impulses was reduced. The flow of non-specific impulses was increased whenever the excitement of the reticular formation increased. A host of differing factors regulated that excitement. Excitatory impulses reached the reticular formation by 'collateral afferents' from all the main sensory paths but, equally importantly, from the cortex. Humoral agents such as carbon dioxide had a like action. On the other hand, the excitement of the reticular formation could be damped down by afferent impulses from the blood pressure receptors of the carotid sinus and elsewhere and, probably more importantly, by impulses from the cortex.

Gradually, research led to changing concepts. A considerable differentiation of function within different parts of the reticular formation became recognized. Sleep may be defined as a recurrent, healthy state of inertia and unresponsiveness, but for purposes of research objective criteria are needed. Constriction of the pupil, rise in electrical skin resistance and slowing of the heart had long been regarded as signs of sleep, but the electroencephalogram (EEG) had become the chief criterion. Characteristic changes in the appearance of the electroencephalogram accompanied sleep, particularly slowing of the rhythms. A great deal of re-thinking was required when account had to be taken of evidence that there were certain periods in the course of incontrovertible sleep during which the EEG was, in some species, similar to that of wakefulness or, in man, similar to that of drowsiness. It has now come to be accepted that there are two different kinds of sleep having sharply differing characteristics which normally alternate during any prolonged period of sleep.[61, 92]

The two kinds of sleep are termed the 'orthodox' phase and the 'paradoxical' phase.

The orthodox phase, sometimes called slow-wave sleep, or fore-brain phase of sleep; often called 'light' sleep by animal research workers, and NREM (non-rapid-eye-movement) sleep by those who have engaged in human research.

The human electroencephalogram in orthodox sleep is characterized

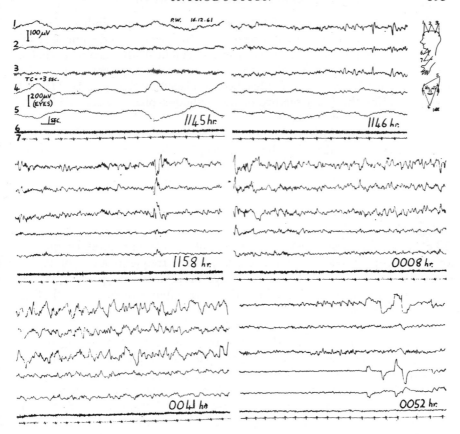

FIG. 1. Successive periods of drowsiness and sleep.

11.45 p.m. Awake but drowsy, alpha rhythm in channel 3, slow, rolling eye movements in channels 4 and 5.

11.46 p.m. Stage I orthodox sleep. Slow, rolling eye movements still present but alpha rhythm is lost and 4 – 6 c/sec waves predominate.

11.58 p.m. Stage II orthodox sleep. Bursts of fast waves (sleep spindles) at about 14 c/sec and brief, high voltage slow wave complexes.

00.08 a.m. Stage III orthodox sleep. The sleep spindles are somewhat slower in frequency and a general slowing and increase of voltage of the background EEG is present.

00.41 a.m. Stage IV orthodox sleep. High voltage waves at about 1 c/sec dominate the EEG. The EEG potentials can be seen also in channels 4 and 5. Channel 6 appears as before in the form of a thick trace owing to innumerable little muscle spikes. The heart rate is regular.

00.52 a.m. Paradoxical sleep. The EEG is of low voltage. Channels 4 and 5 reveal rapid eye movement potentials (also visible in channel 1). A few waves of alpha frequency are visible in channel 3. In channel 1 are a few muscle spikes and, just prior to the burst of eye movements, a few 'saw-toothed' waves at 2 – 3 c/sec. Channel 6 now reveals much diminished muscle tension and in channel 7 the heart rate appears irregular.

(From Oswald) [92].

by high voltage slow waves of 1–6 c/sec and brief sleep spindles of about 12–14 c/sec. The heart-rate and respiration are regular, and some skeletal muscle-tone is retained. There is little movement of the face or eyeballs. Dreaming is not usually described after awakening therefrom. The classification of Stages A to E[76] has been replaced by Stages I, II, III and IV to describe the EEG picture of the orthodox phase of sleep.[23] These stages are illustrated in Fig. 1.

The paradoxical phase, sometimes termed low voltage fast sleep, activated sleep, hind-brain phase of sleep, archi-sleep; 'deep' sleep by animal research workers, and sometimes 'light', REM or rapid-eye-movement sleep ('PMO' of French workers) by those who have studied human sleep.

The appearance of the EEG varies with the species but in man low voltage rhythms of 4–6 c/sec predominate, with occasional alpha rhythm at 10 c/sec. Characteristic 'saw-tooth' waves of 2–3 c/sec are often prominent over the frontal areas and tend to precede the frequent bursts of rapid, jerky eye movements.[11] These rapid-eye-movements are present in the newborn human.[109] In the adult, they are often concurrent with fine twitches of the body.[3]

During orthodox sleep the cat may lie with its chin resting on its paws, but it rolls over flaccid during the paradoxical phase. The transition from orthodox to paradoxical sleep in the human is also marked by a sudden loss of skeletal muscle tone.[9, 56] In man, the monosynaptic reflex which can normally be elicited by electrical stimulation of afferent nerves is practically abolished,[53] while, in the cat, electrical stimulation of the pyramidal tract no longer evokes movement, suggesting that there is a definite inhibition of movement exerted at the spinal level. Erection of the human penis accompanies this phase of sleep,[36] during which the heart-rate, respiration and blood pressure undergo sharp and frequent fluctuations,[117] the skin electrical resistance becomes maximal,[47] and the evoked electrocortical responses to clicks become small.[131] The cat's cerebral blood flow increases and the total activity of visual cortex neurones and pyramidal tract neurones increases to rival that of wakefulness, though the discharge patterns are quite different.[30, 31]

The neonate spends more of its total sleep in the paradoxical phase,[109, 121] a rapid decrease occurring during infancy, especially in ruminants.[111] Paradoxical sleep usually occupies a total of 20 to 25 per cent of the night in the adult human and recurs about five times a night.

The Depth of Sleep

Simple observation long suggested that there were different 'depths' of sleep. Some confusion at first arose as to whether paradoxical sleep should be called 'light' or 'deep'. It is now realized that neither adjective is appropriate.

Muscle relaxation is much greater during paradoxical sleep, as if it were deeper. Yet bodily movements occur more often.[96] It was found more difficult to provoke awakening in animals when they were stimulated electrically within the reticular formation during paradoxical sleep. By contrast, electrical stimulation of the cerebral cortex more readily causes behavioural arousal during paradoxical sleep.[54] The severely sleep-deprived man, when allowed to sleep, takes an excess of Stage IV orthodox sleep,[12, 128] as if this kind of sleep were deeper. By contrast, other very sleepy people who have been suddenly deprived of amphetamine to which drug they have long been addicted will readily fall asleep, but when they do so they take an excess proportion of paradoxical sleep.[99]

When meaningless, auditory stimuli are used it is as difficult to awaken a human from paradoxical sleep as from Stage IV of orthodox sleep. When, however, potentially meaningful stimuli are used it remains difficult to cause awakening from Stage IV of orthodox sleep but easy to cause awakening from paradoxical sleep.[130] If we consider responsiveness to external stimulation, then the readiness with which such responses occur depends upon the index of response being used, and the type of stimulation and the time of the night.[128] It is thus inadvisable to use the adjectives 'light' or 'deep' in regard to sleep unless it be specified what kind of stimulus and what type of response are being considered.

The independence of the two phases of sleep is suggested by their contrasting physiological characteristics, the abruptness of the alternation from one to another and by an apparent distinct need for each. Upon passing from wakefulness to sleep the normal human passes into the orthodox phase. When, therefore, an individual is deliberately awakened at the onset of each period of paradoxical sleep, and subsequently allowed once more to fall asleep, he passes each time into orthodox sleep and becomes selectively deprived of paradoxical sleep. Under these conditions the frequency with which paradoxical sleep periods appear increases very sharply, and when undisturbed sleep is again permitted a significant excess of paradoxical sleep is taken, as if in compensation.[22, 59, 64, 87, 112] By contrast, repeated interruption of orthodox sleep does not have the effect of increasing the 'pressure' towards paradoxical sleep, but if selective deprivation of State IV orthodox sleep is carried out by deliberate stimulation, then on subsequent nights an increased proportion of the night is spent in Stage IV.[1]

What Promotes Sleep?

Obviously, lack of sufficient recent sleep tends to make people sleepy, but there exists also a powerful internal or circadian rhythm, the nature of which is not understood, but which promotes sleepiness when the customary time for retiring approaches.[67] Despite ample opportunity for daytime sleep, workers starting upon night shifts are at first less efficient at complex tasks.[132] Big individual differences exist in the ease with which new rhythms can be established.[67] Those who travel long distances by air become acutely aware of the impossibility of at once adjusting to a new diurnal pattern.

Novelty of stimulation promotes wakefulness and conversely monotony leads to sleepiness. Monotony can be imposed by rhythmic stimulation: sleep is then especially liable to occur, even if the eyes are glued open.[41, 90] The sleep-inducing effects of prolonged and monotonous vehicle driving are considerable and have been investigated among truck drivers in Czechoslovakia.[8] Travis and Kennedy[119] devised an apparatus to overcome this problem. An electrode over the supraorbital muscle was monitored in such a way that when the rate of energy output from the muscle electrical spikes fell below a critical level a warning device operated which stimulated the subject. When subjects wearing this apparatus engaged continuously on a two-hour task in which they had to operate a hand control, rather as a lorry driver does, they gradually became bored and began to make errors. There were frequent episodes when alertness had fallen dangerously and, with it, muscle tension. At these times they were automatically alerted, the sequence of events being particularly common in subjects who had not had a good night's sleep.[65]

The Pre-Sleep Period

The sequence of wakefulness passing into drowsiness and thence into orthodox sleep is accompanied by a decline in efficiency often spoken of as a decline in 'vigilance' and believed to be associated with a decrease in the facilitatory non-specific impulses ascending from the reticular formation to the cerebral cortex. During drowsiness simple, repetitive movements requiring no new decisions can continue but the precision with which they are executed becomes impaired.[89] Equally, the precision of mental life becomes impaired and it becomes difficult to distinguish between fantasy and reality. During drowsiness hypnagogic hallucinations arise. These may be of any sense modality, of any degree of complexity and occur concurrently with inward musings which, if deliberately written down upon sudden awakening, often reveal themselves as nonsense phrases, frequently containing neologisms.[70, 91] It is believed that the hypnagogic hallucinations (which are not infrequently of faces) form the basis of some childhood nocturnal terrors.

It is normal for adults to experience what Weir Mitchell[82] called 'sensory shocks'. Most frequent is the sensation of falling, succeeded by a subjective impact and accompanied by a sudden bodily jerk. These are sometimes accompanied by feelings of 'electric' sensations flowing abruptly through the body, by a sudden auditory experience such as a musical note or a pistol shot or a sudden visual experience such as a flash of light. There may be a complaint that the body suddenly seemed to swell up or to become hot. These momentary experiences generally occur when there is a Stage I EEG picture and are followed by immediate awakening.[88]

Symonds[118] suggested that the jerks were related to myoclonic epilepsy, a possibility rejected by Mitchell[82] and Oswald.[88] The phenomenon occurs so frequently in normal people, and without those electroencephalographic signs that customarily accompany phenomena classed as epilepsy, that there would seem no justification for linking it with epileptic disorders. On the other hand, drowsiness does sometimes promote the appearance of EEG spike phenomena commonly associated with epilepsy. There are individual differences and whether or not EEG spikes are activated depends upon the stage of sleep as well as upon the individual; paradoxical sleep tends to be accompanied by suppression of spike discharges in some but not all people.[14, 114]

As the drift towards sleep continues the loss of contact with reality becomes more profound, the hypnagogic imagery becomes less discontinuous so that if now the individuals are awakened they may describe 'dreams', namely sequential adventures which differ little in content from those which will be described if the individual is awakened from paradoxical sleep later in the night.[37]

Some people will deny these varied phenomena of drowsiness. Many will deny the sudden bodily jerks, despite what their wives or husbands say. The dream experiences are not alone in being forever lost unless immediately recorded upon deliberate awakening. It would appear that people do not easily form memories of those things which were in their minds when they were not fully awake. Various commercial interests have promoted 'sleep learning' machines. These are merely tape recorders which will play students' lessons during the night. Simon and Emmons[115] reviewed the studies that had been made of supposed sleep learning and concluded that they were all unreliable. They themselves carried out a series of experiments in which the EEG of volunteers was recorded throughout the night while tape-recorded auditory material was played from time to time. They showed conclusively that while a small amount of recall of material presented during Stage I was possible, once Stage II of orthodox sleep was reached subsequent recall was not possible.[116] The decline in efficiency and responsiveness that is characteristic of sleep would appear to extend to those cerebral responses which must be assumed to underlie the formation of new engrams or traces in the memory stores. The difficulty of recalling hypnagogic hallucinations and dreams (see below) can thus be understood.

Dreaming

In the first weeks of life the human infant spends less total time asleep than is commonly supposed, namely some 12 to 17 of the daily 24 hours. By the end of the fourth month he has doubled the proportion of his sleep which is taken at night.[68, 102] It was while observing the sleep of babies that an hourly periodicity of restlessness was observed by Aserinsky and Kleitman.[2] Human adults were then studied and the presence of recurrent periods of sleep with a low voltage EEG and rapid eye movements was observed.[23] After nearly 200 awakenings from these periods of sleep, which we would now term paradoxical sleep, Dement and Kleitman[24] reported 80 per cent of instances where dreams were recalled. When they awakened the same volunteers from periods of orthodox sleep only 7 per cent of occasions elicited reports of having just been dreaming.

Choosing a group of persons who claimed never to dream and another group who claimed frequently to dream, Goodenough et al.[42] carried out all-night recording of sleep with awakenings once more from the paradoxical and the orthodox phases, and were able to confirm that dreaming was associated with the periods of sleep accompanied by rapid eye movements, even in those people who believed that they never dreamed. It was concluded that the latter class of person forgets his dream, or refers to it simply as 'thinking' because he may not recall any bizarre or ridiculous features in its content. The longer the duration of paradoxical sleep that has elapsed just prior to wakening, the longer the dream narrative obtained upon awakening.[25] Delay of only a few minutes after the end of a period of paradoxical sleep causes a precipitous fall in the amount of content recallable.[133]

We spend some 20 to 25 per cent of an average night in paradoxical sleep throughout the whole of which we are probably dreaming. The recent knowledge has made it possible for numerous experimental studies of dreaming to be carried out and renders obsolete many older reports. It was formerly said, for example, that people did not dream in colour, but awakenings from periods of paradoxical sleep indicate that the great majority of dreams contain colour experiences.[10, 63] Former reports that dreaming ceased after various kinds of brain injury were based upon daytime recall and in the case of, for example, leucotomy, we now know from nocturnal awakenings that the older reports were not merely inadequate but incorrect.

The psychiatrist will be struck particularly by the very large proportion of the night spent in dreaming, amounting to something of the order of two hours. It is clear that when a patient recounts his dreams to a psychotherapist he is describing only a very small fraction of the total dreams of the night. To what degree his report truly represents the experiences of the night and to what extent they may be distortions or daytime fantasies must remain uncertain. The dream accounts may serve to inform the experienced clinician of the patient's personality but cannot be relied upon as indications of what actually occurred during the night. It is not difficult to understand why psychotherapists of widely differing persuasions have found dreams which illustrate the particular theoretical positions which they hold.

Freud[39] stated that, 'It is an unconscious impulse that creates a dream in order to bring about instinctual satisfactions in an hallucinatory fashion.' Whatever may be the merits of this conception in regard to the dream content, there can be little doubt that we should give priority to the physiological mechanism underlying paradoxical sleep, during which dreaming seems always to be present, rather than to purely psychological mechanisms. In the experiments mentioned previously involving selective awakening from paradoxical sleep the explanation originally put forward by Dement[22] was in terms of a 'need to dream'. This explanation has now been abandoned by that author, as well as by others, in favour of a physiological explanation. The experiments of Jouvet et al.[59] in which 'pontine' cats, which lacked a cerebral cortex and which could hardly be said to dream, were shown apparently to compensate for selective deprivation of paradoxical sleep, indicate the inadequacy of purely psychological theories. The implications of the recent research on sleep and dreaming for psychoanalytic theory have been examined by Fisher.[35]

Can external stimuli influence dream content? Dement and Wolpert,[25] among other things, sprayed sleeping volunteers with water and then observed that, after awakening, dreams of rain were sometimes related. Berger[10] found that externally spoken words were usually incorporated in a disguised form based upon their sound rather than their sense. He used a careful technique to rule out the possibility of an observer falsely judging incorporation to be present. The presence of incorporation of the external stimulus was decided by a judge's ability to select the correct stimulus from a short list of possibles. Clear evidence of such incorporation was found. Thus, when the name, 'Robert, Robert' was spoken during a girl's dream she subsequently described a dream of a 'rabbit' which had, 'looked distorted'. Robert—a distorted rabbit. When the name, 'Jenny, Jenny' had been spoken during a dream the subsequent dream report contained the passage, 'I dreamed that I was opening a safe with a jemmy'. When the stimulus, 'Gillian, Gillian' (the name of an ex girl-friend) was used it was followed by the report of a dream of, 'an old woman who came from Chile'. She was a Chilean (Gillian), an old woman (an ex girl-friend).

External stimuli during the course of paradoxical sleep may therefore not cause awakening but may be woven into the dream adventure. In the case of stimulation during orthodox sleep it has been shown that stimuli which are of personal significance for the sleeper more easily provoke either full awakening or an EEG arousal response (K-complex) than do stimuli lacking personal significance. Again, meaningful spoken words issuing in the normal forwards manner from a tape recorder more often provoke K-complexes in the EEG than will the same words played backwards alternately with the names played forwards. It would appear as if some sort of scrutiny of incoming sensory input is still possible during sleep and that meaningless stimuli are rejected, whereas some slight response is made to meaningful ones, as if to permit assessment of whether full awakening would fulfil some biological need.[98]

Most of those who have studied dream reports would concede the presence of a fair amount of sexual symbolism even if less convinced than Freud of its universality. The regular accompaniment in man and certain animals of penile erections during paradoxical sleep raises the question of whether the dream content provokes the erection or whether some physiological mechanism responsible for the erection may also lead to a tendency towards sexual manifestations in mental life. In normal young male adults, sexual dreams culminating in orgasm with seminal emission are by no means infrequent, whereas such emission does not occur during waking life in the absence of genital manipulation. The dream itself is usually of a frankly sexual nature though occasionally it may appear a prosaic one while yet containing symbols for sexual activity, such as the climbing of ladders.[45] The work of Jouvet[61] has indicated those parts of the brain which are concerned with the control of paradoxical sleep, the so-called 'limbic' system.[86] They are areas of the brain which are also believed to be concerned with the control of sexual behaviour. There may therefore be some sort of irradiation of neural excitement during paradoxical sleep which is responsible for an element of sexual activity. Other links between the physiology of paradoxical sleep and sexual behaviour have been reported.[32, 95]

Sleep Deprivation

Interest attaches to the various means whereby experimental human psychoses can be produced. One is by deprivation of sleep. We do not know what restitution sleep accomplishes for us, but it may be supposed that some sort of chemical imbalance within the nervous system gets corrected. Quantitative changes of performance after sleep deprivation have been demonstrated by Williams et al.[129] and Wilkinson.[125, 127] Sleep deprived individuals are unable to *sustain* their attention, so that if required to respond repeatedly to a steady stream of incoming information they frequently either fail to respond at all or fail to respond appropriately. It is as if they lapsed momentarily and repeatedly into sleep. It becomes extremely difficult to keep them awake and it is necessary constantly to introduce some element of novelty into their environment and the activities on which they are engaged. The sleep-deprived individual has difficulty in coping with multiple data and when required to solve problems in which knowledge of past events could be utilized, he tends to engage in stereotyped behaviour and to ignore information provided by the past.[43] Writers on the subject of political interrogation and persuasion[51, 75] have emphasized how the interrogators deliberately deprive prisoners of sleep in order to facilitate their acceptance of confessions of past wrongs. The fact that sleep-deprived men have difficulty in calling upon and utilizing memories of past events may significantly contribute to false confessions.

Sleep deprivation produces interesting qualitative changes in mental life. Within sixty hours speech becomes intermittently rambling, with repetitions and mispronunciations. From time to time the speaker will stray off into some apparently irrelevant nonsense as if he were participating in a dream conversation. Illusions are common. Surfaces of walls appear to shimmer or oscillate. Inert objects are from time to time seen as human beings, sometimes threatening. Sounds may seem harsh or distant in quality. Visual hallucinations begin to occur, thus one man kept seeing old women peering at him. They would vanish, the legs before the head, as he drew near. He would look furtively behind him after passing and see them once again. Auditory hallucinations of an elementary nature, such as the sound of dogs barking or of lorries passing, are frequent. The attitude of sleep-deprived volunteers towards those who are in charge of them and who keep them awake may become progressively paranoid, an attitude betrayed in their speech by slips of the tongue. Thus one volunteer spoke of the experimenter as 'exquisitor' which he later explained meant to him an inquisitor able to inflict exquisite pain. Another, in the middle of a card game, volunteered the information that he intended to hire a bodyguard to protect him from 'them'—'they are the ones who caused all the trouble in the last year'. In a substantial proportion a psychosis with systematic paranoid delusions appears. The individuals may afterwards describe how they felt like robots with strange feelings in the body. They may indulge in silly laughter or maintain unusual postures. The individual may believe (and act accordingly) that he is a secret agent or that some organization, having nefarious designs upon his person or family, is encircling him.

One volunteer[12] experienced hallucinatory voices while a water tap was running. During the morning he was given a cup of coffee and became convinced that it had contained a drug responsible for his strange experiences, notably his visual hallucinations. He walked along a main city street behind a companion, peering and pointing at the latter's jacket, saying that he saw handwriting on it. He insisted that his companion stop and take off the jacket in the street for closer inspection. In a long account, written the following day, and after a good night's sleep, he divulged the content of his delusions that had been responsible for his behaviour. At the lunch table he had felt that he and his companion were put well away from other people and had believed that he heard people talking about them both and using the word 'pariah'. He felt sure that he had been given a drug so that, although subjectively he was speaking in a normal voice, others must be aware of what he was saying because the drug was somehow making him shout. During the afternoon he was constantly doubtful what he should do with this knowledge that he had gained, namely that he must have been drugged. When, during lunch, a waiter brought two jugs of water to his table it was a further indication that drugs had been administered in the table salt. He noticed a bitter taste in his mouth. During the afternoon he made abortive attempts to telephone one of the experimenters in order to reveal that he had discovered the secret. In the late afternoon one of the experimenters handed some papers over to the other and wrote a pencil note on one. To the volunteer this was a note stating that he had discovered about the drug, although later in the evening he concluded it must have been a message saying that his companion was mentally unbalanced. His talk became strange and he himself felt puzzled that one of the experimenters did not acknowledge his repeated hints that he had discovered the drugs. While being driven in a car he felt very frightened, listening to the conversation between one of the experimenters and the companion volunteer. The conclusion dawned that his companion was being taken away to be locked up after having been hypnotized, for he was being made to move his limbs on command (actually this was to keep him awake). A word game was played to help maintain wakefulness but he grew suspicious of this and when given the word 'train' he replied, 'Glasgow', for it dawned on him that his companion must be about to be put in prison for some fires that had occurred in some trains in Glasgow some months before. He was noted by the experimenter to look frightened and to stare fixedly, making queer and evasive answers to questions such as, 'discovering the unknown', 'the guilty one', 'the characters are different'. As is usually the case, a single, full night's sleep led to elimination of the psychotic behaviour and thinking.

Many such illustrative reports of psychotic behaviour during sleep deprivation have appeared.[12, 16, 78, 84, 120] Bliss et al.[13] reported that lysergic acid diethylamide produced visual hallucinations more easily when volunteers were sleep-deprived and Koranyi and Lehmann[69] that chronic schizophrenic patients suffered a return of active psychotic symptoms when deprived of sleep.

In order to perform normal waking activities, the sleep-deprived individual has to make a tremendous effort and mobilize all his reserves. Wilkinson[126] found that sleep-deprived individuals able to perform with an efficiency comparable to that of control days were able to do so only when having much higher muscle tension than the normal. Hasselman et al.[46] found that the usual small rise of adrenalin and noradrenalin in the urine caused by muscular work was very much greater under conditions of sleep-deprivation.

Luby et al.[77] found biochemical evidence of response to sleep-deprivation as to a stressor agent, revealed by an intracellular increase in the specific activities of adenosine triphosphate, adenylic acid and fructose-1,6-diphosphate. It was reported by Mandell et al.[79] that an indole substance previously known to be released by corticotrophin injections can be found in the urine of sleep-deprived persons at times which correspond to an increase in the secretion of 17-hydroxycorticosteroids.

At the present time, although it is realized that two different kinds of sleep exist, psychological deficits peculiar to deprivation of each alone have yet to be confirmed. The initial report by Dement[22] of psychological changes peculiar to deprivation of paradoxical sleep was not confirmed. Dewson et al.[26] have demonstrated physiological changes arising from paradoxical sleep deprivation, affecting the recovery cycle in cortical responses evoked by acoustic stimuli.

2

Sleep Disorders

Idiopathic Narcolepsy

Idiopathic narcolepsy is characterized by undesired and recurrent sleepiness which overwhelms the individual especially at times when he is bored, such as when riding on trains or buses, sitting in lectures, while on guard duty or at the office desk. There is usually a definite onset, frequently with weight gain, and most commonly in the 10 to 30 years age-group. In addition to sleepiness the classical features include: (i) cataplectic attacks, namely attacks in which sudden emotion causes a brief loss of muscle tone in either a part or the whole of the body; (ii) sleep paralysis, namely experiences of awakening from sleep and having a strong desire to move, yet being unable to do so for periods of as much as a minute or so; and (iii) vivid dream-like experiences of hypnagogic hallucinations.

Understanding of the condition has recently advanced owing to the report of Rechtschaffen et al.[107] that, unlike the normal person, the narcoleptic passes from ordinary drowsiness, not into Stage II of orthodox sleep, but into paradoxical sleep (Fig. 2). In other words, the narcoleptic tends to pass very quickly into the condition in which vivid dreams occur. He does so within a few moments of having been fully awake and oriented, and it is therefore not surprising that elements of recent reality are often woven into his dreams. There is some evidence that paranoid symptoms arise more often among narcoleptics than in the general population. This might be partly due to amphetamine usage but also to the repeated intrusion of dream elements into their waking life. Not only are the vivid dream reports of daytime narcoleptic sleep now more easily understood, but the paralysis of skeletal musculature in paradoxical sleep is clearly relevant to sleep paralysis and to cataplexy. The patient may fall asleep in his chair at home and dream he is in that same chair but that some headless monster is about to attack him. He struggles to move but finds himself paralysed. It is an extremely vivid experience with interweaving of fantasy and reality.

The cataplectic attacks are described as sudden responses to fear, to anger, to laughter (the patient may say that she always has to sit down when expecting a funny story), startle, or a feeling of triumph—thus one patient of mine has collapsed more than once while playing table tennis and when in the act of making a winning smash. Consciousness is retained and it would seem as if cataplectic attacks represent a sort of partial state of paradoxical sleep with only some of the bodily changes. Jouvet and Delorme[62] have described experiments with cats in which lesions localized

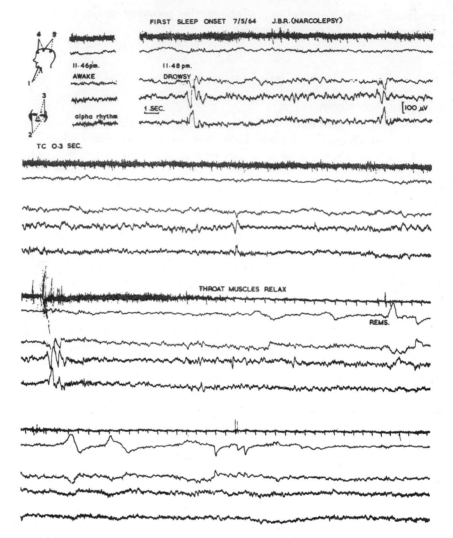

FIG. 2. Sleep onset in a narcoleptic patient. After about a minute of drowsiness with low voltage EEG slow waves (and no sleep spindles) there is an abrupt passage into paradoxical sleep with loss of muscle tone and the appearance of rapid eye movements (REMs).
(From Evans and Oswald.) [29]

to the locus coeruleus resulted in paradoxical sleep from which some of the usual features were missing.

The daytime sleep episodes commonly last about fifteen minutes. If one appears within a short space of time after a previous bout of sleep then, as if some priority for paradoxical sleep has been satisfied, the patient will pass into orthodox sleep, as in any case happens at night when the initial period of paradoxical sleep has lasted its usual fifteen minutes or so. The latter duration can be doubled if the patient has swallowed 5 grams of laevo-tryptophan about fifteen minutes before retiring.[29] It is thus possible that idiopathic narcolepsy may reflect a disorder of brain amine metabolism. Dextroamphetamine sulphate 10 to 70 milligrams per day has for long been the standard treatment but facilitates paranoid symptoms and tends to lose its effect with time. It is probably best not taken regularly but only prior to occasions of special importance.

Insomnia

An indication of the frequency of insomnia is provided by the consumption of hypnotic drugs. Ten per cent* of all National Health Service prescriptions by general practitioners in England and Wales are for hypnotics.[81] In the Australian scheme, whereby prescribed drugs are available cheaply to patients, 12·6 per cent of prescriptions are for hypnotic drugs.[17] McGhie and Russell[80] conducted a survey in Scotland in which completed questionnaires were received from 2,446 persons having an age and social class distribution similar to that of Scotland as a whole. Over a quarter of those of middle age stated that they regularly took some pharmaceutical preparation in order to promote sleep and this figure rose to some 45 per cent of elderly women. Women of all ages complained much more about their sleep than men. They often complained of lying awake and feeling unable to fall asleep, of frequent night wakening and of feeling that their sleep had been only light. In both sexes the complaints about sleep grew more common with advancing years. The effect of age was noted too by Weiss *et al.*,[122] who gathered data from over 100 general medical out-patients, 100 psychiatric clinic out-patients of similar age and social class, and 100 healthy controls. The frequency of complaints about sleep among the medical and 'healthy' groups was the same and was only one quarter of the incidence among the psychiatric patients. Married people complained more often of sleep difficulties than the unmarried, possibly reflecting a tendency to worry over greater responsibilities.

There is little doubt that some neurotic individuals exaggerate the extent to which they are unable to sleep. Indeed, one might say that just as in a former generation the regular evacuation of the bowels was regarded as of prime importance for health, so today there is an unnecessary concern for regularly having some eight hours of sleep. Schwartz and her colleagues[49, 113] have investigated a number of chronic psychoneurotic individuals who claimed not to sleep at all. Patients went to bed in a laboratory and rapidly passed into a state of behavioural sleep accompanied by the characteristic EEG. They remained unmoved by signals to which they had previously said they would respond, snored and were oblivious of persons entering the room. From time to time during the night they would

---

* In the U.S.A. 'from 1952 to 1963, the retail sales of sedatives and tranquilizers increased 535 per cent' (*Health, Education and Welfare*, 1967. A Report to the President on Medical Care Prices. Washington, D.C., Superintendent of Documents.)

stir, open their eyes and announce triumphantly that they were still awake, while in the morning they would rouse and say that they had not closed their eyes all night.

It should not be supposed that there are not patients with very severe and genuine insomnia. Hypomanic patients frequently arise in the early hours of the morning and rush around the house singing. Patients with mania may hardly sleep at all. The obverse picture of severe depressive illness (autonomous melancholia) is characteristically accompanied by a complaint of waking in the early hours of the morning and of lying ruminating upon various morbid themes or of rising from bed and pacing to and fro. The insomnia of these patients is quite genuine and has been confirmed by all-night EEG recordings.[43a, 96] The traditional view, namely that these patients tend to awaken early in the morning rather than have difficulty in falling asleep at night, is sometimes questioned, but the clinician will continue to be guided by the patients' complaints, which are generally those of early morning wakening, rather than by results obtained from laboratory procedures. The patients might, for example, remember their wakefulness of the early morning more vividly if it were characterized by a greater degree of misery than wakefulness upon retiring.

There seems little doubt, however, that the greater majority of sufferers from insomnia are vulnerable members of society who feel anxious and insecure in the face of life's difficulties and for whom insomnia is a recurrent manifestation of minor distress. Even if we are disinclined to believe that they sleep as little as they say, we cannot assume that their complaints of poor quality sleep are without foundation. Monroe[83] carried out a physiological study of the differences between the sleep of healthy volunteers who considered their sleep to be of good quality and the sleep of healthy volunteers who considered it to be of poor quality. The heart-rate and the rectal temperature were lower during the night among the good sleepers, which is not surprising. Electrical skin resistance normally rises steeply with sleep and might have been expected to be greater among the good sleepers: it was, however, higher among the poor sleepers during the course of the night. Such observations serve to remind us that we have yet much to learn of the true basis of sleep's restitutive action.

In the study of McGhie and Russell the persons answering the questionnaires belonged to a variety of social clubs. The objection might be made that the high frequency of complaints of poor sleep in their sample was an artifact—that perhaps people who are gregarious and extroverted and join clubs may sleep worse than the average. Costello and Smith,[18] using nurses' scores of the times at nights during which patients were judged to be asleep (when not receiving hypnotic drugs), compared the sleep of a sample of patients who had been selected because of extreme scores for extroversion on the Maudsley Personality Inventory with the sleep of a sample whose scores indicated extreme introversion. The extroverts, by the nurses' judgements, were found to have slept 50 per cent more than the introverts. The findings of McGhie and Russell therefore cannot at present be questioned on the grounds that their samples were unusually extroverted.

Nightmares, Sleep-talking and Sleep-walking

Night terrors can arise during drowsiness with hypnagogic hallucinations and are also sometimes associated with abrupt awakening from the

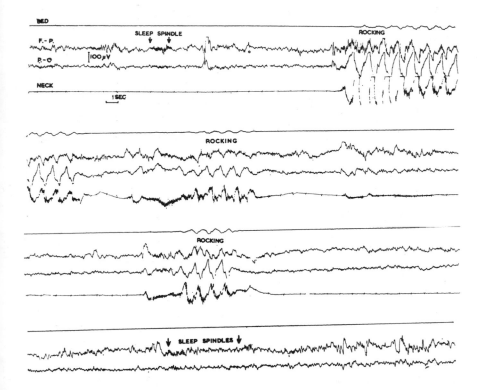

FIG. 3. Recorded during a nightmare, some ten minutes after sleep onset. The excerpts are continuous. Muscle artifacts indicate facial twitches. The characteristic rapid eye movements (REMs) and low voltage 2 – 6 c/sec EEG waves of paradoxical sleep continue despite the groans. Recent reality is woven into the dream—'Help, doctor'. This narcoleptic patient had received oral laevo-tryptophan 5 grams 30 minutes previously.
(From Evans and Oswald.) [29]

orthodox phase of sleep. However, most true nightmares arise in the course of paradoxical sleep. They are terrifying or distressing dreams, frequently associated with a feeling of weight upon the chest which interferes with breathing, together with a feeling of helpless paralysis. Many writers, including Freud, have drawn attention to this feeling of paralysis. The dreamer feels himself swept helplessly towards some terrifying fate, he struggles to move but finds his limbs divorced from his conscious efforts. He may cry out or mutter, his face may twitch (Fig. 3), but he is unable to move until full awakening occurs. The paralysis can now be understood from our knowledge of the physiology of paradoxical sleep. There is evidence too that nightmares occur more frequently when there is

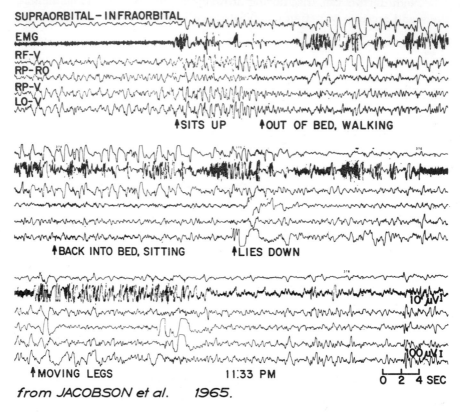

FIG. 4. A sleep-walking incident. Note the persistence of EEG slow waves. R = right, L = left, F = frontal, P = parietal, O = occipital, V = vertex.
  (From Jacobson et al.[57] Copyright 1965 by the American Association for the Advancement of Science.)

an increased 'pressure', as it were, towards paradoxical sleep. In a number of studies where there has been an increased duration of paradoxical sleep in the whole night and when it has tended to come on abnormally early during the night on account, for example, of the withdrawal of drugs, nightmares have been frequent.[29, 72, 97]

Sleep talking is common but there are big individual differences. Usually only mumbling occurs and it is difficult to record what is actually said. Sleep talking is more commonly associated with interruptions of orthodox sleep by major bodily movement, at which time the utterances generally refer to recent events and current situations associated with little emotion.[105] There were many war-time reports of restless sleep following combat experience. Soldiers would shout and hurl themselves around their beds. Sometimes they would leap out of bed and attack imaginary enemies, diving in panic at the sound of a passing aeroplane, and responding only incoherently to question.[100] They are disoriented; mundane reality fails to make much impression upon the troubled fantasy world in which they re-live former experiences.

Recently, Jacobson *et al.*[57] have used biotelemetry and reported upon nine incidents of sleep-walking and sixty-five incidents of sitting up among known sleep-walkers. All such episodes began during periods of orthodox sleep, usually Stages III or IV. Most incidents occurred during the first few hours of the night. The sleep-walkers appeared indifferent to their environment, with open eyes and blank expressions, their move-ments appearing rigid. There was complete amnesia for the incidents by the morning. Their EEGs showed continuance of slow wave activity during the periods of somnambulism. When the periods were brief, very slow delta waves sometimes continued throughout (Fig. 4), though in longer incidents a lower voltage tracing containing rhythms closer to those of wakefulness occurred.

It has been recognized by the law that homicide may be committed during sleep-walking. A case was quoted by Hopwood and Snell[55] of a man who battered his wife to death with a shovel. An English jury at Essex Assizes (19th February 1962) accepted a defence plea that homicide was committed during sleep. Podolsky[104] cited a case of 1878 in Scottish law where a man was acquitted of killing his 18-year-old son on the grounds that the deed was committed during sleep. Podolsky[103] described the case of a sixteen-year-old girl who was said to have dreamed that burglars were in the house attacking her family, she seized two guns and fired, killing a brother, her father, and injuring her mother.

The Syndrome of Periodic Somnolence and Over-eating.

A variety of reports has appeared[20, 40, 66, 74] of patients who were said to sleep for eighteen or more hours per day with brief intervals during which they would awaken, attend to toilet activities and eat voraciously. Most of the cases have been males, particularly during adolescence. It cannot be said that the published reports together indicate a nosological entity. The physiological features of sleep have not been described in support of the contention of excessive sleeping. Critchley[20] assumed the presence of sleep in some of his patients, despite widely-dilated pupils and 'hypermotility'. Many of the cases described by Critchley and others have manifested psychological disorders—confusion, incoherence of speech, restlessness, occasional evidence of hallucinations, periods of euphoria and various schizophreniform features.

The 'attacks' described have ranged in duration from one or two days to twelve weeks or more, sometimes recurring frequently over as many as twenty years or more. Recurrent and self-limited illnesses characterized by psychotic features, inertia and impaired responsiveness are familiar to psychiatrists. It seems likely that many of the cases described by neurologists might well have been subsumed under such diagnoses as schizo-affective, periodic[19] or cycloid[73] psychoses. One of the cases of Critchley[20] was a man with left cerebral atrophy, and Rosenkötter and Wende[110] made a diagnosis of sub-acute encephalitis when describing a case. It may be noted that Pai,[101] having studied sixty-seven cases of young males subject to excessive 'sleep' and to over-eating in some cases, was of the opinion that the two symptoms were coincidental and both hysterical in nature.

Enuresis

This is not the place for a lengthy discussion of enuresis but the author would accept the view that most enuretic children are children who lie near the end of a normal distribution in age of nocturnal bladder control, rather than that such children are either suffering from an organic disorder or enuretic as a symptom of psychological conflict.[5]

The common statement that enuretic children sleep more 'deeply' will be seen to be meaningless in the light of the previous discussion concerning depth of sleep. There is at the present time no rational basis for the treatment of enuretic children by amphetamine or other drugs.

Enuresis occurs predominantly during the orthodox phase of sleep.[28,48] The actual wetting of the bed is frequently preceded by and accompanied by bodily restlessness. There is evidence that simple conditioning can occur during orthodox sleep.[6] This would support, as a rational form of treatment, the use of an alarm or buzzer to cause awakening when the bed is made wet.[123, 124] One may regard the ringing of the bell (brought about by the escape of urine) as the unconditioned stimulus, arousal would form the unconditioned response, visceral afferent impulses from the nearly full bladder, which immediately preceded the bed-wetting and arousal, could be regarded as the conditioned stimuli. The conditioned response of arousal can thus be understood eventually to follow upon the visceral afferents from the full bladder without the intervention of a bell.

Other Sleep Disorders

It is here appropriate to refer to yawning, even though one can hardly regard it as abnormal. Its relation to sleep is realized by all but its significance is uncertain.[4]

It is also doubtful whether one should regard snoring as an abnormality of sleep, though there is an extensive and amusing history of patent devices for its treatment. Snoring occurs in orthodox sleep only.[33] Individual snores cause brief sleep disturbance but repeated snores soon allow habituation.[34] Snoring occurs through vibration of the thin edge or velum of the posterior faucial pillars. It takes place when there are critical positions of tongue and soft palate, depending also on the thickness and tone of the nasopharyngeal musculature and the head position—sleeping on the back causes the rear of the tongue to fall backwards and, like nasal obstruction, predisposes to snoring.

Bruxism, or tooth-grinding, is said to occur in about ten per cent of the population. The individuals grind their teeth during their sleep, causing some damage to the teeth. Reding et al.[108] studied twelve such persons.

Some children and occasional adults engage in violent rhythmic body rocking or head-banging during the night. It is most common as a prelude to sleep in infants of eight to twenty-four months of age, frequently accompanying the teething period and apparently serving as a comfort habit, comparable to thumb-sucking and not an indication of any abnormality of personality.[71] Rhythmic bodily movement always promotes relaxation and sleep.[89] Other infant primates engage in body rocking as a comfort habit when separated from their mothers and, if the separation is prolonged, the habit may persist into later life.[21] Nocturnal body rocking among human infants appears first as a prelude to sleep but with time it occurs actually during sleep. Among institutionalized children, especially mental defectives, it may persist during both the night and the day.

The rhythmic movement, which can be of great violence, may last for only a few seconds or may continue for minutes at a time. The sleeper may turn his body violently from side to side or, having raised himself on to his hands and knees, he may rock his body to and fro, banging his head violently against the pillow or bed-head. The episodes tend to be more frequent at times of life stress. The individual is almost never aware that he has engaged in these, and they cause more inconvenience, by reason of the noise created, to the remainder of the family and immediate neighbours than to the patient. In children, the movements may be accompanied by rhythmic crooning noises. The electroencephalogram usually shows the continuing appearances of sleep, though there tends to be a shift towards faster frequencies (Fig. 5). The rhythmic movements can occur during either the paradoxical phase of sleep or the orthodox phase of sleep.[92]

If one regards the rhythmic rocking movement as a comfort habit learned in infancy then one must wonder whether it is occurring in sleep because of some concurrent unhappy thoughts. Sleep-walking, enuresis and bruxism can, like rhythmic rocking movements, all occur during the orthodox phase of sleep, facts which would lend some support to the belief that mental life can occur during the orthodox phase of sleep, even though dreaming is most particularly associated with the paradoxical phase. Foulkes,[38] from a careful study of reports given by volunteers who were awakened from both the paradoxical and the orthodox phases of sleep, concluded that mental life was present in both. The quality of the mental life reported, however, differed. Awakenings from orthodox sleep tended to be associated with reports of 'thinking', particularly about recent actual events, whereas awakenings from paradoxical sleep more often

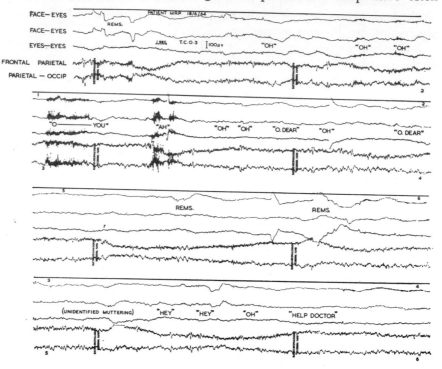

FIG. 5. The EEG signs of Stage II sleep are present with spindles and slow wave complexes. F.–P. = fronto-paretal EEG, P.–O. = parieto-occipital EEG. Suddenly the sleep of this 20-year old man is broken by rhythmic whole-body rocking which causes artifact in the two EEG channels and the 'neck' channel (muscle potentials are visible in the latter). The bed movement recorder (top channel) shows the movements to cease, then to recommence, to cease, to recommence and then to cease once more.

The segments of record are continuous. The spindles disappear for an interval but despite the violent exercise only fleeting traces of EEG alpha rhythm can be seen and sleep spindles return within less than half a minute of the end of rocking.

(From Oswald.) [94]

elicited accounts of 'dreaming' in which mental life was characterized by a greater degree of fantasy, of imagery and emotion.

Drugs and Sleep

The barbiturate drugs reduce the frequency of movements during sleep.[52, 96] Barbiturates and amphetamine share the property of reducing the proportion of the night spent in paradoxical sleep.[96, 106] The demonstration of some neurophysiological effects common to these drugs, contrary to the orthodox view that they were opposite in their action, accorded with the clinical observation by psychiatrists that amphetamine and a short-acting barbiturate in combination did not cancel one another out, but tended, in some people, to have a euphoriant effect sufficient to promote the appearance of addiction. Tranylcypromine[72] and alcohol[44] also reduce the proportion of the night spent in paradoxical sleep.

The effects of drugs on sleep decrease with repeated administration.[7, 97] It would seem that drugs like amphetamine and barbiturates, by their long-continued usage, may become, in some way, woven into the brain chemistry so that, although their initial effects are lost, they are now essential for normal neurophysiological function. When the drugs are then withdrawn, abnormalities of function appear (Fig. 6), which may take

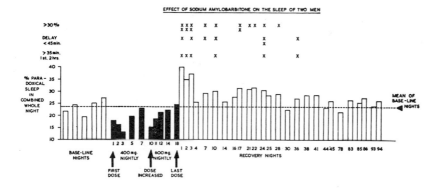

FIG. 6. Effect of sodium amylobarbitone on the sleep of two men who serve as their own controls. The hypnotic drug initially causes suppression of paradoxical sleep. Withdrawal provokes a rebound increase. The time scale is not linear.

Where either or both volunteers spent over 30 per cent of the whole night in paradoxical sleep, had a delay of less than 45 minutes between first falling asleep and first rapid eye movements of paradoxical sleep, or spent more than 35 minutes of the first two hours of sleep in the paradoxical phase, a star has been placed over the night concerned. It will be noted that the stars appear only after drug withdrawal and persist into the sixth recovery week.

(From Oswald and Priest.) [97]

as long as two months to resolve,[97, 99] a fact of obvious relevance to the widespread consumption of such drugs for periods of years at a time.

Conclusion

The recent considerable studies in basic knowledge about sleep have as yet, led to only limited contributions of clinical importance. They have, however, provided knowledge of basic brain function, and as this grows and is linked with neuropharmacological studies of the sleep process, clinical applications will eventually follow.

REFERENCES

1. AGNEW, H. W., WEBB, W. B., and WILLIAMS, R. L., 1964. The effects of stage four sleep deprivation. *Electroenceph. clin. Neurophysiol.*, **17**, 68.
2. ASERINSKY, E., and KLEITMAN, N., 1955. A motility cycle in sleeping infants as manifested by ocular and gross bodily activity. *J. appl. Physiol.*, **8**, 11.
3. BALDRIDGE, B. J., WHITMAN, R. M., and KRAMER, M., 1965. The concurrence of fine muscle activity and rapid eye movements during sleep. *Psychosom. Med.*, **27**, 19.
4. BARBIZET, J., 1958. Yawning. *J. Neurol. Neurosurg. Psychiat.*, **21**, 203.
5. BARBOUR, R. F., BORLAND, E. M., BOYD, M. M., MILLER, A., and OPPÉ, T. E., 1963. Enuresis as a disorder of development. *Brit. med. J.*, ii, 787.
6. BEH, H. C., and BARRETT, P. E. H., 1965. Discrimination and conditioning during sleep as indicated by the electroencephalogram. *Science*, **147**, 1470.
7. BELLEVILLE, R. E., and FRASER, H. F., 1957. Tolerance to some effects of barbiturates. *J. Pharmacol. exp. Ther.*, **120**, 469.
8. BENA, E., HOSKOVEC, J., and STIKAR, J., 1962. *Psychologie a Fyziologie Řidiĉe*. Prague: Nakladatesvi dopravy a spoju.
9. BERGER, R. J., 1961. Tonus of extrinsic laryngeal muscles during sleep and dreaming. *Science*, **134**, 840.
10. BERGER, R. J., 1963. Experimental modification of dream content by meaningful verbal stimuli. *Brit. J. Psychiat.*, **109**, 722.
11. BERGER, R. J., OLLEY, P., and OSWALD, I., 1962. The EEG, eye-movements and dreams of t he blind. *Quart. J. exp. Psychol.*, **14**, 183.
12. BERGER, R. J., and OSWALD, I., 1962. Effects of sleep deprivation on behaviour, subsequent sleep, and dreaming. *J. ment. Sci.*, **108**, 457.
13. BLISS, E. L., CLARK, L. D., and WEST, C. D., 1959. Studies of sleep deprivation-relationship to schizophrenia. *Arch. Neurol. Psychiat., Chic.*, **81**, 348.
14. CADILHAC, J., and PASSOUANT, P., 1965. L'influence des différentes phases du sommeil nocturne sur les décharges épileptiques chez l'homme. In *Neurophysiologie des États de Sommeil*. Ed. Jouvet, M. Paris: Centre National de la Recherche Scientifique.
15. CAIRNS, H., 1952. Disturbances of consciousness with lesions of the brain-stem and diencephalon. *Brain*, **75**, 109.
16. CAPPON, D., and BANKS, R., 1960. Studies in perceptual distortion: opportunistic observations on sleep deprivation during a talkathon. *Arch. gen. Psychiat.*, **2**, 346.
17. COMMONWEALTH DIRECTOR-GENERAL OF HEALTH, 1965. *Annual Report, 1964-65*. Canberra.
18. COSTELLO, C. G., and SMITH, M., 1963. The relationships between personality, sleep and the effects of sedatives. *Brit. J. Psychiat.*, **109**, 568.
19. CRAMMER, J. L., 1959. Periodic psychoses. *Brit. med. J.*, i, 545.
20. CRITCHLEY, M., 1962. Periodic hypersomnia and megaphagia in adolescent males. *Brain*, **85**, 627.
21. DAVENPORT, R. K., and MENZEL, E. W., 1963. Stereotyped behaviour of the infant chimpanzee. *Arch. gen. Psychiat.*, **8**, 99.
22. DEMENT, W. C., 1960. The effect of dream deprivation. *Science*, **131**, 1705.

23. DEMENT, W. C., and KLEITMAN, N., 1957. Cyclic variations in EEG during sleep and their relation to eye movements, bodily motility and dreaming. *Electroenceph. clin. Neurophysiol.*, **9**, 673.
24. DEMENT, W. C., and KLEITMAN, N., 1957. The relation of eye movements during sleep to dream activity, an objective method for the study of dreaming. *J. exp. Psychol.*, **53**, 339.
25. DEMENT, W. C., and WOLPERT, E. A., 1958. The relation of eye movements, body motility and external stimuli to dream content. *J. exp. Psychol.*, **55**, 543.
26. DEWSON, J. H., DEMENT, W. C., WAGENER, T., and NOBEL, K., 1967. Rapid eye movement sleep deprivation: a central-neural change during wakefulness. *Science*, **156**, 403.
27. ECONOMO, C. VON, 1926. Die Pathologie des Schlafes. *Hand. norm. path. Physiol.*, **17**, 591.
28. EVANS, J. I. (1966). Personal communication.
29. EVANS, J. I., and OSWALD, I., 1966. Some experiments in the chemistry of narcoleptic sleep. *Brit. J. Psychiat.*, **112**, 401.
30. EVARTS, E. V., 1962. Activity of neurons in visual cortex of cat during sleep with low voltage fast EEG activity. *J. Neurophysiol.*, **25**, 812.
31. EVARTS, E. V., 1965. Relation of cell size to effects of sleep in pyramidal tract neurons. In *Sleep Mechanisms*. Eds. Akert, K., Bally, C., and Schadé, J. P. Amsterdam: Elsevier Publishing Co.
32. FAURE, J., and BENSCH, C., 1962. Mésencéphale et 'post-réaction-E.E.G.' dans le comportement lié à la vie endocrinogénitale du Lapin. *Rev. neurol.*, **106**, 197.
33. FISCHGOLD, H., and SCHWARTZ, B. A., 1961. A clinical, electroencephalographic and polygraphic study of sleep in the human adult. In *The Nature of Sleep*. Eds. Wolstenholme, G. E. W. and O'Connor, M. London: J. & A. Churchill Ltd.
34. FISCHGOLD, H., SCHWARTZ, B. A., and DREYFUS-BRISAC, C., 1959. Indicateur de l'etat de présence et tracés électroencéphalographiques dans le sommeil nembutalique. *Electroenceph. clin. Neurophysiol.*, **11**, 23.
35. FISHER, C., 1965. The relationship of instinctual drives to physiological processes. Part III: Implications for psychoanalytic theory. *J. Amer. psychoanal. Ass.*, **13**, 271.
36. FISHER, C., GROSS, J., and ZUCH, J., 1965. Cycle of penile erection synchronous with dreaming (REM) sleep. *Arch. gen. Psychiat.*, **12**, 29.
37. FOULKES, D., and VOGEL, G., 1965. Mental activity at sleep onset. *J. abnorm. soc. Psychol.*, **70**, 231.
38. FOULKES, W. D., 1962. Dream reports from different stages of sleep. *J. abnorm. soc. Psychol.*, **65**, 14.
39. FREUD, S. (1933). *New Introductory Lectures on Psychoanalysis*. New York: W. W. Norton.
40. GALLINEK, A., 1954. Syndrome of episodes of hypersomnia, bulimia and abnormal mental states. *J. Amer. med. Ass.*, **154**, 1081.
41. GASTAUT, H., and BERT, J., 1961. Electroencephalographic detection of sleep induced by repetitive sensory stimuli. In *The Nature of Sleep*. Eds. Wolstenholme, G. E. W., and O'Connor, M. London: J. & A. Churchill Ltd.
42. GOODENOUGH, D. R., SHAPIRO, A., HOLDEN, M., and STEINSCHRIBER, L., 1959. A comparison of dreamers and nondreamers; eye movements, electroencephalograms and the recall of dreams. *J. abnorm. soc. Psychol.*, **59**, 295.

43. GOODNOW, J. J., RUBENSTEIN, I., and SHANKS, B. L., 1959. The rôle of past events in problem solving. *J. exp. Psychol.*, **58**, 456.

43a. GRESHAM, S. C., AGNEW, H. W., and WILLIAMS, H. L., 1965. The sleep of depressed patients. *Arch. gen. Psychiat.*, **13**, 503.

44. GRESHAM, S. C., WEBB, W. B., and WILLIAMS, H. L., 1963. Alcohol and caffeine: effect on inferred visual dreaming. *Science*, **140**, 1226.

45. HALL, C. S., 1953. *The Meaning of Dreams*. New York: Harper.

46. HASSELMAN, M., SCHAFF, G., and METZ, B., 1960. Influences respectives du travail de la température ambiante, et de la privation de sommeil sur l'excrétion urinaire de catécholamines chez l'Homme normal. *C.R. Soc. Biol., Paris*, **154**, 197.

47. HAWKINS, D. R., PURYEAR, H. B., WALLACE, C. D., DEAL, W. B., and THOMAS, E. S., 1962. Basal skin resistance during sleep and 'dreaming'. *Science*, **136**, 321.

48. HAWKINS, D. R., SCOTT, J., and THRASHER, G., 1967. Relationship of enuresis in children to level of sleep. (To be published.)

49. HELD, R., SCHWARTZ, B. A., and FISCHGOLD, H., 1959. Fausse insomnie. *Presse méd.*, **67**, 141.

50. HESS, W. R., 1944. Das Schlafsyndrom als Folge dienzephaler Reizung. *Helv. physiol. pharmacol. Acta.*, **2**, 305.

51. HINKLE, L. E., and WOLFF, H. G., 1956. Communistic interrogation and indoctrination of 'Enemies of the State'. *Arch. Neurol. Psychiat., Chic.*, **76**, 115.

52. HINTON, J. M., 1963. A comparison of the effects of six barbiturates and a placebo on insomnia and motility in psychiatric patients. *Brit. J. Pharmacol.*, **20**, 319.

53. HODES, R., and DEMENT, W. C., 1964. Depression of electrically induced reflexes ('H-reflexes') in man during low voltage EEG 'sleep'. *Electroenceph. clin. Neurophysiol.*, **17**, 617.

54. HODES, R., and SUZUKI, J., 1965. Comparative thresholds of cortex, vestibular system and reticular formation in wakefulness, sleep and rapid eye movement periods. *Electroenceph. clin. Neurophysiol.*, **18**, 239.

55. HOPWOOD, J. S., and SNELL, H. K., 1933. Amnesia in relation to crime. *J. ment. Sci.*, **79**, 27.

56. JACOBSON, A., KALES, A., LEHMANN, D., and HOEDEMAKER, F. S., 1964. Muscle tone in human subjects during sleep and dreaming. *Exp. Neurol.*, **10**, 418.

57. JACOBSON, A., KALES, A., LEHMANN, D., and ZWEIZIG, J. R., 1965. Somnambulism: all-night electroencephalographic studies. *Science*, **148**, 975.

58. JEFFERSON, G., and JOHNSON, R. T., 1950. The cause of loss of consciousness in posterior fossa compression. *Folia psychiat. neerl.*, **53**, 306.

59. JOUVET, D., VIMONT, P., DELORME, F., and JOUVET, M., 1964. Étude de la privation sélective de la phase paradoxale de sommeil chez le chat. *C.R. Soc. Biol., Paris*, **158**, 756.

60. JOUVET, M., 1962. Recherches sur les structures nerveuses et le mécanismes responsables des différentes phases du sommeil physiologique. *Arch. ital. Biol.*, **100**, 125.

61. JOUVET, M., 1965. Paradoxical sleep—a study of its nature and mechanisms. In *Sleep Mechanisms*. Eds. Akert, K., Bally, C., and Schadé, J. P. Amsterdam: Elsevier Publishing Co.

62. JOUVET, M., and DELORME, F., 1965. Locus coeruleus et sommeil paradoxal. *C.R. Soc. Biol., Paris*, **154**, 895.

63. KAHN, E., DEMENT, W. C., FISHER, V., and BARMACK, J. E., 1962. Incidence of color in immediately recalled dreams. *Science*, **137**, 1054.

64. KALES, A., HOEDEMAKER, F. S., JACOBSON, A., and LICHTENSTEIN, E. D., 1964. Dream deprivation: an experimental reappraisal. *Nature, Lond.*, **204**, 1337.

65. KENNEDY, J. L., and TRAVIS, R. C., 1948. Prediction and control of alertness II. Continuous tracking. *J. comp. Physiol. Psychol.*, **41**, 203.

66. KLEINE, W., 1925. Periodische Schlafsucht. *Mschr. Psychiat. Neurol.*, **57**, 285.

67. KLEITMAN, N., 1963. *Sleep and Wakefulness*. Chicago: University of Chicago Press.

68. KLEITMAN, N., and ENGELMANN, T. G., 1953. Sleep characteristics of infants. *J. appl. Physiol.*, **6**, 269.

69. KORANYI, E. K., and LEHMANN, T. G., 1960. Experimental sleep deprivation in schizophrenic patients. *Arch. gen. Psychiat.*, **2**, 534.

70. KRAEPELIN, E., 1906. Über Sprachstörungen im Traume. *Psychol. Arb.*, **5**, 1.

71. KRAVITZ, H., ROSENTHAL, V., TEPLITZ, Z., MURPHY, J. B., and LESSER, R. E., 1960. A study of head-banging in infants and children. *Dis. nerv. Syst.*, **21**, 3.

72. LE GASSICKE, J., ASHCROFT, G. W., ECCLESTON, D., EVANS, J. I., OSWALD, I., and RITSON, E. B., 1965. The clinical state, sleep and amine metabolism of a tranylcypromine ('Parnate') addict. *Brit. J. Psychiat.*, **111**. 357.

73. LEONHARD, K., 1961. Cycloid psychoses—endogenous psychoses which are neither schizophrenic nor manic-depressive. *J. ment. Sci.*, **107**, 633.

74. LEVIN, M., 1936. Periodic somnolence and morbid hunger; a new syndrome. *Brain*, **62**, 494.

75. LIFTON, R. J., 1961. *Thought Reform and the Psychology of Totalism: a Study of Brain Washing in China*. New York: Norton.

76. LOOMIS, A. L., HARVEY, E. N., and HOBART, G. A., 1937. Cerebral states during sleep as studied by human brain potentials. *J. exp. Psychol.*, **21**, 127.

77. LUBY, E. D., FROHMAN, C. E., GRISELL, J. L., LENZO, J. E., and GOTTLIEB, J. S., 1960. Sleep deprivation: effects on behaviour, thinking, motor performance, and biological energy transfer systems. *Psychosom. Med.*, **22**, 182.

78. LUBY, E. D., GRISELL, J. L., FROHMAN, C. E., LEES, H., COHEN, B. D., and GOTTLIEB, J. S., 1962. Biochemical, psychological and behavioral responses to sleep deprivation. *Ann. N.Y. Acad. Sci.*, **96**, 71.

79. MANDELL, A. J., SABBOT, I. M., MANDELL, M. P., and KOLLAR, E. J., 1964. The stress responsive indole substance in sleep deprivation. *Arch. gen. Psychiat.*, **10**, 209.

80. McGHIE, A., and RUSSELL, S. M., 1962. The subjective assessment of normal sleep patterns. *J. ment. Sci.*, **108**, 642.

81. MINISTRY OF HEALTH, 1964. *Recent N.H.S. prescribing trends. Reports on Public Health and Medical Subjects No. 110*. London, H.M.S.O.

82. MITCHELL, S. W., 1890. Some disorders of sleep. *Int. J. med. Sci.*, **100**, 109.

83. MONROE, L. J., 1967. Psychological and physiological differences between good and poor sleepers. *J. abnorm. Psychol.* (in press).

84. MORRIS, G. O., WILLIAMS, H. L., and LUBIN, A., 1960. Misperception and disorientation during sleep deprivation. *Arch. gen. Psychiat.*, **2**, 247.

85. MORUZZI, G., and MAGOUN, H. W., 1949. Brain stem reticular formation and activities of the EEG. *Electroenceph. clin. Neurophysiol.*, **1**, 455.

86. NAUTA, W. J. H., 1958. Hippocampal projections and related neural pathways to the mid-brain in the cat. *Brain*, **81**, 319.

87. OKUMA, T., FUJIMORI, M., and HAYASHI, A., 1964. An electrographic study on the modification of the sleep cycle pattern by repeated arousal stimulation in both man and cats (the study on sleep, III). *Fol. psychiat. neurol. jap.*, **18**, 63.

88. OSWALD, I., 1959. Sudden bodily jerks on falling asleep. *Brain*, **82**, 92.

89. OSWALD, I., 1959. Experimental studies of rhythm, anxiety and cerebral vigilance. *J. ment. Sci.*, **105**, 269.

90. OSWALD, I., 1960. Falling asleep open-eyed during intense rhythmic stimulation. *Brit. med. J.*, i, 1450.

91. OSWALD, I., 1962. *Sleeping and Waking*. Amsterdam: Elsevier Publishing Co.

92. OSWALD, I., 1964. Physiology of sleep accompanying dreaming. In *The scientific basis of medicine annual reviews*. Ed. Ross, J. P. London: The Athlone Press.

93. OSWALD, I., 1966. *Sleep*. Harmondsworth, England, Penguin Books Ltd.

94. OSWALD, I., 1966. Sleep Mechanisms: some recent advances. *Int. J. Neurol.*, **5**, 187.

95. OSWALD, I., ASHCROFT, G. W., BERGER, R. J., ECCLESTON, D., EVANS, J. I., and THACORE, V. R., 1966. Some experiments in the chemistry of normal sleep. *Brit. J. Psychiat.*, **112**, 391.

96. OSWALD, I., BERGER, R. J., JARAMILLO, R. A., KEDDIE, K. M. G., OLLEY, P. C., and PLUNKETT, G. B., 1963. Melancholia and barbiturates: a controlled EEG, body and eye movement study of sleep. *Brit. J. Psychiat.*, **109**, 66.

97. OSWALD, I., and PRIEST, R. G., 1965. Five weeks to escape the sleeping pill habit. *Brit. med. J.*, ii, 1093.

98. OSWALD, I., TAYLOR, A. M., and TREISMAN, M., 1960. Discriminative responses to stimulation during human sleep. *Brain*, **83**, 440.

99. OSWALD, I., and THACORE, V. R., 1963. Amphetamine and phenmetrazine addiction: physiological abnormalities in the abstinence syndrome. *Brit. med. J.*, ii, 427.

100. PAI, M. N., 1946. Sleep-walking and sleep activities. *J. ment. Sci.*, **92**, 756.

101. PAI, M. N., 1950. Hypersomnia syndromes. *Brit. med. J.*, i, 522.

102. PARMELEE, A. H., WENNER, W. H., and SCHULZ, H. R., 1964. Infant sleep patterns from birth to 16 weeks of age. *J. Pediat.*, **65**, 576.

103. PODOLSKY, E., 1959. Somnambulistic homicide. *Dis. nerv. Syst.*, **20**, 534.

104. PODOLSKY, E., 1964. Somnambulistic homicide. *Amer. J. Psychiat.*, **121**, 191.

105. RECHTSCHAFFEN, A., GOODENOUGH, D. R., and SHAPIRO, A., 1962. Patterns of sleep talking. *Arch. gen. Psychiat.*, **7**, 418.

106. RECHTSCHAFFEN, A., and MARON, L., 1964. Effect of amphetamine on the sleep cycle. *Electroenceph. clin. Neurophysiol.*, **16**, 438.

107. RECHTSCHAFFEN, A., WOLPERT, E. A., DEMENT, W. C., MITCHELL, S. A., and FISHER, C., 1963. Nocturnal sleep of narcoleptics. *Electroenceph. clin. Neurophysiol.*, **15**, 599.

108. REDING, G. R., RUBRIGHT, W. C., RECHTSCHAFFEN, A., and DANIELS, R. S., 1964. Sleep pattern of tooth-grinding: its relationship to dreaming. *Science*, **145**, 725.

109. ROFFWARG, H. P., DEMENT, W. C., and FISHER, C., 1964. Preliminary observations of the sleep-dream pattern in neonates, infants, children and adults. In *Monographs on Child Psychiatry No. 2*. Ed. Harms, E. New York: Pergamon Press.

110. ROSSENKÖTTER, L., and WENDE, S., 1955. EEG-Befunde beim Kleine-Levin-Syndrom. *Mschr. Psychiat. Neurol.*, **130**, 107.

111. RUCKEBUSCH, Y., 1963. *Recherches sur la regulation centrale du comportement alimentaire chez les Ruminants.* Lyon: Imprimerie BOSC Frères.

112. SAMPSON, H., 1965. Deprivation of dreaming sleep by two methods. *Arch. gen. Psychiat.*, **13**, 79.

113. SCHWARTZ, B. A., GILBAUD, G., and FISCHGOLD, H., 1963. Études électro-encéphalographiques sur le sommeil de nuit. *Presse méd.*, **71**, 1474.

114. SCHWARTZ, B. A., GUILBAUD, G., and FISCHGOLD, H., 1964. Single and multiple spikes in the night sleep of epileptics. *Electroenceph. clin. Neurophysiol.*, **16**, 56.

115. SIMON, C. W., and EMMONS, W. H., 1955. Learning during sleep? *Psychol. Bull.*, **52**, 328.

116. SIMON, C. W., and EMMONS, W. H., 1956. EEG consciousness and sleep. *Science*, **124**, 1066.

117. SNYDER, F., HOBSON, J. A., MORRISON, D. F., and GOLDFRANK, F., 1964. Changes in respiration, heart rate and systolic blood pressure in human sleep. *J. appl. Physiol.*, **19**, 417.

118. SYMONDS, C. P., 1953. Nocturnal myoclonus. *J. Neurol. Neurosurg. Psychiat.*, **16**, 166.

119. TRAVIS, R. C., and KENNEDY, J. L., 1947. Prediction and automatic control of alertness. I. Control of lookout alertness. *J. comp. physiol. Psychol.*, **40**, 457.

120. TYLER, D. B., 1955. Psychological changes during experimental sleep deprivation. *Dis. nerv. Syst.*, **16**, 293.

121. VALATX, J. L., JOUVET, D., and JOUVET, M., 1964. Evolution électroencéphalographique des différents états de sommeil chez le chaton. *Electroenceph. clin. Neurophysiol.*, **17**, 218.

122. WEISS, H. R., KASINOFF, B. H., and BAILEY, M. A., 1962. An exploration of reported sleep disturbance. *J. nerv. ment. Dis.*, **134**, 528.

123. WICKES, I. G., 1958. Treatment of persistent enuresis with the electric buzzer. *Arch. Dis. Childh.*, London, **33**, 160.

124. WICKES, I. G., 1963. Enuresis. *Brit. med. J.*, ii, 1199.

125. WILKINSON, R. T., 1960. The effect of lack of sleep on visual watch-keeping. *Quart. J. exp. Psychol.*, **12**, 36.

126. WILKINSON, R. T., 1961. Effects of sleep-deprivation on performance and muscle tension. In *The nature of sleep.* Eds. Wolstenholme, G. E. W., and O'Connor, M. London: J. & A. Churchill Ltd.

127. WILKINSON, R. T., 1963. Aftereffect of sleep deprivation. *J. exp. Psychol.*, **66**, 439.

128. WILLIAMS, H. L., HAMMACK, J. T., DALY, R. L., DEMENT, W. C., and LUBIN, A., 1964. Responses to auditory stimulation, sleep loss and the EEG stages of sleep. *Electroenceph. clin. Neurophysiol.*, **16**, 269.

129. WILLIAMS, H. L., LUBIN, A., and GOODNOW, J. J., 1959. Impaired performance with acute sleep loss. *Psychol. Monographs*, **73**, No. 14.

130. WILLIAMS, H. L., MORLOCK, H. C., and MORLOCK, J. V., 1966. Discriminative responses to auditory signals during sleep. *Psychophysiol.*, **2**, 208.

131. WILLIAMS, H. L., TEPAS, D. I., and MORLOCK, H. C., 1962. Evoked responses to clicks and electroencephalographic stages in man. *Science*, **138**, 685.

132. WITTERSHEIM, G., GRIVEL, F., and METZ, B., 1958. Application d'une épreuve de choix multiple avec enregistrement continu des réponses des erreurs et des temps de réaction a l'étude des effets sensori-moteurs de l'inversion du rythme nycthéméral chez l'Homme normal. *C.R. Soc. Biol.*, Paris, **152**, 1194.

133. WOLPERT, E. A., and TROSMAN, H., 1958. Studies in psychophysiology of dreams. *Arch. Neurol. Psychiat.*, Chic., **79**, 603.

IX

SENSORY DEPRIVATION

PHILIP SOLOMON

M.D.

Clinical Professor, Department of Psychiatry Harvard Medical School

* AND

A. MICHAEL ROSSI

PH.D.

*Associate in Psychology, Department of Psychiatry
Harvard Medical School*

1

Introduction

Sensory deprivation is a term that conjures up dramatic associations in the minds of many people. Early research results initiated unbridled speculations in the professional literature, and these speculations often were presented as facts in the popular press. Consequently, fact and fancy are still blended in the minds of many, and the true nature of the research results is often not clearly understood.

The purpose of this chapter is to provide the reader with an overview of: the development of interest in this field; the methodological problems involved; findings obtained in research carried out with human subjects; theories for explaining the results; and applications to the fields of medicine and psychiatry.

2

History

In the early 1950s the conjunction of developments in political, social and scientific spheres created the necessary condition to attract widespread attention to sensory deprivation research. The relative suddenness and intensity of this attention led to the erroneous impression that interest in the effects of reduced sensory input was born *de nouveau* at that time.

Such a phenomenon has often occurred in the history of science. Interests or facts may exist for long periods of time with no general recognition until the right intellectual climate, or *Zeitgeist*, is created; then suddenly what is old for some becomes new for many. For centuries, knowledge that reduced exteroceptive stimulation can affect the psychological functioning of man has been included in the texts of all major religions in their accounts of persons seeking isolation in order to control their thoughts and feelings and to achieve new experiences. Throughout history, there has been periodic interest in the effects of relatively barren environments on individuals who were lost, shipwrecked, deserted, in solitary confinement, and in other similar circumstances.[152]

The beginnings of a critical interest in the effects of reduced sensory input can be discerned in the philosophies of Locke ('tabula rasa'), Condillac ('sentient statue') and others who assumed the empiricist position in their epistemological theories. Many students who first become introduced to these philosophies begin to speculate on the consequences of development within a barren environment. Would Condillac's sentient statue think at all without stimulation or would it think about nothing? While this type of subtle differentiation is a favoured source of student debates, it has its counterpart in modern scientific discussion concerning the effect of sensory deprivation: Does sensory deprivation lead to a decrease in reticular activating system (RAS) functioning and consequent loss of consciousness (so that the person does not consciously think at all) or does sensory deprivation lead to a disruption of thought processes in an alert person (so that the person thinks about nothing coherently)?

Like practically all questions relating to mental functioning, the question of the effects of reduced sensory input remained within the province of philosophical discussion and speculation until the nineteenth century. During that century, gigantic steps were taken that eventually brought these questions into the scientist's laboratory for resolution. The discovery of the electrical nature of the nervous impulse, Helmholtz's measurement of the speed of the nervous impulse, Fechner's development of psychophysical methods, and Pavlov's delineation of the conditional reflex were but a few of the highlights in the development of the belief that sensory processes—'the very stuff of the human mind'[21]—could be brought into the laboratory for control and measurement.

The development of scientific interest in the effects of reduced exteroceptive stimulation can be traced through the following preliminary investigations: early studies on the effects of sensory deficits; studies on perceptual and cognitive performances under monotonous conditions; studies on the effects of early isolation or deafferentation in animals; discovery of the non-specific activating system and the alerting function of exteroceptive stimuli; studies of infants reared in impoverished environments; and the identification of a curiosity or exploratory drive.

The cumulative results of this research provided the foundation for Hebb's theory on the functioning of the central nervous system,[99] which ascribed an important role for exteroceptive stimulation in the efficient functioning of the organism. This theory led to research on the effects of reduced exteroceptive stimulation in Hebb's laboratory at McGill University in Montreal around 1950. There seems little doubt that if the results of that research had been reported at any other time, they would have been received with the usual restraint and caution by the scientific community. However, the results actually were reported at a time when the United States was in the throes of its 'McCarthy era' and when reports of 'brainwashing' of political and war prisoners in Korea and elsewhere began to be widespread. The intellectual climate of that time was one in which fears were openly expressed that some powerful, sinister techniques had been developed to control the human mind and that Orwell's *1984* society[173] might soon be a reality. Extreme isolation of the individual was believed to be one of the techniques employed in forceful indoctrinations.

It was within this intellectual climate that the first reports of the McGill studies on sensory deprivation became known, and the catalytic action on the development of interest in sensory deprivation that resulted is attested to by the phenomenal increase in sensory deprivation research over the past decade. Within a few years of the first McGill report, several centres of sensory deprivation research developed across the United States including one at Princeton under Vernon,[242, 243] one at Harvard under Solomon,[51, 147] and one at the National Institutes of Mental Health under Lilly.[135, 136] The research literature increased at such a pace that attempts to synthesize and integrate the results became outdated by the time they were published. The result of all this activity is that a comprehensive and up-to-date understanding of the effects of sensory deprivation is difficult to attain even by those fully immersed in the field.

3

Methodological Problems

Attempts to study the effects of sensory deprivation in a scientific manner have been hampered by difficult methodological problems. Many of these problems exist in almost every other area of psychiatric research, but some are unique here. One should be aware of the nature and extent of these problems and the consequent need for caution in interpreting reported research results.

Heterogeneity of terms and lack of precise terminology plague the field of sensory deprivation research. The literature includes at least twenty-seven different terms that have been used more or less synonymously with 'sensory deprivation'.[25] They range from simple variations (e.g.; stimulus deprivation, sensory reduction) to those which reflect quite divergent conceptual levels and theoretical frames of reference (e.g., perceptual isolation, social isolation). The latter divergencies also are discernible in the types of experimental environments that have been employed by different investigators.

It is ironic that in the one area of psychiatric research where it might be expected that uniformity of experimental conditions would prevail

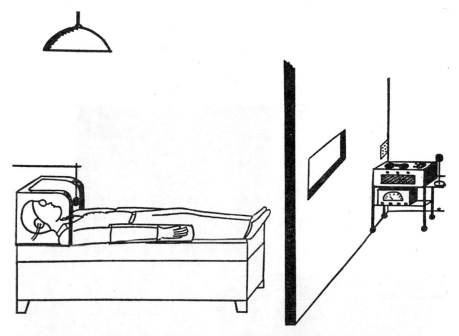

Fig. 1. Experimental conditions containing many of the usual features used in short-term sensory deprivation research. The subject is instructed to remain quiet and motionless; cardboard cylinders enclose the arms from elbows to beyond the finger-tips; soft gloves are worn; halved ping-pong balls cover the eyes to diffuse light; earphones convey white noise to block out ambient sounds. (Reprinted by permission from Goldberger, L. and Holt, R. R. (1961). Experimental interference with reality contact: individual differences. In P. Solomon, *et al.* (eds.) *Sensory Deprivation.* Harvard University Press: Cambridge, Mass.)

from laboratory to laboratory, uniformity is the exception and not the rule. The expectation of uniformity follows from the usage of such terms as sensory deprivation which call to mind environments absolutely free from exteroceptive stimuli. Conceptually, any two environments absolutely free of exteroceptive stimuli would have little or no basis for differences. Yet, in practice, the experimental environments that have been employed have produced only partial reduction of stimuli, and, as a result, the experimental environments sometimes differ markedly. Consider, for example, the differences in the two experimental environments presented in Plates I and II. While such environments have in common a reduction of exteroceptive stimuli, *the very reduction in the amount of stimuli increases the importance of differences in the remaining stimuli.* To date, there have been very few attempts to identify what residual stimuli remain in the experimental environments and to evaluate their roles in producing effects of these environments.

A perusal of Figs. 1 and 2 will call to mind a host of methodological problems inherent in keeping subjects in such environments for any

HYDROHYPODYNAMIC ENVIRONMENT

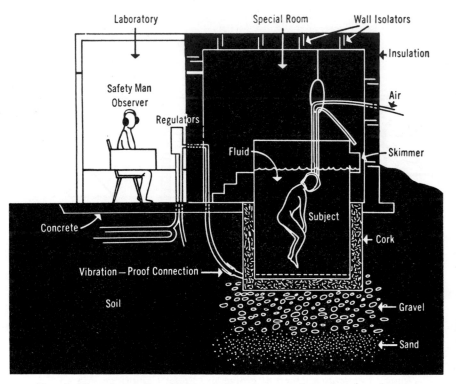

FIG. 2. Experimental conditions believed to produce the most intense form of sensory deprivation in normal, intact subjects. Water is kept at body temperature. (Reprinted by permission from J. Shurley, (1963). *Proceedings of the Third World Congress of Psychiatry*, Vol. 3. Univ. Toronto Press: Toronto, Canada.)

extended period of time. For example, subjects get hungry, have elimination needs, and have itches. The problem of how the experimental subject's needs may be satisfied without interfering with sensory deprivation has not been fully solved. In fact, the difficulties in attempting to keep subjects in such environments for more than a few hours have resulted in a state of affairs in this area of research that may be generalized as follows: the longer the period of sensory deprivation, the less severe the sensory deprivation conditions and the fewer the number of subjects studied. Thus, studies of extended periods of sensory deprivation have the limitation of utilizing less severe reduction of exteroceptive stimulation, and the use of few subjects limits the generalizations possible. On the other hand, studies which utilize short periods of sensory deprivation, while using more drastic reduction of sensory input and more subjects, may be said to be analagous to studies of food deprivation in which subjects are without food for just a few hours.

An additional methodological problem in this area of research is that of obtaining measures of subjects' psychological functioning during sensory deprivation. Two general solutions to this problem have been employed, but neither is satisfactory. One is to obtain the measures during sensory deprivation while keeping the interference with sensory deprivation as little as possible. The other is to utilize 'before-after' measures only. The former solution is not satisfactory because even minimal interference during sensory deprivation provides stimulation of one sort or another, and the effects of this stimulation cannot be fully evaluated. The latter solution is not satisfactory because some effects may dissipate rapidly after sensory deprivation, or may be periodic so that they may not be present at the end of the experiment.

Other problems are those inherent in most psychiatric research: subject selection, adequate controls, experimenter expectations, appropriateness of measures employed, and so on.

For the above reasons, generalizations and conclusions regarding the effects of sensory deprivation must be made cautiously at the present time.

4

Affective Changes

It will be recalled that the impetus for the recent upsurge of interest in sensory deprivation was research carried out in Hebb's laboratory at McGill University.[19, 20, 105, 106] This research was designed primarily to investigate the effects of reduced sensory input on cognitive functioning. A serendipitous finding, and one that was primarily responsible for attracting the widespread attention, was that some subjects experienced markedly unpleasant affective changes as well as cognitive impairments. This finding has been replicated time and again in subsequent studies employing many different experimental conditions and procedures. The exact nature of the affective changes and their intensity, duration, and relationship to personality and experimental variables have not yet been fully explicated. However, that reduced sensory input does affect the emotions as well as the intellect appears to be an established fact.

Negative Changes

When affective changes occur in normal subjects in sensory deprivation, the changes tend to be negative. During the initial period of exposure to the experimental conditions, subjects appear to relax and look forward to the opportunity to be free of extraneous stimulation and task demands. They expect to spend the time in concentrated thought on such subjects as school assignments, future plans, and so forth. However, after a brief period of such thought, they find it difficult to engage in directed thinking, and their minds begin to wander. They soon become bored and tend toward alternating periods of sleep-wakefulness.[20, 42, 148, 190, 201, 207] When unable to escape into sleep, subjects' boredom increases and leads to restlessness and irritability,[201, 207, 214, 282] brooding,[207, 282, 288] depression,[214, 282, 288] and attempts to seek self stimulation.[111, 235] During this period, subjects' inability to control thought processes becomes more pronounced,[14, 31, 69, 79, 135, 147, 148, 214, 257, 288] and anxiety develops.[31, 69, 134, 147, 148, 214, 257] More often, subjects will search for some form of stimulus to alleviate their feelings, and, in the process of this search, they become increasingly sensitive to residual internal stimuli.[31, 135, 209] Dwelling on somatic stimuli in the context of anxiety leads to body-image distortions[31, 50, 51, 71, 81, 134, 147, 214, 257, 279 287, 288] and feelings of depersonalization.[81, 135, 279] Fears and thought processes become more bizarre, and hallucinations may occur.[40, 71, 134, 135, 207, 287, 288] At this stage, subjects with weak personality structures (particularly those with paranoid tendencies) may manifest overtly psychotic symptoms.[31, 71, 135, 148, 214]

In general, the effects described above tend to be short-lived and completely reversible shortly after termination of the sensory deprivation exposure, and the frequency of specific reactions tends to be inversely proportional to the severity of the reaction. For example, boredom occurs almost universely, while overtly psychotic reactions are observed only rarely. The low frequency of the more extreme reactions undoubtedly is related to the fact that almost all studies employ volunteer subjects who have been psychiatrically screened and who have been informed that they would be released from sensory deprivation at any time upon request. In approximately 90 per cent of these studies, there have been subjects who have been discomforted enough to require early release,[207] and it is reasonable to assume that the incidence of extreme negative affect changes would be much higher if all subjects were forced to stay in sensory deprivation and if more psychiatrically vulnerable subjects were used.

Positive Changes

It will not be surprising to note that wide individual differences have been found in affective reactions to sensory deprivation. What may be surprising is that, with very few exceptions, positive affective changes have not been observed to occur in normal subjects. The exceptions have been a few subjects who were vaguely reported to have 'enjoyed' the experience and a few who were reported to have felt elation or euphoria after having first experienced many of the negative affects mentioned above.[31, 71, 111, 181, 282]

In contrast to normal subjects, psychiatric patients exposed to sensory deprivation have been reported to have experienced positive affect changes, and these changes have sometimes persisted after termination of the study.[1, 2, 3, 10, 11, 34, 39, 45, 77, 78, 96] Some patients have been said to experience an improvement in motivation with an increased need to socialize,[10, 11, 45, 78] a loosening of defences,[3, 45, 78] a subsidence of pathological symptoms (depressive ruminations, hallucinations, etc.),[3, 39, 45, 96] and an increased awareness of inner conflicts and anxieties.[3, 45, 78] Apparently as a consequence of improved ego functioning, these patients are described as more receptive to psychotherapy following their sensory deprivation experience.[3, 10, 11, 45, 78]

Personality Variables

There have been many attempts to identify relationships between personality variables and reactions to sensory deprivation. These attempts have led to some of the most contradictory results in the sensory deprivation literature. For almost every study that reports a positive relationship between a specific personality characteristic and a specific reaction to sensory deprivation, there is another study that reports either no relationship or a negative relationship between the same personality characteristic and reaction.

For example, it has been reported that subjects who tolerate sensory deprivation conditions best are those who: have sound egos;[111, 199, 200] have schizoid traits;[40, 87, 96] are emotionally dependent;[115, 257] are emotionally independent;[130] have high feminine interest patterns;[30, 86, 115] have low feminine interest patterns;[235] have a need for conformity;[164] have a need for autonomy;[130] are males;[50, 175, 176] are females;[214, 250, 251] have low pain thresholds;[174a, 174b] have high pain thresholds;[174] are field-dependent;[41, 211] are field-independent;[133] and so on.

Many of these differences undoubtedly reflect variations in experimental conditions, measuring instruments, and population samples. A review of this literature would support few generalizations at the present time. One could say, however, that whatever relationships exist between personality variables and reactions to sensory deprivation, they will not be identified by the use of some simple paper-and-pencil personality test. There has been no consistency in the results of studies that have employed tests such as the Minnesota Multiphasic Personality Inventory, [115, 130, 164, 174, 257, 288] the Edwards Personal Preference Test, [115, 130, 164, 174, 257, 288] or the Myers-Briggs Type Indicator.[196, 225] One could also make the rather obvious statement that among normals, subjects with the most stable personalities will best tolerate the stress of sensory deprivation.

5

Hallucinations

The occurrence of hallucinations during sensory deprivation has received the widest publicity. The original McGill study found that all subjects experienced some type of visual perception,[20, 106] and most subsequent research has found that at least some subjects report visual and auditory perceptions in the absence of patterned exteroceptive visual and auditory stimuli.[289] However, an unfortunate concurrence of events has led to a widespread misunderstanding of the nature of the auditory and visual perceptions experienced by subjects in sensory deprivation. The first report described them as being similar to 'having a dream while awake', and examples included integrated scene-like imagery.[20] While these results were being circulated, a particularly vivid description of bizarre, extended hallucinations experienced during sensory deprivation was reported by another investigator.[135] The conjunction of the two reports led to a general belief that all visual and auditory perceptions experienced during deprivation were vivid, integrated hallucinations. Thus, when succeeding research reported that a substantial percentage of subjects experienced auditory and visual perceptions, this was interpreted to mean that a substantial percentage of subjects had experienced hallucinations in the psychiatric sense. Such an interpretation is erroneous.

Definitions

Part of the confusion is related to different uses of the term 'hallucination' by sensory deprivation researchers and by others outside this research field. Many of the latter define 'hallucination' to mean a belief in a reasonably vivid, integrated perception that occurs in the absence of appropriate stimuli. Many of the researchers, however, define 'hallucination' to mean simply a report of a visual or auditory experience during sensory deprivation conditions. Thus a bare statement by a subject that he 'sees spots before his eyes' would be reported as an hallucination in many studies, and the reader of the report often reaches a mistaken idea of the nature of the subject's experience.

An attempt to avoid this misunderstanding has led to the coining of the phrase, 'reported visual (or auditory) sensation',[163] to describe sensory perceptions that have no known exteroceptive stimuli. While advantageous for some purposes, this phrase has the disadvantage of making no distinction between the various kinds of experiences being reported. The result is that the phrase sometimes is used indiscriminately in the same report to refer to either hallucinations, illusions, daydreams, fantasies, or retinogenic phenomena,[289] thus producing the same confusion that attended the

indiscriminate use of the term 'hallucination' to describe the same phenomena.

The absence of a standard, differentiating terminology makes it
exceedingly difficult to gain a clear understanding of the nature of subjects'
perceptual experiences during sensory deprivation.[129, 229, 276] In the discussion that follows, the term 'imagery' will refer to all reports of mental
experiences during sensory deprivation which have no known exteroceptive
stimuli, and the term 'hallucination' will be used in its usual sense.

Frequency

The occurrence of imagery ranges from a percentage of 0 in some
studies[9, 229, 248] to 100 in others,[20, 80] with a median of approximately
forty for all studies. In recent years with an increase in adequate controls,
the median has dropped to less than 20 per cent[276] and, if these reported
images are dichotomized into reports of brief, meaningless images (e.g.,
spots, flashes of light, vague sounds) and reports of more integrated meaningful scenes (e.g., objects, people, conversations), the median percentage of
subjects reporting the latter imagery during recent years has been less than
10 per cent. Since the latter reports often include other mental experiences
(e.g., daydreams, fantasies, illusions, psychosomatic delusions)[149] in
addition to hallucinations, it is reasonable to assume that the percentage of
subjects who report hallucinations is well below 10 per cent. It must be
recalled, however, that most subjects have been psychiatrically screened
and allowed to terminate the experiment upon request, and these factors
must have some effect on the frequency of reported hallucinations.

Level of Arousal

It would have theoretical significance to know whether hallucinations
during sensory deprivation occur during high or low levels of arousal, and
there has been a variety of hypotheses offered on the probable relationship
between arousal level and hallucinations.[64, 72, 204] Three general hypotheses concerning this relationship may be stated as follows: (*i*) A normal
central nervous system in an alert state will begin generating its own
stimuli (e.g., hallucinations) in the absence of exteroceptive stimuli in
order to maintain an optimal level of arousal; (*ii*) In the absence of cues
normally available in a variegated sensory environment, an organism will be
less accurate in gauging either its level of arousal or its experiences, so that
experiences occurring during drowsy and sleep states (hypnogogic
phenomena and dreams) may be misinterpreted as occurring during an
awake state (hallucinations); (*iii*) A prolonged absence of exteroceptive
stimuli leads to a breakdown of reality-testing, and primitive fears and
ideas take on the appearance of reality in hallucinations.

The lack of differentiating terminology, mentioned above, makes it
difficult to interpret most available data bearing on this question. It
seems that the majority of all imagery reported during sensory deprivation

9

occurs during awake states,[289] but most of the reports are of experiences that apparently are due to increased sensitivity to interoceptive stimulation, and this sensitivity would be expected to be heightened during awake states in an environment devoid of exteroceptive stimuli. In studies which focused directly on hallucinations[189, 190, 266, 269] it was found that the experiences reported and rated as hallucinations occurred during all levels of arousal, but those occurring during awake states were not different from perceptions that would follow from increased sensitivity to interoceptive stimuli (e.g., inner ear noise), while those occurring during sleep states were more integrated and complex. These results are most consistent with hypothesis (ii), above. However, the few detailed accounts of what undoubtedly were true hallucinations occurring during sensory deprivation[71, 148] developed during a panic state and are most consistent with hypothesis (iii), above. It seems evident that the relationship between arousal level and hallucinations during sensory deprivation is a complex one which will be understood only after much more research.

Experimental Variables

It has been reported that the frequency of reported imagery is increased by: instructions indicating that such reports are expected[117, 162, 172, 175, 176] or that they are a mark of intelligence;[116] having subjects lie prone rather than sit;[155] having subjects report continuously during a session rather than postpone reports for a post-session interview.[163] The frequency of reported imagery has not been found to be affected by the introduction of intermittent light stimulation,[51, 248] or by the extent of allowable body-movements,[46] and the vividness of controlled imagery was found not to increase during sensory deprivation.[197]

Personality Variables

There have been no definitive relationships established between personality variables and reported imagery during sensory deprivation. Research results indicate that subjects who give the highest number of imagery reports are suggestible,[31] intelligent,[80] and anxious.[288] However, in other studies, no relationship was found between number of imagery reports and: anxiety,[155] scores on the Minnesota Multiphasic Personality Inventory, or the Edwards Personal Preference Scale,[222, 288] or sex.[8, 133, 155, 175, 250, 293]

6

Physiological Effects

Most investigators assume that psychological disturbances observed during sensory deprivation are reflections of disturbances in physiological functioning. Although this assumption is amenable to direct test, there have been relatively few studies of the physiological effects of sensory deprivation. Most of the work that has been done has employed the electro-encephalogram (EEG) in studying the effects of sensory deprivation on brain activity. These studies have yielded reasonably consistent results which will be discussed below. The remaining work has focused primarily on circulatory, respiratory, and glandular activity. Definite patterns of results are difficult to discern in the latter work, because of the small number of studies and differences in specific measures and experimental conditions.

EEG Measures

The first study of changes in brain activity during sensory deprivation was carried out at McGill University, and the results of that study indicated that reduced sensory input leads to a slowing of alpha waves with an increase in voltage.[104] This progressive slowing of alpha during sensory deprivation has been observed in many subsequent studies,[4, 41, 42, 83, 84, 132, 133, 151, 202, 213, 237, 238, 240, 282, 285, 286] and it is consistently found in animals that have undergone deafferentation by surgical or chemical means.[7, 18, 75, 76, 110, 150, 178, 249] The most extensive recent work in this area has been carried out by Zubek and his colleagues at Manitoba University in Canada.[272, 273, 275, 282, 286] Results obtained in one of their studies are presented in Fig. 3 where a clear slowing of alpha frequency can be seen to have occurred during prolonged exposure to sensory deprivation.

However, this effect is not found to occur universally,[167] and it appears that the effect can be ameliorated by: repeated exposures;[91, 132, 133] a 'set' to perform a task;[237, 238] personality;[41, 42] and exercise.[272] The importance of exercise is emphasized in the finding that prolonged body immobilization alone can lead to a decrease in alpha frequency.[286]

Other EEG changes that have been observed to occur during sensory deprivation are increases in delta,[104, 213] theta,[213, 282, 286] and beta[41, 42] activity. However, these results tend to be isolated and require further confirmation.

Most investigators have found that the slowing of brain activity continues after sensory deprivation for periods ranging from hours[104, 213] to weeks.[132, 285] It is of interest to note that the existence of these effects tend to parallel the existence of decreased motivation.[277]

Skin Potential Measures

Skin potential changes have been studied in the belief that they are related to level of arousal with increases in skin conductance accompanying increases in arousal. The first study to obtain galvanic skin response (GSR) measures from subjects in sensory deprivation found that skin conductance increased over several days of sensory deprivation.[247] However, the results of succeeding studies have been that skin conductance decreases during the first hour or two of exposure,[42, 91, 167, 210, 293] after which it may either slowly increase for the remainder of the session[167] or

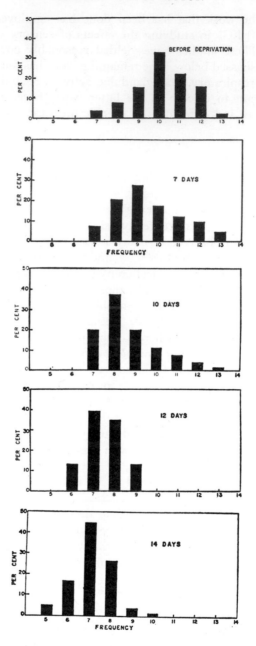

Fig. 3. Progressive shift in frequency spectrum occurring in 300-second occipital lobe tracings obtained from one subject at intervals over a prolonged period of perceptual deprivation. (Reprinted by permission from Zubek, J. P., Welch, G., and Saunders, M. G. (1963). Electroencephalographic changes during and after 14 days of perceptual deprivation. *Sci.*, **139**, 490.)

remain relatively constant until close to the end of the session, when it may sharply increase.[91]

There have been several studies comparing GSR changes during different sets of experimental conditions. The results of these studies suggest that skin conductance (level of arousal) is lower in subjects isolated: without a vigil task rather than with such a task;[225] with knowledge of duration of the session rather than without such knowledge;[48] singly rather than in groups of three;[208] and, in total darkness and silence rather than with either a light or sound source.[293] However, other studies have reported no differences in GSR changes during experimental conditions differing in combinations of visual and auditory deprivation,[133] or during sensory deprivation and control conditions.[294]

Biochemical Measures

The few studies of the effect of sensory deprivation on biochemical measures have yielded interesting, but inconclusive results. Adrenaline and noradrenaline excretion in the urine was found in two studies to increase substantially during sensory deprivation,[147, 203] but no consistent change in output was found in other studies.[42, 284] A pituitary-thyroid stimulating hormone, 17-ketogenic steroids, and 17-ketosteroids were found to increase during sensory deprivation in a recent study.[294] No change in excretion of 11-oxycorticoids was found in one study,[161] but the interpretation of this finding is clouded because no correction was made for the fact that the subjects remained in a recumbent position which would ordinarily lead to a decreased excretion rate.[287] Obviously, more research has to be done in this area before any definite conclusions can be drawn regarding the effect of sensory deprivation on biochemical measures.

Other Physiological Measures

Studies of other physiological changes occurring during sensory deprivation have been sporadic and inconclusive. Oral temperature and basal metabolic rate were found not to change significantly during sensory deprivation.[104] Respiratory activity has been found either not to change significantly throughout a session,[48, 167, 202, 211, 294] or to decrease only during the first few hours.[54, 91, 104, 209] Similarly, circulatory activity has been found either not to change significantly throughout a session,[48, 104, 294] or to decrease only during the first few hours.[91, 209, 211] One study reported a sharp increase in circulatory and respiratory activity toward the conclusion of a twenty-four-hour session.[91]

The subjects in two studies were found to have decreased in body weight during sensory deprivation. A mean weight loss of approximately 3·5 lb was reported to have occurred in subjects after four days of sensory deprivation in one study,[247] and a mean weight loss of 5 lb was reported to have occurred in subjects after two days of sensory deprivation in another study.[127]

Threshold Changes

There have been several interesting studies carried out to determine the effect of sensory deprivation on sensory thresholds. The first of these reported a suggestive but not significant increase in cutaneous sensitivity in subjects who had undergone several days of sensory deprivation.[58] Most of the subsequent work in this area has been conducted at Manitoba University in Canada.

It has been reported that tactual acuity increases not only during a week of sensory deprivation,[274] but also during a week of visual deprivation alone.[280] Moreover, it was found in these studies that the increased sensitivity lasts from one to seven days after the deprivation is terminated. These effects are clearly evident in Fig. 4 from Zubek's studies. Similar results were found to occur during deprivation of patterned vision alone

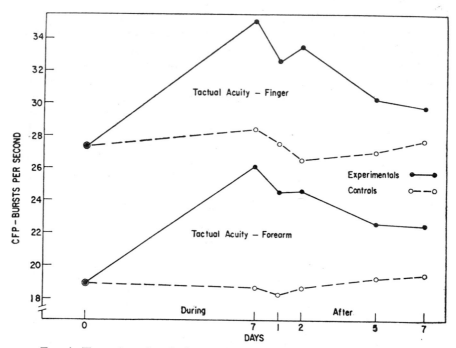

FIG. 4. Tactual acuity during and after a prolonged period of visual deprivation. Experimental and control groups each contained 16 subjects. Critical frequency of percussion (CFP) is the frequency at which successive jets of air pressure are perceived as a constant pressure. (Reprinted by permission from Zubek, J. P., Flye, J., and Aftanas, M. (1964). Cutaneous sensitivity after prolonged visual deprivation. *Sci.*, **144**, 1591.)

(light source present, but eye coverings prevent the perception of patterns); however, neither the increase in tactual acuity nor the persistence of after-effects were as pronounced as those found under the previous conditions.[281]

In a study carried out at Princeton University, it was found that pain sensitivity increases after several days of sensory deprivation (darkness and silence), and that the increase persists for several days after termination of exposure.[245] However, a *decrease* in pain sensitivity was found in a study employing slightly different conditions of sensory deprivation (darkness and unpatterned sound), and the authors suggest that the white noise used to produce the unpatterned sound may have served as an analgesic.[278] Subsequently, the latter investigators found an increase in pain sensitivity in subjects exposed to a week of visual deprivation alone,[280] and in other subjects exposed to a week of patterned-vision deprivation alone.[281] In both of the latter studies, the increased pain sensitivity persisted for a day or two after termination of exposure.

A recent study at Manitoba University laboratories disclosed an increase in auditory discrimination following a week of visual deprivation alone, and the increase persisted for a day after termination of exposure.[60] In this same study, no change was found in absolute auditory thresholds.

Relation to Psychological States

There have been few extensive attempts to relate physiological changes to concurrent psychological states during sensory deprivation. Continuous GSR measures were collected from subjects in one study, and it was found that these measures correlated with subjects' accounts of their affective states.[201] In a comparison of two normal and two schizoid subjects, it was found that the normal subjects maintained a higher level of skin conductance (level of arousal) throughout sensory deprivation, and they also reported being more uncomfortable during the session.[40] Psychiatric patients who showed a slowing of EEG alpha during sensory deprivation performed more poorly on several subtests of the Wechsler Adult Intelligence Scale than patients who did not have such slowing.[84]

EEG records collected over several hours of sensory deprivation[148, 189, 190] have been consistent with reports that subjects drift in and out of sleep during their exposure to reduced sensory input. However, attempts to relate the body of data on physiological changes to the body of data on psychological changes are premature, because both sets of data show large individual difference effects and were collected under widely different experimental conditions.

7

Perceptual-Motor Effects

When the subjects were released from sensory deprivation in the original McGill studies, they complained that they had difficulty in focusing their eyes, that objects appeared to have fuzzy outlines, colours appeared more saturated than usual, objects appeared to be two-dimensional, colour contrast was heightened, and objects appeared to move during head and eye movements.[20, 106] These subjective accounts were quite dramatic and they stimulated others to seek more objective measures of these perceptual-motor deficits. The initial attempts to find objective measures were not particularly successful, and in recent years there has been a decrease of research focusing on this problem. The main difficulty seems to be the instability of results obtained with specific perceptual-motor tasks from one study to another.

Out of the multitude of tasks used in this area of research, only four were found to be adversely affected by sensory deprivation when used in more than one study. These four were figure-ground differentiation,[71, 278] depth perception,[246, 278, 282] colour discrimination,[246, 278] and visual vigilance.[278, 282] In single studies, performances were found to be adversely affected on colour adaptation,[58] autokinesis,[58] figural after-effects,[58] and the Muller-Lyer illusion.[71]

Performances were found to be impaired in some studies and un-affected in others on mirror-drawing,[207, 246] size-constancy,[58, 71, 278, 282] phi-phenomenon,[58, 171] pursuit-motor,[71, 246] auditory-vigilance,[166, 278] and the perception of visual speed.[68, 69, 73, 101, 106]

In one study, performances were found not to be affected on Critical Flicker Fusion, brightness constancy, shape constancy, and the Necker-Cubes.[58]

Obviously, it is not easy to discern a pattern in this conglomeration of data at the present time. It does appear that the dramatic perceptual-motor deficits that were reported in the early literature are neither universal nor strong enough to yield a consistent pattern of results on objective tests. However, results show strong individual difference effects, and there is little doubt that some individuals do experience pronounced perceptual-motor impairments during sensory deprivation. It is a problem common to all areas of sensory deprivation research to identify which individuals are strongly affected by reduced sensory input and to determine why these should be so affected when others are not.

It should be noted that when performances on perceptual-motor tasks are affected by sensory deprivation, the effects are short-lived, usually dissipating within an hour after termination of exposure.[58, 71, 106]

8

Cognitive Effects

In the discussion of affective changes above, it was mentioned that subjects experience difficulty in controlling their thoughts during sensory deprivation. Many investigators have reported that subjects complain of being unable to engage in sustained concentration and that their minds 'go blank'.[20, 71, 207, 214, 283, 288] The frequency and similarity of these subjective reports in so many different studies leaves little doubt that sensory deprivation does interfere with cognitive efficiency, but attempts to develop objective measures of the cognitive deficits have not met with much more success than the attempt to develop objective measures of perceptual-motor deficits.

Intellectual Efficiency

The typical study in this area has employed a battery of intelligence-test items, and the typical findings have been that sensory deprivation leads to an impairment of performance on some items and not on others. These results are difficult to interpret because individual intelligence-test items are not very reliable or valid,[47] the pattern of impairments within a single study has not always been meaningful, and the patterns of impairment have varied from study to study.

Over two dozen specific test items have been used in this area of research, and impairments of performance have been found on most of them in one study or another. For example, impairments have been found on tests of numerical facility,[278] verbal fluency,[278] abstract reasoning,[278] space relations,[278] and completion of a number series.[207] However, other studies have found no impairments of performance on these same test items.[20, 166, 283]

Impairments of performance were found to occur on some test items that have been used in only one study (e.g., successive subtraction,[166] inductive reasoning,[166] digit symbol,[278] logical deductions[79]), but the instability of results obtained with test items that have been used in more than one study indicates that caution is required in interpreting isolated findings.

Of all the test items that have been used in more than one study, only one has consistently demonstrated an impairment of performance (anagrams)[20, 207] and five have consistently demonstrated no change in performance (arithmetic problems,[20, 79, 207, 288] multiplications,[20, 207] making a word from jumbled letters,[20, 207] digit span,[40, 79, 278, 288] and verbal reasoning[278, 283]).

There have been at least two hypotheses offered to explain the discrepancy between the consistency in subjective accounts of cognitive impairments and the lack of consistency in impairments on specific test items. One is that the subjective impairments are the results of a multivariable interaction including the severity of experimental conditions, length of time in sensory deprivation, personality factors, instructions and expectations, so that it is to be expected that different patterns of impairments would be found in different studies.[24] Another is that the test items used in most of the research were highly structured and tapped well-practiced intellectual functions, so that impairments would be evident only in those subjects who experienced a high degree of cognitive disorganization.[230] These authors suggest that less structured tests might be more consistent in demonstrating cognitive impairments, and they present results showing that the length of stories told in response to Thematic

Apperception Test cards decrease during sensory deprivation, a result that they attribute to decreased ability to concentrate.[228, 230]

Learning

There have been relatively few studies of the effects of sensory deprivation on learning ability, and the results of these have been inconclusive. In the first study, it was found that rote-learning of lists of adjectives improved during sensory deprivation.[242] However, in later studies, it was found that rote-learning of lists of adjectives or three-letter words was neither improved nor impaired during sensory deprivation.[9, 243, 283] Performances on learning tasks requiring recall and recognition, were found to be impaired in one study,[283] but not in another.[278] Finally, the results of a recent study indicate that retention of meaningful prose is improved during sensory deprivation.[86]

It is evident that the present data are insufficient to determine the effects of sensory deprivation on learning ability.

9

Susceptibility to Propaganda

One of the sources of general interest in sensory deprivation was its suspected involvement in forceful indoctrinations, i.e., 'brainwashing'. It may be surprising, then, to learn that very little research has been carried out to determine whether sensory deprivation does indeed increase one's susceptibility to propaganda.

One of the original McGill studies focused on this problem.[19] In one part of this study, subjects in sensory deprivation were given the opportunity to listen to a series of short records simply by requesting them. The records contained various material (repetitions of a sixteen-bar chorus, soap commercials, etc.) which control subjects had rated as boring and uninteresting. The subjects in sensory deprivation made many more requests to hear the records than control subjects, and the investigator concluded that persons subjected to perceptual limitations will voluntarily listen to material which ordinarily they would avoid.

In the second part of this study, subjects again were given the opportunity to hear a series of records simply by requesting them, and, again, it was found that subjects in sensory deprivation made many more requests to hear the records than control subjects. This time, however, the records contained ninety-minute talks on the validity of psychical phenomena (telepathy, ghosts, etc.). Attitude scales administered before and after exposure to the records indicated that the sensory deprivation subjects experienced a greater change in attitude toward a more favourable point of view of psychical phenomena than did control subjects.[19, 207]

It was found in another study that subjects in sensory deprivation made significantly more requests than control subjects for short recorded talks on Turkey which were couched in terms diametrically opposed to subjects' attitudes toward Turkey.[165] It was also found in this study that the subjects who had the most extreme attitudes (favourable or unfavourable) toward Turkey experienced the greatest shift in attitudes after hearing the records during sensory deprivation.

Another investigator selected subjects whose initial attitudes toward Turkey were neutral, and then had these subjects listen to a tape-recording of pro-Turkey propaganda during sensory deprivation. He found that these subjects experienced a greater change toward a favourable attitude than control subjects who had heard the recording outside of sensory deprivation.[227]

In two other studies, subjects in sensory deprivation made multiple-choice judgements on the number of tones in a rapidly presented series, and they were given misleading feedback on the answers supposedly given by a group of others making the same judgements. In both studies, subjects in sensory deprivation were greatly influenced by the 'judgements of the group', but no more so than control subjects.[165, 215] An interesting finding was that subjects with the lowest intelligence of the sensory deprivation group were significantly more influenced by 'group judgements' than subjects with the lowest intelligence in the control group.[215]

No strong conclusion regarding the effects of sensory deprivation on susceptibility to propaganda can be drawn from these few studies. However, a tenuous conclusion which seems warranted is that during reduced sensory input there is an increase in interest and willingness to hear material that otherwise would not receive attention. This is a vital, but not sufficient, condition for propaganda to become effective. In view of the obvious importance of this area of sensory deprivation research, it is natural to believe that the paucity of studies is due to the controversial issues that would arise in an extended research programme aimed at changing the attitudes ('brainwashing') of subjects.

10

Stimulus-Hunger

Inherent in the term 'sensory deprivation' is the idea that reduced sensory input deprives the human organism of something it requires in order to function effectively, i.e., that prolonged reduced sensory input produces a 'stimulus-hunger'. The concept of a stimulus-hunger is not unique to sensory deprivation research, since it was used in Ribble's report of 'stimulus-feeding' needs in infants,[182] Hilgard's description of a 'reservoir of responses' that are elicited by inappropriate stimuli in the absence of appropriate stimuli,[107] and Hebb's postulating a biological need for stimulation.[99]

The great majority of the research on sensory deprivation has been aimed at evaluating the deleterious effects of stimulus-hunger rather than at a direct demonstration of its existence and the identification of variables which affect its intensity quantitatively. The obvious value of the latter studies would be in the introduction of greater clarity in the evaluation of research results obtained in different laboratories using different experimental procedures. There are so many apparently contradictory results that have been reported in this field of research. This state of affairs is not surprising in view of the absence of any standard means of evaluating the effectiveness of any specific set of experimental conditions in producing stimulus-hunger or of evaluating how a specific set of procedures may either ameliorate or intensify the stimulus-hunger. An analogous situation would exist if a multitude of studies were undertaken in many different laboratories on the deleterious effects of *partial* food-hunger (all research so far has been on *partial* sensory deprivation) with no knowledge or control over the caloric value of foods still available to subjects, the metabolic rates of subjects, and so on.

A few preliminary studies have recently been undertaken to develop objective measures of a stimulus-hunger and to identify which stimulus characteristics are most effective in satisfying the hunger. A theoretical framework for such studies, based upon methodologies used to develop measures of other biological drives, has recently been offered by Jones.[122]

In his own work Jones has found that initial response rates for light flashes increase with length of sensory deprivation,[120, 121, 123] and this finding is consistent with a stimulus-hunger drive that increases with length of deprivation time. A similar finding has been reported in many studies carried out with isolated animals in which auditory, visual or tactual stimuli were used as reinforcements for an operant response.[15, 29, 30, 66, 153, 177, 187, 256]

Another series of studies has been aimed at the development of an objective measure of the intensity of the aversive properties of stimulus-hunger. In this series, subjects were given the opportunity to earn time-off from their scheduled stay in sensory deprivation by continuously pressing a small button. The hypothesis was that button-pressing would increase with an increase in stimulus-hunger. Results indicated that the kinesthetic and proprioceptive feedback involved in button-pressing was not rewarding in itself[192] but it was positively related to negative descriptions of the sensory deprivation experience,[192] the amount of time-off reward offered,[193] decreases in self-rated well-being,[194] and experimental conditions designed to produce an increase in discomfort.[195]

Some indirect evidence of a stimulus-hunger drive is discernible in results which demonstrate that subjects who are most stressed by sensory deprivation as determined by physiological measurements also respond most for auditory and visual stimuli,[291] and subjects who ask for early release also respond more for visual stimuli than subjects who are able to complete their scheduled stay in sensory deprivation.[244] The recent development of a Sensation-Seeking-Scale holds promise of identifying individuals who normally have different amounts of the stimulus-hunger drive.[292] If this promise is fulfilled, it should be possible to control this important variable in future sensory deprivation research.

A few studies have been carried out to determine which stimulus characteristics best feed the stimulus-hunger. The results of one of these studies indicate that informative stimuli are more rewarding than those simply characterized by variety or complexity.[121] The results of another study verify the finding that meaningful sequences of stimuli are more rewarding than less meaningful sequences, but they also indicate that less meaningful sequences of stimuli are more rewarding in sensory deprivation than in control situations.[191]

Although there has been relatively little research done in this area, the results are encouraging. The development of objective measures of the stimulus-hunger drive and its quantitative strength will do much to increase the experimental rigour of future sensory deprivation research and to make comparable the results obtained in many different laboratories using many different procedures.

11

Theories

It has been said that sensory deprivation is a field of research devoid of theory.[100, 241] Despite the fact that the original studies at McGill University were stimulated by Hebb's theory of psychology, the great bulk of subsequent research has been carried out to establish empirical relationships and not to test hypotheses derived from theory. The accumulated results of sensory deprivation research occasionally are discussed in terms of how well they fit theories originally formulated to integrate data collected in other fields of research, but these discussions are more akin to speculating than to theorizing.

The theories that have been mentioned in this regard usually are referred to under three headings: cognitive, psychoanalytic, and neurophysiological. These theories are not mutually exclusive, and the same data often can fit all three types equally well. This, in addition to a paucity of sensory deprivation studies which have been specifically designed to test hypotheses derived from the theories, makes it impossible to say which type of theory best fits the present facts.

Cognitive

The cognitive theories formulated by Bruner, Werner, and Piaget often are mentioned in the discussion of sensory deprivation results.[26, 70, 87, 129] As applied to sensory deprivation, the cognitive theories are based on the premise that perception operates on a system of probabilities and not on a system of invarient stimulus-response relationships. In the development of the perceptual processes, the individual must learn strategies to evaluate afferent inflow, strategies which will result in a cognitive model of the environment in which there is stability and recurrent regularities. Thus the individual is able to extrapolate or interpolate information from cues and to predict events. For example, new sensory input emanating from something red, shimmering, smoking, and causing turbulations in the air above it will be perceived by an efficient cognitive model as 'probably hot which will burn if touched'.

An additional function of a cognitive model is to select for attention from the multitudinous stimuli usually present, those stimuli which probably are most important for the satisfaction of the individual's needs. This function of the cognitive model can be likened to programming the centrifugal portion of the reticular activating system. Without the programme, there would be no selective gating of incoming impulses, and the individual would attempt to attend to all impinging stimuli with the result that his perceived world would be similar to the 'big, booming, buzzing, confused world'[119] of the neonate.

Once developed, the cognitive model and its strategies are constantly monitored and corrected by feedback information. Since the cognitive model creates a stable world for the individual, an unhampered evaluation process is considered essential even in the moment-to-moment adaptation to the environment. Interference with the evaluation process, such as that occurring during delayed auditory and visual feedback experiments, leads to anxiety and a dominating need to adjust feedback to model.

A sensory deprivation environment provides too few sensory cues for the individual to establish probabilities for accurate perception, and it interferes with the feedback evaluation process by diminishing the amount of feedback. Hence, the individual's cognitive processes become disorganized, and this leads to distorted perceptions (hallucinations, body-image distortions, etc.), anxiety, panic, and other deleterious effects found to occur during sensory deprivation.

Psychoanalytic

Psychoanalytic theory often has been invoked as an explanation of the effects of sensory deprivation.[12, 79, 81, 82, 128, 152, 179] According to the theory, one of the primary functions of the ego is to provide mastery over the external environment. Indeed, its chief *raison d'être* is to enable the individual to 'deal with external reality'. When exteroceptive stimuli are greatly reduced, as during sensory deprivation, this function of the ego goes into abeyance, and more primitive, hitherto repressed, psychic processes become dominant. 'Secondary process' thinking (logical, organized, reality-oriented), a property of the ego, is abrogated, and 'primary process' thinking (irrational, disorganized, wish-dominated) supervenes. The result is a tendency toward cognitive deficits, emergence of infantile wishes and fears, hallucinations, and general panic in some individuals, particularly those who fear the experience of losing control over their impulses.

In addition to the absence of exteroceptive stimuli, *per se*, there are other features of the laboratory conditions in sensory deprivation experiments that facilitate a general regression of psychic processes. Rapaport[179] has pointed out the similarity of sensory deprivation experimental procedures to those psychoanalysts who use it to facilitate regression clinically, e.g., the patient is required to lie on a couch in a quiet room, facing away from the therapist toward a wall or ceiling, to free-associate, and to entrust himself to the therapist. All these conditions are magnified during sensory deprivation, and regression is even more encouraged by the complete dependence of the subject on the experimenter for the satisfaction of such basic needs as feeding, toileting, and physical safety. Kubie[128] has pointed out that regression probably is maximally encouraged in those studies which employ a water-tank with the water kept at body-temperature, because these conditions closely simulate the womb and the amniotic fluid. It may be noted that maximum deleterious effects usually are found in those studies employing a water-tank to create sensory deprivation.[31, 135, 209]

Neurophysiological

The application of neurophysiological theory to sensory deprivation results has been based on the central role of the reticular activating system (RAS) and the hypothalamus in the efficient functioning of the central nervous system (CNS).[65, 104, 138, 205] The central core of the RAS lies between the brain stem and the thalamus, and it is linked with the corticofugal system and the centrifugal system which permits it to monitor all sensory input.

'If one conceives of the reticular formation as a kind of barometer for both input and output level, a structure serving as a sort of homeostat regulating or adjusting input-output relations, then it is a short step to the assumption that it has an adaptation level. Psychologically, this would be reflected in a suitably high or low level of attention or anticipatory set. However, with exceptional conditions of sensory deprivation, literally a void would be created with vigorous striving for necessary stimulation to keep the RAS and, in turn, the cortex, going on an activated basis so that one's past or present may be reviewed. Without such stimulation, boredom, inactivity, and, ultimately, sleep, prevail.'[138]

The RAS also is considered to carry out an important function in the selective gating of incoming impulses (i.e., selective attention).[103] Thus, drastically reduced sensory input leads not only to lowered arousal but also to loss of selective attention. The result is that the individual's thoughts become dominated by residual stimuli, which leads to excessive preoccupation with somatic stimuli, stimulus-bound thinking, body-image distortions, and so on. The individual may begin hallucinating in an attempt to stimulate the RAS to maintain a more optimal level of arousal.

The most thorough application of neurophysiological theory to results obtained in studies of reduced variation in sensory input (e.g. boredom, monotony, sleep, etc.) has been done by Fiske and Maddi,[65] and the most thorough application of the theory to results obtained in sensory deprivation research has been done by Schultz.[205]

12

Clinical Implications

There is much to be learned about the specific effects of sensory deprivation, and the reasons for these effects. Research in this area is hampered by serious methodological problems, results have not always been consistent, and conclusions vary. However, despite these problems, the accumulated facts leave little doubt that monotonous, sensorily-deprived environments can lead to disorganization of thought processes and negative affect changes in normal individuals.

The implications for psychiatric practice may be questioned on the grounds that such extreme conditions rarely are found beyond laboratory walls. While it is true that such extreme conditions are rare, it is equally true that most of the laboratory research has been carried out under relatively benign conditions, including the use of short periods of isolation and healthy, young, volunteer subjects who have been psychiatrically screened and allowed to terminate the experiment on request. It is reasonable to assume that prolonged, involuntary exposure to even moderately monotonous and reduced sensory input by less mentally healthy people (who may be simultaneously facing other sources of stress such as bereavement or physical disability) can lead to even more deleterious psychological dysfunctioning than that seen in laboratory settings. Furthermore, it would be expected that symptoms would develop slowly and insidiously rather than suddenly and dramatically as in the laboratory, and this slow progression may make the relationship between the dysfunction and the reduced sensory environment less obvious.

In the discussion which follows, the purpose is to present illustrative, broad areas of clinical applications rather than detailed descriptions of individual instances. A comprehensive discussion of all applications is not feasible because the range of medical and psychiatric practice is broad and reduced sensory environments may be found almost anywhere. The authors invite the reader to use his own ingenuity in drawing inferences concerning the possible involvement of such environments in problems presented by his own patients.

Military and Industrial Psychiatry

As military and industrial tasks have become more automated, the role of the worker has become more passive and restricted, and the environments in which he functions have been efficiently designed to keep out 'distracting stimuli'. The role of this reduced sensory input in the production of accidents and errors of judgement is receiving increased attention. Research has been carried out on task efficiency during prolonged exposure to the restricted environments found in submarines,[125, 126, 188, 259] modern military aircraft[28, 91, 97, 98, 212] and space vehicles.[33, 49, 62, 63, 90, 92, 142, 157, 170, 198, 218, 236]

Reduced sensory input also has been implicated in plane crashes due to 'grey-out'[17, 23, 35, 36, 102] and in truck and auto crashes on long trips over monotonous superhighways.[140, 141, 156, 217] The deleterious effects of long periods of isolation in prisoners has been investigated,[27, 89, 154, 232, 239, 253] as well as the possible occurrence of such effects in fall-out shelters.[5, 38, 59, 80]

The ability of small groups to live together harmoniously and to work efficiently during long periods of isolation (e.g., during Antarctic expeditions) also has been a subject for much investigation.[61, 88, 158, 159, 168, 200]

The anecdotal literature on changes occurring in the psychological functioning of military personnel who have been lost, marooned, or imprisoned and isolated for extended periods[112, 113, 114, 137, 143, 234] has recently been thoroughly reviewed.[152]

Psychiatric Consultation

Psychiatrists often are asked to consult on psychiatric symptoms appearing in patients under treatment for some general medical problem. The 'rest and quiet' that often is prescribed as part of a treatment programme is sometimes overdone; it then becomes tantamount to a prescription for sensory deprivation. The psychiatric consultant who is aware of this is better able to discriminate between symptoms that arise from the treatment conditions and those that arise from other sources of stress or intrapsychic conflict. It is likely that many mild, transient, psychotic-like states that are seen in the course of the practice of medicine are due, at least in part, to sensory deprivation. Some of these conditions are discussed below. They all are characterized by one or more of the following: confusion, disorientation, irritability, anxiety states amounting in some instances to panic, illusions, and, rarely, delusions and hallucinations. The medical practitioner in these cases, often seems to think of 'hysteria' or 'schizophrenia'; the psychiatrist recognizes the evidences of an organic psychotic state and recommends a search for feasible causes such as toxic conditions, drug overdosage or sensitivity, traumatic states, endocrine or metabolic abnormalities, circulatory disturbances, or CNS pathology. Such a search is no doubt indicated in most instances; the authors would merely emphasize that sensory deprivation is another condition to keep in mind, alone, or in combination with some other.

Neurology. Patients with a variety of neurological diseases in which respiratory paralysis occurs, such as poliomyelitis, polyneuritis, and myesthenia gravis, sometimes are confined in tank-type respirators for long periods of time. These patients may develop symptoms very much like those reported in sensory deprivation research,[134, 146, 149, 231] and these symptoms often can be alleviated by creating a variegated sensory environment for the patient. Sensory deprivation conditions created during medication and treatment of a patient with paraplegia has been described.[118] It is of interest to note that confinement in a tank-type respirator was one of the methods used to create sensory deprivation in a laboratory setting.[147, 148, 257, 288]

Medicine. Hospital routines sometimes are disrupted by patients who wander through corridors and wards during the quiet of night. These patients usually are found to be confused and disoriented for time and place. Prolonged hospitalization with its attendant rest, solitude, and social isolation is coupled with visual and auditory deprivation during the night to produce sensory deprivation conditions. These conditions are most likely to occur with chronic invalids, especially cardiac cases where the prescription of absolute rest is overdone, but sensory deprivation conditions also may occur during acute illnesses which require extreme quiet and isolation.

Ophthalmology. The disturbance described as 'black patch psychosis' has received much attention over the years.[16, 85, 255] This is a disturbance that occurs postoperatively in patients who have undergone cataract or other eye operations and who have both eyes patched. The obvious relation between the postoperative treatment and sensory deprivation has been discussed fully.[264, 269, 270] The incidence of this condition has dropped from 7 per cent to 1 per cent with the provision of greater sensory stimulation during the postoperative period.[264]

The occurrence of blindness of any kind can lead to severe restrictions in mobility as well as the loss of sensory input. The occurrence of subsequent emotional disturbances may be a reaction to the general sensory deprivation as well as to the blindness, *per se*.[139]

Orthopaedics. Patients with orthopaedic problems often are immobilized for long periods by body casts, head tongs and other apparatus. The mental disturbances that may accompany this form of sensory deprivation have been outlined elsewhere.[254] Therapeutically, they have often been quickly dissipated by the provision of frequent visitors, radio, television, and other sources of stimulation. However, it should be recalled that mental disturbances have been found to occur with immobilization alone.[286]

Surgery. The intricate and complicated surgery that has become possible in recent years has often brought with it the need for prolonged isolation and immobilization in postoperative 'recovery rooms'. Patients have been known to develop 'postoperative psychosis' under such conditions, and their general excitement, attempts to tear off bandages, and other abnormal forms of behaviour have seriously interfered with their recovery.[20a, 60a, 127a, 177a] The psychiatric consultant may wish to recommend the provision of more exteroceptive stimulation in the recovery room, perhaps music, or more individual attention from the nurse or a relative.

Mental Hospital Psychiatry

Not too many years ago, treatment in many mental hospitals consisted simply of isolating the mentally ill in bare, unfurnished rooms. The gradual deterioration that so often occurred in patients can now be partially attributed to the sensory deprivation conditions. Modern mental hospitals provide a variety of treatment programmes that have proved effective. It is now common knowledge that almost any new treatment programme administered energetically can produce therapeutic gain in mental hospital patients. The usual explanation is that patients respond to personal attention or to the therapist's expectations that a particular treatment will be beneficial. However, it may well be that new treatments provide patients with new and varied stimulation, and that it is this stimulation itself which is beneficial nonspecifically.

Developmental Psychiatry

The results of sensory deprivation research with adults have complemented the results obtained in research on children which demonstrate a basic need for stimulation.[182, 223, 224] Retardation of intellectual and emotional growth resulting from development within sensorily deprived environments has been amply demonstrated also in animal studies[67, 93, 94, 95, 124, 169, 183, 184, 185, 233] and anecdotal case histories.[13, 52, 53, 55, 56, 57, 74, 108, 109, 144, 145, 226, 261, 262, 263]

Geriatric Psychiatry

The deterioration of psychological functions in the elderly undoubtedly is influenced by biochemical and neurological changes occurring during the ageing process. However, cultural patterns and physical limitations often force the elderly to spend large portions of their time in sensorily deprived environments, and this deprivation may play some role in the psychological deterioration.[6, 32, 160] It is of interest that the pattern of intellectual deficits that was found in a battery of tests administered to young subjects in sensory deprivation was almost identical to the pattern of deficits found when the same battery was administered to a group of elderly persons not subjected to laboratory sensory deprivation.[283]

Psychiatric Treatment

There have been some direct studies of the therapeutic effects of sensory deprivation when used with psychotic patients. Some of the results of this research have been presented above in the discussion of affective changes. While not conclusive, the research does suggest that brief periods of sensory deprivation, combined with a follow-up therapeutic programme, can provide additional gain in the treatment of some psychotic and depressed patients.[1, 2, 34, 39, 77, 96, 186] It would seem that these patients become more aware of their illnesses during sensory deprivation, thus making for better motivation for psychotherapy.[3, 10, 11, 45, 78] It should be noted, however, that sensory deprivation alone would not be expected to produce lasting improvements. On the contrary, if it did, the 'back-wards' and solitary confinement cells in antiquated mental hospitals would have led to psychological health instead of psychological deterioration.

13

Summary

Sensory deprivation, a new research area in psychology and psychiatry, investigates the effects of limiting sensory input in volunteer human subjects. Though there have been comparable anecdotal observations of a similar nature for many years, laboratory experimental work is scarcely a decade old.

Following an historical review, this chapter discusses the many methodological problems that have beset the field and that have often produced contradictory results from different laboratories. The effects of sensory deprivation are presented as affective changes, hallucinations, physiological effects, perceptual-motor effects, cognitive effects, susceptibility to propaganda, and stimulus-hunger.

Three theoretical explanations are offered to account for the observed phenomena: cognitive, psychoanalytic, and neurophysiological.

The clinical implications fall into the following categories: military and industrial psychiatry, psychiatric consultation (neurology, medicine ophthalmology, orthopaedics, surgery), mental hospital psychiatry, developmental psychiatry, geriatrics, and psychiatric treatment.

This chapter was written with the support of ONR contract No. 1866(29); ONR Contract Authority NR 142-115.

REFERENCES

1. ADAMS, H. B., 1964. Therapeutic potentialities of sensory deprivation procedures. *Intern. ment. Hlth. Res. Newsltr.*, **6**, 7.
2. ADAMS, H. B., CARRERA, P. N., COOPER, G. D., GIBBY, R. G., and TOBEY, H. P., 1960. Personality and intellectual changes in psychiatric patients following brief partial sensory deprivation. *Amer. Psychol.*, **15**, 448. (Abstract.)
3. ADAMS, H. B., ROBERTSON, M. H., and COOPER, G. D., 1963. Facilitating therapeutic personality changes in psychiatric patients by sensory deprivation methods. Paper read at XVII Intern. Congr. Psychol., Washington, D.C.

4. AGADZHANIAN, N. A., BIZAN, IU. P., DORONIN, G. P., and KUZNETSOV, A. G., 1963. Change in higher nervous activity and in some vegetative reactions under prolonged conditions of adynamia and isolation. *Z. vysshei nerv. Deiatel'nosti*, **13**, 953.

5. ALTMAN, J. W., SMITH, R. W., MYERS, R. L., McKENNA, F., and BRYSON, S., 1960. Psychological and social adjustment in a simulated shelter—a research report. Amer. Institute for Research. (Contract No. CDR-SR-60-10.) Office of Civil and Defense Mobilization, November.

6. ANDERSON, J. E., Ed., 1956. *Psychological aspects of aging*. Washington, D.C.: Amer. Psychol. Ass.

7. ARDUINI, A., and HIRAO, T., 1959. On the mechanism of the EEG sleep patterns elicited by acute visual deafferentation. *Arch. Ital. Biol.*, **97**, 140.

8. ARNHOFF, F. N., and LEON, H. V., 1963. Sex differences in response to short-term sensory deprivation and isolation. *Percept. mot. Skills*, **17**, 81.

9. ARNHOFF, F. N., LEON, H. V., and BROWNFIELD, C. A., 1962. Sensory deprivation, the effects on human learning. *Science*, **138**, 899.

10. AZIMA, H., and CRAMER, F. J., 1956. Effects of partial isolation in mentally disturbed individuals. *Dis. nerv. Syst.*, **17**, 117.

11. AZIMA, H., and CRAMER-AZIMA, F. J., 1957. Studies on perceptual isolation. *Dis. nerv. Syst.* (Monogr. Suppl.), **18**, 1.

12. AZIMA, H., VISPOS, R. H., and CRAMER-Azima, F. J., 1961. Observations on anaclitic therapy during sensory deprivation. In *Sensory deprivation*. Eds. Solomon, P., *et al*. Cambridge, Mass.: Harvard Univ. Press.

13. BAKWIN, H., 1942. Loneliness in infants. *Amer. J. Dis. Child.*, **63**, 30.

14. BARNARD, C. W., WOLFF, H. D., and GRAVELINE, D. E., 1962. Sensory deprivation under null gravity conditions. *Amer. J. Psychiat.*, **118**, 921.

15. BARON, A., and KISH, G. B., 1962. Low intensity auditory and visual stimuli as reinforcers for the mouse. *J. comp. physiol. Psychol.*, **55**, 1011.

16. BARTLETT, J. E. A., 1951. A case of organized visual hallucinations in an old man with cataract and their relation to the phenomenon of the phantom limb. *Brain*, **74**, 363.

17. BENNETT, A. M. H., 1961. Sensory deprivation in aviation. In *Sensory deprivation*. Eds. Solomon, P., *et al*. Cambridge, Mass.: Harvard Univ. Press.

18. BETELEVA, T. G., and NOVIKOVA, L. A., 1960. Electrical activity of various regions of the cerebral cortex and reticular formation after olfactory deafferentation. *Pavlov. J. higher nerv. Activity*, **10**, 109.

19. BEXTON, W. H., 1953. Some effects of perceptual isolation in human subjects. Unpublished doct. dissert., McGill Univer.

20. BEXTON, W. H., HERON, W., and SCOTT, T. H., 1954. Effects of decreased variation in sensory environment. *Canad. J. Psychol.*, **8**, 70.

20a. BLACHY, P. H., and STARR, A., 1964. Post-cardiotomy delirium, *Amer. J. Psychiat.*, **121**, 371.

21. BORING, E. G., 1950 *A history of experimental psychology*. New York: Appleton-Century-Crofts, Inc.

22. BREMER, F., 1935. 'Cerveau isole' et physiologie du sommeil. *C. R. Soc. Biol. Paris*, **118**, 1235.

23. BROWN, R. H., 1957. Empty-field myopia and visibility of objects at high altitudes. *Amer. J. Psychol.*, **70**, 376.

24. BROWNFIELD, C. A., 1964. Deterioration and facilitation hypotheses in sensory deprivation research. *Psychol. Bull.*, **61**, 304.

25. 1965. *Isolation: clinical and experimental approaches*. New York: Random House.

26. BRUNER, J. S., 1961. The cognitive consequences of early sensory deprivation. In *Sensory deprivation*. Eds.: Solomon, P., *et al*. Cambridge, Mass. Harvard Univ. Press.

27. BURNEY, C., 1952. *Solitary confinement.* New York: Coward-McCann.
28. BURNS, N., and KIMURA, D., 1963. Isolation and sensory deprivation. In *Unusual environments and human behavior.* Eds. Burns, N., Chambers, R., and Hendler, E. New York: MacMillan.
29. BUTLER, R. A., 1957. The effect of deprivation of visual incentives on visual exploration motivation in monkeys. *J. comp. physiol. Psychol.*, **50**, 177.
30. BUTLER, R. A., and ALEXANDER, H. M., 1955. Daily patterns of visual exploratory behavior in the monkey. *J. comp. physiol. Psychol.*, **48**, 247.
31. CAMBARERI, J. D., 1958. The effects of sensory isolation on suggestible and non-suggestible psychology graduate students. *Dissert. Abstracts*, **19**, 1813. Doctoral dissert., Univer. of Utah.
32. CAMERON, D. E., 1941. Studies in senile nocturnal delirium. *Psychiat. Quart.*, 1.
33. CAMERON, D. E., LEVY, L., BARTH, T., and RUBENSTEIN, L., 1961. Sensory deprivation: effects upon the functioning human in space systems. In *Psychophysiological aspects of space flight.* Ed. Flaherty, B. E. New York: Columbia Univ. Press.
34. CHARNY, I. W., 1963. Regression and reorganization in the 'isolation treatment' of children: a clinical contribution to sensory deprivation research. *J. child Psychol. Psychiat.*, **4**, 47.
35. CLARK, B., and GRAYBIEL, A., 1957. The break-off phenomenon. *J. aviat. Med.*, **58**, 121.
36. CLARK, B., NICHOLSON, M. A., and GRAYBIEL, A., 1953. Fascination: a cause of pilot error. *J. aviat. Med.*, **24**, 427.
37. CLEVELAND, S. E., REITMAN, E. E., and BENTINCK, C., 1963. Therapeutic effectiveness of sensory deprivation. *Arch. gen. Psychiat.*, **8**, 455.
38. CLEVELAND, S. E., SHEER, D., and REITMAN, E. E., 1963. Effects of fallout shelter confinement on family adjustment. *Arch. gen. Psychiat.*, **8**, 38.
39. COHEN, B. D., ROSENBAUM, G., DOBIE, S. I., and GOTTLIEB, J., 1959. Sensory isolation: hallucinogenic effects of a brief procedure. *J. nerv. ment. Dis.*, **129**, 486.
40. COHEN, S. I., SILVERMAN, A. J., BRESSLER, B., and SHMAVONIAN, B. M. 1961. Problems in isolation studies. In *Sensory deprivation.* Eds. Solomon P., *et al.* Cambridge, Mass.: Harvard Univ. Press.
41. COHEN, S. I., SILVERMAN, A. J., and SHMAVONIAN, B. M., 1962. Neurophysiological humoral and personality factors in the response to sensory deprivation. In *Proceedings of the Third World Congress of Psychiatry.* Ed. Cleghorn, R. A. Toronto: Univ. of Toronto Press.
42. 1962. Psychophysiological studies in altered sensory environments. *J. psychosom. Res.*, **6**, 259.
43. COHEN, W., 1958. Some perceptual and physiological aspects of uniform visual stimulation. Washington, D.C.: Res. & Dev. Div., Office of the Surgeon General, Dept. of the Army, *Progress report*, 1.
44. 1962. Some perceptual and physiological aspects of uniform visual stimulation. *Final Tech. Rept.*, Univ. of Buffalo, New York, February. (Contract No. DA-49-007-MD-866. Research and Development Div., Office of the Surgeon General, Dept. of the Army.)
45. COOPER, G. D., ADAMS, H. B., and GIBBY, R. G., 1962. Ego strength changes following perceptual isolation. *Arch. gen. Psychiat.*, **7**, 213.
46. COURTNEY, J., DAVIS, J. M., and SOLOMON, P., 1961. Sensory deprivation: the role of movement. *Percept. mot. Skills*, **13**, 191.
47. CRONBACH, L. J., 1949. *Essentials of psychological testing.* New York: Harper and Brothers.

48. CULVER, C. M., COHEN, S. I., SILVERMAN, A. J., and SHMAVONIAN, B. M., 1964. Cognitive structuring, field dependence-independence, and the psychophysiological response to perceptual isolation. In *Recent advances in biological psychiatry*. Ed. Wortis, J., vol. 6. New York: Plenum Press.

49. CUNNINGHAM, C., 1959. The effects of sensory impoverishment, confinement and sleep deprivation. *J. Brit. Interplanetary Society*, 17, 311.

50. DAVIS, J. M., McCOURT, W. F., COURTNEY, J., and SOLOMON, P., 1961. Sensory deprivation, the role of social isolation. *Arch. gen. Psychiat.*, 5, 84.

51. DAVIS, J. M., McCOURT, W. F., and SOLOMON, P., 1960. The effect of visual stimulation on hallucinations and other mental experiences during sensory deprivation. *Amer. J. Psychiat.*, 116, 889.

52. DAVIS, K., 1940. Extreme social isolation of a child. *Amer. J. Sociol.*, 45, 554.

53. 1947. Final note on a case of extreme isolation. *Amer. J. Sociol.*, 52, 432.

54. DAVIS, R., 1959. Somatic activity under reduced stimulation. *J. comp. physiol. Psychol.*, 52, 309.

55. DENNIS, W., 1938. Infant development under conditions of restricted practice and of minimum social stimulation: a preliminary report. *J. genet. Psychol.*, 53, 149.

56. 1941. Infant development under conditions of restricted practice and minimum social stimulation. *Genet. Psychol. Monogr.*, 23, 143.

57. DENNIS, W., and DENNIS, M. G., 1951. Development under controlled environmental conditions. In *Readings in child development*. Ed. Dennis, W. New York: Prentice-Hall.

58. DOANE, B. K., MAHATOO, W., HERON, W., and SCOTT, T. H., 1959. Changes in perceptual functions after isolation. *Canad. J. Psychol.*, 13, 210.

59. DONALDSON, J., MAGNUSON, K., McHUGH, L., NINER, R., WATT, F., WILLIAMS, B., and ZINK, A., 1959. Psychological aspects of confinement in fallout shelters. *J. Psychol.*, 47, 163.

60. DUDA, P., and ZUBEK, J. P., 1965. Auditory sensitivity after prolonged visual deprivation. *Psychon. Sci.*, 3, 359.

60a. EGERTON, N., and KAY, J. H., 1964. Psychological disturbances associated with open heart surgery. *Brit. J. Psychiat.*, 110, 433.

61. EILBERT, L. R., and GLASSER, R., 1959. Differences between well and poorly adjusted groups in an isolated environment. *J. appl. Psychol.*, 43, 271.

62. FAUBION, R. W., and TINNAN, L. M., 1963. *Evaluation of small space station habitability: a seven-day confinement study*. SID 63-913. Downey, Calif.; North American Aviation, Inc.

63. 1963. *Evaluation of the standard orbital vehicle habitability: a four-day confinement study*. SID 63-376. Downey, Calif.: North American Aviation, Inc.

64. FISKE, D. W., 1961. Effects of monotonous and restricted stimulation. In *The functions of varied experience*. Eds. Fiske, D. W., and Maddi, S. Homewood, Ill.: Dorsey Press.

65. FISKE, D. W., and MADDI, S. R., Eds., 1961. *The functions of varied experience*. Homewood, Ill.: Dorsey Press.

66. FOX, S. S., 1962. Self-maintained sensory input and sensory deprivation in monkeys: a behavioral and neuropharmacological study. *J. comp. physiol. Psychol.*, 55, 438.

67. FREDERICSON, E., 1951. Effects of infantile experience upon adult behavior. *J. abnorm. soc. Psychol.*, 46, 406.

68. FREEDMAN, S. J., 1961. Sensory deprivation and the perception of visual speed. *Acta Psychologica*, 19, 562.

69. FREEDMAN, S. J., and GREENBLATT, M., 1960. Studies in human isolation. I. Perceptual findings. *USAF med. J.*, 11, 1330

70. 1960. Studies in human isolation. II. Hallucinations and other cognitive findings. *USAF med. J.*, **11**, 1479.

71. FREEDMAN, S. J., GRUNEBAUM, H. V., and GREENBLATT, M., 1961. Perceptual and cognitive changes in sensory deprivation. In *Sensory deprivation*. Eds. Solomon, P., *et al.* Cambridge, Mass.: Harvard Univ. Press.

72. FREEDMAN, S. J., GRUNEBAUM, H. V., STARE, F. A., and GREENBLATT, M., 1962. Imagery in sensory deprivation. In *Hallucinations*. Ed. West, L. J. New York: Grune and Stratton.

73. FREEDMAN, S. J., and HELD, R., 1960. Sensory deprivation and perceptual lag. *Percept. mot. Skills*, **11**, 277.

74. FREUD, A., and BURLINGHAM, D., 1944. *Infants without families*. New York: Intern. Univ. Press.

75. GALKIN, V. S., and SPERANSKI, A. D., 1935. Cited in *Selected works*. Pavlov, I. P. (English translation.) Moscow: Foreign Languages Publishing House.

76. GELLHORN, E., 1958. The influence of curare on hypothalamic excitability and the electroencephalogram. *EEG clin. Neurophysiol.*, **10**, 697.

77. GIBBY, R. G., and ADAMS, H. B., 1961. Receptiveness of psychiatric patients to verbal communication: an increase following partial sensory and social deprivation. *Arch. gen. Psychiat.*, **5**, 366.

78. GIBBY, R. G., ADAMS, H. B., and CARRERA, R. N., 1960. Therapeutic changes in psychiatric patients following partial sensory deprivation. *Arch. gen. Psychiat.*, **3**, 33.

79. GOLDBERGER, L., and HOLT, R. R., 1958. Experimental interference with reality contact (perceptual isolation): method and group results. *J. nerv. ment. Dis.*, **127**, 99.

80. 1961. A comparison of isolation effects and their personality correlates in two divergent samples. *WADC Tech. Rept. No. 61-417.*

81. 1961. Experimental interference with reality contact; individual differences. In *Sensory deprivation*. Eds. Solomon, P., *et al.* Cambridge, Mass.: Harvard Univ. Press.

82. GOLDFRIED, M. R., 1960. A psychoanalytic interpretation of sensory deprivation. *Psychol. Rec.*, **10**, 211.

83. GORBOV, F. D., MIASNIKOV, V. I., and IAZDOVSKI, V. I., 1963. Strain and fatigue under conditions of sensory deprivation. *Z. vysshei nerv. Deiatel'-nosti, Pavlov.*, **13**, 585. (In Russian.)

84. GREENBERG, I. M., and POLLACK, M., 1965. Occipital slow wave EEG activity: Intellectual deficits in psychiatric patients. Paper presented at VI Intern. Congr. EEG Clin. Neurophysiol., Vienna.

85. GREENWOOD, A., 1928. Mental disturbances following operation for cataract. *J. Amer. Med. Ass.*, **91**, 1713.

86. GRISSOM, R. J., SUEDFELD, P., and VERNON, J., 1962. Memory for verbal material: effects of sensory deprivation. *Science*, **138**, 429.

87. GRUNEBAUM, H. V., FREEDMAN, S. J., and GREENBLATT, M., 1960. Sensory deprivation and personality. *Amer. J. Psychiat.*, **116**, 878.

88. GUNDERSON, E. E. K., 1963. Emotional symptoms in extremely isolated groups. *Arch. gen. Psychiat.*, **9**, 362.

89. GUTSCH, A., 1962. Mental disturbances in solitary confinement. *Allg. Z. Psychiat.*, **19**, 1. (In German.)

90. HANNA, T. D., 1962. A physiologic study of human subjects confined in a simulated space vehicle. *Aerospace Med.*, **33**, 175.

91. HANNA, T. D., BURNS, N. M., and TILLER, P. R., 1963. Behavioral and physiological responses to varying periods of sensory deprivation. BuMed. Subtask MR005. 13-1006.6. Air Crew Equipment Laboratory, U.S. Naval Air Material Centre, Philadelphia, February.

92. HANNA, T. D., and GAITO, J., 1960. Performance and habitability aspects of extended confinement in sealed cabins. *Aerospace Med.*, **31**, 399.

93. HARLOW, H. F., 1953. Mice, monkeys, men, and motives. *Psychol. Rev.*, **60**, 23.

94. 1958. The nature of love. *Amer. Psychologist*, **03**, 673.

95. 1962. The heterosexual affectional system in monkeys. *Amer. Psychologist*, **17**, 1. ·

96. HARRIS, A., 1959. Sensory deprivation in schizophrenia. *J. ment. Sci.*, **105**, 235.

97. HAUTY, G. T., 1958. Conditions peculiar to a closed ecological system in space. *Air Univer. Quart. Rev.*, **10**, 89.

98. HAUTY, G. T., and PAYNE, R. B., 1958. Fatigue, confinement, and proficiency decrement. In *Vistas in astronautics*. Eds. Alperin, M., Stern, M., and Wooster, H. New York: Pergamon Press.

99. HEBB, D. O., 1949. *The organization of behavior. A neuropsychological theory.* New York: Wiley.

100. 1961. Sensory deprivation: facts in search of a theory. *J. nerv. ment. Dis.*, **132**, 40.

101. HELD, R., and WHITE, B., 1959. Sensory deprivation and visual speed: an analysis. *Science*, **130**, 861.

102. HENRY, J. P., 1958. Aviation biology. *J. aviat. Med.*, **28**, 171.

103. HERNANDEZ-PEON, R., SCHERRER, H., and JOUVET, M., 1956. Modification of electrical activity in the cochlear nucleus during 'attention' in un-anesthetized cats. *Science*, **123**, 331.

104. HERON, W., 1961. Cognitive and physiological effects of perceptual isolation. In *Sensory deprivation*. Eds. Solomon, P., *et al.* Cambridge, Mass.: Harvard Univ. Press.

105. HERON, W., BEXTON, W. H., and HEBB, D. O., 1953. Cognitive effects of a decreased variation in the sensory environment. *Amer. Psychologist*, **8**, 366. (Abstract.)

106. HERON, W., DOANE, B. K., and SCOTT, T. H., 1956. Visual disturbances after prolonged perceptual isolation. *Canad. J. Psychol.*, **10**, 13.

107. HILGARD, E. R., 1948. *Theories of learning.* New York: Appleton-Century-Crofts.

108. HILL, J. C., and ROBINSON, B., 1929. A case of retarded mental development associated with restricted movements in infancy. *Brit. J. med. Psychol.*, **9**, 268.

109. HILL, K. T., and STEVENSON, H. W., 1964. Effectiveness of social reinforcement following social and sensory deprivation. *J. abnorm. soc. Psychol.*, **68**, 579.

110. HODES, R., 1962. Electrocortical synchronization resulting from reduced proprioceptive drive caused by neuromuscular blocking agents. *EEG clin. Neurophysiol.*, **14**, 220.

111. HOLT, R. R., and GOLDBERGER, L., 1961. Assessment of individual resistance to sensory alteration. In *Psychophysiological aspects of space flight.* Ed. Flaherty, B. E. New York: Columbia Univ.

112. HOWARD, R. A. Down in the North: an analysis of survival experiences in Arctic areas. *ADTIC Publication No. A-103.* Maxwell AFB, Ala.: Air University.

113. 999 survived: an analysis of survival experiences in the Southwest Pacific. *ADTIC Publication No. T-100.* Maxwell AFB, Ala.: Air University.

114. Sun, sand, and survival: an analysis of desert survival experiences during World War II. *ADTIC Publication No. D-102.* Maxwell AFB, Ala.: Air University.

115. HULL, J., and ZUBEK, J. P., 1962. Personality characteristics of successful and unsuccessful sensory isolation subjects. *Percept. mot. Skills*, **14**, 231.

116. JACKSON, C. W., JR., and KELLY, E. L., 1962. Influence of suggestion and subjects' prior knowledge in research on sensory deprivation. *Science*, **132**, 211.

117. JACKSON, C. W., JR., and POLLARD, J. C., 1962. Sensory deprivation and suggestion: a theoretical approach. *Behav. Sci.*, **7**, 332.

118. JACKSON, C. W., JR., POLLARD, J. C., and KANSKY, E. W., 1962. The application of findings from experimental sensory deprivation to cases of clinical sensory deprivation. *J. Amer. Med. Sci.*, **243**, 558.

119. JAMES, W., 1890. *Principles of Psychology*. New York: Henry Holt and Co.

120. JONES, A., 1961. Supplementary report: Information deprivation and irrelevant drive as determiners of an instrumental response. *J. exp. Psychol.*, **62**, 310.

121. —— 1964. Drive and incentive variables associated with the statistical properties of sequences of stimuli. *J. exp. Psychol.*, **67**, 423.

122. —— 1964. How to feed the stimulus hunger—problems in the definition of an incentive. Paper presented at Amer. Psychol. Ass.

123. JONES, A., WILKINSON, J., and BRADEN, I., 1961. Information deprivation as a motivational variable. *J. exp. Psychol.*, **62**, 127.

124. KING, J. A., 1958. Parameters relevant to determining the effects of early experience upon adult behavior of animals. *Psychol. Bull.*, **55**, 46.

125. KINSEY, J. L., 1953. Report of psychiatric studies on Operation Hideout. *U S. N. Med. Res. Lab.*, **12**, 1.

126. KINSEY, J. L., and MURPHREE, H. E., 1955. Claustrophobic reactions to some stresses of the submarine service. U.S. Naval Research Laboratories, New London, Conn. *Report No. 262.*

127. KITAMURA, S., 1964. Studies on sensory deprivation. II. 3: On the estimation of the body image. *Tohoku Psychologica Folia*, **22**, 69.

127a. KORNFELD, D. S., ZIMBERG, S., and MALM, J. R., 1965. Psychiatric complications of open heart surgery. *N. E. J. Med.*, **273**, 287.

128. KUBIE, L., 1961. Theoretical aspects of sensory deprivation. In *Sensory deprivation*. Eds. Solomon, P. *et al.* Cambridge, Mass.: Harvard Univ. Press.

129. KUBZANSKY, P. E., and LEIDERMAN, P. H., 1961. Sensory deprivation: an overview. In *Sensory deprivation*. Eds. Solomon, P. *et al.* Cambridge, Mass.: Harvard Univ. Press.

130. KUBZANSKY, P. E., 1958. Methodological and conceptual problems in the study of sensory deprivation. *Amer. Psychologist*, **13**, 334. (Abstract.)

131. KUZNETSOV, O. N., and LEBEDEV, V. I., 1965. A contribution to the problem of pseudopsychopathology under conditions of isolation with sensory deprivation. *Z. Nevropat. Psikhiat. Korsakov*, **65**, 386. (Russian.) Translation in *Soviet Psychol. Psychiat.*, **4**, 32 (1965).

132. LEBEDINSKY, A. V., LEVINSKY, S. V., and NEFEDOV, Y. G., 1964. General principles concerning the reaction of the organism to the complex environmental factors existing in spacecraft cabins. Paper presented at XV Intern. Aeronaut. Congr., Warsaw, September. Translated from Russian by NASA, TTF-273.

133. LEIDERMAN, P. H., 1962. Imagery and sensory deprivation, an experimental study. Aerospace Med. Div. *Rept. No. MRL-TDR-62-28*, May.

134. LEIDERMAN, P. H., MENDELSON, J. H., WEXLER, D., and SOLOMON, P., 1958. Sensory deprivation: clinical aspects. *Arch. int. Med.*, **101**, 389.

135. LILLY, J. C., 1956. Mental effects of reduction of ordinary levels of physical stimuli on intact, healthy persons. *Psychiat. Res. Rept.*, **5**, 1.

136. LILLY, J. C., and SHURLEY, J. T., 1961. Experiments in solitude in maximum achievable physical isolation with water suspension of intact healthy persons. In *Psychophysiological aspects of space flight*. Ed. Flaherty, B. E. New York: Columbia Univ. Press.

137. LINDEMANN, H., 1958. *Alone at sea*. New York: Random House.

138. LINDSLEY, D. B., 1961. Common factors in sensory deprivation, sensory distortion, and sensory overload. In *Sensory deprivation*. Eds. Solomon, P. *et al*. Cambridge, Mass.: Harvard Univ. Press.

139. McANDREW, H., 1948. Rigidity and isolation: A study of the deaf and the blind. *J. abnorm. soc. Psychol.*, **43**, 476.

140. McFARLAND, R. A., 1957. Psychological and psychiatric aspects of highway safety. *J. Amer. med. Assoc.*, **163**, 233.

141. McFARLAND, R. A., and MOORE, R. C., 1957. Human factors in highway safety: a review and evaluation. *N.E.J. Med.*, **792**, 256.

142. McKENZIE, R. E., HARTMAN, B. O., and WELCH, B. E., 1961. Observations in the SAM two-men space cabin simulator. III. System operator performance factors. *Aerospace Med.*, **32**, 603.

143. McKIE, R., 1953. *The survivors*. New York, Bobbs-Merrill.

144. MANDELBAUM, D. G., 1943. Wolf-child histories from India. *J. soc. Psychol.*, **17**, 25.

145. MASON, M. K., 1942. Learning to speak after six and one-half years of silence. *J. speech Disorders*, **7**, 295.

146. MENDELSON, J. H., and FOLEY, J. M., 1956. An abnormality of mental function affecting patients with poliomyelitis in a tank-type respirator. *Trans. Amer. Neurol. Ass.*, **81**, 134.

147. MENDELSON, J., KUBZANSKY, P., LEIDERMAN, P. H., WEXLER, D., DuTOIT, D., and SOLOMON, P., 1960. Catechol amine excretion and behavior during sensory deprivation. *Arch. gen. Psychiat.*, **2**, 147.

148. MENDELSON, J. H., KUBZANSKY, P. E., LEIDERMAN, P. H., WEXLER, D., and SOLOMON, P., 1961. Physiological and psychological aspects of sensory deprivation—a case analysis. In *Sensory deprivation*. Eds. Solomon, P., *et al*. Cambridge, Mass.: Harvard Univ. Press.

149. MENDELSON, J., SOLOMON, P., and LINDEMANN, E., 1958. Hallucinations of poliomyelitis patients during treatment in a respirator. *J. nerv. ment. Dis.*, **126**, 421.

150. MEYER, J. S., GREIFENSTEIN, F., and DEVAULT, M., 1959. A new drug causing symptoms of sensory deprivation. *J. nerv. ment. Dis.*, **129**, 54.

151. MIASNIKOV, V. I., 1964. Electroencephalographic changes in persons isolated for long periods. *Cosmic Research*, **2**, 133.

152. MILLER, S. C., 1962. Ego autonomy in sensory deprivation, isolation and stress. *Int. J. Psychoanal.*, **43**, 1.

153. MOON, L. E., and LODAHL, R. M., 1956. The reinforcing effect of changes in illumination on lever pressing in the monkey. *Amer. J. Psychol.*, **69**, 288.

154. MORELLO, M., 1959. A study of the adjustive behavior of prison inmates to incarceration. *Dissert. Abstr.*, **19**, 2149.

155. MORGAN, R. F., and BAKAN, P., 1965. Sensory deprivation hallucinations and other sleep behavior as a function of position, method of report, and anxiety. *Percept. mot. Skills*, **20**, 19.

156. MOSLEY, A. L., 1953. Hypnagogic hallucinations in relation to accidents. *Amer. Psychologist*, **8**, 8. (Abstract.)

157. MOTOBAYASHI, F., and SUGIMOTO, S., 1964. Space flight and the lack of sensory stimulation. *Japanese J. Aerosp. Med. Psychol.*, **1**, 82.

158. MULLIN, C. S., 1960. Some psychological aspects of isolated Antarctic living. *Amer. J. Psychiat.*, **117**, 323.

159. MULLIN, C. S., and CONNERY, H. J., 1959. Psychological study at an Antarctic IGY station. *USAF med. J.*, **10**, 290.

160. MUNNICHS, J. M. A., 1964. Loneliness, isolation and social relations in old age: A pilot survey. *Vita Humana*, **7**, 228.

161. MURPHY, C. W., KURLENTS, S., CLEGHORN, R. A., and HEBB, D. O., 1955. Absence of increased corticoid excretion with the stress of perceptual deprivation. *Canad. J. Biochem. Physiol.*, **33**, 1062.

162. MURPHY, D. B., and MYERS, T. I., 1962. Occurrence, measurement, and experimental manipulation of visual hallucinations. *Percept. mot. Skills*, **15**, 47.

163. MURPHY, D. B., MYERS, T. I., and SMITH, S., 1963. Reported visual sensations as a function of sustained sensory deprivation and social isolation. *Research Memorandum*, U.S. Army Leadership Human Research Unit (HUMRRO,) November.

164. MYERS, T. I., 1965. The isolation experience. Unpublished manuscript cited in *Sensory restriction*. Ed. Schultz, D. New York: Academic Press.

165. MYERS, T. I., MURPHY, D. B., and SMITH, S., 1963. The effect of sensory deprivation and social isolation on self exposure to propaganda and attitude change. *Amer. Psychologist.*, **18**, 440. (Abstract.)

166. MYERS, T. I., MURPHY, D. B., SMITH, S., and WINDLE, C., 1962. *Experimental assessment of a limited sensory and social environment.* Summary results of the HUMRRO U.S. Army Leadership Research Unit. Monterey, Calif., February.

167. NAGATSUKA, Y., and KOKUBUN, O., 1964. Studies on sensory deprivation. II. Part 1. Introductory remarks and results of polygraphic records. *Tohoku Psychologica Folia*, **22**, 57.

168. NARDINI, J. E., HERRMANN, R. S., and RASMUSSEN, J. E. 1962. Navy psychiatric assessment program in the Antarctic. *Amer. J. Psychiat.*, **119**, 97.

169. NISSEN, H. W., CHOW, K. L., and SEMMES, J., 1951. Effects of restricted opportunity for tactual, kinesthetic, and manipulative experience on behavior of chimpanzee. *Amer. J. Psychol.*, **64**, 485.

170. OGLE, D. C., 1957. Man in a space vehicle. *USAF med. J.*, **8**, 1561.

171. ORMISTON, D. W., 1958. The effects of sensory deprivation and sensory bombardment on apparent movement thresholds. *Amer. Psychologist*, **13**, 389. (Abstract.)

172. ORNE, M. T., and SCHEIBE, K. E., 1964. The contribution of non-deprivation factors in the production of sensory deprivation effects: The psychology of the panic button. *J. abnorm. soc. Psychol.*, **68**, 3.

173. ORWELL, G., 1949. *Nineteen Eighty-Four*. New York: Harcourt Brace.

174. PETERS, J., BENJAMIN, F. B., HELVEY, W. M., and ALBRIGHT, G. A., 1963. A study of sensory deprivation, pain, and personality relationships for space travel. *Aerospace Med.*, **34**, 830.

174a. PETRIE, A., COLLINS, W., and SOLOMON, P., 1958. Pain sensitivity, sensory deprivation and susceptibility to satiation. *Science*, **128**, 1431.

174b. 1960. The tolerance for pain and for sensory deprivation. *Amer. J. Psychol.*, **73**, 80.

175. POLLARD, J. C., UHR, L., and JACKSON, C. W., JR., 1963. Studies in sensory deprivation. *Arch. gen. Psychiat.*, **8**, 435.

176. 1963. Some unexpected findings in experimental sensory deprivation. The psycho-pharmacologic interaction of a placebo-potentiated suggestion. Paper read at Amer. Psychol. Ass., St. Louis.

177. PREMACK, R., COLLIER, G., and ROBERTS, C. L., 1957. Frequency of light-contingent bar pressing as a function of the amount of deprivation for light. *Amer. Psychologist.*, **12**, 411. (Abstract.)

177a. PRIOLEAU, W. H., 1963. Psychological considerations in patient isolation on a general surgical service. *Amer. Surg.*, **29**, 907.

178. RANDT, C. T., and COLLINS, W. F., 1960. Sensory deprivation in the cat. *Arch. Neurol.*, **2**, 565.

179. RAPAPORT, D., 1958. The theory of ego autonomy: a generalization. *Bull. Menninger Clin.*, **22**, 13.

180. RASMUSSEN, J. E., 1963. Psychologic discomforts in 1962 Navy protective shelter tests. *J. Amer. Dietetic Ass.*, **42**, 109.

181. REED, G. F., 1962. Preparatory set as a factor in the production of sensory deprivation phenomena. *Proc. Roy. Soc. Med.*, **55**, 1010.

182. RIBBLE, M. A., 1943. *The rights of infants.* New York: Columbia Univ. Press.

183. RIESEN, A. H., 1961. Stimulation as a requirement for growth and function in behavioral development. In *Functions of varied experience.* Eds. Fiske, D. W., and Maddi, S. R. Homewood, Ill.: Dorsey Press.

184. 1961. Excessive arousal effects of stimulation after early sensory deprivation. In *Sensory deprivation.* Eds. Solomon, P., *et al.* Cambridge, Mass.: Harvard Univ. Press.

185. 1961. Studying perceptual development using the technique of sensory deprivation. *J. nerv. ment. Dis.*, **132**, 21.

186. ROBERTSON, M. H., 1961. Sensory deprivation and some therapeutic considerations. *Psychol. Rec.*, **11**, 343.

187. ROBINSON, J., 1957. Light as a reinforcer for bar pressing in rats as a function of adaptation, illumination level and direction of light change. *Amer. Psychologist*, **12**, 411. (Abstract.)

188. ROHRER, J. H., 1961. Interpersonal relationships in isolated small groups. In *Psychophysiological aspects of space flight.* Ed. Flaherty, B. E. New York: Columbia Univ. Press.

189. ROSSI, A. M., FURHMAN, A., and SOLOMON, P., 1964. Sensory deprivation: arousal and rapid eye movement correlates of some effects. *Percept. mot. Skills*, **19**, 447.

190. 1967. Level of arousal and thought processes during sensory deprivation. *J. abn. Psychol.*, **72**, 166.

191. ROSSI, A. M., NATHAN, P., HARRISON, P., and SOLOMON, P. Effect of meaningfulness on operant responding for visual stimuli during sensory deprivation. Unpublished manuscript.

192. ROSSI, A. M., and SOLOMON, P., 1964. Button pressing for a time-off reward during sensory deprivation: I. Compared to activity reward. II. Relation to descriptions of experience. *Percept. mot. Skills*, **18**, 211.

193. 1964. Button pressing for a time-off reward during sensory deprivation. III. Effects of varied time-off rewards. *Percept. mot. Skills*, **18**, 794.

194. 1964. Button pressing for a time-off reward during sensory deprivation: IV. Relation to change in ratings of well being. *Percept. mot. Skills*, **18**, 520.

195. 1964. Button pressing for a time-off reward during sensory deprivation: V. Effects of relatively comfortable and uncomfortable sessions. *Percept. mot. Skills*, **19**, 803.

196. 1966. Effects of sensory deprivation on introverts and extraverts: a failure to find reported differences. *J. Pyschiat. Res.*, **4**, 115.

197. ROSSI, A. M., STURROCK, J. B., and SOLOMON, P., 1963. Suggestion effects on reported imagery in sensory deprivation. *Percept. mot. Skills*, **16**, 39.

198. RUFF, G. E., 1959. Experimental studies of stress in space flight. *Amer. J. Psychiat.*, **115**, 1109.

199. RUFF, G. E., and LEVY, E. Z., 1959. Psychiatric research in space medicine. *Amer. J. Psychiat.*, **115**, 793.

200. RUFF, G. E., LEVY, E. Z., and THALER, V. H., 1959. Studies of isolation and confinement. *Aerospace Med.*, **30**, 599.

201. 1961. Factors influencing the reaction to reduced sensory input. In *Sensory deprivation*. Eds. Solomon, P., *et al*. Cambridge, Mass.: Harvard Univ. Press.

202. SATO, I., and KOKUBUN, O., 1965. Studies on sensory deprivation. III. VI: On the results of the polygraphic records. *Tohoku Psychologica Folia*, **23**, 72.

203. SCHAEFER, K. E., 1964. Counteracting effects of training in geometrical constructions on stress produced by maximal sensory isolation in water immersion. *Aerospace Med.*, **35**, 279. (Abstract.)

204. SCHEIBEL, MADGE, E., and SCHEIBEL, A. B., 1962. Hallucinations and brain-stem reticular core. In *Hallucinations*. Ed. West, L. J. New York: Grune and Stratton.

205. SCHULTZ, D. P., 1965. *Sensory restriction*. New York: Academic Press.

206. SCOTT, T. H., 1954. Intellectual effects of perceptual isolation. Unpublished doct. dissert., McGill Univ.

207. SCOTT, T. H., BEXTON, W. H., HERON, W., and DOANE, B. K., 1959. Cognitive effects of perceptual isolation. *Canad. J. Psychol.*, **13**, 200.

208. SHAPIRO, D., LEIDERMAN, H., and MORNINGSTAR, M. E., 1964. Social isolation and social interaction: A behavioral and physiological comparison. In *Recent advances in biological psychiatry*. Ed. Wortis, J., vol. 6. New York: Plenum Press.

209. SHURLEY, J. T., 1960. Profound experimental sensory isolation. *Amer. J. Psychiat.*, **117**, 539.

210. SILVERMAN, A. J., COHEN, S. I., and SHMAVONIAN, B., 1959. Investigations of psychophysiologic relationship with skin resistance measures. *J. psychosom. Res.*, **4**, 65.

211. SILVERMAN, A. J., COHEN, S. I., SHMAVONIAN, B. M., and GREENBERG, G., 1961. Psychophysiological investigations in sensory deprivation. *Psychosom. Med.*, **23**, 48.

212. SIMONS, D. G., 1958. Pilot reactions during 'Man high II' balloon flight. *J. aviat. Med.*, **29**, 1.

213. SMITH, S., 1962. Clinical aspects of perceptual isolation. *Proc. Roy. Soc. Med.*, **55**, 1003.

214. SMITH, S., and LEWTY, W., 1959. Perceptual isolation using a silent room. *Lancet*, ii, 342.

215. SMITH, S., MURPHY, D. B., and MYERS, T. I., 1963. The effect of sensory deprivation and social isolation on conformity to a group norm. *Amer. Psychologist*, **18**, 439. (Abstract.)

216. SMITH, S., MYERS, T. I., and MURPHY, D. B., 1963. Conformity to a group norm as a function of sensory deprivation and social isolation. *Research Memorandum*, U.S. Army Training Centre, Human Research Unit (HUMRRO), Presidio of Monterey, Calif., November.

217. SOFFER, A., 1956. Dangers of inactivity during automobile travel. *Amer. J. med. Sci.*, **229**, 475.

218. SOLOMON, P., 1961. Motivations and emotional reactions in early space flights. In *Psychophysiological aspects of space flight*. Ed. Flaherty, B. E., New York: Columbia Univ. Press.

219. SOLOMON, P., KUBZANSKY, P., LEIDERMAN, P. H., MENDELSON, J. H., and WEXLER, D., 1959. Meetings: sensory deprivation. *Science*, **129**, 221.

220. SOLOMON, P., KUBZANSKY, P. E., LEIDERMAN, P. H., MENDELSON, J., TRUMBULL, R., WEXLER, D., Eds., 1961. *Sensory deprivation*. Cambridge, Mass.: Harvard Univ. Press.

221. SOLOMON, P., LEIDERMAN, P. H., MENDELSON, J., and WEXLER, D., 1957. Sensory deprivation: a review. *Amer. J. Psychiat.*, **114,** 357.

222. SOLOMON, P., and MENDELSON, J., 1962. Hallucinations in sensory deprivation. In *Hallucinations.* Ed. West, L. J., New York: Grune and Stratton.

223. SPITZ, R. A., 1954. 'Hospitalism': an inquiry into the genesis of psychiatric conditions in early childhood. In *Psychoanal. Stud. of Child.* Vol. 9. New York: Intern. Univ. Press.

224.   1955. 'Hospitalism': a follow-up report. In *Psychoanal. Stud. of Child.* Vol. 10. New York: Intern. Univ. Press.

225. STERN, R. M., 1964. Electrophysiological effects of the interaction between task demands and sensory input. *Canad. J. Psychol.*, **18,** 311.

226. STONE, L. J., 1954. A critique of studies of infant isolation. *Child Develop.*, **25,** 1.

227. SUEDFELD, P., 1964. Attitude manipulation in restricted environments: I. Conceptual structure and response to propaganda. *J. abnorm. soc. Psychol.*, **68,** 242.

228. SUEDFELD, P., GRISSOM, R. J., and VERNON, J., 1964. The effects of sensory deprivation and social isolation on the performance of an unstructured task. *Amer. J. Psychol.*, **77,** 111.

229. SUEDFELD, P., and VERNON, J., 1964. Visual hallucinations during sensory deprivation: a problem of criteria. *Science*, **145,** 412.

230. SUEDFELD, P., VERNON, J., STUBBS, J. T., and KARLINS, M., 1965. The effects of repeated confinement on cognitive performance. *Amer. J. Psychol.*, **78,** 493.

231. SWARTZ, J., 1960. Emotional reactions of patients and medical personnel to respiratory poliomyelitis. *Ment. Hyg.*, **44,** 97.

232. TAYLOR, A. J. W., 1961. Social isolation and imprisonment. *Psychiat.*, **24,** 373.

233. THOMPSON, W. R., and HERON, W., 1954. Effects of restricting early experience on problem-solving capacity of dogs. *Canad. J. Psychol.*, **8,** 17.

234. TIIRA, E., 1955. *Raft of despair.* New York: Dutton.

235. TRANEL, N., 1962. Effects of perceptual isolation on introverts and extroverts. *J. Psychiat. Res.*, **1,** 185.

236. ULVEDAL, F., SMITH, W. R., and WELCH, B. E., 1963. Steroid and catechol amine studies on pilots during prolonged experiments in a space cabin simulator. *J. appl. Physiol.*, **18,** 1257.

237. VAN WULFFTEN-PALTHE, P. M., 1958. Sensory and motor deprivation as a psychopathological stress. *Aeromedical Acta*, **6,** 155.

238.   1959. Sensory and motor deprivation as a psychopathological stress. *Folia psych. neur. neurochirug.*, **62,** 407.

239.   1959. Experimental results in solitary confinement. *Riv. Med. Aero.*, **22.**

240.   1962. Fluctuations in level of consciousness caused by reduced sensorial stimulation and by limited motility in solitary confinement. *Psychiat. Neurol. Neurochirug.,* **65,** 377.

241. VERNON, J., 1963. *Inside the black room.* New York: Clarkson N. Potter.

242. VERNON, J., and HOFFMAN, J., 1956. Effect of sensory deprivation on learning rate in human beings. *Science*, **123,** 1074.

243. VERNON, J., and MCGILL, T. E., 1957. The effect of sensory deprivation upon rote learning. *Amer. J. Psychol.*, **70,** 637.

244.   1960. Utilization of visual stimulation during sensory deprivation. *Percept. mot. Skills*, **11,** 214.

245.   1961. Sensory deprivation and pain thresholds. *Science*, **133,** 330.

246. VERNON, J., MCGILL, T. E., GULICK, W. L., and CANDLAND, D., 1959. Effect

of sensory deprivation on some perceptual and motor skills. *Percept. mot. Skills*, **9,** 91.

247. 1961. The effects of sensory deprivation on some perceptual and motor skills. In *Sensory deprivation*. Eds. Solomon, P., *et al*. Cambridge, Mass.: Harvard Univ. Press.

248. VERNON, J., MARTON, T., and PETERSON, E., 1961. Sensory deprivation and hallucinations. *Science*, **133,** 1808.

249. VILLABLANCA, J., 1962. Electroencephalogram in the permanently isolated forebrain of the cat. *Science*, **138,** 44.

250. WALTERS, C., PARSONS, O. A., and SHURLEY, J. T., 1964. Male-female differences in underwater sensory isolation. *Brit. J. Psychiat.*, **110,** 290.

251. WALTERS, C., SHURLEY, J. T., and PARSONS, O. A., 1962. Differences in male and female responses to underwater sensory deprivation: an exploratory study. *J. nerv. ment. Dis.*, **135,** 302.

252. WALTERS, R. H., CALLAGAN, J. E., and NEWMAN, A. F., 1963. Effect of solitary confinement on prisoners. *Amer. J. Psychiat.*, **119,** 771.

253. WALTERS, R. H., and HENNING, G. B., 1961. Isolation, confinement, and related stress situations: some cautions. *Aerospace Med.*, **32,** 431.

254. WATTERSON, D. J. Visual imagery and inaction. Unpublished manuscript.

255. WEISMAN, A. D., and HACKETT, P., 1958. Psychosis after eye-surgery: establishment of a specific doctor-patient relation in the prevention and treatment of 'black-patch' delirium. *N.E.J. Med.*, **258,** 1284.

256. WENDT, R. H., LINDSLEY, D. F., and ADEY, W. R., 1963. Self-maintained visual stimulation in monkeys after long-term visual deprivation. *Science*, **139,** 336.

257. WEXLER, D., MENDELSON, J., LEIDERMAN, P. H., and SOLOMON, P., 1958. Sensory deprivation; a technique of studying psychiatric aspects of stress. *Arch. Neurol. Psychiat.*, **79,** 225.

258. WEYBREW, B. B., 1961. Human factors and the work environment. II. The impact of isolation upon personnel. *J. occupational Med.*, **3,** 290.

259. WEYBREW, B. B., and PARKER, J., 1960. Bibliography of sensory deprivation, isolation, and confinement. *Memo. Rept. No.* 60-1. U.S. Naval Med. Res. Lab., New London, Conn.

260. WHEATON, J. L., 1959. Fact and fancy in sensory deprivation studies. *Aeromedical Reviews*, No. 5–59. Brooks AFB, Texas: Air Univ.

261. ZINGG, R. M., 1940. More about the 'Baboon boy' of South Africa. *Amer. J. Psychol.*, **53,** 455.

262. 1940. Feral man and extreme cases of social isolation. *Amer. J. Psychol.*, **53,** 487.

263. 1941. India's Wolf children. *Sci. Amer.*, —, 135.

264. ZISKIND, E., 1958. Isolation stress in medical and mental illness. *J. Amer. med. Ass.*, **168,** 1427.

265. 1964. A second look at sensory deprivation. *J. nerv. ment. Dis.*, **138,** 223.

266. 1964. Significance of symptoms of sensory deprivation experiments due to methodological procedures. In *Recent advances in biological psychiatry*. Ed. Wortis, J., vol. 6. New York: Plenum Press.

267. 1965. An explanation of mental symptoms found in acute sensory deprivation: researches, 1958–63. *Amer. J. Psychiat.*, **121,** 939.

268. ZISKIND, E., and AUGBURG, T., 1962. Hallucinations in sensory deprivation—method or madness? *Science*, **137,** 992.

269. ZISKIND, E., GRAHAM, R. W., KUNINOBU, L., and AINSWORTH, R., 1963. The hypnoid syndrome in sensory deprivation. In *Recent advances in biological psychiatry*. Ed. Wortis, J., vol. 5. New York: Plenum Press.

270. ZISKIND, E., JONES, H., FILANTE, W., and GOLDBERG, J., 1960. Observations on mental symptoms in eye patched patients: hypnagogic symptoms in sensory deprivation. *Amer. J. Psychiat.*, **116**, 893.

271. ZUBEK, J. P., 1963. Pain sensitivity as a measure of perceptual deprivation tolerance. *Percept. mot. Skills*, **17**, 641.

272. 1963. Electroencephalographic changes after prolonged sensory and perceptual deprivation. *Science*, **139**, 1209.

273. 1963. Counteracting effects of physical exercises performed during prolonged perceptual deprivation. *Science*, **142**, 504.

274. 1964. Behavioral changes after prolonged perceptual deprivation (no intrusions). *Percept. mot. Skills*, **18**, 413.

275. 1964. Behavioral and EEG changes after 14 days of perceptual deprivation. *Psychon. Sci.*, **1**, 57.

276. 1964. Effect of prolonged sensory and perceptual deprivation. *Brit. Med. Bull.*, **20**, 38.

277. 1967. Physiological and biochemical effects. In *Sensory deprivation*. Ed. Zubek, J. P., New York: Appleton-Century-Crofts.

278. ZUBEK, J. P., AFTANAS, M., HASEK, J., SAMSON, W., SCHLUDERMANN, E., WILGOSH, L., and WINOCUR, G., 1962. Intellectual and perceptual changes during prolonged perceptual deprivation: low illumination and noise level. *Percept. mot. Skills*, **15**, 171.

279. ZUBEK, J. P., AFTANAS, M., KOVACH, K., WILGOSH, L., and WINOCUR, G., 1963. Effect of severe immobilization of the body on intellectual and perceptual processes. *Canad. J. Psychol.*, **17**, 118.

280. ZUBEK, J. P., FLYE, J., and AFTANAS, M., 1964. Cutaneous sensitivity after prolonged visual deprivation. *Science*, **144**, 1591.

281. ZUBEK, J. P., FLYE, J., and WILLOWS, D., 1964. Changes in cutaneous sensitivity after prolonged exposure to unpatterned light. *Psychon. Sci.*, **1**, 283.

282. ZUBEK, J. P., PUSHKAR, D., SAMSON, W., and GOWING, J., 1961. Perceptual changes after prolonged sensory isolation (darkness and silence). *Canad. J. Psychol.*, **15**, 83.

283. ZUBEK, J. P., SAMSON, W., and PRYSIAZNIUK, A., 1960. Intellectual changes during prolonged isolation (darkness and silence). *Canad. J. Psychol.*, **14**, 233.

284. ZUBEK, J. P., and SCHUTTE, W. Urinary excretion of adrenaline and noradrenaline during prolonged perceptual deprivation. Unpublished manuscript.

285. ZUBEK, J. P., WELCH, G., and SAUNDERS, M. G., 1963. Electroencephalographic changes during and after 14 days of perceptual deprivation. *Science*, **139**, 490.

286. ZUBEK, J. P., and WILGOSH, L., 1963. Prolonged immobilization of the body: changes in performance and the electroencephalogram. *Science*, **140**, 306.

287. ZUCKERMAN, M., 1964. Perceptual isolation as a stress situation. *Arch. gen. Psychiat.*, **11**, 255.

288. ZUCKERMAN, M., ALBRIGHT, R. J., MARKS, C. S., and MILLER, G., 1962. Stress and hallucinatory effects of perceptual isolation and confinement. *Psychol. Monogr.*, **76**, No. 30 (Whole No. 549).

289. ZUCKERMAN, M., and COHEN, N., 1964. Sources of reports of visual and auditory sensations in perceptual isolation. *Psychol. Bull.*, **62**, 1.

290. 1964. Is suggestion the source of reported visual sensations in perceptual isolation? *J. abnorm. soc. Psychol.*, **68**, 655.

291. ZUCKERMAN, M., and HABER, M. M., 1965. Need for stimulation as a source of stress response to perceptual isolation. *J. abn. Psychol.*, **70**, 371.

292. ZUCKERMAN, M., KOLIN, E. A., PRICE, L., and ZOOB, I., 1964. Development of a Sensation-Seeking Scale. *J. consult. Psychol.*, **28**, 477.
293. ZUCKERMAN, M., LEVINE, S., and BIASE, D. V., 1964. Stress response in total and partial perceptual isolation. *Psychosom. Med.*, **26**, 250.
294. ZUCKERMAN, M., PERSKY, H., HOPKINS, T. R., and MURTAUGH, T., BASU, G. K., and SCHILLING, M., 1966. Comparison of stress effects of perceptual and social isolation. *Arch. gen. Psychiat.*, **14**, 356.

X

HALLUCINATIONS

LOUIS JOLYON WEST*

M.D.

*Professor and Head, Department of Psychiatry, Neurology, and Behaviora
Sciences, University of Oklahoma School of Medicine, Oklahoma City, Oklahoma*

1

Historical

Hallucinations were defined by Bleuler as 'perceptions without corresponding stimuli from without.' Hinsie and Shatsky's *Psychiatric Dictionary* calls the hallucination 'an apparent perception of an external object when no such object is present'. A complete historical survey of the subject of hallucinations clearly reflects the development of scientific thought in psychiatry, psychology, and neurobiology. By 1838, Esquirol had pointed out the significant relationship between the content of dreams and of hallucinations, and had done much to distinguish the latter from other phenomena in psychopathology. In the 1840s, Moreau of Tours described the occurrence of hallucinations under a wide variety of conditions (including psychological and physical stress), as well as their genesis by such drugs as stramonium and hashish. He pointed out that there are basic similarities in the function of dream and delirium, a surprisingly modern concept.

Brierre de Boismont in 1853 described many instances of hallucinations associated with intense concentration, or musing, and occurring in mental disease. In the last half of the nineteenth century studies of hallucinations continued. Those in France were particularly oriented in terms of psychopathology, and from this came Janet's marvellously lucid descriptions of hallucinosis during somnambulism and other dissociative reac-

* At present (1967) Fellow at the Center for Advanced Study in the Behavioral Sciences, Stanford, California. Preparation of this manuscript was supported in part by the Fellowship, for which the author is deeply grateful.

tions. Perhaps the most simple and yet enduring conceptions were those evolved by Galton. And Hughlings Jackson's brilliant formulation of the hallucination as a release phenomenon is perhaps the greatest single milestone along the way.

During the first three decades of the twentieth century, a spirited interest in hallucinations continued. Freud's concepts of conscious and unconscious ideation made the content of dreams and hallucinations take on an enormous new significance. Hallucinations were linked to the theory that infants normally hallucinate the objects and processes of gratification. This notion has recently been disputed, but the 'regression' hypothesis is still widely accepted, presumably by those who find it clinically useful. During the same period, Mourgue, in France, and Morton Prince, in the United States, worked out theories of hallucinations that were more broadly psychobiological than Freud's, but that had more points in common with the formulations of Freud than with each other.

The medical and scientific literature has continued to contain many references to hallucinatory phenomena, so that by 1932 Mourgue found more than a thousand publications to review.[34] During the next twenty years there was a rather surprising decrease of interest in the subject, but attention has been revived by the recent upsurge of work on hallucinogenic drugs.

The first major neurophysiologic disinhibition theory of dreams and hallucinations was proposed by Hughlings Jackson. Jackson was interested in the relationship of sensory input to the *form* of the illusion. Evarts was one of the first to note a possible relationship between the disruption of information input and the very *occurrence* of disinhibition phenomena of the special senses (particularly in the visual system) in his early experiments with LSD-25.[14, 15] It was Evarts' description of the visual and other 'de-afferentation' of the *rhesus macacque* heavily overdosed with this (then) new and powerful hallucinogen that inspired me to broaden my own clinical investigations of hallucinations in the psychoses, toxic deliria, dissociated states, hypnosis, and sleep deprivation, and to study their relationship to dreams. It was also Evarts who suggested to me at that time the relevant significance of the newly-reported experiments of Hebb and his co-workers[21] on the depatterning of sensory input with resultant hallucinosis in many subjects.

2

A Theory of Hallucinations

The general theory of hallucinations here proposed (which I have elsewhere termed the 'perceptual release theory') is based on Jackson's, and rests upon two fundamental assumptions. The first, well stated by Gerard,[19] is that life experiences affect the brain in such a way as to leave permanent neural traces, templates or engrams. Ideas and images derive from the involvement of these engrams in complex neural circuits. Such circuits subserve the neurophysiology of memory, thought, imagination and fantasy. Papez[35] suggested, and MacLean[27] and others have elucidated, how the emotions or affects associated with these intellectual and perceptive functions are mediated through connections with the limbic system or 'visceral brain', thus permitting a dynamic interplay between perception and emotion through transactions that take place largely at unconscious levels. Magoun[29] and others[24, 28] have shown that, in so far as conscious awareness can now be explained neurophysiologically, it is regulated through a general arousal process mediated by the ascending midbrain reticular activating system. Analyses of the relationships of hallucinations to neurological syndromes, and to brain stimulation experiments in neurosurgical patients, have shown the importance of the temporal lobes and such functionally relevant areas as the cingulat egyrus.[4, 13]

The second basic assumption is that the total personality, as represented by structural, instinctive and acquired functions, is best understood in relation to dynamic psychobiological forces that continually emanate from inside and outside the individual. This dynamic field of force (which may be usefully conceptualized in terms of transactions among systems and information theory) exerts an integrating and organizing influence upon memory traces and thus affects the patterns whereby sensory engrams are woven into images, fantasies, dreams or hallucinations, and also the emotions associated with these patterns. The balance that exists between the internal, instinctual forces and the external environmental forces has been described in the language of ego psychology by Rapaport.[37] Thus, we would expect that cultural factors and psychodynamic factors would indeed be of major importance in determining the actual form and emotional meaning of hallucinations. Such a concept also requires us to maintain respect for the phenomenological rather than the mechanistic comprehension of an hallucinatory experience.

Our brains are bombarded constantly by sensory impulses. Most of these sensations are excluded from consciousness in a dynamically selective fashion. The exclusion is accomplished through the exercise of integrative mental mechanisms which permit the small field of awareness to hold selected areas of psychic content in clear focus. In this way, the work of concentration may be defined as a scanning and screening process, serving to keep out of consciousness everything that is not needed or wanted. In psychoanalytic conceptual terms, this work involves principally the digital-type functions of the neocortical structures. It may be contrasted with the way in which unconscious instinctual and affective life (Freud's 'primary process') involve principally the analogue-type functions of the paleocortical structures. In conditions of good psychological health these two sets of functions are highly integrated with each other. Their malintegration as a mechanism in schizophrenia has been proposed by Rosenzweig.[39]

During normal wakefulness the input of information through the sensory pathways serves a basic function in maintaining the organization of scanning and screening activity. As long as it is working well, scanning and screening exclude from awareness not only information from the internal and external environments that is undesired or low-priority or relatively static, but also the vast bulk of information already stored within the brain in the form of perceptual traces and their derivations and inter-relations. Some of this information can be brought into awareness in the service of memory. Many children and a few adults can screen in and scan perceptual memory traces with great clarity, thereby permitting eidetic or near-eidetic imagery.

What happens when sensory input is diminished or impaired? Its *organizing* effect upon the screening and scanning mechanism then decreases. Simultaneously, as a rule, there is a decrease in the *stimulating* effect of sensory input on the ascending midbrain reticular activating system (through neural connections to the reticular formation from the major sensory pathways rising through the brain stem), and as a result arousal and awareness diminish. But it is possible, under a variety of circumstances, for great reduction or impairment of sensory input to be accompanied by a residual awareness of considerable degree. In such instances, when the usual information input level no longer suffices completely to inhibit their emergence, the perceptual traces may be 'released' and re-experienced in familiar or new combinations. Some people are able to control this perceptual release to an astonishing degree. Coleridge[10] described this quality in himself (presumably even without benefit of opium), saying, 'My eyes make pictures when they are shut.'

Released perceptions ordinarily do not become conscious with hallucinatory vividness. In fact, there appear to be two prerequisites for their emergence even into clear awareness. First, there must be a sufficient general level of arousal for awareness to occur; second, the particular perception-bearing circuits must fire and reverberate sufficiently to command awareness.

Under certain circumstances these latter conditions can be brought about through direct stimulation of the circuits; Penfield and Jasper[36] describe this in cases of focal temporal lobe seizures (occurring either spontaneously or under the neurosurgeon's electrode). Under other circumstances, there must be a decrease in the forces that ordinarily dominate consciousness and inhibit the release of recorded percepts. These inhibiting forces require for their maintenance a total sensory input possessing certain quantitative, qualitative and time-related characteristics.

An oversimplified but perhaps helpful model of these conditions pictures a man in his study, standing at a closed glass window opposite the fireplace, looking out at his garden in the sunset. He is absorbed by the view of the outside world. He does not visualize the interior of the room in which he stands. As it becomes darker outside, however, images of the objects in the room behind him can be seen reflected dimly in the window glass. For a time he may see either the garden (if he gazes into the distance) or the reflection of the room's interior (if he focuses on the glass a few inches from his face). Night falls, but the fire still burns brightly in the fireplace and illuminates the room. The watcher now sees in the glass a vivid reflection of the interior of the room behind him, which appears to be outside the window. This illusion becomes dimmer as the fire dies down, and, finally, when it is dark both outside and within, nothing more is seen. If the fire flares up from time to time, the visions in the glass reappear.

In perceptual release, the daylight (sensory input) is reduced while the interior illumination (general level of arousal) remains bright, and images originating within the rooms of our brains may be perceived as though they came from outside the windows of our senses.

The theory thus holds that a sustained level and variety of sensory input normally is required to inhibit the emergence of percepts or memory traces from within the brain itself. When effective (attention commanding) sensory input decreases below a certain threshold, there may be a release into awareness of previously recorded perceptions through the disinhibition of the brain circuits that represent them. If a general level of cortical arousal persists to a sufficient degree, these released perceptions can enter awareness and be experienced as fantasies, illusions, visions, dreams, or hallucinations. The greater the level of arousal, the more vivid the hallucinations will be.

3

Conditions Related to Hallucinations

Sleeping and Dreaming

The ways in which the reticular formation of the brain stem acts as a regulatory and integrating system for these relationships are still under intensive study. Since levels of arousal during sleep and wakefulness also are mediated via reticular formation activity, let us consider sleeping and dreaming. As a person falls asleep, he passes through a zone in which awareness of the environment is decreased but in which the level of cortical arousal (which falls less rapidly) remains sufficiently high to permit some appreciation of reality. Under these circumstances occur the hypnagogic phenomena.

Common hypnagogic hallucinations may be visual (scenes from the previous few hours appear) or auditory (one's name is called, or a knock is heard at the door). A frequently occurring kinesthetic hypnagogic hallucination is the sensation of loss of support or balance, perhaps accompanied by a fragmentary dream of missing a step or stumbling, and followed immediately by a jerking reflex recovery movement that may even jolt the sleeper back into wakefulness.

With progressive loss of contact with the environment, sleep begins and is at first dream-free, with large slow waves on the EEG (Stage IV). Sensory stimuli either from without (e.g., noise or cold) or from within (e.g., dyspepsia, anxiety), plus the basic ninety-minute fluctuation in the sleep-state, periodically bring the sleeper into the zone for spontaneous perceptual release (emergent Stage I EEG with rapid eye movements or REM) in which case dreaming will take place. This occurs several times every night, probably in all normal people, so that perhaps 12 or 15 per cent of an average man's eight hours of sleep is taken up with five or six dreams, each of about ten minutes' duration. At the time of awakening, the sleeper again returns through the zone of perceptual release, often experiencing dreams that increase in intensity, and perhaps having hypnopompic hallucinations. This concept of the relationship of dreaming to depth of sleep has been confirmed by the findings of Dement and Kleitman[12] and many others.

An analogy might be that our dreams, like the stars, are shining all the time. We do not often see the stars because by day the sun shines too brightly, and by night we sleep. Suppose, however, that during the day there be an eclipse of the sun, or that we choose to be watchful a while after sunset or a while before sunrise, or that we awaken from time to time on a clear night to look at the sky; then the stars, like our dreams, though often forgotten, may always be seen.

Kubie[26] has made reference to the concept of a continuous information processing activity, the 'preconscious stream', which is influenced by both conscious and unconscious forces continually, and which constitutes the matrix of dream content. The dream is an experience during which, for a few minutes, the individual has some awareness of the stream of data being processed. Hallucinations in the waking state are undoubtedly the same.

Level of Arousal

What of the relationship between level of arousal in the brain and information processing during the waking state? The functions of consciousness apparently reach an optimal point in relation to level of arousal, beyond which they disorganize progressively as arousal increases excessively. The presence of marked arousal (caused, for example, by extreme anxiety or by chemical stimulation of the brain) is accompanied by a picture of marked disturbance of concentration. Again, contact with external reality is impaired, this time by excessive input (input-overload) which 'jams the circuits', and spontaneously dissociative phenomena occur. Finally, as arousal reaches overwhelming proportions, the hallucinations of full-blown delirium or psychotic excitement may appear with frightening vividness, intensity, and emotional accompaniment. Even greater arousal might result in generalized cortical seizure phenomena. This relationship between arousal and a variety of functions has been suggested by Burch and Greiner.[9]

Sensory Isolation

In sensory isolation experiments, information input via the special senses is artificially depatterned or reduced. If the subject remains alert, he is likely to experience vivid fantasies and perhaps hallucinations. The findings of Hoffman and Vernon[22] suggest that a slight amount of stimulation of the hallucinated modality enhances the likelihood of the hallucination's appearance. If stimuli are markedly reduced, and the level of arousal is high, the hallucinations should be especially vivid and emotionally charged. There are numerous factors encountered in an experimental sensory isolation situation that can influence the experience.

Prolonged Wakefulness

In 1883, Galton[18] declared, 'The cases of visions following protracted wakefulness are well-known, and I have collected a few of them myself'. Progressive sleep loss appears to cause a decreased capacity for integrating perceptions of the external environment, as described by West et al.[43] Hallucinations probably occur inevitably if wakefulness is sufficiently prolonged, and the presence of excessive arousal due to anxiety is likely to hasten or enhance hallucinatory production. The disorganizing effect of excessive wakefulness has been exploited in extorting false confessions from prisoners, many of whom experience hallucinations during prolonged sleep deprivation. Other experience with sleep-deprived subjects suggests that fleeting hallucinations begin after two or three days without sleep, and that after 100 to 120 sleepless hours a progressive personality disorganization will develop gradually and be marked by periods of hallucinosis and, in some cases, by a reappearance of previously existing psychopathology.[7]

The Mystic

The mystic achieves hallucinations by gaining control of his own dissociative mechanisms, perhaps through autohypnosis. Such individuals can accomplish an astonishing withdrawal of contact from the environment by prolonged intense concentration (e.g., gazing into the ink pool). The hallucinations occurring under such circumstances may be of the scenario type, in which the subject's soul seems to leave his body either to view himself (autoscopic hallucination) or to be transported to new surroundings. Or, the hallucinations may take the form of visual imagery endowed with unique meaning. For example, the *Yantra* is a special visual hallucination of a coloured, geometrical image related to the more general Mandala form described by Jung. It appears at a level of trance corresponding to that of *Samadhi* in Yoga. It has been explained by Ahlenstiel and Kauffman[2] as 'an adequate expression of the ecstacy which cannot be translated into concepts'. The universality of designs and patterns in human hallucinatory experience is very likely related to structural aspects of the visual system.

Hypnosis

Ordinary experimental hypnotic and posthypnotic suggestions of hallucinations are well known. The hypnotically entranced subject (who can be described as a person in a controlled dissociative state) may on occasion also experience spontaneous hallucinations in the absence of specific suggestions.[41]

Monotony

Prolonged monotony or fixation of attention may lead to diminished responsiveness to the environment with a general effect similar to that of absolute reduction of stimulation or of hypnotic trance. Under these conditions occur dissociative phenomena such as 'highway hypnosis'. Similar phenomena that occur among flyers have been called 'fascination' or 'fixation'. During prolonged, monotonous flight, normal flyers may experience visual, auditory and kinesthetic hallucinations. For example, the pilot may suddenly feel that the plane is in a spin or a dive or that it is upside down. A kinesthetic hallucination such as this can be so vivid that the pilot will attempt 'corrective' manoeuvring of the aircraft, with potentially tragic results. The designation of such episodes as 'vertigo' in the literature on aviation medicine is incorrect and misleading.

Disease of Sensory Input

Many other examples of hallucinations related to decrease or impairment of sensory input will come to mind from clinical experience. Bartlett[5] compares visual hallucinations in cases of cataracts with phantom limb syndromes, citing 'absence of normal stimuli from the periphery (as) being an important factor in both syndromes'. It is well known that auditory hallucinations may occur in individuals having a progressive loss of hearing, musical perceptions being not uncommon.[38] A most interesting case of combined visual and auditory hallucinations in a patient with both progressive cataracts and otosclerosis was recently observed by the author. Hallucinations of the phantom limb are probably normal phenomena, arising as the projection of an experientially established template in the absence of long-accustomed input from the missing part. The relative differences in significance of usual sensations from such a part may cause the phantom to be distorted in proportion or in size.

Mental Set

Although the role of expectation or mental set is still being studied in relation to perception, there can be no doubt of the significance of these factors in determining the nature of hallucinated objects. It may be that the psychophysiologic basis for *recognition* requires the subconscious preparation of a perceptual template (a previously seen object, for example) against which to match the incoming information for identification, significance and meaning in terms of past experience. If some real but unrecognized object is present the perceptual template or engram emerges as an illusion; in the absence of a reality object, it is perceived as an hallucination. This accounts for the specificity of collective visions when they occur. For example, among survivors at sea, several will see the same nonexistent ship projected against the blank screen of empty sea and sky.[3]

Multiple Causes

Multiple causes undoubtedly play an *additive* role in bringing about the symptoms of the psychoses, which are so often like waking dreams, and in which hallucinations, usually auditory, may figure prominently. Furthermore, sub-hallucinogenic doses of LSD will quickly produce hallucinations when administered to moderately sleep-deprived subjects, or to subjects in a state of sensory isolation. Continuing attempts (such as those by Deckert)[11] are being made at our Oklahoma City laboratories to discover whether bioelectric findings such as electroencephalographic changes, rapid lateral eye movements, subvocal speech activity and galvanic skin changes, show patterns in dreams similar to those occurring in sensory isolation, sleep deprivation, LSD intoxication, hypnotically induced hallucinations and clinical syndromes featuring hallucinosis. For surely, in clinical cases of acute psychotic reactions with hallucinosis, we can see combinations of factors at work: genetic and cultural predispositions; excessive arousal with anxiety or panic; autointoxication through stress, exhaustion, sleep loss and haemoconcentration; and dissociative mechanisms that impair or distort the reception of information from a frightening or threatening interpersonal environment.

4

Chemically Induced Hallucinations

General

Finally, we can consider hallucinations produced by chemical means that derive from metabolic disturbances, that are engendered inside the body, or that originate from outside the body. Available data support the concept that hallucinations elicited by drugs appear through the perceptual release mechanism. Dramatic abreactions of intense experiences from the recent past, complete with hallucinatory recall, can be brought about by narcosynthesis which reproduces the conditions of perceptual release. Hallucinations during induction of (and emergence from) general anaesthesia are well known and can be explained on the same basis.

It is not necessary that an hallucinogenic chemical impair sensory input specifically by *decreasing* synaptic transmission through raising the resistance to the passage of electrochemical impulses. It might just as easily produce its effects by markedly *increasing* synaptic transmission, thus disrupting the orderly input of information and resulting in a 'jamming of the circuits'. This effect can also be achieved by information input overload of the type described by Miller.[31]

Hallucinogenic drugs are substances that, administered in pharmacological doses (not toxic overdoses), create gross distortions in perception without causing loss of consciousness. These distortions frequently include hallucinations. Such compounds also are likely to exert profound effects on mood, thought and behaviour. These resemble the disturbances seen in naturally occurring psychoses. Some hallucinogens have been termed 'psychotomimetic' or 'psychotogenic' on this account.

Scientists and clinicians have sometimes deliberately taken these compounds as a means of enabling themselves to empathize better with severely ill psychiatric patients. Also, in experimental psychopathology it has been hoped that the study of chemically induced model psychoses would lead to a better understanding of phenomena found in clinical practice. Meanwhile, certain therapists have defined psychotogens as 'psychedelic' or mind-realizing substances, useful to expand perceptual and experiential horizons in the treatment of a variety of patients with alcoholism, rigid personality patterns, frigidity, etc.

The psychological changes produced by these chemicals have sometimes been described as a 'loosening of ego structure', 'dissolving of ego boundaries', or 'disrupting of ego defences'. Such changes may include the experiencing of thoughts, feelings, and perceptions that are usually outside the individual's awareness ('unconscious' or 'repressed'). Persons who are unusually suggestible, emotionally labile, and unusually aware of their own reactions and the reactions of others are likely to be particularly affected. Feelings of transcendence of ordinary experience and distortions in time perception have also been reported.

An increasing number of people are taking various hallucinogenic substances (marihuana, lysergic acid diethylamide (LSD), psilocybin, dimethyltryptamine, etc.), frequently acquired through illegal channels and employed without medical supervision, in order to participate in special group experiences having cult-like characteristics. While these are often recalled by the participants in terms of great enthusiasm, the unintoxicated observer finds little in the way of verbal or non-verbal communication to account for the joyous sense of communion so often described. Not infrequently (especially with LSD) a severe emotional disturbance will result from the drug. This is referred to by psychedelic afficionados (among the 'hippies') as 'a bad trip'. Occasionally, such 'bad trips' lead into persistent psychotic syndromes (e.g., prolonged delirious reactions, catatonic excitements or stupors) following the administration of these substances. Of course, there are also many 'good trips' that do not come to the psychiatrist's attention, but that include hallucinations.

Electrophysiological changes associated with the administration of psychotogens may be useful in understanding their mechanisms of action. Whether recorded from the cortex or the depths of the brain, most of the hallucinogens move spontaneous electrical activity of the central nervous system toward an alert or arousal pattern. Cortical alerting patterns are consistently found with active congeners, but these are apparently dependent on intact lower brain stem cortical connections, while non-psychotogenic congeners can produce an alerting effect even with these connections severed, thus suggesting action at the level of midbrain or higher subcortical sites. Persistent hippocampal electrical changes, resembling those seen in orienting, have been found with low dosage of LSD. Marrazzi[30] has employed trans-synaptic excitability as a criterion, measuring evoked cortical potentials from a homologous area on the opposite hemisphere.

Many chemicals that are alerters of the electrocorticogram inhibit or reduce the transcalosal evoked potential. This suggests that what appears by some electrical criteria to be an increase in excitability may actually be functional inhibition of opposing systems. Winters[45] has described a continuum of reticular-cortical excitability from arousal to excitatory-occlusive blocking and disorganization under the influence of certain excitatory drugs, with staring and hallucinatory-like posturing of experimental animals during the maximum drug effect.

These observations conform with the general proposition previously stated, that the combination of cortical arousal and impaired or distorted information input leads to emergent awareness of ongoing information processing by the brain (the so-called preconscious stream), which is then appreciated by the individual in experiences ranging from fragmentary images to well developed scenarios.[44] The combination of LSD's effects as a sensory poison (it alters retinal cell excitability and electrochemical activity at the sensory synapses) and as a cortical arouser, may well account for its hallucinogenic characteristics.

Biochemical research in the area of mechanisms of action of the hallucinogens has been growing, but consistent correlates have not yet been established. This may, in part, be because one is dealing with a large number of biochemical phenomena, perhaps different for each drug in spite of similarities in their induced behavioural changes. In addition, the theoretical biochemical models being explored are not easily integrated with behavioural models; the clinician is more likely to feel comfortable when considering formulations from neurophysiology. Such words as 'alerting' and 'arousal', which appear to have meaning in both the physiological and behavioural realms (even though they may refer to both related and nonrelated phenomena) are not as available in current neurochemical theory.

A number of the hallucinogens apparently undergo metabolic conversions to more active compounds in the body. Recent studies on enzymes and urinary metabolites suggest that 6-hydroxylation converts the indole alkylamines to psychoactive metabolites. Mescaline apparently is less active than the products of its oxidative deamination, the trimethoxyphenylethanol and aldehyde. Psilocybin is hydrolysed to psilocin quite rapidly. The significance of the oxy and hydroxy metabolites of LSD has not yet been evaluated.

The major theme in research on the biochemical mechanisms of the action of hallucinogens centres around their effects on various postulated neurohormones, including 5-hydroxytryptamine (5-HT or serotonin). norepinephrine, dopamine, histamine, acetylcholine, and a brain polypeptide called 'substance P'. A series of studies of the interaction of LSD and serotonin could be used as representative of this approach.

A marked antagonism between LSD and serotonin in their effects on peripheral structures was first observed by Gaddum; LSD blocked the smooth muscle contraction effect of serotonin. Because of the structural similarities of these and other substances, it was subsequently postulated by Woolley[46] that antimetabolites of serotonin (whether naturally occurring or artificially administered) may prevent the normal functions of serotonin from being accomplished, with psychopathological results. After Brodie[8] demonstrated that serotonin levels were not depleted by LSD and that the reserprine-produced depletion of brain serotonin was not altered by LSD pre-treatment, he postulated that LSD blocked serotonin receptor sites. However, a number of more potent blockers of serotonin's action on peripheral structures were subsequently synthesized in the lysergic acid series, but these blocking agents were not hallucinogenic.

More recent studies by Giarman and Freedman[20] and co-workers showed that LSD produces a consistent increase in the particle-bound fraction of serotonin, but the nonpsychotomimetic lysergic acid congeners are not as effective. These increases are greatest in the brain stem, mesencephalon, hypothalamus, and medial thalamus. That these changes may be significant is suggested by the fact that alterations in the LSD effects on autonomic and behavioural variables are produced by pre-treatment with drugs, such as monoamine oxidase inhibitors and reserpine, which respectively increase and decrease brain amines. Similar studies of drug effects on total brain levels, regional distribution, and bound-free partitioning of serotonin and norepinephrine have been carried out with the use of the indole alkylamines and mescaline.

Acetylcholine has been implicated in the action of some hallucinogens. LSD has been shown to be an inhibitor of both pseudocholinesterase and true cholinesterase. The piperidylglycolates are antagonists of the action of acetylcholine on smooth muscle and are structurally similar to acetylcholine. Histamine levels in the brain have been shown to be reduced by LSD but the bound form appears to be increased.

A recent chemical theory of psychosis and psychotogens is related to the presence of methyl groups in both mescaline (a trimethylated hydroxyphenylethylamine) and the N, N-dimethyltryptamines (methylated at nitrogen). Mescaline can be related to catecholamine metabolites, and the substituted tryptamines have the potential of coming from tryptophan. These characteristics have suggested to Smythies[42] and others that hypermethylation of naturally occurring amines may make them more accessible to the central nervous system, which would result in the conversion of a peripherally active compound to one that, following hypermethylation, would penetrate the blood-brain barrier, becoming centrally active and perhaps psychotogenic.

The search for these hypermethylated compounds in the urine of psychotics has been unrewarding except for the recent finding of Friedhoff and Van Winkle[17] of dimethyoxyphenylethylamine in the urine of schizophrenics in much higher incidence than in normals. They have also shown that this substance is made from DOPA by liver from schizophrenic patients. Although at first reported to produce catatonia in cats, dimethyoxyphenylethylamine in rather large dosages in man did not prove to be psychotogenic, although it was *not* given in the presence of a monoamine oxidase (MAO) inhibitor, an experiment that should be attempted.

Another interesting series of experiments by Kety and others,[25] related to the hypermethylation hypothesis, indicated that loads of methionine (and other methyl donors) and tryptophan (following pretreatment with an MAO inhibitor) produced excerbations of symptoms in schizophrenics. Whether this was a complex toxic psychosis instead of an exacerbation of the underlying disease remains to be fully explored.

Recent demonstrations of increased amine stores produced by hallucinogens may explain the chemical basis for their neurophysiological excitation of those brain stem and hypothalamic systems associated with arousal, information scanning, regulation of readiness, and ability to integrate sensory information. As neurochemical horizons expand, in all likelihood such broad categories as 'amines' and such parameters as 'amount' will give way to more specific physiochemical findings, with behavioural phenomena being the final common pathway of a number of different underlying mechanisms.

The pharmacological screening techniques for potential psychotogenic compounds are of interest. Animal tests include check lists of behaviour patterns, covering such items as aggressivity, excitement, and sociability. More standardized criteria for effects on animal behaviour include performance tests like rope climbing and pole walking; activity levels in an activity wheel; blocking of learned avoidance responses and depression of positive instrumental responses; indicators of emotionality such as urination and defecation in a strange environment; copulation time; and changes in body temperature, because some psychotomimetics produce hyperthermia. Psychotogenic substances have also been found to affect such behaviours as web-spinning patterns in spiders and swimming patterns in Siamese fighting fish. Of course the most sensitive and pertinent technique for evaluation of these substances is the response of the human experimental subject. Care must be taken to control for placebo and mental set or suggestive effects. Other efforts to get at these phenomena in man include questionnaires, interviews, and observations by trained observers.

There are four major chemical classes of hallucinogens: the indole alkaloid derivatives, the piperidine derivatives, the phenylethylamines, and the cannabinols.

Indole Alkaloids

Tryptamine derivatives. The simplest of these substances is tryptamine, which has no hallucinogenic effect. Its N, N-disubstituted derivatives, perhaps having easier access to the brain, comprise several active members of the series.

N, N-Dimethyltryptamine is found, together with bufotenine (which is N-dimethyl serotin), in the Caribbean cahobe bean, chewed by certain natives to produce religious visions, and in the seeds of the domestic morning glory plant, used for hallucinatory experiences in the United States.

Various homologues have been synthesized, including N, N-diethyl-; N, N-dipropyl-; and N, N-diallyl tryptamine.

The *hydroxylated* N, N-dimethyltryptamines are also active. Among these are the 4-hydroxy (psilocin) and its phosphorylated derivative (psilocybin, found in the ritually employed hallucinogenic mushroom *Psilocybe mexicana* of southern Mexico); the 5-hydroxy (bufotenine, originally isolated from the skin of toads) and its more active 5-methoxy derivative; and the 6-hydroxy-N, N-dimethyltryptamine.

Dimethyltryptamine is psychotogenic at 1 mg per kilogramme levels (administered intramuscularly); effective dosages of the others vary. Psilocybin and psilocin produce affects at 4 to 8 mg in man. A recent addition to the tryptamine family is -methyltryptamine, which has been shown to be effective at a dosage level of 20 mg in man.

Harmine, harmaline, and ibogaine. A drug with a three-ring aromatic system (harmine) and its related dihydro derivative (harmaline) are isolated from shrubs and used by South American Indians to produce hallucinatory states. The indole alkaloids with a larger ring structure include ibogaine, used by African natives to remain motionless for as long as two days while stalking, but producing confusion, drunkenness, and hallucinations if taken in large doses.

Lysergic acid diethylamide (LSD). The ergot alkaloids were originally isolated from a grass and rye fungus and were thought to be responsible for the convulsions, mental confusion, and gangrenous changes in the lower limbs associated with the periodic outbreaks of St Anthony's fire caused by infected rye in the Middle Ages. All ergot alkaloids can be hydrolysed to ysergic acid, and various derivatives of this compound have been developed. The diethylamide was synthesized by Stoll and Hofmann in 1938; in 1943 it was discovered by Hofmann to be a potent hallucinogen.

LSD is more than 8,000 times more potent on a dosage basis than mescaline. Less than 0·3 g has caused death in status epilepticus of a 7,000-pound elephant. This remarkable substance is by far the most powerful psychotogenic agent known, effective at levels as low as 1 μg

(0·000 001 g) per kilograms of body weight in man. Originally used experimentally to produce an artificial psychosis resembling an acute schizophrenic reaction lasting several hours, it has rapidly become widely employed as a psychedelic agent by a variety of practitioners, and the basis for a growing cult of sorts.

The temporary perceptual and cognitive effects caused by a dose of 100 to 500 μg of LSD may be accompanied by almost any type of psychopathology. Suicidal attempts have been known to occur if panic or depression is predominant. Many individuals manifest some degree of subjective euphoria and a sense of great mental clarity or comprehension following the initial marked sympathomimetic effects of the drug, although objectively they may be confused, uncoordinated, hallucinating, and disoriented. Upon recovery, there is often a feeling of being reborn after a profoundly moving and significant experience, and there is often a sense of deep camaraderie with others who were present and participating in the ceremony.

Overdoses of substances like LSD may produce delirium or (rarely) convulsions. The phenothiazines, especially the high dosage group (promazine, chlorpromazine, chlorprothixine, thioridazine) are quite effective antidotes to the effects of these drugs and are preferable to the barbiturates and minor tranquillizers. Thioridazine may be the medication of choice if convulsions are feared in a given case.

Prolonged psychopathological reactions to LSD (that is, lasting more than 24 to 48 hours) are usually viewed as latent psychiatric disorders precipitated or exacerbated by the drug experience. However, some current research indicates that biochemical effects of LSD on the brain may last much longer, and in cases of repeated high dosage may be cumulative or even irreversible. Such an illness at present can only be treated basically the same way as in regular clinical practice, according to symptomatology. Recent reports suggest that chromosomal changes similar to those produced by radiation may be caused by LSD, and that taken during early pregnancy it may increase the likelihood of birth defects, while in late pregnancy premature labour may be precipitated.

Brief recurrences (known as 'flashbacks') of LSD symptomatology may be experienced weeks or months after the last dose was taken. The precipitating factors responsible for such a recrudescence are not known at the present time.

Piperidine derivatives. Both belladonna- and stromonium-containing anticholinergic compounds, such as atropine, scopolamine, and hyoscyamine, have been known for centuries to produce organic psychoses with hallucinations. Cocaine, belonging to this same family, produces hallucinations and thought disorders if taken in toxic doses. These agents are perhaps not properly termed hallucinogens (as previously defined) because the effects depend on overdosage. However, a number of compounds have been synthesized and tested recently by Abood and others[1] in which the substituted glycolic acid side chains are *meta* instead of *para* to the nitrogen of the piperidine ring. These changes have resulted in a large series of psychotogens including 1-methyl-3-piperidylcyclopentylphenylglycolate (the most powerful) and Ditran (the best known). These compounds can cause delusional thinking, disorientation, and hallucinations.

Another recently synthesized piperidine derivative that has generated much interest is Sernyl. Originally it was thought to be an analgesic or an agent which prevented sensory impulses from reaching nerve centres. Various research groups subsequently described its effects in lower doses as mimicking the primary (Bleulerian) signs of schizophrenia, including flattened affect, thought disorder, and emotional withdrawal, without the secondary signs, such as delusions and hallucinations. This was considered to be due to a peculiar effect on the sensory synapses.

More recent work has led to other reports of behavioural aberrations induced by Sernyl, including phenomena resembling those resulting from sensory deprivation.

Phenylethylamines

Mescaline. The most significant member of this group is the trimetho-xyphenylethylamine, mescaline, named after the Mescalero Apaches, who developed the cult of peyotism. Mescaline is the major active component of the buttons from the peyote cactus *Lophophora williamsii*. Today these peyote buttons are chewed by Indians of a number of tribes in the south-western United States to induce hallucinatory states in their religious rituals. The standard employment of peyote buttons in ceremonies of the Native American Church makes control of their distribution difficult, since freedom of religion is involved.

Mescaline must be administered in high dosage to achieve a full effect, usually 0·5 to 0·6 g orally. The experience is usually ushered in by one to three hours of flushing, vomiting, cramps, sweating, and other autonomic phenomena, followed by several hours (two days in some cases) of visual hallucinations (often colourful), depersonalization, and distortions of time.

The remarkable sensory and introspective effects of mescaline have long fascinated psychopathologists: both S. Weir Mitchell and Havelock Ellis reported personal experiences with it more than seventy years ago. Aldous Huxley, in his *Doors of Perception*, described mescaline intoxication as providing a voyage to the antipodes of the mind.

Amphetamines. Another phenylethylamine group, the amphetamines, should be mentioned in passing, although the therapeutic and addictive properties of these sympathomimetic amines are properly discussed more extensively elsewhere. Chronic administration of large amounts of amphet-amine may result in a psychosis with delusions, hallucinations, and dangerous behaviour, accompanied by distortions in reality testing. Sleep deprivation, due to the drug's analeptic effects, may contribute to the syndrome. Such reactions usually remit promptly upon withdrawal of the amphetamine, although treatment (including phenothiazine medication) may be required.

Adrenochrome. A trihydroxyindole called adrenochrome (an oxidation product of adrenaline), has been reported by some workers to be hallucinogenic in intravenous dosages of 0·5 mg. Based on these reports (including the supposed discovery of the presence of increased amounts of this and related metabolites in body fluids of psychiatric patients), an adrenochrome theory of schizophrenia was advanced by Hoffer and Osmond. More recent studies have failed to confirm the proposition that adrenochrome is an autogenous psychotogenic substance. However, other, more elaborate work on the role of biogenic amines in the human brain may yet prove to be of significance in the search for hallucinogenic or psychotogenic substances related to errors of metabolism in man.

Cannabinols. Although they have been well known since ancient times as perceptual distorters, the members of this psychically active drug family are perhaps not properly defined as hallucinogens. Called hashish, bhang, kif, marihuana, and various other names, these hemp-derived alkaloids produce excitation, vivid imagery, euphoria, and occasionally depression and social withdrawal. More major effects, such as disorientation and true hallucinations, usually occur only with overdosage or prolonged use. The smoking of marihuana (the active agent of which is tetrahydrocannabinol) in cigarette form ('sticks' or 'joints') has become quite common in Britain and the United States among many groups ranging from criminals to professional musicians to college students (who call it 'weed', 'pot', 'tea', 'grass', or 'Mary Jane'). Recent surveys at major American universities indicate that 20 to 60 per cent of the student body had used marihuana at least once during the previous year.

Psycho-Social Aspects

The growing use of hallucinogens is worthy of special attention from the psycho-social point of view. Near many a college campus one may find small gatherings of young people in relatively characteristic costumes quietly talking of liberal causes, pop art, and avant garde theatre, intermixed with periods of incoherence or sustained staring, against a background of modern jazz music (especially 'rock and roll', 'folk rock', or 'acid rock'; oriental music such as flute and sitar recordings from India are also becoming popular), while smoking 'pot', or perhaps sharing a mutual semi-mystical experience under the influence of black market LSD. The observer wonders if this isn't a modern, secular, pharmacologically more sophisticated version of peyotism in the Native American Church, where groups of Indians under the influence of mescaline wait together through the night for intermittent religious visions.

The issue of marihuana is often discussed under drug addictions, perhaps improperly so, since it is not truly an addicting substance. Nevitt

Sanford[40] has commented 'Only an uneasy Puritanism could support the practice of focusing on the drug addicts (rather than on our five million alcoholics) and treating them as a police problem instead of a medical one, while suppressing harmless drugs such as marihuana and peyote along with the dangerous ones.' On the other hand, it cannot be denied that some antisocial activities include marihuana intoxication as an accompaniment, and that many addicts to substances like heroin and many of those who now use LSD started out by using marihuana. Nevertheless there are those who believe that marihuana should be legalized and made available freely on a commercial basis, like alcohol, for those who wish to use it. With the phenomenal spread in the use of marihuana now taking place in the United States, this issue is likely to become increasingly important.

LSD presents a somewhat different problem, one of importance to medicine and social psychiatry. The use of LSD is increasing, in spite of stringent restrictions upon its distribution, since it is easily synthesized from commercially available starting materials and a growing demand exists. The drug seems to have a particular fascination for intellectuals from the middle and upper classes, many of whom have organized a whole way of life around its use.

It would be an oversimplification to say that all those who are involved in LSD cults of one kind or another are necessarily motivated by a pathological desire to withdraw from reality. The experience is too variable and too complex for such an explanation to hold true; contacts with many LSD users convince the observer that their motives range widely. These motives may include an adventuresome desire to seek new experiences, a craving for shared forbidden activity in a group setting to provide a sense of belonging, a manifestation of adolescent and postadolescent rebelliousness, a simple search for sexual opportunities, a genuine attempt to achieve greater self-understanding and self-fulfilment, the exercise of a truly mystical bent in persons with a philosophical orientation inclined toward the transcendental, and, as Blum[6] has described it, the search for fulfilment of a private utopian myth.

Clinical Use

In addition, of course, there is the inevitable variety of clinical psychiatric patients who are searching for treatment or relief through the use of chemicals. Their desire may be related not only to a magical hope for cure, enhanced by the reputation of a substance as mysterious and extraordinary as LSD, but also to a very understandable human wish for a short cut to therapeutic insight, with considerable saving of time, money, and suffering.

The physician may be tempted in some such cases to go along with the subject's request for one or more treatments with LSD (if, when, and where its use is still legal). Before yielding to this temptation, however, he would do well to remember that there are other therapeutic manoeuvres, such as hypnosis and the Amytal interview, which have been employed to bypass conscious resistance or temporarily modify ego structure, and for which there were once high hopes indeed. Although valuable, these methods have in the long run been found to be of limited general application.

In the use of LSD, as in all instances where powerful drugs are employed, it is important for the clinician to have behind him a solid understanding of both pharmacological and psychodynamic factors, sufficient experience to evaluate the effects of the treatment, and a clear cut formulation of clinical indications and contraindications for the use of the medication in question. There is also a growing impression that repeated large doses of LSD in certain individuals may lead to apparently irreversible personality changes. Whether this is related to some poorly understood 'biochemical scarring', or to the dangers of over-exposure to one's own primary process (normally unconscious) ideation, remains to be seen.

In respect to indications and contraindications, the therapeutic use of LSD and other hallucinogens certainly remains unclear. Among the conditions for which LSD therapy has been tried are alcoholism, narcotic addiction, homosexuality, criminal behaviour, various neurotic symptoms, schizophrenia, and resistance in psychotherapy. However, many of these experiments are characterized by vagueness of the therapeutic rationale and poorly controlled clinical conditions. This, in addition to the rare but disturbing prolonged psychotic reactions to these drugs, has led to serious questions about their usefulness in treatment and makes their place in the psychopharmaceutical armamentarium dubious to say the least. Yet the possibility remains that certain individuals may benefit from controlled psychotic-like experiences in which primary process information floods the awareness to produce a self-realizing effect. Therefore, careful clinical research on the therapeutic potentialities of substances like LSD should continue.

5

Schizophrenia

In closing it should be emphasized that there are significant differences between experimental hallucinations and those of psychiatric patients. The visual hallucinations of schizophrenia usually appear suddenly and without prodromata; those of mescaline and LSD are heralded by unformed visual sensations, simple geometric figures, and alterations of colour, size, shape, movement and number. Certain visual forms (form-constants) almost invariably present during the development of the drug-syndromes, are rarely seen in schizophrenic hallucinations.

In schizophrenia, hallucinations occur in a psychic setting of intense affective need or delusional preoccupation, and these features are either spontaneously reported or can be obtained through brief questioning. The mescaline and LSD hallucinations appear to develop independently of such emotional conditions, or else they produce their own affective alterations.

Schizophrenic hallucinations may be superimposed on a visual environment that appears otherwise normal, or, more rarely, they may appear with the remainder of the environment excluded. The drugs produce diffuse distortions of the existing visual world. One could liken this distinction to the changes of visual agnosia.

Schizophrenic hallucinations are generally seen with the eyes open; those of mescaline and LSD are more readily seen with the eyes closed or in darkened surroundings.

In searching for schizophrenic patients who experience true visual hallucinations one is struck by their rarity, compared with those who have auditory hallucinations. A rough estimate of the frequency of visual hallucinations on the receiving wards of large state hospitals is that such hallucinations occur in fewer than 5 per cent of schizophrenic patients. Other studies suggest a higher incidence, but there is no doubt that visual hallucinations in schizophrenia occur far less often than do auditory hallucinations. The same disproportion probably holds true for most of the hallucinatory syndromes accompanying other functional psychoses, and at least in the early stages of many delirious reactions and alcoholic hallucinosis as well.

Feinberg[16] offers the following possible explanations:

1. That the neurophysiologic system underlying visual memory and images is less susceptible to derangement by, or involvement in, the schizophrenic process than is the system underlying verbal memory and images.

2. That stimulation in the auditory environment is more fleeting and transitory than is that of the visual world. Relatively prolonged periods of exposure to the same stimuli are common in vision, but infrequent in audition. The visual background is one of patterned stimuli; the auditory background is, in general, less structured. Thus, the latter may be considered more ambiguous and hence more open to misinterpretation, or reconstruction, in the direction of affective need.

3. That the information that must be communicated, for delusional reasons, is more readily expressed in words than in pictures. It is easier to hear, 'You are a wicked person,' or 'You are a specially chosen person,' than it is to conjure up a visual image which would convey the same message.

Morgenbesser[33] has suggested that hallucinations in schizophrenia may represent, in part, an attempt to find support for delusional beliefs through sensory data. He hypothesizes that the schizophrenic is confronted with a situation in which a delusional idea is primary, for reasons which are unknown to us. Unable to give up this idea, but recognizing the absence of supporting evidence, the patient manufactures the required evidence through hallucinations. In this sense, hallucinations might be considered restitutional in that they restore the normal relationship between sense data and belief. However, this explanation would not encompass hallucinatory phenomena which appear unrelated to delusional material, or those that seem to occur prior to the establishment of delusions.

Auditory sense data, i.e., verbal material, may be simpler and more effective than pictorial data for supporting delusional beliefs. It is noteworthy that the majority of visual hallucinations in schizophrenics are of stereotyped content, primarily religious, obvious in their implications, and requiring little interpretation.

Isakower[23] has suggested that auditory hallucinations are pre-eminent because they represent criticism by the super-ego. The super-ego develops through the incorporation into the psychic structure of normative values previously expressed through the verbal prohibitions or commands of the parents. In hallucinations, the super-ego speaks with these voices to an individual beset by the eruption into consciousness of intolerable impulses.

It is by no means certain, however, that verbally expressed censure is more potent than censure that is visually perceived, i.e., in facial expressions. Furthermore, Modell[32] has objected to Isakower's formulation on the grounds that hallucinated voices frequently give helpful advice or assist in decisions, and in this manner represent executive, or ego, rather than super-ego, functions.

An alternative explanation, offered by Feinberg[16] is that the trauma or events responsible for the development of schizophrenic reactions in later life occur at a critical period of development, and that this period coincides with the organization of that aspect of the ego concerned with verbal functioning or language mastery. 'Ego' is used according to its specialized psychoanalytic sense, and includes the psychic processes that mediate between inner needs and external reality. The perceptual apparatus is particularly important in this regard. The critical period presumably occurs between the first and third years of life. Such an hypothesis requires an assumption that the organization of visual functions of the ego is largely completed by the end of the first year. Recent work on dreams in infants supports this possibility.

REFERENCES

1. ABOOD, L. G., and BIEL, J. H., 1962. Anticholinergic psychotomimetic agents. *Int. Rev. Neurobiol.*, **4**, 218.
2. AHLENSTIEL, H., and KAUFFMAN, R., 1952. Über die Mandalaform des 'Linearen Yantra'. *Schweiz. Z. Psychol., Anwend.*, **11**, 188.
3. ANDERSON, E. W., 1942. Abnormal mental states in survivors, with special reference to collective hallucinations. *J. Roy. Nav. M. Serv.*, **28**, 361.

4. BALDWIN, M., 1962. Hallucinations in neurologic syndromes. In *Hallucinations*. Ed. West, L. J. New York: Grune and Stratton.
5. BARTLETT, J. E. A., 1951. A case of organized visual hallucinations in an old man with cataract, and their relation to the phenomena of phantom limb. *Brain*, **74**, 363.
6. BLUM, R., ed., 1965. *Utopiates*. New York: Atherton Press.
7. BRAUCHI, J. T., and WEST, L. J., 1959. Sleep deprivation. *J. Amer. med. Assn.*, **171**, 11.
8. BRODIE, B. B., and COSTA, E., 1962. Some current views on monoamines. *Psychopharmacol. Serv. Cent. Bull.*, **2**, 1.
9. BURCH, N. R., and GREINER, T. H., 1957. A bioelectric scale of human alertness: concurrent recordings of the EEG and GSR. In *Explorations in the physiology of emotions*. Eds. West, L. J. and Greenblatt, M. *Psych. Res. Rept.*, **12**, 1960.
10. COLERIDGE, S. T., 1912. A day dream. In *Complete poetical works*. Ed. Coleridge, E. H. New York: Oxford University Press.
11. DECKERT, G. H., 1964. Pursuit eye movements in the absence of a moving visual stimulus. *Science*, **143**, 1192.
12. DEMENT, W., and KLEITMAN, N., 1957. Cyclic variations in EEG during sleep and their relation to eye movements, body motility, and dreaming. *EEG and Clin. Neurophysiol.*, **9**, 673.
13. ESQUIROL, J. É. D., 1938. *Des maladies mentales*. Paris, Bailliére.
14. EVARTS, E. V., 1954. Personal Communication.
15. EVARTS, E. V., 1957. A review of the neuro-physiological effects of lysergic acid diethylamide (LSD) and other psychotomimetic agents. *Ann. N.Y. Acad. Sci.*, **66**, 479.
16. FEINBERG, I., 1962. A comparison of the visual hallucinations in schizophrenia with those induced by mescaline and LSD-25. In *Hallucinations*. Ed. West, L. J. New York: Grune and Stratton.
17. FRIEDHOFF, A. J., and Van Winkle, E., 1965. A biochemical approach to the study of schizophrenia. *Amer. J. Psychiat.*, **121**, 1054.
18. GALTON, F., 1883. *Inquiries into the human faculty and its development*. London: Macmillan and Co.
19. GERARD, R. W., 1955. The biological roots of psychiatry. *Amer. J. Psychiat.*, **112**, 81.
20. GIARMAN, N. H., and FREEDMAN, D. X., 1965. Biochemical aspects of the actions of psychotomimetic drugs. *Pharmacol. Rev.*, **17**, 1.
21. HERON, W., BEXTON, W. H., and HEBB, D. O., 1953. Cognitive effects of a decreased variation in the sensory environment. *Am. Psychologist.*, **8**, 366.
22. HOFFMAN, J., and VERNON, J., 1956. Sensory deprivation. *Science*, **123**, 3207.
23. ISAKOWER, O., 1939. On the exceptional position of the auditory sphere. *Internat. J. Psycho-Analysis*, **20**, 340.
24. JASPER, H., and AJMONE-MARSAN, C., 1950. Thalamocortical integrating mechanism. *A.R.N.M.D. Proc.*, **30**, 480.
25. KETY, S. S., 1957. The pharmacology of psychotomimetic and psychotherapeutic drugs. *Ann. N.Y. Acad. Sci.*, **66**, 417.
26. KUBIE, L. S. Personal Communication.
27. MACLEAN, P. D., 1955. The limbic system ('visceral brain') and emotional behavior. *Arch. Neurol. Psychiat.*, **73**, 130.
28. MACLEAN, P. D., 1955. The limbic system ('visceral brain') in relation to the central gray and reticulum of the brain stem. *Psychosom. Med.*, **17**, 355.
29. MAGOUN, H. W., 1952. An ascending reticular activating system in the brain stem. *Arch. Neurol. and Psychiat.*, **67**, 145.

30. MARRAZZI, A. S., 1964. The generality of cerebral synaptic drug responses and its relation to psychosis. *Recent Adv. Biol. Psychiat.*, **6**, 1.

31. MILLER, J. G., 1960. Personal Communication—Subsequently published as: Information input overload and psychopathology. *Am. J. Psychiat.*, **116**, 695.

32. MODELL, A., 1958. Hallucinatory Experiences in Schizophrenia. *J. Am. Psychoanal. A.*, **6**, 442.

33. MORGENBESSER, S., 1962. Personal Communication to Feinberg, I.: A comparison of the visual hallucinations in schizophrenia with those induced by mescaline and LSD-25. In *Hallucinations*. Ed. West, L. J. New York: Grune and Stratton.

34. MOURGUE, R., 1932. *Neurobiologie de L'hallucination*. Brussels, Lamertin.

35. PAPEZ, J. W., 1937. A proposed mechanism of emotion. *Arch. Neurol. Psychiat.*, **38**, 725.

36. PENFIELD, W., and JASPER, H., 1954. *Epilepsy and the functional anatomy of the human brain*. Boston, Little, Brown and Co.

37. RAPAPORT, D., 1958. The theory of ego antonomy: a generalization. *Bull. Menninger Clin.*, **22**, 13.

38. ROSANSKI, J., and ROSEN, H., 1952. Musical hallucinations in otosclerosis. *Confinia. Neurol.*, **12**, 49.

39. ROSENZWEIG, N., 1955. A mechanism in schizophrenia; a theoretical formulation. *Amer. med. Assn. Arch. Neurol. Psychiat.*, **74**, 544.

40. SANFORD, N., 1965. Foreword. In *Utopiates*. Ed. R. Blum. New York: Atherton Press.

41. SCHNECK, J. M., 1953. Hypnotic hallucinatory behavior. *J. clin. exp. Hypnosis*, **1**, 4.

42. SMYTHIES, J. R., 1960. Recent advances in the biochemistry of psychosis. *Lancet*, i, 1287.

43. WEST, L. J., JANSZEN, H. H., LESTER, B. K., and CORNELISON, F. S., 1962. The psychosis of sleep deprivation. *Ann. N.Y. Acad. Sci.*, **96**, 66.

44. WEST, L. J., Ed., 1962. *Hallucinations*. New York: Grune and Stratton.

45. WINTERS, W. D., and SPOONER, C. E., 1965. A neurophysiological comparison of GHB with pentobarbital in cats. *Electroenceph. Clin. Neurophysiol.*, **18**, 287.

46. WOOLLEY, D. W., 1962. *The biochemical bases of psychoses*. New York: Wiley.

XI

MODEL PSYCHOSES

Elliot D. Luby

M.D.

Associate Director
Professor of Psychiatry and Law

AND

Jacques S. Gottlieb

M.D.

Director, Professor and Chairman
Dept. of Psychiatry

From the Lafayette Clinic
and
Wayne State University School of Medicine
Detroit, Michigan

Laboratory models in psychiatry have been difficult to create. Animals provide experimental paradigms which are only partially applicable to man and there is an understandable reluctance to expose man to conditions which might evoke an irreversible psychosis. Models are useful conceptual tools, however, and during the past two decades attempts have been made in laboratories all over the world to produce transient, reversible psychoses in humans in order to relate the genesis of these states to naturally occurring disease. The strategy proposes that psychotomimetic states, no matter how induced, might have as their basis disturbed physiology, biochemistry or psychodynamics which will lead to the uncovering of comparable pathology in schizophrenia. At the same time drugs which reverse these laboratory psychoses might be useful in the treatment of the real process.

That these are gratuitous assumptions, both Elkes[1] and Hollister[2] have emphasized, particularly in drug induced models. The differences between the LSD state and schizophrenia, for example, are obvious to the clinician and even to the schizophrenic patient to whom the drug has been administered.[3] Nevertheless, the model psychosis has much to commend it as a research strategy recognizing that its purpose is not the momentary, precise duplication of a disease, which required years for its evolution and whose content is determined by a complex of psychosocial variables. If we can define persisting and common patterns of disturbance and defect in schizophrenia, techniques which create analogous approximations in control subjects can lead to testable hypotheses about the nature of such disturbance and defect. Sleep deprivation, sensory isolation and Sernyl do not make non-psychotic subjects schizophrenic, but the phenomenology of these models is, in part, similar to the naturally occurring disease.

There are certain parameters of disordered functioning in schizophrenia which appear to be primary defects, not culturally determined or restitutional. Shakow's[4] now classic studies on set clearly indicate that the chronic schizophrenic is unable to attend to the relevant input in his sensory field. Chapman and McGhie[5] observed the distracting effect of extraneous stimuli on the perceptual motor performance of their patients. The gating mechanisms which allow for the selective inhibition of peripheral and unessential stimuli both internally and externally generated are somehow not operative. Loosening and fragmentation of associations together with overinclusive thinking and concreteness are probably related to this gating or attention fault inasmuch as words and ideas only peripherally or even randomly related tend to be put together without contextual constraint. With each resurgence of schizophrenic disorganization a peculiar emptying out of affect occurs together with a decreasing ability to link such affect with its correlative series of thoughts or events. Although depersonalization can be found in other psychopathologic states, we consider that it may underlie the other manifestations of schizophrenia. The profound disruption of body image in many patients can hardly be ignored as an insignificant finding.

Having established these signs and symptoms as a diagnostic constellation, how do the models approximate them and what useful hypotheses do they provide for us? Sleep deprivation, sensory isolation and drug induced psychoses will be considered in this context.

1

Sleep Deprivation

Sleep deprivation affords a unique opportunity for the psychiatrist to follow the development of a psychosis *in statu nascendi*. Certain psycho-dynamically determined behavioural patterns emerge early while more severe presumably metabolically based symptomatology is a consequence of the prolonged sleepless state. Such behaviours are determined by the premorbid personality structure of the subject, his relationship to the investigator, techniques used to maintain wakefulness, and whether the experiment is run in an isolated or group setting. The Harvard students of Gifford and Murawski[6] were sleep deprived for only twenty-four hours under both grouped and isolated conditions. During that brief period fears of passivity, of being overwhelmed and assaulted and a need to maintain distance from the investigators were characteristic reactions of all subjects. This anxiety was more effectively managed in the group setting which provided the support and stimulation to cope with drowsiness in addition to outlets for aggression and acting out. A primary conflict centred around the drive to sleep and the motivation to remain awake with conformity to the expectation of peers and experimenters. Although group support was anxiety reducing in some areas it was anxiety arousing in others.

In one of our groups of four young men, homosexual concerns emerged rather early.[7] These were controlled by an intense preoccupation with heterosexual fantasy and conversation about wives and girl friends. One night in the peculiar splitting of consciousness which occurs in sleep deprivation one of the men amorously embraced a coat tree and began to dance with it around the room. He became furious when interrupted until he suddenly recognized the harsh, inanimate, totally unfeminine configuration of his dancing partner. He then reported being convinced that he was dancing with his wife and was astonished to find that he was in a kind of wish fulfilling waking dream. Another subject in the same experiment grew more morose, irritable and withdrawn with the passage of each tortured, wakeful hour.

Finally in a monumental panic, he called his wife and urged her to contact the FBI inasmuch as he was certain that he was going to be mutilated and dismembered. Of psychodynamic interest was his delusional belief that his car had been stolen despite the fact that it was clearly visible in the parking lot. He remained paranoid for two weeks after termination of his ordeal. The progression from vague fears of being homosexually overwhelmed to heterosexual preoccupation and finally to paranoid restructuring of reality could clearly be observed.

The phenomenology of the sleep deprived state is characterized by changes in thinking, perception, affect, mood and motor activity. The truly psychotic phase usually requires 100 hours before its gross manifestations become evident. The earlier period is not without some striking behavioural disturbances, however. The expected drowsiness is usually intense during the down part of the diurnal cycle often becoming agonizing around 3 a.m. Between 48 and 72 hours subjects will start to lose conversational or perceptual sets and begin to respond to intrusive, internal cues. During these lapses or microsleeps, material having the same cognitive structure of the dream erupts into consciousness and a kind of splitting of consciousness may occur. For instance a disc jockey in the middle of a discussion about his dinner suddenly grew glassy eyed and mumbled almost incoherently a reportorial account of a fire. When aroused, he felt certain that he had just observed a burning building and was telephoning an account of the inferno to his station. At the same time he knew that he was in a room talking to the investigator.

Bodily sensations of an unusual and frightening nature are reported by almost all subjects. Depersonalization experiences are quite common as feelings of floating, body deadness or detached self-observation. Extremities become increasingly heavy and difficult to move as though they were weighted with lead. Pressure bands develop around the head particularly in the occipital region so that subjects wryly mention that they are wearing a skull-cap. The sensation is so compelling that they repeatedly touch the back of the head certain that they are wearing a hat. Beyond 100 hours, despite constant reality confrontation this becomes an unshakable 'hat delusion'.

Visual imagery is remarkably similar to that produced by LSD. Burning, itching eyes, blurred vision and diplopia occur first. Then illusional misinterpretation of real objects is seen. A street sign in the distance appears to be human or the floor seems to waver and shimmer. These illusional distortions are viewed with detachment and insight in the beginning but later come to be accepted with considerable affect. For example, one man saw smoke seeping out from under a door but laughed because he was aware of its unreality. The following day he saw it again and felt it necessary to open the door to be assured that there was no fire in the next room. Finally subjects describe fascinating geometric patterns on the floor, walls or ceiling, become frightened by monstrous faces in the window, or vague and shadowy forms flitting about. The eerie and peculiar feeling of being enclosed by cobwebs or netting is also reported. At 180 hours the record seeking disc jockey was startled by flashes of blue light which seemed to shoot out of the walls. Auditory hallucinations are rare although one of Berger and Oswald's[8] subjects heard voices while a water tap was running. When he turned off the water to hear them better, the voices ceased.

Cognitive disorganization begins with a general slowing of thought processes with word searching. Subjects cannot maintain seriatim thinking and stray from topic to topic. Amusing spoonerisms are haltingly mouthed. Speech tends to become incoherent with confused mumbling which fades into dozing silence. Dream thoughts are interspersed with secondary process thinking as though there were a failure in repression. New learning is interfered with because the attentional or set impairment will not allow for the acquisition of new memories.

Regulation and control of affect is frequently disturbed. Loud explosive laughter which is sometimes inappropriate or at least over-reactive can be heard. A number of men become easily annoyed and irritable. This may escalate to outbursts of seemingly unprovoked rage. Such hostile outbursts may be part of a paranoid resolution. As an example a subject suddenly threw down his cue while playing pool and began to choke his partner. After forcible disengagement he bitterly complained that the assault was necessary because the partner was making a fool out of him. Another subject kicked in the side of a phone booth 'because it made him feel better'. He was a discharged marine whom we later discovered had a long history of sociopathic behaviour. Striking out at attendants who prodded them awake was not uncommon but was also responsive to the harshness of the attendants' behaviour.

At 100 hours or beyond the sleep deprived person appears utterly weary, grim and slowed. At this time the real psychosis appears. West et al.[9] described their subjects in these terms. 'Faces become elongated and immobile; the brow is furrowed with the effort to hold open drooping lids during drowsy periods of growing intensity; at such times the subject looks for all the world like a patient having a myasthenic crisis. During periods of greater alertness there is a hollow eyed suspicious stare, so typical that we have dubbed it 'the Mindzenti look' after pictures taken of the tragic cardinal at his trial and public confession of being a spy following a presumed period of prolonged interrogation and sleep deprivation'.

Clouded-delirium-like states are also observed. Here the Jungian phrase 'waking dream' applies. The dream cycle seems to break through and the subject walks about responding to his private dream material as though it were real and public. Our disc jockey, although pacing around with eyes open, felt as though he were on a black cloud, weightlessly floating among a group of ballet dancers whose forms he could barely perceive. He repeatedly 'blacked out' but would automatically continue certain behaviour as playing records, yet suddenly 'awaken' with no memory of what he had done just moments before. The most frightening manifestation of an organic delirium was seen in a college student who became disoriented for name, place, and time. The delirium cleared following sleep but he remained cognitively slowed for one month and was unable to pass his final examinations. Sleep deprivation is hardly an innocuous procedure.

How eagerly and with what satisfaction do subjects greet the bed. There is a sense of accomplishment at having endured the trial, even an enhancement of masculinity. Within seconds they are deeply asleep and can only be aroused with great difficulty. Berger and Oswald[8] using EEG criteria (Loomis et al., 1937) for sleep depth nicely demonstrated that significantly more time was spent in the deepest levels of sleep (stage 4) by subjects during the night following termination of the sleep deprived period. The two also measured paradoxical sleep or dream time and to their surprise found a significant increase in this sleep phase on the second post experiment night. The majority of subjects sleep for 12 to 14 hours and awaken refreshed and seemingly whole again. A few continue to have serious psychiatric symptoms for two weeks to a month following the experiment. No disquieting long-term changes have been observed.

Sleep deprivation profoundly affects peripheral physiology reflecting central alterations in autonomic balance. The results seem clearly dependent upon the demands made upon the subject during psychophysiologic recording. If he is allowed to rest comfortably, muscle tension, galvanic skin response (GSR), heart rate, palmar sweating and blood pressure gradually fall as the period of deprivation is lengthened. Ax and Luby[10] proposed that prolonged sleeplessness is accompanied by a reduction in central sympathetic reactivity manifested most dramatically by a paradoxical fall in diastolic blood pressure in response to a pain stimulus given on the fourth day as demonstrated in Fig. 1.

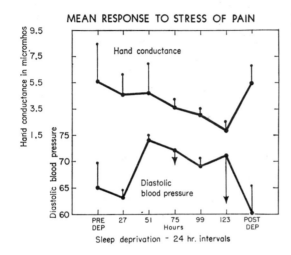

FIG. 1. Galvanic Skin response (GSR) represents the change in hand conductance to a pain stimulus and is depicted in the graph by the vertical lines.
(Reproduced by permission from Amer. med. Assn. Arch. gen. Psychiat., 1961, 4, 55–59.)

On preceding days diastolic pressure had risen in reaction to this stimulus. Malmo and Surwillo[11] made their subjects perform a tracking task and found that levels of physiologic activation increased progressively in order to maintain the arousal necessary for adequate performance. Wilkinson[12] discovered a similar phenomenon in his subjects who were required to perform an adding task. Increased levels of muscle tension correlated inversely with impaired function as measured by both speed and accuracy. Thus when sleep is lost higher levels of muscle tension are necessary to maintain arousal adequate for efficiency. Thus a sleep deprived person will require increasing levels of autonomic arousal in order to perform a perceptual motor task, but if left alone, his autonomic activation will progressively decrease as the experiment continues.

The biochemical correlates of sleep deprivation occur in energy production systems. Luby and Frohman[13, 14] studied adenosine triphosphate (ATP) and adenosine disphosphate (ADP) turnover in the erythrocyte by means of labelled radioactive phosphorus.

High energy phosphate formation as measured by the specific activity of ATP was stimulated in the initial phase of sleep deprivation. Levels of the adenine phosphates paradoxically fell and remained low throughout the experiment. Between 72 and 100 hours the mechanisms associated with energy production began to fail and ATP specific activity dropped precipitously. These peripheral studies may reflect events in the neuron, although of course, they may simply be a manifestation of muscular exertion.

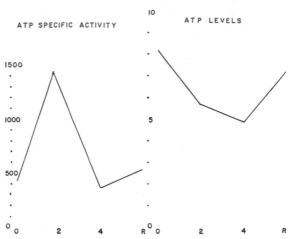

FIG. 2. ATP specific activity counts per milligram per minute expressed in the thousands. ATP levels in milligrams per cent.
(Reproduced by permission from *Ann. N. Y. Acad. Sci.*, 1962, **96**, 71–78.)

Increased catechol amine output might also be anticipated as a consequence of sleep deprivation. Despite Tyler's[15] negative findings, Hasselman,[16] utilizing more sophisticated biochemical techniques, reported that the usual rise in epinephrine and norepinephrine excretion caused by muscular exertion was markedly enhanced by sleep deprivation. The pituitary adrenal axis seems variably affected, again dependent upon the demands for the subjects' performance. When he is allowed to rest, the secretory reactivity of the pituitary adrenal axis is reduced.[6] Work that requires sustained attention and arousal increases the secretory reactivity of this endocrine system.

Electroencephalographic changes seem to parallel the biochemistry. The early stages of sleep deprivation are characterized by an increase in cerebral irritability which may even result in epileptic like manifestations in certain predisposed people.[17] Beyond 48 hours the irritability diminishes and the EEG tends to flatten out. Alpha rhythm also disappears and stimuli which normally block it paradoxically elicit it. Lapsing in the performance of a perceptual motor task is related to the dropping out of alpha, a shift to lower frequencies, dilatation of finger vessels and dozing.[18] Rapid changes in EEG rhythm from alpha to delta and back may occur with drowsing and reawakening.

The characteristic psychological performance deficits of sleep deprivation are a result of brief periods of drowsing or lapsing which intensify with passage of sleepless time. Lapses can be predicted seconds prior to their occurrence through a shift in EEG rhythm from alpha to theta and a concomitant rise in finger pulse volume. Decrements in perceptual motor efficiency occur only during lapses, while remaining within a normal or modal range during alert intervals. Williams, Lubin and Goodnow[18] showed that the sleep deprived do poorly on experimenter paced tasks while those that are self paced decline minimally in accuracy because the subject has the time to respond between lapses.

The lapse as a period of non-reactivity is similar to the 'automatic resting response' which Kimble[19] noted in the performance of fully aroused subjects working under conditions of massed practice. Automatic resting is attributed to the development of reactive inhibition by Hull[20] which then reaches a threshold or critical level. Within the framework of learning theory, reactive inhibition is regarded as a negative drive state. It accumu-

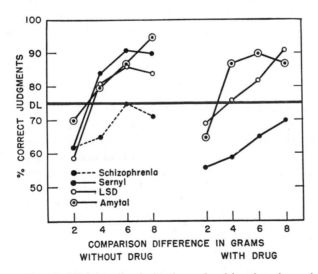

FIG. 3. Weight discrimination of schizophrenic and drug groups.
(Reproduced by permission from *Amer. med. Assn. Arch. gen. Psychiat.*, 1959, **81**, 363–69.)

lates during work and depresses performance, since the making of a response sets up a tendency not to repeat the response. It is assumed to be a temporary inhibition of response which dissipates during rest. Reminiscence is defined as the improvement in performance associated with the dissipation of reactive inhibition by rest. Resting allows for the dissipation of reactive inhibition enabling the motivated subject to continue his work until the threshold is once again reached. According to Cohen *et al.*[21] those as yet undetermined central changes which occur in sleep deprivation tend to accelerate the accumulation of reactive inhibition and to interfere with its dissipation.

Cohen, Grisell and Ax[21] required sleep deprived subjects to perform the pursuit rotor and reversed-digits tests. These perceptual motor tests, described elsewhere,[21] are employed to obtain indices of the accumulation and dissipation of reactive inhibition.

The results of the pursuit-rotor test are presented in Fig. 3. In the first 48 hours all subjects showed a gain from pre-rest to post-rest scores. This increment dropped out at 48 hours, however, and finally at 120 hours the post-rest score became lower than the pre-rest. Following sleep both scores rose and the post-rest time on target returned to the 'normal' pattern of superiority over the pre-rest.

Pursuit-rotor deficits in the sleep-deprived state can be attributed to the build-up of reactive inhibition to intolerable levels beyond 48 hours of wakefulness. From this point on, the subject's ability to tolerate cumulating reactive inhibition is impaired and brief involuntary lapses in perceptual motor functioning occur. These lapses may serve as subject-produced rest periods which function to dissipate the inhibition so that none is left for the experimental rest period and hence, no post-rest increment (reminiscence) in performance results. A more detailed explanation of this hypothesis is given by Cohen, Grisell, and Ax.[21]

The reversed-digits writing test reflects a similar phenomenon. All four subjects showed within-trial declines in output during sleep deprivation in excess of that seen on the pre- and post-tests. Scores on the last 30-sec unit of the work period were consistently below those of the initial unit. The variability among the 30-sec unit of each work period can be considered as a measure of the tendency to engage in lapses. This variability is an indication of unevenness of performance which other investigators have related to periods of no response. Fig. 4 indicates that variances almost doubled at 48 hours compared to the predeprivation test day and then redoubled at 72 hours.

Lapses, or periods of nonresponding, which may function as temporary dissipators of accumulated reactive inhibition, apparently increase as sleep deprivation is prolonged. With prolonged wakefulness, experimentally introduced rest is of no value in reducing the lapse rate and a point is reached where post-rest functioning becomes appreciably worse than pre-rest. Thus, both subject-produced and experimenter-produced resting were inadequate to reduce the levels of reactive inhibition which had accumulated at 120 hours in sleep deprived subjects, and phenomena suggesting negative reminiscence effects were obtained. Lapsing and the accumulation of reactive inhibition have neurophysiologic and probably metabolic correlates. Their precise definition remains to be determined but our preferred formulation is that the lapse is a restitutive event occurring because of central depletion of the chemical energy necessary for alerting and sustained perceptual motor functioning. Lapses

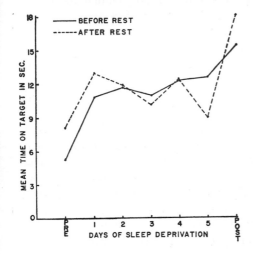

Fig. 4. Rotary pursuit performance of ten sleep-deprived subjects. (Reproduced by permission from the *Proceedings of the Third World Congress of Psychiatry*, Univ. Toronto Press, 1963.)

reach their peak intensity and frequency when phosphate esterification becomes depleted and central sympathetic responsivity is considerably diminished.

The behavioural consequences of sleep deprivation can also be understood within the framework of the lapse hypothesis. Initially, however, anxiety associated with fears of passivity and surrender are engendered by the dynamics of the experimental setting. This is generally controlled by preoccupation with heterosexuality but may extend to a more regressive, paranoid resolution. As the days of sleeplessness continue, it becomes more difficult to maintain attention on the external world. Perhaps attention to external sensory input requires greater sympathetic arousal and mobilization of energy resources than attention to internal stimuli, possibly because the external source necessitates more active and effortful scanning and orientating reactions.

The sleep-deprived subject, with his energy resources depleted, will then be likely to react predominantly to internal stimulus cues, especially during periods where 'lapses' or brief periods of drowsiness occur. The subject's behaviour at these times can be compared with other conditions in which there is faulty filtering of input and inability to narrow attention or to maintain repression. Moving from one frame of reference to another is admittedly hazardous, but the speculation can be made that maintenance of attention, reticular and sympathetic arousal, and mobilization of high energy phosphorylation are closely interrelated phenomena.

Cohen and Grisell[22] attempting to correlate certain performance tasks with energy production, discovered that there was a significant relationship between increased ATP specific activity in response to insulin and the ability to perform a work output task demanding sustained attention. This relationship was present in both non-psychotic control subjects and in schizophrenic patients. Callaway and Dembo[23] coined the phrase 'narrowing of attention' to describe the filtering out of peripheral stimuli (peripheral in terms of time, space, or meaning) and correlated this with the level of central sympathetic activity. Thus ability to mobilize ATP with associate sympathetic arousal may be crucial for sustaining attention and filtering sensory input.

How can these changes in energy production occurring in the sleep deprivation model be related to schizophrenia? Frohman and Gottlieb[24, 25] have reported impairment in the ability of chronic schizophrenic patients to increase ATP turnover and to shift from the synthetic hexose monophosphate shunt to the high energy Emden-Meyerhof scheme of metabolism in adaptive response to an insulin stressor. The origins of such a defect are obscure but it may be the result of sustained, overwhelming anxiety, a genetically determined enzyme lesion, or inadequate exposure to stressors in childhood as a consequence of maternal overprotection. The last interpretation is suggested by the work of Beckett et al.,[26] showing a relationship between the severity of a defect in intracellular energy transfer mechanisms and symptomatology, chronicity, premorbid characteristics, and early parent-child relations.

2

Sensory and Perceptual Isolation

Our Canadian colleagues initiated the imaginative research on the effects of reduction of environmental stimulation upon humans. American and British research groups seized upon the techniques as a way of studying information processing and brain function and in the twelve years following the McGill experiments developed an enormous literature in the area. Phrases utilized to describe the precise nature of this work have included sensory and perceptual as input labels, while isolation, deprivation and restriction have characterized the experimental operation. It would appear meaningful following Shurley,[27] to apply the term deprivation to experimental settings involving immature animals and confining the use of isolation to those situations in which mature organisms participate. In adult human research, following Kubzansky,[28] the phrase sensory isolation should be attached to conditions of reduction of sensory input in one or all modalities to the lowest possible level. Perceptual isolation best depicts the condition of depatterning or disorganization of sensory input while the total level remains fairly normal.

Sensory deprivation studies have dramatically demonstrated the importance of stimulation to the immature organism. Animals so deprived become hyperexcitable, have a low seizure threshold and motor dysfunction when exposed to a normal environment.[29] Harlow's,[30] now legendary monkeys, emerged from their barren and impoverished infancy as grossly defective adults without the capacity to relate to peers and a peculiar ignorance of the instrumental acts of sexuality. Bruner[31] predicted that such early deprivation would produce a disturbance in sensory gating and the ability to occlude unessential or irrelevant stimuli. According to Bruner, sensory deprivation results in an inadequate construction of environmental models and a disturbance in information processing because of the absence of early learning against which new experiences can be compared probably along a reward punishment continuum. On a cellular level there is good evidence that essential enzyme systems fail to develop when appropriate stimuli are absent at critical growth periods. These deprivation induced defects are apparently irreversible. A human analogue would be the institutionalized maternally deprived infants described by Spitz[32] who were observed to be apathetic and marasmic. Although the neurophysiologic systems which mediate affect are present at birth, they require maternal stimulation in order for appropriate response patterns to evolve.

The syndromes which sensory and perceptual isolation induce in humans are more related to the concept of model psychosis. Beginning with the work of Bexton, Heron, and Scott,[33] a succession of studies have evinced certain hardcore data. With diverse experimental operations essentially similar phenomenologic states ensued.

The McGill group placed volunteer subjects in a small, air conditioned, cubicle covering their eyes with translucent goggles and forearms with cotton gloves. Lilly[34] and Shurley,[35] in separate experiments, immersed their subjects in a tank of water at body temperature, requiring them to wear darkened breathing masks. Mendelson and Foley[36] observed respirator psychoses in patients with bulbar poliomyelitis. Wexler et al.[37] restricted normal subjects for eight hours in a tank type respirator. Zubek[38] immobilized his people in a coffin-like wooden box. This variously elicited isolation state produces tedium, boredom, anxiety, less controlled thinking, revery, blurring of body boundaries, difficulty in sequential thinking and vivid visual imagery. The imagery may subsequently be interpreted as occurring outside of the subject and as real. Many subjects terminate the experiment prematurely and few are desirous of repeating the experience. Not all of the changes are in a deficit direction inasmuch as a performance facilitation cluster has been reported by Myers.[39] Heightening of simple sensory acuity, enhanced learning and memory, greater desire for significant information associated with more persuasive effects of that information are also consequences of sensory isolation.

The electroencephalographic and peripheral physiologic responses to sensory and perceptual isolation move in the direction of reduced arousal.

After fourteen days of isolation combined with exposure to unpatterned light and white noise, there was a downward shift in EEG frequencies in the alpha range of Zubek's[40] subjects. This slowing effect persisted for several days following the procedure and was accompanied by decrements in motivation. A tendency for subjects to sleep has also been described. The GSR as in sleep deprivation, gradually diminishes, unless panic supervenes, indicative of reduction in central sympathetic activation.

Not all of the phenomena of sensory isolation are explicable in terms of a stimulus reduction theory. Psychodynamic factors powerfully influence subject behaviour in a variety of ways. The experimental setting with its novelty, ambiguity and aloneness is in itself evocative of anxiety at first exposure. The immobilization coupled with the absence of input around which to focus alerting and orienting responses elicits feelings of passive surrender, vulnerability and finally fears of either homosexual or heterosexual assault. Subjects analogize the stillness and monotony to their conceptions of the experience of dying. Freedman, Grunebaum and Greenblatt[41] correlated tolerance of isolation to the vague concept of ego strength. The studies of Goldberger and Holt[42] demonstrated, however, that externally oriented, field dependent subjects were the least adaptive and the least tolerant of the experiment. In this connection, we[43] have observed that chronic schizophrenic patients who can hardly be characterized as having ego strength were remarkably comfortable in sensory isolation and even appeared to enjoy the procedure.

In addition to the psychodynamically determined behavioural constellations, the specific productions of subjects were closely linked to the suggestions given by the experimenter in his preparation of subjects. This was demonstrated by Pollard, Uhr, and Jackson.[44] Subjects were placed in the sensory deprived situation but were given a placebo and the minimal experimental instructions referred to a 'drug experiment'. The usual bizarre, dramatic effects did not occur. Discomfort and anxiety were reported but the subjects stayed for an average of 6·5 of the maximum 8 hours. When the experimental instructions described the study in terms of 'sensory deprivation' and referred to other studies, more unusual effects were reported. The 'suggestion group' spoke more, on more different topics and seemed more disturbed than the 'drug study group'. This potent influence of suggestion on the results has been verified by other workers. Recruitment of subjects, relationship with experimenter and terms like 'panic buttons' make up a social psychology that affects the subjects' expectations.

Pollard, Uhr, and Jackson[44] also investigated the effect of repeating the experience. The second trial, separated by about a week, was quite different from the first. The repetition provoked less anxiety and fewer effects. Subjects spoke less, on fewer topics and experienced less discomfort. A similar decline in 'production' occurred in the latter half, as opposed to the first half of each session.

Sensory isolation can be compared to sleep deprivation in several respects. The early behavioural changes are a consequence of the dynamics of the relationship between subject and researcher, together with the peculiar nature of the experimental setting. Fears of passive surrender and homosexual assault progress to panic and paranoid outcome and, in some, to termination of the procedure. As time in isolation increases, vigilance and arousal cannot be maintained in the absence of adequate input to the reticular core, EEG alpha diminishes in frequency, GSR falls and the subject begins to experience hypnogogic reveries. Body boundaries are disrupted and because there is no external reality against which to assess these internally generated productions, they are experienced as outside and real.

This notion is comparable to the model of Inglis[45] in which he postulates that deterioration of cognitive functioning under the isolation condition occurs because the problem solving organism is deprived of the stimulus manifold against which his perceptions and solutions can be continuously checked.

The schizophrenic patient, as opposed to the control subject, has a reception-interpretation system which is geared down and unable to accommodate the usual flow of input stimulation without distractibility or distortion. He has already acquired the capacity to tolerate his autistic productions and is not as disturbed by them as is the non-psychotic subject. The isolation setting then may be one which presents to the schizophrenic subject a more balanced relation between input load and reception-interpretation capacity. Schizophrenic withdrawal may represent an attempt by the patient to reduce input overload, resulting in a form of learned, self-imposed sensory isolation.

3

Psychotomimetic Drugs

The relationships between schizophrenia and the psychotomimetic effects of drugs are admittedly tenuous. As Elkes[1] has forcefully pointed out there is an enormous difference between the highly personal and meaningful auditory hallucinations of the schizophrenic person and the patterned visual hallucinations of the LSD experience. The remarkable effects of LSD, however, stimulated a renaissance of biological investigation in schizophrenia, particularly in the search for the toxic factor as exemplified by Hoffer's[46] adrenolutin and Heath's[47] taraxein. How comforting it would be to find a substance which would unify our conflicting and disparate conceptions of this elusive disease. In terms of the renewed interest in the biology of schizophrenia and in other respects, the drug model has been useful and should not be completely disparaged as having no relevance to the real problem or as 'self deluding'.[2]

To illustrate this point of view the rather striking psychosis produced by 1-(1-phenylcyclohexyl) piperidine monhydrochloride (Sernyl)[48] led to a number of interesting formulations about its mechanism of action and a corollary hypothesis about schizophrenic deficit. Sernyl was initially developed as an anaesthetic and came into our hands when Meyer and Greifenstein[49] reported a number of postoperative psychoses associated with its use. Our initial studies with it were prompted by a desire to observe the effects of 'interoceptive' sensory isolation resulting from administration of the drug at dosage levels which permitted the subject to remain awake and communicate.

When given intravenously to control subjects at a dose level of 0·1 mg/kg the drug produced a predictable series of changes mimicking the primary symptoms of schizophrenia. Initially, alteration of body image occurred with a loss of body boundaries and a profound sense of unreality. Then feelings of estrangement and loneliness ensued, sometimes associated with an intensification of dependency needs and attachment to the observer. Progressive disorganization of thought, inability to maintain a set, loss of goal ideas, impairment of abstract thinking, blocking, neologizing, negativism and hostility all followed. Some subjects became catatonic and many had dream-like experiences in which they felt as though they were in a different setting at a different time. Genuine hallucinations were not characteristic effects of the drug.

Since distortions of body image and depersonalization were universal reactions to Sernyl and occurred just prior to the other deficits in thinking and affect, it was hypothesized that the effect of the drug was mediated through the reduction of proprioceptive feedback or impairment of the central integration and interpretation of input from this sensory modality. Experiments were next set up by Rosenbaum et al.,[50] to provide data with respect to this hypothesis, employing performance tasks which were considered to depend on an intact proprioceptive feedback system. These included measures of attention (reaction time), motor function (rotary pursuit learning), and proprioceptive acuity (weight discrimination). The effects of Sernyl on the tasks were compared with those of lysergic acid diethylamide (LSD) and amobarbital. In addition, a criterion group of chronic schizophrenic patients was tested without drugs in an attempt to find how closely the performance of control subjects under each of the drugs approximated that of schizophrenic patients. The results clearly demonstrated that Sernyl produced severe impairments beyond those attributable to sedation (as seen by comparison with amobarbital) or to some general psychotomimetic factor (as indicated by comparison with LSD). Also, Sernyl was the only drug to produce the level and pattern of deficits shown by the criterion group of schizophrenic subjects. The same results were found by Cohen et al.,[51] with tasks involving symbolic and sequential thinking.

The inference was drawn that Sernyl results in schizophrenic-like primary attention and cognition deficits, while LSD simulates secondary phenomena (e.g., hallucinations). The findings were regarded as consistent with the hypothesis of a disturbance in proprioceptive feedback mechanisms in both the Sernyl state and in chronic schizophrenia.

With the hypothesis in mind that Sernyl acts through a disruption in body feedback systems, and that such a disturbance already exists in schizophrenia, it was decided to observe the effects of Sernyl in schizophrenic subjects. The results were quite vivid. Sernyl produced profoundly disorganized regressive states in these patients. Their thought disorders were greatly intensified and considerable affective expression was stimulated. It was as though the acute, agitated phase of the illness had been reinstated. Chronic patients generally became more assertive, hostile and unmanageable. Unexpectedly, the behavioural changes persisted from four to six weeks after Sernyl injection in these patients.

Since the administration of Sernyl accentuated schizophrenic symptoms, we concluded that the drug touched upon some fundamental aspect of the disease. Tentatively, we believe this feature to involve central integration of body input or a disturbance in the proprioceptive feedback system.

Having observed that chronic schizophrenic patients tolerated sensory isolation with so much less tension and discomfort than control subjects, and in view of the possible intimate relation between the Sernyl state and schizophrenia, it was considered instructive to observe the reactions of Sernyl injected control subjects under sensory isolation conditions. The data consisted of immediate observations of the subjects and their retrospective accounts of the experience. The results reported by Cohen et al.,[52] indicated that the manifest psychotomimetic phenomena usually produced by Sernyl under non-isolation conditions were markedly attenuated under isolation. The subjects were not asleep and were able to report on their experiences, at least retrospectively, as 'nothingness' and 'total emptiness'. The state was analogized with 'death'. Compared to non-isolation experiences with the drug, the subjects felt calm and self-controlled.

Our conclusion was that the usual psychotomimetic effects of Sernyl required exteroceptive inputs for their arousal. It occurred to us that the Sernyl engendered state resembled schizophrenia to the extent that subjects under the drug tolerated sensory isolation in a manner similar to that reported by Cohen et al.,[43] as characteristic of schizophrenic patients Perhaps both the model psychosis of Sernyl and the clinical psychosis of schizophrenia produce a disturbance in the capacity of the organism to filter and interpret a normal sensory input load. This handicap results in generalized aversion to the complex and dynamic influx that is characteristically provided by the normal sensory environment.

We do not believe that the disturbance is at a receptor or spinal cord site, as evidenced by the fact that the patellar reflex is enhanced.[48] A more central system responsible for the integration of exteroceptive with body feedback inputs is probably operative, perhaps at a thalamic or cortical level.[53] The appropriate adaptive accommodation of exteroceptive inputs requires that the central system be intact. When it is not intact, the organism will seek and prefer more simplified and monotonous environments, and will withdraw from those that are more complex and changing.

4

Related Research

In our sleep laboratories Caldwell and Domino[54] have done all night sleep recordings on a population of twenty-five chronic schizophrenic patients. In this group of twenty-five patient subjects, ten had no scorable delta wave activity indicating a virtual absence of stage IV sleep. The mean percentage of stage III was also significantly reduced. The other sleep

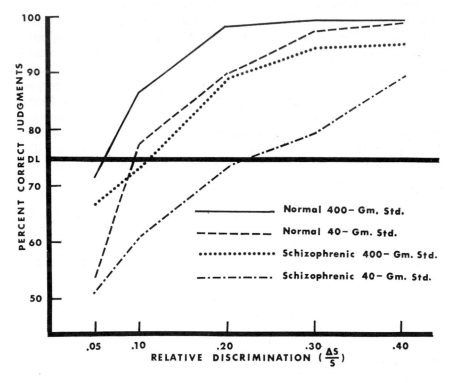

Fig. 5. Weight discrimination of normals and schizophrenics at two intensities.
(Reproduced by permission from *J. abnorm. Psychol.*, 1965, **70**, 446–50.)

stages including I-REM were present in the same amount in both schizophrenic and control subjects. Luby and Caldwell[55] then sleep deprived four of the delta deficient group for eighty hours. Their tolerance for the procedure and the slight improvement in relatedness and thinking was surprising. Most impressive was the observation that only a minimal increase in the delta waveband occurred on the sleep night following the vigil in these schizophrenic subjects. The physiology of delta wave or slow sleep is poorly understood but cortical structures do seem to be involved. Do the slow recovery cortical neurons believed by Moruzzi[56] to be responsible for the plastic activity of the CNS restitute during delta wave sleep? It is his contention that we sleep in order to permit recovery of the synapses which 'learn', not those which are necessary for routine transmission of impulses along inborn pathways. Such recovery may not only be necessary in the energy production systems of these neurons, but also may require reorientation of macromolecular proteins providing for an erasure or 'readout' of redundant information accumulated during the day.[57] In the delta impoverished group, the inhibitory or reticular deactivating complex described by Hernandez-Peon[58] could be nonfunctional dooming certain chronic schizophrenics to a persistent state of hyperalertness. These are highly speculative assumptions considering our rather preliminary knowledge of sleep physiology.

An additional extension of our model psychosis research has been the further investigation of the validity of the proprioceptive hypothesis by Rosenbaum et al.[59] If there is indeed a proprioceptive or reafferent feedback disorder in schizophrenia, it should be observable in perceptual motor functioning. A series of weight discrimination tasks were devised and given to matching groups of schizophrenic patients and control subjects. Weight discrimination thresholds were found to be significantly elevated in the schizophrenic group correlating with the severity of the psychopathology and most evident at the lighter weight intensity. The schizophrenics showed significantly greater improvement than normals with the heavier weights (see Fig. 5). According to Rosenbaum et al.,[59] 'The results support the hypothesis of a schizophrenic deficit in proprioceptive acuity and suggest that this deficit is the result of insufficient proprioceptive feedback.'

5

Discussion

All model psychoses may be conceptualized as resulting from disruption in the central processing or from interference with the normal sensory influx from body or distance receptors. The experimental findings of the effects of sleep deprivation, sensory isolation, psychotomimetic drugs and a combination of drugs and sensory isolation require some unifying hypothesis having relevance to the problem of schizophrenia. Schizophrenia is far more than a concatenation of primitive avoidance responses, explicable in terms of the anachronisms of libido theory. A major defect in the transmission and processing of sensory and internally generated, ideational input is present resulting in a profoundly distorted self experience, inept blocking of irrelevant or redundant signals and unstable set-shifting.

Intrusions arise from the 'noise' aspects of a perceptual set, chance distractions in the surround or irrelevancies from the past which cannot be screened. The disarticulated set in schizophrenia was demonstrated electroencephalographically by Jones et al.,[60] who found by means of the auditory evoked response that schizophrenics remained preoccupied with the physical difference between two tones in the absence of assigned symbolic or instrumental significance. The facilitation or inhibition of an afferent stimulus is probably dependent upon its approach-avoidance or neutral meaning and according to Hernandez-Peon,[61] the reticulo fugal influences of the central core of the brain stem mediate this function. This non-specific arousal system together with its elaborate thalamic and cortical connections, is at this point, the neurophysiologic construct to which this filter function can best be attributed. The relationship between delta wave sleep, maintenance of attention during waking hours and recovery of high energy phosphorylation in the neuron deserves further study. We have already drawn parallels between central sympathetic activation, arousal, narrowed attention with associated sensory inhibition or facilitation, and mobilizable ATP.[62] We now would attempt to establish a link between these processes and so called slow sleep.

The importance of altered experience of self and external world in schizophrenia has not been sufficiently emphasized. These perceptual changes rather than representing a point of difference between drug models and schizophrenia are remarkably similar to those induced by drugs. Restitutional symptoms can be understood as attempts to explain and give meaning to these perceptual distortions. Freedman and Giarman[63] in a comparison of drugs and natural psychoses points out that 'the drugs and clinical states set up a "search for synthesis", and the motives and capacities of subjects and patients to achieve this are obviously of importance if one is to assess outcomes and compare and contrast these states'.

Perceptual confusion and flooding apparently induce not only synthesis (psychotic insight) but also aversive behaviour in schizophrenic patients. The patient wishes to simplify his world as much as he possibly can, suggesting that his stimulus filtering and interpretation capacity is diminished.

Conceivably the defect may be similar to that produced by Sernyl and involve the disruption or reduction of body input transmission and integration. In Kubie's[64] parlance, when the subject's image of himself, 'the I', is destroyed, the ability to assess external reality or the 'not I' is lost. As Federn[65] suggested, depersonalization may be the core of schizophrenia, and disturbed body input transmission or integration may be its basis. In our hypothesis such disturbed neural integration in schizophrenia might result either from the presence of an inhibitor substance or from a defect in energy production.

Analogous situations in the animal can be produced by psychotomimetic drugs such as Sernyl or by lesions in lateral midbrain involving tracts mediating touch, proprioception, and pain. Sernyl has been shown by Lees[66] to be an uncoupling agent. It may thus reduce available energy stores, although admittedly other uncoupling drugs do not produce psychotomimetic effects. That Sernyl has profound action on central reception and integration of body input is evidenced by the work of VanMeter et al.[67] and Domino.[53] At the cortical level both axosomatic and axodendritic synapses are partially blocked by the drug. There is also evidence for depression of the diffuse thalamic projection system.

Recent work on destruction of lemniscal pathways in the cat by Sprague, Chambers, and Stellar[68] might lend additional support to our hypothesis. When the sensory afferent systems mediating proprioception, pain, and touch in these animals were cut, severe behavioural changes occurred. The cat was rendered incapable of attending to or making adaptive responses to relevant stimuli associated with eating, sexuality, or defence. Emotionality was diminished and the cats seemed flat and automaton-like. At times they appeared to be hallucinating.

Our preoccupation with proprioceptive or reafferent feedback may not be justified inasmuch as the regulation of all sensory systems is probably impaired in schizophrenia. The altered experience of self, however, may be primary to the thought disorder, psychotic synthesis, and avoidance behaviour and must be appreciated in any treatment consideration.

6

Clinical Applications

It cannot be sufficiently emphasized that the hospital must provide a special kind of environment or milieu for the fragmented schizophrenic. The workers in that milieu from the doctor to nurse to attendant to janitor should be fully cognisant of the distorted, jumbled, Daliesque world of the patient. The structure of the ward as determined not only by the behaviour of personnel but also its physical setting has to provide simplicity, stability, certainty, and interested neutrality. Psychotic symptoms can be appreciably reduced by diminution of sensory input, particularly that which is complex, contradictory or affectively loaded. Thus, occasional seclusion can be utilized not as a form of retributive control but as a technique of eliminating disturbing, emotionally charged afferent bombardment which the patient is poorly equipped to integrate.

Scheduling must be definite and followed through with a consistency that allows for few surprises. It is even useful to have a blackboard upon which daily activities can be listed and bulletin boards for posting memos, names of patients, calendars, and mementoes of the day which can be inspected repeatedly by the patients.

In the process of resocialization it may be necessary to guide a patient to a table, give him a fork and teach him once again how to eat.

Because of the fundamental dysidentity disturbance, patients require the trappings which reinforce self-knowledge, as a wallet, identification bracelet and familiar clothing. The dehumanizing nature of hospital garments and the humiliation of being stripped and forced to look like all other patients decidedly add to the alienation and confusion. Finally a nurse does not, like the patient's mother, pursue him relentlessly in an effort to break into his world and involve him in hers. His need for temporary withdrawal and privacy is respected. It will soon disappear as the psychosis subsides.

In essence then, provide the floridly psychotic patient with cohesive structure, the presence of external controls to neutralize his aggression and repetitive reorientation to a world which his perceptual apparatus has grotesquely altered. In some respects our management of the acute schizophrenic person is comparable to that which we would provide for a patient in a delirium. Beyond a doubt, dedicated and capable nurses with some awareness of the subjective schizophrenic experience are among the most powerful therapeutic forces in the hospital.

We apply the same general principles to individual psychotherapy. It should be structured and sufficiently concrete to avoid ambiguity. During the period of psychotic panic, the patient is seen daily but for brief periods on the ward or in his room. Tolerance for such dyadic contact is sensitively gauged and never overextended. The focus is on his subjective experience, his feelings about hospitalization and his treatment. Uncertainty, doubt, misgiving and suspicion are constantly clarified in an attempt to nurture a positive and trusting relationship.

We are in agreement with Freeman, Cameron and McGhie[69] who suggest that such interviews be conducted face to face with the patient in a position where he can clearly see everything around him. All extraneous communication or input should be avoided while the content of the therapist's productions should be simple, direct and, at times, repetitive. Sitting behind a perplexed and terrified schizophrenic or forcing him into a supine position is unconscionable. In the same connection, passively waiting for him to provide interview material presents him with a burden he cannot assume and results in greater disorganization.

The use of antipsychotic drugs need not be detailed here. With the possible exception of paranoid males who sometimes experience a paradoxical panic, the majority of acute schizophrenic patients are helped by the drugs. Not only do these drugs reduce anxiety but they also block painful sensory flooding.

Within six weeks the majority of acute schizophrenic patients respond to such an approach and demonstrate significant evidence of restitution. The structure is then loosened and the patient given increasing autonomy. With the subsidence of panic and the disappearance of delusions and hallucinations, attempts can be made to engage him more vigorously in one-to-one psychotherapy. Here again this is a sector psychotherapy with the focus on the precipitants of the illness and the meaning of the psychotic behaviour.

REFERENCES

1. ELKES, J. E., 1961. Schizophrenic disorder in relation to levels of neural organization: the need for some conceptual points of reference. In *The chemical pathology of the nervous system:* Proceedings, Int. Neurochem. Symposium, 3rd Strasbourg, 1958. Ed. Folch-Pi, J. New York: Pergamon Press. pp. 648–65.
2. HOLLISTER, L. E., 1962. Drug induced psychoses and schizophrenic reactions: a critical comparison. *Ann. N.Y. Acad. Sci.*, **96,** 80–88.
3. BLEULER, M., 1959. Comparison of drug induced and endogenous psychoses in man. In *Neuropsychopharmacology:* Proc. of the First Int. Congress of Neuropharmacology. (Rome, Sept. 1958) Eds. Bradley, P. B., *et al.* Amsterdam: Elsevier. pp. 161–65.
4. SHAKOW, D., 1962. Segmental set. *Arch. Gen. Psychiat.*, **6,** 1–17.
5. CHAPMAN, J., and McGHIE, A., 1962. A Comparative study of disordered attention in schizophrenia. *J. Ment. Sci.*, **108,** 487–500.
6. GIFFORD, S., and MURAWSKI, B. J., 1965. Minimal sleep deprivation alone and in small groups. In *Symposium on medical aspects of stress in the military climate.* Walter Reed Army Med. Center, 1964. Washington, D.C.: Govt. Printing Office. pp. 203–09.
7. LUBY, E. D., GRISELL, J. L., FROHMAN, C. E., LEES, H., COHEN, B. D., and GOTTLIEB, J. S., 1962. Biochemical, psychological, and behavioral responses to sleep deprivation. *Ann. N.Y. Acad. Sci.*, **96,** 71–79.
8. BERGER, R. J., and OSWALD, I., 1962. Effects of sleep deprivation on behavior, subsequent sleep and dreaming. *J. Ment. Sci.*, **108,** 457–65.
9. WEST, J. W., JANSZEN, H. H., LESTER, B. K., and CORNELISON, F. S., JR., 1962. The psychosis of sleep deprivation. *Ann. N.Y. Acad. Sci.*, **96,** 66–70.
10. AX, A., and LUBY, E. D., 1961. Autonomic responses to sleep deprivation. *Arch. Gen. Psychiat.*, **4,** 55–59.
11. MALMO, R. B., and SURWILLO, W. W., 1960. Sleep deprivation: changes in performance and physiological indicants of activation. *Psychol. Monogr.*, Gen. and App., **74** (15, whole No. 502).
12. WILKINSON, R. T., 1962. Muscle tension during experimental sleep deprivation. *J. expl. Psychol.*, **64,** 565–71.
13. LUBY, E. D., FROHMAN, C. E., GRISELL, J. L., LENZO, J. E., and GOTTLIEB, J. S., 1960. Sleep deprivation: effects on behavior, thinking, motor performance and biological energy transfer systems. *Psychosom. Med.*, **22,** 182–90.
14. FROHMAN, C. E., and LUBY, E. C., 1965. Some biochemical findings in sleep deprivation. *Symposium on medical aspects of stress in the military climate.* Walter Reed Army Med. Center, 1964. Washington, D.C.: Govt. Printing Office. pp. 203–09.
15. TYLER, D. B., GOODMAN, J., and ROTHMAN, T., 1947. The effect of experimental insomnia on the rate of potential changes in the brain. *Amer. J. Physiol.*, **149,** 185–93.
16. HASSELMAN, M., SCHAFF, G., and METZ, B., 1960. Influences respectives du travail, de la temperature ambiante, et de la privation de sommeil sur l'excretion urinaire de catecholamines chez l'homme normal. *C.R. Soc. Biol.*, **154,** 197.
17. RODIN, E. A., LUBY, E. D., and GOTTLIEB, J. S., 1962. The electroencephalo-

gram during prolonged experimental sleep deprivation. *Electroenceph. Clin. Neurophysiol.*, **14**, 544–51.

18. WILLIAMS, H. L., LUBIN, A., and GOODNOW, J., 1959. Impaired performance with acute sleep loss. *Psychol. Monogr.*, **73** (484), 1–26.

19. KIMBLE, G. A., 1949. An experimental test of a two factor theory of inhibition. *J. Exp. Psychol.*, **39**, 15–23.

20. HULL, C. L., 1943. *Principles of behavior.* New York: Appleton-Century-Crofts.

21. COHEN, B. D., GRISELL, J. L., and AX, A., 1962. The effects of voluntary sleep loss on psychological and physiological functions. *Proc. Third World Cong. Psychiat.* Canada: Univ. of Toronto Press, McGill Univ. Press. pp. 986–91.

22. COHEN, B. D., and GRISELL, J. L., 1963. Some relations between biochemical and schizophrenic subjects. In *Serological fractions in schizophrenia.* Ed. Heath, Robert G. New York: Hoeber Med. Div., Harper and Row. pp. 203–17.

23. CALLAWAY, E., and DEMBO, D., 1958. Narrowed attention. *Amer. med. Assn Arch. Neurol. Psychiat.*, **79**, 74–90.

24. GOTTLIEB, J. S., FROHMAN, C. E., TOURNEY, G., and BECKETT, P. G. S., 1959. Energy transfer systems in schizophrenia: adenosinetriphosphate (ATP). *Amer. med. Assn. Arch. Neurol. Psychiat.*, **81**, 504–08.

25. GOTTLIEB, J. S., FROHMAN, C. E., BECKETT, P. G. S., TOURNEY, G., and SENF, R., 1959. Production of high-energy phosphate bonds in schizophrenia. *Amer. med. Assn. Arch. Gen. Psychiat.*, **1**, 243–49.

26. BECKETT, P. G. S., FROHMAN, C. E., SENF, R., TOURNEY, G., and GOTTLIEB, J. S., 1960. Energy transfer systems and the clinical manifestations of schizophrenia. In *Sci. Papers and Disc. A.P.A. Dist. Br. Pub. I.* Eds. Gottlieb, J. S., and Tourney, G. (Feb. 1960). pp. 278–96.

27. SHURLEY, J. T., 1965. *Symposium on medical aspects of stress in the military climate.* Walter Reed Army Med. Center, 1964. Washington, D.C.: Govt. Printing Office. p. 252.

28. KUBZANSKY, P. E., and LEIDERMAN, P. H., 1961. Sensory deprivation: an overview. In *Sensory deprivation.* Eds. Solomon, Philip, *et al.* Cambridge Mass.: Harvard Univ. Press. pp. 221–38.

29. RIESEN, A. H., 1961. Excessive arousal effects of stimulation after early sensory deprivation. In *Sensory Deprivation.* Eds. Solomon, Philip, *et al.* Cambridge, Mass.: Harvard Univ. Press. pp. 34–40.

30. HARLOW, H. F., 1962. Development of affection in primates. In *Roots of Behavior.* Ed. Bliss, E. L. New York: Harper and Row. pp. 157–66.

31. BRUNER, J. S., 1961. The cognitive consequences of early sensory deprivation. *Sensory Deprivation.* Eds. Solomon, Philip, *et al.* Cambridge, Mass.: Harvard Univ. Press. pp. 195–207.

32. SPITZ, R. A., 1945. Hospitalism: an inquiry into the genesis of psychiatric conditions in early childhood. *Psychoanal. Stud. Child.*, **1**, 53–74.

33. BEXTON, W. H., HERON, W., and SCOTT, T. H., 1954. Effects of decreased variation in the sensory environment. *Canad. J. Psychol.*, **8**, 70–76.

34. LILLY, J. C., 1956. Mental effects of the reduction of ordinary levels of physical stimuli on intact, healthy persons: a symposium. *Psychiat. Res. Rep. Amer. Psychiat. Ass.*, **5**, 1–9.

35. SHURLEY, J. T., 1960. Profound experimental sensory isolation. *Amer. J. Psychiat.*, **117**, 539–45.

36. MENDELSON, J. H., and FOLEY, J. M., 1956. An abnormality of mental function affecting patients with poliomyelitis in a tank-type respirator. *Trans. Amer. Neurol. Ass.*, pp. 134–36.

37. WEXLER, D., MENDELSON, J., LEIDERMAN, P. H., and SOLOMON, P., Sensory deprivation. *Arch. Neurol. Psychiat.*, **79**, 225–33, 1958.

38. ZUBEK, J. P., 1964. Effects of prolonged sensory and perceptual deprivation. *Brit. Med. Bull.*, **20**, 38–42.

39. MYERS, T. I., 1965. Sensory and perceptual deprivation. *Symposium on medical aspects of stress in the military climate*. Walter Reed Army Med. Center, 1964. Washington, D.C.: Govt. Printing Office. pp. 243–51.

40. ZUBEK, J. P., WELCH, G., and SAUNDERS, M. G., 1963. Electroencephalographic changes during and after 14 days of perceptual deprivation. *Science*, **139**, 490–92.

41. FREEDMAN, S. J., GRUNEBAUM, H. V., and GREENBLATT, M., 1961. Perceptual and cognitive changes in sensory deprivation. In *Sensory deprivation*. Eds. Solomon, Philip, *et al.* Cambridge, Mass.: Harvard Univ. Press. pp. 58-71.

42. GOLDBERGER, L., and HOLT, R. R., 1961. Experimental interference with reality contact: individual differences. In *Sensory deprivation*. Eds. Solomon, Philip, *et al.* Cambridge, Mass.: Harvard Univ. Press. pp. 130–42.

43. COHEN, B. D., ROSENBAUM, G., DOBIE, SHIRLEY I., and GOTTLIEB, J. S., 1959. Sensory isolation: hallucinogenic effects of a brief procedure. *J. Nerv. Ment. Dis.*, **129**, 486–91.

44. POLLARD, P. C., UHR, L., and JACKSON, C. W., 1963. Studies in sensory deprivation. *Arch. Gen. Psychiat.*, **8**, 435–54.

45. INGLIS, J., 1965. Sensory deprivation and cognitive disorder. *Brit. J. Psychiat.*, **111**, 309–15.

46. HOFFER, A., and OSMUND, H., 1959. The adrenochrome model and schizophrenia. *J. Nerv. Ment. Dis.*, **128**, 18.

47. HEATH, R. C., MARTENS, S., LEACH, B. E., COHEN, M., and FEIGHLEY, C. A., 1958. Behavioral changes in non-psychotic volunteers following the administration of taraxein, the substance obtained from the serum of schizophrenic patients. *Amer. J. Psychiat.*, **114**, 917.

48. LUBY, E. D., COHEN, B. D., ROSENBAUM, G., GOTTLIEB, J. S., and KELLEY, R., 1959. Study of a new schizophrenomimetic drug—Sernyl. *Amer. med. Assn. Arch. Neurol. Psychiat.*, **81**, 363–69.

49. MEYER, J. S., GREIFENSTEIN, F., and DEVAULT, M., 1959. A new drug causing symptoms of sensory deprivation: neurological, electroencephalographic and pharmacological effects of sernyl. *J. Nerv. Ment. Dis.*, **129**, 54–61.

50. ROSENBAUM, G., COHEN, B. D., LUBY, E. D., GOTTLIEB, J. S., and YELEN, D., 1959. Comparison of sernyl with other drugs. I. Attention, motor function, and proprioception. *Amer. med. Assn. Arch. Gen. Psychiat.*, **1**, 651–56.

51. COHEN, B. D., ROSENBAUM, G., LUBY, E. D., and GOTTLIEB, J. S., 1962. Comparison of phencyclidine hydrochloride (sernyl) with other drugs. II. Symbolic and sequential thinking. *Amer. med. Assn. Arch. Gen. Psychiat.*, **6**, 395–401.

52. COHEN, B. D., LUBY, E. D., ROSENBAUM, G., and GOTTLIEB, J. S., 1960. Combined sernyl and sensory deprivation. *Compr. Psychiat.*, **1**, 6, 345–48.

53. DOMINO, E. F., 1964. Neurobiology of phencyclidine (sernyl), a drug with an unusual spectrum of pharmacological activity. *Int. Rev. Neurobiol.*, **6**, 303–47.

54. CALDWELL, D., and DOMINO, E. F. Unpublished Data.

55. LUBY, E. D., and CALDWELL, D. Unpublished Data.

56. MORUZZI, G., 1966. Significance of sleep for brain mechanisms. In *Brain and conscious experience*. Ed. Eccles, John. New York: Springer Verlag. pp. 338–45.

57. GAARDER, K., 1966. A conceptual model of sleep. *Arch. Gen. Psychiat.*, **14**, 253-60.

58. HERNANDEZ-PEON, R., 1964. Attention, sleep, motivation and behavior. In *The role of pleasure in behavior*. Ed. Heath, Robert G. New York: Harper and Row. pp. 195–217.

59. ROSENBAUM, G., FLENNING, F., and ROSEN, H., 1965. Effects of weight intensity on discrimination thresholds of normals and schizophrenics. *J. Abnorm. Psychol.*, **70**, 446–50.

60. JONES, R. T., BLACKER, K. H., CALLAWAY, E., and LAYNE, R. S., 1965. The auditory evoked response as a diagnostic and prognostic measure in schizophrenia. *Amer. J. Psychiat.*, **122**, 33–41.

61. HERNANDEZ-PEON, R., 1961. Reticular mechanisms of sensory control. In *Sensory Communication*. Ed. Rosenblith, Walter A. Cambridge, Mass.: Massachusetts Institute of Technology. pp. 497–520.

62. LUBY, E. D., GOTTLIEB, J. S., COHEN, B. D., ROSENBAUM, G., and DOMINO, E. F., 1962. Model psychoses and schizophrenia. *Amer. J. Psychiat.*, **119**, 61–67.

63. GIARMAN, N. J., and FREEDMAN, D. X., 1965. Biochemical aspects of the action of psychotomimetic drugs. *Pharmacol. Rev.*, **17**, 1–25.

64. KUBIE, L. S., 1953. The central representation of the symbolic process in psychosomatic disorders. *Psychosom. Med.*, **15**, 1–7.

65. FEDERN, P., 1952. *Ego psychology and the psychoses*. New York, Basic Books.

66. LEES, H., 1961. The effects of 1-(1-phenylcyclohexyl) piperidine hydrochloride (sernyl) on rat liver mitochondria. *Fed. Proc.*, **21**, 306. (Abstract.)

67. VANMETER, W. G., OWENS, H. F., and HIMWICH, H. E., 1960. Effects on rabbit brain of a new drug with psychotomimetic properties. *J. Neuropsychiat.*, **1**, 129–34.

68. SPRAGUE, J. M., CHAMBERS, W. W., and STELLAR, E., 1961. Attentive, affective and adaptive behavior in the cat. *Science*, **133**, 165–73.

69. FREEMAN, T., CAMERON, J. L., and McGHIE, A., 1966. *Studies on psychosis*. New York: International Universities Press. p. 193.

XII

THE NEUROPHYSIOLOGICAL BASIS OF THOUGHT

WILDER PENFIELD
O.M., C.C., M.D., F.R.S.

Honorary Consultant, Montreal Neurological Institute

It was the intention of the Editor that we, who write the chapters of this book, should bring forth 'the facts from the growing points in the field of psychiatry'. He called for a 'personal assessment' and one that is 'practical rather than academic'.

I shall attempt, therefore, with far too little description of the work of others, to set down in personal perspective an outline of localization of function in the brain of man and show which of the localized mechanisms is most intimately related to different aspects of speech, perception, motor skills, conscious control and thought itself. I shall suggest certain hypotheses of interaction and integration. Hypotheses are no more than structural scaffoldings on which to work and build. Psychiatrists and neurologists must use them for what they are.

The human brain and the spinal cord which together constitute the central nervous system can, of course, be looked upon as a functional unit (Fig. 1). But they can also be studied as a collection of functional units coordinated and integrated by a remarkable system of electrical interconnections.

Among the cranial nerves, five provide man with special senses. They have specialized receptor nerve endings in nose and mouth and eye, also in the cochlea and labyrinth of the inner ear. Thus, in addition to somatic sensation which comes to him directly from the body as a whole, man is able to smell and taste, see, hear and balance.

There are many units of automatic action: (*i*) Inborn reflex mechanisms are located in brain stem and spinal cord. These are normally the same for all humans and many of the other mammals. (*ii*) There are also the acquired mechanisms created by the process of conditioning in the cerebral cortex. These provide the automatic machinery that responds to direction by the ever-changing neuronal action which is the counterpart of thought and awareness. Neuronal action may be automatic or conscious. It is based on effective electrical activity in neurones and on conduction along their connections in a meaningful or purposeful pattern. Purpose, in this sense, may, or may not, be automatic.

1

Inborn Reflex Action

There is a great deal of motor activity which is involuntary and dependent on inborn reflex mechanisms in the diencephalon, lower brain-stem and spinal cord. Temperature control is managed by neurone circuits that include small centres of grey matter in the diencephalon. The same is true of sleep, as pointed out by Hess.

Cases of diencephalic autonomic epilepsy demonstrate that there are, within the grey matter covering the third ventricle, centres that control blood pressure, heart rate, vascular dilatation, sweating, salivation, lacrimation, pilomotor reactions, shivering, hiccoughing and yawning (Penfield, 1929).[8]

These are all motor activities dependent on specific reflexes and never activated, as far as my experience goes, by electrical stimulations of the cerebral cortex of patients during operations under local anaesthesia.

The gastro-intestinal system, on the other hand, is clearly influenced by certain areas of cerebral cortex in man. Penfield and Faulk (1955)[16] showed that the cortex covering the insula (Island of Reil) in man is related to sensation and movement in this tract from mouth to rectum.

In the spinal cord, reflex action produces inhibitions and contraction of muscle. It maintains muscle tone and produces reciprocal innervation of agonist and antagonist muscle. Spinal reflexes are, in general, local or segmental. Above the spinal cord, at the level of the lower brain-stem, some of the reflex action begins to exert an influence over the musculature of the whole body. Thus reflex mechanisms in the midbrain wield a powerful control over the posture and the coordinated movement of the whole body. They produce the muscle-tone of standing and the walking rhythms and also the maintenance of positions adopted.

The cerebellum is an outgrowth or dependency of midbrain and pons (Fig. 1). As an organ, it contributes to the smooth accuracy of movement. For example, it is thanks to the cerebellum that the ballet dancer, the gazelle and the bird are able to carry out graceful coordinated action. Its contribution is a secondary one, secondary to voluntary initiation and reflex initiation alike. It does not originate the currents that produce movements but it acts as a perfecting governor.

The mechanical animal, or 'laboratory preparation', that results when the brain has been removed down to the midbrain of cat or monkey, has been used for the analysis of reflexes in lower brain-stem and cord by

Sherrington,[24] Graham Brown and others. This is a 'decerebrate prepara-tion'. When it is kept 'alive' by controlling its temperature artificially, it may be studied for weeks (Bazett and Penfield, 1922).[2] Circulation and respiration continue, but there is no evidence of consciousness or of

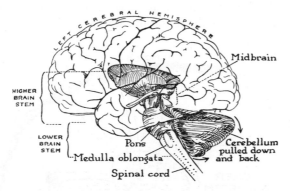

FIG. 1. Left cerebral hemisphere of man. The darkly shaded brain-stem and cerebellum and the spinal cord are shown as they would appear if the hemispheres were removed. The ' higher brain-stem ' may be understood to include the diencephalon, mesencephalon (midbrain) and probably upper portion of metencephalon (pons). The thalamus on each side and the ventrally placed hypothalamus are included in the diencephalon. (Penfield and Roberts, 1959.[22])

capacity to suffer. When a man has a transverse lesion in the midbrain, a somewhat similar situation is produced. There may appear the same types of rigidity in varying patterns, and similar righting reflexes may be present, but there is no evidence of consciousness of any sort.

2

Sensory and Motor Apparatus

The upper end of the brain-stem presents two enlargements of grey matter, the right and the left thalamus. The cerebral hemispheres on each side are the outward projections of the thalamic nuclei. This is suggested by Fig. 2. In Fig. 3, the areas of the cortex covering the left hemisphere are labelled according to their thalamic origins.

It has often been assumed that because the cerebral cortex, from a philogenetic point of view, is a recent development (and because, in man, it is comparatively such a vast ganglionic blanket) that the cortex is responsible for man's intellectual supremacy. This is no doubt true. But it has also been assumed that the cerebral cortex is the end station of the sensory afferents and the origin of the voluntary motor efferents. This is not true. The truth is that there are, in the cortex, separable sensory and motor areas which serve as way-stations to and from the higher brain stem. These are much the same for man and other mammals.

The ganglionic target of the various afferent sensory tracts is in the thalamic nuclei. Auditory, visual and discriminatory-somatic sensation make an essential detour from thalamus out to cortex and back to the end-target in the higher brain-stem, instead of stopping there on first arrival. The currents of pain sensation, however, do not make a cortical

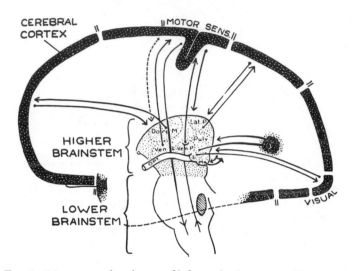

Fig. 2. Diagrammatic scheme of left cerebral cortex to illustrate its direct connections with the underlying thalamic nuclei. The afferent somatic input is shown coming up through the spinal cord and lower brain-stem. Passing through an interruption in the thalamus, it goes on to the sensory convolution of the cortex and back to thalamus. The efferent voluntary output is shown coming through thalamus to motor convolution and on out in the cortico-spinal tract to the muscles (Penfield and Jasper, 1954.[19])

detour. Head and Holmes (1911)[4] showed that the thalamus alone has to do, also, with the ' physiological processes which underlie the crude aspects of sensations of contact, heat and cold'. Thus the eventual *rendezvous* for all forms of sensory information brought to consciousness is in the higher brain-stem.

If the brain and spinal cord are compared to a railway system, the final 'arrival platform' in 'central station' is sub-cortical. The sensory detours to areas on the cortex are no more than way-stations. Incoming traffic stops there, but passes on into the sub-cortical arrival platform. The motor departure platform is likewise sub-cortical. The motor area in the cortex serves as a way-station for outward-bound traffic. Much of the evidence that leads one to think in terms of the foregoing communication parable is to be found in the neurosurgeon's experience with the human cerebral cortex. The space limitation of this chapter forbids description of the evidence (Penfield, 1950[10]; Penfield and Rasmussen, 1950[21]; Penfield, 1958[12]; Penfield and Jasper, 1954[19]; Penfield, 1960[13]).

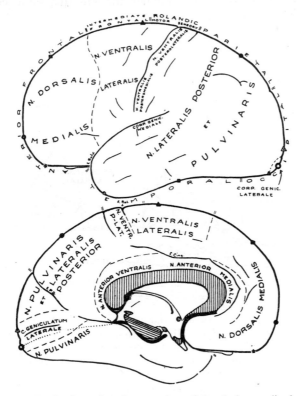

FIG. 3. Projection of nuclear masses of the thalamus (including the geniculate bodies) out to the lateral surface of the left hemisphere (above) and the mesial surface (below). Drawn for man, after extrapolation, from studies of the anthropoid brain made by Earl Walker (1938).[25] The corpus callosum, which is shown as cut across and shaded, is a major tract of direct transcortical connecting fibres.

The location of the sensory areas in the human cortex are outlined in Fig. 4, as worked out by cortical stimulation during operations under local anaesthesia and by planned excisions of cortex in the treatment of focal epilepsy.

It can be stated with certainty that unilateral removal of the cerebral cortex which is adjacent to and surrounds the precentral motor gyrus does not interfere with the ability of an individual to carry out delicate, normally directed voluntary movements in the contralateral limbs. This extirpation of surrounding cortex does, however, remove all trans-cortical connections to that gyrus.

It is necessary, therefore, to conclude that the outgoing efferent stream of electrical potentials, which controls voluntary movement, originates not in the cortex but in a more central area of the higher brainstem. One is forced to assume further that, in this same central area

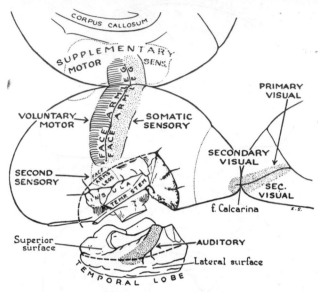

Fig. 4. Primary sensory and motor areas of the human cortex (sensory: dotted, and motor: lined) with some secondary and supplementary areas in the cortex of the lateral surface of the left hemisphere. Localizations are derived from stimulation evidence during operation on conscious patients.

Parts of the mesial surfaces are shown above and on the right. The temporal lobe has been cut and turned down to expose its superior surface (which is ordinarily hidden in the fissure of Sylvius) and the primary auditory area on the transverse gyrus of Heschl. No secondary auditory-sensory area is figured, since our stimulation evidence does not distinguish it from adjacent interpretive cortex shown in Figure 13. (Penfield and Roberts, 1959.[22])

(diencephalon and perhaps mesencephalon) the integration takes place that is pre-requisite to planned movement. This means that a patterned stream of potentials passes out to the motor cortex area (of both hemispheres) as suggested by the broken lines in Fig. 5.

In Fig. 6B, the motor sequence in the primary cortical motor area of man is set down in detail and the length of the segments of the broad line shows the comparative amount of cortex devoted to each body part. The overlying motor homunculus (drawn by Hortense Douglas) demonstrates, in a grotesque but revealing manner, the relative importance of these body parts in the cortical scheme of things. It suggests that the elaboration of complex movements of the hand and fingers in digital skills, and the control of lips and tongue and diaphragm in speaking, constitute the major cortical contribution to motor function.

In Fig. 6A, the artist has pictured the relative extent of the post-central gyrus devoted to each body part. Transcortical connecting nerve fibres

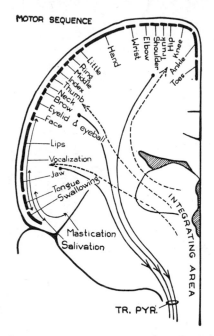

FIG. 5. *Voluntary Motor System.* A diagrammatic cross-section through the right hemisphere along the plane of the precentral gyrus is viewed from in front. The pathway of control of consciously directed movement is suggested as originating somewhere in the grey matter of the higher brain stem. The patterned message passes outward, as shown by the broken lines, to the motor transmitting strip of the precentral gyrus. From there, after elaboration, it continues down the cortico-spinal tract, as shown by the unbroken lines, toward the muscles. (Penfield and Jasper, 1954.[19])

between pre- and post-central convolutions no doubt play an important role in skilful acts. Stimulation of the motor gyrus occasionally (once in four times) produces sensation, and stimulation of the sensory gyrus occasionally produces movement. But removal of motor gyrus devoted to hand and fingers produces paralysis of the part with preservation of discriminatory sensation. Removal of sensory gyrus for hand brings complete loss of discriminatory sensation with preservation of conscious motor control of the part. But the movement has now become awkward. One may surmise, therefore, that the sensory cortex transmits information to higher brain-stem. It contributes much to motor hand-skills, a contribution that is probably direct as well as indirect.

Skills and Conditioning

It is clear that skills of hand and foot and mouth and vocalization are made possible by acquired mechanisms established in the primary (and probably also secondary and supplementary motor) somatic areas of the cerebral cortex.

When well learned, man's skills may be carried out while he is thinking of something else. But in the beginning, during the acquisition of each of the underlying mechanisms, he must focus his attention upon the proposi-

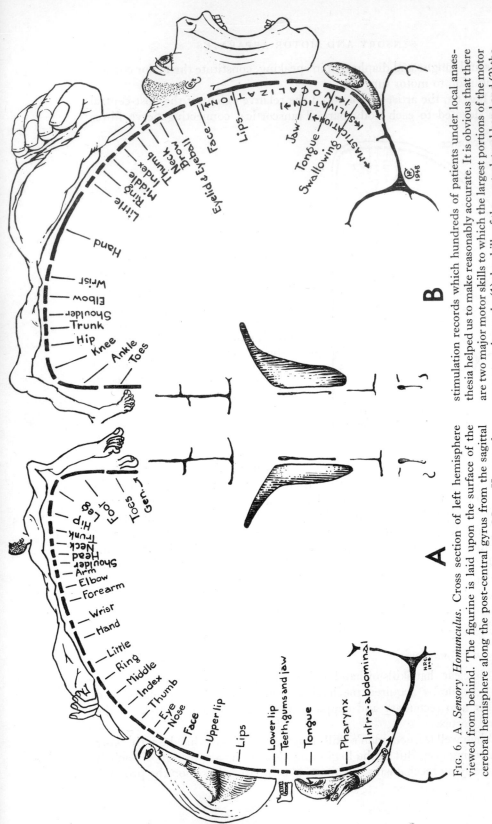

FIG. 6. A. *Sensory Homunculus.* Cross section of left hemisphere viewed from behind. The figurine is laid upon the surface of the cerebral hemisphere along the post-central gyrus from the sagittal fissure above to the fissure of Sylvius below. B. *Motor Homunculus.* Cross-section along the line of the precentral gyrus of the left hemisphere viewed from in front.

The broad broken line on the hemisphere surface of A and B

stimulation records which hundreds of patients under local anaesthesia helped us to make reasonably accurate. It is obvious that there are two major motor skills to which the largest portions of the motor cortex are devoted : (1) the skills of the contralateral hand and (2) the uses of the bilateral muscles of articulation and respiration in speech.

Movement of hand (with fingers) and also sensation of hand (including fingers) is separate from the single digits. The turning of tion. The action and the focusing of attention are always voluntary and conscious in the outset.

These become 'conditioned reflexes', as first understood and described by Ivan Pavlov. Working with dogs, he described learning as a process based on the establishment of conditioned reflexes in the cerebral cortex. He showed that cortical excision would abolish each newly-acquired conditioned reflex. The animal lost what he had learned. In man, such heedless cortical excision as he carried out would have produced hand paralysis, as well, or aphasia. It was not so with the paw, or the bark, of a dog. Pavlov's basic suggestion, however, is valid for man—that learning depends upon the establishment of acquired reflexes in the cerebral cortex and related thalamus.

Conscious Control

In time, such activities as driving an automobile or writing or talking or playing a piano may be carried out subconsciously. Starting and stopping the mechanism, at least, is a conscious act. One may assume that there is usually intermittent conscious guidance. But paying attention to the mechanics of these skills (for example, hitting a golf ball) may, in time, seem to interfere with the expertness of performance.

In this semi-independent activity, I surmise that no part of the cortex is ever acting quite alone without some control through back-and-forth connections from and to the higher brain-stem. We may assume also, as will be pointed out, that conscious direction is never possible without neuronal action in some portion of the diencephalon.

As is suggested in Fig. 2 and Fig. 5, the important nerve fibres that carry impulses to the cortex and away to the medulla and spinal cord are close to each other and run, for some distance, in parallel lines, although in opposite directions. Thus, ordinary pathological lesions interrupt both limbs of the motor efferent stream. This explains why the stream of impulses responsible for planned bodily action was so long considered to originate in the cortex.

Any pathological or surgical interference with a sensory or motor area of cerebral cortex interferes with its use, but the individual is still conscious and may well use other areas of cortex to carry out a selected plan. If the right hand is paralysed or the right field of vision is blind, due to cortical injury, he 'makes do' with the left hand or turns his eyes to expose more of the other side of the retina and so makes use of the normal field of vision remaining to him.

Indeed any area of cerebral cortex can be destroyed or removed without loss of consciousness. But when the higher brain-stem is rendered inactive, there follows immediate unconsciousness. Neuronal action in this central area may be arrested by injury or tumour, by the discharge of an epileptic seizure or by the local loss of circulation during fainting, or by the more normal physiological alteration that comes with sleep.

3

Scientific Approach to the Study of the Brain Mechanisms of Man

Experimental physiologists have made most important contributions to knowledge of the functional anatomy of motor and sensory mechanisms in the animal brain. They have studied the integration of the inborn reflexes and the formation of conditioned reflexes. But there is a whole field of brain problems, that relate to the mind, which can only be studied when man himself is the subject.

Reference to Fig. 7 shows that in lower mammals there is very little

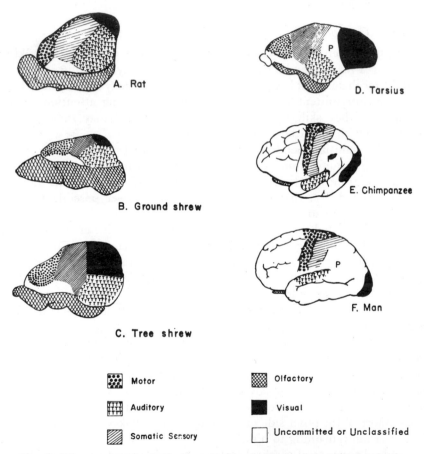

Fig. 7. The mammalian brain from rat to man, prepared by Stanley Cobb to illustrate quickly the vast proportional increase in cerebral cortex not committed to sensory or motor function.

uncommitted or unclassified cortex until, in an ascending scale, the anthropoid ape is reached. It shows further that, passing from chimpanzee to man, a major increase occurs in the uncommitted and unclassified portions of the brain.

Human neurophysiology now constitutes a new science of its own. It is a clinical, rather than a laboratory science. It should never be experimental. But, to the clinician who is willing to wait, chance eventually presents the most perfect experiments for his observation. Modern methods of recording and operating, electrical techniques of stimulating and recording, and the mutual understanding that develops between conscious patient and skilled observer, has opened a scientific approach to the brain's action that forms the physical basis of the mind.

A short discussion of at least four of the methods of study open to the clinician may serve as a preamble to a further consideration of speech, perception and consciousness. (The art of diagnosis, electroencephalography, special radiography, neurocytology, pathology and chemistry are important too, but may not be discussed here.)

The Clinical Lesion

The chance occurrence of a discrete pathological lesion sometimes inactivates one convolution or a group of convolutions of the cerebral cortex. Paul Broca (1861)[3] discovered thus that there was a speech mechanism in the human brain that could be paralysed without other evidence of interference in brain function.

Epilepsy

Epileptic attacks which are due to local explosive discharges of electrical energy may, on occasion, block and thus paralyse a single brain mechanism. On occasion, too, the attack activates a discrete mechanism by its local electrical stimulation. This fact provided Hughlings Jackson with a key to insight into functional localization within the human brain.

If an attack begins in the somatic sensory or motor area, the discharge may cause a tingling, a numbness, or a movement in, for example, the opposite thumb. A Jacksonian march may carry it slowly in any direction across the cortex. If the epileptogenic abnormality happens to originate in the visual grey matter of the cerebral cortex, the first symptom of an attack will be awareness of sudden lights and colours, associated with temporary blindness. Any such minor attack may 'trigger' a major convulsive seizure.

Attacks which begin with discharge in the grey matter within the higher brain-stem have a different character. Here loss of consciousness is apt to be the initial phenomenon. This, and perhaps falling, due to interference with the midbrain standing and postural reflexes, may be all. These small (petit mal) attacks or large (grand mal) attacks, due to higher brain-stem discharge, are easily recognized in the electroencephalographic tracing from the scalp. They are ushered in by rhythmic spike-and-slow-wave changes in the electroencephalogram. Electrical stimulation at certain sites in the diencephalon produces the same form of bilateral EEG wave sequences.

In the cerebral cortex, spread of discharge may be through contiguous grey matter. It may also be by axonal conduction to distant functionally related grey matter. Thus discharge may spread across the corpus callosum to corresponding cortex of the other hemisphere. Or, it may spread from cortex to grey matter in higher brain-stem. In either case, the attack at once becomes a major convulsion.

Cortical Excision

Planned excision of cortical convolutions may, by chance, fulfil all the requirements of a scientific experiment. It is possible to remove convolutions from the brain, leaving the underlying white matter intact and without producing abnormality of circulation in the remaining convolutions. Thus, in selected patients whose epilepsy is due to localized epileptogenic abnormality of the cortex, it is possible to remove the cause.

Cure by such a method must, of course, be balanced against loss of the function of the excised convolutions, if they are still functional. In any case, the surgeon does well to make a preliminary survey of the cortex before removal, mapping out the function of the convolutions with the help of a stimulating electrode. He may also map out the extent of epileptogenic abnormality by means of direct electro-corticography. He must also protect the patient from pain by local anaesthesia, and from anxiety by carrying on calm running conversation with him. Surgery, in any case, should be reserved for selected cases. If a patient can lead a useful, happy life with the help of conservative medication and care, he should not be considered a candidate for craniotomy. But, when medical therapy fails, and if there is evidence of a cortical focus, the chance of a cure by neurosurgery is good.

Electrical Stimulation

The neurosurgeon can use electrical stimulation to reproduce any fit which ordinarily begins in an abnormal epileptogenic area of the cerebral cortex. (The patient will often say, 'That is the way they begin.') But, if he is careful to use a mild stimulus, no after-discharge occurs and no fit follows. The surgeon can also use an electrode to map out the normally responsive functional areas, thus increasing the accuracy and the safety of proposed surgical excision of the epileptogenic areas of cortex. The patient, who is inevitably well aware of the need for accuracy, can talk with him and guide his hand.

In a small book called *The excitable cortex in conscious man* (Penfield, 1958),[12] I undertook to study the significance and the interpretation of cortical stimulations. Some areas of cerebral cortex respond in a positive manner to electrical stimulation. Others do not. But, in all areas, the application of a current interferes temporarily with the normal employment of that area of cortex.

Electrical Interference

While the electrode is applied to an area of cortex, the patient cannot use the functional mechanism of which the area forms a part. While the electrode is producing, for example, flashing lights in one visual field by application to the contralateral occipital cortex, the patient is also blind to lighted objects in the field. While the electrode is causing movement of the right thumb, the patient has lost all control over it. When the electrode is applied to the speech cortex, there is no positive response. The patient is aware of nothing new. But, when he tries to speak, or read, or write, he finds himself aphasic.

TABLE 1

Psychical responses to electrical stimulation
of interpretive areas of cortex

A. *Experiential Flash-Back:* Random re-enactment of a conscious sequence from the patient's past.

B. *Interpretive Signalling:* Production of sudden interpretations of the present experience, such as *familiar, strange, fearful, coming nearer, going away,* etc.

Positive Response

In regard to the positive response, my final conclusion was this: 'The principal cortical areas of the human brain that yield positive responses to gentle electrical stimulation may be placed in three groups: sensory, motor and interpretive. The positive effects of stimulation seem to be due to dromic cortico-fugal conduction to distant but functionally connected nerve-cell groups.'[12]

'Dromic conduction' means passage of impulses from a nerve-cell along its axone, as in normal neuronal activity, to some other cell or cells which may be at a distance. Neuronal action, then, is caused to take place at the next ganglionic station. Conduction to it, in that case, is not by diffuse escape of current. It is axonal and, in a sense, physiological. Thus, stimulation of a sensory area of cortex activates, by its normal linkage, certain ganglion cells in the thalamo-diencephalic target which was discussed above. Stimulation of the motor cortex activates (by efferent conduction) motor nuclei in the lower brain-stem or the spinal cord.

How to interpret the results of electrical stimulation of the cortical speech areas calls for further consideration. The surprisingly different result of stimulating the homologous area of the cortex in the non-dominant hemisphere also needs explanation. The structure of nerve cells and nerve-fibre tracts was, presumably, identical at birth on the two sides. But after the child has learned to speak and to interpret the meaning of his environment, the functioning connections of the adult are obviously quite different on the two sides.

If the electrode has any effect (discoverable by surgeon or patient) when applied to the speech area, the result is interference-aphasia. If it has any effect when applied to the other side, the result is a positive response—either a sudden interpretation of present experience or an equally sudden re-run of a strip of conscious experience from the past.

These are facts, not theories. One conclusion is clear: The initially uncommitted cortex of the temporal regions is programmed by the child during early years of life—programmed for speech, or for perception, but not for both. The functioning connections, that are established while the child is learning to speak and to perceive, are quite different. One must assume that, during the process of learning, the passage of electrical potentials along one (of many possible collateral branches of a neurone and through the junction of that branch with another cell) facilitates that pathway. In time, the facilitation becomes absolute and the linkage of the cell is fixed.

Such are some of the data that have come to light through electrical stimulation of the cortex of the conscious patient. With the new evidence comes the new opportunity, indeed the responsibility, of considering what new light the facts may shed on the nature of thought and consciousness.

4

Frontal Lobes and Planned Initiative

Before discussing the initially uncommitted cortex of the temporal regions further, we may consider the presently unclassified cortex of anterior portions of the frontal lobes. Man's high bulging forehead bears testimony to the comparative enlargement of frontal cortex, since skull growth in each individual is normally a response to the outward thrust of the brain during its rapid growth in the first years of life. The anterior half of the frontal lobe is covered by cortex, the function of which is still difficult to define. It constitutes the cortical projection of the dorso-medial nucleus of the thalamus, as shown in Fig. 3. Posterior to it are the supplementary motor area, the primary motor strip and the anterior speech area (Broca) as outlined in Figs. 9 and 11. There is also a zone between Broca's area (below) and the supplementary motor area (above) where stimulation produces contraversive eye turning. All of these areas of active response to stimulation (back as far as the central fissure) correspond roughly to the cortical projection of the nucleus ventralis lateralis of the thalamus (Fig. 3).

Frontal pole stimulation produces no easily detectable effect. The same is true of frontal pole removal. On the other hand, if the stimulus were strong enough to produce after-discharge and thus an epileptic fit, the first evidence of that fit would be loss of consciousness. We have seen this happen. This is to be explained by the axonal bombardment of grey matter in the higher brain-stem, bombardment of sufficient intensity to cause epileptic discharge there. Spontaneous epileptic fits, which begin with discharge in one frontal pole, characteristically begin with a blank expression, and perhaps turning of the eyes to the opposite side, followed by loss of consciousness. Fits that are caused by initial discharge in the diencephalon begin, as already mentioned, with loss of consciousness. Hughlings Jackson referred to attacks of this sort as 'highest level fits' (Penfield and Jasper, 1947).[17] We have called them centrencephalic seizures.

For our present purposes, let us conclude from this discussion of fits arising in one frontal pole, only that there is a remarkably direct connection between the pole and the highest level of neuronal integration. The unclassified cortex of the frontal poles and the initially uncommitted cortex of the temporal regions have a more direct access to these circuits (as shown by seizure patterns) than do the sensory and motor areas of the cortex (Penfield, 1952).[11]

Hippocrates understood that epilepsy was the great teacher. It was in his lecture on 'The Sacred Disease' that he wrote: 'Through it [the brain] in particular, we think, see, hear and distinguish the ugly from the beautiful, the bad from the good, the pleasant from the unpleasant. . . . To consciousness the brain is messenger.' After twenty centuries, one can only continue to quote these words with wonder. Perhaps Apollo took a hand in the enlightenment of the Father of Medicine, using the patterned fits of 'epilepsia' to teach him the simple truth!

Study of cases in which removal of one or both frontal poles has been carried out should throw some light on function. The same is true of critical study of the effects of leucotomy (the cutting of the projection fibres from thalamus to frontal pole, often referred to as lobotomy).

To this end, seven patients, who were suffering from some form of psychosis, were selected. They were considered by the psychiatrists, Professor Ewen Cameron and Dr. Miguel Prados, to be reasonable candidates for therapeutic leucotomy. It was thought that gyrectomy might serve them as well or better. So, carefully planned and symmetrically placed removals of anterior frontal cortex were carried out in different positions.

The conclusions drawn from the eventual post-operative study were these: the alterations produced in each patient were restricted to the field of personality and intellectual ability. The nearer the removals were to the tip of the pole and the inferior surfaces of the frontal lobes, the less was the evidence of functional loss or change. When the bilateral excisions were placed in a superior position, close to, or including part of the supplementary motor area, the patients were confused, incontinent, apathetic, repetitive. These symptoms disappeared slowly after two to five months. But further conclusions were difficult, as always in such patients, since they were not normal mentally at the start (Penfield, 1947).[9]

12

Somewhat clearer evidence was drawn from study of the results of maximal frontal lobe removals in the treatment of brain tumour or of traumatic epilepsy. These patients had never been subject to any form of psychosis. The general conclusion from study of very large removals of the anterior frontal lobe on either side were as follows:

Insight and capacity for introspection were well preserved. Capacity to follow instructions was unimpaired. But *initiative* and *capacity for self-planned action* were clearly defective. In so far as final conclusion was justifiable, it was determined that 'maximum amputation of right, or left frontal lobe has for its most important detectable sequel impairment of those mental processes which are pre-requisite to *planned initiative*' (Penfield and Evans, 1935).[15]

5

Speech

It was man's capacity to learn and to develop acquired skills that singled him out from other mammals during the later stages of mammalian evolution on this planet. It is not known when, in evolutionary time, he developed dominance for hand movements. At least one can say it was more than three and a half millennia ago. Russell Brain called attention to the fact that in the year 1406 B.C. there were (in the Army of the Children of Benjamin), according to the Biblical record, seven hundred chosen left-handed men who 'could sling stones at an hair breadth, and not miss'. At least 8·7 per cent of the army were left handers. Obviously, at that time, the great majority were right handed. Man probably developed hand dominance as early as the appearance of organized language, but this is pure surmise.

Brain Dominance

Dominance in favour of one extremity is peculiar to man. There is also a far more important cerebral dominance, that for speech. In the great majority of human beings, the left hemisphere is dominant for both hand and speech. But this is not invariable. When I refer to the dominant hemisphere, I shall mean the one in which the speech mechanism is located. Throughout the discussion of speech, I shall draw heavily on the work of others and on our own studies recorded and documented in previous writings (Penfield and Roberts, 1959).[22]

Without quoting statistics, it is enough to say that right-handers, almost invariably, are found to have the speech mechanism in the left hemisphere. Left-handers sometimes have speech in the right hemisphere, sometimes in the left. When there is injury to the cortical motor-area of the right hand at birth, or during early childhood, hand dominance appears on the other side. Speech dominance does not shift with hand dominance unless there is also injury to the major speech area in the cortex or damage to the underlying nucleus in the thalamus.

Aphasia

If a child has already learned to speak, destruction of the speech mechanism in the left hemisphere produces complete aphasia. At the end of about a year of silence, the child begins to speak again and he or she may learn to speak perfectly. The speech mechanism will then be found, newly established, in the other hemisphere. If brain injury occurs after the age of ten or twelve, however, such a complete transference does not take place. The adult, who has become aphasic after a severe brain injury or haemorrhage involving the major speech area, may improve, but he is no longer able to make a complete recovery. He cannot, it seems, set up a completely new mechanism for language in the other hemisphere.

There are probably two reasons for this:

1. The young child has an amazing capacity for acquiring the basic units of the mother tongue (and other secondary languages at the same age, if he is allowed to hear them). He listens and imitates and, in so doing, establishes the neuronal set, the brain-patterning of a language. From six years onward, he can add to his vocabulary with ease in any language already set. But from this time onward, the unilingual child loses progressively the facility of establishing the basic brain-pattern of a new language.

2. The second reason one cannot shift speech to the other side after entering the teens is that the cortex of the non-dominant hemisphere has not been idle. It is not a 'silent area'. It has been progressively 'programmed', before that time, to subserve a different function. It is reasonable to assume, then, that the nerve cells on the right which might have accepted the imprint of a language are too busy after the age of ten or twelve. To express it another way, the interneuronal connections are set finally to serve a different mechanism. The paths of facilitated passage for electrical potentials are fixed parts of the perception mechanism.

This throws some light on the facility for language learning possessed by an individual who hears a second and perhaps a third language before, say, the age of six. He establishes a 'set' for each language (in the dominant hemisphere) and develops a remarkable subconscious 'switch' technique that 'turns on' one 'tongue' at a time. In later years, he can add at will to his vocabulary in any of the languages for which the set has been established, doing it easily and without an awkward accent.

The Blank Slate

Reference to Fig. 7 shows the large extent of the cerebral cortex that has appeared in man between the visual cortex posteriorly and the auditosensory and somatosensory cortex anteriorly. This newly-appearing cortex, in the temporal region, may be used for speech or for the mechanism of perception. At the time of birth, it is not committed in regard to either function. The sensory and motor areas are committed.

Much of the infant's temporal cortex may thus be compared to a clean slate. It will be utilized and written upon as the child grows older and *pays attention* to language and to experience. Speech and perception depend upon acquired ideational mechanisms established by the child in this great zone of cortex. The mechanisms come to serve the adult as an aid to interpretation—interpretation of speech posteriorly on the dominant side (speech cortex), interpretation of experience in the light of the individual's past in the other portions of both sides (interpretive cortex).

Consider the posterior temporal area of the cerebral cortex on the right (non-dominant) side of any adult. This would have been used for speech if that function were not being established on the left: removal of this area on the right, if carried out in adult life, produces no interference with speech. It does, however, produce a loss of awareness of body-scheme and of spatial relationships (Fig. 8). This functional deficit has

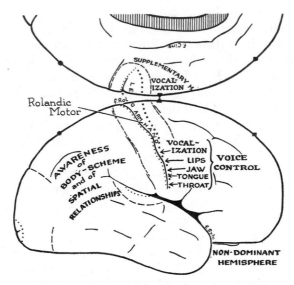

FIG. 8. *Non-dominant hemisphere.* The voice control is the same as on the dominant side. Its removal on either side produces no more than motor difficulty of enunciation. Removal of cortex about the posterior end of the fissure of Sylvius, if complete, produces loss of perception of spatial relationships. (Hécaen, Penfield *et al.*, 1956.[5])

been described by many clinicians and summarized by Critchley. Riddoch (also Brain) referred to it as visual disorientation, Hécaen as *troubles visuo-constructifs* or apractognosia. Patients who have lost this area of the non-dominant cortex are unable to interpret visuo-sensory information, unable to orient themselves in space.

Cortical Speech Areas

Fig. 9 presents the dominant hemisphere. The area, that was used on the other side to orient an individual in space, is here devoted to the ideational transactions of language. It is the major speech area originally described by Wernicke (1874).[26] The anterior speech cortex, as discovered by Broca (1861),[3] must be considered a secondary area. Aphasia follows its removal but it clears up (after months or years, even in the adult) provided the major posterior area of Wernicke is intact. The third speech centre, which we may call supplementary or superior, is still more easily

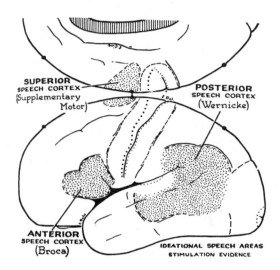

FIG. 9. *Speech areas of dominant hemisphere.* This map is derived from a complete summary of the use of electrical interference to localize speech. (Penfield and Roberts, 1959.[22])

dispensable. It is located in the general supplementary motor area. Aphasia does not continue following its removal for more than a few weeks. In this illustration (Fig. 9) the limits of the speech areas were established by summarizing the evidence derived from a long series of cases in which speech was mapped out by means of electrical interference.

Application of the electrode to a speech area produces no positive phenomena. It does produce aphasia which the patient only discovers when called upon to speak or to read. The type and degree of speech interference is much the same regardless of which of the three areas is subjected to an interfering current. It is equally irresistible. This suggests that the anterior and superior areas have effective axonal entrance into the thalamic nucleus which has its direct connection with the major speech cortex. It suggests, too, that it is axonal conduction (not spread of current) from cortex to thalamus that produces the temporary interference.

Fig. 10 shows, by broken lines, the connection of the posterior cortical speech area of the left hemisphere with the underlying thalamus (pulvinar). A destructive lesion there produces aphasia. But if the lesion is placed more centrally or below, the syndrome of aphasia never appears. Instead, all awareness vanishes and the patient is unconscious. Something analagous occurs as the result of a lesion in the homologous zone in the non-dominant hemisphere. There is loss of perception of space relationships. This, too, can be produced only in cortex and thalamus.

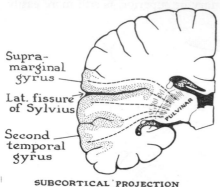

Supra-
marginal
gyrus

Lat. fissure
of Sylvius

Second
temporal
gyrus

SUBCORTICAL PROJECTION
to SPEECH CORTEX

FIG. 10. *Cortico-thalamic connections* – for the posterior cortical area of the speech mechanism in the dominant hemisphere. Similar connections serve the spatial perception mechanism in the non-dominant hemisphere.

These two cortico-thalamic mechanisms (speech and space orientation) can be activated only by neuronal action in the diencephalon. This action corresponds with conscious thinking. We may say it accompanies thought. Here are some of the neurophysiological mechanisms that form the *physical basis of thought*.

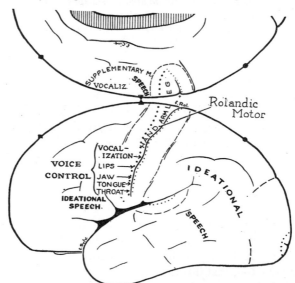

FIG. 11. *Dominant hemisphere* of the human adult. Compare with Fig. 8. There are no indispensable transcortical connections between the cortical speech areas and the motor areas for vocalization and verbal articulation.

Compare now Fig. 11 with Fig. 8. The motor control of throat, tongue, jaw, lips and vocalization has a cortical area on each side. Removal of this sensori-motor area for voice control on the right produces no more than anarthria, to the extent of thickness of speech which tends to clear up in time. Excision of the lower end of the motor strip on the left side we have also carried out (although rarely) in order to remove an epileptogenic focus. This was done first with some misgiving since it was sure also to interrupt whatever direct transcortical connection there might be between the anterior and posterior ideational speech areas. The result was temporary post-operative aphasia, but that cleared up, leaving only anarthria such as would have appeared following removal on the other side. We have never removed any of the major speech cortex because of the fact that speech is never to be forfeited even in exchange for freedom from fits. But we have removed blocks of epileptogenic cortex in various positions all around the major speech area. None of these excisions produced an enduring aphasia. By summarizing them all, a map of the three cortical speech areas was produced. It corresponded closely with the map (shown in Fig. 9) prepared by the method of electrical interference.

It must be clear, therefore, that the anterior and the superior areas of speech cortex play some sort of secondary role, analagous perhaps to the secondary visual cortex and the second somatic sensory cortex and the supplementary motor cortex. Wernicke's (posterior) area, which could be called 'major' or perhaps 'primary', is bounded by the visual cortex behind and in front by the audito-sensory and voice-control areas. Nevertheless, it is clear that transcortical inter-communication (however useful it may be) is not essential for speaking, writing or understanding speech.

The Patterning of Potentials

Suppose one listens to the word 'apple' spoken by a companion—the sound waves activate those nerve cells in the cochlea of the inner ear that correspond with each vibration frequency. The electrical potentials thus evoked make up an afferent auditory stream, a specific message-pattern, which is flashed to the thalamic nuclei and out to the audito-sensory cortex on both sides, then back into the circuits of central integration. There, the potentials can presumably be blocked by inattention. Or they may be sent on to the ideational speech mechanism. An alteration that we may call 'translation' must then take place in the speech mechanism. The message, now altered in its potential pattern, passes back into appropriate circuits of the central integrating system and evokes, in the mind, the idea of a familiar, rounded, coloured, eatable fruit.

If the individual chooses to repeat the word, as a young child is apt to do, a stream of patterned potentials must pass out from the central integrating complex to the voice-control portion of the motor cortex on both sides and so down to the appropriate motor nuclei in the pons and medulla oblongata, causing the word 'apple' to be spoken.

For reading, a similar succession must be hypothecated: Seeing the word 'apple' written on a page, a similar afferent message and translation sequence is set off, beginning this time in the visual system. The light waves activate nerve cells in the retina in a pattern that corresponds with the written word. The message pattern of potentials flashed from retina through thalamus to visual cortex of both sides and back through thalamic nuclei to the central integrating system where the two patterned halves are combined. From there the message of patterned potentials goes out to the speech mechanism. Here it is translated and flashed back into appropriate central integrating circuits. Again the idea of an apple is evoked.

What I have referred to as an 'auditory message-pattern' and a visual 'message of pattern potentials', D. H. Hubel described more aptly, no doubt, as a coded arrangement of nerve impulses. Russell Brain referred cautiously to 'schemata' in the 'realm of speech' and of recognition patterns of nerve impulse.

When an adult listens to words, he comes in time to ignore all of the process described above and is aware only of the succession of ideas evoked. But the child in the learning state is conscious of the sound of the spoken word and the shape of the written word and is excited by the first evocation of the idea. Later, however, by the time the relationship is learned, a conditioned reflex has been set up and the whole process by which the adult derives ideas becomes a subconscious one.

When the affair described above is reversed, the apple itself is presented and the child sees it, speaks the word, learns to write it, quite conscious of each sound and shape. The adult, however, speaks the word on seeing the object, or writes it, oblivious of the mechanism. Thus he is able to focus his attention on meanings or ideas. The important point is that the learner can only acquire a conditioned reflex in the full light of conscious attention.

Attention

A child learns when paying attention. If he is keenly interested at the moment in something else, such as in an idea of his own, a desire of his own, or the appearance of an approaching dog, he will not hear the word 'apple', nor see the word, even if he seems to look at the page on which it is written. He may not see the object if it is placed before him. Active inhibition, of incoming streams of information, is obviously a part of the neuronal mechanism of the focusing of attention. Inhibition or blockade of messages seems to be exerted at some point quite early in the input sequence, a fact that need not be discussed here. Language learning may be looked upon as the process of setting up conditioned reflexes in the uncommitted cortex of the dominant hemisphere. Thus a speech mechanism is created. But there is another brain mechanism which must be created. It serves the purposes of concept perception.

6

Perception and the Interpretive Cortex

Words are symbols. Before a child can speak and understand the meaning of the word that stands for 'apple', whether it is written or spoken, he must have a concept of what an apple is. Indeed perception and speech are normally acquired at the same stage in life step-by-step. During the process, the initially uncommitted cortex is conditioned by the child and his teacher. Thus, the *speech cortex* is conditioned for speech. The remainder of the initially uncommitted cortex (which we have called *interpretive cortex*) is programmed to serve the purposes of perception. Two brain mechanisms are thus being established which, it will be shown, can operate separately. A stimulating electrode, applied to the speech cortex, produces only interference aphasia without loss of non-verbal perception. From the interpretive cortex, positive psychical responses have been obtained, a vastly different phenomenon.

Physical Responses

The word 'psychical', as used here, was borrowed from Hughlings Jackson who recognized that fits, derived from discharges in either temporal region, might have an 'intellectual aura'. He referred to such fits as 'dreamy states'.[6] We may call them psychical seizures. They are of two kinds: (i) One is an illusion during which there is a sudden change in the patient's interpretation of present experience. He calls the environment 'familiar' or 'strange' or 'frightening', etc. Objects may seem to come

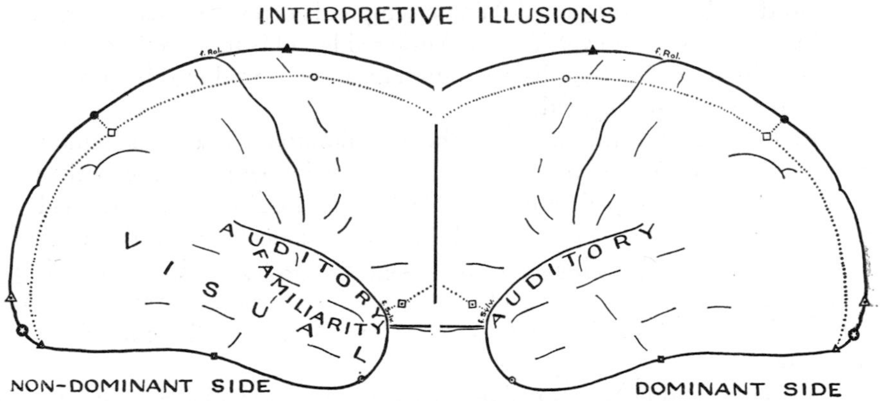

INTERPRETIVE ILLUSIONS

FIG. 12. Summarizing map of areas from which electrical stimulation produced illusions of interpretation. Changed interpretation of things heard (auditory) was produced by stimulation of the first temporal convolution on either side. A change in interpretation of things seen (visual) was produced in the non-dominant side only. The feeling that this had all happened before (*déjà vu*, familiarity) was also produced in the non-dominant side. 'Dominant' means side on which speech was localized. (Mullan and Penfield, 1959.[7])

near or to recede. (*ii*) In the second form, the patient has an hallucination which comes to him like a dream. In it, some previous period of time is re-experienced.

The positive responses that we have produced by stimulation at various points in the interpretive cortex are like these 'dreamy state' fits. We see now that the hallucinations are, in reality, experiential flashbacks from the past; while the illusions are sudden interpretive conclusions about the present. See Table 1.

Interpretive Signals (Fig. 12)

Take as an example of interpretive signalling (Mullan and Penfield, 1959)[7] the following: the patient (on the operating table under local anaesthesia) remarks suddenly, when the electrode is applied to an anterior point on the non-dominant temporal lobe, 'This all seems familiar, as though it happened before and I even know what is coming next'. Under normal circumstances, such a judgement of familiarity often proves to be true. To make that possible, it must follow that there is a mechanism in the brain which enables the individual to make an instantaneous, subconscious review of similar experiences from his past.

Another example: 'People seem to be getting smaller ... you both looked more distant.' In another case, stimulation caused the patient to say that he had a sudden feeling that objects seen were coming closer and that things heard were growing louder. These are common judgements of things that approach or go away.

Illusions that were strictly visual, as well as interpretations of space, were produced when the non-dominant temporal cortex was being stimulated (Fig. 12); rarely, if ever, from the other side. This may well bear some relationship to the fact that disorientation in space is produced by posterior temporal excision on that side.

In one patient, this area on the non-dominant side was removed completely (Fig. 8). In the years that followed operation, the patient's epileptic attacks stopped. He was able to earn his living, but he had a penalty to pay. With his eyes closed, he had no conception of his position in space. On leaving his house in the village, where he lived, he seemed to be well oriented until he turned a street corner. After that he was lost. To get back home, it would be necessary for him to ask the direction from a passerby.

This man had no functional defect except this: he had lost the capacity to construct in his mind a concept of spatial relationships. When called upon to make a drawing, he showed a loss of understanding of the relationships of external objects to each other as well as to himself. The loss (after removal on the non-dominant side, Fig. 8) was as absolute and as discrete as the aphasia would have been if the homologous area of cortex (Ideational Speech in Fig. 11) had been excised on the dominant side.

Experiential Response or Flashback

These responses to electrical stimulation are altogether different. They bear no relation to present experience in the operating room. Consciousness for the moment is double. The patient can discuss the phenomenon. If he is hearing music, he can hum in time to it. The astonishing aspect of the phenomenon is that, suddenly he is aware of all that was in his mind during an earlier strip of time. It is the stream of consciousness flowing again. If music is heard, it may be orchestra or voice or piano. Sometimes he is aware of all he was seeing at the moment. Sometimes he is aware only of the music. It stops when the electrode is lifted. It may be repeated (even many times) if the electrode is replaced without too long a delay.

The details of all examples of experiential response are included in our final summary of them (Penfield and Perot, 1963).[20] This electrical recall is completely random. Most often, the event was neither significant nor important.

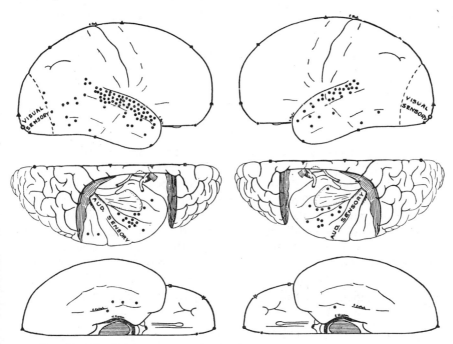

Fig. 13. *Flashbacks*. Points of stimulation that produced experiential responses. Hemisphere partly excised to show superior surface of temporal lobe. (Penfield and Perot, 1963.[20])

When all the points, from which experiential responses were produced, were summarized on a brain map, Fig. 13 resulted. The general distribution is the same as that from which interpretive illusions were elicited. This we have called the 'interpretive cortex'. It avoids the speech area and skirts the visuo-sensory and audito-sensory areas. When the purely visual and purely-auditory experiential responses were summarized, the diagram shown in Fig. 14 was produced. The additional experiences that were both auditory and visual were elicited from points on the first temporal convolution of both sides.

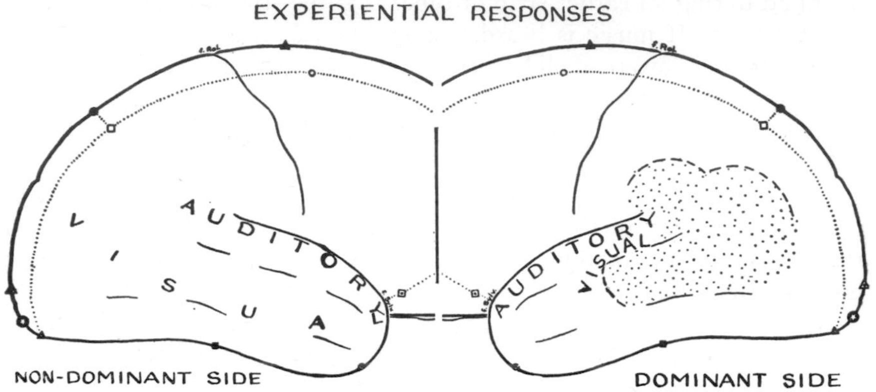

EXPERIENTIAL RESPONSES

FIG. 14. Experiential responses to stimulation shown for the lateral surfaces of both hemispheres. The temporal speech area (compare with Fig. 9) is stippled. The number of experiential responses which are visual in character is much greater on the non-dominant side and nearer the occipital cortex. No positive experiential responses followed stimulation of the speech area. (Penfield, 1966.[14])

These are facts collected from carefully preserved records of craniotomies under local anaesthesia. They have been critically studied and presented on these maps by my associates (Sean Mullan, interpretive illusions, and Phanor Perot, experiential responses). These operations, as I have said, were not planned experiments. But, chance did fulfil, from time to time, all the conditions of controlled experimentation. These are not epileptic phenomena. Ordinarily when the current was switched off during deep stimulation, or the electrode was removed following superficial stimulation, the psychical response stopped instantly. If not, this response was given no localizing value. Experiential responses occurred in forty cases (forty different patients) out of a total series of 1,132 cases surveyed. There was no such response to stimulation in any other area of the brain.

The Uncommitted Cortex

Consider for a moment the two homologous areas of originally uncommitted cortex—ideational speech, Fig. 11, and awareness of spatial relationships, Fig. 8. We may assume that at the time of birth the anatomical detail was identical, right and left. The connections of cortex to thalamus were similar and yet the child makes a different use of the two sides.

It has already been pointed out that if you destroy the ideational speech area on the left at the age, for example, of five years, previously learned speech goes with it. But, it returns to normal after a year or more of aphasia and the major speech area is then (in our experience) established on the right.

Speech is apparently served best by a strictly unilateral mechanism. If there is destruction of the original speech cortex after the age of ten or twelve, we must assume that there are no longer unemployed neurones on the right. The slate that was once blank on the non-dominant side is so no longer. After the age of ten or twelve, the writing on it can no longer be erased. Thus, with the posterior temporal region destroyed on the dominant side, restoration of speech will be no more than partial.

Interpretive Cortex

Let me re-capitulate the evidence from stimulation of the speech cortex and the interpretive cortex. We have had almost no cases of cortical stimulation before the age of ten. But after that time it is apparent that the neuronal paths open to a stimulating electrode in the two areas are quite distinctly different. On the speech side, a gentle current sends axonal impulses from any of the three cortical speech areas to the pulvinar nucleus of the thalamus and blocks the speech mechanism effectively.

On the other (non-dominant) side, a similar current applied similarly, if it has any effect, produces a positive phenomenon. Whether it is an interpretation of the present or a recall of the past, it seems evident that the surgeon's electrode has activated a small part of an automatic mechanism. The mechanism is involved in non-verbal perception. In the right posterior temporal region, it deals particularly with pure visual experiences from the past and with present spatial relationships. On the other hand, the cortex of the first temporal convolution on both sides deals with pure auditory experience and with combined auditory and visual experience.

How does this interpretive mechanism work? What are its parts? One can only give partial answers, of course. It is clear that there is a neuronal record of the stream of consciousness. It seems to be complete and detailed during conscious life from childhood onward. It is not located in the temporal cortex. It is located at a distance from the cortex. One may hazard a guess that the record itself is in the hippocampus of both sides together with their connecting central circuits. Conscious effort gives any individual only limited access to this record. With rare exceptions, it fades progressively to voluntary recall, and may be replaced by memory's generalizations, to be discussed below.

What we have termed the interpretive cortex is apparently used in the subconscious mechanism that summons previous experience for comparison with present experience. The mechanism is constantly employed in scanning the past for similar or related experience. The strips of the stream of previous consciousness that we have been able to summon electrically are largely concerned with visual and auditory phenomena, together with the previously attendant emotions and reactions. (Whether there is a mechanism for recall of other phenomena in life's experience that are predominantly non-auditory and non-visual is not clear.)

Perception

Perception (for the normal adult, and as I have used the term) may be defined as interpretation of present experience in the light of past experience. For example, when someone on the street is recognized as a man, that is the beginning of perception; a general concept has been summoned. When the man speaks, perhaps the sound is familiar. Then the subconscious mechanism signals something like—'heard before'. If that voice had been heard before with fear, the observer would probably feel the fear now. Then comes a more specific recognition. The man is suddenly remembered and details of that man come to mind and with such clarity that one realized exactly what changes have occurred—a different bearing perhaps, a moustache, signs of advancing age. The particular concept of that man, having come clear, is presented now to the speech mechanism where the idea is translated automatically into the name. Both man and name are remembered. They emerge again in consciousness.

7
Relation of Mind to Brain-Mechanism

The programming or conditioning of the uncommitted cortex that goes on in childhood produces two automatic brain-mechanisms that are separable functionally. Their interaction and their relationship to the neuronal action that accompanies conscious thought must now be faced!

A Patient's Introspection

The case of C.H., which has been reported fully elsewhere, brings us directly to this problem. Under local anaesthesia a large part of the left hemisphere of this patient had been exposed. As a guide to cortical excision, I undertook to outline clearly the limits of the major speech area in the temporal region. To that end, one of my associates began showing him a series of pictures. C.H. named each accurately. While this was going on (and without the patient's knowledge), I applied an interfering current by means of an electrode placed on the speech area. When the next picture was shown to him, he remained silent. But he snapped his fingers as though in exasperation. Presently, I withdrew the electrode.

'Now I can talk,' he said, 'butterfly. I couldn't get that word "butterfly" so I tried to get the word "moth".'

It is clear that while the speech-mechanism was temporarily blocked, he could still perceive the meaning of the picture of a butterfly. He made a conscious effort to 'get' the corresponding word. Then, not understanding why he could not do so, he summoned another concept which he considered the closest thing to butterfly. He presented that to the speech-mechanism and 'drew another blank'.

When trying to understand the interdependence of brain and mind, I have often recalled this quiet moment in the operating room. The patient's simple statement startled me. He was calling on two automatic brain-mechanisms alternately and at will. I had it in my power to inactivate one mechanism, that of speech, without altering his ability to use other mechanisms of the brain and certainly without making it difficult for him to think. I could do this at will. *Conscious thought* and *brain action* seemed suddenly within reach of one's understanding.

This patient, wanting to help the surgeon, had turned his complete attention to the task, ignoring all else, even in this strange operating-room environment. We may assume that he was inhibiting all the unrelated streams of sensory information that might otherwise have reached the place from which he was *sending* the patterned potentials that carried the idea of a butterfly to the speech mechanisms. Now that one had some idea of where the mechanisms were, it was necessary to ask where the messages came from, where the pattern was put together.

Somehow the patient had held the line of communication open. He waited. When no answer came, he turned to the non-verbal perception mechanism again, seeking the nearest substitute for butterfly. The concept of moth was forthcoming and he compared it in his mind's eye with the concept of butterfly. Then he sent off a different message, so patterned that it should mean 'moth' to the speech mechanism. When again there was no automatic response, he made a movement of exasperation with his hand.

Now, while C.H. was making this effort to direct the action of his brain, his stream of consciousness was certainly being recorded. It is more accurate to say that the neurone action that accompanied and made possible the stream of consciousness was recorded so that it might be reproduced when summoned consciously or unconsciously. Meanwhile, all the other contemporary neuronal activity came and went without a record, like a million moving lights that twinkle for a moment on as many circuits and go out.

Duality of Approach

In this discussion I have said *he* wanted to help, *he* turned his attention, *he* summoned another concept, *he* chose, *he* presented, *he* was exasperated—as though he and his mind were one while the brain was something else, a machine to be used. I have said *I* was startled, *I* could inactivate his speech mechanism, *I* could do this at will. In all of this, I was clearly thinking of the persons, he and I, as distinguished from brain and brain-mechanisms. There is no other language a scientist can use.

Science has not explained the mind, the person or the personality. A neurophysiologist can study the central nervous system with its inborn reflexes, its lines of communication, and its acquired brain-mechanisms. He can point out the parallelism between the electrical activity in neurones and the changing content of the mind. But he cannot study the mind directly. There is no method.

A biographer may describe the changing behaviour of a man all through life. His objective is to picture what he considers to be a changing personality. He assumes that the person who is the subject of his book is something more than a collection of reflexes, 'something' which looks out of the eyes of his subject, listens through the subject's ears, makes decisions, laughs and weeps. Like the scientist, a biographer must use the language of duality. There is no other way. There is no other way for a man to describe himself or to work out his own belief about his Creator.

Another School

The revelations of biological evolution and the history of the planets serve the purposes of science. But there is another school and a far more ancient scholarship that have to do with social evolution and the history of moral and religious thinking. Wise men, poets, prophets, priests, philosophers and common men have glimpsed spiritual and moral truths that are no less important to man than the discoveries of science. There is a vast accumulation of knowledge that has to do with the nature of man. There are depths of good and bad in human nature. Man is teachable, loyal to ideals and traditions and yet capable of critical and creative thinking.

To say that such characteristics are hidden in a man's genes, chromosomes and nucleoprotein molecules explains nothing. It points merely to one of the approaches which science may make to the problem. When Pavlov's early work was reported, it was said (although not by him) that conditioned reflexes could explain the mind and disprove the spirit of man or God. But the saying was wrong. Pavlov's work threw light on the mechanisms, not on the nature of the mind.

Physicians in general, and psychiatrists in particular, must make a double approach to the problem of man, for there is no thoroughfare of cause and effect between the brain and the mind of man, and there will be none until a new bridge is built. It is our present task to lay a solid footing for a bridge from both sides. But all the while we must bear in mind 'the possibility', to use the words of Sir Henry Dale, 'that man's mind may never be able to achieve for itself an understanding of its own relation to the function of the brain'.

Lord Adrian (1966)[1] spoke for neurophysiologists as a whole when he wrote in a discussion of Consciousness: 'As soon as we let ourselves contemplate our own place in the picture, we seem to be stepping outside the boundaries of natural science.' But, in conclusion, he observed:

'possibly our picture of brain events or of human actions may be changed so radically that in the end they will account for the thinker as well as his thoughts.'

8

Conscious Man

Physicians are called upon to care for the unconscious as well as the conscious. In cases of coma, not due to toxic agents or drugs, the doctor's problem is to discover where the interference with brain function may be located as well as what it is.   In that case, he turns his attention at once to the diencephalon since hemispheral lesions do not produce coma.

Certain brain mechanisms that are operative in human neurophysiology can be studied in mammals which are said to be lower in the scale of evolution. These are the sensory and motor mechanisms. There are also mechanisms which may be called psychical. They are to be studied in conscious man. Speech and perception can now be localized in cortico-thalmic mechanisms. But this is no more than a beginning of understanding.

Consciousness

Neuronal action may be described as the passage of electrical potentials in meaningful patterns over appropriately selected lines of communication within the brain. Since, in some cases, neuronal action clearly accompanies corresponding changes in the content of the mind, the scientific hypothesis is this: All mental phenomena are associated with corresponding neuronal action. On that assumption, then, what has been called 'the stream of consciousness' must be accompanied by a corresponding stream of neurone action.

Sir Charles Sherrington, when addressing a lay audience, gave us a fanciful and often-quoted description of the brain of a man as he wakens from sleep.

'Picture to yourself', he said, 'a scheme of lines and nodal points gathered at one end into a great ravelled knot, the brain. . . . Imagine activity in this shown by little points of light. . . . Should we continue to watch . . . the great top-most sheet of the mass, where hardly a light had twinkled or moved, becomes now a sparkling field of rhythmic flashing light points with trains of travelling sparks hurrying hither and thither . . . Swiftly the head mass becomes an enchanted loom where millions of flashing shuttles weave a dissolving pattern, always a meaningful pattern though never an abiding one. The brain is waking and with it the mind is returning.'

When the mind returns after sleep or after coma, a man is conscious. Consciousness returns. One might object that neither mind nor consciousness can return, since no one can say where they are at any time. But consciousness does return when normal movement returns in certain areas of the brain. While there is light, the stream of light waves that impinge upon the human retina must be forever renewed. There is no light without vibratory movement, and there is no evidence of consciousness without neuronal action.

The content of a man's consciousness is never twice the same. It resembles a melody which must advance to be a melody. In the waking state, the shuttles of the brain weave 'a meaningful pattern' but never 'an abiding one'. The changing content of man's thinking corresponds with continuing neuronal action in meaningful patterns in the higher brain-stem and the cerebral hemispheres. The action is never an abiding one and yet that action is recorded with great fidelity and can be used and recalled in various ways. Consciousness is awareness. The individual is not aware of all that is going on in the brain. He is aware only of what lies within the focus of his attention and here is the heart of the matter.

Sensory Input

The sensory in-flow is remarkably varied. The afferent current of electrical potentials brings into the thalamus, from the special sense organs, the sights and the sounds, the written and the spoken words and all the meanings of social life. Together with the afferent impulses from the body, it makes available a remarkable amount of information of the

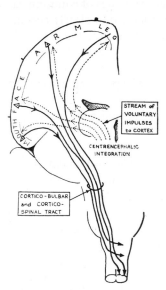

Fig. 15. The *motor path* from neuronal action to muscular contraction. The broken lines show the course of the hypothetical stream of patterned potentials from diencephalon to motor cortex.

environment. But only a small portion of the available information is selected and admitted to consciousness at any one time. By turning or directing his attention, each individual selects for himself, and that is an act one may call voluntary.

Origin of Motor Output

The supposition is inescapable that the efferent stream of potentials, which produces the purposeful use of the motor system, arises within the higher brain-stem (Fig. 15). This directing current passes out to motor cortex and on through medulla or spinal cord to the muscles. Within the diencephalon and the reverberating circuits that link it to the cerebral cortex, the decisive neuronal action takes place. This action must precede the formation of potentials into a meaningful motor pattern. The neuronal action that precedes the pattern formation selects from sensory material and formulates the pattern. This action is an accompaniment of consciousness and thought.

Motor Skills

As already pointed out, man's motor skills can only be acquired in the full light of consciousness, but they rapidly become semi-automatic and even 'subconscious', although they are started and modified and stopped consciously. Conditioned reflexes, it must be remembered, are not established in the cortex alone. They always depend on cortico-subcortical circuits. Thus the cortical area of a learned skill, when it is operating subconsciously, is still not cut off from subcortical interplay. But it is, for the time being, not receiving conscious directives.

Thus it is apparent that the diagram (Fig. 15) is vastly over-simplified. The broken lines, for example, refer to the course of messages that formulate muscular action at times. At other times, they initiate, modify or arrest semi-automatic mechanisms. Here is one example in which what may be called voluntary potentials were recorded.

In the case of a conscious patient whose cerebral cortex was exposed under local anaesthesia, a line of recording electrodes was placed along the precentral gyrus (Jasper and Penfield, 1949).[18] The patient was then asked to squeeze with the opposite hand. The so-called resting beta rhythm of neuronal activity which was being recorded all along the convolution was disturbed only in the hand area. The disturbance disappeared after he had clenched his fist. It reappeared when he was asked to stop clenching. He was then asked to get ready to clench at the word 'now', but not to clench. When the surgeon said 'now', the same disturbance of rhythm occurred at the electrode placed on the hand area (and only there), but there was no hand movement.

Such an observation does not prove anything. It is entirely consistent however, with the hypothesis of electrical potential messages moving out to selected points in the cortex as indicated in Fig. 15. In conclusion, one must accept the fact that the patterned potentials that provide conscious direction to the voluntary motor system emerge from the diencephalon. They cannot conceivably come from anywhere else.

Stream of Consciousness

The psychologist, William James, said of consciousness, 'it flows. A "river" or a "stream",' he added, 'are the metaphors by which it is most naturally described ... the stream of thought, of consciousness, or of subjective life.' But James's description may well be misleading. There is an inevitability about the content of a river that does not characterize consciousness. An observer cannot influence the river as he stands on the bank. He can control the stream of conscious experience. It comes to him out of the future. It passes and moves on into the past. The movement is inexorable, but each individual modifies the content, to some extent. Each man selects for himself. He pays attention to a small portion of the sensory input, admitting that portion to his stream of awareness. The rest vanishes without effect. It 'dries like rain drops off the stones', leaving no neuronal record. Of course there are things no man can exclude from notice. An explosion, near at hand, cannot be denied. It enters consciousness. But even then the man, though frightened, makes his own addition to consciousness. He considers instantly what it means to him. He looks about, discovers how best to escape.

The movement of the stream of awareness continues through each man's waking day until drowsiness intervenes and sleep closes the gates. When he wakes again, he begins to select.

Attention

Even when he seems to be doing nothing, a man's attention ranges. Discomfort, curiosity, interest, desire, purpose, influence his decision, but the focusing of attention is to some extent a voluntary act. There must be, accompanying it, a corresponding neuronal action with currents of potentials moving in appropriate paths. Some of the activity is inhibitory, some activating.

Is this accompanying pattern of neuronal action formed within the diencephalon and do messages emerge to the cerebral cortex like those that serve to direct voluntary motor activity as suggested in Fig. 15? No answer can be given to that question. But the assumption must be made that control of attention has corresponding neuronal action somewhere. Where else can it be?

Attention has been compared to the beam of a searchlight moving about in the darkness. It may focus on the world without or on inner thoughts and fancies. The act of paying attention is much more than the control of a searchlight. It is a part of the neuronal action which corresponds to the whole of the conscious state.

Memory

A neuronal record of the stream of consciousness is made within the brain, as pointed out in Section 6 above. The record apparently includes all that the individual is at any time aware of, things seen and heard in normal detail, things felt and believed. The flashback strips of experience, that have been summoned from the past by electrical stimulation of the interpretive cortex, include, as far as one may judge, all of the individual's awareness, nothing of what he ignored.

The neuronal action, that accompanies each succeeding state of consciousness, leaves its permanent imprint in the brain. It is a trail of facilitation of neuronal connections that can be followed by an electric current many years later with no loss of detail, as though a tape recorder had been receiving it all. For a short time, a man can recall all the detail of his awareness. Then it fades progressively beyond his voluntary reach. But through the brain mechanism of perception the detail can still be recalled.

But man's memory has a much broader meaning than his limited direct access to this detailed record. Most of what a man remembers is made up of subsequent generalizations. He recalls a song but does not remember, perhaps, any of the times he heard it or sang it. He can summon a generalization of a butterfly or a moth and can summon the word symbol for each. The concept is recorded in the perception mechanism. The word is remembered, thanks to the speech mechanism. He uses these mechanisms at will, and what emerges in consciousness he calls a memory. He can think of other things while these two acquired mechanisms are working for him. (This was illustrated by the case of C.H. in Section 7.) He can use the previously established motor skills to write or to speak the word. He can play the piano and do a thousand things that he seems to remember. These skills are based on conditioned reflexes, as speech and perception are. Thus the man, or should one say the mind, selects, and seems to remember so many things.

All of these things that a man remembers were established with materials that once formed a part of his awareness. There is no evidence that any of the things he ignored are stored—at least not in any available form in the central nervous system. Thus a man, in selecting to what he will attend, selects what is to be recorded in numerous mechanisms of the brain.

Concluding Remarks

'Neuronal action', to repeat the definition, 'is the passage of electrical potentials in meaningful patterns over appropriately selected lines of communication within the brain.' But the only neuronal action which leaves a memory imprint is that which was once a part of consciousness. The record, in a strangely complete form, continues to be available to the mechanism for perception. But parts of conscious experience are recorded, too, in other acquired cortico-thalamic units: the speech mechanism and the many conditioned skills a man creates for himself. They are incorporated, too, in the general concepts he builds up.

The conditioned reflex is the basis of learning, no doubt, whether this forms a part of the speech mechanism, the perception mechanism or the skills and the habits that men acquire. These reactions are given permanency by facilitation of paths in the cortex. But none is cortical alone. All are cortico-thalamic.

The selecting and organizing brain-mechanism that must be activated in order to enable a man to think and choose must have its major localization, it seems, at the higher cross roads of neuronal communication. That means the diencephalon.

The infant, during the early months of life, gives evidence of curiosity and of concentration and occasionally individual purpose. He ignores some things stubbornly, attends to others. Thus, in the first two years of life, he begins the task of programming his uncommitted cortex—for speech on one side, for spatial orientation on the other, for the interpretation of new experiences in both sides.

If one thinks of the mind or the spirit as acting with some degree of independence, one can only speak of it as the child, as though the mind and the child were one and the same thing. By selecting to what he will attend, the child conditions his own cortex. Thus, as the years pass, the child, with the help of mother and teacher, may be said to create his own brain mechanisms. Until the day (if that day ever comes) when we understand the nature of the mind, we can only say that man uses his mind to condition and programme his own brain.

A clinician, however scientific and critical he may wish to be, must adopt and use a partly hypothetical plan of how the brain works. The patient cannot wait to listen to the 'ifs' and the 'buts' of opposing views. The physician has no choice. He must put on the cloak of medical competence, however well aware he may be of his limitations, as well as his strengths, beneath the cloak. He should bear in mind what is sure and what is probable. He must be ready to add new evidence and to act on it, learning the while to speak with honest simplicity.

REFERENCES

1. ADRIAN, E. D., 1966. Consciousness. In *Brain and conscious experience*. Ed. Eccles, J. C. New York: Springer-Verlag.
2. BAZETT, C., and PENFIELD, W., 1922. A study of the Sherrington decerebrate animal in the chronic as well as the acute condition. *Brain*, **45**, 185.
3. BROCA, P., 1861. Sur la siège de la faculté du langage articulé. *Bull. Soc. anat. Paris*, 2 Série, **6**, 355.
4. HEAD, H., and HOLMES, G., 1911. Sensory disturbances from cerebral lesions. *Brain*, **34**, 102.
5. HECAEN, H., PENFIELD, W., BERTRAND, C., and MALMO, R., 1956. Syndrome of apractognosia due to lesions of minor cerebral hemisphere. *Archs Neurol. Psychiat., Chicago*, **75**, 400.
6. JACKSON, J. H., 1873. On the anatomical, physiological and pathological investigation of the epilepsies. *West Riding Lunatic Asylum Medical Reports*, **3**, 315.

7. MULLAN, S., and PENFIELD, W., 1959. Illusions of comparative interpretation and emotion. *Archs Neurol. Psychiat., Chicago*, **81**, 269.

8. PENFIELD, W., 1929. Diencephalic autonomic epilepsy. *Archs Neurol. Psychiat., Chicago*, **22**, 358.

9. PENFIELD, W., 1947. Bilateral frontal gyrectomy and post-operative intelligence. *Proc. Ass. Res. nerv. ment. Dis.*, **27**, 519.

10. PENFIELD, W., 1950. The supplementary motor area in the cerebral cortex of man. (Published as part of the 80th and 75th birthday volume for Oskar and Cécile Vogt.) *Arch. Psychiat. Nervkrankh.*, **185**, 670.

11. PENFIELD, W., 1952. Epileptic automatism and the centrencephalic integrating system. *Proc. Ass. Res. nerv. ment. Dis.*, **31**, 513.

12. PENFIELD, W., 1958. *The excitable cortex in conscious man*. Liverpool: Liverpool University Press also Springfield, Ill., Thomas.

13. PENFIELD, W., 1960. A surgeon's chance encounters with mechanisms related to consciousness. *Jl R. Coll. Surg. Edinb.*, **5**, 173.

14. PENFIELD, W., 1966. Speech, perception and the uncommitted cortex. In *Brain and conscious experience*. Ed. Eccles, J. C. New York: Springer-Verlag.

15. PENFIELD, W., and EVANS, J., 1935. The frontal lobe in man: a clinical study of maximum removals. *Brain*, **58**, 115.

16. PENFIELD, W., and FAULK, M. E., Jr., 1955. The insula: further observations on its function. *Brain*, **78**, 445.

17. PENFIELD, W., and JASPER, H., 1947. Highest level seizures. *Proc. Ass. Res. nerv. ment. Dis.*, **26**, 252.

18. PENFIELD, W., and JASPER, H., 1949. Electrocorticograms in man: effect of voluntary movement upon the electrical activity of the precentral gyrus. *Arch. Psychiat. Nervkrankh.*, **183**, 163.

19. PENFIELD, W., and JASPER, H., 1954. *Epilepsy and the functional anatomy of the human brain*. Boston: Little, Brown.

20. PENFIELD, W., and PEROT, P., 1963. The brain's record of auditory and visual experience. A final summary and discussion. *Brain*, **86**, 595.

21. PENFIELD, W., and RASMUSSEN, T., 1950. *The cerebral cortex of man*. New York, Macmillan.

22. PENFIELD, W., and ROBERTS, L., 1959. *Speech and brain-mechanisms*. Princeton: Univ. Press; also (1966) New York: Atheneum.

23. SHERRINGTON, C. S., 1941. *Man on his nature*. New York: Macmillan Co.; Cambridge: Univ. Press.

24. SHERRINGTON, C. S., 1947. *The integrative action of the nervous system*. Cambridge: Univ. Press.

25. WALKER, A. E., 1938. *The primate thalamus*. Chicago: Univ. Press.

26. WERNICKE, C., 1874. *Der aphasische Symptomencomplex*. Breslau: Max Cohn and Weigert.

PART TWO

CLINICAL

XIII

THE CONTRIBUTIONS OF
CLINICAL PSYCHOLOGY TO PSYCHIATRY

H. J. Eysenck
Ph.D., D.Sc.

Institute of Psychiatry, University of London

1

Introduction

It is not possible to write a chapter on the contribution of clinical psychology to psychiatry in the same way as one might write one on the contribution of electroencephalography, or of psychopharmacology. There are two reasons for this. In the first place, psychology is basic to psychiatry in a manner quite different to any other subject. In England, psychiatry is often referred to as 'medical psychology', indicating that psychiatry (or at least a large part of it) is neither more nor less than applied psychology. The establishment of diagnostic categories, and the allocation of patients to the appropriate one; psychotherapy, or the application of psychological methods of treatment to the patient; research into the mechanisms of neurotic and psychotic disorders—these are among the main tasks and duties of both psychiatrists and psychologists, and the proper allocation of duties, spheres of influence and areas of competence is by no means an obvious or an easy one. Precisely because of this close and overlapping relationship, there have been many arguments, discussions, and even legal quarrels between the two disciplines (particularly in the U.S.A., cf. Joint Report, 1960);[63] and there is no agreed line of demarcation between them; arguments rage between the two groups, and no responsible writer of such a chapter can avoid consideration of the issues raised.

In the second place, neither the psychiatric nor the psychological side can be said to present a monolithic outlook; both are riven by dissensions almost as marked as those which separate the two professions.

It will be our duty to present the arguments of all sides involved, but having quite definite views on some of these points the writer can not claim to be impartial. This chapter cannot in the nature of the case present an agreed point of view, which might be acceptable to all clinical psychologists; no such agreed point of view exists at the moment. All that we can claim to have done is to have read and re-read most of the published papers, reports, books and arguments; to have visited large numbers of hospitals, V.A. clinics, child guidance clinics, and other places where clinical psychologists work, both in England and the U.S.A., and to have discussed the main issues with proponents of all the leading schools involved. From all this work, spread over twenty years, have arisen certain conclusions which will be embodied in this chapter; they are purely personal, and would certainly not be subscribed to by many American clinicians; they would perhaps be more acceptable in England (if only because most clinical psychologists here have at one time or other passed through the writer's Department!), but even such a claim might be hard to substantiate. We will give ample references, as well as discussions of opposing views, so that the reader will be able to obtain a less restricted view if he so desires. It seemed better to adopt this method, and warn the reader of its dangers, rather than to pretend to an impossible impartiality and leave all the vital issues undecided and hanging in the air.

2

The Growth of Clinical Psychology

In 1896 Lightner Witmer established the first psychological clinic at the University of Pennsylvania, an event frequently taken to have marked the point of origin of the whole movement. In 1917 the first professional organization for the study of clinical problems was founded (Rosenzweig et al., 1944).[93] In 1931 a symposium on clinical psychology was published by the University of Pennsylvania, which showed how widely his term had become accepted, and to what extent agreement had been reached with respect to the field covered (Brotemarkle, 1931).[10] The further history of clinical psychology in the U.S.A. has been traced elsewhere (Eysenck, 1950),[27] particularly its recent spectacular growth following upon the second world war and the establishment of the Veterans Administration.

In England, pre-war developments were almost entirely in the area of educational psychology; work with adults was hardly done by psychologists at all, and no training courses for such work were available. Eysenck (1950)[29] has discussed the position, and some of the consequences which it had on the relation between psychology and psychiatry; this may be summarized by saying that the two professions had little knowledge of each other, and perhaps little desire to know each other! Some means to bring the two closer together seemed urgently required, and in order to facilitate such a rapprochement, a course of training in clinical psychology was started at the Institute of Psychiatry (Maudsley and Bethlem Royal Hospitals) in 1948, and since then similar courses, though on a smaller scale, have been started in Liverpool, Glasgow, and elsewhere; there are also some courses given by clinics and institutes lacking University affiliation. The Ministry of Health has now laid down regulations governing the grading and definition of clinical psychologists, as well as their remuneration and training. Thus more slowly and less spectacularly than in America, here also a new profession, with defined status and training is coming into being.

Clinical psychology is a profession almost exclusively confined to England and the U.S.A.* As David (1958)[20] has pointed out, 'when compared to the phenomenal expansion of clinical psychology in the United States, continental professional psychologists are far fewer in proportion. Their influence is much more limited and only rarely does a training programme enjoy the broad support commonly attained here. . . . Most continental European "clinical psychologists" tend to be physicians with specialized postgraduate training'.

This 'phenomenal expansion' in the U.S.A. is well documented by Ross and Lockman (1964),[94] in their survey of graduate education in psychology. Fig. 1 shows post-graduate degrees granted by American universities by area of psychology in the academic year 1962-63; it will be seen that clinical (to which should be added counselling) accounts for almost half the doctoral degrees, and a quarter of the masters. When analysed by enrolment during the same year, the figures are even more overwhelming. It is calculated that about half the membership of the American Psychological Association is concerned in one way or another with clinical psychology! This extremely rapid growth has of course produced its problems, which are discussed in a variety of publications (Brophy and Durfee, 1960;[9] Castle and Eickhorn, 1961;[13] Ethical Standards, 1959;[24] Harding and Cravens, 1957;[57] Hathaway, 1958;[58] Kahn and Santostefano, 1962;[64] Levy, 1962;[74] Proposed Standards,1960;[89] Rychlak, 1959;[96] Shakow, 1965)[99] and has led to a lot of heart-searching (Berenda, 1957;[6] Carter, 1965;[12] Small, 1963;[109] Sundberg, 1961;[114] Taylor, 1962;[117] Vance and Volsky, 1962).[119]

This growth in the number of clinical psychologists should be seen in the perspective of psychiatric need and growth of psychiatric personnel (Albee and Dickey, 1957).[1] Their figures show an almost linear growth in the rate of first admissions to state mental hospitals over a twenty-year period; they also show the failure of psychiatry to grow in numbers at anything like the corresponding speed. There is also an equal need for, and likely shortfall of supply, of V.A. psychologists. These figures indicate that even the rapid rise in the number of clinical psychologists in the U.S.A. is not likely in the foreseeable future to catch up with demand, a

---

* Canada is rather similar to the U.S.A. in the structure of its clinical psychology programmes, and will not here be separately treated (Bernhardt, 1961).[7]

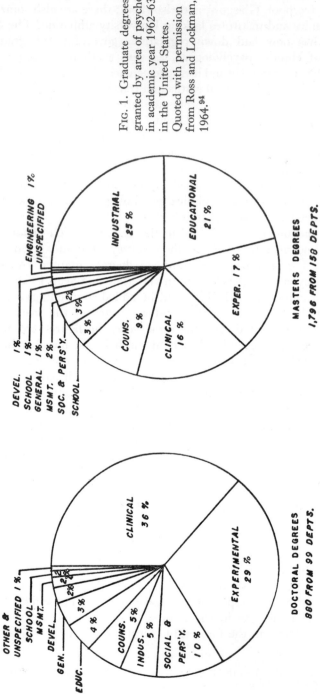

Fig. 1. Graduate degrees granted by area of psychology in academic year 1962–63 in the United States. Quoted with permission from Ross and Lockman, 1964.[94]

demand which is certainly not met by the relatively small expansion of psychiatric services and personnel.

In England there has also been a great increase in the number of clinical psychologists, but financial and other causes have prevented the sort of explosion which has taken place in the U.S.A., and no accurate figures are available. Certainly the absolute figures are still small, and many vacancies exist and cannot be filled in the foreseeable future, unless a greater sense of urgency is shown by Government departments and the University Grants Committee. Details of the English condition are given by Desai (1958),[22] Eysenck (1949,[26] 1950),[27] Franks (1957),[50] Maher (1957),[79] and Summerfield (1958).[113]

The general position on the continent of Europe has already been summarized; detailed accounts can be found in a variety of publications (Froehlich, 1953;[52] Hiltman, *et al.*, 1953;[59] Hout, 1956;[60] Lehner, 1955;[71] London, 1951;[75] Lossen, 1955;[77] Meili, 1955;[81] Mintz, 1958;[83] Misiak and Staudt, 1953;[84] Page, 1938;[85] Simon, 1957;[108] Stern, 1954;[111] Zuckerman, 1954[128]). Slow changes for the better are apparent in West Germany, but the position in the southern countries, such as Italy and France, is still very poor. Denmark and the Scandinavian countries generally are not far behind England, if at all, and are likely to run a course much like that found in this country. Our discussion will not be incomplete if it restricts itself to U.K. and U.S.A. practices as representative of world trends.

3
Different Conceptions of Clinical Psychology

The point has already been made that there are many areas of ongoing discussion and dispute within clinical psychology. It is possible to discern three main camps within this area; three syndromes, as it were, which define different types of approach and different conceptions. These syndromes are not defined with absolute clarity, of course, and they partly overlap and interact—very much as do psychiatric definitions of syndromes. But with all the reservations one might feel inclined to make, nevertheless some meaning attaches to the distinction between the *dynamic*, the *psychometric*, and the *experimental* approaches to clinical psychology, and a brief consideration of the shibboleths characteristic of each may be in order.

The Dynamic Approach

This conception, like the others to be considered, rests on three main foundations; hence it may be referred to as P.I.P.—the projective-interpretative-psychotherapeutic approach. Essentially this is based on the acceptance of a psychoanalytic framework of thought (usually Freudian or neo-Freudian), leading to the practice of psychoanalysis or at least dynamically-oriented psychotherapy. Projective techniques, in particular the Rorschach test, are used—not as psychometric measuring devices, but

TABLE 1

Summary of the Twenty Most Used Psychological Tests in Each of Three Decades

N (1935) = 49
N (1946) = 43
N (1959) = 185

Name of Test	Total Mentions			Total Mention Order			Weighted Scores		Weighted Score Order	
	1959	1946	1935	1959	1946	1935	1959	1946	1959	1946
Arthur Performance	67	29	26	20·5	15·5	3	72	58	28	7·5
Bell Adjustment Inventory	28	26	—	50	18·5	—	37	42	50	19·5
Bernreuter Personality Inventory	30	25	11	46	20	19·5	35	41	52·5	21
Binet-Simon	—	—	11	—	—	19·5	—	—	—	—
Draw-A-Man (Goodenough)	119	36	17	9	3·5	12	194	74	10	3
Draw-A-Person (Machover)	160	—	—	2·5	—	—	360	—	2	—
Gesell Developmental	51	24	20	30	22	8·5	60	45	31·5	17
Goldstein-Scheerer	93	4	—	13	97·5	—	113	4	16	100
Gray Oral Reading	78	32	7	16	8	34·5	98	63	18	6
Healy Picture Completion, I	—	19	17	—	35	12	—	28	—	38·5
Healy Picture Completion, II	27	30	24	53	12	4	31	44	56·5	18
Herring-Binet	—	7	16	—	77·5	14	—	7	—	90
House-Tree-Person	104	—	—	12	—	—	169	—	11	—
Ishihara Colour Blindness	44	30	—	32·5	12	—	46	42	42	19·5
Kent EGY	65	30	—	22·5	12	—	82	50	24	12·5
Kent-Rosanoff Free Association	60	27	6	27·5	17	43	68	36	29	28
Kohs Blocks	67	26	6	20·5	18·5	43	87	47	20·5	15
Kuder Preference Record	108	23	—	11	25	—	166	46	12	16
Kuhlmann-Anderson	—	15	20	—	47·5	8·5	—	25	—	40·5
Kuhlmann-Binet Revision	1	11	19	—	61	10	1	14	—	65·5

Continued

13

Name of Test	Total Mentions			Total Mention Order			Weighted Scores		Weighted Score Order	
	1959	1945	1935	1959	1946	1935	1959	1946	1959	1946
Merrill Palmer	18	22	22	—	28·5	6	26	40	—	22
MMPI	123	29	—	7·5	15·5	—	217	50	8	12·5
Otis Intelligence	—	21	12	15	31·5	17·5	—	38	—	23·5
Otis Self-Administering	80	33	12	15	7	17·5	115	55	14·5	10
Pintner-Patterson Performance	—	12	22	18	54	6	—	20	—	53
Porteus Mazes	72	30	27	18	12	2	84	48	22	14
Roschach	170	34	—	1	5·5	—	424	68	1	4
Rosensweig Picture Frustration Study	70	—	—	19	5·5	—	80	—	25	—
Stanford Achievement	42	34	22	36	5·5	6	56	58	33	7·5
Stanford-Binet	146	43	49	5	1	1	254	112	6	1·1
Stenquist Mechanical Aptitude	—	13	17	17	50	12	—	21	—	48·5
Strong VIB (Men)	74	31	7	17	9	34·5	115	57	14·5	9
TAT	160	36	—	2·5	3·5	—	317	64	4	5
Terman Group	—	11	15	14	61	15	—	13	—	68·5
Thurstone Personality	—	10	14	4	66	16	—	11	—	74
Vineland Social Maturity	82	30	—	14	12	—	130	54	13	11
Visual Motor Gestalt (Bender)	158	12	—	4	54	—	350	15	3	60·5
WAIS	132	—	—	6	—	—	284	—	5	—
Wechsler-Bellevue	123	41	—	7·5	2	—	211	103	9	2
WISC	114	—	—	10	—	—	242	—	7	—

TABLE 1: Tests used by 10 per cent or more of the total sample (N = 185). Quoted with permission of N. D. Sundberg, 1961.[114]

rather as sources of interpretative evaluation; as indicators of dynamic mechanisms, not as classificatory, nosological tests. One might say that this approach is not really in any meaningful sense to be considered as part of clinical psychology, because it does not contain any psychology at all; it is based on psychoanalysis, and uses psychoanalytically-biased procedures which in their construction and validation violate all the rules laid down by academic psychologists. We shall return to this point presently.

The Psychometric Approach

The second school to be considered might be referred to as C.E.S.— the classificatory, evaluative, statistical approach. Here the primary emphasis is on accurate diagnosis, on the precise evaluation, by means of tests, of psychological deficits, and on the statistical investigation of prognostic devices. The test most characteristic of this group is the Minnesota Multiphasic Personality Inventory, with its almost 600 questions, culled with great care from psychiatric practice and from published questionnaires, and analysed statistically against thousands of psychiatric and other control groups. The value of such careful psychometric work is furiously disputed by dynamic psychologists, who argue that all classification does violence to the unique personality structure of the patient— just as psychometricians argue strongly against the careless disregard by the dynamic school of canons of test construction carefully laid down (Campbell, 1960).[11]

The Experimental Approach

The third main school in clinical psychology (T.E.D.) emphasizes the value of psychological *theories*, such as modern learning theory; the importance of the *experimental* approach to clinical questions; and the *dimensional*, as opposed to the categorical, approach to nosological problems. This school has certain criticisms to make of both the dynamic and the psychometric groups, and these will be presented in some detail later. Here we would just like to say that the distinctions between these schools are not of course absolute; psychological tests (particularly intelligence tests) are used by nearly all clinical psychologists, not only by the psychometrists, and all groups would pay at least lip-service to the importance of experiment. It is in the precise understanding of these terms that the schools differ, and in the actual procedures considered as 'tests' or 'research'.

To give some empirical body to this discussion, we may consider the actual tests most widely used by clinical psychologists in America (Sundberg, 1961),[114] Table 1 lists the results of a study of practices in a great variety of places where clinical psychologists live and have their being: 27 Veterans Administration stations, 66 hospitals and institutions, 53 out-patient clinics, 23 counselling centres, and 16 University training clinics. In the total sample there was almost an exact balance between out-patient and in-patient services, and between adults and children (including adolescents) seen for testing. The table presents the 62 tests used by 10 per cent or more of the respondents. The weighted score column gives the total of ratings multiplied by the frequency with which agencies checked these ratings. It will be seen that among the leading ten tests there are four projective techniques and five intelligence tests. The other is the MMPI. A similar list in this country would be much shorter, and would include tests not mentioned here, such as the Matrices or the Nufferno test; diagnostic reading tests used here are of course also quite different. But the top ten tests would all be represented here also, and it is unlikely that an American or Canadian clinical psychologist who dropped in on a ward round or discussion session in this country would be out of his depth.

4

The Clinical Psychologist's Contribution: Psychotherapy

In 1947, the Committee on training in clinical psychology set up by the American Psychological Association reported that they recognized 'the need for preparing the clinical psychologist with a combination of applied and theoretical knowledge in three major areas: diagnosis, therapy and research'. (These areas, of course, resemble in part our three 'school' with their psychometric, dynamic and experimental outlook.) Two main reasons are given for the belief 'that no clinical psychologist can be considered adequately trained unless he has had sound training in psychotherapy'. One is in terms of social need: 'The social need for the increase of available therapists is great. Clinical psychologists are being called upon to help this need. . . .' This argument has been widely criticized on the grounds that we must be careful not to let social need interfere with scientific requirements; that ultimately psychology cannot simply go where social need requires, unless it wishes to be led into a cul-de-sac. A science must follow its course according to more germane arguments than the possibly erroneous conceptions of 'social need'.

That other pressures than that of social need may be more important is indeed recognized by the writers of the report. They say: 'If a social need for therapy exists, then the need for research is even greater.' 'The fact that there is not equal pressure for the latter is mainly due to the excusable but still short-sighted outlook of the public. The universities, with their more far-sighted orientation, have a serious responsibility to develop research interests and abilities in the clinical psychologists they train. The interest should be in research on the laws of human behaviour primarily and on technical devices and therapy secondarily.' Thus the first argument leads inevitably to the second, which is based on therapeutic experience as an indispensable qualification for research.

'Our strong conviction about the need for therapeutic experience grows out of the recognition that therapeutic contact with patients provides an experience which cannot be duplicated by any other type of relationship for the intensity and the detail with which it reveals motivational complexities. A person who is called upon to do diagnostic or general research work in the field of clinical psychology is seriously handicapped without such a background; a person who is called upon to do research in therapy . . . cannot work at all without such a background.'

To a scientist, a statement of this kind must be anathema. It is traditionally conceded that the value of scientific research is judged in terms of its methodology, the importance, within the general framework of scientific knowledge, of the results achieved, and the possibilities that other scientists can duplicate the experiment with similar results. To say that research in therapy (which presumably means research into the process and the effects of therapy) cannot be carried out at all by persons who are not themselves therapists appears to us to take the concept of research in this field right out of the realm of science into the mystical regions of intuition, idiographic 'understanding', and unrepeatable personal experience.

The arguments in favour of including psychotherapy in the clinical psychologist's training course are not very convincing. The writer (Eysenck, 1949)[26] has put forward a number of arguments against the belief that psychotherapy is part of the clinical psychologist's role.

In the first place, it is our belief that in the field of mental illness, no less than in other fields of human endeavour, specialization of function is an inevitable condition for advance. The team of psychiatrist-psychologist-social worker constitutes such a combined attack on a problem, based on specialization of functions. In this team, the psychiatrist is responsible for carrying out therapy, the psychologist for diagnostic help and research design, and the social worker for investigation of social conditions in so far as they affect the case. Nothing but confusion and lowered efficiency all round would follow from an attempt to muddle up these different functions to any significant extent. There are far too few persons competent in their own sphere—be that psychiatry, psychology, or social work—to allow any but the most exceptional to combine several functions. But training courses are run for the average practitioner, not for the rare and isolated genius. It follows that training in clinical psychology should concentrate on those areas in which the psychologist can make his most significant contribution to the psychiatric team.

In the second place, it seems to us that there are quite unanswerable reasons why therapy must be the prerogative of the physician. In this connection, we may quote Dr. D. G. Wright (1948)[124] who points out that 'the psychiatrist's part in defining the kind of pathological processes at work must be decisive. A great many pathological processes have significance only to the physician, and are in the first place illnesses which, although manifested by emotional and mental symptoms, are caused directly by injuries, diseases, and other organic processes in the brain.'

In the third place, we believe that there are many dangers in the acceptance of the therapeutic role which can best be realized by quoting the following sentence from the APA report: 'Psychologists, in our opinion, must come around to the acceptance of some kind of intensive self-evaluation as an essential part of the training of the clinical psychologist. We are not prepared to recommend any special form of such procedures, although some of us believe that whenever possible this should take the form of psychoanalysis. . . .' The reader may more easily see the danger in this recommendation (which itself is an almost inevitable consequence of the premise that clinical psychologists should do therapy) if he glances at the following statement, made by one of the best-known psychoanalysts in this country, whose experience in the field is probably unrivalled: 'The transferences and counter-transferences developing during training analysis tend to give rise in the candidate to an emotional conviction of the soundness of the training analyst's theories' (Glover, 1945).[53] In other words, it is proposed that the young and relatively defenceless student be imbued with the 'premature crystallizations of spurious orthodoxy' which constitute Freudianism through the 'transferences and counter-transferences' developing during his training. Here, indeed, we have a fine soil on which to plant the seeds of objective, methodologically sound, impartial, and scientifically acceptable research! It is because of this implication—no therapy without analysis—more than for almost any other reason that we wish to protest against the inclusion of therapy in the training syllabus of the clinical psychologist.

Our fourth reason for believing that therapy should not form part of the training of the clinical psychologist is closely related to our first belief that a thorough training in research and diagnostic testing is, in itself, a full-time occupation and that the addition of a third type of training would merely result in a lower level of skill and knowledge in all three levels. In our experience, it takes two academic years to train students in diagnostic testing. It takes at least another two years to teach them the fundamental principles of research and statistical method. If part of this time were given over to learning how to fill the therapeutic role, it is difficult to avoid the conclusion that the training in diagnostic testing and in research would be much less complete than it should be. We need only point to the current research reports on psychiatric problems and those affecting clinical psychology to show that the level of research competence is distressingly low; anything mitigating against an improvement in this unsatisfactory state of affairs should at least be considered very carefully.

In the fifth place, it has been our experience that students who are interested in the therapeutic side are nearly always repelled by the scientific flavour of research training, while conversely, the students who are best suited and most successful on the research side betray little interest in active therapy. We feel that the APA Committee dismisses rather too airily this widespread belief that 'the scientific and therapeutic attitudes mix poorly in the same person'. If our experience be borne out by experimental work, which it should be easy to arrange, we suggest that here is a powerful reason for restricting training in clinical psychology to diagnosis and research.

In the sixth place, we believe that stress on the therapeutic function of the clinical psychologist encourages unscientific thinking in the field of selection. 'The ability to carry out effectively the combination of functions called for depends upon the clinical psychologist's being the right kind of person.' It is interesting to note the qualities which the 'right kind of person' must possess, according to the writers of the APA report. He must apparently possess, *inter alia*, superior intellectual ability and judgement, originality, resourcefulness, and versatility, curiosity, insight, sense of humour, tolerance, 'unarrogance', industry, acceptance of responsibility, tact, co-operativeness, integrity, self-control, stability, and a variety of qualities whose operational definition would be even more difficult, such as 'ability to adopt a "therapeutic" attitude'. It would be interesting to know the reliability and validity with which any of these 'qualities' or 'faculties' can be measured or assessed, and to what extent they would characterize the clinical psychologist as opposed to, say, the lawyer, the doctor, the teacher, or any other professional person. As a job analysis, this list is perhaps typical of the 'retreat from science' implicit in the adoption of the 'therapeutic attitude'.

In listing these reasons against the adoption of the psychotherapeutic role by the clinical psychologist, we have omitted what is perhaps the most important. It has been assumed by all sides that psychotherapy does in actual fact do what it is alleged to do, i.e. cure mental disorder, or at least ameliorate it. There is no evidence to support such a view, and much to contradict it (Landis, 1938;[69] Wilder, 1945;[121] Eysenck, 1952;[30] 1965;[42] Zubin, 1953;[126] Levitt, 1957,[72] 1963[73]). It cannot be the purpose of this paper to rehash the evidence; even leading psychoanalysts and psychotherapists have now admitted that there is no acceptable evidence for the contention that psychotherapy has positive effects over and above those of spontaneous remission. (They still maintain, of course, that such evidence will in due course be provided.) Until it is, and it should be noted that the evidence already in existence makes it very unlikely that such proof is likely to be forthcoming, the writer finds it impossible to accept the suggestion that psychotherapy should assume a prominent part in the training and the daily work of the clinical psychologist. By practising an unvalidated and almost certainly ineffective type of therapy the clinical psychologist may succeed in maximizing the area of friction with the psychiatrist, but he is unlikely to make any positive contribution to the latter's work.*

* In view of what will shortly be said in regard to other types of treatment, it should perhaps be added that in this context the term 'psychotherapy' is defined so as to include all types of interpretative, dynamic, or even Rogerian systems; it does not include psychological systems involving re-education, conditioning, or behaviour therapy.

5

The Clinical Psychologist's Contribution: Diagnosis

The possibility of aiding the psychiatrist in the field of diagnosis is regarded by both clinical psychologists and psychiatrists as almost axiomatic; we have already mentioned the enormous amount of time spent on this task, and the great variety of tests used for this purpose. We would like to draw attention to certain logical prerequisites which require to be met before any such claim can be countenanced. In the first place, there is the need for an *agreed* and *valid* system of diagnosis; if the system is arbitrary, invalid, and in dispute, then no help in operating such a system can be of much use to the psychiatrist; what is needed is a new and different system. In the second place, there is need for a proper criterion in assessing the accuracy of psychological diagnostic measures; psychiatric diagnosis has usually been the only criterion, and this may itself be in need of investigation. In the third place, diagnosis must be shown to be closely relevant to type of therapy used; if it is not, then the skill expended in arriving at a 'correct' diagnosis would be wasted. Are these prerequisites in fact met?

It is well known that psychiatric systems of classification are not in any sense based on rational scientific criteria; there is a large element of arbitrariness about the many different systems used, and agreement between different schools is far from marked. Even the most elementary questions have so far remained unanswered; thus there is a great controversy about the respective positions of neurosis and psychosis. Some psychiatrists view these as quite separate disorders, unrelated to each other; others see them as steps along a single continuum of 'regression'. Even the very notion of 'mental diseases' is in doubt (Szasz, 1961),[115] and the classificatory system derived from medical practice is considered quite inapplicable to mental disorders, where a dimensional system of classification is considered more appropriate (cf. discussion in Eysenck, 1960).[35]

Where even the most fundamental aspects of the classificatory system are in doubt, one would not expect much reliability in operating the system. Much work has been done on the inter-psychiatrist reliability of diagnosis; the following references may serve as an introduction to this field: Ash, 1949;[3] Boisen, 1938;[8] Caveny, *et al.*, 1955;[15] Conrad, 1956;[17] Doering and Raymond, 1934;[23] Foulds, 1955,[48] 1965;[49] Goolker, 1956;[55] de Groot, 1958;[56] Hunt, *et al.*, 1953;[62] 1956;[61] King, 1954;[65] Kreitman, 1961;[67] Kreitman, *et al.*, 1961;[68] Mehlman, 1952;[80] Rumke, 1953;[95] Schmidt and Fonda, 1956;[97] Seeman, 1953;[98] Star, 1950;[110] Wallinga, 1956.[120] The outcome seems to be that psychoses, neuroses and organic illnesses can be distinguished from each other with some degree of reliability (although even this is often not very high), but that finer subdivisions cannot be made with any degree of accuracy, and that neurotics are difficult to distinguish from normal controls. These findings are not surprising in view of the somewhat arbitrary nature of the classification used, but they do not suggest that clinical psychologists would be well employed in trying to work to unreliable and probably invalid criteria of this kind.

Even if diagnoses could be made with great accuracy, would this help to determine in any way the treatment of the patient? Bannister, *et al.* (1964)[5] have investigated this question, by noting the treatments given to patients differently classified. Table 2 shows their results. The table was constructed with diagnostic category titles along the top and treatment category titles down the side. Each cell of this matrix thus contains the percentage of patients, out of a total sample of 1,000, with diagnosis X receiving (as their first treatment) treatment Y. Positively significant cells (i.e. cells where the number of patients of the given diagnostic group receiving the named treatment is higher than would be expected by chance) are denoted by asterisks. The table shows that neurotics tend more frequently than chance expectation to receive treatments involving psychotherapy and rare single or rare combination treatments. Psychotics more frequently receive treatment involving E.C.T. Organics more frequently receive Phenothiazines or non-specific treatment.

Schizophrenics more frequently receive Phenothiazines and Long E.C.T. treatment. Affectives more frequently receive treatments involving Antidepressants, but it should be noted that Reactive Depressives resemble them in receiving more Antidepressants and differ from them in that they receive less E.C.T., more Psychotherapy and more rare and rare-combination treatments. Hysterics differ from Anxiety States in being more likely to receive 'Non-specific' treatment. Personality Disorders are distinguished only by being relative favourites for Psychotherapy. Addictions (mainly alcohol) receive primarily Phenothiazines with or without Psychotherapy. The two organic groups (Senile and Other) who are adequately represented, differ little from each other in the treatment they receive.

Bannister, *et al.* summarize their results as follows. (They argue in terms of three levels, the second of which is that level of complexity indicated in the Table we have quoted from their work. Level 1 simply refers to neurotics, psychotics, and organics; level 3 refers to the W.H.O. classification.) They say: 'It is clear from our data that diagnosis and treatment *are* to some degree and at certain levels associated. It is also clear that many variables other than diagnosis must play a vital role in choice of treatment, since there are large areas of no or slight association. Do we conclude then that between diagnosis and treatment "there is a surprisingly high relationship" or that "there is surprisingly little relationship"? The direction of surprise might well be a function of who is viewing the data.

'Kreitman, *et al.* (1961)[68] carried out a study, part of which examined broad diagnostic agreement in relation to broad choice of treatment agreement. The agreement level was significant ($p < 0.01$). But the finding of "a significant association" can be misleading in that, given a sizeable sample, such a finding can emerge from data which still reveal a remarkable

TABLE 2—(Entries in percentages)

Treatment	Schizophrenics	Affectives	Compound	Organic Senile	Organic Pre-Senile	Organic Other	Anxiety State	Hysteria	Reactive Depressives	Personality Disorder	Neurotics Unspecified	Addictions
Short E.C.T.	2·2	14·1	6·8	5·0	0	2·4	0	0	5·4	0	0	0
Phenothiazines	62·6‡	6·5	16·9	50·0†	0	35·7*	15·6	0	7·9	4·4	42·8	38·8‡
Psychotherapy	0	0	0	0	0	0	0	9·5	2·4	26·1‡	0	2·0
Non-specific	1·4	1·4	1·7	20·0	100·0	33·3‡	2·9	23·8‡	8·0	21·7	0	10·3
Antidepressants + Phenothiazines	3·5	22·3†	18·6	10·0	0	2·4	12·8	0	18·8	13·0	0	12·2
Phenothiazines + Psychotherapy	0	0	0	0	0	0	4·3	0	1·9	0	0	18·4‡
Short E.C.T. + Phenothiazines	14·4‡	7·3	22·0†	0	0	2·4	1·4	0	1·0	0	0	0
Antidepressants	0	18·2†	5·1	10·0	0	11·8	4·3	0	19·9†	21·7	0	6·1
Short E.C.T. + Antidepressants + Phenothiazines	1·4	10·6‡	8·5	0	0	0	0	0	3·4	0	0	0
Antidepressants + Phenothiazines + Psychotherapy	0	0·8	3·4	0	0	2·4	5·7	0	4·5*	4·4	28·6	2·0
Antidepressants + Psychotherapy	0	1·1	1·7	0	0	2·4	2·9	4·8	5·0†	0	0	4·1
Long E.C.T. + Phenothiazines	9·4‡	1·1	8·5†	0	0	0	1·4	4·8	0	0	0	0
Short E.C.T. + Antidepressants	0	7·9‡	1·7	0	0	0	1·4	4·8	0	0	0	0
Other Combinations or Rare Treatments	5·1	8·7	5·1	5·0	0	7·2	48·7‡	57·1‡	21·8†	8·7	28·6	6·1
Raw Totals	139	368	59	20	1	42	70	21	201	23	7	49

Note: * = p<0·05   † = p<0·01   ‡ = p<0·001.

TABLE 2: Different types of treatment given to different diagnostic groups (entries in percentages). Quoted with permission from D. Bannister, et al., 1964.[5]

absence of association. In the Kreitman study the authors concluded, "It is gratifying to note, however, that diagnosis was shown to have clear implications for therapy." How do we assess the clarity of the implications and how easily are we gratified?

'One way of describing our present data is in terms of "best prediction". Imagine that at each level of classification a hypothetical predictor makes the best possible guess as to the treatment received by each diagnostic group, i.e. he selects what is in fact the most popular of the fourteen listed treatments for each diagnostic group. Note that here our predictor does not necessarily select significantly associated diagnosis-treatment intersects; he may take advantage of the *general* popularity of certain treatments where these are the "best guess". How often would he have correctly predicted the treatment received by our 1,000 cases? For level of diagnostic classification I he would have guessed correctly 182 times out of 1,000 guesses, for Level II, 329 out of 1,000; for Level III (the W.H.O. classification), 306 out of 1,000. Each time he would have guessed significantly above chance level (which given fourteen treatment categories to allot to is 71·4) but at each level his *absolute* success would be unimpressive. If we reduce the number of treatment categories as shown in Table III and repeat the performance of our hypothetical best guesser on diagnostic classification II, he is now correct in 509 cases out of the 1,000 (chance expectancy 200).

'Within the limits of this sample and this mode of analysis our *tentative* conclusion is as follows. The findings are not consistent with the notion that each particular diagnosis leads logically (or habitually) to a particular treatment. It suggests that variables other than diagnosis may be as important as, or more important than, diagnosis in predicating choice of treatment.'

It seems clear that our three prerequisites for a profitable employment of psychologists in the task of providing psychiatric diagnostic labels are not fulfilled. The principles of classification are largely notional; the criteria used are themselves unreliable; and the usefulness of diagnosis, once achieved, is doubtful. What, under these circumstances, is the accuracy of widely used procedures? Goldberg (1965)[54] has provided us with an illuminating report on the M.M.P.I. Analysing large samples of records, he found that the distinction between neurotics and psychotics was effected with 74 per cent accuracy—as compared with the chance level, which of course is 50 per cent! He also found that simple formulae could make better diagnoses than clinicians using their judgement and experience; clearly the function of the clinical psychologist could be usurped by a computer without loss of validity, and even with some gain!

Rorschach workers sometimes argue that this outcome follows inevitably from the rigid, psychometric construction and validation of the M.M.P.I., and that projective devices, which give more scope to the individuality of tester and patient alike, are liable to be much more accurate. This belief is not supported by the evidence. The writer (Eysenck, 1958)[33] once summarized a review of projective devices as follows: (*i*) There is no consistent, meaningful and testable theory underlying modern projective devices. (*ii*) The actual practice of projective experts frequently contradicts the putative hypotheses on which their tests are built. (*iii*) On the empirical level, there is no indisputable evidence showing any kind of marked relationship between global projective test interpretation by experts, and psychiatric diagnosis. (*iv*) There is no evidence of any marked relationship between Rorschach scoring categories combined in any approved statistical fashion into a scale, and diagnostic category, when the association between the two is tested on a population other than that from which the scale was derived. (*v*) There is no evidence of any marked relationship between global or statistically derived projective test scores, and outcome of psychotherapy. (*vi*) There is no evidence for the great majority of the postulated relationships between projective test indicators and personality traits. (*vii*) There is no evidence for any marked relationship between projective test indicators of any kind and intellectual qualities and abilities as measured, estimated, or rated independently. (*viii*) There is no evidence for the predictive power of projective techniques with respect to success or failure in a wide variety of fields where personality qualities play an important part. (*ix*) There is no evidence that conscious or unconscious conflicts, attitudes, fears, or fantasies in patients can be diagnosed by means of projective techniques in such a way as to give congruent results with assessments made by psychiatrists independently. (*x*) There is ample evidence to show that the great majority of studies in the field of projective techniques are inadequately designed, have serious statistical errors in the analysis of the data, and/or are subject to damaging criticisms on the grounds of contamination between test and criterion.'

Altogether it is the feeling of the writer that the era of the projective technique as the favourite device of clinical psychologists is definitely drawing to a close. Readers who feel that such a conclusion is too strong, may like to be reminded of similar conclusions drawn by well-known psychologists reviewing the same literature. Here is what Cronbach (1949)[18] has to say about the TAT: 'There is little evidence that the TAT protocol, examined for formal characteristics or process variables, is of more diagnostic value than any other sample of verbal behaviour. The test produces meaningful thematic information, but much more research on interpretation is required. Considerable caution is required in interpreting thematic material as a random sample of perceptions and fantasies.' Again, here is another quotation from Cronbach's summary of work on the Rorschach: 'The test has repeatedly failed as a predictor of practical criteria. For those attributes which the Rorschach taps, better projective or objective tests can no doubt be built. The Rorschach's legitimate place appears to be as a wide-band instrument singling out salient aspects of the personality regarding which more data must be obtained. *There is nothing in the literature to encourage reliance on Rorschach interpretations.*'

In 1955, during the International Congress of Applied Psychology, a symposium was held on projective techniques under the writer's chairmanship. The Rorschach test was reviewed by Payne (1955),[87] who came to the following conclusions. Having reviewed the criteria which must be met before a diagnostic scale could be considered useful, he continued: 'A disturbing fact is that I know of no Rorschach scale for any diagnostic condition which fulfils all these requirements. In fact, most existing studies are extremely inadequate indeed . . . we must conclude that there is no positive evidence that the Rorschach is useful in differential diagnosis . . . at the moment there is no evidence that the Rorschach can provide information about conflicts, fantasies and so on, which is useful to the psychiatrist in psychotherapy . . . although a few interesting theoretical findings have emerged from the Rorschach personality studies, there is no evidence that the test is of any practical use at the moment either for describing personality or for predicting behaviour . . . research forces us to the conclusion that there is *no* evidence that the Rorschach can be used to assess whether or not individuals are well or poorly adjusted. Thus, it would appear to have little vaiue in assessing the outcome of therapy.' Payne concludes his survey by saying 'It may be a plausible theory that people's perceptions of ambiguous stimuli, and their associations to such stimuli are a function of their personality. Until some adequate theory is developed to explain precisely how this takes place, and what personality variables are relevant, it seems premature to attempt to put this type of psychological phenomenon to any practical use.'

When confronted with such strong and widespread condemnation of projective techniques on experimental grounds, adherents of these techniques often claim that they possess 'clinical usefulness'. It is easy to see how this illusion may have come about. In an interesting study Davenport (1952)[19] investigated the 'semantic behaviour' of clinical psychologists evaluating TAT records from a heterogeneous group of subjects. The judges had to decide which of a large number of typical interpretative statements applied to which TAT record. The statements were rated for ambiguity by twenty-six other clinical psychologists. Davenport found relatively little agreement among judges in the differential use of the statements with the TAT records; she also found that the judges tended to use statements rated as universal to almost any patient, and avoided the use of more specific statements. She analysed the statements considered to be the most ambiguous and found them to be most heavily loaded with psychoanalytic terminology. In other words it is easy for the projective expert to write a generalized, ambiguous, vague, psychoanalytically tinged descriptive account, which would fit most mentally abnormal subjects; such an account would be acceptable to many psychiatrists and would be considered evidence of the clinical usefulness of the projective device employed. Yet, it appears clear from the evidence that such a report can be written without the writer ever having to see a patient or apply any kind of test to him whatsoever! The illusion of clinical usefulness produced in this fashion cannot be considered acceptable evidence in a scientific sense.

The most recent, scholarly and comprehensive review by Zubin, et al. (1965)[127] comes to conclusions which do not differ notably from the above, and may be taken as definitive; the combination of clinical sophistication and psychometric knowledge demonstrated by these writers is unique in the literature on this subject, and unlikely to be surpassed. Occasional positive reports continue to appear in the literature, but these are almost always technically faulty and guilty of elementary statistical and experimental errors; great caution should be observed in assessing such studies. We must conclude that in this field too a close examination of the clinical psychologist's role in helping the psychiatrist has disclosed a situation where it must be said that much of what is done is of doubtful value. In saying this we do not intend to cast any aspersions on genuinely valuable work, such as that of Wittenhorn (1955),[122] Lorr, et al. (1963)[76] and others who have tried to objectify the judgements on which psychiatrists base their diagnoses, and to subject these to proper statistical treatment; such work finds its proper place under 'research' rather than in this section.

6

The Clinical Psychologist's Contribution: Research

Like motherhood, research is unanimously singled out for praise in the many discussions and conferences which have been held to consolidate opinion on the practice of, and training in clinical psychology (Cttee. on training, 1947;[16] Raimy, 1950;[91] Strother, 1956;[112] Roe, 1959;[92] Bernhardt, 1961[7]); many psychologists consider this the most important area of contribution of their specialty to psychiatry. In principle, this view is unchallengeable; if, as I have tried to indicate, our knowledge of diagnosis and treatment is really so woefully inadequate, then our only recourse must be to further research, and who better qualified to do this research than the psychologist who has to undergo a lengthy period of training in research methodology? In actual fact, there are a number of flies in the ointment.

1. Clinical psychologists are nominally trained in research, but the name 'research' can, and often does, hide many different types of training. The rigour of thinking; the courage to doubt the accuracy and value of any *a priori* premises; the ability to design experiments which will really answer, rather than beg, the question; the knowledge of complex and recondite, but essential statistical procedures; the integration of present empirical work with past theories and experiments—all these essential elements of truly scientific research are only too frequently missing in the training of the clinical psychologist. In America particularly, stress is often on 'service'

rather than on research, and while lip service is paid to research training, the trainee knows as well as does his teacher that future advancement and earnings depend far more on his putative therapeutic skills and mastery of 'dynamic' terminology than on his knowledge of learning theory, statistics, and research design. The extremely low quality of so much clinical research is the most eloquent commentary on this statement; the reader who doubts the truth of this view may be recommended to turn back to our discussion of projective techniques, and consult some of the works there mentioned. On reading these he will encounter hundreds if not thousands of carelessly designed, improperly executed, incorrectly analysed, theoretically worthless, practically useless and scientifically inacceptable pieces of work, for each of which the perpetrator has proudly received the degree of Ph.D. in clinical psychology! What is more, each of these pieces of work has been specially selected as worthy of publication in a scientific journal by leading members of the profession of clinical psychology. To emphasize training in research is clearly not enough; what needs emphasis is the quality of the training received. At the moment there is a wide and almost impassable barrier between the quality and rigour of the work done by experimental psychologists, and that done by clinical psychologists. In the training courses held at the Institute of Psychiatry, we have laid down the rule that Ph.D. research in the clinical field must conform to exactly the same standards as Ph.D. research in any other field; there is no special clinical Ph.D. with relatively low standards, as is only too often the case in America.

2. Good research is anchored in good theory. Looking now, not at the technical quality of clinical research done by psychologists, but at its general value, we find that much of it is vitiated by slavish adherence to *a priori* assumptions taken over from psychiatry. Clinical psychologists often start out by taking for granted assumptions which themselves require proof. Many examples of this have already been given in preceding pages. If we can take it for granted that psychiatric nosology is sound, meaningful and reliable, then the multifarious research on differentiating between categories makes sense. The construction, and most of the research on the M.M.P.I. assumes this; as the assumption is clearly incorrect, all the research done is fundamentally of little value, even though much of it is of reasonable technical competence. If we can assume that unconscious complexes exist and determine abnormal behaviour, and if in addition we can assume that these complexes are reflected in projective-type techniques, then much work in this field would make sense. But the major premises still remain unproven, and extremely unlikely; surely research should not base itself so completely on assumptions, but should rather set about proving or disproving these assumptions? If we can take it for granted that psychotherapy cures, then perhaps much of the detailed work on precisely how different therapists work makes sense. But again the major assumption remains unproven, and little research or discussion is directed

towards it. In other words, clinical psychologists have taken over the psychiatric outlook and assumptions hook, line and sinker, making this the basis of their thinking and their work. In doing this, they have in fact sold their birthright for a mess of pottage.

3. Psychology can make its greatest contribution to psychiatry, not by trying to be as like psychiatry as possible, and by embracing all the beliefs and trends of psychiatry, but rather by making use of its own principles, laws, and methods. If the current system of diagnosis is to be operated, then psychiatrists are the obvious people to operate it; it is difficult to see why psychological devices poorly validated against unreliable criteria, should be of any great assistance. If psychotherapy is to be used, then it is not obvious why the therapists who have worked out this technique should receive much help from psychologists trained in other matters. Psychologists who thus imitate the actions and mimic the methods of psychiatry are not likely, in the nature of things, to make much contribution to it, and the record seems to bear this out—the text-books do not reveal to the searching gaze any spectacular achievement on the part of clinical psychologists which could be said to aid the psychiatrist, improve his work, or contribute to his theoretical system. Clinical psychologists often complain that they are looked down upon by their academic brethren (who consider them beyond the scientific pale) and by their psychiatric colleagues (who fail to appreciate their help). Perhaps the cure is to assert their professional identity, and to try and become, not second-rate, second-class imitations of psychiatrists, but first-rate, first-class psychologists in their own right, bringing to bear on psychiatric problems the accumulated knowledge of academic psychology. This recommendation will be discussed in a later section in so far as it bears on the problem of therapy and of diagnosis; here I will stress rather its application to research. Such fundamental problems as the categorical vs. the dimensional approach to classification (Eysenck, 1960)[35] or the relation between neurosis and psychosis (Eysenck, 1960)[36] should not be regarded as solved by simple acceptance of psychiatric or psychoanalytic practices; they should form the basis of independent psychological research, using the most advanced methods of statistical analysis, such as canonical variate analysis.

4. Such an approach does of course raise the difficult problem of communication. The two problems mentioned above have been attached to the basis of complex statistical procedures, such as criterion analysis (Eysenck, 1950)[28] and discriminant function analysis (S. B. G. Eysenck, 1956;[46] Eysenck, 1952,[31] 1955[32]), with results favouring the dimensional view and the hypothesis that neurosis and psychosis are separate and independent types of disorder. These demonstrations have been passed by as far as psychiatry is concerned, not so much because they are faulty (which they may of course be), but because the statistics used are incomprehensible to all but a handful of psychiatrists. If psychology is to make an independent contribution to psychiatry, then psychiatrists will

have to learn something of the methods, the language, and the statistics used by psychologists. If they do not, then no communication is possible, and what might be a real contribution may be completely lost. Psychiatrists often argue that psychology has no contribution to make to their fundamental problems, but by failing to learn the language in which such contributions can be communicated they automatically ensure that their belief shall be supported; knowing the language of the Rorschach worker, but not that of the experimentalist or the psychometrist, they naturally only respond to the writings of the former, and remain ignorant of those of the latter.

We may conclude that while research certainly must be the most outstanding contribution of the psychologist to psychiatry, this generalization is subject to many qualifications. Quality and direction are all-important, and on both grounds there is cause for disquiet. Furthermore, research findings must be communicated, and here the recipient, be he psychiatrist or clinical psychologist, is often untrained to understand the result, and unwilling to believe it if it conflicts with long-held convictions.

7

The Clinical Psychologist's Contribution: Description

One important function of the clinical psychologist is hardly ever mentioned in discussions of his proper contribution to psychiatry. A vital aspect of psychiatry is the accurate description of the patient, his behaviour, his mental and emotional state, his outstanding traits, his post-operative deficits, and so forth. It is in this field that psychology has a considerable contribution to make. The use of intelligence tests is too well known, and needs too little defence, to be stressed in this chapter; but it provides an excellent example of the increase in accuracy over subjective observation which is possible through psychological devices. Psychiatric observation and description are almost completely subjective and qualitative; the clinical psychologist can and should contribute objectivity and quantitative methodology.

An example may make clear the importance of this contribution. It is widely believed that hysterics are characterized by a strongly marked trait of suggestibility. The writer (Eysenck, 1947)[25] compared hysterics with other neurotics on a wide selection of suggestibility tests, and found no differences between hysterics and other types of neurotics; he did find that neurotics as a whole were more suggestible than normals. It was objected by some psychiatrists that perhaps the tests which sought to objectify the concept of 'suggestibility' did not in fact succeed in embodying the precise meaning that term had for psychiatrists, and accordingly the writer had large samples of neurotics rated for 'suggestibility' by several experienced psychiatrists, at least two of whom knew any particular patient well enough to attempt the rating. It was found that the ratings made by these independent judges did not correlate together to any appreciable extent; whether a particular patient was judged highly suggestible or non-suggestible depended, not at all on his particular character structure or behaviour, but solely on who was carrying out the rating! In other words, psychiatric judgements of this trait carried no assignable meaning whatsoever. Clearly subjectivity cannot go further, and the need for objectification is clear. Whatever may be the defects of the objective tests, at least they are reliable, carry a specified meaning, and can be duplicated by other workers; none of these advantages attaches to the subjective rating.

A similar experiment was carried out by Cattell (1961)[14] who had a large group of subjects rated on 'anxiety'. In spite of the fact that this concept plays a crucial part in the theorizing of most psychiatrists, it was found that correlations between independent raters (all experienced psychiatrists) were disappointingly low, averaging only about 0·2, which indicates only some 4 per cent agreement between the judges! It is clear that when even the most fundamental concepts are so subjectively anchored that no communicable meaning attaches to them, then the objectification of description becomes an important and even a critical task.

The writer has discussed in some detail the problems presented by attempts of this kind (Eysenck, 1960)[37] and the successes and failures of different tests. No attempt can be made here to duplicate this discussion. The reader will find one or two further examples in the section on 'explanation'; there is a clear-cut relation between description and explanation which will be brought out further then. Here we would simply insist that any descriptive statement, such as 'hysterics are more suggestible than other types of neurotics' should be taken as a theoretical statement, rather than as a factual one, until objective evidence can be adduced to translate it into behaviouristic, operational terms. Subjective description will not suffice; it may serve as the starting point of an investigation, but it does not provide the evidence on which the statement must ultimately be judged. Such evidence requires objective measurement, and it is one of the primary functions of the clinical psychologist to provide such evidence.

Description can of course assume many forms and functions. We may wish to use it in the service of nosology, as in the case of the 'suggestible' hysteric; if this theory were in fact true, then we would be able to use measurement of the trait in the service of diagnosis. When translated into objective test results, theories of this kind can provide very accurate diagnostic models; Eysenck, Eysenck and Claridge (1960)[47] and Eysenck and Claridge (1962)[44] have given examples of this procedure, as well as a detailed account of the statistical and experimental problems involved. Description may be used to identify the precise nature of the symptoms complained of, or the positive sources of health and recovery possessed by the patient. Description may be used to measure objectively the outcome of therapy; this is a particularly important aspect of this topic which has been too much neglected. Description may pinpoint precise areas of dysfunction in neurological patients, as well as negative after-effects of different types of operation. Examples of all these uses will be found in the writer's *Handbook of Abnormal Psychology* (Eysenck, 1960),[36] and no further discussion will therefore be given here. Orthodox psychiatry has always recognized the importance of accurate description in neurotic, psychotic and organic disorders, and clinical psychology can help quite considerably to make these descriptions more accurate, more objective, and more reliable.

8

The Clinical Psychologist's Contribution: Behaviour Therapy

Our discussion in the last section has been largely theoretical, and the reference to psychological principles and laws which the clinical psychologist is recommended to apply to his daily work may sound faintly academic. As an example of direct, practical importance, I will turn briefly to behaviour therapy; briefly, because a more extended discussion is given in another chapter of this book. Behaviour therapy (Eysenck, 1959)[34] is a term coined by the writer to denote methods of treatment which are derived from modern learning theory, including methods of desensitization, deconditioning, operant conditioning, and so forth. Detailed accounts are available (Eysenck, 1959,[34] 1960,[37] 1964;[41] Wolpe, 1958;[123] Bandura, 1961;[4] Metzner, 1961;[82] Franks, 1964;[51] Krasner and Ullmann, 1965;[66] Ullmann and Krasner, 1965[118]); as well as a text-book (Eysenck and Rachman, 1965).[45] In addition, a new journal (*Behaviour Research and Therapy*: Pergamon Press) is devoted to this new area of investigation and application.

Behaviour therapy springs directly from a consideration of psychological laws and theories, particularly those of Pavlov, Hull, Skinner, Mowrer, and Miller; it thus constitutes an application of fundamental research methods and results in the fields of human and animal learning and conditioning to the problems of the neurotic and psychotic child and adult. It not only owes nothing to the classical psychoanalytic views, but is in direct contradiction to them both in theory and practice. Thus where psychoanalysis stresses some underlying disease process, and deprecates the treatment of symptoms, behaviour therapy denies the existence of any underlying disease process and advocates the direct treatment of 'symptoms'—erroneously so called because they are symptomatic of nothing. Where psychoanalysis insists on the necessity of 'uncovering' repressed material for a complete cure, and predicts the occurrence of relapse if this is neglected, behaviour therapy disregards this alleged 'repressed' material and denies the likelihood of relapse (Eysenck, 1963).[39] Where psychoanalysis denies the possibility of spontaneous remission, behaviour therapy emphasizes it as a species of experimental extinction, and explains it theoretically (Eysenck, 1963).[40] The contrasts could be multiplied, but those mentioned will suffice to show that here we are dealing with an entirely different type of theory to that traditionally accepted.

Experiments have been performed comparing the efficacy of this new method with that of orthodox psychotherapy (Eysenck and Rachman, 1965;[45] cf. also later papers in *Beh. Res. Ther.*), and the results have on the whole been favourable to behaviour therapy. However, such direct comparisons are not essentially more revealing than actuarial counts are wont to be, and they do not necessarily permit of wide generalization; the fact that Dr. A, using method X, had a significantly greater number of cures than Dr. B, using method Y, may not generalize to Drs. C, D, E and F, using their own variants of methods X and Y. Nor are the reported high proportions of successes credited to behaviour therapy always accepted as proof; alternative explanations are not usually ruled out, however impressive the reports may be. We would rather draw attention to the way that this new theory generates truly scientific research projects, projects which make genuine use of the training and background of the clinical psychologist.

Thus it now becomes possible to design experiments in which the different aspects of the treatment, and their mode of combination, can be investigated. Wolpe's theory assigns importance to the combination of imagined fear-producing object and relaxation; the hypothesis can be tested by having control groups in which subjects practise both the imagining of the feared object and relaxation, but not at the same time; results indicate that training in relaxation, and the imagining of feared objects, are both useless if practised in isolation. Lang and Lazovik (1963)[70] have demonstrated in some brilliant experiments what can be done along these lines, and many others have since extended their work and added considerably to our knowledge (Rachman, 1966;[90] Davison, 1965;[21] Paul, 1964[86]).

Other types of experimentation make possible the direct investigation of certain deductions from learning theory in the therapeutic situation. Thus Yates (1958)[125] showed that the occurrence of tics could be controlled by negative practice; he was able to show that the rate of decline of ticking behaviour could be controlled exactly by variation of amount of practice. Thus when one of the tics was practised twice as much as the others, this particular tic declined in frequency more than did the others, and when one of the tics was practised less than the others, it did not decline in frequency as fast as they did. It is this precise concomitance of the dependent variable with variation in the independent variable that makes this an important experiment; the fact that the patient was cured is interesting but not crucial. Psychiatrists have sometimes ridiculed the procedure by saying that a single case proves nothing, and that spontaneous remission could have been responsible for the cure. To argue thus is to miss the whole point of the experiment, which was not designed to demonstrate the curative value of the method of negative practice, but to show the close dependence of symptom on experimental variation. The fact that such criticisms can be made shows the great gulf that still exists between psychiatry and experimental psychology.

A third example of the application of learning theory principles to psychiatric treatment illustrates the possibilities inherent in the controlled modification of human conduct. Lovibond (1963)[78] found that the bell-and-blanket treatment of enuresis led to relapse in a sizeable number of cases. Arguing that relapses could be regarded as a form of extinction after non-reinforcement, he called to mind the so-called Humphrey paradox, i.e. the well-known fact that extinction is reduced after partial reinforcement during learning, as compared with 100 per cent reinforcement. Using two groups of children, he was able to show that the children receiving the partial reinforcement training did in fact show less relapse than did those receiving the 100 per cent reinforcement. Again, this demonstration has obvious practical implications, but it should be viewed first and foremost as proof of the correctness of the theoretical conceptualization of treatment as conditioning, and relapse as extinction.

The point made could be strengthened considerably by reference to many other experiments, but lack of space makes it necessary to refer the reader to other sources (Eysenck and Rachman, 1965).[45] What can hardly be denied is the fact that behaviour therapy serves as an excellent illustration of the point that clinical psychologists can make a genuine contribution to psychiatry by making use of the principles and laws of psychology, and that in this way they are able to add in a unique manner to psychiatric knowledge and methodology. Again, of course, the question of communication must be raised; psychiatrists are not on the whole knowledgeable about learning theory or conditioning, and theories and methods which are perfectly familiar to the academic psychologist may not be so to the clinical psychologist. We shall revert to this problem in a later section.

One important corollary of what has been said so far may perhaps require pointing up. If the conditioning theory of the aetiology and treatment of neurosis is at all along the right lines, then it immediately suggests a new way of looking at diagnostic testing (Eysenck, 1957).[33] Clearly what is important in this connection is the degree of conditionability of the patient, his speed of extinction of conditioned responses, his tendency to generalize such responses, his autonomic reactivity, and other features of his nervous system related to these concepts. Consequently it would appear much more important to know something about these variables, and to study them in typical laboratory situations, than to subject the patient to Rorschach or M.M.P.I. procedures irrelevant to his treatment, and only of actuarial interest. Unfortunately very little work is being done along these lines at present, but the logic of the situation is unmistakable, and it seems likely that in the future genetic features of the individual's biological make-up will be studied much more intensely than they have been in the past.

This approach to diagnostic testing takes us near to the position of the advocates of the 'single case' type of study, particularly Shapiro (1951,[100] 1957,[101] 1961,[102, 103] 1964).[104] What is suggested here is that each particular patient presents us with a theoretical problem which as scientists we are required to solve. Why does this patient fail to comprehend material which he has read, in spite of an adequate I.Q.? (Shapiro and Nelson, 1955).[106] Is this G.P.I. patient's very poor I.Q. score indicative of low intelligence, or is it due to intellectual fluctuation? (Shapiro, 1957).[101] Is this patient's slowness in cognitive tests due to his being disturbed by the presence of the psychologist? (Shapiro, 1957)[101]. Does this patient find difficulties in learning to read because of failure to learn or failure to retain what he has learned? (Shapiro, 1957)[101]. These and other similar problems have been tackled by Shapiro and his colleagues (Shapiro, *et al.*, 1955,[106] 1959,[107] 1963[105]) in the belief that they should be regarded as specific research problems, and that the answer would involve, not the application of a battery of standard tests, but rather a specially designed experimental investigation. This whole approach is of course closely akin to the clinical attitude of the psychiatrist; its distinctive contribution is (*i*) that it makes quite explicit the hypotheses to be investigated, and the experimental nature of the whole procedure, and (*ii*) that it uses psychological concepts, methods and explanations in the course of the study. It would take us too far out of our way to discuss this trend within clinical psychology in detail, but it is without doubt a promising and important development which may be of considerable use to psychiatry.

9

The Clinical Psychologist's Contribution: Explanation

Clinicians tend to think along empirical lines, and to neglect theories and explanatory concepts. Even when theory apparently plays a dominant part, as for instance in psychoanalysis, it can easily be seen not to be the rigorous type of theory which one is accustomed to in science; at the moment there are dozens of 'dynamic' theories disputing the field, the differences between which are very marked on the verbal level, but which do not seem to give rise to either experimental attempts at clarification or to different methods of treatment. Scientific theories, as Popper (1949)[88] has never ceased to emphasize, must be capable of being falsified if they are to have any real meaning, and 'dynamic' theories, as he goes on to show, simply do not fall into this category. Consequently they cannot be used to furnish the explanatory concepts which psychiatry so urgently needs.

A whole book could be written on the meaning of the term 'explanation' in science, and on the many uses of this term in psychology and psychiatry. Here lack of space forces us to be dogmatic, and consequently we shall merely say quite baldly that explanation is simply reduction to an established system of knowledge relevant to the phenomenon at issue. We explain the fall of the apple and the movement of the planets by reference to the Newtonian system of knowledge of the facts of gravitation; this of course leaves unexplained gravitation itself. Similarly, we can explain the facts of neurosis in terms of the conditioning paradigm, as well as those of spontaneous recovery, reciprocal inhibition, treatment, and so forth. The hypothesis implied in all this may of course be wrong, but it is a scientific hypothesis nevertheless because it is subject to falsification. Thus by appropriate empirical testing we may hope to slough off the incorrect hypotheses and improve the correct ones, making them more and more quantitative as research proceeds. It is our considered opinion that this mode of explanation (as opposed to the purely verbal type offered by the 'dynamic' schools) is the greatest contribution which clinical psychology can make to psychiatry. Explanations have meaning only when they refer back to something that is already reasonably well known, that has been empirically studied for a long time, and the experimental manipulation of which has reached a reasonable degree of expertise. This 'something' can, at the present time, only be found in experimental psychology; it clearly does not exist in psychiatry itself. Psychiatry is an applied science; it must reach back to a fundamental science for its principles and laws. Imperfect as they are, the principles and laws of psychology are the only ones available to psychiatry, and evidence is already available (as in behaviour therapy) that these principles and laws can be of the utmost value both in conceptualizing the problems, furnishing an answer to these problems, and suggesting a solution to the practical issues involved.

An example may make clearer what is meant here. It is well known that schizophrenics are poor learners; in other words, although they may be of equal intelligence to a control group of neurotics or normals, they are inferior in standard tests of learning. This poses the problem of explanation; why are they poorer, and what precisely is the nature of their deficit? The writer has argued that learning has at least two stages: the encoding of the learned material in the C.N.S., and a consolidation period during which this material becomes available to the organism for use (Eysenck, 1965).[43] When massed learning is followed by rest, it is observed that little improvement in performance occurs during learning, but much during the rest (the so-called reminiscence phenomenon). Fig. 2 shows typical curves for pursuit-rotor learning of normal and psychotic subjects; it will be seen that reminiscence (i.e. the difference from last pre-rest to first post-rest trial) is almost non-existent for psychotics, but very large for normals. We might therefore say that psychotics are inferior either in their ability to encode, or in their ability to consolidate. In this experiment the rest pause lasted 10 min; in other studies much longer rest pauses have been used, and it has been found that when these last for 24 hours, or a whole week, psychotics have if anything a greater reminiscence effect than normals (Eysenck, 1961).[38] Thus clearly encoding must have proceeded quite normally, and there cannot have been any permanent defect in consolidation either;

the difference between psychotics and normals appears narrowed down to a much slower process of consolidation in schizophrenics. We now have a much more specific theory of learning deficit in schizophrenics, and we may go on from there to ask even more fundamental questions. What causes slowness in consolidation? Normal subjects who are inferior in cortical arousal can be shown to have poor reminiscence scores, rather like schizophrenics; possibly schizophrenics are defective in reticular formation activating system responses? I have on purpose taken an example where the ultimate answer is not known; it illustrates well how the search for an explanation of a common, every-day observation (schizophrenics learn poorly) can be pursued by reference to psychological principles and psychological knowledge; how it can generate explanatory hypotheses, and how these in turn lead to experiments which generate new and relevant knowledge. Some of this knowledge could already be used for practical

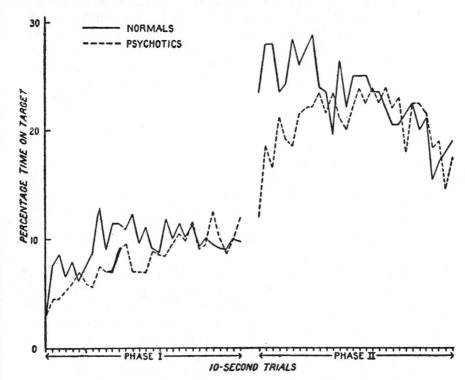

FIG. 2. Learning and reminiscence scores of normal and psychotic subjects on pursuit rotor. Quoted from G. Claridge, in H. J. Eysenck (Ed.), *Experiments in Personality* (Routledge & Kegan Paul).

purposes (such as retraining); some of it can be used for further pursuing the enquiry. The main point to be made is that experimental studies in abnormal psychology should be guided by a search for the explanation of psychiatric observations in terms of better-understood psychological phenomena, laws, and theories. When this is done, psychology renders its most important, most valuable, and most fundamental service to psychiatry.

10

The Clinical Psychologist's Contribution: Teaching

At present, psychiatrists are taught very little psychology. Even in the Institute of Psychiatry, where two out of three papers in the first part of the Diploma in Psychological Medicine (the postgraduate qualification in psychiatry) are on psychology, only twenty lectures are in fact given on the subject, added to which are five lectures on statistics and some twenty hours of test demonstrations. Even when private reading is added, it cannot be pretended that this qualifies the budding psychiatrist to understand and follow psychological research articles, or theory-oriented books, or to actively use concepts and methods of psychology in any meaningful fashion. It is this disproportion between the potential contribution of psychology to psychiatry, and the amount of time devoted to it in the teaching of the psychiatrist, which produces the problem of communication mentioned several times on previous pages. Out of seven years of training, the psychiatrist spends less than a fortnight on psychology; yet psychology is the most relevant and directly useful science from the point of view of his professional competence. Psychology can contribute the main body of knowledge from which explanations of neurotic and psychotic behaviour can spring; psychology can generate suggestions for new methods of treatment based on knowledge rather than hunch and surmise; psychology is in a position to make more accurate and rigorous the measurement of the intellectual deficits and the emotional defects of psychiatric patients; do the facts not suggest that the teachings of psychology should play a much more important part in the training of the budding psychiatrist than they do at present?

We need not confine ourselves to a consideration of the fundamental facts and theories of psychology; at least equally important perhaps is the teaching of the experimental approach to psychological problems, and the hypothetico-deductive method of investigating theoretical problems. Most psychiatrists tend to absorb completely the medical-clinical atmosphere of their early training, and have little teaching in the field of scientific methodology; it is in this field that the clinical psychologist as teacher can perhaps be of particular use—provided of course that he himself has been brought up in the scientific tradition, and has not taken up clinical psychology as a *pis aller*! Many clinical psychologists, particularly in the U.S.A., adopt a service outlook and regard themselves as psychiatrists manqués; they assume all the values and traditions of psychiatry, rather than those of psychology, and would accordingly be quite unable to act as teachers in this way.

In designing special courses in psychology for psychiatrists, teachers have often taken the line that what is taught should be of direct concern and obvious usefulness to the student; consequently they have tended to concentrate on areas such as intelligence testing, projective techniques, dynamic psychology, and so forth. It is our belief that this is the wrong approach entirely, and that what should be taught is rather the central core of psychology—learning theory, perception, conditioning, developmental psychology, animal work, and so forth. We have tried to argue in preceding sections that the main contribution of psychology to psychiatry is precisely in the application of these central sets of concepts, theories, laws and methods to psychiatric problems, and in order to make such an application, or even to understand its import, some knowledge of fundamental psychological principles is obviously required.

So much for our suggestion that teaching of psychology constitutes an important contribution to psychiatry; it cannot be the purpose of this chapter to spell out in detail how this could be done, or what other item of content would have to be left out in order to give more time to psychology. Clearly psychiatrists themselves must decide issues of this kind. Similarly, it has not formed part of our task to suggest who should apply behaviour therapy, psychiatrist or clinical psychologist. Answers to such questions are in part legal, in part a function of traditional values and habits; they can be raised with some advantage, but there is little hope of being able to suggest a universally acceptable answer. Sir Cyril Burt (quoted in Eysenck, 1950)[26] has made the following suggestion: 'Instead of trying to sweep all human and social problems into its net, the profession of medicine should, now as in the past, seek more and more to hand over its outlying fields to specialists appropriately trained. But, of course, increasing specialization will call for increasing co-ordination, increased differentiation for increased integration. The paramount need is for specialist teams.' Such co-ordination and integration demands a greater knowledge on the part of the psychiatrist of the vocabulary and the concepts of psychology; specialist teams must learn to speak each other's language. Psychologists as a matter of course learn a great deal about psychiatry, psychoanalysis, and even neurology and physiology; it is here suggested that this search for knowledge be reciprocated, and it is further suggested that learning what the psychologist is about is no dry-as-dust, purely academic piece of knowledge on the part of the psychiatrist, but is vital for the pursuit of his proper work.

11

Clinical Psychology and Psychiatry: The Future

It is of course impossible for any man to look into the future, but a scientist may cautiously, and with full awareness of the dangers of such an approach, extrapolate current trends into the future. It seems that clinical psychology will in the future follow paths of scientific rectitude rather more than it has done in the past; it will give us, albeit reluctantly, its Freudian dalliance, and it will renounce although with ill grace, its love child, the projective test. Instead it will begin to pay more heed to academic injunctions leading it to scientific virtue, experimental rigour, and theoretical purity. In other words, clinical psychology will begin to grow up, and will cease to delight in irresponsible flights of fancy; it will become the applied branch of a scientific discipline, rather than an artistic adventure. In so doing psychotherapy and routine diagnostic testing will assume less and less importance, and behaviour therapy and the experimental study of the single case will become more and more widespread. It seems reasonably certain that this will be the course of events in England; whether the U.S.A. will hold on to the old and discredited methods very much longer is a question which is impossible to answer from this distance.

It may also be thought that in the future psychiatrists will become more and more knowledgeable about psychology, and that co-operation between clinical psychologists and psychiatrists will become closer and closer. There is evidence of this already, at least in England; in America the fratricidal struggle between the two professions over the legal permission to practice psychotherapy, a struggle having financial but no scientific importance in view of the proven lack of value of this form of treatment, may delay this closer coming together for an appreciable period.

There are certain implications of this development which need to be clearly understood by psychiatrists. Thus in the appointment of clinical psychologists there should be a much more searching demand for academic competence, knowledge of experimental procedures and theoretical sophistication; at the moment, possibly because of the scarcity of clinical psychologists, the ability to apply some of the simpler I.Q. tests is sometimes regarded as a high-grade qualification. Training courses need to be longer and better organized, and some courses, such as those which insist on providing nothing but indoctrination in 'dynamic' notions, should be exorcized completely. There are many other administrative and financial steps which are necessary before clinical psychology can carry out its rich promises, but this is perhaps not the proper place to spell these out in detail.

One point, however, needs to be made with all possible urgency. The psychologist is a laboratory animal; he is crucially dependent on apparatus in his attempts to present stimuli under controlled conditions, and in his attempts to provide detailed measurement of responses. He needs sound-proofed and air-conditioned rooms, as well as extensive apparatus, for the investigation of autonomic and conditioned responses, or for the establishment of thresholds and j.n.d.s. As the E.E.G. expert needs an electroencephalograph, so the psychologist needs his particular equipment. It is useless to expect him to carry out his job properly if conditions are such as to make this impossible; it is not reasonable to expect him to do a scientific job if he is given nothing but a couch, pencil and paper, and some

Rorschach cards. Psychiatrists should be the first to realize the help which the clinical psychologist can give them if he is given the equipment he needs, and they should be the first to press for the provision of such equipment. Hospital boards are often reluctant to provide apparatus for psychologists, simply because in the past psychologists seem to have got by without needing anything of the kind; psychiatrists are in a position to know better, and to help the clinical psychologist to help them better.

So much for the near future, as it were. In the more distant future, I believe it is likely that the boundaries between psychiatrists and clinical psychologists will dissolve more and more into thin air. The evidence shows that however many practitioners of both kinds we train, demand will always outrun supply. Under these conditions the fraternal strife which has so disfigured the American scene becomes more and more senseless, and an attitude of mutual helpfulness more and more desirable. The more psychiatry becomes 'medical psychology', the more closely will it be drawn to psychology, until finally it will be difficult to see the precise nature of the split. Some distinction will of course always remain, due to the fundamentally medical orientation of the psychiatrist, and the fundamentally academic orientation of the psychologist. In their actual work relation, however, training and background orientation will assume less importance than functional factors, such as the question: Who, in this particular situation, can do more for the patient? Who, in relation to this particular problem, is better qualified to set up an experiment? Who, on the basis of his knowledge, can provide a better theory to account for the facts of this case? Functional questions of competence in clinical settings providing for proper team work are less likely to provoke disputes than the legalistic concepts of rival pecking orders so prevalent today.

Whatever may be the right and wrong of the detailed views here discussed, and however mistaken may be the attitudes adopted, and the extrapolations into the future, the writer is convinced that the clinical psychologist will and must become a biologically and behaviouristically oriented scientist, whose contribution to psychiatry is defined and shaped by a proper training in experimental psychology and empirically-based theory. The importance of his contribution will be in inverse proportion to his outward similarity—in function, orientation, and attitude—to the practising psychiatrist. Complete imitation will ensure complete lack of usefulness. Only by being psychologists first and foremost can we bring to bear the contribution of our training and our knowledge to the advantage of psychiatry.

REFERENCES

1. ALBEE, G. W., and DICKEY, M., 1957. Manpower trends in three mental health professions. *Amer. Psychol.*, **12**, 57–70.
2. ANDREWS, T. G., and DREESE, M., 1948. Military utilization of psychologists during World War II. *Amer. Psychol.*, **35**, 533–38.
3. ASH, P., 1949. The reliability of psychiatric diagnosis. *J. abnorm. soc. Psychol.*, **44**, 272–77.
4. BANDURA, A., 1961. Psychotherapy as a learning process. *Psychol. Bull.*, **58**, 144–59.
5. BANNISTER, D., SALMON, P., and LEIBERMAN, D. M., 1964. Diagnosis-treatment relationships in psychiatry: a statistical analysis. *Brit. J. Psychiat.*, **110**, 726–32.
6. BERENDA, C. W., 1957. Is clinical psychology a science? *Amer. Psychol.*, **12**, 725–29.
7. BERNHARDT, K. G. (Ed.), 1961. *Training for research in psychology: the Canadian Opinion Conference, 1960.* Toronto: Univ. Press.
8. BOISEN, A. T., 1938. Types of dementia praecox, a study in psychiatric classification. *Psychiatry*, **1**, 233–36.
9. BROPHY, A. L., and DURFEE, R. A., 1960. Mail-order training in psychotherapy. *Amer. Psychol.*, **15**, 356–60.
10. BROTEMARKLE, R. A. (Ed.), 1931. *Clinical psychology: essays in honor of Lightner Witmer.* Philadelphia: Univ. Press.
11. CAMPBELL, D. T., 1960. Recommendations for A.P.A. test standards regarding construct, trait, or discriminant validity. *Amer. Psychol.*, **15**, 546–53.
12. CARTER, F. F., 1965. Psychological tests and public responsibility. *Amer. Psychol.*, **20**, 123–25.
13. CASTLE, R. L. VAN DE, and EICKHORN, O. J., 1961. Length of graduate training for experimental and clinical psychologists. *Amer. Psychol.*, **16**, 178–80.
14. CATTELL, R. B., and SCHEIER, I. H., 1961. *The meaning and measurement of neuroticism and anxiety.* New York: Ronald.
15. CAVENY, E. L., WITTSON, C. L., HUNT, W. A., and HERMANN, R. S., 1955. Psychiatric diagnosis, its nature and function. *J. nerv. ment. Dis.*, **120**, 367–73.
16. Committee on training in clinical psychology, 1947. Recommended graduate training program in clinical psychology. *Amer. Psych.*, **2**, 539–58.
17. CONRAD, K., 1956. *Beitrag zur Diagnosenstatistik, Fortschritte der Neurologie und Psychiatrie*, **24**, 231–44.
18. CRONBACH, L. J., 1949. Statistical methods applied to Rorschach score: a review. *Psychol. Bull.*, **46**, 393–429.
19. DAVENPORT, B. F., 1952. The semantic validity of T.A.T. interpretations. *J. consult. Psychol.*, **16**, 171–75.
20. DAVID, H. P., 1958. Clinical psychology in other lands. In *Progress in clinical psychology*, vol. 3, pp. 235–47. Eds. Brower, D., and Abt, L. G. London: Grune and Stratton.
21. DAVISON, G. C., 1965. *The influence of systematic desensitization, relaxation and graded exposure to imaginal aversion stimuli on the modification of phobic behavior.* Stanford, unpublished Ph.D. thesis.
22. DESAI, M. M., 1958. Clinical psychology in Britain. *Amer. Psychol.*, **13**, 179.
23. DOERING, C. R., and RAYMOND, A., 1934. Reliability of observation in psychiatric and related characteristics. *Amer. J. Orthopsychiat.*, **4**, 249-54.
24. Ethical Standards of Psychologists, 1959. *Amer. Psychol.*, **14**, 279–82.

25. EYSENCK, H. J., 1947. *Dimensions of personality*. London: Routledge and Kegan Paul.
26. EYSENCK, H. J., 1949. Training in clinical psychology: an English point of view. *Amer. Psychol.*, **4,** 173–76.
27. EYSENCK, H. J., 1950. Function and training of the clinical psychologist. *J. ment. Sci.*, **96,** 1–16.
28. EYSENCK, H. J., 1950. Criterion analysis—an application of the hypothetico-deductive method to factor analysis. *Psychol. Rep.*, **57,** 38–53.
29. EYSENCK, H. J., 1950. The relation between medicine and psychology in England. In *Current trends in the relation of psychology to medicine*. Pittsburgh: Univ. Press.
30. EYSENCK, H. J., 1952. The effects of psychotherapy: an evaluation. *J. consult. Psychol.*, **16,** 319–24.
31. Eysenck, H. J., 1952. *The scientific study of personality*. London: Routledge and Kegan Paul.
32. EYSENCK, H. J., 1955. Psychiatric diagnosis as a psychological and statistical problem. *Psychol. Rep.*, **1,** 3–17.
33. EYSENCK, H. J., 1958. Personality tests: 1950–1955. In *Recent progress in psychiatry*, published by *J. ment. Sci.*, **3.**
34. EYSENCK, H. J., 1959. Learning theory and behaviour therapy. *J. ment. Sci.*, **105,** 61–75.
35. EYSENCK, H. J., 1960. *The structure of human personality*. London: Routledge and Kegan Paul.
36. EYSENCK, H. J. (Ed.), 1960. *Handbook of abnormal psychology*. London: Pitman.
37. EYSENCK, H. J. (Ed.), 1960. *Behaviour therapy and the neuroses*. London: Pergamon Press.
38. EYSENCK, H. J., 1961. Psychosis, drive and inhibition: a theoretical and experimental account. *Amer. J. Psychiat.*, **118,** 198–204.
39. EYSENCK, H. J., 1963. Behaviour therapy, extinction and relapse in neurotics. *Brit. J. Psychiat.*, **109,** 12–18.
40. EYSENCK, H. J., 1963. Behavior therapy, spontaneous remission and transference in neurotics. *Amer. J. Psychiat.*, **119,** 867–71.
41. EYSENCK, H. J., 1964. *Experiments in behaviour therapy*. Oxford: Pergamon Press.
42. EYSENCK, H. J., 1965. The effects of psychotherapy. *Internat. J. Psychiat.*, **1,** 99–144.
43. EYSENCK, H. J., 1965. A three-factor theory of reminiscence. *Brit. J. Psychol.*, **56,** 163–81.
44. EYSENCK, H. J. and CLARIDGE, G., 1962. The position of hysterics and dysthymics in a two-dimensional framework of personality description. *J. abnorm. soc. Psychol.*, **64,** 46–55.
45. EYSENCK, H. J., and RACHMAN, S., 1965. *The causes and cures of neurosis*. London: Routledge and Kegan Paul.
46. EYSENCK, S. B. G., 1956. Neurosis and psychosis: an experimental analysis. *J. ment. Sci.*, **102,** 517–29.
47. EYSENCK, S. B. G., EYSENCK, H. J., and CLARIDGE, G., 1960. Dimensions of personality, psychiatric syndromes, and mathematical models. *J. ment. Sci.*, **106,** 581–89.
48. FOULDS, G. A., 1955. The reliability of psychiatric and the validity of psychological diagnoses. *J. ment. Sci.*, **101,** 851–62.
49. FOULDS, G. A., 1965. *Personality and personal illness*. London: Tavistock.
50. FRANKS, C. M., 1957. Personality theory in Britain. In *Perspectives in personality theory*. Eds. David, H. P. and van Bracken H., New York: Basic Books.

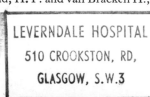

51. FRANKS, C. M., 1964. *Conditioning techniques in clinical practice and research.* New York: Springer.
52. FROEHLICH, C. P., 1953. Psychological testing in West Germany. *Educ. Psychol. Measmt.*, **13**, 548–73.
53. GLOVER, E., 1945. An examination of the Klein system of child psychology. In *The psychoanalytic study of the child*, vol. 1. New York: Internat. Univ. Press.
54. GOLDBERG, L. R., 1965. Diagnosticians vs. diagnostic signs. *Psychol. Monogr.*, **79**, No. 9.
55. GOOLKER, P., 1956. The role of diagnosis in psychiatry. *J. Hillside Hospital*, **5**, 361–67.
56. DE GROOT, M. J. W., 1958. Kwantitatieve benadering van het verzuim door neurosen bij Nederlandse fabrieksarbeiders. *Verhandeling van het Ned. Inst. v. Praeventieve Geneeskunde XXXIII.* Leiden.
57. HARDING, G. F., and CRAVENS, R. B., 1957. Military clinical psychology. *Amer. Psychol.*, **12**, 89–91.
58. HATHAWAY, S. R., 1958. A study of human behavior: the clinical psychologist. *Amer. Psych.*, **13**, 257–65.
59. HILTMAN, H., *et al.*, 1953. *Verlaufs analyse in der psychologischen Diagnostik.* Bern: Huber.
60. HOUT, H. V. D. (Ed.), 1956. *Psychology in Europe. Gawein*, **4**, 53–128.
61. HUNT, W. A., and WITTSON, C. L., 1956. Concurrence in psychiatric diagnosis. *U.S. Armed Forces Med. J.*, **7**, 1605–08.
62. HUNT, W. A., WITTSON, C. L., and HUNT, E. B., 1953. A theoretical and practical analysis of the diagnostic process. In *Current problems in psychiatric diagnosis.* Eds. Hoch, P. H., and Zubin, J. New York.
63. Joint report on relations between psychology and psychiatry, 1960. *Amer. Psychol.*, **15**, 198–200.
64. KAHN, M. W., and SANTOSTEFANO, S., 1962. The case of clinical psychology: a search for identity. *Amer. Psych.*, **17**, 185–89.
65. KING, G. F., 1954. Research with neuropsychiatric samples. *J. Psychol.*, **38**, 383–87.
66. KRASNER, L., and ULLMANN, L. P., Eds., 1965. *Research in behavior modification.* New York: Holt, Rinehart and Winston.
67. KREITMAN, N., 1961. The reliability of psychiatric diagnosis. *J. ment. Sci.*, **107**, 876–86.
68. KREITMAN, N., SAINSBURY, R., MORRISBEY, J., TOWERS, J., and SCRIVENER, J., 1961. The reliability of psychiatric assessment: an analysis. *J. ment. Sci.*, **107**, 887–908.
69. LANDIS, C., 1938. Statistical evaluation of psychotherapeutic methods. In *Concepts and problems of psychotherapy.* Ed. Hinsie, S. E. London: Heinemann.
70. LANG, P. J. and LAZOVIK, A. D., 1963. The experimental desensitization of a phobia. *J. abnorm. soc. Psychol.*, **66**, 519–25.
71. LEHNER, G. F. J., 1955. Psychological training facilities in Austria and West Germany. *Amer. Psychol.*, **10**, 79–82.
72. LEVITT, G. E., 1957. The results of psychotherapy with children: an evaluation. *J. consult. Psychol.*, **21**, 189–96.
73. LEVITT, G. E., 1963. Psychotherapy with children: a further evaluation. *Behav. Res. Ther.*, **1**, 45–51.
74. LEVY, L. H., 1962. The skew in clinical psychology. *Amer. Psychologist*, **17**, 244–49.
75. LONDON, I. D., 1951. Psychology in the U.S.S.R. *Amer. J. Psychol.*, **64**, 422–28.

76. LORR, M., KLETT, C. J., and McNAIR, D. M., 1963. *Syndromes of psychosis.* London: Pergamon Press.

77. LOSSEN, H., 1955. *Einführung in die Diagnostische Psychologie.* Stuttgart: Wolf.

78. LOVIBOND, S. H., 1963. Intermittent reinforcement in behaviour therapy. *Beh. Res. Ther.*, **1**, 127–32.

79. MAHER, B. A., 1957. Clinical psychology in Britain: a laboratory for the American psychologist. *Amer. Psychol.*, **12**, 147–50.

80. MEHLMAN, B., 1952. The reliability of psychiatric diagnosis. *J. abnorm. soc. Psychol.*, **47**, 577–78.

81. MEILI, R., 1955. *Lehrbuch der psychologischen Diagnostik.* Bern: Huber.

82. METZNER, R., 1961. Learning theory and the therapy of the neuroses. *Brit. J. Psychol. Monogr. Suppl.*, **33**.

83. MINTZ, A., 1958. Recent developments in psychology in the U.S.S.R. *Ann. Rev. of Psychol.*, **9**, 453–504.

84. MISIAK, H. and STAUDT, Virginia, 1953. Psychology in Italy. *Psychol. Bull.*, **50**, 347–61.

85. PAGE, J., 1938. Mental disease in Russia. *Amer. J. Psychiat.*, **94**, 859–65.

86. PAUL, G., 1964. *Effects of insight, desensitization and attention in placebo treatment of anxiety.* Urbana, Illinois: unpublished Ph.D. thesis.

87. PAYNE, R. W., 1955. L'utilité du test de Rorschach en psychologie clinique. *Rev. de Psychol. appliquée*, **5**, 255–64.

88. POPPER, K. A., 1948. *The logic of scientific discovery.* London: Routledge and Kegan Paul.

89. Proposed Standards for A.P.A. Directory listings of private practice. 1960. *Amer. Psychol.*, **15**, 110–12.

90. RACHMAN, S. Studies in desensitization: I, II, III. *Behav. Res. Ther.*, to appear.

91. RAIMY, V. C., Ed., 1950. *Training in clinical psychology.* New York: Prentice Hall.

92. ROE, A., Ed., 1959. *Graduate education in psychology.* Washington, D.C.: Amer. Psychol. Ass.

93. ROSENZWEIG, S., ROOK, W. T., and PEARSON, C. B., 1944. Education for clinical psychology. *J. consult. Psychol.*, **8**, 354–59.

94. ROSS, S., and LOCKMAN, R. F. 1964. Survey of graduate education in psychology. *Amer. Psychol.*, **19**, 623–28.

95. RÜMKE, H. C., 1953. De betrekkelijkheid van de psychiatrische diagnose in Nieuwe Studies en Voordrachten. Amsterdam hoofdstuk 7.

96. RYCHLAK, J. F., 1959. Clinical psychology and the nature of evidence. *Amer. Psychol.*, **14**, 642–48.

97. SCHMIDT, H. O. and FONDA, C. P., 1956. The reliability of psychiatric diagnosis: a new look. *J. abnorm. soc. Psychol.*, **52**, 262–67.

98. SEEMAN, W., 1953. Psychiatric diagnosis, an investigation of interperson reliability. *J. nerv. ment. Dis.*, **118**, 541–44.

99. SHAKOW, D., 1965. Seventeen years later: clinical psychology in the light of the 1947 committee on training in clinical psychology report. *Amer. Psychol.*, **20**, 353–62.

100. SHAPIRO, M. B., 1951. An experimental approach to diagnostic psychological testing. *J. ment. Sci.*, **97**, 748–46.

101. SHAPIRO, M. B., 1957. Experimental method in the psychological description of the individual psychiatric patient. *Internat. J. soc. Psychiat.*, **3**, 89–102.

102. SHAPIRO, M. B., 1961. The single case in fundamental psychological research. *Brit. J. med. Psychol.*, **34**, 255–61.

103. SHAPIRO, M. B., 1961. A method of measuring psychological changes specific to the individual psychiatric patient. *Brit. J. med. Psychol.*, **34**, 151–55.
104. SHAPIRO, M. B., 1964. The measurement of clinically relevant variables. *J. psychosom. Res.*, **8**, 245–54.
105. SHAPIRO, M. B., MARKS, I. M., and FOX, B., 1963. A therapeutic experiment on phobic and affective symptoms in an individual psychiatric patient. *Brit. J. soc. clin. Psychol.*, **2**, 81–93.
106. SHAPIRO, M. B. and NELSON, E. H., 1955. An investigation of an abnormality of cognitive function in a co-operative young psychotic. *J. clin. Psychol.*, **91**, 344–51.
107. SHAPIRO, M. B. and RAVENETTE, A. T., 1959. A preliminary experiment in paranoid delusions. *J. ment. Sci.*, **105**, 295–311.
108. SIMON, B., Ed., 1957. *Psychology in the Soviet Union.* Stanford: Univ. Press.
109. SMALL, L., 1963. Toward professional clinical psychology. *Amer. Psychol.*, **18**, 558–62.
110. STAR, S. A., 1950. The Screening of psychoneurotics: comparison of psychiatric diagnoses and test scores at all induction stations. In *Studies in social psychology in World War II*, vol. 4. Stouffer, S. A. Princeton: Measurement and Prediction.
111. STERN, E., Ed., 1954. *Die Tests in der Klinischen Psychologie*, 2 vols. Zurich: Rascher Verlag.
112. STROTHER, C., Ed., 1956. *Psychology and mental health.* Washington, D.C.: Amer. Psychol. Ass.
113. SUMMERFIELD, A., 1958. Clinical psychology in Britain. *Amer. Psychol.*, **13**, 171–76.
114. SUNDBERG, N. D., 1961. The practice of psychological testing in clinical services in the United States. *Amer. Psychol.*, **16**, 79–83.
115. SZASZ, T. S., 1961. *The myth of mental illness.* New York: Hoeber-Harper.
116. TRAPP, G. P. and FIELDS, S. J., 1959. The licensing act in Arkansas: its inception and impact. *Amer. Psych.*, **14**, 95–98.
117. TAYLOR, W. S., 1962. Psychoanalysis revised or psychodynamics developed? *Amer. Psych.*, **17**, 784–88.
118. ULLMANN, L. P. and KRASNER, L., Eds., 1965. *Case studies in behavior modification.* New York: Holt, Rinehart and Winston.
119. VANCE, F. L. and VOLSKY, T. C., 1962. Counseling and psychotherapy. *Amer. Psychol.*, **17**, 565–70.
120. WALLINGA, J. V., 1956. Variability in psychiatric diagnoses. *U.S. Armed Forces Med. J.*, **7**, 1305–12.
121. WILDER, J., 1945. Facts and figures in psychotherapy. *J. clin. Psychopath.*, **7**, 311–47.
122. WITTENHORN, J. R., 1955. *Psychiatric rating scales.* New York, Psychol. Corp.
123. WOLPE, J., 1958. *Psychotherapy by reciprocal inhibition.* Stanford: Univ. Press.
124. WRIGHT, D. G., 1948. Psychiatry and clinical psychology. In *An introduction to clinical psychology*. Eds. Pennington, L. A., and Berg, I. A. New York: Ronald.
125. YATES, A., 1958. The application of learning theory to the treatment of tics. *J. abnorm. soc. Psychol.*, **56**, 175–82.
126. ZUBIN, J., 1953. Evaluation of therapeutic outcome in mental disorders. *J. nerv. ment. Dis.*, **117**, 95–111.
127. ZUBIN, J., ERON, L. D., and SCHUMER, F., 1965. *An experimental approach to projective techniques.* London: J. Wiley and Sons.
128. ZUCKERMAN, S. B., 1954. Some notes on psychology in Germany. *J. clin. Psychol.* **10**, 353–57.

XIV

FAMILY PSYCHOPATHOLOGY AND

SCHIZOPHRENIA

JOHN G. HOWELLS

M.D., D.P.M.

Director
The Institute of Family Psychiatry
Ipswich and East Suffolk Hospital

1

Introduction

Schizophrenia constitutes a long recognized disorder with the most fascinating complex of symptoms in the whole of medicine. Yet international authorities do not agree about its definition, its incidence, or its aetiology.

That there is no agreement about its definition constitutes one of the greatest barriers to the formulation of investigations on it and to the comparison of research work going on in different countries—as the work on family psychopathology and schizophrenia will also demonstrate. Traditional European psychiatry bases its definition on the descriptive work of the German psychiatrists;[1, 2] to them the syndrome manifests a complex of symptoms that makes it unmistakable in most instances. In some European centres, usually with a dynamic orientation, and in the U.S.A., the definition is widened to include many patients who would not conform to the strict criteria of the German psychiatrists. In an attempt to bring order into definition, the Norwegian psychiatrist Langfeldt[3] proposed a classification of psychoses based on two types—'process' and 'non-process' psychoses. 'Process' psychosis covers the organic endogenous type and 'non-process' psychosis covers the remainder. Stephens and Astrup[4, 5] have shown that the former, 'process' psychosis, is accompanied by a poor prognosis. It would seem that 'non-process' psychosis includes

14

the graver types of emotional illness (neurosis), manifesting well-marked abnormal behaviour. Abnormal behaviour can arise from a number of causes—toxic, endocrine, emotional and schizophrenic. Unfortunately, in some quarters abnormal behaviour is always assumed to be due to schizophrenic processes, despite the fact that some of the most alarming behaviour is seen in agitated emotional states. The two, schizophrenia and emotional illness, should not be confused, otherwise the definition of schizophrenia will be greatly widened and embrace non-schizophrenic abnormal behaviour. Sometimes symptomatology overlaps, e.g. that dyspnoea of anaemia overlaps with dyspnoea of cancer of the chest, does not make anaemia and cancer of the chest into two identical conditions. Similarly, some of the symptomatology of severe emotional states, e.g. withdrawal, overlaps with the symptoms of schizophrenia, but this does not make schizophrenia and emotional illness into identical conditions.

Differing definitions of schizophrenia constitutes one of the reasons for the disparities in estimations of the incidence of the condition. In Europe where a definition akin to the 'process' definition of Langfeldt is employed the condition is uncommon. For example, English studies[6, 7, 8] point to the low incidence of schizophrenia. In some countries the condition is diagnosed much more frequently than this.

Definition of the condition and thus more accurate studies of incidence would gain from the isolation of the aetiological factor or factors in this condition. Many formulations are put forward—genetic, constitutional, endocrine, neuropathological, biochemical, toxic and psychological. The latter has hitherto been confined to formulations based on individual psychopathology. It was natural that with the increasing interest in the family its psychopathology should be explored as a possible fundamental aetiological factor. However, work here may be frustrated for the same reasons as operate in the other fields—and one of the most cogent is the failure to arrive at an agreed definition of the condition. Criteria employed in its definition should be clearly stated in every case.

As many views are expressed later in this chapter on family psychopathology in relation to schizophrenia, some common criteria for establishing the value of each must be enunciated at the start. Many parameters of judgement could be used, but space makes it essential to limit them to a few crucial ones. These are:

1. Is the condition under study indubitably schizophrenia?

2. Is the anomaly in family functioning definable by precise criteria?

3. Does the anomaly cause schizophrenia or is it only associated with it? In other words, is a definite link established between the anomaly and schizophrenia. When the anomaly is present, is schizophrenia produced? When the anomaly is removed will the schizophrenia improve?

4. Is this anomaly always present in the family when one of its members is schizophrenic? A representative sample of schizophrenics must be studied.

5. Is this anomaly present in the families of schizophrenics by chance? Thus the need for controlled studies using matched groups of healthy patients, neurotic patients, and schizophrenics.

6. Does the hypothesis satisfy a feature of the illness, its onset in adolescence?

At this point the author should reveal his own hypothesis that provides an alternative for the explanation of the data: (*i*) 'process' schizophrenia is qualitatively different from 'non-process' schizophrenia. The former has an organic aetiology, the latter is severe emotional illness. In the former, 'process' schizophrenia, the perceptual and communication difficulties of the schizophrenic arise due to dysfunction of the intra cerebral organic machinery of thought and communication and not due to external events in the family. (*ii*) In the author's view the anomalies described in this chapter do not constitute all the anomalies associated with emotional illness. Many others are present in healthy families, mildly neurotic families and severely neurotic families ('non-process' schizophrenia). The more disturbed the family the clearer are the anomalies and the greater number there are—as can be seen in studies[9] of hard-core (problem) families. (*iii*) The anomalies of family functioning described in this chapter are coincidental with 'process' schizophrenia and do not cause it; they are found in association with severe neurosis (including 'non-process' schizophrenia), to a lesser extent in mild neurosis, and to some extent in healthy families. The families of 'process' schizophrenics approximate to the families of the population at large; the population at large has marked psychopathology in about 30 per cent of its families and this will therefore be true of the families of 'process' schizophrenia by chance alone. This explains why these anomalies are found coincidently in the families of some 'process' schizophrenics. In the families of institutionalized 'process' schizophrenics, a selection factor may operate to increase the incidence of anomalies—the more disturbed families with the greater number of anomalies can tolerate handicapped members less well and therefore there is an increase of institutionalized 'process' schizophrenics from these disturbed families.

As will be seen a number of anomalies in family functioning are put forward to explain the development of schizophrenia in one of the family members. Space does not allow complete coverage and thus a number of well-known postulations are taken for demonstration, while a number of others, that may prove to be equally valuable, are also briefly mentioned. A number of associated matters are considered and the chapter will conclude with an overall evaluation.

A striking quality of most of the literature on this subject, with a few exceptions, is the lack of clear concepts. Experts on communication, it seems, find it difficult to communicate. Intellectualization, based on a modicum of fact, flourishes. The danger of such vagueness is that it may be interpreted as a cloak for ignorance and the formulations ignored. An even greater danger is that we may assume knowledge when there is none, and elevate the work to the status of mysticism. In putting forward the various viewpoints of the proponents, care has been exercised even to the employment of paraphrase when in doubt, and full references are supplied which the reader is invited to study whenever he is in doubt.

2

Main Studies

The Views of Bowen

Bowen[10] has been admirably clear in stating his views about his family concept of schizophrenia. These are worth outlining in some detail.

Bowen's view, that the schizophrenic psychosis of a patient is a symptom manifesting an acute process involving a triad of the family, arose from clinical research over three and a half years in which schizophrenic patients and their parents lived together on a psychiatric ward at the National Institute of Mental Health, Bethesda, U.S.A. The family unit is regarded as a single organism, and the patient is seen as that part of the family organism through which the overt symptoms of psychosis are expressed.

The initial focus of the study, started in 1954, was on the mother-patient relationship. At this point there was increasing evidence that the mother was an intimate part of the patient's problems, that the mother-patient relationship was a dependent fragment of the larger family problem, and that the father played an important part in it. At the end of the first year the hypothesis was extended to regard the psychosis in the patient as a symptom of the total family problem. This coincided with developing 'family psychotherapy' as a new plan of psychotherapy.

Bowen has come to regard schizophrenia as a process which requires three or more generations to develop. The grandparents are relatively mature, but their combined immaturities are acquired by the one child who is most attached to the mother. When this child marries a spouse with an equal degree of immaturity, and when the same process repeats itself in the third generation, it results in a child, the patient, with a high degree of immaturity.

A constant finding in his families was a marked emotional distance between the parents. Bowen referred to this as 'emotional divorce'. In all the families, the parents have definite patterns of functioning in the emotional divorce' situation. Both parents are equally immature. One denies the immaturity and functions with a facade of overadequacy. The other accentuates the immaturity and functions with a facade of inadequacy. There are some constantly recurring situations which accompany the overadequate-inadequate reciprocity. One is the 'domination-submission issue'. On personal issues, especially decisions that affect both parents, the one who makes the decision becomes the overadequate one and the other becomes the inadequate one.

One of the outstanding characteristics of the family is the inability of the parents to make decisions. The decision to have a child is the most difficult of all decisions in these families. For the mother, the pregnancy becomes a constant frustration between 'promise of fulfilment' and a 'threat that it could never be true'. A significant shift in the husband-wife relationship begins when the wife first knows that she is pregnant. At this point she becomes more emotionally invested in the unborn child than in the husband.

At the birth of the child the mother is securely in the overadequate position to another human being, this human being belonging to her and realistically helpless. She can now control her own immaturity by caring for the immaturity of another—the child. The mother-child relationship is the most active and intense relationship in the family. The term 'intense' describes an ambivalent relationship in which the thoughts of both, whether positive or negative, are largely invested in each other. The mother makes two main demands on the patient, the more forcible of which is the emotional demand that the patient remain helpless. This is conveyed in subtle, forceful ways which are out of conscious awareness. The other is the overt, verbalized, 'hammered home' demand that the patient become a gifted and mature person. Bowen thinks of two levels of process between the mother and the patient. Much of the emotional demand that the patient remain a child is conveyed on an action level and out of conscious awareness of either mother or patient. The verbal level is usually a direct contradiction to the action level. In this reciprocal functioning, Bowen sees similarities between it and Wynne's 'pseudo-mutuality', and Jackson's 'complementarity'.

Prominent features of every mother-patient relationship in these cases are the mother's worries, doubts and concerns about the patient. These are a continuation of the mother's overinvestment that began before the child was born. The subjects of the mother's concern about the patient and the focus of her 'picking on the patient' are the same as her own feelings of inadequacy about herself. The term 'projection' refers to the most all-pervasive mechanism in the mother-child relationship. It has been used constantly by the mother of every patient in her relationship with him. According to Bowen's thinking, the mother can function more adequately by ascribing to her child certain aspects of herself, which the child accepts. This is of crucial importance in the area of the mother's immaturity. The mother then 'mothers' the helplessness in the child (her own projected feelings) with her adequate self, thus, a situation that begins as *a feeling in the mother, becomes a reality in the child*.

Bowen proceeds to throw light on the mechanisms of symptom formation. The 'projection' occurs also on the levels of physical illness. This is a mechanism in which the soma of one person reciprocates with the psyche of another person. An anxiety in one person becomes a physical illness in another. The somatic reciprocation often includes definite physical pathology. A striking series of such reciprocations occur in a mother in response to a rapid improvement in a regressed patient. Within a few hours of each significant change in the patient, the mother develops a physical illness of several days' duration.

The child, Bowen believes, is involved in the same two levels of process as the mother, except that the mother actively initiates her emotional and verbal demands, and the child is more involved in responding to the mother's demands than in initiating his own. In this process, Bowen can see similarity with Bateson's 'double bind' hypothesis. The response of the patient to the mother's demands varies with the degree of functional helplessness of the patient, and the functional strength of the mother. A very helpless and regressed patient will comply immediately to emotional demands and pay little attention to verbal demands. The compliance of an inadequate patient to the mother's emotional demands is almost instantaneous. The patient lives his life as though the mother would die without his 'help', and if the mother died, then he would die too. The child makes his emotional and verbal demands on the mother by exploiting the helpless, pitiful position.

All Bowen's research families have followed the basic patterns of over-adequate mother, helpless patient, and peripherally attached father. Bowen leans strongly to the belief that the essential process is confined to the father, mother, patient triad, rather than to the whole family.

When the child's self is devoted to 'being for the mother' Bowen holds that he loses the capacity of 'being for himself'. He stresses the function of 'being helpless', rather than the fixed 'is helpless' viewpoint. The process in which the child begins to 'be for the mother' results in an arrest in its psychological growth. It can now be seen, how, in Bowen's view, the acute psychosis develops. The rapid growth of the child at adolescence interferes with the functioning equilibrium of the inter-dependent triad. There is an increasing anxiety in all three members. The adolescent period is one in which the growth process repeatedly upsets the equilibrium and the emotional process attempts to restore it. The conscious verbal expressions demand that the child be more grown up. The child's course from adolescence to the acute psychosis is one in which he changes from a helpless child, to a poorly functioning adult, to a helpless patient. Once free of the mother, he faces outside relationships without a self of his own. The psychosis represents an unsuccessful attempt to adapt the severe psychological impairment to the demands of adult functioning. It represents a disruption of the symbiotic attachment to the mother and a collapse of the long-term interdependent father-mother-patient triad.

The patient need not develop a psychosis. Bowen believes that unresolved, symbiotic attachments to the mother varies from the very mild to the very intense, that the mild one causes little impairment, and that schizophrenic psychosis develops among those with the most intense, unresolved attachment. There are a number of ways in which the individual in an intense attachment may find some solution to his dilemma. Certain individuals are able to replace the original mother with a mother substitute. The functional helplessness may find expression in somatic illness. The person with a character neurosis uses a flight mechanism to deal with the helplessness. The patients in Bowen's families attempted to find distant relationships. The psychotic collapse is seen as an effort at resolution that failed.

Bowen's work also led to formulations about the therapy of the schizophrenics. It could be seen that when father was encouraged to be less inadequate and to be a husband in a fuller sense, then the 'emotional divorce' disappeared and the patient lost the symbiotic relationship with the mother. The closer emotionally the parents were to one another, the greater the patient's improvement.

In addition to the above important contribution, Bowen has developed elsewhere[11-14] views about special aspects of the family. His one time collaborators, Dysinger[15-17] and Brodey[18, 19] have elaborated on the work.

Discussion. The work just outlined will be briefly discussed in the light of the six criteria put forward in the introduction.

1. A precise definition of schizophrenia, which would win universal acceptance, is not found in the work.

2. The anomaly in family functioning is clearly expressed, but it is far from being a simple or discrete concept.

3. A link between the anomaly and schizophrenia is not too clearly established. Indeed, the anomaly need not cause schizophrenia; it is a matter of degree of anomaly. There are no experiments on the artificial production of the anomaly and thus of schizophrenia. It is claimed, however, that attenuating the anomaly by treatment aimed at increasing father's participation may improve the patient.

4. It is not known whether the sample was a representative sample of schizophrenics. But the pattern seemed consistent for the group studied.

5. It is not known if the anomaly is present by chance alone as no control groups were employed and studied.

6. An explanation is offered for the age of onset in adolescence—the unsuccessful attempt by the patient to adapt his severe psychological impairment to the demands of adult functioning.

Side issues of the work include the three generation spread of immaturity—noticed by Henry,[20] Mendell and Fisher,[21] and Howells[22] but regarded by these workers as characteristic of emotional illness; the 'see-saw' shift of symptomatology noted also by Howells[23] and regarded as characteristic of emotional illness; double communication between mother and child, noted also by the Palo Alto group; the mechanism of somatic symptom formation; treatment by family group therapy.

If acceptance of Bowen's view has to be made it must be dependent on an assurance that he is studying patients who indubitably suffer from schizophrenia. The anomaly described coincides closely with anomalies described by many workers in the background of emotional illness. His study does not exclude the possibility of many other anomalies being present that are found in the families of the emotionally ill but on which his studies did not focus. His findings would be consistent with his patients being severely emotionally ill, rather than schizophrenic.

The Views of Wynne et al.

Wynne and his collaborators[24-31] have continued the work on families begun by Bowen at the National Institute of Mental Health. These workers have concentrated mainly on schizophrenic illness in which the onset of psychosis occurred acutely in late adolescence or early adulthood. They feel that the striving for relatedness to other human beings may be regarded as a primary feature of the human situation. Another key feature is that every human being strives consciously and unconsciously, in a lifelong process, to develop a sense of personal identity. They consider that the universal necessity for dealing with both the problems of relation and identity leads to three main solutions. These are (*i*) mutuality, (*ii*) non-mutuality, and (*iii*) pseudo-mutuality.

Each person brings to the relations of genuine *mutuality* a sense of his own meaningful, positively-valued identity, and, out of experience of participation together, mutual recognition of identity develops, including a growing recognition of each other's potentialities and capacities.

Many interpersonal relations are not characterized by either mutuality or pseudo-mutuality, but by *non-mutuality*. The interchange of customer and sales clerk, for example, does not ordinarily involve beyond the purchase of merchandize a strong investment in excluding non-complementarity, or in exploring what the relationship has to offer to either person.

Pseudo-mutuality is a miscarried 'solution' of widespread occurrence. This kind of relatedness, in an especially intense and enduring form, contributes significantly to the family experience of people who later, if other factors are also present, develop acute schizophrenic episodes. In pseudo-mutuality emotional investment is directed more towards maintaining the sense of reciprocal fulfilment of expectations, than towards accurately perceiving changing expectations. The relation which persists can not be given up, except under very dire or special circumstances, nor be allowed to develop or expand. Thus the pseudo-mutual relation involves a characteristic dilemma; divergence is permitted as leading to disruption of the relation, and therefore must be avoided; but if divergence is avoided, growth of the relation is impossible.

Wynne and his co-workers believed that within the family of persons who later developed acute schizophrenic episodes, those relations which are openly acknowledged as acceptable have a quality of intense and enduring pseudo-mutuality. In these families the predominant pre-psychotic picture is a fixed organization of a limited number of engulfing roles. Such a family role structure may already be forming in the phantasy life of the parents before the birth of the child, who sometimes is expected to fill some kind of void in the parents' life. Thus these workers believe that non-complementarity has a more intense and enduring threat in the families of schizophrenics than it has in other families in which pseudo-mutuality may also appear. They also think that, in the families of potential schizophrenics, the intensity and duration of pseudo-mutuality has led to the development of a particular variety of shared family mechanisms by which deviations from the family role structure are excluded from recognition or are delusionally re-interpreted. The individual family member is not allowed to differentiate his personal identity either within or outside the family role structure.

Normally, shared cultural mechanisms and codes facilitate the selection of those aspects of communication to which attention should be paid. In contrast, in schizophrenic relations, the shared mechanisms facilitate a failure in selection of meaning. It is not simply that divergence is kept out of awareness, but rather that the discriminative perception of those events which might specifically constitute divergence is aborted and blurred. At this point the views of Wynne and his colleagues show some similarities to the perceptual anomalies referred to by Bateson and his collaborators as the 'double bind' situation.

Pseudo-mutuality must be maintained at all costs. This leads to the maintenance of stereotyped roles in the families of schizophrenics. These roles constrict identity development and contribute to serious crises including psychosis. This is the subject of a later paper.[25]

The potential schizophrenic, Wynne and his colleagues believe, develops considerable skill and an immense positive investment in fulfilling family complementarity and in saving the family, as well as himself, from the panic of disillusion. However, as he approaches chronological adulthood, with the shift or loss of family figures, and exposure to new outside relations more seductive or coercive than earlier ones, there comes a time when he can no longer superimpose the family identity upon his ego identity. Acute schizophrenic panic or disorganization seem to represent an identity crisis in the face of overwhelming guilt and anxiety attendant upon moving out of a particular kind of family role structure. Later, pseudo-mutuality is re-established, in a chronic state, at a greater psychological distance from the family members, with an increasing guilt and anxiety over subsequent moves towards differentiation, and with heightened autism, loneliness, and emptiness of experience. The psychotic episode as a whole represents a miscarried attempt at attaining individuality. He succeeds in attaining independence in some ways, only by withdrawal. In addition the overt psychosis may have a covert function of giving expression to the family's collective, although disassociated, desires for individuality.

In their original work, Wynne and his colleagues formulated a hypothesis which has been the springboard for present research. They believed the fragmentation of experience, the identity diffusion, the disturbed modes of perception and communication, and certain other characteristics of the acute reactive schizophrenic personality structure are, to a significant extent, derived by processes of internalization from characteristics of the family social organization. Thus they have gone on to study the links between family patterns of thought disorder in schizophrenia. They believe, after a number of systematic studies, that it is possible to differentiate individual forms of thinking and to predict the form of thinking that will develop from the patterns of perceiving, relating and communication within the family. This work is described in a series of four papers.[26-29]

Through the use of projective techniques these workers have been able to predict the form of thinking and the degree of disorganization of each patient's offspring from the tests of *other* members of his family, and to match blindly patients and their families. The workers have evolved a classification of schizophrenic disorders which is based upon thought disorder. This classification provides a means of discriminating along two continua, among varieties of schizophrenic and paranoid thinking. They define thought disorder as including not only forms of thinking which are disrupted or *fragmented* by primary process phenomena, but also by quieter, less bizarre, *amorphous* forms of thinking. In their formulation the amorphous thinking schizophrenics have a schizophrenic thought disorder of an especially ominous type.

In another investigation Singer and Wynne[30] have differentiated characteristics of parents of childhood schizophrenics, childhood neurotics, and young adult schizophrenics. This was done through the analysis of the Thematic Apperception Test and the Rorschach. The parents of twenty autistic children were primarily differentiated at a statistically significant level of accuracy from sociologically matched parents of neurotic children. The parents of the neurotic children, half withdrawn and half aggressive, were in turn successfully differentiated into these two groups on the basis of the parental projective tests. The results showed that the disaffiliative tendencies of the parents of the autistic young children were especially significant, while the parents of patients whose schizophrenia did not become overt until late adolescence or young adulthood appeared to let relationships develop that distorted and impaired the focusing of attention and the acquisition of clear meanings. The parents of the acting out children in this series were active and energetic in these relationships, though often with various disturbed moods and impulses, and were relatively well defined and clear in their percepts. Parents of a group of withdrawn neurotic children showed especially sadness, together with serious strivings to maintain relationships. Morris and Wynne[31] match styles of parental communication and schizophrenic offspring in another paper.

Discussion. Comment on the above work in the light of the six criteria is as follows:

1. No clear definition of schizophrenia emerges.

2. The anomaly in family functioning is less clearly defined than by Bowen. The anomaly is diffuse if not separated into a number of unlinked parts. Aspects of it show similarities to the views of Bowen and the Palo Alto group.

3. The direct link between the anomaly and schizophrenia is not clear. There are no experiments in producing the family anomaly and hence schizophrenia. The results of family therapy are not precisely stated; however, it is claimed that from the form of family functioning it is possible to predict the type of schizophrenia.

4. Varieties of the anomaly, it is maintained, are always found in the families of schizophrenics, but it is not known whether the group studied is a representative sample of schizophrenics.

5. It is said that the parents (not the family) of child schizophrenics, adolescent schizophrenics and child neurotics can be differentiated. But the method employed is indirect and imprecise—through the Thematic Apperception Test and Rorschach techniques. The findings would be equally consistent with differing attitudes in parents in different groups of the emotionally ill.

6. An explanation, with similarity to Bowen's view, is offered for the emergence of schizophrenia in adolescence.

Side issues are: types of schizophrenia are differentiated; predictive studies are employed.

Here again acceptance of Wynne's views must depend on an assurance that schizophrenics are under study. All aspects of the anomaly are also found in the families of the emotionally ill and the findings are not inconsistent with his patients being in this state. Other anomalies that may be present to an equal or greater degree are not studied.

The Views of Lidz et al.

Lidz, Fleck, Cornelison and their Yale colleagues have also been responsible for a number of important studies concerning anomalies in patterns of behaviour in the families of schizophrenics. Lidz[32—54] began his interests in the families of schizophrenics in 1949. He studied the histories of fifty patients and found that in only five out of the fifty could the patient be considered to have been raised in a reasonably favourable home, which contained two stable and compatible parents until the patient was eighteen years old. The large majority were impeded by multiple deleterious influences, which were chronically present or frequently recurrent. The paternal influence, according to this gross evaluation, was harmful as frequently as the maternal. In 1952 Lidz commenced a series of investigations on the families of seventeen patients. These studies are collected together in a recent volume.[55]

Fleck[56] gave a progress report in 1960. By then the workers had found that the study of their families shed much light on many schizophrenic manifestations, and that aspects of the parental personalities, and of intrafamilial behaviour of all members, determine much of what they consider characteristic or pathognomonic of schizophrenia.

Some of the characteristic forms of family dysfunction related to schizophrenic manifestations that the workers observed were:

1. Failure to form a nuclear family, in that one or both parents remain primarily attached to one of his or her parents or siblings.

2. Family schisms due to parental strife and lack of role reciprocity.

3. Family skews when one dyadic relationship within it dominates family life at the expense of the needs of other members.

4. Blurring of generation lines in the family, e.g. (*i*) when one parent competes with children in skewed families; (*ii*) when one parent establishes a special bond with a child giving substance to the schizophrenic's claim that he or she is more important to the parent than the spouse; and (*iii*) when continued erotization of a parent-child relationship occurs.

5. Pervasion of the entire family atmosphere with irrational, usually paranoid, ideation.

6. Persistence of conscious incestuous preoccupation and behaviour within the group.

7. Socio-cultural isolation of the family as a concomitant of the six preceding conditions.

8. Failure to educate toward and facilitate emancipation of the offspring from the family, a further consequence of points 1–5.

9. Handicapping of a child in achieving sexual identity and maturity by the parents' uncertainty over their own sex roles.

10. Presentation to a child of prototypes for identification that are irreconcilable in a necessary process of consolidating his own personality.

Further findings in these families were that the siblings, who were of the same sex as the patient, were clearly more disturbed as a group than the siblings of the opposite sex. This led to an examination of the data on the family pathology of the seventeen schizophrenic patients according to their sex. The workers found that schizophrenic males often came from skewed families with passive, ineffectual fathers and disturbed, engulfing mothers; whereas schizophrenic girls typically grew up in schismatic families with narcisistic fathers, who were often paranoid and, while seductive of their daughter, were disparaging of women, and with mothers who were unemphatic and emotionally distant.

More recently, Lidz[57] has reviewed some of the findings from the families of schizophrenic patients to families generally. In lectures given at Tulane University he examined the thesis that the isolated nuclear family, despite its paucity of stabilizing forces, is better suited for preparing its children to live in a society that is rapidly changing its adaptive techniques, than are families with extended kinships systems. The instability of the isolated nuclear family can, however, reach such proportions as to be unable to provide sufficient structuring, security and satisfaction for its members. In his second lecture Lidz proposed that the essential dynamic structure of the family rests upon the parents' ability to form a coalition, maintain boundaries between the generations, and adhere to their appropriate sex-linked roles. Failure to meet these few requisites leads to distortion of the ego structuring of their children. In the last lecture he focuses specifically on the transmission of linguistic meanings. A grasp of the complexities of the acquisition of language and logic by the child suggested the possibility that schizophrenic patients received a faulty and confused grounding in linguistic meanings, as well as in other instrumental techniques, and that both limited their adaptive capacities and permitted them to escape from insoluble conflict, or irreconcilable contradictions, by abandoning the meaning system of their culture. Our children obtain their fundamental training in meanings and logic within the family, and, as irreconcilable conflicts also usually have their roots within the family, it appears essential to scrutinize the family environment in which schizophrenic patients grow up. Investigations have shown that such patients have invariably been raised in seriously disturbed families, which almost always contain at least one unusually disturbed parent. Lidz concluded that it is a tenable hypothesis that schizophrenia is a type of maladaption and malintegration due to deficiencies in acquired instrumental techniques in ego structuring, rather than the cause of some process which disrupts the integrative capacity of the brain.

Discussion. Comments on the six criteria are as follows:

1. Here again Lidz *et al.* must convince psychiatric opinion that their seventeen patients were in fact indubitably schizophrenics.

2. The anomalies of schizophrenic families are several in number, although prominence is given to the child's receiving a confused grounding in linguistic meanings. Even the latter is a broad concept.

3. A clear link between the anomalies present in the family and schizophrenia is not established.

4. Not one anomaly, but one of a number of anomalies are said always to be present in the families of schizophrenics. The anomalies differ in male from female schizophrenics. It is not known if the sample of schizophrenics are representative of all schizophrenics.

5. Controlled studies are not employed, and the possibility of the anomalies being present by chance is not excluded.

6. The hypothesis does not adequately explain the emergence of schizophrenia in adolescence.

Side issues of the work are: concepts of family schism and family skew; a study of the acquisition of logic and language by the child.

A number of the identical anomalies in the parents and families of the emotionally ill have previously been noted by workers. The findings are not inconsistent with the patients being emotionally ill.

The Views of the Palo Alto Group

In 1952 a group of workers commenced a research project at Palo Alto which terminated ten years later, in 1962. From this work one element, the 'double bind' hypothesis, has received a great deal of attention. But the workers themselves, however, regard it as part of a general communicational approach to a wide range of human behaviour including schizophrenia.[58-127] They are particularly concerned with the incongruity in communication.

In the original formulation there were four elements. Haley held that symptoms of schizophrenia were suggestive of an inability to discriminate the Logical Types—a part of communication theory. Bateson added the notion of the 'double bind' hypothesis. Jackson contributed his ideas on 'family homeostasis'—a constancy of the internal environment maintained by an interplay of dynamic forces. Analogies between hypnosis and schizophrenia were added by Weakland and Haley.

It may be useful to repeat here the definition of a 'double bind' from the original paper:[60]

'The necessary ingredients for a double bind situation, as we see it, are:

1. *Two or more persons.* Of these, we designate one, for purposes of our definition, as the "victim". We do not assume that the double bind is inflicted by the mother alone, but that it may be done either by mother alone or by some combination of mother, father and/or siblings.

2. *Repeated experience.* We assume that the double bind is a recurrent theme in the experience of the victim. Our hypothesis does not invoke a single traumatic experience, but such repeated experience that the double bind structure comes to be an habitual expectation.

3. *A primary negative injunction.* This may have either of two forms: (*i*) "Do not do so and so, or I will punish you," (*ii*) "If you do not do so and so, I will punish you." Here we select a context of learning based on avoidance of punishment rather than a context of reward seeking. There is perhaps no formal reason for this selection. We assume that the punishment may be either the withdrawal of love or the expression of hate or anger—or most devastating—the kind of abandonment that results from the parent's expression of extreme helplessness.

4. *A secondary injunction conflicting with the first at a more abstract level, and like the first enforced by punishments or signals which threaten survival.* This secondary injunction is more difficult to describe than the primary for two reasons. First, the secondary injunction is commonly communicated to the child by nonverbal means. Posture, gesture, tone of voice, meaningful action, and the implications concealed in verbal comment may all be used to convey this more abstract message. Second, the secondary

injunction may impinge upon any element of the primary prohibition. Verbalization of the secondary injunction may, therefore, include a wide variety of forms; for example, "Do not see this as punishment"; "Do not see me as the punishing agent"; "Do not submit to my prohibitions"; "Do not think of what you must not do"; "Do not question my love of which the primary prohibition is (or is not) an example"; and so on. Other examples become possible when the double bind is inflicted not by one individual but by two. For example, one parent may negate at a more abstract level the injunctions of the other.

5. *A tertiary negative injunction prohibiting the victim from escaping from the field.* In a formal sense, it is perhaps unnecessary to list this injunction as a separate item since the reinforcement at the other two levels involves a threat to survival, and if the double binds are imposed during infancy, escape is naturally impossible. However, it seems that in some cases the escape from the field is made impossible by certain devices which are not purely negative, e.g. capricious promises of love, and the like.

6. Finally, the complete set of ingredients is no longer necessary when the victim has learned to perceive his universe in double bind patterns. Almost any part of a double bind sequence may then be sufficient to precipitate panic or rage. The pattern of conflicting injunctions may even be taken over by hallucinatory voices.'

The workers conceive the family situation of the schizophrenic as follows:

'1. A child whose mother becomes anxious and withdraws if the child responds to her as a loving mother. That is, the child's very existence has a special meaning to the mother which arouses her anxiety and hostility when she is in danger of intimate contact with the child.

2. A mother to whom feelings of anxiety and hostility towards the child are not acceptable, and whose ways of denying them is to express overt loving behaviour to persuade the child to respond to her as a loving mother and to withdraw from him if he does not. "Loving behaviour" does not necessarily imply "affection"; it can, for example, be set in a framework of doing the proper thing, instilling "goodness" and the like.

3. The absence of anyone in the family, such as the strong and insightful father, who can intervene in the relationship between the mother and child and support the child in the face of the contradictions involved.'

In this situation, the mother of a schizophrenic will be simultaneously expressing two orders of message. To put it in another way, if the mother begins to feel affectionate and is close to her child, she begins to feel endangered and must withdraw from him; but she cannot accept this hostile act and to deny it must simulate affection and closeness with the child. The child must not discriminate accurately between orders of message, in this case the difference between the expression of simulated feelings (one Logical Type) and real feelings (another Logical Type). As a result the child must systematically distort his percept of meta-communicative signals. It is essential to appreciate that the double bind situation is responsible for the inner conflicts of Logical Typing.

The workers give an example. The mother might say, 'Go to bed, you're very tired. I want you to get your sleep.' This overtly loving statement is intended to deny a feeling which could be verbalized as, 'Get out of my sight because I'm sick of you.' This means that the child must deceive himself about his own internal state in order to support mother in her deception. To survive with her he must falsely discriminate his own internal messages, thus upsetting the Logical Typing as well as falsely discriminate the messages of others. The child is punished for discriminating accurately what the mother is expressing, and he is punished for discriminating inaccurately—he is caught in a double bind. It is hypothesized that a child continually subjected to this situation develops a psychosis. A psychosis seems a way of dealing with double bind situations to overcome their inhibiting and controlling effect.

At first the double bind was studied in relation to a two-party situation, but was later extended to involve a three-party case, mother, father and child. The parents of a schizophrenic child formed a special triadic system in the larger family unit. Psychotic behaviour is seen as an attempt to adapt to double bind situations. Psychotic behaviour was seen as a sequence of messages which infringed a set of prohibitions which were qualified as not infringing them. The only way an individual could achieve this was by qualifying incongruently all levels of his communication. At a later stage interest of the workers focused on the many manifestations of incongruent communication in the family.

At the end of ten years of research the group agreed on a statement about the double bind:[79]

'1. The double bind is a class of sequences which appear when phenomena are examined with a concept of levels of communication.

2. In schizophrenia the double bind is a necessary but not sufficient condition in explaining etiology and, conversely, is an inevitable by-product of schizophrenic communication.

3. Empirical study and theoretical description of individuals and families should, for this type of analysis, emphasize observable communication, behaviour, and relationship contexts rather than focusing upon the perception or affective states of individuals.

4. The most useful way to phrase double bind description is not in terms of a binder and a victim, but in terms of people caught up in an ongoing system which produces conflicting definitions of the relationship and consequent subjective distress. In its attempts to deal with the complexities of multi-level patterns in human communications systems, the research group prefers an emphasis upon circular systems of interpersonal relations to a more conventional emphasis upon the behaviour of individuals alone or single sequences in the interaction.'

Discussion. Comments on the six criteria are as follows:

1. Yet again the workers must be able to satisfy psychiatric opinion that they are indubitably studying schizophrenic patients.

2. At first the anomaly of family functioning was isolated as the double bind hypothesis. However, later this concept was greatly broadened to include incongruent communication and to involve a system or pattern of relating.

3. The direct link between the broad and recent description of anomalies and the onset of schizophrenia is far from clear. This applies even to the narrower concept of the double bind. It is not clear why psychosis should be regarded as a way to adjust to a double bind situation; other possibilities are open, e.g. to simulate deafness, or to develop lack of attention; or to accept the whole situation by the parent as a rejection, or the child might interpret the first message as false and the second as the right message and thus there would be no confusion, or the child might see through the total situation—since the double bind is a common situation in everyday life to which he would learn to adjust. The results of the treatment of schizophrenics by the manipulation of the family anomalies are not sufficiently clear to make a reliable judgement possible.

4. The workers imply that the double bind is a necessary but not sufficient condition to cause schizophrenia. Furthermore, they add that the double bind situation may result from schizophrenia. It is not known whether the sample employed is a true representative sample of schizophrenics as a whole.

5. The anomalies could be present by chance in the families of schizophrenics. Controlled studies are not employed. The double bind situation for instance is very common in everyday life. It is also clear that in addition to manifesting or producing double bind situations the parents who do this also have a number of other qualities which may be disturbing to children. It could be argued that these other qualities within the parents are equally significant in producing schizophrenia.

6. Convincing reasons for the development of the illness in adolescence are not given.

Side issues are: work was extended to families of non-schizophrenics; family therapy techniques were developed; interest focused on communication; attention was paid to family homeostasis and hypnosis.

It must be repeated again that the findings are not inconsistent with the individuals studied being emotionally ill. Though attention at first focused on the double bind, many other elements described in the parents and families, including the defective communication have been observed by other workers as being present in the families of the emotionally ill.

3

Other Views

Some of the more recent, but no less important, views on the family process in relation to schizophrenia will be briefly reviewed.

Spiegel[128, 129] has paid much attention to the social roles within families, imposed by the culture. The acculturation process may lead to strain in the family role systems. Role conflict calls forth re-equilibrating processes, either role modification or role distortion. Role distortion is associated with the appearance of symptoms of psychopathology in family members, including psychosis. In an adult, if the role distortion ceases to operate, the symptoms may disappear. However, if in a child, the role distortion operates over a long period of time, the deformation of the underlying personality may be permanent.

Ackerman, a pioneer in family studies, considers the whole spectrum of abnormal mental functioning, including schizophrenia. This latter he links with role playing. Rapid shifts of role, influenced by group stimuli, are often seen. At one pole there is an identification of the self image with the deep bodily surging, unintegrated with the influence of social contacts. And in contrasting group situations there is an identification of the self image with the presumed constraining and hostile, menacing aspects of the surrounding environment, activating the urge to deny the body altogether. The schizophrenic, Ackerman believes,[130] is characteristically apprehensive of loss or destruction of self. If he identifies himself with his bodily drives, he tends to renounce social participation for fear of his own destructive powers, or fear of being injured through the exposure of his body to retaliatory attack. This renunciation is one kind of destruction of self. On the other hand, if the schizophrenic denies his body and identifies himself with the hostile elements of his environment, he again renounces social participation because of his intense hostile feeling towards other persons, whom he blames for the required sacrifices of the vital pleasures of his body. This is again a kind of destruction of self. The schizophrenic's preoccupation with the threat of destruction evoked by closeness to other persons induces withdrawal and resistance to social participation.

Ackerman illustrates this by referring to schizophrenics who automatically assume the mannerisms of the persons by whom they are surrounded—a phase of their uncontrolled obedience to social pressure. Or they may show a bizarre pattern of opposition to these same influences. In any case, in some schizophrenic individuals one does see remarkable shifts in adaptive behaviour, with lightning transitions in role stimulated by the patient's awareness of the hostile or sympathetic climate of the personal environment. Ackerman believes that adolescence is important as the phase in which schizophrenia can be precipitated. The fragility of the personality, the weakness of the repression, the inefficiency of defences, the closeness to basic drives, tend strongly to push into an overt state any latent schizophrenic trends that exist.

Boszormenyi-Nagy[131] considers the problems and mechanisms of close family relationships, the total interactional field of the family, with special emphasis on the determining influence exerted on a schizophrenic patient by the unconscious motivations of other family members. He examines the hypothesis that schizophrenic personality development may in part be perpetuated by reciprocal need complementarities between parents and offspring. His observations are based on the study and intensive psychotherapy of young schizophrenic females, with family therapy in ten cases. In these ten cases, it seemed that the patient was considered sick either because she conformed blindly to her parents' deepest expectations of her, or because she rebelled against them.

Boszormenyi-Nagy believes that it is usually possible to deduce from the parents' reactions to a schizophrenic patient's attempts at separation from them, that they have a great destructive possessiveness and need for symbiotic relatedness to the patient. The parents often seem to be avoiding repetition of the pain of an early loss. Unsatisfied with each other, they bind the child to them, and even parentify him. The willingness of the child to surrender his own autonomous life goals can be accounted for by dynamic forces originating in a specifically thwarted superego structure. The parent unconsciously shapes the child's early internalized value orientation according to his own symbiotic needs. He directs his most important moral injunctions not primarily toward destructive or sexual impulses, but toward any attempt at increased autonomy. He does not condemn sexual impulses per se, but, rather, erotic relationships outside the family. Once the pre-schizophrenic child has developed the counter-autonomous superego structure, he reacts at the most simple trigger signal with painful and perplexing feelings of guilt over any semblance of emancipation. In establishing this pathological split between aspirations toward autonomy and symbiosis the parent must first have used a 'double bind' type of communication. Later, when the patient's own motivational forces lead to resistance against autonomy, the parent's communication may represent only a comment on the patient's impotent internal situation. According to the author, this hypothesis of intrafamilial need complementarity as a psychogenic factor in maintaining schizophrenia, is not meant to supersede or exclude other known explanations. However, he feels that more attention should be paid to the needs of patients' parents as influences in superego formation.

Scott and Ashworth[132] conceive a 'shadow of insanity' which goes to form the attitude by which one member of the family sees and treats another as mad. The behaviour of the person seen as mad is one determinant of the attitude. But the shadow is also fed by potent sources beyond the parents' immediate perception of the patient; sources from the past and from the current social field. In so far as those sources, other than immediate perception, determine the shadow attitude, we may say that one person confers a mad identity on another.

Russell Davis[133–134] carefully reviews the conflicts of the Oedipus Complex which might contribute to the etiology of schizophrenia. He finds that significant elements are a poor relationship between mother and father, or failure of identification with the father, and an abnormal relationship between mother and son. He gives significance to the period when the child is between 10 and 16 years old.

Laing,[135–142] in his work on the families of schizophrenics, amalgamates the influence of existentialism with psychoanalysis and psychiatry. He regards schizophrenia as a social creation and the outcome of what goes on in the family. The symptoms are 'a strategy invented by the person in order to live in what to him has come to be an unlivable situation'. In these family systems liable to produce schizophrenics, 'mystification' is to be found. 'By mystification is meant the *act* of mystifying and the *state* of being mystified.' The *act* of mystifying is to befuddle, cloud and obscure whatever is going on. The *state* of mystification is a feeling of being muddled or confused. The prime function of mystification is to maintain the status quo. Laing sees some affinity between his views and those of Lidz, Wynne, and Jackson and Bateson. With collaborators he is developing an Interpersonal Perception Method for studying dyadic relationships. His concepts have been employed in therapy and good results claimed. Carstairs[143] however claims similar results and maintains that the work of Laing and his own indicate the non-specific response on the part of schizophrenics to an increased amount of personal attention.

Beckett *et al.*[144, 145] studies exogenous trauma in the genesis of schizophrenia. They uncovered a severe intrafamilial pathology with the use of denial and defence mechanisms which led to the obstruction of ego differentiation.

Alanen[146] links pseudo-mutuality, in the sense of Wynne, with the double bind hypothesis.

Like the above workers, Delay *et al.*[147] consider the family as a whole in relation to schizophrenia.

A number of contributors have paid attention to special aspects of the family process in relation to schizophrenia—Kim[148] (speech intrusion), Rosenbaum[149] (counterpart of schizophrenic in his family), Speck[150] (transfer phenomena), Yi-Chuang Lu[151, 152] (comparisons of schizophrenics and non-schizophrenic siblings) and Ferreira[153] (language). Two studies have compared the families of schizophrenics with the families of other clinical groups—Sharp,[154] Stabenau *et al.*[155]

4

Associated Views

All the work discussed above has been concerned with a family triad or a whole family as it relates to schizophrenia. However, we cannot overlook a number of studies concerned with relationships within the family—parent-schizophrenic, mother-schizophrenic and father-schizophrenic.

Parent-Schizophrenic

Conclusions drawn from parent-schizophrenic studies are contradictory, as is illustrated by consideration of some of the studies. Ellison and Hamilton[156] found the mothers overprotective and the fathers over-aggressive. Johnson et al.[145] found physical assault of children by the parents. Wahl[157, 158] found the loss of a parent in childhood or adolescence. Reichard and Tillman[159] described overtly or covertly rejecting mothers and domineering fathers. The work of Tietze,[160] Gerard and Siegel,[161] and Kasanin et al.[162] supported the notion of dominant mothers and passive fathers. Caputo[163] investigated this last possibility and found that it required qualification; they found a hostile atmosphere in the homes of schizophrenics and that both parents contributed to it. Prout and White[164] compared the parents of schizophrenics and those of normal males and found no significant difference between them. Rogler and Hollingshead[165] found that experiences in the childhood and adolescence of schizophrenic persons do not differ noticeably from those of people who are not afflicted by the illness.

Mother-Schizophrenic

Studies of the mother-patient interaction have not brought universal agreement as to its characteristics. Fromm-Reichmann[166] refers to the coldness and rejection of the 'schizophrenogenic mother'. Cheek's[167] recent study tended to support this. Alanen[168] noted that the mother tends to be closer to the schizophrenic son than to her other children, and 'possessively protects' him; with their schizophrenic daughters the mothers tended to be aloof. Hill[169] conceived of a mother-child symbiosis which developed into a pathological interdependence that did not allow growth. Limentani[170] and Lyketsos[171] have considered the symbiotic relationship pattern. Searles[172, 173] refers to the pathological symbiotic tie of mother and child. Beavers et al.[174] report a difference between the mothers of schizophrenics and non-schizophrenics on three elements in an interview. Zuckerman et al.[175] compared the mothers of schizophrenics and normals, and on only one out of twenty-three comparisons was there a significant difference—and this they put down to chance. It might have been expected that psychotic mothers would affect the adjustment of their children. Gardner's[176] and Preston's[177] findings are contrary to this expectation.

Father-Schizophrenic

The father-schizophrenic relationship has received less attention in the literature. The small amount of literature produced on this relationship is contradictory—some describe it as passive and ineffectual, others as harsh and dominating—this observed in a recent review by Cheek.[178]

Age Group

Some work has concentrated on the age group at which pathological processes are likely to lead to schizophrenia. Foudraine[179] in an able review considers the material relevant to schizophrenia in childhood in the literature produced up to 1960. Since then there have been contributions by Waring,[180] McCord et al.,[181] Becker,[182] and a series of interesting papers on childhood loss by Hilgard et al.[183–87] Early adolescence has been given significance by Russell Davis.[133–134]

Child Psychosis

Most of the above work refers to adult schizophrenia. Naturally much attention has been given to the family background and family relationships of child psychotics. Kanner's[188] views on the parents of the autistic child require no elaboration. Goldfarb's[189] views on parental perplexity are recently linked to his management of schizophrenic children. The subject has been reviewed by O'Gorman[190] and again by Bender[191] in companion volumes in this series.

Community Care

The schizophrenic might be causing the anomalies observed in family functioning. His care in the family and the impact he has on it has been the subject of a number of studies—Brown et al.,[192–193] Grad and Sainsbury,[196] Goldberg,[197] Deyking,[198] Evans et al.[199] and Cheek.[200] Rogler and Hollingshead[165] found that the impact of schizophrenia on the family depends on the sex of the person afflicted. Faris and Dunham[201] and Hare[202] have observed that city areas in which social isolation is most marked are rich sources of schizophrenic patients; it may be that schizophrenic patients drift to such areas.

5

Conclusion

The studies reviewed hitherto will be assessed in the light of the six criteria put forward in the introduction, with particular attention to the four main studies.

1. None of the studies puts forward a clear definition of schizophrenia by which the subjects under study were selected and which would find unquestioned acceptance by psychiatrists. Visitors from Europe and the U.S.A. attending clinics in the other's areas must be impressed with the wide differences in establishing criteria for the diagnosis of schizophrenia. To the writer the careful criteria for the diagnosis of schizophrenia, based on European psychiatry would be met only by a fraction of the patients seen under treatment as schizophrenics in family orientated centres in the United States; the remainder, though having a severe degree of pathology, appear to be severely emotionally ill but not schizophrenic.

Thus, should this view be substantiated, the findings of studies on these patients would be relevant to emotional illness, but not to schizophrenia. It is essential to have agreement about the criteria for the diagnosis of schizophrenia before findings can be compared and deductions drawn from the studies.

2. The anomalies of family functioning said to be associated with the production of schizophrenia in a family member are not always a single, simple, discrete concept; sometimes they are broad, sometimes fragmented into a number of parts, and sometimes several in number. There is a general broad agreement that defects of inter-personal communication are involved. But the authorities do not agree about the precise nature of the significant anomalies of communication; the greater the number of conflicting theories, the more likely they are all to be wrong. Also, the defects of communication noted may of course result from the illness and not be the cause of it. In the main, the workers concentrate on one anomaly and take little account of many other co-existing anomalies that may be present; these co-existing anomalies might be equally significant in causing schizophrenia.

3. The direct link between the anomaly of family functioning and schizophrenia is not well established in any of the studies. In no instance is the anomaly experimentally produced in order to cause schizophrenia. The results of treatment to relieve the schizophrenia through removal of the anomaly are not convincing.

4. Most of the workers claim that the anomaly noted is always present in the families of the schizophrenics studied; some maintain it varies with the sex of the schizophrenic. However, it is not demonstrated that a representative sample of schizophrenics are under study.

5. The possibility that the anomalies exist by chance alone is not excluded in any of the studies by adequate controls.

Should the English epidemiological studies be correct, approximately a third of the population are significantly emotionally disturbed. Should schizophrenics come from a representative group of families of the population at large, then in a third of families of schizophrenics family psychopathology will be found by chance alone. Furthermore, disturbed families are less likely to cope with schizophrenic members, and thus institutionalized schizophrenics will be present from such families in greater numbers, i.e., a selection factor may also be operating.

It may be that the psychopathological mechanisms described in the families of schizophrenics may also be found in non-schizophrenic families. Emotional divorce, immaturity, inadequacy, ambivalence, projection, pseudomutuality, stereotyped roles, family schisms, family skews, parental strife, family isolation, distortion of meaning, the double bind, unloving parents, incongruent communication, mystification, are elements found in non-schizophrenic families. Control studies will say to what extent. Experience with problem families, would suggest that all pathological mechanisms are more manifest in severely emotionally disturbed families—but do not necessarily give rise to schizophrenia.

6. Why does schizophrenia appear in late adolescence, although family trauma has been bearing on a sensitive organism for a number of years? Some answers are offered. Bowen sees it as a clash of strength between parent and child in adolescence. Wynne sees it as a matter of different processes: 'disaffiliation' in childhood psychosis and distortion of meaning in adult schizophrenia. Ackerman enumerates some special factors in adolescence. But other possibilities remain, which are not incompatible with an organic etiology; many physical conditions are tied to an age of onset.

As was mentioned in the introduction the above six questions are not exhaustive. For instance, whilst on the one hand it can be argued that the family psychopathology has causal significance for schizophrenia, it can also be held that the schizophrenia causes family psychopathology. It would be strange if such a severe and perplexing disorder did not have some effect on the family state; this must be specially true of childhood psychosis, where one sees the sad disappointment and puzzlement of a mother at the lack of response from her child. Again, it must be adequately explained why one member of the family develops schizophrenia rather than another and also why that family member develops schizophrenia rather than some other clinical condition.

But, whether the manifest pathology is caused by events within the individual or outside him in the family is the essential question. The workers previously mentioned see processes at work in the family that distort communication, perception and meaning. An equally large group of worker, e.g. McGhie and Chapman,[203—205] see distortions resulting from interference with the intracerebral organic machinery of thought and communication. Such distortions are observed in organic brain lesions, dementia, acute toxic delirious states and the model psychoses. Thinking in metaphor, for example, can be a defence from the intrusions of fellow family members, or result from organic perceptual difficulties. Two other views are possible as explanations of the perceptual anomalies. First that an underlying constitutional weakness in the individual is released by emotional stress emanating from the family. Secondly, that an existing constitutional weakness in a family member provokes a family reaction which may be harmful, but need not necessarily be so; the important and careful study of Pollin et al.[206] on identical twins may support this view. These possibilities need further exploration. An admirable review of possible etiologies of schizophrenia is found in Rosenthal.[207]

The author leans to the view that the anomalies, noted by the workers on family psychopathology reviewed here, are found with additional anomalies in the families of the emotionally ill, and, by chance, in the families of schizophrenics; these anomalies are not significant in the aetiology of schizophrenia, which is caused by intracerebral organic factors.

The studies, however, are not wasted. Despite their present inconclusive nature, the studies undertaken up to date may be the springboard for further conclusive research. Should it even be established, according to the views of the writer, that the patients under study are not schizophrenics, a great deal will have been learnt from these painstaking and ingenious studies about the psychopathology of emotionally disturbed individuals and families.

REFERENCES

1. KRAEPLIN, E., 1899. Zur Diagnose und Prognose der Dementia Praecox. *Allg. Z. Psychiat.*, **56,** 254.
2. BLEULER, E., 1911. Dementia Praecox oder Gruppe der Schizophrenein. In *Handbuch der Psychiatrie.* Ed. Aschaffenberg, G. Leipzig and Wien.
3. LANGFELDT, G., 1937. *The prognosis in schizophrenia and the factors influencing the course of the disease: a katamnestic study, including individual re-examination in 1936.* London: Oxford Univ. Press.
4. STEPHENS, J. H., and ASTRUP, C., 1963. Prognosis in 'process' and 'non-process' schizophrenia. *Am. J. Psychiat.*, **119,** 945.
5. STEPHENS, J. H., and ASTRUP, C., 1965. Treatment outcome in 'process' and 'non-process' schizophrenics treated by 'A' and 'B' types of therapists. *J. nerv. ment. Dis.*, **140,** 449.
6. PEMBERTON, J., 1949. Illness in general practice. *Br. med. J.*, i, 306.
7. COUNCIL OF THE COLLEGE OF GENERAL PRACTITIONERS, 1958. Working party report. *Br. med. J.*, ii, 585.
8. KESSELL, W. I. N., 1960. Psychiatric morbidity in a London general practice. *Br. J. prev. soc. Med.*, **14,** 16.
9. HOWELLS, J. G., 1966. The psychopathogenesis of hard-core families. *Am. J. Psychiat.*, **122,** 1159.
10. BOWEN, M., 1960. *A family concept of schizophrenia. The etiology of schizophrenia.* New York: Basic Books.
11. BOWEN, M., 1957. Family participation in schizophrenia. Paper presented at Annual Meeting, Am. Psychiat. Ass., Chicago, May, 1957.
12. BOWEN, M., 1959. Family relationships in schizophrenia. In *Schizophrenia—An integrated approach.* Ed. Auerback. New York: Ronald Press.
13. BOWEN, M., DYSINGER, R. H., and BASAMANIA, B., 1958. The role of the father in families with a schizophrenic patient. Paper presented at 114th Annual Meeting of Am. Psychiat. Ass., San Francisco.
14. BOWEN, M., DYSINGER, R. H., BRODEY, W. M., and BASAMANIA, B., 1957. Study and treatment of five hospitalized family groups each with a psychotic member. Paper presented at Annual Meeting of Am. Orthopsychiat. Ass., Chicago.
15. DYSINGER, R. H., and BOWEN, M., 1959. Problems for medical practice presented by families with a schizophrenic member. *Am. J. Psychiat.*, **116,** 514.
16. DYSINGER, R. H., 1961. The family as the unit of study and treatment. *Am. J. Orthopsychiat.*, **31,** 61.
17. DYSINGER, R. H. A study of relationship changes before onset of abruptly beginning schizophrenic psychosis. Unpublished material.
18. BRODEY, W. M., 1959. Some family operations with schizophrenia. *Archs gen. Psychiat.*, **1,** 379.

19. BRODEY, W. M., and HAYDEN, M., 1957. Intrateam reactions: their relation to the conflicts of the family in treatment. *Am. J. Orthopsychiat.*, **27**, 349.

20. HENRY, J., 1951. Family structure and the transmission of neurotic behaviour. *Am. J. Orthopsychiat.*, **21**, 800.

21. MENDELL, D., and FISHER, S., 1967. An approach to neurotic behaviour in terms of a three generation family model. In *Theory and practice of family psychiatry*. Howells, J. G. Edinburgh: Oliver and Boyd.

22. HOWELLS, J. G., 1967. *Theory and practice of family psychiatry*. Part I. Edinburgh: Oliver and Boyd.

23. HOWELLS, J. G. Family psychiatry. This volume (chapter xxiv).

24. WYNNE, L. C., RYCKOFF, I. M., DAY, J., and HIRSCH, S. I., 1958. Pseudomutuality in the family relations of schizophrenics. *Psychiatry*, **21**, 205.

25. RYCKOFF, I., DAY, J., and WYNNE, L. C., 1959. Maintenance of stereotyped roles in the families of schizophrenics. *Archs gen. Psychiat.*, **1**, 93.

26. WYNNE, L. C., and SINGER, M. T., 1963. Thought disorder and family relations of schizophrenics. A research strategy. Reprinted. In Howells, J. G., 1967, *Theory and practice of family psychiatry*. Howells, J. G. Chapter 43. Edinburgh: Oliver and Boyd.

27. WYNNE, L. C., and SINGER, M. T., 1963. Thought disorder and family relations of schizophrenics. II. A classification of forms of thinking. *Archs gen. Psychiat.*, **9**, 199.

28. SINGER, M. T., and WYNNE, L. C., 1965. Thought disorder and family relations of schizophrenics. III. Methodology using projective techniques. *Archs gen. Psychiat.*, **12**, 187.

29. SINGER, M. T., and WYNNE, L. C., 1965. Thought disorder and family relations of schizophrenics. IV. Results and implications. *Archs gen. Psychiat.*, **12**, 201.

30. SINGER, M. T., and WYNNE, L. C., 1965. Differentiating characteristics of parents of childhood schizophrenics, childhood neurotics and young adult schizophrenics. *Am. J. Psychiat.*, **120**, 234.

31. MORRIS, G. O., and WYNNE, L. C., 1965. Schizophrenic offspring and styles of parental communication. *Psychiatry*, **28**, 19.

32. LIDZ, R. W., and LIDZ, T., 1949. The family environment of schizophrenic patients. *Am. J. Psychiat.*, **106, 332.**

33. LIDZ, R. W., and LIDZ, T., 1952. Therapeutic considerations arising from the intense symbiotic needs of schizophrenic patients. In *Psychotherapy with schizophrenics*. Eds. Brody, E. B., and Redlich, F. C. New York: International Univ. Press.

34. LIDZ, T., 1958. Schizophrenia and the family. *Psychiatry*, **21**, 21.

35. CORNELISON, A., 1960. Casework interviewing as a research technique in a study of families of schizophrenic patients. *Ment. Hyg.*, **44**, 551.

36. LIDZ, T., CORNELISON, A., FLECK, S., and TERRY, D., 1957. The intrafamilial environment of the schizophrenic patient: I. The father. *Psychiatry*, **20**, 329.

37. FLECK, S., CORNELISON, A., NORTON, N., and LIDZ, T., 1957. The intrafamilial environment of the schizophrenic patient: III. Interaction between hospital staff and families. *Psychiatry*, **20**, 343.

38. LIDZ, T., CORNELISON, A., FLECK, S., and TERRY, D., 1958. The intrafamilial environment of the schizophrenic patient: II. Marital schism and marital skew. *Am. J. Psychiat.*, **114**, 241.

39. LIDZ, T., FLECK, S., CORNELISON, A., and TERRY, D., 1958. The intrafamilial environment of the schizophrenic patient. IV. Parental personalities and family interaction. *Am. J. Orthopsychiat.*, **28**, 764.

40. FLECK, S., FREEDMAN, D. X., CORNELISON. A.. LIDZ, T., and TERRY, D.,

1966. The understanding of symptomatology through the study of family interaction. In *Schizophrenia and the family*. Chapter IX. New York: International Univ. Press.

41. LIDZ, T., CORNELISON, A., TERRY, D., and FLECK, S., 1958. The intra-familial environment of the schizophrenic patient. VI. The transmission of irrationality. *Archs Neurol. Psychiat.*, **79**, 305.

42. SOHLER, D. T., HOLZBERG, J., FLECK, S., CORNELISON, A., KAY, E., and LIDZ, T., 1957. The prediction of family interaction from a battery of projective tests. *J. proj. Techniques*, **21**, 199.

43. LIDZ, T., SCHAFER, S., FLECK, S., CORNELISON, A., and TERRY, D., 1962. Ego differentiation and schizophrenic symptom formation in identical twins. *J. Am. psychoanal. Ass.*, **10**, 74.

44. FLECK, S., LIDZ, T., CORNELISON, A., SCHAFER, S., and TERRY, D., 1959. The intrafamilial environment of the schizophrenic patient: Incestuous and homosexual problems. In *Individual and familial dynamics*. Ed. Masserman, J. New York: Grune and Stratton.

45. LIDZ, T., FLECK, S., ALANEN, Y., and CORNELISON, A., 1963. Schizophrenic patients and their siblings. *Psychiatry*, **26**, 1.

46. FLECK, S., LIDZ, T., and CORNELISON, A., 1963. Comparison of parent-child relationships of male and female schizophrenic patients. *Archs gen. Psychiat.*, **8**, 1.

47. FLECK, S., 1962. Psychiatric hospitalization as a family experience. *Spec. Treat. Situations*, **1**, 29.

48. LIDZ, T., CORNELISON, A., SINGER, M. T., SCHAFER, S., and FLECK, S., 1966. The mothers of schizophrenic patients. In *Schizophrenia and the family*. New York: International Univ. Press.

49. LIDZ, T., CORNELISON, A., and FLECK, S., 1966. The limitation of extra-familial socialization. In *Schizophrenia and the family*. New York: International Univ. Press.

50. LIDZ, T., 1962. The relevance of family studies to psychoanalytic theory. *J. nerv. ment. Dis.*, **135**, 105.

51. LIDZ, T., and FLECK, S., 1965. Family studies and a theory of schizophrenia. *The American family in crisis*. Des Plaines, Ill.: Forest Hosp. Publications.

52. LIDZ, T., WILD, C., SCHAFER, S., ROSMAN, B., and FLECK, S., 1963. Thought disorders in the parents of schizophrenic patients: A study utilizing the object sorting test. *J. psychiat. Res.*, **1**, 193.

53. ROSMAN, B., WILD, C., RICCI, J., FLECK, S., and LIDZ, T., 1964. Thought disorders in the parents of schizophrenic patients: A further study utilizing the object sorting test. *J. psychiat. Res.*, **2**, 211.

54. LIDZ, T., and FLECK, S., 1960. Schizophrenia, human integration and the role of the family. In *Etiology of schizophrenia*. Ed. Jackson, D. New York: Basic Books.

55. LIDZ, T., FLECK, S., and CORNELISON, A. R., 1966. *Schizophrenia and the family*. New York: International Univ. Press.

56. FLECK, S., 1960. Family dynamics and origin of schizophrenia. *Psychosom. Med.*, **22**, 333.

57. LIDZ, T., 1964. *The family and human adaptation*. London: Hogarth.

58. BATESON, G., 1955. A theory of play and fantasy. *Psychiat. Res. Rep.*, **2**, 39–51.

59. BATESON, G., 1956. The message 'this is play'. In Second Conference on Group Processes. New York; Josiah Macy Jnr., Fnd.

60. BATESON, G., JACKSON, D. D., HALEY, J., and WEAKLAND, J. H., 1956. Toward a theory of schizophrenia. *Behavl Sci.*, **1**, 251–64.

61. BATESON, G., 1958. Language and psychotherapy, Frieda Fromm-Reichmann's last project. *Psychiatry*, **21**, 96–100.
62. BATESON, G., 1958. *Naven*, 2nd ed. with new chapter. Stanford, Calif.: Univ. Press.
63. BATESON, G., 1958. Schizophrenic distortion of communication. In *Psychotherapy of chronic schizophrenic patients*. Ed. Whitaker, C. Boston: Little, Brown and Co.
64. BATESON, G., 1958. Analysis of group therapy in admission ward. In *Social psychiatry in action*. Ed. Wilmer, H. A. Springfield, Ill.: Thomas.
65. BATESON, G., 1959. Anthropological theories. *Science*, **129**, 334–49.
66. BATESON, G., 1959. Panel review. In *Individual and familial dynamics*. Ed. Masserman, J. H. New York: Grune and Stratton.
67. BATESON, G., 1959. Cultural problems posed by a study of schizophrenic process. In *Schizophrenia, an integrated approach*. Ed. Auerbach, A. A.P.A. Symposium 1958. New York: Ronald Press.
68. BATESON, G., 1958. *The new conceptual frames for behavioral research*. Proceedings of the Sixth Annual Psychiatric Institute, Princeton.
69. BATESON, G., 1960. Minimal requirements for a theory of schizophrenia. *Archs gen. Psychiat.*, **2**, 477–91.
70. BATESON, G., 1960. The group dynamics of schizophrenia. In *Chronic schizophrenia: Explorations in theory and treatment*. Eds. Appleby, L., Scher, J. M., and Cumming, J. Glencoe, Ill.: Free Press.
71. BATESON, G., 1960. Discussion of Families of schizophrenic and of well children; method, concepts and some results, by Samuel J. Beck. *Am. J. Psychiat.*, **30**, 263–66.
72. BATESON, G., 1961. The biosocial integration of behavior in the schizophrenic family, and The challenge of research in family Diagnosis and Therapy. Summary of panel discussion: I. Formal research in family structure. In *Exploring the base for family therapy*. Eds. Ackerman, N. W., Beatman, F. L., and Sanford, S. New York: Family Service Assoc.
73. BATESON, G., ed., 1961. *Perceval's narrative, a patient's account of his psychosis*, 1830–32. Stanford, Calif.: Univ. Press.
74. BATESON, G. Structure and the genesis of relationship, Frieda Fromm-Reichmann Memorial Lecture. *Psychiatry*. (In press.)
75. BATESON, G., 1962. Exchange of information about patterns of human behavior. *Symposium on information storage and neural control*. Houston, Texas. (In press.)
76. BATESON, G., 1962. Communication theories in relation to the etiology of the neuroses. *Symposium on the etiology of the neuroses*. Society of Medical Psychoanalysis, New York. (In press.)
77. BATESON, G., 1962. Problems of credibility and congruence in applying computational methods to problems of peace, delivered at the Spring Joint Computer Conference, American Federation of Information Processing Societies, San Francisco.
78. BATESON, G. The prisoner's dilemma and the schizophrenic family. (To be published.)
79. BATESON, G., JACKSON, D. D., HALEY, J., and WEAKLAND, J. H., 1963. A note on the double bind—1962. *Family Process*, **2**, 154.
80. ERICKSON, M. H., HALEY, J., and WEAKLAND, J. H., 1959. A transcript of a trance induction with commentary. *Am. J. clin. Hyp.*, **2**, 49–84.
81. FRY, W. F., 1958. The use of ataractic agents. *Calif. Med.*, **98**, 309–13.
82. FRY, W. F., 1959. Destructive behavior on hospital wards. *Psychiat. Q.*, Supplement No. 33, Part 2, 197–231.

83. FRY, W. F., and HEERSEMA, P., 1963. Conjoint family therapy: A new dimension in psychotherapy. In *Topic. Prob. Psychother.*, **4**, 147–53.

84. FRY, W. F., 1962. The schizophrenogenic who? *Psychoan. psychoan. Rev.*, **49**, 68–73.

85. FRY, W. F., 1962. The marital context of an anxiety syndrome. *Family Process.*, **1**, 245–52.

86. FRY, W. F. *Sweet Madness: A Study of Humor.* Palo Alto, Calif.: Pacific Books. (In press.)

87. HALEY, J., 1955. Paradoxes in play, fantasy, and psychotherapy. *Psychiat. Res. Rep.*, **2**, 52–58.

88. HALEY, J., 1958. The art of psychoanalysis. *Psychiat. Res. Rep.*, **15**, 190–200.

89. HALEY, J., 1958. An interactional explanation of hypnosis. *Am. J. clin. Hyp.*, **1**, 41–57.

90. HALEY, J., 1959. Control in psychoanalytic psychotherapy. *Progress in Psychotherapy*, **4**, 48–65.

91. HALEY, J., 1959. An interactional description of schizophrenia. *Psychiatry*, **22**, 321–32.

92. HALEY, J., 1959. The family of the schizophrenic: A model system. *Am. J. nerv. ment. Dis.*, **129**, 357–74.

93. HALEY, J., 1960. Observation of the family of the schizophrenic. *Am. J. Orthopsychiat.*, **30**, 460–67.

94. HALEY, J., 1960. Control of fear with hypnosis. *Am. J. clin. Hyp.*, **2**, 109–15.

95. HALEY, J., 1961. Control in brief psychotherapy. *Archs gen. Psychiat.*, **4**, 139–53.

96. HALEY, J., 1961. Control in the psychotherapy of schizophrenics. *Archs gen. Psychiat.*, **5**, 340–53.

97. HALEY, J., 1962. Whither family therapy? *Family Process*, **1**, 69–100.

98. HALEY, J., 1962. Family experiments: A new type of experimentation. *Family Process*, **1**, 265–93.

99. HALEY, J., Marriage therapy. *Archs gen. Psychiat.* (In press.)

100. HALEY, J. *Strategies of psychotherapy.* New York: Grune and Stratton. (In press.)

101. JACKSON, D. D., 1956. Countertransference and psychotherapy. In *Progress in psychotherapy*, Vol. 1, pp. 234–38. Eds. Fromm-Reichmann, F., and Moreno, J. L. New York: Grune and Stratton.

102. JACKSON, D. D., 1957. A note on the importance of trauma in the genesis of schizophrenia. *Psychiatry*, **20**, 181–84.

103. JACKSON, D. D., 1957. The psychiatrist in the medical clinic. *Bull. Am. Ass. med. Clinics*, **6**, 94–98.

104. JACKSON, D. D., 1957. The question of family homeostasis. *Psychiat. Q.*, Supplement No. 31, Part 1, 79–90.

105. JACKSON, D. D., 1957. Theories of suicide. In *Clues to suicide*. Eds. Schneidman, E., and Farberow, N. New York: McGraw-Hill.

106. JACKSON, D. D., 1958. The family and sexuality. In *The psychotherapy of chronic schizophrenic patients*. Ed. Whitaker, C. Boston: Little, Brown and Co.

107. JACKSON, D. D., 1958. Guilt and the control of pleasure in schizoid personalities. *Br. J. med. Psychol.*, **31**, 124–30.

108. JACKSON, D. D., BLOCK, J., BLOCK, J., and PATTERSON, V., 1958. Psychiatrists' conceptions of the schizophrenogenic parent. *Archs Neurol. Psychiat* **79**, 448–59.

109. JACKSON, D. D., 1959. Family interaction, family homeostasis and some implications for conjoint family psychotherapy. In *Individual and familial dynamics*. Ed. Masserman, J. New York: Grune and Stratton.

110. JACKSON, D. D., 1959. The managing of acting out in a borderline personality. In *Case studies in counseling and psychotherapy*. Ed. Burton, A. New York: Prentice-Hall.

111. JACKSON, D. D., and WEAKLAND, J. H., 1959. Schizophrenic symptoms and family interaction. *Archs gen. Psychiat.*, **1**, 618–21.

112. JACKSON, D. D., ed., 1960. *The etiology of schizophrenia*. New York: Basic Books.

113. JACKSON, D. D., 1961. The monad, the dyad, and the family therapy of schizophrenics. In *Psychotherapy of the psychoses*. Ed. Burton, A. New York: Basic Books.

114. JACKSON, D. D., SATIR, V., and RISKIN, J., 1961. A method of analysis of a family interview. *Archs gen. Psychiat.*, **5**, 321–39.

115. JACKSON, D. D., and SATIR, V., 1961. Family diagnosis and family therapy. In *Exploring the base for family therapy*. Eds. Ackerman, N., Beatman, F., and Sherman, S. New York: Family Service Ass. of America.

116. JACKSON, D. D., and WEAKLAND, J. H., 1961. Conjoint family therapy, some considerations on theory, technique, and results. *Psychiatry*, **24**, 30–45.

117. JACKSON, D. D., 1962. Action for mental illness—What kind? *Stanford med. Bull.*, **20**, 77–80.

118. JACKSON, D. D., 1962. 'Interactional psychotherapy' and 'Family therapy in the family of the schizophrenic.' In *Contemporary psychotherapeis*. Ed. Stein, M. I. Glencoe, Ill.: Free Press.

119. JACKSON, D. D., 1962. Psychoanalytic education in the communication processes. In *Science and psychoanalysis*. Ed. Masserman, J. New York: Grune and Stratton.

120. JACKSON, D. D., and HALEY, J. Transference revisited. (To be published.)

121. JACKSON, D. D., and WATZLAWICK, P. The acute psychosis as a manifestation of growth experience. *A.P.A. Res. Rep.* (In press.)

122. WEAKLAND, J. H., and JACKSON, D. D., 1958. Patient and therapist observations on the circumstances of a schizophrenic episode. *Archs Neurol. Psychiat.*, **79**, 554–74.

123. WEAKLAND, J. H., 1960. The double-bind hypothesis of schizophrenia and three-party interaction. In *The etiology of schizophrenia*. Ed. Jackson, D. D. New York: Bsaic Books.

124. WEAKLAND, J. H., 1961. The essence of anthropological education. *Am. Anthrop.*, **63**, 1094–97.

125. WEAKLAND, J. H., 1961. Review of E. H. Schein, I. Schnier and C. H. Barker, *Coercive Persuasion*, Norton, New York, 1961. *J. Asian Studies*, **21**, 84–86.

126. WEAKLAND, J. H., 1962. Family therapy as a research arena. *Family Process*, **1**, 63–68.

127. WEAKLAND, J. H., and FRY, W. F., 1962. Letters of mothers of schizophrenics. *Am. J. Orthopsychiat.*, **32**, 604–23.

128. SPIEGEL, J. P., and BELL, N. W., 1959. The family of the psychiatric patient. In *The handbook of American psychiatry*. Ed. Arieti, S. New York: Basic Books.

129. SPIEGEL, J. P., 1964. Conflicting formal and informal roles in newly acculturated families. In *Disorders of communication*, vol. 42. Ed. Rioch, D. M. New York: Ass. for Res. in Nervous & Mental Disease.

130. ACKERMAN, N. W., 1958. *The psychodynamics of family life*. New York: Basic Books.

131. BOSZORMENYI-NAGY, I., 1962. The concept of schizophrenia from the perspective of family treatment. *Family Process*, **1**, 103.

132. SCOTT, R. D., and ASHWORTH, P. L., 1965. The 'axis value' and the transfer of psychosis. *Br. J. med. Psychol.*, **38**, 97.

133. DAVIS, D. R., 1961. The family triangle in schizophrenia. *Br. J. med. Psychol.*, **34**, 53.

134. DAVIS, D. R., 1964. Family processes in mental illness. *Lancet*, i, 731.

135. LAING, R. D., 1961. *The divided self*. London: Tavistock Publications; Chicago: Quadrangle Press.

136. LAING, R. D., 1962. *The self and other*. London: Tavistock Publications; Chicago: Quadrangle Press.

137. LAING, R. D., 1962. Series and nexus in the family. *New Left Rev.*, **15**, May–June.

138. LAING, R. D., and COOPER, R. D., 1964. *Reason and violence. A decade of Sartre's philosophy—1950–1960*. London: Tavistock Publications; New York: Humanities Press.

139. LAING, R. D., and ESTERSON, A., 1964. *Sanity, madness and the family. Vol. 1. Families of schizophrenics*. London: Tavistock Publications; New York: Basic Books.

140. LAING, R. D., 1965. Mystification, confusion and conflict. In *Intensive family therapy*. Eds. Boszormenyi-Nagy, I., and Framo, J. L. New York: Harper and Row.

141. LAING, R. D., PHILLIPSON, H., and LEE, A. R., 1966. *Interpersonal perception*. London: Tavistock Publications.

142. ESTERSON, A., COOPER, D. G., and LAING, R. D., 1965. Results of family-orientated therapy with hospitalized schizophrenics. *Br. med. J.*, ii, 1462.

143. CARSTAIRS, G. M., 1966. Family-orientated therapy with hospitalized schizophrenics. Correspondence. *Br. med. J.*, i, 49.

144. BECKETT, P. G. S., *et al.*, 1956. The significance of exogenous traumata in the genesis of schizophrenia. *Psychiatry*, **19**, 137.

145. JOHNSON, A. M., GRIFFIN, M. E., WATSON, J., and BECKETT, P. S., 1956. Studies in schizophrenia at Mayo Clinic. *Psychiatry*, **19**, 143.

146. ALANEN, Y., 1960. Some thoughts on schizophrenia and ego development in the light of family investigations. *Archs gen. Psychiat.*, **3**, 650.

147. DELAY, J., DENIKER, P., and GREEN, A., 1957. Le milieu familial des schizophrenics. *Encéphale*, **46**, 189.

148. KIM, K., 1964. *Study of emotion in family transactions of schizophrenics—Speech intrusion and interpersonal anxiety*. Paper presented at annual meeting of American Psychiatric Association.

149. ROSENBAUM, G. P., 1961. Patient-family similarities in schizophrenia. *Archs gen. Psychiat.*, **5**, 120.

150. SPECK, R. V., 1965. The transfer of illness phenomenon in schizophrenic families. In *Psychotherapy of the whole family*. Friedman, A. S., *et al.* New York: Springer.

151. LU, Y. C., 1962. Contradictory parental expectations in schizophrenia. *Archs gen. Psychiat.*, **6**, 219.

152. LU, Y. C., 1961. Mother-child role relations in schizophrenia. *Psychiatry* **24**, 133.

153. FERREIRA, A. J., 1960. The semantics of the context of the schizophrenic's language. *Archs gen. Psychiat.*, **3**, 128.

154. SHARP, V. H., GLASNER, S., LEDERMAN, I. I., and WOLFE, S., 1964. Sociopaths and schizophrenics—A comparison of family interactions. *Psychiatry*, **27**, 127.

155. STABENAU, J. R., TUPIN, J. T., WERNER, M., and POLLIN, W., 1965. A comparative study of families of schizophrenics, delinquents and normals. *Psychiatry*, **28**, 45.

156. ELLISON, E. A., and HAMILTON, D. M., 1949. Hospital treatment of dementia precox. *Am. J. Psychiat.*, **106**, 454.

157. WAHL, C. W., 1954. Some antecedent factors in family histories of schizophrenics. *Am. J. Psychiat.*, **110**, 668.

158. WAHL, C. W., 1956. Some antecedent factors in the family histories of schizophrenics in the U.S. Navy. *Am. J. Psychiat.*, **113**, 201.

159. REICHARD, S., and TILLMAN, C., 1950. Patterns of parent-child relationships in schizophrenia. *Psychiatry*, **13**, 247.

160. TIETZE, T., 1949. A study of the mothers of schizophrenic patients. *Psychiatry*, **12**, 55.

161. GERARD, D. L., and SIEGEL, J., 1950. The family background of schizophrenia. *Psychiat., Q.* **24**, 47.

162. KASANIN, J., KNIGHT, E., and SAGE, P., 1934. The parent-child relationship in schizophrenia. *J. nerv. ment. Dis.*, **79**, 249.

163. CAPUTO, D. V., 1963. The parents of the schizophrenic. *Family Process*, **2**, 339.

164. PROUT, C. T., and WHITE, M. A., 1950. A controlled study of personality relationships in mothers of schizophrenic male patients. *Am. J. Psychiat.*, **107**, 251.

165. ROGLER, L. H., and HOLLINGSHEAD, A. B., 1965. *Trapped: Families and schizophrenia.* New York: Wiley.

166. FROMM-REICHMANN, F., 1948. Notes on the development of treatment of schizophrenics by psychoanalytic psychotherapy. *Psychiatry*, **11**, 263.

167. CHEEK, F. E., 1964. The 'schizophrenogenic mother' in word and deed. *Family Process*, **3**, 155.

168. ALANEN, Y. O., 1958. The mothers of schizophrenic patients. *Acta psychiat. scand.*, **124**, 1.

169. HILL, L. B., 1955. *Psychotherapeutic intervention in schizophrenia.* Chicago: Univ. Press.

170. LIMENTANI, D., 1956. Symbiotic identification in schizophrenia. *Psychiatry*, **19**, 231.

171. LYKETSOS, G. C., 1959. On the formation of mother-daughter symbiotic relationship patterns in schizophrenia. *Psychiatry*, **22**, 161.

172. SEARLES, H. F., 1958. Positive feelings in the relationship between the schizophrenic and his mother. *Int. J. Psycho-Analysis*, **39**, 569.

173. SEARLES, H. F., 1959. The effort to drive the other person crazy. *Br. J. med. Psychol.*, **32**, 1.

174. BEAVERS, W. R., BLUMBERG, S., TIMKIN, K. R., and WEINER, M. F., 1965. Communication patterns of mothers of schizophrenics. *Family Process*, **4**, 95.

175. ZUCKERMAN, M., OLTEAN, M., and MONASHKIN, I., 1958. The parental attitudes of mothers of schizophrenics. *J. consult. Psychol.*, **22**, No. 4.

176. GARDNER, N. H., 1949. The later adjustment of children born in a mental hospital to psychotic mothers. *Smith Coll. Stud. soc. Work*, **19**, 137.

177. PRESTON, G. H., and ANTIN, R., 1932. A study of children of psychotic parents. *Am. J. Orthopsychiat.*, **2**, 231.

178. CHEEK, F. E., 1965. The father of the schizophrenic. *Archs gen. Psychiat.*, **13**, 336.

179. FOUDRAINE, J., 1961. Schizophrenia and the family. A survey of the literature 1956–1960 on the etiology of schizophrenia. *Acta psychother.*, **9**, 82.

180. WARING, M., and RICKS, D., 1965. Family patterns of children who become adult schizophrenics. *J. nerv. ment. Dis.*, **140**, 351.

181. McCORD, W., PORTA, J., and McCORD, J., 1962. The familial genesis of psychoses. *Psychiatry*, **25**, 60.

182. BECKER, E., 1964. Infant development and schizophrenia: New theoretical perspectives. *Int. J. soc. Psychiat.*, Special ed. 1, 1.
183. HILGARD, J. R., NEWMAN, M. F., and FISK, F., 1960. Strength of adult ego following childhood bereavement. *Am. J. Orthopsychiat.*, **30**, 788.
184. HILGARD, J. R., and NEWMAN, M. F., 1963. Early parental deprivation in schizophrenia and alcoholism. *Am. J. Orthopsychiat.*, **33**, 409.
185. HILGARD, J. R., and NEWMAN, M. F., 1963. Parental loss by death in childhood as an etiological factor among schizophrenic and alcoholic patients compared with a non-patient community sample. *J. nerv. ment. Dis.*, **137**, 14.
186. HILGARD, J. R., and NEWMAN, M. F., 1961. Evidence for functional genesis in mental illness: Schizophrenia, depressive psychoses and psychoneuroses. *J. nerv. ment. Dis.*, **132**, 3.
187. HILGARD, J. R., and FISK, F., 1960. Disruption of adult ego identity as related to childhood loss of a mother through hospitalization for psychosis. *J. nerv. ment. Dis.*, **131**, 47.
188. KANNER, L., 1949. Problems of nosology and psychodynamics of early infantile autism. *Am. J. Orthopsychiat.*, **19**, 416.
189. GOLDFARB, W., 1968. The therapeutic management of schizophrenic children. In *Modern perspectives in international child psychiatry*. Ed. Howells, J. G. Edinburgh: Oliver and Boyd.
190. O'GORMAN, G., 1965. The psychosis of childhood. In *Modern perspectives in child psychiatry*. Ed. Howells, J. G. Edinburgh: Oliver and Boyd.
191. BENDER, L., 1968. The nature of shildhood psychosis. In *Modern perspectives in international child psychiatry*. Ed. Howells, J. G. Edinburgh: Oliver and Boyd.
192. BROWN, G. W., CARSTAIRS, G. M., and TOPPING, G., 1958. Post hospital adjustment of chronic mental patients. *Lancet*, ii, 685.
193. BROWN, G. W., 1959. Experiences of discharged chronic schizophrenic patients in various types of living groups. *Millbank mem. Fund Q.*, **37**, 105.
194. BROWN, G. W., MONCK, E. M., CARSTAIRS, G. M., and WING, J. K., 1962. Influence of family life on the course of schizophrenic illness. *Br. J. prev. soc. Med.*, **16**, 55.
195. BROWN, G. W., 1966. Measuring the impact of mental illness on the family. *Proc. R. Soc. Med.*, **59**, 18.
196. GRAD, J., and SAINSBURY, P., 1966. Problems of caring for mentally ill at home. *Proc. R. Soc. Med.*, **59**, 20.
197. GOLDBERG, E. M., 1960. Parents and psychotic sons. *Br. J. psychiat. soc. Wk*, **5**, 1.
198. DEYKING, E., 1961. The re-integration of the chronic schizophrenic patient discharged to his family and community as perceived by the family. *Ment. Hyg.*, **45**, 235.
199. EVANS, A. S., BULLARD, D. M., and SOLOMON, M. H., 1961. The family as a potential resource in the rehabilitation of the chronic schizophrenic patient: A study of 60 patients and their families. *Am. J. Psychiat.*, **117**, 1075.
200. CHEEK, F. E., 1965. Family interaction patterns and convalescent adjustment of the schizophrenic. *Archs gen. Psychiat.*, **13**, 138.
201. FARIS, R. E. L., and DUNHAM, H. W., 1939. *Mental disorders in urban areas*. Chicago: Univ. Press.
202. HARE, E. H., 1956. Family setting and the urban distribution of schizophrenia. *J. ment. Sci.*, **102**, 753.
203. McGHIE, A., and CHAPMAN, J., 1961. Disorders of attention and perception in early schizophrenia. *Br. J. med. Psychol.*, **34**, 103.

204. CHAPMAN, J., and McGHIE, A., 1962. A comparative study of dysfunction in schizophrenia. *J. ment. Sci.*, **108,** 487.
205. McGHIE, A., CHAPMAN, J., and LAWSON, J. S., 1964. Disturbances in selective attention in schizophrenia. *Proc. R. Soc. Med.*, **57,** 419.
206. POLLIN, W., STABENAU, J. R., and TUPIN, J., 1965. Family studies with identical twins discordant for schizophrenia. *Psychiatry*, **28,** 60.
207. ROSENTHAL, D., ed., 1963. *The Genain quadruplets.* New York: Basic Books.

XV

THE SYMPTOMATOLOGY, CLINICAL FORMS AND NOSOLOGY OF SCHIZOPHRENIA*

A. V. Snezhnevsky

Director, Institute of Psychiatry, Academy of Medical Sciences, Moscow, USSR

1

Introduction

The symptoms and course of schizophrenia were known long before the condition was identified as an independent illness. Ancient medical descriptions of the various forms of melancholia, mania, dementia and hallucinosis include observations on several states which would today be attributed to schizophrenia.

The first half of the nineteenth century appeared to be dominated by a search for a concept of a common psychosis, and there gradually emerged the description of a certain consecutive course of the schizophrenic process, which was not at that time defined. The patterns of development of the different forms of this disease and its identification within its modern nosological boundaries were established by Morel (in the simple form)[40] and Magnan (*Le delire chronique a evolution systematique progressive, syndrome episodique des hereditaire*).[38] Further clinical investigations into specific features of separate form, such as the catatonic and hebephrenic, are associated with the name of Kahlbaum.[26] Subsequently a very comprehensive description of schizophrenia was presented by Kraepelin,[30, 31] who summarized its characteristic symptoms. But Kraepelin dealt only very generally with the separate schizophrenic states, and with their inter-relationships and subsequent transitions. He restricted himself to delineations of the main forms and the typology of its terminal stages, classifying forms of development as simple, paranoid, circular, agitated, depressive-paranoid and depressive-stuporose.

* Translated by Dr. B. Petrousbaia, Herrison Hospital, Dorchester, and the author's translator.

The extreme polymorphism of clinical symptoms in schizophrenia was one of the stimuli to the search for its inherent, original patterns, and to the attempt to isolate the primary schizophrenic disturbance. E. Stransky[57] called this disturbance 'intrapsychic ataxia'. E. Bleuler[6] developed the idea further. He defined the main disturbance in schizophrenia as an associative splitting and also described several supplementary symptoms. Bleuler's concept laid a foundation for subsequent persistent searches for the primary schizophrenic disturbance. It must be noted, however, that Wernicke[62] was originally responsible for the concept of an unknown primary psychological disturbance as lying at the root of the different psychopathological states. He spoke in anatomico-physiological terms of a concept of sejunction, i.e. a disturbance of conduction at the transcortical segment of the sensori-motor arc. It was Griesinger[20] who propounded the idea of a fundamental disturbance as a source of the multiplicity of symptoms.

Contemporaneously with Bleuler, Berze[5] discussed the concept of a fundamental schizophrenic disturbance. According to him the essence of the disturbance lay in a weakening in the volitional sphere, of the psychocerebral lowering of inherent strength. This resulted from a lessening of tonus issuing from subcortical levels. The latter evoked a disturbance in the receptive and efferent spheres, thus causing a hypotonus of the consciousness, i.e. the fundamental schizophrenic disturbance.

Later the notion of a primary schizophrenic disturbance became progressively purely psychological. This phase included Gruhle's idea of a disturbance in the motivational synthesis of deliberate psychological acts, Beringer's[3] concept of a weakening in the intentional acts and the concept of Schilder[49] and Storch[55] of primitive thinking in schizophrenia.

French psychiatry also assumed that the essence of the main schizophrenic disturbance resided in a splitting, which was termed discordance by J. Chaslin[9] and disintegration of personality by H. Ey.[17] In Italy, Lugarro stressed the dissociation of mental activity.

Soviet literature in the search for the specific diagnostic criteria necessary for differential diagnosis also emphasized a hypothetical, primary schizophrenic process. Sluchevsky[54] discussed an ataxic antagonism arising in the sphere of feeling, thinking and volition. A. D. Zurabashvili[64] also spoke of ataxia, or mental disautomatization as taking place physiologically as well as psychologically, and expressed as a disruption of the coordination of activity between the two hemispheres, and an intracortical disturbance at synaptic levels.

K. Conrad[11, 12] considered such purely organic pathological investigations to be valueless. He thought that throughout the present century the problem of the concept of schizophrenia has been the lack of a coherent interconnected system uniting the multiform symptoms of the disease. There were still merely long catalogues of separate symptoms. Making use of Gestalt psychology he attempted to integrate the great variety of symptoms and he clarified, in the development of schizophrenia, trema, apophrenia and apocalyptic subjective experiences (Greek terms). But Conrad's evaluation of the clinical picture of schizophrenia was only partially correct.

The search for a primary schizophrenic disturbance was accompanied by the gradual emergence of the concept of psychopathological syndromes. This characterized both clinical psychiatry in general and the study of schizophrenia in particular. At the beginning of the twentieth century Hoche,[21] Cramer[13] and Bonhoeffer[7] began to develop the idea of a symptom-complex, i.e. a syndrome, as a pre-determined reaction of the brain to certain noxious agents. French psychiatrists in particular employed the notion of the syndrome very widely. This teaching on the psycho-pathological syndromes was foreshadowed in the middle of the nineteenth century. Several psychopathological syndromes were described as distinct and separate entities in *General Psychopathology* by Emminghaus[16] who regarded syndromes as examples of pathological unity at a higher level of complexity than the symptom. Jackson[23] also used the concept of a syndrome in his *Forms of Insanity*. Korsakoff[34] in his *Handbook of Psychiatry*, isolated and delineated six independent psycho-pathological syndromes. In Russia Scherback[48] also sustained the concept of psycho-pathological syndromes and regarded them as a reaction of the brain to traumatic agents. I. G. Orshansky described in his *General Psychiatry*, a series of psychopathological syndromes and subdivided them into simple and complex types. K. Jaspers[24] in his *General Psychopathology*, identified four independent groups of syndromes. Later in Kraepelin and Lange's *Textbook of Psychiatry* the latter defined eight such groups. In his paper on 'Forms and Manifestations of Insanity', K. Kraepelin[32] also employed the concept of syndromes as independent reaction types, which he termed 'registers'.

Empirical experience in the clinical evaluation of schizophrenia gradually promoted the concept of catatonic, paranoid, hallucinatory-paranoid, depressive and oneiroid syndromes as independent but inter-connected symptom complexes. By the 1940's the existence of schizo-phrenic syndromes had become fully accepted (A. S. Kronfeld[26]) and in the following years O. V. Kerbikov[29] isolated seventeen independent syndromes.

K. Schneider[50] also attempted to relate the symptoms of schizophrenia in interconnected formulations ('symptomverbände'), and isolated three such groups. The first group consisted of an altered concept and alienation of the self together with 'the sounding of ideas', the second involved general sensory, somatic hallucinations and affective disturbances, and the third consisted of primary delusions of significance.

As already mentioned the concept of psychopathological syndromes has been intensively explored in France. On a comparative basis Ey[17] and Rouart[18] attempted to create a scale of syndromes, akin to the 'registers' of Kraepelin reflecting the depth of the psychic disturbance. They established a sequential gradation of syndromes of neurotic, paranoid, oneiristic, synaesthetico-pathologic, affective, amentive-stuporose, schizophrenic, dissociative and dementive. According to Ey and Rouart[18] the dynamism of the earlier syndromes is intense, but lessens with progression, whilst manifestations of psychic weakness increase in proportion. Ey and Rouart developed Jackson's concept of 'plus' and 'minus' disturbances—the more dynamic the pathological positive disturbances, the less the weight of the disease.

Nevertheless, the study of psycho-pathological syndromes, including those of schizophrenia, is still far from complete, and lacks any unified classification. At times the classification appears quite arbitrary and there is frequent confusion between syndrome and forms of the disease, or between syndrome and symptoms. Attempts have been made to synthesize the concept of the primary schizophrenic disturbance on the one hand and of schizophrenic syndromes on the other (A. S. Kronfeld[36] and A. D. Zurabashvili).[64]

2

Symptomatology

Before outlining the symptomatology of schizophrenia it seems useful to dwell on the meaning of syndrome and symptom as based on theoretical views, in medicine and the natural sciences (I. V. Davidovsky,[15] L. A. Abramyan,[1] S. S. Schwartz,[52] G. Svechnikov,[60] S. E. Zak and V. V. Agudov.[2])

A symptom (a sign) is an expression of a disturbed function of an organ or system within the organism. The detection of one symptom is insufficient for the diagnosis or for the understanding of its pathogenesis. The disease is never expressed by one sign or feature only, but always by clusters of several interrelated symptoms, which constitute syndromes. The clinical manifestations of a syndrome are determined by the specificity of its pathogenesis, or, in other words, by the pathokinesis of the pathogenic process.

A syndrome (symptom-complex, clinical picture, state) is a biological functional formation. It is a single interconnected system within the larger formation, and in its turn consists of parts, which are its symptoms. At any given moment any functional structure, pathological structures included, is static; over a segment of time it is dynamic. Any process, including the pathological one, is always directed towards the future. Elements produced in the past, in this case symptoms, and elements in the transition into the future, always co-exist and are specifically interrelated within the functional structures. An evolution of a structure is accompanied by an increasing complexity of its constituent elements, and by a transformation of its interrelationships. The clinical study of the changes in symptoms within a functional system and of their interrelationships offers possibilities for prognostication in the development of the disease.

A clinical study of schizophrenia as of any other progressive disease reveals at any given segment of time continuous changes in the clinical picture and a movement within it of interrelationships between the symptoms. As a result of the unfolding of the disease, at any given moment the syndrome is altered and transformed into a new one. In other words, as the disease develops, there is a successive progression of states, of syndromes, which are, however, always functionally interconnected in a significant manner. A study of any disease requires not only a knowledge of its aetiology but an application of the movement of its syndromes, of the patterns according to which one state is transformed into another. The aetiology of the disease and of the successive progression of its syndromes reflect the various aspects of the pathological process. Consequently, we may say that certain pathological processes correspond to certain successively changing states.

Thus, the study of schizophrenia implies not only the study of its syndromes but also a study of the patterns of the successive changes in the disease, i.e. a demonstration of the stereotype in the development of the disease. It also presupposes an investigation of the static states. A thorough investigation of the static states is necessary for the determination of preceding changes and the prognosis of succeeding changes, i.e. for the establishment of connections in the dynamic flow of the disease.

The departments of psychiatry of the Central Institute for Postgraduate Training and of the Institute of Psychiatry of the Academy of Medical Sciences of the U.S.S.R. undertook a continuous study of over 5,000 schizophrenic patients in the period 1951-66. As a result they isolated the following syndromes as occurring during the course of the disease: (*i*) asthenic; (*ii*) affective; (*iii*) pseudo-neurotic; (*iv*) paranoial; (*v*) hallucinatory; (*vi*) hallucinatory–paranoid (the syndrome of Kandinsky-Clerambault); (*vii*) paraphrenic; (*viii*) catatonic; (*ix*) terminal, polymorphic state, which is relatively stable.

This investigation confirmed that schizophrenia is not characterized by amnestic, convulsive or psycho-organic syndromes, nor by exogenous states of clouded consciousness, such as delirium, amentia, or the twilight states.

The successive development of these syndromes reflects an increasing intensity of the psychic disturbance in schizophrenia. In other words, the order in which these syndromes are listed represents an attempt to establish a scale of increasing severity of the mental disturbance, and to establish also a quantitative as well as a qualitative assessment of the clinical state. This scale does not enumerate discrete and firmly demarcated disturbances, but implies a continuous development of progressively intense stages. The syndromes change not only with the development of the process, but also as the result of the appearances of new elements or symptoms, and of changes in the pattern of their inner interrelationships.

Over a short period one observes a clinical picture corresponding clearly to one or other type of syndrome. But over a long period one sees a continuous, ever-changing succession of clinical patterns. The syndrome represents the temporary parameters within a continuous process. It may thus be regarded as a temporary 'focal point' which expresses the qualitative features of the process at a given time. The continuous and the temporary forms of the pathological disturbance are inseparable.

There are no firm boundaries between separate symptoms. For instance, according to the degree of evolution of schizophrenia, genuine hallucinations may be transformed into pseudo-hallucinations, or obsessional manifestations may become increasingly automatic (D. Oseretskovsky).[43] Rituals may gradually lose their original phobic character and become impulsive stereotyped actions deprived of inner content. According to Friedmann some obsessions may change into delusions. A flow of visual images may be transformed into a flow of visual hallucinations, and fantastic delusions may become dream-like.

This, however, does not mean that any psychopathological symptom may be indiscriminately transformed into any other as the process develops.

The transformation of symptoms is determined by the nature of the psychic process. Thus genuine verbal hallucinations may be transformed into pseudo-hallucinations, but only of the verbal type. Obsessional movements may evolve into stereotyped automatic acts; obsessional ideas into delusions, and visual paraidolias into visual hallucinations.

Such transitions occur within the syndrome system, and reflect its development. The modification of former symptoms takes place contemporaneously with the emergence of fresh ones.

K. Jaspers[24] related psycho-pathological symptoms to primary process as being final and indivisible. He drew an analogy between symptoms and chemical elements. But the inner structures of the symptoms are expressed in their capacity for change.

The term syndromes is not used in the plural fortuitously. Each of the syndromes listed above may emerge in different forms during the course of schizophrenia. Thus, asthenic syndromes occur predominantly with hyperaesthesic or adynamic components; affective syndromes may be in the form of manic or depressive states. A depression may be adynamic, agitated, anxious or dysphoric, whilst a manic state, in its turn, may be exalted, aggressive, hypomanic, sthenic or with heightened drives, or silly and expressive of facile foolishness. Pseudo-neurotic states may be expressed in obsessions, depersonalization, synaesthopathia, hypochondria or dysmorphic phobias. Paranoial states sometimes take the form of overvalued ideas, or may be either systematized or fragmented or may emerge finally as delusional moods, 'Wahnstimmung'.

Hallucinosis may be characterized mainly by genuine verbal hallucinations, or merely by pseudo-hallucinations. Hallucinatory-paranoidal states are dominated either by a prevalence of delusions or by pseudo-hallucinations. They may present complete or incomplete forms of Kandinsky-Clerambault syndrome. Paraphrenic subjects may be fantastically hallucinated, or may, on the other hand be megalomaniac or fantastically confabulated. Catatonic states may be predominantly excitatory or negativistic or stuporose.

These variants do not exhaust the list of possible schizophrenic syndromes. Although some schizophrenias are relatively stable and become spontaneously transformed into more complex states in a slow, gradual, non-remitting way, there are others which display complexity from the start. The latter normally develop in the form of attacks with periodic remissions. In such cases the onset is characterized by immediate complex syndromes. Paranoial states are accompanied by affective disturbances and become acute paranoia. Depression may be characterized by anxiety or by depressive-paranoid states, a depressive-hallucinosis or pseudo-hallucinosis, or fantastic depressive-hallucinosis, the last being the depressive oneiroid delusion of Cotard. The manic syndrome may be complicated by fantastic delusions, pseudo-hallucinations or oneiroid or catatonic disturbances. Paraphrenias set in violently with fantastic, hallucinatory or confabulatory content and frequently attain a dream-like, oneiroid clouding of consciousness.

This second major group of schizophrenias is distinguished from the first group by the vivid, colourful picturesqueness of its expression and by the intensely sensory character of its delusions and hallucinations. The ideational content is unstable, completely inconsistent and accompanied by a general heightened agitation. The clinical picture is characterized by extreme dynamism.

By contrast with the first groups the changes in the relationships between the separate symptom elements remain incomplete. For instance the affective disturbance may continue to dominate the clinical picture, despite the development of paranoid, hallucinatory manifestations or of the Kandinsky–Clerambault symptoms.

Nevertheless both types show a consistency in their sequential unfolding and in their scale of severity. In both groups the onset is manifested by asthenia which then proceeds to affective, delusional, hallucinatory-delusional and catatonic phenomena. But in the development these transitions take only days or weeks in the case of attacks of periodic and of the schub-type of schizophrenia whereas in the continuous (1st Group) forms they take months or even years.

The occurrence of dynamic syndromes which are complex from the start may be observed not only in the shift-like schizophrenia (schub-type) and in periodic schizophrenia, but is also seen in certain circumstances in the development of the continuous non-remitting schizophrenias. In many cases the transition of paranoia into paranoid-hallucinosis and then into paraphrenia or catatonia may be acute and transitory and be differentiated from attacks of the periodic schizophrenia only with great difficulty. These sudden and transient states may also be found in the early stages of malignant hebephrenia in the young. Krafft-Ebing[33] described such episodes as occurring during transitions from paranoia into paranoid states and from paranoid into paraphrenic. There are also cases in which the schizophrenia proceeds for a long period with systematized paranoid delusions and with marked schizophrenic personality changes, but also with episodically acute attacks. During the latter the delusions assume a more sensory and richly fantastical content and are accompanied by heightened affect.

From the foregoing emerges the fact that it is impossible to draw strict boundaries between a galloping process and one with sluggishly shifting syndromes. The two cases show different expressions, of different structures, at a different pace in a way that seems analogous to an isomerism in schizophrenic disturbances.

In the process of a wide-range epidemiological survey of more than five thousand patients we isolated almost a hundred different states. These, however, were only variants of the nine syndromes listed above. Each of them found expression within the specific limitations of the inherent psychic process, i.e. in a manner reminiscent of the 'levels' of Jackson or the 'registers' of Kraepelin.

Symptoms that contribute to the different schizophrenic syndromes may be pathologically productive, or so called positive. Alternatively they may be negative symptoms, expressive of 'flaws', defects and disintegration. Both types combine as a unit, exhibiting organic interdependence and constituting the elements of a syndrome structure.

However, although they form a unit, the positive and the negative disturbances are not equivalent to each other. In simple schizophrenia as well as in remissions after acute attacks, negative symptoms may sometimes emerge alone without coincident positive ones. I. F. Ovchinnikov[42] has pointed out that the positive and the negative symptoms are disposed as if on two levels. The positive is the higher level and is characterized by a marked variability. This level may be expressed in a hundred different forms and appears to depend upon pathogenic factors which are as yet not understood. The lower or negative level by contrast is invariable. We are familiar with only two of its aspects: an inner psychic disharmony and a reduction in the energy potential.

Negative disturbances emerge almost from the onset of the illness and are initially expressed in a change in the subject's psychic structure. As the disease progresses the personality of the patient becomes more and more altered. It may become deeply schizoidal and alien to the patient's premorbid character. Such acquired personality disharmony may be expressed in developing introversion and a tendency to reflection, and increasing loss of spiritual empathy with others, an emotional flattening combined with emotional fragility (the metaphor of 'wood and glass' may be appropriate), a lability in the awareness of the self-consciousness and of the outer reality, a progressive rationalization, rigidity and stereotypy of thought, a progressive break in external relationships, a growing stereotypy of behaviour with pedantry and rigidity, an absence of mental flexibility, a loss of the sense of activity, a passive submissiveness to circumstances and an insufficient integration of drives and attitudes.

The initial light disturbances of this type resemble psychopathic states, and point to changes at the highest levels of personality. But their progressive intensification amounts to a defect, and a regression of personality.

As the disease progresses such disturbances are manifested in varying degrees of intensity, and are accompanied by varying degrees of reduction of energetical potentials (Conrad).[12] This reduction of energy is seen in mental productivity and activity as well as in the emotional sphere. In the more malignant cases this loss of mental energy, or deficit of psychic activity, assumes the dominant character in the clinical picture of schizophrenia.

The invariability of the negative disturbances is very clearly demonstrated during contemporary therapy with modern psychotropic drugs. As a result of therapy the positive disturbances undergo some degree of change and become more rudimentary. In some cases they may disappear altogether, and modern therapy may create a barrier to the emergence of certain features, for instance, of catatonia. The negative disturbances, however, are refractory to therapy and do not change. They may, nevertheless, become usually to a certain extent compensated.

The inverse ratio between positive and negative mental disturbances described by Jackson[23] is almost invariably confirmed in schizophrenia. The less the change in personality in a schizophrenic, the more dynamic are the positive disturbances. This is especially vividly demonstrated in the attacks of the shift-like (schub-type) forms of the disease.

The emotional changes which occur as continuous swings of elation and depression fade with the reduction of energy potential. Depression becomes increasingly adynamic, while the manic states grow less euphoric, but become more continuously and purely states of excitement. The circular form is later expressed in regular swings of agitation with temporary accentuations of positive productive symptoms alternating with periods of calm.

In cases of a more slowly progressive growth of negative disturbances in the 'schub'-type of schizophrenia both sensory delusions and hallucinations and affective changes are given a much poorer expression than in cases of periodic schizophrenia in which there is a paucity of the negative, lower 'register' manifestations. Where the negative changes are slowly progressive, the clinical picture of acute attacks becomes increasingly of the cliché type. With each attack there is a diminishing dynamism and a lessening sensory and affective tension. The clinical picture in general approaches that of the continuous form of schizophrenia.

In those cases of simple schizophrenia which display rapid and profound development of personality changes and a very early reduction of energy potential, the positive disturbances are very scanty. It is well known that this form is characterized by poor positive productive symptoms.

When schizophrenia commences in adolescence and progresses in 'schub' attacks with subsequent marked reduction in dynamism during the remissions, the residual positive symptoms also become stereotyped and poor in energy, most frequently in the form of obsessions. The patients seem to capitulate to them; they come to accept their existence as a matter of course.

The dependence of the expressed positive symptoms upon the level of energy potential is indirectly revealed by the use of psychotropic drugs. The lowering of the psychical activity and of general mental tonus as a result of neuroleptic therapy, leads to an improvement and sometimes to a complete, though perhaps temporary, disappearance of many of the positive symptoms. By contrast the use of stimulating, thymotropic, drugs may greatly increase the intensity of many positive schizophrenic disturbances.

When schizophrenia begins in adult life it usually proceeds with slowly progressive changes of personality. Transitions of positive disturbances also occur at this age gradually. Each syndrome attains its full development and its complete pathological organization. A marked reduction in the energetic potential is deferred to a much later period.

The personality disharmony, or change in inner structure, is less clearly and less intensely expressed in schizophrenia of the later age groups. In such cases the development of the positive disturbances progresses rather rapidly, with an early appearance of paraphrenic delusions and frequently with a fantastic and megalomaniac content. In comparison with the younger patient, there is an insignificant reduction in energy potential.

In the terminal stages of the continuous (Group 1) forms of schizophrenia, however, the reduction of energy reaches its maximum. At this period the emergence of new positive symptoms ceases. The psychosis markedly loses its structure, and the level of its organization falls significantly. It disintegrates into a ruin. At this stage the patient's individual traits become obliterated and there ensues a nosological isomorphism. The terminal clinical picture in such schizophrenics resembles that of the terminal stages of some cases of idiopathic epilepsy (V. M. Morozov).[41]

The vanishing of the 'nucleus' of the personality also approximates the terminal stages of continuous schizophrenia and of idiopathic epilepsy to the terminal stages of severe organic psychoses, e.g. of general paralysis of the insane, Huntington's chorea, Pick's disease, and senile and arteriosclerotic dementia. But in the latter cases, if not interrupted by premature intercurrent diseases, the development of the main disease process leads to the organic destruction, decerebration, and death of the brain tissue, whereas in the course of the continuous schizophrenia, and in some cases of idiopathic epilepsy, there sooner or later appears a certain degree of adaptive inhibitive process and relative stabilization. It is probable that this is established by a maximal deduction from the energy potential as an expression of the organism's adaptive mechanisms.

According to S. P. Botkin and I. P. Pavlov[44] the reduction in the energetical potential is related to the phenomenon of 'break'. In the terminal stages of schizophrenia this 'break' becomes a defensive mechanism.

In the course of benign, continuous schizophrenia the adaptive inhibition develops significantly earlier, i.e. in the pseudo-neurotic or paranoidal phases, or more frequently in the paranoid or paraphrenic phases. In the 'schub' forms of schizophrenia there are again slow but nevertheless permanently increasing personality changes, which may, however, become arrested at any level and thereby lead to stabilization. In all such cases the manifestations of psychic weakening are present in different degrees.

The emergence of adaptive process is determined by the nosological nature of schizophrenia and suggests possibilities of recovery, even in the rare cases of malignant and potentially fatal catatonia. This is most likely if therapy is instituted at an early stage. It would appear that therapeutic success depends on the therapy being coincidental with the adaptive mechanisms. This principle also applies to the steadily developing process of progressive general paralysis even in its terminal stages.

The variability of the positive symptoms do not merely depend upon the impact of negative disturbances but is also directly dependent upon the patient's age, level of maturation and degree of mental development.

In early childhood the positive schizophrenic symptoms manifest themselves in perversions of instincts and defensive reactions, in disturbances of sleep, in panic fears of everyday objects, in stereotyped movements, in obsessional motor activity, in autistic drives to phantasy formations, etc. (T. Simson,[53] G. E. Sukhareva,[59] A. N. Chekhova,[10] B. Kothe[35] and others). Maudsley[39] pointed out that verbal hallucinations and paranoid delusions do not occur in childhood.

Neither is adolescence typified by systematized paranoid delusions. Delusions of adolescence are fragmentary and auditory hallucinations normally predominate over delusions. The structure of schizophrenic symptoms is polymorphic and catatonic syndromes tend to occur early.

Older age groups are characterized by systematized paranoid or paraphrenic disturbances, fantastic hallucinosis and confabulations. By comparison with the younger age groups the structure of the manifested syndromes is, therefore, more completely organized.

Various degrees of catatonic-oneiroid disturbances are prevalent in the clinical pictures of periodic and schub-type of schizophrenia. The older age group is more likely to be characterized by fantastic delusions of destruction or nihilism, i.e. by the delusions of Cotard.

In addition, the clinical manifestations of schizophrenia depend to a significant extent on sex and constitutional endowment of the individual, as well as on socially determined characteristics. These, however, are predominantly related to the variable positive disturbances. Nevertheless, the influence of sex is also manifested in the intensity of evolution of negative manifestations. Thus, the malignant forms of continuous schizophrenia of adolescence are encountered more frequently in the male, and periodic schizophrenia in the female.

Despite the considerable differences in the varieties of negative and positive schizophrenic symptoms, they always tend to form a unity, and thereby give rise to the typically constructed syndromes, for instance, schizophrenic asthenia, depression, or obsessional or paranoidal states.

Digressing for a moment, if psychological syndromes are considered beyond the facts of the disease, they represent merely abstract conceptions (V. Kandinsky).[27] For instance the forms of psychic disturbances may be defined in context of inherent characteristics of the structure and functions of the brain. By the bedside, however, the physician describes only the nosologically expressed syndromes. He names, for instance, not simply asthenia, but a neuroasthenia, or an organic arterio-sclerotic asthenia, or schizophrenic asthenia, and so on; he does not diagnose dementia in general but for instance, an epileptic, or senile dementia, or dementia of general paresis.

As has already been mentioned the very polymorphism of schizophrenic manifestations directed investigators to an attempt to isolate the primary disturbance. The ultimate significance of all the proposed definitions (sejunction, splitting, discord, dissociation, intrapsychic ataxia or antagonistic ataxia) appears to be equivalent.

In biology we find more and more facts which point to the relative independence, an autonomy of separate structures, for example, the cell or the elements, that compose more complex systems. The autonomy of these separate constituent elements ensures their selective and goal directed functioning (I. A. Akmurin, N. F. Vedenov, Y. V. Skachkov).[47] The high degree of adaptability of the central nervous system and the speed and precision of its function also depend upon the significant autonomy of the lower controlling centres and systems (N. Bernstein).[4]

That similar automatization takes place in the sphere of mental activity has been stressed by many psychiatrists, e.g. by Maudsley,[39] Ribot,[46] Korsakoff[34] and others. Any psychic or mental act is stereotyped, organized, and systematized. This is true of simple acts such as walking and of the increasingly complex acts of reading, talking, writing, everyday or professional thinking, remembering, or motor activity. Without such automatization no goal directed creative would be possible. It would be impossible to assimilate and master new situations or to adapt continuously to the constantly changing conditions of life. Automatization of mental processes forms a new kind of a functional organ (A. A. Ukhtomsky).[61] These autonomous mental processes represent independent elements contributing towards the organized and goal-directed functioning of the whole complex mental system.

Thus, many schizophrenic disturbances may be looked upon as manifestations of a weakened, detached activity of the functionally autonomous organs. This includes obsessions, mentism, verbal hallucinations, and pseudo-hallucinations, many features of the Kandinsky-Clérambault syndrome, involutary fantasies and others. Regarded in this way sejunction, intra-psychic ataxia, splitting and dissociation admit of a new explanation, which is, however, close to the automatism concept of French psychiatry. But this, and other aspects, however, do not explain the nature of the primary disturbance. They remain figurative concepts. They may be justified only as useful descriptions of schizophrenic characteristics and may help in differentiation from disturbances inherent in other diseases. In particular they may help in differentiation from organic cases with specific, coarse diffuse damage and gradual destruction of the entire psychic system.

From the viewpoint of the pathophysiology of the higher nervous activity, detached activity of separate mental organs may be the result of a focus of pathological inert excitation, e.g. in the Kandinsky-Clérambault syndrome, or of inert inhibition. A. Ivanov-Smolensky[22] has used inert inhibition of the subcortical vegetative centres to explain the presence of prolonged vegetative disturbances which persist even after a reactive depression has passed.

3

Clinical Forms

Many investigators have reported that long-term observations of large groups of schizophrenic patients demonstrate definite differences in inter-relationships of their pathological states, and the stereotypes of their development. We can clearly distinguish a main group of patients with continuous transitions of the positive manifestations during the whole course of the disease, beginning with asthenic states and ending with terminal deterioration. There is a concurrent development of consistently negative disturbances, which at times effect a considerable reduction in psychic energy. Secondly, there is a large group of patients in whom the process proceeds very slowly for long periods of time, with negative disturbances that are mainly psychopathic in type. In these there is only a moderate reduction in the energetical potential, especially in the initial stages of the disease, and it is frequently accompanied by distinct positive disturbances, for example pseudo-neurotic or paranoial. Such a slowly developing process may be interrupted from time to time by comparatively short attacks. The clinical course of the attacks is characterized by a galloping development of complex schizophrenic syndromes, and in some cases even by attacks of the simple lucid type of catatonia. After each attack there is an intensification of the negative disturbances, usually with residual positive symptoms. This is the schub type of schizophrenia.

In the third, less numerous group, the disease proceeds almost exclusively in the form of attacks, with complex, galloping syndromes. The clinical picture is dominated by affective disturbances, a prevailing sensory character in delusions and a definite tendency to oneiroid clouding of consciousness. Between the attacks the negative disturbances preserve a light psychopathic character. They show little or no tendency to intensification. This is the recurrent or periodic form of schizophrenia, schizo-affective psychosis or oneirophrenia.

The nature of the course and manifestations of these typical basic psychotic forms gives each of them a claim to independent existence, but there are also demonstrable transitional forms which connect them with a continuous chain. Thus we find cases that can only with the greatest difficulty be attributed to either the undoubted schizo-affective psychosis of the circular, depressive-paranoid and oneiroid catatonic type, or to the manic-depressive psychoses. An example is provided by cases where the first attack is in the form of an oneiroid catatonia, while the subsequent ones are in the form of the typical depressive or manic phases, with clear remissions between the attacks. Sometimes it is no less difficult to decide whether the case belongs to the group of periodic schizophrenias or to the schub type. The difficulty arises either because of relatively scanty personality changes after the acute attacks or because of the considerable dynamism of the attacks or because of the similarity of the attacks. Examples of such difficulties may be experienced where despite their atypical character, the attacks occur intermittently at definite times of the year.

Those forms of schizophrenias that are transitional between the continuously-progressive and the schub-type vary according to the evolution of the process. They include first types which are gradually acquiring a continuous form, and, secondly, cases where gradual and stable pseudo-neurotic or paranoidal disturbances, more rarely with hallucinations, are transformed into circular ones with somewhat subdued phases of affective disturbance. With these we may also classify cases which are scarcely capable of differentiation from remissions and in which there is a very slow progressive process with residual obsessional and paranoid features, occurring after the experience of a 'schub'. This is often very lightly expressed and recovered only with difficulty under anamnesis.

The inter-relationships between the basic forms of the psychoses and their transitional variants are as follows. (The main forms are given in *italics*; the transitional in ordinary print.)

Continuous-progressive schizophrenia: obliterated, latent forms with a favourable, continuous course; indefinitely long remissions after attacks (schubs), proceeding in the form of schizophrenic shifts (schubs) with a tendency to a progressive and continuous course.

Schizophrenia, proceeding in the form of shifts (*schubs*): proceeding with deep remissions and intermissions, but with a prevalence of hallucinatory-delusional or catatonical disturbances during attacks. Circular schizophrenia with a continuous change of phases. Chronic mania.

Recurrent schizophrenia (*schizo-affective psychoses, oneirophrenia*). Atypical cases of manic-depressive psychosis.

Manic-depressive psychosis. Cyclothymia (ambulatory cases of manic-depressive psychosis).

The main groups of the typical psychoses may be internally differentiated by cases which do not go beyond the nosological boundaries, but which are engendered by certain deviations in the stages of the pathogenic mechanism. Within the manic-depressive group of psychoses, as examples of such varieties, may be found those which progress slowly in the manic or only in the depressive phases or in the double phases. Another form is the typical alternation of depressive and manic states. Within the framework of periodic (recurrent) schizophrenia certain variants are more frequently encountered, e.g. the circular or the depressive-paranoid, often with oneiroid clouding of consciousness at the height of the attack. Sometimes there is an alternation of manic, depressive, or depressive paranoid attacks. Oneiroid catatonia is an extreme variety of this type of psychosis, which approaches the schub type.

Schizophrenia proceeding in the form of 'schubs' also exhibits differential features. The attacks may occur in the form of acute paranoia, acute hallucinosis, acute Kandinsky-Clerambault syndrome, acute paraphrenia or lucid catatonia. The remissions between the attacks are characterized by personality deterioration of various degrees, by the presence or absence of residual positive disturbances, by variable frequency of recurrences and by a variation in type.

The varieties of continuous-progressive schizophrenias are determined first of all by the pathogenetic role of age. The principle of age influence as proposed by Kahlbaum[25] is still valid here. Continuous schizophrenia beginning at puberty or adolescence progresses as simple schizophrenia or hebephrenia. In adults it takes the form of dementia paranoides of different intensities, and in the older age groups there is a prevalence of paraphrenic disturbances. The stages of development (i.e. paranoiac, paranoid, paraphrenic or catatonic) change rapidly in the young. Very frequently the boundaries are indistinct. In the adults they are clearly demarcated whilst in old age different manifestations of paraphrenia predominate. In continuous schizophrenia the variants are analogous with isomers, with a predominance of delusional and hallucinatory forms. Such varieties may be manifested in the forms with schubs.

Although the age is especially important in the incidence of continuous schizophrenia, it does not determine any selectivity of special forms, i.e. periodic, continuous or the 'schub'-type. However, every schizophrenic form may occur at any age, a fact which indirectly demonstrates the versatile adaptability of its pathogenesis.

After Kraepelin's isolation and delineation of the manic-depressive psychosis and dementia praecox, all the variety and variability of the schizophrenic features mentioned above have served to create unsurmountable obstacles to the general formulation of a perfect psychiatric nosology of schizophrenia. This led to the employment of the terms independent psychosis—atypical, periodic, cycloid, schizo-affective, mixed psychoses and so on. Actually, they were known previously and even before the acceptance of Kraepelin's classification. S. S. Korsakoff described them under the Russian term 'vesanias'.

The absence of clear boundary differentiation between schizophrenia and manic-depressive psychoses caused Kleist and Leonhard[37] to consider them jointly, but with a number of subdivisions. Basing their views on contemporary symptomatology, they distinguished twenty-two separate diseases.

Both statistics and dynamics have shown that there can be no strict boundaries between the manic-depressive psychosis and schizophrenia and this forced K. Conrad[11, 12] to speak of a common endogenous psychosis with different forms of development: circular, periodic, continuous, progressive, etc.

According to modern concepts schizophrenia and the manic-depressive psychosis represent two extreme poles of an essential lesion in mental activity. But it is difficult to establish any limit or clear-cut boundary between the two (L. Brilluen). Indeed when studying large groups of patients it becomes impossible to draw such a boundary. It has already been noted that it is often difficult to decide whether a patient suffers from a circular schizophrenia or from a manic-depressive psychosis; or in the schub-form or in the periodic form. Neither the study of the static clinical picture nor the course of the disease can assist the diagnosis, and such transitional cases are customarily termed atypical.

However, along with the existence of a significant number of atypical transitional or mixed forms, there is even a greater number of undeniably typical cases of the disease, considered both statistically and developmentally. In spite of the occurrence of the atypical forms, the statistics and the dynamics of the typical forms indicate the presence of distinct and inherent pathogenesis and pathokinesis.

The continuance of transitional states and the presence of intermediate forms does not exclude discreteness. But it does not justify the view that there is possibly one disease comprising the manic-depressive psychosis and all forms of schizophrenias. The entire group of similar diseases, including the transitional types, may be looked upon as a genus of diseases, the genus of essential psychoses, which are perhaps justifiably described as endogenous or hereditary psychoses. They may include different and nosologically independent types together with taxonomically transitional groups. H. Ey,[17] for instance, classified schizophrenia, paranoia and paraphrenia as one genus of diseases.

A similar position has recently been established in respect of the group of exogenous and organic psychoses. Recent clinical investigation has established that together with acute psychoses with course organic disturbances and lesions, there exists a transitional group. This group is typified by a protracted course without either symptoms of clouded consciousness or gross organic changes, i.e. an exogenous-organic group. Another example is the senile arterio-sclerotic psychoses which are the transitional forms of two independent diseases, the senile and the arterio-sclerotic dementias.

Nor are there any strict boundaries between the endogenous psychoses and the exogenous ones, e.g. of toxic, infective, traumatic or grossly organic type. Typical psychoses of this group with a typical picture of delirium, amentia, twilight states and clouding of consciousness of the psycho-organic syndrome, are constantly associated wih cases of exogenous psychoses by origination, but with clinical features to a certain degree similar to endogenous psychoses—various pleomorphic and rapidly developing schizophrenic forms and affective disturbances coexisting with distinct symptoms characteristic of purely exogenous disease. Such cases may be considered as endogenous modifications of psychogenetically exogenous psychoses. Quite frequently we see patients in whom, after an attack of an exogenous psychosis with an endogenous clinical picture, the subsequent development of the disease reveals endogenous disturbances, occurring periodically or spontaneously without any external noxious factors.

In other cases such later manifestations acquire a profound character. A psychosis which develops in direct response to the impact of an exogenous noxious factor and which is initially expressed in purely exogenous form may during succeeding attacks exhibit the clinical picture and course of a continuous schizophrenic process, i.e. a picture of provoked schizophrenia. In contrast there may be cases with typical symptoms of a gross, progressive, organic psychosis.

In such instances the initial psychotic manifestations may be indistinguishable from those of endogenous psychosis of schizophrenia or manic-depression, and yet the subsequent course shows a gradual transition into a distinctly organic process of arteriosclerosis or senile dementia. Bostroem[8] described similar developments with progressive paralysis or cerebral syphilis.

At present it is still uncertain whether such transitions are determined by constitutional and hereditary factors or by the specificity of the noxious agents(weaker ones may evoke an endogenous reaction and a severer one an exogenous reaction (Specht)[56] In the present context, however, it is important to stress that such transitions from exogenous and endogenous psychoses do exist. The fact is that together with the typical exogenous and organic psychoses there exist exogenous-endogenous and endogenous-exogenous psychoses.

Similar conditions may be observed with psychogenic asthenic states. The presence of a predisposition may modify such asthenia into obsessional or depressive forms (Jaspers).[24] Examples include transitions from endogenous to psychogenic psychoses, and instances of endo-reactive depression, psychogenic paranoia and psychogenic hallucinosis.

The pathogenesis and pathokinesis of certain exogenous psychoses suggests that these are models of distinct forms of schizophrenia. Acute alcoholic psychoses with delirium tremens and hallucinosis may occur as in schizophreniform schubs (shifts), if there are some preceding mental changes induced by the influence of alcohol.

The emergence of acute alcoholic psychoses as well as the development of schubs is facilitated by the action of supplementary noxious agents. As in schizophrenia alcoholic hallucinosis may occur initially in episodic forms and finally merge into a chronic state with transformation into the Kandinsky-Clerambault syndrome. A similar condition may be seen with alcoholic paranoidal disturbances. As in schizophrenia they may set in acutely and then become chronic psychotic states, as, for instance, with alcoholic delusions of jealousy.

The similarity in the pathokinesis of exogenous psychoses and of remittent schizophrenia may produce certain extremely clear characteristics during their course. The development of acute attacks of exogenous psychoses and of schizophrenia leads but rarely to exhaustion and death. As a rule at the level of the profound mental clouding of consciousness or of oneiroid schizophrenia there ensues adaptive inhibition. In some instances of similar types of psychoses adaptive inhibition may develop earlier, during the concurrent emergence of other states resembling both, e.g. hallucinatory, delusional, affective or asthenic states. Moreover, in both states a transition into chronicity is possible, e.g. into chronic hallucinosis, chronic alcoholic delusions or a transition into schizophrenia progressing by means of schub into continuous form.

The same noxious factor, be it exogenous or endogenous, may precipitate nosologically different disease. Syphilis may be the cause of several nosologically independent diseases, namely of general paralysis, syphilitic endarteritis, cerebral gumma, tabes dorsales or acute syphilitic psychoses. The same is true of alcohol which may cause delirium tremens, acute hallucinosis, acute or chronic paranoia or the Korsakoff syndrome.

The nosological independence of such disease is determined by their aetiological and pathogenetic unity. And the specificity of the latter is determined by the total character of the organism (heredity, constitution and initial pre-morbid state).

Certain inner prerequisites are necessary for the emergence of exogenous psychoses and the essential psychoses. For instance in infectious psychoses disturbances of psychic activity are observed in nearly all cases of typhus. In the course of the other infections, psychoses occur only in isolated cases. This correlation confirms the oft-stated dictum that the weaker the exogenous traumatic factor, the greater the significance of endogenous predisposition in the production of mental disturbances.

'An analysis of aetiological factors in any individual illness should always be an analysis of external ecological and internal factors, such as immunity, age, somatotype, constitution etc. In the final analysis it is precisely the inner factors (summed up historically in the philo-onthogenesis) which determine the occurrence of the disease. And it is these which communicate their attributes to the clinical and morphological manifestations' (I. Davidovsky).[14]

4

Conclusion

Initially mental disturbances were studies from the standpoint of general pathology. The concept of common psychosis prompted the investigators to examine general features, manifestations and developments common to all mental diseases. The second historical stage was characterized by the study of separate diseases and their individual clinical pictures and developments. This inevitably led to the unilateral diagnoses and the isolation of strict boundaries contrary to nature in general. It led to the concept of specificity of symptoms as inherent in a single disease, i.e. to what is now called nosological dogmatism (I. Davidovsky).[14]

The task of overcoming such unilateral concepts, which were also related to mechanistic concepts of causality, began in the first decade of the twentieth century (Hoche,[21] Bonhoeffer).[7] These concepts are still in the process of reorganization. Modern psychiatry still experiences critical problems stemming from a lack of synthesis between the general pathological and the specific characteristics of psychoses. They are expressed mainly as discrepancies in the evaluation of mental states in patients, in the interpretation of psychopathological concepts and in an absence of a generally accepted nosological classification.

In relation to schizophrenia as well as other mental diseases, synthesis may be attained as a result of comprehensive investigations. This is true of investigations at all levels of vital activity of the diseased organism, i.e. by multi-disciplinary methods. One should employ clinical, pathophysiological, social, epidemiological and all forms of available biological methods. As our experience has shown, the state of our knowledge of the clinical picture of schizophrenia is far from perfect. We have not sufficiently investigated the early forms of schizophrenia as manifested in adult and adolescent years, and more especially in childhood.

In many cases we are unable to exclude the previous occurrence of early attacks, of the first schub or 'break down' in very early childhood (M. Yudin,[63] N. Streltsova).[58] The symptomatology of early schizophrenia is fairly well known, but we do not know its syndromology. We have far from wholly investigated the symptomatology and syndromology of early childhood schizophrenia and of its comparative forms in childhood, puberty, adolescence and adult and old age. Our knowledge of the remissions of the 'schub'-type and recurrent schizophrenia is far from being complete. We do not know their relationships and specificity of factors in correlation with intermissions in phases of manic-depressive psychoses. If we have achieved a certain success in the prognosis of the three main forms of schizophrenia (the continuous-progressive, the schub-type and the recurrent), our prognosis of the subsequent development of each of these forms in an individual patient remains still unreliable and lacking in authenticity. We have just begun a systematic study of transitional forms of schizophrenia, especially those which are nearer to the junction of periodical schizophrenia and manic-depressive psychosis.

In evaluating the patient's clinical states and the patterns of evolution of the disease, a constant correlation should be made of the impact of modern therapy. There is as yet a lamentably inadequate study of the role of the therapeutic pathomorphosis in both its clinical and biological aspects.

Clinico-genetic investigations with schizophrenia are complex and labour consuming. Experience has confirmed that comparative investigations of the hereditary factors of each of the three main forms of schizophrenia are more effective. They are inseparable from the study of inheritance of various personality deviations and disharmonies. This was initiated by Kretschmer's investigations and by those of M. Yudin[63] in the Soviet Union.

These studies have shown that psychopathic personalities and their psychopath-like varieties in the relatives of schizophrenic patients do not coincide with the clinical picture of psychopathy as described by Kraepelin, Schneider,[51] Gannushkin,[19] Petrilowitsch[45] and others. They appear to have their own clinical typology which has not yet been investigated. Their genetic relationships to the schizophrenic process requires careful and intensive study.

Clinical and clinico-genetical studies are inseparable from large-scale epidemiological investigations. These studies should not be limited only to the determination of the prevalence of schizophrenia in the population and the conditions facilitating their occurrence. They should include the study of their clinical expression, specificity in the course of the disease, the influence of heredity and of external factors. Epidemiological investigations should include the evaluation of the efficacy of inpatient and outpatient treatment, and the possibilities and limitations of social rehabilitation.

Psychopathology should be explored by the comparative method of the specific features of separate mental processes in patients with different forms of schizophrenia and at different stages of development of these forms. To the present time the clinicians and the psychologists have contented themselves merely with descriptions of the characteristics of a changed personality and of schizophrenic deterioration. Precise definitions of both these states do not exist.

Clinical investigations into the nature of schizophrenia are inseparable from biological studies. The latter may be accomplished only by strict selection of material which is comparable in its expression and development. Experience has shown that biological studies should be most productive if we study similar clinical states and their characteristics in patients at the various levels of vital activity and functioning, e.g. neurophysiological, physiological and morphological levels.

There exist abundant up-to-date results of biological studies at all these levels. Among these we have data regarding conditioned and unconditioned reflex activity, disturbances of spatial synchronization of activity of the different parts of the brain, the presence of various abnormal metabolites in the blood and other biological fluids of schizophrenics, etc. However, this wealth of information remains at the level of empirical laboratory data and has not as yet been united into a satisfactory working hypothesis.

Consequently the results of biological investigations are still unable to resolve the problem of the nature of the primary and secondary schizophrenic processes of cerebral origin. There is the utmost need to direct the future research into biological as well as clinical fields.

REFERENCES

1. ABRAMYAN, L., 1966. *Problems of Philosophy*, **10.**
2. AGUDOV, V., 1967. *Problems of Philosophy*, **1.**
3. BERINGER, K., 1924. *Zschrft. Neurol. Psychiatr.*, **93.**
4. BERNSTEIN, N., 1965. *Problems of Philosophy*, **10.**
5. BERZE, J., and GRUHLE, M., 1929. *Psychologie der Schizophrenie.*
6. BLEULER, E., 1911. Dementia Praecox oder Gruppe der Schizophrenien. *Aschafenburgs Handbuch der Psychiatrie.*
7. BONHOEFFER, K., 1912. Die Psychosen un Gefolge von Akuten Infektionen. *Aschafenburgs Handbuch der Psychiatrie*, vol. 3, part 1.
8. BOSTROEM, A., 1930. Die Progressive Paralyse. *Handbuch Bumke*, **8.**
9. CHASLIN, 1912. *Element de semiologie et clinique mentales.*
10. CHEKHOVA, A., 1963. 'The course of schizophrenia beginning in childhood.'
11. CONRAD, K., 1959. *Der Nervenartzt.*
12. CONRAD, K., 1966. *Die beginnende Schizophrenie*, 2nd. ed.
13. CRAMER, 1910. *Allgemeine Zeitsch. f. Psychiatrie*, **67.**
14. DAVIDOVSKY, I., 1962. *The problems of causation in Medicine* (Aetiology).

15. DAVIDOVSKY, I., 1966. *Gerentology.*
16. EMMINGHAUS, M., 1878. *Allgemeine Psychopathologie.*
17. EY, H., 1958. *Der Nervenartzt,* **29.**
18. EY, H., and ROUART, 1936. *Essai d'application des Principes de Jackson à une Conception Dynamique de la Neuro-Psychiatrie.*
19. GANNUSHKIN, N., 1933. *Psychopathic Clinics.*
20. GRIESINGER, W., 1845. *Pathologie und Therapie d. Psychischen Krankheiten.*
21. HOCHE, 1912. *Zeitschr. Neurol. Psych.,* **12.**
22. IVANOV-SMOLENSKY, A., 1952. *I. P. Pavlov's teachings in Pathological Psychology.*
23. JACKSON, J. H., 1931. *Selected writings of John Hughlings Jackson,* vol. 2.
24. JASPERS, K., 1953. *Allgemeine Psychopathologie.* 6th ed.
25. KAHLBAUM, K., 1874. *Die Katatonie.*
26. KAHLBAUM, K., 1897. *Lehrbuch der Psychiatrie.*
27. KANDINSKY, V., 1890. *Relating to the question of alienation.*
28. KEDROV, B., 1966. *Problems of Philosophy,* **12.**
29. KERBIKOV, O., 1949. *Acute Schizophrenia.*
30. KRAEPELIN, 1923. *Psychiatrie,* vol. 3, part 2.
31. KRAEPELIN, 1923. Die Erscheinungsformen des Irrenseins. *Zschrft. Neurol. Psychiat.,* **62.**
32. KRAEPELIN and LANGE, 1927. *Psychiatrie,* **1.**
33. KRAFFT-EBING, 1897. *Lehrbuch der Psychiatrie.*
34. KORSAKOFF, S., 1901. *A course in psychiatry,* vols. 1 and 2.
35. KOTHE, B., 1957. *Uber Kindlische Schizophrenie.*
36. KRONFELD, A., 1940. Problems of Syndromology and Nosology in Contemporary Psychiatry. *Transactions of the Gannushkin Institute,* **5.**
37. LEONHARD, K., 1960. Die Atypischen Psychosen und Kleists Lehre von Endogenen Psychosen. *Psychiatric der Gegenwait,* vol. 2.
38. MAGNAN, V., 1893. *Lecons Clinique sur les Maladies Mentales.*
39. MAUDSLEY, H., 1867. *Physiology and pathology of mind.*
40. MOREL, B., 1860. *Traite des Maladies Mentales.*
41. MOROZOV, V., 1964. *Psychiatry, Neurology and Medical Psychology,* **7.**
42. OVCHINNIKOV, 1966. *Problems of Philosophy,* **9.**
43. OZERETSKOVSKY, D., 1950. *Obsessional States.*
44. PAVLOV, I., 1951. *Complete collected works,* vol. 5, part 3, No. 2.
45. PETRILOWITSCH, H., 1960. *Abnorme Personlichkeiten.*
46. RIBOT, 1892. *Les Maladies de la Memoire,* 8th ed.
47. SKACHKOV, Y., 1966. *The Communist,* **16.**
48. SHCHERBACK, A., 1901. *Clinical lectures in nervous and mental disorders.*
49. SCHILDER, 1924. *Medizinische Psychologie.*
50. SCHNEIDER, K., 1942. *Die Schizophrenien Symptonverbande.*
51. SCHNEIDER, K., 1950. *Die Psychopatischen Personlichkeiten,* 9th ed.
52. SCHWARTZ, S., 1965. *Problems of Philosophie,* **2.**
53. SIMSON, T. P., 1948. *Schizophrenia of early childhood.*
54. SLUCHEVSKY, I., 1955. Aetiology and Pathogenesis of Schizophrenia. *Transactions of the all Union Conference in Memory of Birth of Korsakoff.*
55. STORCH, A., 1922. *Das Archaisch-primitive Erleben und Denken der Schizophrenen.*
56. SPECHT. *Zentralblatt Neurol. Psych.,* **19.**
57. STRANSKY, E., 1914. *Lehrbuch der Allgemeinen und Speziellen Psychiatrie.*
58. STRELTSOVA, N., 1964. *The Korsakoff Journal of Neuropathology and Psychiatry,* **64,** 1.
59. SUKHAREVA, G., 1937. *Clinics in schizophrenia of childhood and adolescence.*
60. SVECHNIKOV, G., 1966. *The Communist,* **14.**

61. UKHTOMSKY, A., 1954. Notes on the Physiology of the Nervous System. *Collected Works*, No. IV.
62. WERNICKE, 1860. *Grundriss der Psychiatrie.*
63. YUDIN, M., 1941. Schizophrenia as a Primary Defect—Psychosis. *Papers of the Central Psychiatric Institute*, 2.
64. ZURABASHVILI, A., 1964. *Contemporary problems in psychiatry.*

XVI

PSYCHOANALYSIS: AN EVALUATION

ROBERT B. WHITE,

M.D.

Professor of Psychiatry,
The University of Texas Medical Branch at Galveston

1

Introduction

Since the 1940s, psychoanalysis has greatly expanded its scope of interest and activity to many areas beyond the treatment of neuroses, thereby improving therapeutic procedures and clarifying a variety of concepts while making important contributions to numerous fields outside of clinical psychoanalysis proper. This expansion has included studies of human and animal subjects in the psychological laboratory, observational studies on the development of infants and children, and research on family structure, family pathology, and therapy. Analytic principles have also been applied to the study of the organization of the mental hospital, sociology, industrial organization, labour-management relations, child care, pediatric practice, psychosomatic conditions, group therapy, and hypnosis. Psychoanalytic therapeutic procedures have been further extended to the treatment of borderline states, schizophrenia, and manic-depressive psychosis. Efforts have been made to correlate analytic observations with those from ethology and the developmental psychology of Piaget. As Alexander[1, 3] and his co-authors have noted, this broadening of analytic interests began in the 1920s and 1930s, but there has clearly been a remarkable extension of such efforts in the last two decades.

From its beginnings, psychoanalysis has been frequently criticized as being an imprecise endeavour not warranting the status of a scientific discipline. Bailey,[5] for instance, has recently noted: 'Naturally Freud hoped that some of his speculations might turn out to be true . . . , but that it was largely through the use of . . . interesting sophistries (that) he deluded himself and his followers into believing that he had been correct after all, so that today he is practically deified by them (in ways that have) . . . done great damage to psychiatry as well as to our civilization in general.' Eysenck[41] has expressed doubt that psychoanalytic therapy alleviates neurotic symptoms any more effectively than supportive care by general practitioners, custodial care in state hospitals, or the simple passage of time with no treatment at all.

Prior to the last twenty years or so, analysts have tended to maintain a parochial reluctance to heed the challenge of such critics, to grapple with the difficult task of systematizing their theory, or to expose their therapeutic techniques to systematic scientific scrutiny. There was, up to a point, good sense in this reluctance to stretch the varied and novel discoveries of analysis on to the Procrustean bed of the methods of laboratory research or neatness of a prematurely fixed theory. But, in the past two decades, increasing numbers of analysts have begun to feel that the ways of the naturalist clinician from which psychoanalysis stemmed should not continue to be the sole method for proceeding further. Edward Glover,[63] noting the difficulty involved in applying to psychoanalytic therapy the controls and research methods usual in science, commented: 'This difficulty is unavoidable but not insuperable: it can be met by sustained application of such scientific checks as *are* appropriate to the special conditions of psychoanalysis.' He further notes: '. . . there is . . . a tendency *not* to apply to the data of observation or to the methods of interpretation such scientific controls as *are* available. The consequence is that a great deal of what passes as tested (psychoanalytic) theory is little more than speculation, varying widely in plausibility.'

In 1939, Heinz Hartmann[70] began a long sustained effort to systematize and bring better order into psychoanalytic theory, an effort reported in a series of papers[71] some of which were written in collaboration with Kris and Loewenstein.[72] David Rapaport,[114-116] Schafer,[133] and Gill[61] have made similar contributions. As these and other analysts attempted to order psychoanalytic concepts, Anna Freud and her collaborators,[17, 54-58] Spitz,[150-154] Peter Wolff,[173, 175] Winnicott,[170-172] Bowlby,[23-25] Benjamin,[12-15] Escalona,[40] Melanie Klein,[85-88] Jacobson,[80] and others have enriched the fund of psychoanalytic knowledge from treatment or direct observation of infants and children. Helen Sargent,[127-132] Robert Wallerstein,[158-164] and colleagues[32, 66, 77, 98-101, 118, 119] at The Menninger Foundation have taken up Glover's challenge by subjecting psychoanalytic therapy to rigorous, quantitative research in an ingenious method that gives hope of being true both to the rich complexity of psychoanalytic clinical experience and to the canons of scientific methodology. George Klein,[83, 84] Holt,[74-76] Fisher,[48-51] Miller,[106] Altshuler,[4] Ernest Hartmann,[69] and others have reconsidered psychoanalytic concepts in the light of experimental studies from the laboratory on perception, sensory isolation, or dreaming. Harlow's[67, 68] experiments on monkeys have supplemented psychoanalytic observations about maternal deprivation. The bold investigations of Masters and Johnson[105] on sexual behaviour have been used by Sherfey[145] to modify a variety of psychoanalytic assumptions about female sexuality. Erikson[39] and others have applied the findings of ethology[96, 97, 157] to analytic notions about aggression and inborn instinctual behaviour. Peter Wolff[174] has co-ordinated the concepts of Piaget with many psychoanalytic assumptions. The ferment among psychoanalytic researchers is illustrated in recent comments by George Klein:[84] '. . . excepting a few recent faint stirrings, there has not been since Freud's lifetime a *single* advance in the investigative or research methodology used by psychoanalysts—not one advance in dealing with psychoanalytic protocols for research purposes.'

Klein's criticisms seem extreme in the light of the Menninger study and other recent studies that use sound movies as an instrument for objective study of psychotherapy. Nevertheless, Klein correctly points to a significant problem when he comments:

'In no field (other than analysis) is it presumed that raw data can be carried around as part of one's memory; it is especially funny when the claim is made by analysts who are capable of forgetting where they parked their cars on any given day.'

Roy Schafer[133] has emphasized the constructive dissatisfaction among analysts with the fragmented and unintegrated state of many aspects of psychoanalytic theory:

'Any student of the psychoanalytic literature on a single basic concept or a single clinical entity must be, if he is receptive to all he reads, bewildered'; and furthermore, 'He will also be made aware that . . . there is no far reaching and exact consensus in any specific area of Freudian psychoanalytic thought—not on instinct theory or ego psychology, not on hysteria or schizophrenia, not on technique or criteria for treatment and termination, and so forth. There is consensus on many important details but not on broad generalizations and their interrelations.' Schafer also notes: 'if psychoanalysis is to be a science, the psychoanalyst's role can never be restricted simply to gathering further data, as some conservative theorists today propose or imply; psychoanalysts must always be equally concerned with how to think about data, with refining their notions of what constitutes data, with articulating data in new ways, and, by such means, with gathering data beyond the ken of older ways of thinking.'

Although some critics continue to insist that analysis is dead, the lively ferment in analytic thinking and research should make it permissible for analysis to reply to its more vituperative critics by borrowing Mark Twain's apt comment about an erroneously published notice of his death: 'The reports of my death are greatly exaggerated.'

If, then, psychoanalysis is by no means dead, what is its current state of health? To bring my reader abreast of the many new developments in recent years, I shall use as my main scaffolding the psychoanalytic schema of stages of personality development in order to summarize Erikson's newer psychosocial concepts and to illustrate their relationship to traditional psychosexual views. This scaffolding is outlined in Table 1.

TABLE 1. Schematic Outline of Stages of Personality Development

	PSYCHOSOCIAL STAGES	PSYCHOSEXUAL STAGES	RADIUS OF SIGNIFICANT OTHERS AT EACH STAGE
I	TRUST VS. MISTRUST	ORAL	MATERNAL PERSON
II	AUTONOMY VS. SHAME, DOUBT	ANAL-URETHRAL, MUSCULAR	PARENTAL PERSONS
III	INITIATIVE VS. GUILT	PHALLIC-LOCOMOTOR (OEDIPAL)	BASIC FAMILY
IV	INDUSTRY VS. INFERIORITY	LATENCY	NEIGHBORHOOD, SCHOOL AND PLAYMATES
V	IDENTITY VS. IDENTITY DIFFUSION	PUBERTY	PEER GROUPS AND OUT-GROUPS; MODELS OF LEADERSHIP
VI	INTIMACY VS. ISOLATION	GENITALITY OR ADULTHOOD PROPER	PARTNERS IN FRIENDSHIP, SEX, COMPETITION, COOPERATION
VII	GENERATIVITY VS. STAGNATION		DIVIDED LABOR, SHARED HOUSEHOLD, SPOUSE AND CHILDREN
VIII	INTEGRITY VS. DESPAIR		MANKIND AND SOCIETY GENERALLY

(Adapted from Erikson, 1959)

The section on the first or oral stage of personality formation will serve as a base from which to range into recent work on the observational studies of early infancy and the mother-infant relationship, and studies on the etiology and treatment of schizophrenia and the manic-depressive psychoses. The third (oedipal) stage of development and, to some extent, the second (anal) stage will be used to lead us into psychoanalytic work on family dynamics, family pathology, and family therapy. After discussing the remaining stages of personality development, we will turn to recent advances in research in psychoanalytic therapy and a variety of other problems, such as laboratory studies on perception, sensory deprivation, and dreaming, and extensions of analytic insights to problems outside of the clinician's consulting room.

These are the major new frontiers of psychoanalysis as I see them. I trust that my efforts to summarize some rather fully and to note others more briefly will convey the vigour with which psychoanalysis is expanding its work and leaving behind its parochial tendencies of past years to follow its own way while in good measure ignoring its critics and remaining aloof from other fields of behavioural science.

2

The Development of Personality

Starting from different points of view and using different methods for gathering data, Rene Spitz[153, 154] and Erik Erikson[37, 38] have arrived at remarkably similar positions concerning the step-wise manner in which personality structure unfolds under the influence of the interplay between environmental factors and biologically given maturational potentials. Both authors build on the basic Freudian views that personality formation occurs in a regular, step-wise progression of definable stages from earliest infancy to adulthood and that disturbances in early childhood are crucial determinants of both emotional health and pathology.

Although analysts have always acknowledged the importance of the earliest oral and anal stages of the first three years of life, they have tended to give primary emphasis to the oedipal period from about three to six years of age as being crucial to later emotional health or illness. Unquestionably, one of the outstanding trends in psychoanalytic thinking today is the emphasis on the earliest months of life and the mother-infant relationship as important determinants of the major and pervading tone of later mental health. The findings of a wide variety of analysts including Melanie Klein, Anna Freud, Winnicott, Bowlby, Erikson, and others point compellingly to the great importance of the developmental phase of earliest infancy, a consensus arrived at by investigators who have differed in their observational methods and ways of conceptualizing their findings.

The Concept of Epigenesis

Working from the original observations of Freud, both Spitz and Erikson have independently concluded that the epigenetic principle, so central to embryological concepts of prenatal physical development, can with profit be expanded in its application to postnatal psychological development. The ground plan of the embryo, if not disturbed by intercurrent pathological influences, ensures an orderly unfolding of various organ systems, each with its particular and unique time of ascendancy. A similar principle ensures the step-wise unfolding of personality structure in the growing child, an unfolding that occurs when his innate tendency to mature psychologically is met by what has been called variously a facilitating environment (Winnicott),[172] mutuality of regulation between parents and child (Erikson),[37, 38] adequate stimulus-nutriment (Rapaport),[115] or aliment (Piaget).[112, 113]

Embryological and psychoanalytic concepts about development coincide on two other points: (*i*) the earlier in life that disturbing influences impinge on the development of the organism, the more widespread and pervasive will be the impairment and distortions of later stages; and (*ii*) each stage, like that of embryological development, involves phase specific vulnerabilities for each particular budding attribute. Each particular capacity must be met by adequate environmental conditions if it is to emerge at its appointed time or remain forever stunted or distorted to some degree. Furthermore, the unfolding of new attributes at each stage must be satisfactorily completed if growth of succeeding attributes at later stages is not to be jeopardized; impairment at phase one prejudices the developments of stage two; impairment at stages one and two imposes still further handicaps for development at stage three, and so on. In this fashion early faults in development may lead to an ever greater accrual of psychological vulnerabilities as development proceeds. Later, more healthful influences may, of course, compensate for earlier deficiencies.

Analysis further emphasizes that for genetically sound children (and this includes the vast majority of infants) the crucial factor that determines personality development is the quality of parental care and family organization, especially the quality of maternal care in the first year or two of life. Erikson[37] states:

'The healthy child, given a reasonable amount of guidance (by loving parents who are reasonably at peace with each other), can be trusted to obey inner laws of development, laws which create a *succession of potentialities for significant interaction* with those who tend him.' He further goes on to state: 'Personality . . . (develops) according to steps predetermined in the human organism's readiness to be driven toward, to be aware of, and to interact with, a widening social radius, beginning with the dim image of a mother and ending with mankind. . . .'

The Psychosexual Point of View

With these general concepts of development in mind, let us now discuss the analytic conceptualization of the specific developmental phases of personality. Initially, Freud described the oral, anal, phallic (or oedipal) stages of early childhood; the latency phase of late childhood; adolescence; and adulthood proper. Freud's designation of developmental stages as being psychosexual in nature reminds us that sexual (and also aggressive) drives are of central importance to personality formation and that man begins life with no innate morality and precious little capacity to tolerate frustration, impose delay on biological urges, be guided by moral precepts, or exercise restraint and judgement. Man must, step by step, evolve from the egoistic need of the child for immediate gratification of urges to the more stable, self-confident capacity of the adult to tolerate frustration and give thoughtful and moral direction to his acts. To do this he must slowly develop capacities to master his own body, his wishes, and the world in which he lives. Furthermore, he must develop the capacity for mature give and take with others like him. The term 'psychosexual' is only a technical shorthand to specify certain important sexual attributes of the major way stations in this journey. In his emphasis on biological drives, Freud seemed at times to underemphasize the complexities of the actual interactions between offspring and parents in the course of the child's journey to maturity. Those who are not familiar with all of Freud's writings often conclude that analysts consider the process of personality development primarily a struggle of the child with his instinctual urges. Although giving great weight to the biological drives and the conflicts they cause, Freud, from his earliest papers on, recognized the importance of environmental factors. As early as 1905[59] he emphasized the significance of '. . . the purely human and social circumstances of our patients' and commented, 'Above all, our interest will be directed towards their family circumstances.' It has remained for later workers to give special emphasis to the social factors in development, notably Heinz Hartmann, Rapaport, and Erikson.

Let us now describe the various stages of development of personality in both their psychosexual and psychosocial aspects.

The Oral Stage (Freud) or the Stage of Trust versus Mistrust (Erikson)

To the infant, the environment is the mother and his first taste of the kind of world into which he has been pushed comes from the mother's breast and the manner in which she holds, caresses, coos, cuddles, suckles, and cares for him. Because biologically the mouth cavity is initially the most sensitive body area and so much of the infant's experience is centred on the nursing interactions with the mother, Freud designated the first year or so of life as the oral stage. Furthermore, because the nursing experience is, under optimal circumstances, so patently a sensuous, erotic interlude for the child *and* the mother, this stage is designated as the first of the several psychosexual stages. Further reasons for designating the oral stage as psychosexual can be found in the obvious contribution behaviour patterns of this stage make to both mature and perverse adult sexuality; kissing, nibbling, 'love bites,' and sucking in normal love play for example, and the prominence of sucking and biting in various perversions.

These same stages of infantile development can be considered from the viewpoint of psychosocial concepts that Erikson has proposed as a complement to, *not a replacement for*, the psychosexual concepts. Because of the human infant's extended period of helplessness, the major adaptive tasks of the mother-infant twosome falls to the mother who, as Spitz[154] puts it, must act as an 'auxiliary ego,' performing for the baby those adaptive tasks that are beyond his limited capacities. By a kind of emotional lend-lease, she extends to the baby her more organized and adequate ego capacities of perception, accurate judgement, and skilful ability to alter the environment to provide food, warmth, cleanliness, body care and so on, functions which the baby can as yet not arrange for himself. In Erikson's[37] terms, the mother-child relation must also involve an adequate degree of 'mutuality of regulation' if the baby is to get the food and experience he needs to grow and if the mother is to be able to sense properly what he needs and provide it in the right amounts at the appropriate time. Thus, between a healthy mother and a healthy baby, a highly personalized set of communications develop and a mutual steering each of the other evolves. Concerning this stage and the importance of mutuality between mother and infant, Erikson[37] notes:

'As the newborn infant is separated from his symbiosis with the mother's body, his inborn and more or less co-ordinated ability to take in by mouth meets the mother's more or less co-ordinated ability and intention to feed him and to welcome him. At this point he lives through, and loves with, his mouth; and the mother lives through, and loves with, her breasts.
'For the mother this is a late and complicated accomplishment highly dependent on her development as a woman; on her unconscious attitude toward the child; on the way she has lived through pregnancy and delivery; on her and her community's attitude toward the act of nursing—and on the response of the newborn. To him the mouth is the focus of a general first approach to life. . . .'

In this fashion, Erikson clearly indicates the continuity between traditional psychosexual concepts and his more recent psychosocial views. Erikson[37] goes on to note that the infant not only takes in stimuli and food through his mouth, but also takes in, that is, internalizes or incorporates, environmental stimuli through visual, tactile, olfactory, and auditory modes of perception. Adequate stimuli must be provided in a variety of ways in order to facilitate and stimulate adequate physiological and psychological development. Furthermore, these stimuli must be delivered in the proper intensity, at the right times, and in the correct sequence. Otherwise, the infant's capacity to respond may change into a lethargic withdrawal—even stupor. This calls for a sensitive attunement of the mother's behaviour with the baby's needs—a mutual regulation of each other. Where the baby has special sensitivities and inborn vulnerabilities, such mutual regulation may be difficult even for loving and attentive mothers.

Erikson goes on to describe how mutuality between mother and baby may break down if the mother, from conflicts within herself or within her family, is unable adequately to understand the needs that the infant indicates by his various signals such as crying, restlessness, and so on. She may become erratic in her care as she anxiously changes formulae or alternately comforts or lets the baby cry it out. The deprived baby may 'find his thumb and damn the world,' as Erikson states, or if deprivation becomes more extreme he may in despair withdraw into lethargy. Such failures in the capacity of the mother and the child to attune themselves to each other seem especially disturbing to infants born with a sensitive nature. The schism that results when mutuality breaks down between him and his mother may become the model for later serious disturbances in his ability to relate adequately to people in general, particularly so if early frustrations are not compensated for by more nurturant experiences in later stages of childhood.

16

Since even the best of mothers fail in some degree to meet adequately all of an infant's needs, and since every baby must in time be weaned and lose his position as the being who is central in the mother's life, every person retains from this inevitable infantile loss a dim sense of having been deprived, abandoned, and having lost a blissful state of unity with the mother. This gives all mankind a 'dim but universal nostalgia for a lost paradise' and some residue of basic mistrust and sense of inner division into a good and an evil, greedy self. Erikson goes on to state:

'... *the firm establishment of enduring patterns for the balance of basic trust over basic mistrust* is the first task of the budding personality and therefore first of all a task for maternal care. But it must be said that the *amount of trust* derived from earliest infantile experience does not seem to depend on absolute *quantities of food or demonstrations of love* but rather on the *quality* of the maternal relationship. Mothers create a sense of trust in their children by that kind of administration which in its quality combines sensitive care of the baby's individual needs and a firm sense of personal trustworthiness within the trusted framework of their community's life style. (This forms the basis in the child for a sense of identity which will later combine a sense of being "all right," of being oneself, and of becoming what other people trust one will become.) Parents must not only have certain ways of guiding by prohibition and permission; they must also be able to represent to the child a deep, an almost somatic conviction that there is a meaning to what they are doing.'

In general, Spitz agrees with Erikson but has specified in greater detail several crucial nodal points of development in the first eighteen months of life: (*i*) the smiling response at about the age of three months that indicates the beginnings of social responsiveness; (*ii*) stranger anxiety and apprehension over loss of the mother when she is too long absent in the second half of the first year; and (*iii*) the capacity for semantic communication in the middle of the second year.

Melanie Klein[85-88] (see also, Segal)[143] has developed a different set of concepts about mental functioning in infants during the earliest months of life. Basing her views on the fantasies of older children and adults, she postulates that even *very* young infants have a primitive capacity to perceive and dimly differentiate an image of the mother in the earliest weeks and months of life, and to engage in remarkable fantasies of devouring and destroying the mother out of ruthless need for her. In turn the infant develops vivid fantasies that the mother now is a vengeful and potentially murderous persecutor inside the child's body where she rips and tears his insides in retaliation for his cannibalistic wish to eat and destroy her. Although there is a great controversy in analysis about the validity of Klein's views, there is no question that children from about the age of two on are clearly capable in moments of rage of having such fantasies which seem so bewildering or unbelievable to grown-ups who have never carefully observed the workings of the minds of children. Those analysts who work with deeply regressed psychotics find such bizarre infantile fantasies in their patients with great regularity as Searles,[138] Guntrip,[64] Fairbairn,[43, 44] Sechehaye,[139-142] and many others have repeatedly documented.

Whatever the eventual outcome may be of this controversy over Kleinian views on the infant stages of psychological functioning, Klein has done a great service in calling to our attention the crucial importance of the earliest mother-child relationship and the important degree to which childhood fantasies as well as actual experience in the first year or so of life determines later psychological health or illness, especially predisposition to malignant schizoid, schizophrenic, and manic-depressive psychoses. It seems to me very likely that forthcoming publications by Schafer[133] and Burnham et al.[26] may provide ways to reconcile some of the confusion and controversy between Melanie Klein's concepts and those views on ego formation and early stages of personality development that are more generally accepted (at least in America).

It is on the basic issue of the crucial impact of mothering that Melanie Klein, Winnicott, Bowlby, Guntrip, Fairbairn, Erikson, Spitz, Anna Freud, and many others all agree. The overwhelming importance of proper maternal care as a necessary condition for adequate physical and emotional development of infants has been clearly documented by Spitz,[150-154] who has described in detail the steps and processes through which children withdraw into psychotic conditions when they are subjected to severe deprivation of maternal care in infancy. Harlow[67, 68] has demonstrated very similar effects from maternal deprivation experimentally imposed on monkeys. Winnicott[172] has postulated that schizophrenia is largely due to an 'environmental failure' imposed by inadequate mothering in infancy.

Searles, who has written most extensively on the subject of schizophrenia, is in agreement with Winnicott,[170, 172] Guntrip,[64] Fairbairn,[43] Balint,[8] Rosenfeld,[124, 126] Rosen,[123] and others who feel that pathological qualities or inadequate quantities of mothering are crucial etiological factors in schizophrenia. The experiences of childhood that contribute to the etiology of manic-depressive states as well as the psychoanalytic therapy of these states have been studied by Scott,[136] Rosenfeld,[125] Gibson,[60] Guntrip,[65] and others.

Balint[8] has noted that the successful psychoanalytic treatment of the schizophrenic or schizoid patient depends largely on the therapist's ability to provide in his therapeutic approach the conditions necessary for the patient to regress to very infantile levels of experience and make a 'new beginning' in his transference relation to the analyst as his mother. Sechehaye[139 -142] has described an analytic technique for the treatment of the chronic schizophrenic. Using 'symbolic realization,' she provides the patient in symbolic ways with maternal care such as one would give an infant. After recovering from chronic schizophrenia, one of her patients, Renee (Sechehaye),[139] wrote an autobiographical account of her psychotic experience and the curative effects of her therapist's actions. Renee describes how she felt like a bewildered, terrified infant, at times consumed with jealous rage when her therapist was attentive to other patients. At those times, Renee would suddenly find the world had become unreal and she would be overwhelmed by frightening hallucinations. When Sechehaye would be attentive to her, Renee states, '. . . beautiful and living reality reappeared and I felt an invigorating contact with her.' But the patient could again lose contact with reality: 'if . . . Mama (Mrs Sechehaye) was annoyed with me. . . .' Her transference relation to the therapist as a mother was: '. . . the well spring, the source of normal reality perception.' The observations of Spitz, Erikson, Anna Freud, and Melanie Klein suggest that Renee's experience is very much like that of the infant as maternal care makes it possible for him to develop realistic perception, independence, and trust in the early months of his life. Renee further notes, '. . . meanwhile I succeeded in strengthening myself to such a point that at the end of two years I was able to oppose Mama and even—something unheard of—to defend myself when she chose to be annoyed with me. And without losing reality! In the matter of stable and valid perception, I had become independent.' Again, this parallels closely the actual events that we observe in the course of development of children as they become independent of the mother. Finally, Renee reached the point where, '. . . reality became more real, more rich, and I (became) more social and independent. Now I can accept Mrs Sechehaye in her own right. I love her for herself and I am eternally grateful to her for the priceless treasure she has granted me in restoring reality and contact with life.'

Searles,[138] Rosen,[123] Rosenfeld,[124, 126] Winnicott,[170] and Balint[8] have also given full accounts of this intense emotional give and take between patient and therapist in the course of psychotherapy with the schizophrenic. Freeman et al.[53] and Burnham et al.[26] have described the organization of the mental hospital necessary to provide adequate care for severely psychotic patients.

Most psychoanalytic observers agree that the role of maternal care in the etiology of childhood mental illness must be considered in its relation to the infant's specific needs and capacities to respond to mothering. Some mothers can provide adequately for reasonably responsive children, but fail badly with a child whose idiosyncratic needs and sensitivities are beyond the range to which the mother can respond. It seems possible that some children are born with such severe inherent peculiarities and defects in their capacities to respond to mothering that few, if any, mothers could provide the care needed to nourish the child's emotional growth. And it seems very likely that even the healthiest infant will fail to flourish if grossly deprived of adequate mothering.

Longitudinal studies illuminate the interplay between inborn defects of adaptive capacity in the baby and environmental factors in creating vulnerability to mental illness. Fish et al.[45-47] studied sixteen infants who were randomly selected at a well baby clinic and examined them periodically from the age of one month to ten years. At the age of one month, three infants were found to have serious, seemingly inborn defects in adaptive capacities and on this basis were predicted to have a high vulnerability to the later development of schizophrenic disturbances, the prediction being based on the presence of extreme unevenness in development as measured clinically and by standardized tests of child development. All came from families with a high incidence of social or psychiatric pathology. At the age of ten years the children were comprehensively studied by 'blind' examiners. The three children who had been predicted at age one month to be vulnerable to the later development of schizophrenia were all seriously disturbed at age ten. The one who was judged most vulnerable at age one month was grossly psychotic; the other two suffered respectively from paranoid schizophrenia and a psychopathic state with schizoid emptiness and detachment. The thirteen infants who had been judged as not especially vulnerable were, at age ten, normal or at worst neurotic. Fish concludes that environmental factors play a relatively less important role when there are severe and apparently inborn defects in development; in cases showing few or no early defects, environmental factors play a more important role in determining the outcome.

Spitz[154] has further illuminated the interplay of inborn sensitivities and vulnerabilities with environmental conditions in determining development. He found that eczema in infants results from the interplay of specific inborn sensitivities of the skin of the infant with specific conflicts in the mother, both factors being necessary to produce the eczema. The mothers of eczematous babies showed an unusually high degree of thinly veiled hostility coupled with great overt anxiety about the welfare of their babies. They did not like to touch their children and often had a friend diaper, bathe, or feed their child. On the one hand they were concerned about the fragility and vulnerability of their children, but, on the other hand, they often inflicted such dangerous acts on their children as dropping an open safety pin in the infant's cereal, tying a bib so tight the child turned blue, or consistently and intolerably overheating the baby's cubicle on the plea that he might catch cold.

In the light of the work of Spitz,[153, 154] Benjamin,[12-15] Mahler,[102] and others, the nature-nurture issue turns out to be a meaningless question. To determine meaningfully the current or future state of health or disease of the child, one must examine the kinds of conflicts in the mother, how they interact with the inborn characteristics of the child, and at what stages of development and in what kind of family atmosphere they occur. Only when we begin to ask far more sophisticated questions than those of nature versus nurture can we possibly hope to get meaningful answers to the many intricate riddles of human development and behaviour.

I have lingered long in my treatment of the first stage of personality development because this has been such an important recent focus of psychoanalytic interest. Let us now move on to a consideration of the other stages of development.

The Anal Stage (Freud) or the Stage of Autonomy versus Shame and Doubt (Erikson)

From about the midpoint of the second year onward, orality wanes in importance as the musculature generally and the anal and urethral zone and sphincters in particular move to a central position in the child's emotional life. As his musculature becomes better coordinated, the child becomes able to act with purpose and to communicate with accuracy. He can say no or yes and mean it, hold on to people and things with tenacity, or push them away with determination. The anal zone now replaces the mouth as the body area of special erogenous sensitivity. Bowel functions become the centre of fantasies of eliminating people cruelly or turning loose of them tenderly and confidently, of fantasies of coercively retaining his hold on them out of anxiety, or of holding to them lovingly. In our culture, bowel functions often become an arena of conflict as the child is taught to deposit faeces only at certain times and in certain places. The mother still remains the central person in the child's life, although the father and siblings now begin to enter the child's widening radius of meaningful people. The psychosexual aspects of this stage are apparent in his fantasies of being sexually penetrated anally or of giving birth through that orifice. When indulged and stimulated too much or frustrated too harshly, the child may become unable to relinquish these sensuous anal pleasures and fantasies and they may persist into adulthood as anal perversion or an egocentric infatuation with bowel function.

The interplay of parental control with the fantasies and wilful urges of the child at this stage will determine whether the youngster comes to feel pride and confidence in his autonomous capacities for self-imposed discipline or a shame-ridden overdependence on parental authority that stems from a deep dread of being unable to exercise adequate self-control. Such conflicts may lead to obsessional preoccupation with uncontrollable thoughts or self-imposed compulsive overcontrol that makes paralysing rigidities out of potential virtues. In this way, the conscience begins to function and the seeds may be planted for later obsessive-compulsive neuroses. Erikson[37] comments on this stage from the psychosocial point of view:

'The over-all significance of this stage lies in the maturation of the muscle system, the consequent ability (and doubly felt inability) to coordinate a number of highly conflicting action patterns such as "holding on" and "letting go," and the enormous value with which the still highly dependent child begins to endow his autonomous will.'

Noting that at this stage '. . . mutual regulation between adult and child now faces its severest test,' Erikson goes on to state that toilet training done too early or too harshly will rob the child of the opportunity to develop an autonomous sense of self-willed control over his body and mind. He may regress under such circumstances to the babyish ways of the oral period or enter into a battle of wills with the mother. Therefore, this stage is decisive for determining the ratio between love and hate in the child, between cooperative willingness to learn and stubborn wilful disobedience, and for the development of a sense of self-control without loss of self-esteem. The events of this stage will determine whether he accrues a sense of autonomy and pride in his ability to control himself or a pervasive sense of shame and doubt that he can ever exercise self-restraint because *he* wants to. A firm sense of trust from the first stage is essential to development of confidence in his own autonomous abilities in this second stage. Parental firmness must now protect him from frightening experiences of loss of self-control; yet it must not coerce unduly lest it undermine his self-esteem and budding independence.

Erikson[37] notes the difficulties that arise when experts attempt to educate parents about the care of children:

'. . . when it comes to human values, nobody knows how to fabricate or manage the fabrication of the genuine article. My own field, psychoanalysis, having studied particularly the excessive increase of guilt feelings beyond any normal rhyme or reason, and the consequent excessive estrangement of the child from his own body, attempted at least to formulate what should *not* be done to children. These formulations, however, often aroused superstitious inhibitions in those who were inclined to make anxious rules out of vague warnings. Actually, we are learning only gradually what exactly *not* to do with *what kind* of children at *what* age. . . .'
He goes on to say: 'The sense of autonomy which arises, or should arise, in the second stage of childhood, is fostered by a handling of the small individual which expresses a sense of rightful dignity and lawful independence on the part of the parents and which gives him the confident expectation that the kind of autonomy fostered in childhood will not be frustrated later. This, in turn, necessitates a relationship of parent to parent, of parent to employer, and of parent to government which reaffirms the parent's essential dignity within the hierarchy of social positions. It is important to dwell on this point because much of the shame and doubt, much of the indignity and uncertainty which is aroused in children is a consequence of the parents' frustrations in marriage, in work, and in citizenship.'

The Phallic Stage (Freud) or Stage of Initiative versus Guilt (Erikson)

This period between the ages of about three years and six years is designated in psychosexual terms as the phallic stage, a stage that culminates in the crucial oedipal conflict. Until the last few decades, many analysts considered this phase the central factor in the later development of mental illness. The neuroses and disturbances of sexual identity were looked upon as conflicts over the incestuous wishes and their accompanying dread of castration that regularly characterize the oedipal conflict. The psychoses were considered the result of regression to more primitive modes of functioning in order to avoid insurmountable oedipal conflicts through return to earlier phases of development. Most analysts today consider the pre-oedipal stages of development to be the major locus of conflicts and disturbances that predispose to malignant pathology.

It is necessary to contrast the impacts of isolated traumatic events that occur in a generally adequate mother-child situation with those impacts that result from a pervasive traumatic atmosphere. By and large, isolated frustrations and deprivations do not have lasting disturbing effects on a child when they occur in the context of a generally healthy family. On the other hand, even isolated instances of trauma can be devastating to a child who has a long-standing uncertainty of his mother's love or who is caught in the throes of serious and long-standing family tensions. It is the corrosive effects of long-continued family tensions that severely damage the young child.

Despite newer concepts that modify and lessen the importance of the oedipal conflict, this phallic or oedipal period is unquestionably pivotal in the etiology of neurosis and the formation of personality traits.

The sexual aspects of this period are obvious from several characteristics of the child at this stage: (*i*) his intense emotional investment in the genital zone and oedipal fantasies; (*ii*) his great curiosity about sex organs, his own body, and that of others; (*iii*) his preoccupation with questions about sexual intercourse, pregnancy, birth and death; (*iv*) his concern at realizing that some people possess a penis and some do not. His imagination is vivid and his comprehension of facts inadequate. The pressure of sexual and aggressive urges create bewildering oedipal fantasies of incest, pregnancy, and violent bodily retaliation. Out of castration anxiety, the child represses his oedipal urges. In the place of passionate attachments and violent rivalries with parents, the child now identifies with them. From this identification, the conscience, or superego, arises. If all goes well, the predominant identification is with the parent of the same sex and the child's personality receives the appropriate stamp of masculinity or femininity. Self-imposed guilt replaces the fear of parental punishments as the youngster prepares himself for the next stage, the latency period—that lull that precedes the psychological storms of puberty and adolescence. The hallmark of the child's growth at this oedipal age is his increasing independence from his mother as the central figure in his life and the expansion of his world of meaningful relations to include father, brothers, sisters, teachers, and other children and grown-ups.

This internalization of parental controls is one of the important ways in which the child becomes a person in his own right—a reliable, stable, self-disciplined social being. Adelaide Johnson[82, 95] and her collaborators have vividly described how 'lacunae' in the superego of parents are internalized by their children who then become delinquent or perverted, carrying out thereby the unconscious delinquent or perverse longings of the parents, who, despite all their protests to the contrary, derive vicarious satisfaction from the child's aberrant behaviour that they have subtlely, covertly encouraged.

In terms of the psychosocial point of view, this is the stage of initiative versus guilt. Erikson[37] describes this conceptualization as follows:

'Having found a firm solution of his problem of autonomy, the child of four and five is faced with the next step—and with the next crisis. Being firmly convinced that he *is* a person, the child must now find out *what kind* of a person he is going to be.' He further notes: 'It is at this stage of initiative that the great governor of initiative, namely, *conscience*, becomes firmly established. Only as a dependent (being) does man develop conscience, that dependence on himself which makes him, in turn, dependable; and only when thoroughly dependable with regard to a number of fundamental values can he become independent and teach and develop tradition.'

The child now tends automatically to feel guilt for thoughts as well as deeds, often making little distinction between the reality of the two. Although the capacity to feel guilt is a cornerstone of adult morality, the child, in his anxious wish to rid himself of guilt-laden oedipal fantasies, may overdo it. His conscience may become uncompromising beyond ithe degree to which parents intend. An overly harsh conscience can lead to lasting resentments toward the parents who the child comes to feel have deprived him of his freedom and initiative. In this regard Erikson[37] states:

'For the conscience of the child *can* be primitive, cruel, and uncompromising as may be observed in instances where children learn to constrict themselves to the point of over-all inhibition; where they develop an obedience more literal than the one that the parent wishes to exact; or where they develop deep regressions and lasting resentments because the parents themselves do not seem to live up to the new conscience which they have fostered in the child. One of the deepest conflicts in life is the hate for a parent who served as a model and executor of the conscience but who (in some form) was found trying to "get away with" the very transgressions which the child can no longer tolerate in himself.'

Before childhood can end and the adolescent journey to true adulthood can begin, the child must ready himself for the discipline of the school years while learning to inhibit his restless energies and oedipal wishes. Erikson comments:

'For those sinister oedipal wishes (so simply and so trustingly expressed in the boy's assurance that he will marry mother and make her proud of him and in the girl's that she will marry father and take much better care of him), in consequence a vastly increased imagination and, as it were, the intoxication of increased locomotor powers, seem to lead to secret fantasies of terrifying proportions. The consequence is a deep sense of *guilt*—a strange sense, for it forever seems to imply that the individual has committed crimes and deeds which, after all, were not only not committed but also would have been biologically quite impossible.'

This third, or oedipal, stage of development leads us to recent work on the structure, pathology, and therapy of families. At this stage, the family unit comes to have a very obvious impact on the child and vice versa. That the family atmosphere is a highly important influence on personality development of the child from birth on has been made clear by Lidz et al.[94] and Singer and Wynne,[146-148,176,177] and others. Family pathology and dynamics are mentioned here simply to emphasize that the effect of family forces becomes abundantly apparent in the life of the oedipal child. In the oral period, the child developed a sense of worth from his relation with the mother who valued him for his inherent value. In the anal period, the mother's care allowed the child's sense of individuality and autonomy to flourish. If all of these complicated events that occur largely in the dyadic mother-infant relation facilitate rather than cripple development, then the infant can become a child actively participating in the family unit. In the two decades since World War II, the study of the processes of interaction and communication within the family unit has become of increasing interest to numbers of psychoanalysts such as Jackson,[79] Searles,[137] Ritvo,[117] and Laing.[92, 93] We will take special note of the work of Singer and Wynne,[146-149, 176, 177] Bowen,[21, 22] and others at the National Institute of Mental Health, and Lidz[94] and his co-workers at Yale.

As Lidz et al.[94] note, Flugel studied family dynamics in 1921 and Spitz in 1937 but the main stream of analysis displayed little interest in the systematic study of the family unit until after World War II. Furthermore, Lidz states that recent studies have required considerable revisions of psychoanalytic theory to take into account the 'pervasive and decisive role of the family in personality development and human adaptation.'

In the extended study of seventeen families, each with a young adult schizophrenic offspring, Lidz et al.[94] found that every area of interaction within the family was faulty in some respect. They concluded that schizophrenia most likely resulted from the inability of the parents to establish a family unit capable of providing the emotional, experiential nutriment essential for the healthy development of their child. Like Winnicott, Lidz concluded that schizophrenia is an emotional deficiency disease. Whereas Winnicott emphasized deficiencies of maternal care, both the Yale study and those of Singer and Wynne broaden the concept to include family deficiencies in psychological nurturance and transmission of basic adaptive techniques, especially techniques of clear thought and communication.

In discussing the etiology of schizophrenia, Lidz et al.[94] emphasize emotional deprivation imposed on the child by the father as well as the mother, stating that 'fathers who are still seeking mothering or who require constant feeding of their narcissism provide little parental nurturance. They fail to stimulate a son's masculine efforts or to provide an adequate identification model. A daughter's femininity is too dangerous (to the father) either during the oedipal transition or later with the onset of her puberty to permit any intimacy that is not seduction.' Lidz cites a variety of schizophrenia engendering family influences such as failure to reward and inculcate problem solving through logical and lucid verbal communication, discouraging the child's efforts to socialize with age mates because activities outside the family are considered dangerous, and obstructing the influence of teachers because the mother experiences any emotional attachment of the child to other people as abandonment and rejection of her. Lidz concludes that schizophrenia results from a deficiency in family structure that grossly impairs the process of enculturation in the child, especially failure to provide the child with the ability to think and communicate clearly.

Wynne and Singer[146-149, 176, 177] have studied the disordered style of communication and interpersonal relations in thirty-five families, each of which had an offspring that was either psychotic, borderline, or neurotic. Each family member and the family as a unit were studied in depth, both clinically and by psychological tests. On the basis of blind interpretations of these tests, the researchers made surprisingly accurate predictions about the dynamics and pathology of each family, the nature and severity of illness in its patient member, and which patient came from which family. The details of this study are too lengthy to describe further, but it should be noted that a variety of these predictions proved valid at a very high level of statistical significance. These workers concluded that it is the total constellation of psychologically helpful or pathogenic forces in the family which determines the development of the child. For example, the impact of a severely confused, inconsistent mother might be ameliorated by a clear-thinking, orderly father—or the impact of a very sick mother might be increased by a passive, detached father who assumes little importance in the lives of his children. Various combinations of maternal and paternal pathology have different effects on children of different ages and of different sexes or temperament. In a provocative discussion of whether or not seemingly organic deficits in muscular coordination, perception, and so on were inborn or were the result of early psychonoxious influences, these authors conclude that early influences are the major factors.

They cite some of their earlier research to support the idea that stressful experience in infancy and childhood might create enduring neurophysiological alterations that affect psychological functioning. They suggest that intense traumatic experiences at stages of special vulnerability in early development could account for the persistent behaviour in severe schizophrenics that often seems to be organic or inborn.

They also give thoughtful consideration to whether or not parental concern over having a severely disturbed child might cause the disorders in family functioning so often seen in these families. They present convincing evidence that it is primarily the impact of disturbed family influences that damages the child rather than the impact of a congenitally unresponsive or disturbed child that affects the family. They do feel, however, that pathology in the child, once it is initiated, adds to the total family problem.

Studies by a number of other analysts are in essential agreement. Boatman and Szurek[19] have conducted investigations of family disturbances and have taken a forthright stand that schizophrenia in childhood is the result of pathological parental care and family dynamics. They feel this is not a condition caused to any significant degree by inborn, biological factors, and conclude:

'. . . that the psychotic disorder is the result . . . of the postnatal experience of each particular child early in life in interaction with significant adults who were themselves in conflict . . .'

Noting that fine motor skills used in complex ritualistic movements are as reliable indicators of neuromuscular development as performance on standardized tests, they state that, '. . . *we have seen few if any schizophrenic children who showed maturational lags or spurts which were wholly determined by physiological or genetic somatic factors.*'

They describe how many parents behave toward their emotionally ill child as if he were more stupid or younger than he actually is. Such parents send childishly simple letters to children who are quite able to read well, or they dress their children in clothes that are too small or too childish. Some parents clothe their disturbed offspring in ill-fitting, unattractive hand-me-downs and then express anger or concern because the child lacks interest in his personal appearance. One mother complained of her son's indifference to her shows of affection. She would plead with or order her reluctant child to give her a goodbye kiss, but as soon as he would move toward her to do so, the mother would begin to talk to someone else. The child's kiss would fall on the half-turned face of the mother who was now obviously more interested in another person than in him. When the child responded to this rebuff by biting the mother and spitting at her, she immediately became again attentive to him, but now in anger. She threatened never to return to see the child, but in the next moment renewed her efforts to get the child to say he loved her. This confusing style of communication and relating has been described as the double bind (Bateson *et al.*),[9] mystification (Laing),[92] the effort to drive another person crazy (Searles),[138] or pseudo-mutuality (Wynne).[178]

Boatman and Szurek comment that often neither parent seems able to provide the very disturbed child with any clear distinction between safe and dangerous behaviour or between 'feeling' and 'doing'. Destructive behaviour of the child is often tolerated as being just playful. Sometimes it is allowed because the parent who feels unable to stop the child is unconsciously wishing to break things too, or fears that stopping him will harmfully frustrate him. Such parents often are unable to tolerate strong displays of feelings in the child and become more childishly emotional at such moments than the child himself is. Sometimes the child's demands, even unreasonable ones, are indulged; at other times, legitimate requests are met with rage and punishment.

Concerning the etiology of schizophrenia and other severe disturbances of children, they state:[19]

'The nature of the stress appears to lie in the anxiety of the parental persons about basic sensual impulses. The timing is in the earliest months and years of life, the period of greatest developmental vulnerability. The duration is more or less constant. The intensity is greatest at periods that coincide closely with the onset and exacerbations of the child's severest symptoms and that almost always follow periods of identifiable increased strain for one or both parents and between them. It is our strong impression that the pathologic moments for the child are ones in which the executive function of the parent has been strained to or near the breaking point.'

It is now time to return to the discussion of psychosexual and psycho-social stages of development and complete our consideration of them before branching out to consider research on psychoanalytic treatment and various experimental studies from the psychological laboratory that have been conducted by analytic investigators.

The Latency Period (Freud) or the Stage of Industry versus Inferiority (Erikson)

From the psychosexual point of view, the resolution of the oedipal complex culminates in the repression of infantile sexuality. From the ages of about six to twelve years, sexual urges are significantly lessened as the energies formerly channelled into sexual fantasies and activities are now diverted into the more socialized activities, learning and the discipline of education. In R. W. White's[169] terms, the child now develops an increasing sense of 'competence' and a rewarding sense of mastery that compensates for the loss of the prerogatives of childhood.

Concerning this stage, Erikson[37] notes, '. . . now it is time to go to school.' He goes on to comment:

'Nothing could better express the fact that children at this age do like to be mildly but firmly coerced into the adventure of finding out that one can learn to accomplish things which one would never have thought of by oneself, things which owe their attractiveness to the very fact that they are *not* the product of play and fantasy but the product of reality, practicality, and logic; things which thus provide a token sense of participation in the real world of adults.'
He concludes:
'. . . and while all children need their hours and days of make-believe in games, they all, sooner or later, become dissatisfied and disgruntled without a sense of being useful, without a sense of being able to make things and make them well and even perfectly; this is what I call the *sense of industry*. Without this, the best entertained child soon acts exploited. It is as if he knows and his society knows that now that he is psychologically already a rudimentary parent, he must begin to be somewhat of a worker and potential provider before becoming a biological parent. . . . He develops industry, that is, he adjusts himself to the inorganic laws of the tool world. He can become an eager and absorbed unit of a productive situation. To bring a productive situation to completion is an aim which gradu-ally supersedes the whims and wishes of his idiosyncratic drives and personal disappointments. As he once untiringly strove to walk well, and to throw things

away well, he now wants to make things well. He develops the pleasure of *work completion* by steady attention and persevering diligence.'

Puberty and Adolescence (Freud) or the Stage of Identity versus Identity Diffusion (Erikson)

The rudimentary sense of sexual identity, of basic maleness and femaleness, that accrued to the child at the end of the oedipal period, must now be re-evaluated, revised, and consolidated by the adolescent as the sexual urges of puberty break the relative calm of the latency period. Traditional psychoanalytic views have emphasized problems at this stage concerning masturbation, homosexual experimentation, and heterosexual ventures. The larger context of the psychosocial notion of identity formation provides us with complementary, enriching points of view of this stage of development. In this regard Erikson[37] notes:

'The integration now taking place in the form of the ego identity is more than the sum of the childhood identifications. It is the inner capital accrued from all those experiences of each successive stage, when successful identification led to a successful alignment of the individual's *basic drives* with his *endowment* and his *opportunities*. In psychoanalysis we ascribe such successful alignments to "ego synthesis"; I have tried to demonstrate that the ego values accrued in childhood culminate in what I have called a *sense of ego identity*. The sense of ego identity, then, is the accrued confidence that one's ability to maintain inner sameness and continuity (one's ego in the psychological sense) is matched by the sameness and continuity of one's meaning for others. Thus, self-esteem, confirmed at the end of each major crisis, grows to be a conviction that one is learning effective steps toward a tangible future, that one is developing a defined personality within a social reality which one understands. The growing child, must, at every step, derive a vitalizing sense of reality from the awareness that his individual way of mastering experience is a successful variant of the way other people around him master experience and recognize such mastery.

'In this, children cannot be fooled by empty praise and condescending encouragement. They may have to accept artificial bolstering of their self-esteem in lieu of something better, but what I call their accruing ego identity gains real strength only from whole-hearted and consistent recognition of real accomplishment, that is, achievement that has meaning in their culture. . . .

'The emerging ego identity, then, bridges the early childhood stages, when the body and the parent images were given their specific meanings, and the later stages, when a variety of social roles become available and increasingly coercive. A lasting ego identity cannot begin to exist without the trust of the first oral stage; it cannot be completed without a promise of fulfilment which from the dominant image of adulthood reaches down into the baby's beginnings and which creates at every step an accruing sense of ego strength.'

Commenting on the clannish tendency of the adolescent to adhere rigidly and intolerantly to the code of his peer groups, Erikson[37] attributes this characteristic to the adolescent's need for '*defense against a sense of identity diffusion*, which is unavoidable at a time of life when the body changes its proportions radically, when genital maturity floods body and imagination with all manners of drives, when intimacy with the other sex approaches and is, on occasion, forced on the youngster, and when life lies before one with a variety of conflicting possibilities and choices. Adolescents help one another temporarily through such discomforts by forming cliques and by stereotyping themselves, their ideals, and their enemies.' He adds, 'It is difficult to be tolerant if deep down you are not quite sure that you are a man (or a woman), that you will ever grow together again and be attractive, that you will be able to master your drives, that you really know who you are, that you know what you want to be, that you know what you look like to others, and that you will know how to make the right decisions without, once for all, committing yourself to the wrong friend, sexual partner, leader, or career.'

In traditional psychosexual terms, the next stage of development is adulthood. Although psychoanalysis has always recognized the great importance of such nodal points of adulthood as courtship, career choice, marriage, parenthood, the climacteric, and senility, it has remained for Erikson[37, 38] to conceptualize systematically specific stages in the life cycle of the adult. He divided adulthood into three stages:

1. Intimacy versus Isolation.
2. Generativity versus Stagnation.
3. Integrity versus Despair.

The Stage of Intimacy versus Isolation

Concerning the stage of intimacy versus isolation, he states:[38]

'Thus, the young adult, emerging from the search for and the insistence on identity, is eager and willing to fuse his identity with that of others. He is ready for intimacy, that is, the capacity to commit himself to concrete affiliations and partnerships and to develop the ethical strength to abide by such commitments, even though they may call for significant sacrifices and compromises. Body and ego must now be masters of the organ modes and of the nuclear conflicts, in order to be able to face the fear of ego loss in situations which call for self-abandon: in the solidarity of close affiliations, in orgasms and sexual unions, in close friendships and in physical combat, in experiences of inspiration by teachers and of intuition from the recesses of the self. The avoidance of such experiences because of a fear of ego loss may lead to a deep sense of isolation and consequent self-absorption.'

He goes on to note: 'The danger of this stage is that intimate, competitive and combative relations are experienced with and against the self same people. But as the areas of adult duty are delineated, and as the competitive encounter, and the sexual embrace, are differentiated, they eventually become subject to that *ethical sense* which is the mark of the adult.'

Concerning the dangers of inadequate resolution of this stage of growth, he further comments:

'The danger of this stage is isolation, that is the avoidance of contacts which commit to intimacy. In psychopathology, this disturbance can lead to severe "character-problems". On the other hand, there are partnerships which amount to an isolation *à deux*, protecting both partners from the necessity to face the next critical development—that of generativity.'

The Stage of Generativity versus Stagnation

Regarding this developmental stage, Erikson[38] states:

'Generativity, then, is primarily the concern in establishing and guiding the next generation, although there are individuals who, through misfortune or because of special and genuine gifts in other directions, do not apply this drive to their own offspring. And indeed, the concept generativity is meant to include such more popular synonyms as *productivity* and *creativity*, which, however, cannot replace it.

'It has taken psychoanalysis some time to realize that the ability to lose oneself in the meeting of bodies and minds leads to a gradual expansion of ego-interests and to a libidinal investment in that which is being generated. Generativity thus is an essential stage on the psychosexual as well as on the psychosocial schedule. Where such enrichment fails altogether, regression to an obsessive need for pseudo-intimacy takes place, often with a pervading sense of stagnation and personal impoverishment. Individuals, then, often begin to indulge themselves as if they were their own—or one another's—one and only child; and where conditions favour it, early invalidism, physical or psychological, becomes the vehicle of self-concern. The mere fact of having or even wanting children, however, does not "achieve" generativity. In fact, some young parents suffer, it seems, from the retardation of the ability to develop this stage. The reasons are often to be found in early childhood impressions; in excessive self-love based on a too strenuously self-made personality; and finally (and here we return to the beginnings) in the lack of some faith, some "belief in the species," which would make a child appear to be a welcome trust of the community.'

The Stage of Ego Integrity versus Despair

Of this final stage in the life cycle, Erikson[38] states:

'Only in him who in some way has taken care of things and people and has adapted himself to the triumphs and disappointments adherent to being, the originator of others or the generator of products and ideas—only in him may gradually ripen the fruit of these seven stages. I know no better word for it than ego integrity.' Integrity, he states, '. . . is the acceptance of one's one and only life cycle as something that had to be and that, by necessity, permitted of no substitutions: it thus means a new, a different love of one's parents.'

A sense of integrity is further described as a dignified willingness to defend one's own life style and culture combined with tolerance and understanding of those that may be different. Of the state that results from inadequate negotiation of this last stage, Erikson[38] comments:

'The lack or loss of this accrued ego integration is signified by fear of death: the one and only life cycle is not accepted as the ultimate of life. Despair expresses the feeling that the time is now short, too short for the attempt to start another life and to try out alternate roads to integrity. Disgust hides despair, if often only in the form of "a thousand little disgusts" which do not add up to one big remorse . . .' In closing, he says: 'And it seems possible to further paraphrase the relation of adult integrity and infantile trust by saying that healthy children will not fear life if their elders have integrity enough not to fear death.'

3

Research on Psychoanalytic Therapy

Thus far, I have summarized Erikson's[37, 38] psychosocial concepts to show how they expand psychoanalytic theory of personality development and complement the traditional psychosexual concepts of psychological growth. A more detailed account of how psychosocial concepts aid in understanding the life cycle of individuals can be found in Erikson's[36] study of the life of Luther and my own recent re-formulations of the psycho-dynamics of the Schreber Case.[165, 166] We have also explored the importance of the mother-infant relation and the family organization in personality growth.

It is appropriate now to turn from the etiological factors in mental disorders to the therapeutic. In discussing psychotherapy, I shall consider primarily recent research on the psychotherapeutic process, beginning with The Menninger Project, the most ambitious study of psychotherapy undertaken to date.

The Menninger Psychotherapy Research Project

Begun in 1954 and still in progress, this study conducted by Sargent, Wallerstein, Robbins, and a number of collaborators has been reported in a series of papers beginning in 1956.[32, 66, 77, 98–101, 118, 119, 127–132, 158–164] The research studies the course and outcome of treatment of forty-two patients undergoing intensive psychotherapy, half being treated by formal psychoanalysis and half by various forms of less intensive psychoanalytic psychotherapy. The project is based on a variety of generally accepted psychoanalytic concepts such as: (*i*) mental illness is caused by unconscious intrapsychic conflicts that largely result from pathogenic childhood experiences; (*ii*) intrapsychic conflict occurs between instinctual drives (sexual and aggressive) and the controlling, defensive, and adaptive functions of the ego as well as the moral strictures of the superego; (*iii*) symptoms occur when stresses within the person and between him and the environment upset the balance between his instinctual drives and his ego controls and defences to a degree that repressed drives threaten to break into conscious awareness or overt expression and behaviour; (*iv*) symptoms reveal important characteristics of the pathogenic inner conflict as well as the ways in which the patient characteristically copes with conflict.

The data used in this study is that information (including psychological test data) routinely gathered in the course of the regular diagnostic evaluation and psychotherapeutic treatment conducted on all cases at The Menninger Foundation. After therapy is concluded, additional information is obtained from research interviews with the patient, his family, and his therapist as well as from re-administration of psychological tests. The research is done in three parts:

1. The Initial Study, done following the period of diagnostic evaluation and before therapy starts.
2. The Termination Study, conducted as soon as therapy ends.
3. The Follow Up Study, performed two years after treatment has ended.

An outstanding feature of this research is that it is conducted in such a way that it does not impinge on the natural course of the treatment. Neither patient nor therapist knows that a given case is to be part of the study until after treatment ends. Then, with the permission of therapist and patient, the Termination Study and later the Follow Up Study are conducted by the research staff. The data for the Initial Study is the information routinely obtained by the clinical staff on all cases at Menningers. At termination of treatment psychological tests are repeated and all notes on the case made by the clinical staff are added to the information obtained from the research interviews with patient and therapist. On follow up, psychological tests are re-administered and an intensive series of six or eight hours of interviews are conducted with the patient and his family. Thus, a massive amount of information is obtained on each case.

. Before therapy starts, the research staff assesses the information on the patient along a series of twenty-four variables, the Patient Variables. These include age, sex, degree of anxiety, type of symptoms, nature of intrapsychic conflict, ego strength and defences, intellectual and emotional assets, motivation for change, and so on. The researchers then make a series of about fifty predictions as to the kind of treatment that will be recommended by the clinical staff and the problems that will arise in therapy such as transferences, resistances, prognosis, and the like. These predictions are set down in a formal, if-then-because, model together with the reasons for each prediction and the information that is deemed necessary to confirm or refute the prediction when the termination and follow up studies are conducted. An example of a prediction made concerning a patient who came for treatment of guilt engendering hostile feelings toward an adopted child so intense that she had to return the child to the adoption agency is as follows: '*If* this patient is treated by psychoanalysis, and *if* she resolves her conflicts with regard to femininity and motherhood, *then* she will behave differently and be able to handle a child of her own (whether adopted or natural) *because* to the extent that a resolution of unconscious conflicts occurs via the expressive interpretative aspects of psychoanalysis, there is an at least proportional change in symptoms, character traits, and life style.'

At the time of termination and follow up, all data on the case are re-evaluated to assess changes in the patient and the outcome of the predictions made before treatment began. The information is systematically evaluated as to thirty-eight Treatment Variables such as the form of treatment actually used, basic techniques that the therapist followed, subject matter discussed in therapy, qualities and skills of the therapist, climate or atmosphere of the treatment relationship, major transference themes and resistances, and so on. In addition, the case is looked at from the viewpoint of seven Situational Variables such as the patient's cultural and socioeconomic background, type of interpersonal relations between him and family members or colleagues, marital relationship, occupation, recreational activities, physical health, etc.

In this way, the interplay of variables in the patient, his life circumstance, and his treatment can be interrelated and the process and outcome of therapy better understood. In addition to the study of each case and the predictions made on it, patients are compared with each other on those of the three sets of variables that allow for quantification. This quantitative aspect to the study is done by the method of paired comparisons, a method which this research group feels offers great promise in reducing complex clinical information to measurable terms. By such quantification, sophisticated statistical methods can be introduced into psychotherapy research in ways that, as Wallerstein[164] has noted, '. . . are faithful to the usual canons of scientific work, yet appropriate to the subtlety and complexity of clinical phenomena under scrutiny.'

By translating clinical judgements into '. . . verifiable predictions based on clearly stated assumptions',[158] prior to treatment, this project attempts to overcome one of the weakest points of most clinical research, *post hoc* reasoning by means of which almost any outcome can be rationalized. Since the research is conducted by a staff that is completely independent of the clinicians engaged in the treatment, the project avoids contaminating research views on the one hand or distorting the treatment from its natural course on the other.

Such a longitudinal study involves a tremendous amount of sustained, hard work. From the several hundreds of typewritten pages of raw data that have been amassed on each case, the research group abstracts a summary of about fifty pages in length. From this, a ten-page interpretative synthesis is made which states in most parsimonious form the over-all understanding of the case, the changes that have taken place in the patient, and conclusions reached about predictions that were made and hypotheses advanced.

By the paired comparison method, each case is compared with every other and, from this ranking procedure, patients are given an ordinal ranking on each member of the three sets of variables. A profile can thus be constructed so that patients can be easily compared as to any one or group of variables in each of the three sets. The Initial Study and the Termination Study have been completed on all forty-two of the patients and the Follow Up Study, on thirty-five. The comparison of patients with each other on the twelve quantifiable patient variables has been finished.

An example of a profile rating a patient on these variables is shown in Table 2.

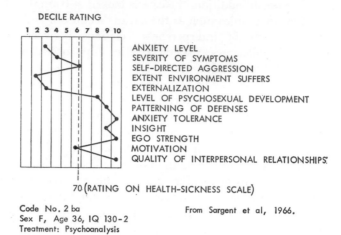

TABLE 2. Patient Profile, Menninger Project

DECILE RATING

1 2 3 4 5 6 7 8 9 10

ANXIETY LEVEL
SEVERITY OF SYMPTOMS
SELF-DIRECTED AGGRESSION
EXTENT ENVIRONMENT SUFFERS
EXTERNALIZATION
LEVEL OF PSYCHOSEXUAL DEVELOPMENT
PATTERNING OF DEFENSES
ANXIETY TOLERANCE
INSIGHT
EGO STRENGTH
MOTIVATION
QUALITY OF INTERPERSONAL RELATIONSHIPS

70 (RATING ON HEALTH-SICKNESS SCALE)

Code No. 2 ba   From Sargent et al, 1966.
Sex F, Age 36, IQ 130-2
Treatment: Psychoanalysis

This research design allows the use of sophisticated statistical processes involving modern computer techniques and will be described in a forth-coming publication by Sargent *et al.*[131] In this monograph, she points out that the great amount of clinical data gathered on each of their cases 'all but defies efforts at quantitative analysis.' She notes that many analysts feel that quantitative procedures such as those used in this research do grave injustice to the subtlety and richness of clinical events. She feels, however, that the proper application of the paired comparison method provides a technique whereby elusive clinical phenomena can be quantified, subjected to statistical manipulation, and studied in ways that are both precise *and* relevant to psychoanalytic practice. She concludes: 'At the very least we have demonstrated that powerful methods of quantification can be so designed that they pose a clinically congenial judgemental task for the psychoanalytically trained clinician—a task that he can willingly execute in relation to the material of psychoanalytically conceptualized treatment processes.'

Another aspect of The Menninger Project is noteworthy. These researchers are not attempting to prove that psychoanalytic treatment is better or worse than other forms of therapy; they are attempting only to see if a group of experienced analysts using readily available clinical data can make valid predictions about psychoanalytic treatment and if these predictions, the incorrect as well as the correct, can clarify the complicated processes of psychotherapy. Having stated in advance their predictions and how they were arrived at, the researchers are in a good position to retrace their reasoning after they learn the outcome on a case.

By retracing their steps, they hope to learn as much from their incorrect predictions as from their correct ones. In summary they state,[160] 'The goal of this project . . . is the development of a consistent and comprehensive set of hypotheses about what determines change in psychotherapy . . . which can subsequently be verified, refuted, or modified in detail.' They hope thereby 'to achieve a comprehensive set of propositions . . . that will allow the setting up of experiments and . . . of process and outcome studies that will systematically test these propositions.' The research has demonstrated that the clinical material of psychoanalysis can be put to the test of prediction and quantification. All of psychiatry wishes this research group well in its continuing efforts to analyse its mountainous supply of data. The tenacity and courage with which they have set about their enormous task sets a standard that only a few will dare to emulate. Although the research group is, as yet, cautious in stating any conclusions, the following tentative results can be gleaned from their numerous papers:

1. In the hands of experienced clinicians, clinical psychoanalytic data can be used to make meaningful predictions about psychotherapy.

2. Clinical data can be organized making possible their quantitative as well as qualitative analyses.

3. Patients are surprisingly willing to participate in intensive research interviews despite the anxiety that it causes them.

4. If performed tactfully by skilled clinicians, intensive research study of patients who have undergone analytic therapy is not likely to be harmful to patients.

5. The clarity with which patients can describe what it was in their treatment that helped them does not necessarily correlate with the degree of benefit the patient has obtained. For example, some very inarticulate patients, who were definitely benefited by therapy, could only make such comments as, 'I don't know what it was that made me change. I don't even remember what we were talking about most of the time. But after a while I began to feel and act differently.' Other patients who were much less benefited were able to speak in vivid detail about the events of treatment with what seemed to be a good grasp of the meaning of those events.

6. Some patients who were treated with supportive psychotherapy without achieving much, if any, insight, had considerable relief from symptoms, lessening of disordered patterns of behaviour, and growth of personality, although they were often totally unable to describe how this improvement had taken place.

7. Both patient and therapist are more willing to discuss the treatment freely with the research team if they feel that it was successful. If they were disappointed with the outcome, their accounts of what occurred in treatment tend to be halting, disjointed, and full of glaring inconsistencies. In such circumstances, both the patient and the therapist usually talk more about their disappointment and

frustration with the results than about what actually happened within the treatment itself.

8. Such a research study is threatening to the therapist who treats the patient. He almost always feels his professional ability and his personal worth are being made vulnerable to criticism by the researchers.

The Psychotherapy Research Project of the Hampstead Child Therapy Clinic

Anna Freud and her numerous collaborators at the Hampstead Clinic in London are conducting a systematic study of the process and outcome of psychoanalytic treatment of children. Begun over ten years ago, this project has recently been described in detail by Bolland and Sandler.[20] An essential feature is the systematic classification of the clinical data contained in the weekly treatment reports of each case. According to a predetermined scheme for classification, the events in treatment are indexed at weekly intervals so that various similarities among cases can easily be found from the massive amount of information that accumulates on each case. Data are classified into such categories as object relations, fantasies, ego defences, superego effects, symptoms, qualities of the treatment situation, therapeutic techniques, and so on. Manuals have been devised to standardize the indexing of clinical material by different therapists. As in The Menninger Project, each patient is rated on a variety of factors so that a developmental profile can be made in accordance with the method devised by Anna Freud.[58] Bolland and Sandler[20] have recently reported on the study of one case which illustrates various aspects of the process of treating children psychoanalytically as well as the research methods that have been developed at the Hampstead Clinic.

Other Research Projects on Psychoanalytic Treatment

A variety of other research projects on psychoanalytic treatment are under way. Pfeffer[109-111] has conducted a systematic follow-up study of patients treated by Freudian techniques. Paul Bergman,[16] Shakow et al.,[33, 144] Carmichael,[29] Cohen,[31] Scheflen,[134, 135] and English[35] have used sound movies and one-way vision screens to study the detailed operations of psychoanalytic therapy. These later studies have examined the behaviour of the therapist as well as the responses of the patients. These 'microscopic' studies of the minute-to-minute details in the analytic process promise to complement the broader, more 'macroscopic' study of the Menninger group.

4

Other Recent Psychoanalytic Studies on Various Problems

Social Psychiatry, Group Therapy, Psychosomatics, Hypnosis, and Drug Therapy

The impact on patients of the social organization of the mental hospital has been the focus of researches of Stanton and Schwartz,[155] Caudill,[30] Main,[103, 104] and others.[156, 168] This area of study will be pursued further in the forthcoming monograph by Burnham, Gibson and Gladstone.[26] The many dimensions of social and community psychiatry have been looked at by Caplan,[27, 28] Hume, [78] and Bellak,[11] and recently reviewed in Bellak's handbook.[10] Group psychotherapy has been enriched by Bion,[18] Foulkes,[52] Ezriel,[42] and others. Advances in psychosomatic medicine have stemmed from the work of Alexander and French,[2] Knapp,[89, 90] Engel,[34] and Balint.[7] Hypnosis in both its clinical application and its relation to psychoanalytic theory has been explored by Gill and Brenman.[62] The studies of Parsons[108] and others in sociology have both fed and been fed by psychoanalysis.

Although drugs have been enthusiastically used by general psychiatrists to treat schizophrenia and manic-depressive states, analysts have been reluctant to combine analysis with drug therapy. Among them, only Ostow[107] has written extensively on the use of antidepressants and tranquilizers as an adjunct to psychoanalytic treatment, although more recently lithium carbonate has been suggested as potentially helpful in the psychotherapeutic management of mania by White *et al.*[167]

Work of The Tavistock Group

In the area of social psychiatry, workers associated with the Tavistock Clinic and Institute of Human Relations bear special mention. Analysts associated with this group have worked on various issues far removed from the free associations of the patient on the couch. Deserving particular notice is the work of Bion[18] on group therapy and group dynamics, Bowlby,[23] Winnicott,[171] Heinicke and Westheimer,[73] and others on infant and child care, Balint[6] on the education of general practitioners in psychotherapy, Jaques[81] on problems of labour-management relations through his many years of experience as social analyst with the Glacier Company, and Robertson[120–122] on the reaction of pediatric patients to being hospitalized.

Laboratory Experiments Relevant to Psychoanalysis

Finally, we turn to the various laboratory studies on perception sensory isolation, dreaming, and social isolation in monkeys. Since these are topics covered elsewhere in this volume, I only note them as areas of importance to psychoanalysis and call attention to the comprehensive review of the work on sensory deprivation by Miller[106] who correlated these laboratory findings to the enrichment of psychoanalytic ego psychology. Also to be noted are the papers by Holt,[74-76] George Klein,[83, 84] and Fisher[49, 50] in which they have made significant contributions to analytic theory—contributions derived in part from their laboratory experiments.

5

Summary

My task was to evaluate psychoanalysis so that students and workers in other areas might have some notion of its present status. My emphasis has largely been on research rather than clinical application. In my opinion, this emphasis properly reflects the most significant activity in psychoanalysis today. The general procedures of analytic treatment are well known and have in their essence remained little changed for some years. Anyone wishing to familiarize himself with them in greater detail should turn to the succinct summary by Kubie.[91] He outlines the clinical procedures involved in conducting an analysis and describes what the experience of analysis is for the patient. He also discusses the kinds of patients for whom analysis is indicated, the frequency of sessions and the duration of treatment, the nature of free association and transference, and the use of dream interpretation. He discusses problems concerning the relationship between the analyst and the physician who refers a case to him as well as the relation of the analyst to the patient's family. He describes the training necessary to become an analyst and answers a host of other questions that any informed person might raise about the clinical practice of analysis.

Where do the various studies cited in this paper point? In what direction is analysis moving? How can one evaluate its present status? Clearly, analysis is having a great impact on clinical psychiatry—seemingly more so in the United States than in England or Europe. In America, a large percentage of chairmen of departments of psychiatry are analysts. Analytic concepts of personality formation and psychotherapy comprise a major segment of psychiatric training for medical students and residents and, clearly, are a major moulding factor in determining prevailing psychiatric opinion. Equally evident is a marked trend toward more rigorous research rather than the previous, almost sole reliance on naturalistic clinical observations. The National Institute of Mental Health and a variety of private foundations such as the Ford Foundation, the Field Foundation, the Commonwealth Fund, and others have been important sources of financial support to research, both in the United States and England.

Through the work of Erikson and others, social and family factors have now become generally recognized in psychoanalytic thinking as co-determinants of behaviour alongside the more traditional emphasis on intrapsychic and unconscious conflicts. The crucial importance of early life is a major theme and this emphasis has spawned numerous studies that promise to clarify the nature-nurture question. As more refined methods evolve to determine inborn patterns of autonomic response and sensory receptivity, we will very likely find that experiences in the earliest months of life may give a fixed and even irreversible stamp to basic neurophysiological processes, much like the imprinting process that the ethologists have brought to our attention. Here, I predict, we will find the ever elusive answer to the question of the seemingly organic factors in schizophrenia and manic-depressive disorders.

Studies on child development have already influenced the care of pediatric patients in ways that lessen the traumatic effect of prolonged hospitalization on children. Family therapy promises a treatment modality for disturbed children that is less expensive and time consuming than child analysis. Long-term, traditional psychoanalytic therapy continues to offer the most hope of radical correction of problems stemming from severe neuroses and character disorders. Although the time and expense required for psychoanalysis of children or adults prevents it from being an answer to the widespread need for psychotherapeutic help, the application of analytic insights to the fields of social and community psychiatry has been a step in this direction.

Research on psychoanalytic treatment and the increasing intercourse between analysis and a variety of other areas, ranging from sociology and community psychiatry to the experimental laboratory, stimulate many new and exciting activities in psychoanalysis today. These demonstrate quite clearly that, despite occasional reports to the contrary, psychoanalysis is very much alive!

REFERENCES

1. ALEXANDER, F., EISENSTEIN, S., and GROTJAHN, M., Eds., 1966. *Psychoanalytic pioneers*. New York: Basic Books.
2. ALEXANDER, F., and FRENCH, T. M., 1948. *Studies in psychosomatic medicine*. New York: Ronald Press.
3. ALEXANDER, F., and SELESNICK, S. T., 1966. *The history of psychiatry*. New York: Harper and Row.
4. ALTSHULER, K. D., 1966. Comments on recent sleep research related to psychoanalytic theory. *Arch. gen. Psychiat.*, **15**, 235.
5. BAILEY, P., 1965. *Sigmund the unserene*. Springfield, Ill.: Charles C. Thomas.
6. BALINT, M., 1957. *The doctor, his patient and the illness*. New York: Internat. Univ. Press.
7. BALINT, M., 1961. Training for psychosomatic medicine. In *Advances in psychosomatic Medicine*. Eds. Jores, A., and Freyberger, H. New York: Robert Brunner.
8. BALINT, M., 1965. *Primary love and psycho-analytic technique*. New York: Liveright.
9. BATESON, G., JACKSON, D. D., HALEY, J., and WEAKLAND, J. H., 1956. Toward a theory of schizophrenia. *Behav. Sci.*, **1**, 251.

10. BELLAK, L., Ed., 1964. *Handbook of community psychiatry and community mental health.* New York: Grune and Stratton.

11. BELLAK, L., 1964. The comprehensive community psychiatry program at City Hospital. In *Handbook of community psychiatry and community mental health.* Ed. Bellak, L. New York: Grune and Stratton.

12. BENJAMIN, J. D., 1959. Prediction and psychopathologic theory. In *Dynamic psychopathology in childhood.* Eds. Jessner, L., and Pavenstedt, E. New York: Grune and Stratton.

13. BENJAMIN, J. D., 1961. The innate and the experiential in child development. In *Lectures on experimental psychiatry.* Ed. Brosin, H. W. Pittsburgh, Pa.: Univ. Press.

14. BENJAMIN, J. D., 1961. Some developmental observations relating to the theory of anxiety. *J. Amer. Psychoanal. Assn.*, **9,** 652.

15. BENJAMIN, J. D., 1965. Developmental biology and psychoanalysis. In *Psychoanalysis and current biological thought.* Eds. Greenfield, N. S., and Lewis, W. C. Madison: Univ. Wisconsin Press.

16. BERGMAN, P., 1966. An experiment in filmed psychotherapy. In *Methods of research in psychotherapy.* Eds. Gottschalk, L. A., and Auerbach, A. H. New York: Appleton-Century-Crofts.

17. BERGMANN, T., and FREUD, A., 1965. *Children in the hospital.* New York: Internat. Univ. Press.

18. BION, W. R., 1961. *Experiences in groups.* New York: Basic Books.

19. BOATMAN, M. J., and SZUREK, S. A., 1960. A clinical study of childhood schizophrenia. In *The etiology of schizophrenia.* Ed. Jackson, D. D. New York: Basic Books.

20. BOLLAND, J., SANDLER, J. et al., 1965. *The Hampstead psychoanalytic index* New York: Internat. Univ. Press.

21. BOWEN, M., 1960. A family concept of schizophrenia. In *The etiology of schizophrenia.* Ed. Jackson, D. D. New York: Basic Books.

22. BOWEN, M., 1965. Family psychotherapy with schizophrenia in the hospital and in private practice. In *Intensive family therapy.* Eds. Boszormenyi-Nagy, I., and Framo, J. L. New York: Hoeber Medical Division, Harper and Row.

23. BOWLBY, J., 1952. *Maternal care and mental health.* Geneva, Switzerland: World Health Organization.

24. BOWLBY, J., 1958. The nature of the child's tie to his mother. *Int. J. Psychoanal.*, **39,** 350.

25. BOWLBY, J., 1960. Separation anxiety. *Int. J. Psychoanal.*, **41,** 89.

26. BURNHAM, D. L., GIBSON, R. W., and GLADSTONE, A. I., 1968. *Schizophrenia and the need-fear dilemma.* New York: Internat. Univ. Press (In press.)

27. CAPLAN, G., 1961. *An approach to community mental health.* New York: Grune and Stratton.

28. CAPLAN, G., 1964. *Principles of preventive psychiatry.* New York: Basic Books.

29. CARMICHAEL, H. T., 1966. Sound-film recording of psychoanalytic therapy: a therapist's experiences and reactions. In *Methods of Research in Psychotherapy.* Eds. Gottschalk, L. A., and Auerbach, A. H. New York: Appleton-Century-Crofts.

30. CAUDILL, W., 1958. *The psychiatric hospital as a small society.* Cambridge, Mass.: Harvard Univ. Press.

31. COHEN, R. A., and COHEN, M. B., 1961. Research in psychotherapy: a preliminary report. *Psychiatry*, **24,** 46.

32. COYNE, L. (In Press). The quantitative measurement of change. (To appear in *J. abnor. Psychol.*)

33. DITTMANN, A. T., STEIN, S. N., and SHAKOW, D., 1966. Sound motion

picture facilities for research in communication. In *Methods of research in psychotherapy*. Eds. Gottschalk, L. A., and Auerbach, A. H. New York: Appleton-Century-Crofts.

34. ENGEL, G. L., 1962. Somatic consequences of psychological stress: I. Compensated states; conversion reactions; pain. In *Psychological development in health and disease*. Engel, G. L. Philadelphia: W. B. Saunders.

35. ENGLISH, O. S., HAMPE, W. W., BACON, C. L., and SETTLAGE, C. F., 1961. *Direct analysis and schizophrenia*. New York: Grune and Stratton.

36. ERIKSON, E. H., 1958. *Young man Luther*. New York: W. W. Norton and Company.

37. ERIKSON, E. H., 1959. Identity and the life cycle. *Psychol. Issues*, **1**, No. 1.

38. ERIKSON, E. H., 1963. *Childhood and society*. 2nd ed. New York: W. W. Norton and Company.

39. ERIKSON, E. H., 1965. Psychoanalysis and ongoing history: problems of identity, hatred and nonviolence. *Amer. J. Psychiat.*, **122**, 241.

40. ESCALONA, S., and HEIDER, G., 1959. *Prediction and outcome*. New York: Basic Books.

41. EYSENCK, H. J., 1965. The effects of psychotherapy. *Int. J. Psychiat.*, **1**, 99.

42. EZRIEL, H., 1950. A psycho-analytic approach to group treatment. *Brit. J. med. Psychol.*, **23**, 61.

43. FAIRBAIRN, W. R. D., 1954. *An object-relations theory of the personality*. New York: Basic Books.

44. FAIRBAIRN, W. R. D., 1963. Synopsis of an object-relations theory of personality. *Int. J. Psychoanal.*, **44**, 224.

45. FISH, B., 1957. The detection of schizophrenia in infancy: a preliminary report. *J. nerv. ment. Dis.*, **125**, 1.

46. FISH, B., 1959. Longitudinal observations of biological deviations in a schizophrenic infant. *Amer. J. Psychiat.*, **116**, 25.

47. FISH, B., SHAPIRO, T., HALPERN, F., and WILE, R., 1965. The prediction of schizophrenia in infancy: III. A ten-year follow-up report of neurological and psychological development. *Amer. J. Psychiat.*, **121**, 768.

48. FISHER, C., and DEMENT, W. C., 1963. Studies on psychopathology of sleep and dreams. *Amer. J. Psychiat.*, **119**, 1160.

49. FISHER, C., 1965. Psychoanalytic implications of recent research on sleep and dreaming. I. Empirical findings. *J. Amer. Psychoanal. Assn*, **13**, 197.

50. FISHER, C., 1965. Psychoanalytic implications of recent research on sleep and dreaming. II. Implications for psychoanalytic theory. *J. Amer. Psychoanal. Assn*. **13**, 271.

51. FISHER, C., GROSS, J., and ZUCH, J., 1965. Cycle of penile erection synchronous with dreaming (REM) sleep: preliminary report. *Arch. gen. Psychiat.*, **12**, 29.

52. FOULKES, S. H., 1964. *Therapeutic Group Analysis*. New York: Internat. Univ. Press.

53. FREEMAN, T., CAMERON, J. L., and McGHIE, A., 1958. *Chronic schizophrenia*. New York: Internat. Univ. Press.

54. FREUD, A., and BURLINGHAM, D., 1943. *War and children*. New York: Internat. Univ. Press.

55. FREUD, A., and BURLINGHAM, D., 1944. *Infants without families*. New York: Internat. Univ. Press.

56. FREUD, A., 1951. Observations on child development. *Psychoanal. Study Child*, **6**, 18.

57. FREUD, A., 1953. Some remarks on infant observation. *Psychoanal. Study Child*, **8**, 9.

58. FREUD, A., 1965. *Normality and pathology in childhood*. New York: Internat. Univ. Press.

59. FREUD, S., 1953. Fragment of an analysis of a case of hysteria (1905). In *The standard edition of the complete psychological works of Sigmund Freud*, vol. 7. Freud, S. London: Hogarth Press.

60. GIBSON, R., 1963. Psychotherapy of manic depressive states. *Psychiat. Res. Rep. Amer. Psychiat. Assn.*, **17**, 91.

61. GILL, M. M., 1963. Topography and systems in psychoanalytic theory. *Psychol. Issues*, **3**, No. 2

62. GILL, M. M., and BRENMAN, M., 1959. *Hypnosis and related states.* New York: Internat. Univ. Press.

63. GLOVER, E., 1956. *On the early development of mind.* New York: Internat. Univ. Press.

64. GUNTRIP, H., 1961. *Personality structure and human interaction.* New York: Internat. Univ. Press.

65. GUNTRIP, H., 1962. The manic depressive problem in the light of the schizoid process. *Int. J. Psychoanal.*, **43**, 98.

66. HALL, B. H., and WALLERSTEIN, R. S., 1960. Operational problems of psychotherapy research: third report: II. Termination studies. *Bull. Menninger Clin.*, **24**, 190.

67. HARLOW, H. F., 1962. The heterosexual affectional system in monkeys. *Amer. Psychol.*, **17**, 1.

68. HARLOW, H. F., ROWLAND, G. L., and GRIFFIN, G. A., 1964. The effect of total social deprivation on the development of monkey behavior. *Psychiat. Res. Rep. Amer. Psychiat. Assn.*, **19**, 116.

69. HARTMANN, E. L., 1966. The D-state: a review and discussion of studies on the physiologic state concomitant with dreaming. *Int. J. Psychiat.*, **2**, 11.

70. HARTMANN, H., 1958. *Ego psychology and the problem of adaptation*, (1939). New York: Internat. Univ. Press.

71. HARTMANN, H., 1964. *Essays on ego psychology.* New York: Internat. Univ. Press.

72. HARTMANN, H., KRIS, E., and LOEWENSTEIN, R. M., 1964. Papers on psycho-analytic psychology. *Psychol. Issues*, **4**, No. 2.

73. HEINICKE, C. M., and WESTHEIMER, I. J., 1965. *Brief separations.* New York: Internat. Univ. Press.

74. HOLT, R. R., 1962. A critical evaluation of Freud's concepts of bound vs. free cathexis. *J. Amer. Psychoanal. Assn.*, **10**, 475.

75. HOLT, R. R., 1965. Ego autonomy re-evaluated. *Int. J. Psychoanal.*, **46**, 151.

76. HOLT, R. R., 1965. A review of some of Freud's biological assumptions and their influence on his theories. In *Psychoanalysis and current biological thought*. Eds. Greenfield, N. S., and Lewis, W. C. Madison: Univ. Wisconsin Press.

77. HORWITZ, L., and APPELBAUM, A. (Submitted for publication.) A hierarchical ordering of assumptions about psychotherapy.

78. HUME, P. B., 1964. Principles and practice of community psychiatry: the role and training of the specialist in community psychiatry. In *Handbook of community psychiatry and community mental health*. Ed. Bellak, L. New York: Grune and Stratton.

79. JACKSON, D. D., 1961. The monad, the dyad, and the family therapy of schizophrenics. In *Psychotherapy of the psychoses*. Ed. Burton, A. New York: Basic Books.

80. JACOBSON, E., 1964. *The self and the object world.* New York: Internat. Univ. Press.

81. JAQUES, E., 1964. Social-analysis and the Glacier Project. *Hum. Relat.*, **17**, 361.

82. JOHNSON, A. M., and SZUREK, S. A., 1952. The genesis of antisocial acting out in children and adults. *Psychoanal. Quart.*, **21**, 323.

83. KLEIN, G. S., 1965. On hearing one's own voice: an aspect of cognitive control in spoken thought. In *Psychoanalysis and current biological thought.* Eds. Greenfield, N. S., and Lewis, W. C. Madison: Univ. Wisconsin Press.

84. KLEIN, G. S., 1966. Perspectives to change in psychoanalytic theory. (Paper presented at conference of Psychoanalysts of the Southwest, Galveston, Texas, March, 1966—to be published.)

85. KLEIN, M., 1937. Love, guilt, and reparation. In *Love, hate and reparation.* Eds. Klein, M., and Riviere, J. London: Woolf and Hogarth Press.

86. KLEIN, M., 1950. *The psycho-analysis of children.* 3rd ed. London: Hogarth Press.

87. KLEIN, M., HEIMANN, P., and MONEY-KYRLE, R. E., Eds., 1955. *New directions in psycho-analysis.* New York: Basic Books.

88. KLEIN, M., 1957. *Envy and gratitude.* New York: Basic Books.

89. KNAPP, P. H., 1963. Short-term psychoanalytic and psychosomatic predictions. *J. Amer. Psychoanal. Assn.*, **11**, 245.

90. KNAPP, P. H., MUSHATT, C., and NEMETZ, S. J., 1966. Collection and utilization of data in a psychoanalytic psychosomatic study. In *Methods of research in psychotherapy.* Eds. Gottschalk, L. A., and Auerbach, A. H. New York: Appleton-Century-Crofts.

91. KUBIE, L. S., 1950. *Practical and theoretical aspects of psychoanalysis.* New York: Internat. Univ. Press.

92. LAING, R. D., 1965. Mystification, confusion, and conflict. In *Intensive Family Therapy.* Eds. Boszormenyi-Nagy, I., and Framo, J. L. New York: Hoeber Medical Division, Harper and Row, Publishers.

93. LAING, R. D., and ESTERSON, A., 1964. *Sanity, madness and the family.* New York: Basic Books.

94. LIDZ, T., FLECK, S., and CORNELISON, A. R., 1965. *Schizophrenia and the family.* New York: Internat. Univ. Press.

95. LITIN, E. M., GIFFIN, M. E., and JOHNSON, A. M., 1956. Parental influence in unusual sexual behavior in children. *Psychoanal. Quart.*, **25**, 37.

96. LORENZ, K., 1965. *Evolution and modification of behavior.* Chicago: Univ. of Chicago Press.

97. LORENZ, K., 1966. *On aggression.* New York: Harcourt, Brace and World.

98. LUBORSKY, L., and SARGENT, H. D., 1956. The psychotherapy research project of The Menninger Foundation: V. Sample use of method. *Bull. Menninger Clin.*, **20**, 263.

99. LUBORSKY, L., FABIAN, M., HALL, B., TICHO, T., and TICHO, G., 1958. The psychotherapy research project of The Menninger Foundation: second report: II. Treatment variables. *Bull. Menninger Clin.*, **22**, 126.

100. LUBORSKY, L., 1962. Clinicians' judgments of mental health: a proposed scale. *Arch. gen. Psychiat.*, **7**, 407.

101. LUBORSKY, L., 1962. The patient's personality and psychotherapeutic change. In *Research in psychotherapy*, vol. 2. Eds. Strupp, H. H., and Luborsky, L. Washington, D.C.: Amer. Psychol. Assn.

102. MAHLER, M. S., 1952. On child psychosis and schizophrenia: autistic and symbiotic infantile psychoses. *Psychoanal. Study Child*, **7**, 286.

103. MAIN, T. F., 1957. The ailment. *Brit. J. med. Psychol.*, **30**, 129.

104. MAIN, T. F., 1958. Mothers with children in psychiatric hospitals. *Lancet*, ii, 845.

105. MASTERS, W. H., and JOHNSON, V. E., 1966. *Human sexual response.* Boston: Little, Brown and Company.

106. MILLER, S. C., 1962. Ego-autonomy in sensory deprivation, isolation and stress. *Int. J. Psychoanal.*, **43**, 1.
107. OSTOW, M., 1962. *Drugs in psychoanalysis and psychotherapy.* New York: Basic Books.
108. PARSONS, T., 1964. *Social structure and personality.* New York: Free Press.
109. PFEFFER, A. Z., 1959. A procedure for evaluating the results of psychoanalysis: a preliminary report. *J. Amer. Psychoanal. Assn.*, **7**, 418.
110. PFEFFER, A. Z., 1961. Follow-up study of a satisfactory analysis. *J. Amer. Psychoanal. Assn.*, **9**, 698.
111. PFEFFER, A. Z., 1963. The meaning of the analyst after analysis: a contribution to the theory of therapeutic results. *J. Amer. Psychoanal. Assn.*, **11**, 229.
112. PIAGET, J., 1952. *The origins of intelligence in children.* New York: Internat. Univ. Press.
113. PIAGET, J., 1954. *The construction of reality in the child.* New York: Basic Books.
114. RAPAPORT, D., 1951. *Organization and pathology of thought.* New York: Columbia Univ. Press.
115. RAPAPORT, D., 1958. The theory of ego autonomy: a generalization. *Bull. Menninger Clin.*, **22**, 13.
116. RAPAPORT, D., 1960. The structure of psychoanalytic theory. *Psychol. Issues*, **2**. No. 2.
117. RITVO, S., McCOLLUM, A. T., OMWAKE, E., PROVENCE, S. A., and SOLNIT, A. J., 1963. Some relations of constitution, environment and personality as observed in a longitudinal study of child development: case report. In *Modern perspectives in child development.* Eds. Solnit, A. J., and Provence, S. A. New York: Internat. Univ. Press.
118. ROBBINS, L. L., and WALLERSTEIN, R. S., 1956. The psychotherapy research project of The Menninger Foundation: first report: I. Orientation. *Bull. Menninger Clin.*, **20**, 223.
119. ROBBINS, L. L., and WALLERSTEIN, R. S., 1959. The research strategy and tactics of the psychotherapy research project of The Menninger Foundation and the problem of controls. In *Research in psychotherapy*, vol. I. Eds. Rubinstein, E. A., and Parloff, M. B. Washington, D.C.: Amer. Psychol. Assn.
120. ROBERTSON, J., 1953. Film: *A two-year-old goes to hospital.* 16 mm. Snd. 45 mins. English or French. London: Tavistock Clinic; New York University Film Library.
121. ROBERTSON, J., 1958. Film. *Going to hospital with mother.* 16 mm. Snd. 45 mins. English or French. London: Tavistock Institute of Human Relations; New York University Film Library.
122. ROBERTSON, J., 1958. *Young children in hospitals.* New York: Basic Books.
123. ROSEN, J. N., 1964. The study of direct psychoanalysis. *Psychiat. Res. Rep. Amer. Psychiat. Assn.*, **19**, 41.
124. ROSENFELD, H., 1963. Notes on the psychopathology and psychoanalytic treatment of schizophrenia. *Psychiat. Res. Rep. Amer. Psychiat. Assn.*, **17**, 61.
125. ROSENFELD, H., 1963. Notes on the psychopathology and psychoanalytic treatment of depressive and manic-depressive patients. *Psychiat. Res. Rep. Amer. Psychiat. Assn.*, **17**, 73.
126. ROSENFELD, H., 1965. *Psychotic states.* New York: Internat. Univ. Press.
127. SARGENT, H. D., 1956. The psychotherapy research project of The Menninger Foundation: first report: II. Rationale. *Bull. Menninger Clin.*, **20**, 226.
128. SARGENT, H. D., 1956. The psychotherapy research project of the Menninger Foundation: first report: III. Design. *Bull. Menninger Clin.*, **20**, 234.

129. SARGENT, H. D., MODLIN, H. C., FARIS, M. D., and VOTH, H. M., 1958. The psychotherapy research project of The Menninger Foundation: second report: III. Situational variables. *Bull. Menninger Clin.*, **22,** 148.

130. SARGENT, H. D., 1961. Intrapsychic change: methodological problems in psychotherapy research. *Psychiatry*, **24,** 93.

131. SARGENT, H. D., COYNE, L., WALLERSTEIN, R. S., and HOLTZMAN, W. H., 1966. (Submitted for publication.) An approach to the quantitative problems of psychoanalytic research.

132. SARGENT, H. D., HORWITZ, L., WALLERSTEIN, R. S., and APPELBAUM, A., 1966. Prediction in psychotherapy research: a method for the transformation of clinical judgments into testable hypotheses. (To appear in *Psychol. Issues.*)

133. SCHAFER, R., 1968. *Aspects of internalization.* New York: Internat. Univ. Press. (In press.)

134. SCHEFLEN, A. E., 1961. *A psychotherapy of schizophrenia: direct analysis.* Springfield, Ill.: Charles C. Thomas.

135. SCHEFLEN, A. E., 1966. Natural history method in psychotherapy: communicational research. In *Methods of research in psychotherapy.* Eds. Gottschalk, L. A., and Auerbach, A. H. New York: Appleton-Century-Crofts.

136. SCOTT, W. C. M., 1963. The psychoanalytic treatment of mania. *Psychiat. Res. Rep. Amer. Psychiat. Assn.*, **17,** 84.

137. SEARLES, H. F., 1965. The contributions of family treatment to the psychotherapy of schizophrenia. In *Intensive family therapy.* Eds. Boszormenyi-Nagy, I., and Framo, J. L. New York: Hoeber Medical Division, Harper and Row.

138. SEARLES, H. F., 1965. *Collected papers on schizophrenia and related subjects.* New York: Internat. Univ. Press.

139. SECHEHAYE, M., 1951. *Autobiography of a schizophrenic girl.* New York: Grune and Stratton.

140. SECHEHAYE, M., 1951. *Symbolic realization.* New York: Internat. Univ. Press.

141. SECHEHAYE, M., 1956. *A new psychotherapy in schizophrenia.* New York: Grune and Stratton.

142. SECHEHAYE, M., 1963. Principles and methods of symbolic realization. *Psychiat. Res. Rep. Amer. Psychiat. Assn.*, **17,** 40.

143. SEGAL, H., 1964. *Introduction to the work of Melanie Klein.* New York: Basic Books.

144. SHAKOW, D., 1960. The recorded psychoanalytic interview as an objective approach to research in psychoanalysis. *Psychoanal. Quart.*, **29,** 82.

145. SHERFEY, M. J., 1966. The evolution and nature of female sexuality in relation to psychoanalytic theory. *J. Amer. Psychoanal. Assn*, **14,** 28.

146. SINGER, M. T., and WYNNE, L. C., 1963. Differentiating characteristics of the parents of childhood schizophrenics, childhood neurotics, and young adult schizophrenics. *Amer. J. Psychiat.*, **120,** 234.

147. SINGER, M. T., and WYNNE, L. C., 1965. Thought disorder and family relations of schizophrenics. III. Methodology using projective techniques. *Arch. gen. Psychiat.*, **12,** 187.

148. SINGER, M. T., and WYNNE, L. C., 1965. Thought disorder and family relations of schizophrenics. IV. Results and implications. *Arch. gen. Psychiat.*, **12,** 201.

149. SINGER, M. T., and Wynne, L. C., 1966. Principles for scoring communication defects and deviances in parents of schizophrenics: Rorschach and TAT scoring manuals. *Psychiatry*, **29,** 260.

150. SPITZ, R. A., 1945. Hospitalism. An inquiry into the genesis of psychiatric conditions in early childhood. *Psychoanal. Study Child*, **1,** 53.

151. Spitz, R. A., 1946. Hospitalism: a follow-up report. *Psychoanal. Study Child*, **2**, 113.

152. Spitz, R. A., 1957. *No and yes*. New York: Internat. Univ. Press.

153. Spitz, R. A., 1959. *A genetic field theory of ego formation*. New York: Internat. Univ. Press.

154. Spitz, R. A., 1965. *The first year of life*. New York: Internat. Univ. Press.

155. Stanton, A. H., and Schwartz, M. S., 1954. *The mental hospital*. New York: Basic Books.

156. Talbot, E., Miller, S. C., and White, R. B., 1964. Some antitherapeutic side effects of hospitalization and psychotherapy. *Psychiatry*, **27**, 170.

157. Tinbergen, N., 1953. *The Herring Gull's world, a study of the social behavior of birds*. London: Collins.

158. Wallerstein, R. S., and Robbins, L. L., 1956. The psychotherapy research project of The Menninger Foundation: first report: IV. Concepts. *Bull. Menninger Clin.*, **20**, 239.

159. Wallerstein, R. S., and Robbins, L. L., 1958. The psychotherapy research project of The Menninger Foundation: second report: I. Further notes on design and concepts. *Bull. Menninger Clin.*, **22**, 117.

160. Wallerstein, R. S., and Robbins, L. L., 1960. Operational problems of psychotherapy research: third report: I. Initial studies. *Bull. Menninger Clin.*, **24**, 164.

161. Wallerstein, R. S., 1963. The problem of the assessment of change in psychotherapy. *Int. J. Psychoanal.*, **44**, 31.

162. Wallerstein, R. S., 1964. The role of prediction in theory building in psychoanalysis. *J. Amer. Psychoanal. Assn.*, **12**, 675.

163. Wallerstein, R. S., 1966. The psychotherapy research project of the Menninger Foundation: an overview at the midway point. In *Methods of research in psychotherapy*. Eds. Gottschalk, L. A., and Auerbach, A. H. New York: Appleton-Century-Crofts.

164. Wallerstein, R. S., 1966. The psychotherapy research project of The Menninger Foundation: a semifinal view. (Presented to plenary session of the Third Conference on Research in Psychotherapy, June 4, 1966, Chicago, Illinois.)

165. White, R. B., 1961. The mother-conflict in Schreber's psychosis. *Int. J. Psychoanal.*, **42**, 55.

166. White, R. B., 1963. The Schreber case reconsidered in the light of psychosocial concepts. *Int. J. Psychoanal.*, **44**, 213.

167. White, R. B., Schlagenhauf, G., and Tupin, J. P., 1966. The treatment of manic depressive states with lithium carbonate. In *Current psychiatric therapies*, vol. 6. Ed. Masserman, J. H. New York: Grune and Stratton.

168. White, R. B., Talbot, E., and Miller, S. C., 1964. A psychoanalytic therapeutic community. In *Current psychiatric therapies*, vol. 4. Ed. Masserman, J. H. New York: Grune and Stratton.

169. White, R. W., 1963. Ego and reality in psychoanalytic theory. *Psychol. Issues*, **3**, No. 3.

170. Winnicott, D. W., 1958. *Collected papers*. New York: Basic Books.

171. Winnicott, D. W., 1965. *The family and individual development*. New York: Basic Books.

172. Winnicott, D. W., 1965. *The maturational processes and the facilitating environment*. New York: Internat. Univ. Press.

173. Wolff, P. H., 1959. Observations on newborn infants. *Psychosom. Med.*, **21**, 110.

174. Wolff, P. H., 1960. The developmental psychologies of Jean Piaget and psychoanalysis. *Psychol. Issues*, **2**, No. 1.

175. WOLFF, P. H., 1966. The causes, controls, and organization of behavior in the neonate. *Psychol. Issues*, **5**, No. 1.

176. WYNNE, L. C., and SINGER, M. T., 1963. Thought disorder and family relations of schizophrenics: I. A research strategy. *Archs gen. Psychiat.*, **9**, 191.

177. WYNNE, L. C., and SINGER, M. T., 1963. Thought disorder and family relations of schizophrenics: II. Classification of forms of thinking. *Arch. gen. Psychiat.*, **9**, 199.

178. WYNNE, L. C., RYCKOFF, I. M., DAY, J., and HIRSCH, S. I., 1958. Pseudo-mutuality in the family relations of schizophrenics. *Psychiatry*, **21**, 205.

XVII

EXISTENTIAL ANALYSIS

GION CONDRAU

Professor of Psychotherapy
University of Fribourg
Switzerland

AND

MEDARD BOSS

Professor of Psychotherapy
University of Zürich,
Switzerland

1

Introduction

Ever since analytical psychotherapy was established by Sigmund Freud, a pioneering and revolutionary development in the history of medicine, attempts have repeatedly been made to abandon the impersonal, objective approach of a medical science based solely on the principles governing the natural sciences, in favour of a total approach. Freud's greatest achievement is to have discovered that in every treatment of an ailing human being the encounter between physician and patient, and the nature of this interpersonal relationship, play a crucial role. This decisive advance has met with practical success in the treatment of the patient, and enthusiastic therapists have achieved positive results because of it. However, on the theoretical side, many investigators got nowhere because they did not advance to those other basic psychotherapeutic principles, which transcend the approach of the natural sciences in the understanding of man's nature.

In the last few years only, psychotherapy has broken fresh ground. The psychotherapists have found new points of departure for their work in the existential-ontological ideas of contemporary philosophical thinkers, in particular of Martin Heidegger.[27, 28] For the first time psychotherapy has become aware of a conception of man's nature that means to liberate man from the bondage of speculative subject-object relationship and 'causal' connections. Seeing that man now appears as fellow-man, with whom we are in communion and whose concerns and distresses are already components of our own inner scheme of the world, there can be no longer any question of interpreting the phenomena that confront us in illness, as being other than what they really are. From the standpoint of the method, Freudian[25] psychoanalysis remains the basis of this psychotherapeutic approach. Nevertheless, it is just this philosophical reorientation in our conception of man's nature that opens up new ways of approaching the patient, which have hitherto been closed.

It is rather astonishing that psychotherapists nowadays are concerned about philosophy, and they are sometimes blamed for doing so. Doctors regard it as a betrayal of the natural scientific origin of medicine, while philosophers consider it an unwarranted and incompetent intrusion into an alien field of inquiry. However, all these critics are overlooking that every human mode of thought and every action, including medical science, and also psychiatry and psychotherapy, rest on pre-scientific, philosophical premises.

To be sure, these philosophical presuppositions were, up to very recently, neither thought about as such nor debated, but were merely taken as self-evident. Traditional medicine and psychiatry are based, of course, on the Western European philosophical foundation laid down by René Descartes (1596–1650). He established the scientific dualism of body (*res extensa*) and mind (*res cogitans*). Bodies are comprehended under the category of quantity, and their laws can be unequivocally expressed in terms of mathematics. In this way the basis was laid for the amazing development and expansion of our knowledge of the physical universe. Therefore it is perfectly understandable that medical science, which is mainly concerned with the human body, welcomed with open arms this new theory, which seemed to guarantee such positive results. However, it was precisely the successes owed to this method by medicine that lured medical men into the erroneous notion of seeking to understand the human being in its entirety and in all its manifold aspects, from a purely quantitative aspect. With its concept of 'man the machine', medical science celebrated its most glorious triumphs and, in so doing, at the same time stumbled into a blind alley.

For us the most important reaction against the exclusively physical-mechanistic approach of classical medical science occurred at the end of the nineteenth century, when the psychological treatment of many hitherto undefined types of illness became part of ordinary therapeutic procedure.

This new method of treatment grew out of the startling, empirical findings of investigators like Charcot, Janet, Breuer and Freud. At the same time there was an increasing tendency to understand the nature of man in its totality; this approach was most typically represented in philosophy by the work of Dilthey. He amplified Kant's apperception: perceiving, feeling and willing and all of man's available modes of relating to the world are in this way comprised in the human subject as an inalienable unity. With these basic conceptions as starting-points there developed the unitary-and-structural psychology (Driesch, Kruger, Kohler, Wertheimer, Koffka, Spranger), as well as the personalist psychology of William Stern. The unity of body and mind is not thought of in any static way by Dilthey, but it is accomplished in the course of a continuous interplay; it is a continuous becoming, an 'appropriation-to-the-self', and it is dynamically understood. It is precisely this dynamic understanding of the unified field of reciprocal corporeal and mental influences that involves the possibility of dysharmony. The problems dealt with in psychiatry stem from this dysharmony, from this plasticity of psycho-physical behaviour. Moreover, the line, as it were, where these psycho-physical problems emerge became thought of as the boundary of medical science and psychology and also as their line of intersection. The very possibility of an active psychotherapy of the neuroses shows sufficiently, for example, that mental and corporeal events not only interplay with each other, but that the human being does not, in fact, consist of body and mind only, seeing that 'the organism is from the outset always something different and much more than merely organism, the mind is always something more than merely mind. The human being is and remains a unity. It does not split up into body and mind; rather, the body is already mind, the mind already body. From the empirical standpoint, of course, body and mind are by no means identical, but are reciprocally dependent peripheral concepts. However, they are purely theoretical entities. Only in this way is it possible to understand that an important turning-point in one's life can entail a modification on the somatic plane, and how a somatic change can also bring about a major transformation in one's personal life history.'[1] This new insight into the body-mind relationship, into the nature of man and of his being-in-the-world, has its roots, as mentioned above, in the philosophy of Martin Heidegger,[27, 28] especially in his fundamental, ontological investigation *Sein und Zeit* (1927). Heidegger is one of a group of philosophical thinkers whose works, despite their occasional divergences, are all subsumed under the collective designation of 'Existential Philosophy'. It so happens that the existential concept (the notion of 'existence') was not introduced into philosophy for the first time by these thinkers. Metaphysics has always been concerned with the concept of existence, although, to be sure, in a different way from Heidegger. Scholastic philosophy, for example, speaks of existence as distinct from essence. The scholastic notion of existence is, however, not at all identical with the concept of existence as propounded by Heidegger, since it points not to the accomplishment of the *human* existence, but indicates rather the actuality of every being, of every essence.

2

Historical Development of Existentialism as a Philosophy

'Existentialism', as it is called, became a stylish philosophy after the Second World War, its main centre being France, from where it spread throughout Western Europe exerting an influence on art, literature and life in general. Müller[41] is right in maintaining that these circumstances must not obscure the fact that the German founders of the so-called existential philosophy, 'who wrote their decisive works long before the transitory style of "existentialism", had a more profound and more genuinely lasting influence, without which it would be impossible to conceive the kind of philosophical thinking now practised in Germany.' However, existential philosophy is commonly given an even earlier date of birth and a place of origin outside Germany, the Danish theologian and thinker Søren Kierkegaard[34] (1813-55) being regarded as its originator. In opposition to the dialectical formalism of Hegel, Kierkegaard invokes the inner experience as the real and authentic reality of the human being, of its true self, not to be grasped by the subjective reason, and this reality he calls 'existence', an expression having a metaphysical-religious relevance. To Hegel's 'Welvernunft' (the reason immanent in the world) Kierkegaard opposes the antirational, the irrational. Nevertheless, it has to be emphasized that existential philosophy does not mean merely an irrational, emotional form of apperception, nor must it be equated with irrationalism. If rationalism claims that everything real must be discernible by the reason and that there is nothing rationally unknowable for the human mind, then this very claim is just as irrational and as incapable of demonstration by the reason, as the opposing assertion that there is nothing to be known by the reason. The Dasein (existence, in the sense of being-there) can not be proved. Even so, it can be known—by way of revelation (Schelling). Kierkegaard shifts the main emphasis from pure knowledge to *realization*, from consciousness to being (Gabriel)[26]. What Kierkegaard is concerned with here is the intellectual formulation of the spiritual existence of man, 'the fact that man in the act of reflecting actively discloses himself to himself, that he carries out in the act of thinking what he is thinking, e.g., he does not merely think for an instant: Now you have to be attentive every instant, but really is attentive every instant . . . .'

In this idea of Kierkegaard's concerning existence already appear certain points of departure which were later to prove significant in existential psychotherapy. To exist 'does not mean to be finished, to exist means to become'. The inner development of the self occurs in the free actions of the individual, in which he realizes his self. 'Since in the active freedom of the individual existence arises'—says Gabriel[26]—'literally as a leap into existence, it is not possible to let the existence of the self, of the actual inner being, follow from external premises and be derived from them. Hence the leap. This leap is made by the individual in his freedom. It is a leap into the dark. It is the venture of becoming. And therefore this venture is a decision. Spiritual reality or existential spirit is, according to Kierkegaard, rooted in spontaneous decision.' The way leads from the 'cogito' to the 'sum'. Existence thus wins its ecstatic character. I ec-sist, I am 'outside' myself.

The human being who does not attain to the realization of the absolute self, who remains caught in, so to say, the realm of relativity, this relative man succumbs to the 'sickness unto death', to total despair over himself, to absolute self-dissolution.

Human freedom, according to Kierkegaard, is ambiguous. There is a freedom to be and a freedom not to be. 'Not-being, however, generates anxiety'; man fears not-being, for which he can, through his being free, decide. Anxiety is the reality of freedom. For this reason we in our daseinsanalytical investigations of the problems of anxiety and guilt in human existence have also devoted our main attention to Kierkegaard's discussion of anxiety (Condrau).[17] It was the treatise on anxiety that gave birth to the existential philosophy.

The modern existential philosophers, however, invoke Kierkegaard less than they do Edmund Husserl (1859–1938), who in 1913 published his *Ideen zu einer reinen Phänomenologie*[29] (*Reflections on a pure phenomenology*). In this work he was interested to attend to the things themselves and to see and to understand the given without any prior conditions. This given is designated phenomenon, that which immediately manifests itself. The phenomenological method consists in the demonstration and the clarification of that which is given. The subject-matter of the phenomenological philosophy is the interrelationships underlying being (in the sense of essential nature, essence), its procedure is the description of being. It is not concerned with the merely sensuous and empirical seeing of a thing, but with an apprehension of the being as the self-disclosing. This being, however, is for the most part hidden.

Martin Heidegger (1889–   ) may probably be regarded as the founder and chief proponent of modern existential philosophy, although he himself considers this designation as inapt for the content, form and intention of his philosophical procedure. 'Existential philosophy' would give rise to the idea that his philosophy was in the first instance a philosophical anthropology, which Heidegger in *Sein und Zeit*[27] (*Being and Time*) decisively rejects. The daseinsanalysis, or existential analysis, of Martin Heidegger inquires into the meaning of being as such. Man possesses a primordial understanding of being. 'Being' is for us self-evident, we employ the words 'is' or 'are' with an assurance that excludes any kind of doubt about the notion of 'being'. This understanding of being is a prerogative of man only, it is not shared by the animals and plants, let alone inanimate nature. On this basis man reveals himself as the field of lumination of being—as the openness of being. This approach, as we have said, is quite essentially distinct from that which, from the anthropological viewpoint, inquired into the nature of man. The question why man is a feeling, thinking and acting being, and what is the nature of his awareness of, or his attunement with, anxiety, guilt, sickness and death, are reduced to the inquiring into 'the peculiar character of precisely the being of man'. Man can never be apprehended in his wholeness, which is always more than the individual, but also something other than the sum of everything individual, from the standpoint of the environing world, that is to say, from the standpoint of beings (Seiende). As long as he is understood in one aspect only, the spiritual or the material, he is, owing to the neglect of the other aspect, simultaneously misunderstood.

Anthropology sought to overcome this onesidedness, but, owing to its anthropocentricity, got into a blind alley in its endeavour to demonstrate the relationship of man to the world. Whereas the philosophical anthropologies proceed from man, and thence seek to understand the world, Heidegger[28] always sees man in relationship to being. 'Are we really on the right path toward the essence of man, if, and as long as, we make a sharp distinction between man as a living being among others and plants, animals and God? We can proceed in this way, of course, and we can in this fashion locate man within beings as a particular being among others. In so doing we shall always be able to make correct assertions about the human being. However, we must also have no illusions about the fact that man thereby remains thrust into the realm of animalitas, even if we do not equate him with the animal, but credit him with a specific difference setting him apart from the animal. We always think, in principle, of *homo animalis*, even when anima is formulated as *animus sine mens*, and this, in turn, later on, as subject, person, mind.'

Even man's body is something essentially different from an animal organism. 'The aberration of biologism is not overcome by superimposing the mind on the body of man and the spirit on the mind and the existent on the spirit and lauding the spirit more loudly than before, only to allow everything to lapse back into the living of life as such, with the admonitory assurance that thinking, with its rigid concepts, annihilates the stream of life and that the thinking of being disfigures existence. The fact that physiology and physiological chemistry are able scientifically to investigate the human being as an organism does not prove that the essence of man is based on this "organic" element, that is to say, on this scientifically explained body. This is as little to the point as saying that the essence of physical nature is contained in atomic energy. It could very well be that nature presents only one of its sides for technical manipulation and mastery by man and that its essence is completely concealed. No, the essential nature of man does not consist in being an animal organism, nor can this inadequate definition of man's essence be dealt with and compensated by equipping man with an immortal soul or with reason or with a personality. In every case, being (essence), and that on the basis of the same metaphysical scheme, is passed over.'[28]

Heidegger repeatedly defends himself against the reproach that his questioning of the theoretical anthropologies and one-sided definitions of man signifies a nihilistic devaluation of man. 'Because, in all the above, a position is everywhere taken up against what mankind considers exalted and sacred, this philosophy teaches an irresponsible and destructive "nihilism". What, after all, is "more logical" than this, that whoever in this way denies everywhere that which is truly being, takes the side of not-being and so proclaims mere nothingness as the meaning of reality? . . . But does the "against", which is produced by thinking in relation to what is usually meant, necessarily point to mere negation and to the negative principle?' The vulnerable point on which Heidegger very definitely lays his finger is the granting of absolute status to a one-sided elucidation of man's essential nature, the assignment of value, which he calls 'the greatest blasphemy imaginable against being'. Therefore the question can no longer be: *What* is man, but how *is* man. If we say of man that he possesses an understanding of being, then we are bound to ask what exactly is the case with this 'being'. From the inquiry into the being of man we arrive at the inquiry into 'being pure and simple', and so at the fundamental problem of all philosophy. In other words: the question of being is itself already a part of the nature of being, that is to say, out of being come the questions about being itself: 'it has a relationship to itself.' Being, however, does not remain freely hovering, but all being is the being of particular beings. 'Being means, then, that beings and world have burst open to themselves and, as it were, have broken out of an inchoate and undifferentiated, dead lump, into themselves, that is, into the variegated manifoldness of beings.'[28]

Heidegger sees the human being in his relationship to being in such a way that the human being signifies the openness of being. The 'essence' of existence (Dasein) lies in its actual existence (Existenz); 'man has (or is) an essence such that he is the "there" (the "da" in Dasein), that is, the openness of being'. This standing in the openness of being is called by Heidegger the ec-sistence of man. This ec-sisting does not reply to the question whether man really is or not, but to the question as to the 'essence' of man. Ec-sistence, however, is not the reification of an essence, but a relationship to the openness of being. Every existence (Dasein) has its *world*; being-in-the-world is the basic constituent of existence (Dasein). The 'in', however, does not have a spatial meaning; rather the 'being-in' constitutes the character of beingness of existence; 'world is a character of existence (Dasein) itself'. ' "World" means in that definition not a realm of beings, but the openness of being.'

Also, every individual discernment of things is grounded in the original understanding of being; primordial world-openness renders possible not only the knowledge of existing things, but also provides understanding for the other human beings who, in accordance with their nature as existence (Dasein) are in the world equally with me. The world of existence is shared, interpersonal world. Man can in an unmediated way understand himself and the fellow human beings and things confronting him. Before we discuss the significance of the Daseinsanalysis of Heidegger for psychotherapy, we should like to refer briefly to the leading ideas of other existential philosophers. This is all the more indicated as their points of departure are fundamentally at variance both in relation to the phenomenological understanding of human existence and in relation to the subject-object dichotomy, which is removed in Heidegger's concept of being-together (Mit-Sein).

Jean Paul Sartre (1905–   ) in his major work *L'être et le néant*[43] (1943), as well as in numerous plays, presents his basic ideas; he conceives existence in a way that is still entirely subjectivistic. It is sometimes asserted that Sartre's position is the closest to that of Heidegger. In reality, there is hardly a thinker who has so misunderstood and falsely interpreted Heidegger as he has done. The fundamental experience of being, in Sartre's view, consists in a general state of loathing, disgust, expressed in his novelistic journal *La nausée*[45] (1938). Whereas the existentialism of Kierkegaard has distinctly Protestant features and that of Marcel even bears a specifically Catholic stamp, Sartre's approach is unequivocally atheistic, which appears to be explainable from the antithesis to the Deistic notion of God, a typical product of the Enlightenment. In addition, Sartre was no doubt more inspired by Nietzsche than by Kierkegaard—with whose writings he is doubtless familiar.

Sartre's influence on the development of psychotherapy has been, if it has been an influence at all, very slight. He is credited with the elaboration of his own phenomenology of the body (under the influence of Marcel) and the enunciation of principles for an existential psychoanalysis, but his significance has probably remained confined more to the literary and political scene in France. Sartre's antitheological ethics have had a special resonance; he preaches here an unbridled moral scepticism. The sole moral norm is: to act in accordance with one's freedom. All vital earnestness is to be spurned as dishonest, being-together is nothing but the endeavour to master the Other Existence (Dasein) manifests itself in the freedom to which man is 'condemned'. 'Man is free, man is freedom.'[44]

Another French philosopher, Gabriel Marcel (1877–   ) is closer to Kierkegaard in his approach than is Sartre, although—in contrast to Sartre—he was not familiar with the works of the Dane when he was elaborating his own philosophy. Marcel's ideas were presented mainly in the Metaphysical Journals[35] (*Journaux métaphysiques*) in 1927 and 1935 and finally in their continuation *Présence et Immortalité*[36] in 1960. Like all existential philosophers, he too rejects the dichotomy between subject and object, between thinking and being, mind and body, I and Thou. However, like Sartre, Marcel has not been able to get rid of the objective materiality of the body; both philosophers assign to the human body an objective-instrumental character. In the case of Marcel this approach derives from the antithesis of being and having [Etre et Avoir]. Existence is made intelligible by a phenomenological analysis of having. Existence is inseparable from embodiment. The union of mind and body is perhaps not essentially different from the union of mind with the other existing things of the world.

However, what does this mean but that there is mind *and* body, mind and world, that they are even in the realm of possession, to 'be had'? This 'having', though, always points to a subjectivism, whether there is involved a possessing having (avoir-possession) or an implied having (avoir-implication). In both cases one notes a *qui* which has a *quid*. Thus the overcoming of the subject-object dichotomy, on which the French phenomenologists pride themselves, has in fact become at least dubious. Here not only Marcel but also Sartre and the other proponents of 'phénomenologie existentielle' appear to have misunderstood Heidegger's being-in-the-world. The statement of these contemporary anthropologists, including also A. de Waelhens,[46] P. Ricoeur,[42] Merleau-Ponty[40] among others, to the effect that man *has* and *is* his body at the same time, is unacceptable. If we attempt to take both points of this statement seriously, we must switch from an 'instrumentalist' horizon of understanding—within which one sees only utilitarian objects—to a horizon of understanding of being within which the essence of being human is disclosed in an existential sense. In other words, 'to have' and 'to be' do not actually refer here to a twofold character of man's relation to his physical sphere itself, but only to two possible and different mental approaches to this relation.

While Marcel[38] has *de facto* concerned himself very little with questions of psychotherapy and psychoanalysis and has brought medicine only peripherally within his field of discussion, the German existential philosopher Karl Jaspers (1883–   ) became known for his clearly negative attitude towards psychoanalysis. He himself started as a psychiatrist and achieved international renown with his *General Psychopathology*[30] (1913). The *Psychology of Philosophical Outlooks*,[31] which appeared in 1919, constituted the transition to philosophy, his work in this field being crowned by the three-volume *Philosophy*[32] in 1932. Jaspers was probably most markedly influenced by Kant, but also by Spinoza and Schelling. The problem of the philosophy of Jaspers is the theme of reason and existence. We must consider (recollect ourselves), experience from the peripheral situation of time, what we are; what in mythic language means 'mind' (or 'soul') signifies in the philosophy of Jaspers existence. The intellectual ascertainment of existence is illumination of existence. When Heidegger speaks of understanding of being, Sartre of self-creation, what Jaspers is concerned with is being-the-self. This self-being, the illumination of existence, occurs, as we have said, in the break-through, in peripheral situations, in struggle and in guilt, in suffering, in death, in freedom and in communication. 'What man is and can become has its ultimate origin in the experience, appropriation and overcoming of peripheral-situations.'[30] In the peripheral situation alone we really do know how things stand with us, that we are in fact limited, finite, but look into the infinite, the boundless which closes around our existence (Dasein) as a horizon. "To experience peripheral situations and to exist are the same thing.'[31] In the face of death 'as the point of my existence (Dasein) that rigidifies me', we are torn out of our empirically accustomed field of existence and are exposed to all existence (Dasein). We lie open, stripped, there. In such a radical openness we experience who we are, what we can do, since we can do nothing more. Then all masks fall away, all artificial façades are torn away, all seeming, all appearing vanish. Here the being (Sein) of man as he is emerges. Jaspers is concerned with self-experience, self-perception in the face of transcendence, self-realization out of the relation to the whole, unconditioned and infinite encompassing the existence (Dasein).

Of outstanding significance in the realm of self-realization is communication. No one can encounter himself in the mind wholly by himself, he needs communication with others, he needs ex-pression—as a medium of his own self-realization. In addressing and in being addressed both partners to a dialogue come home, together, to themselves, each to his existence. Psychotherapy, however, is called by Jaspers[33] 'planned communication'. Owing to his hostile and unobjective criticism of psychoanalysis, there has unfortunately been no chance of opening a discussion which could have been productive both for philosophy and for psychotherapy.

The case is quite different with Martin Heidegger. Psychotherapy has gained from his writings more than a new outlook on man and an elucidation of our understanding of illness. In personal talks and in seminars in Zürich, in the last few years, he has made himself increasingly acquainted with the endeavours of psychiatrists and psychotherapists and has given them an opportunity to put Daseinsanalysis on a firm scientific basis.

3

Analysis of Dasein

There are good reasons for supposing that Martin Heidegger's *Analysis of Dasein* is more appropriate to an understanding of man than the concepts which natural science has introduced into medicine and psychotherapy. If this kind of approach does come closer to human reality than the approach of natural science, it will be able to give us something we have hitherto not been able to find in psychoanalytic theory: an understanding of what we are really doing (and of why we are doing it in just this way) when we treat a patient psychoanalytically, such understanding to be based on insights into the essence of human being. A deeper understanding of our practices could not but have a beneficial effect on them.

Analysis of Dasein urges all those who deal with human beings to start seeing things and thinking about them from the beginning, so that they can remain in the presence of what they immediately perceive and do not get lost in 'scientific' abstractions, derivations, explanations, and calculations estranged from the immediate reality of the given phenomena. It is of paramount importance to realize from the outset that the *fundamental difference which separates the natural sciences from the Daseins analytic or existential science of man is to be found right at this point.*

No one, perhaps, has yet been able to formulate the basic working principle appertaining to all natural sciences more poignantly than Sigmund Freud when he characterized the approach of his psychology as follows: Our purpose is not merely to describe and classify phenomena, but to conceive them as brought about by the play of forces in the mind, as expressions of tendencies striving towards a goal, which work together or against one another. In this conception, the trends we merely infer are more prominent than the phenomena we perceive.

In sharp contradiction to this natural-scientific approach to man's nature, the existential understanding of man and his world demands that we look at the phenomena of our world themselves, as we are confronted by them. In other words, Daseinsanalytic statements never seek to be anything more than 'mere', albeit severely strict, careful and subtle descriptions and expositions of the essential aspects and features of all things: inanimate objects, plants, animals, human beings just as they disclose themselves immediately in the light of the Daseinanalyst's awareness.

The existential approach is faithful to the given phenomena in its own way and has a fundamental strictness in its descriptions and its exposition of their immediately perceived meanings which is at least equal to the so-called exactness of the natural sciences. If today the label 'Daseinsanalysis' or 'Existentialism' is also claimed by so many rather obscure, confused, and confusing psychologies, analysis of Dasein itself should not be blamed.

Analysis of Dasein categorically refrains from imposing some arbitrary idea of being and reality—however customary or 'self-evident'—on the 'particular being' we call 'man'. We must be able to abstain from forcing man into any preconceived and prejudicial categories, such as 'soul', 'psyche', 'person', or 'consciousness'. We must choose an approach which enables us to be alert in order to see how man appears in his full immediacy.

Man's primordial 'being-in-the-world' is not an abstraction but always a concrete occurrence. His being-in-the-world occurs and fulfils itself only in the manifold particular modes of human behaviour and of man's different ways of relating toward things and fellow beings. This kind of being presupposes a unique openness of man's existence. It has to be an openness into which the particular beings which man encounters can disclose themselves as the beings they are, with all the context of their meaningful references. How else could man relate to things in the sensible and efficient way he actually is capable of if his relationships towards them were not primarily of the nature of illuminating, of disclosing and understanding the meaning of what he encounters, whether this disclosure of the things of his world occurs as seeing or hearing them, smelling or tasting them, feeling them, thinking or dreaming of them, or as handling them unreflectingly?

Contemporary child psychology has shown how the emotional attitude of the mother is crucially important for the new-born child, even more than the quantity and quality of the milk he receives from her. If understanding of what is encountered were not of the essence of human nature, this importance would be hard to explain. The mother can be importantly 'meaningful' to the infant in this interpersonal sense only if his initial relationship to her is one of opening up and discovering meaning— in this case the meaning of being sheltered or loved by her. Of course, the child cannot, as yet, articulate his understanding in thoughts and abstract notions. For a long period of time, his meaning-disclosing encounters remain of a nature which psychology and biology up to now have tended to describe with such incomprehensible and distorting terms as 'empathic', 'instinctual', and 'reflexive'. Nevertheless, they too are fundamentally an understanding and disclosing of the meaning and references of encountered particular beings.

Man's primary and immediate understanding of things as what they are naturally includes the possibility of also misunderstanding them— taking a rope for a snake at first sight, for instance. A possible misunderstanding of something is no argument against, but rather one for, the designation of man's being-in-the-world as primary and fundamental understanding and elucidating. Even in such a mistaken perception, there still is understanding of something as something, though an erroneous one.

4

Differences Between Existential Analysis and Psychoanalysis

Comparing Daseinsanalytic thinking about human existence with the understanding of man prevailing in psychoanalysis we elucidate the relationship which, we believe, exists between the two. To avoid unnecessary confusion, however, we think it wise to distinguish from the outset between two entirely different matters, both of them labelled 'psychoanalysis'. On the one hand, and primarily, psychoanalysis denotes a specific method of medical treatment, with its own, though unreflected, tacit understanding of man; on the other hand, the term refers to a psychological theory derived secondarily from the method of treatment. The two ways of understanding man inherent in psychoanalytic therapy and theory differ so much from each other that they amount, at times, to a clear-cut contradiction, especially with regard to their most important features. This is the reason why we have to study their respective relationships to Existential Analysis separately.

Psychoanalysis as a psychological theory is, according to Freud's own statements, a 'speculative superstructure', a 'rational foundation for—medical efforts, gradually developed', any part of which 'can be abandoned or changed without loss or regret the moment its inadequacies have been proved', it is an 'artificial structure of hypotheses' which would probably be 'blown away' *in globo* by the progress of science. Above all, however, psychoanalytic theory is expressly intended to form part of the realm of the natural sciences. Freud's intentions in this regard are unequivocal. Indeed, as we have pointed out, few, if any, have ever been able to formulate the general working principle of the traditional natural sciences in keener terms.

The philosophical faith which supports Freud's assertions consists in the prescientific presuppositions which form the basis of all the natural sciences. They may be summarized as follows:

1. There is an external, 'real' world, existing in itself, independent of man.

2. 'Real' can be only what can be measured, calculated, and thereby established with certainty. Reality is the totality of those objects which constitute the world.

3. The relations between the particles of every object as well as the connections between one entire object to all the others are predictable causal connections; thus the chain of these relations of causes and effects is always an unbroken one.

4. Finally, everything that is 'real' fits into the three dimensions of space and into a temporal order derived from the movements of the sun and the other stars.

Freud transferred the above-mentioned natural-scientific approach into his theory of man. He supposes the existence of a 'psyche', which he compares with a microscope, telescope, or a photographic camera. The psychic apparatus is moved by an assumed energy called 'libido'. Psychic manifestations always have the character of wishes. 'Only a wish is able to set the (psychic) apparatus in motion', Freud states in the *Interpretation of Dreams*.

The sole aim of all the processes going on within the psyche is like motor discharge of energy into the external world, in order that the apparatus may maintain itself so far as possible without excitation. For 'accumulation of excitation is felt as unpleasure—diminution of excitations as pleasure'.

It is easy to see that the basic categories within which Freud built his scientific psychology have their roots in the philosophies of Descartes and Kant. It is not surprising, then, that Freud cites Kant in connection with a statement concerning the subjective conditioning of perceptions, the distortions of reality thereby introduced, and the fundamental unrecognizability of the perceived things as such. Here is proof, given by Freud himself, that all sciences rest upon predetermined philosophic bases, as we have stated before.

Above all, these philosophical presuppositions of the natural sciences —applied unreflectingly by Freud to the science of man—led from the start to a mental destruction of the unity of the psychoanalytical situation in all of Freud's theoretical considerations. In the actual situation of psychoanalytical therapy, patient and therapist are together in caring about the same phenomena which disclose themselves in the light of their existences. Freud's theory, however, dissects this union into the medical observer and the observable object. And this dissection by no means stops with this first step. A second one follows immediately, with the postulate of a body-psyche dichotomy. The patient's 'psyche' is assumed to reside somewhere 'in' the observed human object, and to be worldless at the start.

Freud had gained an immediate and primary understanding of man through his discovery and practice of psychoanalysis. But he destroyed this primary understanding when he introduced his theoretical construction. To realize the extent of his destruction, we have only to compare the two pillars of psychoanalytical *practice* with their counterparts in his *theory*. On the one hand, 'transference' and 'resistance' testify Freud's deep understanding of man; on the other hand, his theoretical formulations distort this understanding to the extent that understanding is lost. Transference and resistance indisputably refer to actual phenomena of inter-human relationships. Observation confirms over and over again how right Freud was when he stated that if the analyst allows the patient time, devotes serious interest to him and acts with tact, a deep attachment of the patient to the analyst develops of itself. Nor can any analytical observer deny Freud's discovery that all patients in psychoanalytic treatment strongly resist total recognition of themselves. Every experienced analyst, therefore, will fully agree with Freud's observation that the pathological factor is not the patient's ignorance itself, but the root of this ignorance in his inner resistances; both are abstractions, intellectual reductions of specific features of the human existence and of modes of relating to objects of a physical and mental nature. This is the reason why such notions do not lead to a full understanding of any kind of human behaviour.

Psychoanalytic theory has of course undergone a great many modifications in the course of half a century. The most important ones were introduced by Freud himself. Many other valuable theoretical contributions were made by Freud's disciples, by those inside as well as outside the orthodox psychoanalytical school. The main objection of analysis of Dasein regarding all these psychoanalytical extensions of, and additions to, Freud's theory of man, however, would have to point to their common lack of a basis for a real understanding of the possibility of man's having 'personal' relations to objects of an external world which are determined by his 'partial instincts'; or for man's entering into reciprocal social relations with his fellow human beings; or for man's being involved in social processes and his being formed thereby. As long as we do not understand man's essential nature as being of a meaning-disclosing, elucidating character, we remain unable even to understand how someone is able to perceive a fellow man as a fellow man and enter into relationships.

There is no other way out of the confused situation of our contemporary pyschology in general and of the psychoanalytic theory in particular than to re-evaluate one basic psychoanalytic conception after another in the light of a more adequate understanding of man.[12]

The difference between the psychoanalytic and the existential analytic perception of neurosis is best proved by Freud's doctrine of the neuroses with 'hysterical conversion'. Freud thought that in all hysteria cases certain ideas had been prevented from being 'discharged' normally, i.e. into conscious actions. In such cases, the 'affect' of these ideas, according to Freud, may be 'strangulated' and undergo 'a transformation into unusual somatic innervations and inhibitions'. For this assumed psychic process, Freud coined the term 'hysterical conversion': a certain portion of our mental excitation is normally directed along the paths of somatic innervation and produces what we know as an 'expression of the emotions'. Hysterical conversion exaggerates this portion of the discharge of an emotionally cathected mental process; it represents a far more intense expression of the emotions, which has entered upon a new path.

Freud's concept of hysterical conversion is of more than historical interest; it is the key concept supporting the gigantic theoretical structure of present-day 'psychosomatic medicine', at least insofar as it pays tribute to psychoanalytic theory. Yet if we look more closely, we notice that the concept of hysterical conversion provides a very weak and uncertain foundation for both the psychoanalytic theory of neurosis and psychosomatic medicine. Freud himself questioned the nature of the concept he coined. He realized that it is impossible to imagine a functional connection between two such utterly and essentially different objects as those implied by such terms as 'body' and 'psyche'. With admirable candour, he confessed that the leap from the mental to the physical remains a mystery.

To break the deadlock created by the concept of 'hysterical conversion', we reflect again on the Daseinsanalytic understanding of man. Here it is clear that all psychic 'things'—conscious and unconscious thoughts, fantasies or emotions, body functions and body organs—do not, in fact, exist as primarily separate phenomena, nor is there such a thing as an illness which exists by itself. *The* stomach and *the* stomach illness, *the* thoughts and *the* general paralysis are unreal abstractions. On the other hand, *my* arm, *my* stomach, *our* instincts, *your* thoughts are real. Mention of my, your, or their *being ill*, refers to reality. The possessive pronouns of the daily language point to an existence which persists and unfolds in a life history. They refer to a human being never exhaustively described by reference to his 'possessions', whether these are thought of as the constantly changing 'substance' of his 'body' or his equally inconstant instincts, feelings, fantasies and thoughts. Nor is man identical with the sum of all these objectifications. If so, it would be impossible to see how feelings, thoughts or parts of the body could ever belong to an individual as *his* feelings, thoughts or body-parts. Furthermore, if man were essentially an extant object among other mundane objects, an organic conglomeration of physical and psychic things, how could such a thing ever be 'touched' by another in such a way that he could perceive it, understand it, where it might even 'move' him? Lastly, how could such a 'thing' ever encounter a fellow human being and become aware of him as that particular being?[5]

To suffer from hysteria or from an organ-neurosis means that one gives up the freedom and openness to the world in every way. Those world-relations which are prevented from being realized appropriately in an intentional, interpersonal manner must carry themselves out in the dark, mute spheres of existence where there are no thoughts or words, i.e., primarily in the somatic realm. In such cases, the relationships which are not openly admitted come forth and remain within the sphere of the body and provoke instead of vibrating. Such an existence is bound to show a pathological inflation as well as distortion of its corporality. This is true for all the hysterical and some of the organ-neurotic symptoms. Other organ-neurotic symptoms can arise even if there is no possibility of relating. The whole existence of a person is one-sidedly—and more or less exclusively—reduced to one kind of relation to the world. Then the whole melody of this man's life has to be played on one string. Even if this *one* possibility of relating is admittedly open, it still amounts to an exorbitant demand on, and overtaxing of, one possibility. The somatic realms which belong to this possibility of relating to the world also start to function in a pathologically exaggerated manner.

All adequate investigations of the existence of ulcer patients, for instance, present the following picture. These patients' relations to fellow humans and to things are one-sidedly and exaggeratedly oriented toward seizing, overpowering, and taking possession. They want to subjugate everything they encounter and to rob it of its individuality. The condition of such patients is—for external and internal reasons—so completely and excessively reduced and narrowed down to this one relationship to the world that their somatic realm behaves in the same way. Stomach and duodenum belong specifically to the world-relation of seizing and overpowering. These parts of the body (owing to motility, hydrochloric acid, pepsin and the enzymes of the pancreas) really attack the food which has been grasped and cut up by the teeth. They dissolve and demolish food particles so that they make part of the physical realm.

It is still possible to distinguish organ-neurotic symptoms daseinanalytically from hysterical ones. It is true that, in hysterical symptoms, too, the patient confines his carrying out of certain world-relations to his bodily sphere. But he does it in the form of gestures, even if their meaning is unconscious. Nevertheless, gestures—the word has the same root as 'gestation'—always are meant to bring something forth, to disclose something. Gestures are full of meaning in relation to one or the other partner. Hysterical behaviour occurs within a comparatively open sphere of communication and interpersonal relations. It even needs the physical presence of other people, since it addresses itself in some way or other much more obviously to spectators—is much more 'narrative' and more impressive—than organ-neurotic symptoms. But the original character of being with things and fellow men is by no means lost in the latter symptoms either. It is merely more thoroughly disguised. Here, existence is no longer carried out in gestures which unabashedly appeal to an audience of concrete fellow human beings, but it is muted and seemingly uncommunicative.

In other words, the kind of symptoms—whether hysterical or organ-neurotic—do not depend on the type of world-relation which is arrested in the somatic sphere. What matters is the degree of concealment, how far a given world-relation was deflected from its appropriate manner of being carried out openly in willed, responsible interpersonal behaviour. For this reason, it is possible for each particular behavioural phenomenon to retreat to the realm of the hysterical language of gestures, or to the even more hidden realm of organ-neurotic phenomena. What matters most, however, is that both categories of symptoms have revealed themselves to us in a new light. We have seen that each hysterical and each organ-neurotic bodily symptom belongs immediately to one or another meaningful relationship toward something. The afflicted bodily spheres fluctuate, so to speak, from the outset in those relationships, although in a pathological way.

5

The Views of Existentialism on the Concepts of Neurotic and Psychotic Disorders

The daseinsanalytical understanding of illness can no longer be oriented on a speculative definition of the neuroses—let us say, as disturbances of the instincts, drives and affects—whose inadequacy has its cause in undemonstrable premises. To be sure, it still sounds heretical nowadays to question the actual presence of drives or instincts or even to expose the 'affects' as mere abstractions and pure figments of thought. All the same, up to the present no investigator has succeeded in demonstrating the factual presence of these drives and affects, let alone in localizing them. However, the splitting up of the human being (Dasein) into a mind (psyche), a body and an external world, as is done by scientific psychology, on closer examination turns out to be a purely intellectual construction. It is then obvious that consequently psychoanalytical concepts like the libido, the instinctual mechanisms, repression and regression, the play of psychodynamic forces, and projection become superfluous in the daseins-analytical-phenomenological way of understanding the human being.

Special importance is assigned in the psychoanalytical theory to the hypothesis of an 'unconscious' within the psychic apparatus. When people speak of 'depth psychology' what they mean is a psychology which does not remain at the level of the 'consciousness', but penetrates into the 'depths' of the 'unconscious'. Freud concedes without further ado that the unconscious is not empirically demonstrable; for this reason later on, he speaks not of a psychological, but of a 'metapsychological' concept.

If we, on the basis of the daseinsanalytical understanding of the human being, have arrived at the conviction that other persons and things show themselves in the meaning-disclosing light of our existence simply as what they are, then the assumption of the presence of an 'unconscious' becomes superfluous. It is unnecessary to assume that a specific 'ideational content' of possibly unpleasant character would be forced down from the consciousness into the unconscious; not to mention the fact that it would remain, in any case, always inexplicable how such a process should operate, unless we want to deform the human being, making it into a mere material object, comparable, for instance, to a piece of furniture with different drawers. The truth is that man emerges into the illuminated world-openness and always relates in one way or another to the phenomenon showing itself immediately in the openness of its existence (Dasein), as such, and not merely to 'inner-psychic copies' of it. Man has a fundamental property, the power to perceive things, and this power primordially includes both a being-open over against what confronts him, and a capacity to close himself up against what confronts him. Man can reflectively linger, in a thematic sense, over a thing. However, he also has the capacity to close himself up against his perception of his relation to a fellow human being. Even in warding off a connection with a fellow human being, and precisely in doing so, he has never only repressed an isolated psychic drive or a representation into the 'unconscious' system of a psyche. Rather, even in the case of such a warding off of an interpersonal relationship, one is immediately there in the presence of the fellow human being concerned and is ineluctably committed to the relationship to him.[10]

Also, all the new versions of the 'unconscious'—even if they are far removed from the original Freudian or Jungian idea—are not able to obscure the fact that what we have here is an abstract, hypothetical and artificial concept, corresponding to nothing demonstrable and not capable of furthering our understanding of human phenomena in any way.[18]

The assumption of an unconscious became necessary for psychoanalytical theory so that within it hidden forces and energies could be subordinated to psychic phenomena and 'explained' on the basis of such phenomena. As opposed to this, Daseinsanalysis is phenomenologically oriented; it is not concerned with 'explaining', with a deduction of Something from something Else, but with laying clear, revealing. Daseins-analysis does not seek to prove anything at all, but 'merely' tries to show and understand the immediately perceptible phenomenon in its full meaning-content. The natural scientific deductive demonstration is a progression from one to the other, in a continuous causal sequence. From the standpoint of interpretative understanding, what is involved is un-mediated (immediate) grasping of the whole that is to be understood. Thus it can be said that where we are after the understanding of a 'meaning', the classical natural scientific and mathematical procedures of deduction and induction are henceforth out of the question. While psychoanalysis inquires about the play of forces lying at the basis of the neurosis, and the causes to be assumed behind its appearances, Daseinsanalysis searches for the meaning or meaning-content of the pathological behaviour.

The choice of the illness or the form of the neurosis is, then, in short, dependent on the intensity with which specific world-relationships are admitted or warded off. The case is quite different concerning the choice of organ. Here the decisive role is not played by the degree of knowing admission or rejection of conflict-fraught phenomena, but by the given special meaning-content of the affected organ. The symbolic thinking prevalent in the doctrine of psychoanalysis is responsible for the introduc-tion of the concept of the organ idiom into medicine, taking for granted that this idiom, this code, is not immediately understandable, but has to be deciphered first, like the symbolic language of dreams. The stomach ulcer was interpreted as 'hunger for a sense of security'; asthma signified sym-bolically anxiety in the face of loss of sense of security and defiance; the asthma attack became an outcry against the mother or a cry for her. However, the exact observation and elucidation of the psychosomatic illnesses confirmed neither a symbolic nor a conflictual organ specificity. Rather, the choice of organ is determined from the given special type of disturbed vital relation. We can acquire a better understanding of the patient suffering from heart or stomach trouble only if we know how the heart or the stomach figure physically in the milieu of a given life.

To be sure, a physical organ does not accompany, for instance, every 'psychic' quality, every mood, vicariously jumping in and announcing in its organic idiom, as it were, the 'situs' or the essential nature of the illness. Rather, both the heart and the sex organs can express the bodily aspect of love. The heart, however, is also the seat of hate, sorrow, anxiety, courage or timidity. In a state of joyful expectancy it beats faster, in a state of fright it almost stops. In still another way the stomach is related to the situation in which food is taken in and digested, which for the man with an ulcer means that he is always trying to cope with more than is in keeping with his existential possibilities. Many other examples could be given; such a medical-psychological understanding of human illness is applicable to the entire field of medicine.

While the existence (Existieren) of neurotics and psychosomatic patients is to a great extent accessible to a human understanding and does not appear entirely alien even to the layman, the relationship to the world of mentally disturbed persons, especially that of schizophrenics, is often judged to be empathically inaccessible and deranged, infantile or retrograde. Scientific pathology is lacking of an understanding of psychoses and is content to classify them according to symptoms and types of development, to study their causes and laws. Freudian theory is based on the hypothesis that a mental illness is a consequence of a predominance of the 'id', by which the 'ego' would be compelled to retreat 'from a portion of reality'. A psychosis is said to deny reality and to seek to take its place. While a neurosis represents the conflict between the ego and the id, a psychosis signifies the analogous outcome of such a disturbance in the relations between ego and external world.

By contrast, Daseinsanalysis stresses the point that failure is unavoidable in any attempt to understand the optical and auditory hallucinations of the schizophrenic as mere sensory delusions without any reality-value or even as results of metabolic changes, and indeed all psychological attempts at explanation are bound to fail. The patients themselves are convinced that the reality of their experiences is quite different in nature. Being-human in the true sense of the word includes the appropriation of all the potentialities of behaviour, and opening-up to what confronts one, which is given to man as such and constitutes his essence. Frequently, the radically rejected potentialities of relation and development that have not yet been appropriated, along with the human and environmental phenomena appearing in their light, as well as the corresponding, and merely instilled, defensive behaviour, can only be perceived from an uncanny, alien 'realm of spirits', in the shape of precisely those phenomena which psychiatry is accustomed to call 'hallucinations'. Everything that the patients refuse to face stares at them now as 'hallucinatory', monstrous, visages and pries into their most hidden selves.[8] The potentialities of development of the sensuous-erotic life, for instance, can only be lived out by the patients in the shape of psychotic 'sensory delusions', which always indicates an especially intensive, indeed complete 'self-closure' and 'not-letting-oneself-be-used' when confronted by these phenomena.[9]

Both the exponents of a 'somatogenesis' and the interpreters of 'psychogenesis' are guilty of a decisive self-misunderstanding when they seek to understand the nature of schizophrenia, one group making organic findings into a 'foundation' of psychiatry and the other making its psychodynamic considerations into a 'depth' psychology. Wanting to regard any sort of somatic processes as the basis of any kind of perceiving-understanding human mode of behaviour in the only really fundamental sense—that one sees the latter as caused, or derived from the former, or the former as being manifested in the latter—is to go astray in the abyss of a kind of intellectual magic and to assume an inconceivable transformation of material things into meaning-perceiving intellectual acts. But, again, the psychogenetic, psychodynamic, depth-psychological approaches can not penetrate into the real depths of phenomena, because they themselves stop at the shallow level of vague, never ascertainable assumptions of psychic structures and of forces lying behind the observed phenomena.[13] On the other hand, in the schizophrenic break-down man is usually so overwhelmed and swamped by alien-seeming external factors that, wholly sacrificed to the excess of new contents of awareness, he is caught and totally subjugated by them. Such a happening leads to a break-down and tearing-open of a self-being that had always been dependent, precarious, and hardly viable. Such a complete subjection of the existence (Dasein) to something perceived amounts, however, to a proximity to the latter, a proximity which out of itself condenses the perceived meaning-content into the appearance of a sensorily present phenomenon. For this reason, it is observed that schizophrenic patients become increasingly helpless when they are confronted by what they perceive and this reveals itself to them in ever more corporeal shape and becomes a direct physical threat. At first such a thing can occur as a compulsive having-to-think of something. Soon, however, it emerges in the shape of delusions and hallucinations. The transition from a relatively reserved, intellectual, representational, recalling, imagining visualization of something into its hallucinatory, oppressive, palpable, sensuous-perceptible being-present, corresponds to the given stage of break-down of an existence in the face of an emergent meaning-content. The excessively great, but also unfree proximity of a hallucinatory visibility and audibility makes clearly understandable the immediate, unquestionable knowledge of the full meaning of what is seen and heard. A corresponding, if only transitory, immediate certainty can also be observed in the intensive 'emotionalism' of normal people.

An insight into this profound complexity of a 'schizophrenic symptom' prevents us at the same time, however, from cherishing the deceptive hope of ever being able to explain it 'genetically', and to think of it as caused by organic cerebral processes, somatic disturbances or by psychic, environmental impressions. At best, we shall be able to take the individual somatic and psychic findings, ascertained before or during schizophrenic hallucinations, as the possible means which attune a person to this or that world-situation, that is always a co-constituent of his existence (Dasein), and hold on to it there, in certain circumstances, in a way that is pathologically restrictive or liberating.

6

The Impact of Existential Analysis on Psychotherapy

There is no doubt that dascinsanalytical interpretation is not only compelling us to undertake theoretical modifications of our theory of illness, but is also of decisive significance for psychotherapeutic practice. At first, it seemed as if Daseinsanalysis differed from psychoanalysis only, or mainly, on the theoretical plane; however, it has become increasingly clear that theory and practice can never be wholly separated. Thus, for practical psychotherapy, it is not a matter of indifference what anthropological theory lies at the basis of a treatment.

An example may be adduced in support of what has been said above: A young bookkeeper suffered from an intense case of writer's cramp, which threatened his whole future career. Every time he attempted to write his right hand became painfully cramped. His writing became so illegible that after a short time the patient was obliged to give up this work. The writing inhibition of this patient made its first appearance while he was in school, when he was seeking in secret to copy a test. During puberty, and again a few years later, the symptom became more obvious in connection with an incipient acquaintance with a girl.

Psychoanalysis, according to Freud, sees in writer's cramp, as in every sort of inhibition, a functional restriction of the ego, an excessive eroticization of the organs used, in this case, for the function of writing. He writes: 'We have, quite generally speaking, arrived at the insight that the ego function of an organ is damaged when its sexual significance increases. It then behaves, if we may venture a rather scurrilous comparison, like a cook who does not care to work at the stove any longer because the master of the house has become her lover. If writing, which consists in letting fluid run out of a tube on to a piece of white paper, has assumed the symbolic significance of coitus. . . .', becomes inhibited, 'because it is as if one would carry out the prohibited sexual act. The ego renounces these functions incumbent on it in order not to be obliged to proceed to yet another repression, in order to evade a conflict with the id.'

For our patient this, then, would mean that the right hand, required for writing, abdicated its ego function owing to its charging with sexual libido. At this juncture we merely point out the dubiousness of an interpretation of writing as a symbol of sexual union. Interpretations of symbols are a part of the psychoanalytical basic premise, according to which our main attention is to be devoted not to the phenomenon, but to drives 'assumed' to be behind phenomena. Perhaps, however, one is required to ascribe to a thing an additional symbolic content only where one has already essentially restricted its full meaningful and referential relations. In the case of our patient, we learn immediately that when he writes he gets a cramp in the hand. At first we see no sign of any sexual charging, we see nothing of a renouncing ego and nothing of a symbol. If we want to get at the phenomenon of writer's cramp, we have to try to understand the meaningful content of this symptom. In this quest we are assisted by the three indications constituting his 'illness' that are offered by the patient: the writing, the hand, the cramp.

Accordingly we shall first have to concern ourselves with the meaning-content of writing, if we want to grasp the meaning of writer's cramp. Writing signifies informing, making known, getting in touch. Informing means that I am sharing something with another person. This 'something' is a part of me, I share myself with another, or I share myself with another in respect of a matter. Information means accordingly being-open primordially for another, for a fellow human being. What is written is, in addition, a firmly laid down announcement of something. In writing man reveals himself in a definitive, largely irreversible fashion. He sets forth his position; he commits himself. While the spoken word can be forgotten or taken back, what is written is binding. It can no longer be denied, reinterpreted, altered. 'Let me have that in writing' is what people demand of one another, whenever they want to nail down a statement, and make it stick. The significance of writing as information, announcement, has even been experimentally confirmed, by demonstrating that writing movements of those suffering from writer's cramp have been executed without effort when the patients were under the impression the writing instrument was not making any mark.[22]

The fact that the symptom of cramp manifested itself precisely in the *hand* is explained, no doubt, by the fact that writing is a function of the hand. But the meaning-content of the hand is not exhausted in the function of merely writing. The hand is also used for all sorts of other actions—it grasps, it seizes, with it we hold on to things, it furnishes us with support, it is indispensable for life. The hand can strike out in hate, it can stroke tenderly in a mood of love. We speak of the strong hand of a father and the tender hand of a mother, of the generous hand of the benefactor, of the corrective hand of the educator. In writer's cramp the hand is inhibited, its free capacity to play is restricted, hampered. In this disturbance there is immediately revealed, however, the constriction of the world-openness of the patient, that world-openness of which the hand is part. This constriction of the world-openness is experienced as *cramp*. When we said every world-relation was always attuned, that means here: the world-relation of interpersonal being-open is attuned in the sense of cramp. The cramp is the opposite of freedom. Cramp means tension, compulsion, unfreedom. The cramped person surrounds himself with an armour, he is not emotionally open to things, but sealed, encapsulated. Our patient spoke very significantly of a 'confected shape' into which he had been squeezed.

The human shape of the patient was so rigidified that he was able to live his life only in a very deficient form of being-together, in the solitude of one exiled and isolated, like the existence (Dasein) of a sado-masochistic patient suffering from a cramped defensive state of mind described by Boss.[2] Like this patient our cramped writer was 'squeezed into a purely personal egoistic standpoint and constrained to merely utilitarian actions, cut off both from his environment and from the inner world of his feelings, and from the ground of his existence (Dasein).'[2] He was separated from the world of his own feelings, in order to allow himself to be determined by the world of things, professional advancement, money (a book-keeper!). Characteristic of him was anxiety in the face of loving attitudes, the onset of feeling into his intellectualistic world. Feelings, human sensitivity and capacity to love were present, to be sure, somewhere in the patient, but immured within him.

This cramped state of our patient included a catastrophic relation to the *body*. Everything concerning the creatureliness of the patient had, from childhood been outlawed as sinful by a puritanical upbringing that was hostile to the instinctual life. A brutal, alcoholic father and a soft, weak mother, who gave him no feeling of security, had seen to it that the patient never got to know about the realm of interpersonal love and of the body.

The patient went through an analysis lasting two and a half years. Externally this analysis did not differ essentially from a classical psychoanalysis, in that the patient—as in psychoanalysis—was asked to lie down on a couch and to tell everything that came into his mind at that moment. At first the therapist confined himself to listening to him in that state of free-hovering attentiveness recommended by Freud and to drawing his attention to inner resistances wherever these appeared. He came regularly to his sessions, three times a week, with neither the number of sessions nor the frequency representing a daseinsanalytical deviation from the procedure followed in psychoanalysis. In both cases rules should not be rigid but adapted to circumstances and to individual patients.

It is occasionally asserted that daseinsanalytical psychotherapy is not technically different from Freudian psychoanalysis. For example, Rollo May[39] writes that Medard Boss is 'a thorough-going Freudian in his technique, using couch, free association, and the other methods of classical psychoanalysis'. This is correct only to the extent that 'technique' is understood solely as the external procedure of analysis. However, in so far as one also counts as part of the method the behaviour of the analyst, the technique of dream interpretation, permitting and denying, the processing of the material, Daseinsanalysis can surely no longer be put on the same footing with psychoanalysis. It is equally wrong to state that 'therapists with the existential viewpoint can and do belong to different schools of practice'. To be sure, Daseinsanalysis does not claim to be a school of its own; it seeks to induce the leading schools of therapy to come to terms with their own principles. In point of fact, however, all psychotherapeutical approaches which do so, and really go into the essential nature of man and his illness, are obliged not only to drop their theoretical ballast, but in most cases to alter their practice in accordance with the new understanding.

Space does not allow to present a complete survey of the technique of daseinsanalytical psychotherapy. Thus, only two deviations from Freudian psychoanalysis will be mentioned: namely, the treatment of 'acting out' and the interpretation of dreams.

In the treatment Daseinsanalysis can do more than interpret the acting out of the patients as behaviour indicating resistance, as psychoanalytical theory does. Freud still thought that in the analysis the patients would try 'to act something, to repeat in life what they ought only to remember, to reproduce as psychic material and to retain on the psychic plane'. But, Daseinsanalysis sees the 'acting out' of the patient not simply as resistance to memories, but understands in it the same immediate and genuine appearance of newly emerging possibilities of relation that is found in intellectual thought. What is involved here is not necessarily a wanting to 'repress' memories. Rather, in many cases, the analysand in his acting out dares to take his first step towards his own unfolding. In other words: he catches up with a possibility of behaviour that was previously not permitted and never got to be lived out. The result is that the admitting, granting of the acting out, can be therapeutically most beneficial.

The analytical self-opening of a neurotically constricted patient becomes possible only when the doctor permits the patient to enter into those modes of behaviour in which the latter actually finds himself. These modes of behaviour, in the case of patients who are seriously ill, are not the conceptual, intellectual-linguistic possibilities of relating possessed by normal adults. For this reason, as in the relationship between the infant and his mother, an authentic interpersonal relation corresponding truly to the natural constitution of the patient can often emerge only in a wordless gesture language, perhaps at times exclusively in a permissive silence and simple presence-there (Dasein). In the psychotherapeutic treatment of small children it is not possible to dispense with allowing the patient to act-out, and the same applies to daseinsanalytical treatment, seeing that the neurotic by his nature has remained, to a great extent, at the developmental stage of the infant. For the same reason Daseinsanalysis treats with causal-genetic explanations and deductions following from the psychoanalytical 'Why'?, in order to replace this question with the provocative question 'Really why not?' The 'Why' question demands too much of the analysand, while with the permissive 'Why not' question it is made possible, often for the first time, for the patient to rid himself in the analysis of at least certain inhibitions imposed on him by the external world. Of course we take for granted the fact that such a permissive approach presupposes in the analyst himself a high degree of maturity and sense of responsibility, and obliges him never to slip himself into the unfreedom of childish or compulsively egoistic behaviour.

Daseinsanalysis is distinguished from *Freud*ian conceptions in the interpretation of *dreams* just as clearly as in the handling of the transference and the acting-out. Daseinsanalysis speaks of 'interpretation' ('Auslegung') of dreams and by that means 'interpreting' in the sense of 'grasping the meaning of the immediately emerged dream phenomena'. When psychoanalysis speaks of dream interpretation, it means an 'explanation', a reduction to something else of hidden meaning, supposed to be behind what is presented. Such 'explanation' presupposes that the 'meaning' of the dream does not reveal itself as such, but remains at first veiled, and has to be deciphered like a secret script. *Freud*, however, supplies no justification for such a procedure. The whole assumption of the so-called psychoanalytical dream-distortion serves only the purpose of making dreams correspond to a pre-conceived theory. But, existential analysis maintains that dreams are not to be regarded as some sort of objects detached from a person, nor can they be compared with other objects fashioned by a person. Rather, a human being, whether dreaming or waking, always remains in some sort of percipient state regarding the things and fellow human beings confronting him. For this reason, the daseinsanalytical-phenomenological interpretation of dreams speaks neither of 'latent dream ideas', nor of a 'dream censorship', nor does it speak of symbols or dream figments. Also, it recognizes no justification for distinguishing dream interpretations on an 'object relation' from those on a 'subject relation', nor does it believe in the theory of the dream as a wish fulfilment. If we judge our dreams not from an external, alien standpoint, but we allow the dream phenomena to be simply in their immediate givenness, it is obvious that what we dream is perceived neither as images nor as symbols. We experience what confronts us in dreaming as real entities: a thing as a real thing, an animal as a real animal, a human being as a real human being, a ghost as a real ghost. In our dreams we are in a world just as authentic and palpable as that of our waking life, and in both worlds we live out our existence (Dasein) in our relations and in our behaviour towards the things and fellow human beings confronting us.[4]

7

The Significance of Existentialism and Existential Analysis for Psychiatry

Insights into the nature of human existence can become a major foundation of psychiatry in its efforts to liberate patients from the bonds of their psychotic, neurotic and psychosomatic symptoms. We even maintain that without such knowledge no psychotherapist will succeed at all.

Another question affecting psychotherapeutic practice in detail is in what way we can induce our patients to share in the insight into their human nature, which would allow them to overcome anxiety and oppressive guilt. To be sure, we shall never get anywhere with an intellectual appeal to reason and understanding, or with invocations of the modern slogan word 'existence'. That would mean a step backward to the psychotherapy of Freud's time. After all, it is not our patients' heads and intellects that are sealed up and cut off by anxiety, but rather their hearts. Therefore, all words, even the cleverest, remain for them mere sound and fury signifying nothing.

As psychotherapists we have to abstain from influencing our patients by maxims and dogmas. Our function is a modest one, the removing here and there of a little stone, of an obstacle. The highest aim of psychotherapy is and remains to enable our patients to a being-able-to-love-and-trust, which can overcome all oppressive anxiety and guilt, as mere misunderstandings cleared away. Such trust can and may be regarded as the most mature kind of human love. However, our mentally and emotionally disturbed patients can get to this point only by means of a human maturing process. Normally, this would happen if the corporeal concrete experience of a sufficient never-failing maternal love were present. Our patients would not become ill if they had not lacked this. But this harmful missing out never depends solely on mothers, but just as much on the widely varying needs for love in the children. In psychotherapy the rule is to allow the patient to make up for the loss of the indispensable maternal love that was adapted to the nature of the child. The psychoanalytical situation is the arena of selfless authentic love, and from here the patient can gradually emerge out of childish reserve into ever more mature possibilities of love, and this can occur spontaneously, in so far as the patient is furnished by nature with the corresponding potentialities of development. For this purpose the psychotherapist is bound to credit the spiritual or religious experiences of his patients that come up in the treatments with the same primordial quality, authenticity and reality, as the phenomena of the so-called instinctual sphere. He must be on his guard against demoting these things, for the sake of a prejudice of the secondary psychoanalytical theory, to the status of merely derived products of sublimation of libido.

But not only in theory and practice can one distinguish between Daseinsanalysis and psychoanalysis. The therapeutic goal too requires correction. To Freud man's nature originates from a pleasure-ego, wants to satisfy sexual instincts and preserve itself. He believed that early, primitive man, and especially children exemplified the more or less unadulterated, primary, guiltless 'naturalness' of man—a naturalness obligated only to the 'pleasure principle'. Modification of the pleasure principle is forced on man by the external world; but this modification is called the 'reality principle', which is secondary, according to Freud. It occurs because the individual would perish (and would be unable to have any kind of satisfaction) if he did not consider the given realities of the external world. One part of this adaptation to external reality is the child's acceptance of the moral demands his parents make on him. Eventually, the superior force of external reality results in the child's psychic incorporation of these and other demands and prohibitions which originally came from outside. The final result of this theory is Freud's 'Super-Ego', or conscience. Once the super-ego has been formed, it becomes a source of guilt feelings. Hence, man experiences feelings of guilt every time he violates, or intends to violate, one of the seven commandments. Characteristically enough, Freud in all his papers never spoke of guilt as such, but only of guilt feelings. He expected psychoanalysis to liberate the patient from neurotic thralldom and allow him to return to his 'original naturalness'. So he would no longer be inhibited by feelings of guilt, but would have the guarantee of guiltless enjoyment.

In contrast to Freud, Existential Analysis is accepting guilt feelings, not only as secondary, externally determined ones which can be removed by psychoanalysis. From the standpoint of analysis of Dasein, man is primarily guilty. His primary guilt commences at birth. For it is then that he begins to be in debt to his Dasein, by not being able to carry out all the possibilities of life. Man remains guilty in this sense, i.e. indebted to all the demands that his future keeps in store for him until his last breath. Also, as we have pointed out, every act, every decision, every choice, involves the rejection of all other possibilities which also belong to a human being at a given moment. In this twofold sense, he must always remain behind, so to speak. This is as much a part of fundamental human nature as the other *existentialia*. Man's existential guilt consists in his failing to carry out the mandate to fulfil all his possibilities. Man is aware of existential guilt when he hears the never-ending call of his conscience. This essential inevitable being-in-debt is guilt, and not merely a subjective feeling of guilt, which is disguised in a neurotic way. Because of existential being-in-debt (experienced as guilt), even the most skilfully conducted psychoanalysis cannot free man of guilt. Actually, not one single analysand could be found who has been transformed into a really guiltless person by psychoanalytic treatment. The worst result an analysis could accomplish in this regard would be to deafen a patient to the pangs of his conscience, and this would not be to his advantage. Being liberated from guilt by psychoanalysis, is an antiquated myth.

Psychotherapy, however, can accomplish something else. It can elucidate the past, present and future of a patient's life to the point where he becomes thoroughly aware of his existential being-in-debt. This enables him to acknowledge his debt, to say 'yes' to it and take it upon himself. He becomes aware of his possibilities by listening to the call of his conscience; he can take over responsibility and stand by himself.

Once a person has been freed from his essential and existential being-in-debt, he no longer experiences neurotic feelings of guilt. The latter did not originate in himself, but derived from a foreign and crippling mentality which his educators forced upon him. He had to live up to modes of life which were alien to him, but he could not shake them off. Such neurotic feelings of guilt continually increase existential guilt as well, since they result in a steadily increasing debt in regard to a fulfilment of one's own existence. As a result, the call of conscience becomes increasingly persistent. But the patient, caught in acquired moralistic concepts, misunderstands this voice as a demand to follow even more rigidly this mode of living. Only analysis can break this vicious circle.

If a patient reaches the goal of Daseinsanalysis, that is, if he freely accepts his debt to his existence, he reaches at the same time the goal Freud had in mind—full capacity for work and enjoyment. But he will no longer use these capacities in the service of egotistic power—or pleasure—tendencies. Rather he will let all his possibilities of relating to the world be used as the luminated realm into which all he encounters may come to its fulfilment.

8

Conclusion

'Since the existential analytical conception of illness is based on a totally different anthropological concept from the one underlying psychoanalysis, its aims must also be different. The essential significance of the analysis of Dasein of Martin Heidegger for psychiatry does not consist solely in the clarification of merely theoretical or technical details and individual problems. More important than this, and something that only renders possible this kind of understanding, are two fundamental aids offered to the doctor by analysis of Dasein.

Heidegger in *Sein und Zeit* (*Being and Time*)[27] describes two possibilities of behaviour, which may serve as invaluable guidance for the psychotherapist's attitude to his patients, when he speaks of 'intervening' and of 'anticipating' care. Intervening care is acting for the other. The latter steps back, in order to take up what has been done for him as something ready-made and available, or he dispenses with it entirely. In such care the other can become dependent and dominated, be this dominance tacit or not, and concealed from the dominated one or not. This intervening, solicitous care determines the being-together to a great extent, and it affects mainly the treatment of what is present at that moment. In contrast to this, is the possibility of a type of care which does not intervene so much for the other but anticipates him in his ability-to-be, does not relieve him of concern, but in fact gives it back to him. This type of care helps the other to become free for his concern.

If the psychotherapist takes to heart these statements of Heidegger as to how he ought to behave towards his patients, he has already gained the decisive point of view underlying a truly effective therapeutic intervention. Above all, however, the doctor regains a new respect for everything confronting him by absorbing the discoveries of the analysis of Dasein. He also becomes spontaneously aware of the reality presenting itself to him. In an age of radical reduction of all things to the level of calculable elementary particles and quanta of energy, there is special need for an understanding of the 'Being-in-the world'.

REFERENCES

1. BINSWANGER, L., 1953. *Grundformen und Erkenntnis menschlichen Daseins.* 2. Aufl. Zürich: Niehans.
2. BOSS, M., 1952. *Sinn und Gehalt der sexuellen Perversionen.* 2. Aufl. Bern und Stuttgart: Huber.
3. BOSS, M. 1952. Die Bedeutung der Daseinsanalyse für die Psychologie und die Psychiatrie. *Psyche,* **6.**
4. BOSS, M., 1953. *Der Traum und seine Auslegung.* Bern und Stuttgart: Huber.
5. BOSS, M., 1954. *Einführung in die Psychosomatische Medizin.* Bern und Stuttgart: Huber.
6. BOSS, M., 1954. Mechanistic and holistic thinking in modern medicine. *Amer. J. Psychoanal.,* **14.**
7. BOSS, M., 1957. 'Daseinsanalysis' and Psychotherapy. In *Progress in psychotherapy.* New York: Grune and Stratton.
8. BOSS, M., 1959. Martin Heidegger und die Aerzte. In *Martin Heidegger-Festschrift.* Pfullingen: Neske.
9. BOSS, M., 1959. Psychotherapeutischer Beitrag zur Schizophrenielehre. *Congress Report,* II Int. Congr. Psychiatry, Zürich.
10. BOSS, M., 1961. Daseinsanalytische Bemerkungen zu Freuds Vorstellung des 'Unbewussten'. *Zschr. Psycho-somat. Med.,* **7.**
11. BOSS, M., 1962. The conception of man in natural science and in daseinsanalysis. *Comprehensive Psychiatry,* **3.**
12. BOSS, M., 1963. *Psychoanalysis and daseinsanalysis.* New York: Basic Books.
13. BOSS, M., 1963. Gedanken über eine schizophrene Halluzination. *Schweiz. Archiv f. Neurologie, Neurochirurgie und Psychiatrie,* **91.**
14. BOSS, M., 1964. Psychosomatics and Existentialism. *Proc. Third Wld Congr. of Psych.,* **3.**
15. CONDRAU, G., 1960. Die psychotherapeutische Begegnung mit Schuld und Schuldgefühlen. *Praxis,* **21.**
16. CONDRAU, G., 1961. Psychotherapie eines Schreibkrampfes. *Zschr. Psychosomat. Med.,* **7.**
17. CONDRAU, G., 1962. *Angst und Schuld als Grundprobleme der Psychotherapie.* Bern und Stuttgart: Huber.
18. CONDRAU, G., 1963. *Daseinsanalytische Psychotherapie.* Bern und Stuttgart: Huber.
19. CONDRAU, G., 1963. *Einführung in die Psychotherapie.* Solothurn: Antonius.
20. CONDRAU, G., 1964. *Psychosomatik der Frauenheilkunde.* Bern und Stuttgart: Huber.
21. CONDRAU, G., 1965. Daseinsanalyse. In *Psychotherapie und religiöse Erfahrung.* Stuttgart: Hrsg. W. Bitter, Klett.
22. CONDRAU, G., 1965. *Die Daseinsanalyse von Medard Boss und ihre Bedeutung für die Psychiatrie.* Bern und Stuttgart: Huber.
23. CONDRAU, G., 1965. Die philosophischen Grundlagen der Psychotherapie. *Schweizer Rundschau,* **64.**
24. CONDRAU, G., 1966. Angst und Schuld im menschlichen Dasein. *Wege zum Menschen,* **18.**
25. FREUD, S., 1948–52. *Gesammelte Werke.* London: Imago.
26. GABRIEL, L., 1951. *Existenzphilosophie von Kierkegaard bis Sartre.* Wien: Herold.
27. HEIDEGGER, M., 1947. *Uber den Humanismus.* Frankfurt a.M.: Klostermann.
28. HEIDEGGER, M., 1957. *Sein und Zeit.* 8. Aufl. Tübingen: Niemeyer.
29. HUSSERL, E., 1913. *Ideen zu einer reinen Phänomenologie und phänomenologischen Philosophie.*

30. JASPERS, K., 1913. *Allgemeine Psychopathologie.*
31. JASPERS, K., 1919. *Psychologie der Weltanschauungen.*
32. JASPERS, K., 1932. *Philosophie.* 3 Bde.
33. JASPERS, K., 1959. *Der Arzt im technischen Zeitalter.* Schweiz, Aerztezeitung.
34. KIERKEGAARD, S., 1957. *Gesammelte Werke.* Düsseldorf, Köln: Diederichs.
35. MARCEL, G., 1927, 1935. *Journaux métaphysiques.*
36. MARCEL, G., 1935. *Etre et Avoir.*
37. MARCEL, G., 1956. *Was erwarten wir vom Arzt?* Stuttgart: Hippokrates.
38. MARCEL, G., 1960. *Présence et Immortalité.*
39. MAY, R., 1959. The existential approach. *American Handbook of Psychiatry,* vol. 2. New York: Basic Books.
40. MERLEAU-PONTY, M., 1945. *Phénoménologie de la perception.* Gallimard.
41. MÜLLER, M., 1964. *Existenzphilosophie im geistigen Leben der Gegenwart.* 3. Aufl. Heidelberg: Kerle.
42. RICOEUR, P., 1949. *Philosophie de la volonté.* Paris: Montaigne.
44. SARTRE, J. P., 1946. *L'existentialisme est un humanisme.*
43. SARTRE, J. P., 1943. *L'Etre et le néant.*
45. SARTRE, J. P., 1938. *La nausée.*
46. WAELHENS, A., DE, 1950. La phénoménologie du corps. *Rev. philos. de Louvain,* **48.**

XVIII

MORITA'S THEORY OF NEUROSIS AND ITS APPLICATION IN JAPANESE PSYCHOTHERAPY

Kazuyoshi Ikeda, M.D.

Professor of Psychiatry
Kyushu University
Japan

1

The Theory of Nervosity

History

Morita's theory of nervosity[11, 12] and his psychotherapy (Morita therapy) were originated in 1918 by Dr S. Morita, then professor of Tokyo Jikeikai Medical College and were evolved by Dr M. Shimoda, emeritus professor of Kyushu University, Dr T. Kora and others.

It should be specially emphasized that this theory was the direct result of Morita's thinking on the question of a new aetiology for the development of a neurosis. As outlined in this paper, he introduced some characteristic ideas into the construction of the theory and his therapeutic practice, based on his profound knowledge of Buddhism.

Since then, this theory has been practised and re-examined extensively at his own University and at Kyushu University, and by some psychiatrists practising privately. Recently many Japanese psychiatrists have begun to pay more attention to it. The seventh issue of the *Japanese Journal of Psychiatry*, for instance, was a special one and consisted entirely of a report on Morita's theory and its practice; what follows is derived from my own contribution.[4] At the formal session of the Joint Meeting of the Japanese and American Psychiatric Associations, in 1963, Dr Nomura and the writer read reports about Morita therapy and its socio-cultural background.[5, 13]

Outside Japan, Dr Jacobson discussed Morita's theory in its report on Japanese psychiatry and psychotherapy in the *American Journal of Psychiatry 1952*.[8] Dr Kondo, one of the staff of Jikeikai Medical University wrote a report on it in the *American Journal of Psychoanalysis 1953*.[9] In 1958 Dr Kato read a report about this therapy at one of the sections of the International Congress of Psychotherapy in Spain.

Definition of Symptoms and Aetiology

In the earlier days when Morita first formulated his theory, the term neurasthenia had been generally used in Japanese medical practice, but contained ambiguities. The essential meaning of neurasthenia, proposed by Dr Beard in 1869, is the state of irritable exhaustion or enfeeblement of the central nervous system. Every chronic somatic disease and natural physiological fatigue, therefore, may produce this symptom. Following the trend prevalent in Germany in those days, attempts were made to treat this condition by biological means ignoring the real psychogenesis of the disorder. But there are many cases of so-called neurasthenia which have no special somatic cause and do not improve in spite of such treatment or long rest. Morita discovered that in some cases the symptom evolved through certain psychogenic mechanisms unrelated to exhaustion or enfeeblement of central nervous system and belonging to the same psychopathological unit. As the starting point of his theory he named such symptom-complexes, 'nervosity'. The following four important factors have been pointed out by Morita in the evolution of nervosity.

Premorbid personality. The symptoms of nervosity easily appear in people who have the character traits similar to those of the introvert postulated by Jung and called the 'hypochondriacal temperament' by Morita. The central pattern of this personality is, according to Dr Shimoda, the tendency towards insufficient feeling about the self. Such people, therefore, are hypersensitive, highly perfectionistic and idealistic in their acts and thoughts, attend easily to their own psychic and somatic phenomena and often believe that their normal physiological phenomena are due to serious disease or weakness (hypochondriacal interpretation).

According to Morita this tendency is the normal expression of the human drive for living and is not fundamentally abnormal. Moreover one of the cardinal points of his theory is that, as we discuss later, this character of patients who suffer from nervosity is accepted by Morita as probably part of the normal patterns of human existence. This view of the human being, in one sense optimistic and in another pessimistic, is the guiding principle of his unique psychotherapy.

Psychic interaction. Fundamentally this means the interaction between attention and sensation; for instance, the more keenly one pays attention to a sensation, the more poignantly it will be felt. At the same time, attention will be fixed more strongly to the sensation, thus often lowering its function and developing naturally into the vicious circle of attention and sensation.

People of hypochondriacal temperament usually direct their attention to their own mental or physical condition and function, or to social behaviour. Further, they come to believe that their normal physiological disturbances are abnormal or pathological (hypochondriacal interpretation) and so develop the intrapsychic interaction. Once this mechanism does start, autosuggestion, anticipated anxious expectation and so on may together reinforce this process.

The psychological situation from which nervosity patients are suffering, therefore, are the states that are seen in normal people. The important difference between the patient and the normal people is that the former interprets his condition intuitively to be something abnormal, harmful to his existence and tries to get rid of them in vain. The difference might be, so to speak, quantitative.

Hypochondriacal experience. This is one of the experiences which acts as a precipitating factor and releases the psychic interaction. This unpleasant, unfavourable experience occurs usually accidentally in the daily life of a patient and compels him to doubt or reflect upon his physical or mental health, or his interpersonal behaviour. Most people have such experiences in their lives, but only those of hypochondriacal temperament develop psychic interaction; most people can deal efficiently with such experiences, thus avoiding fixation.

The three factors mentioned above constitute the formal psychogenic elements of this neurosis, and are demonstrated in Fig. 1.

Contradiction of thoughts. This refers to the irresoluble contradiction which exists between emotion and intelligence, understanding and conviction, objective and subjective facts, and so on. It is, in other words, the mistaken attitude of always trying to reconcile, in an intellectual way, one's irrational and illogical emotions rationally and logically. For example, a patient, in attempting to reconcile the eventual inevitability of death with his natural fear of it, finds himself in an impasse, not amenable to intellectualization. By putting it out of his mind, he persuades himself that the problem is solved. This is one of the well-known obstacles, very difficult to manage, often observed in practising the discipline of Buddhism.

In the development of nervosity, this fourth factor plays a counteracting role which increasingly excites the psychic interaction. The patient, for instance, may sometimes become conscious of the existence of this cycle and begin to turn in the opposite direction to minimize his symptoms. His family, friends, and even his doctor may advise him 'not to worry about it', or 'not to pay too much attention to it', although it is something he is already quite naturally worrying about.

This counteracting suppression, or denial of his symptom, is the most important dynamic factor which energizes the psychic interaction and makes it possible for it to continue and develop for a long time. Without such counteraction the cycle of interaction would not develop to the degree of a neurotic disturbance.

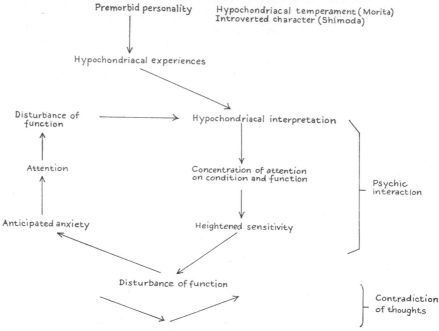

FIG. 1. Development of Symptom.

Comparison with Psychoanalysis

It would be useful to follow the above brief explanation of the psychogenic mechanism of nervosity postulated by Morita and, to make it more clear, compare it with Freud's theory using the terminology of dynamic psychiatry.

As is well known, the psychoanalytic theory of neurosis and personality development postulates conflicts between functionally different mental layers, for example, between Id and Ego, Ego and Superego, and so on. According to Freud, these conflicts often threaten the whole integration of personality, the result being felt by the Ego usually as anxiety. To maintain personality integrity or to avoid its further disintegration, the Ego adopts many kinds of defence mechanisms against this anxiety. The sum of these characteristic defence techniques adopted unconsciously by the Ego decides the pattern of neurotic disorders. This is the psychoanalytic theory of neurosis simply summarized.

If Morita's theory is described in the frame of the psychoanalytic hypothesis, nervosity does not arise in the conflicts between the Ego and the Id or Superego, but just within the structure of the Ego itself. It is within one of the most important parts of the Ego, broadly its intellectual function, that the dynamics of the possible development of Morita's process can be found, especially in those people of hypochondriacal temperament.

The origin of Morita's neurosis, therefore, exists nearer to consciousness, in the relatively superficial layer of the psyche—in Ego function—while the psychogenesis according to Freud should be found in the deep and unconscious layer of the psyche. Or using the conception of ego psychology postulated by Federn,[1] one could say that the pathogenesis of nervosity is an example of the overstrengthening of ego boundary cathexes. These differences naturally characterize both the symptoms of nervosity and Morita's therapy. As might be supposed from such a pathogenesis, the development of this neurosis increases suddenly at the age of adolescence when the Ego function differentiates rapidly and thus becomes more unstable.

One of the important conclusions, which might be deduced from comparing these two theories, is that Morita's theory is not inconsistent with the other and vice versa, but each restricts the field of neurosis covered by the other theory. Here the writer cannot agree that the development of every neurosis can be explained by the psychoanalytic hypothesis, much less by Morita's theory or by any other theory of neurosis. We have arrived at this position in the practice of both psychoanalytic treatment and Morita therapy. This is also the reason for both theories and therapeutic practices co-existing in our clinic. We treat some by the psychoanalytic method and some with Morita therapy according to each one's psychopathology. Of course, considering the nature of psychic process, it is probable that the symptoms of nervosity might overlay the others although the reverse seems unlikely.

Differential Diagnosis of Nervosity

These comparative considerations of his theory in the context of psychoanalytic theory were not enough in Morita's theoretical discussion and he discussed in his books, though insufficiently, the important problem of the differential diagnosis of nervosity.

As mentioned above, the writer believes that not only are there many neuroses which may be explained clearly by the psychoanalytic hypothesis, but also some others explainable by Morita's mechanism and perhaps others. Nervosity is differentiated by carefully considering the following points.

Premorbid personality. The hypochondriacal temperament may be found in many cases.

Hypochondriacal experience. Some patients can easily remember the precipitating factor from which their complaints began; in others it can be elicited only in the course of repeated interviews, and in others not at all.

Of course the psychic interaction may begin without any direct traumatic experience.

Development of symptoms. This is very important; often it will be possible to trace the gradual development of symptoms in the life history of patients through the psychic interaction, autosuggestion and contradiction of thoughts. Sometimes they are recognized by the patient or might become evident to him through the therapeutic instruction of his therapist. One can also rule out this diagnosis by finding different developmental processes.

Present status. (*a*) *Types of nervosity.* Morita classified three clinical subgroups—simple nervosity (neurasthenic state), obsessive phobic state and paroxysmal state. Their occurrence in 821 cases in the Psychiatric Clinic of Kyushu University between 1928–37 are shown in Fig. 2.[10]

FIG. 2

The Symptoms of Nervosity

Symptom	Case	%
A. NEURASTHENIC STATE (515 CASES)		
Feeling of pressure on the head	217	41·8
Poor memory	186	35·8
Disorder of sleep	159	30·6
Headache	99	19·1
Physical and mental fatiguability	45	8·7
Dizziness	44	8·5
Poor concentration	45	8·7
Difficulty in thinking, making decisions and understanding	37	6·6
Impotence	34	6·5
Langour	30	5·8
Feeling of clouding of consciousness	27	5·2
Irritability	27	5·2
Tinnitus	25	4·8
Nocturnal emission	25	4·8
Tension feeling in shoulder	24	4·6
Premature ejaculation	18	3·5
Abnormal sensation	15	2·9
Gastro-intestinal complaints	15	2·9
B. OBSESSIVE PHOBIC STATE (262 CASES)		
Fear of disease	85	32·4
Fear of people	43	16·4
Fear of blushing	33	12·6
Fear of dirt	26	9·9
Persistent doubting	26	9·9
Fear of ugliness	15	5·7
Persistent unwelcome thoughts	14	5·3
Fear of committing crime	11	4·2

Fear of being watched closely	..	..	..	8	3·1
Fear of acting	..	..	..	7	2·7
Fear of pointed things	..	..	..	5	1·9
Fear of bacteria	..	..	..	6	2·3
Fear of spaces..	..	..	..	4	1·5
Fear of high places ..	..	..	..	3	1·1

C. PAROXYSMAL STATE (40 CASES)

Fit of palpitation	..	..	..	23	57·5
Fit of difficulty in breathing	..	..	8	20·0
Fit of dizziness	..	..	..	6	15·0
Fit of vomiting	..	..	..	4	10·0

The terms 'phobia' and 'obsessive neurosis' are so popular that one usually thinks only of those neuroses caused by Freud's mechanism. Morita used the terms to describe subgroups of his neurosis without sufficiently considering the theoretical relationship between his and Freud's theories. This greatly confused the discussion between practitioners of the psychoanalytic and of Morita's techniques at the Japanese Psychiatric Association meeting in 1935 and subsequently. They could reach no common conclusion as a result of describing similarly named, but psychopathologically different, symptoms.

The obsessive phobic state mentioned above is caused by ego dysfunction and differs clinically from those phobic and obsessive compulsive neuroses described by Freud.[2] The former usually begins with obsessive thinking (as deduced from the function of the ego), often accompanied by secondary obsessive feeling and compulsive behaviour and especially characteristics 1, 2, 3 below.

(b) Symptomatology.

1. Content of symptom is clear and definite.

Of course the symptoms of nervosity may change during the patient's life, but at any one time they are relatively clear and definite. The clinical features of other neuroses in which the symptoms are ambiguous, often unclear to the patient himself, floating and changing from time to time, will not usually be observed.

2. The qualitative nature of the symptom is within the limit of normal physiology and psychology.

It is not always easy to decide the limit of normal and abnormal, but if one observes the irrational and bizarre symptoms which are often found in phobic or obsessive neuroses caused by Freud's mechanism, one can differentiate them from nervosity.

3. The intensity of symptom fluctuates logically according to the changing environment of the patient.

4. Anxiety and depression are, in nervosity, of a secondary nature.

So-called anxiety and depressive feeling observed in the patient with nervosity can be recognized as being originally reactive or secondary to certain thoughts, interpretations or anticipations. It might be more correct to use the word fear instead of anxiety, since the symptom is really different from that of real free floating, objectless anxiety often observed in Freud's neuroses. Similarly, depression in nervosity is also different from that of endogenous depression. They may and must be differentiated clinically.[3]

5. Insight.

Patients with nervosity usually have clear insight into their disease and its symptoms.

6. There are big differences between subjective complaints and objective disturbances. Of course, the former is usually more severe than the latter.

7. The attitude of the patient towards treatment is usually very earnest.

The factors mentioned above must be considered as a whole. In general, patients suffering from nervosity give us the impression of being intelligent, moderate and obedient people.

2

Morita Therapy

Fundamental Principle of Morita Therapy

As may be supposed from the psychopathology of nervosity mentioned above, three important therapeutic factors must be realized throughout the whole process of treatment, (*i*) developing patient's insight of his own personality, (*ii*) breaking up of the psychic interaction, and (*iii*) solution of contradiction of thoughts.

For this purpose, specially schemed therapeutic situation including physical work and necessary instructions is introduced. Using the technique of direct, intellectual approach on the one hand, the therapy tries, on the other, to make the patient jump over the limit, where the intellectual approach usually comes to a deadlock, by his self conviction acquired through the therapeutic experience.

Stages of Treatment

First stage: *Period of absolute bed rest* (4–10 *days*). The realization of the therapeutic factor (c) is particularly aimed at in this stage. The patient is prohibited from reading, writing (except diary), speaking or doing anything to pass away the time and is deprived of stimuli from the outer world, left alone to think about anything that emerges from his mind without resisting it, thus minimizing the room for contradiction of thoughts and letting the psychic interaction work as purely as possible.

By continuing this attitude strictly, the psychic interaction which had never declined as long as the contradiction of thoughts had counteracted against it, begins to recede into the background, that is, feeling of ennui and desire for work appear in the mind of the patient usually by 5–7 days. This sort of absolute rest also plays the role of stimulating activity of patients who have in fact no organic disturbance. During this period, the patient is asked to write a diary about whatever he likes, within an hour before his sleep. The content of the diary often gives important information to the therapist and enables him to give necessary instructions at the adequate moment, or to modify the subsequent treatment procedure. Instructions are given verbally or written in the diary.

This period is also important as an aid to diagnosis; while the patient suffering from nervosity can usually conform to the instructions, the other patients suffering from, for instance, hysteria, early schizophrenia or depression, often cannot accept this rest, or continue it without feeling ennui at all.

Second stage: *Period of light work* (1–2 *weeks*). This is the stage in which the patient passes from rest to work. Breaking up of psychic inter-action cycle (b) must be achieved mainly through the patient's act, which has necessarily no direct relation with symptoms. This method for solving spiritual problems using the attitude directed to the relatively simple but realistic physical conduct, has been well known in the process of Buddhist religious training. Of course the technique of this therapy has nothing to do with Buddhism. The kind of work may be decided according to the situation of the hospital, but in general the work which necessitates the concentration of attention and the result of which may be seen by a patient, for instance, polishing of the glass cover of a microscope, is desirable at this stage. The work is requested to be done perfectly disregarding the quantity achieved. At first, the quantity of the work should be so arranged that it leaves the patient still wanting to do something more.

Third stage: *Period of moderate work* (2–4 *weeks*). This period is the extension of the previous one. The patient is allowed to perform some moderately heavy work, but physical work is still desirable. Reading, speaking and every communication with the outerworld must still be prohibited. The patient, therefore, continues his physical work in a psychologically isolated environment.

After making sure that the subjective symptoms have disappeared and that normal life is possible in spite of some symptoms still remaining, treatment passes to the next period. The whole term of treatment usually depends on the duration of this third stage.

Fourth stage: *Period of preparing for normal life* (1–3 *weeks*). This final stage is to prepare the patient for a return to a complex social life. All therapeutic restrictions are taken off at the beginning of this period. The patient is encouraged to go out of the hospital for shopping, for meeting with his friends or for staying at his home for a few days.

The necessary instructions and interpretations given by the therapist vary from case to case, from stage to stage, but of course have to be derived from fundamental therapeutic principles.

Recovery

The process of recovery also varies from patient to patient. It appears, however, that there are three essential courses of recovery. In one type, the patient achieves insight suddenly, often during the second or third stage. From that point on the recovery is rapid. In the second type, improvement begins almost immediately and continues gradually to the final goal. In the third type, recovery is achieved with some relapses (Fig. 3).

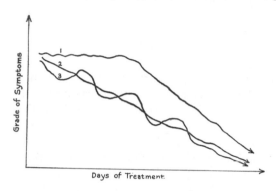

FIG. 3. Courses of Recovery.

There are also many mild cases who might be treated as out-patients using the standard method mentioned above, but modified to a simple one.

Results

The two examples of the result of treatment are shown in Fig. 4 and Fig. 5.

FIG. 4.
Results of treatment (1951)

	No. of Cases	Cured	Improved	Unchanged	Stopped treatment	Complicated by other diseases
Simple nervosity	38	30	2	2	3	1
Obsessive phobic state	60	44	5	4	5	2
Paroxysmal state	7	6	1	0	0	0
Total per cent (per cent)	105	80 (76·2)	8 (7·6)	6 (5·7)	8 (7·6)	3 (2·9)

Days of treatment
The longest   180 days
The shortest   13 days
Average   73 days

FIG. 5
Results of Morita Therapy (1959)

	No. of Cases	Cured	Improved	Unchanged
Nervosity	27	20 (74·1 %)	7	
Anxiety neurosis	2		2	
Phobia	3		3	
Hypochondriasis	2		2	
Conversion hysteria	1		1	
Total	35	20 (57·1)	15	

Days of Treatment
Over 3 months   7
1–3 months   28

The above Fig. 4, which includes many out-patients, shows the statistics presented by the writer in 1951, and referred to by Jacobson in his report.[8] Fig 5 shows the result obtained reported at the Annual Meeting of the Japanese Psychiatric Association 1959, and includes only in-patients and also eight cases of neurosis caused by so-called Freud's machanism, treated by this method. That the results obtained by this treatment differs according to the kind of neuroses, as might be supposed theoretically, has already been pointed out by us. [6, 7]

All reports about the result of this therapy which have been published in Japan have quoted cure rates of 60–70 per cent.

REFERENCES

1. FEDERN, P., 1953. *Ego psychology and psychoses.* London: Imago.
2. IKEDA, K., 1956. Obsessive symptoms of neuroses. In *Progress of psychiatry.* Tokyo: Medical and Dental Publishing Co.
3. IKEDA, K., 1958. Psychopathological Study on Anxiety. *Annual Report of Education Faculty*, Kyushu University, No. 5.
4. IKEDA, K., 1959. Morita's nervosity and Morita therapy. *Jap. J. Psychiat.*, **1.**
5. IKEDA, K., 1963. Psychotherapy in Japan, *Proceedings of the Joint Meeting of the Japanese Society of Psychiatry and Neurology and the American Psychiatric Association.*
6. IKEDA, K., and SAKURAI, T., 1959. *Annual Report of the Japanese Psychiatric Association.*
7. IKEDA, K., SASAKI, Y., and KURAUCHI, K., 1955. Study on neuroses. *The Kyushu Neuro-Psychiatry*, **4.**
8. JACOBSON, A., 1952. Japanese psychiatry and psychotherapy. *Am. J. Psychiat.*, **109**, 4.

9. KONDO, A., 1953. Morita therapy, a Japanese therapy for neuroses. *Am. J. Psychoanal.*, **13.**

10. MIKURIYA, I., 1938. *The statistics of nervosity.* Memorial Report for the late Prof. Morita.

11. MORITA, S., 1921. Therapy of Neurasthenia and Nervosity. *Japanese Psychiatric Association.*

12. MORITA, S., 1928. *Pathogenesis and therapy of nervosity.* Memorial Report for Prof. Kure, Tokyo.

13. NOMURA, A., 1963. Morita Therapy. *Proceedings of the Joint Meeting of the Japanese Society of Psychiatry and Neurology and the American Psychiatric Association.*

XIX

THE PAVLOVIAN THEORY IN PSYCHIATRY: SOME RECENT DEVELOPMENTS*

K. K. Monakhov,

Chief of Laboratory of Neurophysiology
Institute of Psychiatry,
Academy of Medical Sciences of the USSR,
Moscow

1

Introduction

Pavlov's theory has attracted the attention of many investigators for over fifty years. Though Pavlov himself worked with animals only, his theory has been applied both by himself and by others to the study of both normal and abnormal human behaviour.

During the last fifty years, for a number of reasons, the popularity of Pavlov's theory has been waxing and waning. Sometimes the application of Pavlovian techniques brought many new results as, for example, in Ivanov-Smolensky's studies of different groups of mental patients. His findings encouraged others to work in a similar direction. But this approach gradually lost its appeal because of its limited possibilities; new technical advances were needed. Science had to go beyond the mere study of peripheral stimuli and responses in order to acquire an understanding of the functioning of the central nervous system. However, neurophysiology itself has only recently become preoccupied with the integrated functioning of the organism-as-a-whole, whereas previously it studied only isolated functions and/or structures. In the study of the physiology of the human brain the basic task is to find practical applications in medicine, in education and in applied psychology, of the newly discovered regular activities of the brain. Only in the early stages of its development can brain research do without a comprehensive theory. Later a theory is needed to explain brain activity as an integrated functioning and as the expression of the

*Translated by Dr Robert Pos, University of Toronto.

highest form of adaptation of the organism. To many investigators Pavlov's theory fits this purpose and this may account for a renewed interest in it. The question arises, of course, as to whether Pavlov's concepts have become obsolete in the light of modern neurophysiology as they were evolved at an early stage of our knowledge in this field. This paper will attempt to show that they are not obsolete. Let us first examine some of Pavlov's basic concepts.[28–33]

The conditioned reflex, or temporal bond, is viewed as the mechanism for the most subtle and flexible adaptation of the organism to its environment on one hand, and for the internal regulations within the organism, on the other.

However, the conditioned reflex is not an isolated phenomenon, but an expression of the integrated functioning of the brain-as-a-whole.

Finally, the organism does not represent an isolated system, and its functioning can be understood only as the product of continuous interaction between organism and environment.

We believe that one of Pavlov's most important contributions is his attempt to study, for the first time, life-experience through neurophysiological methods, thus establishing a physiological approach to normal and abnormal psychological functions, which previously had constituted the sole realm of psychology. We do not believe that Pavlov's teaching represents the ultimate truth, but we tend to feel that there are not many other (if any) theories which enable us to study the higher integrated nervous activity in such a logical fashion and on the basis of physiological methods.

Because of his interest in psychiatry, Pavlov attempted to apply his concepts based on the results of his work with animals, to clinical syndromes, by regarding them as multiple pathological variations of the functions which he had subjected to physiological investigations. His first work on this subject was *Psychiatry as an aid to the Physiology of the Cerebral Hemispheres* published in 1919. Pavlov's interest in psychological phenomena (though he did not allow the use of psychological formulations) brought him to the Psychiatric Clinic in Leningrad where he attempted to apply his early experimental findings to psychopathological functioning. This in turn focused his attention on pathological behaviour in animals and led to his research into the experimental neuroses of animals. The results of this, once again, were applied to the understanding of human psychopathology.

A physiologist's first trip into the Field of Psychiatry, On neuroses in men and animals, An attempt to interpret the symptomatology of hysteria in a physiological way, Passivity feelings and the ultraparadoxical phase and *An attempt to interpret the obsessive neurosis and paranoia in a physiological way* were all published between 1927 and 1934, and contributed a great deal to the further development of the investigation of mental activity in men.

In the meantime Professor Ivanov-Smolenski, following in the footsteps of Pavlov, began to investigate the higher nervous activity in psychiatric patients. Such work by him, as well as by others, is still continuing.

Basic Concepts of Higher Nervous Activity

In order to understand Ivanov-Smolenski's[13] work we will first consider briefly some of the basic concepts of higher nervous activity. In the Pavlovian sense, the concept of 'excitation' applies to the integrated total state of the central nervous system, if the organism is in the process of acting or responding. The Pavlovian concept of 'inhibition' applies when no acting or responding is taking place. These concepts should not be confused with the neurophysiological concepts of excitation and inibition which pertain to individual units, or groups of units, in the central nervous system itself and not to the nervous system as a whole.

In terms of Pavlovian inhibition, a distinction is made between 'active inhibition' which is thought to arise as the result of special training, and 'passive inhibition' resulting from the suppression of one activity by another, or from exhaustion. Unfortunately, so far there have been few detailed investigations into the neurophysiology of the integrated processes of inhibition and excitation, so that little information about their neurophysiological nature is available. It should be understood that the functional state of the nervous system, at any given moment, is thought to represent a complex integrated combination of both inhibition and excitation and that the equilibrium between these processes shifts continuously and changes from moment to moment.

The higher nervous processes are generally given three attributes:

1. *The intensity of the nervous process.* This refers to the strength, or intensity of the conditioned response, as well as to the length of the latency period in an excitatory process between stimulus and response. In an inhibitory process, it refers to some form of measurement indicating how stable the non-reacting to a stimulus is.

2. *The flexibility of the nervous process* indicates how easily a process of positive conditioning or excitation can be replaced by one of negative conditioning or inhibition, and vice versa.

3. *The equilibrium of the nervous process.* This indicates how far there is a lack of predominance of the positive over the negative conditioning, or vice versa, during a certain conditioning procedure. It may or may not indicate a more generalized tendency of the organism.

Pavlov viewed the central nervous system in terms of certain functional levels, a theoretical approach which was further developed by Ivanov-Smolenski, who sees the higher nervous activity as the result of interaction between the first and the second signal system and the functional activity of the subcortical structures. Pavlov defined 'the first signal system' as the functional system which receives and deals with the immediate concrete stimuli or signals, such as light, sound, interoceptive stimuli, etc. 'The second signal system', which is considered to be specific for the human being, handles symbols usually in the form of words, whether heard, seen, written, spoken or thought. Through it the outside world is interiorized.

This system plays, of course, a very significant role in human communication and in interaction with the environment. Pavlov thought that the subcortical structures were the source of energy for cortical activity, though at different times he assumed a direct participation of the subcortex in the establishment of conditioned reflexes, even when he could not yet have been aware of the important cortical-subcortical connections, which came to light in the more recent investigations of the reticular system. Further investigation of the importance of subcortical-cortical connections for conditioned brain activity may also contribute significantly to our understanding of the higher nervous activity. In this activity the function of conditioned closure, i.e. the ability to form new temporal bonds, is, of course, of primary importance.

When dealing with both healthy and ill people we always find, of course, an already established system of conditioned reflexes developed during previous life experience. This system may be interfered with by a pathological process in some way or another and in different degrees of severity. Yet, in general, the state of the pre-existing system of conditioned reflexes is not estimated by the usual clinical methods of investigation of higher nervous activity, except perhaps, for certain psychological tests, such as the word association test, or the clinical method of free association, which may be analysed with Pavlovian methods. Rather, the methods of investigation are designed to determine the capacity of the brain to form new temporal connections. It is not difficult to establish a conditioned reflex in a normal waking person, but in certain physiological states, such as sleep, or during some activity in which an individual is engaged, we fail to establish conditioned reflexes. In the first case (sleep) the cortex is in a state of inhibition, while in the second (activity) the involved structures spread inhibition to structures not so engaged (external inhibition by induction).

In mental disorders the function of conditioned closure may be affected in different degrees. Not only may there be a failure to establish new temporal bonds within a constantly changing environment, but there may be also an inadequate usage of previous experience, which in normal individuals is constantly being related to newly established conditioned reflexes. These disorders of conditioned closure in the mentally ill may be caused by many different factors in varying combinations, such as unfavourable environmental conditions, psychological traumata, and overstrain and exhaustion of the nervous system resulting from working conditions, or insufficient rest. But they may be caused also by acute or chronic pathological processes, such as infections, intoxications and metabolic disorders.

Environmental conditions may be 'unfavourable' in the sense that most, if not all, people would react to them by becoming distressed. In this case the pre-existing system of conditioned reflexes contains a widely shared, or 'cultural', set of temporary bonds. But the conditions may also be 'unfavourable' in a more individual sense corresponding to a more unique set of life-experiences of the individual.

The breakdown in the function of conditioned closure may proceed along different lines depending not only on the various causes, but also on previous life experience, i.e. the pre-existing system of conditioned reflexes, and, finally, on the complexities of the conditioned reflexes involved in the process of breakdown. This complexity of conditioned reflexes may be illustrated by the following three aspects. First of all the character of the conditioned stimulus itself: to which system is it addressing itself? Is the stimulus 'direct' or 'concrete', i.e. addressing the first signal system? Or is it 'symbolic' or 'indirect', i.e. addressing the second signal system? What is its modality or its modalities, what is its physical intensity? Secondly: which type of reinforcement has been used? Electrocutaneous stimulation, a verbal order, etc. Again, the absolute intensity of the reinforcing stimulus is of great importance. Thirdly, the character of the response which enables us to detect the presence or absence of a temporal connection. It should not be forgotten that the conditioned response always consists of many components reflecting the participation of various organ-systems, such as respiratory, cardio-vascular, motor, or speech components. That is, a response is always a reaction of the organism-as-a-whole representing a particular, integrated, combined state of inhibition and excitation. In some instances one or another component may be manifest, but more commonly several components can be observed. For example, in attempting to establish a motor reflex we may fail to register a movement, yet the respiratory, or cardio-vascular, component will indicate the presence of a conditioned reaction.

Having stressed the state of the nervous system at any given moment as an integrated particular balance of excitation and inhibition; the intensity, flexibility and equilibrium as the three aspects of the higher nervous processes; the ability to establish new temporary bonds and their relation to the pre-existing system of conditioned reflexes; and, finally, the complexities of the conditioned reflex in terms of the characteristics of the stimulus, the reinforcement and the response—we should now state that pathological processes may involve changes in all these respects. Space does not permit us to discuss the possible disorders to the fullest extent. Therefore, we shall limit discussion to the well-known method of conditioning of the motor reaction with verbal reinforcement, a method developed by Ivanov-Smolenski.

Conditioning of the Motor Reaction

The procedure is as follows: a visual or auditory stimulus is presented to the subject accompanied by the verbal order of the experimenter 'press the button'. The particular button is a part of a reflexometer, which measures the strength of the muscular movement, and which is within reach of the subject. The verbal order 'push the button' is considered as reinforcement. If after a few trials the subject pushes the button before this verbal order is given, a second verbal order, 'you are doing all right', is given as further reinforcement. The conditioned reflex is considered to be stable if within ten trials the subject pushes the button before the verbal order 'push the button' is presented. In normal subjects, as a rule, the temporary bond is established within two or three trials.

A failure to establish a conditioned reaction in patients with 'catatonic schizophrenia' was first described by R. A. Grekker in 1911.[10] In more recent days and with somewhat different methods many investigators, notably Ivanov-Smolenski and his co-workers, also studied conditioned closure in schizophrenic patients. They noticed that this function is most seriously affected in cases of catatonic stupors, though even in these patients new temporal connections can be established with the aid of special techniques. In these patients the formation of the conditioned reflex, as well as the conditioned reflex itself, remain nevertheless different, i.e. abnormal. In patients with purely paranoid and hallucinatory-paranoid syndromes of schizophrenia temporary connections can be more easily established, though they often remain inhibited. This function is seriously impaired in advanced schizophrenic deteriorations: both negative (inhibitory) and positive (excitatory) temporal connections are formed very slowly and they remain unstable. Positive connections often disappear in spite of reinforcement, though they may be restored in a further experiment. A similar pattern may also be found in oligophrenia and certain dementias (e.g. general paresis, epilepsy). In manic-depressive psychosis the pattern is again different. In manic states the positive connections appear more readily, but often disappear, apparently under the influence of a very vivid and unstable orienting reflex (negative induction of external inhibition). Yet, in these states, negative or inhibitory connections can only be established with difficulty and, frequently, not at all. In depressive states the formation of new positive temporal bonds is retarded and unstable, but inhibitory connections are easily provoked.

In involutional depressions both the positive (excitatory) and the negative (inhibitory) temporal connections are only established with difficulty, but once present they seem to be inert, that is, they can hardly be changed, so that the flexibility of the higher nervous processes seems affected.

Studies with this particular method (which has found widespread use in the USSR) have thrown an interesting light on the function of closure of temporary bonds, and on the way in which this function is disturbed in a number of mental illnesses. Generalizations are possible as to the function of closure, but should eventually be supported by further investigations through a variety of different methods.

With the use of this method, however, it has also been found that in many mental diseases the equilibrium between excitation and inhibition is disturbed, in that, as a rule, there is a predominance of the inhibitory processes, i.e., a rather diffuse inhibition, apparently involving many different situations in which the system under study, i.e. the motor system, may be involved. This phenomenon may be interpreted as a defensive mechanism which protects the brain against excessive strain and exhaustion.

When studied with the above described methods, the interaction between the first and second signal systems, which plays such an important role in higher nervous activity, is also found to be affected in the mentally ill, in various ways and to different degrees.

Although the results of these studies have given us some idea of disordered higher nervous activity in various mental illnesses, they tell us nothing about their pathogenesis. However, they have provided the clinician with some objective criteria in evaluating a mental illness. While the work of Ivanov-Smolenski *et al.* on a particular kind of conditioned reflex activity has given us a sensitive indicator of the state of a mental illness, it unfortunately does not tell us anything about the neurophysiological phenomena in the core of the nervous system. Technical advances, especially in the field of electronic recording devices, have made this type of further research possible. At the same time this necessitated the development of new scientific methods of data acquirement and analysis.

Electrical Activity

In an effort to obtain information about the electrical activity during various conditioning procedures, a number of research workers began attempts to study the electrophysiological phenomena of the brain during the performance of various kinds of higher nervous activity.

One of the first publications on this subject came from Laptev (1941),[16] who concluded that neither the complexity of the biopotentials on the surface of the brain, nor their constant changeability permits us to evaluate any specific changes taking place during the conditioning process. Livanov (1951).[19] however, pointed out that Laptev's work showed an uneven distribution of electrical activity during the course of conditioning; he was able to observe in a number of cases a reciprocal relationship between the motor and the visual areas of the brain. In 1945 a publication by Livanov and Polyakov revealed the presence in the brains of rabbits of synchronized rhythms during conditioning with repetitive stimulus; this synchronization apparently arose long before the appearance of the conditioned response, e.g. motor response. As this synchronization emerged in almost all brain structures it was named 'the generalized synchronization of rhythms'. Livanov felt that synchronization of brain rhythms was one of the essential features of the conditioning process. Later he studied the distribution of this phenomenon.

More recent works by other authors described a double-phased bioelectrical reaction, during the development of conditioned bonds, i.e. a primary phase of desynchronization of electric activity followed by secondary phase of synchronized slow wave activity (M. I. Vinogradov and V. S. Vorobjeva, 1954;[38] A. M. Maruseva and L. A. Tchistovitch, 1954;[23] Gastaut *et al.* 1957;[5] E. F. Polezhaev, 1959;[35] R. S. Mnukhina, 1957,[24] and others).

Other workers established the existence of temporary bonds between certain electrical brain activities, as, for example, the blocking of rhythm by light, and some non-specific stimulus in this respect, as, for example, sound (e.g. Morell and Jasper, 1956).[26] These temporary connections, though conditioned in nature, cannot be called conditioned reflexes in the strict Pavlovian sense because their biological significance, including their adaptive value, is not yet clear.

The study of evoked potentials during conditioning processes has also received attention. Some authors (Hernandez-Peon *et al.*, 1956;[11] Peimer, 1958)[34] reported an increase in amplitude of these potentials (for example as a response to light after the stimulation had been linked for a period with a reinforcement stimulus, such as a verbal order); while others found a marked decrease (Roitbakh, 1958;[36] Kogan, 1958).[14] It is Mnukhina's opinion (1964)[25] that evoked potentials decrease at the beginning of conditioning, whereas they increase at later stages.

Spatial Inter-relationship

While all such studies are making interesting contributions toward our knowledge of the electrical activity of the brain, particularly of the cortex, and especially during the establishment of temporary bonds, they do not reveal the mechanism of the conditioned reflex itself. They tell us something about localized or general events, i.e. diffusely occurring electrical phenomena in the brain during conditioning, but they fail to inform us about the topographical spatial inter-relationships which take place in the brain as-a-whole during the conditioning process. However, since 1945 (Livanov and Polyakov)[18] and more specifically in their recent publications (Livanov, 1962a,[20] 1962b).[21] Livanov and his co-workers have been paying attention to these spatial relationships. This approach has greater appeal, for in final analysis the conditioned reflex remains a connection of two, or several, functions, requiring a complicated topographical co-ordination and integration of total brain functioning. Therefore, the question is not that of specific electrical activity of a particular brain area, nor that of diffusely occurring activity, but that of a consistently occurring relationship between the activity of several, if not all, brain areas.

An initial approach to this very complicated problem may be an attempt to correlate the electrical activity of a number of brain regions in a quantitative fashion, as an expression of conditioned closure.

Research shows that, initially, during the conditioning process there is a considerable similarity in the electrical activity of a great many brain areas, but this similarity becomes gradually restricted to the brain areas which are most directly concerned with the conditioned functioning. This pertains both to positive (excitatory) conditioning as well as to negative (inhibitory) conditioning or extinction.

In Livanov's laboratory this type of work has been carried further with the aid of the toposcope in the process of data collection, and through computer analysis of the data obtained (Livanov, 1962;[20, 21] Glivenko, Korolkova and Kuznetsova, 1962).[9] During the conditioning process in rabbits electrical activity is registered with the fifty leads of the toposcope. The electrical activity in those fifty points is continuously represented in fifty columns the height of which varies with the voltage. These columns are recorded by a movie camera with a filmspeed of 24 frames/sec., so that only low frequencies of electrical activity can be analysed. The increases and decreases in the height of each column are measured manually, and indicated with + or − in terms of an increase or a decrease. These data are then put on punch tape, which is later fed into a computer. The computer is programmed to compare the electrical processes in each of the fifty points with those in the other forty-nine. Thus it can be established how far the electrical processes in each of the fifty points work in a synchronous fashion with each other, or in other words, whether slow rhythms are shared (without indicating which rhythms or with which amplitude).

With the help of this method it was established that there is a spreading synchrony of slow rhythm electrical brain activity during the conditioning process as compared with the pre-experimental record, which reaches its maximum just before the establishment of the temporary bond, after which a reversal of this development takes place. As the method of analysis did not indicate the topographic details of the synchronization process, but analysed quantitatively synchrony over the surface of the brain-as-a-whole, it was only indicated that the conditioning process is accompanied by an increasing spatial synchronization over the brain surface, but not how this synchronization was distributed. Further and more refined methods of data acquisition and analysis are under way in Livanov's laboratories (Livanov et al., 1964;[22] Gavrilova et al., 1964,[8] 1965).[7]

This work indicates, however, that the widespread synchronization involves areas of the cortex which do not seem to be immediately concerned with the establishment of the particular conditioned reflex (which was a motor reaction). To clarify this issue somewhat further, the following experiments were carried out in our laboratory at the psychiatric Institute of the Academy of Medical Sciences in Moscow. In a group of normal subjects a conditioned motor response was established on the sound of a bell—the subject was ordered to push a button on hearing the bell. The strength of the motor-response was recorded with the reflexometer while the electrical activity of the primary visual and the motor cortex was registered.

Following this procedure ten subjects were given two further series of experiments. During the first series they were instructed not to push the button when hearing a first signal (a buzz), but to press it when hearing a second signal (the bell), to which they had been conditioned previously. In this experiment, therefore, the two signals were of different significance, i.e. the first one inhibitory and the second one excitatory. In the second following series the subjects were told that a first signal (a buzz) would forewarn them of the second one (the bell), to which they had been conditioned. Here the first signal had an 'activating' significance rather than an inhibitory one. One monopolar recording was obtained from the visual cortex and one from the motor cortex and these were analysed for intensity of alpharhythm'8–12 c/sec with the Nihonkohden 2-channel frequency analyser. The amount of alpha-activity in the visual and in the motor cortex were compared and this relationship within the ten subjects was correlated.

The first correlation pertains to a pre-experimental recording, i.e. before any conditioning took place. The correlation between the alpha rhythm of the two cortical areas was found to be 0·7 for the ten subjects.

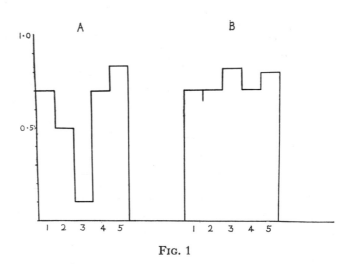

FIG. 1

Fig. 1 represents findings in the inhibitory (A) and activating experiments (B). The first correlation (1) in both figures is the pre-experimental one. In 'A' the next correlation (2) is computed for the situation immediately after the verbal instruction ('do not push the button on the buzz') is given followed by measurements on one second, after the inhibitory buzz (3), then one second before the bell (4), and finally just before the motor response (5). In 'B' the second correlation (2) represents again the correlation for the moment after the activating verbal instruction, then for one second after the activating buzz (3), one second before the bell (4), and finally just before the motor response (5). Under the condition in which the inhibitory variant is explained we find a decrease from 0·7 to 0·5 in the correlation. Application of the first (inhibitory) signal leads to a still greater decrease in the correlation co-efficient to 0·1, whereas the application of the conditioned signal restores it to a level of 0·7. In the second set of experiments the instruction does not cause any significant change in the correlation. Application of the activizing signal causes an increase to 0·8. Before the second conditioned signal is given it returns to 0·7. In both types of experiments the subjects tend to develop a relationship between the visual and motor cortex in terms of alpha rhythm of a more similar nature (correlation 0·8).

It is interesting to note that the correlation obtained in these experiments were only positive, i.e. the relationship between the visual and motor cortex tended to change in the same direction. However, if chlorpromazine is administered, it was found that the correlation coefficient for the spontaneous pre-experimental activity is negative, being 0·4. The first inhibitory instruction causes a decrease in the co-efficient and an appearance of a positive value. The first signal (buzz) hardly changed the correlation within significant levels, but the co-efficient increased to + 0·3 just before the application of the conditioned signal (bell). In the activating type of experiment, we see an increase of the co-efficient following the activizing verbal instruction with a change to a positive value. But the first signal (buzz) causes once again a negative correlation which increases before the introduction of the conditioned signal (bell). Negative correlation indicates that in the comparison of visual and motor area there is a shift in the amount of alpha frequency in an opposite direction from values found in positive correlation.

These experiments showed that the computed correlation between the electrical activity in the cortical areas responsible for the realization of the conditioned reflex is related to the particular characteristics of the conditioning process involved. We did not obtain any information about the original conditioning process, as this conditioned reflex is immediately present as if 'ready made' after the preliminary instruction.

Therefore further experiments were carried out. The conditioned motor reflex was established in normal subjects with a single light signal followed by the order 'press the button'. The evoked potentials (i.e. following the visual signal) in the occipital, motor and frontal areas of the brain were registered. An average response for each area was obtained through the method of superimposing the records of every subject obtained from ten consecutive lightsignal applications. The curves were digitized and thus an average curve for the entire group of subjects, eight in total, was computed. Finally the correlation co-efficient was calculated for two areas at a time, leading to three sets of correlation co-efficients.

Fig. 2 demonstrates the obtained results. The curves of the average potentials, from the moment of the conditioned stimulus to that of the conditioned response, was divided into three sections, i.e. the initial phase, the middle phase and the phase immediately preceding the execution of the

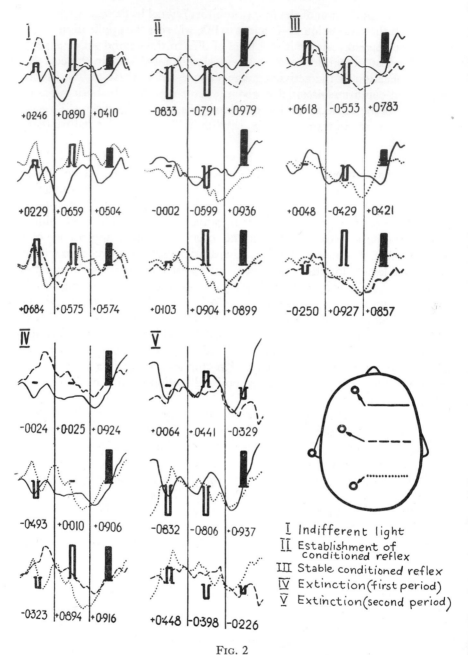

I Indifferent light
II Establishment of
   conditioned reflex
III Stable conditioned reflex
IV Extinction (first period)
V Extinction (second period)

FIG. 2

response. This was done to give us some idea of the dynamics of the correlation co-efficient in the interval between the conditioned stimulus and
response.

The figure shows five sets of columns (I, II, III, IV, V). Each column contains three sets of curves, each of which expresses the average curve of two brain areas, together with the correlation co-efficients between these two curves in the initial middle and pre-response phases. Column I represents the situation in which light stimulation is offered without reinforcement, i.e. as an indifferent stimulus. The third phase of each two curves of this recording period shows a certain level of correlation between the electrical activity in the three brain regions. This particular correlation increases at the initial stage of conditioning (column II) as compared with the pre-experimental condition (column I), i.e. it reaches high values in the stage of establishment of the conditioned response, when the motor response is already present, but not yet in a stable form. Column III shows the level of correlation at the stage in which the reflex can be considered to be stable. Here the correlation in the pre-response phase of the record between the frontal and the occipital areas decreases (from + 0·936 to +0·421). The correlation between the frontal and the motor area is also somewhat reduced, while the correlation between the motor and occipital areas still remains very high. It can be seen in the fourth column (i.e. during extinction) that the correlation co-efficients are increasing once more. But, if extinction is continued even after the conditioned response to the signal is no longer witnessed (column V), the correlation between the frontal and the motor areas, and between the motor and the occipital areas, is significantly changed, whereas a high correlation between the frontal and the occipital areas remains.

Thus we obtained some impression of the correlation dynamics relating the electrical activity of three brain areas during the periods of formation, stabilization and extinction of the conditioned reflex.

Cortical Mechanisms

According to Livanov spatial synchronization, i.e. similarity of electrical activity in spatially different structures, occurs on the basis of equalized lability or, in other words, on the basis of similar functional states in different brain areas. We may assume that spatial synchronization reflects the fact that separate brain areas become linked in a functional way.

Gavrilova (1965)[7] regarded this phenomenon as a cortical-subcortical interaction, mainly due to the reticular substance influencing the cerebral cortex. However, without rejecting the functional significance of this system, or systems, we would like to focus on the cortical mechanism of this phenomenon itself. Even if we assume that spatial synchronization is caused by the influence of the subcortical structures (and we could base this assumption on data obtained from stimulation of, or lesions in, the reticular substance, as in Jasper's hypothesis about primary and secondary cortical synchronization) there is no reason to dismiss the cortex itself as playing an active role in this process. Many authors confirmed this, for example, Kogan (1958)[14] who studied the cortex, after isolating it by under-cutting from the subcortical structures, and found indications of cortical mechanism of slow diffuse generalized activity. Burns (1958),[2] Ingvar (1955),[12] Kristiansen and Courtois (1949),[15] Echlin (1949)[4] also reported data on isolated cortical slabs and stated that bioelectrical potentials in these areas could be obtained. On the basis of their animal experiments, N. U. Belenkov and V. D. Tsirkov (1961)[1] pointed out that convulsive discharges could spread at a cortical level without the participation of the subcortex. F. I. Serkov, R. F. Makulkin and V. V. Ruseev (1960)[37] came to the conclusion that the possibility exists for alpha-like activity to spread through cortical structures which were isolated from the thalamus along intra-cortical pathways.

We carried out some experiments in rabbits on cortical slabs which were completely free from neurogenic connections with the rest of the brain. Blood supply was maintained through vessels of the pia-mater. After 2–2½ hours no electrical activity in its usual form could be registered for all practical purposes. We then stimulated the surface electrically; evoked electrical activity was registered at two points one of which was located a few millimeters away from the stimulating electrodes and the other at a greater distance.

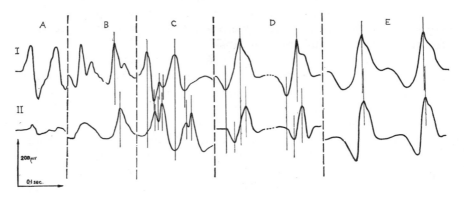

FIG. 3

Fig. 3 illustrates one of these experiments. The electrical activity which occurred soon after stimulation at the point close to the stimulating electrode (I) resembled convulsive discharges and continued even after cessation of the stimulation (A). At that moment no activity could be registered at the remote electrode (II), but some time later activity was recorded even there (B) though there was little similarity in the activities at the two points. When the evoked activity of the slab continued, we could observe that the morphology of the waves at the two points became similar (G). The synchronous activity got more and more in-phase (D), leading eventually to similar and in-phase activity (E). This spatial synchronization occurring in completely isolated brain structures indicates that it took place through a cortical mechanism. It may be assumed that a cortical mechanism mediates the spread of this form of activity or, more precisely, tunes the cortical elements into the rhythm and form of the evoked activity. It seems that the functional state of the cortex may be tuned to the functional state in a particular area.

Spatial Synchronization

We assumed that spatial synchronization reflects functional correlations which unite various brain structures, as shown in previous experiments. This study using the correlation method, may now be interpreted in the following way.

When we look at the average response curves obtained when applying the external stimulus only without reinforcement, i.e. as an indifferent visual stimulus (see Fig. 2, column I), we can observe a high correlation between the visual and motor areas during the first phase of the experiment, decreasing slightly toward the end of the curve. This is likely to be caused by the appearance of the orienting reflex which often has a marked motor component. In the initial phase of the experiment the correlation between the occipital and frontal areas appears to be low, then increases during the middle phase, and again slightly, during the final phase. Somewhat similar correlation dynamics can be observed between the frontal and the motor areas.

In considering these average curves of evoked potentials obtained with an indifferent light stimulus, we may assume that the first analysis takes place in the visual analyser with the motor analyser participating and with the frontal area joining in during the second phase. Since no other stimulation, or further stimulation, is offered the co-ordinated functioning of these areas is not necessary any more. This may account for the fact that the correlation of the electrical activity of these areas is reduced in the third phase.

Fig. 2, unfortunately, represents only curves of the mean of ten trials at a time, with column II representing the establishment of the conditioned reflex and column III representing the stabilization thereof. It seems reasonable to assume that the correlations undergo certain changes during each period of ten trials, yet with this form of data analysis, the dynamics of the development remain obscure in this detail. We can, however, see that the curves obtained during the establishment of the conditioned reflex show in the initial recording phase (column II) a cessation of the correlation between the motor and visual areas and between the frontal and occipital areas, as compared with the corresponding recording phase in the previous situation (column I). At the same time the correlation between the frontal and motor areas has become high and negative. During the second part of this recording period a negative correlation between the frontal and visual areas emerges, while the correlation between the frontal and motor areas remains at the same high negative level. However, the positive correlation between the visual and motor areas increases significantly during the middle phase of this recording period (column II). These dynamics can be understood in terms of negative induction, which spreads to other areas of the brain from the system responsible for the conditioned closure, i.e. the functional combination of the visual and motor analyser. As to the third phase of this recording period (column II), i.e. just before the response is provoked, the correlation between all three brain areas is high, indicating that it is necessary to combine the function of all these structures into one integrated operation.

During the extinction procedure we find a tendency to very low, or moderately high, negative correlations between the motor and visual areas and the motor and frontal areas. Probably this kind of correlation did not emerge right away, but developed gradually as the extinction procedure progressed. During the middle phase of this record (column IV), following the stimulation, there was a high positive correlation between the visual and the motor areas and no correlation of significance between the other areas. Apparently co-ordination of the functions of visual and motor analysers still existed without participation of the others. At the moment of execution of conditioned motor response, the functional co-ordination of all areas should be optimum. For, even if there is a lack of activity in the motor system in terms of output, this in itself results from intense brain activity. It is remarkable that during the third phase the nature of the correlation was similar both during the establishment of the conditioned reflex and during extinction, whereas the correlation dynamics in both instances during the first and second phase were different. This indicates that the processes leading to positive or negative responses are different in nature, though in both cases the integrated functioning of the whole system is necessary just before the realization of the response.

The analysis presented here is in no way final and further experiments are necessary. However, it allows us to conclude that the correlation method used provides an opportunity to investigate the processes of higher nervous activity in the central core of the nervous system where conditioning takes place, i.e. in the central apparatus of the conditioned reflex, and to test the well-known concepts of the Pavlovian School against objective experimental data.

We have to conclude that the occurrence of similarity in the electrical activity of various brain areas, or 'spatial synchronization', is directly related to conditioned reflex mechanisms.

2

Clinical Applications

Although the conditioned reflex method is a rather sensitive method in the clinical assessment of mentally ill patients, it is not always a practical method of reaching conclusions, as it is very time consuming. Furthermore, the creation of *new* conditioned reflexes under laboratory conditions, does not tell us much about the pre-existing system of conditioned reflexes in these patients. Therefore we chose yet another method of investigation in an attempt to test already existing reflexes and to determine their characteristics in both the healthy and the ill.

We assume that every subject acquires a complex system of conditioned reflexes in the course of his individual life experience. Electrical manifestations of localized brain activity fail to provide a sufficiently clear demonstration of the mechanism of the conditioned reflex. As we pointed out before, a more adequate method of investigation of these mechanisms and of the functional organization of this system is the study of functional connections which exist between the electrical activity of various brain regions. Spatial synchronization can be viewed as a manifestation thereof. Pavlov, as is well known, regarded the cerebral cortex as a system made up of the central parts of the analysers. This system constantly analyses the external and internal signals in order to adapt the organism to the environment by means of conditioned reflexes. Therefore the data obtained by electrophysiology on the interaction of analysers within the integrated cerebral system are of great importance.

Gavrilova (1958)[6] demonstrated that the interaction between the visual and auditory analysers as characterized by their bioelectrical reactivity (the so-called method of reactivity curves, introduced by Livanov (1944)[17] undergoes changes in various tests undertaken with the same subject. In some cases the reactions in the visual cortex to repetitive light-flashes of increasing brightness would be intensified, in other cases diminished. Gavrilova interpreted these phenomena either as a summation of excitation of the auditory and visual analyser (positive interaction), or as negative induction of the visual analyser by the auditory one, or a supraliminal inhibition due to the combined influence of the two stimulations, which has led to a reduced effect (negative interaction). She also reported on the different manifestations of this interaction in various other areas of the cerebral cortex. In the same subject sound intensified a reaction to light in some areas, while it reduced them in others. This apparently depends on the existing functional state in the structures under consideration, as well as on the physical intensity of the stimulus applied.

Most subjects from a group of schizophrenic patients showed negative interaction if auditory and visual stimuli were combined, and Gavrilova concluded that this pointed to a reduced function of the cortex as a whole. There were also certain differences depending on the particular form of the disease in question. In epilepsy a positive interaction predominated, in the post-ictal phase negative interaction predominated, indicating the broad generalization of the excitation process. In senile dementia there were far less changes in the electroencephalographic reactions to repetitive visual stimulation, as well as less interaction between analysers. This, presumably, is due to atrophic changes. This work showed that the close interaction between various analysers can be tested electroencephalographically.

What happens to the interaction between analysers if only one is stimulated, i.e. if only one modality of stimulation is applied? Borisova, a research worker in our laboratory, analysed the changes in alpha, beta, delta and theta activity of the encephalogram of various areas of the brain, when only a single visual or auditory stimulus was applied. From the data obtained could be compiled, a map of the areas in which statistically significant changes of these rhythms took place in response to the applied stimulus (Fig. 4). *A* in this figure represents the distribution of the

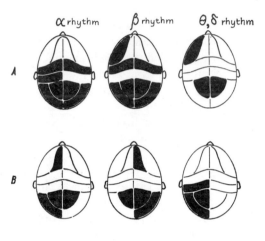

FIG. 4

different rhythms as they significantly changed after stimulation in normal subjects. *B* shows the same situation in a group of patients with the oneiroid catatonic form of schizophrenia.

Puskina took yet another approach to the same general problem. Her procedure consisted of applications of 2-sec lightflashes over a 10-second period, followed by a 10-second interval, then a 10-second period of 3-sec lightflashes, an interval, 4-sec lightflashes, and so on till 15-sec lightflashes with finally periods of 18, 20 and 24 sec lightflashes. The photic driving response was counted in terms of the percentage of the total number of flashes in each frequency. During the experiment the visual cortex was studied as well as the frontal, temporal and parietal areas. It was demonstrated (Fig. 5) that responses to lightflashes of different frequencies occur not only in the area of the analyser to which the stimulation is addressed, but also in other analysers, although the degree of their participation was different. In normal subjects there was a response in the occipital lobe to all frequencies, but mostly in the range of the alpha rhythm.

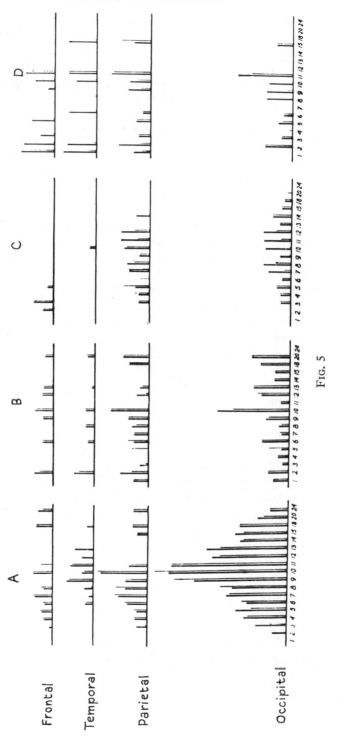

Fig. 5

The parietal, temporal and frontal lobes in normals usually respond to a lesser degree, and not to all rhythms.

This normal pattern of response, which reflects the integrated functioning of the brain under the experimental circumstances, was found to vary in the different stages of paranoid schizophrenia, as represented in B, C and D of Fig. 5. A is the normal pattern. Here is reflected the disruption of normal interdependencies between the brain areas. In the first stage (Fig. 5, B)—the paranoid stage—in which only delusions occur, the occipital lobe is found to respond to all frequencies, but to a lesser degree, that is the percentage index only is down. However, the temporal and frontal areas show considerable differences from the normal pattern towards less responsiveness, which becomes even more marked in the paranoid hallucinatory phase (Fig. 5, C). Then it can be observed that the temporal lobe is almost completely locked out of the unitary functional system, which is normally present in the reaction to the experimental stimuli. The same pertains to the frontal lobe, although to a somewhat lesser degree. In the still more advanced paraphrenic stage (Fig. 5, D) a peculiar functional disconnection pattern can be observed, in that some frequencies were well reproduced, while there was no response to others.

Therefore, the investigations described, demonstrate that the brain, when exposed to certain stimulations, does not respond only through a particular corresponding analyser, but also through analysers not immediately involved; the brain functions as an integrated system. Burns and Smith (1962)[3] indeed reported that a response to a stimulus can be registered in practically any point of the brain irrespective of the stimulus' modality. Even a simple situation like this supports the notion of unitary brain functioning.

Whereas the study of the electroencephalogram has not been rewarding in the study of schizophrenia when the functional interrelations between brain areas have been neglected, the study of the brain function as an integrated system permits us to see differences between normal subjects and those in various phases of schizophrenia, reflected in their gross psychopathological features. At this stage we are unable to conclude whether this disturbance in the integrated functioning of the brain is a direct, or primary, expression of the schizophrenic process, or whether it represents a secondary phenomenon, i.e. an expression caused by the schizophrenic process. Be that as it may, in schizophrenia there are disturbances of this kind in the activity of the brain, and this in turn makes necessary the study of the systemic aspects of electrical reactions, that is the study of their spatial distribution, in an attempt to discover regularly and consistently occurring phenomena and to relate these to the process of normal and abnormal higher nervous activity.

From Puskina's experiments we learned that a particular spatial pattern of electrical responses occurred in the cerebral cortex when a particular set of visual stimuli was applied. However, under normal physiological circumstances, the cerebral cortex is exposed to a very complex and ever changing set of stimulations, which not only provoke all sorts of electrical responses, but also maintain a certain level of arousal and may trigger off existing conditioned reflexes. The question occurred to us whether it would be possible to recognize a 'physiological base line' amidst this complicated and continuously changing set of stimulations (leading to an equally complicated and continuously changing set of electrical responses in varying patterns of spatial relationships); i.e. whether an average pattern of spatial relationships between the electrical activities of different cortical areas could be detected.

We therefore studied the distribution of the alpha rhythm in different brain areas, choosing alpha rhythm because it is not only easily identifiable, but is considered as 'the rhythm of inattention'. Data were obtained from two groups of normal subjects (Fig. 6, N_1 and N_2), as well as from groups of patients suffering from the three stages of paranoid schizophrenia (Fig. 6, I : paranoid form, II : hallucinatory-paranoid form, III :

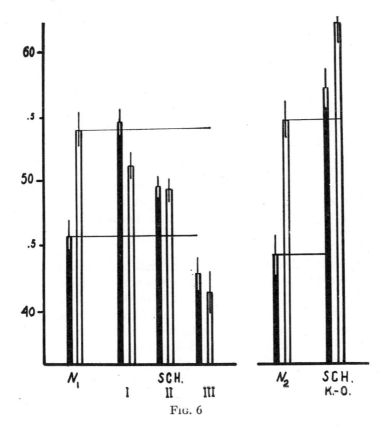

Fig. 6

paraphrenic form) and a group suffering from catatonic oneiroid schizophrenia (an acute form of catatonic schizophrenia with lowered awareness,

19

occurring during periodic schizophrenia and not to be confused with periodic catatonia) (Fig. 6, K. – 0.).

In the analysis of our data we attempted to estimate the synchronization, i.e. the in-phase, of the alpha rhythm in different areas of the brain, as compared with that in the occipital area. If all the leads were synchronized, this was indicated by 100 per cent; if few were synchronized this was indicated by the appropriate percentage as an index of diffuse brain synchronization in terms of occipital alpha rhythm. In order to compute this index different leads were compared with a number of 4-second samples of occipital recordings which contained good alpha rhythm.

Fig. 6 demonstrates our results. The black columns refer to the right hemisphere, the white columns—to the left. The two series of normal subjects (N_1 and N_2) did not lead to indices of statistical significance.

The index of alpha-synchronization for the left hemisphere was significantly higher than that for the right hemisphere. In the paranoid form of paranoid schizophrenia (I) there was a significant increase in the index for the right hemisphere and a decrease in the index for the left hemisphere, which, however, was not statistically impressive. Yet the relationship between the right and the left side, which in normal subjects seem to indicate a dominance in alpha synchronization of the left over the right, was reversed in the paranoid stage of paranoid schizophrenia, with a right sided dominance. In the paranoid-hallucinatory stage of the illness (II) we found no dominance of one side over the other, but, in comparison with the normal group, the index for the left hemisphere was significantly lower, the right significantly higher. In the paraphrenic stage (III) again, no dominance was observed, but we found the indices for both sides to be significantly lower than it was in the preceding stage and in the normal group. In the catatonic oneiroid form of schizophrenia (K.-0.) we found indices of alpha synchronization, which both in the left and right hemisphere were significantly higher than in the normal control group, yet the relation between the right and the left side remained the same as in normals.

Thus the index differs between normal and schizophrenic subjects, between the different stages and/or forms of schizophrenia. We must point out, however, that these results cannot be used in reverse, i.e. to diagnose which particular stage or form of schizophrenia an individual patient belongs to, for this investigation indicates only statistical tendencies, which occur within a particular clinically defined group.

We extended our analysis in order to calculate an index not for the brain as-a-whole, but for three specific areas, i.e. the frontal, precentral (motor) and parietal areas. This index illustrates quantitatively the synchronization of alpha rhythm of these areas with the occipital region. Fig. 7 demonstrates that the parietal (P), precentral (Pr) and frontal (F) areas are showing decreasing indices in that order, whereas in oneiroid catatonia (Sch) this tendency is reversed. Thus it has been shown that not only reactive changes in electrical activity spread over the cortex beyond their primary analysers as an expression of systemic brain activity, but that a similar systemic aspect can be found also in the spontaneous background activity, which is not restricted to one particular area either. This kind of spatial synchronization may well provide us with useful information about the general state of the brain.

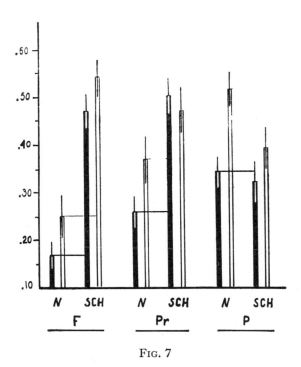

FIG. 7

Morozova (1965),[27] a research worker in our laboratory, carried out a similar study of spatial synchronization of alpha waves in subjects of 65–85 years of age, who, for all practical purposes, could be judged to be normal. Spatial synchronization of the alpha rhythm in this age group was different from that of younger subjects. Fig. 8 shows, under A, the two age groups compared for the index of the brain as a whole (general index), while under B is shown the index pertaining to the individual brain areas frontal (F), precentral (Pr), parietal (P) (specific index). In comparison to young people a significant increase in the general index of the right hemisphere and a decrease in the left hemisphere is found in old people. In the left hemisphere the specific indices are all significantly lower than in the younger age group, whereas in the right hemisphere there is a significant difference in the frontal area only where, in older people, the index is higher.

Studies of higher nervous activity intensity, flexibility, equilibrium, etc. comparing younger age groups with older ones, revealed that amongst older people the processes of excitation is less intensive, that the processes of passive inhibition predominate and that the flexibility of the nervous processes is reduced. If we compare these findings with our own it may be

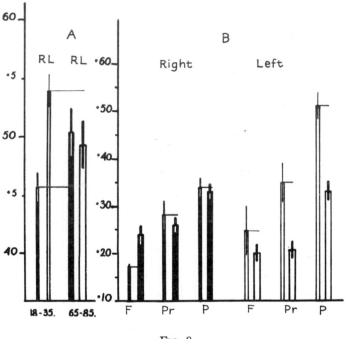

Fig. 8

that our findings reflect this weakening of higher nervous processes. But our data may also be meaningful beyond the consideration of simple nervous processes. The more complicated thought processes are similarly associated with the phenomenon of spatial synchronization, as was shown through Gavrilova's experiments (Livanov's Laboratory, 1965). With the use of the toposcopic method she demonstrated that mental arithmetic leads to an increase of spatial correlations between various brain areas, particularly in the anterior-frontal parts. Similar tests in schizophrenic patients showed poorer spatial co-ordination when compared with normals.

The described method of study of the cortical electrical activity, therefore, enables us to estimate the state of the processes of higher nervous activity, while characterizing and continuously stressing the brain activity as a unitary integrated functional system. This is particularly important for research into the pathogenesis of schizophrenia, which, as we all know, continues to be one of the most crippling and widespread mental illnesses.

On the basis of the manifold clinical-physiological, anatomical and other investigations we may assume that schizophrenia is not the result of hyperfunction or hypofunction of a particular structure. It appears to represent mostly a disturbance in the systemic activity of the brain-as-a-whole, leading to very complex disturbances of the higher nervous activity. The total activity of the integrated brain system is in continuous reciprocal relationship with environmental and internal conditions and, therefore, dependent on them. However, this relationship cannot be regarded as a simple deterministic system, but rather as a system which follows the laws of probability. In our investigations, this led to the acceptance of statistical methods, but also to a continuous re-interpretation of our statistical data. If the unitary activity of the normal brain in response to certain stimuli is expressed in certain organizational patterns of the intracerebral functional connections, then it seems that in schizophrenia these patterns occur in a random fashion more often or that they may follow altogether different functional organizational patterns. These pathophysiological situations may express themselves in observable behaviour manifestations, delusions, hallucinations, or indeed the entire set of schizophrenic phenomena.

3

Conclusion

If we regard the electrical processes of the brain as an expression of the system which lies at the basis of manifest behaviour, and if we consider the pattern of inter-connections between these electrical processes as one of the main characteristics of this system, then we may expect that clinical manifestations of mental illness correlate with abnormalities in these patterns of electrical inter-connections. This is what we attempted to demonstrate in the final part of this paper. We did not attempt to correlate in detail the data presented with clinical symptomatology. The aim of this paper has been to argue the main rationale for this type of method in the research of higher nervous activity. We have also pointed out areas in psychiatry where research based on Pavlov's theory has taken place.

REFERENCES

1. BELENKOV, N. U., and TSIRKOV, V. D., 1961. *J. Higher nerv. Activity*, **11**, 512.
2. BURNS, D. B., 1958. *The mammalian cerebral cortex*. London.
3. BURNS, D. B., and SMITH, G. R., 1962. *J. Physiol.*, **164.**
4. ECHLIN, F. A., 1949. *E.E.G. Clin. Neurophysiol.*, **1**, 265.
5. GASTAUT, H., ROGER, A., DONGIER, S., and REGIS, H., 1957. *J. Higher nerv. Activity*, **7**, 185.
6. GAVRILOVA, N., 1958. *Korsakov J. Neuropath. Psychiatry*, **58**, 351.
7. GAVRILOVA, N., 1965. *Korsakov J. Neuropath. Psychiatry*, **65**.
8. GAVRILOVA, N., ASLANOV, A., and DZUGAEVA, C., 1964. *J. Higher nerv. Activity*, **14**, 3.

9. GLIVENKO, E., KOROLKOVA, T., and KUZNETSOVA, G., 1962. *J. Physiol. USSR*, No. 4, 384.
10. GREKKER, R., 1911. Doct. Thesis. St. Petersburg.
11. HERNANDEZ-PEON, R., SCHERRER, H., and JOUVET, M., 1956. *Science*, **123,** 331.
12. INGVAR, D. H., 1955. *Acta Physiol. Scand.*, **33,** 151.
13. IVANOV-SMOLENSKI, A. G., 1958. *Papers of the Institute of Higher Nervous Activity*, **5,** 3.
14. KOGAN, A. B., 1958. *J. Physiol. USSR*, **44,** 810.
15. KRISTIANSEN, K., and COURTOIS, G., 1949. *E.E.G. Clin. Neurophysiol.*, **1,** 263.
16. LAPTEV, 1941. 1st Conference of Moscow Society of Physiol., Biochem., Pharmac., p. 135.
17. LIVANOV, M. N., 1944. *Rep. Acad. Sci. USSR, Biol. Series*, 331, 339.
18. LIVANOV, M. N., and POLYAKOV, K. L., 1945. *Rep. Acad. Sci. USSR, Biol. Series*, 286.
19. LIVANOV, M. N., 1951. In *The teachings of I. P. Pavlov in theoretical and practical medicine.*
20. LIVANOV, M. N., 1962. *The E.E.G. researches into the Higher Nervous Activity*, 174.
21. LIVANOV, M. N., 1962. *Biological aspects of cybernetics.* Academy of Sciences of the USSR.
22. LIVANOV, M. N., GAVRILOVA, N., and ASLANOV, A., 1964. *J. Higher nerv. Activity*, **14,** 185.
23. MARUSEVA, A. M., and TCHISTOVITCH, L. A., 1954. *J. Higher nerv. Activity*, **4,** 482.
24. MNUKHINA, R. S., 1957. *J. Higher nerv. Activity*, **7,** 608.
25. MNUKHINA, R. S., 1964. The E.E.G. researches into conditioned reflex reactions.
26. MORELL, J., and JASPER, H., 1956. *E.E.G. Clin. Neurophysiol.*, **8,** 1229.
27. MOROZOVA, T. V., 1965. *Korsakov J. Neuropath. Psychiatry.*, **65.**
28. PAVLOV, I. P., 1930. *Arch. Internat. Pharmacodynamie Therapie*, **38,** 222.
29. PAVLOV, I. P., 1932. *Bull. Battle Greek Sanitorium* and *Hospital Clinic.*
30. PAVLOV, I. P., 1933. *L'Encephale*, **28,** 285.
31. PAVLOV, I. P., 1933. *J. Psychologie*, 849.
32. PAVLOV, I. P. ,1937. *J. ment. Sci.* Nos. 31–35. See also *Complete collected works*, **80,** 187, **3.**
33. PAVLOV, I. P., 1952. *Complete collected works*, **3,** 347.
34. PEIMER, I. A., 1958. *J. Physiol. USSR*, **44,** 829.
35. POLEZHAEV, E. F., 1959. *J. Trans. USSR Acad. Sci.*, **126,** 909.
36. ROITBAKH, A. I., 1958. *2nd Conference on Questions of Electrophysiology of CNS*, 106. Moscow.
37. SERKOV, F. I., MAKULKIN, R. F., and RUSEEV, V. V., 1960. *J. Physiol. USSR*, **46,** 408.
38. VINOGRADOV, M. I., and VOROBJEVA, V. A., 1957. *Rep. Univ. Leningrad*, No. 4. p. 97.

XX

LEARNING THERAPIES

JOSEPH WOLPE

M.D.

Professor of Psychiatry
Temple University Medical Center, Philadelphia, Pa.

1

Introduction

The general aim of psychiatric treatment is to replace unadaptive behaviour patterns by adaptive ones. Psychiatric methods can be broadly divided into those intended to procure change by direct action on neural structures by chemical or physical agents like drugs, hormones, electroshock or surgery; and those comprising indirect (behavioural) manoeuvres. The latter constitute the field of *psychotherapy*. Since the changes psychotherapy achieves depend on experiences, it seems self-evident that learning is their basis. But in most psychotherapies the unlearning of unadaptive behaviour is not usually a primary therapeutic target, and occurs, when it does, as an incidental by-product of the patient's transactions with the therapist. In this chapter we shall be concerned with methods of psychotherapy whose primary aim is to obtain specific behaviour change on the basis of experimentally established principles of learning. Such methods, widely known as 'behaviour therapy',[13, 33] are of course mainly applicable to those kinds of unadaptive behaviour that owe their existence to learning. Pre-eminent among them are the neuroses.

It is important to state that learning therapies are not offered as mere supplements to the widely popular psychoanalytic systems of therapy. Rather, they challenge these systems at their very roots and bid fair to replace them. There has never been any scientifically acceptable support for psychoanalytic theory. The causal role in neuroses of the basic mechanisms it postulates, such as repression, castration anxiety, and resistance is quite without validation. Psychoanalysts have done nothing to meet the challenge of the critical surveys that have been appearing for half a century.[12, 15, 46, 54, 65, 76] Similarly, in the practical matter of treatment of neurosis, psychoanalytic therapy has never been shown to deserve the status of 'the best therapy available'. Long ago, Eysenck[11a] showed that its results were no better than those obtained by relatively simple traditional methods consisting mainly of reassurance, explanation, persuasion, and suggestion, either separately or in combinations. A study of the American Psychoanalytic Association has provided data of an even more distinctly negative character.[5, 41] Of cases regarded as *completely analysed*, only 60 per cent were rated either recovered or much improved after therapy that was administered, on the average, three or four times a week for three or four years (about 650 sessions). As will be shown later in this chapter, behaviour therapy seems to do a great deal better than this, on the very criteria that Knight[30] suggested for the use of psychoanalysts.

2

The Nature of Neurotic Behaviour

An objective experimental approach to what is called neurotic behaviour, reveals that both in animals and in man it has all the attributes of learned behaviour. In the experimental neuroses of animals, the neurotic behaviour is similar in detail to that observed in the situation of conflict or noxious stimulation by which the neurosis has been precipitated. When noxious stimulation is applied to a cat by electrifying the grid on the floor of a small cage, it elicits a variety of reactions, like clawing, vocalizing, mydriasis, piloerection, tachypnoea and others that vary from case to case. The shock is administered several times, and thereafter, when the animal is put back into the experimental cage on any number of later occasions (without ever again being shocked) it shows precisely those reactions that were elicited by the shock.

Stimuli in the experimental situation, because of their contiguity with the shock, have acquired the power to evoke responses like those that the shock evoked.

If these responses were present at all times or in a variety of situations unrelated to the experimental situation, it might seem that some physical change in the nervous system was their basis. But because they constantly occur at greatest intensity in the experimental cage, at lesser strength in the experimental room, and still less in other rooms in correlation with their pegree of resemblance to the experimental room, it seems clear that the behaviour has become connected by learning to the stimuli of the experimental situation, and by generalization to other situations resembling it.

The most marked and constant responses in the neurotic animals are, as indicated above, *autonomic*, predominantly responses of the sympathetic division of the autonomic nervous system—and we refer to them as 'anxiety'. They are intense responses, and fail to undergo extinction no matter how often or for how long the animal is placed in the experimental cage. If the animal were rational about the matter he would sooner or later 'realize' that there is no longer any likelihood of being shocked—and perhaps, like a human neurotic patient, he does; but realization *per se* does not abolish anxiety, *because it is based on learning at a subcortical level of neural integration*, which is not likely to be undone merely because thinking, a cortical affair, has changed.

Repeated evocation of the neurotic responses without reinforcement by shock might be expected to produce extinction—the progressive diminution of strength that is usually observed when responses are repeatedly evoked without reinforcement. But this, as indicated above, does not occur in the case of the neurotic anxiety responses, for reasons that have been discussed in some detail elsewhere.[68] It has, however, been found that if one can arrange for a stimulus to a neurotic response to be acting on the animal at the same time as other stimuli are evoking relatively strong responses incompatible with anxiety, the anxiety evocation will be inhibited; and each time this happens the habit strength of the anxiety responses will be to some extent diminished. When one tries to feed a neurotic animal in the experimental cage where he was shocked, one finds his eating response to be completely inhibited even though he may have been starved for a day or two beforehand. But if one then offers the food on the floor of the experimental room and in other rooms that more or less resemble the experimental room, one eventually finds a place where the anxiety is weak enough not to inhibit eating. When the animal eats in that place, each portion of food seems to be followed by diminution of anxiety, which before long ceases to be manifest. It is then possible to procure feeding in a room somewhat more like the experimental room. Through a succession of steps, eating is finally rendered possible in the experimental cage, where also the anxiety response is progressively diminished by feeding. Apparently, a progressive conditioned inhibition of anxiety is developed on the basis of individual occasions of its *reciprocal inhibition*.

Human neuroses are like those of animals in all essential respects. There are no differences that can not be attributed to the different and more complex organization of the human organism. I have elsewhere discussed in some detail nine points of similarity between animal and human neuroses,[73] but only the most basic of these need be referred to here.

In human cases, as in animal, autonomic responses of an anxiety pattern usually dominate a neurosis. These responses can almost invariably be related to specific stimulus antecedents if a sufficiently diligent behavioural analysis of the case is made. Sometimes there is also an undercurrent of continuous anxiety that does not have discrete antecedents (so called 'free-floating anxiety'). There is reason to believe that this is anxiety conditioned to pervasive aspects of experience ranging from space, time and general awareness of the 'self' at the most ubiquitous extreme, to such less pervasive elements as light and shade contrasts and amorphous noise. The specific stimuli to which the patient responds with anxiety can generally be found upon investigation to have been present either in the situation in which the neurosis was originally conditioned, or else in later situations where second order conditioning has occurred. For example, in a forty-year-old man, a cardiac neurosis was in the first place precipitated by the alarming sensations produced by an attack of paroxysmal tachycardia. One day, months later, while he was driving his car, an attack of anxiety was set off by a succession of extrasystoles; and this was the beginning of an agoraphobia which underwent extensions and modifications through other conditioning events during the following ten years.

It has for long been customary to label neurotic anxiety reactions 'phobias' when clear stimulus antecedents can be identified. But there are many patients who do not enter the consulting room stating, 'I have a fear of so-and-so,' but instead, complain of difficulty in adjusting to work situations, of sexual problems, of incompatability with people, of blushing, of attacks of asthma, of stuttering, and of many other difficulties. In almost all of these cases investigation reveals anxiety to be the basis of the presenting complaint, and definite stimulus antecedents to the anxiety can be determined. Thus, most other neuroses, whether they present as personality problems, psychosomatic disorders, or compulsions, turn out to be essentially phobias in disguise.

Human neurotic reactions are generally as resistant as those of the animal to attempts to extinguish them through repeated evocation by the stimuli to which they have been conditioned, but the counter-conditioning method whose effectiveness in animals is exemplified above has turned out to be widely applicable to human neuroses. The therapeutic use of feeding is only an instance of what has turned out to be a general principle—*the reciprocal inhibition principle of psychotherapeutic effects*. If any response inhibitory of anxiety can be made to occur in the presence of anxiety evoking stimuli it will on each occasion weaken the conditioned connection between these stimuli and the anxiety responses. In the following account, the main emphasis will be on the utilization of this principle; but reference will also be made to some applications of experimental extinction and operant conditioning.

3

Methods: Counterconditioning (Reciprocal Inhibition)

This group of methods was foreshadowed by Guthrie,[24] but they owe their concrete realization to the animal experiments described above. They have been systematically described by Wolpe[68] and Wolpe and Lazarus.[75] An introductory text[16] is also available. Their use is mainly, but not exclusively, in connection with the elimination of neurotic anxiety response habits. The first task of the therapist is always to ascertain the stimulus antecedents of neurotic responses. Virtually any stimulus that does not bespeak a

real threat may be conditioned to neurotic anxiety. The strategy of behaviour therapy requires an accurate knowledge of the stimulus-response
relationships relevant to the patient's neurotic habits.

A careful history is taken of the circumstances of onset of each neurotic
habit, and of any experiences that may later have led to its intensification or
amelioration. Consideration is also given to pre-existing sensitivities that
might have favoured the development of a particular neurotic reaction.
For example, an uneasiness in motor cars resulting from an accident
might predispose to an automobile phobia following a later accident. A
detailed survey is made of factors that influence the neurotic reactions at
present. Thereafter, in order to obtain a broad conspectus of the patient as
a functioning organism, a detailed life history is taken. This includes all his
early relationships and performances at home and at school, his later
educational experiences, his work life, his social life, and his sexual life
from his first awareness of sexual responding. Further data are obtained by
administering certain questionnaires, of which the most useful have been
the short Clark-Thurstone Inventory[64] and a Fear Survey Schedule.[74]
All this information is preliminary to active therapy.

Before applying specific emotional reconditioning techniques it is
usual for the therapist to give the patient a picture of his neurosis as being
due to unfortunate emotional learning and to set the stage for the therapeutic enterprise as a co-operative effort. Adaptive and unadaptive fears
are distinguished. Obscurities are clarified. Misconceptions, such as of the
harmfulness of masturbation, are corrected; and reassurance is given
where necessary.

The selection of techniques depends in the first place on the character
of the neurotic habits. On the whole, the most urgent and incapacitating
area of disturbance will be treated first, but there are sometimes tactical
reasons for varying this rule. It is usually good practice, where applicable,
to give early attention to anxieties whose treatment requires changed motor
behaviour in the assertive or sexual areas, because the crucial therapeutic
events here take place in the life situation. Treatment of phobia-like
anxieties is introduced a little later, and then continues in parallel with the
foregoing methods.

The Use of Assertive Responses

The term 'assertive' covers behaviour involving the expression of
practically all feelings other than anxiety, on the assumption—strongly
supported by experience—that such expression tends to inhibit anxiety
responses. The patient has difficulty in expressing himself where it is
reasonable and right to do so because he is inhibited by anxieties that are
aroused in him in relation to other persons. He may, for example, when
unfairly imposed upon by others be prevented by such anxieties from doing
anything about it, even though he feels injured and annoyed. The therapist
instigates the outward expression of this just annoyance and goes on to

show him in detail how to carry it out. When other kinds of emotional expression like affection, admiration, revulsion, are inhibited by fear, their expression is likewise taught and encouraged. Salter[53, 55] advocates the fullest exploration and exploitation of situations which lend themselves the expression of the affectional feelings, and also promotes expression of minor emotional responses by directing the patient to focus on immediate stimuli and to verbalize his emotional responses to them—e.g. 'I like your scarlet scarf'.

A type of patient for whom assertive training is indispensable is the one whose early training has over-emphasized social obligations and made him feel that the rights of others always come before his own. An example is a thirty-eight-year-old woman who on being divorced invited her sister to live with her. The sister was extremely dependent and turned out to be a millstone around her neck, but it took her two years to summon the courage to ask her sister to leave. In the course of these two years the patient had a continuous conflict between the impulse to expel her sister and a conditioned fear of hurting her feelings if she did so. The high anxiety level produced by this conflict[18] led to a conditioning of new neurotic reactions of a phobic pattern.

The new reactions required the application of a desensitization technique (see below), but the first task was to train her in appropriate assertiveness. After the reasonableness of this was explained to her, she was given one or two examples relating to previous patients. She grasped the idea, and the next day for the first time phoned a neighbour to turn down the television set which had frequently been turned on loud at 6 o'clock in the morning. This was followed by a succession of other acts that built up a general habit of adaptive assertiveness—refusal to contribute to causes that she did not favour, complaining about unsatisfactory service in restaurants, giving compliments when indicated. In correlation with this development was a progressive increase of emotional ease, and the growth of an attractive self image.

The instigation of assertive behaviour seems to succeed on the basis of a summation between the action tendency connected with the patient's spontaneous reaction to a situation (e.g. resentment), and the coaxing and goading of the therapist towards action in the same direction. A total action potential is thus produced that is great enough to overcome the inhibitory effects of the anxiety and reciprocally to inhibit the latter. In the course of the same operations, another learning process also goes on—the operant conditioning of the motor acts of assertion, which are reinforced by such rewarding consequences of these acts as the lowering of anxiety levels and the attainment of reasonable goals previously out of reach.

The Use of Relaxation Responses

It is a belief of common folklore that an anxious person may feel better if he can relax; but not until the classic studies of Edmund Jacobson[26] was it demonstrated that relaxation inhibits the autonomic responses characteristic of anxiety. Its effects on pulse rate, blood pressure, respiration, and galvanic skin response are the precise opposite of those of anxiety. Jacobson went on to treat neurotic and other patients by giving them very extensive training in relaxation, and then instructing them to relax at all times as many muscles as were not in use (differential relaxation). It would appear that when improvement occurs in neuroses by this method it is because persistent relaxation provides a means of reciprocal inhibition of anxiety aroused by stimuli that appear in the course of daily life; and if there are repeated reciprocal inhibitions of the anxiety responses to a particular family of stimuli, conditioned inhibition of the anxiety responses to these stimuli will progressively develop. A disadvantage of this method is that it usually requires 50–150 training sessions and a great amount of home practice by the patient. Another disadvantage is that its deconditioning effects depend on uncontrolled encounters with the stimuli to neurotic reactions.

Both of these disadvantages are circumvented by the procedure known as *systematic desensitization*. A modest amount of relaxation training generally suffices; and the therapist has full control of the introduction of the stimuli that evoke the anxiety that the relaxation is meant to inhibit. Desensitization is almost exclusively applied to overcoming neurotic responses to stimulus situations that do not call for changed motor behaviour patterns on the part of the patient—in contrast to assertive behaviour (see above).

For the purposes of systematic desensitization, the instruction in relaxation is usually given during the last fifteen minutes of each of about half-a-dozen sessions. It is on the lines laid down by Jacobson, but much less detailed and meticulous. Usually, relaxation of the arms is shown at the first lesson, and later lessons deal with face and jaws, tongue and neck, shoulders, trunk, and inferior extremities, respectively.

The essence of the desensitization procedure is the presentation of anxiety-arousing stimulus situations *to the imagination* of the deeply relaxed patient. Since stimuli that would evoke anxiety strongly would destroy the relaxation, the therapist must introduce only weak stimuli. To ensure this, he prepares *anxiety hierarchies*. These are lists of anxiety-arousing situations ranked according to the amount of anxiety they arouse. The lists are separated according to their subject-matter. Thus, a particular patient might have a space hierarchy (e.g. agoraphobia), a rejection hierarchy, and a scrutiny hierarchy. In a scrutiny hierarchy, anxiety would usually increase as a function of the number of people watching the patient performing, for example, a religious rite.

At the first desensitization session, the weakest item from a hierarchy (e.g. being watched by a single witness) is briefly presented to the patient's imagination, and the presentation is repeated several times until it ceases to bring forth any trace of anxiety. Then the next item (e.g. being watched by an audience of two) is presented and similarly handled. The procedure is repeated with each subsequent item. (In the example given, the size of the audience would increase by ones only at first; later increments would be larger according to a simple power function.[71]) Eventually, even the 'strongest' hierarchy item loses its ability to evoke anxiety.

The crucial point is that the desensitization effect transfers to the corresponding real situation. The correspondence is frequently strikingly exact, but some quantitative variations have been pointed out by Rachman.[50]

It is hardly surprising that systematic desensitization is ineffective in the 10 or 15 per cent of individuals who are not disturbed by imagined situations that disturb them in reality. In them desensitization can only be accomplished by plying them with real stimuli, and it is then called 'desensitization *in vivo*'.

The parallel between systematic desensitization and the therapeutic experiments on animals outlined above is clearly evident. Nevertheless, it cannot be taken for granted that the procedure itself is the basis of change, and not some other feature of the therapeutic transaction. And even if change is related to the procedure, it cannot be taken for granted that all the phases of it are necessary to the production of such change. Recently, a number of controlled experimental studies have been performed to explore these uncertainties.

Two studies have been concerned with the question whether there is any specific effectiveness in the procedure or whether any changes obtained can be attributed to suggestion or 'transference'. Using phobias for harmless snakes as their subject matter, Lang, Lazovik, and Reynolds[32] showed that systematic desensitization of fifteen or more items of a snake hierarchy was significantly superior to 'pseudotherapy' in which the patients were given interpersonal insights which they had been told would lead to the resolution of their phobias. Paul[43] found that psychoanalytically oriented therapists obtained significantly better results in students suffering from fears of public speaking when they used systematic desensitization than when they used their own accustomed kind of insight therapy or a support and suggestion schedule. These studies provide good support for the presumption that special therapeutic effects are yielded by the desensitization procedure.

But granting such potency in relation to the procedure as a whole, the question must still be posed whether all parts of it are necessary for the therapeutic effects, or whether some of its components are really redundant. Davison[10] and Rachman,[49, 50] working respectively with snake phobias and spider phobias, compared the effects of systematic desensitization with those of relaxation training without scene presentations on the one hand, and systematic scene presentations without relaxation on the other. In both of these studies the evidence showed a significant superiority for desensitization.

Another question which merits formal study is whether the hierarchical presentation of scenes is really necessary. I have repeatedly found that if scenes relatively high in a hierarchy are presented to patients in the usual way (i.e. for a few seconds at a time), the anxiety level does not decrease even after a dozen or more presentations. Rachman[49] gave three patients with spider phobias ten two-minute exposures to the most disturbing item of the hierarchy during each of ten sessions, without obtaining improvement in any of them.

The Use of Other Agents for Imaginal Desensitization

Emotive Imagery. This is a variant of desensitization introduced by Lazarus and Abramovitz[37] for treating children's phobias. The patient is made to imagine phobic stimuli in contexts in which pleasant emotional excitement is also aroused. If the excitement is strong, it evidently inhibits the anxiety and thus progressively stronger phobic stimuli can be introduced, on the basis of the usual kind of hierarchy.

One of their cases was a twelve-year-old boy who had a marked fear of darkness. He shared a room with his brother, and at night had a light shine constantly next to his bed. He was especially afraid in the bathroom which he only used if another member of the household accompanied him. Attempts at relaxation training failed. The child had a passion for two radio serials, 'Superman' and 'Captain Silver'. He was asked to imagine that Superman and Captain Silver had appointed him their agent. Lazarus and Abramovitz describe subsequent developments as follows:

The therapist said, 'Now I want you to close your eyes and imagine that you are sitting in the dining-room with your mother and father. It is night time. Suddenly, you receive a signal on the wrist radio that Superman has given you. You quickly run into the lounge because your mission must be kept a secret. There is only a little light coming into the lounge from the passage. Now pretend that you are all alone in the lounge waiting for Superman and Captain Silver to visit you. Think about this very clearly. If the idea makes you feel afraid, lift up your right hand.'

An on-going scene was terminated as soon as any anxiety was indicated. When an image aroused anxiety, it would either be represented in a more challengingly assertive manner, or it would be altered slightly so as to prove less objectively threatening. At the end of the third session, the child was able to picture himself alone in his bathroom with all the lights turned off, awaiting a communication from Superman.

Apart from ridding the child of his specific phobia, this treatment appeared to have diverse beneficial effects on his personality. A follow-up eleven months later revealed that the gains had been maintained.

Non-Aversive Electrical Stimuli. Some years ago an exceptionally severe agoraphobia in a young woman who failed to learn muscle relaxation was completely overcome by the use of electrically induced forearm flexion.[67, 68] Hierarchical stimuli were presented to the imagination of the patient. When she signalled that the image was clear, a weak faradic pulse was delivered, upon which she flexed her forearm. Usually, fifteen to twenty-five flexions were required to eliminate the anxiety reaction from a particular scene. She was eventually able to travel overseas without anxiety. Five years later her recovery had been fully maintained.

At the time this case was treated, it was thought that the recovery was due to the competitive inhibition of anxiety by a well-channelled motor response. That explanation may prove to be correct, but it is thrown into some doubt by the observation[45] that weak galvanic stimuli that evoke only passive muscle contraction can inhibit anxiety. I have recently found that this is sometimes also true of galvanic stimuli too weak to produce any visible muscle response, but strong enough to be distinctly felt by the patient. Possibly, change is due to conditioned inhibition based on external inhibition.

These stimuli are used for desensitization as follows: Two strips of saline-soaked gauze are made to encircle the forearm about three inches apart, and their ends are held together by alligator clips attached to the poles of the stimulating apparatus, which is essentially a 90-volt dry cell in series with a 50,000 ohm variable resistance. The patient, sitting in a comfortable chair with eyes closed, is asked to imagine the 'weakest' scene from a hierarchy and to raise the index finger of his other hand as soon as the image is clear. Two or three galvanic stimuli are then delivered to his forearm in quick succession. As soon as possible, he again visualizes and raises his finger, and is again shocked. As a rule, after ten to thirty presentations of a scene, the anxiety response to it is completely eliminated; and then the therapist introduces the next scene in the hierarchy, and so on.

The Use of the Patient's Emotional Responses to the Therapist

It is well recognized that all traditional forms of psychotherapy (i.e. therapies other than behaviour therapy) produce lasting beneficial changes in at least some patients. The incidence of such changes seems to bear no relation to the techniques employed.[31, 63] A reasonable supposition, that has yet to be tested, is that the basis of the changes is the arousal in the patient by the therapeutic situation of certain emotional responses that inhibit the anxiety responses to verbal stimuli that crop up during the interviews.

These effects are fortuitous in that the therapist does not regulate the stimuli that are introduced. Therapeutic effects of this nature can of course occur in the sessions of behaviour therapists just as in those of others. But the behaviour therapist often also takes additional advantage of any 'anti-anxiety' emotions that the interview situation may evoke, using them to inhibit the anxiety of stimuli systematically introduced from hierarchies. Sometimes imaginal stimuli are used, and in patients who cannot learn deep relaxation these emotions seem to afford a basis for desensitization.

More often, real stimuli are used to bring about desensitization *in vivo*. For example, in the case of a lawyer whose practice had long been restricted by a fear of making mistakes under the scrutiny of other people, a two-dimensional hierarchy was constructed, ranking mistakes according to their 'seriousness', and audiences according to their threat. Then the patient was instructed to make speeches in the consulting room before a 'mild' audience and to introduce a minor mistake. A little anxiety was aroused by this; and then the same speech was repeated four times in the course of which the anxiety aroused by the mistake declined to zero. Increasingly 'serious' mistakes were serially introduced, and then, later, more threatening audiences were used. Progressive diminution of anxiety in real public-speaking situations followed these manoeuvres.

The Use of Sexual Responses

Sexual responses are, as might be expected, mainly used for overcoming habits of anxiety response to various aspects of situations. Their therapeutic application has so far been largely to male sexual inadequacy, but they have also at times been used to treat frigidity.[75] In the latter condition systematic desensitization is generally more appropriate.[35]

In male sexual inadequacy, usually manifest as impotence or premature ejaculation, sexual responses can be used only in those cases (fortunately, the majority) who retain sexual feeling responses. The therapist needs to obtain an exact picture of the range of factors that evoke anxiety in the patient in the sexual situations, and to determine a situation in which the anxiety level is very low. He then instructs the patient to tell his sexual partner that his impotence is due to automatic habits of fear engendered by unfortunate past experiences, and that her co-operation will enable him to overcome these fears. She must permit him, without ridicule or pressure, to take lovemaking no farther than he can go with minimal anxiety, on repeated occasions. The patient is directed not to go beyond a particular stage of the sexual approach until it ceases to evoke any anxiety, and to treat each subsequent stage similarly. Through advances in this stepwise manner, with frequent opportunities, normal intercourse becomes possible in a few weeks. Wolpe and Lazarus[75] found the mean time span to be eight weeks in thirty-one cases of whom twenty-one achieved an entirely satisfactory functional result, and six others limited but significant functional improvements. Though this mode of treatment is very simple in principle, details are important and the exact strategy always has to be adjusted to the individual case.

Avoidance Conditioning

Avoidance (aversive) conditioning is the application of the reciprocal inhibition principle to the overcoming of responses other than anxiety.

It is employed largely to treat obsessional behaviour. The agents commonly used have been strong faradic stimulation of the forearm, and nausea induced by such drugs as apomorphine, either of which must be administered in an appropriate time relation to the stimulus to which avoidance conditioning is desired. Much better accuracy is obtained with the electrical stimulus.[47] Avoidance conditioning has produced beneficial effects in a wide range of obsessional and compulsive states.[52, 68] Several writers have reported its application to transvestism.[3, 4, 22] In homosexuality, in contrast to the largely negative pioneer study by Freund,[21] favourable experiences with the use of aversion have recently been reported.[8, 17, 28] Feldman and MacCullough[17] papers describe the effects of a technique of shocking the patient while a homosexual figure is projected on to a screen in front of him and terminating the shock at the appearance of an attractive female figure. There are some homosexual cases in which aversive techniques fail, and it is likely that among them are those that are based on general interpersonal anxiety, which should of course be treated by deconditioning the anxiety, after which nothing further may be needed.[59]

Avoidance conditioning has also been applied with limited success to the treatment of drug habits, especially alcoholism.[61] Recent modifications of technique, employing curare-like drugs, seem to offer the prospect of rapidly achieving abstinence in a high percentage of cases[9] but some follow-up observations have indicated that abstinence is not always sustained and is sometimes restricted to the beverage used in the treatment.[58] It is possible that additional success may result from treatment programmes that do not neglect endogenous stimuli to drug habits ('craving').[72]

4

Methods: Experimental Extinction

Experimental extinction is the breaking of a habit through repeated performance of the relevant response without reinforcement. The therapeutic use of extinction was formally introduced by Dunlap[11] under the name 'negative practice'. The method was never widely used, partly, it may be presumed, because of the dominance of psychoanalytic theory, but recently there has been renewed interest in it, especially with regard to the treatment of such motor habits as tics. Very large numbers of deliberate evocations of the undesired movement are encouraged, and in correlation with these, spontaneous evocations progressively lessen.[51, 62, 78]

There are certain procedures that are sometimes successful in eliminating neurotic anxiety response habits and that have features in common with experimental extinction but appear almost certainly to be based on some other mechanism. The essence of these is that the patient is exposed to anxiety-arousing stimuli either in reality or in imagination *at the greatest possible intensity*—'flooding'.[19, 39, 57] Persistence with this kind of strategy leads, in some patients, to a rather rapid decline in the anxiety response habit; but some do not benefit, and others are made worse. A case of agoraphobia who had failed to respond to systematic desensitization was markedly improved after the strongest moral pressure had persuaded her to go alone on an hour-long flight on a commercial aircraft. But there are at present no reliable means of predicting in whom these measures will succeed, and in the absence of such means their use should be advocated only when practically everything else has failed.

The fact that the severe anxiety of experimental neuroses does not diminish with prolonged evocation[40, 66, 68] really makes it seem unlikely that when improvement occurs it is due to experimental extinction. Rachman[49] found no improvement in patients with phobias for spiders to whose imagination he presented the most fearful possible image for two-minute periods, ten times per session for ten sessions. Similar cases given systematic desensitization did significantly better. But Wolpin and Raines[77] obtained practically as good a result in two snake phobias exposed to the maximum phobic stimulus as in two others who received systematic desensitization. Their difference from Rachman may lie in the fact that they employed longer durations of exposure—up to fifteen minutes; but if so it would be difficult to explain it on the basis of extinction, for Rachman's patients had a longer total period of unreinforced evocation of anxiety (200 minutes as against about 100 minutes). It seems that another mechanism should be sought—such as the possibility that conditioned inhibition may be based on transmarginal (protective) inhibition.[23, 44]

5

Methods: Operant Conditioning

The foregoing techniques are all essentially directed at the elimination of undesirable habits, but in some instances the conditioning of positive new habits has been involved as well. For example, in assertive training, where the primary aim is the counterconditioning of unadaptive anxiety to people, there is at the same time the development of motor habits of assertion on the basis of operant conditioning. Each successful act of assertion is reinforced immediately by such practical results as obtaining a concession from a superior, and by reduction of anxiety; and later by the commendation of the therapist. But there are other cases in which new motor habits need to be established even where anxiety is not involved. An example is enuresis nocturna.[29, 38] In recent years, formal operant conditioning manoeuvres have had an increasing role in such contexts. Anorexia nervosa has been successfully treated by following eating by social rewards such as the use of a radio or receiving company, while withdrawing these rewards when the patient fails to eat.[2]

Many varieties of psychotic or socially deviant behaviour have been treated on the same principle and a good many of the reports of treatment have been collected by Eysenck,[15] Franks,[20] and Ullman and Krasner.[60] Major and lasting changes have been brought about in the behaviour of chronic schizophrenic patients, some of whom had been in hospital for ten years or more. For example, in a 47-year-old woman Ayllon[1] broke a long-standing habit of wearing about 25 lbs of clothing by refusing her entry into the dining room unless her weight was reduced by 2 lbs from the level at which she presented herself. She could achieve this by removing some clothing, and the act of doing so was reinforced by the rewarding con-sequences of going into the dining room. Within about three months the weight of clothes she wore had fallen to 3 lbs and subsequently remained stable at that weight. Habits of over-eating, stealing food, and hoarding towels were eliminated from this patient by other operant conditioning schedules.

Promising results have also attended exploratory applications of oper-ant conditioning techniques to delinquent behaviour.[6, 56] The former authors treated forty adolescent delinquents by a simple reinforcement procedure. A three-year follow-up study of twenty of them revealed a significant reduction in the frequency and severity of crime in comparison with a matched-pair control group. Burchard and Tyler[6] produced a marked decrease in the 'destructive and disruptive behaviour' of a thirteen-year-old delinquent boy by systematically isolating him when he performed in an antisocial way and by rewarding socially acceptable behaviour.

6

Evaluation of Behaviour Therapy

Behaviour therapy is distinguished from conventional types of psycho-therapy in aiming its procedures directly towards changing behaviour that is deemed unadaptive. The therapist perceives a clear relation between his clinical manoeuvres and therapeutic change; and if particular operations fail to produce the expected changes, he switches to others. But while every deliberate move he makes accords with his experimentally established principles, he recognizes that, like other therapists, he also obtains *non-specific therapeutic effects* in some patients due to their emotional responses to him (see p. 566), and that the contribution of these must be taken into account in any evaluation of results.

Statistical Data

Uncontrolled Outcome Data. Only extensive controlled studies could give us an accurate picture of the relative efficacy of behaviour therapy and other therapies. At present, all comparisons between different methods on the basis of large-scale clinical statistics are unsatisfactory because of the uncontrolled composition of the material. The studies by Arnold Lazarus[33] and myself,[68] giving our personal results to a combined total of over 600 unselected patients, have shown that almost 90 per cent of patients *who afford themselves a fair exposure to the techniques* either recover or improve markedly on R. P. Knight's[30] five criteria—symptomatic improvement, increased productiveness, improved adjustment and pleasure in sex, improved interpersonal relationships, and ability to handle ordinary psychological conflicts and reasonable reality stresses. Among my own patients the mean number of interviews has been about thirty.

These results are only provisionally comparable with the 60 per cent 'cured' or 'greatly improved' patients among those *completely analysed*, in the study of the Central Fact-finding Committee of the American Psycho-analytic Association.[5, 41] These patients were treated an average of four times a week for three to four years, i.e. about 700 sessions. The enormously greater number of sessions per patient than is required for behaviour therapy seems unlikely to be merely a statistical artifact. It should be realized that behaviour therapists accept *all* neurotic patients that present them-selves for treatment, while psychoanalysts generally reject those they regard as unlikely to benefit.

Regarding the question of the durability of the therapeutic changes achieved by conditioning methods, all skilled behaviour therapists agree that resurgence of neurotic reactions is rare. In 1958 I reported that among forty-five patients followed up for periods ranging from two to seven years there was only one relapse. I have on file about a dozen cases who have maintained their recovery for twelve to seventeen years, without symptom substitution or resurgence of their original reactions. Recurrence of a neurosis, whenever it has been found, has always been traceable to new learning; and has never seemed to be the spontaneous eruption of 're-pressed emotional forces'.[69]

Controlled Comparative Outcome Studies. The studies under this heading have all involved systematic desensitization. The first, by Laza-rus,[34] compared the results of treating phobias, mainly claustrophobia, acrophobia, and sexual phobias, by two different forms of group therapy. The patients were separated into pairs that were matched as far as possible, and then by the toss of a coin one member of a pair was placed in a de-sensitization group, and the other in a conventional 'dynamic' group. After twenty-one sessions, 72 per cent of the patients in the desensitization groups had recovered, and only 12 per cent of those in the 'dynamic' groups.

At the University of Illinois, Paul[43] carried out an experiment that ingeniously isolated the effects of desensitization from non-specific therapeutic effects. His subjects were members of a public speaking class who had severe fears of the public speaking situation. He obtained the services of five experienced psychotherapists whose 'school' affiliation ranged from Freud to Sullivan, and who were paid for their time at stan-dard rates. Forty-five subjects were subdivided into three groups of fifteen that were equalized in various respects, and there were also two untreated control groups, of which one—a 'contact control group'—was given the expectation of later treatment. The three experimental groups were treated respectively by insight therapy, a suggestion and support procedure called 'attention-placebo' therapy, and systematic desensitization which the therapists had to be trained to administer. Each therapist treated nine patients—three by each of the three methods—and each patient received five therapeutic sessions. The results favoured systematic desensitization on a variety of measures, and most significantly in decrease of psycho-physiological responses. In terms of conventional clinical ratings, 86 per cent of the patients treated by desensitization were much improved and 14 per cent were improved. In the insight group 20 per cent were much improved and 27 per cent improved. In the attention-placebo group none were much improved and 47 per cent improved; and in the contact control only 17 per cent were improved.

Lang, Lazovik and Reynolds[32] treated students showing severe phobic reactions to harmless snakes by systematic desensitization, and compared them with two control groups—one that received no treatment and another that received 'pseudotherapy' consisting of relaxation training followed by interviews focusing on problems of 'living', with the patient in a state of relaxation. Subjects in whom fifteen or more hierarchy items were desensitized improved significantly more than either of the control groups.

Working independently, on spider and snake phobias respectively, Davison[10] and Rachman[49, 50] found that subjects to whom the whole desensitization sequence of procedures was applied showed significantly more improvement than either those receiving relaxation training without scene presentations or others to whom scenes were presented without relaxation.

In all of the foregoing studies, the subjects were in one way or another *invited* to participate in treatment. The first controlled study to deal with patients who applied for treatment spontaneously has recently been reported by Norah Moore.[42] Using a balanced incomplete block design (which uses the patients as their own controls) she found that in cases of asthma reciprocal inhibition therapy had a significantly greater effect on objectively measured improvement of respiratory function than either relaxation alone or relaxation combined with suggestion.

Altogether, while much remains to be done, and, indeed, investigation of the field is still at a very early stage, it seems fair to state that the specific effectiveness of at least one or two procedures of the learning therapies is more firmly established than anything in all of the conventional modes of psychotherapy.

REFERENCES

1. AYLLON, T., 1963. Intensive treatment of psychotic behavior by stimulus satiation and food reinforcement. *Behav. Res. Ther.*, **1**, 53.
2. BACHRACH, A. J., ERWIN, W. J., and MOHR, J. P., 1965. The control of eating behavior in an anorexic by operant conditioning techniques. In *Case studies in behavior modification*. Eds. Ullman, L., and Krasner, L. New York: Holt, Rinehart and Winston.
3. BLAKEMORE, C. B., THORPE, J. G., BARKER, J. C., CONWAY, C. G., LAVIN, N. I., 1963. The application of faradic aversion conditioning to behavior therapy in a case of transvestism. *Behav. Res. Ther.*, **1**, 29.
4. BLAKEMORE, C. B., 1960. The application of behavior therapy to a sexual disorder. In *Experiments in behavior therapy*. Eysenck, H. J. p. 165. New York: Pergamon Press.
5. BRODY, M. W., 1962. Prognosis and results of psychoanalysis. In *Psychosomatic medicine*. Eds. Nodine, J. H., and Moyer, J. H. Philadelphia, Lea and Febiger.
6. BURCHARD, J., and TYLER, V., 1965. The modification of delinquent behavior through operant conditioning. *Behav. Res. Ther.*, **2**, 245.
7. CAMPBELL, D., SANDERSON, R. E., and LAVERTY, S. C., 1964. Characteristics of a conditioned response in human subjects during extinction trials following a single traumatic conditioning trial. *J. Abnorm. Soc. Psychol.*, **68**, 627.
8. CLANCY, J., 1965. *Personal communication*. College of Medicine, University of Iowa.
9. CLANCY, J., VANDERHOOF, E., and CAMPBELL, P., 1966. Evaluation of an aversion technique as a treatment for alcoholism. *Quart. J. Stud. Alc.* (In press.)
10. DAVISON, G. C., 1965. The influence of systematic desensitization, relaxation, and graded exposure to imaginal aversive stimuli on the modification of phobic behavior, *Ph.D. Dissertation*, Stanford University.
11. DUNLAP, K., 1932. *Habits, their making and unmaking.* New York: Liveright.
11a. EYSENCK, H. J., 1952. The effects of psychotherapy. *J. Consult. Psychol.*, **16**, 319.
12. EYSENCK, H. J., 1953. *The uses and abuses of psychology.* London: Penguin Books.
13. EYSENCK, H. J., 1959. Learning theory and behavior therapy. *J. ment. Sci.*, **105**, 61.
14. EYSENCK, H. J., 1960. *Behavior therapy and the neuroses.* New York: Pergamon Press.
15. EYSENCK, H. J., 1965. *Experiments in behavior therapy.* New York, Pergamon Press.
16. EYSENCK, H. J., and RACHMAN, S., 1965. *The causes and cures of neurosis.* San Diego: Knapp, and London: Kegan Paul.
17. FELDMAN, M. P., and MacCULLOCH, M. J., 1965. The application of anticipator avoidance learning to the treatment of homosexuality. 1. Theory, technique and preliminary results. *Behav. Res. Ther.*, **2**, 165.
18. FONBERG, E., 1956. On the manifestations of conditioned defense reactions in stress. *Bull. Soc. Sci.*, Lettr. Lodz. **7**, 1.125.
19. Frankl, V., 1960. Paradoxical intention: Logotherapeutic techniques. *Amer. J. Psychother.*, **14**, 520.
20. FRANKS, C. M., Ed. 1964. *Conditioning techniques in clinical practice and research.* Springer, New York.
21. FREUND, K., 1960. Some problems in the treatment of homosexuality. In

Behavior therapy and the neuroses. Eysenck, H. J. New York: Pergamon Press.

22. GLYNN, J. D., and HARPER, P., 1961. Behavior therapy in a case of transvestism. *Lancet*, i, 619

23. GRAY, J. A., 1965. *Pavlov's typology*. Oxford: Pergamon Press.

24. GUTHRIE, E. R., 1935. *The psychology of learning*. New York: Harper.

25. HULL, C. L., 1943. *Principles of behavior*. New York: Appleton-Century Crofts.

26. JACOBSON, E., 1938. *Progressive relaxation*. Chicago: Univ. Press.

27. JACOBSON, E., 1964. *Anxiety and tension control*. Philadelphia: Lippincott.

28. JAMES, B., 1962. A case of homosexuality treated by aversion therapy. *Brit. Med. J.*, i, 768.

29. JONES, H. G., 1960. The behavioral treatment of enuresis nocturna. In *Behavior therapy and the neuroses*. Eysenck, H. J. New York: Pergamon Press.

30. KNIGHT, R. P., 1941. Evaluation of the results of psychoanalytic therapy. *Amer. J. Psychiat.*, **98**, 434.

31. LANDIS, C., 1937. A statistical evaluation of psychotherapeutic methods. In *Concepts and Problems of Psychotherapy*. Hinsie, L. New York: Columbia Univ. Press.

32. LANG, P. J., LAZOVIK, A. D., and REYNOLDS, D. J., 1965. Desensitization, suggestibility and pseudotherapy. *J. abnorm. Psychol.*, **70**, 395.

33. LAZARUS, A. A., 1953. New methods in psychotherapy: a case study. *S. African Med. J.*, **33**, 660.

34. LAZARUS, A. A., 1961. Group therapy of phobic disorders by systematic desensitization *J. abnorm. Soc. Psychol.*, **63**, 504.

35. LAZARUS, A. A., 1963. The results of behavior therapy in 126 cases of severe neuroses. *Behav. Res. Ther.*, **1**, 69.

36. LAZARUS, A. A., 1963. The treatment of chronic frigidity by systematic desensitization. *J. nerv. ment. Dis.*, **136**, 272.

37. LAZARUS, A. A., and ABRAMOVITZ, A., 1962. The use of 'emotive imagery' in the treatment of children's phobias. *J. ment. Sci.*, **108**, 191.

38. LOVIBOND, S. H., 1963. The mechanism of conditioning of enuresis. *Behav. Res. Ther.*, **1**, 17.

39. MALLESON, N., 1959. Panic and phobia. *Lancet*, i, 225.

40. MASSERMAN, J. H., 1943. *Behavior and neurosis*. Chicago: Univ. Press.

41. MASSERMAN, J. H., 1963. Ethology, comparative biodynamics and psychoanalytic research. In *Theories of the mind*. Ed. Scher, J. New York: Free Press.

42. MOORE, N., 1966. Behavior therapy in bronchial asthma: a controlled study. *J. Psychosom. Res.*, **9**, 257.

43. PAUL, G. L., 1966. *Insight vs. desensitization in psychotherapy: an experiment in anxiety reduction*. Stanford: Univ. Press.

44. PAVLOV, I. P., 1927. *Conditioned reflexes*. London: Oxford Univ. Press.

45. PHILPOTT, W. M., 1964. *Personal communication*.

46. RACHMAN, S., 1963. *Critical Essays on Psychoanalysis*. Oxford: Pergamon Press.

47. RACHMAN, S., 1965. Aversion therapy: chemical or electrical? *Behav. Res. Ther.*, **3**, 289.

48. RACHMAN, S., 1965. Studies in desensitization—I. The separate effects of relaxation and desensitization. *Behav. Res. Ther.*, **3**, 245.

49. RACHMAN, S., 1966. Studies in desensitization—II. Flooding. *Behav. Res. Ther.*, **4**, 1.

50. RACHMAN, S., 1966. Studies in desensitization—III. Speed of generalization. *Behav. Res. Ther.*, **4,** 7.
51. RAFI, A. A., 1962. Learning theory and the treatment of tics. *J. Psychosom. Res.*, **6,** 71.
52. RAYMOND, M. J., 1956. Case of fetishism treated by aversion therapy. *Brit. Med. J.*, ii, 854.
53. SALTER, A., 1949. *Conditioned reflex therapy.* New York: Creative Age Press.
54. SALTER, A., 1952. *The case against psychoanalysis.* New York: Holt.
55. SALTER, A., 1966. *Personal communication.*
56. SCHWITZGEBEL, R., and KOLB, D. A., 1964. Introducing behavior change in adolescent delinquents. *Behav. Res. Ther.*, **1,** 297.
57. STAMPFL, T., 1965. Quoted by London, P. *The modes and morals of psychotherapy.* New York: Holt, Rinehart, and Winston.
58. STAPLES, F., 1966. *Personal communication.*
59. STEVENSON, I., and WOLPE, J., 1960. Recovery from sexual deviations through overcoming nonsexual neurotic responses. *Amer. J. Psychiat.*, **116,** 737.
60. ULLMAN, L. P., and KRASNER, L., 1965. *Case studies in behavior modification.* New York: Holt, Rinehart, and Winston.
61. VOEGTLIN, W. L., and LEMERE, F., 1942. The treatment of alcohol addiction. *Quart. J. Stud. Alc.*, **2,** 717.
62. WALTON, D., 1961. Experimental psychology and the treatment of a ticqueur. *J. Child Psychol.*, **2,** 148.
63. WILDER, J., 1945. Facts and figures on psychotherapy. *J. Clin. Psychopath.*, **7,** 311.
64. WILLOUGHBY, R. R., 1934. Norms for the Clark-Thurstone Inventory. *J. Soc. Psychol.*, **5,** 91.
65. WOHLGEMUTH, A., 1923. *A critical examination of psychoanalysis.* London: Allen and Unwin.
66. WOLPE, J., 1952. Experimental neurosis as learned behavior. *Brit. J. Psychol.*, **43,** 243.
67. WOLPE, J., 1954. Reciprocal inhibition as the main basis of psychotherapeutic effects. *Am. Med. Assn. Arch. Neurol. Psychiat.*, **72,** 205.
68. WOLPE, J., 1958. *Psychotherapy by reciprocal inhibition.* Stanford: Univ. Press.
69. WOLPE, J., 1961. The prognosis in unpsychoanalyzed recovery from neurosis. *Amer. J. Psychiat.*, **117,** 35.
70. WOLPE, J., 1961. The systematic desensitization treatment of neuroses. *J. nerv. Dis.*, **132,** 189.
71. WOLPE, J., 1963. Quantitative relationships in the systematic desensitization of phobias. *Amer. J. Psychiat.*, **119,** 1062.
72. WOLPE, J., 1965. Conditioned inhibition of craving in drug addiction: a pilot experiment. *Behav. Res. Ther.*, **2,** 285.
73. WOLPE, J., 1967. Parallels between human and animal neuroses. In *Comparative psycopathology*, Zubin, J., and Hunt, H. F. (Eds.). New York: Grune and Stratton.
74. WOLPE, J., and LANG, P. J., 1964. A fear survey schedule for use in behavior therapy. *Behav. Res. Ther.*, **2,** 285.
75. WOLPE, J., and LAZARUS, A. A., 1966. *Behavior therapy techniques.* London: Pergamon Press.
76. WOLPE, J., and RACHMAN, S., 1960. Psychoanalytic 'evidence': a critique based on Freud's case of Little Hans. *J. nerv. ment. Dis.*, **131,** 135.
77. WOLPIN, M., and RAINES, J., 1966. Visual imagery, expected roles and extinction as possible factors in reducing fear and avoidance behavior. *Behav. Res. Ther.*, **4,** 25.

78.   YATES, A. J., 1958. The application of modern learning theory to the treatment
        of tics. *J. abnorm. soc. Psychol.*, **56**, 175.

XXI

THEORY AND PRACTICE OF GROUP HYPNOSIS, OR COLLECTIVE HYPNOSIS, IN THE USSR*

N. V. IVANOV

Professor
Gorki Medical Institute
USSR

1

Introduction

At the 1965 Congress of Hypnosis and Psychosomatic Medicine L. Chertok[4] pointed out that the study of hypnosis in most European countries had developed extremely slowly. This was due to a negative attitude towards hypnosis, dating from the turn of the century and the rise of rational psychotherapy and psychoanalysis. In the USSR, by contrast, hypnosis was intensively explored and taught, especially in its application to groups. This has furnished an abundance of material which forms the basis of this paper on the theory and practice of group hypnosis. It should be stressed that only the scientific literature of Socialist countries has been drawn upon and no attempt has been made to cover the numerous investigations and reports that have appeared in the West.

The Russian equivalent of the term group hypnosis is *collective hypnosis*,† which is preferred for reasons to be explained below.

---

* Translated by Dr. B. Petrovskaia, Herrison Hospital, Dorchester.

† Translator's Note. In the translation the English terms 'group hypnosis' and 'group hypnotherapy' will be used but the original preferred term should be borne in mind.

The fact that Soviet psychotherapy has experienced no crisis in the field of hypnology can be linked with the historical tendency that was pointed out by V. I. Lenin that, 'in its main trends progressive thought in Russia is fortunately based on solid materialistic traditions'. In the teaching of hypnosis the materialistic tradition has stimulated a constant search for the physiological basis of hypnotic phenomena. Hypnosis was defined as a state capable of explanation in terms of organic phenomena and the natural sciences. This attitude ensured a lively and continuous scientific interest in hypnosis at a time when it was considered in the West to be pseudo-scientific or frankly mystical.

The first quarter of the twentieth century saw a rich accumulation of data testifying to the therapeutic value of hypnosis (V. M. Tokarsky[37, 38] and V. M. Bechterev[1, 2] and his colleagues). In the 1930s I.P. Pavlov[21] formulated his fundamental concept which regarded the hypnotic state as a 'partial sleep' in which irradiated sleep inhibition coexisted with still actively functioning foci of arousal. It is these zones of wakefulness that permit 'rapport', as they can be stimulated by suggestion. The 'word of command' is in itself an adequate stimulus of the secondary signal system; it operates in isolation from all other influences and becomes an absolute irresistibly acting stimulus. Thus it continues to operate as an active stimulus even after the subject has returned to a state of complete general wakefulness.

In 1937 K. I. Platonov[22] who shared I. P. Pavlov's views, wrote, 'we sometimes hear that psychotherapy should be experiencing a crisis, but this is not so in reality. Psychotherapy is only beginning to develop, and it should be all the more valuable and significant because of its materialistic foundations'.

This scientific materialistic attitude towards psychopathological mechanisms, based on organic and physiological laws, should ensure that psychotherapy is highly reliable and significant.[22]

It is on this basis that Soviet psychotherapists have been intensively investigating hypnosis and this has naturally encouraged a rational methodology in 'group hypnotherapy'.

Scientific investigation of group methods dates from 1904 when there appeared a report by I. V. Viasemskii[41] who had carried out hypnosis on a group of five or six alcoholics. This was termed hypnotherapy for alcoholism. His practice was to induce a state of hypnotic trance in the whole group by hypnotizing each subject in turn. In this way he was able to make use of the phenomenon of mutual influence among the patients in order to reinforce their suggestibility.

2

Theory of Group Therapy and of Group Hypnosis

Historical differences in the social order of Western countries and of the USSR resulted in certain differences in the development of scientific concept. In this respect let us consider the nature of personality and in particular what kinds of experiences are pathogenic in character and which are likely to respond to psychotherapeutic measures.

On reading Western philosophy and psychology, we can easily see that in the West harsh and traumatic agents are responsible for man's anxiety concerning his social experiences both present and future. It is no accident, for instance, that his fear for existence and social survival inflict upon him a constant psychic tension and lead him into a neurotic flight from reality. This is emphasized by the existentialists as being the primary, central factor in the essence of man. 'The reason for his anxiety lies in man's very existence in the world as it is' (M. Heidegger).[7]

Soviet sociologists consider that the cause of Western man's prevailing fear is to be found in his social conditions. In Western society man is forced to struggle for his individual position in society and from this there arise the primary factors that determine his peculiar isolation and alienation. Western man is surrounded more by competitors than co-workers. From this it follows that the actual conflicts engendering neuroses are the conflicts between his personality and the competitive environment.

This accounts for the specific problems of psychotherapy. In order to help the patient escape from his neurosis it is necessary to relieve his personality from the traumatic social pressures which cause his constant psychic tension. In Western countries this has given rise to the popularity of those methods of group psychotherapy which resolve social rather than clinical problems.

It would appear that the psychotherapeutic group should compensate at least temporarily for the subject's uncertainties of social existence. It assumes the psychological value of alleviating the patient's burdens of social responsibility and stressful mode of coping with life, inasmuch as within the group he re-examines his pressing problems and thereby appears to clarify them. Thus the primary value of the group appears to be more corrective than therapeutic. For instance, it is stated in Y. W. Klapman's[10] monograph that the group should represent to the patient 'a second society' in which he should re-experience his relationships with his environment from scratch.

Naturally there is no place for hypnosis in groups which emphasize the re-enacting of interpersonal relationships among its members. This is one of the reasons why group hypnotherapy has not been widely used in the West, in spite of the popularity of a number of other forms of group therapy.

By contrast the Soviet psychotherapists' attitude to essential personality problems is fundamentally different. Under the socialist order the more important social needs of personality are catered for by the Government. For the Soviet man there is no emphasis on his concern for and uncertainty about the future. Broad opportunities of education, full employment and social security eliminate his anxiety for existence and survival.

The actual factors which lead to the evolution of neuroses are usually purely psychogenic. These result in the break-down of co-ordination within the higher nervous system and thus lead to functional disorders. Therefore the dominant experience of the neurotic lies in his awareness of his illness. His affective overvaluation of difficulties creates excessive and unnecessary anxiety, and this in turn accentuates the severity of his illness. All this manifests itself as an actual situation and not as a symbolic manifestation of fundamental, nuclear personality tendencies. In such cases the basic task of psychotherapy consists of correcting and influencing the patient so as to give him an adequate appreciation of his illness and to mobilize the strengths of his personality and its defences to combat and overcome his illness. The execution of this plan lies strictly within a purely clinical sphere. The goal of the organized therapeutic group is not the establishment of a second society, but rather the facilitation of purely therapeutic measures which aim at changing the patient's attitude towards his illness and the elimination of his symptoms. By virtue of its specific therapeutic methods hypnosis can be used par excellence within the group situation. The patient on his part comes to accept hypnotherapeutic methods as completely and indisputably rational procedures.

Thus the preference of Soviet clinicians for group hypnotherapy is determined by their different theoretical approach to group psychotherapy.

These differences in definition also give rise to different views about the basic nature of psychodynamic mechanisms at work in group psychotherapy. In the West and in the United States the emphasis is on the dominant role of interpersonal relationships operating within the group. Their main goal is to achieve the intrapsychic equilibrium between the id, the ego and the superego by means of catharsis, i.e. analytically. Ultimately this process is psychoanalytic. It is directed towards the discovery of the basic causes of illness, namely the uncovering of the various complexes that have been forced into the subconscious.

The Western emphasis on establishing proper interpersonal relationships among members of the group imparts to the physician merely the role of observer. He participates only occasionally to modify the trend of the group discussion. Such an attitude generally precludes the introduction of hypnotherapeutic measures by the physician since he would then acquire a more active and controlling role.

Under the socialist order a predominant significance is assured by the organization of the collective with its characteristic specific goals. At all stages in his personality development the Soviet man is decisively influenced by the collective, which determines his main patterns of action and personality relationships. This illustrates the important psychological truth that any environmental influences become much more significant for the personality if they are supported by the collective.

In its psychotherapeutic application this principle determines the advantages enjoyed by the physician if his therapy is directed not at a single individual, but at a group of patients who have been brought together on account of similarities in their clinical characteristics. The physician's tasks of explaining, modifying and correcting are directed towards the group. They therefore carry more weight in a group situation than in a setting of personal contact. The content of the therapist's addresses to the group are received by the group as a serious scientific exposition, and accepted more readily by its members. Because of their collective awareness its efficacy is enhanced.

The therapeutic group promotes a conscious re-evaluation of subjective experiences involved in the illness and a pre-requisite is experienced psychiatric guidance. In other words the goal of a therapeutic group is a modification of personality attitudes, and the physician's function is guidance and direction, since only he can expertly appreciate and comprehend the psychotherapeutic problems. The organization of the group under a dominating or guiding physician greatly facilitates the use of hypnotherapeutic methods because the group does not counter but reinforces his function in the therapeutic process.

The obligatory guiding role of the therapist does not, of course, minimize the positive effect of mutual contact among the patients. They are encouraged actively to discuss the meaning of their illness as presented to them by the physician. Moreover, their close mutual contact gives each of them an opportunity to observe for himself the various degrees of improvement that takes place in others. These observations are so vital to the creation of a calm and beneficial psychotherapeutic atmosphere within the group. As has been pertinently remarked by V. A. Giliarovsky[6] a patient will always prefer to believe another patient rather than the physician.

The theoretical premises described above are used to determine the particular constitution of the therapeutic groups and their organization on the basis of common pathogenic categories of illness.

When the group has been constituted the psychotherapeutic sessions begin with an obligatory preliminary talk by the physician. During this there is a gradual explanation of the material necessary for the mobilization of personality. Then follows a general discussion of the data that have been presented and finally the physician proceeds to group hypnosis of all members simultaneously.

We may now assume that the place of group hypnotherapy has been clearly defined and finally assured within the general science of psychotherapy.

Even during the early exploratory stages of the study of hypnotism the possibility of simultaneous hypnosis of a group was suggested (A. Moll)[17] but although Liebault Wetterstrand[44] and Vogt[42] all noted the advantages of the reinforcement of suggestion within a group, the method did not become popular. A. Moll himself did not consider this method as suitable because it cut across the physician patient relationship of professional secrecy and allowed the patients to learn about each others problems.

Since Pratt[25] wrote on the organization of therapeutic groups and V. M. Bechterev[1] introduced the obligatory preliminary address and discussion by the physician, certain inherent advantages of group hypnotherapy have secured for it an assured place. For the Soviet clinician group hypnotherapy is not a method used in isolation but is one component in a system of psychotherapy. Such a course includes preliminary parallel work with each member of the group in private as well as the explanatory address to the whole group.

The Hungarian psychotherapist Volgyesi[43] shares similar views and elaborates his system of active and complex psychotherapy, asserting that this 'aspires to the combination of verbal (intellectual-logical and suggestion) and somato-therapeutic methods'. Thus he regards hypnotherapy as one element in general psychotherapy. However, these views have not yet found general complete acceptance. The French psychotherapist L. Chertok[4] believes that in some situations the positive results of group hypnosis may be partly due to the fact that the group protects its members from an unconscious fear of hypnosis. He does not claim any specific inherent features in group hypnotherapy. Another view is expressed by the German psychotherapist D. Muller-Heyemann,[19] who admits certain advantages in simultaneous hypnosis of several patients including that of economy of the physician's time, but he does not recommend mutual contact of patients and prefers them to be in separate cubicles. He also seems to deny that there is any specific value in group hypnotherapy. However, he is strongly in favour of and attributes inherent positive characteristics to the practice of autogenic training.

3

The Practice of Group Hypnotherapy

Physiological Foundation

The acceptance by Soviet psychotherapists of Pavlov's[21] fundamental concept of hypnosis as partial sleep inaugurated an intensive study of some physiological correlates of hypnotic states. Convincing data concerning the identity of physiological substrata of natural and of hypnotic sleep have been obtained. Some of these physiological correlates permit of explanations for the phenomena of suggestibility, rapport and the extent of influences during a hypnotic seance.

B. N. Birman,[3] who was Pavlov's closest student, provided the experimental demonstration of the presence in hypnosis of localized, active, wakeful zones in the cerebral cortex. These constitute the physiological correlates of rapport. He also showed that the degree of suggestibility is determined by the regularity of phase states. The paradoxal phase is of decisive importance. As a consequence of this paradoxal phase the weaker stimulus of the word appears more powerful than direct stimuli either conditioned or unconditioned.

V. E. Roshnov[27] carried out a series of investigations into the dynamics of the phase states during deepening hypnotic sleep. He has demonstrated that such phase states are present at all stages of hypnosis but that with the deepening of sleep the number of the vascular reactions increases and thus reflects the phase state. Plothysmographic experimental methods were used. The enhanced effect of word stimuli becomes more marked whilst the conditioned reflex responsiveness to direct stimuli clearly lessens. It has been shown that there is a simultaneous increase in the selectivity of rapport. Thus there are many more positive conditioned responses to the words of the physician than to those of other persons. However, even at the stage of somnambulism rapport is not completely limited to the hypnotizing physician, but may relate to other persons, and I. O. Narbutowich[20] has demonstrated experimentally that the reaction to certain extraneous direct stimuli also occur.

The essential practical clinical conclusions derived from experimental data are:

1. The presence of phase states at all stages of hypnosis, including the lightest ones, permits and justifies the use of therapeutic suggestion at any stage of hypnosis; the depth of sleep is an important but not the sole determinant of the efficacy of suggestion.

2. Selectivity of rapport testifies to the fact that even in the deepest somnambulism the assimilation, acceptance and fulfilment of suggestion do not represent automatic obedience. To the contrary it points to a specific process of inner remaking and elaboration of the suggested data and the subsequent fulfilment takes place as a result of this working through.

The experimental physiological research conducted by A. G. Ivanov-Smolenskii[9] and his colleagues I. V. Strelchuk,[34] L. B. Gakkell[5] and F. P. Majorov,[15] has produced a wealth of material on the influence of the word as an adequate stimulus of the second signal system which creates new foci of excitation in the cortex. These new foci of activity are prepotent, and by the mechanism of negative induction or by disruption of the dynamic stereotype eliminate the pathodynamic zones that determine the illness. In practice it was these data that led to a realization of the need to create such new foci of cortical activity. Their clinical counterpart would be fresh experiences presented in the process of psychotherapy. They should counteract the morbid factors. The resultant positive affective significance of these new factors endows them with the force necessary to eliminate the illness.

20

The Hungarian psychotherapist Volgyesi[43] shares the opinion that hypnotherapy has as its goal 'the establishment and reinforcement of new conditioned reflex connections', and that 'therapeutic hypnosis represents an inter-cortical dynamic process in which the active neocortex of the physician comes to substitute itself for the passive neocortex of the patient'.

The physiological data demonstrate that one of the essential problems of hypnotherapy is to evolve such suggestions which will offer intensive, prepotent emotional experiences to the personality. The setting of group hypnotherapy carried with it some additional specific features which serve to reinforce and enhance this affective experience.

Methodology of Suggestion

The fundamental requirements for group hypnotherapy are a clear, systematic and sequential exposition and explanation during the physician's preliminary talks and during the subsequent suggestion introduced step by step in the seances.

As early as 1899 A. A. Tokarsky[37] formulated the requirement of such a structured sequential set of suggestions, which would provide a uniform planned system. This principle is still practised in Soviet hypnotherapy. The suggestion offered at the beginning of a course of therapy should be of a general nature, and 'have a sense of improvement in general' (Tokarsky).[37] The content of the suggestion should be continued and deepen in intensity during each seance and also from one seance to another. They should also introduce new material which in its turn will be continued, amplified and reinforced in the succeeding seances.

The explanations in the preliminary talk and conferences are also conducted step by step according to a planned sequence. At first they stress the importance and rationale of organizing the patients in a given group. Then follows a gradual exposition of the pathogenesis and evolution of illness. Finally, there is an explanation of those features of the therapeutic regimen which spring from the nature of the illness and from the peculiarities of a given group. Gradually the right attitude towards the illness is defined and its value stressed. Clear instructions are given and should be carried out punctiliously. The significance and value of these elucidated precepts is again discussed and emphasized. At the stage of formulating suggestions one of the most important considerations is to reflect and reinforce those already dealt with by the physician and the group. In this way a planned and structured system of suggestions is carried out in logical sequence to increase the potency of suggestion as a whole.

The address to the conscious 'ego', inherent in Soviet psychotherapy, necessitates the use of motivated suggestions. V. V. Sprimon (1887)[32] asserted that 'the methods of suggestion are various and should be suited to each given case. Very often words of command do not suffice, and it becomes necessary to discuss, rationalize, persuade or even furnish proofs to the subject, since his individuality continues to operate even while he is in hypnosis as it does in reality'.

At the end of the nineteenth century and during the first quarter of the present century it was generally believed that the degree of suggestibility depended entirely on the depth of sleep. For this reason much of psychotherapeutic research concentrated upon methods of deepening the hypnotic sleep, and hence greater opportunities for employing concrete, imperative suggestions. Much has been achieved in this sphere, for example, by the interesting experiments of K. I. Platonov[24] and I. S. Sumbajev.[35] These experiments have shown that suggestions employing concrete imagery are much more completely fulfilled than those of an abstract logical character. However, the employment of such concrete imagery has its limitations, since they can be applied only to the more easily suggestible subjects.

Paralleled to this trend in research, problems of motivated suggestion were being investigated. Several reports convincingly demonstrated the effectiveness of formulations which dwell upon the need to change symptomatology, and especially those which logically modify the affective experiences of the patient. Naturally, in group hypnotherapy situations motivated suggestions are the most suitable variants owing to their logical structure.

In this respect K. I. Platonov[22] elucidated specific physiological mechanisms. He stated that 'verbal influences should be motivated and as far as possible linked to the cause. . . . This is necessary in order to create broader and more numerous zones of stimulations in the higher levels of the brain'. . . and that, therefore, 'this method is less primitive than it is usually thought to be when it is considered as pursuing the narrow aims of symptomatic therapy'.

S. S. Libich[14] examined the conditions which increase the effectiveness of suggestions in collective hypnosis and formulated the following requirements.

1. Suggestion should be sufficiently broadly framed that each patient can select from it that which he needs for himself.

2. The general suggestion should touch on typical features of the disease which are to some extent common to all the members of the group.

3. Suggestions should be expressed in concrete imagery, but should only outline—as if to hint at—the decision which should then be taken by the patient.

S. S. Libich[14] proposes to use 'unities of suggestion'. The complex content of any given suggestion should be subdivided with a series of elementary formulations, thus allowing the patients themselves to reconstruct the whole content from these units to suit their own individual needs.

When we come to discuss the psychotherapy of neuroses we shall give examples of how to construct suggestions for a group.

Degree of Suggestibility

At the present time we may take it as proved that the efficacy of suggestions is not proportional to the depth of hypnotic sleep. Many cases have been cited in which the physician has obtained a radical disappearance of a symptom in this state, only to find that the symptom recurs very soon or is substituted by some other symptoms. Therefore, complete recovery is not necessarily achieved in the stage of somnambulism. Yet, sometimes a suggestion offered during the lightest sleep proves radically curative. From this it follows that the mechanisms which determine the effectiveness of suggestions are not identical with those that determine automatic obedience. They must represent some other specific processes which depend upon the physician/patient contact. In the course of this contact it is the personality of the patient which plays such a vital part in the selection and assimilation of suggestion, and it is the inner working through or reshaping of the suggestion which determines its acceptance.

We are aware of the importance of the phase states as the essential condition for carrying out suggestion, but to our regret we do not know what constitutes all the circumstances which determine the acceptance of suggestion by the individual. The physician often has recourse to the methods of trial and error, sometimes acquiring considerable influence over the patient, at other times temporarily losing it. Thus his work with patients represents for the physician a specific process of plastic adaptation to the patient's state at particular stages of the dynamics of his illness. In the final analysis the acceptance and fulfilment of the suggestion depends on the integration of fine nuances in the reciprocal relationships between the physician and the patient during a seance.

In individual hypnotherapy this integration varies considerably from seance to seance. This variability of pattern due to the nature of individual therapeutic sessions is very familiar to every hypnotherapist. In group hypnotherapy, however, there evidently emerges some factor which stabilizes the tendency to variability. We believe this factor to be the quiet, benevolent atmosphere within the group which is felt by and favourably influences the patient from the moment of his arrival at the therapeutic session. This atmosphere is peculiarly capable of modifying that individual anxiety tension which the sick man brings with him. In the group the patient immediately becomes to some extent distracted and then merges his sufferings with the organized work of the group in participating in the discussions of the material presented by the therapist. By the beginning of the hypnotic seance the sick man has already developed the anticipation and preparedness which is pre-requisite to an adequate acceptance of suggestion.

We always emphasize the significance of uniformity in the conditions in which hypnotherapy should be conducted. It is necessary to maintain identical circumstances and settings for the seances, to ensure similar poses and postures in the patients, to employ similar methods in the induction of sleep, and so on. But in this connection we often overlook the fact that during a personal contact with the physician, whilst relating his experiences and anxieties, the patient brings with him something new each time—new factors which disturb the requirements of uniformity during hypnotherapy. Hence in individual therapy the physician does not always succeed in establishing the patient's transition from emotional excitement and complaints to the desired optimum, beneficial calm in which the patient becomes entirely capable of accepting suggestion. In this respect the conditions within a therapeutic group usually offer certain advantages in that the very inclusion of the patient in the uniform group activity leads to his gradual and speedy acquiescence in the benevolent, calm, psychotherapeutic group atmosphere as a prelude to hypnosis.

The patient often comes convinced that only deep hypnosis can help him, but the group settling tends to overcome this restiveness. The group promotes the reinforcement of suggestibility and the readier acceptance of suggestion by the individual. The modification of this resistance is very difficult in individual hypnotherapy. In the group, however, the patients observe various intensities of sleep in each other and see for themselves the extent of improvement in those who experience only light hypnosis. These observations induce a change of attitude and deepen their suggestibility. Therefore group hypnotherapy produces additional beneficial factors which tend to reinforce acceptance of suggestion and thereby enhance the effectiveness of conducted hypnotherapy.

Suggestion and Personality in Group Hypnotherapy

The hypnotherapeutic seance is a channel for the physician's contact with the patient. A. Moll[17] has defined the relationship developing in hypnosis as an individual contact, but more precisely it should be regarded as a contact with various degrees of participation.

The physician always retains the leading role, but the patient engages in activity that is peculiar to himself. This is evident in his selection of suggested formulations or in the appearance of an antagonistic tendency towards unacceptable suggestions. The inner remaking through the processes of selection, acceptance and elaboration gives the patient an opportunity to endow the suggestion with fresh nuances which are dependent upon his individual patterns and relationships. One may quote a vivid example in which the patient reproduces his personal life experiences in a dream after the physician had offered only a general theme in the suggestion.

In individual hypnosis the physician's suggestion is too closely influenced by the immediate content of the patient's distress. His approach is therefore constructed as his suggestions must be directed towards the amelioration of his subject's complaints. In group hypnotherapy the suggestions may be more general. They are not entirely restricted to the feelings which the patient voices during a given session, and as a result there is greater scope for the patient to add fresh and individual elements to the content of the suggestion. Thus the physician can take more account of the patient's individual and varied activity. The patient, in his turn, can fulfil not only the specific instructions that are suggested, but can also carry out formulations carried out by his own individual elaborations. Thereby the effectiveness of suggestion is enriched.

The data adduced above have been amply proved by the experiments of the Czechoslovak psychotherapist I. Strelchuk[34] who demonstrated the presence of a spontaneous moment when the patient chooses and exhibits spontaneous behaviour, whereas the suggestion itself has prompted only a general tendency. An obvious positive aspect of group hypnotherapy is seen in this release of 'capacity' exercised by the subject in carrying out suggestions.

A special feature of interpersonal contact in group hypnotherapy is the fact that the patient subconsciously feels a certain subordination in his attitude towards the physician. This attitude is seen in the majority of cases especially in the initial stages of treatment, causing some distrustfulness towards the forthcoming seances. These phenomena are most marked in individual hypnotherapy, when the patient is left face to face with the therapist.

In group hypnotherapy there soon develops a feeling of community, which in turn fosters a favourable acceptance of the hypnotic situation. This is another positive feature of the collective group method. We shall not dwell here upon another characteristic of group situations, namely that the fear of hypnosis which so often operates at the beginning of individual hypnotherapy, usually rapidly disappears in a group. This fact has been recorded by almost all group hypnotherapists.

Since the content of a forthcoming suggestion partially reflects previous discussions and suggestions, the patient approaches the hypnotic seance already partially mobilized to receive it. This facilitates the patient's inner working through of the material suggested, and permits greater efficiency. Here we observe the beneficial influence of previous psycho-therapeutic measures, which have reinforced the personality and enhanced its defence mechanisms. Attention has been drawn to these facts by the English psychotherapist D. Hartland in his report to the International Congress on Hypnosis in 1965.

Shortcomings of Group Hypnotherapy

It may be questioned whether group hypnotherapy has any advantages in comparison with individual hypnotherapy. In cases where there has been a weakening of the immediate personal contact between the patient and the physician, can the latter ameliorate the patient's anxious complaint? at any given session as well in a group setting as in an individual sessions We may ask whether all the advantages of group method described above compensate for what is inevitably lost in a collective situation, by virtue of the greater distance between the therapist and the subject. Is the physician's personality too far removed from the experiential contact of the patient in group sessions?

These doubts would be justified if the contact between the physician and patient were restricted to hypnotherapeutic seances alone. But these doubts no longer arise if the treatment is organized in such a way that each group participant enjoys preliminary individual interviews with the therapist to support and maintain their psychotherapeutic relationship. This individual contact is enriched by material which has emerged at group sessions and which can and should be further utilized by the therapist at subsequent individual therapeutic interviews.

On the other hand the individual interviews enable the physician to elucidate the finer psychodynamic points involved. Later he should present this material and explain it positively in a form relevant to the group as a whole. This approach encourages the patient.

A serious risk which may be encountered in a group is the result of a lessening of a keen interest and the development of an attitude of commonplace matter-of-factness, which the patient rapidly senses. It lowers his affectivity and personal interest, and may even make him indifferent as to whether he attends the sessions regularly or with the necessary keen personal involvement. This may lead to the loss of the most important factor in collective hypnotherapy.

Certain other types of patients may also present substantial obstacles to the smooth and effective conduct of group hypnotherapy. Some may be characterized by a histrionic demonstrativeness, others may be inherently suspicious towards hypnotherapy, while others still may entertain a conviction that nothing can help them in their illness. They may be prevailed upon to give group hypnotherapy a chance, but may then tend to wish to prove that no improvement is occurring or can occur. They continue in their obstinate attempts to prove to the therapist and to others present that the group does not suit them. They seem to regard the group situation as an attack upon, or threat to, their individual integrity and dignity. Whilst remaining with the group they may deliberately obstruct instructions and advice. For instance, during the hypnotic seance these individuals may stubbornly insist on keeping their eyes open, indulge in motor restlessness or complain that they are uncomfortable.

In the majority of cases these refractory manifestations can be overcome if the physician ignores the patient's behaviour, especially in the early stages of a course, or perhaps if he casually and calmly remarks to such a patient 'Never mind . . . it will soon pass . . .'. When the physician assumes outward indifference and lightly ignores the patient, this same patient usually becomes an active and positive participant in group work at a later stage.

With less amenable refractory subjects there are greater difficulties in introducing them to, and involving them in, a group. Some may even stop attending. In such cases additional individual psychotherapeutic interviews may bring about the desired co-operation within the group.

But patients with a tendency to convulsive reactions, hysterical seizures or impulsive cries are contraindicated for selection to a group. They should be included only if preliminary individual psychotherapy has succeeded in removing the disturbing symptom.

4

Group Hypnotherapy of Neuroses

Within the present paper it would be impracticable to attempt detailed account of the Soviet attitude to neurosis. We shall confine ourselves to quoting the views of V. N. Mjassischev.[16] Mjassischev shared both Pavlov's views and his conclusions based on experimental findings regarding the role of personality and the structure of neuroses.

According to Mjassischev[16] 'Neuroses are psychogenic disorders resulting from unresolved conflicts between the personality and significant aspects of reality. These conflicts are intolerable and produce in the patient severely painful subjective experiences. These may be based on his failures in the struggle for existence, unsatisfied demands, unattained goals, unrewarded efforts or irreparable losses. His failure to reach a rational and productive solution results in his psychic and physiological disruption or disintegration'.

The physiological disruption results from a persistent neuronal overexcitation or overinhibition of the higher nervous system or to different degrees of their combination resulting in motor overactivity. These processes determine the presence and extent of functional disorders. In Pavlov's definition neuroses are a manifestation of a breakdown in the integrative functioning of the higher cortical activity.

In a systematically planned course of group hypnotherapy the clinician can isolate and define these disrupted manifestations and then control them by means of psychotherapeutic measures aimed towards reintegration. These measures are embodied in the physician's preliminary discussions and in the subsequent carefully structured hypnotic suggestion.

Let us now consider the actual characteristics of the basic, constituent stages of a hypnotherapeutic course and of the content of corresponding suggestions.

1. The patients are organized with a therapeutic group for the purpose of instructing and familiarizing them with the nature of their illness. They should be convinced that they can be cured because their illness is functional and this should be proved to them in medical terms. From the start it is inculcated into neurotic patients that their illness is based on a disturbance of equilibrium by the disrupted fundamental processes of the higher nervous system, and that therefore their common aim within the group must be a re-establishment of a desired normal functioning. This

method justifies the organization of the therapeutic group and dictates to the physician the necessity to use suggestion to induce a feeling of calm and quietness, a lessening of the central excitation and irritability and an enhancement of a general sense of wellbeing.

2. This is followed by discussions of the problems relating to the causation and evolution of the disease process. The physician uncovers the presence and significance of the anxiety or depressive manifestations or, for instance, of egocentric hypochondriasis and so on, and shows how the presence of these factors serves to perpetuate the illness.

At this stage it is again suggested to the patients that they must cultivate a calm, quiet and optimistically expectant attitude towards their illness, according to the precept 'However difficult it may be for me right now, I *know* that I shall get better, because I understand that my illness is functional'. The actual variants of the hypnotic formulations and suggestion are determined by the individual characteristics and attitudes of patients in a given group. The psychopathological attitudes are gradually eliminated by appropriate therapeutic means according to a careful plan.

3. We then proceed to a consideration of how to produce a reversal of neurotic processes. The patient is made to turn his attention from his characteristic egocentric emphasis on his illness and to focus it upon the recognition of the various emerging signs of recovery. At this stage of the course, the suggestions are aimed at reinforcing the patient's emphasis on some specific aspects of his recovery. It is usually observed at this stage that the patient's distress appears to recede, and that he joyfully states that his symptoms have become milder and less frequent. His conviction that he is on the way to recovery is thus further reinforced.

In formulating the suggestion it is useful to cite the patient's own comments and expressions as precisely as possible, without specifically referring to the persons present at the time in the group. As a result the patient clearly recognizes that the therapist has by now ameliorated his own peculiar painful experiences and a reinforcement of suggestibility is further secured.

4. Often in the preliminary talks the physician discusses with the patient his mode of life and the traumatic experiences that have caused the neurosis, and which at this stage still hinder his progress towards the recovery. At this stage suggestion again reinforces the need for a calm and quiet subsequent wakeful state. The patient's interest is diverted from those difficulties and problems to which he had succumbed and his resistance to the traumatic memories is built up, until his awareness of his past stressful and painful experiences is finally eliminated.

5. Lastly, the stage is reached in which the patient is given active instruction in specific methods of combating his neurotic symptoms and of distracting himself from them. This necessary training is achieved by the mobilization of personality in the direction of modifying and correcting psychopathological patterns and by further enhancement of his self

assurance and an encouragement of greater social participation and purposefulness. These instructions in specific means of combating his illness is an obligatory stage in the course.

By means of discussions and suggestion instruction is given in systematic and intensive autosuggestion. The patient should create in his own mind a specific, individual formula of self-encouragement by autosuggestion. By means of this formula he consolidates his progress between the sessions; this is not practised during the seances.

In practice the effectiveness of such autosuggestions is secured if the following conditions are accepted.

1. The creation by the patient of his own formula that tends to some degree to minimize the significance of morbid experiences, e.g. of an obsessive thought.

2. An active transformation of the patient's morbid thoughts into those which create visual imagery or other affectively charged associations, and which permit the patient to exclude any awareness of morbid phenomena even if temporarily.

At these final stages the therapist has trained the patient in efficient methods of autosuggestion and emphasizes the need for them and reinforces their effectiveness from seance to seance. This is linked to a reinforcement of the personality.

The timing of introduction and application of fresh material depends upon the therapeutic development. Fresh material does not counter the preceding suggestion but rather serves to enrich the therapist's methods and in the end leads to significant positive results.

5

Organization of Group Hypnotherapy in the USSR

The basic form of organized group hypnotherapy is widely used in our country, and is practised in neuropsychiatric dispensaries. These institutions serve not only those with clearly delimited psychological disorders but also those with a wide variety of peripheral borderline conditions. In particular they also offer effective hypnotherapeutic group treatment for chronic alcoholism.

The structure of hypnotherapeutic treatment of the alcoholic is also organized in a strict programme of clearly recognized stages.

1. The initial stage is aimed at the elimination of the subjectively painful withdrawal symptoms.

2. Then follows an elaboration of a negative attitude towards alcohol.

3. Finally, there is a reinforcement of resistance to alcohol, of consolidating abstinence and of long term avoidance of—aversion to—situations in which a ready availability of alcohol may prove too tempting to the patient.

The basic hypnotherapeutic methods which we have outlined above are also practised in a number of specialized therapeutic departments for neuroses, e.g. in the Psychotherapeutic Department of one of the Moscow Neuro-psychiatric Hospitals under Professor M. S. Lebedinskii[12] and Assistant Professor G. K. Tarasov;[36] in the department for treatment of neuroses in the Bekhterev Neuro-psychiatric Institute in Leningrad under Professor V. N. Mjassischev[16] and Doctors R. A. Sachepizckii,[28] S. S. Libich[14] and A. Y. Straumit[33]; in the Department for Neurosis in Kharkow under Professor A. N. Shagam,[29] as well as in the Kharkow Psychotherapeutic Clinic under Professor I. Z. Velvovskii,[39] attached to the Chair of Psychotherapy of the Ukrainian Advanced Medical Training Institute. This latter offers group hypnotherapy in a sanatorium—spa environment. Similar therapeutic spa-sanatoria are also found in Kiev, Sljausk, in the Crimea and in Sochi in the Caucasus.

Group hypnotherapy is also practised in a number of units attached to clinics for internal diseases in general hospitals, and thus may be applied in cardio-vascular and gastro-enterological syndromes in which powerful neurogenic factors are known to operate. We may also mention their usefulness in the early stages of hypertension, paroxysmal tachicardia, stenocardia, bronchial asthma and moderate hyperthyroidism.

In tuberculosis sanatoria group hypnotherapy is employed to ameliorate anxiety associated with the primary condition and also to mitigate certain untoward effects of specific, organic methods of treatment.

Success is also obtained with organized hypnotherapy of selected patients suffering from purely neurological disorders. In such cases group hypnosis may attain a symptomatic relief of various sensory dysfunctions, such as causalgia or phantom limb syndrome. It is also used to aid the patient in his re-adaptation to the new way of life brought about by his illness.

Gynaecologists may utilize hypnotherapy for the treatment of menopausal disorders, menstrual disorders, pruritis, psychogenic hypogalactia etc.

In each of the foregoing spheres hypnotherapy adapts itself and evolves specific characteristics in courses of exploration, discussion and suggestion. But a detailed account of these latter systems is beyond the scope of the present paper and we have contented ourselves with only a brief mention of the basic variants of group hypnotherapy as practised in our country.

REFERENCES

1. BECHTEREV, V. M., 1911. *Hypnosis, suggestion and psychotherapy and their therapeutic value.* St. Petersburg.
2. BECHTEREV, V. M., 1928. *A new method of collective therapy of chronic alcoholics.* A collection of papers dedicated to the XXXth anniversary of work of Professor Brustein, C.A. Moscow, Leningrad.

3. BIRMAN, B. N., 1930. Psychotherapy as Social Reflexotherapy of Neurotic Illness. *J. Contemp. Psychoneurol.*, Nos. 4–6.
4. CHERTOK, L., 1959. *L'Hypnose. Probleme theoritique at pratique.* Paris.
5. GAKKELL, L. B., 1960. *Human neuroses.* A Manual of Neurology in several volumes, vol. 6. Moscow.
6. GILIAROVSKY, V. A., 1927. Collective Psychotherapy of Neurotics. *Moscow Med. J.*, No. 7.
7. HEIDEGGER, M., 1941. *Sein und Zeit.* Halle a.d. Saale, 5 Ausfl, p. 180.
8. IVANOV, N. V., 1959. *Psychotherapy in neuro-psychiatric dispensaries.* Moscow.
9. IVANOV-SMOLENSKII, A. G., 1952. *Notes on the pathophysiology of the higher nervous activity.* 2nd ed. Moscow.
10. KLAPMAN, Y. W., 1948. *Group psychotherapy. Theory and practice.* London.
11. KRASNICH, S. A., 1954. *An experiment in the application of psychotherapy in a hospital for somatic diseases.* Gorki.
12. LEBEDINSKII, M. S., 1959. *Notes on psychotherapy.* Moscow.
13. LEONHARD, K., 1963. *Individual therapie der neurosen.* Ycha.
14. LIBICH, S. S., 1966. Special characteristics of collective psychotherapy in small groups. Collected papers *Problems of psychotherapy.* Moscow.
15. MAJOROV, F. P. 1950. Physiological characteristics of the somnambulistic phase of hypnosis. *Physiol. J. USSR,* **36,** No. 6, 649.
16. MJASSISCHEV, V. N., 1960. *Personality and neuroses.* Leningrad.
17. MOLL, A., 1892. *Der Rapport in der Neurosen.* Leipzig.
18. MORENO, J. L., Ed. 1945. *Group psychotherapy. A symposium.* New York.
19. MULLER-HEYEMANN, 1957. *Psychotherapie.* Berlin.
20. NARBUTOVICH, I. O., 1958. Researches into selective rapport in hypnosis. Collected papers *Problems of psychotherapy.* Moscow.
21. PAVLOV, I. P., 1951. *Twenty years of experiments in objective studies of the higher nervous activity.* 7th ed. Moscow.
22. PLATONOV, K. I., 1935. Towards a New Foundation in Psychotherapy. *J. Neuropath. Psychiatry Psychol. Hyg.,* No. 11.
23. PLATONOV, K. I., 1937. General Considerations of Means towards a Materialistic Foundation of Psychiatry. *Trans. Krasnodar med. Inst.*
24. PLATONOV, K. I., 1962. *The word as a physiological and therapeutic factor.* 2nd ed. Moscow.
25. PRATT, Y. H., 1906. The home sanatorium treatment of consumption. *Johns Hopkins Hospital Bull.,* **17.**
26. ROSHNOV, V. E., 1954. *Hypnosis in medicine.* Moscow.
27. ROSHNOV, V. E., 1958. Problems of Physiological Characteristics of Various Depths of Hypnotic Sleep. Collected papers *Problems of psychotherapy.* Moscow.
28. SACHEPIZCKII, R. A., 1966. Interpersonal relationships between physician and patient in the process of psychotherapy. Collected papers *Problems of psychotherapy.* Moscow.
29. SHAGAM, A. N., 1966. Data relating to the theory of psychotherapy. Collected papers *Problems of psychotherapy.* Moscow.
30. SLAVSON, S. K., 1947. *The practice of group therapy.* London.
31. SLAVSON, S. K., 1956. *The fields of group psychotherapy.* New York.
32. SPRIMON, V., 1887. Hypnotic suggestion as a means of treating neuroses. *J. med. Rev.,* **27,** 102.
33. STRAUMIT, A. Y., 1966. Problems in idiopathogenetic Psychotherapy. Collected papers *Problems of psychotherapy.* Moscow.
34. STRELCHUK, I. V., 1966. Cited from Bassin, F. V. and Roshnov at the International Congress on Hypnosis and Psychosomatic Medicine (1965). Ref. *Korsakov J. Neuropathol. Psychiatry,* No. 2.

35. SUMBAJEV, I. S., 1946. *Theory and practice of psychotherapy*. Irkutsk.
36. TARASOV, G. K., 1966. Problems of effectiveness of psychotherapy in small groups. Collected papers *Problems of psychotherapy*. Moscow.
37. TOKARSKY, V. M., 1890. *Therapeutic application of hypnosis*. Moscow.
38. TOKARSKY, V. M., 1889. *Problems of possible harmful influence of hypnosis*. St. Petersburg.
39. VELVOVSKII, I. Z., 1964. Some aspects of the introduction of psychotherapy into spas and sanatoria services to the sick. Collection of papers *One hundred years of Berjosorsky (The Birches) Mineral Waters*. Khartov.
40. VISH, I. M., 1959. *Psychotherapy of certain neuropsychiatric and somatic disorders*. Leningrad, Tambov.
41. VJASEMSKII, I. V., 1904. Alcoholism and its Treatment by Hypnotherapeutic Suggestion. *Korsakov J. Neurol. Psychiatry*, No. 1–2.
42. VOGT, O., 1894–95. Zur Kenntnis des Wesens und der Psychologischen. Bedentung der Hypnotisnms. *Zeitschrift fur Hypnotisnms*.
43. VOLGYESI, 1959. *Uber aktiv-Komplexe Psychotherapie und die Bewegung*. Schule der Kranken. Berlin.
44. WETTERSTRAND, L., 1893. *Hypnotism and its application to practical medicine*. (Translated into Russian from Swedish.)

XXII

THE PLACEBO RESPONSE

ARTHUR K. SHAPIRO

M.D.

Clinical Associate Professor
Department of Psychiatry
The New York Hospital—Cornell Medical Center
(Payne Whitney Psychiatric Clinic)
525 East 68th Street
New York, N.Y. 10021

1

Pre-Scientific Medicine

Psychological factors, always important in medicine, were recognized as early as the period of Hippocrates. Galen estimated that sixty per cent of patients had symptoms of underlying emotional rather than physical origin. This figure is close to the contemporary estimate of fifty to eighty per cent. Despite Galen's and Hippocrates' acumen, none of the drugs they used were of any use. Treatment was not only primitive, unscientific, and for the most part ineffective, it was often shocking and dangerous.[115, 116]

Patients took almost every known organic and inorganic substance—crocodile dung, teeth of swine, hooves of asses, spermatic fluid of frogs, eunuch fat, fly specks, lozenges of dried vipers, powder of precious stones, bricks, furs, feathers, hair, human perspiration, oil from ants, earthworms, wolves, and spiders, moss scraped from the skull of a victim of violent death, and so on. Blood from every animal was prepared and administered in every way, and was used to treat every conceivable symptom and disease. Almost all human and animal excretions were used.

Some famous treatments that were used for centuries included: the Royal Touch, Egyptian mummy, unicorn's horn, bezoar stone and mandrake Theriac contained 37—63 ingredients, mattioli 230, and required several months to concoct. Galen's elaborate pharmacopoeia, all worthless, contained 820 substances. Medical reasoning was primitive: Lung of fox, a long-winded animal, was given to consumptives. Fat of bear, a hirsute animal, was prescribed for baldness. Mistletoe, a plant that grows on the oak which cannot fall, was specific for the falling sickness.[71a] The injury of a wounded person was cured by sympathetic powder which was applied to the bloodstained garment, and by sympathetic ointment when applied to the implement inflicting the wound. Throughout medical history patients were purged, puked, poisoned, punctured, cut, cupped, blistered, bled, leeched, heated, frozen, sweated and shocked.[28, 41-43, 76, 115, 116]

Though medicine was in the finest scientific, religious, cultural, and ethical traditions throughout history, one may wonder how physicians maintained their position of honour and respect. The appearance of useful drugs or procedures was infrequent and usually forgotten by succeeding generations. For thousands of years physicians prescribed what we now know were useless and often dangerous medications. This would have been impossible were it not for the fact that physicians did help their patients.

Today we know that the effectiveness of these procedures and medications was due to psychological factors often referred to as the placebo effect. Since almost all medications until recently were placebos, the history of medical treatment can be characterized largely as the history of the placebo effect.

The first major contribution to the end of Galenism and to the beginnings of scientific medical treatment often is attributed to Sydenham in the seventeenth century. He is credited erroneously with demonstrating that cinchoma bark (which contains quinine) was specific only for fevers of malarial origin, and not for all febrile infections.[12, 28] Cinchoma bark often has been thought of as the first drug that was not a placebo, because previously there had been no way to distinguish a placebo from a non-placebo. The placebo effect, however, continued to be the norm of medical treatment even after the beginning of modern scientific medicine seven or eight decades ago.[115, 116]

These considerations led to the famous admonition: *Treat as many patients with the new remedies while they still have the power to heal.*

2

Modern Medicine

Modern medicine no longer relies chiefly upon psychological factors, placebo effects, or the doctor–patient relationship. Today there are an increasing number of specific and predictable drugs and medical procedures. Although psychological factors may be minimized, they cannot ever be excluded. Of course, if the dosage of a drug is high enough all patients will react with toxicity or even death, regardless of psychological factors. But such predictability is of little medical use because the majority of clinically useful drugs are prescribed in dosages which are far below the toxic level. Most drugs are useful only in a range in which psychological factors or placebo effects are important.[119]

Despite these advances the placebo effect is an important component of modern medicine. Many papers have demonstrated the importance and magnitude of the placebo effect in every therapeutic area.[5, 6, 9, 12, 22, 24, 25, 28, 49, 59, 68, 82, 115–117, 121, 122, 144, 149] Placebos can be more powerful than, and reverse the action of, potent active drugs.[149] The incidence of placebo reactions approaches 100 per cent in some studies. Placebos can have profound effects on organic illnesses, including incurable malignancies.[119] Placebos can often mimic the effects of active drugs.[68] Uncontrolled studies of drug efficacy are reported effective four to five times more frequently than controlled studies.[22, 23] Placebo effects are so omnipresent that if they are not reported in controlled studies it is commonly accepted that the studies are unreliable. Increased appreciation of placebo effects is reflected in the speculation that the major medical achievement of the last decade will be recorded by future historians as the development of methodology and controlled experimentation.

The importance of the placebo effect continues to be underestimated because it is human frailty to be able to appreciate the shortcomings of others more easily than our own.[116, 117] Hofling found that three times as many physicians thought that their colleagues used placebos more than they did.[49] The tendency of physicians to project the use of placebos on other physicians was confirmed in a study by the author. In addition physicians tended to define the placebo by excluding what they did from the definition.[133] Defensiveness in the attitudes toward placebos and placebo effects is also reflected in the history and definition of the word *placebo*.[117, 120, 121, 127]

3

Definition of Placebo

The history of the placebo begins with the Hebrew Bible. The first word of Psalm 116:9 is 'Ethalekh'. It was translated into the Latin Bible as 'placebo', which is derived from the Latin verb 'placere' meaning to please.[87] Placebo was the initial word of the first antiphon and entered the English language in the twelfth century by becoming the name commonly given to the vespers for the dead, a custom no longer followed whose meaning is now obscure.[10]

The placebo took on a secular meaning in the fourteenth century, and its connotation gradually became derisive during the next several centuries. It was used to describe a servile flatterer, sycophant, toady, and parasite. This usage derives from depreciation of the professional mourners who were paid to 'sing placebos' at the bier of the deceased in substitution for the family whose role it was originally.

Before proceeding, errors in the etymology of the placebo have to be clarified because they have influenced all later histories. Few people realize that medical dictionaries have limited their definitions of the placebo to inert or inactive drugs only during the last seventeen years.[8] In recent medical dictionaries definitions have expanded. They are now more like the original definition that appeared in the 1785 edition of *Motherby's New Medical Dictionary*:[85] 'A commonplace method or medicine.' It is interesting that this original definition is either overlooked or misquoted as 'a commonplace method of (*sic*) medicine'. The distinction between *of* and *or* is important. The former limits the definition to medicine whereas the latter includes methods and medicine. Although the original definition included all therapies, as medical theory and practice changed in the nineteenth century, the term became limited to medicine. This continued until seventeen years ago when, medical dictionaries, in part by happenstance, began to limit the definition to inert substances. Such interpretation has influenced the thinking of many physicians and non-physicians who conceive of the placebo only as inert. In recent medical literature and dictionaries definitions have expanded. My proposed definition, which I believe fulfils historic and heuristic criteria, follows:

A *placebo* is defined as any therapy (or that component of any therapy) that is deliberately used for its nonspecific psychologic or psychophysiologic effect, or that is used for its presumed specific effect on a patient, symptom, or illness, but which, unknown to patient and therapist, is without specific activity for the condition being treated.

A *placebo*, when used as a control in experimental studies, is defined as a substance or procedure that is without specific activity for the condition being evaluated.

The *placebo effect* is defined as the non specific psychologic or psychophysiologic effect produced by placebos.

In other words, a therapeutic procedure may be given with or without knowledge that it is a placebo. It would include treatments given in the belief that they are not placebos but which actually are placebos by *objective* evaluation. The placebo may be inert or active and may include, therefore, all medical treatment, no matter how specific or how administered. It may take the form of oral and parenteral medication, topical preparations, inhalants, and all mechanical, surgical, psychotherapeutic, and other therapeutic techniques. It may include psychiatric treatments such as psychotherapy, psychoanalysis, psychochemotherapy, I.C.T., E.C.T., neurosurgery, and so on. It would include a treatment which produced symptoms or side effects which were not specific for that treatment. A placebo may or may not result in a placebo effect, and the effect may be favourable or unfavourable—that is, positive or negative.

This definition makes no assumption about which treatments are placebos, or about the mechanism of placebo action. These issues are left open because the placebo effect is a multidetermined phenomenon which is not yet understood.[116, 119–121, 128–132] The definition is a phenomenological statement which avoids becoming tautological. It provides a good model for research, a structure into which variables can be put for testing, and makes possible independent assessment about which everyone can agree.

The placebo was used originally as a pejorative and derisive epithet to describe the treatment of others, and not knowingly or deliberately prescribed by physicians. Today, the criterion for placebo treatment is based on more than opinion about what is effective treatment. It is based on, or should be based on, scientific methodology and principles of controlled evaluation. This criterion is justified historically, linguistically, dynamically, and heuristically. Other alternatives result in many difficulties.[122, 123, 127]

Although the definition may prove to be too inclusive, for heuristic reasons it would be premature at the present time to make specific exclusions. It is likely that various placebogenic factors will be reliably isolated in the future. When everything is known about the placebo and placebo effect there will probably no longer be a need for the definition, except in etymologies of obsolete terms, but this is yet a desideratum for the future.

4

Recent Interest in Placebo Effect

Recent interest in the placebo effect began about 1953, and was accelerated by the introduction of the tranquilizing drugs in 1955. The number of papers on the placebo effect has increased each year since that time; the number of papers published since 1960 totals more than all previous years combined. This development is reflected in the increased use of statistics, placebos, double blind procedure, and other controls in recent studies. Whereas controlled studies appeared infrequently in medical literature before 1950, today they are the norm.[7, 51, 116, 119–121, 124, 126, 128, 130–132]

Patient-Physician Relationship

The physician's role in society is unique. He performs and combines functions that have always been important to mankind—that of healer, priest, and scientist.[55] These attributes facilitate the tendency of patients to relate unrealistically to physicians. These tendencies have been referred to as *transference*, which is usually thought of as a process whereby a patient's feelings (such as love, hatred, trust, distrust) unconsciously attached to significant persons in the past (usually parents or parent surrogates), are displaced on to the physician in the present.

Most patients have a readiness for a positive transference or relationship to the physician. It is probably related to satisfactory early infantile and childhood experiences with parents and parent surrogates which establish future patterns of behaviour in the adult. Individuals who expect succour and comfort despite hunger, fright, and discomfort are probably one group of positive placebo reactors. Hope and optimism reflected in positive placebo reactions is probably an indication of a health potential in the patient.

The patient's transference potential may be apparent in the initial interview. He may be hostile, servile, compliant, rebellious, co-operative, or suspicious. He may not take the medication that is prescribed, or he may distort the instructions. He may report dramatic relief of symptoms or describe alarming side-effects, that is, positive and negative placebo effects.

The patient's transference relationship with the doctor, and the doctor's countertransference relationship with the patient are important elements in placebo reactions, the direction of placebo reactions (positive, negative, or absent), and influence the outcome of all treatment. Although the concept of transference is difficult to demonstrate experimentally, it is most frequently referred to as being important in the placebo effect. It may be referred to as the doctor-patient relationship, rapport, warmth, trust, faith, empathy, and so on.[24, 25, 49, 82, 96, 115, 116, 128, 144, 149] This concept is a qualitative description of a process. Further understanding requires detailed experimental analysis of the elements that contribute to this gross phenomenon. An analysis of the elements in the patient and physician that contribute to placebo effects might contribute some of these details.

Patient

Personality. Various investigators have attempted to relate placebo effects to the personality of the patient. Placebo reactors have been characterized as compliant, religious, hypochondriac, anxious, less educated, and frequently using cathartics;[69] disturbed and likely to react to drugs with atypical reactions;[146] anxious;[6, 19, 25, 32, 62, 102] depressed; [25, 32] dependent;[62, 69] ideational;[1] neurotic;[19] extroverted;[7] and so on.[29, 45, 51, 60, 66, 73, 75, 84, 86, 102, 111, 130–132, 141, 143]

The attempt to relate placebo effects to the personality of the patient has not been successful. Traits found in one study have not been confirmed in other studies done under different conditions. It is possible that no definitive trait exists. If they do exist, sundry contaminating variables will have to be isolated before they become apparent.

Of these variables, the nature of the placebo stimulus has not yet been considered. Some personality variables appear to describe patients for whom a placebo in the form of a drug would be culturally appropriate, for example, patients of a lower social class. For another, a psychotherapeutic placebo stimulus might be more appropriate. Recognition of this factor is a precondition for any attempt to understand the role of personality in the patient's reaction to placebos. The poor correlation among various studies offers some support for this hypothesis.

The placebo stimulus variable might explain other contradictory results that follow.

Sex, age and intelligence. Conclusions about the relationship between placebo effects and sex, age, and intelligence are not possible at the present time because the results of several studies are contradictory.[6, 119, 120, 132]

Some studies report that females have more placebo effects than males; [1, 4, 32, 89,] others that there is no difference between the sexes.[7, 69, 102, 111, 141] While in some studies youth correlated positively with placebo effects;[32, 66, 132, 141] in others, it correlated negatively,[69, 89] or did not correlate either negatively or positively.[1, 7, 19, 45, 60, 62, 102, 140]

Suggestion and suggestibility. The most extensively investigated factor has been the concept of suggestion. This approach is popular because the concept is important in theories of hypnosis, and because of the ease with which tests of suggestibility can be devised, discrete experiments designed, factors manipulated, and data analysed. During the years the meaning of the term has expanded to include many diverse phenomena including the placebo effect. Unfortunately, correlations among tests of suggestibility and between these tests and personality traits are contradictory. The placebo effect does not appear to correlate with tests of suggestibility.[38, 140] The placebo effect is more complex than simple suggestion. Suggestibility in the laboratory is a somewhat different phenomenon from the placebo effect in a clinical situation.[127] This probably applies to hypnosis. Despite these differences, potential factors held in common, such as clinical and experimental situations, hypnosis, placebo effects, suggestion, persuasion, and so forth, warrant further investigation.[36, 63]

Projective tests. The results of Rorschach and other psychological tests were inconclusive or contradictory in several studies.[1, 32, 38, 45, 53, 60, 62, 69, 71, 75, 102, 132, 144]

Psychiatric diagnosis. Placebo reactions are not related to whether patients are neurotic or psychotic,[45, 65, 66, 111] although the intensity and range of such reactions may be greater in psychotics.[132] Reported placebo effects range between 18 and 67 per cent for various diagnostic categories. Placebo effects are reported more frequently in patients with symptoms of anxiety and depression.[115, 116]

Constancy of placebo effects. Severe illness and chronic symptoms do not preclude response to placebos[6, 19, 48, 96, 102, 111, 132, 141] although short duration of illness has been related to positive placebo effects.[7, 141] The response is believed to be short-lived by some investigators and long-lasting by others.[6, 25] Favourable prognoses may characterize patients with positive placebo responses.[25, 46, 47, 131, 137, 148] Inconstant placebo reactors are usually more frequent than constant positive or negative placebo reactors. Studies usually report a greater incidence of positive placebo reactions than negative reactions.[32, 45, 69, 146] Patients who fail to respond to a placebo in one study may respond in another study.[96, 150] Reactions to placebos are generally not uniform, constant, or predictable.[40, 65, 66, 150]

Anxiety. The factor most frequently reported to be characteristic of placebo reactors is that of manifest, unelaborated, free-floating anxiety.[6, 19, 25, 32, 35, 62, 69, 102, 112, 116, 128, 146] Beecher in anaesthesiology, Castiglioni in history, Malinowski in anthropology, and Parsons in sociology believe that suggestibility increases with increased stress. Hysterics with *la belle indifference*, or without manifest anxiety, are reported to react poorly to placebos. These patients traditionally have been thought to be the most suggestible of all patients. This surprising finding, especially if replicated, tends to confirm the importance of anxiety in placebo reactions. Patients without anxiety, such as sociopaths and obsessive compulsives, generally have poor prognoses and would be expected to be poor placebo reactors. Anxiety, agitation, and panic is thought to be generally a favourable prognostic sign. Schizophrenic patients with marked anxiety, in homosexual panic or with schizo-affective features, patients with agitated depression, and neurotics with manifest anxiety are among such patients. Anxiety is a favourable prognostic sign in psychotherapy, psychopharmacotherapy, insulin treatment, and lobotomy.

It is often stated that interpretations of unconscious conflicts during psychotherapy produce anxiety. During these periods of successful interpretation, insight, the *ne plus ultra* of psychotherapy, occurs. In appropriate amounts, anxiety also facilitates learning and conditioning. There is no doubt left by a review of the literature that anxiety is an important element associated with placebo effects.

Negative and nonplacebo reactors. The negative and nonplacebo reactor have not been well characterized. Some researchers report that psychotic patients have more frequent negative placebo reactions than neurotic patients,[19] but this claim is disputed by others who report little difference in the reactivity of psychotics and nonpsychotics.[66, 132] Negative reactors are described as vague, nonspecific, hard to pin down about their history, and not responding to treatment,[19] and as more rigid and controlled but with less personality deviation than reactors.[146] One author questions the adjustment of the individual as an important attribute of the placebo reactor.[66]

The results of a recent preliminary study by the author indicates that nonreactors are rigid, authoritarian, stereotypic, tend to use the mechanism of denial, and are not psychologically oriented. More reactive patients respond to the placebo. Positive reactors rely more on outer stimuli; negative reactors rely more on inner stimuli, and tend to have more paranoid and masochistic traits.[132, 134]

Motivation, learning and conditioning. Motivation, learning, and conditioning, to the extent that they are independent of transference and other factors mentioned in this paper, contribute to placebo effects. This is a new area of research and investigation.[24, 25, 31, 32, 35, 60, 63, 65, 66, 69, 143, 149, 151]

Faith. The importance of faith is reflected in the fact that one of the major, best educated, religious groups in the United States is able to deny the rational efficacy of any treatment or medicine, and to assign all treatment benefits to faith. Faith is frequently mentioned in vague terms such as trust and faith in the doctor, confidence in the treatment, expectation and anticipation of relief, previous experience with treatment and doctors, fame and popularity of a treatment and so on. When coupled with the patient's magic expectation, we get back to important elements in the doctor-patient relationship and transference.[19, 24, 25, 31, 32, 35, 49, 59, 65, 66, 82, 91, 107, 116, 141, 148]

Catharsis. Catharsis can occur in every therapy; in psychotherapy because the patient talks, in nonverbal medical treatment through symbolism and displacement. Catharsis leading to guilt reduction is one of the constants in the history of medical treatment.[58, 67, 88, 101, 119–121]

The history of medicine is filled with procedures or substances which have important symbolic meaning. In every era methods of depletion were widely used: emetics, enemas, purges, stomachics, sweating, salivating, bleeding, leeching, cupping, lancing, trephination, starvation, and dehydration. Methods of depletion and expulsion, manipulation of internal body wastes and vital fluids may relieve symptoms by symbolically expelling bad thoughts and ego-alien impulses.[33] The discomfort of submitting to these procedures and the ingestion of many vile substances may assuage and expiate considerable guilt.[18, 67] Today, in our edified and verbal culture, these primitive methods are on the wane. The same expression and relief of symptoms may occur when patients verbally express conflictual and guilt-ridden thoughts and feelings in the free, nonjudging, and accepting atmosphere of the doctor's office. The alimentary and other primitive methods of catharsis have been superseded by a more intellectual and appropriate verbal catharsis. But the fundamental mechanism may be the same.[11, 25, 39, 44, 58, 80, 88]

Defence mechanisms. Placebo effects can be discussed as defence mechanisms such as repression, regression, displacement, substitute symptom formation, obsessions, compulsions, denial, distortion, projection, flight into health, and so on.[20, 21, 25, 33, 34, 45, 49, 75, 113, 114, 116, 124, 128]

Uncontrolled and nonspecific factors in medical, psychiatric, or psychoanalytic treatment can produce placebo-effects by reassuring patients about their idiosyncracies, fantasies, fears of loss of control and potential insanity, guilt and so on. The mechanism includes inexact and incomplete interpretation and other nonspecific factors that are a part of all treatment.[128] Conflictual impulses may be displaced by the physician on to a carefree vacation, thus gratifying impulse but decreasing anxiety and guilt.[33] Countertransference is another factor.[3, 61]

Medicine may provide the same outlet for anxiety as does drinking, eating, and smoking. A patient may express his need to be cared for by a physician by requesting medication or reporting hypochondriacal symptoms because he feels unworthy of love for himself as a person because of guilt. Some patients cannot express needs for dependency except by requesting and taking medicine.

The ritual of taking medicine, like the conventional ten drops in one half glass of water, one half hour before meals and at bedtime, can decrease symptoms because of the anxiety reducing effects of obsessive-compulsive activity. Medicine may provide the patient with repetitive reminders of other reassuring aspects of the physician-patient relationship. The response of patients to medicine or placebo, whether positive, negative, or absent, may communicate important nonverbal responses to treatment.[121, 124, 128]

The use and effectiveness of any defence depend on the character of the patient, the abilities and character of the physician, and the situation in which treatment occurs.

Other Factors. Other important placebogenic factors expectation and anticipation of relief,[35] knowledge of and experience with the treatment,[1] previous experience with doctors, fame and popularity of the treatment,[128] possibilities of spontaneous remission or cure,[119] and so on.

Physician

Despite recognition throughout history that the relationship between the physician and patient was an important determinant of response to medical treatment, the responsibility of the patient for these effects has always been emphasized. Recent study of how physicians contribute to placebo and therapeutic effects has resulted in general agreement that the psychosociology of the physician is a crucial variable in therapy.

The mechanism will be referred to as iatroplacebogenics, a term describing the study of placebo effects produced by physicians.[128]

Iatroplacebogenesis can be direct or indirect. Direct refers to placebo effects produced by the direct effect of the physician's attitude to the patient, treatment, and results of treatment.

Direct iatroplacebogenesis. Attitude toward patients refers to the therapist's interest, warmth, liking, sympathy, empathy, neutrality, disinterest, hostility, and rejection.

The importance of the physician's interest is indicated by a survey in which the physician's personal interest—not his competence—was the main determinant of whether patients' like their doctors.[93]

Twenty-one studies reported that the psychotherapist's interest in the patient is associated with acceptance for treatment, less frequent drop-outs, and successful outcome of treatment.

Patient-physician expectations are important in therapy. Goldstein reports that therapists' favourable feelings to patients are related to the therapists' expectation of improvement and the patients' attraction to the therapist, and influence the obtained improvement.[35]

Strupp has demonstrated in many studies that the therapists' liking or disliking of patients is associated with the therapists' evaluation of the patients' personality, motivation, maturity, insight, anxiety, clinical status, diagnosis, treatment goals, proposed techniques, improvement expected, and mutual beliefs of the patient and therapist.[138]

Interest in the patient is related to the amount of feeling expressed in therapy by the patient, the therapist's understanding of the patient's behaviour, and to common factors in inexperienced and experienced therapists. It may be related to the frequent observation that therapists are often more successful as beginners than when experienced.

Interest in the patient has been related to successful psychochemotherapy in five studies.

Psychologists who are interested in their patients or subjects are more persuasive, elicit better conditioning and learning, higher intelligence scores, and better Rorschach records.

The interest of the investigator in the subject affects surgery in dogs, gastric acid secretion, metabolic changes, laboratory procedures, and the galvanic skin response. It has been described as a crucial variable for successful psychotherapy in summaries reported at national research conferences on psychotherapy,[90, 139] as the cornerstone of Rogerian nondirective therapy,[103] behaviour therapy,[64] in psychotherapy and psychoanalysis,[128] psychochemotherapy,[128] placebo effects,[128] the success of shamans and quacks,[58] and the saving of derelicts by the Salvation Army.[50]

The primary and direct effect of the healer's interest in the patient is on reduction of guilt. It is also associated with increased potentials for learning, conditioning, suggestibility, catharsis, and it stimulates other factors that have been correlated with placebo effects.

Attitude toward treatment, such as a therapist's faith, belief, enthusiasm, conviction, commitment, optimism, interest, positive and negative expectations, scepticism, disbelief, and pessimism about treatment, has been established by research as a nonspecific factor in most therapies. Supporting data for this notion was first reported in a study of the use and success of psychochemotherapy in 1956.[16] Most, though not all, subsequent studies confirmed this report—12 studies of psychochemotherapy, 7 studies of psychotherapy, and 2 studies of hypnosis. Interest in treatment may explain the success of younger therapists and experienced therapists who have a reputation for success with particular patients or problems.

Although it is difficult to differentiate between the therapist's interest in the patient and treatment, several studies suggest that the therapist's interest in treatment is frequently primary and leads to a secondary interest in the patient.

The primary and direct effect of the therapist's interest in the treatment is the mobilization of the patient's hope and optimism.

Attitude toward results refers to the interest of the investigator which results in data distortion caused by random observer effects and by intentional or unintentional nonrandom observer bias.

Observer bias has been extensively studied by Rosenthal.[104] One of his early experiments was a study of rat learning. Experimenters were told that their rats had been specially bred for either brightness or dullness, although rats in both groups were actually genetically pure strains. The results were that experimenters obtained significantly better learning from rats that they thought were bright than did experimenters who believed that their rats were dull.

This is not an isolated study. The data has been consistent in more than twenty different experiments involving several thousand subjects.

Rosenthal has presented data relating the sources of experimenter bias to the experimenter's hypotheses, expectations, motivation, and prestige, instances of cheating, recording and computational errors (more biased experimenters tending to make more and larger errors in the direction of their hypotheses), early data returns, nonspecific factors in the pre-data-gathering interaction (greeting, seating, instructing), verbal conditioning, visual and verbal cues, several similar personality characteristics of experimenter and subject, and so on. The behaviour and personality of the successful biaser were strikingly similar to characteristics of the successful psychotherapist. Possibly relevant to supervision in psychotherapy was the finding that the biasing phenomenon was successfully communicated by senior to assistant experimenters, who were employed as data collectors and actually performed the experiments, without the senior telling the assistant experimenters about the nature of the study.

Rosenthal's conclusion is that 'experimenters obtain the results that they want or expect,' and 'that human beings can engage in effective and influential unprogrammed and unintended communication with one another. The subtlety of this communication is such that casual observation of human dyads is unlikely to reveal the nature of this communication process'.

The direct effect of an interest in results is a nonrandom intentional or unintentional observer bias. Data are influenced, communicated, distorted, and then used to confirm hypotheses.

Conclusion. The therapist's interest in the patient, treatment, and results is related to success in treatment and placebo effects. The evidence includes many clinical studies of many patients with varying diagnoses and backgrounds, and treated with different methods by many therapists with diverse orientations and experience. The generality of the evidence is supported by similar findings in clinical and experimental psychology, and by the observations and conclusions of many physicians, psychotherapists, psychologists, and other investigators. It includes the placebo effect, brief and long psychotherapy, psychoanalysis, hypnosis, psychochemotherapy, insulin coma treatment, projective tests, general medical treatment, and experimental, and laboratory data. The evidence is no longer isolated, fragmentary, or quantitative, and has reached a qualitative stage which has established the generality of the phenomena.

All of these placebogenic or psychologic factors may now interact with the potential specific effects of various therapies. A second conclusion is that there is a complex interaction between the therapist's interest in the patient, treatment, and results. The explanation of how these factors influence results is not clear. It is also not clear which factors are primary or secondary or how these factors are related to each other as cause and effect. For example, a therapist may be interested in the treatment of a patient, expect success, and then like the patient. The patient may react to the therapist with similar feelings, and in turn, stimulate the therapist with more interest in the patient, greater enthusiasm for the treatment, and increased expectation of favourable results. All of these factors may contribute to the final success of therapy.

Indirect iatroplacebogenics. The physician's interest in his treatment and his patient is a necessary component of almost every specific therapy, has a synergistic effect on most therapies, and often produces psychological or placebo effects in and of itself. Although the concept of direct iatroplacebogenics has been demonstrated in many studies, another mechanism, indirect iatroplacebogenesis, perhaps the most subtle and extensively used mechanism, has not been considered adequately in the literature. This concept may also help explain the complex interaction described previously.[124, 128]

The physician's interest may be indirect, subtle, and paradoxical. An interest in a theory and method of treatment, as opposed to an interest in the patient, may produce placebo effects. This occurs when the patient displaces the interest from the therapy to himself and experiences the physician's interest in his treatment as a personal one. Thus, placebo effects are produced or augmented when the physician is prestigeous, dedicated to his theory and therapy, especially if it is of his own innovation, or if he is a recent convert; and when the therapies are elaborate, detailed, expensive, time-consuming, fashionable, esoteric, and dangerous.

In another paper data were presented in support of the concept of indirect (and direct) iatroplacebogenesis. Data included evidence from the history of medicine, psychopharmacology, case histories of patients treated with psychochemotherapy and psychoanalysis, many clinical and experimental studies, and observations about therapeutic and placebo effects.

The conclusion was reached that the placebo effect is probably a multidetermined phenomenon, but that iatroplacebogenesis may parsimoniously help explain many observations about therapeutic and placebo effects. The concept is supported by its general applicability to many therapies. It is probably more important in some forms of therapy than others. It may function as a prerequisite or catalyst for therapies which involve psychological factors or interpersonal relationships, for example, the evidence that specific effects occur in psychochemotherapy when the iatroplacebogenic atmosphere is favourable.

Situation

In addition to patient and physician, the treatment situation produces and influences placebo effects. Situational variables include staff attitudes, subject and patient population, treatment procedure, and miscellaneous factors.

Staff. Staff attitudes, expectations, biases, conflicts, and harmony of the staff can influence placebo effects.[2, 13, 35, 49, 74, 81, 97, 116, 135, 136, 145, 147] A placebo effect can be reduced from 70 to 25 per cent if the nurse's attitude toward the placebo injections is communicated to the patient.[145] In another study patients treated with placebos improved more than patients on tranquilizers. The authors attributed this result to the bias of the nurses against psychochemotherapy and for habit-training psychotherapy. The authors observed that nurses crushed, dissolved, and tasted the tablets in order to distinguish between placebo and active agent.[2, 19]

The continued decrease of patients in state mental hospitals since 1955 has been attributed to the tranquilizing drugs which were introduced in that year. But some authors have concluded that drugs were less important than changes in the character of attendants, nurses, and physicians, factors such as increased numbers, greater interest, optimism and so on.[74, 97] The behaviour of staff can influence patient behaviour; for example, disturbed patient behaviour has been attributed to staff conflict.[97, 135, 136]

Changes associated with research activity can produce improvement in 80 per cent of patients.[96] The bias of investigators has been noted previously to influence clinical and experimental results.[4, 6, 13, 16, 22, 52, 82, 116] Research, while attempting to control variables, often introduces other variables.[14, 30, 60, 95, 96] The changes caused by the research are difficult to evaluate. It is not easy for researchers to observe objectively when they are involved in the process of being observed.[52, 81, 96]

Subject and patient population. Subjects used for clinical and experimental drug studies are often volunteers who are assumed to be a normal control group. Several studies have demonstrated that this assumption is untenable because volunteer subjects may have a high incidence of pathology.[70, 92, 94] The converse was found in another study which concluded that volunteer subjects were less ill or as normal as control nonvolunteer subjects.[99] The degree of normality or abnormality appears to depend on the population studied.[15, 92, 94, 99]

Treatment procedure. Patients do not react uniformly to different treatment procedures.[149] Reaction to size, colour, and shape of tablets or capsules varies.[54, 72] Patients may dissolve and taste tablets if they are suspicious that it is a placebo.[19] Several investigators have reported that up to 50 per cent of patients do not take their medication or follow instructions about dosage.[27] In another study, improvement with placebos was attributed partly to one group of patients receiving a sweet placebo tablet, while another group on active drug received a bitter tablet.[2] It is possible that a prescription of *exactly* nine drops of liquid medication would be more effective than the conventional and casually prescribed ten drops. Even greater psychologic response, and placebo effects, would be expected with injections, various complicated procedures, and impressive machines.

Miscellaneous factors. Spontaneous remission, transient everyday symptoms, new social group formation, change of environment, and many changes due to environmental factors can be attributed to placebos or treatment.[35, 60, 71, 96, 97, 110, 135, 149] Sometimes placebos and the general environment are as effective if not more so than tranquilizing drugs in improving chronically hospitalized patients.[97] Psychologic factors inter-acting with social forces within the environment influence response to treatment on a metabolic and psychiatric ward.[96, 135] The transfer of psychotic patients from a state hospital to an intensive treatment hospital for lobotomies can result in considerable improvement in the behaviour of patients prior to the surgery. The mood of a group, influenced by many factors, affects placebo responsivity.[60] Placebo effects are increased in some subjects when they are tested as a group compared with individual testing.[60] Placebo reactivity is related to type of referral.[45] Untreated patients may be influenced favourably by treated patients.[81] Merely filling out questionnaires can increase the number of responses which can then be attributed erroneously to placebos.[30]

Patients may react differentially to private or clinic treatment or to treatment at a famous university centre compared with an informal private clinic. It is not known how patients differ in their response to physicians and personnel who are intimate or informal, busy or unhurried, matter-of-fact or involved, or supporting or rejecting. Studies of the psychosocial influences on psychiatric treatment have appeared recently in medical literature. The relationship between placebo effects and these important factors have not yet been explored.

5

Use of Placebos in Treatment

The attitudes of physicians toward the use of placebos in treatment was reviewed in a previous paper.[117] Before 1960 the opinions of nonpsychia-trists toward the use of placebos in treatment ranged between extremes of for and against, with the majority favouring their use. Psychiatrists were predominantly against their use. Since 1960 psychiatrists have accepted the use of placebos in treatment.[133a] The use of placebos in treatment is com-plex and a simple or absolute answer is not possible. Although the knowing or unknowing use of placebos is inevitable at the present time, encourage-ment should be given to the use of specific and rational therapy whenever possible.

Indications

Some of the less controversial indications for the use of placebos are:

for patients with degenerative, malignant, or incurable diseases for which there is no available specific treatment; for patients hospitalized for prolonged investigation who become impatient while undergoing tests; for patients with a confusing clinical course placebos can be substituted for drugs which may contribute obfuscating symptoms; for weaning postoperative patients from opiates to prevent habituation; for elderly or chronic patients who have become accustomed to taking medication of questionable value, to differentiate psychological from nonpsychological side effects in psychochemotherapy.[117, 124] Least controversial is the use of placebos as a control in research in the evaluation of therapy, although some investigators have questioned the ethics and legality of using placebos even here.

Precautions

Placebos should be used only if the indications are carefully examined. The physician should be cautious about their use when aware of hostility, contempt, and other negative feelings toward demanding and difficult patients. Placebos should not be used when the physician can think of nothing else to give. Patients may sense the underlying attitude of the doctor and their response to treatment or placebo can vary accordingly.

Inert vs Active Placebos

Opinions differ about whether to use inert or active placebos.[122, 123, 127] Active placebos, in full or inadequate dosage, such as phenothiazene tranquilizers, can have serious consequences, for example, agranulocytosis, hepatitis, and allergic responses.[125] If an active placebo is used the drug should always be a safe one. But the physician should guard against attributing favourable results to an active drug which is used as a placebo.

6

Evaluation of Therapies

Recognition and study of the placebo effect has contributed to improved methodology in clinical evaluation of therapeutic agents. Although many of the problems and difficulties in evaluation have not been solved, major advances have been achieved.

Single-Blind Procedure

Methods of clinical evaluation have had a varied and checkered history.[9] One of the earliest techniques has been referred to recently as the single-blind procedure. In this method, the physician or investigator knows that control substances are being used and which patients are receiving them. Only the patient is unaware. The control substance is usually an inert placebo.

Double-Blind Procedure

But single-blind studies frequently produce spurious results because of bias that occurs when the investigators know to which groups patients have been allocated.[128] The double-blind procedure, in which neither patient nor physician (or others treating or evaluating) know to which groups patients have been assigned, was thus evolved. Although the earliest use of such procedures goes back to the beginning of the twentieth century[100, 148] they did not become popular until recently. Since 1960 the double-blind procedure has been the norm for most well-designed studies.

Triple-Blind Procedure

The triple-blind procedure, more euphemistic than descriptive, has been used in two ways. Some investigators have attempted to exclude or minimize placebo effects by conducting a preliminary study with placebos. Placebo reactors are then excluded from the definitive study which follows. But as mentioned previously, placebo effects may occur in as high a percentage of cases in the definitive study as occurred in the preliminary study. A second use of this term refers to blindness about the design of the study. Only investigators who do not treat patients or evaluate outcome are aware of the design.

Exact Placebos

It is important that a placebo control mimic all the physical characteristics of the experimental substance. Patient, physician, or investigator may uncover the code if the placebo does not resemble the experimental drug, or have the same taste, consistency, rate of dissolving in water, and so on.

Active Placebos

The placebo control should mimic all the telltale side-effects of the experimental substance. A more sophisticated study would employ an active placebo. A placebo control into which active but incidental ingredients are introduced (such as atropine to produce xerostomia) is referred to as an active placebo. Without an active placebo, physician and staff usually can distinguish between experimental and control groups, and the double-blind procedure then actually becomes a single-blind procedure.[118]

Limitations of the Double-Blind Procedure

The use of the double-blind procedure limits the possibility of erroneous acceptance of a drug as effective when in fact it is ineffective. However, the double-blind procedure may result in rejection of an effective drug. This comes about because physicians or staff may be too conservative or anxious about their evaluations and fail to recognize true differences between placebo and active drug response.[83]

Some investigators believe that objective experiments do not exist.[17, 37, 56, 57, 106, 108] It has prompted suggestions that every experiment be done by an enthusiast and sceptic, that the investigator's bias about expected results be specified in the paper, and various suggestions about how to make methodology more rigorous and foolproof.[17, 26, 35, 37, 57, 77–79, 98, 104–106, 108, 109, 119, 142]

7

Conclusion

Therapy will be impaired if physicians are unaware of placebo effects. Therapeutic effects will be attributed to specific procedures which unknown to the physician are caused by placebo effects. The therapist's credulity about the efficacy and specificity of the procedure will be exaggerated. And it will encourage the use of one technique for all patients. Therapists who rely on one technique will be unable to treat many patients; some may be hurt because of inappropriate treatment; and specific indications for a therapeutic procedure will be obfuscated. Awareness of placebo effects will enable clinicians to better evaluate the effects of therapy, contribute to the development of more flexible and appropriate procedures, and make therapy more comprehensive, resourceful, and effective. The recognition that these factors contribute to the treatment process will improve studies by investigators, and may help clarify unsolved problems of specificity in many therapies.

It is important to remember that despite the massive evidence in support of the concepts of placebogenesis and iatroplacebogenesis, the evidence is based primarily on retrospective data. Careful prospective studies will be necessary for clarification of the primacy, relevancy, and validity of these concepts.

Medical history is largely the history of the placebo effect: *Those who forget it are destined to repeat it.* Garrison observed that 'whenever many different remedies are used for a disease, it usually means that we know very little about treating the disease, which is also true of a remedy (*sic*) when it is vaunted as a panacea or cure-all for many diseases'.[28] If we keep these thoughts in mind we may avoid the problem which the compiler of the *Paris Pharmacologia* insightfully observed a century ago: 'What pledge can be afforded that the boasted remedies of the present day will not like their predecessors, fall into disrepute, and in their turn serve only as a humiliating memorial of the credulity and infatuation of the physicians who recommended and prescribed them.'[43]

REFERENCES

1. ABRAMSON, H. A., JARVIK, M. E., LEVINE, A., KAUFMAN, M. R., and HIRSCH, M. W., 1955. Lysergic acid diethylamide (LSD-25). XV. The effects produced by substitution of a tap water placebo. *J. Psychol.*, **40**, 367.

2. BAKER, A. A., and THORPE, J. G., 1957. Placebo response. *Am. med. Assn Arch. Neurol. Psychiat.*, **78**, 57.

3. BARCHILON, J., 1958. On countertransference 'cures'. *J. Am. Psychoanal. Assn*, **6**, 222.

4. BEECHER, H. K., 1952. Experimental pharmacology and measurement of the subjective response. *Science*, **116**, 157.

5. BEECHER, H. K., 1955. The powerful placebo. *J. Am. med. Assn*, **159**, 1602

6. BEECHER, H. K., 1959. *Measurement of the subjective response*. New York: Oxford Univ. Press.

7. BLACK, A. A., 1966. Factors predisposing to a placebo response in new outpatients with anxiety states. *Brit. J. Psychiat.*, **112**, 557.

8. *Blackiston's new Gould medical dictionary*, 1st ed., 1949. Philadelphia: Blackiston.

9. BULL, J. P., 1959. The historical development of clinical therapeutic trials. *J. Chron. Dis.*, **10**, 218.

10. *The catholic encyclopedia*, vols **2, 7, 8.** 1911. New York: Gilmary Society.

11. DE GRAZIA, S., 1952. *Errors of psychotherapy*. New York: Doubleday and Co.

12. DURAN-REYNALS, M. L., 1946. *The fever bark tree*. New York: Doubleday and Co.

13. EISSEN, S. B., SABSHIN, M., and HEATH, H., 1959. A comparison of the effects of investigators' and therapists' attitudes in the evaluation of tranquilizers prescribed to hospital patients. *J. nerv. ment. Dis.*, **128**, 256.

14. EKMAN, P., 1961. Research therapy. *J. nerv. ment. Dis.*, **133**, 229.

15. ESECOVER, H., MALITZ, S., and WILKENS, B., 1961. Clinical profiles of paid normal subjects volunteering for hallucinogenic drug studies. *Am. J. Psychiat.*, **117**, 910.

16. FELDMAN, P. E., 1956. The personal element in psychiatric research. *Am. J. Psychiat.*, **113**, 52.

17. FELDMAN, P. E., 1963. Non-drug parameters of psychopharmacotherapy the role of the physician. In *Specific and Non-Specific Factors in Psychopharmacology*. Ed. Rinkel, M. New York. Philosophical Library:

18. FENICHEL, O., 1954. *Brief psychotherapy in the collected papers of Otto Fenichel*. New York: W. W. Norton and Co.

19. FISHER, H. K., and OLIN, B. M., 1956. The dynamics of placebo therapy: A clinical study. *Am. J. Med. Sci.*, **232**, 504.

20. FORRER, G. R., 1964. The therapeutic use of placebo. *Mich. Med.*, **63**, 558.

21. FORRER, G. R., 1964. Psychoanalytic theory of placebo. *Dis. Nerv. Syst.*, **25**, 655.

22. FOULDS, G., 1958. Clinical research in psychiatry. *J. ment. Sci.*, **104**, 259.

23. FOX, B., 1961. The investigation of the effects of psychiatric treatment. *J. ment. Sci.*, **107**, 493.

24. FRANK, J. D., 1958. Some effects of expectancy and influence in psychotherapy. In *Progress in Psychotherapy*, vol. 3. Eds. Masserman, J. H., and Moreno, J. L. New York: Grune and Stratton.

25. FRANK, J. D., 1961. *Persuasion and healing*. Baltimore: The Johns Hopkins Press.

26. FRIEDMAN, N., KURLAND, D., and ROSENTHAL, R. (In Press). Experimenter

behavior as an unintended determinant of experimental results. *J. Proj. Tech.*

27. GARETZ, F. K., 1962. A comparison of urine phenothiazine test results with prescribed medication dosage. *Am. J. Psychiat.*, **118**, 1133.
28. GARRISON, F. H., 1921. *An introduction to the history of medicine.* Philadelphia: W. B. Saunders.
29. GARTNER, Jr, M. A., 1961. Selected personality differences between placebo reactors and non-reactors. *J. Am. Osteopath, Assocn*, **60**, 377.
30. GLASER, E. M., and WHITLOW, G. C., 1954. Experimental errors in clinical trials. *Clin. Sci.*, **13**, 199.
31. GLIEDMAN, L. H., GANTT, H., and TEITELBAUM, H. A., 1957. Some implications of conditional reflex studies for placebo research. *Am. J. Psychiat.*, **113**, 1103.
32. GLIEDMAN, L. H., NASH, JR, E. H., IMBER, S. D., STONE, A. R., and FRANK J. D., 1958. Reduction of symptoms by pharmacologically inert substances and by short-term psychotherapy. *Am. med. Assn Arch. Neurol. Psychiat.*, **79**, 345.
33. GLOVER, E., 1931. The therapeutic effect of inexact interpretation: A contribution to theory of suggestion. *Internat. J. Psychoanal.*, **12**, 397.
34. GLOVER, E., 1952. Research methods in psychoanalysis. *Internat. J. Psychoanal.*, **23**, 403.
35. GOLDSTEIN, A. P., 1962. *Therapist-patient expectancies in psychotherapy.* New York: The Macmillan Co.
36. GOLDSTEIN, A. P., 1966. Psychotherapy research by extrapolation from social psychology. *J. Counsel. Psychol.*, **13**, 38.
37. GREINER, T., 1962. Subjective bias of the clinical pharmacologist. *J. Am. med. Assn*, **181**, 120.
38. GRIMES, F. V., 1948. The nature of suggestibility. In *Studies in psychology and psychiatry.* Ed. Stafford, J. W. Washington: Catholic University.
39. GUMPERT, G., 1963. Witch-doctor 'psychiatrists'. *SK&F Psych. Report*, **9**, 2.
40. HAGANS, J. A., DOERING, C. R., ASHLEY, F. W., and WOLF, S., 1957. The therapeutic experiment. *J. Lab. Clin. Med.*, **9**, 282.
41. HAGGARD, H. W., 1929. *Devils, drugs and doctors.* New York: Harper and Bros.
42. HAGGARD, H. W., 1933. *Mystery, magic and medicine.* New York: Doubleday Doran and Co.
43. HAGGARD, H. W., 1934. *The doctor in history.* New Haven: Yale Univ. Press.
44. HALEY, J., 1963. *Strategies of psychotherapy.* New York: Grune and Stratton.
45. HANKOFF, L. D., ENGELHARDT, D. M., FREEDMAN, N., MANN, D., and MARGOLIS, R., 1960. Denial of illness. *Am. med. Assn. Arch. gen. Psychiat.*, **3**, 657.
46. HANKOFF, L. D., ENGELHARDT, D. M., and FREEDMAN, N., 1960. Placebo response in schizophrenic outpatients. *Arch. gen. Psychiat.*, **2**, 33.
47. HANKOFF, L. D., FREEDMAN, N., and ENGELHARDT, D. M., 1958. The prognostic value of placebo response. *Am. J. Psychiat.*, **115**, 549.
48. HARGREAVES, G. R., HAMILTON, M., and ROBERTS, J. M., 1958. Treatment of anxiety states: II Clinical trial of benactyzine in anxiety states. *J. ment. Sci.*, **104**, 1056.
49. HOFLING, C. K., 1955. The place of placebos in medical practice. *Gen. Pract.*, **11**, 103.
50. HOLMES, O. W., 1891. *Medical essays, 1842-82.* Cambridge, Mass.: The Riverside Press.
51. HONIGFELD, G., 1964. Non-specific factors in treatment: 1. Review of

placebo reactors. II. Review of social-psychological factors. *Dis. nerv. Syst.*, **25**, 145; 225.

52. HOUSTON, W. R., 1938. Doctor himself as therapeutic agent. *Ann. Int. Med.*, **11**, 1416.

53. HULL, C. L., 1933. *Hypnosis and suggestibility.* New York: Appleton-Century.

54. *J. Am. med. Assn*, 1955. Placebos (Editorial). **159**, 780.

55. JASPERS, K., 1965. *The nature of psychotherapy.* Chicago: Univ. Press.

56. KELLY, M., 1962. The tempestuous winds of fashion in medicine. A College of Medicine Lecture, State Univ. Iowa, College of Med., Iowa City, *Arch. Int. Med.*, **110**, 287.

57. KETY, S., 1961. The academic lecture. The heuristic aspect of psychiatry. *Am. J. Psychiat.*, **118**, 385.

58. KIEV, A., 1964. The study of folk psychiatry. In *Magic Faith and Healing.* Ed. Kiev, A. London: Collier-Macmillan Ltd.

59. KLOPFER, B., 1957. Psychological variables in human cancer. *J. Proj. Tech.*, **21**, 331.

60. KNOWLES, J. B., and LUCAS, C. J., 1960. Experimental studies of the placebo response. *J. ment. Sci.*, **106**, 231.

61. KOLB, L. C., and MONTGOMERY, J., 1958. An explanation for transference cure: Its occurrence in psychoanalysis and psychotherapy. *Am. J. Psychiat.*, **115**, 414.

62. KORNETSKY, C., and HUMPHRIES, O., 1957. Relationship between effects of a number of centrally acting drugs and personality. *Am. med. Assn Arch. Neurol. Psychiat.*, **77**, 325.

63. KRASNER, L., 1962. Therapist as social reinforcement machine. In *Research in Psychotherapy.* Eds. Strupp, H. H., and Luborsky, L. Washington: American Psychological Assoc.

64. KRASNER, L., 1964. Societal and professional implications of the behavior therapies. Paper presented at the First International Congress on Social Psychiatry, London, England.

65. KURLAND, A. A., 1957. The drug placebo—its psychodynamic and conditional reflex action. *Behav. Sci.*, **2**, 101.

66. KURLAND, A. A., 1958. The placebo. In *Progress in psychotherapy*, vol. 3. Eds. Masserman, J. H., and Moreno, J. L. New York: Grune and Stratton.

67. LaBARRE, W., 1964. Confession as Catholic therapy in American indian tribes. In *Magic Faith and Healing.* Ed. Kiev, A. London: Collier-Macmillan Ltd.

68. LASAGNA, L., LATIES, V. G., and DOHAN, L. J., 1958. Further studies on the 'pharmacology' of placebo administration. *J. Clin. Invest.*, **37**, 533.

69. LASAGNA, L., MOSTELLER, F., VON FELSINGER, J. M., and BEECHER, H. K., 1954. A study of placebo response. *Am. J. Med.*, **16**, 770.

70. LASAGNA, L., and VON FELSINGER, J. M., 1954. The volunteer subject in research. *Science*, **120**, 359.

71. LEHMANN, H. E., and KNIGHT, D. A., 1960. Placebo-proneness and placebo-resistance of different psychological functions. *Psychiat. Quart.*, **34**, 505.

71a. LENNOX, W. G., 1957. The centenary of bromides. *New England J. Med.*, **259**, 887.

72. LESLIE, A., 1954. Ethics and practice of placebo therapy. *Am. J. Med.*, **16**, 854.

73. LIBERMAN, R., 1962. An analysis of the placebo phenomenon. *J. Chron. Dis.*, **15**, 761.

74. LINN, E. L., 1959. Sources of uncertainty in studies of drugs affecting mood, mentation or activity. *Am. J. Psychiat.*, **116**, 97.

75. LINTON, H. B., and LANGS, R. J., 1962. Placebo reactions in a study of LSD-25. *Arch. gen. Psychiat.*, **6**, 369.
76. MAJOR, R. H., 1955. *Classic descriptions of disease*. Springfield: C. C. Thomas.
77. MASLING, J., 1959. The effects of warm and cold interaction on the administration and scoring of an intelligence test. *J. Consult. Psychol.*, **23**, 336.
78. MASLING, J., 1960. The influence of situational and interpersonal variables in projective testing. *Psych. Bul.*, **57**, 66.
79. McGUIGAN, J. F., 1963. The experimenter: A neglected stimulus object. *Psychol. Bul.*, **61**, 421.
80. MEERLOO, J. A. M., 1958. The essence of mental cure. *Am. J. Psychoth.*, **12**, 42.
81. MEZAROS, A. F., and GALIGHER, D. L., 1958. Measuring indirect effects of treatment on chronic wards. *Dis. Nerv. Syst.*, **19**, 1.
82. MODELL, W., 1955. *The relief of symptoms*. Philadelphia: W. B. Saunders.
83. MODELL, W., and HOUDE, R. W., 1958. Factors influencing clinical evaluation of drugs. *J. Am. med. Assn*, **30**, 2190.
84. MORISON, R. A. H., WOODMANSEY, A., and YOUNG, A. J., 1961. Placebo response in an arthritis trial. *Ann. Rheum. Dis.*, **20**, 179.
85. MOTHERBY, G., 1795. *A new medical dictionary or general repository of physics*. 4th ed. London: J. Johnson.
86. MULLER, B. P., 1965. Personality of placebo reactors and nonreactors. *Dis. Nerv. Syst.*, **26**, 58.
87. MURRAY, J. H., 1933. *A new English dictionary on historical principles*. Oxford: Clarendon Press.
88. MURRAY, J. M., 1964. Psychotherapeutic aspects of shamanism on St. Lawrence Island, Alaska. In *Magic, faith and healing*. Ed. Kiev, A. London: Collier-Macmillan Ltd.
89. O'BRIEN, J. R., 1954. Is liver a 'tonic'? A short study of injecting placebos. *Brit. Med. J.*, ii, 136.
90. PARLOFF, M. B., and RUBINSTEIN, E. A., 1958. Summary of research problems in psychotherapy conference, 1958. In *Research in Psychotherapy*. Eds. Rubinstein, E. A., and Parloff, M. B. Washington: American Psychological Assoc.
91. PARSONS, T., 1951. *The social system*. Glencoe, Ill.: The Free Press.
92. PERLIN, S., POLLIN, W., and BUTLER, R. N., 1958. The experimental subject. *Am. med. Assn Arch. Neurol. Psychiat.*, **80**, 65.
93. POLANSKY, N., and KOUNIN, J., 1956. Clients reactions to initial interviews. *Hum. Rel.*, **9**, 237.
94. POLLIN, W., and PERLIN, S., 1958. Psychiatric evaluation of 'normal control' volunteers. *Am. J. Psychiat.*, **115**, 129.
95. RASHKIS, H. A., 1960. Cognitive restructuring: Why research is therapy. *Am. med. Assn Arch. gen. Psychiat.*, **2**, 612.
96. RASHKIS, H. A., and SMARR, E. R., 1957. Drug and milieu effect with chronic schizophrenics. *Am. med. Assn Arch. Neurol. Psychiat.*, **77**, 202.
97. RATHOD, N. H., 1958. Tranquilizers and patients' environment. *Lancet*, i, 611.
98. REZNIKOFF, M., and TOOMEY, L. C., 1959. *Evaluation of changes associated with psychiatric treatment*. Springfield: C. C. Thomas.
99. RICHARDS, T. W., 1960. Personality of subjects who volunteer for research on a drug (Mescaline). *J. Proj. Tech.*, **24**, 424.
100. RIVERS, W. H. R., 1908. *The influence of alcohol and other drugs on fatigue*. London: Edw. Arnold.

101. RIVERS, W. H. R., 1924. *Medicine, magic and religion.* London: Macmillan and Co.

102. ROBERTS, J. M., and HAMILTON, M., 1958. Treatment of anxiety states. *J. ment. Sci.*, **104**, 1052.

103. ROGERS, C. R., 1957. The necessary and sufficient conditions of therapeutic personality change. *J. Consult. Psych.*, **21**, 95.

104. ROSENTHAL, R., 1963. On the social psychology of the psychological experiment: The experimenter's hypothesis as unintended determinant of experimental results. *Am. Sci.*, **51**, 268.

105. ROSENTHAL, R., 1964. Letter to the editor. *Behav. Sci.*, **9**.

106. ROSENTHAL, R. (In press). Experimenter effect in the interpretation of data. In *The experimenter in psychological research.* New York: Appleton-Century Crofts.

107. ROSENTHAL, D., and FRANK, J. D., 1956. Psychotherapy and the placebo effect. *Psychol. Bul.*, **55**, 294.

108. ROSENTHAL, R., PERSINGER, G. W., MULRY, R. C., VIKAN-KLINE, L., and GROTHE, M., 1964. Emphasis on experimental procedure, sex of subjects and the biasing effects of experimental hypotheses. *J. Prog. Tech.*, **28**, 470.

109. ROSENTHAL, R., PERSINGER, G. W., VIKAN-KLINE, L., and FODE, K. L., 1963. The effect of early data returns on data subsequently obtained by outcome-biased experimenters. *Sociometry*, **26**, 487.

110. SABSHIN, M., and RAMET, J., 1956. Pharmacotherapeutic evaluation and the psychiatric setting. *Am. med. Assn Arch. Neurol. Psychiat.*, **75**, 362.

111. SAMUELS, A. S., and EDISEN, C. B., 1961. A study of the psychiatric effects of placebo. *J. Louisiana Med. Soc.*, **113**, 114.

112. SCHAPIRO, A. F., 1955. Psychological factors in evaluation of hypertensive drugs. *Psychosom. Med.*, **17**, 291.

113. SCHMIDEBERG, M., 1939. The role of suggestion in analytic therapy. *Psychoanal. Rev.*, **26**, 219.

114. SCHMIDEBERG, M., 1958. Values and goals in psychotherapy. *Psychiat. Quart.*, **32**, 234.

115. SHAPIRO, A. K., 1959. The placebo effect in the history of medical treatment-implications for psychiatry. *Am. J. Psychiat.*, **116**, 298.

116. SHAPIRO, A. K., 1960. A contribution to a history of the placebo effect. *Behav. Sci.*, **5**, 109.

117. SHAPIRO, A. K., 1960. Attitudes toward the use of placebos in treatment. *J. nerv. ment. Dis.*, **130**, 200.

118. SHAPIRO, A. K., 1960. A browsing double-blind study of iproniazid in geriatric patients. *Dis. Nerv. Syst.*, **21**.

119. SHAPIRO, A. K., 1963. The psychological use of medication. In *The psychological basis of medical practice.* Eds. Lief, H. I., Lief, V. F., and Lief, N. R. New York: Harper Bros.

120. SHAPIRO, A. K., 1964. Factors contributing to the placebo effect: Implications for psychotherapy. *Am. J. Psychoth.*, **18**, 73.

121. SHAPIRO, A. K., 1964. Etiological factors in the placebo effect. *J. Am. med. Assn*, **187**, 712.

122. SHAPIRO, A. K., 1964. An historic and heuristic definition of the placebo. *Psychiatry*, **27**, 178.

123. SHAPIRO, A. K., 1964. Rejoinder. *Psychiatry*, **27**, 178.

124. SHAPIRO, A. K., 1964. Placebogenics and iatroplacebogenics. *Med. Times*, October.

125. SHAPIRO, A. K., 1964. Rational use of psychopharmaceutic agents. *N.Y. State J. Med.*, **64**, 1084.

126. SHAPIRO, A. K., 1966. The curative waters and warm poultices of psychotherapy. *Psychosomatics*, **7**, 21.

127. SHAPIRO, A. K. (Submitted for publication). Semantics of the placebo.

128. SHAPIRO, A. K. (Submitted for publication). Iatroplacebogenics.

129. SHAPIRO, A. K. (In preparation). Placebo response and prognosis.

130. SHAPIRO, A. K. (In preparation). Problems in the measurement of placebo effects.

131. SHAPIRO, A. K. (In preparation). Correlates of the placebo response.

132. SHAPIRO, A. K. (In preparation). Attributes of the positive, absent, and negative placebo reactor.

133. SHAPIRO, A. K. (In preparation). Questionnaire survey of the attitudes toward a definition of placebo.

133a. SHAPIRO, A. K. (In preparation). Attitudes toward the use of placebos.

134. SHAPIRO, A. K. (In preparation). The meaning and treatment of negative placebo reactors.

135. SHOTTSTAEDT, W. W., PINSKY, R. H., MACKLER, D., and WOLF, S., 1959. Prestige and social interactions on a metabolic ward. *Psychosom. Med.*, **21**, 132.

136. STANTON, A. H., and SCHWARTZ, M. S., 1954. *The mental hospital.* New York: Basic Books.

137. STEINBROOK, R. M., JONES, M. B., and AINSLIE, J. D., 1966. Suggestibility and the placebo effect. *J. nerv. ment. Dis.*, **140**, 87.

138. STRUPP, H. H., 1960. *Psychotherapists in action.* New York: Grune and Stratton.

139. STRUPP, H. H., and LUBORSKY, L., 1962. *Research in psychotherapy.* Washington: American Psychological Assoc.

140. STUKAT, K., 1958. *Suggestibility—a factorial and experimental analysis.* Stockholm: Algrist e Wilsell.

141. TIBBETS, R. W., and HAWKINS, J. R., 1956. The placebo response. *J. ment. Sci.*, **102**, 60.

142. TROFFER, S. A., and TART, C. T., 1964. Experimenter bias in hypnotist performance. Abstract. Laboratory of Human Development, Stanford University, California.

143. TROUTON, D. S., 1957. Placebos and their psychological effects. *J. ment. Sci.*, **103**, 344.

144. UHLENRUTH, E. H., CANTOR, A., NEUSTADT, J. O., and PAYSON, H. E., 1959. The symptomatic relief of anxiety with meprobamate, phenobarbital and placebo. *Am. J. Psychiat.*, **115**, 905.

145. VOLGYESI, F. A., 1954. 'School for patients' hypnosis therapy and psychoprophylaxis. *Brit. J. Med. Hypnotism*, **5**, 8.

146. VON FELSINGER, J. M., LASANGA, L., and BEECHER, H. K., 1955. Drug-induced mood changes in man. 2. Personality and reactions to drugs. *J. Am. med. Assn.* **157**, 1113.

147. VON MEHRING, O., and KING, S. R., 1957. *Renovating the mental patient.* New York: Russel Sage Foundation.

148. WHITEHORN, J. C., 1958. Psychiatric implications of the 'placebo effect'. *Am. J. Psychiat.*, **114**, 662.

149. WOLF, S., 1959. The pharmacology of placebos. *Pharm. Rev.*, **11**, 689.

150. WOLF, S., DOERING, C. R., CLARK, M. L., and HAGANS, J. A., 1957. Chance distribution and the placebo 'reactor'. *J. Lab. Clin. Med.*, **49**, 837.

151. WOLF, W., 1950. Effects of suggestion and conditioning on the action of chemical agents in human subjects—the pharmacology of placebos. *J. Lab. Clin. Med.*, **29**, 100.

XXIII

CLINICAL PERSPECTIVES
IN PSYCHO-PHARMACOLOGY*

JEAN DELAY

Professeur de Clinique des Maladies Mentales et de l'Encéphale de la Faculté de Médecine de Paris, membre de l'Académie Nationale de Médecine.

and

PIERRE DENIKER

Professeur agrégé de Neuro-psychiatrie à la Faculté de Médecine de Paris, Médecin de l'Hôpital Sainte-Anne.

By psychopharmacology, which is only ten years old, we mean the knowledge about and the research on all the chemical agents having the property of influencing behaviour in general, and man's mental state in particular. In a general clinical survey, we shall mainly study psychopharmacology in its psychiatric applications and particularly the pharmaco-dynamic exploration of the personality and the various chemotherapies of mental diseases.

From the historical point of view, research about medications for the mind, is as ancient as medicine and therapeutics. However, it must be acknowledged that up to the present, this research remained fruitless, so far as true drug therapy of the major psychoses is concerned. In the same way, the collective or individual use of substances inducing euphoria, intoxication or hallucinations appears to be as old as civilization, even though it seems that in the past the use was less widespread than it is now.

If psychopharmacology has recently become a particular medical discipline, it is probably due to three more or less concurring advances. The first is the pharmacological exploration of the psyche, which makes it

* Translated by Maria-Livia Osborn, Research Assistant, The Institute of Family Psychiatry, Ipswich.

possible to change, almost at will, in a pre-determined way, the mental state for diagnostic or psychotherapeutic purposes. Secondly, a renewal of interest caused by research on the possible existence of a material substratum for certain mental diseases; this substratum could be a biochemical lesion generating abnormal pathogenic metabolites. These findings have been made plausible by the discovery of infinitesimal doses of 'hallucinogenic' substances and made possible by the advances in intimate chemistry of the brain. Lastly and most important, new aspects of psychiatric chemotherapy have achieved the methods of biological treatment, particularly the treatment of psychotic diseases, formerly regarded as incurable.

These are, then, the three aspects of psychopharmacology that we shall consider in the limited space of this paper: general problems of definition and classification, pharmaco-dynamic explorations of the psyche, research in the biochemical substratum of psychoses, psychiatric chemotherapies and lastly the shaping of future prospects.

1

Problems of Classification and Nomenclature

Among the general problems of methodology in psychopharmacology, the crossroads of many disciplines, the problem of definition and classification is unquestionably important.

On the one hand, a tentative classification based on *chemical structures* is made difficult by the fact that, for the same type of psychotropic action, different compounds are found which have nothing in common; for instance major tranquillizers or neuroleptics are found among phenothiazines, reserpinic or butyrophenones; anti-depressant drugs are either tricyclic compounds or hydrazines.

On the other hand, a *purely pharmacological* classification is inconvenient because in psychopharmacology, instead of proceeding from the animal to the man, research workers were often obliged to do the reverse: starting from clinically observed effects, they tried to select experimental tests or, more exactly a battery of tests, which would allow them to predict what effect a drug would have on man, and to select the most efficient compounds that would produce that effect. In this way psychopharmacology based on prediction and selection was born, an important contribution to basic pharmacology.

The research workers have succeeded empirically in establishing classifications, the main categories of which are essentially *clinical* categories based on the most important type of effect on man: sedative effects, stimulating effects, or effects disturbing mental activity. Within their main divisions, it is possible to define some sub-groups, which correspond with a particular type of effect correlating experimental and clinical data; such sub-groups are, for instance, the hypnotics, the tranquillizers, the anti-depressants etc. .... Lastly, in each sub-group, we find some basic chemical structures, which are of particular value.

In short, a practical and modern classification, which could be used by both clinicians and basic scientists might be useful on three levels: (*i*) On the clinical level, in which the main types of effect on man are described; (*ii*) on the psychopharmacological level proper, in which are indicated the operational patterns corresponding to both experimental data and clinical observations for certain types of medications and drugs; (*iii*) on the level of structural chemistry, in which, as we shall see, a classification has retained a certain interest.

We may hope that in future better knowledge of the mechanisms of psycho-physiological effects and biochemical metabolism will allow us to establish a more rational classification. Despite the complexity of these two mechanisms, which are both involved in this classification, the data already acquired about biogenous amines and their role in certain nervous structures enable us to think that eventually it will be possible to have notions simple enough to be easily used as a principle of classification.

For the moment, we shall limit ourselves to describe, as an example, the principles of the classification we have proposed, and which have been adopted by both pharmacologists and clinicians. This method of classification, which is essentially clinical, is based upon the *principal* effect of the compounds upon mental 'tone', this 'tone' being considered as the *resultant* of the levels of alertness and of mood.

Modern drugs and medications are thus divided into three main groups:

> The *psycholeptics*, which lower the psychological tone;
> The *psycho-analeptics*, which increase this tone;
> The *psycho-dysleptics*, which disturb mental activity.

1. The psycholeptics are divided into (*i*) depressants of alertness, or *hypnotics*, and (*ii*) sedatives of mood, or tranquillizers. Among the latter, we can differentiate the neuroleptics or major tranquillizers, characterized by neurological, extrapyramidal and vegetative effects quite specific to them, setting them apart from the *minor tranquillizers*, which could be compared with classic sedative drugs.

2. The psycho-analeptics too are divided into two subgroups: *stimulants of alertness*, or anti-hypnotics, such as the phenamines and their derivatives, and *stimulants of mood* or anti-depressants, whether they are imipramine derivatives or belong to the group of monoamine-oxydase inhibitors. Classic stimulants are classified in this group.

3. The psycho-dysleptics include the drugs which produce disturbed or deviant forms of mental activity. These are the 'hallucinogenic' or better *oneirogenic* drugs, which cause a system of dreams, as well as the compounds which give birth to 'oneirism' with mental confusion.*

---

* Such are Ditran (a mixture of benzylates of piperidyl) and 7360 RP which is a phenothiazine inducing delusion.

This classification is shown in Table 1, where the clinical aspect of the main types of psychotropic action is shown in the left column; in the middle column are listed the main psychopharmacological types to which we shall return when dealing with operational definitions; and in the right column are described the chemical structures, the importance of which will be discussed later.

TABLE 1

Classification of psychotropic drugs

A—*PSYCHOLEPTICS*		
(a) acting upon alertness (noo-leptics)	1—*Hypnotics:*	barbiturics non-barbiturics
	2—*Neuroleptics:*	phenothiazines reserpincs butyrophenones
(b) acting upon mood (thymo-leptics)	3—*Tranquillizers:*	meprobamate diazepines, etc.
B—*PSYCHO-ANALEPTICS*		
(a) stimulating alertness (noo-analeptics)	1—*Alertness amines:*	phenamines and derivatives
(b) stimulating mood (thymo-analeptics)	2—*Anti-depressants:*	tricyclics hydrazines IMAO etc.
C—*PSYCHO-DYSLEPTICS*		
disturbing mental activity	*Hallucinogenics* or oneirogenics	Mescaline Lysergamide Psilocybine

First of all, let us remember that it is convenient to apply this system of classification only with flexibility and taking dosages into account. Because, even though some categories are symmetrically opposed to each other as the hypnotic drugs and the stimulants, or even as mere antidotes—the neuroleptics counter-acting the hallucinogenic drugs—, other limits are less clearly defined, for example, small doses of hypnotics may have a sedative action; small repeated doses of dysleptics may have the same action as psychostimulants, and again high doses of analeptics may be psycho-pathogenic.

Another consideration, which in future may have to be taken into account, is the possible finding of compounds that, thanks to their properties will 'span' categories in the classification. Some tranquillizers with basic stimulating structures have already been found, such as the benzhydrol derivatives; some sedatives of the diazépine group have paradoxical effects upon mood, such as an anti-depressant action, which has been observed.

Research is already orientated towards a synthesis of molecules of complex action. After observing that neuroleptics and analgesic drugs reinforce each other's efficiency, a phenomenon called 'neuroleptanalgesy', the researchers looked for structures which would not be a mixture of compounds, but a combination of them. On the other hand, as the associations of neuroleptics and anti-depressant drugs are more and more frequently used in psychiatry, the researchers are trying to find complex molecules which would produce the effect of both. But we must admit that until now no decisive advances have been made in this field; although drugs in association, far from nullifying each other, add to their respective effect, the combination of opposite properties in the same chemical structure has not yet been achieved.

2

Investigations in Pharmacodynamics

Although certain procedures such as narco-analysis date back to the Second World War, the techniques of pharmaco-dynamic investigation are among the first rank acquisitions of modern psychopharmacology. Despite the little attention paid to them, these techniques have possibilities of fruitful investigation in store.

These experiments, as it is well known, consist in administering a single dose—repeatedly or not—of different agents capable of altering the level of alertness and consciousness and even of introducing a series of dreams. These experiments indicate very well the 'acute' effect of the compounds used. However, the usefulness of repetition of these trials is limited by a progressive slackening of their effects (tachyphilaxy) in the case of the amphetamines, or by mere need for caution, in the case of oneirogenic drugs.

Narco-analysis. Barbituric subnarcosis, an agent of narco-analysis, allows us to lower alertness, and thus makes it easier to examine the psyche and investigate the subconscious. Moreover, the subnarcosis has a favourable effect—although transitory—upon disruption of mood; this is used in diagnosis to reduce inhibition and depression, and thus to facilitate the exteriorization of depressing thoughts. However, we must remember that subnarcosis has some effect upon neurological extra-pyramidal symptoms, temporarily reducing them. Care should be taken, therefore, not to confuse them with hysterical manifestations.

Amphetamine experiments. The reverse experiment, using intravenous amphetamine injections employed in the so-called 'weck-analysis', induce a keen intellectual stimulation, making speech and memorizing easier and thus allows the investigation of mutism, resistances and amnesia. The 'amphetaminic shock' is also an efficient treatment for symptoms of hysterical conversion. But, amphetamine administered parenterally has also a stimulant effect and thus has been used for diagnostic aims in cases of atypical depressions as it produces improvement in neurasthenic forms, but aggravates depressive psychosis.

Amphetaminic subnarcosis. Nowadays, it is possible to associate and combine the two above-mentioned tests, thanks to the technique of amphetaminic subnarcosis.* Thus it is possible to act upon the level of alertness and consciousness, upon intellectual activity and memory, or upon mood, by inducing euphoria, to facilitate a more precise psychiatric diagnosis and to discover individual psycho-biographical elements, which can be used in psychotherapy.

'Chemical psycho-analysis' is on principle repudiated by the most strict Freudians, who see in it the intervention of an artificial factor, alien to the real relationship between patient and psychotherapist. For this reason it is necessary that the psychotherapist using these pharmacodynamic procedures should have an exact knowledge of them, he should be cautious and should not forget objectivity and common sense. These conditions observed, 'brief psychotherapy' can be employed for the treatment of some emotional disorders, of some sexual neuroses and some psychosomatic symptoms. Freud himself said that he was interested in 'psychological methods' because, in his days, there were 'no other ones', but he had foreseen the time when psychiatrists would have learned how to 'have a direct influence, through the use of special chemical substances, upon the amount of energy and its localization in the mental apparatus'.†

However, pharmacodynamic investigations of the personality are invaluable tools of research, which should be used as a routine examination in modern psychiatric services. It would be unfortunate if, to adhere to a doctrine, young psychiatrists should renounce them on principle.

Oneiroscopy. There is also a special investigation process, called oneiroscopy, which involves the use of an hallucinogenic compound, and particularly psilocybine. This technique is of interest inasmuch as it can induce a dreaming activity without sleep allowing the subject to memorize and analyse each detail of the dream. Of course, this method is to be advised only when other means have failed; and it goes without saying that the test will be repeated as seldom as possible as each session provides the psychiatrist with considerable psychological material.

It has been agreed too that, as a rule, the infinite repetition of this sort of experiment upon volunteers is to be avoided. However, from Moreau de Tours onwards, specialists have gathered psycho-pathological information of inestimable value by practising auto-observation. Besides the antidotic property of the neuroleptics, which anyway will reverse these artificially induced effects has made the practice of these experiments much easier and more legitimate.

It is indeed unfortunate that nowadays there should be a misuse

---

* By using amobarbital with methylamphetamine.

† S. Freud, *An outline of psychoanalysis.*

outside medicine, of hallucinogenics, but this is no concern of ours, since these abuses are quite independent of the medically controlled use of these drugs. Besides we must remember that modern research on psycho-dysleptics plays a great part in the renewal of interest on work on the biochemical substratum of the psychoses. The finding of the hallucino-genic properties—with infinitesimal doses—of LSD 25 has given new interest to the research on abnormal natural metabolites, which, even in very small quantities, can induce psychopathological states.

3

Perspectives of Biochemical Psychiatry

Here, we are led to examine a particular aspect of psychochemistry: the mental disorders of 'dysmetabolic' origin. It could be argued whether this field is part of psychopharmacology, but as drug action and biochemical abnormalities eventually occur through the body metabolism and the nervous structures, it is logical not to dissociate them completely. An example of this close relationship is the antidotic effect of *triphosphoric adrenosine* (A.T.P.) to the neuroleptics, in both man and animal.

Another example is *glutamic acid*, initially considered, as a metabolite of the nervous cells, for the treatment of deficiency psychoses. Even though the initial hypothesis has not been confirmed by recent works on levoglutamine, it is nevertheless true that this acid and its salts often act as psychic stimulants, maybe on account of their acid p(H).

On the other hand, it is known that decisive advances have been made in the treatment of metabolic mental deficiency typified by *phenylpyruvic oligophrenia*, which is due to a well defined disorder in the metabolism of amino-acids. Recent clinical works have proved that patients kept on special diets, in which the quantity of phenylalamine was rigorously determined, showed a complete reversal of both psychic and physical symptoms.

Great advances have also been made in identifying mental disorders caused by the *porphyrins*. Thus, states formerly described as mental confusions, as 'schizophrenias', and especially as 'hysterical states', can now be attributed to their real cause, and receive a more suitable treatment.

The etiology of schizophrenia, whose genetic factors are yet to be confirmed, has led, of course, to numerous biochemical researches, many of which are still proceeding. This research could be divided in two groups: the endeavour to find in the schizophrenic patients' body fluids (and possibly in those of their parents') abnormal pathogenic substances, to be defined later; and the attempt to modify the patient's metabolism in order to produce either improvement or aggravation of psychotic symptoms, and hence infer the nature and seat of an etiological dysmetabolic disorder. One of the hypotheses currently accepted by several research groups is that of an abnormality in the *transmethylation* of biogenous amines in schizophrenia. A compound extracted from schizophrenic patients' urine, or from members of their families, reveals a 'pink spot' when subjected to electrophoresis. This corresponds to an abnormal, dimethylated dopamine derivative, the dimethoxyphenylethylamine, which has been experimentally proved to be pathogenous, when inoculated into volunteers. Simultaneously, other research workers have tried to influence the metabolism of cerebral amines with amino acids or methionine (bearing methyl) and through the action of monoamine oxydase—they seem to have observed concomitant and transistory aggravation of the patient's mental state.

This work, however encouraging for research, cannot yet be considered as having reached firm conclusions. Meanwhile it is not unrealistic to foresee that research on the metabolism of cerebral amines will lead to important findings in the near future. Indeed too many seem to reach the same conclusion. In the biochemistry of certain mental disorders, we know that a manic fit (an acute manic episode) involves a massive elimination of 5-hydroxyindolacetic acid (5HIAA), a phenomenon which does not occur in other states of agitation. Whilst there is no comparable study in the melancholic states, the complete study of the metabolites of the catecholamines is not yet achieved. As for the effect of the main psychiatric drugs, it is generally agreed that neuroleptic drugs fixate (phenothiazine) or displace (reserpinic) the bioamines of the intraneuronal granules; in the same way, anti-depressant drugs assist the storage of mono-amines (IMAO), or increase the sensitivity of the tryptamino receptors (imipraminic). Lastly, we are becoming better acquainted with the chemical mechanisms characteristic of the nervous structures, through which drugs act; the neuroleptics have particular effect upon the striated centres and it has been demonstrated that extra-pyramidal diseases are accompanied by modification of the metabolism of neurogenic amines in the sub-cortical structures, the chemical mechanism of which is already known.

From the clinician's point of view, it is quite reasonable to think that in future research on the 'biochemical lesions' responsible for mental disorders will require close co-operation between biochemists and psychiatrists. The exact diagnostic classification of the psychic manifestations is here as important as the accuracy and reliability of chemical analysis. Moreover, although it involves delicate ethical problems, it cannot be denied that the best way of ascertaining whether a chemical compound found in a sick organism is really pathogenic, is to administer it to healthy volunteers.

4

Chemotherapy of the Psychoses

For many of us, the introduction of chemotherapy in the treatment of the psychoses has contributed to giving psychopharmacology its own individuality.

As we have seen, the drugs effective in the major psychoses have varied chemical structures, but can be classified into two main groups: the neuroleptics on the one hand, and the anti-depressants on the other. Although quite different and often opposed in their effects, these two types of medication have several characteristics in common: first, their action is bound to a certain degree of nervous impregnation, and they should be used for a continuous period; second, their action is manifest through therapeutic effects and, at the same time, through certain *neurological effects*, often unobtrusive, but rarely absent, which point to impregnation; lastly, they seem to have an essentially *deferring* action on the disorder in question, therefore the treatment must be prolonged for as long as the treated disease is present.

Neuroleptics

The neuroleptics were the first to be used after the discovery of chlorpromazine. Their therapeutic effect is accompanied by a tendency to produce characteristic psycho-motor, extra-pyramidal and neuro-vegetative syndromes. Most compounds answering this definition are to be found in the phenothiazine groups; their strength varies according to the nature of the radicals tied to the benzolic nucleus, but they are differentiated mostly by the length and the structure of the lateral chain. The aliphatic chains correspond especially to sedative effects, with akinetic and

TABLE 2

The main neuroleptic phenothiazines.

1—*Phenothiazines with a lateral aliphatic chain:*

Chlorpromazine	(Largactil)	} halogenic derivatives
Triflupromazine	(Vesprin)	
Promazine	(Sparine)	
Acépromazine	(Plegicil)	
Levomepromazine	(Nozinan)	

2—*Phenothiazines with a piperazinic lateral chain:*

Prochlorpemazine	(Tementil)
Thiopropazate	(Dartal)
Perphenazine	(Trilifon)
Dixyrazine	(Esocos)
Thioproperazine	(Majeptil) sulfamide derivative
Butyrylperazine	(Rendolectyl)-butyryl derivative
Trifluoperazine	(Terfluzine) } fluor derivatives
Fluphenazine	(Moditen or Desyner)

3—*Phenothiazines with a piperidinic lateral chain:*
    Mepazine (Pacatal)
    Thioridazine (Melleril)
    Propericiazine (Neuleptil)

neuro-vegetative neurological symptomatology; the piperazinic chains provide 'uninhibitor' compounds, if not stimulants, which allow maximum hyperkinetic effects with a minimum of vegetative modifications; lastly, the piperidinic chains produce substances easy to manage, as they have few side effects, but are certainly less active.

With the phenothiazines, reserpine should be mentioned, nowadays less used, but with a differential analogy of action with chlorpromazine, by which we recognize the individual and characteristic general action of the neuroleptics.

More recently, the *butyrophenones* have been introduced—a group of equal interest. Its prototype, haloperidol, possesses a powerful sedative action simultaneously with marked anti-hallucinatory properties. The discovery of these substances followed that of the neuroleptics in general, but it must be stressed that these therapeutic and neurological properties of the butyrophenones have confirmed their value. Thus it could be said that all psychotropic drugs having anti-psychotic effects and inducing vegetative and extra-pyramidal manifestations, are neuroleptics; while sedative drugs stripped of neurological effect are tranquillizers, with much more limited indications for the treatment of the major psychoses.

Recent facts have reinforced this point of view. Until 1964, all true neuroleptics were found in the following three chemical structures: phenothiazines, reserpinics and butyrophenones. But in the last two years, different formulae have been successfully offered, especially some derivatives of iminodibenzyle (dibenzothiazepine), thioxanthene derivatives (thiothixene), procainamide derivatives (metoclopramide) etc. All these compounds have the same effects as the neuroleptic prototypes on psychoses, and the same specific neurological manifestations.

What is the future of this group of neuroleptics, whose list is already long and varied? We might compare it with the antibiotics whose numerous forms have made it possible to find more powerful, easier to manage or more specific compounds. We have seen that the effects peculiar to each type of neuroleptic are a guide in the choice of indication; in addition the introduction of new compounds has made it possible to reduce, bit by bit, the number of cases resistant to chemotherapy. It is well known that the best indication for neuroleptics are states of excitement and psychotic agitations and that thanks to the neuroleptics, a great change has taken place in the atmosphere of psychiatric services and in the care of patients. The neuroleptics are effective in acute and subacute psychoses (except in endogenous depressions, to be discussed later) and also in chronic psychoses formerly considered incurable. But if we consider, for instance, the case of schizophrenic psychoses, we must admit that the neuroleptic are effective mostly in psychotic 'seizures', in hallucinatory or delirious episodes, when deficiency symptoms of inertia or of athymia have a poor response to the drug. Indeed there has been great progress in psychopharmacology by the introduction of the neuroleptics with uninhibiting

TABLE 3

Psychophysiological characteristics of the neuroleptics

Experimental data	Clinical data

1. *Causing a particular state of psychomotor indifference*

Reversible hypersomnia by trivial stimuli (E.E.G. of physiological sleep with spreading of the initial stages, rarity of the rapid rhythms of wakefulness and great number of slow waves. Absence of spindles.)

Experimental data	Clinical data
Decrease of spontaneous and induced locomotor activity.	Rarity and slowness of movements hypo- or amimia.
Inhibition of conditioned and learned reflexes.	Psychic indifference, decrease of initiative. Emotional and affective neutrality. No gross alteration of consciousness or intellectual faculties.

2. *Efficacy in excited and agitated states*

Experimental data	Clinical data
Tranquillizing of naturally aggressive animals.	Efficiency in manic syndrome.
Action upon the sham-rage of decorticated animals.	Effect upon excitement and psychotic agitation in general.
Suppression of the hyperkinesia of the 'IDPN turning mice' without narcoses nor paresia.	Action upon aggressivity and impulse.

3. *Gradual reduction of acute and chronic psychotic disorders*

Experimental data	Clinical data
Antagonism towards psychodysleptics or hallucinogenic drugs.	Anti-confusional, anti-hallucinatory and delirious actions.
Preventive and reducing action on 'experimental psychoses'.	Disinhibitory or stimulating action in schizophrenia.
No effect upon experimental neuroses.	

4. *Production of vegetative and extra-pyramidal syndromes*

Modifications of thermic regulations, of the pulse, of blood pressure, peristalsis, secretions and metabolism.

Anti-emetic action

Experimental data	Clinical data	
Catalepsy (according to the species)	Akinetic syndrome	of the
Tremors. Paroxystic dyskinetic and buccal hyperkinetic disorders (in monkeys)	Hyperkinetic syndrome durable or transitory Hypertonic syndrome	post- encephalic type

5. *Principal subcortical effects*

Experimental data	Clinical data
Action upon the reticular system.	Action upon psychotic syndromes in relation to diencephalic pathology.
Diencephalic accumulation of labelled phenothiazines and displacement of serotonin by reserpine.	Side-effects, cf. 4 above.
Experimental meso-diencephalic lesions.	

TABLE 4

General characteristics of the anti-depressants.

Clinical data	Experimental data
1. General behaviour	
Thymo-analeptic action upon depressive mood after a regular delay (10–15 days) with the possibility of inversion of mood.	Motor hyperactivity of animals (of the amphetaminic type). No action upon conditioned reflexes.
2. Vigil function	
Reduction of sleep (after initial drowsiness with tricyclic derivatives).	Potentialization of the hypnotics.
3. Extra-pyramidal effects	
Corrective action on neuroleptic akinesia and anti-parkinsonian action on akinesia.	Anti-neuroleptic action, specially anti-reserpinic (upon the ocular syndrome of the animal).
4. Vegetative actions	
Chiefly orthostatic hypotension (Hypertensive thrusts so called paradoxical). Retarded peristalsis and decreased salivation. Inhibition of sexual functions.	Hypotension. Activation of sexual functions (MAOI).
5. Convulsant action	
Activation of E.E.G. in epileptics (tricyclics). Convulsions with high dosage and in predisposed patients.	Anti-convulsant with useful doses. Convulsant with high dosage.
6. Biological actions	
Anti-pyridoxine action	Inhibition of monoamine-oxidase or increase of sensitivity to tryptamino-receptors.

effect (piperazinic phenothiazine, butyrophenone, thiothixene), and the therapeutic combination of antidepressants, or shock-therapy, with neuroleptics. Possibilities for research in this field are still open.

Anti-depressants

The anti-depressants are quite different from the neuroleptics. But here again, the varieties of chemical structures forces us to resort to an essentially clinical definition: the anti-depressants are characterized by their therapeutic property in the treatment of depression, which they can correct (thymo-analeptic action) and even reverse (thymo-reversive action). This therapeutic effect is accompanied by neurological effects which, though slighter than those induced by the neuroleptics, are, nevertheless, worth noting: these are vegetative effects (slackening of peristalsis, of salivation and often of arterial hypotension), and extra-pyramidal effects, characterized by small intention tremor and slight dysarthria, as well as anti-Parkinsonian effect (on akinesia), and an anti-neuroleptic effect.

These general properties are quite common to chemical substances with very different structure and biological properties, which can be classified into two groups: in the first one are the tricyclic derivatives, typified by imipramine; in the second, the monoamine-oxydase inhibitors, which are mostly hydrazines.

The tricyclic derivatives are largely used, even by general practitioners, for the treatment of depressions and related disorders. Imipramine remains the referential drug, compounds with greater sedative effect have been produced with the introduction of amitryptiline and trimeprimine, the most stimulating compound being represented by chlorimipramine.

The M. A. O. inhibitors are more delicate in management, particularly for possible effects on blood pressure (hypotension, and hypertension,

TABLE 5

Main anti-depressant drugs

Tricyclic derivatives of imino-dibenzyle	Imipramine (Tofranil) Desimipramine (Pertofran) Chlorimipramine (Anafranil) Amitriptyline (Laroxyl, Elavil) Nortriptyline (Flurostyl) Trimeprimine (Surmontil)
Hydrazines	Isoniazide (Rimifon)—non MAOI
	Iproniazide (Marsilid) Nialamide (Niamide) Isocarboxazide (Marplan) Hydrazino-octane (Ximaol) Phenelzine (Nardelzine–Nardile) Iproclozide (Sursum) Pheniprazine (Catron)*
Non-hydraziniques	Tranylcypromine (Tylcyprine, Parnate) Etryptamine (Monase)*

* No longer on the market.

wrongly called 'paradoxal') and anti-vitaminic effects (nephritis, stomatitis), but they are invaluable in those cases of depression that do not respond to iminodibenzyle derivatives, and in certain cases of asthenic neuroses, in which their effect is comparable to that of hormones.

It must be noted that these two types of anti-depressants have in common convulsive potentialities, latent in most of them, which, however, could lead experimental research towards the new compounds with quantitative or qualitative superiority.

However, it must be admitted that anti-depressants have not reached the power and the quick action of the electro-shock, which remains the best treatment for serious or emergency cases of depression, while the anti-depressants are specially suitable for prolonged therapy in the chronic or recurring forms, so frequent in old people. Far from opposing each other, the two methods are complementary, but it can be assumed that eventually a drug as powerful, effective and safe as E.C.T. will be produced, even though it has not quite yet been achieved.

Another possibility of developing the anti-depressant chemotherapies is in the field of neurosis, a less serious but much more frequent mental disorder than the psychoses. The results observed in the treatment of certain obsessional neuroses by imipramine, and the treatment of cases of psychoasthenia by iproniazide, already indicate an open field of research, which is far enough from the symptomatic treatment by classic sedatives or by modern tranquillizers. It is quite probable that the drugs stimulating mental energy in any of its aspects will be greatly developed in the future.

5

Risks, Shortcomings and Future Aims

In this survey of the main chemotherapies in psychiatry, we have mentioned the advances that could be made in each category; it is desirable that neuroleptic compounds should become even more numerous, that they should become more powerful, more specific in action, and easier to use; in the same way, the research field is open to the production of anti-depressant drugs with the same efficiency as E.C.T. and capable of meeting the requirements of individual responses.

Again, from the nosographic point of view, those mental disorders which have least benefited from the new treatments could be listed. Thus we have shown that those forms of schizophrenia, such as forms of 'athymia', as well as old chronic forms, present serious problems of therapeutic research.

In the same way, deficiency psychoses— mental retardation and deterioration—constitute an almost unexplored field of research. However, a cautious use of tranquillizers and of stimulants has already resulted in limited but appreciable symptomatic improvements in a number of cases.

Research on new drugs affecting memory and learning is already on the programme of some laboratories. The curiosity caused by experimental administration of ribo-nucleic acid, the substratum of genetic 'memory', is not satisfied, but work is progressing with other substances, such as Pemoline-magnesium, which we know to be related to amphetamine, and has re-kindled interest in the amphetaminic trials for investigating disorders of memory.

It is quite probable that the neuroses in general will greatly benefit from progress in psychopharmacology; we have sketched the perspectives of the anti-depressant drugs. In cases of anxiety, tension or stress, the current attitude of the therapist—whether a specialist or not—seems to be the prescription of tranquillizers, in ever increasing quantity. It is a way of shirking the analysis of the disorder and disguising it, more or less without going to the bottom of the trouble whether psychological or merely physical.

This leads us to consider the possible abuse of psychotropic drugs and medications. Some years ago, the American Congress, perturbed by the consumption of tranquillizers in the United States, initiated an investigation on the usefulness and abuse of these compounds which, it seemed, absorbed a considerable part of the national income. The only practical conclusion was to restrict to medical prescription a larger number of substances. This tendency is to be found in the rules of all modern countries. It must be stressed that the dangers of modern psychotropic drugs derives mostly from their use outside medicine and without medical advice.

It must also be emphasized that the most useful drugs in psychopharmacology are those with the least drug dependence, or toxic effects. Particularly the neuroleptics, or major tranquillizers, have no euphoric effects to cause drug-addiction, and it can even be questioned whether their systematic association with classic narcotics would not further reduce the dangers of addiction, when their use is necessary. The anti-depressant drugs effecting depressive states, could produce after the bout of depression, slight excitation, but despite this they do not cause drug addiction. This is probably due to the type of psychic disorder for which this type of medication is prescribed, as it is well known that cases of melancholia, classically tested with laudanum, would only exceptionally turn to drug addiction.

So the notion of 'special' type of disorder can never be emphasized too much, regarding the risks of drug addiction. Whether it depends on individual psychological factors, or on social climate, drug craving plays a part too often forgotten; drug dependence leads to their abuse and changes the most ordinary drug into a dangerous poison, like the barbiturates and the hypnotics, the phenamines and even the tranquillizers, which the drug addict's inventive mind has contrived to combine with alcohol to obtain reactions similar to those of the psychodysleptics.

Of course, it is also easy to obtain a greater number of substances, the use and fancy associations of which could not be foreseen. A sad example is the recent collective addiction to hallucinogenic drugs, which are completely alien to medical use. Only strict and all embracing regulation will enable us to fight these abuses without withdrawing from the practitioner all the weapons of modern psychopharmacology.

In concluding about the perspectives in psychopharmacology, we could say that in the future there will be no great revolution, as this has already taken place, by the discovery of efficient means for the chemical control of behaviour and for the medical treatment of mental disorders. Considering how the chemotherapy of psychoses started, it can be said that its progress has been due to one principle—that of medical treatment for madness—aided by innovations in chemistry and pharmacology. And we have reasons to believe that it will be the same in the future.

REFERENCES

1. *Actualités de thérapeutique psychiatrique*, 1963. By a group of twelve authors. Paris: Masson.
2. BORDELEAU, J. M., Ed., 1961. *Système extra-pyramidal et neuroleptiques*. International Symposium at Montreal, 1960. Editions Psychiatriques.
3. BRADLEY, P., DENIKER, P., and RADOUCO-THOMAS, C., Eds., 1959. *Neuro-psychopharmacology* I. Proceedings of the Congress at Rome, 1958. Elsevier.
4. BRADLEY, P., FLUGEL, F., and HOCH, P., Eds., 1964. *Neuro-psychopharmacology*, III. Proceedings of the Congress at Munich, 1962. Elsevier.
5. Conference on depression and allied states, McGill University, 1959. *Canadian Psychiat. Assn. J.*, **4**. Special suppl, p. 197.
6. DELAY, J., 1950. *Méthodes biologiques en clinique psychiatrique*. Paris: Masson.
7. DELAY, J., and DENIKER, P., 1961. *Méthodes chimiothérapiques en psychiatrie*. Paris: Masson.
8. DENIKER, P., 1957. *Hibernothérapies et médicaments neuroleptiques*. Paris: Doin.
9. DENIKER, P., 1966. *La psycho-pharmacologie*. P.U.F.
10. GARATTINI, S., and GHETTI, V., Eds., 1957. *Psychotropic drugs*. Proceedings of the International Symposium of Milan, 1957. Elsevier.
11. *International Symposium on Chlorpromazine and Neuroleptic Drugs, Paris, 1955*. Encéphale, 1956. Special issue.
12. KLINE, N. S., Ed., 1958. *Psychopharmacology frontiers*. Symposium of the 2nd World Congress of Psychiatry, 1957. New York, Little, Brown and Co.
13. LEWIN, L., 1928. *Les paradis artificiels*. French translation by Payot.
14. *Neuro-psychopharmacology* IV. 1966. Proceedings of the Congress at Birmingham, 1964. Elsevier.
15. RINKEL, M., and DENBER, H., Eds., 1958. *Chemical concepts of psychosis*. Symposium of 2nd World Congress of Psychiatry, 1957. McDowell-Obolensky.
16. ROTHLIN, E., Ed., 1961. *Neuro-psychopharmacology*. II. Proceedings of the Congress at Basle, 1960. Elsevier.

17. *Round-table on Psychopharmacology*. 1963. Presided by Delay, J., Proceedings of 3rd World Congress of Psychiatry, 1961. Vol. 3, 431–62. Toronto: Univ. Press.

18. UHR, L., and MILLER, J., 1960. *Drugs and behaviour*. New York: John Wiley and Sons.

XXIV

FAMILY PSYCHIATRY

John G. Howells
M.D., D.P.M.

The Institute of Family Psychiatry
Ipswich and East Suffolk Hospital, Ipswich

Family Psychiatry[5, 7, 8] is a new theoretical and practical system for the clinical practice of psychiatry, whereby the family group replaces the individual as the functional unit. Thus, individual psychiatry taking the adult as the functional unit (adult psychiatry), the child as the functional unit (child psychiatry), or the adolescent as the functional unit (adolescent psychiatry), is made obsolete by this new system.

Family psychiatry in its clinical application is an approach which takes the family as the unit for the organization of practice. Taking the family as the unit, in the author's system, applies to the referral plan, to the explanation of symptomatology, to the procedures of investigation, to the recording of data, and to the processes of therapy. The family is the focus of endeavour throughout; the aim is to produce an harmonious, healthy, well adjusted family.

Interest in the family and its psychiatry does not always coincide with the system of family psychiatry—the two should not be confused. For instance, in the movement to understand the individual in terms of his family dynamics, the emphasis is on the individual. But in family psychiatry the emphasis is on the family group as a single unit, the individual is only one of its many elements. Again much has been written about the technique whereby an individual may be treated within his family group, family group therapy. But in family psychiatry the family group itself is the object of therapy and this technique is but one of a number of techniques of a larger system of family therapy. Also, interest has concentrated on the possible association of schizophrenia with family dynamics. But in family psychiatry schizophrenia is one part only of the whole spectrum of clinical disorders which are considered on the principle that the family should be the unit of study.

1

Theoretical Aspects of Family Psychiatry

General

Family psychiatry is a revolt from the present tendency to over-concentrate on individual intrapsychic events alone. It restores balance by giving significance also to events outside the individual; the most cogent are within the family, and others lie in society. Thus account is taken of the individual intrapsychic, family and social events.

Humanity flowing in a stream from the Past, through the Present into the Future, might appear at first glance to be made up of a multitude of individuals. Closer observation, however, shows that they coalesce into groups. These groups, the families, expand, individuals split off and new groups are formed. But for the coalescing groups, the families, the flow of humanity would stop; through these groups humanity propagates itself and nurtures and trains its new members. Hence the family is the most significant unit in society. In his life span the individual normally experiences two groups, his family of origin as a child, and his family of adoption later. Such groups, family groups, are so tightly formed and have such a continuous history as to claim to be the basis on which society is built.

The choice of a functional unit in psychiatry is between the individual, the family, or society. The first and most important reason for choosing the family as the unit relates to its special significance as mentioned above in the emotional life of the individual and society as the unit for child rearing. A child's emotional health or sickness is dependent on the quality of the influences coming from the individuals closest to it in its formative years, usually the other family members (for example, see the photograph facing p. 660). Thus the family has special significance in the emotional life of people. Furthermore, sick young members of sick families are prone as adults to make sick families of their own later on and thus perpetuate the sick unit from generation to generation. Thus, even more significant than its being the unit for child care, is its function as the originator of more families. The family is the begetter of families.

The second reason for choosing the family as the unit relates to its position midway between the individual and society. The sick individual, sick family, and sick society, are indivisible. All elements of the field of forces in the life space have equal significance as phenomena, but due to special factors in clinical psychiatric practice, the sick family is the best vantage point from which to work, and ignores neither the individual nor the society.

The third reason for taking the family as the unit relates to its size; it is a manageable small group in society. Occasionally, the family is not the significant unit in child rearing, e.g. it may be an institution, or the greater family, the clan. Were these anomalies widespread, they would have led to the acceptance of a larger social group as the functional unit, and thus to a less manageable systematization of psychiatric services; it is fortunate that the optimum group for child rearing is a group manageable in psychiatric practice. As an element in the total field of forces in the life space, the family can claim no more significance than other elements, e.g. the individual, or the community, or the culture. But in psychiatric practice it is certainly the most meaningful and convenient unit.

Rarely, a sick person does not indicate a sick family, but without exception it still means family involvement. Take the extreme case of a sick person joining a family. Immediately the family is involved. The family have accepted him as a member for motives of its own. The family itself may become ill, or could become the best agent for producing health in him. The family is still the significant unit.

When, as it is usual, a sick member indicates a sick family, the members of the family are not all sick to the same degree; the interplay of factors producing pathology from the past and present life experiences do not strike each family member equally. But whatever the degrees of pathology in individual members, there is family involvement and family psychiatry is the method of choice in their resolution.

Family psychiatry does not overlook intrapsychic events and individual procedures; it embraces both. The individual is an element in the family and all aspects of his structure and functioning must be encompassed. He gains new significance when seen against the background of family and society. Individual procedures of referral, investigation and treatment are elements in the system of family psychiatry, but, again, given new significance when related to the whole.

Family psychiatry does not impose a rigid conformity in interpreting phenomena, e.g. the Freudian, Jungian systems can be retained by its adherents. But, by revealing a larger canvas it exposes traditional views to a new scrutiny. Re-evaluation may lead to new philosophies which can be embraced as readily in family psychiatry. Nor does it limit psychiatric practice to one clinical syndrome. All are embraced—delinquency, psychopathy, psychosomatic disease, neurosis, psychosis, and mental retardation. The core of the system, the essential principle, is that the family is always the functional unit. Thus any existing psychiatric service, whatever its case material, system, facilities, location or philosophy, is capable of adaption to and gaining from family psychiatry.

Like the 'individual psychiatrist', the family psychiatrist is dependent upon the findings of the basic scientists, but in addition he must absorb the relevant work of sociologists, social workers, developmental, experimental, industrial, cultural and social psychologists, cultural and social anthropologists, ethnographers, and historians.

What It Is Not

The central idea of family psychiatry—the family as the unit in clinical practice—because of its novelty provokes, as is to be expected, the usual resistances to the acceptance of a new concept. For instance, it calls for a shift in conceptualization. Moreover, progress implies criticism of previous practice; the advance may be explained away by saying that it has always been practised without the critic understanding its true nature.

A common misconception is to assume that family psychiatry means using the family background of an individual *to help that one person*. It takes various forms which can be illustrated from the management of a child patient. Hitherto in the children's field, emphasis has been placed on the intrapsychic functioning of the child, and little prominence given to the present environmental influences. Fantasies have been assumed to be more important than on-going traumata, even in therapy. The parents' involvement in starting and maintaining the child's illness has not been appreciated. The child has been regarded as an isolated sick individual for whose care the parents require advice and reassurance *in order to help the child*. This is classical, old-time child guidance and *child psychiatry*. Sometimes the involvement of the parents in the child's illness is perceived, but is often limited by concentrating on the mother-child relationship alone—*child and mother psychiatry*. Less often, attention is given to the involvement of both parents in the child's condition. This may lead to adjusting the joint parental attitude or ameliorating the parental illness *in order to help the child—child and parent psychiatry*. An advance from this position sees the child as a part of a family situation, parents and sibs, that requires adjustment *in order to help the child–child and family psychiatry*. But, *family psychiatry* sees the child's illness as a part of family illness. It gives no more, but no less, attention to the presenting child in the procedures of investigation, than it does to the remaining family members. It aims to produce a healthy family including a healthy child. Throughout, the family, and not the individual, is the functional unit.

Sometimes family psychiatry is thought of as a procedure which studies specific events in the family background which may have *given rise to illness* in one person. Prominence is given to such events as divorce, 'broken home', hospital admission, the mobility of the family, etc. But family psychiatry sees these as incidents in a long, wide, family life experience. Divorce, for instance, may be an attempt to solve the family's problems; it is the end product of a whole group dynamic process and the reaction of the individual to it has significance only against this far wider background.

Again, family psychiatry may be thought of as a measure which takes account of *the effect on* the family of mental illness in one family member. But this is but a part of the whole picture. Account must, of course, be taken of such matters as the different attitudes towards a sick person in sick and healthy families, the motives for the care of the patient in the family, family attitudes leading to the individual's hospital care, the ability of the family to co-operate in treatment, the contribution of the family in causing the patient's illness; the family may be equally sick and it may require help in its own right. Understanding will come from the study of the family as a unit. It is not a matter of the patient *and* his family, but of the patient as *part of* his family.

Due to the great interest in the new technique of *family group therapy*, this is sometimes thought to embrace the whole of family psychiatry. In fact, family group therapy is just one of the many measures employed in family therapy, the treatment of the family. Family therapy in turn is just one aspect of the total system of family psychiatry. To practice family group therapy alone is a severe limitation to the practice of family psychiatry.

The quest for the factors responsible for *schizophrenia* has focused attention on family psychopathology as the possible causal agent. There is such interest in this aspect of family psychopathology that it might be thought to be the whole of family psychiatry. It has led to prominence being given to the management of this one clinical condition in family practice and overlooking the value of family psychiatry in the management of a wide variety of other clinical conditions. Indeed, there is controversy as to the contribution of family psychopathology in schizophrenia and to the efficacy of resolving family psychopathology in its treatment. Whatever contribution family psychiatry has to make in schizophrenia, it has a more certain place in the management of the far commoner and equally destructive condition of emotional disorder, or neurosis.

Advantages of Family Psychiatry

Family psychiatry pays attention not only to intrapsychic events, but also brings into prominence extrapsychic events in the family and social environment of the individual. Individual, family and social psychiatry are indivisible. The door is opened to new outlooks, procedures of investigation and methods of treatment.

An outstanding advantage of family psychiatry is the economy of the procedure. The information so carefully garnered to help one member of the family is precisely the information required, with small additions, to assist all the members of the family. Often the same measures of treatment will help the whole family group.

Again, within families there are 'see-saw' movements; as one member of the family improves so another deteriorates. It is possible to treat one member of the family to the disadvantages of the remainder. What profit to a family if one member improves while the others become liabilities? Such happenings will not be apparent unless attention is paid to the whole family.

Furthermore, when the co-operation of the whole family is obtained, there are no impediments introduced by absent members who often feel criticized by implication.

At every level of clinical practice, referral, investigation and treatment, many advantages accrue over the traditional individual procedures.

The *referral* service allows for the acceptance of patients of any age group and of any clinical category. The presenting patient may be the least ill. Behind him are equally or more disturbed additional family members. Family psychiatry does not neglect them.

Symptomatology in an individual, a part of the family, or the whole family, is not explained in terms of obscure theoretical formulations, but as an inevitable consequence of the life experience of the whole family group. Clarity can replace concepts that hitherto by their unreality have confused clinical practice.

In the procedures of *investigation* much more attention is paid to the stresses bearing on the individual than in traditional procedures. These invariably arise within the intimates of the presenting patient—often within the family. Thus all possible foci of stress are brought into the investigation. It is soon apparent that it is not a matter of individual psychopathology, but a situational psychopathology involving the whole family. This new investigatory approach has been an impetus to the development of new facilities for investigation—new psychometric techniques, and the useful family group diagnosis.

The processes of *treatment* are enormously enhanced by accepting the family as the functional unit. New methods of treatment have emerged which are more effective than traditional procedures and can be employed when traditional methods are inoperative. Even individual psychotherapy is enhanced if the therapist bears in mind that he is involved in a great deal more than just the individual patient and his psychopathology; if he casts his horizon to the family his individual techniques are improved. Dyadic procedures are more in use. Family group therapy, sometimes termed conjoint therapy, has emerged as a profitable and promising method of treatment. Vector therapy[8] devised by the author repatterns the field of forces in the life space to bring relief and benefit to individuals and families. Greater attention to the impact of the community and culture on the family creates opportunities in the field of preventive psychiatry. By producing a healthy family, a healthy platform is developed which will maintain the health of all the family members.

Lastly, a new area for research has emerged. The infant is born and nourished in a group situation; much more attention is given to the evaluation of the group forces bearing on the infant throughout his formative years. Light is thrown too on those members of the family who are often neglected—father, siblings, etc. The family is a sub-unit of the community, and increasing attention is given in research to the family's involvement with the community, culture and society. Other areas thrown into relief include: the reason behind the referral of a particular individual patient; the family's contribution in the aetiology of clinical conditions; the generation to generation spread of family psychopathology pointing to the familial rather than the hereditary transfer of neurosis; anomalies of family functioning which throw up new areas for investigation (e.g. one healthy member in an otherwise unhealthy family).

A Family Model

Humanity flows through time. The past reaches the present and flows on into the future. This is a dynamic process of which we are a part, and which we perceive from within the process. Individuals usually coalesce into small loose groups, the families in the time-space continuum. Time passes, and individuals break off from the families to form new families; and these again pass on into time, coalescing and breaking up. These coalescing groups, the families, need description. They are complex. Categorisation is essential so that an understandable description can be communicated to others. To be able to encompass them calls for some frame of reference, which should take account of the separate functioning parts of the family and the family as a whole.

Furthermore, the family is an everchanging, flowing dynamic entity. To grasp change is usually beyond our conceptualization. Therefore we freeze the family process at one moment in time, usually our first contact with the family, and describe what we see. We must be careful to add dynamism to this static picture.

Life development is not smooth, nor is human development—hence pain, anguish and incompetence. For the clinician, description is more than a theoretical exercise. For sick families he needs a conceptual framework that will allow assessments to be made, therapy to be planned and the outcome to be predicted.

Furthermore, a clinician has to pay special attention to the emotional aspects of the family. It must be confessed that emotion and emotional disorder are concepts not easy to define. Emotion is perhaps the best word we have. Attempting more precise definitions in our present state of knowledge may be disadvantageous. Emotional phenomena are real enough.

A study of relevant authorities, the requirements of the situation, and clinical experience, would suggest that a satisfactory conceptual framework must embrace the following:

1. The individual as an amalgam of the physical and emotional; his whole functioning in health and disease, at all times of life.

2. Reciprocal interactions in the family involving individuals, dyads, family coalitions and the whole family.

3. The family as a small group with a structure and properties—roles, leadership patterns, qualities, standards, etc.

4. The material structure of the family.

5. The family as a sub-system of society and endowed with social properties. The family is an entity in a field of forces and thus there is a transactional process that includes all family elements, the extended family, community and culture.

6. The historical development of the family. Thus the time sequence of past, present and future.

7. The family as a unit of change—its dynamism, its flow, the process.

8. Family functioning and dysfunctioning, health and pathology.

9. Flexibility to allow for different sizes, states and conditions.

10. Practicality that allows the framework to be expanded for research, or contracted according to the dictates of the day to day work.

Labelling of families as clinical or other categories is to be avoided. Labelling has a disadvantage of concentrating upon one element, which by chance has come into focus, and thus of giving that element disproportionate attention. In individual psychiatry, for instance, such labels as anxiety neurosis, obsessional neurosis, depression, etc. have focused upon the presenting symptom in the individual, and has led to a situation where the symptom itself is regarded as the illness, and scarce attention is given to the rest of the psychopathological processes within the individual. Such labels limit description. It is the whole *process* in individual, family and society which has to be understood and described and then re-patterned to bring health, efficiency and competence into the individual, family and social system.

The author has suggested[8] that the above can be satisfied in a fifteen-dimensional approach to the family. Five dimensions are each described at three consecutive time periods, the past, the present and the future. The five are those of the individual dimension, the relationship dimension, the group properties dimension, the material circumstances dimension, the family-community interaction dimension.

Usually, a family description starts with the present in its five dimensions. To understand the present in the light of what has gone on before then requires a description of the past in five dimensions. Ideally it should be completed with a description of the future in its five dimensions; in our present stage of knowledge this is only predictable within crude limits, e.g. that a university career is possible, a marriage breakdown likely, or financial difficulties a probability.

The analysis of a simple three member family is taken for illustration.

1. *The individual dimension* can diagrammatically be represented as follows:

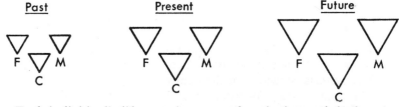

Each individual's life experience as a functioning and dysfunctioning social being is evaluated from conception through its intra uterine experience to birth, infancy, childhood, adolescence and adulthood.

2. But the individual is not a motionless monument. He *relates* all the while within the family group. Father interacts on mother, mother on father, father on the child and the child on father, mother on the child and the child on the mother. This, then, is a dynamic situation. Minute by minute, hour by hour, day by day, we have the cut and thrust of daily living. This family experience can be seen in the present, and it also has a past, and will inevitably have a future. The study of interaction between persons embraces relationship, the standing of one person to another, and communication, the process of connection between persons. *The relationship dimension* is depicted with arrows as follows:

3. The family members make a small group and thus all that is true about small group dynamics will also be true of the family. The family is a small group with characteristics common to all small groups; it also has special characteristics of its own. It has to be described in terms of its structure, group transaction, family roles, cohesion and general qualities. This will apply not only now, but has applied in the past and will apply in the future. The *Group Properties Dimension* can be diagrammatically represented as follows:

4. The family, too, lives in *material circumstances*. They have a house of a certain size in a particular neighbourhood, with a garden, or otherwise. They have a certain diet, a certain income and with certain recreational facilities, etc. They have these circumstances now, they differed in the past, and they will differ again in the future. The *Material Circumstances Dimension* can be diagrammatically represented by:

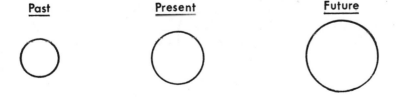

5. This dynamic group of individuals in its material circumstances *reacts with the community*, and the community in turn reacts with the family. This dimension encompasses more than the title suggests. *Neighbourhood* is that part of the social system closest to the family. The body of people living in the same area is termed '*the community*'. Beyond the community in the social system is the *culture*—a large body of people with shared values and meanings. Humanity makes up the total social system or *society*. Thus this dimension is concerned with the interaction of the family with the total social system, embracing family-neighbourhood, family-community, family-culture, and family-social system interaction. The term 'family-community interaction' is adopted for convenience.

This interaction normally takes place at two levels, the level of the individual and the level of the group. The individual reacts with the extended family outside, with friends, neighbours, workmates, schoolmates, chance acquaintances, and all these individuals in turn react on the individuals in turn react on the individual in the family. But more than this, the group as a whole reacts with the social system as a whole. In the social system the family is expected to subject itself to the dictates of society. To the family, the social system is symbolized by the term 'they'— 'they' being the subtle, intangible community or public opinion. All the while 'they' formulate principles and precepts which are imposed upon the family. 'They' convey what they feel about this or that or other issues through the mass media of communication, the press, radio, television, etc. All the while, the family is under the scrutiny of 'they', and feels impelled to conform to the standards of 'they'.

This situation applies now, also applied in the past and will apply again in the future. The *Family Community-Interaction Dimension* can be represented by the following diagram:—

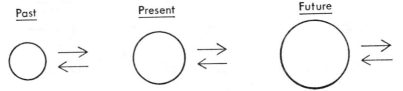

In the next diagram it is now possible to bring together the five dimensions in each of the three time sequences.

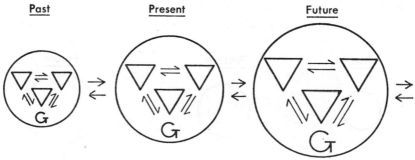

Not only is the individual dependent on the past for health, but also for pathology. This is a matter not only of genetic endowment, but also of generation to generation communication which may determine pathology and the expression of pathology. Thus the family description must include *health and pathology* in its fifteen dimensions.

Family description should thus be based upon fifteen dimensions encompassing the dynamic flow through time as a healthy and pathological unit. Labels are avoided. The *process* is all important.

Thus are met all ten conditions mentioned above as essential to a family model.

Conclusion

In the pages that follow the author asserts that the usual pattern of psychiatric practice should be that of family psychiatry, and he puts forward a system for its practice.

Clinical work as has been explained is based upon a theory of family functioning, a theory which is still incomplete. In many areas knowledge is sparse or absent. Work on the family that can be incorporated into family psychiatry has been reviewed elsewhere.[8] An indispensable aspect of theory is to develop a conceptual model of the family; the one put forward here is a simple one and one that will do as a start to our efforts in conceptualization. Clinical progress in family psychiatry too, while definite, is still at an early stage. More experience and knowledge are required. Thus, the contributions on clinical practice that follow represent aspirations to solve the many problems in this area; they record progress to date, and point to targets for the future.

2

The Practice of Family Psychiatry

Introduction

Every psychiatric service should be a *family psychiatric* service, accepting the family as the functional unit. Both out-patient and in-patient services should be based on the family as the unit. The organization of a service in family psychiatry will now be described in the light of the author's many years of experience at the first hospital department organized for family psychiatry. Starting in 1949, the department (now the Institute of Family Psychiatry) developed his concepts by 1957 to the point when family psychiatry was the only clinical approach employed. In this department it is not a side activity or an experimental tool, but a day-to-day service in family psychiatry for the full range of clinical conditions in a geographical area.

Family psychiatry has not only a theoretical basis to explain the sick family, but also a system for the practice of psychiatry whereby the family

22

is always the target of the referral service, of the procedures of investigation and of the processes of therapy. The presenting member, irrespective of age or clinical condition, is regarded merely as an indicator of family psychopathology. Thus, after accepting the presenting member, all the remaining family members are investigated and later treated—the aim is to produce an emotionally healthy family.

Emotional illness (neurosis) is common in the community and many studies[1] support the view that about 30 per cent of the population require treatment because of it. Family psychiatry is the ideal way to organize a service for emotional illness and the greater part of the out-patient service should be devoted to it. However, psychosis is much less common and its incidence in the population is not greater than 0·5 per cent. It is believed by some that family psychopathology may be responsible for the etiology of psychosis—using this term to mean 'process', 'endogenous', or 'true' psychosis, as employed in Europe. Whatever the truth of its etiology, it certainly has repercussions on the family circle. Psychosis is best dealt with by a separate special clinic in the out-patient service of the department of family psychiatry; its own in-patient service should be attached to it and this is usually large as psychosis tends to require lengthy management.

There are many points of departure from which to develop a family psychiatric service. Starting with an adult service, or an adolescent service, or with a service devoted to a specific clinical category, it is possible in time to arrive at a reformulation in terms of family psychiatry. In the case of the department noted here, development started with a child psychiatric service, and ended up with a family psychiatric service embracing all age groups and clinical categories.

The account of the organization of a service in family psychiatry will describe:

> Symptomatology of family dysfunctioning
> The presenting family member
> Referral service from the family
> Family investigation
> Family therapy.

Symptomatology of Family Dysfunctioning

Clinical syndromes in psychiatry should be considered in the context of the family. In emotional illness, it is strikingly true that symptomatology is an expression of family psychopathology. Some would claim the same position for psychosis; at the least the family influences it, and psychosis in time, has repercussions on the family. Mental retardation must certainly be considered in the context of the family.

For the purposes of this section the psychiatric field is divided into three parts—emotional illness, psychosis, and mental retardation. Psychosis is subdivided into organic psychosis (acute and chronic) and functional psychosis (schizophrenia and manic-depression).

Emotional illness because of its frequency and gravity is given pre-eminent attention here. Emotional illness is a far commoner condition than schizophrenia; it is not a minor illness, it can have drastic repercussions on the life of the individual and the family, and can, and does, lead to death in a significant number of people each year; in the United Kingdom 30,000 people attempt suicide every year and 5,000 succeed. Furthermore, emotional illness is so interwoven with the matrix of the family as to be the condition reflecting its psychopathology most sensitively and responding most clearly to beneficial changes in its dynamics.

(a) *Emotional Illness* (i) *Symptomatology as a family expression.* Usually, the family is responsible for the emotional stress, the emotional illness that results from it and its choice of symptom.

An emotional symptom is always the expression of the psychopathology of the whole family. Symptomatology for which obscure and symbolic explanations have been given becomes easily comprehensible when seen in the context of the family. The following example will help to make this clear. A boy of 12 suffers from anorexia; for the first few years of his life he was brought up by two grandmothers who lived with his family. The maternal grandmother was permissive and did not believe that a child should be forced to eat. The other held as firmly that a child should eat what was put before it. The strict grandmother forced the child to rebel against her, the other grandmother offered him a way to express his rebellion. So the child refused to eat. When the strict paternal grandmother left the family, her son, the boy's father, inherited her role and tried to force the child to eat the food he did not like. Thus his symptoms continued. As can be seen, a family creates the emotional stress, the emotional illness, and the particular manifestation of the disorder—the choice of symptom.

(ii) *Expression in any dimension.* The instance just related concerns a symptom, a manifestation of dysfunction, in an *individual*, but as surely symptoms can show at any *facet of the family*. But by tradition interest has been focused on the individual. However, stress may arise in the family in any of its dimensions and at any point in a dimension. As clouds gather in the sky due to a complex of variables, so do strains within the family. Thus symptomatology can appear in any or all of the five dimensions of the family—the individual, the relationship, the group, the material circumstances and the family-community interaction. Careful examination may show that they invariably appear in all. It should not be overlooked that the family-community dimension is a frequent source of stress, and least under the control of the family. However a family group may not manifest dysfunction equally throughout its system. One dimension, or one aspect of it, may show disproportionate dysfunction due to the 'set' of the emotional events at that time.

Not only do present events dictate choice of symptomatology, but so do those from the past. Symptoms may be transmitted from generation to generation. A previous generation imposes a symptom on the next, or the following generation finds itself caught in precisely the same set of circumstances as the former. Thus, every symptom has to be understood as a manifestation of past and present family dysfunctioning, or as a resultant of both.

(iii) *Classification of symptoms.* It is usual to subdivide emotional disorder in the individual into certain clinical categories—anxiety states, obsessional, hysterical states, etc. This practice has grave weaknesses. It pays attention to the presenting symptom, often elevates this to the status of a disease, and limits the description of the process. The *process* is all-important and cannot be covered by one or many labels. Each process is made up of such a combination of circumstances as to be unique to itself.

(iv) *Choice of particular symptom.* The choice of symptom is a reflection of family dysfunctioning. The individual's choice is dictated by his life experience in the family, e.g. an angry family evokes anger in a child. The choice of expression in a relationship is similarly determined, e.g. physical hostility may be taboo and verbal hostility alone possible in that family. The material changes in the family can take place only within the limits set by its condition. Group manifestations are a family expression, e.g. sulking may be an expression of hostility in a particular family. The community interaction may determine symptomatology, e.g. that fear be controlled by obsessional ritual, or that sexual taboos be imposed. Again, gastric ulceration is a common symptom in Western civilization, but not in primitive communities.

(b) *Psychosis.* Psychosis, or insanity, strictly defined means 'a condition of the mind'. It is still an open question whether this condition is one of the mind rather than of the cerebrum. By common usage, the term psychosis has come to be used for abnormal states of mind with well described symptomatology some of which is of unknown etiology. These states of insanity include organic psychosis (acute and chronic) and functional psychosis (manic-depressive psychosis and schizophrenia). Of organic psychosis as a family disorder the literature is silent. Manic-depressive psychosis has passing mention. Schizophrenia in relation to family psychopathology, on the other hand, has had massive coverage; nearly half the literature on the psychiatric aspects of the family deals with it. This is excessive and disproportionate.

(i) *Schizophrenia* A family psychiatric service concerned only with schizophrenia covers only a small part of the whole field. Pemberton,[11] found that of patients suffering from mental illness in his general practice, 93·6 per cent presented with neurosis, 6·1 per cent with psychosis. On the assumption that 30 per cent[1] of individuals attend a general practitioner with mental illness, only approximately 2 per cent of his total patients are psychotic. Psychosis covers a number of conditions, senile dementia, manic-depressive psychosis and schizophrenia. Thus the percentage of schizophrenia may be as small as 0·5 per cent. That this is so is suggested by the study by Kessell[10] who in a general practice found only three psychotic patients. A wider definition, as employed for instance in the United States, might embrace 10 per cent of the population—still much the smaller part of the 30 per cent. Schizophrenia in relation to family psychopathology is evaluated in Chapter XVI.

(ii) *Manic-depressive psychosis*. Manic-depressive psychosis, one of the functional psychoses, has received some small attention in the literature. Depressive psychotic states should not be confused with reactive neurotic depression, which is much more frequent in the population at large. The stress to which the depression is reactive may be easily overlooked, assumed absent, and an unwarranted diagnosis of psychotic depression made, which will thus expand its statistical significance. In this chapter reactive depression is considered under emotional disorder. Finley and Wilson[2] consider some of the characteristics of the family of manic-depressives.

(iii) *Organic psychosis*. Organic psychosis, a term covering such conditions as the delirious states, toxic states, drug intoxication, and the chronic states of dementia, should certainly be linked with family pathology. For instance, alcoholism and drug addiction, which lead to acute organic states, are truly comprehensible only as manifestations of family pathology; concentration on the offending addict leads to the intolerable family dynamics from which he suffers to go unassessed; his treatment in isolation is largely futile. Rarely is the agony of family life so manifest as in these conditions—should the observer care to look at the family. Dementia, a handicap as serious as schizophrenia, can also be aggravated by wrong family attention and can in turn be a burden to the family.

(c) *Mental Retardation*. Much less attention has been given to mental retardation than to schizophrenia in relation to the family.

But the family is important in the aetiology of mental retardation. Adverse home influences can lead to pseudo feeblemindness; lack of stimulation and deprivation can have the same effect. Emotional illness can retard intellectual functioning leading to poor school and work performance. Degrees of real retardation are worsened by the adverse family climate.

Not only do families contribute to mental retardation, they also react to it. Wrong attitudes may develop which are damaging to both the handicapped member and to the family. The more disturbed the family, the lower its toleration of a handicapped member, and therefore the more likely it is to seek institutional care for him. Thus socialization of the retarded in institutions should include giving the retarded those ingredients of family care which hitherto have been absent in his home life. Should the retarded improve because of these institutional influences, care must be taken not to return him to his previously adverse home, unless the family dynamics have changed to his favour. Thus substitute family care may be preferable.

The retarded reacts to the whole family and not just to the mother. The whole family deprives him, rejects him and needs guidance in his management.

The Presenting Family Member

Emotional stress, within or without the family, may set up emotional symptoms, as has been described, in all or any of its dimensions.

The family is sick as a whole; yet it rarely presents at a psychiatric service as a complete unit. An individual may be referred as the 'presenting' patient, the 'propositus', the 'indicating' patient, the 'identified' patient, or the 'manifest' patient. What determines that a fragment of the family, an individual, a dyad, or a part of the family is sent for treatment rather than the whole? The understanding of the mechanisms concerned with the referral of one member or part of the family throws light on the correct arrangement of referral agencies and the organizations of the psychiatric service. It exposes important aspects of the psychodynamics of the family, it underlines the central thesis of family psychiatry—that the family is a social unit specially meaningful for psychiatry.

Some of the mechanisms determining the ascertainment of a fragment of the family will be briefly reviewed.

Organization of services. Should the psychiatric service in a certain area be based on adults or children or adolescents, then only that particular age group finds its way to the service, while equally disturbed, or more disturbed, members of the family cannot be seen because they are in a different age group. Thus the shape of the service determines who comes from the family. Equally the patient may produce symptoms that demand the attention of that agency and fit its special interest.

The state of the family dynamics. This varies from moment to moment in the life history of the family. In families there are 'see-saw' movements. The person 'down' at a moment in time is likely to be the prepositus. At a conclusion of a brilliant survey of the exclusive treatment of a child patient, a therapist observed that, at conclusion of the child's treatment, the mother had become severely depressed and was now the inmate of a mental hospital; the dynamics of the family had changed to the mother's disadvantage, and she had become the prepositus.

Vulnerability of a family member. One family member may be so placed as to be specially vulnerable to stresses within the family. More than this, these family members may have constellations of personality characteristics which make them vulnerable to a particular stress. In addition ordinal position, sex gender, or age, may be important for vulnerability.

A child may be the only child, the first, second, next youngest and youngest. Although the investigations on ordinal position appear contradictory, when groups are studied, the child's ordinal position in a particular family may yet be highly significant, but understandable only in that unique set of circumstances.

The sex of a child may lead to vulnerability. In families there may be a tendency for parents to reject one gender while accepting the other. Again, this may only become apparent when evaluated as part of the psychodynamics of a particular family. Sex may also be a factor in determining the attitudes of siblings.

The age of a family member may be the cause of vulnerability. The writer has observed that in some problem families a mother may pay a child a great deal of attention for the first two years, because of her own emotional needs for an emotional 'lollypop'. At the age of two or three, as the child makes demands on the mother, he is rejected and another infant sought. Thus, at an early age the child is accepted, later rejected. Similarly, parents talk of difficulties in acceptance of and in relating to their offspring when they are children or adolescents. Old age is anathema to some families.

Anniversary reactions. Individuals may not fall ill with equal regularity throughout the year. There are peak periods, e.g. Fowler[3] reports a higher incidence of suicide amongst the Mormons of Salt Lake City at Christmas. This is probably not unique to Salt Lake City. Not only may there be dates, seasons, months or significance to whole populations, but also to individuals. Furthermore, the individual breakdown may reflect a family's association with that moment in time. The significance of the time may not be apparent to an onlooker, as it has meaning only in terms of the life experience of a particular individual or family. The range and variety of possible stresses in the past is great.

Family motivation. The family may make use of an individual family member; it can, for instance, punish a member by sending him for psychiatric treatment, can express guilt through him, or use him in a crisis as a means for getting assistance.

Of the many motivations setting in motion family dynamics, some of the most intriguing are those causing the role of scapegoat to be given to a family member. The member becomes the 'butt' for the family. A mother, for example, may imply to her children 'things go wrong so much because of the feeble father you have'. Frazer[4] observes that the evil of which a man seeks to rid himself need not be transferred to a person; it may equally well be transferred to an animal or a thing. Similar means have been adopted to free a whole community from diverse evils afflicting it.

Communicated symptomatology. Two or more individuals in a family may share common symptomatology to such an extent that they will be referred together to a psychiatric service. The members may be beset by a common stress, as in the case of two elderly sisters who had lived closely together for many years, and who, on hearing that their house was to be sold, walked quietly into the sea hand in hand and drowned together. The members of a coalition may borrow symptomatology from one another by imitation or suggestion. A paranoid person can persuade another of a common enemy and draw him into his delusional system. This manifestation is common in neurotic patients. In psychotic patients it is termed communication insanity, induced insanity, or *folie à deux*.

Attention-giving symptoms. From time to time a member of a family will manifest symptoms which are striking, call attention to themselves, or have considerable 'nuisance value'. Thus another family member, the family, or a community agency will seek his referral. Some examples of striking symptoms are tics, speech disorders, hysterical symptoms and skin conditions. A child with encopresis, enuresis, or awkward behaviour will come quickly to attention, while an equally disturbed, but apathetic, listless, depressed child may be overlooked.

Referral as a sign of health. Insight into one's own emotional state is found to be inversely proportional to the degree of the disturbance. Thus highly disturbed family members avoid, 'can see no point in', or obstruct, referral to psychiatric services. Less disturbed family members, on the other hand, can 'see the point' and come as the family's representative. Paradoxically, individual psychiatry can lead to a concentration of effort on those least disturbed in the family.

Referral Service from the Family

(a) *General.* Emotional stress usually from within the family, but sometimes from without, sets up family psychopathology. Its manifest strains, as has been described earlier, are seen in symptoms that appear in any or all its dimensions. However, due to the mechanisms just discussed a part only of the family may be referred.

The referral service aims to collect the whole family, either initially or ultimately. The whole family may present at first, but more frequently it is an individual, a dyad, or part of a family. An individual of any age group of clinical category may be accepted at the beginning; the referral may consist of a dyad, e.g. marital partners, or mother and child, or father and child; part of a family may come, e.g. mother and children. The personal element first presenting may or may not be the most sick part of the family. Psychopathology in any element is nearly always an expression of dysfunction in the whole family group. In all circumstances the ideal ultimate aim is the referral of the total family.

(i) *Intake clinics based on dimensions.* Signs of pathology can arise at any facet of the family group—in any of its dimensions—in the individual, in the relationships, in its group processes, in its material circumstances, and in its social interactions. Thus intake clinics can be based on any one, or on all dimensions. *Individuals* naturally concentrate on their own discomfort and tend to seek help themselves: agencies make use of this ready referral. Thus a referral service can be based on the individual with intake clinics for all age groups—child, adolescent, adult and geriatric. A referral service could also concentrate on *relationships*—e.g. the marital, parent-child, or sibling-sibling. In practice, the last two are usually associated with a children's intake clinic; it may be useful to establish a marital problems intake clinic to gather in marital problems, a common feature of disturbed families. Establishing an intake clinic for the *family group* is valuable; with increasing understanding of family psychopathology this will become in time the method of choice; it must never, however, be inferred that only the group as a whole will be accepted by the service. Intake clinics based on poor *material circumstances* are already a feature of countries with well developed welfare systems. In advanced countries problem, or hard-core, families find their way to such clinics. If the psychopathological nature of their disability is accepted, in future they will be referred to family group intake clinics. *Family-community* interaction may break down at many points, engendering problems which require clinics to cope with them, e.g. delinquency clinics.

(ii) *Intake clinics based on clinical categories.* Not only may a family show signs of disruption in any dimension, but it may also present with varying types of psychopathology—neurosis, psychosomatic symptoms, delinquency, psychosis. The family or the intermediary must acknowledge that any such manifestation anywhere in the family is accepted as a good reason for referral to the family psychiatric service. Thus a service could base its intake clinics on clinical categories, instead of on signs of pathology in family dimensions—or on both.

(iii) *Direct and indirect referral.* The family members may be aware of the need for psychiatric help. Frequently, however, the significance of this phenomenon escapes the family and meaning is given to it only by agencies in close touch with the family. Thus help may be sought directly by the family or indirectly through family agencies. Agencies tend to be selective in their interests and thus a number are required before a complete ascertainment service is given to the family.

Direct referrals from the family to a psychiatric service carry the advantage of speed. They carry the disadvantage of possible wrong selection of specialist service and by-pass the agencies that can give continuous support, both before and after specialist help. All requirements can be met if the psychiatric service offers direct help in an emergency, but usually accepts families through agencies only.

Referral agencies, responsible for indirect referral, can be conveniently divided into medical and social, and the latter into statutory and voluntary bodies. Some of the main medical referral agencies are family doctors, family nurses, polyclinics, hospital departments, departments for the care of the handicapped, and school clinics. Some of the main social referral agencies are child care agencies, workers attached to legal courts, industrial welfare officers, church workers, moral welfare workers, marriage guidance services, housing departments, school welfare officers, and government assistance officers.

In some countries medical agencies with associated welfare agencies are ready to offer continuous observation and support of families in what they regard as essentially a medical problem—family psychopathology. Thus, whatever the manifestations of dysfunction, they become the main referral channel to the psychiatric service. The continuous medical coverage is given through a family doctor and the continuous welfare coverage either by a home nursing visitor with experience of physical, emotional and social problems, or by an all-purpose social worker with similar experience. These services are supported by specialist medical and social agencies. A vital condition for success is that the workers offering a continuous service should be trained to see the significance of emotional phenomena.

In other countries medical agencies concern themselves with the more obviously medical problems, e.g. psychosomatic manifestations, neurosis and psychosis, while leaving to social agencies other conditions of social importance, e.g. alcoholism, anti-social behaviour, poor material circumstances and child neglect. There is little doubt that these latter conditions are basically personality problems and arise out of individual and family psychopathology. However, these conditions giving rise to social difficulties do come to the notice of social agencies and may then be referred to the psychiatric service. Thus here there are two main referral channels, medical and social.

A community should assure itself that symptomatology in any dimension of a family, in any social class, can readily come to the attention of one or more designated agencies, trained to ascertain psychopathology, and with clear links with the psychiatric service, which will help them with problems beyond their capacity.

(b) *Intake Procedure.* The request for assistance arrives from the referral agency at the family psychiatric service. It may consist of a request in elucidating a problem that subsequently will be dealt with by the agency itself, or for help in management of a problem, or for both elucidation and management.

Ideally, the whole family should be referred from the beginning and thus there would be no need for clinics with special functions in relation to age groups or clinical categories. Until understanding of family psychopathology is widespread, to insist that nothing less than a whole family will be accepted, would lead to severe curtailment of the service. Neither agencies nor families have a high degree of understanding of family psychopathology. Indeed, in general, understanding in families correlates with the degree of stability. Thus, the more disturbed families, in most need of help, would be neglected.

Whatever the family or the agency offers should initially be accepted, whether it be an individual member, the whole family, or part of it. The department of family psychiatry can then itself work to achieve the desired aim of involving the whole family.

Usually, a family psychiatric service receives an individual, the presenting member, who is the starting-off point of investigation. In areas accustomed to the traditional individual psychiatric approach, it may be necessary to remind referral agencies that the service accepts individuals of all age groups by establishing in-take clinics for children, adolescents, adults, and the aged. These may be just 'clinics on paper', for administrative convenience and have no separate time or facilities. In large departments it may be convenient for the in-take clinics to actually exist, so that slightly different facilities can be set up for the examination of the presenting patient. Again, some departments may wish to establish special in-take clinics for certain clinical categories of patients, either as a reminder to referral agencies, or out of convenience to itself, e.g. for marital problems, delinquency, psychosis, psychosomatic states, alcoholism, etc. Even small units may find it useful to separate patients with 'process' schizophrenia from the remainder by having special in-take clinics for them. Some departments will have in-take clinics based both on age groups and clinical categories. Whatever the starting point, every in-take clinic leads to the same final point—involvement of the whole family.

Effective work begins with the establishment of rapport. Thus a pleasant letter should convey to the patients the time and date of the *appointment*. It can be accompanied by a brochure giving information likely to be required before attendance. Care should be taken to see that the right member or members of the family receive the correct appointment. Patients should be received by a welcoming receptionist in the waiting area. It enhances rapport again if contact by telephone is handled by an accommodating, considerate telephonist.

An invaluable institution is that of the *evening clinic*. Patients quite unable to attend regularly during the day may be able to do so in the evening. It has advantages for the mother, who is able to leave her children with her husband. It has obvious advantages to husbands in not interfering with their work programme. Thus members of the family otherwise elusive can be brought into investigation and treatment. It is sometimes the only time when a complete family can easily attend together and is thus a popular time for family group diagnosis.

A steady flow of referrals keeps the clinical staff at optimum efficiency, and for this a *waiting list* is required. Urgent cases should be seen at once and the remainder need not wait more than two weeks.

A psychiatric service should give a rapid diagnostic service, or it will hamper the activities of other agencies. If, however, it accepts for prolonged treatment all the cases requiring it, then, with the staff available, a long waiting list will soon accumulate. *Selection* of cases for treatment is essential, as it allows the available staff to be used to the best advantage, prevents the accumulation of a long waiting list and lets patients pass directly from diagnosis to treatment—a highly desirable practice. Accumulating a long waiting list does not allow any more patients to be treated, as treatment limited by the capacity of the therapeutic service. Families that cannot be passed from the diagnostic to the treatment service are dealt with by referral back to the referral agency for supportive work.

Family Investigation

The general aim of the investigation is to obtain a complete picture of the family's functioning and dysfunctioning, assets and liabilities, described under five dimensions in the historical sequence of the past, the present and the future.

A procedure is followed which starts with the *presenting patient*, or part of the family, and then moves to the *whole family* which is examined by individual, dyadic, or family interviews, group supplemented by *special procedures*.

At the end of the investigation a *formulation* is possible which describes family functioning and dysfunctioning and outlines the programme of treatment. Achievement of rapport with individual and family is the golden road to obtaining information.

(a) *The Presenting Individual Patient.* The initial step at interview is to establish whether or not he has a mental illness, emotional or psychotic. The following evaluation of the individual is undertaken: (*i*) a history of the complaint or presenting problem, (*ii*) a systematic exploration for symptomatology following a schema devised for this purpose, (*iii*) a mental examination on another schema devised for the purpose.

Having elucidated the present malfunctioning of the individual, the next step is to build up a picture, following a schema devised for this purpose, of the life experience of the individual from conception to date, including his present personality. Some of the information is collected by questionnaire. Psychometric examinations add to the personality profile.

In a small minority of cases the presenting problem will appear to have a whole or partial organic basis. Thus, at times, there may be need for physical examination, supplemented by pathological, encephalographic, radiological examinations, etc.

Should a child be the presenting patient, much of the information will come from the parents. In addition, the child may undergo play observation or play diagnosis, in playrooms equipped for this purpose.

Now it is possible to answer the question, 'Has the presenting patient a mental illness, and if so, is this an emotional illness or psychosis?' A positive diagnosis of an emotional illness leads (*i*) to the next stage of exploring and describing the family psychopathology of which it is a part as described below, and (*ii*) to the psychiatrist conveying his finding to the referral agency. At times the investigation ends at this point because it may have revealed a non-psychiatric problem, or because the patient can be dealt with by the referring agency. In the event of a positive diagnosis of 'process psychosis', the patient is transferred to the special clinic for this condition.

(b) *The Presenting Family*. Occasionally the whole family presents itself at the initial interview. More often only one family member does so and the remaining members are gathered in over time as rapport develops; with unco-operative families this may take several months. A few families will never be seen as a whole, but even with only part of a family, practising family psychiatry to the possible limit will lead to more realistic assessments than individual psychiatry.

A complete family assessment contains information under five dimensions.

1. Description of each *individual* on the lines outlined above for the presenting patient, and including functioning and malfunctioning in the time sequence of past and present. Interview procedures are supplemented by questionnaires, psychometric examinations and play examination of children.

2. Description of all *relationships* in the family both in the past and in the present. Interview procedures are supplemented by psychometric procedures and by special charts that depict the intimate emotional relationships of each member of the family in his early years.

3. Description of the family's *group properties* in the past and the present.

4. Description of the family's *material circumstances* in the past and the present. Interview procedures are supplemented by questionnaires.

5. Description of *family-community interaction* both past and present.

The information is obtained as the result of interviews with individual family members, dyadic interviews and family group diagnosis. The plan must be flexible enough to use the type of interview most useful at that moment in time and best able to produce the required information. Individual interviews are especially useful with (1), (2) and (4) above, dyadic interviews with (2) above and family group diagnosis with (2), (3), and (5) above.

Usually the same team of clinical workers should be employed throughout the investigation of one family. The division of labour is as follows. Psychiatrist and social worker undertake the interview procedures with an individual or a family; the areas to be covered are apportioned to each. Questionnaires and charts are the responsibility of the social worker. The clinical psychologist conducts all psychological procedures. Play observation and play diagnosis is the function of the child therapist.

Individual interviews usually last for 50 minutes, dyadic for 90 minutes and family group for two hours.

All the information obtained is passed into a master file. Each clinical worker in addition keeps *progress notes* on his work with the family.

(c) *Special Procedures*.

(i) *Family Group Diagnosis* is a procedure whereby all the members of the family who are meaningful in the family's situation at that moment are interviewed together. This may involve two or three generations. It may include nannies, lodgers, etc. present in the family at that time. The aim of the procedure is to get a first-hand picture of the dynamics of the family. Family group diagnosis is a procedure of such value that it is certain that it will have an established place in psychiatric practice, and indeed should rarely be overlooked in the exploration of the family dynamics. The true situation in the family will not usually emerge until a few interviews have passed.

Family group diagnosis should not be confused with family group therapy. Many family groups are termed therapeutic, when in fact they consist almost exclusively of an exploration of the family dynamics. At the same time diagnosis may sometimes lead to family therapy. Furthermore, family group diagnosis may be an essential first step in vector therapy and run parallel with it.

Family group diagnosis may be conducted by one clinical worker; it seems that it is easier to establish rapport in this way. Our experience has been that there are more advantages than disadvantages in using one competent worker for family group work. Others maintain that it is better to have a team exploration of the family group. The difficulty that arises in practice is that the loyalty of the family may be fragmented by individuals attaching themselves to different members of the exploring team. Furthermore, communication between members of the exploring team may be faulty, thus there is no unity of decision. A useful procedure is to take the material obtained by one interviewer and subject it to a team analysis.

(ii) *Play Procedures* are utilized for observation and diagnosis with children either as individuals or groups. In this department the work is the responsibility of occupational therapists who have had two years' full time post-graduate training and experience both with normal and disturbed children. A schema has been devised for analysing the functioning of the child as the result of play observation. In play diagnosis, by using a variety of play media, the child is encouraged to reveal the dynamics of the family as he sees them.

(iii) *Psychological Procedures* are developing which may give quick and accurate ways of assessing aspects of the family. The Family Relations Indicator (F.R.I.)[9] is already a valuable adjunct to clinical procedures.

(iv) *Questionnaires* are not given immediately at first attendance; they are found to be more effective once rapport has been established. They cover the more historical material and constitute a way by which information can be quickly obtained about dates and events that are unexceptional. The questionnaire can be filled up either at attendance at the department, or at home, depending on the circumstances. Sometimes the patient requires the guidance of a secretary. At other times the social worker may find it useful to run through the questionnaires with the patient and thus use it as a controlled interview.

(v) *Charts of Relationships* give a diagrammatic record of the

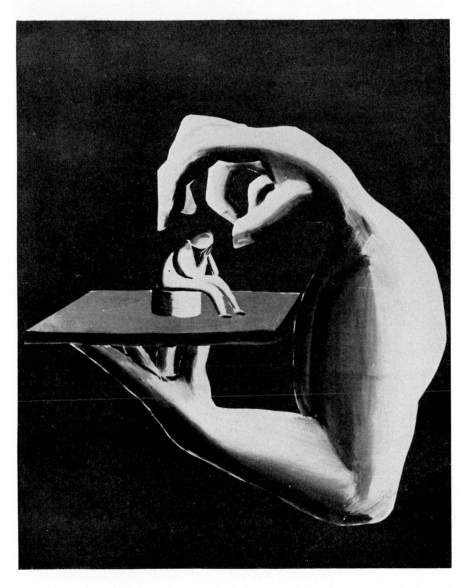

' Family Care ' is the title of the above painting, which epitomizes the feelings of many adolescents about their families. The central figure, the adolescent, is insignificant, dejected, overpowered and restricted to a grey platform. A parental hand above threatens, envelops and is strong; the hand is where the head should be and might belong to the head of the family. The lower parental hand gives some support, but does not counter the other parent. The two hands, the parents, are in strong union.

The artist has used considerable skill to convey strong feelings with great economy; proportions have been distorted, so as to emphasize feeling; the colours, black and white, are apposite to the task of depicting icy gloom.

'What goes on?' One of the cards of common family situations taken from the Family Relations Indicator.[9]

duration and number of relationships in which a family member was involved in his first fifteen years. It includes relationships within and without the child's nuclear family.

(vi) *In-patient Observation* may be required from time to time to establish a diagnosis in an individual family member. It may be profitable, when circumstances permit, to admit a whole family for rapid evaluation.

(vii) A regular *consultation service* should be supplied by neurologists, physicians, and pediatricians.

(d) *Formulation*. In an ideal exploration time is allowed to achieve a complete description of family functioning. In practice a formulation may have to be made before this point is reached. The formulation describes what is known about the family to date in terms of both its assets and liabilities. The department may be required only to convey this formulation to the referring agency who may then be able to plan its own treatment programme for the family. Frequently the department alone has the facilities necessary to effective treatment. From the formulation it plans its own treatment programme. Diagnosis may continue parallel with treatment, and information goes on being added to the cumulative master file.

(e) *Records*. One confidential master file for each family is kept in a locked cabinet in the department. Each clinical worker adds to the file, and has access to the information in it.

The material can be *collected* in one of the following ways:

1. On every occasion any member of the family is seen by any clinical worker, the master file is at hand and information obtained as a result of that contact is added in writing to the master file at the appropriate place.

2. Information in the master file is itemized under code numbers. Each paragraph of the interview report is itemized and given the appropriate code number. Each paragraph is then entered under its code number in the master file by a secretary.

3. An interview can be taped, the material typed, analysed under the coding system and added by the secretary to the master file.

4. Mechanical recording.

Family Therapy

(a) *General*. From investigation the family moves to treatment by the same clinical team and in the same department. By adjusting the treatment caseload to what is possible with available resources, the family can pass from investigation to treatment without a waiting period. In therapy, as in all other aspects of family psychiatry, the family is the unit. The purpose of treatment is to produce a healthy family unit. This end is achieved by a variety of means deployed to improve the family unit. Treatment may involve a number of family members simultaneously, or the family as a whole.

Whenever possible, the whole family must be involved in the treatment process. This does not mean the employment of family group therapy alone, but applies to all the therapies appropriate to the task at that time. Treatment may have to proceed with an individual, or with only a part of the family; this may be so because of inability to involve the whole family, or because of the dictates of the treatment situation at that moment. But if only a part of a family is under treatment, the rest of the family is not overlooked, and the aim does not change; to adjust the whole family is still the target.

Treatment need not wait until the whole family group presents itself. Some help can be offered to those who are available, and the opportunity to involve the rest of the family may come later.

Diagnosis and therapy run parallel to some extent. From the sending of the initial appointment onward there is potential for therapy in everything that is undertaken.

Treatment may be based on the out-patient setting, the in-patient unit, or the home.

A routine follow-up contact with the family can reinforce previous procedures, offer continuing support and may, with the detachment of time, allow a realistic appraisal of the extent and techniques of clinical effort.

Family therapy is not exclusively a clinical activity. Liaison with a host of family health and welfare agencies can enhance the scope and effectiveness of therapy.

Within family psychiatry, the term family therapy, treatment of the family, embraces any procedure employed to adjust the family.

Three main procedures are available in family therapy:

1. Family psychotherapy by various techniques, which seeks a direct change in the individual, the dyad or the family group.
2. Vector therapy, which seeks to produce a more harmonious pattern of emotional forces within the life space of the family.
3. Promoting a salutiferous community, which creates the optimum emotional environment for the family.

Sometimes there is an emphasis on one, rather than another, but all forms of therapy can exist together; in the ideal case all three forms are in use. The treatment programme must at all times be flexible to meet the ever-changing demands of the family situation. This applies to the choice of individual, dyadic or family group approach in psychotherapy, or whether psychotherapy or vector therapy should be the approach to be employed at that moment.

(b) *Family Psychotherapy.* It may be useful to define some of the terms employed: *Family psychotherapy* means treatment of the psyche of the family. Family psychotherapy can be practised with an individual (*individual therapy*) a dyad (*dyadic therapy* or joint therapy), as a whole family (*family group therapy* or conjoint family therapy), a number of families treated together (*multiple family therapy*), and a non-family group (*group therapy*). *Multiple Impact Psychotherapy* describes an intensive approach developed by the Galveston group of workers in the U.S.A.

In view of the attention given to the new technique of family group therapy, it should be emphasized that it is only one of the procedures of psychotherapy, which again is only one section of family therapy; its exclusive use leads to gross limitation of family therapy.

In our experience the utmost degree of flexibility is required in selecting a therapeutic procedure. Sometimes one may start off with family group therapy, later fragment the family into dyadic therapy, or individual therapy, then bring the family together again. In another instance, one may start off with individual therapy and end up with family group therapy. Family therapy is still being undertaken in individual therapy as long as the target is the family psychopathology and the aim to produce a healthy family.

(i) *Individual Psychotherapy.* In *individual* psychotherapy, the attempt is made to effect an adjustment in the personality of the individual family member. One or more adults or children may be under therapy at one moment. Many techniques can be employed from psychoanalysis to brief therapy. All of them can be encompassed by family psychiatry. In our own practice we use two forms of psychotherapy, (a) supportive therapy, aimed at adjusting the individual and family to stresses and strains in the present, and (b) prolonged psychotherapy which aims at an analysis of the whole life experience of the individual, and interprets it in terms of the real meaning of the emotional events to that person. A close relationship between patient and therapist makes possible the resolution of those adverse situations in the past which are at the root of present disturbance, and so a reintegration of the personality is effected.

(ii) *Dyadic Therapy. Dyadic* therapy involves the management of two people together in therapy. The commonest grouping would be that of husband and wife. Other groupings may be father and child, or mother and child, or even two children. The way in which the material is analysed can depend upon the viewpoint of the therapist, and again family psychiatry can encompass any approach. This method may be supplementary to others or be the method of choice at a particular stage of treatment.

(iii) *Family Group Therapy. Family group* therapy is a procedure for the therapy of the family as a unit. It is not just a procedure for the treatment of an individual through a family group experience. The aim is to treat the family through a group experience. Traditional group therapy brings together individuals from a number of families; the aim here too is to use a group experience to help individuals. Family group therapy is a valuable new technique in psychiatry. Nevertheless, it has its limitations, and as little is known about it as of individual psychotherapy, the way is still uncertain. The main principle is that the assets of the family are mobilized in order to overcome its liabilities.

Family group therapy has elements in common with group therapy and individual therapy; it also differs from both.

The family group has a strong identity which reaches from the past and extends into the future. It existed as a group before therapy, and will go on after it. It is a heterogenic group of both sexes and of all age groups. It is subject to strong influences from the extended family group. Its members have learnt rigid patterns of behaviour in relation to one another. Each member of the family has strong meaning for the others. Powerful emotions can be aroused in it, for good or ill. Yet the family group has features in common with any small group, and thus its therapy has some elements in common with group therapy.

Family group therapy has also features in common with individual therapy—for example, transference, countertransference, resistance, affective changes and catharsis. But in family group therapy, the number of relationships is greater and the therapist is part of a web of communication.

Family group therapy is the procedure of choice for any emotional disturbance. Its biggest limitation is that not all the family members may be at a stage in their relationship with the psychiatric service, where they can agree to attend. Problems of transference may militate against a group coming as a whole; an experienced family therapist can, however, overcome most of these problems. The effectiveness of this form of therapy is dependent on a number of factors. The less the degree of family disturbance, the more rewarding, naturally, is the therapy; with our present knowledge, even the best therapists may have difficulty in resolving a severe degree of family emotional disorder. Problems of the present resolve very satisfactorily; problems with deep roots in the past are resistant. A high degree of disturbance in one family member may be suggested as an indication for the time saving procedure of individual therapy; but family therapy would be as effective, as the remaining near-healthy members can be mobilized as assets in therapy.

Family group therapy is a particularly valuable technique in conjunction with vector therapy; even in the most resistant families, insight can develop to the point when the family can accept adjustment which will change the intra and extra family dynamics to their favour. In the writer's experience family group therapy is not a profitable procedure for 'process' schizophrenia. Equally good results can be obtained with all other clinical categories, including the psychopath, the alcoholic, and those with severe anomalies. In general, the younger the family members, the more effective the therapy.

The family group usually meets in the clinic setting. They can meet informally in a comfortable circle of chairs, or seated around a table. All members of the family of any age group, including infancy, are present. Each family member is allowed equal voice; this is one of the matters that the group members come to learn in time. Less than $1\frac{1}{2}$ hours is unlikely to be worthwhile and more than $2\frac{1}{2}$ hours is likely to be exhausting. At first the picture obtained of the group is false; with time the true life situations emerge.

Family therapy usually takes place in an out-patient clinic. Few clinics offer a service in the family's home. It is held by some that therapy in the clinic is a less artificial situation than therapy in the home, where it creates embarrassment to the family by provoking the interest of the neighbours, and where distractions are many. Others claim that the home, as the family's natural setting, is more revealing, that it is easier to collect family members together there, and that it offers less distractions than a clinic. Therapists feel safer in their own clinic setting and claim that it offers a controlled environment, which makes diagnosis easier. Probably the main determining factor in choice of setting is the time factor; it saves therapeutic time to bring the family to the clinic.

It is not always clear what constitutes a family group. The family group in therapy should consist of those who are involved together in an emotionally significant way. Thus the functional, rather than the physical group, is important, e.g. in a particular set of circumstances, a lodger may be a more important father figure for the family than a husband; a nanny may be a more important mother figure than the natural mother. Thus, added to the nuclear family, there may be grandparents, siblings, neighbours, friends, servants, etc. Always, the approach should be flexible—in the course of therapy the group may need to shrink or to expand.

It is one of the dangers in psychiatry to assume that if a group of people meet together to talk, then some good may come of it; it is equally possible for ill to come of it. Thus, if a family group is to meet together for therapy, it should be expected that some new factor is operating. This new factor is the personality of the therapist. The therapist has the task of being the convener of the setting, its chairman, its catalyst, the representative of healthy community opinion, and of instilling courage that can lead to change. In addition he introduces the art of psychotherapy, which starts by imparting to the group the significance of emotional events, the significance of its family emotional life now, the significance of the past emotional events that interact with the present events; he then uses the particular strengths of a section of the family together with his own to resolve the particular weakness of the rest of the family. The therapist has a loyalty to the family as a unit and this will be tested. He will meet dependence, transference and resistances, old friends from individual psychotherapy.

Another matter of organization is that concerning the choice of employing one therapist or several. Sometimes economics dictate the choice of one only. At first, therapists new to the field have difficulty in shifting loyalty from one person to a group. Yet all have had experience of such a loyalty within their own families; such a shift is possible once the group idea is grasped and habit given time to work. The handling of group loyalty is one of the skills necessary to a family therapist. Having a number of therapists carries the danger of each forming an attachment to an individual family member and setting up rivalries. On the other hand, if more therapists are introduced more dilution is obtained of family disturbance. The greatest problem in having multiple therapists is maintaining adequate communication between them; the difficulties are considerable. It has been argued that a number of therapists are collectively wiser and more skilled. But an experienced individual therapist should have the skill to manage alone, and is usually of one mind.

The following illustrates the need to be flexible in a family group therapy and to allow fragmentation when required. A father, mother and daughter meet together for family group therapy. At one moment father becomes silent, anxious and restless; the group makes no progress. The father then asks that he be allowed to see the therapist alone. When he does so, he relates that some time ago he had an affair with a third party. He ends by wondering whether this information should be imparted to the family group. Discussion may show that two plans should be considered, (i) that the material imparted is of no significance to the family group, and therefore need not be divulged, (ii) that the material is of significance to the wife, who, the patient feels, may suspect the situation. He asks for a meeting between the therapist, the wife and himself, as he feels that the matter needs resolution. Husband, wife and therapist meet—dyadic therapy. Again the couple wonders whether the information should be imparted to the family group. They decide that the event has no significance for the adolescent daughter and they do not wish to introduce the material to the group. Or, they may decide that the daugther may already suspect this relationship, is worried about it, and the matter should be divulged. Thus the therapist, father, mother and daughter meet to discuss the situation. Thereafter family group therapy continues.

A complete change, or a complete stabilization of the family members may not be required to effect a considerable improvement in a family situation. For example a highly disturbed, rigid, obsessional father, with a highly abnormal attitude toward sexual matters, as the result of free discussion in family group therapy finds himself able to see that the son should have the freedom to leave the family, and secondly to adopt the values of the community, rather than the values of the father. Father's personality is not changed, but by releasing his son and giving him a dispensation on the matter of sexual values, his son gains immeasurably in his own emotional life.

Follow-up studies of family psychotherapy are superficial or nonexistent. Problems of evaluation which are considerable in individual psychotherapy, are even greater in family psychotherapy. Much of family psychotherapy amounts to the evaluation of family dynamics without any clear benefit to the family. However, careful research could show that family group therapy is not only the most potent form of group therapy, but also one with advantages over individual therapy. The need for research is evident.

The literature on family group therapy is considerable. Most of it is devoted to the treatment of schizophrenia by means of family group procedures. The papers about it, together with the papers on family process in relation to schizophrenia, constitute probably two thirds of the literature on the psychiatry of the family. Many of the papers are concerned with the management of a 'primary' adolescent family member through a family group; to the writer this does not constitute therapy as the aim should be to improve not one person only, but the whole family unit. This has come about because family groups with an adolescent member are easier to manage than those with children. Furthermore, schizophrenics emerge in considerable numbers in adolescence.

Elsewhere[8] the literature on family therapy is reviewed.

(iv) *Additional Therapeutic Procedures.* In addition to the above, any of the following may be employed to assist in achieving the aims of family psychotherapy.

1. *Group therapy* treats together a number of individuals from different families. Groups may be male, female or mixed. They may be of any age group—children, adolescents and adults. They may meet formally for intensive therapy, or informally in a club setting. One or more therapists may be employed, and the clinical material is interpreted according to the school of thought of the therapists.

2. In *multiple family therapy* one or many, even over a hundred families, are treated together. Naturally it is less easy to be precise in the manipulation of each family's dynamics among so many. Thus it is best employed in supportive therapy over situations common to many families. Such a large group however, can employ powerful suggestion.

3. *Play therapy* for children. A young child can communicate only through play; an older child may spontaneously verbalize to the therapist. The play medium appropriate to the child's age, sex and inclination is supplied. Play therapy is used to corroborate information obtained through one medium, by that disclosed by another. The first aim is usually to establish rapport, for which much play material is utilized. Thereafter systematic observation of the child takes place in the play situation; this gives a base-line for comparison later on. Play diagnosis follows. The aim here is to encourage the child to reveal his problems as he knows them, and to express what he knows about himself and his relationships within the family, the school and the neighbourhood. Play therapy is the final technique, and is employed for one of the following reasons:

(*i*) to support the child while the family is receiving treatment; (*ii*) to support the child when the family environment cannot be changed, or when he cannot be separated from it; (*iii*) to help to separate the child from his family, for either short or lengthy periods; (*iv*) to make a change in the child's personality. The relationship between therapist and child is the most potent therapeutic medium. Within the safety of this relationship, the child expresses his fears, guilt and hate, and, sharing these with the therapist, is encouraged to healthier reactions. With adolescents art therapy is often a useful medium.

4. *Physical methods* are required to supplement the above procedures, e.g. anti-convulsants for an epileptic patient, hypnotics to induce sleep, or sedation to reduce anxiety.

5. *Home therapy*. This may be merely domiciliary visiting, seeking information and giving reassurance, or it may be the base for family group therapy.

6. *A day hospital* programme for children, adolescents, or adults. The accommodation can often be shared with in-patients.

7. *Residential care*. This must be supplied for the emotionally ill in all age groups—children, adolescents, adults and the aged. Thus with the in-patient, whether accompanied by his family or not, no evaluation is made or procedure undertaken without relating it to the context of his family. This does not mean that the individual must always remain in contact with his family. His particular need may be to escape from it; this manipulation will be undertaken more effectively if evaluated in terms of the total situation of his family. The individual may be withdrawn from his traumatic environment and subjected, sometimes for a number of years, to intensive milieu therapy, i.e. a potent form of vector therapy. It is unlikely to be effective unless the remainder of the family group are co-operative; they may need adjustment before the individual member can return to it or agree that on discharge he joins another family group. At times the family group may need to join the in-patient unit on a day basis or the whole family be admitted for intensive care. This leads to a flexible use of in-patient facilities—sometimes for an individual, a dyad, a part, or the whole family. The admission procedures involves a family evaluation, as do the ward regime and discharge procedures. The out-patient and in-patient management should be a continuous whole. Members of the family are not mere 'visitors' they are participants in the clinical process.

Where after-care is supplied away from home, a whole range of community facilities becomes necessary—hostels, special boarding schools, cottage homes, foster homes, work rehabilitation units, supervised accommodation for the aged, etc.

For patients with psychosis, organic and functional, there should be separate accommodation catering for all age groups. These patients are improved by institutional care, but are rarely cured by it. An efficient after-care service can reduce the re-admission rate.

8. In some countries severely disturbed families, problem or 'hard-core' families, are housed in *settlements* for which there is a special provision of welfare services.

(v) *Selection of Families for Family Psychotherapy* Few units are so well staffed as to be able to apply family therapy to all their families. Thus selection becomes necessary. In general, units deploy their facilities to give optimum value. So therefore the families selected are those with a degree of disturbance likely to respond in a reasonable period of time, to the treatment offered by the facilities available. Families with young children have young parents; young parents have not been emotionally ill as long as older people, and thus respond more readily to treatment. The younger the children when the family is stabilized, the more they profit. The number of children in the family is a factor in selection; the greater their number the greater the benefit that will accrue to society by improving their emotional health. In all families, whatever the degree of disturbance, efforts should always be made to bring relief to the children, the coming generation.

As an approximate index it can be said of the department noted here that one-third of cases are closed after advice and assessment and the expression of an opinion to the referring agency. A third are accepted for supportive therapy, with co-existing vector therapy. Another third are accepted for prolonged psychotherapy in association with vector therapy.

However hard-pressed a service, it is of the utmost importance that at least some cases are given the fullest measure of investigation and treatment. It is only in this way that knowledge is accumulated and techniques are improved. Unless intensive work is entered into, work becomes superficial; thus there is no self-improvement. Given good work with a small number of families, the work with the remainder of the families, although it may be curtailed, will never be superficial.

(c) *Vector Therapy. Definition.* A vector denotes a quantity which has direction. Force, including emotional force, is a quantity with direction and therefore can be represented by a vector. Furthermore, as direction is a property of a vector and direction implies movement, it results in a dynamic situation.

Vector therapy effects a change of the emotional forces within the life space to bring improvement to the family within the life space.

The forces in the life space can be thought of in terms of fields of force. Within these fields there are potent forces, continually bearing, for good or ill, on families. These forces if positive, harmonious and constructive promote wellbeing, but have to be counterbalanced, or removed should they be negative, disharmonious and destructive. These fields of force are (*i*) within the individual, (*ii*) outside the individual and within the family, (*iii*) outside the individual and the family and within society.

Vector therapy can involve:

1. A change in the *magnitude* of the emotional force, e.g. father's aggression may be diminished.

2. A change in the *direction* of the emotional force with no change in its magnitude, e.g. father abuses mother instead of child.

3. A change in the *length of time* during which the emotional force operates, e.g. father works away from home, spends less time at home and his aggression has less duration.

4. A change in the *quality* of the emotional force when one force replaces another, e.g. father treats his son with kindness instead of with aggression.

To effect these changes, the sources of the emotional forces may have to be moved, e.g. by father going out to work; or the object of the forces may have to move, e.g. the child goes to a boarding school to avoid father's aggression.

Vector therapy not only nullifies the effect of *past* traumata, but also, by producing optimum conditions for emotional growth now, it prevents traumata in the *present*.

Psychotherapy as a special instance of Vector Therapy. An individual moving in time through his life space encounters emotional influences that help to make him an integrated healthy person, but in varying degrees he may meet adverse emotional influences that make for disintegration and ill health. In either event, account has to be taken of the quality of the influence, its force, its direction and the time during which it operates.

Faced with a disintegrated individual, reintegration is possible by mobilizing a set of influences in the present that may still nullify the effects of the previous influences. This can be done (*i*) by the mobilization of intense, precise, beneficial emotional influences from a therapist acting over a short period of time in the interview situation, i.e. by psychotherapy, a special instance of vector therapy; or (*ii*) by mobilizing less intense emotional influences of a general nature known to be beneficial over a long period of time outside the interview, i.e. by vector therapy. Thus, for example, a child disintegrated by being deprived of the right kind of emotional care, instead of being subjected to psychotherapy, is placed in a foster home selected for its ability to provide the right care. In the latter case, benefit comes from a new set of beneficial vectors able to act over a long period of time.

In a given instance, intra and extra interview procedures can be employed together, i.e. psychotherapy and vector therapy are complementary. As an example at a simple level, consider the young infant of a highly anxious, ill-adjusted mother, put to the breast and, because of the disharmonious influence from mother, being unable to feed. Direct psychotherapy might effect a change in the mother's personality, so that in time she may be able to mother her infant adequately. The situation can also be broken into by a simple rearrangement of the people who provide the emotional influences playing on the child in the feeding situation. The stable young father who stands by, little imagines that he has a part to play in the feeding situation; but by placing the infant on the bottle, and allowing the well-adjusted father to feed him, the infant can have a happy and satisfying feeding experience. By the use of vector therapy a change of forces has been effected and a disharmonious situation has become harmonious. Psychotherapy is worthwhile for the mother as a long term project. The infant is best served by the immediate satisfying relationship in the arms of his father. *Thus both psychotherapy and vector therapy have a part to play, they are complementary.* Indeed, psychotherapy is a special instance of vector therapy.

The Application of Vector Therapy. To be effective, a number of general considerations have to be borne in mind when practising vector therapy.

There must be a reliable *appraisal* of what is going on within the family. By using family group diagnosis, supplemented by individual methods of investigation, it should be possible to achieve an accurate picture of the family situation in its five dimensions. Unless this picture is accurate the forces bearing within and without the family will be incorrectly adjusted and a poor therapeutic result obtained.

The family must *co-operate* with insight. Insight springs from understanding. This may be induced by individual, dyadic or family group sessions.

Again, the manipulation of forces is concerned with changing the emotional rather than the material events within the family. *Emotional prescriptions* are required for emotional ills.

Also, just as damage to the family is produced by negative influences working over a period of time, so it becomes necessary for reparative work to allow *time* for the positive influences to bring results.

Furthermore, therapy should not concentrate on any one member of the family, but should aim at helping the *whole family*. The maximum benefit comes from the utilization of services for all family members at the same time—a total front programme.

But, as *childhood* is the period of maximum personality development, it is obvious that special attention, if not priority, will be given in vector therapy, to families containing early age groups.

Forces bearing on family members may sometimes be changed within the family without separating the individual member from the family. At other times, partial *separation*[6] may be required, e.g. day foster care, day hospital care. Sometimes semi-permanent or permanent separation may be essential, e.g. foster care, adoption or boarding school care. The most skilful use of vector therapy may occasionally allow a family to fragment and, subsequently, for new and better families to be formed from the fragments.

To effect vector therapy calls for organized *facilities*, i.e. a service to supply its requirements, e.g. to advise nursery or day foster care for an infant is of no avail unless these facilities exist. Facilities must supply treatment in emotional terms to satisfy an emotional need. It is fundamental to vector therapy that facilities compensate for, or improve, bad personal relationships. The most important therapeutic agent available in the community is a relationship between a well-adjusted individual and another. Thus it is necessary to mobilize those who are emotionally healthy at the points where they can be of maximum assistance to the unhealthy. The strong must help the weak. To bring the right people to the right place may necessitate a re-allocation of rewards and prestige.

Exact assessment of family dynamics is now a reality. The social worker, using interview techniques, can aim at targets different from psychotherapy—effecting rapport with the family, developing insight in the family, prompting the family to action causing change in their favour in the field of forces, and deploying those family agencies which can help to produce and sustain the changes.

The complete fulfilment of aims is never achieved in any field. In this field the results are encouraging and sometimes spectacular. Benefit will accrue with each succeeding generation. Vector therapy can be employed with family psychotherapy, and at times when psychotherapy is unavailable or unavailing.

(d) *A Salutiferous Society*. The third approach to family therapy calls for consideration of the author's concept of a salutiferous, health promoting, society.[7] In the long term this is the most effective help in the service of society, the family and the individual.

The author sees society as a vast field of forces in which elements are loosely defined—culture, community, neighbourhood, family, individual; these elements are indivisible and essentially each element has equal significance. The emotional forces within the life space produce degrees of wellbeing or harm and they can be repatterned to promote either. Understanding of this potential for change in either direction allows the conscious selection of repatterning of emotional forces towards bringing wellbeing to society and to the elements within it. Thus a reshaping over the generations of the emotional stratum of society has great opportunities for society's emotional self-improvement. This is the ultimate goal of vector psychiatry of which family psychiatry is a part.

How repatterning could succeed in the field of emotional health is thrown into relief by comparison with an analogous field, that of physical health. A vast study of society over many generations has identified items that promote physical health, e.g. clean milk, well fitting shoes, clean air, a balanced diet, pure water, etc., and items that are antagonistic to it. Those items promoting health are retained, those antagonistic to it are changed. Thus a repatterning takes place.

Similarly, a close study of the emotional stratum of society will reveal multitudinous items that can promote emotional health, e.g. non-guilt producing morality, less coercion, less destructive competitiveness, measures inducing group acceptance of individuals, avoidance of isolation, secure family life, wanted children, etc. Items antagonistic to emotional health should be changed; those conducive to emotional health should be retained. Here again a repatterning can take place.

Thus a vast study of society is required, embracing every aspect of its functioning—organizations, institutions, roles, standards and aims. Every one of its multitudinous facets should be examined to assess its value in promoting emotional health. Over the generations increasing self improvement will result in a salutiferous society that supplies optimum conditions for emotional health in itself and its elements—culture, community, neighbourhood, family and individual.

Conclusion

Much thought and print has been expended in attempting to define health. It is easier to feel it than to define it. Its correlates are easy to delimit and describe—emotional and physical wellbeing, the capacity of adjust to life stresses, the ability to co-operate with others, unselfish actions born of security, efficiency, and productivity. All these indicate harmonious functioning in the individual—what he feels is the comfortable state of 'being happy'.

Most definitions of health are in terms of the individual; it may be more realistic to attempt it in terms of society, which ultimately dictates the state of its element, such as families and individuals within it. It might be thought that society is only sick in the sense that it contains a number of sick people. It is more correct to say that society itself is sick and therefore must contain a number of sick individuals. Forces within society at the moment are arranged in a pattern that provokes emotional illhealth which flows from one generation to the next. Society carries within it the capacity for health because its fields of force carry the potential for rearrangement. This fact makes clinical endeavour worthwhile. Health and 'normal' behaviour must not be confused. The normal, usual, statistically average, state of emotional functioning in society is far from 'health'. With each succeeding generation it is hoped that the emotional norm will increasingly approximate to health—a state of affairs slowly and hardly achieved in the field of physical health.

The clinician has as his endeavour the production of health. In family psychiatry the goal is a healthy family, with, of course, healthy individuals, a task always limited by the fact that social illhealth pulls the family towards conformity to its norms. Over the generations small gains in the rearrangement of the vectors will have a cumulative effect on society. Gains can be made at individual, family and social levels, and the process is indivisible. For the present, the family is the vantage point. Progress can be made only at the speed with which knowledge develops. But clinical effort carries the prospect of new insight; research and clinical work go hand in hand.

REFERENCES

1. Council of College of General Practitioners, 1958. Working Party report. *Brit. med. J.*, ii, 585.
2. FINLEY, C. B., and WILSON, D. C., 1968. The relation of the family to manic-depressive psychosis. In *Theory and practice of family psychiatry*. Ed. Howells, J. G. Edinburgh: Oliver and Boyd.
3. FOWLER, H. B., Personal Communication.
4. FRAZER, J. G., 1927. *The golden bough*. New York: Macmillan.

5. HOWELLS, J. G., 1962. The nuclear family as the functional unit in psychiatry. *J. Ment. Sci.*, **108,** 675.

6. HOWELLS, J. G., 1963. Child-parent separation as a therapeutic procedure. *Am. J. Psychiat.*, **119,** 922.

7. HOWELLS, J. G., 1963. *Family psychiatry*. Edinburgh: Oliver and Boyd.

8. HOWELLS, J. G., 1968. *Theory and practice of family psychiatry*. Edinburgh: Oliver and Boyd.

9. HOWELLS, J. G., and LICKORISH, J. R., 1967. *Family relations indicator*. 2nd, new ed. Edinburgh: Oliver and Boyd.

10. KESSELL, W. I. N., 1960. Psychiatric Morbidity in a London General Practice. *Brit. J. prev. soc. Med.*, **14,** 16.

11. PEMBERTON, J., 1949. Illness in general practice. *Brit. med. J.*, i, 306.

XXV
COMMUNITY PSYCHIATRY

by

MAXWELL JONES,

C.B.E., M.D., M.R.C.P.E., D.P.M.

Physician Superintendent, Dingleton Hospital
Melrose, Scotland

1

Introduction

Community Psychiatry

Community psychiatry is a somewhat vague concept and depends to some extent on the meaning of the term community. Howe[8] says 'The most frequently found definitions of community treat it mainly as a territorial entity although with the proviso that there can also be "functional" communities, based not on geography but on the functions people perform'. Under this concept of a functional community one could include an industrial concern or a hospital or the members of the Mental Health Association.

In the same context the term therapeutic community has come to be associated with the social aspects of treatment within a hospital setting but there is no reason why the term should not apply equally to the social therapeutic factors in the environment outside the hospital. Immediately one is in difficulty regarding the terms 'social' and 'community' and it would seem that one would convey much the same meaning by the phrases 'social aspects of treatment within a hospital setting' or 'community aspects of treatment within a hospital setting'. Even if one is to restrict the term community psychiatry to the practice of this discipline outside psychiatric hospitals there is inevitably confusion because the lines of demarcation between the hospital and the outside community are being increasingly blurred as psychiatry and other disciplines become involved in treatment extramurally.

At the same time, bodies associated essentially with extramural practice such as private psychiatrists, family doctors, local authorities and other welfare agencies are becoming increasingly more involved in hospital practice. The complexity is heightened by the fact that disciplines other than the traditional medical ones are becoming more important in psychiatric practice. This applies particularly to the behavioural sciences but in the field of preventive psychiatry, educationalists, town planners, architects, ministers, business managers, government officials and many others have a significant part to play. It is considerations such as the above which have led to a great deal of confusion regarding the terms community psychiatry and social psychiatry. If a distinction is to be made at all then it would seem logical to limit the term community psychiatry to the practice of psychiatry in the community outside the hospital.

There have been many attempts to define the term community psychiatry and some of these have been brought together in a U.S. Government publication.[6] All these definitions state or imply that community psychiatry is concerned with psychiatry practised in relation to groups of people (specified in one definition as larger than a family unit) but do not state whether these groups are intramural or extramural or both. The implication is more towards the latter as for instance in the point of view put forward by the Division of Community Psychiatry Columbia University School of Public Health and Administrative Medicine.[6] 'As a subspeciality, its approach to those aims focuses on a multiplicity of relationships between individuals and their social world which it strives to elucidate and upon which its patterning and provision of services is based. These services are directed toward comprehensive coverage whereby a co-ordinated network of differentiated services is available to meet the diverse mental health needs of all members of a community.' Here we are getting away from the idea of a 'sick' person and moving towards ideas of mental hygiene and preventive psychiatry. Some psychiatrists dislike the tendency for psychiatry to widen its parameters to include such areas of involvement and feel that we should restrict our practice to the 'sick' person. The important factor would seem to be the *nature* and extent of such involvement and its limitation to such skills as the psychiatrist may possess. Whatever the purists may feel it seems inevitable that psychiatry should expand its area of involvement as a consequence of its increasing collaboration with other disciplines particularly into spheres of behavioural science and education. Gerald Caplan (1964)[4] has had an important influence in developing the theory of community psychiatry and applying it to the fields of prevention and training.

2

Social Psychiatry and Community Psychiatry

Definitions

It is difficult to make any clear distinction between the terms community psychiatry and social psychiatry and the terms are often used synonymously. It would seem to me that Social Psychiatry is a more generic term than Community Psychiatry which, as already indicated, might be said to confine itself to the practice of psychiatry in the community. A study of the literature does little or nothing to clear up the confusion. The Division of Community Psychiatry, Columbia University School of Public Health and Administrative Medicine has this to say,[6] 'Community psychiatry and social psychiatry are often used interchangeably and, we believe, with considerable justification. We recognize many areas of overlap between the two. However, in distinguishing between them, we think that community psychiatry tends to signify a greater emphasis on applied practice at the community level, as well as the investigations and programme evaluations which underlie and keep shaping its service operations, while social psychiatry has come to connote a more exclusive emphasis on theory and research rather than practice. Therefore, community psychiatry, in encompassing both, is viewed as the more comprehensive designation.' In apparent contradiction the Department of Psychiatry, University of Texas Southwestern Medical School states,[6] 'Social psychiatry is the application and extension of psychiatric knowledge and insights reciprocally with other behavioural science fields and the use of the product in increasing the understanding of total human functioning and the practical use of such knowledge; e.g. in community psychiatry and community mental health.'

Jurgen Ruesch,[21] in an excellent review of the subject, describes social psychiatry as the issue of the union of social disciplines with psychiatry and goes on to say that social psychiatry is not unified by a set of activities as much as by a point of view, and then lists as points of view the sociological and anthropological, the epidemiological and the ecological, the preventive and the therapeutic. To this list I would be inclined to add the educational and even the governmental and business management points of view. If one accepts that social psychiatry must concern itself with prevention then clearly there is no end to the new parameters which can be seen as significant factors in the development and prevention of mental illness.

For my part I am content to leave social psychiatry as a comprehensive concept including all social, biological, educational, philosophical and other factors which may modify psychiatric practice in the direction of a more equilibrated society with less mental illness.

As no one is in a position to say how far social psychiatry will contribute to society and its problems in the future it would be better to leave a precise definition of social psychiatry to the future as it evolves.

Some people may feel that the term social psychiatry is too restricting even if used in this comprehensive way. The term psychiatry implies medical training and the medical model. If psychiatry is going to be optimally influenced by the social and educational forces which surround it then the psychiatrist will have to be a much more widely informed and generically trained individual than he at present is. The medical model presupposes treatment at the level of the individual—the doctor patient relationship. Psychiatry has widened this to include the group and to some extent the community particularly through the family. A modification of the social structure of hospitals to improve communications and decision making has also occurred but the focus is still on a 'sick' person. This is a perfectly legitimate and desirable state of affairs and is epitomized by the social psychiatry and psychotherapy section of the Royal Medico Psychological Association with its headquarters in London. However, many people think that there is a need for a multi-disciplinary meeting of people who are selectively independent, that is not seeking membership for its own sake. In this way general topics such as automation, town planning, old age, etc. can be discussed on a broader frame of reference than by limiting the discussion to the question of 'sickness'. In this context one of the problems of our time is the narrow frame of reference used by the medical profession. One example of this is the present structure of hospitals where communications are frequently quite unsuitable for the task in hand, and where the authority of the doctor frequently blocks appropriate two-way communication. However, in this context international organizations such as the recently formed International Association for Social Psychiatry represents one of many influences which are helping to foster a multi-disciplinary approach to psychiatry.

Hospital Treatment

In January, 1962, the Ministry of Health presented to Parliament, a Hospital Plan for England and Wales,[1] which indicated that the 152,000 beds occupied by psychiatric patients in 1960 would be reduced to 92,000 in 1975, a decrease of forty per cent, or, put in terms of beds per thousand of population, a decrease of 3·3 beds to 1·8 beds.[25]

The plan anticipates a steady increase in the number of psychiatric units attached to general hospitals and a rapid decrease in the number of mental hospitals with 1,000 beds or more. There were sixty-nine such hospitals in 1960 and the plan is to reduce the number of such hospitals to twenty-six. No one seriously suggests the disappearance of mental illness as a major problem or even a reduction in the incidence of mental illness. The expectation is that many patients now treated in hospital will, in future, be treated at home or by some form of community care. There has been much scepticism about the validity of the statistics and basic assumptions made by the Ministry of Health in 1962. Rehin and Martin[20] made an exhaustive study of the Hospital Plan and concluded: 'the authors of this broadsheet have been unable to find any evidence which suggests that either its assumptions or its possible consequences have been systematically examined.' They made a strong case for a more circumspect approach to the problem of community care and recommended the development of a number of model areas in which different patterns of services are built up and their consequences assessed. In their opinion, far too much has been taken for granted and there has been little study to date of the problems created by community psychiatry in general. For example, family doctors can be very reluctant to assume the responsibility which will inevitably rest on their shoulders if patients now treated in hospital are to be treated in the home. Much will depend on the support which the Local Authority services are able to provide, but such support varies immensely from one region to another. It would seem that it will be many years before the correct balance has been established between what psychiatric problems can most effectively be treated in hospital and what problems are more effectively handled in the community.

Treatment in the Community.

Too little is as yet known about the effect that community treatment may have on families of patients who are being kept at home. Grad and Sainsbury[7] have produced some important findings but they are far from conclusive. Talking about psychiatric geriatric patients they were cautious not to generalize from their findings but there was some evidence to indicate that the families of elderly patients treated at home were affected adversely compared with families of patients who were being treated in hospital. Wing and Brown[27] have also done important research in this area.

Another factor which affects the outcome of community treatment is the skill of the personnel involved. Social workers have a long experience of community work and their training prepares them for such a role. Psychiatrists would seem to be less well prepared for work in the community and it is not enough for mental hospital doctors to treat patients in their homes in much the same way as they would were they resident in the hospital ward. Clearly the question of training in community psychiatry calls for a great deal more attention than it has so far received, particularly from the medical profession. This situation is receiving far more attention in the US than it is in the UK. There are at present eight schools of community psychiatry in the US where psychiatrists, social workers, psychologists and other suitably qualified people are being trained in community psychiatry. The best known of these programmes are in Harvard under Gerald Caplan, at Columbia under Viola Bernard, and at the University of California under Portia Bell Hume.

Development of Community Psychiatry in Britain and in the USA.

This is not to suggest that the transition from traditional psychiatry to community psychiatry is any more advanced in the US than it is in the UK. On the contrary, Britain had been developing community psychiatry for a decade before the publication of the final report of the Joint Commission on Mental Illness and Health, *Action for Mental Health* in 1961.[2] This publication must be seen as a milestone in the development of American psychiatry and was a prelude to frantic activity on the part of the

Federal and State authorities to correct the haphazard state of affairs in American psychiatry. The majority of American psychiatrists are employed in private practice and the State hospitals have always had a very difficult time in finding sufficient numbers of adequately trained medical staff. Moreover, the rewards of private practice are two or three times as great as those attained by psychiatric practice when employed by the State. Huge Federal grants, matched by State funds, are now being made in an attempt to create community clinics which will provide treatment for the lower income brackets which has been largely lacking in the past. Many people may feel that community psychiatry is developing far too rapidly in the United States.

In Britain, the evolution of community psychiatry has been gradual and in large measure has reflected the development of social services in response to an increasing sensitivity to the social needs of the population. In fact, it might be said that the emergence of community psychiatry in Britain reflects this overall social growth more than any particular initiative on the part of psychiatry. In America, such a social evolution is less apparent, and one cannot escape the feeling that to some extent the 'fashion' of community psychiatry has been artificially encouraged by the outpouring of huge amounts of Federal money. Despite the difference in the social and political factors in the two countries, there seems little doubt that community psychiatry has come to stay and the developments in the one country will help the other, and vice versa. As an example of this mutual advantage in exchange of ideas, child guidance clinics, which started in the US many years ago have had an indirect but important effect on community psychiatry in both countries. This is particularly true in the US where child guidance clinics are often community supported and grow out of a deeply felt community need. This contrasts sharply with what is at present happening with the development of community clinics for adults in the US, where the incentive is coming from Federal and State Departments rather than from the community itself. In an excellent article on the present and future of community psychiatry in the US, Wedge and Boonin[26] state: 'In summary, it seems fair to say that a handful of local programmes have represented the operational realization of the community health concept, that the massive infusion of Federal funds has immensely stimulated hopes and plans on the State and local levels which fly the flag of community programmes, but that the operational expression of community psychiatry concepts has achieved minimal reality. For the most part the effect of the legislation, planning, and financing which has been stimulated by the community concept has been to support the development of professional facilities located, of course, in community settings, rather than to stimulate the community towards active responsibility for its own members. While these developments represent some progress over the practice of shipping alienated people out of the community and institutionalizing their alienation, they do not fulfil the requirements of the community concept. Indeed, they may impede development of attitudes to social responsibility by substituting professional services to persons defined as "patients" for action to help community members find a place for themselves even as they receive professional attention which is itself designed to support reintegration of the person with his society.'

The situation in the US is in striking contrast to the situation in the USSR as described by Isidore Ziferstein[28, 29] who spent fifteen months studying psychiatry in the Soviet Union. He comments on the relatively small number of hospitalized psychiatric patients in the USSR which amounts to about 220,000 in the entire country. In Russia, as in Britain, it would seem that community psychiatry has evolved as a natural outgrowth of the culture characteristics of the country. To quote from Ziferstein:[29] 'The Soviet psychiatrist's concept of society as a therapeutic community is a direct outgrowth of his collective upbringing and life-experience. His active collectivist approach in treating his patients is in keeping with the ideals of interpersonal relationships of his collective society-ideals which stress mutual aid and the central role of the collective in the security system of the individual, in the satisfaction of his material and emotional needs, and in the furthering of his growth and development.'

In the USSR hospitals tend to be located in the districts which they serve so that they do not lose contact with their families and friends. The hospitals are small, with 300 to 400 beds, and the patients are returned to the community clinic or dispanser, as it is called in the USSR, as soon as is possible. Psychiatrists working in the USSR would seem to have very much more authority than is the case either in the US or the UK. It would seem that they have the authority to ensure that patients, on returning to work, are placed in work suited to their particular condition or to ensure that appropriate housing arrangements are made and so on. Their views are also important in the fields of education, the effects of automation on the mental health of workers, and in other areas. It is important to remember that the number of doctors per capita is considerably higher in the USSR than in the US or UK. Moreover, there are no social workers in the Soviet Union and this task is taken over by a special category of nurse.

It is difficult to view ideological differences dispassionately but whether we like it or not it would seem that community psychiatry in the USSR has many advantages over both the US and the UK. Perhaps the greatest of these is the effectiveness of the peer group. It would seem that many problems, which in Britain or America would be dealt with by the psychiatrist or his team, are dealt with in the Soviet Union as social problems, to again quote Ziferstein:[29] 'This is a direct result of the widespread practice of involving the peer group in the solution of personal problems. Soviet pedagogues and sociologists maintain that pre-delinquent behaviour, school difficulties, work and similar problems are handled more effectively by the combined support, help, censure, and pressure of the peer group than by the behavioural scientist. As a result of the significant role played by the peer group in the rearing of the young, a predominantly peer-superego may be replacing the usual parental superego.'

3

The Future of Community Psychiatry

It is difficult to foresee what these developments mean for the future of psychiatrists. The medical man has been pre-eminent in hospitals, which an unkind critic might say have been built round the needs of the medical profession. As psychiatry moves from the hospital to the community the authority of the doctor tends to be challenged. It has already been stated that the social worker has a much longer tradition in community service and a better training for such work. Unless the psychiatrist comes to be fully conversant with the society in which the patient lives he cannot reasonably be expected to play a leadership role in this sphere. There is no doubt that he has a contribution to make but it is of a very special kind and it is unlikely that, as things are at present, he has the knowledge and training to mobilize the potential resources for treatment which are available in every community.

There are at present in Britain examples of community psychiatry services which have been developed from the mental hospital which has co-ordinated its services along with those of the local authority and the family doctors.[15] Alternatively, schemes have been developed in which the local authority has taken the initiative and co-ordinated the services of psychiatrists and family doctors in their area.[13, 24] The fact is that the problem of leadership in such areas is still a matter which is decided by the conditions peculiar to any one programme. The position of the medical officer of health in such schemes remains rather obscure. It may be that the future medical officer of health will be given a far better training in community psychiatry than is at present the case. The control of infectious diseases and specialization in bacteriology, sanitary engineering, etc. have left the medical officer of health with a far less important role than was formerly the case. Indeed it might be argued that this particular branch of medicine has become largely superfluous. It may be that more adequate training in community psychiatry might go a long way to increase the importance of the Medical Officers of Health.

Another complicating factor in the development of community psychiatry is the blurring of the margins between 'wellness' and 'illness'. Psychiatrists can no longer hope to see only definite 'cases' of mental illness. Many problems referred to them are essentially social rather than psychiatric. In this context the role relationship between the psychiatrist and the social worker is becoming blurred. Many cases do not call for the intervention of the psychiatrist at all, and this creates a very different set of circumstances to those which have prevailed in mental hospitals in the past.

The future of community psychiatry will depend on many factors, amongst the most important of which are (*i*) the extent to which local authorities accept their new responsibility and the possible regionalization of the local authority system. (*ii*) The future organization of social workers. (*iii*) Family doctors and the extent to which they are prepared to play a psychiatric role. (*iv*) The role of the psychiatrist in the community and his training for such work; and (*v*) Concepts of the therapeutic community in the hospital, and in the community.

Local Authorities

The psychiatrist is a relative newcomer in the field of community psychiatry and local authorities have had a long association with the needs of social and psychiatric casualties. Before the advent of the National Health Service Act in 1946,[19] the treatment of mental illness had been in part the concern of local authorities. In Britain, the large mental hospitals had been built mainly in the latter half of the nineteenth century and were financed and maintained by governing bodies representing county councils, or county boroughs, acting independently or in combination. In 1948, the responsibility for the treatment of the mentally ill in the mental hospitals and elsewhere became the concern of the Ministry of Health through its Regional Hospital Boards.[19] The local authorities retained their concern with prevention and after-care and, when necessary, for the admission of patients to a mental hospital in an emergency. In 1959, it became the responsibility of the local authorities to provide adequate facilities for after-care in the fields of mental illness and retardation.[17]

Different authorities have carried out their responsibilities in different ways and some excellent programmes have been developed. Certain programmes contrast in many ways with the more usual hospital-based pattern. Instead of a community service developing through out-patient departments, day hospitals, night hostels, etc., into the community, we have the local authority establishing community services which link up with the mental hospital and the psychiatrist, when this is thought necessary. In the former case leadership lies largely with the psychiatrist, whereas in the latter (local authority) case it lies primarily with the social worker. It is understandable if social workers employed by local authorities are a little surprised at the enthusiasm with which psychiatrists have welcomed the advent of community psychiatry. A scheme like that at West Ham, in London[13, 14] epitomizes a broad approach to problems which contrasts with the more specific psychiatric model, based usually on a mental hospital. With a population of approximately 160,000, West Ham tries to apply principles of positive mental health in addition to meeting the functions which are obligatory under the 1959 Mental Health Act.[17] Their programme is based on dynamic principles of family psychiatry, as developed by Howells.[9a,b,c,] Psychiatric social workers represent the main treatment staff. In contrast to the practice of traditional psychiatry, which tends to view the 'sick' person as an individual, they try to see the patient within the family matrix. As they put it, if one member of the family is singled out to carry the symptoms then when he is 'cured' or removed from the family, another member may succeed to the role of the disturbed individual. Wherever possible they attempt to see the 'case' as a symptom of a sick family and involve the family in treatment rather than focusing on the patient in isolation. 'Psychiatric Social Workers have an advantage in their knowledge of dynamic processes and a readiness to proceed at the rate at which the relatives are prepared to go. They should also, through their training, be better able to cope with problems resulting from the fact that the psychopathology of our patients is in some degree present in every "normal individual". A knowledge of this enables the trained psychiatric social worker to avoid the danger either of denying or evading the recognition of these processes or of becoming personally involved when carrying out case work in problems of personal relationships.'

At West Ham there is an establishment for twelve qualified psychiatric social workers to be appointed gradually as the scheme develops. There are three part-time psychiatrists employed jointly by the Regional Hospital Board and the Local Authority. The other staff is employed solely by the ocal Authority and includes two full-time psychologists and one lay sychotherapist.

There is at present a Government Committee studying the possible reorganization of local authorities and their report should be before Parliament within the next two years. It is impossible to foretell what these recommendations will be but it seems pretty certain that one of the major goals will be to achieve much better integration of local authorities and central Government services than is at present the case. As an example, it would appear desirable that hospitals, family doctors, and health services run by the local authority, should all come under one integrated scheme. However, such a change immediately raises the question of leadership. At present, each of the three services are administered by medical men but the regions of the three services do not coincide and, quite understandably, no one organization wishes to lose its sovereignty. It will be extremely interesting to see what happens to psychiatry when these developments materialize.

It would seem that the university departments of social medicine are more alive to possible future developments in the field of community psychiatry than are the departments of psychiatry. Departments of social medicine may well produce a training for the future medical officer of health which will give him a right to assume leadership in a new regionalized local authority system. There is no evidence as yet that in the training of the undergraduate doctor, or of the psychiatrist, sufficient attention is being paid to these developments. How far a new type of medical officer of health, trained for integrated local authority services which are being planned, will be able to co-ordinate his field of activity with those of education, recreation, industrial development, and so on, is impossible to say at this stage. One would like to think that the study of leisure, problems of retirement, and so on, will not be entirely neglected by the medical profession. The present trend in Britain would seem to indicate that the psychiatrist is not likely to play as important a part in community psychiatry as will the medical officer of health if trained to lead the integrated services of hospital, family doctors and health services at present run by the local authority. The psychiatrist will certainly have an important part to play in his own speciality within such an integrated service, but will be utilized more in the role of the consultant than as a leader of a multi-disciplinary team. The fact is that the part that the psychiatrist of the future will play in community psychiatry still rests to some extent with the leaders in the professions and particularly the university professors.   The indications at present are that psychiatry will be unprepared to play a leadership role in community psychiatry as it emerges following the reorganization of the local authority system.

Social Workers

To be a psychiatric social worker in a scheme such as that at West Ham, which is fairly typical of many other developments throughout the country, involves important changes compared with the role of a psychiatric social worker in the mental hospital. The future organization of social work in Britain is in a state of flux and it is not yet clear whether social workers will come under one large organization or whether they will remain separated into different professional groups according to training. Nor is it yet clear what reorganization will emerge where the local authorities themselves are concerned. If the local authorities became regionalized this may bring about a better and more effective integration of social services. How such services will link up with family doctors and with the hospitals under the National Health Service, remains to be seen. Nevertheless, the establishment of mental health co-ordinating committees, which bring together local authorities, hospitals, and family doctors, is a step in the right direction. The fact is that social workers are divided into many professional groups and integration of medical social workers, psychiatric social workers, probation and child care services, etc., is going to be very difficult. Again the question of leadership stands in the way of easy integration and one must await the findings of the Seebohm Committee to see how the social work profession itself views this problem. An integrated social work service would appear to be an essential prelude to the integration of the health services and local authorities. One can only hope that social workers who have played such an essential part in the development of social services in Britain will rise to the occasion and set an example for other professions. Their training and social sensitivity would seem to justify an optimistic attitude. It would seem that if community psychiatry is to become truly effective much will depend on the leadership which social work can give.

Family Doctors

The family doctor in Britain is an invaluable link in the chain of community psychiatry. Virtually every patient has a family doctor and the vast bulk of referrals to psychiatrists come through the general practitioner. In addition, on discharge it is the established practice to send a letter from the hospital to the family physician outlining what has been attempted in hospital and what drugs and other treatment is recommended for his post-hospital stage. Many cases are handled by the family doctor and never reach the psychiatrist. How far the family doctor is prepared for this psychiatric role is a moot point and at the present it depends rather more on the personality of the doctor than on any formal training which he has received as an undergraduate. Professor McKerracher,[16] at the University of Saskatchewan, has emphasized the importance of training doctors to play a psychiatric role in much the same way as they handle obstetrics, minor surgery, etc. in general practice. His work has aroused considerable interest and it may be that as community psychiatry develops, McKerracher's views will come to be much more accepted and imitated than at present. The more usual practice in Britain is to arrange courses of instruction for family doctors and Balint[3] has done much to pioneer on the job training for general practitioners.

There seems to be a very strong case for family doctors to bring their current problems to psychiatrists in an open seminar so that there can be a free exchange of views with appropriate learning. This would seem to have many advantages over the more passive role relationship between teacher and pupil in the lecture type of programme. With the change in social organization which seems to be imminent in the health service and local authority services, the family doctor will become increasingly important. Already family doctors are aware to a greater extent than before of the value of co-operating with district nurses, health visitors, social workers, and so on. There seems to be a very strong case for the adequate preparation of the family doctor for community psychiatry in his training as an undergraduate. As yet, medical schools seem to be poorly equipped to provide this type of training.

The Role of the Psychiatrist in the Community

The community psychiatrist is in a stage of uneasy transition from his hospital to his community function. At the same time his hospital role is changing. In the last two decades the social aspect in psychiatry has come to play an increasingly important part. Preoccupation with the clinical, organic and psychoanalytic aspects of psychiatry have been modified by an increasing awareness of the importance of the social factor. In essence, the doctor/patient relationship, the traditional basis of the medical model, has been widened to include all personnel who can contribute in any way to the benefit of the patient. In this metamorphosis a sharp distinction between doctor and patient, treater and treated, no longer prevails. A doctor may still be the leader of the therapeutic team co-ordinating the efforts of his colleagues and acting as their spokesman, but in certain circumstances his leadership role is in question. As an example, the psychiatrist may not be as closely in touch with a ward population as the nurse.

If the social forces in that patient community are to be mobilized for treatment and a ward meeting instituted, it may be that the nurse is a more appropriate leader of this meeting than the doctor. In such a situation patient leadership becomes an important factor and at times it may be apparent that the patient leadership is more important than the staff leadership. We will come back to the question of ward meetings later. Our concern here is to demonstrate how the simple explicit model of doctor/ patient relationship is being extended in the areas of treaters and treated. The distinction between these two areas is much less definite and distinct than it was a decade or two ago. The leadership role of the doctor, often based on little more than his professional standing in society, is being questioned. On the other hand, the passive, dependent role of the patient to whom treatment is 'given' is being modified in favour of a more active participant and 'therapeutic' role. Nor can the patient be seen as a 'case'; to study him in isolation is to ignore the social forces of which his symptoms represent one of the end products. As is well known, a family may retain some degree of equilibrium and manage to survive as a social unit at the expense of one of its members who becomes 'sick'. Thus, starting with the simple concept of doctor/patient relationships we have to consider ever-widening parameters in the areas of 'treaters' and 'treated' and in the process completely new concepts of role relationships begin to emerge. Are the psychiatric skills of the doctor as important as the social environment of the ward or the climate in the patient's family environment? Group treatment carried out by the psychiatrist or any other adequately trained person may be relatively unproductive if the social climate in the hospital as a whole is opposed to such a form of treatment.[10]

We are bringing the world of the 'treaters' and 'treated' into much closer approximation and finding that each has a lot to learn from the other. Such a tradition inevitably creates a great deal of anxiety, because at first sight it appears to imply a loss of status in the 'treater' group and a much more complex role with increased responsibility in the 'treated' group. In fact, we are disturbing deeply entrenched cultural characteristics which are often outside consciousness. People have always felt a deep need to turn to someone for protection against the fear of death. Ideas of immortality or rebirth have this quality, which is seen in pure culture in the concept of an omnipotent God. Much of this mystique surrounds the image of the physician and many people would agree that this is an important aspect of the physician's role. Society wants to believe that the medical profession has enormous and ever increasing skills.

The growing expectation of life is ample evidence of the increasing medical control over disease. At the same time there is a persistent theme that even the aging process may be modified so that man may not only increase his span of life but even defeat the process of aging itself. All established institutions such as the Church, the family, the hospital and the neighbourhood, to mention only a few, are being re-examined with a view to making them more effective in the light of modern knowledge and needs. People are beginning to think in a more global sense but unfortunately such a world view of events is as yet possible only to a few exceptional individuals.[5] However, the crisis created by the atomic age and the possibility of world destruction creates a new urgency and a stimulus for man to study himself not only in terms of individual, group or national needs, but in relation to man as a totality. With the idea of over-killing we can no longer afford to think of war as a means of destroying or modifying the effect of our enemies on ourselves. Even the man in the street is becoming aware that his economy, way of life, and security, are bound up with events in other parts of the world. The segregation issue in the United States has obvious links with the racial issues in Africa and Asia. Ideas of the 'rightness' of the American way of life and the need to protect the Vietnamese from the evils of Communism are no longer accepted by a large body of public opinion. At the same time there is a growing awareness of the evils which can form part of any industrial system.

The industrial model, applied to undeveloped countries, tends to destroy the stability of their existing culture and superimposes ideas and values which in the older industrial countries have taken centuries to evolve. To meet such enormous changes man is evolving new techniques and ideas and, hopefully, a growing identification with man as a global concept rather than living in a world limited to self and one's immediate contacts. The peace demonstrations in various parts of the world, the self-destruction by burning of Buddhist monks, the impossibility of accepting in any absolute form the ideologies propounded either by the US or the USSR, are a few of the factors which seem to be producing a barely audible voice of 'world opinion'. I have developed this concept of widening parameters of self-awareness in order to emphasize that in the state of flux which the world finds itself in, it is not surprising to find similar development of self-examination in the field of medicine.

Training the psychiatrist for work in the community. Ideally, one would like to see training for community psychiatry starting in the undergraduate years, and already some American medical schools are giving a combined medical and social science degree. How far such a move will counteract the effect that the traditional medical training has on the young student, remains to be seen. In a general hospital training setting, the young doctor tends to develop a feeling of his own omnipotence in the treatment field which often excludes any great sensitivity to the opinions of other professional personnel and unfortunately often excludes the patient too. Such a tendency is, of course, reinforced by the patient's own expectations which, quite understandably, would like the doctor to 'cure' him and the traditional attitude where the patient puts himself entirely in the hands of the doctor. What would seem to be needed is some common background and experience in the behavioural sciences for the undergraduate training of doctors, nurses, occupational therapists, social workers, catering officers, and so on.

The development of a behavioural science dimension in undergraduate training will take time and in the foreseeable future it would seem that training in community psychiatry must be largely on the job training in hospital as an addition to an existing training programme. In our experience, perhaps the best opportunity for such an experiment is in the multidisciplinary setting of a ward meeting where patients and all staff who come in contact with the patients meet daily in a ward setting. In this type of meeting the patients are encouraged to talk about their feelings, both about the staff and about their own day to day problems. Through time, such meetings can become a very valuable medium for the expression of not only conscious but, to some extent, latent material. In the staff meeting which should properly follow the ward meeting, there is an ideal opportunity for teaching. Everyone has been exposed to the same social situation and people will react according to their training, personality and sensitivity. In fact, this staff meeting can become a very valuable learning experience, not only in terms of what has happened in the staff/patient interaction, but also in terms of staff/staff interaction where various rivalries and emotional problems inevitably become manifest. It is possible to teach in such a meeting, not only borrowing from the psychoanalytic field where manifest and latent content can be discussed, but also to some extent make people aware of group processes, ego defences, transference, counter-transference, and so on. There is also the day-in day-out examination of what we are doing and why we are doing it, and this inevitably leads to a very valuable discussion of roles and role relationships, not only within the staff but also in terms of the patient.

New models of training situations relevant to social psychiatry are beginning to appear. The industrial psychologist's sensitivity training seems to have very much in common with the staff training meetings in a therapeutic community. In fact, it is difficult to see what is particularly new about the sensitivity training approach. More important perhaps is the 'living-learning' situation. By the living-learning situation is meant the utilization of a difficult interpersonal relationship situation for training purposes. The important thing is that the situation is used while the emotions are still active, and not in the retrospective way which characterizes most supervision of social work home visits or a psychiatrist's supervision of a student in a diadic treatment relationship. In the living-

learning situation the people involved in some emotionally toned interaction are brought into a face-to-face confrontation as soon as possible
after the incident occurs or even during the crisis situation. To bring about
such a confrontation usefully requires considerable skill on the part of at
least one of the parties involved. For example, a senior nurse may become
angry at an incident in a ward involving a patient and a junior staff member.
Traditionally, such a situation would be left unresolved, the junior staff
member reprimanded or supported, and the situation would 'end' by some
unilateral decision or statement being made by the senior nurse. In the
circumstances, nothing is learnt and a great deal of bad feeling is engendered with no opportunity to work through this feeling except by recourse
to one's own peer group where the inevitable hostility towards authority
figures is reinforced. Whenever possible we are attempting to use such
situations for training purposes. Thus, in the situation we have mentioned,
the senior nurse, the junior staff member, patient or patients, and other
people who are involved, would be asked to discuss what had happened as
they perceived it. Almost invariably it will be found that the situation has
many facets and may well originate in some rivalry, misunderstanding, or
carry-over from past situations. Even at the most superficial level it is
almost certain that misunderstandings will come to light and at the very
least the senior staff will become aware of unresolved tensions within the
ward situation. More usually, however, a considerable lessening of tension
occurs by merely discussing the episode and trying to understand what
factors have contributed to the intense feeling which is so often engendered.
As the staff become more familiar with group methods and the patients
themselves are more acculturated it is possible to have quite searching
analysis of what lies behind behaviour, with the emergence of latent
content, ego defences, transference, countertransference, and so on. We
believe that this is one possible way of carrying out a part of training in
community psychiatry but it requires considerable expenditure of time
and a skilled group worker to carry it out successfully.

The simple extension of such ideas can be seen in the admission of a
new patient to a ward. If the admission interview is carried out with the
patient, his relative, or relatives, one or two nurses from the admission
ward, social worker and any other relevant personnel, it becomes a spontaneous group and the staff become aware of the patient and his family as
people with emotional problems and personality attributes which is a very
different matter to reading about the same patient from the doctor's case
notes. Moreover, at the end of the interview the patient can be taken to the
ward along with his relatives by a nurse who has already got some feeling
for the situation and who intuitively tends to use this information to
introduce the new patient to appropriate peers and also to win over the
family to a more sympathetic attitude towards the patient and a greater
willingness to participate in family group treatment.

In brief, it would seem that there is much to be said for carrying out part of the training in community psychiatry as an extension of ordinary psychiatric training which doctors and other disciplines already receive by the introduction of a more specific training in group dynamics and a more sensitive awareness of the feelings of other people. In addition, there is the need for some instruction in social organization and awareness of the concept of a therapeutic culture which can be built up through time by the daily analysis of what people are doing and why they are doing it. It is our belief that people trained in this way over a period of at least a year are much more comfortable in social situations and show much greater awareness of the social environment and skill in using it. They become more sensitive to the feelings of other people and more ready to listen to not only other professional and non-professional personnel, but to the patients and their relatives. In other words, we feel that a training of this kind is equally relevant to intra- and extramural practice of psychiatry.

The current training that the average young doctor, nurse, occupational therapist, etc. receives in psychiatry, does not adequately prepare people for the new field of community psychiatry and allied mental health practices. We believe that a more specific training will emerge through time but in the meantime we feel that a training along the lines outlined above will go a long way to preparing the various disciplines for practice in mental health clinics and in the field of community psychiatry.

Concepts of the Therapeutic Community in the Hospital and in the Community

Community psychiatry can be looked at from various points of view, such as the epidemiological, ecological, or sociological, or certain aspects of the subject can be taken in isolation, such as suicide, crisis situations, problems of retirement, and so on. The concept of the therapeutic community has grown up along with many aspects of community psychiatry and may be considered by some to have a particular relevance in this field. No attempt will be made to give a detailed account of therapeutic community concepts here and my own ideas have been brought together in book form (Jones, 1952 and 1962).[11, 12]

If one assumes that the patient population in hospital has certain treatment potentials which can be developed under constant medical and professional supervision, then one has to set up a structure whereby the patient contribution can be maximized. The immediate objection can be raised that the patients are ill and it is unfair or unrealistic to expect them to help in treatment and make decisions involving a good deal of responsibility; in any case, this is the job that the staff is paid to do.

This question of elaborating the role of a patient to one of therapist is, I think, one of the fundamental tenets of therapeutic community procedure. This concept is often mistakenly seen as handing over ultimate responsibility to the patients. This, in my opinion, is not practicable and what one wishes is to give the patients optimal responsibility compatible with their overall capacity at any one time, and in no sense does the staff or the doctor in charge relinquish his ultimate authority which merely remains latent to be invoked when necessary. It is the application of this principle which calls for considerable experience and skill. As an example, a community may be functioning at a fairly high level of effectiveness and the patients may be able to take over a considerable amount of responsibility and then, on a particular day, four or five of the most responsible and successfully treated members leave, to be replaced by four or five new patients who may be in the state of considerable disorganization. The loss of patient leadership within the ward and the effect of the new intake may be such that the ward functioning is materially altered and the staff have to play a much more active and controlling role than they were previously doing. This is not fundamentally different to what happens in an individual or a group treatment session when the lack of ego strength or anxiety level is such that the therapist feels it necessary to be largely supportive for a time.

I am talking about patient responsibility of a higher order than one usually understands by the term 'Patient government'. Patient government is usually restricted to decisions on relatively minor matters of ward organization and activities. What I have in mind, is decisions shared with the staff and involving such matters as the discharge of patients or transfer to other wards, or what disciplinary action should be taken in the case of deviant behaviour. This sharing of serious responsibility with the staff is, I think, one of the most important ways in overcoming the lack of confidence, low self-estimate, and overdependency which all too frequently is characteristic of the psychiatric patient in the hospital ward. This responsibility can also be carried over to the patient's work role. It is ideal if one can also do production work for the hospital community and have patient foremen, timekeepers, etc.

If one is fortunate enough to have the freedom to build up a therapeutic community from the point of view of the patients' social and treatment needs, then a structure which deviates markedly from the more usual pattern may emerge. The familiar hierarchical hospital social structure is essentially staff-centred and often is determined by traditions from the past which have little relevance to current treatment methods and practices. As an example, one finds that in a ward where the patients have a great deal of identification with responsible roles and with treatment, they will come to the aid of the night nurse in the event of disturbed patient behaviour, instead of leaving it entirely for the staff to deal with. In this context also, the patients come to feel much more able to bear with highly disturbed behaviour among their peers because the community meetings help them to understand the meaning of the disturbed behaviour and gives them a better idea of how to relate in a helpful and understanding way to the sick member.

I am leading up to what I think is fundamental in any therapeutic community of the kind I have in mind. I believe that daily ward or community meetings with all patients and staff is essential and this meeting should be followed by a staff meeting, preferably lasting thirty to sixty minutes, where the interaction between staff and patients in the community meeting can be discussed. The daily examination of ward behaviour and current problems means that the patients become aware of the factors which lie behind behaviour and learn a great deal about each other's problems. In any type of hospital, they are forced to relate to other patients and staff at ward level whether they like it or not, and it seems reasonable to try to help them to have a positive role to play and a better insight into what is going on in themselves and in those around them. In my experience, it is possible to get patients and staff at all levels to appreciate some of the phenomena that occur on the ward and in the daily ward meetings. The progression that occurs in these meetings through time has many points in common with ordinary group treatment. In the first instance, the patients in the community meeting tend to look to the staff for leadership and are glad when some general topic is raised which has no personal significance. As time progresses, they begin to talk about some of their deeper feelings and to test out the staff reactions in this direction. Assuming adequate skills on the part of the staff, they become used as transference figures with advantage to the treatment process. The same applies to the transference on to various members of the patient population. The concepts of manifest and latent content, the unconscious, and ego defences, come to be understood in much the way that occurs in a small group. It may be necessary to have additional seminars for the assistant nurses who are less well-trained than the other staff members and to whom the change of role implicit in this discussion is greater than that required of any other staff member. For the staff meeting, concepts, like feedback from informal staff-patient groups, and difficulties occurring during the night between patients and night staff can usefully be communicated to the group. Ideally, one would hope that nursing personnel rotate so that the night staff have opportunity to participate in the learning experience afforded to the day staff, more particularly the morning shift.

The meetings I am describing are clearly less specifically therapeutic and more concerned with everyday behaviour and ward management than is the typical therapeutic group of six or eight patients of a selected kind. Nevertheless, I think that the community meetings of up to eighty patients and staff have a particular place in hospital therapy, particularly in bringing about the establishment of what one might call a 'therapeutic culture'. By this, I mean that the day-after-day examination of the problems existing on a ward and the consideration of the roles of all staff members and of the patients leads through time to considerable modification of the ward structure. Not only that, but the traditional attitudes and beliefs can come in for scrutiny and we are in a position to ask ourselves why we do what we do, when we do it.

4

Conclusion

I have already indicated in discussing the training of the psychiatrist for work in the community that it is my belief that the therapeutic community affords an excellent setting in which to learn community psychiatry. The fact is that as yet most training in psychiatry occurs in hospital but will, through time, occur increasingly in a community setting. As yet, most teachers in psychiatry, and, for that matter, in social work, tend to be associated with the department in which they work and have relatively little contact with the field. It would seem that considerable changes are called for before we can arrive at an integrated social structure in the area of community psychiatry. Some of these problems have already been touched on and one must hope that whatever social organization emerges it will prove to be more appropriate for the task in hand than has the social organization which pertains in most psychiatric hospitals.

It is my belief that the principles and skills arising out of the practice of community therapy in hospital can be transferred to the outside community. Whether this belief is justified or not, time alone will tell. It is, I think, appropriate to end with a note of caution. Simmons,[23] writing on the impact of social factors upon adjustment within the community, states: 'A final concept worthy of comment is the fact that it has not seemed possible for a socio-cultural system anywhere to sustain itself as a total society and also to safeguard the normality and the mental health of all its membership. In every social system some members are sacrificed either because they cannot fit into the selective slots of the system, or they pay with the price of scars on their lives, or by their lives, for the good or for the folly of the whole, as in warfare, for example. It would probably be a spurious psychiatric hope to anticipate that any possible form of milieu manipulation would be able to produce a millennium of fulfilment for every member. Let us hope that community psychiatry may not permit itself to become committed to such a Utopian goal. The realities of community life are much too formidable for that.'

REFERENCES

1. *A hospital plan for England and Wales.* 1962. Comnd. 1604. London: H. M.S.O. Jan.
2. *Action for Mental Health.* 1961. Final Report of the Joint Commission on Mental Illness and Health. New York: Basic Books.
3. BALINT, M., 1960. *The doctor, the patient, and the illness.* London: Pitman.
4. CAPLAN, GERALD, 1964. *Principles of preventive psychiatry.* London: Tavistock Publications.
5. CHISHOLM, BROCK, 1959. *Can people learn to learn?* London: Allen and Unwin.

6. *Concepts of community psychiatry.* 1965. U.S. Dept. of Health Education and Welfare. Washington, D.C.: U.S. Government Printing Office.

7. GRAD, J., and SAINSBURY, P., 1966. Evaluating the community psychiatric service in Chichester. *Milbank Memorial Fund Quarterly*, **44**, 246.

8. HOWE, L. P., 1964. The Concept of the Community. *Handbook of community psychiatry and community mental health.* Ed. Bellak, Leopold. New York: Grune and Stratton.

9a. HOWELLS, J. G., 1962. The Nuclear Family as a Functional Unit in Psychiatry. *J. ment. Sci.*, **108**, 675.

9b. HOWELLS, J. G., 1963. *Family psychiatry.* Edinburgh: Oliver and Boyd.

9c. HOWELLS, J. G., 1968. *Theory and practice of family psychiatry.* Edinburgh: Oliver and Boyd.

10. JONES, MAXWELL, 1968. Group work in mental hospitals. *Brit. J. Psychiat.*, In press.

11. JONES, MAXWELL, 1952. *Social psychiatry.* London: Tavistock Publications. The same book was published in the U.S.A. as *The therapeutic community.* New York: Basic Books, 1953.

12. JONES, MAXWELL, 1962. *Social psychiatry in the community, in hospitals and in prisons.* Springfield, Ill.: Chas. C. Thomas.

13. KAHN, J. H., 1963. Community responsibilities for Mental Health. In *Trends in the mental health services.* Eds. Freeman, H., and Farndale, J. Oxford: Pergamon Press.

14. KAHN, J. H., 1962. *A community mental health service based on principles of family psychiatry.* W.H.O. Seminar on Mental Health and the Family. Athens, 1962.

15. MACMILLAN, D., 1961. Community Mental Health Services and the Mental Hospital. *Wld ment. Hlth*, **13**, 1.

16. McKERRACHER, D. G., SMITH, C. M., COBURN, F. E., and McDONALD, I. M., 1965. General-practice psychiatry. *Lancet*, ii, 1005.

17. *Mental Health Act.* 1959. London: H.M.S.O.

18. MENZIES, I. E. P., 1961. *The functioning of social systems as a defence against anxiety.* Tavistock Pamphlet No. 3. London: Tavistock Publications.

19. *National health service Act.* 1946. London: H.M.S.O.

20. REHIN, G. F., and MARTIN, F. M., 1963. Psychiatric Services in 1975. *PEP*, **29**.

21. RUESCH, J., 1965. Social psychiatry, an overview. *Arch. gen. Psychiat.* **12**, 501–09.

22. REVANS, R. W., 1964. *Standards of morale.* London: Oxford Univ. Press.

23. SIMMONS, L. W., 1966. Impact of social factors upon adjustment within the community. *Am. J. Psychiat.*, **122**, 990.

24. SUSSER, M. W., 1960. *Report on the mental health services for the City of Salford, 1959.*

25. TOOTH, G. C., and BROOKE, E., 1961. Trends in the mental hospital population and their effect on future planning. *Lancet*, i, 710.

26. WEDGE, B., and BOONIN, N., 1966. The present and future of community psychiatry. In *Current psychiatric therapies.* Ed. Masserman, Jules H. New York and London: Grune and Stratton.

27. WING, J., and BROWN, G. W., 1964. Morbidity in the community of schizophrenics discharged from London mental hospitals in 1959. *Brit. J. Psychiat.*, **110**, 10.

28. ZIFERSTEIN, I., 1965. Direct observations of psychotherapy in the U.S.S.R. *Sixth Internat. Congr. of Psychotherapy*, London, 1964. Selected lectures, pp. 150–160. New York: S. Karger.

29. ZIFERSTEIN, I., 1966. The Soviet psychiatrist's concepts of society as a therapeutic community. In *Current psychiatric therapies*. Ed. Masserman, Jules.
New York and London: Grune and Stratton.

XXVI

TRANSCULTURAL PSYCHIATRY

E. D. WITTKOWER

Department of Psychiatry,
McGill University, Montreal

with the assistance of

DR P. E. TERMANSEN

1

Definitions

Cultural psychiatry is the field of psychiatry which concerns itself with the frequency, causation, and nature of mental illness, and the care and aftercare of the mentally ill within the confines of a given cultural unit. The term *trans*-cultural psychiatry, which is an extension of cultural psychiatry, denotes that the vista of the scientific observer extends beyond the scope of one cultural unit on to others, whereas the term *cross*-cultural is applied to comparative and contrasting aspects of psychiatry in any of the areas named.

In the light of our present knowledge, transcultural psychiatry is predominantly a field of research though there are also practical applications. It is obvious that understanding of the cultural background of his patients in his own culture greatly assists the practicing psychiatrist in handling his patients, that a white, Euro-American psychiatrist has some difficulty in understanding the behaviour of an African bush Negro, whose attitudes, beliefs, and value orientations are remote from his own, and that in planning mental health services, cultural considerations have to be taken into account. It is hoped that knowledge of socio-cultural variables, noxious to mental health will continue to assist in the reduction of mental illness.

An essential prerequisite for understanding the cultural aspects of abnormal thought, feeling, and behaviour, is a knowledge of the effects of differences in cultural environments on normal personality development. As an area of research, this is regarded as the domain of cultural psychologists and anthropologists. International psychiatry, which concerns itself with such comparative aspects of psychiatry as teaching, training facilities, hospital administration, and treatment problems due to shortage of qualified psychiatrists and drugs, may also be separated off from the immediate research interest of transcultural psychiatry.

In short, transcultural psychiatric research may be defined as the contributions which psychiatrists and social scientists can make to the understanding of mental abnormality against different cultural backgrounds.

Culture has been defined as 'the sum total of the attitudes, ideas, and behaviour shared and transmitted by the members of society' or briefly by the same author (Linton)[31] as 'social heredity'. As regards mental illness, the relativity of what is regarded as normal or abnormal from culture to culture must be borne in mind. Behaviour which is considered as normal in one culture is not necessarily considered as such in another. *Mental illness* may be defined as behaviour that would be regarded as abnormal by trained observers everywhere, irrespective of the culture in which it is observed.

Man influences culture and culture influences man. The way in which human beings learn and embody the culture in which they live can be understood in terms of various concepts. In psychoanalytic terms, the interrelationship between culture and personality can be conceived as follows. Certain basic drives exist universally. Every human being is hungry, thirsty, eats, drinks, urinates, defecates, loves, and hates. These are biological needs, biological functions, instincts, feelings and impulses. However, the degree and quality of some of these urges, the prohibitions imposed on them by the key figures in the family and the inhibitions blocking their expression are subject to variations from individual to individual. This is equally true for cultures. Precept and example within the family circle have their counterpart in the mores of a society. There is a continuum of cultures ranging from those whose members are predominantly guided by external authority to those whose members have incorporated external authority in terms of morality, sense of duty, sense of obligation, and control of aggressiveness; and there is a continuum of cultures ranging from those whose members freely express instinctual drives, impulses and feelings to those whose members are severely inhibited in instinctual and emotional expression.

These differences can be accounted for only by due regard to cross-cultural differences in infant handling, child upbringing, and other socio-cultural influences. Intensity and nature of maternal care of the infant vary a great deal between different cultures. There are differences in the scheduling and the duration of breast feeding. Babies may be swaddled, tied to their mother's back, held against their mother's breast or wheeled in a baby carriage with only occasional body contact with the mother. Toilet training may be strict or lenient and a display of early genitality may be frowned upon or treated with indulgence. Moreover, cultural values are imparted to the growing child by teaching, by reward, and by punishment.

2

Methodology

There are two major approaches to the field of transcultural psychiatry: those focused on quantitative differences and those focused on qualitative differences of mental disorders in contrasting cultures. Both types of studies may be started off either from the psychiatric or from the social science point of view. That is, the scientific observer may have been able to demonstrate differences in the frequency and/or nature of mental disorders at two or more culturally different observation posts and may ask himself whether and how these differences can be explained in terms of socio-cultural variables or the scientific observer may choose locations of his research according to socio-cultural factors, e.g. adherence to tradition versus culture change and may ask himself to what extent, if at all, these factors affect the frequency and nature of mental disorders. Or the investigator may leave the field of clinical psychiatry altogether and may submit to cultural comparison effectiveness of social institutions in dealing with attitudes towards, and emotional responses to such universal phenomena as death, disablement, physical illness or mental illness. Examples of this last type of research are comparative studies concerning the impact of disablement of the father on the family carried out in Canada and Peru by (Castro)[5] and comparative studies concerning the impact of prolonged serious illness of one child on the family carried out in three Canadian sub-cultures by Ellenberger and Saucier[13] under the auspices of the Section of Transcultural Psychiatric Studies at McGill University, Montreal.

Methodologies of transcultural psychiatric research consist of application of the same investigative technique to persons of contrasting cultures, either by the same observer or by different observers. These observers may be psychiatrists, anthropologists, social workers, psychologists, or a team composed of representatives of any of these disciplines. For obvious reasons most psychiatric observations in primitive societies have in the past been made by cultural anthropologists, ill equipped in psychiatric knowledge or, if enterprising enough to leave the security of the office or analytic couch, by psychiatrists ill equipped in anthropological knowledge. Since there are few psychiatrists or anthropologists who competently straddle both fields, team co-operation becomes a logical necessity. Such team co-operation entails one of the major problems of all inter-disciplinary research, namely the dovetailing of data obtained by different disciplines— different in the primary focus of interest, in their theoretical orientation and in the methodologies employed.

The common research tools of transcultural psychiatric research are those of clinical interviews, field surveys and observations (interviews with key informants, home visits and census examinations), hospital, law and government records, psychological tests, questionnaires and psycho-analytic techniques. At the present time, psychiatrists dominate the field of transcultural psychiatric research with respect to clinical observations. Emphasis in the future is expected to be on collaboration between psychiatrists and social scientists.

3

Clinical Issues

A comprehensive survey of all the ramifications of the field of transcultural psychiatry is not possible in the space available. Instead, some of the fundamental issues which have been raised will be discussed in the light of our present knowledge.

Mental disorders in primitive cultures

The myth that mental disorders are confined to nations of advanced cultures has long been exploded. Such simple hunting and gathering tribes as the Siriono of Bolivia (Holmberg),[22] and the Ojibwa of Wisconsin (Hallowell)[19] can produce and maintain unresolved severe states of anxiety among their members. Even well integrated, stable, traditionally oriented, and by no means primitive communities, like the Hutterites, have been shown to be by no means ideally mentally healthy (Eaton and Weil).[11] Moloney's[35] report on the Okinawans as being relatively immune to psychosis has been refuted (Wedge;[52] Hankoff)[20]. However, it is still possible to maintain the position that, as far as mental health is concerned, some cultural environments may be more favourable than others.

Total frequency of mental disorders

One of the basic questions which transcultural psychiatry has raised has been that of possible significant differences between different cultures in the total frequency of mental disorders. Statistics are available which show that the total incidence of mental illness in so-called primitive societies is lower than in advanced societies. For instance, Carothers[3] states that 'certified lunatics' in England and Wales in 1938 were four per one thousand population; while at roughly the same time, there were in the Gold Coast 0·3 per thousand (Tooth).[50] These and other statistics should be regarded with utmost caution, (a) because they are based on hospitalized patients, and mental hospitals are scarce in many underdeveloped countries, (b) because customarily the mentally ill in many of these countries turn to native healers rather than physicians, if they seek help at all, (c) because tolerance for the mentally ill within the community in many of these countries is, so long as they are not socially disturbing, great and (d) because grossly disturbed and disturbing psychotics are often left to die or are disposed of by their fellow tribesmen. As the above comments have indicated, comparative studies of total frequencies of mental disorders in contrasting cultures are fraught with methodological difficulties. Hospital admission rates, fail to give information on the issue, and only a few reliable comparative field studies such as Leighton's Nova Scotian,[27] and Nigerian[28] studies, and Lin's Formosan study[30] are available. Suggestive evidence exists that the total frequency of mental disorders varies from society to society and is in some preliterate societies even higher than in civilized ones (Field).[14]

Relative frequency of mental disorders

With respect to the question of differences in the relative frequency of mental disorders between different cultures, it must again be stated that the data thus far accumulated does not warrant any definite conclusions. On methodological grounds more convincing evidence has been submitted regarding differences in the relative frequency of mental disorders on comparison of sub-cultures within the same overall culture than on crosscultural comparison.

However, some generalizations can be attempted:

1. Diagnostic labels developed and employed in advanced countries are not necessarily applicable to so-called primitive societies, be it certain American Indians (Devereux),[9] certain groups of African Negroes (Tooth;[50] Carothers;[3] Field)[14], or certain groups of Arabs (Parhad).[40]

2. The borderline between neurotic and psychotic states in preliterate peoples is ill-defined and atypical states are fairly common.

3. Schizophrenia is ubiquitous. It is still debatable whether any particular way of life or culture predisposes to an increase in its frequency.

4. Infectious psychoses are frequent in areas where risks of exposure are high and medical services are inadequate.

5. Most observers agree, (1) that depressive states are rare in so-called primitive societies, such as the preliterate native populations of Java (Kraepelin),[24] Kenya (Carothers),[3] Nigeria (Leighton),[28] South Africa (Laubscher)[26] and Haiti (Bordeleau)[2] and that if they occur at all, feelings of guilt and self-reproach are uncommon (Stainbrook;[48, 49] Tooth).[50]

This alleged rarity of depressive states may be a mere artifact due to the well-known fact that in primitive societies, for a variety of reasons, only grossly emotionally disturbed and socially disturbing patients are taken to the few available mental hospitals whereas quiet, retarded depressives are usually retained in, and looked after by, the extended family. This view is borne out by M. J. Field's[14] recent observations in which she noted the presence of depressives in considerable numbers among the Ashanti at religious shrines in Ghana. It has also been suggested that the 'sick role' of depressives is not acknowledged in African society—there are indeed no words for depression in their languages (Margetts)[32]—and that hypochondriacal manifestations, may conceal depressive symptomatology.

Conversely, if true, the rarity of depressive states may be accounted for by the protective effect of the extended family against mourning over object loss (Stainbrook),[49] by the effectiveness of funeral rites in working through object loss, by the effectiveness of projective mechanisms as a defence against depression, and by a predominance of a collective (clan) super-ego in preliterate societies versus a predominance of an individual super-ego in Western-type societies. Contrariwise it has been hypothesized that 'psychotic depression is generally more frequent among those persons who are more cohesively identified with their family, kin groups, communities, and other significant groupings' (Cohen).[6]

6. Suicide rates are unusually high in Japan, Sweden, Denmark, and Switzerland, and are alleged to be low in African Negroes who, however, if emotionally disturbed, are apt to wander off into the jungle or bush and never come back (Laubscher;[26] Shelley and Watson;[46] Aubin).[1] It must be emphasized again, however, that comparative ratings of suicide must be interpreted with the greatest of caution. Socio-cultural attitudes and beliefs profoundly influence the way in which the cause of death is recorded. Even within Western countries it is extremely difficult to obtain figures on suicide rates which are comparable.

7. Consensus exists that in less developed countries hysterical reactions are much more common than in highly developed countries while obsessional neuroses have been reported as rare in various underdeveloped countries (Vahia;[51] Gaitonde).[16] The rarity of the latter could be attributed to the disinclination of obsessive-compulsives all over the world to consult psychiatrists, to the mitigating effect of lenient early toilet training on morality development, to externalization of a threatening conscience in the form of popular beliefs and superstitions, and to absorption of obsessional defences in culture dictated rituals.

8. Psychosomatic disorders such as gastric ulcer, high blood pressure and bronchial asthma which are usually attributed to the hurly-burly of Western civilization are by no means uncommon in African natives or the rural population of India. The expression of psychological distress in somatic terms is indeed characteristic of peoples anywhere in the world where illiteracy rates are high and formal education is unknown.

9. The diagnosis of sexual perversion depends, of course, on social conventions. If in a society, homosexuality is institutionalized, as in some Arabic societies (Parhad),[40] homosexual behaviour is obviously not a sign of sickness, and if in a society, as in the Urubi Indians in Eastern Brazil (Carstairs)[4] it is customary to go about naked with a ribbon tied around the penis, a gentleman thus attired can hardly be accused of indecent exposure. The inference may be drawn that identical behaviour in different societies may be based on different psychodynamics.

Cultural factors as stress

Considerable debate has centred around the question of which cultural factors are likely to be stressful. In general, those factors likely to affect mental health adversely are (*i*) those due to *existing* value orientations, (*ii*) those due to *co-existing* value orientations, and (*iii*) those due to *changing* value orientations.

1. The hurly-burly life of North American cities with its emphasis on speed, achievement, and success would appear to be more stressful than, for instance, life on some Pacific island where food is sufficient or abundant, where authority and other social pressures are minimal, and where time-lessness reigns supreme (Spiro).[47] Other cultural stresses inherent in exist-ing value orientations arise from traditional family structure, role and status of women and sibling rank. The example of India may be given. In the traditional Indian household the father is the absolute ruler and his wife an obedient servant. If a woman happens to be barren, she is subject to contempt. As far as children are concerned, boys are welcomed but girls are unwanted. This constitutes a serious handicap for girls throughout their lives. The eldest son is in a privileged position but has to bear heavy responsibilities, especially if the father dies early. Marriages are arranged by the parents without consulting the partners concerned. These marriages are usually concluded at a very early age when men and women alike are ill prepared for their sexual roles. The whole subject of sex is severely tabooed. On marrying, the young woman moves into the house of her husband's parents where she is kept under the mother-in-law's thumb. She will not be able to assert herself until her son marries and she can take out on her daughter-in-law the humiliations which she herself has suffered.

2. Stresses due to co-existing value orientations are exemplified by the interaction of racial, ethnic and religious minorities with the dominating majority of the population. Instances of this nature are familiar to all. Less familiar are perhaps the psychological effects of migration, voluntary and enforced, in many parts of the world (Fried;[15] Seguin).[45] A higher fre-quency of mental disorders in immigrants as well as migrants has been observed by many, notably Eitinger;[12] Malzberg,[33, 34] Murphy,[36, 37, 38] and Odegaard.[39] In areas such as Israel and Singapore where immigrants constitute a large proportion of the population their hospitalization rates may be relatively low (Murphy).[37]

3. All over the world there is a change of value orientation towards Westernization. The traditional joint family is replaced by the Western-type nuclear family, tribal units are breaking up, religious allegiances are being abandoned, and there is an intensive drive towards education along with increasing industrialization. The intense nationalism which is charac-teristic of many of the developing countries has brought in its wake con siderable political, economic and social change.

Symptomatology of mental disorders

Differences in the symptomatology of mental disorders in different cultures has received considerable attention by researchers in transcultural psychiatry. It has been pointed out that, in general, the definition of what constitutes a symptom is subject to cultural variations and that identical symptoms have different meanings in different cultures on account of differences in culturally shared beliefs.

As stated before, gross hysterical reactions such as hysterical blindness, hysterical deafness, hysterical convulsions and hysterical paralysis which were common in Euro-American countries two or three decades ago but have since almost disappeared, are frequent in many so-called primitive societies. Their frequency, for instance, in rural India has been attributed to deficient repression and their recession in Western Europe and North America to the emancipation of women and to an increasing sophistication of the population. Common among hysterical reactions in these societies are vague aches and pains, functional visceral disorders (autonomic dysfunctions), and sensations of heat (reported from countries as far apart as India and Nigeria) which are based on prevailing folk beliefs. Acute anxiety reactions of short duration are more common in primitive societies than in advanced societies. These anxiety states are often precipitated by failure to perform customary rites and attributed to the wrath of the gods or to bewitchment. They are often accompanied by incoherence of thought amounting to confusion and by delusional and hallucinatory activity. By and large, in comparison with Euro-Americans, emotional involvement and tendencies to put morbid impulses culminating in homicidal attempts into action are greater in primitive societies (Carothers;[3] M. J. Field;[14] Collomb).[7, 8]

Differences are much more subtle as regards psychotic behaviour. The example of schizophrenia may be given. It is obvious that the content of schizophrenic delusions is influenced and coloured by cultural beliefs. It has been stated that schizophrenia in primitive African societies (Gordon)[18] is quieter than in the Western world—'a poor imitation of European forms'—and it has been reported that there is less 'method in the madness' of schizophrenic patients in India (Hoch)[21] than in Euro-American patients, that Indian patients are less aggressive and Southern Italian patients are more aggressive, more expressive and more affectionate than patients in the United States and that social withdrawal is one of the last symptoms to appear in these Italian schizophrenics (Parsons).[41]

This may appear a hodgepodge of observations illustrative of the present state of transcultural psychiatry. However, if one tries to bring order into disorder and to explain the various observations which have been made, the following tentative suggestions may be offered: (*i*) The lack of aggressiveness in Indian schizophrenics, disputed by some writers, may be related to the premium set by Indian culture on control of emotion in general and of anger and aggressiveness in particular; (*ii*) The barrenness of the clinical picture in preliterate African negroes may be due to the paucity of their cultural and intellectual resources and their difficulties in dealing with abstractions as we know them (Yap);[54] and (*iii*) The maintenance of social contacts in Southern Italian schizophrenics may be related to their traditional sociability and gregariousness, greater family solidarity and lack of strong feelings of guilt about being ill and being hospitalized (Parsons).[41]

Unusual symptom patterns

Some of the unusual symptom patterns which have been observed in different cultures constitute the so-called culture bound disorders. Some of the more well known of these disorders are possession states, Windigo, Koro, Tarantism, Latah and Amok. There is no doubt that culture specific elements have an important patho-plastic effect on these disorders, but it is also true that there is a remarkable similarity in some of them, designated differently in disparate societies, and it therefore seems reasonable not to regard them as unique culture phenomena but rather as culture determined variance of known psychiatric disorders.

In accordance with the beliefs of people in primitive societies, outside agencies may take possession of individuals and replace their 'soul'. These possession states may be transient or of prolonged duration. Temporary states of possession during religious ceremonies have been reported from many parts of the world. Typical, also of others, are the possession states which occur during voodoo ceremonies in Haiti. Suddenly, activated by the wild rhythm of the drums and encouraged by the priest, the houngan, a member of the congregation passes into a trance state. His face appears empty, he stares into space, and he acts and speaks like the god that possesses him. Remarkable feats, which otherwise seem impossible, such as climbing a palm tree upside down, have been performed in this condition and convulsive seizures often occur. Possession states in the setting of voodoo ceremonies, by and large, are culturally sanctioned institutionalized phenomena which occur in suggestible persons living in a culture which fosters submissiveness and hence suggestibility (Wittkower;[53] Douyon).[10] Possession states such as these usually end when the voodoo ceremony is over. By contrast, states of possession by ancestors, gods and animals, and enactments of reincarnation have been reported from the Far East, from India and from other parts of the world. These are of prolonged duration and amount to a mental illness. An example of this kind of disorder is Kitsunetsuki (Yonebayashi)[55] known to occur in certain areas of Japan where the social structure is feudal in nature and attitudes of superstition and ignorance prevail. Based on features of Shintoism, people affected in this manner are believed to be possessed by foxes and are said to change their facial expression accordingly. A whole family may be thus afflicted; if they are, they are feared and shunned by the whole community.

The main feature of this disorder and of similar disorders, as stated previously, is 'soul' replacement, i.e. the intrusion of an outside agent into the self. Its counterpart is 'soul' projection. The belief is held in many primitive societies that temporarily, for instance, during sleep, the soul may leave the body and wander off. A disorder based on such belief is Susto (magic fright) which has been reported from various South American countries especially from Peru (Gillin;[17] Leon;[29] Rubel;[44] Ponce).[42] It usually occurs in children or adolescents, is often precipitated by a frightening experience and is characterized by intense anxiety, hyperexcitability, and a state of depression accompanied by considerable loss of weight. The patients believe that their soul has been separated from their body and has been kidnapped and absorbed by the earth. Treatment consists of invocation of the absent soul, of propitiatory offerings to the earth and of rubbing a guinea-pig on the naked body of the patient followed by sacrifice of the guinea-pig to the earth.

There is another group of culture specific mental disorders which are unrelated to soul replacement and soul projection. An example of this kind of disorder is Koro (Yap;[54] Rin),[43] a mental derangement which appears to occur only in South Eastern Asia, and particularly among the inhabitants of the Malay Archipelago and among the Southern Chinese who immigrated to this region. It resembles castration anxiety so common in the West, but differs in the manner in which the threat to the genitals is experienced, and in the manner in which the irrational fear is dealt with by the patient and members of his family. In Koro, the patient is afraid that his penis will retract into his abdomen and that as a result of this he will die. To prevent withdrawal of the penis, the patient holds the penis in a vice-like grip. He is assisted in this by his wife, friends, or relatives, who may clamp the penis in a wooden box or tie a red string around it. Psychodynamically, the presenting symptom both in the East and the West is presumably based on an unresolved oedipal conflict, but as Rin[43] has pointed out, it is also deeply rooted in fundamental Chinese concepts of sexuality. Moreover the susceptibility of the Chinese to symbolic castration threats may be related to their oral orientation and to fear of oral deprivation.

Treatment of mental disorders

As regards the treatment of the mentally ill, in many parts of the world, in primitive and not so primitive societies, the bulk of the mentally ill, or at least a substantial proportion of them are looked after by non-medical personnel. They are treated by quacks, herbalists, religious healers and cult groups. The choice of these non-medical healers is by no means solely determined by scarcity of trained psychiatrists, but also by prevailing etiological concepts. The nature of these etiological concepts has been explored. If the belief is held that mental disturbances are due to evil spirits, demons, or sorcery, persons believed to be in possession of supernatural powers are likely to be consulted. The personalities of these native healers, the procedures which they adopt, and the psychodynamics involved in their treatment have been studied. In keeping with African and

Indian cultural requirements, procedures such as family participation in the treatment of the mentally ill in hospitals, in village settlements, have been employed and appraised in their effectiveness (Lambo;[25] Kohl-meyer).[23] Reasons for resistance to Western psychotherapeutic measures, such as psychoanalysis, in some countries have been explored and reasons for preference for such procedures as Morita therapy in Japan have been given. Modification of Western type group therapy, based on cultural considerations, have been experimentally introduced in Latin countries. Noteworthy are investigations regarding doctor-patient relationship and management of the mentally ill in contrasting cultures. Somatic forms of treatment are of course, universally used, provided that equipment and drugs are available. As yet little is known about the differential response to phrenotropic drugs in different cultures.

Care of the mentally ill in primitive societies is characterized by the employment of treatment procedures based on animistic beliefs. In order to illustrate the features of such procedures and beliefs, the practices in Western Nigeria will be described in some detail.

In Western Nigeria, as in many other parts of the world, the mentally ill were cared for until recently by native healers whose systems of treat-ment are either secular or religious in nature.

The *secular system* consists of a network of treatment centres operated by traditional healers (onishegun) whose lore has been passed from father to son for many generations. These treatment centres are like small private hospitals. The healer may use his own house for the accom-modation of his patients or he may have specially constructed huts adjacent to his home. Usually about a dozen psychotic patients are accommodated; in addition the healer may run a large out-patient department for patients with milder psychological disorders. Many healers insist on having in-patients accompanied by near relatives who prepare his food and give him nursing care. This practice enables the healer to establish and the patient to maintain contact with his relatives.

In the case of unmanageable psychiatric patients, relatives may ask for a home visit by healers who have a considerable proficiency in applying shackles and manacles. They also employ magical devices which they believe will make their words become so powerful that the disturbed patient will do as he is commanded. Having arrived at the treatment centre in shackles, usually in the company of a horde of relatives, disturbed psychotic patients are rapidly sedated by a strong infusion of Rauwolfia root. Not infrequently they remain in deep comatose sleep for twenty-four hours. Such prolonged sleep therapy may be extended over a week or two until the acutely disturbed behaviour has been controlled. The dosage is then reduced and shackles are removed. Some patients are retained in shackles partly because their condition requires it and partly, as malicious rumour has it, so that they cannot run away without paying the healer's quite substantial fee.

The treatment is largely herbal; physiologically active plants such as Rauwolfia and an opium related poppy as well as others which have solely a placebo effect are used. In addition, a wide variety of healing rituals are employed in the treatment. In neurotic patients it may consist entirely of rituals among which animal sacrifice figures prominently. Usually a goat will be slaughtered. Important elements in the sacrificial ritual are gestures indicating that the patient's uncleanliness is being transferred to the scapegoat. After the throat of the animal has been slit, its blood and selected body parts are placed in a calabash and deposited at the crossroads where the offended spirit is expected to consume it and be placated. Many patients feel greatly relieved after the sacrifice. Elaborate discharge rituals are put into operation to prevent a return of the disease.

As stated before, the treatment is quite expensive. Should patients or their relatives be unable to pay the fees, male patients after their recovery are requested to work on the healer's cocoa farm until the debt has been paid while unattached female patients may become one of the numerous wives of the healer.

The key figure in the *religious system* of therapy is the diviner-priest, the father-of-mysteries, the *babalawo*. Babalawo are usually highly intelligent men endowed with sometimes remarkable instinctive psychological acumen and understanding. As part of their training they must memorize a vast body of literature—verses, songs and stories—which present the history, folklore medicine and wisdom of the Yoruba people. This literature is used for divination. The process of divination and the meaning of it for the culture as a whole is a highly complex subject. May it suffice to state that palm-nuts thrown into the air and caught afterwards are used for divining purposes and that, as one of the impressive features of the procedure, guidance, prophecy and therapeutic advice are given without interviewing the client or patient. As regards the care of the mentally ill, the functions of the babalawo consist of prescribing sacrifice, of giving advice and of divining, i.e. diagnosing the patient's needs, difficulties and problems and of directing him towards initiation into one or another of the diverse cult groups.

These cult groups fall into two general classes, cults which feature masquerade dances which are generally for men, and those which feature possession and are generally for women. The initiation into these cults is secret and expensive. During the process the particular protecting spirit for the individual is revealed. The initiate receives special emblems and secret objects. He becomes integrated within a highly supportive group. Most cults have annual festivals that may last for a week or two and it is during these annual festivals that the masquerade dances and possessions take place.

The effectiveness of these treatment procedures cannot be doubted. In fact, some African psychiatrists are convinced that in mental disorders which are deeply rooted in cultural beliefs they are more effective than Western scientific methods.

Factors which can be identified as of curative value are: (*i*) the usage of potent drugs, such as Rauwolfia, as mentioned before, and more often than not, of placebos; (*ii*) rationalization of fears of unknown origin, e.g. 'Sopono, the Smallpox god, has inflicted this on you'; (*iii*) suggestion reinforced by the high prestige of the native healer resulting in repression; (*iv*) projection of internal badness on to vicious deities; (*v*) displacement of internal badness, be it sin or sickness, on the scapegoat or any other sacrificial animal; (*vi*) displacement of target of attack, i.e. the killing of an animal in lieu of a person; (*vii*) penance by sacrifice of objects of considerable monetary value; and (*viii*) group support as in the religious cults described.

Treatment procedures employed in other primitive societies include such measures as ventilation of worries and conflicts, release of repressed impulses as in highly erotic movements and aggressive actions in voodoo ceremonies, a kind of shock treatment—throwing cold water on the victim in Thailand, and hypnotic procedures in Afghanistan. A brief example of a patient treated by a native healer in Ghana may be given. This patient consulted the native healer on account of impotence. The healer divined the patient and came to the conclusion that the patient's impotence was due to his sister who was a witch. The sister was called in; she admitted that she was a witch and that she had stolen her brother's testicles. She had buried them in an ant heap. 'But then the ants will have eaten up your brother's testicles', the healer said. 'No', the sister replied, 'they can't have done this because I put them into a tin box'. They all went to the ant heap, took out the tin box, which of course was empty, and returned the testicles to the rightful owner who lived happily ever after.

4

Summary and Conclusions

As a field of systematic scientific research, transcultural psychiatry is a new field. During the last few years, interest in this field has grown considerably. There are still very few centres in the world which devote themselves specifically to the study of this subject. Difficulties encountered in the development of transcultural psychiatry as a field of research include the reluctance of psychiatrists to leave the security, emotional and financial, of their practice at home for the hazardous experience of research in underdeveloped countries, the sparsity of research workers, be they psychiatrists or anthropologists, who are interested in and capable of going beyond the boundaries of their own discipline and are open-minded enough to cooperate with representatives of other disciplines, and the heavy expense entailed by transporting research teams to foreign countries. There is an urgent need for trained personnel in any of the disciplines involved, willing and suitable to carry out the job.

Methodological difficulties are still of much concern to workers in the field of transcultural psychiatry. Some of the research procedures which have been employed are open to serious objections. Attempts to bridge psychiatric and social science concepts have thus far not been fully successful.

It should be emphasized that the approach in cultural and transcultural psychiatry is clearly and deliberately segmental. The research worker in our field focuses his eyes on the cultural dimension of psychiatry, but he is, and should be, aware of the fact that his observations deal with only one aspect of a much bigger problem. To obtain a comprehensive view of normal and abnormal human behaviour, genetic, biological and individual psychological parameters of the total process have to be taken into account. It is believed that the psychiatrist who encompasses all the parameters named does a better job in dealing with his patients than someone whose vista is restricted.

For some time to come, the main focus of research in the field of transcultural psychiatry will probably be on the relation of family structure and group value systems to mental health and illness, and the psychological and psychopathological effects of culture change with special emphasis on those due to industrialization, and on the emotional disturbances produced by voluntary and enforced population shifts.

With respect to treatment of the mentally ill, it would be a serious mistake to assume that all knowledge rests with the technologically advanced, scientifically oriented societies. We may be able to learn a good deal from procedures adopted by healers in primitive societies.

REFERENCES

1. AUBIN, H., 1952. *L'homme et la magie*. Paris.
2. BORDELEAU, J. M., 1963. Medecine et psychiatrie haitienness. *Transcult. Psychiat. Res. Rev.*, **15,** 58.
3. CAROTHERS, J. C., 1953. *The African mind in health and disease: a study in ethnopsychiatry.* W.H.O. Monograph Series No. 17.
4. CARSTAIRS, G. M., 1964. Cultural differences in sexual deviation. In *Pathology and treatment of sexual deviation.* Ed. Rosen, I. London: Oxford Univ. Press.
5. CASTRO, R., 1962. The impact of sudden, severe disablement of the father upon the family. *Review and Newsletter*, **12,** 49–53.
6. COHEN, YEHUDI A., 1961. *Social structure and personality.* New York: Holt, Rinehart, and Winston.
7. COLLOMB, H., 1964. Psychosomatic conditions in Africa. *Transcult. Psychiat. Res. Rev.*, **1,** 130.
8. COLLOMB, H., and AYATS, H., 1962. Les migrations au Senegal: etude psychopathologique. *Cahiers d'Etudes Africaines*, **2,** 570–98.
9. DEVEREUX, G., 1961. Mohave Ethnopsychiatry and Suicide: The Psychiatric Knowledge and the Psychic Disturbances of an Indian Tribe, *Bulletin* 175. Washington, D.C.: Smithsonian Institution Bureau of American Ethnology.

10. DOUYON, E., 1965. La crise de possession dans le Vaudou Haitien (Trance in Haitian Voodoo). *Transcult. Psychiat. Res. Rev.*, **11**, 155–59.

11. EATON, J. W., and WEIL, R. J., 1955. *Culture and mental disorders*. A Comparative Study of the Hutterites and Other Populations. Glencoe, Ill.: Free Press.

12. EITINGER, H., 1958. *Psychiatriske Undersekelser Blant Flyktninger*. Oslo: Norge.

13. ELLENBERGER, H., SAUCIER, J-FRS, and WITTKOWER, E. D., 1964. Phases types de l'adaptation familiale à la maladie Physique prolongee d'un enfant. *Canad. Psychiat. Assn J.*, **9**, 322–30.

14. FIELD, M. J., 1960. *Search for security: an ethnopsychiatric study of rural Ghana*. Evanston, Ill.: Northwestern Univ. Press.

15. FRIED, J., 1959. Acculturation and mental health among Indian migrants in Peru. In *Culture and mental health*. Ed. Opler, M. New York: Macmillan.

16. GAITONDE, M. R., 1958. Cross-cultural study of the psychiatric syndromes in out-patient clinics in Bombay, India and Topeka, Kansas. Paper presented at the 114th Meeting Amer. Psychiat. Assn, San Francisco.

17. GILLIN, J., 1956. Cross-cultural aspects of socio-cultural therapy. *Estud. Anthropolog.*, 343–52.

18. GORDON, H. L., 1934. Psychiatry in Kenya Colony, *J. Ment. Sci.*, **80**, 167.

19. HALLOWELL, A. J., 1955. *Culture and experience*. Pennsylvania: Univ. Press.

20. HANKOFF, L. D., 1958. *Newsletter*, **4**, 19–21.

21. HOCH, E., 1961. *Review and Newsletter*, **11**, 65–71.

22. HOLMBERG, A. R., 1950. *Nomads for the long bow*, Publication No. 10. Washington, D.C.: Smithsonian Institute of Social Anthropology.

23. KOHLMEYER, W. A., and FERNANDES, X., 1963. Psychiatry in India: family approach in the treatment of mental disorders. *Transcult. Psychiat. Res. Rev.*, **15**, 36–38.

24. KRAEPELIN, E., 1904. Vergleichende Psychiatrie. *Zentralblatt für Nervenheilkunde und Psychiatrie*, **27**, 433–37.

25. LAMBO, T. A., 1956. Neuropsychiatric observations in the Western Region of Nigeria, *Brit. med. J.*, ii, 1388.

26. LAUBSCHER, B. J. F., 1937. *Sex, custom and psychopathology: a study of South African pagan natives*. London: Routledge and Kegan Paul.

27. LEIGHTON, A., 1959. *My name is Legion*. New York: Basic Books.

28. LEIGHTON, A., 1962. *Conference Report:* First Pan-African Conference, Abeokuta, Nigeria, Nov 12th to 18th, 1961. Ibadan, Nigeria: Government Printer.

29. LEON, CARLOS A., 1965. 'El Espanto': Sus Implicaciones Psiquiatricas. *Transcult. Psychiat. Res. Rev.*, **11**, 45–48.

30. LIN, TSUNG YI., 1953. A study of the incidence of mental disorder in Chinese and other cultures. *Psychiatry*, **16**, 313–36.

31. LINTON, R., 1956. *Culture and mental disorders*. Springfield, Ill.: Charles C. Thomas.

32. MARGETTS, E., 1959. The psychiatric examination of native African patients. *Review and Newsletter*, **6**, 32–34.

33. MALZBERG, B., and LEE, E. S., 1956. *Migration and mental disease*. New York: S.S.R.C.

34. MALZBERG, B., 1962. Migration and mental disease among the white population of New York State 1949–51. *Hum. Biol.*, **34**, 89.

35. MOLONEY, J. C., 1962. *The battle for mental health*. New York: Philosophical Library.

36. MURPHY, H. B. M., 1955. *Flight and resettlement*. Paris: UNESCO.

37. MURPHY, H. B. M., 1959. Social change and mental health. In *Causes of mental disorder: a review of epidemiological knowledge*. New York: Milbank Memorial Fund.
38. MURPHY, H. B. M., 1965 Migration and the Major Mental Disorders: A. Re-appraisal. In *Mobility and Mental health*. Ed. Kantor, M. Springfield, Illinois: C. C. Thomas.
39. ODEGAARD, O., 1932. *Emigration and insanity*. Copenhagen.
40. PARHAD, L., 1965. The cultural-social conditions in a psychiatric out-patient department in Kuwait. *Int. J. soc. Psychiat.*, **11**, 14–19.
41. PARSONS, A., 1961. Some comparative observations on ward Social Structure: Southern Italy, England and the United States. *Review and Newsletter*, **10**, 65–67.
42. PONCE, O. VALDIVIA., 1965. Historia De La Psiquiatria Peruana (History of Peruvian Psychiatry). *Transcult. Psychiat. Res. Rev.*, **11**, 41–43.
43. RIN, H., 1965. KORO. *Int. J. soc. Psychiat.*, **11**, 7.
44. RUBEL, A. J., 1964. The epidemiology of a folk illness: Susto in Hispanic America. *Ethnology*, **3**, 268–83.
45. SEGUIN, C. A., 1956. Migration and psychosomatic disadaptation. *Psychosom. Med.*, **18**, 404.
46. SHELLEY, H. M., and WATSON, W. H., 1936. Investigation concerning mental disorder in Nyasaland natives, with special reference to primary aetiological and other contributory factors. *J. ment. Sci.*, **82**, 701.
47. SPIRO, M., 1959. Cultural heritage, personal tensions and mental illness in a South Sea Culture. In *Culture and mental health*. Ed. Opler, M. New York: Macmillan.
48. STAINBROOK, E., 1952. Some characteristics of the psychopathology of schizophrenic behavior in Bahian society. *Proc. Am. Psychiat. Assn*, **109**, 330–335.
49. STAINBROOK, E., 1954. A cross-cultural evaluation of depressive reactions. In *Depression*. Eds. Hoch, P. and Zubin, J. New York: Grune and Stratton
50. TOOTH, G., 1950. *Studies in mental illness on the Gold Coast*. Col. Res. Pub No. 6. London: H.M.S.O.
51. VAHIA, N., 1963. Cultural differences in the clinical picture of schizophrenia and hysteria in India and the United States. *Transcult. Psychiat. Res. Rev.* **14**, 16–18.
52. WEDGE, B. M., 1952. Occurrence of psychosis among Okinawans in Hawaii. *Amer. J. Psychiat.*, **109**, 255–58.
53. WITTKOWER, E. D., 1964. Spirit possession in Haitian Vodun Ceremonies. *Acta Psychother.*, **12**, 72–80.
54. YAP, P. M., 1951. Mental diseases peculiar to certain cultures: a survey of comparative psychiatry. *J. ment. Sci.*, **97**, 313–27.
55. YONEBAYASHI, T., 1964. Kitsunetsuki (Possession by Foxes). *Transcult. Psychiat. Res. Rev.*, **1**, 95–97.

XXVII

GENERAL PRINCIPLES OF CONSTRUCTION OF PSYCHIATRIC HOSPITALS*

P. SIVADON

Medical Director of 'La Verrière'
Professor of Psychiatry at the University of Bruxelles
Paris, France

1

Introduction

In becoming differentiated, modern psychiatric practice has multiplied its methods of treatment. Until recently, the asylum was the most important, and practically the only, means of hospitalization for mental patients. Hospital services and private clinics were usually content with receiving acute cases so that they could select those who, after short term treatment, could take up once more a normal life while the others were confined to the asylum.

Within the last thirty years, under the influence of a veritable revolution brought about by the advent of effective therapeutic techniques, two ideas have developed, that of diversified services and that of continuity of care. These two requirements, partly contradictory, have found a solution in team practice for a definite area.

The specialization of clinical and auxiliary services means the provision, side by side with the psychiatric hospital now reserved for the active treatment of progressive diseases, of outpatient centres, domiciliary care, after care and rehabilitation, psychiatric services in general hospitals, day hospitals, and sheltered workshops, as well as special institutions for the retarded, the senile, the epileptic, the drug addicts, the antisocial psychopaths, etc.

On the other hand, so that this diversification should not produce

*Translated by Maria-Livia Osborn, Research Assistant, The Institute of Family Psychiatry, Ipswich.

an indiscriminate transfer of patients from one service to another, the whole system should be co-ordinated by a single team. But this team cannot remain efficient unless it is of small size and responsible for a relatively small catchment area, covering only a well-defined section of the population. This division could be based on a geographical area; it could equally well be defined by membership to an organization or to a profession (ex-Service associations, insurance companies, etc.).

However, it is practically impossible to study the general principles of construction of the psychiatric hospital without carefully defining its role in relation to the other clinical and auxiliary services depending on the same team, the section of the population it serves, and the type of function for which it is intended. It is impossible to fashion a tool for treatment without an exact knowledge of the way in which it is going to be used.

Therefore we shall limit our purposes to the study of the psychiatric hospital, a medical service for mental patients whose condition requires hospitalization and allows active treatment, with the understanding that other services are provided for prevention and after-care, for out-patients' treatment, for the feeble minded, the stabilized patients, the psychopaths, etc.

This study will embrace the description of hospital functioning and in particular the role of the personnel.

Having had the privilege, during the last ten years, on one hand of collaborating in the studies of the World Health Organization[1] on psychiatric architecture, and on the other of developing the programme for a completely new psychiatric hospital based on those studies, I will describe this hospital, now completed, which is a concrete example of one of the possible solutions to the problems presented by our subject.

Thus, in the first part of this chapter, we will look at the general principles of construction and functioning of a psychiatric hospital. In the second part we will describe the solutions adopted at the Institute Marcel Rivière, the private psychiatric hospital sponsored by the Mutuelle Générale de l'Education National at La Verrière, Mesnil-Saint-Denis, near Paris.

2

General Principles

Let me repeat that we are dealing with a hospital service, which is part of a whole system of diversified psychiatric institutions.

In this framework, the psychiatric hospital is no more than a link in a chain, or, more exactly, an element in a network which must be put at the disposal of certain patients at certain times during the course of their illness. The hospital, as we see it, must not receive all the patients, nor keep any of them as a permanent measure. The majority of mental patients can and must be treated as ambulant both in general hospitals and in private clinics. And the feeble minded, as well as certain chronic patients, should be able to benefit from organizations that can manage and eventually develop their residual power of adaptation; this demands different techniques.

The hospitalization of the mental patient is increasingly dependent on positive indications, rather than on negative. The mental patient is hospitalized because he needs to be separated from the conditions of his everyday life, and not because society cannot endure him any longer, because his condition demands some collective therapeutic activities, and not because one does not know what to do with him. But as soon as his condition does not positively benefit from hospitalization, the latter must be replaced by other methods.

The psychiatric hospital must be a medical service characterized by therapeutic facilities which can be realized only within it, and nowhere else.

Provided that hospitalization is not 'wasted' nor utilized 'in the absence of anything better', or 'awaiting another solution', or simply unnecessarily prolonged, one can see to it that it offers to the patient an important concentration of therapeutic facilities.

But even more than a place offering a concentration of therapeutic facilities, the psychiatric hospital must be in itself an 'instrument of healing' as visualized by Esquirol.

It is here that the psychiatric hospital differs from the general hospital. Mental illness is characterized by difficulty in meaningful relationships with things and people, this difficulty corresponds to a disorganization of the personality. The therapeutic facilities concentrated in the hospital aim to reorganize this personality, but the hospital structure itself must be favourable to the resumption of meaningful relationships with things and people.

One could treat personality disturbances by many other means than those offered by the psychiatric hospital, but the latter allows the utilization to a therapeutic end, of a medical and social environment whose characteristics can be changed by the doctor. It cannot be stressed enough: the psychiatric hospital is a therapeutic tool, therefore it is an institution managed and organized in such a way that, within it, each patient can benefit from relationships controlled and eventually modified by the doctor. These conditions of existence offered to the patient satisfy a double need; on the one hand to readjust the behaviour to assist personality readjustment, on the other hand to create a secure climate which will allow the assimilation of patterns of behaviour experienced within the hospital.

This supposition admits on the one hand that it is possible to encourage a reorganization of behaviour making use of a material and social structure; on the other hand, that a behaviour experienced in a secure situation tends to be assimilated and reproduced in other situations.

Experience shows very adequately the soundness of these propositions

Better still, it appears that patterns of behaviour developed in situations analogous to those in everyday life can be assimilated and subsequently transferred to normal living. Only in this way we can explain the therapeutic value of the majority of techniques using the reduction of conflicts at the phantasy level (symbolic realization, 'rêve eveillé', psychodrama, etc.).

The psychiatric hospital so conceived differs on many points both from the general hospital and the traditional asylum. It must provide a kind of world in miniature, complex enough to embrace various conflicting situations, but also simple enough for human interrelations to be clear. Therefore there is an advantage in removing anything which encumbers its economic and administrative functioning (avoiding for instance agriculture and, if one can, laundering services).

3

Siting

This microcosm cannot be inserted in the middle of an urban centre. The less structured the environment, the better will be its internal cohesion. On the other hand, it is most important that it should be sited in the immediate proximity of that section of the population which it serves. This is to avoid the feeling of insecurity associated with long distances and inconvenience of admission and of visiting. It is also necessary that it should be located in an area which permits an easy recruitment of staff, therefore having a sufficient population density and offering easy liaison with the cultural, educational and commercial centres. Lastly, let me repeat that the psychiatric hospital, as we envisage it, is part of a system of services complementary to each other. It is therefore necessary that it should be both distinct from these institutions and sufficiently near to them (outpatient centres, clubs for discharged patients, sheltered communities, etc.). All this leads to the choice of areas in the so-called immediate outskirts, putting the hospital at a distance that can be covered by journeys of less than thirty minutes, emphasizing on the one hand its autonomy and on the other its belonging to the demographic area which it serves.

It is often pointed out that land at the periphery of towns is scarce and expensive, as it is usually devoted to market gardening or to residential quarters, when not already taken up by industrial development. The psychiatric hospital has as much priority as the market gardens and the middle class residential developments. It is a question of providing a place of residence for beings who are biologically impaired. What is good enough for vegetables and well-to-do people should not be a luxury for sick human beings. In fact, it is not desirable to build a psychiatric hospital on ground on which animals and vegetables do not prosper well. A microclimate is, in practice, determined essentially by its flora. Among the invigorating elements in the proposed plan for the hospitalized patient, a vigorous natural environment represents a contribution not to be neglected.

4

Size

Here is an essential aspect. The size, in practice, is in proportion to demographic density and to the structuring of space put at the disposal of the community. These two factors to a great extent, determine human interrelationships. Moreover, they have an important economic significance.

Let us examine this aspect through three points : the social, the economic and the architectural.

From the *social point of view*, it matters that the total population of the hospital community should constitute a group forming a social field,* that is to say so constituted that the behaviour of each individual in it should influence the whole and reciprocally be modelled by it. It should be possible to divide the whole field into separate fields, forming coherent groups interacting with other fields in the whole system.

The size must be big enough to allow these subdivisions and small enough to avoid break-up and failure of group relations, which would involve the danger of isolation for the individual, and of loss of independence by the separate fields.

The model aimed at is that of a living organism, that is to say a group with precise limits and internal stability resulting from the perpetually renewed resolution of conflicts between stability factors and variability factors : general rules on one hand and specific application on the other; traditions and innovations; hierarchic authority and democratic participation; internal cohesion of the sub-groups and involvements of them in a wider whole, etc.

Communication must be easy, yet require effort, that is to say that at certain levels it must be direct and immediate, at other levels it must demand an effort to make sure of a correct transmission. Closely knitted groups favour immediate communication. Larger groups, and even more the institution as a whole, demand special attention, and at times require technical expedients, to assure a total and correct diffusion of information indispensable to the cohesion of the group.

A human group is considered to have 'authentic' relationships when all information may be transmitted 'face to face', that is to say from individual to individual without a written or mechanical intermediary. This authenticity, the mark of closely knitted and homogeneous groups, becomes impossible when the group reaches about 500 people. At least, this is what the ethnologists have found. (Levi-Strauss.)[4]

* Social field in the sense of Lewin's definition—Translator's note

Therefore if one wishes to have at one's disposal a system offering the whole gamut of possible means of communication, one must visualize a group of staff and patients of about 500 people, provided that it can be divided into sub-groups of smaller size.

From the *economic point of view* one must consider two contradictory factors. On one side, the larger the institution, the easier is the exploitation of technical equipment and the possibility of buying at lower prices. On the other side, over certain levels of complexity, an institution can only retain its coherence at the price of a multitude of controls. The various studies undertaken on the optimum size of hospitals have proved that those of about 400 beds attain the best economic return, and that the latter decreases progressively over 500 beds.

The World Health Organization[3] recommends that the size of the psychiatric hospital should be between 250 and 1,000 beds, which represents a vast margin. Here we have limits, beyond which it is advisable not to trespass and within which it is possible to find an optimum in relation to particular local factors (feasibility of staff recruitment, needs of the population, land available, etc.). But when there is no restriction of choice, it seems that one must limit the patients to about 250–300 (to which must be added the staff) if one wishes to achieve a group having at its disposal all the levels of complexity useful to therapy, without exceeding the limits of social and economic coherence.

Levels of integration in human groups

The problem of the overall size of the hospital is connected to the size of its internal structures.

According to its progress or regress, the mental patient becomes capable of adjustment to groups of different sizes. However, it is beneficial to offer him the possibility of alternating between solitude and human contacts.

He will find solitude in a single room, or at least in a cubicle in which he can place his personal possessions and his familiar belongings. Solitude, for a patient, like for a child, cannot be endured unless it is peopled by material mementoes (photographs, personal papers and books, etc.) and unless the nearness of reassuring persons is easily felt. It is particularly reassuring to be within calling distance of a nurse.

The group is perceived only if it does not exceed certain dimensions. In practice one distinguishes small groups of between three and nine people (more than the Parcae*; less than the Muses†, as the Ancients used to say), large groups of between twenty and thirty people, small communities of between 80 and 100 people and large communities in which, as we have seen, the optimum dimensions are between 250 and 1,000 people.

---

* Parcae—the three fates of Roman mythology—Translator's note.
† Muses—nine sisters, goddesses of Learning and the Arts—Translator's note

These various types of social units are to be found empirically in the various organized groupings (youth movements, the army, etc.), the number varies according to the case, but most usually it fluctuates around 7, 30, 90 and 350. It is a curious fact that these social units correspond to the cycles of time within which we function; the week, the month, the quarter and the year.

It was long before I made this perhaps fortuitous comparison, that I adopted for the construction of the Psychiatric Hospital at La Verrière the unit of treatment of thirty beds divided into small groups, the village of three units, making ninety beds, and the whole concern of 330 beds.

The number seven for the small group corresponds also to the idea of 'span', that is to say the number of objects which one can enumerate at a glance without counting them (perceptive span) or which one can remember after a single presentation (immediate memory span). This little group corresponds also to the size of an average family: parents, children and grandparents, and it seems that its perception imprints itself in a particularly forceful way on everyone's mind.

The number thirty is well known to educators as representing the maximum number of pupils in a class that can be controlled without effort. Florence Nightingale, who, over a century ago, codified for the first time nursing techniques, estimated at thirty patients the unit of care. And this, in fact, is the maximum number of patients that can be entrusted to a nursing team, if the aim is to give each patient regular attention.

The group of 80 to 100 corresponds without doubt to a less precise, but nevertheless indisputable fact. It is at this level that the figure of the chief stands out best, near enough to make his influence felt directly, yet usually far enough to avoid provoking opposition. Hundred corresponds to the Roman Army unit.

The superior unit, between 250 and 1,000 corresponds to an economic unit. Its size justifies the existence of autonomous services and the provision of expensive items: a laboratory, a library, a theatre, etc.

5

The Architectural Space

To favour, on the one hand, the alternation of isolation and group life, and on the other the belonging to groups of various sizes, it is up to the architect to devise formulations capable of variety.

At La Verrière hospital the following formula has been adopted:

Three hundred single rooms are distributed in ten pavilions of thirty beds each—these ten pavilions are grouped in three villages: the first two villages are of three pavilions each (90 beds), the third village consists of four pavilions (120 beds). The pavilions of each village are so arranged that they delimit a kind of internal common enclosure. This inner area, relatively small, rectangular, gives a sense of peaceful security to the inhabitants of the surrounding pavilions. It is the collective 'territory' whose instinctive importance to most animals is well known.

The size and shape of these reassuring areas deserve further study. They are determined by purely aesthetic consideration. By ethological dictates, it seems that their size must be restricted enough for easy supervision at a glance, and large enough for a manoeuvre of escape or aggression in case of danger. The territory is in fact a kind of psychological fortress, intended as a protection against an eventual attacker. The most reassuring shape seems to be the rectangle, because the spatial references of man are related to two axes, frontal and sagittal, on which his organism is built. Man can appreciate with approximation the displacing of an object in relation to himself only in relation to two perpendicular lines. A diamond shaped space, on the other hand, is very perturbing, because it confuses any precise estimation of other people's movements.

As contrast is the surest means of highlighting a characteristic, it is enough to provide a vast diamond shaped area side by side with the rectangular and confined shape of the village, to confer to the latter a reassuring value immediately perceivable.

Whatever the adopted formula, the principle lies in the well-known fact that people tend to congregate more willingly in places surrounded by anxiety provoking spaces. Of course, shape and dimensions are one aspect only of the social value of an area, but they are precisely the aspect that the architect cannot neglect.

In the psychiatric hospital, the patient should be given the opportunity of finding again a certain degree of autonomy of behaviour through various milieux where he can exercise various modes of human relationships. These milieux must be discontinuous so that the patient should make the effort necessary to integrate them. In assimilating various milieux the patient builds his personal identity. The evolutive stages which he must be allowed to overtake, can in fact be schematized as follows:

Undifferentiated activities in a family type milieu represented by the pavilion.

Differentiated activities by variable attachment to various other milieux of different structure.

Interiorization of various modes of adaptation experienced within the hospital, and integration of differentiated patterns of behaviour in a general schemata constituting the personality. This integration gives the patient a beginning of autonomy and helps him to free himself by relating to the environment.

It is important to understand that the utilization made of the material environment to therapeutic ends, postulates the attachment of the patient to this environment and, to cure him, the necessity to free him from it by the interiorization of a variety of relationship patterns.

At a more general level, one finds the problems of object relation on which psycho-analysis insists: interiorization of modes of relationship with the mother or the mother-substitutes to allow successive separations.

Because of this, it is advisable that, as soon as he has re-established satisfactory contacts within his pavilion, the hospitalized patient should be provided with different places where he can learn new modes of relationship. He will then go to another building for physiotherapy sessions, to a third for work, to yet another for entertainment.

But, to avoid the inconvenience of a multiplicity of pavilions, which should be grouped in three villages, all other activities should be concentrated in two main centres: the *Medical Centre* and the *Social Centre*.

The Medical Centre

The concentration of the principal technical facilities in the same part of the hospital satisfies a double need.

On the one hand, the importance of these facilities and their cost do not allow their duplication at various points in the establishment. It must be possible to use them almost continuously, and therefore they must be at the disposal of the whole hospital.

On the other hand, these facilities make particular architectural demands which do not harmonize with those of residential areas, or with the style of the Social Centre. The set-up of the Medical Centre recalls that of a traditional hospital of medicine or surgery. There one finds waiting rooms, consulting rooms, patient-lifts, and laboratories; it is like the polyclinic of the hospital.

Finally from the administrative point of view, it functions during the day only. In fact, the Medical Centre has no hospital beds: the staff, the heating and the lighting follow a time-table similar to that of an office, whereas the hospitalization areas function without interruption.

In the Medical Centre are to be found: the pharmacy and the biological laboratories; equipment for radiology and electroencephalography; psychological laboratories; facilities for medical records and scientific research; special consulting facilities for the use of the in-patients, and eventually for out-patients: general psychiatry, psychotherapy, relaxation, cardiology, gastroenterology, gynaecology, dentistry, etc.

Physical medicine services could also be included within it: psychomotor re-education, kinetic therapy, electrotherapy and hydrotherapy. It is important to differentiate these latter activities, which are strictly clinical, from play and sport activities, which have their place in the outbuildings of the Social Centre. Therefore the services for physical medicine include halls of various sizes for individual and group exercises, but not sport fields.

It is sometimes useful to provide the passages between the Medical Centre and one or several treatment pavilions with corridors covered for weather protection, so that patients can be comfortably taken by trolly from their beds to the various laboratories.

The Social Centre

While the activities of the Medical Centre are under the strict control of the doctors and their direct collaborators, those of the Social Centre are left to the spontaneity of the in-patients. Patients do not go to the Medical Centre unless they are summoned there; but they are encouraged to frequent the Social Centre and to participate as much as possible in the activities organized there.

The Social Centre consists of an hostelling section and a cultural section.

In the hostelling section are situated the kitchens and the dining rooms for the patients and for the staff. It might be useful, and it is the solution that we have adopted at La Verrière, to offer to the patients the choice of taking their meals in their own pavilions, or in the common dining room. At the beginning of their stay it is preferable that they should eat in groups with a family atmosphere, therefore within their pavilions. But before long they will progress in the organization of their behaviour and so differentiate the places of their various activities. Meeting people in the restaurant, or in the cafeteria at coffee time, allows them to widen their social horizon.

The staff dining room must be separated from that of the patients. Meals are times of relaxation, during which all professional preoccupations should be set aside.

In the Social Centre there are also several halls for meetings, games and various occupations. However, these halls, of varying sizes, should be relatively small, to facilitate the activities of groups of about three to twelve people. A musical auditorium, serving also as a theatre for psychodrama, can also be provided, and a theatre, a library, a discotheque, a ladies' and a gentlemen's hairdresser, a shop where newspapers, stationery and toilet articles may be purchased. A special hall must be reserved for the meetings of the patients' club. At La Verrière a mixed association, of half patients and half nursing staff, is in charge of the organization of most cultural activities: editing a paper, organizing shows and conferences, fairs and fêtes. Public from outside is usually invited to these functions, so encouraging the hospital opening on life outside.

Various workshops, making possible simple expressive activities (drawing, modelling) as well as elaborate works (mechanics, printing), are provided at various points in the hospital, so sited as to encourage as much as possible the differentiation of behaviour through a distribution of the activities throughout the area.

Personality organization consists mostly of a modulation of behaviour and its distribution in time and space. The spacial aspect of this distribution is of direct concern to our purpose.

The Social Centre must be organized taking into consideration the cultural habits of the population it serves. Very often, its various components are distributed around a place of worship, or a square. A sports field should complete the ensemble.

When the hospital is at a distance from a town with hotel facilities, it is very desirable to provide, within the hospital itself, a reception centre for patients' families and for foreign visitors. The acclimatization of an anxious patient, on the evening of his arrival, will often be facilitated if he knows that the relative who accompanied him will spend the night nearby, and he will see him again on the following morning. The relative himself will leave less worried if he has spent the night in the hospital. Of course, strict regulations must prevent anybody from staying at the reception centre for more than a few nights.

So we have, distributed in the area, three residential villages totalling ten pavilions, a Medical Centre and a Social Centre.

This complex, purposely diversified, must be strongly co-ordinated and the reception and administration pavilion sees to this. All information must converge on a single point and be co-ordinated and eventually spread by a central organ under the direct control of the officers of the establishment.

At La Verrière Hospital we have realized this centralization in the following manner:

The reception pavilion consists of: the office of the medical superintendent and his clerical staff; the office of the administrative officer and his clerical staff; the reception office; the office of the matron; the central surveillance post; the post office.

The medical superintendent, the administrative officer and the matron are the people in charge of management and supervision of the establishment. A general office is near their offices. The reception service is used both as an enquiry and an administration office. Visitors and new in-patients are directed to it. This service has the double function of receiving, informing and directing them, and also of allocating the patients to the various pavilions.

The central surveillance post is placed on the first floor, so situated to allow direct visual supervision of most of the hospital. Again, at night, entries and exits at main doors are supervised by a television circuit. This post functions without interruption night and day. It mans the telephone switchboard with the outside. It is furnished with a system of internal telephones which provides, in addition to the external telephone, direct communication with each pavilion.

A personal radio-call system makes possible through portable receivers, to call at any moment persons urgently needed (doctors on duty, matron, ambulance, etc.). A control board monitors the whole lighting system of the establishment, gives the alarm in case of faults in the heating system, in the water distribution, etc.

During the night, this surveillance post consists of a team of some highly qualified nurses, who are in intertelephonic contact with the pavilions' night staff and can intervene at the least incident.

Thus, while the hospital is widely spread out and its various functions are differentiated as much as possible, the central surveillance post insures its co-ordination and supervision in an utterly centralized manner.

The reception pavilion includes also the post office: collection and distribution of the mail, long distance telephoning, handling of parcels and postal orders, etc.

Some architectural problems

When an architect unfamiliar with psychiatric hospitals visits one of these establishments, his curiosity is usually orientated towards a certain number of problems which he imagines to be specific to psychiatry. These problems are mostly about protection of openings (doors and windows), means of supervision, safe apparatus. Sometimes, he will also take an interest in colours. Let us examine these problems.

Doors and windows. Until a few years ago, doors and windows in psychiatric hospitals were so fashioned that the patients could not use them freely nor oppose the use that the staff wanted to make of them. Also the windows were usually barred and secured by special locks. Doors would open to the outside, so that the patient could not block them from the inside. They were made of solid materials and their locks were formidable.

In fact, and despite the therapeutic progress which has reduced almost all agitation states, it is still necessary to be able to control the escape of certain patients and in particular to prevent them from throwing themselves out of the windows. For this reason the use of windows the opening of which can be controlled by the staff is recommended together with doors which can be locked. The best solution is a bolt allowing the patient to lock himself in, but which can be worked from the outside with a special key. The basic principle is as follows: agitation and aggression (against oneself or others) are directly related to anxiety—whatever increases anxiety, increases danger.

The patient is best appeased by according him space for himself, which he can lay out with personal objects and to which he can control the entry. It may become necessary to prevent an unruly patient from leaving his room. Thus, it is useful to provide a removable locking device, which can be omitted as necessary.

Methods of supervision. In several modern psychiatric hospitals, the main aim was to allow the staff to see everything while protected, and at the same time to see without being seen. It is obvious that this formula is the most apt to increase the feeling of insecurity of the patient and therefore to aggravate both his inhibition and his aggression. Spy-holes, viewing devices, one-way glass partitions and a thousand other inventions designed to put the patient in an inferior position in respect to the supervising staff, should be abolished forthwith.

The best way to supervise a patient is to be with him and, when he is alone, to give him means to call and the assurance that he will be answered at the first call. Mental patients are not delinquents who try to escape from their guards, they are human beings who are afraid. They need a reassuring presence, this could be a motherly nurse or a nurse who is calm and strong. But nothing can aggravate their fear as much as a sparse and timid staff who hide behind protective secrecy to spy on them, in case they should transform their creativity into dominant, if not violent, attitudes.

Quite simply: with mental patients it is not possible to replace a protecting human presence with spying instruments, however modern. The worst of these systems has been installed recently in a so-called 'modern' establishment, where close circuit television allows a single supervisor to check on the behaviour of several hundred patients, in the same way as displays of large stores are guarded against thieves.

The same measures of supervision can be reassuring or distressing, according to the way in which they are used. It seems to me that the principle which must guide the use of means of supervision is as follows: when an apparatus isolates the patient from the staff, hiding the latter until the former feels himself watched, there is a risk of increasing anxiety. But when an apparatus lets the patient know that the staff is present and eventually available, this apparatus is reassuring. For example, an internal telephone making possible communication between the patient's room and the surveillance post is reassuring if the patient can hear the nurse's voice, as well as the latter hearing that of the patient. A viewing device is reassuring if the patient sees his nurse's face when she looks at him.

Any measure allowing the staff to check on the patient's presence and behaviour, must also give him the secure feeling of a benevolent presence, otherwise it will be anxiety producing and therefore a source of danger. The supervision of a mental patient follows the same rules as the supervision of a young child: the aim is not to control him by a glance, but to be able to help him at his least request. In short, the staff must be seen and heard by the patients even more than the patients by the staff.

Safety. The same principles are applicable to this problem. Material apparatus which absolutely eliminates any danger of violence and suicide does not exist. But numerous studies have agreed that this danger is directly bound to fear and to anxiety originating in a feeling of rejection and desertion.

It can be said that every safety measure has been tried; bare or padded cells; patients stripped of all clothes or restrained by a strait-jacket; unbreakable glass and furniture fixed to the walls; nothing has ever resisted for long to the aggressive impulses of the patient. But, it has been known since Pinel that by replacing the shackles and the chains by a bit of human warmth, often one changes in a spectacular way attitudes which seemed most hopeless.

However, should nothing be prevented? Without doubt, it is better to put unbreakable or at least reinforced glass in rooms where agitated and confused patients are to be placed. But we must not forget that an aggressive patient, who has been unable to vent his aggression on a window-pane, will vent it more dangerously on another object or on a person. Breaking windows represents for the patient the solution to a problem. It is not enough to prevent this happening, the patient must be allowed to express himself in another way.

The problem of lift-cages and of patients throwing themselves out of windows is solved when single storey pavilions are adopted. If not, the usual safety regulations of residential premises are generally sufficient.

At La Verrière Hospital, no special precautions have been taken except for the fitting of reinforced glass in a number of rooms. The furniture, however, is of the same type as that found in good hotels. The architecture includes large glass covered bays, and certain parts of the Social Centre are partitioned by glass alone. Patients can find all that is needed for wounding themselves and for suicide: sharp tools, trees from which to hang and pools to drown themselves in. But, without doubt, the presence, or the absence, of these materials does not increase, or decrease, the frequence and gravity of aggression. It is the psychological atmosphere of the establishment that matters, this atmosphere is essentially related to the presence and emotional stability of the staff.

If a patient takes a dangerous instrument, or a jar of drugs, with the intent of killing himself, he was tempted to do so not so much by seeing these things, as by the feeling of insecurity provoked by the negligence or the carelessness of the nurses who have omitted to put these objects out of his reach.

Decorative details, shapes, colours and materials have seldom been the subject of research.

Mental patients benefit from the opportunity offered to them to choose the décor of their environment. But it is equally important to encourage their adaptation to an imposed environment. Therefore some areas (for example the bedroom and the workshops) could be decorated by the patients, while others (dining room, communal living room) should be unchangeable. As Piaget says, adaptation entails bipolarity: assimilation, through which the subject manages the environment in relation to his own structure, and adaptation by which he models himself in relation to the demands of the environment.

In regard to *shapes*, let us remember that their choice is between two incompatible extremes: the circular and the rectangular. Biologically, it seems that circular shapes are those of the body, or of mobile objects, while rectangular shapes are those of the framework, within which body or mobile objects move. By its rounded shape, but also because it is built on two rectangular axes, the human body is at ease in handling rounded objects in a rectangular frame. The grounds laid out for physical exercises are rectangular, while the objects banded within it are rounded.

The impression of movement, or stillness, in the environment is produced by alternating, or combining, round and square elements. In nature, as Cézanne[2] has said, everything is finally reduced to a sphere or a cube. The curve has movement but is elusive, the rectangle has stillness but is reassuring. On the other hand diamond shapes and spirals are particularly disorientating. They are invaluable to highlight, by contrast, the more reassuring character of round and square shapes in their proximity.

These ideas, still not fully proved, can meanwhile be utilized in architecture, and more particularly in hospital environments. Rounded furniture in rectangular premises constitutes the very type of a reassuring environment. Rectangular furniture in a diamond shaped area gives a feeling of ambiguity. A circular boundary is bearable only if it includes rectangular landmarks.

In the psychiatric hospital there must be a careful choice between orientating and disorientating features.

Colours too influence behaviour. It is known that red usually brings an increase in muscular tone and aggressive attitudes, while blue brings about relaxation and appeasement.

But this idea has no practical use, as it is the impact of a colour and not its persistence which provokes these reactions. But practical use can be made of colour alternation or contrast; monotony encourages disinterest and sleep; contrast, or unexpected alternation, maintains alertness.

A very intense polychromy can satisfy the double need of contrast and continuity. It is true that some colours are depressing and others gay. But our knowledge in this field is still incomplete.

Materials are equally important. Those which are traditional and so-called 'living', because they usually derive from the living world (woods, skins, wool, fibres and lianas, bone, etc.) are usually accepted best. The same applies to materials derived from the earth transformed by fire: terra-cotta, ceramics, and glass. The feeling of security, in the guise of an impression of comfort, is often bound to the use of these materials, while a cold picture is presented by more modern media, such as concrete, metal and plastic materials. However, the fact still remains that we can enliven our environment by the combination of traditional and modern, their alternation and contrast.

6

Conclusion

Until recently the architecture of psychiatric hospitals was dictated by the double need for safety and economy. It was a matter of housing the maximum number of patients with the minimum staff, and the latter to be used to the best advantage.

The present psychiatric hospital is no longer conceived as a place of custodial care, but as an environmental system, artificially contrived to help the re-education of the mental functions of those under its care. Its architecture, therefore, should reproduce, in a smaller scale, that of a normal town, where it is possible to control human relationships, regulate the utilization of space and time, manage situations, the therapeutic value of which produces equilibrium between safety factors and freedom.

Far from looking for a special architecture for mental patients, the planner of a modern psychiatric hospital must aim to develop, as in town planning, a simplified but normal environment, in which the patient will be able to face once more the difficulties of real social life, to be found in the hospital in symbolic forms easier to master.

REFERENCES

1. BAKER, A., DAVIES, R. L., and SIVADON, P., 1959. Psychiatric services and architecture. *Public Health Papers* No. 1. Geneva: W.H.O.
2. CÉZANNE, P., quoted by Brion, M. in *Art abstrait*, page 16. Albin Michel.
3. Community Mental Hospital, 1953. W.H.O. Technical Report No. 73.
4. LEVI-STRAUSS, C., 1958. *Anthropologie structurale—les critères de l'authenticite.* Plon.

AUTHOR INDEX

This index covers both volumes of the Modern Perspectives in Psychiatry series, the figure in bold type denoting the volume of the entry.

SUBJECT INDEX

This index covers both volumes of the Modern Perspectives in Psychiatry series, the figure in bold type denoting the volume of the entry.

CONTENTS OF MODERN PERSPECTIVES IN CHILD PSYCHIATRY